W9-CFB-333

WHO WAS WHO IN THE CIVIL WAR

WHO WAS WHO IN THE CIVIL WAR

JG
PRESS

Published by
World Publications Group, Inc.
140 Laurel Street
East Bridgewater, MA 02333
www.wrldpub.com

Copyright © 2011

10-ISBN: 1-57215-816-6
13-ISBN: 978-1-57215-816-0

Printed in China by Toppan Leefung Printing Limited

PAGE 1: Patriotic Union song of 1861.

PAGE 2: Clockwise from top: Stonewall
Jackson and his home; Ulysses S Grant;
Robert E Lee; and William T Sherman

PAGE 3: Famous Union commanders: (top
row left to right) Gen George H Thomas,
Gen Philip Kearney, Gen Ambrose E
Burnside, Gen Joseph Hooker, Gen John A
Logan, Gen George G Meade, Gen George B
McClellan; (middle row left to right) Gen
Irwin McDowell, Gen N P Banks, Gen Philip
H Sheridan, Gen Ulysses S Grant, Gen
William T Sherman, Gen William S
Rosecrans, Gen Daniel E Sickles; (bottom
row left to right) Admiral David G Farragut,
Gen John Pope, Gen Benjamin F Butler, Gen
Winfield S Hancock, Gen John Sedgwick,
Admiral David D Porter.

BELOW: Famous Confederate generals (left to right) John B Hood, Richard Stoddert Ewell, Braxton Bragg, Albert Sydney Johnston, Wade Hampton, E Kirby Smith, Jubal A Early, A P Hill, Stephen D Lee, Richard H Anderson, John B Gordon, Theophalus S Holmes, William G Hardee, Joseph E Johnston, Samuel H Buckner, James Longstreet, Leonidas Polk, Robert E Lee, Nathan B Forrest, P G T Beauregard, Thomas J (Stonewall) Jackson, Samuel Cooper, J E B Stuart, Richard Taylor, J C Pemberton, D H Hill.

Editor's Preface

There are probably many good reasons for America's seemingly insatiable interest in the Civil War, but surely one of the most important has to do with the war's intense *personality*. Personality, that is, in the literal sense, for the many actors who played central roles in this greatest of our national epic dramas were nothing if not individually fascinating. They ran the gamut of human types – from the noble to the venal, from the brilliant to the ludicrously incompetent, from the brave to the cowardly. Many of them were animated by passions so extreme that they were at times driven to extremes of behavior, some to atrocity, others to something approaching saintliness.

Yet – and this may be what truly makes them fascinating – they were all far more complex and multi-dimensional than sentimental mythology would have us believe. Like all real human enterprises, the Civil War was no theatre of humours: it was fought by living, flesh-and-blood people, men and women whose characters were filled with all the quirks and contradictions that the human estate entails.

Thus the courtly, sedate Robert E. Lee had in his nature at least some elements of bloodthirsty rashness that would not have seemed out of place in a Western gunslinger. The wise and visionary Lincoln was also a sly politician and a somewhat meddlesome armchair strategist. W. T. Sherman, whose name is to many Southerners still a synonym of military barbarity, was a man who detested war, had more sympathy for the Southern cause than most of his Union colleagues, and offered his defeated foe, J. E. Johnston, such generous surrender terms that they were repudiated by Congress. Heroic battlefield nurses Clara Barton and Dorothea Dix both had difficult personalities and questionable administrative skills. The war's most legendary bungler, Ambrose Burnside, was also famous among his contemporaries for his unfailing charm and engaging humility. The flamboyant Jeb Stuart, that "gay knight-errant of the elder time," was in private the most sobersided and conventional of husbands. Whether the brilliant Stonewall Jackson was altogether sane was a question that bemused at least a

few of those who knew him well. Such examples could be multiplied almost indefinitely.

Knowing human details about the men and women who played important roles in the Civil War in no way diminishes our regard for them. On the contrary, it both heightens our admiration for their accomplishments and serves to make us more sympathetic towards their failures and shortcomings. At the same time, it vastly increases our understanding both of them and of the war itself.

Yet the very fact that our understanding of the war is so heavily rooted in our sense of its personalities also has its penalties. Our histories of the war, even the most summary and general, fairly bristle with names, many of which keep reappearing in confusingly various contexts. It is no wonder that casual readers sometimes have difficulty in keeping track of all the players. And the problem is compounded in all those formal military histories which observe the hallowed – if inexplicable – martial convention of almost always providing the exact rank of every army and navy officer mentioned and almost never giving their first names (thereby leaving it to the reader to puzzle out just which Lee, Porter, Johnston, Davis, Anderson, Reynolds, Smith, Hill, Cooke, etc. the author might have in mind).

This book, *Who Was Who in the Civil War*, has been designed to assist non-expert readers in negotiating the sometimes complex shoals of Civil War biography. It contains approximately 520 profiles – many illustrated – of the period's most prominent figures, men and women, military and civilian. The entries vary in length

according to the importance of the subject. The longest entries run to over 1000 words; the shortest, brief vitae, are sometimes less than 50. The authors' criteria for judging the relative importance of a subject almost always have to do with the subject's relationship to the war itself. Thus, for example, James Garfield and Benjamin Harrison receive rather brief entries, not because these future presidents were unimportant in other contexts but simply because their roles in the Civil War were comparatively minor. On the other hand, in a few cases where individuals' future lives and works were largely determined by their Civil War experiences, their postwar careers are dealt with in somewhat more detail: Clara Barton, whose battlefield experiences ministering to sick and wounded soldiers led to her founding of the American Red Cross, is a case in point.

At the risk of laboring the obvious, perhaps it is worth adding that readers of this volume should bear in mind that it is essentially a companion book, one meant to be read in conjunction with other historical works rather than instead of them. Although it is true that the reader will find the broad outlines of Civil War history presented piecemeal in a various key biographies – mainly those of Lincoln, Jefferson Davis, Lee, Grant, and Sherman – the book was never intended to double as a general history of the period. Thus, while it takes pains to try to identify the major campaigns and battles in which all its military subjects participated, it rarely attempts to give more than cursory descriptions of any of the actions so noted. And the same is true of its treatment of political, economic, and social events. In short, its purpose to serve as a useful supplement to general histories, to do precisely what most of them, by their very nature, cannot hope to do as well. If it succeeds in this aim, its authors and its editor will be well pleased.

OPPOSITE: Robert Shaw at Fort Wagner.

BELOW: Abraham Lincoln.

legislator in the 1840s he helped to confirm Massachusetts's opposition to slavery. He founded the *Boston Whig* (1846) and ran as a Free-Soiler as Martin Van Buren's vice presidential candidate (1848). In the U.S. Congress (1859-1861) he skilfully headed the House Committee on the State of the Union. In the crucial post of U.S. minister to Great Britain (1861-1868), he successfully maintained England's (and thus Europe's) neutrality, a feat regarded as the diplomatic equivalent of winning a major military victory at home. He helped to arbitrate the U.S. government's *Alabama* Claims against Great Britain for war damages (1871-1872) and eventually retired to Massachusetts.

Abercrombie, John Joseph
(1798-1877) Union general

Tennessee-born Abercrombie was graduated from West Point in 1822 and fought in the infantry in the Seminole and Mexican wars. Commissioned at Union colonel in 1861, he commanded a brigade in the Peninsular Campaign. As a brigadier general he led Abercrombie's Division in the defense of Washington and defended the Fredericksburg depots. After retiring from the regular army in June 1865 he served on courts martial.

Adams, Charles Francis
(1807-1886) U.S. diplomat

The son of President John Quincy Adams, he was educated at Harvard and became a writer on politics and history. As a state

Charles Francis Adams

Daniel Weisiger Adams

Adams, Daniel Weisiger
(1821-1872) Confederate general

A Kentucky-born lawyer-politician, he settled in Natchez, Mississippi, and later in New Orleans. Weisinger commanded the 1st Louisiana Regulars at Shiloh, then led a brigade at Perryville, Murfreesboro and Chickamauga. Wounded and captured at Chickamauga, he was exchanged in 1864. He commanded the District of Central Alabama during the final months of the war. After a brief postwar exile in England, he returned to New Orleans to practice law.

Alexander, Edward Porter
(1835-1910) Confederate general

A Georgia-born graduate of West Point, he taught at the academy, helped develop the army's "wig-wag" system of flag signals and served in the Pacific Northwest before resigning during the secession crisis. Commissioned a captain in the Confederate

Edward Porter Alexander

army in May 1861, Alexander developed a reputation as one of its most resourceful and energetic officers. First as a staff officer, later as an artillerist, he fought at First Bull Run, Fredericksburg and Gettysburg and commanded James Longstreet's artillery at Knoxville, the Wilderness, Spotsylvania and Cold Harbor. Alexander's influential *Military Memoirs of a Confederate* appeared in 1907.

Allen, Henry Watkins
(1820-1866) Confederate general

A Louisiana planter and legislator, Allen had only recently returned from extensive European travels when the Civil War broke out, whereupon he joined the Confederate army. He was wounded at Shiloh in 1862 and fought at Vicksburg in 1862-63. He led the Louisiana Brigade at Baton Rouge in 1864. His wounds there prevented further field service, but he proved an outstanding governor of Louisiana (1864-1865): he restored the state's shattered economy by establishing trade routes through Mexico to beat the Union blockade and negotiated Confederate General Kirby Smith's surrender. He died in Mexico.

Ames, Adelbert
(1835-1933) Union general

A native of Maine, he was seriously wounded at First Bull Run 10 weeks after his West Point graduation (and earned a Congressional Medal of Honor for gallantry). He fought in the Peninsular and Antietam campaigns and at Fredericksburg and Chancellorsville. As a brigadier general he led divisions at Gettysburg, then in Virginia and North Carolina in 1864-1865). He was Mississippi's governor (1868-1870, 1874-1876) and US Senator (1870-1874). He engaged in milling and manufacturing in the North and, after serving in the Spanish-American War, retired to Massachusetts.

Anderson, "Bloody" Bill
(d. 1864) Confederate guerrilla

His band of near-criminals looted Centralia, Missouri, on September 27, 1864, hijacked a train and murdered 24 unarmed Federals and two civilians on board. Two hours later Anderson's gang ambushed a

ABOVE: Adelbert Ames (seated, l.) served in both the Civil and Spanish-American wars.

RIGHT: Confederate General George B. Anderson, mortally wounded at Antietam.

Union cavalry detachment, killing 124 of 147 troopers in what became known as the Centralia Massacre. Pursuing Federals caught and killed Anderson near Richmond, Missouri, in later October.

Anderson, George Burgwyn
(1831-1862) Confederate general

He was graduated from the University of North Carolina at age 17, then entered West Point, from which he was graduated in 1852. Anderson resigned from the U.S. Army in 1861, entered Confederate service and commanded a North Carolina regiment at First Bull Run. He led a brigade of North Carolina troops during the battles of the Seven Days in 1862. Wounded in the ankle at Antietam in September, he died of the effects of an amputation of his foot on October 16, 1862.

Joseph Reid Anderson

Anderson, Joseph Reid
(1813-1892) Confederate general

A Virginia-born West Point graduate, he bought the Tredegar Iron Works (Richmond, Virginia) in 1858 after serving for a time in the Virginia legislature. In August 1861 he was made major of artillery in the Confederate army while still running the ironworks, which were considered vital to the Confederacy's military armaments. In September 1861 he was promoted to brigadier general and given command of the District of Cape Fear. In 1862 he was wounded at Frayser's Farm while leading the 3rd North Carolina Brigade on the Peninsula; no longer fit for field duty, he resigned and returned to the ironworks in 1862.

Anderson, Richard Heron
(1821-1879) Confederate general

This West Point graduate and 20-year army veteran resigned from frontier service in March 1861 to join the 1st South Carolina infantry. A brigadier general by July, he fought steadily with the Army of Northern Virginia, distinguishing himself particularly in the Peninsular Campaign and at Chancellorsville and, from May to October 1864, commanding General James Longstreet's corps at Spotsylvania, Cold Harbor, Petersburg and Richmond. After the war he worked for the South Carolina railroad and as a state phosphate inspector.

Anderson, Robert
(1805-1871) Union general

An 1825 West Point graduate, the Kentucky-born Anderson fought in the Seminole and Mexican wars and taught artillery tactics at the military academy. He commanded the U.S. garrison in Charleston Harbor, South Carolina, during the secession crisis and became the "hero of Fort Sumter" when Confederate forces bom-

barded the harbor citadel in April 1861. Promoted to brigadier general in May, he commanded Union forces in Kentucky during the period of that state's so-called neutrality. Anderson retired on a disability in October 1863. He returned to Fort Sumter on April 14, 1865, for the ceremonial raising of the U.S. flag there.

Andrews, John Albion
(1818-1867)
Governor of Massachusetts

Born in Maine and a graduate of Bowdoin College, he became a lawyer in Boston and was outspoken in his opposition to slavery. A Republican, he was elected governor of Massachusetts in 1860, taking office in 1861 and retaining it throughout the Civil War (and until his death in 1867). He was prompt and effective in lending his support to the Union war effort – the Massachu-

Robert Anderson

BELOW: Fort Sumter in April 1861

setts 6th Regiment was the first major armed force to arrive in Washington after President Lincoln's call for volunteers – and Andrews's Massachusetts remained a pillar of Union strength throughout the remainder of the war.

Armistead, Lewis Addison
(1817-1863) Confederate general

Born in North Carolina to a respected military family, he attended West Point and fought in the Mexican War. He resigned his U.S. Army commission in 1861 and entered Confederate service. He led a brigade in "Pickett's Charge" at Gettysburg that is said to have made the deepest penetration in the Federal line; he died in this action. Union General Winfield Scott Hancock, Armistead's close friend, led the defending troops in this part of the line, and later Hancock had the sombre duty of sending Armistead's spurs to his family. On the spot where Armistead fell is a monument marking what has come to be called "the high tide" of the Confederacy.

Armstrong, Frank Crawford
(1835-1909) Confederate general

Born in Indian Territory, he joined the regular army and fought on the western frontier, taking part in the Utah Expedition with the 2nd U. S. Dragoons. In August 1861 he resigned from the United States Army and joined the Confederate forces, fighting at Wilson's Creek, Missouri. Promoted to brigadier general in April 1863, he fought at Stones River, Tullahoma, Chickamauga, Knoxville and in the Franklin and Nashville Campaign. Following the war, he served as a U.S. Indian inspector (1885-1889) and commissioner of Indian affairs (1893-1895).

Armstrong, Samuel Chapman
(1839-1892) Union officer

Born in Hawaii, where his parents had gone as missionaries, he was attending Williams College when the Civil War

LEFT: Frank Crawford Armstrong

broke out. He volunteered for Union service and was commissioned a captain in August 1862. In 1864 he was made a colonel with the 9th Regiment, made up of African-Americans, and was breveted a brigadier general in November 1864. Because of his experiences with the black troops, he was made an agent of the Freedmen's Bureau after the war. This led him to found the Hampton Institute (1868), and he spent the rest of his life working to educate African-Americans.

Ashby, Turner
(1828-1862) Confederate general

The grandson of a Revolutionary War officer, he was born in Fauquier County, Virginia, where he became a planter and grain dealer in the Shenandoah Valley. An influential local politician, Turner favored slavery but opposed secession, and in 1859 he raised a volunteer company and led it to Harpers Ferry to defend Virginia against John Brown. When Virginia seceded, he again raised and led a mounted troop to Harpers Ferry, staying to scout. As part of the 7th Virginia Cavalry after June 1861, his men defended the upper Potomac border, participating in First Bull Run. A daring intelligence-gathering expedition to Chambersburg, Pennsylvania, undertaken in disguise in the spring of 1862 cemented his growing reputation for courage and resourcefulness. As Stonewall Jackson's cavalry commander, he played an important role in the Jackson's Shenandoah Val-

OPPOSITE: William W. Averell (seated).

BELOW: Turner Ashby.

ley Campaign in 1862. Joining Jackson at Front Royal, he displayed exceptional leadership on picket and scouting duty and fought at Winchester. He was promoted to brigadier general in May of that year. He was killed in a rearguard action protecting Jackson's retreat from the Valley on June 6.

Augur, Christopher Colon
(1821-1898) Union general

A New York native, Augur saw Mexican War and frontier service after graduation from West Point. Appointed a brigadier general in the Union army, he fought on the Rappahannock (capturing Fredericksburg in April 1862) and was wounded at Cedar Mountain. As a major general he was second-in-command in Nathaniel Banks's 1862 New Orleans Campaign. He later commanded the District of Baton Rouge, the Department of Washington and XXII Corps. In his 20-year postwar army career he directed operations against the Indians and was Reconstruction commander of the Department of the Gulf.

Averell, William Wood
(1832-1900) Union general

This New York-born West Point graduate was a pre-war Indian fighter. In the Civil War he was one of the Army of the Potomac's more accomplished young cavalry leaders, bringing the Union cavalry its first taste of success in the engagement at Kelly's Ford in March 1863. He was one of General George Stoneman's lieutenants at Chancellorsville (May 1863), but General Joseph Hooker relieved him of command for apparent lack of aggressiveness. He served in the Shenandoah Valley Campaign of Philip Sheridan (1864), who also relieved Averell of command for the same reason. After the war he served as U.S. consul general in Canada (1866-69), then became wealthy as a manufacturer and inventor of industrial products.

Ayres, Romeyn Beck
(1825-1888) Union general

This New York-born West Point graduate, having served in the Mexican War and on the frontier, was promoted to captain in the U.S. Army in May 1861. He fought at First Bull Run, Yorktown, Lee's Mill, Williamsburg, Gaines's Mill, South Mountain, Antietam, Fredericksburg, Chancellorsville, Gettysburg and the Wilderness. He was wounded at Petersburg and breveted a major general for war service. He remained in the army after the war.

Babcock, Orville
(1835-1884) Union officer

Born and raised in a small Vermont town, he entered West Point in 1857 and was graduated third in his class four years later. He saw action with a Union engineer unit on the Virginia Peninsula in the spring of 1862 and won appointment as chief engineer of the Left Grand Division of the Army of the Potomac later in the year.

Babcock joined Ulysses S. Grant's staff in 1864 as an aide-de-camp and took part in the Wilderness, Spotsylvania and Cold Harbor battles and in the siege of Petersburg. Grant had great confidence in his abilities, employing him as a courier, to collect information and to survey positions, and it was Babcock whom Grant sent

Orville Babcock (right), a longtime associate of Ulysses S. Grant

to conduct Robert E. Lee to the McLean house for the surrender on April 9, 1865.

Babcock served as Grant's private secretary for several years after the war. In the 1870s he became associated with the group of corrupt government officials known as the "Whiskey Ring" and accepted costly presents from one of the ring leaders, John McDonald, the Internal Revenue Service supervisor in St. Louis. In December 1875 a grand jury indicted Babcock for conspiracy to defraud the IRS. Grant stood by him, insisting he could not be guilty. Swayed by Grant's defense, the court returned a verdict of not guilty in February 1876.

Babcock re-entered public service briefly, then retired to Florida. He was accidentally drowned at Mosquito Inlet, Florida, on June 2, 1884.

Bagby, Arthur Pendleton
(1832-1921) Confederate officer

He was graduated from West Point in 1852 and served on the frontier before quitting the army to practice law in Texas. Commissioned a major in the 7th Texas in 1861, Bagby participated in the New Mexico Campaign and in the defense of Galveston. He commanded a brigade during the Red River Campaign of 1864 and saw action at Mansfield and Pleasant Hill. He returned to his Texas law practice after the war.

Bailey, Joseph
(1825-1867) Union general

This Ohio-born lumberman became a captain in the Union's 4th Wisconsin Cavalry in July 1861 and became an engineer of defense at New Orleans in December 1862. He was breveted a brigadier general in June 1864 for his successful efforts to save Nathaniel Bank's fleet in the Red River Campaign and won the Thanks of Congress. Promoted to brigadier general in November 1864, he held various posts as an engineer before resigning in July 1865. He was sheriff of Newton County, Missouri, when he was killed in 1867.

Bailey, Theodorus
(1805-1877) Union admiral

This New Yorker became a midshipman in 1818 and earned his first independent command during the Mexican War. He commanded U.S.S. *Colorado* in the blockade of Pensacola; in the sloop-of-war *Cayuga* he was second-in-command under Admiral David Farragut at New Orleans in April-May 1862 and accepted the city's surren-

Theodorus Bailey (above) and (right) Alpheus Baker

der. From November 1862 he led the East Gulf blockading squadron in intercepting 150 blockade runners. Ill health forced him to a shore command in September 1864. He retired as a rear admiral in 1866.

Baker, Alpheus
(1828-1891) Confederate general

Born in South Carolina, Baker was a delegate to Alabama's secession convention. He entered Confederate service and in March 1862 fought at New Madrid and Island No. 10. He was captured in this latter action and was exchanged in September 1862. He was wounded during the Vicksburg Campaign. Promoted to brigadier general in March 1864, he fought in the Atlanta Campaign at Resaca and at Ezra Church. In January 1865 he was sent to Mobile and then fought at Bentonville. He practiced law after the war.

Baker, Edward Dickinson
(1811-1861) Union officer

A childhood immigrant from England, he settled in Illinois and in 1835 established a law practice in Springfield. There he became an intimate of Abraham Lincoln. He became a state legislator and U.S. Representative (1845-1846, 1849-1851). He moved to San Francisco (1852) and achieved such a political reputation on the West Coast that Oregon Republicans solicited him for a U.S. Senate seat (1860-1861). A skilled orator, he helped to deliver both of these states in the election of 1860 to Lincoln, to whom he was now an advisor. Baker at first declined a brigadier general's commission in 1861 to remain in the Senate, but it was as a colonel of the 71st Pennsylvania that he was killed at Ball's Bluff in October 1861.

Baker, LaFayette Curry
(1826-1868) U.S. secret service chief

This New Yorker, a San Francisco Vigilante and State Department detective, was a Union special agent throughout the war, reaching the rank of brigadier general. His intelligence-gathering against Confederates, conspirators and bounty-jumpers often involved unconstitutional searches and arrests, in addition to spectacular work behind enemy lines. Baker organized the pursuit and capture of John Wilkes Booth.

LaFayette Curry Baker

Baker, Laurence Simmons
(1830-1907) Confederate general

This West Point graduate left frontier Indian fighting to join the cavalry of his home state, North Carolina, in May 1861. He fought in the Army of Northern Virginia in the Peninsular, Antietam and Fredericksburg campaigns of 1862 and the Gettysburg Campaign of 1863. He assumed a North Carolina territorial command in 1864 as a brigadier general. Paroled soon after his surrender in 1865, he farmed in Virginia and, after 1878, worked as a railroad agent.

Banks, Nathaniel Prentiss
(1816-1894) Union general

Massachusetts-born Banks was a career politician: he would represent no less than five political parties in 10 Congresses (1853-1891) and was an able governor of Massachusetts (1858-1860). Commissioned a major general in May 1961, he commanded the Department of Annapolis, led V Corps during the Shenandoah Valley Campaign of 1862 and, leading II Corps, made a con-

troversial and unsuccessful attack at Cedar Mountain in August of that year. Replacing B.F. Butler as commander of the Gulf Department late in 1862, he assisted Ulysses S. Grant in opening the Mississippi: his leading role in the capture of Port Hudson (July 1863) earned him the Thanks of Congress. He resigned after leading the ill-fated Red River Campaign of 1863-1864, though his superiors, notably Henry Halleck, were probably even more responsible for the operation's failure.

Barker, Mrs. Stephen
Sanitary Commission worker

She accompanied her husband, a Massachusetts regimental chaplain, to the war. A nurse attached to the 1st Heavy Artillery at Fort Albany for two years, she became the Sanitary Commission superintendent of several Washington hospitals in 1864 and in the last years of the war lectured widely to raise funds for the commission. After the war she was active in veterans' relief.

Mrs. Stephen Barker, one of the most noted Sanitary Commission workers

William Barksdale

Barksdale, William
(1821-1863) Confederate general

This Tennessee-born lawyer served in the Mexican War and ran a pro-slavery newspaper. He was a Democratic Congressman in 1861, but he resigned in January and subsequently joined the Confederate army. He served at First Bull Run and in the Peninsular Campaign, at Antietam, Fredericksburg, Chancellorsville and Gettysburg. He commanded a brigade in Lafayette McLaws's division of James Longstreet's Corps; the brigade saw particularly heavy fighting and became known as "Barksdale's Mississippi Brigade." He was both wounded and captured at Peach Orchard, Virginia, and died the following day from his wounds.

Barlow, Francis Channing
(1834-1896) Union general

He was a Harvard-educated New York lawyer and writer. Despite several serious wounds requiring long recuperations, Barlow fought in many major eastern theater battles and campaigns between 1862 and 1865: the siege of Yorktown, Fair Oaks, Antietam, Chancellorsville, Gettysburg, the Wilderness, Spotsylvania, Cold Harbor, Petersburg and Sayler's Creek. He was appointed a brigadier general in September 1862. Resuming his law career after the war, Barlow was a prominent anti-corruption reformer; as New York attorney general (1871-1873) he prosecuted William "Boss" Tweed.

Barnard, John Gross
(1815-1882) Union general

A Massachusetts native and West Point graduate, he was a career army engineer and coastal defence specialist who superintended the fortification of New York, Mobile and San Francisco, among other ports. During the Civil War, as chief engineer of Washington, D.C., and the Union armies, he designed Washington's defenses, supervised Union positioning at First Bull Run and in the Peninsular Campaign of 1862 and briefed General W.T. Sherman for the Carolinas Campaign of 1865. He retired from the army in 1881. Barnard published many works on engineering and science.

Barnum, Henry A.
(1833-1892) Union general

This New York-born teacher and lawyer was commissioned a captain in the Union army on the same day in May 1861 that he attempted to enlist as a private. He fought at First Bull Run and Blackburn's Ford before being wounded and captured at Malvern Hill. Released in June 1862, he was made a colonel in September 1862. He fought at Gettysburg, was wounded at Lookout Mountain and was the first Union officer to enter Savannah in December 1864. He was awarded the Medal of Honor

John Gross Barnard, the Federal army's chief engineer

in 1865 and was breveted a major general. He served as New York inspector of prisons after his resignation from the army in 1866.

Barringer, Rufus
(1821-1895) Confederate general

A North Carolina-born legislator in the Whig Party, Barringer was against secession, but he went with his state and was commissioned a captain in the Confederate army in May 1861. He fought on the Peninsula, at Second Bull Run, Antietam, Fredericksburg and Chancellorsville, and was wounded at Brandy Station. Promoted to brigadier general in June 1864, he was captured at Sayler's Creek on April 3, 1865, but was released in July. He practiced law and ran a plantation after the war. Both Stonewall Jackson and D. H. Hill were his brothers-in-law.

Barry, John Decatur
(1839-1867) Confederate officer

A native of North Carolina, he enlisted in the home state regiment that later became the 18th North Carolina. Elected captain in that regiment in April 1862, he fought throughout the Seven Days' Battles of late June and early July, in the Second Bull Run Campaign in August and at Antietam in September.

E.P. Alexander, in his *Military Memoirs of a Confederate* (1907) identified Barry, by then a major, as the officer who gave the fatal order to fire on Stonewall Jackson and his retinue at dusk on May 2, 1863, during the Battle of Chancellorsville. Jackson had just completed the rout of the Federal right wing and meant to press on that night for a junction with R.E. Lee that might have led to a decisive defeat for the Army of the Potomac. Seriously wounded in the fusillade, he died eight days later.

Barry commanded the 18th North Carolina on the Gettysburg Campaign and participated in Pickett's Charge on the third day of the battle. He briefly commanded a brigade at Cold Harbor in June 1864 and again for a short time during the closing days of the war.

He edited a newspaper in Wilmington, North Carolina, during the two years that remained to him after the war.

Barry, William Farquhar
(1818-1879) Union general

Born in New York, this West Point graduate served on the frontier, in the Mexican War and in the Seminole War. He fought at

First Bull Run and was appointed a brigadier general in August 1861. He served as chief of artillery in the Peninsular Campaign and fought at Yorktown, Gaines's Mill, Mechanicsville, Charles City Crossroads, Malvern Hill and Harrison's Landing. He was chief of artillery of the defenses of Washington (1862-1864) and became W.T. Sherman's chief of artillery in March 1864. He remained in the regular army after the war and headed the army's artillery school at Fort Monroe for 10 years, dying a colonel on active duty.

Barton, Clara
(1821-1912) Humanitarian

A farmer's daughter, born near Oxford, Mass., Clara (Clarissa Harlow) Barton grew up as virtually an only child, for her next elder sibling was seven years her senior. Her public-spirited father, Stephen Barton, a veteran of Anthony Wayne's Indian campaigns, served as a selectman

William Farquhar Barry (above) and (below) John Decatur Barry

and state legislator. Her mother, Sarah Stone, and her older brothers and sisters attended to her primary education. As partial repayment, she skillfully nursed her brother David through a two-year illness, tending him day and night, almost without respite, with a toughness and stamina that would see her through many hard times on Civil War battlefields.

Independent and willful even as a girl, Barton went to work as a schoolteacher at the age of 15. For a decade she superintended a school for the children of North Oxford millhands. She studied at the Liberal Institute in Clinton, N.Y., in 1851 and, after a period of recuperation from a nervous ailment, accepted an unusual teaching position in Bordentown, N. J., for Barton offered to teach without salary for three months if the town agreed to provide, in return, a free education for all its children. The Bordentown school flourished under the Barton system. Indeed, it expanded so rapidly that the town officials decided it could no longer be entrusted to a woman's management, and when they

LEFT: Clara Barton.

BELOW: Clara Barton tended Union troops wounded in the 1861 Baltimore riots.

Washington's Armory Square Hospital was far better equipped than most of those in which Clara Barton served.

hired a male principal to supervise Barton's activities she angrily resigned.

Moving to Washington, D.C., in 1854, Barton obtained a clerkship in the U.S. Patent Office and settled in the capital. On the outbreak of Civil War in April 1861 she became one of the first volunteers to minister to the Union sick and wounded, collecting medical supplies and providing nursing care for the casualties of the 6th Massachusetts, a militia regiment caught in a riot in Baltimore as it made its way to Washington.

After the Union defeat at the First Battle of Bull Run/Manassas in July, Barton advertized in a Massachusetts newspaper for provisions for the sick and wounded, and she received such enormous quantities that she set up her own distribution agency. By July 1862 she had obtained the surgeon general's permission to work in the front lines.

Only five feet tall, frail and slightly built, with prominent features and a mass of thick brown hair, she became a familiar figure in Army of the Potomac camps and field hospitals, handing out medicines and comforts and providing nursing care. The troops soon came to call her "the angel of the battlefield."

She operated almost entirely on her own, a free lance with no connection with the private aid agencies such as the Sanitary Commission or with the army itself, though for one period she bore the semi-official title of supervisor of nurses for the Army of the James. She carried her work to Charleston, S.C., during siege operations there in 1863 and set up in Fredericksburg during Ulysses S. Grant's Wilderness and Spotsylvania campaigns in 1864.

At President Lincoln's request, Barton organized a postwar search for missing soldiers. She also lectured widely on her wartime experiences. In 1869, her health again failing, she went abroad, only to find herself caught up in the Franco-Prussian war of 1870-71. She collected and distributed supplies throughout the battle zone under the auspices of the International Red Cross of Geneva and won acclaim from both sides in the conflict.

Returning home in 1873, she launched an eight-year campaign to establish an American branch of the Red Cross. In its isolationist way, the U.S. had refused to sign the Geneva Convention, impeding efforts to establish an American branch. Barton worked tirelessly to overcome political and bureaucratic difficulties. She saw the organization into formal existence in May 1881, became its first director and remained at the head of the American Red Cross for the next 23 years.

As she always had done, Barton kept the levers of control firmly in her own hands and expended much of her considerable energy in the field, insisting on visiting the scenes of calamity herself and seeing personally to the distribution of Red Cross assistance. She went to Turkey after the Armenian massacres of 1896. She delivered supplies to Cuban war zones in 1898. At the age of 79 she spent six weeks tending the ill and homeless in Galveston, Texas, after a devastating flood there. She disliked delegating authority, still less sharing it, and earned a well-deserved reputation as a poor manager. As a result, the American Red Cross failed to grow as an organization, membership and fundraising both lagging significantly during the last years of Barton's leadership.

After a long struggle, largely over control of finances, the board of the American Red Cross finally forced Barton aside, though she fought for her perquisites almost to the last. In the end, it took an act of Congress to bring about the reorganization and reform that left her powerless and allowed the Red Cross to expand. She resigned the directorship in June 1904 and spent the last eight years of her life in Glen Echo (outside Washington), where she died, in her 91st year, on April 12, 1912.

Edward Bates (far right) attends the 1862 cabinet meeting at which Lincoln announces his Emancipation Proclamation.

Bate, William Brimage
(1826-1905) **Confederate general, governor of Tennessee.**

Bate, a Mexican War veteran, ardent secessionist and public servant in his native Tennessee, rose from private in the Confederate army's 2nd Tennessee to major general in four years. He was wounded three times during a career that included fighting at Shiloh, Stones River, Chattanooga and Missionary Ridge and in both the Atlanta and Franklin and Nashville campaigns. He was later a powerful Tennessee Democrat, serving as governor (1882-1886) and U.S. Senator (1886-1905).

Bates, Edward
(1793-1869) **Union attorney general**

Virginia-born Bates moved to St. Louis in 1814 and there became a lawyer and moderate Republican. He gained a national reputation presiding over the River and Harbor Improvement Convention in Chicago (1847) and continued thereafter at the forefront of national politics as a Free-Soil Whig; he was considered as a Republican presidential nominee in 1860. As Abraham

Lincoln's attorney general (1861-1864), he proposed establishing the Mississippi naval fleet, but he eventually lost his initial influence by opposing West Virginia statehood, Union military policies and what he considered to be the erosion of constitutional rights. He resigned in November 1864 and spent his last years opposing radicals in Missouri.

Baxter, Henry
(1821-1873) **Union general**

Born in New York, Baxter was commissioned a captain in the Union army in August 1861 and was promoted to brigadier general in March 1863. At Fredericksburg he led a regiment that crossed the river to try to eliminate the Confederate sharpshooters and was wounded. He went on to fight at the Wilderness, Dabney's Mills and Five Forks and was wounded two more times. After the war he served as U.S. minister to Honduras (1866-1869).

Beale, Richard Lee Turberville
(1819-1893) **Confederate general**

A Virginia lawyer, legislator and Congressman (1847-1849), Beale joined the Confederacy's "Lee's Light Horse" in 1861 and won rapid promotions fighting in every Army of Northern Virginia cam-

paign – including the Peninsular Campaign, Second Bull Run, Fredericksburg and Gettysburg. His repeated resignations in 1862-1863 were refused. In March 1864 his troops intercepted Ulric Dahlgren, a Union officer carrying evidence of an assassination plot against Jefferson Davis. He returned to his Virginia law practice and political career after the war.

Richard Lee Turberville Beale

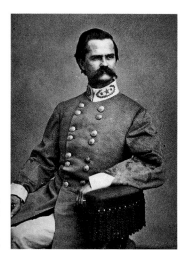

Beauregard, Pierre Gustave Toutant

(1818-1893) Confederate general

Born into a prosperous old Creole family in St. Bernard Parish, Louisiana, he attended school in New Orleans, obtained a West Point cadetship and was graduated from the military academy in 1838, second in his class. Commissioned into the engineer corps, he worked on fortifications, primarily in the New Orleans area, in the early years of his career. In 1846 he went to Mexico as an engineer on General Winfield Scott's staff and was wounded at Chapultepec the following year.

Beauregard returned to engineering duties after the Mexican War, overseeing drainage works around New Orleans, navigation improvements to the mouths of the Mississippi River and the construction of the New Orleans custom house. Appointed superintendent of West Point, he served just five days (early in 1861) before his outspoken secessionist sympathies led to his recall. He resigned his U.S. commission on February 20, 1861, and accepted an appointment as a brigadier general in the Confederate army, with command of the defenses of Charleston, South Carolina.

Small, animated, of soldierly bearing and courtly manner, he became the new Confederacy's first hero as the result of his role in the assault on Fort Sumter. Before dawn, April 12, at the expiration of a surrender ultimatum, he opened the bombardment on the Federal harbor fort, forcing the garrison's capitulation some 34 hours and 4,000 shells later. The Sumter success gained him command of one of the two field armies forming in northern Virginia. On June 1 he took charge of the army assembling at Manassas, 30 miles from Washington. Beauregard received much of the credit for the Confederate victory at the Battle of First Manassas/Bull Run, leading from the front while Joseph E. Johnston, who outranked him, fed reinforcements from his own Shenandoah army into the battle. This victory of July 21 raised Beauregard higher than ever in public esteem. Jefferson Davis soon approved his promotion to full general.

Transferred to the western theater early in 1862, he served as A. S. Johnston's second in command at the Battle of Shiloh, succeeding Johnston when he fell mortally wounded on the afternoon of April 6. Beauregard actually wired news of a decisive victory to Richmond that evening, but the Federal forces under Ulysses S. Grant rallied the next day, counterattacked and

Pierre Gustave Toutant Beauregard

turned an apparent Confederate victory into a serious setback. Beauregard retreated to Cornith, Mississippi., where he fell victim to a siege and then to the collapse of his health. When he returned from a long sick leave, Davis removed him from the western command and reassigned him to the coastal defenses of Georgia and the Carolinas. There, his forces checked Union attacks on Charleston in 1863.

Beauregard's military reputation rested on his ability to defend static positions. Critics found him lacking in the qualities of

coolness, enterprise and vision necessary for success on a fluid battlefield. Nevertheless, he led his small command to an open-field victory over the Federal Army of the James at Drewry's Bluff, Virginia, in May 1864 and kept the James army bottled up in Bermuda Hundred while Grant moved down from the Rapidan. After Grant's crossing of the James in June, Beauregard conducted a successful initial defense of the strategic communications center of Peters-

burg, repulsing repeated attacks until Lee finally recognized the threat and sent the Army of Northern Virginia to his assistance. When Grant's Petersburg initiative ended in a siege, Lee absorbed Beauregard's command. Toward the war's end Beauregard returned to the West, where he became Johnston's second-in-command, serving through the Carolinas Campaign. He surrendered with Johnston in late April 1865.

After the war Beauregard turned down offers of senior commands in the Rumanian and Egyptian armies. He headed the New Orleans, Jackson & Mississippi Railway for five years, managed the Louisiana lottery and, in 1888, became commissioner of public works in New Orleans. Among his extensive writings on military affairs were *Report on the Defense of Charleston* (1864) and *A Commentary on the Campaign and Battle of Manassas* (1891).

Bee, Bernard Elliott
(1824-1861) Confederate general

Born in South Carolina, he moved with his family to Texas and obtained a West Point cadetship in 1841. Bee was graduated in 1845, fought in the Mexican War and served on the frontier throughout the 1850s. Resigning in March 1861, he entered Confederate service and took command of a brigade in Joseph E. Johnston's army in June. It was Bee who gave Thomas J. Jackson his *nom de guerre* during the First Battle of Bull Run, July 21, 1861. "Look at Jackson's brigade," he cried, "it stands like a stone wall! Rally behind the Virginians!" Wounded shortly thereafter, he died the next day.

Beecher, Henry Ward
(1813-1887) Clergyman and reformer

Brother of Harriet Beecher Stowe and himself an outspoken opponent of slavery (although he advocated allowing it to wither away in the slave states), he was probably the best-known Protestant minister of his day. During the violence that overran Kansas in 1854-59, carbines were shipped to the anti-slavery proponents in boxes marked "Bibles" to disguise their true contents. These weapons came to be known as "Beecher's Bibles" because Beecher had publicly declared that there was "more moral power in one of these in-

ABOVE: The First Battle of Bull Run.

BELOW: Henry Ward Beecher, with his sister, Harriet Beecher Stowe, the author of the novel *Uncle Tom's Cabin*.

struments so far as the slaveholders were concerned than in a hundred Bibles." Pastor of the Plymouth Congregational Church in Brooklyn, N.Y., since 1847, he became editor of the *Independent* in 1861. A series of lectures he delivered in England in 1863 is credited with doing much to gain British sympathy for the Union cause.

William Worth Bellknap

Belknap, William Worth
(1829-1890) Union general

A New York native, he was graduated from Princeton, practiced law and served in the Iowa legislature. Belknap obtained a U.S. commission in the 15th Iowa in December 1861 and fought at Shiloh, Corinth and Vicksburg. He commanded a brigade during W. T. Sherman's Atlanta Campaign. Charged with corruption as President Ulysses S. Grant's secretary of war (1869-1876), he resigned before he could be brought to trial. The charges eventually were dropped.

Bell, John
(1797-1869) Southern statesman

He was born in Nashville and became a prominent lawyer there. As a U.S. Representative (1827-1841) he at first supported Andrew Jackson; after a subsequent rift, he led the Tennessee Whigs for 20 years. He was briefly President William Henry Harrison's secretary of war (March-September 1841). His moderation alienated Southerners during his U.S. Senate career (1847-1859) and doomed his presidential candidacy on the Constitutional Union ticket in 1860. He worked to keep Tennessee in the Union, but was finally forced to recommend a Confederate alliance.

Benham, Henry Washington
(1813-1884) Union general

This Connecticut-born West Point graduate served as an army engineer in the Mexican War. In the Civil War he commanded a Union brigade in the occupation of western Virginia and later (April 1862) played a role in the capture of Fort Pulaski, Georgia. Charged with disobedience for ordering a disastrous attack at Secessionville (June 1862), he was relieved of command and his brigadier general's rank. Reappointed brigadier general (February 1863), he worked as an army engineer, and redeemed his reputation by constructing pontoon bridges during the Chancellorsville Campaign and at Franklin's Crossing. He is perhaps best remembered for building the famed James River bridge in 1864. He remained in the regular army until 1882.

Benjamin, Judah Philip
(1811-1884) Confederate statesman

Born in St. Thomas, British West Indies, the son of Jewish parents, he moved with his family to Charleston, where he attended a local academy before going north to Yale at the age of 14. He left after two years without taking a degree. Returning to the South in 1828, he accepted a job with a merchant in New Orleans. He meanwhile studied law, opened a practice and began to rise rapidly in the profession.

Benjamin's participation in the case of the brig *Creole* solidified his growing reputation. His brief, which reviewed the status of slavery under U.S. and international

The first Confederate cabinet, 1861: Judah Benjamin (4 o'clock position) was the Confederate attorney general.

law, was reprinted and widely read. For a time he ran a sugar plantation but encountered financial difficulties and soon returned to law and its near relation, politics. He served in the Louisiana legislature and in 1852 won election to the U.S. Senate as a Whig. The political crisis over slavery turned him gradually toward the Democratic party, which he formally joined in 1856.

Upon Abraham Lincoln's election to the presidency in 1860 Benjamin became one of the strongest supporters of secession. He resigned from the Senate in early February 1861 after Louisiana left the Union, and within a few weeks he accepted Jefferson Davis's offer of the Confederate States' attorney generalship. He got on well with Davis from the start, and in September 1861 Davis appointed him secretary of war, succeeding the ineffectual Leroy P. Walker. Within a few months, Benjamin had become one of the most unpopular men in the South, blamed for the Confederacy's first defeats, at Roanoke Island, North Carolina, and forts Henry and Donelson in the Kentucky-Tennessee theater.

A congressional investigating committee, in search of a scapegoat, found Benjamin responsible for the loss of Roanoke Island. Davis stood by him staunchly, easing the pressure on him slightly in early March 1862 by naming him secretary of state. Benjamin seemed to lack political in-

Judah Philip Benjamin

stincts, and some of his political problems were of his own making. In one famously clumsy instance he quipped that Confederate soldiers were barefoot not because the army failed to supply them with shoes but because they traded their footwear for whiskey.

Benjamin did not appear to mind being the object of almost universal dislike. He was, and remained, one of the most clear-sighted of Confederate leaders. He became one of the first to discard the hallowed Southern political principle of states' rights, recognizing that it served as a brake on the central authority's ability to wage war. States' rights policies on conscription and taxation, he argued, would lead to the Confederacy's ruin. He had no particular interest in preserving the institution of slavery: in 1864 he campaigned in favor of educating slaves, drafting them into the Confederate military forces and sending them into combat. In return, slave veterans would be granted their freedom.

William Plummer Benton saw most of his Union army service in the West.

The proposal outraged most Southerners. "If we didn't go to war to save our slaves what did we go to war for?" Senator Robert Hunter asked. In January 1865 Benjamin sent a diplomatic emissary to England to offer general emancipation in return for British intervention and the raising of the Federal blockade. But the offer came too late, and the Confederacy's last diplomatic gambit ended in failure. As for Benjamin, he narrowly survived censure by congress, the Confederate senate dividing evenly in February on the resolution that he had not been "a wise and prudent Secretary of State."

It hardly mattered by then. Benjamin lasted in office as long as Robert E. Lee did, fleeing south with Davis in April 1865. He took leave of the presidential party in Charlotte, North Carolina, and made good his escape to England. Penniless, he studied for the English bar and supported himself with journalism, specializing in articles on international relations. His Lincoln's Inn colleagues waived the three-year rule and admitted him to practice in June 1866, after only five months of study. He gradually built a successful practice, which he continued until failing health forced his retirement in 1883. He died in Paris the following year.

Benning, Henry Lewis
(1814-1875) Confederate general

A Georgian, Benning was for 40 years a Columbus, Georgia, lawyer and legislator. An early and extreme secessionist, he attended the Nashville Convention in 1850 and his state's secession convention; on the Georgia supreme court (1853-1859) he ruled the state and federal supreme courts to be "coordinate and co-equal." In his Civil War career he fought with distinction, if not brilliance, throughout the war, after April 1863 as a brigadier general. "Old Rock" led a brigade at Antietam, Fredericksburg, Gettysburg, Chickamauga and the Wilderness, where he was seriously wounded. He recovered to fight at Petersburg and Appomattox. Fort Benning, Georgia, is named after him.

Benton, William Plummer
(1828-1867) Union general

Maryland-born, he was a judge and lawyer when he was commissioned a colonel in the Union army and fought from April until August 1861. Mustered out, he re-enlisted in September 1861 and fought under General John Frémont in Missouri and Kansas. He was appointed a brigadier general in April 1862 and fought at Pea Ridge and Vicksburg. He went on to serve in Tennessee, the Gulf, southeast Missouri and Baton Rouge. He was breveted a major general March 1865.

Berdan, Hiram
(?1823-1893) Union officer

This New York-born mechanical engineer was known as the best rifle shot in the country long before the Civil War. He also invented a repeating rifle. Commissioned a colonel of the 1st U.S. Sharpshooters in November 1861, he was breveted a brigadier general after Chancellorsville and a major general after Gettysburg. Having antagonized many who had dealings with him – he was regarded as "unscrupulous" – he resigned January 2, 1864. He went on to develop much new military technology.

Mary Ann Ball Bickerdyke

Bickerdyke, Mary Ann Ball
(1817-1901)
Sanitary Commission worker

As an Illinois widow supporting three children, she began to practice "botanic" medicine in 1859. At the onset of the war she began ministering to Illinois volunteers. "Mother" Bickerdyke worked throughout the war, evacuating the wounded from Fort Donelson, then running field hospitals with Ulysses S. Grant's army in Tennessee and Mississippi and with W. T. Sherman's in the Chattanooga and Atlanta campaigns. Resourceful and efficient, she set up army laundries and tirelessly nursed, foraged and cooked through 19 battles. Her colorful personality and Northern fundraising tours made her the most famous Sanitary Commission worker of the war. She later engaged in charitable ventures in San Francisco before retiring to Kansas with a Congressional pension in 1887.

Birney, David Bell
(1825-1864) Union general

Son of a prominent abolitionist, he became a Philadelphia lawyer. In response to the looming crisis, in 1860 he studied military manuals and joined the militia; in 1861 he raised a Pennsylvania regiment. He led a brigade in the Peninsular and Second Bull Run campaigns. Succeeding Philip Kearny's division command, he then fought at Fredericksburg and Chancellorsville. At Gettysburg he assumed command of III Corps after General Daniel Sickles was wounded. He died from the effects of malaria the following year.

Birney, James Gillespie
(1792-1857) Abolitionist leader

Born in Kentucky, he practiced law there and in Alabama and began working to restrict slavery and the slave trade. Back in Kentucky in 1832 he became ever more outspoken in his opposition to slavery, and in 1836 he founded an abolitionist newspaper, the *Philanthropist*. In 1840 and 1844 he was the presidential candidate for the abolitionist Liberty Party.

William Birney

Birney, William
(1819-1907) **Union general**

Born in Alabama, he was active in the revolution of 1848 while in France and was made a professor at Bourges. Like his father, James G. Birney, he was fervently opposed to slavery. Commissioned a captain in the Union army in May 1861, he fought at First and Second Bull Run, Chantilly and Fredericksburg, and he helped the Union to regain parts of Florida in 1864. He also helped to raise seven African-American regiments that went to the field. Breveted a major general and mustered out in August 1865, he served as attorney for the District of Columbia after the war.

Blackwell, Elizabeth
(1821-1910) **Physician**

The first-ever woman medical school graduate (Geneva College, New York, 1849), this Englishwoman helped to found a women's infirmary (1857) and medical college (1868) in New York. Her initiative in organizing women's relief work in 1861 led to the establishment of the Sanitary Commission; she trained Union nurses throughout the Civil War. She lived in

Elizabeth Blackwell

England after 1869, retiring in 1876. Her promotion of sanitation and preventive medicine were important contributions to public health.

Blair, Francis Preston Jr.
(1821-1875)
Union statesman and general

Kentucky-born Blair organized the Free-Soil (1848) and Republican parties in Missouri and achieved national prominence as a Unionist orator, as a state legislator and as a U.S. Congressman in the 1850s. He saved Missouri and Kentucky for the Union by seizing the St. Louis arsenal in May 1861.

Blair participated in the Yazoo expedition, Vicksburg and, as a major general and corps commander, the Chattanooga and Atlanta campaigns. He turned Democrat after opposing Reconstruction policies and was a U.S. Senator (Missouri, 1871-1873).

Blair, Montgomery
(1813-1883)
Lawyer, Union postmaster general

Son of a prominent political leader, Francis P. Blair, he was graduated from West Point (1835) but resigned his commission in 1836 to become a lawyer. A moderate on the slavery question, he represented Dred Scott in the Supreme Court. Having become a Republican, he was named postmaster general by President Lincoln and organized the army's postal system during the Civil War. Suspect because of his Southern and Democratic past, he was forced out of office in 1864 by more radical Republicans; after the war he went back to the Democratic Party. The Blair family home, across from the White House, was purchased by the U.S. government in 1942 and is now used to house high-ranking foreign visitors.

Blenker, Louis
(1812-1863) Union general

Born in Germany, Blenker participated in the 1848 revolution and was forced to leave Germany, coming to the United States in 1849. He was commissioned a colonel in the Union Army in 1861, and his regiment covered the Union retreat at First Bull Run. He was appointed a brigadier general

in 1861, and in March 1862 he led a division of German brigades in a difficult six-week march from George McClellan's Army of the Potomac command to join John Frémont in West Virginia, subsequently

ABOVE: Louis Blenker (left center), leader of German-American Troops.

BELOW: Francis Preston Blair, Jr., has been credited with saving Missouri and Kentucky for the Union.

taking part in several battles in the Shenandoah Campaign of 1862. Discharged on March 31, 1863, he died on October 31, 1863, of injuries he sustained from an earlier fall from his horse.

Blunt, James Gilpatrick
(1826-1881) Union general

This Maine-born doctor practiced in Ohio and then moved on to a political career in Kansas, where he was a supporter of John Brown. Appointed a lieutenant colonel in the Union army in July 1861, he was promoted to major general in November 1862. He fought successfully with the Army of the Frontier at Cane Hill and Prairie Grove, captured Fort Van Buren and then suffered a sharp defeat at Baxter Springs. He beat back Sterling Price's Raid in Missouri, ending the Confederate threat in the West. He was mustered out in July 1865.

Bonham, Milledge Luke
(1813-1890) Confederate general

Born in South Carolina, Bonham fought in the Seminole War and in the Mexican War. A lawyer by training, he was named to Congress as a states-rights Democrat to finish out the term of his cousin, Preston Brooks. He chose to serve under General P. G. T. Beauregard in the initial firing at Fort Sumter, was appointed a brigadier general in the Confederate army in April

Milledge Luke Bonham

1861 and fought at Fairfax, Centreville, Vienna and First Bull Run. He resigned in January 1862 to serve as governor of South Carolina (1862-1864). He was reappointed brigadier general on February 20, 1865, to serve under General Joseph Johnston until the surrender. After the war he was a Democratic politician, legislator and railroad commissioner.

Bonneville, Benjamin Louis Eulalie de
(1796-1878) Union officer, explorer

French-born, he was brought to the U.S.A. as a child. He was a West Point graduate (1815) and became publicly known for his western exploratory expedition (1831-1836); his journal was later used by

Washington Irving to write *The Adventures of Captain Bonneville* (1843). He fought in the Mexican War, retired from active duty in September 1861 due to disabilities but continued to command recruiting and mustering activities in Missouri throughout the war. He was a breveted brigadier general and served until 1866.

Booth, John Wilkes
(1838-1865) Lincoln's assassin

He was born and raised on a farm near Bel Air, Maryland, one of a large family. An active child, good-looking, athletic and adventurous, Booth received an irregular

Benjamin Louis Bonneville

John Wilkes Booth

From the outbreak of the Civil War, Booth was a zealous Southern sympathizer and a great supporter of slavery, though he made no effort to enlist in the Confederate army and fight for his beliefs. He viewed the war as a simple struggle between freedom and tyranny; Edwin Booth thought him "insane" on the subject. By 1864 Booth had hatched a plot to kidnap President Lincoln and carry him away to Richmond, where he could be held hostage to force a successful end to the war.

His acting now took second place to conspiracy. He recruited two former Confederate soldiers and a onetime Roman Catholic seminarian, John Surratt, who had been a dispatch rider for the Confederacy. Surratt's mother, Mary, kept a boarding house in Washington, and it provided an occasional meeting place for the conspirators. By early 1865 he had recruited three more men, including Lewis T. Powell, also known as Payne, a near-destitute Confederate veteran of the Battle of Gettysburg.

The conspirators planned a March 20 abduction of Lincoln as he drove to the Soldier's Home on Washington's outskirts, but the president failed to turn up. Fearing the authorities had found them out, the group separated. In early April, Robert E. Lee surrendered the Army of Northern Virginia, effectively ending the war and making the notion of kidnapping Lincoln irrelevant. Booth decided instead to kill him.

He learned at midday on April 14 that Lincoln was to attend a performance of the English farce *Our American Cousin* at Ford's Theatre that evening. He assigned two remaining members of his band the tasks of killing Vice President Andrew Johnson and Secretary of State William Seward. Booth himself entered the presidential box shortly after 10 p.m., raised his pistol and shot Lincoln in the head. He leaped down from the box on to the stage, shouting "*Sic temper tyrannis!* The South is avenged!" He broke his left leg in the fall but managed to escape the theater and flee the city. Johnson was not attacked, but Powell (a.k.a. Payne) assaulted and seriously injured Seward. Lincoln died on the morning of April 15.

Booth evaded capture for nearly two weeks. Dr. Samuel Mudd, a Maryland physician, set his broken leg. He crossed into Virginia on April 23. Early on the 26th his pursuers trapped him in a barn. When he refused to surrender the barn on fire. A shot rang out. Pulled mortally wounded from the burning barn, Booth died a few hours later.

education and preferred passing the day with Chesapeake Bay watermen to going to school. Stage-struck like others in his family, he made his acting debut at age 17 at the St. Charles Theater in Baltimore.

In 1857-58 Booth played minor roles at the Arch Street Theater in Philadelphia, where his failure to learn his parts adequately made him unpopular with audiences. He soon achieved distinction, however, especially in Shakespearean roles. In 1860, on tours of the South, the Southwest and finally the North, he became an acknowledged star.

He acted in Boston and Washington, D.C., in 1862-63, and his reputation rose steadily. Even his brother, Edwin Booth, a much more famous actor, saluted him as one of America's great young stage talents. His repertoire included *Richard III*, in which he played a realistic and widely admired royal death scene, *Hamlet, Romeo and Juliet* and popular favorites such as *The Robbers* and *The Corsican Brothers*.

John Wilkes Booth murders Lincoln in Fords' Theatre, April 14, 1865

His accomplices were quickly rounded up. Four of them, including Mary Surratt, were convicted of conspiracy by a military tribunal and hanged. Mudd received a sentence of life imprisonment. (He was later pardoned.) Though the government claimed Booth had been in conspiracy with Jefferson Davis and the Confederate government, no evidence of such a link was ever found.

A poster offering rewards for the capture of Booth and two others

Boyd, Belle
(1844-1900) Confederate spy

Born Isabelle Boyd in Martinsburg, Virginia (now West Virginia), she attended Mount Washington Female College in Baltimore and was in due course formally presented to Washington, D.C. society. Returning to Martinsburg at the outbreak of the war, she traded on her considerable presence to elicit military information from occupying Union soldiers and pass it to the Confederates. Her charm was such that when she shot and killed an abusive Union soldier there was no question of her being punished for the act. As a courier to P. G. T. Beauregard and T. J. Jackson after autumn 1861, she was especially useful for her equestrian skill and intimate knowledge of the local terrain. She became a Confederate heroine in May 1862 by signalling Jackson's troops to accelerate their advance to save the bridges at Front Royal. Three times arrested, she escaped to England carrying Confederate dispatches in 1864 and was again captured. She subsequently married her captor, Union Lieutenant Samuel Wylde Hardinge, Jr., in London. He died soon afterward, and to support herself she wrote a dramatic (and unreliable) account of her espionage career (1865) and became an actress. Making her stage debut in Manchester, England, in 1866, she then toured the U.S. until she remarried in 1869. She took to the stage again after her third marriage in 1886, when, once again in financial straits, she began presenting popular dramatic recitals of her wartime adventures. She died while on tour.

Bradley, Amy Morris
(1823-1904)
Educator, Sanitary Commission worker

A New England teacher, she joined the 5th Maine as a nurse at First Bull Run, then

supervised Sanitary Commission hospital ships throughout the Peninsular Campaign. After December 1862 she transformed Camp Distribution, a squalid convalescent camp near Alexandria, Virginia, into a clean, efficient operation and edited the *Soldiers' Journal*, which disseminated practical information to Federal troops. She later established schools for the poor in Wilmington, North Carolina, and retired in 1891.

ABOVE: Mathew B. Brady, the world's first great war photographer.

OPPOSITE TOP: Belle Boyd, perhaps the most famous Southern spy.

OPPOSITE BOTTOM: Mathew Brady in the field (wearing straw hat).

Brady, Mathew B.
(1823-1896) Photographer

Established as a New York portrait photographer by 1843, he early worked in daguerreotype, publishing the *Gallery of Illustrious Americans* (1850) and winning numerous international prizes. He adopted the new photographic wetplate technology in the mid-1850s and opened a successful Washington, D.C., studio in 1858. Early in the Civil War he sought Lincoln's authorization to photograph camp and battle scenes. Accompanying Federal troops with cumbersome wetplate cameras, often at great personal risk, Brady and his assistants compiled a documentary record of 3500 photographs that preserves some of our most enduring and valuable images of the conflict. His career collapsed after the war, and he died in poverty.

Braxton Bragg

Bragg, Braxton
(1817-1876) Confederate general

Bragg, a North Carolinian, was graduated from West Point in 1837, fought in the Seminole War and saw distinguished service in Mexico, where he won acclaim for the performance of his battery at Buena Vista in February 1847. He resigned from the army in 1856 to become a planter in Louisiana.

Appointed a brigadier general in the Confederate army in February 1861, he commanded the coastal defenses between Mobile and Pensacola. He helped Albert Sidney Johnston reorganize the Army of Tennessee in northern Mississippi in the early spring of 1862 and led Johnston's right wing at Shiloh in April. Promoted to full general shortly after the battle, he took charge of the Army of Tennessee in June. In late August, Bragg launched his invasion of Kentucky, with the political aim of drawing the state into the Confederacy. After the drawn battles of Perryville (October 1862) and Stones River (December 1862-January 1863) he withdrew to Tullahoma, the campaign a failure.

Federal forces under William J. Rosecrans maneuvered Bragg out of Tullahoma, and then out of Chattanooga, in the summer of 1863. Bragg attacked Rosecrans along Chickamauga Creek on September 19 and 20, driving the Federals back to Chattanooga with heavy losses. This was potentially a great victory, but Bragg failed to exploit his initial advantage. Instead of pressing the attack, he drew his army up into the hills above Chattanooga and besieged the city.

U.S. Grant reopened a supply line into Chattanooga in October and launched a breakout attempt on November 23. Two days later the Confederate center on Missionary Ridge collapsed, forcing Bragg to retreat into north Georgia. Joseph E. Johnston relieved him of command of the Army of Tennessee on December 2.

Bragg's difficult personality compounded his lack of battlefield success. Irritable, disputatious, dyspeptic, he made many enemies among the senior officers and inspired little affection in the ranks. Senior subordinates such as James Longstreet, D. H. Hill and William Hardee had no confidence in him. "The tone of the army among its higher officers toward the commander was the worst conceivable," Longstreet's aide, G. Moxley Sorrel, wrote of the period after Chickamauga. "Bragg was the subject of hatred and contempt, and it was almost openly so expressed."

Bragg served as an adviser to President Jefferson Davis through most of 1864. He returned to the field toward the war's end and fought his last battle against W. T. Sherman's forces in North Carolina in March 1865. He joined Davis in his attempt to escape Union forces; taken prisoner on May 9, he was paroled shortly thereafter.

He worked as a civil engineer in Texas and Alabama after the war, served a four-year term as Alabama's commissioner of public works and supervised a harbor improvement scheme at Mobile. He died in Galveston, Texas.

Branch, Lawrence O'Bryan
(1820-1862) Confederate general

Born into a well-to-do family in North Carolina, of which state his uncle was the governor, he became a journalist, lawyer and Democratic Congressman before the war. He had initially been an advocate of moderation in the South, but he joined the secessionists and enlisted in the Confederate army. He served as quartermaster and paymaster of the North Carolina troops and was made a brigadier general in November 1861. He fought at Hanover Courthouse, in the Seven Days' Battles and at Second Bull Run and Harpers Ferry. He was killed at Antietam.

Brannan, John Milton
(1819-1892) Union general

Born in Washington, D.C., Brannan was a West Point graduate who served on the frontier and in the Mexican and Seminole wars. Appointed a Union brigadier general in September 1861, he fought at Pocotaligo, Hoover's Gap and Chickamauga; led the St. John's River expedition; was chief of artillery for the Army of the Cumberland; and was at Mission Ridge, Dalton, Resaca, Dalls, Kenesaw Mountain, Chattahoochee, Peach Tree Creek, Atlanta and Jonesboro. He remained in the regular army until his retirement in 1888.

Breckinridge, John Cabell
(1821-1875) Confederate general and secretary of war.

He was born near Lexington, Kentucky, into a politically powerful Deomcratic family. After graduation from Centre College and studying law at Transylvania University, he practiced law in Iowa and Kentucky. He joined the 3rd Kentucky Volunteers too late to fight in the Mexican war and returned to Kentucky to begin a political career. As a U.S. representative (1851-1855), he established a national reputation with his funeral oration for Henry Clay (1852). He was President James Buchanan's vice president (1857-18610 and ran against Abraham Lincoln in 1860 as the candidate of the breakaway Southern Democrats. In the U.S. Senate (March-September 1861) he unsuccessfully promoted compromise, then helped to organize Kentucky's provisional Confederate government. He joined the Confederate army as a brigadier general in November 1861. Natural leadership outweighing his inexperience, Breckinridge commanded the reserve corps with distinction at Shiloh and, promoted to major general, led a division at Stones River. He fought in the Vicksburg Campaign, unsuccessfully attacked Baton Rouge and fortified Port Hudson. He later commanded divisions at Chickamauga and Missionary

John Cabell Breckenridge

Ridge. Summoned to the Shenandoah Valley, he fought at Cold Harbor. In Jubal Early's Washington Raid in the summer of 1864 he fought at Martinsburg and Monocacy. He served as the Confederate secretary of war after February 1865 and advised J. E. Johnston during surrender negotiations. He returned from foreign exile in 1868 and resumed his Lexington law practice and developed railroads.

Breckinridge, Margaret E.
(?1832-1864)
Sanitary Commission worker

Born in New Jersey, she came from a family divided between Confederate and Union sympathies, her most notable relation being to her cousin, Confederate General John Breckinridge. She was an agent with the Sanitary Commission and a nurse from 1862, serving under Ulysses S. Grant. She also ran a boat carrying aid between St. Louis and Vicksburg. She died in July 1864 from exhaustion and typhoid fever.

Margaret E. Breckenridge

Brooke, John Mercer
(1826-1904) **Confederate naval officer**

This Florida-born Annapolis graduate became the Navy's chief of ordnance and hydrography; he invented a deep-sea sounding device used to map the topography of the ocean's bottom. Joining the Confederate navy, he helped in the reconstruction of the USS *Merrimack* into the ironclad vessel CSS *Virginia*. He was also known for his invention of the Brooke Gun, a rifled cannon shaped like the Parrott gun but differing in its reinforcing band of iron rings. After the war Brooke taught at the Virginia Military Institute.

Brooke, John Rutter
(1838-1926) **Union general**

He joined the Union's infamous 4th Pennsylvania Infantry in 1861, which claimed its discharge and returned home rather than fight at First Bull Run. Brooke re-enlisted and fought in the Peninsular Campaign, Antietam, Fredericksburg, Chancellorsville, Gettysburg, the Wilderness, Spotsylvania and Cold Harbor, there sustaining

wounds that ended his field career. In the regular army, after 1866, he served in the Spanish-American war, commanded the Department of the east and retired as a major general in 1902.

Preston Brooks

Brooks, Preston
(1819-1857)
South Carolina Representative

He was a Democratic member of the House of Representatives (1853-57) when, in 1856, Senator Charles Sumner of Massachusetts, an impassioned anti-slavery proponent, delivered a speech in the Senate that criticized Brooks's uncle, Senator Andrew P. Butler of South Carolina. Two days later (May 22) Brooks came upon Sumner seated at his desk in the Senate and beat him severely with his cane. Sumner was so seriously injured that it was over three years before he could return to take his seat in the Senate.

Brooks, William Thomas Harbaugh
(1821-1870) **Union general**

An Ohio-born West Point graduate, Brooks fought in the Indian wars and under Robert E. Lee in the Mexican War. He fought with the Army of the Potomac in the Peninsular, Antietam and Rappahannock campaigns, commanded the District of the Monongahela (June 1863-April 1864), led a division at Cold Harbor and Drewry's Bluff and X Corps at Petersburg, before resigning in ill-health in June 1864. He farmed in Alabama after the war.

Brown, John
(1800-1859) **Abolitionist**

He was born in Torrington, Connecticut, into a family with a history of mental instability: Brown's mother died insane when he was only 8 years old. His father, an itinerant handyman and jack of several trades, supported the abolition cause and worked for a time on the underground railroad. He moved often in John's early years, finally settling in Hudson, Ohio.

Brown absorbed a little learning in the Hudson school, took up the trade of tanner and married Dianthe Lusk in 1820; the couple had seven children before she died in 1831. Less than a year later he married again, a 16-year-old named Mary Anne

John Brown (below) and (opposite) *en route* to his execution

Day. They produced 13 more children over the following 21 years.

He set up a tannery in Richmond, Pennsylvania, in 1825 but could not settle down. He moved some 10 times over the next three decades, pursuing various vocations, including shepherd, land speculator and farmer. He failed at everything he tried. Beset by lawsuits, he turned away from his own affairs to ponder larger issues, especially, and obsessively, slavery.

By the early 1850s he was indulging in visions of slave insurrections. Long an abolitionist like his father, he now began to dream of setting up a mountain base from which runaway slaves and their white sympathizers could sortie for terror raids against the slaveowners. In May 1855, responding to calls from several of his sons who had emigrated to Kansas, he went west to join the fight for free soil.

Brown arrived with a wagonload of weapons and settled in Osawatomie, Kansas, where, in the spring of 1856, he planned retaliation for the sacking of Lawrence by pro-slavery bands. In May, Brown and his sons carried out the cold-blooded murder of five Kansan settlers thought to be pro-slavery.

He returned east in the autumn of 1856. Old acquaintances thought he looked old, won, slightly deranged; the found him monomaniacal on the subject of slavery. "With an eye like a snake, he looks like a demon," the widow of one of the murdered men said of him. Nevertheless, respectable abolition circles embraced Brown. Emerson called him "a pure idealist of artless goodness," Several prominent Massachusetts abolitionists, the so-called "Secret Six," supplied him with money, arms and moral support, and he began recruiting men to join him in fomenting a slave uprising.

"One man and God can overturn the universe," Brown said. He chose the U.S. arsenal at Harpers Ferry, Virginia, as his first target. Renting a farm a few miles away, he laid final plans for the raid and assembled a band of 21 accomplices. He set out on the evening of October 16. The first casualty was the bridge watchman on the Baltimore & Ohio railroad – a free black, as it happened. Brown's little army took possession of the Harpers Ferry arsenal and seized several hostages, including one slaveholder.

Word of the raid spread quickly, and by midday of October 17 militia forces arrived and drove Brown's guerrillas into the shelter of the armory buildings. A detachment of U.S. Marines under Army Lt. Col. Robert E. Lee marched into Harpers Ferry that night and stormed the arsenal the next morning. Ten of the raiders were killed; Brown, slightly wounded, was captured and taken to Charles Town, Virginia, to be tried for treason.

"I believe that to have interfered as I have done, in behalf of His despised poor, is no wrong, but right," Brown told the Virginia court. He was convicted anyway, and sentenced to be hanged. On December 2, 1859, he rode in a wagon atop his own oak coffin to the scaffold outside Charles Town. He seemed to welcome his martyrdom. "I John Brown am now quite certain that the crimes of this guilty land will never be purged away but with blood," he wrote in a note to his jailer. Upon his death he became a saint to many Northern abolitionists and a demon to almost all Southerners. The blood purge he had foretold began at Fort Sumter, 17 months later.

Brown, Joseph Emerson
(1821-1894)
Confederate governor of Georgia

Born in South Carolina and educated at the Yale Law School, Brown was a Georgia legislator and judge. As a secessionist governor of Georgia (1857-1865) he reformed the militia and seized forts Pulaski and Jackson (January 1861) and the Augusta arsenal. A strong states' rights advocate, he opposed Jefferson Davis's centralization of the Confederate government. Georgians denounced his short-lived Republicanism during Reconstruction as opportunistic but later elected him U.S. Senator (Democrat, 1880-1891).

Brownell, Kady
(b.1842) **Vivandière**

The daughter of a British soldier, she was born in South Africa. She accompanied her American husband to war carrying the regimental colors and, wearing trousers under her skirts, fighting alongside the men. She fought with her husband's Rhode Island regiments at First Bull Run and New Bern. General Ambrose Burnside signed her discharge, and she received an army pension. Her last years were spent in poverty and obscurity.

Brownlow, William Gannaway
(1805-1877)
Tennessee Unionist and governor

A Virginia-born itinerant preacher, Brownlow became an influential Tennessee newspaperman, eventually editing the state's premier Whig journal, *Knoxville Whig* (1849-61). He supported slavery but joined the eastern Tennessee Unionists in 1861. Briefly imprisoned by the Confederates for treason in 1861-1862, he was a vocal Unionist lecturer, throughout the war. He was later Tennessee's Republican governor (1865-1869) and U.S. Senator (1869-1875).

Buchanan, Franklin
(1800-1874) **Confederate admiral**

Born in Maryland, Buchanan served in the U.S. Navy and helped to plan the U.S. Naval Academy under Navy Secretary George Bancroft in 1845. He served in the Mexican War, and went with Commodore Matthew Perry's expedition to China and Japan (1852-1855). He headed the Washington Navy Yard from 1859 to 1861. He resigned from the U.S. Navy in 1861 and accepted a commission as a captain in the Confederate navy, taking command of

the Chesapeake Bay Station in 1862. He was in command of the CSS *Virginia* – the rebuilt USS *Merrimac* – and was wounded in the course of capturing the USS *Congress*. In the Battle of Mobile Bay in August 1864 he was in command of the Confederate squadron that was defeated by Admiral Farragut: he was wounded in the action. He became president of Maryland State Agricultural College after the war.

Buchanan, James
(1791-1868)
15th president of the United States

After graduation from Dickinson College, he established a successful law practice in his native Pennsylvania and launched a Democratic political career. He sat in the U.S. House (1821-1831) and Senate (1834-1845) and served as U.S. secretary of state

Kady Brownell

James Buchanan

(1844-1849, negotiating the treaty ending the Mexican War); he was minister to Russia (1831-1834) and Great Britain (1852-1856). A states' rights advocate who nevertheless opposed secession, he was elected U.S. president in 1856 on a platform of conciliation. His indecisiveness when Fort Sumter was threatened and Southern states seceded left his successor, Abraham Lincoln, facing imminent war upon his inauguration in 1861. Buchanan was, however, a vocal Union advocate throughout the war.

Buckner, Simon Bolivar
(1823-1914) **Confederate general**

A farmer's son, born in Kentucky, he was graduated from West Point in 1844, taught at the academy, and fought in Mexico in 1846 and 1847. He saw frontier duty in the Minnesota and Arkansas territories before resigning from the army in 1855 to go into business.

Buckner did well in real estate and construction in Chicago. He moved to Louisville in 1858, where he continued to build the small fortune he had started in the North. Though he was not politically active, he drafted a militia bill which the Kentucky legislature adopted in March 1860. At the same time, the legislators appointed Buckner inspector general of state forces with the rank of major general. By early 1861 he had raised, trained and armed a militia of 61 companies. In May the state issued a declaration of neutrality in the Civil War, and Buckner negotiated a sort of non-belligerent agreement with George McClellan, who commanded Federal troops north of the Ohio River. The agreement fell apart after a few weeks. Buckner resigned his militia command in July, though at first he declined a commission in the Confederate army. When Confederate forces occupied Columbus, Kentucky, he urged the Confederates to withdraw; he also opposed the Kentucky legislature's decision to abandon the state's policy of neutrality.

With Kentucky drawn into the war, Buckner moved to obtain a brigadier general's appointment in the Confederate army. Sent to Fort Donelson in Tennessee early in 1862, he succeeded to command there when the two ranking officers fled their posts after being brought under siege by Ulysses S. Grant. When Grant called on Buckner to surrender, he asked for terms. He and Grant had been friends in the old army and Buckner expected favorable treatment. But Grant demanded unconditional surrender. Though this surprised and angered Buckner, he had no choice in the matter. The Federals held him prisoner until August, when he was exchanged.

He led an infantry division during Braxton Bragg's invasion of Kentucky and saw action at Perryville in October. At the year's end Jefferson Davis sent him to Mobile to strengthen that port city's defenses. He returned to Bragg's army in time to command a corps at Chickamauga. He afterward commanded the Department of Louisiana, and he helped negotiate the

Simon Bolivar Buckner

surrender of the transmississippi armies in May 1865.

Buckner settled in New Orleans after the war and became head of an insurance company there in 1866. Returning to Kentucky in 1868, he edited the Louisville *Courier* and became active in Democratic politics, serving as governor of the state from 1887 to 1891.

Buckner kept up a long friendship with Grant, despite their unhappy encounter at Fort Donelson: he was a pallbearer at Grant's funeral. He died in January 1914, the last of the high-ranking Confederate generals. His son Simon Bolivar Buckner Jr. was killed commanding the 10th Army at Okinawa in 1945.

Buell, Don Carlos
(1818-1898 Union general

Born in Ohio and raised in Indiana, Buell was graduated from West Point in 1841 and reported to the 3rd Infantry as a second lieutenant. He saw service in the Seminole War in Florida and fought in Mexico – at Monterey, Contreras and Churubusco – in 1846 and 1847.

Appointed a brigadier general of volunteers in May 1861, Buell helped organize the Army of the Potomac and commanded an infantry division under George McClellan. In November, succeeding William T. Sherman, he took command of the Department of the Ohio, with responsibility for organizing and training a new field army.

Buell's task was to advance into east Tennessee, a stronghold of Union sentiment and therefore of particular political interest to President Lincoln. As Ulysses S. Grant moved on forts Henry and Donelson, Buell advanced with the 50,000-man Army of the Ohio to Bowling Green, Kentucky, and then into central Tennessee. He occupied Nashville without a battle on February 24, 1862.

Buell received orders in March to advance south to Savannah, on the Ten-

Don Carlos Buell

nessee River, and his leading division arrived in time to save Grant from a possible defeat during the first day of the Battle of Shiloh, April 6. His reinforcements on the second day forced the Confederate retreat south to Corninth.

He marched east in July and August, repairing the railroad as he went, but could not reach Chattanooga before Braxton Bragg's Army of Tennessee occupied the place. He responded to the Confederate invasion of eastern Kentucky by falling back all the way to Louisville. On October 8, at Perryville, he engaged Bragg's army and fought a drawn battle. Buell was relieved of command when he failed to pursue the retreating Confederates aggressively. William Rosecrans replaced him on October 30.

A military commission investigated Buell's conduct but made no recommendations. He remained in limbo for more than a year, "awaiting orders" in Indianapolis, before the government discharged him as a major general of volunteers in May 1864. He resigned his regular army commission the following month.

Buell, whose reputation as a good military organizer survived the wreck of his

ABOVE: Buell took Nashville in 1862.

RIGHT: Abraham Buford.

career, may have been a victim of his association with McClellan. He was viewed as opposed to the Lincoln administration, and even Grant's recommendation could not convince the government to restore him to duty.

Buell settled in Kentucky after the war. He headed a mining concern and worked as a pension agent in Louisville in the 1880s. He died at Rockport, Kentucky.

Buford, Abraham
(1826-1894) Confederate general

A Kentucky native, Buford was graduated from West Point in 1841. He served on the frontier and fought in Mexico. He resigned in 1854 to raise cattle and horses in Kentucky. Entering the Confederate army in September 1862, he fought at Stones River and commanded a cavalry brigade under N. B. Forrest. He returned to horsebreeding after the war. The death of his wife and his son, coupled with a series of financial setbacks, led Buford to take his own life.

John Buford

Buford, John
(1826-1863) **Union general**

A Kentucky native, he was graduated from West Point in 1848 and saw extensive service on the frontier during the 1850s. Buford took charge of a Union cavalry brigade at the outset of the Second Bull Run Campaign in August 1862 and proved a first-rate cavalry commander. He led the cavalry screen that intercepted Confederate forces moving toward Gettysburg on July 1, 1863. Buford's decision to hold McPherson Ridge until Federal infantry could arrive both precipitated the great Gettysburg battle of July 1-3 and helped to secure its favorable outcome for the Union. He came down with typhoid fever in the autumn on 1863 and died from its effects on December 16.

Bulloch, James Dunwoody
(1823-1901) **Confederate naval officer**

This Georgian served in the U.S. Navy from 1839 to 1854, resigning to command a mail service steamer. As a wartime Confederate naval agent, he served in England and France outfitting such raiders as the *Alabama*, *Florida*, *Shenandoah* and *Stonewall*. After the war he stayed in Liverpool, England, as a cotton merchant. In later years he wrote a book about the Confederacy's secret foreign service (1894).

Burnett, Henry Lawrence
(1838-1916) **Union officer**

This Ohio lawyer enlisted in the Union army in 1861 and fought in Missouri and Kentucky. In 1863 he became judge advo-

cate of the Department of the Ohio. He prosecuted the white-supremacist Knights of the Golden Circle in Indiana, Chicago conspirators to free Confederate prisoners at Camp Douglas and Abraham Lincoln's assassins. In later life he was a prominent Republican strategist, a Cincinnati and New York lawyer and a federal district attorney.

Burns, John Lawrence
(1793-1872)
"The Old Hero of Gettysburg"

An ageing veteran of the War of 1812 and the Seminole and Mexican wars. Burns persistently tried to enlist with the Federals at the beginning of the Civil War. Repeatedly rejected, he doggedly accompanied the army as a teamster until he was sent home to Gettysburg, Pennsylvania, and appointed to the local constabulary. He joined in the fighting as a sharpshooter on all three days of the Battle of Gettysburg and was wounded three times. He became a folk hero, and Congress eventually voted him a pension.

Burnside, Ambrose Everett
(1824-1881) **Union general**

Born in Liberty, Indiana, and raised there in modest circumstances, he received an adequate education in the village seminary but could not afford to go on to college. He was working as a tailor's apprentice when his father won election to the Indiana senate and, through political influence, obtained a West Point appointment for him. He was graduated in 1847, 18th in a class of 38 cadets.

Burnside saw routine duty on the frontier and served in the garrison of Fort Adams, Rhode Island, before resigning in 1853 to open a factory for the production of a breechloading carbine he had invented. He drove the venture into bankruptcy in 1857. His friend George McClellan found a place for him on the Illinois Central Railroad, and he rose quickly to become its treasurer. When war came in April 1861 Burnside organized the 1st Rhode Island

John Lawrence Burns, "The Old Hero of Gettysburg"

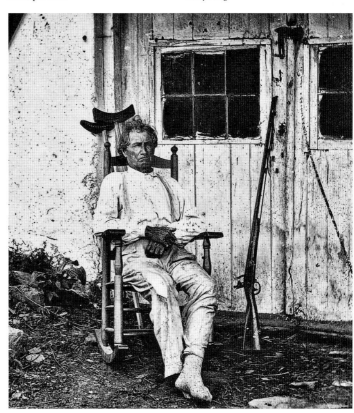

ABOVE: Ambrose Burnside and his staff.

BELOW: Ambrose Everett Burnside.

regiment. He commanded a brigade at the First Battle of Bull Run in July.

His genial nature and agreeable manners made him many friends, including President Lincoln, and his connections brought him rapid advancement in the army. In February 1862 he commanded the land forces in the capture of Roanoke Island, North Carolina, then went on to take New Bern in March and Beaufort in April. Recalled to Virginia in midsummer, he led McClellan's right wing at Antietam in September. His inept performance before what became known as "Burnside's Bridge" may have cost McClellan a decisive victory at Antietam.

In November, Lincoln relieved McClellan and put Burnside in his place as commander of the Army of the Potomac. Burnside had protested that he was not qualified for the assignment, and events proved him all too correct. He was in turn relieved after the disastrously mismanaged Battle of Fredericksburg on December 11-15 and its low comedy aftermath, the famous "Mud March" of mid-January 1863, in which his whole army became so enmired in rain-sodden ground that it could not get back across the Rappahannock to resume the fight with the Rebels.

Burnside, six feet tall, handsome, famous for his flamboyant whiskers (he gave the word "sideburns" to the language), was unlucky as well as inept. The government bought more than 55,000 of his carbines during the war, but all the profits went to the creditors who had taken over his patents. He was ill-served by his subordinates at Fredericksburg, some of whom were conspiring to see him removed from command. Yet, unlike many other failed commanders, he took full responsibility for his operations and refused to blame anyone but himself for the Fredericksburg debacle.

In March 1863 he took charge of the Department of the Ohio and launched offensive operations against the enemy behind the fighting line. In May, Burnside arrested former Congressman Clement Vallandigham, a prominent Democratic critic of the war effort, and saw him into exile with scant regard for his civil rights. He also suppressed the Chicago *Times* newspaper, an action Lincoln soon repudiated.

On the other hand, Burnside did attain a measure of success with military operations in the department. He led the little Army of the Ohio to Knoxville, Tennessee,

in early September, withstood a siege there, repulsed a general assault on November 29 and saw the Confederates withdraw early in December.

In early 1864 he returned to the Virginia theater to serve as a corps commander under Grant and Meade. He led the IX Corps in the battles of the Wilderness, Spotsylvania and Cold Harbor in May and June. At Petersburg, in late June, a Pennsylvania officer sold him on the notion or mining the Confederate stronghold at Elliott's Salient. The 511-foot-long main shaft ended with two lateral galleries filled with 8,000 pounds of black powder. The mine worked beautifully, the detonation burying parts of two enemy regiments in a crater 170 feet long, 80 feet wide and 30 feet deep. But the follow-up assault was bungled in the classic Burnside manner. The IX Corps reported 4,000 casualties, and Burnside left the army on leave. He was not recalled.

Burnside enjoyed considerable postwar success. He accepted the presidencies of two railroads, became a director of a steamship company and won election as governor of Rhode Island in 1866, 1867 and 1868. He served in the U.S. Senate from 1875 until his death on September 13, 1881.

Butler, Benjamin Franklin
(1818-1893) **Union general**

He was born in Deerfield, New Hampshire. Dramatic and effective as a speaker, Butler became a nationally influential Massachusetts criminal lawyer and Democratic politician. Always a figure of controversy, he supported Jefferson Davis, then the

Southern candidate, J. C. Breckinridge, in the 1860 presidential campaign. Following the outbreak of the war, his 8th Massachusetts helped to garrison Washington after the fall of Fort Sumter. Commanding the District of Annapolis, he peacefully occupied Baltimore in May 1861, soon thereafter being promoted to major general. He was then disastrously engaged at Big Bethel before turning south, taking forts Hatteras and Clark and, in May 1862, New Orleans. He was an arbitrary and corrupt military governor there: he confiscated Southerners' bullion on deposit with the French consul, hanged a man for taking down a

Burnside commanding his brigade at the First Battle of Bull Run

Union flag and issued the notorious "Woman Order" declaring that any woman insulting a Federal soldier would be treated as a prostitute. Removed from his New Orleans command in December 1862 after international protests, Butler took over the Army of the James, but his incompetence at Petersburg and Fort Fisher finally cost him that command as

Burnside at Fredericksburg, his first great military disaster

Benjamin Franklin Butler (seated, left center) and his staff

well. Butler is considered typical of the politically appointed generals who made such a dubious military contribution to the Union. As a Radical Republican Congressman (1867-1875, 1877-1879) he was instrumental in impeaching President Andrew Johnson. He became governor of Massachusetts (1883) after numerous unsuccessful campaigns, and in 1884 he was the National Party's unsuccessful presidential candidate.

Daniel Buttlerfield

Butterfield, Daniel
(1831-1901) Union general

A New York merchant, Butterfield led the first Union regiment to reach Virginia. He fought with distinction in the eastern theater: a brigadier general by September 1861, he earned a Medal of Honor for action at Gaines's Mill. He was chief of staff to generals Joseph Hooker and George Meade in 1863-1864, and led a division in W. T. Sherman's March to the Sea in 1864. He wrote the music for the war's most haunting melody: "Taps." After the war his extensive business interests encompassed shipping, railroads and banks.

Cabell, William Lewis
(1827-1911) Confederate general

This Virginian West Point graduate served in the quartermaster corps on the frontier and participated in the Utah Expedition (1858-1860). He organized the Confederate quartermaster, commissary and ordnance departments and was quartermaster to P. G. T. Beauregard and both Albert and Joseph Johnston. He fought at Iuka and was wounded at Corinth and Hatcher's Ridge. As a brigadier general commanding northwest Arkansas troops, he organized outstanding cavalry brigades. Captured at Marais des Cygnes in October 1864, he was imprisoned for the duration of the war. After 1872 he was a lawyer and railroad executive in Dallas, where he served four terms as mayor.

Calhoun, John Caldwell
(1782-1850) Southern statesman

He grew up in upcountry South Carolina, the son of a modestly prosperous homesteader and small slaveholder. His father, a state legislator, held strong states' rights views and opposed ratification of the federal Constitution. Young Calhoun ran the family farm for a time after his father died in 1796, then went on to study at Yale. He was graduated in 1804, read law in Connecticut and South Carolina and was admitted to the bar in 1807.

Calhoun built a successful law practice and, in 1811, married into a wealthy lowland South Carolina planter family. His wife's property, added to his own small holdings, made him financially independent and enabled him to enter public life full time. He launched his political career in 1807 with a speech denouncing British violations of American maritime rights. Cal-

John Caldwell Calhoun

houn won election to the South Carolina legislature in 1808 and to the U.S. Congress two years later. There he joined the "War Hawks" faction that agitated for war with Britain in defense of American maritime rights.

Though a supporter of the treaty of Ghent that ended the war in 1815, Calhoun lobbied for the development of a navy that would be strong enough to protect American maritime interests. He also called for a larger standing army, government support of industry, taxpayer funding on internal improvements and a national bank – positions associated with politicians who favored strong national power at the expense of states' rights. He became secretary of war in the James Monroe administration in 1817 and served in that office for more than seven years.

A powerful debater, Calhoun developed a reputation as an eloquent and persuasive public speaker, He gradually turned his talents toward a defense of states' rights against what he took to be encroachments of the federal government. He won election to the vice presidency in 1824, even though his views had begun to diverge from those of the president, John Quincy Adams. He was elected to a second term in 1828, this time with Andrew Jackson at the top of the ticket.

He and Jackson soon quarrelled, both on political and personal grounds. At the same time, South Carolina stepped up its opposition to tariffs aimed at protecting Northern manufacturers. Tariffs, the South's argument ran, caused further damage to the region's cotton economy, already in decline after several years of low prices. Calhoun argued that the federal govern-

ment had overstepped its constitutional bounds in imposing high tariffs on foreign factory goods.

This view led eventually to his theory of nullification, which held that the constitutional compact gave a state the right to declare null and void any federal law it deemed unconstitutional. "It is the Constitution that annuls an unconstitutional act," Calhoun wrote. "Such an act is itself void and has no effect." Calhoun resigned from the vice presidency in a flareup over the tariff dispute in 1832 and returned to the Senate, where he began a 20-year defense of his nullification theory.

A compromise averted a national crisis over tariffs, but Calhoun's nullification doctrine formed the theoretical underpinning for the secessionist arguments of the following political generation. The issue of slavery because the next great states' rights battleground, and Southerners turned to Calhoun to defend that "Peculiar Institution." Abolition "strikes directly and fatally, not only at our prosperity, but our existence as a people," he said in 1836.

Calhoun served in the Senate until 1843, when he resigned to take up direct management of his plantation. He returned to Washington as President John Tyler's

secretary of state in 1844 and regained his Senate seat the following year. His last Senate speech argued that Henry Clay's conciliatory bill regulating slavery in the territories (the measure became the Compromise of 1850) offered insufficient guarantees to the South. He died March 31, 1850, 11 years before nullification evolved into secession. More than any man of his time, Calhoun articulated the constitutional, political and moral assumptions that led the South out of the Union, and the nation into civil war.

Cameron, Simon
(1799-1889) Union secretary of war

Born in Lancaster County, Pennsylvania, he was early apprenticed to a printer, became a newspaper editor and, by 1824, was the publisher of the influential Harrisburg *Republican*. Various other business interests made him rich and paved the way for his entry into politics. His corrupt dealings as a commissioner for settling Winnebago claims in 1838 led to his being satirically called "The Great Winnebago Chief." He won James Buchanan's old

Simon Cameron

Senate seat as a coalition candidate in 1845. As U.S Senator (1845-1849, 1857-1861, 1867-1877) and as the organizer and highly effective party boss of his state's Republican Party (1855-1877), he dominated Pennsylvania politics for 30 years. He traded his support for Abraham Lincoln in 1860 for a cabinet post: Lincoln reluctantly honored this ill-advised promise (made by his subordinates) and named Cameron as his first secretary of war. In office Cameron presided over massive fraud and corruption in appointments and procurement, attracting widespread complaints. Equally embarrassing to the administration, he publicly advocated freeing and arming the slaves. He received a Congressional censure, and, probably to get him our of Washington, Lincoln appointed him minister to Russia in January 1862. Cameron resumed his Senate career after the war as a Radical Republican. A consummate politician dedicated to patronage rather than issues, he was particularly powerful during President Ulysses S. Grant's administration. Cameron delivered his Senate seat and state political empire to his son, James Donald Cameron, in 1877 and retired to his Pennsylvania farm.

Campbell, John Archibald
(1811-1889)
Jurist and Confederate statesman

In 1861 Campbell, a Georgian, resigned after an eight-year term on the U.S. Supreme Court, during which he had actively sought to avert the war. He was subsequently the Confederate assistant secretary of war and administrator of the conscription law (1862-1865). He was a commissioner at the Hampton Roads Peace Conference (January 1865). In later years he was one of the nation's leading lawyers, practicing in New Orleans.

Canby, Edward Sprigg
(1817-1873) **Union general**

He was graduated from West Point in 1839 and fought in the Seminole war in Florida and in Mexico. Canby held New Mexico for the Union in 1861, even though he lost the only battle of the campaign. He commanded troops in New York City in the wake of the 1863 draft riots there. Forces under Canby captured Mobile, Alabama, in April 1865; he received the surrender of the last two Confederate field armies in May. Canby later commanded U.S, forces in the Pacific Northwest. Modoc Indians murdered him during a parley in 1873.

Capron, Horace
(1804-1885) **Union officer**

Capron was born in Massachusetts. He hoped to go to West Point but failed to obtain an appointment, so he turned to scientific and large-scale farming. President Millard Fillmore appointed him a special Indian agent. He obtained a commission as a lieutenant colonel in the Union cavalry in December 1862 and served in many posts, ending as commander of a regiment in VI Cavalry Corps and breveted a brigadier general. After the war he resumed his career in farming and cattle-breeding. In 1867 he was named U.S. commissioner of agriculture. He was esteemed for his progressive farming techniques and served as an advisor to the Japanese on the development of agriculture on Hokkaido Island (1871-1875).

Horace Capron (right) and (below) Edward Sprigg Canby

Carleton, James Henry
(1814-1873) Union general

A Maine native, Carleton fought in the Aroostook War and began a long army career by joining the dragoons in 1839. His frontier and western service continued through the Civil War, In spring 1862 he raised the "Californian column" and led it to New Mexico, and as a brigadier general (April 1862) he commanded the Department of New Mexico (1862-1865). He died while on active duty in 1873.

Carr, Eugene Asa
(1830-1910)
Indian fighter and Union general

Carr was a New Yorker and West Point graduate whose 40-year career as an Indian fighter was interrupted by the Civil War. He fought for the Union with distinction at

Eugene Asa Carr

Wilson's Creek, Pea Ridge (winning a Medal of Honor), Port Gibson and Champion's Hill. He also led divisions in the Vicksburg Campaign and Mobile Campaign and commanded the District of Little Rock. His later cavalry operations against the Indians, who dubbed him "War Eagle," made him famous.

Carrington, Henry Beebee
(1824-1912) Union general

This prominent Ohio lawyer and abolitionist reorganized the state militia in 1857. In 1861 nine Ohio militia regiments saved western Virginia for the Union before volunteers could be organized. During the war he recruited 100,000 troops in Indiana and directed the controversial trials of the Sons of Liberty and the Louisville guerillas. He retired from the army in 1870. He thereafter wrote *Battle of the American Revolution* (1876) and other military and historical works.

Carroll, Anna Ella
(1815-1893) Union pamphleteer

She was the daughter of a leading Maryland Democrat. By the 1850s she had emerged as a leading polemicist of the Know-Nothing Party, lecturing widely and writing for Millard Fillmore's 1856 presidential campaign. She moved to Washington D.C., at the outbreak of the war to support Maryland's Unionists. Encouraged by a war department official, she published several substantial pamphlets and justifying Lincoln's wartime assumption of executive prerogative. She spent the rest of her life unsuccessfully demanding payment for that service and for military strategy she claimed to have supplied the government, notably for Ulysses S. Grant's Tennessee River naval operations.

Christopher (Kit) Carson

Carson, Christopher
(1809-1868)
Union officer and Indian fighter

In 1826 "Kit" Carson ran away from his native Kentucky and, in New Mexico and on southwestern expeditions, learned trapping and Indian fighting. He became famous as John C. Frémont's guide on his first expedition of exploration in 1842 and, after accompanying Frémont's second and third expeditions, became a national hero for his exploits fighting under Frémont and Philip Kearny in the Mexican War. He was later a Taos, New Mexico, Indian agent (1853-1860). In 1861 he organized a New Mexico regiment and spent the Civil War fighting Indians in New Mexico and Texas. Breveted a brigadier general in 1865, he resigned from the army in 1867.

Carter, Samuel Powhatan
(1819-1891) Union general

A Tennessee native and Princeton College graduate, Carter became a midshipman in 1840 and was graduated from Annapolis in 1846. Seconded to the war department in 1861, he served the Union throughout the war in the army and eventually held the unique double rank of major general and rear admiral. He organized the first eastern Tennessee Union volunteers and, as a brigadier general (May 1862), held a series of field commands in the Ohio and Cumberland Armies, finally commanding XXIII Corps. He is perhaps best remembered for leading the first successful Union cavalry raids of the war in the upper Tennessee Valley in December 1862. He returned to the navy after the war, served as Annapolis commandant of cadets (1877-1880) and retired in 1881.

Casey, Silas
(1807-1882) Union general

A Rhode Island-born career infantryman, he was graduated from West Point and participated the Seminole and Mexican wars and fought on the frontier. His *Casey's Tactics* (1862) was long a standard infantry manual. He was wounded in the Peninsular Campaign, then commanded the defense of Washington, D.C. (1862-1865) and trained troops. From 1863 to 1865 he superintended examinations of prospective officers of black troops. He retired in 1868.

Silas Casey

Joshua Lawrence Chamberlain

Cass, Lewis
(1782-1866) Statesman

A veteran of the War of 1812, he was an Ohio lawyer and legislator who rose to national prominence negotiating Indian treaties as governor of Michigan Territory (1813-1831). Cass served as U.S. secretary of war (1831-1836) and U.S. Senator (Michigan, 1845-1848). He ran for president in 1848. A strong Unionist, he was secretary of state (1857-60). His diplomatic successes were clouded by his resignation over President James Buchanan's failure to reinforce the Charleston forts, despite the impending war.

Chamberlain, Joshua Lawrence
(1828-1914) Union general

Born in Brewer, Maine, and educated at Bowdoin College and Bangor Theological Seminary, he was professor of rhetoric at Bowdoin when the Civil War broke out. In August 1862 he obtained a commission as a lieutenant colonel in the Union army's 20th Maine.

Chamberlain fought at Shepherdstown Ford immediately after Antietam and at Fredericksburg in December 1862. He took command of the 20th Maine in May 1863 and led it on the Gettysburg Campaign. In a decisive action, Chamberlain's regiment held the extreme Union left on Little Round Top against repeated Confederate assaults on the second day of Gettysburg, July 2, 1863.

He led the 20th Maine at Spotsylvania in May 1864 and commanded a brigade in the June 18, 1864, assault on Petersburg. Severely wounded in that battle, he returned to the army in the autumn of 1864 and fought at Five Forks on April 1, 1865, and throughout the Appomattox Campaign. Ulysses S. Grant chose Chamberlain to receive the formal surrender of the Confederate infantry at Appomattox on April 12, 1865.

After the war, Chamberlain was four times elected governor of Maine. From 1871-83 he was president of Bowdoin College, and in 1900 he obtained the patronage appointment of surveyor of the port of Portland, Maine.

Chamberlain's memoir of the last campaign, *The Passing of the Armies*, appeared in 1915, the year after his death. He died from complications of the wound he had received at Petersburg in 1864.

Chase, Salmon Portland
(1808-1873)
Union secretary of the treasury

This New Hampshire native and Dartmouth College graduate made his name as a Cincinnati lawyer who defended escaped slaves. He helped to found the Free-Soil (1848) and Republican parties (1854), served as U.S. Senator (1849-1855, 1860) and state governor (1855-1859) and attended the Washington Peace Convention (1861). As Lincoln's secretary of the treasury (1861-1864), Chase successfully financed the war with the help of private financiers, though he was forced to issue unsecured "greenback" paper currency. He also created the national banking system (1863). Dissatisfied with what he considered to be Lincoln's administrative incompetence and undue moderation in prosecuting the war, Chase became the center of a disloyal anti-Lincoln cabinet faction. Nevertheless, after Chase resigned, Lincoln appointed him to the U.S. Supreme Court (1864-1873).

Salmon Portland Chase

Mary Boykin Miller Chesnut

Chesnuts, Mary and James
Confederate notables

Born into the fourth generation of a family of Camden, South Carolina, planters, James Chesnut, Jr. (1815-1885), earned a degree at Princeton, studied law and returned home to enter politics. Sitting in the state legislature almost continuously from 1841 to 1858, he became an ardent secessionist. As a U.S. Senator (1858-November 1860) he was renowned as a fine orator and defender of slavery. He helped to draft South Carolina's secession ordinance and the permanent Confederate constitution and sat in the Confederate provisional congress (1861). He was an aide-de-camp to P. G. T. Beauregard at Fort Sumter and First Bull Run, and was later an aide-de-camp and a trusted adviser to Jefferson Davis (1862-1864). Requesting field service and appointed a brigadier general, he commanded the South Carolina reserves. He returned to state politics after the war.

James Chesnut, Jr.

as a brigadier general in the Confederate army in May 1861. He was wounded at Shiloh and again at Baton Rouge; he was also captured at the latter battle and was held prisoner until October 1863. Unable to walk properly because of his wounds, he resigned after being exchanged as a prisoner. He became governor of Mississippi (1863-1865). After the war he returned to his law practice and to resume the farming of his plantation.

Clark, Meriwether Lewis
(1809-1881) **Confederate colonel**

Named for the Meriwether Lewis who had made the famous expedition with his father, William Clark, he was graduated from West Point (1830) and served in the Black Hawk and Mexican wars. A civilian

Meriwether Lewis Clark (above) and (below) Thomas James Churchill

As the daughter of a South Carolina governor and U.S. Senator, Mary Boykin Miller Chesnut (1823-1886) was immersed in politics from childhood. She met James Chesnut, Jr., when she was a 13-year-old Charleston schoolgirl and married him four years later. The Chesnuts were at the center of Southern political life, and throughout the Civil War Mary Chesnut kept a detailed diary of the history unfolding around her. Cultured, intelligent, and compassionate, she created one of the most sensitive chronicles of the wartime Confederacy. It was published as *Diary from Dixie* (1905).

Churchill, Thomas James
(1824-1905) **Confederate general, governor of Arkansas**

This Kentucky native and Mexican War veteran was an Arkansas planter and postmaster. In 1861 he raised the 1st Arkansas Mounted Riflemen and fought at Wilson's Creek: he surrendered his outnumbered and poorly equipped force at Arkansas Post. He fought in the Red River Campaign of 1864 and at Jenkins's Ferry. He surrendered reluctantly in Texas in 1865. Churchill was later Arkansas's state treasurer (1874-1880) and governor (1881-1883)

Clark, Charles
(1810-1877) **Confederate general, governor of Mississippi**

Born in Cincinnati, Ohio, Clark moved to Mississippi in about 1830 and served in that state's legislature. He fought in the Mexican War. He accepted an appointment

engineer when the Civil War broke out, he accepted a commission as a major in the Confederate army in March 1862. He held staff positions in charge of artillery under generals Sterling Price and Braxton Bragg and ended the war as an inspector for the Confederate Ordnance Department. After the war he was both the commandant of cadets and a professor at Kentucky Military Institute.

Clark, William Thomas
(1831-1905) Union general

A Connecticut-born Iowa lawyer, he raised an Iowa regiment and fought at Shiloh, Corinth, Port Gibson and Champion's Hill. He was General James

Cassius Marcellus Clay

McPherson's adjutant general during the Vicksburg and Atlanta campaigns and ended the war commanding a division in Texas. He was "the last of the carpetbaggers" in Texas (1868-1872), then was expelled from Congress for vote-rigging. He achieved more lasting success as a Galveston banker and federal tax agent.

Clay, Cassius Marcellus
(1810-1903) Union diplomat

The son of slave-owning Kentucky planters, Clay became a staunch abolitionist while a student at Yale. Back in Kentucky, he founded a crusading abolitionist journal, *True American* (1845), served with distinction in the Mexican War and established a strong emancipation party in his state. He was a confidant of Abraham Lin-

coln. On his way to a ministerial posting in Russia (1862-1863) he briefly suspended his diplomatic appointment to consider an army commission but refused to fight until slavery was abolished. In Russia (1863-1869) he helped to negotiate the purchase of Alaska. He lived as a recluse in Kentucky in his later years.

Clay, Henry
(1777-1852) Statesman

He had three years of education in a frontier school before moving with his family from his native Hanover County, Virginia, to Richmond. He worked there as a store clerk, then in more congenial surroundings as a clerk in the chancery court. Taking up the study of law in 1796, he gained a license to practice within a year and, having moved to Lexington, Kentucky, soon built a successful practice, specializing in criminal law.

Clay entered public life in 1798 with a speech against the Sedition Act. He served in the Kentucky legislature from 1803-06 before shifting his base to the new national capital at Washington, D.C., in 1806 to serve out an unexpired U.S. Senate term. After a brief return to Kentucky, he re-entered the Senate in 1809. There he took up issues of trade and internal improvements and became a forceful advocate for the protection of American maritime rights.

Leaving the Senate again, he entered the House of Representatives and won election

Henry Clay

A pro-Democratic election cartoon of 1844 portrays Whig Henry Clay as an anglophilic aristocrat.

as House speaker in 1811. As an influential member of the "War Hawk" faction in Congress, he helped push the James Madison administration into war with Britain in 1812. Later in the decade he declined an offer to be secretary of war and began to fix his ambitions on the presidency.

Clay helped push through the Missouri Compromise in 1820, a temporary solution to the first great Congressional impasse over slavery. The compromise, simple enough in theory, maintained the sectional balance by admitting Maine as a free state and Missouri as a slave state, leaving 12 states in each column. The Compromise of 1820, as the measure was alternatively known, stilled – but did not dismiss – the slavery debate for a full political generation.

Clay retired briefly from politics, then returned to Congress in 1823 and again became House speaker. He made the first of his three unsuccessful bids for the presidency in 1824. When that disputed election went to the House of Representatives, Clay threw his vote to John Quincy Adams. He joined Adams's cabinet as secretary of state, leading to charges he had sold his support in a "corrupt bargain." Clay served four rather quiet years in the Adams cabinet. In 1833 he re-entered the Senate and became a bitter opponent of Adams's successor in the White House, the Tennessee Democrat Andrew Jackson.

Despite his frequent criticisms of those in power and his long-term feud with Jackson, Clay retained an ability to forge compromise agreements on complex issues. In 1824, for example, in the House, he had pushed through the highest tariff in America's short history. Yet eight years later, in alliance with John Calhoun, he headed off the Nullification crisis by securing passage of a compromise tariff measure that managed to appease both extremes.

The Mexican War of 1846-47 set off the slavery debate anew. Vast new western territories were America's spoils of victory over Mexico. In 1849-50 Clay, now known as "The Great Compromiser," worked to resolve the dispute that flared over the bid of one of these new territories, California, to enter the Union as a free state.

To assuage Northern opinion, Clay proposed the gradual emancipation of slaves, and he warned Southerners of the perils of secession. The Compromise of 1850 provided for California to be admitted as a free state and for the Utah and New Mexico territories to decide their future status by local vote. Slavery would be abolished in the District of Columbia. The federal government would rigorously enforce the Fugitive Slave Law – meaning federal agents would aggressively seek out runaway slaves and return them to their owners.

In its way, the compromise was a remarkable achievement. But it soon fell apart under the extraordinary stresses of the sectional conflict. The agreement could satisfy nobody for long: the Kansas-Nebraska Act of 1854 and the U.S. Supreme Court ruling in the Dred Scott case in 1857 wrecked Clay's handiwork and strengthened radicals on both sides of the Mason-Dixon line. But before these events, Clay had died (1852), still doing his best to reconcile the irreconcilable.

Clayton, Powell
(1833-1914) Union general

This Pennsylvania-born civil engineer was commissioned a captain in the Union cavalry in May 1861. He repulsed General

Powell Clayton

John Marmaduke at the Post of Pine Bluff, Arkansas. After being mustered out in August 1865, he settled in Arkansas and became a "carpetbag" politician. He was a Republican governor of that state (1868-71) and then became its U.S. Senator (1871-77), amidst charges of faulty election procedures. The charges were eventually dropped, and from 1879 to 1905 he was the U.S. ambassador to Mexico.

Cleburne, Patrick Ronayne
(1828-1864) Confederate general

This Irishman served in the British army before emigrating to the U.S. in 1849. Established as a Little Rock, Arkansas, druggist and lawyer, he helped to muster

Patrick Ronayne Clayburn

volunteers before the Civil War, He organized the Yell Rifles for the Confederacy in 1861 and seized the Little Rock arsenal. This "Stonewall Jackson of the West" performed impressively at Shiloh (promoted to brigadier general), Richmond, Kentucky (wounded) and Perryville. As a major general (December 1862), he led divisions at Stones River, Chickamauga and Chattanooga, fighting W. T. Sherman at Missionary Ridge. He commanded William Hardee's Corps in the Atlanta Campaign. He was killed in action at Franklin, Tennessee, in November 1864.

Cobb, Howell
(1815-1868) Confederate general)

He was born on a plantation in Jefferson County, Georgia, into a wealthy and socially prominent family. After attending Franklin College (later the University of Georgia), he was solicitor general of the western circuit (1837-1841). As a Democratic U.S. Representative (1843-1851, 1855-1857) he urged the extension of the Missouri Compromise line to the Pacific. His famous "Southern Address" (January 1849) and energetic campaigning incurred the implacable emnity of Southern Rights Democrats by leading Georgia to support the Union, but his moderation also won him Northern support, and he was elected speaker of the House (1849-1851). In this office he presided over the compromise debates of 1850. He served as governor of Georgia (1851-1853) and as his friend James Buchanan's secretary of the treasury (1857-1860). After Lincoln's election he became a secessionist. He chaired the Montgomery Convention in February 1861 and was president of the provisional Confederate congress. He organized the 16th Georgia and, despite his lack of military training,

Howell Cobb

had a distinguished war career. As a brigadier general he fought at Shiloh, Seven Pines, the Seven Days' Battles, Second Bull Run and Antietam; he commanded Georgia's reserve forces and, promoted to major general, the District of Georgia. His troops accepted the surrender of George Stoneman in Macon in 1864. He himself surrendered at Macon, where he established himself as a lawyer, planter and opponent of radical Reconstruction after the war. His brother, lawyer and author Thomas Reade Rootes Cobb (1823-1862), was killed at Fredericksburg.

Philip St. George Cocke

Cocke, Philip St. George
(1809-1861) Confederate general

This Virginia-born West Point graduate managed his many plantations in Mississippi and Virginia before the war. He was commissioned a brigadier general in the Virginia militia in April 1861 and then was mustered into the Confederate army as a colonel. He fought at First Bull Run and Blackburn's Ford and was named a brigadier general in October 1861. Forced to resign from the army in ill health, he committed suicide in December 1861.

Colquitt, Alfred Holt
(1824-1894) Confederate general

The son of a Georgia Senator and secessionist, Colquitt was graduated from Princeton College and settled in Monroe, Georgia, as a lawyer, planter and extreme states' rights politician. He served as a staff officer during the Mexican War. He led the

Confederate army's 6th Georgia in the Peninsular Campaign and, promoted to brigadier general (September 1862), led Colquitt's brigade at Antietam, Fredericksburg, Chancellorsville, the Wilderness, Spotsylvania and Petersburg, where he surrendered. His greatest victory was at Olustee (February 1864), where he stopped the Union incursion into Florida. After the war he returned to his plantation: he was Georgia's governor (1876-1882) and U.S. Senator (1882-1894).

Colston, Raleigh Edward
(1825-1896) Confederate general

Born and educated in Paris, France, he came to America in 1842. He left the French faculty of Virginia Military Institute in 1861 to join the 16th Virginia Infantry. He fought in the Peninsular Campaign, led a division at Chancellorsville and took part in the defense of Peters-

burg. He was commanding at Lynchburg when the war ended. He was paralyzed on a Sudanese expedition after six years in the Egyptian army and returned to a desk job in the U.S. War Department.

Connor, James
(1829-1883) Confederate general

A successful Charleston, South Carolina, lawyer, he served as a U.S. district attorney and wrote several legal works in the 1850s. He prompted the convening of the state's secession convention. He fought for the Confederacy with distinction at First Bull Run and joined the 22nd North Carolina in fighting on the Peninsula (he was seriously wounded at Gaines's Mill) and at Chancellorsville and Gettysburg. He was promoted to brigadier general (June 1864) and commanded brigades during the Peters-

Alfred Holt Colquitt

A. H. Colquitt

James Connor

ABOVE: John Esten Cooke

burg Campaign and the Shenandoah Valley Campaign of Sheridan: the loss of a leg ended his field service. He resumed his law career after the war. As South Carolina's attorney general (1876-1877) he established the legality of the Wade Hampton's right to be governor, despite the protests of the carpetbagger incumbent.

Cook, Philip
(1817-1894) Confederate general

A graduate of the University of Virginia law school, he was a Georgia lawyer and state senator. Cook fought for the Confederacy with the 4th Georgia in the Seven Days' Battles and at Antietam, Fredericks-

burg and Chancellorsville, earning steady promotions. After returning briefly to the state legislature (1863-1864), he fought with Jubal Early in the Shenandoah Valley in 1864. Several times wounded, he was finally captured by Union forces at Petersburg in April 1865. Resuming his law practice after the war, he served as U.S. Representative (1873-1883) and as Georgia's secretary of state (1890-1894)

Cooke, John Esten
(1830-1886) Confederate general

This Virginian became a nationally known writer in the 1950s for his poems, essays and fiction (particularly *The Virginia Comedians*, 1854), much of his work treating colonial Virginia themes. An ardent

secessionist, he served in the army throughout the war. He was J. E. B. Stuart's ordnance officer and Robert E. Lee's inspector general of the horse artillery. He surrendered with Lee at Appomattox, and later returned to his farm to write. Cooke published biographies of Stonewall Jackson (1863) and Lee (1871), among other books about the war.

Cooke, John Rogers
(1833-1891) Confederate general

A Missouri-born, Harvard-educated engineer, he resigned after six years of U.S. Army frontier duty in 1861 to raise a Confederate light artillery company. Cooke fought at First Bull Run, Seven Pines, Fredericksburg, Bristoe Station and the Wilderness, suffering several wounds. His father, Philip St. George Cooke (1809-1895), was a Union general. Cooke was a Richmond merchant and powerful Virginia Democrat after the war.

Cooke, Philip St. George
(1809-1895) Union general

This Virginia-born West Point graduate was involved in Indian fighting and served on the frontier, in the Mexican war and on the Utah Expedition before he was appointed brigadier general in the Union army in November 1861. He led a number of cavalry divisions in combat until June 1862, then served on court martial duty service until August 1863. He was in charge of

Philip St. George Cooke

the army's recruiting service after 1864. He retired a major general in 1873. His son (John R. Cooke), nephew (John Esten Cooke) and son-in-law (Jeb Stuart) all fought for the Confederacy.

Cooper, Joseph Alexander
(1823-1910) Union general

An uneducated Tennessee farmer, this Mexican War veteran vigorously opposed secession at the Knoxville Convention in 1861. His military abilities were revealed by

Joseph Alexander Cooper

the war: he recruited and trained Union troops in eastern Tennessee: earned rapid promotions (brigadier general, July 1864) fighting at Stones River, Chickamauga and Chattanooga; led a division at Atlanta; and participated in eastern Tennessee operations toward the war's end. He became a Knoxville tax collector (1969-1879) and later farmed in Kansas.

Cooper, Samuel
(1798-1876) Confederate general

A New Jersey-born West Point graduate, Cooper was a Washington, D.C., staff officer for much of his long military career. He became adjutant general of the army in 1852. His administrative experience proved invaluable when his Southern ties and sympathies led him to become the Confederate army's highest ranking officer in 1861. He served as adjutant- and inspector-general throughout the war. He saved and surrendered the historically valuable Confederate War Department records. After the war he retired to his Virginia estate.

Corcoran, Michael
(1827-1863) Union general

Irish-born, Corcoran served with the Irish Constabulary in 1845 and then came to the U.S. in 1849. He entered the New York militia, and, soon after the Civil War began, he narrowly avoided a court martial for his refusal to serve in the guard honoring Britain's Prince Albert when he came to the U.S. on a state visit. He was captured and imprisoned for a year after First Bull Run and, after his exchange (August 1862), was promoted to brigadier general. He is known for raising a brigade called the Corcoran Legion. He was killed in December 1863 when his horse accidentally fell on him.

Corse, Montgomery Dent
(1816-1895) Confederate general

A veteran of the Mexican War and the Gold Rush, this Virginian banker enlisted in the

Samuel Cooper

ABOVE: Fort Corcoran, one of the fixed defenses of Washington, D.C., was named in honor of Michael Corcoran. Shown here: one of the fort's heavy batteries.

LEFT: Montgomery Dent Corse.

Confederate army's 17th Virginia. He fought at First Bull Run, on the Peninsula and at Second Bull Run and Antietam. Promoted to brigadier general (November 1862), he took over George Pickett's brigade and fought in the battles of Fredericksburg, Gettysburg, Chickamauga and the Wilderness and in the Appomattox Campaign. He was captured at Sayler's Creek and briefly imprisoned, returning to his Alexandria bank after his release.

Cox, Jacob Dolson
(1828-1900)
Union general, governor of Ohio

He was a Canadian-born Ohio lawyer, legislator and radical antislavery activist before the war. Cox fought for the Union in the Kanawha Valley and Antietam campaigns. As major general (October 1862) his commands included divisions in the Atlanta and Franklin and Nashville campaigns. He was later a single-term Ohio governor (1866-1867), Congressman (1876-1878) and dean of the Cincinnati Law School (1881-1897). A prolific author, he wrote extensively and authoritatively about the Civil War.

Crawford, Samuel Wylie
(1829-1892) Union general

After medical training at the University of Pennsylvania, he enlisted as an army surgeon (1851) and served in the Southwest. He fought for the Union as a commissioned officer throughout the Civil War. He led a battery at Fort Sumter and, as a brigadier general (April 1862), fought at Winchester, Cedar Mountain, South Mountain and Antietam, where he was badly wounded. He led the Pennsylvania Reserves division at Gettysburg, fought in

Samuel Wylie Crawford (fourth from right) fought almost continuously from Fort Sumter to Appomattox.

all the Potomac Army operations of 1864-1865 and witnessed the Appomattox surrender. He retired from active duty in the regular army in 1873.

Crittenden, John Jordon
(1787-1863) Southern statesman

A Kentucky lawyer and politician, he was a U.S. Senator most years between 1835 and 1861. He achieved national prominence in the 1840s; he served as U.S. attorney general (1841. 1850-1853) and strongly opposed the Mexican war and the Kansas-Nebraska Act (1854). An anti-secessionist, he supported Lincoln and worked to keep Kentucky in the Union. In December 1860 he offered the Senate the Crittenden Compromise, proposing the extension of the Missouri Compromise line to the Pacific, but this peace-keeping measure was rejected by both sides. He returned to Kentucky to promote that state's neutrality, and sat in the U.S. Congress until his death.

Crook, George
(1829-1890) Union general

Crook was a West Point graduate from Ohio who interrupted his outstanding career as a northwest explorer and Indian fighter to serve the Union with distinction in the Civil War. He fought at South Mountain and Antietam; promoted to brigadier general (August 1863) he led a cavalry division at Chickamauga. He engaged in operations against Confederate bridges and railroads in West Virginia early in 1864, then joined the Shenandoah Valley Campaign of Sheridan, fighting at Winchester, Fisher's Hill and Cedar Creek. As a major general, he led a cavalry division in the Appomattox Campaign. His later Indian fighting included the Sioux War (1876) and operations against Geronimo in the Sierra Madre. He was celebrated (and sometimes criticized) for the fairness with which he dealt with Indians.

Cullum, George Washington
(1809-1892) Union general

A New Yorker, this West Point graduate and career army engineer (1833-1874) specialized in harbor fortifications. During the Civil War he held Union staff positions under Winfield Scott (1861) and Henry Halleck (1861-1864) and was chief engineer of the Departments of the Missouri and Mississippi. He was long associated with West Point (as superintendent, 1864-1866) and wrote a monumental biographical register of academy graduates from 1802 to 1889. He published many other works on engineering and military history.

Cumming, Alfred
(1829-1910) Confederate general

A Georgia-born West Point graduate and career officer, Cumming participated in the Utah Expedition (1858-1860), resigning from frontier duty in January 1861 to join the Confederate army. He commanded a Georgia arsenal, then joined the 10th Georgia. Wounded at Malvern Hill and Antietam, he was promoted to brigadier general and led the Alabama Brigade at Mobile before helping in the attempt to relieve the Vicksburg siege. Captured and exchanged, he led his reorganized brigade at Missionary Ridge and in J. B. Hood's corps in the Atlanta Campaign. He was wounded at Jonesboro and discharged. After the war he farmed in Georgia.

RIGHT: Alfred Cumming.

BELOW: The harbor fortification expert George Washington Cullum served as a superintendent of West Point.

ABOVE: Newton Martin Curtis, the winner of both the Medal of Honor and the Thanks of Congress. He was also the author of a well-regarded personal war memoir titled *From Bull Run to Chancellorsville*, which was published in 1906, and was a noted figure in New York State politics.

Curtis, Newton Martin
(1835-1910) Union general

Curtis was a New York farmer who fought as a Union captain at First Bull Run. Steadily promoted, he fought at Cold Harbor, Petersburg and Fort Fisher, where he was badly wounded. He eventually earned a brigadier generalship, a Medal of Honor and the Thanks of Congress. Later a noted social reformer, he was a New York assemblyman, Congressman (1891-1897), customs inspector, and treasury agent. He wrote *From Bull Run to Chancellorsville* (1906).

Curtis, Samuel Ryan
(1805-1866) Union general

This West Point graduate and civil engineer worked on major road and river projects in the 1830s and raised Ohio volunteers for the Mexican War. He resigned his Iowa Congressional seat (1856-1861) to join a state regiment at the outbreak of the Civil War. As commander of the Union's Army of the Southwest in 1862, he fought at Pea Ridge, then commanded successively the Departments of the Missouri, Kansas and the Northwest. He stopped Sterling Price's Missouri raid (September-October 1864).

William Barker Cushing, who single-handedly destroyed the big Confederate ironclad ram *Albemarle*

George Armstrong Custer

Cushing, William Barker
(1842-1874) Union naval officer

He resigned while still a senior at Annapolis but was reinstated in the U.S. Navy in October 1861. Commanding the USS *Ellis* (1862) and USS *Monticello* (1863-1865), he performed brilliantly in Florida and the Carolinas. He destroyed the formidable Confederate ram *Albemarle* in a daring night torpedo attack made in a small boat in October 1864, and he led an heroic but doomed assault by sailors on Fort Fisher in January 1865.

Cushman, Pauline
(1835-1893) Union spy

Born in New Orleans and raised in Michigan, she became an actress in New York at age 17. She was fired from a Kentucky theatrical production in March 1863 after toasting the South onstage at the behest of Confederate sympathizers in the audience. The Federals soon sent her south to gather military intelligence. She was arrested in possession of military maps near Braxton Bragg's Tullahoma headquarters and sentenced to death; spared by the Confederates' retreat from Shelbyville, she passed valuable information to W. S. Rosecrans. Notoriety had ended her usefulness as a spy, but she capitalized on her adventures by lecturing (wearing Federal uniform) in the North. Her later years were troubled, and she committed suicide.

Custer, George Armstrong
(1839-1876) Union general

Custer's grandfather, a Hessian mercenary officer named Kuster, settled in Pennsylvania after the Revolutionary war. His may have been the example that fired Custer's childhood ambition to be a soldier. Custer's father, a blacksmith and farmer who migrated westward to Ohio, did nothing to discourage his hopes and saw to

Pauline Cushman

it that he received sufficient education to qualify for a West Point cadetship.

Never much of a hand with the books, Custer was graduated 34th in the 34-man class of 1861 and proceeded directly to the battlefield. He fought with the Union's 5th Cavalry at Bull Run and later served on the staffs of Philip Kearney, William F. Smith and George McClellan. During the Peninsular Campaign of 1862 one of his staff assignments involved supervision of balloon reconnaissances. Promotion came extraordinarily swiftly, and Custer won his brigadier's star after leading a spirited cavalry charge at Aldie in June 1863. He commanded the Michigan Brigade of the 3rd Cavalry Division at Gettysburg, taking part in a sharp encounter with Wade Hampton's Confederate cavalry on the second day of the battle.

Tall, lithe, with ringletted yellow hair, he was always something of an exhibitionist, cutting a figure that some found dashing and others absurd: in his elaborate uniform he looked "like a circus rider gone mad," Theodore Lyman thought. Yet he was undeniably courageous, excelling in such hell-for-leather operations as Philip Sheridan's raid toward Richmond in May 1864, during which he advanced to within four miles of the Confederate capital.

Custer accompanied Sheridan to the Shenandoah Valley in September 1864 and took part in the battles of Winchester and Fisher's Hill. Promoted to command of the 4,600-man 3rd Cavalry Division, he routed the Confederates on October 9 in what became known as the Woodstock Races: he

forced the pursuit of the beaten enemy for more than 25 miles. Ten days later, at Cedar Creek, Custer's division, along with that of Wesley Merritt, held off Jubal Early's infantry long enough for the disorganized Federals to reform and for Sheridan to complete his famous ride and lead them to victory (a feat dramatized in Thomas Buchanan's poem "Sheridan's Ride").

Custer returned, along with Sheridan, to the Army of the Potomac in early 1865 and fought at Dinwiddie Courthouse and Five Forks at the beginning of the Appomattox Campaign. In his greatest triumph, he led the advance in Sheridan's relentless final pursuit of Lee's army westward to Appomattox and received the first flag of truce from the Army of Northern Virginia. In a farewell order to his division shortly after Lee's surrender, he claimed his command had captured 111 pieces of artillery, 65 battle flags and 10,000 prisoners.

Custer served in Texas in the immediate aftermath of the war and later became lieutenant colonel of the 7th Cavalry. His first experience fighting Indians came against the Cheyenne in the spring of 1867. On November 27, 1868, Custer attacked and destroyed a large Cheyenne village on the Washita River in the Oklahoma territory, a bitter and bloody defeat that forced the Cheyenne to return to their reservation.

From 1871 to 1873 he served with the regiment in garrison in Elizabethtown, Ky., where he wrote his well-regarded memoir *My Life on the Plains*. It showed another, more thoughtful side of Custer, as did his efforts to reform the Bureau of Indian Affairs, then riddled with corrup-

tion. He returned to the plains with the 7th Cavalry in 1873. The regiment had its first encounters with hostile Sioux guarding the Northern Pacific Railroad.

Custer set out on his last campaign on June 22, 1876, moving up the Rosebud River toward the headwaters of the Little Big Horn. On the morning of June 25 he divided his force into three parts and prepared for offensive operations against Sioux and Cheyenne war parties known to be in the vicinity. He himself led five companies up the right bank of the Little Big Horn and into a trap. A Sioux force of some 2,500 warriors ambushed his command and, after three hours of fighting, killed every man in it.

that revolutionized naval armaments, the best known being the "Dahlgren gun": a cast-metal smoothbore cannon with a distinctive shape – thick at the breech and tapering to the muzzle. When the Civil War broke out he became head of the Washington Navy Yard in April 1861 when Captain Franklin Buchanan resigned that post to join the Confederacy. In 1862 Dahlgren was promoted to captain and named head of the navy's Ordnance Bureau. In July 1863 he was promoted to rear admiral and assigned command of the South Atlantic Blockading Squadron. He helped seal off Charleston, South Carolina, captured Savannah, Georgia, and in February 1865 led the Union fleet that entered Charleston harbor. He remained on active duty with the navy until his death. He was the father of Ulric Dahlgren.

Dahlgren, John Adolphus Bernard
(1809-1870) Inventor, Union admiral

He was born in Philadelphia where his father was serving as the Swedish consul. At 16 he joined the U.S. Navy as a midshipman and after spending many years at sea and working for the coast survey he was assigned in 1847 to the navy's ordnance bureau at Washington, D.C. During his years there he invented several weapons

John Adolphus Dahlgren

Dahlgren, Ulric
(1842-1864) Union officer

An admiral's son, he abandoned his law studies to enter the Union army at the beginning of the war. Dahlgren was Franz Sigel's chief of artillery during the second Bull Run Campaign and later served on the staffs of Ambrose Burnside, Joseph Hooker and George Meade. He lost a leg to amputation after being wounded at Gettysburg in July 1863. Dahlgren was

killed near Richmond on the Kilpatrick-Dahlgren Raid of March 1864, of which he was co-commander. Plans for an assassination attempt on Jefferson Davis and his cabinet were allegedly found on his body. Though Union authorities claimed the papers had been forged, recent research suggests they may have been authentic.

Ulric Dahlgren

Dana, Napoleon Tecumseh Jackson
(1822-1905) Union general

This West Point graduate and Mexican war veteran was a Minnesota banker after 1855. He fought for the Union at Ball's Bluff and led a brigade on the Peninsula and at Antietam, where he was seriously wounded. Promoted to major general, he commanded Philadelphia's defenses during the Gettysburg Campaign and led a successful expedition against the Texas coast late in 1863. He resigned his command of the Department of Mississippi in May 1865. His later business interests included western mining and railroads.

Davidson, John Wynn
(1823-1881) Union general

A West Point graduate and career cavalry-man, this Virginian fought on the frontier and sustained severe wounds in Indian

Edmund Jackson Davis

fighting. He declined a Confederate commission in 1861, instead joining the Federals. He fought in the Peninsula, held Missouri field commands and led a cavalry division in the Little Rock expedition, finally serving as chief of cavalry of the Division of the West Mississippi in 1865. He remained in the army after the war and died while still on active service.

Davis, Edmund Jackson
(1827-1883)
Union general, governor of Texas

A Texas judge stung by losing an election for the secessionist convention, Davis organized a Texas Unionist regiment in Mexico. He joined the 1st Texas Cavalry in October 1862 and, although he had spent much of the rest of the war in Louisiana, unsuccessfully attacked Laredo in 1864. Elected governor of Texas (1869-1873), he presided over a notoriously dictatorial and corrupt carpetbag administration. He afterward remained a leading Texas Republican and lawyer.

Davis, George
(1820-1896)
Confederate attorney general

Descended from a distinguished North Carolina family, he was graduated as valedictorian from his state university at 18 and practiced law. Actively anti-secessionist, he participated in the Peace Conference in Washington in February 1861 but afterward denounced its recommendations. He was a Confederate senator (1862-1864), then served as the C.S.A.'s attorney general. He resumed his law practice after the war.

Davis, Jefferson
(1808-1889) Confederate president

Born in Kentucky, the 10th child of a modestly prosperous settler who had led a troop of irregular cavalry during the Revolutionary War, Jefferson Davis grew up on a plantation created out of the canebrakes and deep woods of the Mississippi frontier. He returned to Kentucky for his education, studying at a Roman Catholic seminary (where he came close to renouncing his family's Baptist Protestantism) and later at Transylvania University. His older brother, Joseph, with a better head for business than their father, acquired a fortune as a cotton planter and raised the family to social prominence in Mississippi. His influence gained Davis an appointment to the U.S. Military Academy, from which he was graduated in 1828, a year ahead of Robert E. Lee.

Davis spent the next seven years in remote garrison posts in Wisconsin and Illinois. He saw action (as did Abraham Lincoln, an Illinois militia volunteer) in the Black Hawk War of 1832. In 1835 he married, against her family's wishes, the daughter of one of his garrison commanders, future President Zachary Taylor. Resigning in the face of Taylor's disapproval, he took his bride to Mississippi, to a small plantation he called Brierfield. Three months later she was dead of a fever, and for the next decade Davis lived an obscure, lonely life as a planter.

During these years he read widely in political theory and, on his own and in long discussions with Joseph, formed a political philosophy rooted in a deep attachment to the Southern system of plantation slavery. He met the attacks of the increasingly influential abolitionist movement with pure states' rights arguments of a kind that, ironically, would be turned against him as president of the Southern Confederacy.

He ended his period of retirement,

Jefferson Davis, the president of the
Confederate States of America

abruptly in 1845, with marriage to Varina
Howell, daughter of a prominent Mississippi planter, and an entry into politics.
With his brother's encouragement, he ran
successfully for Congress in 1845 but resigned after only a few months in Washington to accept command of a regiment of
Mississippi volunteers bound for Mexico.
He led the regiment in a critical stand that
may have won the Battle of Buena Vista
(1847) for the Americans. The exploit
attracted wide notice and heightened
Davis's already high opinion of his own
military abilities. He returned to Washington later in 1847 as a Senator. He soon became known as a staunch defender of the
"peculiar institution" (slavery) and an
advocate of its extension into the new territories seized from Mexico after the war.

Davis served as secretary of war during
the Pierce administration (1853-57), then
returned to the Senate, where he became
something of a force for moderation,
though he remained bitterly opposed to
any political adjustments that would inter-
fere with slavery in the territories. Davis
became a familiar figure on the Senate floor
during the slavery debates of the late 1850s,

a tall, slender, impressive figure, though
often a frail one (he suffered greatly in the
late 1850s from a painful eye disease, neu-
ralgia and other ailments). Opposing secession, Davis urged some form of compromise on radical Southerners right up to
the newly-elected Lincoln's declaration
that he would not permit any expansion of
slavery into the territories.

He resigned his Senate seat on January

21, 1861, and followed Mississippi into the
Confederacy. He hoped to be made commander-in-chief of the Confederate
armies, Instead, on February 18, he was inaugurated as provisional president of the
Confederate States of America, a compromise choice. The new government confirmed him in the presidency the following
year.

Davis led a thoroughly unprepared and
ill-equipped nation into war. The Southern
states lacked the industrial and financial
base to sustain a long conflict, and Union
blockade gradually choked off supplies
from the outside world. Davis's political
and diplomatic skills proved to be margi-
nal. At home, states' rights radicals
opposed his taxation and conscription in-
itiatives. Abroad, he found himself unable
to find allies – particularly European allies
– to aid the Southern cause.

Inflexible, hot-tempered, in ill health
(his wife described him as "a mere mass of
throbbing nerves"), Davis quarrelled with
many senior military and political leaders,
particularly with General Joseph E. Johnston and his own vice president, Alexander
Stephens. He often supported mediocre
soldiers such as Braxton Bragg at the expense of Johnston and other more capable
men, but he never quarreled with Robert E.
Lee: Lee and Davis remained in sympathy
to the end. From 1863 on, a majority in the
Confederate Congress opposed him, and
he never inspired much liking among
ordinary Southerners.

BELOW: Davis and his cabinet get a briefing
from Robert E. Lee.

OPPOSITE: Davis's inauguration in
Montgomery, Alabama, in 1861.

In 1864-65, with the Confederacy crumbling, he proposed to draft 40,000 slaves and free them at the successful conclusion of the war, a suggestion that provoked outrage throughout the South. He resisted any proposal for a negotiated peace that fell short of full independence, and this intransigence ultimately condemned the South to much misery. The end came swiftly in April 1865. Davis left Richmond on April 3 just ahead of Union occupation forces (including black troops) and fled into the Deep South where word of Lee's surrender reached him. A Federal cavalry detachment captured him near Irwinville, Georgia, on May 10.

The U.S. government held him for two years as a state prisoner at Fortress Monroe but never bought him to trial. Released on May 13, 1877, Davis returned to his beloved Mississippi. He gradually recovered his health (though not his fortune; he was an inept businessman) and settled on a friend's estate on the Gulf of Mexico, where he wrote his two-volume *The Rise and Fall of the Confederate Government* (1878-81). He died in New Orleans on December 6, 1889.

Varina Howell Davis and husband

Davis, Jefferson Columbus
(1828-1879) **Union general**

Born in Indiana, he served in the Mexican War as a private and then stayed in the regular army. He was at Fort Sumter during the bombardment in April 1861 that ignited the Civil War. From that time on he fought for the Union in many battles – Wilson's Creek, Pea Ridge, Corinth – and by May 1862 he was a brigadier general. Upset over a rebuke from his commander, General William Nelson, he killed Nelson with a revolver. Thanks to political pressures, Davis was never punished and was allowed to return to active command. He led forces all the way through the Atlanta Campaign, the March to the Sea and the Carolinas Campaign. After the war he stayed on in the regular army, serving in Alaska and in the war against the Modocs.

Union General Jefferson Columbus Davis (at desk, left)

Davis, Varina Howell
(1826-1906) **Wife of Jefferson Davis**

Born in Mississippi, she married Jefferson Davis in 1845 and forged an intellectual and political partnership with him. She was an ambitious and successful Washington hostess during his years in the federal government in the late 1840s and 1850s. As First Lady of the Confederacy she was controversial because of her Northern ancestry and political influence. She supported herself in later life as a New York-based magazine writer and published a memoir of her husband (1890).

Deas, Zachariah Cantey
(1819-1882) **Confederate general**

A wealthy South Carolina-born cotton broker, Deas served in the Mexican War. Signing on with the Alabama Volunteers when the Civil war began, he spent $28,000 in gold to arm his men with Enfield rifles (he was paid back in Confederate bonds). He was wounded at Shiloh and served at Stones River, Chickamauga, Missionary Ridge and in the Atlanta Campaign and the Franklin and Nashville Campaign. He tried to stop W. T Sherman's March through Georgia. He went back to selling cotton after the war.

George Washington Deitzler

Deitzler, George Washington
(1826-1884) Union general

Born in Pennsylvania, Deitzler farmed and agitated as a Free-Soiler in Kansas, smuggling guns from the East. Arrested by pro-

Frederick Tracey Dent

slavery forces, he was charged with treason but released. He was commissioned a colonel in a pro-Union Kansas unit in 1861. He served at Wilson's Creek and was promoted to brigadier general in November 1862. He resigned due to ill health in 1863 but returned to command the Kansas State Militia when Sterling Price invaded the state in 1864.

Dent, Frederick Tracy
(1821-1892) Union general

This Missouri-born West Point graduate was a classmate and brother-in-law of Ulysses S. Grant. Dent first served in the Mexican War, then in the West as an Indian fighter. In 1863 he took command of a regiment in the Army of Potomac and in 1864 helped to suppress the Draft Riots in New York. As a lieutenant colonel he served as an aide de camp to Ulysses S. Grant (1864-1865). In 1865 he served as military governor of Richmond, Virginia. He retired as a colonel in the regular army in 1883.

Denver, James William
(1817-1892) Union general

By 1861 Denver had been a midwestern teacher, lawyer and newspaper editor; a California secretary of state and Congressman; and a Kansas Territory governor,

James William Denver

besides fighting in the Mexican War. As a brigadier general he commanded the Federal troops in Kansas, held commands in the Army of the Tennessee and fought at Shiloh and Corinth. He resigned in March 1863 to practice law in Washington, D.C. Denver, Colorado, was named after him.

De Trobriand, Philip Regis Denis de Keredern
(1816-1897) Union general

Born in France into a noble family, he was a poet and writer who married while visiting the U.S. He joined the "Guards Lafayette" and later fought with the Army of the Potomac. He was named a brigadier general in January 1864 and was breveted major general in 1865. He took his father's title (baron) in 1874 but remained with the regular U.S. Army until 1879. He wrote (in French) a oft-cited account of his experiences.

Devens, Charles
(1829-1891) Union general

A Harvard-educated lawyer and Massachusetts public school official and orator, Devens became a commander in the Army of the Potomac in 1861. He was appointed a brigadier general in April 1862. Wounded at Ball's Bluff, Fair Oaks and Chancellorsville, he also fought at Fredericksburg and Cold Harbor and took part in the advance on Richmond in 1864-65. He returned to Massachusetts, where he sat on the state supreme court (1873-1877, 1881-1891). He was U.S. attorney general (1877-1881). Camp Devens, Mass., is named for him.

Charles Devens

Dewey, George
(1837-1917) Union naval officer

George Dewey

This Vermont-born Annapolis graduate was a young naval lieutenant in 1861. During the war he held junior commands on the old side-wheeler USS *Mississippi* at New Orleans and Port Hudson, on David Farragut's lower Mississippi flagship, the steam sloop *Monongahela*, and on the steam frigate *Colorado* at Fort Fisher, and he later served on the Atlantic blockade duty. As a commodore commanding the Asiatic squadron, he achieved international fame for the great victory at Manila Bay in 1898 that established the United States a major Pacific naval power: his instruction to his flagship captain ("You may fire when you are ready, Gridley") became a household phrase. He returned home a hero, and the rank of admiral was created to honor his achievement.

Dibrell, George Gibbs
(1822-1888) Confederate general

Born in Tennessee, Dibrell was a farmer and merchant before the war. Although he was against secession, he enlisted as a private for the Confederacy, eventually

Dix, Dorothea Lynde
(1802-1887) Social reformer

Born in Hampden, Maine, of parents barely competent to raise a family, she moved into her grandmother's home in Boston at the age of 10. Resourceful and determined, Dix saw to the education of her younger brothers and, at the age of 14, began to earn her own living as a schoolteacher in Worcester, Massachusetts. She returned to Boston in 1821 to establish a girls' school and ran it successfully until 1834, when a tubercular illness forced her to give up the work.

Dix taught for a time in a private home, but ill health drove her to seek treatment abroad. Returning to the U.S. after 18 months in England, she took over a Sunday School class of women inmates in a jail in East Cambridge, Massachusetts. What she found there – filth, overcrowding, no distinction between insane persons and criminals – prompted her to launch what would become a two-year study of conditions of the insane in asylums, prisons and alms houses in Massachusetts. The findings appalled her. Conventional wisdom still held that insanity was a moral defect, deserving of punishment rather

LEFT: Dorothea Lynde Dix.

BELOW: George Gibbs Dibrell.

being promoted to lieutenant colonel under Felix Zollicoffer. When his regiment chose not to re-elect him, he raised his own cavalry regiment to harass the Federals behind their lines. He joined General Nathan B. Forrest in the Stones River Campaign (December 1882-January 1863), and in July 1863 he took command of Forrest's former brigade. He led this unit at Chickamauga, during W. T. Sherman's March to the Sea and in the final days of the Carolinas Campaign. He was a successful businessman after the war and also served in the Congress.

Divers, Bridget
Union army nurse

This vigorous Irishwoman accompanied her husband to war with the 1st Michigan Cavalry. A vivandière, nurse and Sanitary Commission agent, "Michigan Bridget" frequently fought with her regiment, riding a government horse and replacing fallen comrades in battle. At Cedar Creek she rode through enemy lines. After the war she remained with the army as a laundress on the frontier.

than treatment. Dix reported on men and women confined "in cages, closets, cellars, stalls, pens; chained, naked, beaten with rods, and lashed into obedience."

She presented her findings to the Massachusetts legislature in January 1843: they caused a sensation. She convinced influential political leaders to stir public opinion to support the cause of reform, and as a result, Massachusetts thoroughly overhauled its system. Over a three-year period in the mid-1840s Dix traveled more than 10,000 miles to carry on her investigations in some 20 states, beginning with New Jersey, where she founded a state asylum. New asylums were built elsewhere, and others improved; eventually, most states adopted more humane methods of treatment.

Dix took her reform crusade abroad to Canada, Europe and Japan. She helped bring about reform of Scotland's lunacy laws and renovated the Channel Islands' system for treatment of the insane. She went on to tour hospitals and asylums in Holland, Norway, Russia, Greece and Italy.

With the coming of war in America she turned her attention to the army camps, nursing sick and wounded soldiers with her characteristic energy, single-mindedness and attention to details. President Abraham Lincoln appointed her superintendent of women nurses on June 10, 1861, a position she retained until the end of the war, despite considerable criticism of her organizational abilities. She eventually oversaw the recruitment, placement and training of some 2,000 volunteers who cared for the Union war wounded.

Some people found Dix, dour, difficult, cold and distant. "I have no particular love for my species," she once said, "but own to an exhaustless fund of compassion." One of the best known of Civil War nurses, Louisa May Alcott, thought her "a kind old soul, but very queer and arbitrary." She established the strictest of standards for her nurses, though these sometimes had little to do with medicine. She accepted only homely women between the ages of 30 and 45 and required applicants to submit certifications of health and character. "I am plain-looking enough to suit you, and old enough," one prospective volunteer wrote her. "I never had a husband and am not looking for one – will you take me?"

Dix carried on a running battle with hospital administrators, the army medical bureau and the U.S. Sanitary Commission, a volunteer agency that provided a broad range of services to the troops. The secretary of war finally intervened in October 1863, giving the army surgeon general the power to appoint nurses and subordinating Dix's volunteers to hospital medical officers.

She resumed her work on behalf of the insane after the war, despite recurring tuberculosis and other illnesses. She had "the grasp of intellect, the fertility of resources, and the indomitable force of will that go to the make-up of a great statesman, or a great commander," someone said of her. Toward the end of her life, her health ruined, she moved into the asylum she had founded at Trenton, New Jersey. She died there on July 17, 1887.

Dix, John Adams
(1798-1879) U.S. treasury secretary and Union general

After fighting in the War of 1812 as a boy of 14, he served in the army until 1828. In a meteoric Democratic political career he was New York's secretary of state (1833-1839) and U.S. Senator (1845-1849). As Abraham Lincoln's first secretary of the treasury (January-March 1861), he laid a sound basis for financing the war and issued the famous "American Flag Dispatch": ordering the arrest of a revenue cutter in New Orleans, he directed, "If anyone attempts to haul down the American flag, shoot him on the spot." As a Union major general, he later held territorial commands, ending the war in command of the Department of the East. He was later U.S. minister to France (1866-1869) and served as governor of New York (1873-1875).

Dodge, Grenville Mellen
(1831-1916) Union general

Born into an old Massachusetts family, he trained as an engineer and, after conducting western railroad surveys, settled in Iowa in 1853. As a Union volunteer, Dodge held a series of commands in the Armies of Southwest Missouri and the Tennessee. He was wounded at Pea Ridge and Atlanta. His most important contribution to the Union army, however, was the construction of bridges and railroads. After the war he became one of the country's major railroad builders. His most notable achievement was the completion of the Union Pacific Railroad while serving as its chief engineer (1866-70). He subsequently built thousands of miles of railroads in the West and Southwest and, after 1900, in Cuba.

John Adams Dix

OPPOSITE: Some Sanitary Commission workers at Fredericksburg in 1864

Donelson, Daniel Smith
(1801-1863) Confederate general

A West Point graduate, Donelson was a planter, militiaman and Democratic state legislator in his native Tennessee. An ardent secessionist, he built Fort Donelson while in the provisional army. As a Confederate brigadier general (July 1861), he led brigades in West Virginia, under Robert E. Lee at Charleston and under Braxton Bragg at Perryville, Stones River and Shelbyville. In January 1863 illness forced him to a territorial command, and he commanded the Department of East Tennessee. Sources disagree on the place and circumstances of his death.

Doubleday, Abner
(1819-1893) Union general

A native of New York state, he trained as a civil engineer, was graduated from West Point and fought in the Mexican and Seminole wars. On garrison duty, he aimed the Federals' first shot from Fort Sumter. He won successive promotions through the Shenandoah Valley Campaign of 1862. As a brigadier general (February 1862) he fought at Second Bull Run and led divisions at South Mountain, Antietam and Fredericksburg. Promoted to major general, he temporarily led I Corps when

Abner Doubleday

Stephen Arnold Douglas

its commander, John Reynolds, was killed at Gettysburg. He was denied the permanent command, however, and served out the war in administration. He retired from the regular army in 1873. Historians agree that Doubleday had nothing of significance to do with baseball, although he is popularly credited with "inventing" the game in 1839.

Douglas, Stephen Arnold
(1813-1861) U.S. statesman

Born in Brandon, Vermont, he settled in Illinois in 1833 and quickly established himself in local politics. Active, acute and articulate, he organized the state's Democratic party and from 1934 to 1842 was a public prosecutor and state legislator, secretary of state, and supreme court judge. In the U.S. Congress (1843-1847) and Senate (1847-1861), his brilliant oratory made "the Little Giant" the nation's foremost advocate of compromise in the prewar years. With Henry Clay, he was instrumental in forging the Compromise of 1850, and his chairmanship of the Committee on Territories put him at the heart of the national debate on slavery. He originated the doctrine of popular sovereignty

during the Kansas-Nebraska Act debates (1854) and ensured its incorporation in the acts organizing the territories of Utah and New Mexico. His advocacy of popular sovereignty diminished his Northern support, and his denunciation of the proslavery Lecompton constitution in Kansas (1857) made him unpopular in the South. During his successful Senate race in 1858, his debates with Lincoln propelled Douglas's unknown opponent to national prominence. In 1860 the Northern Democrats nominated Douglas for the presidency after the party split at the Charleston convention. He publicly supported Lincoln after the election and finally abandoned his compromise stance after the attack on Fort Sumter. He died of typhoid fever on a northwestern tour to rally support for the war.

Douglass, Frederick
(c. 1817-1875) Abolitionist

Douglass was born into bondage in Talbot County, Maryland, and lived in his grandmother's slave cabin until he was five or six years old, when he went into the home of

his father, a plantation overseer. At the age of eight Douglass was sent to the family of Hugh Auld of Baltimore. There his mistress gave him the rudiments of an education before Auld, hearing of his progress, prohibited any further schooling.

Auld put Douglass to work in the family shipyard in Baltimore but also hired him out to a farm where, working as a field-hand, he endured much abuse. Douglass hatched a plot to escape, but his plans were discovered. He was sent to jail and subsequently put up for auction, but in the end his master decided not to sell him, and he eventually returned to his labors in the Baltimore shipyard.

Douglass made his break from slavery in 1838. He fled the shipyard, safely reached free territory and settled in New Bedford, Massachusetts, with his freedwoman wife, Anna Murray. Though he had learned the caulker's trade in Baltimore, Douglass was barred, because of his race, from working at it in New Bedford. He managed to earn a subsistence as a stevedore and common laborer.

He began his career in public life around this time, speaking out on matters of race at

LEFT: Frederick Douglass.

BELOW: Black Union infantry.

abolition meetings. In 1841 he went to work for the Massachusetts Anti-slavery Society as a lecturer. By 1843, under the auspices of the American Anti-Slavery Society, he was traveling extensively in the Northern states as a lecturer for the abolition cause.

Partly to refute charges that he had invented his slave background, Douglass wrote his famous autobiography in 1844. Published the following year, it contained details such as his master's precise name and address, that exposed him to the possibility of arrest and a return to slavery. He thus went abroad in 1845, continuing his lecturer's work in England, Scotland and Ireland. An English sympathizer purchased his freedom, and he returned in 1847 with sufficient funds to found and edit an antislavery journal, the *North Star*, which he published for 16 years.

Douglass continued to agitate for abolition through the 1850s. In 1859 the authorities accused him of taking part in the John Brown conspiracy. Though he had refused to join the Harpers Ferry venture – "You'll never get out alive," he told Brown – he found it expedient again to go abroad for a time. But he shortly returned, and when war broke out in 1861 he issued an immediate call for the arming of slaves.

From the beginning, Douglass saw the war as a crusade against slavery. He persuaded President Lincoln to allow blacks to fight for the Union. "Give them a chance," he asked. "I don't say they will fight better than other men. All I say is, give them a chance." Douglass saw military service as a means to full acceptance for blacks. "Once let the black man get upon his person the letters U.S.; let him get an eagle on his button, and a musket on his shoulder and bullets in his pocket, and there is no power on earth which can deny he has earned the right to citizenship," he said. Douglass helped to raise the 54th and 55th Massachusetts infantry regiments, and two of his sons were non-commissioned officers in the famous 54th Massachusetts, which lost nearly half its complement in an assault on Fort Wagner, South Carolina, in July 1863.

Douglass remained in demand as a lecturer after the war. He founded another journal, *The New National Era*, and campaigned for full civil rights for the South's freed slaves. In 1877 President Rutherford B. Hayes appointed him U.S. marshal for the District of Columbia; he was the first black to hold that office. From 1889 to 1891 he served as U.S. minister to Haiti. Douglass remained a powerful spokesman for civil rights for blacks until his death.

Drayton, Thomas Fenwick
(1808-1891 Confederate general

A South Carolinian, he was graduated from West Point with Jefferson Davis and spent eight years as an army engineer before returning home to farm. He was a railroad president in 1861. He proved an ineffectual field commander as a Confederate brigadier general at Port Royal and elsewhere. After Antietam and brief court martial duty, he was relegated to inactive field commands in Arkansas and Texas. He failed as a Georgia planter and worked as an insurance agent in later life.

Thomas Fenwick Drayton

Alfred Nattie Duffié

Duffié, Alfred Nattie
(1835-1880) Union general

French-born, Duffié had fought in Senegal, Algiers and the Crimea and had won medals for valor during the French campaign against Austria in 1859. He came to the U.S. in 1861 specifically to join the Union cavalry. Promoted to brigadier general in 1863, Duffié played an important role in cavalry actions throughout the war in the East. He was mustered out in August 1865 and later saw diplomatic service.

Basil Wilson Duke

Samual Francis Du Pont

Duke, Basil Wilson
(1838-1916) Confederate general

This Kentucky-born lawyer was an active secessionist in Missouri and was almost hanged by the Union as a spy before he enlisted in his brother-in-law John H. Morgan's "Lexington Rifles." Duke was wounded at Shiloh, was captured in the Ohio raid of 1863 and was promoted to brigadier general in 1864 after his release. In 1865 Duke's cavalry brigade escorted Jefferson Davis from Charlotte, North Carolina, until his capture two weeks later in Georgia. Duke wrote about the Civil War in later years and worked as a lawyer, politician and editor.

Du Pont, Samuel Francis
(1803-1865) Union admiral

Born in Bergen Point, New Jersey, Du Pont began his 50-year navy career in 1815. Commanding the sloop-of-war *Cyane* during the Mexican War, he cleared Mexican forces from the Gulf of California. He helped to organize the naval academy at Annapolis (established 1850),

recommended the navy's adoption of steam power (1851) and in 1855 was prominent on the controversial naval efficiency board that found 201 officers to be incompetent. He headed the Commission of Conference that planned Union naval strategy and operations early in the Civil War (June 1861). As a flag officer, he was appointed (September 1861) the first commander of the South Atlantic Blockading Squadron, at 75 vessels the largest fleet ever commanded by a naval officer at that time. He enforced the blockade in 13 of 14 stations and in a brilliant operation captured Port Royal (November 1861), giving the Federals a southern base and himself earning the Thanks of Congress and a promotion to rear admiral. In coastal operations he seized ships, forts and islands, occupied the Georgia sounds and took Jacksonville and St. Augustine. In April 1863 he suffered a severe setback at Charleston, where the fleet of monitors and ironclads assigned to him suffered much damage in an unsuccessful attempt to take the city. Du Pont thereupon asked to be relieved of his command and spent the rest of the war on boards and commissions. Du Pont Circle in Washington, D.C., is named for him.

Early, Jubal Anderson
(1816-1894) Confederate general

He was born in Franklin County, Virginia. After graduation from West Point he fought in the Seminole War and then resigned to become a Virginia lawyer and Whig state legislator. He volunteered for garrison duty during the Mexican War. Having opposed secession, he nevertheless joined the Confederate army and led the 24th Virginia at First Bull Run. As a brigadier general, he fought in the Peninsular Campaign (wounded at Williamsburg) and Second Bull Run. He commanded a division at Antietam and Fredericksburg and, after being promoted to major general (January 1863), at Chancellorsville, Gettysburg, the Wilderness and Spotsylvania. He led a Corps at Cold Harbor. After

Jubal Anderson Early

May 1864, promoted to lieutenant general, he held an independent command in the Shenandoah Valley, leading raids and other operations as far north as Pennsylvania. He marched on the Union capital in Early's Washington Raid (June-August 1864), but his advance was delayed by the fighting at Monocacy, and when he resumed his advance he found Washington reinforced by two Union corps and was forced to retreat. Defeated by Philip Sheridan at Winchester, Fisher's Hill and Cedar Creek, and routed by George Custer at Waynesboro in March 1865, "Old Jube" was finally relieved of his command in response to mounting public pressure. He resumed his Lynchburg law practice in 1867. He never took the oath of allegiance, but continued to promote the Confederate cause in a war memoir (1866; expanded into an autobiography, 1912) and as president of the Southern Historical Society. He later worked for the Louisiana lottery.

Eaton, John Jr.
(1829-?) Union officer

A New Hampshire native, he entered Union service as chaplain of the 27th Ohio in August 1861. In November of the following year Ulysses S. Grant chose him to

John Echols

direct aid programs for freed slaves in the departments of Tennessee and Arkansas. The War Department used Eton's operation as a model when it established the Freedman's Bureau in 1865; he served as bureau commissioner for Washington, D.C., Maryland and Virginia and ended the war a brevet brigadier general. After the war, Eaton held office briefly as U.S. commissioner of education and later was president of Marietta College in Ohio and Sheldon Jackson College in Utah.

Echols, John
(1823-1896) Confederate general

Echols attended Virginia Military Institute and was graduated from Harvard, returning to Virginia to practice law in 1843. Settling in Monroe (now West Virginia), he became a secessionist and attended the state secession convention. He led the Confederate 27th Virginia at First Bull Run and was wounded at Kernstown. As a brigadier general (April 1862), he fought in the Shenandoah Valley Campaign of Jackson and at New Market and Cold Harbor. He also commanded the West Virginia Department and the District of Southwest Virginia. He surrendered in 1865 after accompanying Jefferson Davis to Augusta. His later business interests included banking and railroads.

Edmonds, Sarah Emma Evelyn
(1841-1898) Union soldier

As a runaway adolescent disguised as "Frank Thompson," she sold Bibles in rural Canada. While living in Michigan she assumed the same identity to join the Union's 2nd Michigan Infantry in 1861. She fought in the 1861-1862 Potomac Army campaigns, deserting in Kentucky in 1863. Her *Nurse and Spy in the Union Army* (1865) made her famous. Pensioned by the army in 1884, she spent her last years as a nurse.

Oliver Edwards

Edwards, Oliver
(1835-1904) Union general

Edwards owned a foundry in Illinois, but he returned home to Massaachusetts in 1861 to serve as an adjutant to Union General Darius Couch. He led a regiment on the Peninsula, at Fredericksburg and at Gettysburg. He led a brigade during the New York Draft Riots and fought at the Wilderness and Spotsylvania and in Philip Sheridan's 1864 Valley Campaign. At Sayler's Creek his men captured Confederate generals Richard Ewell and Curtis Lee, their staffs and an entire Confederate brigade. He was promoted to brigadier general in 1865. He was a manufacturer and inventor after the war.

Ellet, Charles, Jr.
(1810-1862)
Engineer, Union naval officer

A native of Pennsylvania, he was a civil engineer famed for designing and building suspension bridges. He also urged the construction of dams and reservoirs to control floods and to foster navigation on the rivers of the American West. In 1855 he published *Coast and Harbour Defences*, in which he proposed construction of "ram boats" – ships with heavy iron prows that could be driven into the hulls of enemy ships. Both the Union and Confederate navies built many of these ram-boats, and in spring 1862 Ellet, by then commissioned an officer in the Union navy, led a fleet of nine ram-boats down the Mississippi River; the operation succeeded in opening the river past Memphis, but Ellet died of wounds received in the action.

Elliott, Washington Lafayette
(1825-1888) Union general

Born in Pennsylvania and the son of a famous naval officer, Elliott failed graduation from West Point and enlisted in the regular army, serving in the Mexican War until he fell ill. He then served on the frontier until appointed a captain in 1861. During the Civil War he fought at Wilson's Creek, New Madrid and Island No. 10 and took part in the siege of Corinth. He was wounded at Second Bull Run. He was breveted a major general for his war services and remained in the regular army until 1879. He later worked in California as a banker.

Ellsworth, Elmer Ephraim
(1837-1861) Union officer

As a young Chicago clerk Ellsworth organized a company of Zouaves, troops known for their exotic Algerian-inspired costumes and flamboyant drill: they performed at the White House in 1860. In May 1861 his New York Zouave regiment helped to take Alexandria, where he was killed in a dispute over a Confederate flag. A friend and election aide of Abraham Lincoln, Ellsworth was the first prominent Union casualty of the war.

Elzey, Arnold
(1816-1871) Confederate general

This Maryland-born West Point graduate served on the frontier, in Seminole War, in the Mexican War and as an Indian fighter. Forced by the Rebels to surrender the U.S.

arsenal in Augusta, Georgia in 1861, he personally brought his troops to Washington, then resigned and accepted a commission with the Confederate forces. He fought at First Bull Run and suffered a head wound at Gaines's Mill (Cold Harbor) in 1862. Although unable to fight, he returned to duty as a major general in December 1862 and commanded the Department of Richmond. He went back into the field as General J. B. Hood's chief of artillery in the Tennessee Campaign. He spent his postwar years peacefully tending to the work on his farm in Maryland.

Ericsson, John
(1803-1889) Marine engineer, inventor

Swedish-born Ericsson joined a corps of mechanical engineers at age 13 and was a Swedish army surveyor before emigrating to England in 1826. There he began his remarkably fertile career as an inventor and engineer, developing, among many other projects, the transmission of power by compressed air, steam boilers, underwater warship engines, screw propellers, a steam

Elmer Ephraim Ellsworth

locomotive (which lost in competition with George Stephenson's Rocket in 1829), and rotary engines. After moving to the U.S. in 1839, he introduced the screw propeller to boats on inland waterways. He designed the steam sloop *Princeton* (1844), the first warship with underwater propellers. In a rare setback, his hot air-powered ship, the *Ericsson*, failed commercially in 1851. In 1861 he revolutionized warship technology with the USS *Monitor*, an ironclad vessel with a revolving gun turret. Based on a design Ericsson had made in 1854, the *Monitor* was built in only 100 days and launched in January 1862. After

John Ericsson

an accident-plagued voyage along the coast, she achieved an historic victory over the CSS *Merrimac* (March 9, 1862). Ericsson received the Thanks of Congress. He went on to design other ironclads for the Union and for foreign countries. He later developed the torpedo technology introduced during the Civil War, as well as heavy guns, superheated steam and the hot air (or gas) engine.

Etheridge, Anna Blair
(b.1844) Union army nurse

"Gentle Annie" enlisted with the Union's 2nd Michigan and tended Michigan regiments throughout the war, often working under fire and once being wounded. Union General Philip Kearny died before fulfilling his intention to appoint her a sergeant major, but she earned the Kearny Cross for bravery. She worked for the government after the war.

Evans, Clement Anselm
(1833-1911) Confederate general

This George-born judge and legislator fought on the Peninsula, at Fredericksburg, Gettysburg, the Wilderness, Petersburg and Appomattox. He was promoted to brigadier general in 1864 and commanded J. B. Gordon's old brigade both in Jubal Early's Washington raid and during Philip Sheridan's Valley Campaign. Moved by the violence he witnessed at Fredericksburg, Evans became a Methodist preacher after the war. He was active in veterans' organizations and wrote about the war.

Evans, Nathan George
(1824-1868) Confederate general

Born in South Carolina and a graduate of West Point, Evans was an Indian fighter before he resigned in 1861 and joined the South Carolina army after the bombardment of Fort Sumter. "Shanks" Evans's career as a cavalry officer began well: he played an important role in the victory at First Bull Run, and he led the Confederate force at Balls Bluff, for which he won the formal thanks of the Confederate congress and a gold medal. In command of the so-called "tramp brigade," he fought at Second Bull Run, Antietam and Vicksburg. But in 1863, after being tried for drunkenness and disobedience, he was relieved of his command, despite being acquitted. In 1864 he returned to the field, only to sustain serious injuries after falling from his horse. He was a school principal in Alabama after the war.

Evarts, William Maxwell
(1818-1901) Union public official

Born in Boston, he became a prominent lawyer in New York City and joined the new Republican Party. In 1860 he was secretary of the Union Defense Committee, a moderate group that argued against a definitive split between North and South. In 1863 and again in 1864 he was dispatched by the Union government to England to use his influence and talents to persuade the British to stop building and equipping shops for he Confederate navy. After the war Evarts served as one of the government prosecutors of Jefferson Davis and as one of President Andrew Johnson's defense lawyers during his impeachment trial; his legal and oratorical abilities are credited with keeping Johnson from being convicted of the impeachment charges. Johnson showed his appreciation by appointing him U.S. attorney general (1867-68). In later years Evarts was one of the most prominent lawyers in America, and he served President Hayes as secretary of state (1877-81).

ABOVE: Richard Stoddert Ewell.

BELOW: The remains of Ewell's corps surrenders, April 1865.

Everett, Edward
(1794-1865)
Clergyman, statesman, orator

A classics professor at Harvard and eventually the university's president, Everett also held many high government offices, including U.S. Congressman (1824-1834), governor of Massachusetts (1835-1839), minister to Great Britain (1841-1845) and U.S. Senator (1853-1854). He was noted for brilliant oratory. His many wartime speeches rallied Northern support for the government and were judged by some to be his primary achievement; perhaps the most famous was his two-hour speech preceding Lincoln's brief Gettysburg Address.

Ewell, Richard Stoddert
(1817-1872) Confederate general

Born in Georgetown, D.C., this West Point-trained career officer participated in Indian fighting and the Mexican War. Despite his Unionist sympathies, he became a Confederate brigadier general in June 1861. Ewell was a "fighting" commander. He led the second brigade at First Bull Run; as a major general he won victories at Winchester and Cross Keys and participated in the Peninsular Campaign and at Cedar Mountain and Second Bull Run. Despite the loss of a leg (August 1862), he led the Second Corps as a lieutenant general at Gettysburg, the Wilderness and Spotsylvania. Commanding the Department of Henrico, he was captured by Philip Sheridan at Sayler's Creek in April 1865. He was a Nashville farmer after the war.

Thomas Ewing, Jr.

Ewing, Thomas Jr.
(1829-1896) Union general

A Kansas lawyer and antislavery activist who helped to keep Kansas a free sate, he attended the 1861 Peace Convention in Washington. He resigned from the state supreme court to join the Union army in 1862, fought in Arkansas and commanded the Border District (where he issued the famous Order No. 11, which depopulated western Missouri in order to eradicate the guerrillas) and at St. Louis. He was a prominent Ohio (and, after 1881, New York) lawyer and politician after the war.

Democratic, then as a Republican. Enlisting as a Union private in 1861, he was soon promoted to captain. He led a regiment in the Iron Brigade at Second Bull Run and was wounded and captured at Gettysburg. Promoted to brigadier general in 1863, he resigned soon after, becoming governor of Wisconsin from 1886 to 1872, then serving as consul in England and Paris and then as ambassador to Spain (1880-1882).

Farnsworth, Elon John
(1837-1863) Union general

This Michigan native left the Utah Expedition against the Mormons to join the Union's 8th Illinois Cavalry in September 1861. He fought in every regimental operation (some 41 engagements) until his death, meanwhile serving as acting chief quartermaster of IV Corps and later as General Alfred Pleasanton's aide-de-camp. Farnsworth was killed while courageously leading a doomed cavalry charge, ordered by General H. J. Kilpatrick on the third day at Gettysburg, four days after his promotion to brigadier general.

Fairchild, Lucius
(1831-1896) Union general

Born in Ohio, Fairchild joined the California Gold Rush in 1849, then returned to Wisconsin to hold public office, first as a

Lucius Fairchild

Farragut, David Glasgow
(1801-1870) Union admiral

Born in Tennessee, orphaned young, educated in Washington, D.C., and Pennsylvania, he entered the U.S. Navy in 1810, when he was nine, and went to sea the following year in the frigate USS *Essex*. In 1812 the captain of the *Essex*, Farragut's guardian, David Porter, gave the 12-year-old midshipman his first command, a prize of war taken in the Pacific Ocean. Farragut sailed the vessel safely and without incident across the Pacific to the Chilean port of Valparaiso.

After the War of 1812 he served in the Mediterranean for five years. There had not been time for much formal education,

BELOW: David Glasgow Farragut.

OPPOSITE: Farragut on *Hartford*'s quarterdeck (top) and (below) a view of Mobile Bay's Fort Morgan.

so he resumed his studies during a nine-month period ashore with the American consul in Tunis. In fact, Farragut always tended to pick up knowledge wherever it was available: in the 1820s, while living in New Haven, he attended lectures at Yale, and he audited lectures at the Smithsonian Institution during a tour of duty in Washington.

Farragut served in the West Indies and in the South Atlantic and commanded the sloop *Saratoga* on blockade duty off Vera Cruz during the Mexican War. He spent many years on shore duty, much of it in Norfolk, Virginia, where he met his first

Edward Ferrero

wife, who died in 1840, and his second, whom he married three years later. In 1854 the navy sent him west to establish a shipyard at Mare Island, California, and he received the coveted promotion to captain the following year.

Unemployed at the outbreak of the Civil War, he went into a brief period in limbo in New York: the authorities evidently considered his loyalty suspect – he was Tennessee born, with Virginia connections by marriage. He finally received an active appointment on January 9, 1862, when he was given command of the Gulf Blockading Squadron.

Farragut launched the initial Union effort to open the Mississippi on April 18,

1862. "As to being prepared for defeat, I certainly am not," he had written his wife. "I hope for success; shall do all in my power to secure it, and trust to God for the rest." Six days later, on the night of April 23-24, he sailed his flotilla past the guns of Confederate forts Jackson and St. Philip, fought a sharp battle with Confederate warships and captured New Orleans. The victory earned him a promotion to rear admiral and confirmed him as the pre-eminent Union naval commander. It came as he approached his 50th anniversary of naval service.

In 1862 and 1863 Farragut commanded the naval forces in the combined operations against Vicksburg, which finally fell to Ulysses S. Grant's besieging army on July 4, 1863. He sailed to New York City in his flagship, the steam sloop *Hartford*, to a hero's welcome in August. The Navy secretary, Gideon Welles, said of Farragut that he would "more willingly take great risks to obtain great results than any officer in either army or navy." After several months of rest, he returned to the Gulf of Mexico early in 1864 to plan a daring assault on the Confederate defenses in Mobile Bay.

His fleet moved against the Alabama harbor forts early on August 5, 1864. Despite mines – then known as torpedoes – in the channel and an accurate fire from the forts, he pressed on. One of his monitors, *Tecumseh*, struck a torpedo and sank. ''Torpedoes ahead," someone called from the sloop-of-war *Brooklyn*, next ahead of Farragut's flagship. "Damn the torpedoes," he replied. Soon the fleet was safely into Mobile Bay. There followed a fierce battle with the defending Confederate fleet, but eventually all the Rebel ships and forts surrendered. The South had lost the use of its greatest remaining port.

Farragut returned to New York City at year's end. Failing health prevented him from taking command of the naval forces assembling to attack Wilmington, North Carolina, the last Confederate port to remain open. After a convalescent leave, he served briefly on the James River in Virginia and was one of the first Northern officers to enter Richmond after the fall of the Confederate capital on April 3, 1865.

Promoted to full admiral in July 1866, he was the first to hold that rank in the U.S. Navy's history. Farragut commanded the European Squadron in 1867 before going into semi-retirement. He never fully recovered from a severe heart attack in 1869. He died on August 14 of the following year in the commandant's house at the navy yard in Portsmouth, New Hampshire.

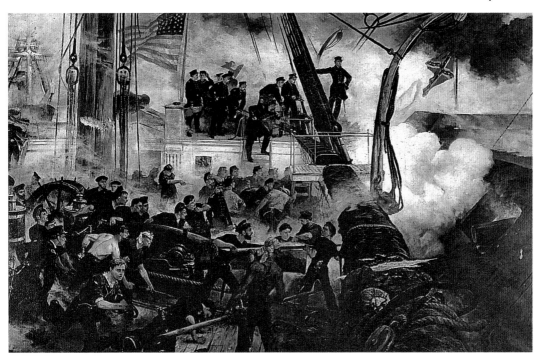

Ferrero, Edward
(1831-1899) Union general

This Spanish immigrant, a New York dancing instructor and militiaman, fought under Ambrose Burnside in North Carolina, led Potomac Army troops from Second Bull Run through Fredericksburg and joined Ulysses S. Grant's army at Vicksburg and Knoxville. He won notoriety at the Petersburg crater by abandoning his black division after ordering them to charge.

Fessenden, James Deering
(1833-1882) Union general

A Bowdoin College graduate and Maine lawyer, he recruited sharpshooters and trained Union volunteers in Virginia in 1861. He was David Hunter's aide-de-camp in the Carolinas in March 1862. He fought at Charleston in spring 1863 and later in the year at Lookout Mountain and Missionary Ridge. His distinguished contribution to the Atlanta Campaign was rewarded with a promotion in administrative posts. While on Hunter's staff Fessenden organized the first black Union regiment, which the authorities, however, disbanded. As a Portland, Maine, lawyer he was later register of bankruptcy (1868-1878).

Finley, Jesse Johnson
(1812-1904) Confederate general

This Tennessee-born lawyer served in the Seminole War, was an Arkansas legislator, a mayor of Memphis, a Whig politician and a judge before he enlisted in the Confederate army in 1862. Appointed a brigadier general in 1863, he fought in Kirby Smith's

Clinton Bowen Fisk

Farragut on *Hartford* during the duel with Fort Morgan in Mobile Bay

Kentucky Campaign, at Chickamauga and in the Atlanta Campaign. He was wounded at Resaca and Jonesboro. He served in the U.S. Congress and Senate after the war.

Fisk, Clinton Bowen
(1828-1890) Union general

A New York-born banker, Fisk was wiped out by the Panic of 1857. A friend of both Ulysses S. Grant and Abraham Lincoln, he joined the Union forces in Missouri and was eventually breveted a major general for war service. After the war Fisk was appointed to the Freedman's Bureau and went on to open an African-American school in Nashville, chartered as Fisk University in 1867. From 1881 to 1890 he was president of the Board of Indian Commissioners. A Methodist and temperance leader, in 1888 he was a presidential candidate for the Prohibition Party.

Floyd, John Buchanan
(1806-1863) Confederate general

Born in Blacksburg, Virginia, and educated at the College of South Carolina, he practiced law and politics and won election to

John Buchanan Floyd

Andrew Hull Foote

Fogg, Isabella
Sanitary Commission worker

She joined a Maine regiment as a nurse when her son enlisted in 1861. Fogg served the Potomac Army in field hospitals, the hospital ship *Elm City* and behind the lines in the Peninsular and Antietam Campaigns and at Fredericksburg, Chancellorsville, Gettysburg and the Wilderness. In January 1865 she was permanently disabled by a fall sustained on a hospital ship.

Foote, Andrew Hull
(1806-1863) Union admiral

The son of a Connecticut Senator, he became a midshipman in 1822 and, as a deeply religious man, worked during his naval career for temperance and other reforms (he was instrumental in abolishing the navy's spirit ration in 1862). He wrote and lectured against the slave trade in the 1850s. From August 1861 to May 1862 he commanded the Union's upper Mississippi naval operations, building the river flotilla and fighting at forts Henry and Donelson. Invalided and promoted to rear admiral, he then directed the bureau of equipment and

Foote's Mississippi fleet bombarding Island No. 10. This Confederate stronghold fell on April 7, 1862.

the Virginia governorship in 1850. Floyd served as President James Buchanan's secretary of war from 1857 until the end of 1860, when he resigned to try his fortunes with the new Confederacy. Commissioned a brigadier general in 1861, he was in command at Fort Donelson, Kentucky, when Union forces under Ulysses S. Grant attacked in February 1862. Floyd turned the fort over to his next in command and fled before the Federals captured the place. Jefferson Davis relieved him of his command.

recruiting. Foote died of illness in June 1863 en route to assume command of Samuel Du Pont's squadron off Charleston, South Carolina.

Forbes, Edwin
(1839-1895) War artist

He was a New York artist sent by *Frank Leslie's Illustrated Newspaper* to illustrate the Potomac Army's operations. Forbes stayed in the field from 1861 to 1864, sending back a series of sketches of camps and battlefields. Later etched as *Life Studies of the Great Army* (1876), these Civil War sketches remained the highlight of his long career as an illustrator and artist.

Force, Manning Ferguson
(1824-1899) Union general

Born in Washington, D.C., he became a lawyer. He was appointed a Union major in 1861 and fought at Fort Donelson, Shiloh and in the Vicksburg Campaign. Promoted to brigadier general in August 1863, he served in W. T. Sherman's 1864 Meridan and Atlanta campaigns. He was shot in the face just outside Atlanta, but he continued to serve in the March to the Sea. He was eventually (1892) awarded the Medal of Honor for his actions at Atlanta. After the war he was a lawyer, judge and writer.

Forney, William Henry
(1823-1894) Confederate general

This North Carolina-born lawyer had served in the U.S. Army in the Mexican War but in 1861 accepted a commission as a captain for the Confederates. During his career he was wounded at Dranesville, Williamsburg, Salem Church and Gettysburg. He was captured while in the hospital after Williamsburg, and then again at Gettysburg. Though permanently crippled after Gettysburg, he was appointed a brigadier general after his release and fought at Petersburg, Hatcher's Run, High Bridge, Farmville and Appomattox. He was a legislator after the war.

Forrest, Nathan Bedford
(1821-1877) Confederate General

His father, a blacksmith who settled on the Tennessee frontier in 1806, died when he was 16, leaving him to be the sole support for a large family. Forrest had scant education but a surplus of native wit; starting as a farm laborer and building on a small livestock trading business, he bought cotton plantations in Arkansas and Mississippi and gradually amassed a fortune.

In 1849 Forrest moved to Memphis, and for a time was an alderman there. He had had no military training, so when war

broke out he enlisted as a private in a Confederate cavalry regiment that he raised and equipped at his own expense. By October 1861 he had risen to lieutenant colonel's rank and had taken command of the regiment. During his first major campaign, at Fort Donelson in February 1862, he argued against surrender of the besieged garrison and, when his arguments failed, led his troopers, with several hundred volunteers from other units, through the Union lines to escape the doomed fort.

Seriously wounded at the Battle of Shiloh in April 1862, he recovered and embarked on a career that would make him one of the greatest cavalry raiders of the Civil War. His first foray, in the midsummer of 1862, took him to Murfreesboro, Tennessee, where he surprised the Federal garrison, captured 1,000 prisoners, destroyed or carried off supplies valued at $1 million and wrecked a long stretch of railroad. Operating from west Tennessee in 1862-63, he raided Ulysses S. Grant's supply lines and seriously impeded his drive on Vicksburg. When Federal forces brought Forrest to bay at Parker's Crossroads, Tennessee, on the last day of 1862, he is reputed to have ordered his cavalry, "Charge them both ways!" In the event,

An Edwin Forbes sketch shows Union troops re-forming at Antietam.

Nathan Bedford Forrest

hard-pressed Confederate troopers kept the two Federal wings from meeting long enough to escape.

In the spring of 1863 Forrest broke up a Federal raid styled after one of his own deep penetrations. After a long, exhausting chase he caught Union Colonel Abel Streight's cavalry at Cedar Bluffs, Alabama, and, through a ruse that involved marching his men and guns in a circle, convinced Streight to surrender his 1,500 troopers to one-third as many Confederates.

He fought at Chickamauga in September 1863 and in the aftermath of the battle clashed with the Confederate commander in Tennessee, Braxton Bragg. After investigating the incident, C.S.A. President Jefferson Davis declined to lay blame on either officer, but he promoted Forrest to major general and transferred him to another command, where he soon resumed his independent and highly successful raiding.

In April 1864 Forrest's command carried out the infamous massacre of black troops who had tried to surrender at Fort Pillow, Tennessee. Though Forrest denied ordering the killings, he earlier had threatened the Federals with no quarter, a tactic he often used to encourage the enemy to give up. In this instance, the Confederates carried out the threat, killing several dozen black soldiers in cold blood.

From June to November 1864 Forrest led a series of raids on W. T. Sherman's lines of communication and fought several defensive battles against large Federal forces dispatched to track down and destroy him. Sherman vowed to stop Forrest "if it costs ten thousand lives and bankrupts the federal treasury," but his executants were scarcely up to the task. Forrest routed a Federal force with nearly twice his numbers at Brice's Cross Roads, Mississippi, on June 10, capturing 2,000 men, 16 guns and 250 wagons. A month later, again heavily outnumbered, he fought a drawn battle against A. J. Smith's Federals at Tupelo, losing nearly 1,100 men before Smith, low on ammunition and rations, retreated to Memphis to refit. When Smith

returned to the chase, Forrest, in an audacious raid, rode into Memphis with 2,000 men on August 21 and just missed taking two Union generals prisoner before he retired. In October and November, in one of his most successful raids, another foray into west Tennessee, he destroyed four gunboats, 14 river transports and 20 barges, and took or burned nearly $7 million-worth of property.

Forrest commanded the Confederate cavalry in J. B. Hood's disastrous Tennessee Campaign of late 1864 and returned to independent operations after the destruction of Hood's army in December. Promotion to lieutenant general came to him in February 1865, though by then his troops were so worn down by fighting and hunger that they had lost much of their effectiveness. In March and April Forrest could not stop Union General James H. Wilson's raid to Selma, Alabama, perhaps his only important failure of the war. On May 4 his troops were surrendered.

"I went into the army worth a million and a half dollars and came out a beggar," Forrest said. He suffered personal losses too. One of his seven brothers was killed commanding a brigade at Okolona, Mississippi, in February 1864; a second died of pneumonia in Confederate service. Forrest returned to his cotton interests after the war and, for a time, served as president of a railroad that eventually went bankrupt. He had a brief postwar involvement with the Ku Klux Klan in Tennessee, holding office as its Grand Wizard from 1867 to 1869.

Tall, lithe, powerful, mild in repose but fiercely – some said maniacally – aggressive in battle, Forrest had an instinctive genius for soldiering. His colloquial formula for battlefield success, "Get thar fust with the most men," is widely quoted, but the notion that he was uniformly coarse of speech and manner is myth. Someone once asked Gen. Joseph E. Johnston to name the war's preeminent soldier. Johnston answered: "Forrest, who, had he had the advantages of a thorough military education and training, would have been the great central figure of the Civil War."

Fowle, Elida Barker Rumsey
(1842-1919) Philanthropist

Too young to enlist as an army nurse, she developed a private wartime relief effort, visiting camps and hospitals and raising money by performing concerts with her fiancé, John Fowle. The pair founded the Soldiers' Free Library in Washington, D.C., and became such famous field nurses that they were married before a joint session of Congress in March 1863. After the war she performed charitable works in New York and Boston.

Fox, Gustavus Vasa
(1821-1883)
Union assistant navy secretary

An Annapolis graduate, Fox resigned from the navy in 1856 and became a manufacturer in his native Massachusetts. In April 1861 he headed a volunteer expedition to reinforce Fort Sumter, arriving in time to observe the bombardment and evacuate the Federals after their surrender: Lincoln commended this operation. The post of first assistant secretary of the navy was created for him, and throughout the war Fox proved an indispensable planner of naval operations. He proposed David Farragut for the New Orleans command and supported the adoption of the ironclad *Monitor*. He afterward returned to his Massachusetts business career.

Franklin, William Buel
(1823-1903) Union general

This Pennsylvania-born West Point graduate was a surveyor in the Mexican war and on Stephen Kearney's Rocky Mountain expedition. Appointed a colonel in May 1861 and promoted to brigadier general three days later, he fought at First Bull Run, in

William Buel Franklin

the Peninsular Campaign and at Antietam. He was blamed by Ambrose Burnside and the Committee on the Conduct of the War for his part in the Union's disaster at Fredericksburg. He was wounded at Pleasant Hill in April 1864 and then was captured that July by Jubal Early's men, only to escape a day later. He never served in the field after his capture but remained in the army until 1866. He was vice-president of the Colt's Fire Arms Manufacturing Company until 1888, then held various public offices.

Frémont, John Charles
(1813-1890) Union general

Raised in South Carolina, he joined the army's topographical corps and began his explorations of the western frontier. In his first major independent expedition he employed Kit Carson as a guide along the route of the Oregon Trail (1842). His spectacular 1843-1844 expedition through Oregon, Vancouver, Nevada, New Mexico and Utah made him a national hero. These explorations were important first steps in settling the western territories. His expedition members formed the "California Battalion" during the Mexican War and helped to secure California, where he was briefly governor (1847). He became rich during the Gold Rush and later led expeditions to identify railroad routes. In 1856 he was the Republican and Know-Nothing presidential candidate. From July 1861 he commanded the Union army's Department of

John C. Frémont (left), as the 1864 Radical Democratic candidate

the West, a difficult job made worse by the flamboyance, recklessness and corruption of his administration and by his excessively harsh policies toward slave-holders (which precipitated his removal). Sent abruptly to the Mountain Department in March 1862, Frémont failed to stop T. J. Jackson in his Shenandoah Valley Campaign of 1862 and was relieved of his command in June when he refused to serve under his old adversary, John Pope. The favored candidate of the Radical Republicans to oppose Lincoln in 1864, he withdrew from the race in September. After the war his fortunes and reputation declined steadily: he went bankrupt as the president of the Memphis and El Paso Railroad (1865-1873). He did, however, serve as a territorial governor of Arizona (1878-1883).

French, William Henry
(1815-1881) Union general

A Maryland-born West Point graduate, he fought in the Seminole and Mexican wars. He held Union commands in the Gulf and in Washington's defenses in 1861-1862 and fought on the Peninsula and at Antietam, Fredericksburg, Chancellorsville and Gettysburg. He lost his command of III Corps after misjudgements in the Mine Run Campaign (1863), ending his wartime field service.

William Henry French

Frietschie, Barbara Hauer
(1766-1862) Patriot

Barbara Frietschie (Fritchie), as she was popularly imagined

She was the widow of a Frederick, Maryland, glovemaker. According to popular legend, as T. J. Jackson's troops marched out of the border town of Frederick en route to Antietam in September 1862, this 95-year-old patriot defiantly waved a Union flag, winning Jackson's respect. Upon hearing this story, John Greenleaf Whittier composed his 1863 poem "Barbara Fritchie," which made her a national heroine. There is, however, scant evidence that the incident ever took place.

Fry, Birkett Davenport
(1822-1891) Confederate general

He practiced law in his native Virginia and California and was an Alabama businessman before the war. A Mexican War veteran, he joined the Confederate army's 13th Alabama infantry in 1861. Fry was repeatedly wounded (at Seven Pines, Antietam, Chancellorsville and Gettysburg): at Gettysburg he was captured while leading a brigade in Pickett's Charge. Exchanged in April 1864 and promoted to brigadier general, he fought at Drewry's Bluff and Cold Harbor. He later commanded the District of Augusta. After the war he was a cotton trader in Alabama and Virginia.

Birkett Davenport Fry

Gamble, Hamilton Rowan
(1798-1864)
Union governor of Missouri

A Virginia-born Missouri legislator and judge, he left retirement in 1861 to become provisional governor in June when secessionist officials fled the state. Gamble

James Abram Garfield

opposed the government's draft of soldiers as unconstitutional but led a Union-funded militia against Southern-guerrillas, keeping Missouri free and in the Union. He died in office amid bitter controversy over emancipation.

Garfield, James Abram
(1831-1881) **Union general and 20th president of the United States**

Garfield worked his way through an impoverished childhood, was graduated from Williams College and became a teacher and lay preacher. He left the Ohio legislature (1859-1861) for the Union army's 42nd Ohio in 1861 and earned rapid promotions, leading brigades at Middle Creek, Pound Gap and Shiloh. He was William Rosecrans's chief of staff in the Chickamauga Campaign before resigning as a major general in December 1863 to sit in the U.S. Congress (1863-1880). He was a Republican Party loyalist who earned a reputation for his advocacy of sound finance policy. A compromise candidate, he was elected U.S. president in a close election in 1880. He was assassinated by a disappointed office-seeker in July 1861.

Garnett, Richard Brooke
(1819-1863) **Confederate general**

A Virginian West Point graduate and career officer, he saw fighting in the Seminole and Mexican wars and frontier service before resigning to join the Confederate army in 1861. He led the Stonewall Brigade under T. J. Jackson in the Shenandoah Valley Campaign of 1862 but was relieved of his command for ordering his brigade's withdrawal at Kernstown in March. He commanded George Pickett's brigade in the Maryland Campaign and his own brigade at Fredericksburg. He was killed in Pickett's Charge at Gettysburg.

Kenner Garrard

Garrard, Kenner
(1828-1879) **Union officer**

This Kentucky-born West Point graduate was captured in April 1861 by Southern sympathizers while in San Antonio, Texas, and then paroled. He was commissioned a colonel in the Union army in 1862 and fought at Fredericksburg, Chancellorsville and Gettysburg, in the Rappahannock and Mine Run campaigns and at Covington and Nashville. He was breveted major general for war service. He resigned in 1866, worked in real estate and studied history after the war.

Gary, Martin Weatherspoon
(1831-1881) **Confederate general**

This South Carolina-born lawyer was a secessionist leader. As a commissioned captain in what became known as the Confederate army's Hampton Legion, he fought in various battles, including First Bull Run, the battles of the Peninsular Campaign, Second Bull Run, Antietam, Fredericksburg, Chickamauga, Knoxville and Appomattox. Appointed a brigadier general in May 1864, Gary was the last Confederate general in Richmond before its fall. He escorted Jefferson Davis to Cokesbury, South Carolina, where one of the last cabinet meetings was held at the house of Gary's mother. He was a legislator after the war.

Getty, George Washington
(1819-1901) **Union general**

Born in Washington, D.C., this West Point graduate was a veteran of the Seminole and Mexican wars. He commanded Union artillery batteries in the Peninsular Campaign and at South Mountain and Antietam. As a brigadier general he led a division at Fredericksburg. He constructed entrenched lines at Norfolk and Portsmouth and suffered severe wounds in the Battle of the Wilderness, recovering to participate in the Shenandoah Valley Campaign of Philip Sheridan, the Petersburg siege and the final pursuit of Robert E. Lee. He retired from active service in 1883.

George Washington Getty

John Gibbon

Gibbon, John
(1827-1896) **Union general**

This Pennsylvania-born West Point graduate served in the Seminole War and on the frontier. He joined the Union army even though three of his brothers chose to fight with the Confederate forces. He began as General Irvin McDowell's chief of artillery and was made a brigadier general in May 1862. He fought at Gainesville, Second Bull Run and Antietam; at South Mountain his command was named the Iron Brigade. He was wounded at both Fredericksburg and Gettysburg. After his recovery after Gettysburg, he fought at the Wilderness, Spotsylvania, Cold Harbor, Petersburg and Appomattox. He was promoted to major general in 1864 and continue in the regular army until 1891. He spent most of his years after the war on the frontier and led the relief column to Little Big Horn in 1876; it arrived in time to bury George Custer and all his men.

Gillmore, Quincy Adams
(1825-1888) **Union general**

This Ohio-born West Point graduate was an engineer and teacher at West Point before being appointed the Union's acting chief engineer on the Port Royal expedition to South Carolina in 1861. He was injured after falling from his horse in pursuit of Jubal Early in the Shenandoah Valley in 1864. After his recovery he served on various boards and commissions. He became especially well known for the 400 medals – the Gillmore Medal of Honor – he personally issued to the enlisted men who had served under him in Charleston, South Carolina, in a vain effort to recapture Fort Sumter. (The fort surrendered only on April 14, 1865.) After the war, he remained in the regular army, wrote several engineering texts and was president of the Mississippi River Commission.

Gilson, Helen Louise
(1835-1868)
Sanitary Commission worker

A Massachusetts native, she organized a local soldier's aid society before joining the Sanitary Commission in 1862. She began her field work in the Peninsula and accompanied the Potomac Army for two years. She specialized in organizing contraband and freed blacks to provide services to Union troops. Taking over the City Point hospital in Virginia in June 1864, she reorganized a crude operation into a model of efficiency.

Goldsborough, Louis Malesherbes
(1805-1877) **Union naval officer**

He joined the navy as a boy in 1816 and saw action in the first Seminole War and in Mexico. Appointed to command the Union's Atlantic Blockading Squadron in September 1861, Goldsborough led Union naval forces in the successful joint operation with A. E. Burnside along the North Carolina coast in February 1862. He came in for heavy criticism in May 1862 when his James River flotilla failed to capture Rich-

Quincy Adams Gillmore

Helen Louise Gilson

mond. In September, largely as a result of this criticism, he asked to be relieved. Goldsborough held administrative appointments in Washington until the last months of the war, when he commanded the European Squadron. He retired in 1873 after 57 years of service.

Gordon, John Brown
(1832-1904) **Confederate general**

Gordon practiced law in Alabama and was developing coal mines in his native Georgia in 1861. An untrained but gifted officer, he fought with the Confederacy's 6th Ala-

bama and then with a Georgia brigade at Seven Pines, Malvern Hill, Antietam, Chancellorsville, Gettysburg and Spotsylvania. Appointed a major general, he led the failed assault on Fort Stedman at Petersburg. His wife, Fanny Haralson Gordon, accompanied him in the field throughout the war. Later, as a popular Democratic U.S. Senator (1873-1880, 1891-1897) and state governor (1886-1890), he promoted Georgia's industrial and commercial development so successfully that he became a revered figure in the state.

Gorgas, Josiah
(1818-1883)
Confederate general, chief of ordnance

This Pennsylvania-born West Point graduate studied military units in Europe before fighting in the Mexican War. He resigned from the U.S. Army in April 1861 and joined the Confederates as chief of ordnance. Appalled at the lack of supplies, by 1863 he had gotten the ordnance bureau running successfully, and by November 1864 he was promoted to brigadier general. After the war he served as chancellor of Sewanee College and president of the University of Alabama. He was the father or William C. Gorgas, who later became the surgeon general.

Granger, Gordon
(1822-1876) Union general

This New York-born West Point graduate served in the Mexican War, and on the frontier as an Indian fighter. He was appointed a major general in the Union army in 1862. Among other battles, he fought at Wilson's Creek, New Madrid and Island No. 10, Tullahoma, Chickamauga, Missionary Ridge, Knoxville and Mobile. He remained in the regular army after the war and died while on duty.

Grant, Ulysses Simpson
(1822-1885) Union general, 18th president of the United States

A tanner's son, born Hiram Ulysses Grant at Point Pleasant, Ohio, he grew up in modest circumstances. His hard-working father eventually attained a degree of prosperity, enabling him to attend school regularly until the age of 17. Hating the tannery, he worked on his father's farm, where he became a master handler of horses. Grant loved animals and disapproved of killing them, even for food. He once explained his distaste for chicken by saying he could not bring himself "to eat anything that goes on two legs."

He arrived at West Point in 1839. Listed incorrectly as Ulysses S. Grant, he dropped Hiram, adopted his mother's maiden name of Simpson and retained the new designation for the rest of his life. His cadet career was uneventful. Commissioned in 1843, he served in Missouri and Louisiana. In 1846-47 he fought in Mexico, earning citations for bravery, and performed ably as quartermaster in Winfield Scott's army during the march on Mexico City.

Grant married Julia Dent in 1848. Assigned to remote Pacific Coast garrisons

ABOVE: Ulysses Simpson Grant.

OPPOSITE: A haggard Grant after the grisly Battle of Cold Harbor.

where she could not follow, he was miserable, lonely and increasingly bibulous. Higher authority reprimanded him for his heavy drinking, and he resigned from the service in 1854, evidently to avoid being dismissed.

He was a failure in civil life. Unable to make farming pay, he was reduced during one difficult period to selling firewood for a living. In 1860 he went to work as a clerk in his brothers' dry goods store in Galena, Illinois. The advent of the Civil War changed Grant's fortunes at a stroke. In June 1861 he obtained a commission in the Union army as colonel of an Illinois volunteer infantry regiment. By September he had risen to brigadier in command of the Cairo military district. "Be careful," his father wrote. "You're a general now; it's a good job, don't lose it."

In early 1862 Grant set out on the Kentucky-Tennessee River Campaign that would first make him famous. Moving swiftly, with gunboat support, he captured Fort Henry and then Fort Donelson – the latter the most important Union victory of the war to date. At Shiloh, in April, he allowed his army to be surprised and nearly routed, but he recovered on the second day and drove the Confederates from the field. In the aftermath of bloody Shiloh Lincoln rejected calls for his removal. "I can't spare this man," the president said. "He fights."

Quiet and shy, unprepossessing in appearance, Grant proved himself over the next year to be a bold and brilliant strategist and a master of the logistical problems of war. In spite of his early trials, he seemed to be without fear of failure. His campaign against Vicksburg, the fortress city controlling the Mississippi River, ended on July 4, 1863, with the surrender of the city. It was probably the war's pivotal Union victory. In November Grant lifted the siege of Chattanooga, Tennessee, decisively defeating the Confederates under Braxton Bragg at Missionary Ridge.

Lincoln appointed Grant commander-in-chief of all the Union armies in March 1864. Making his headquarters in the field with the Army of the Potomac, Grant moved against Robert E. Lee in Virginia while W.T. Sherman, his successor in Tennessee marched into Georgia towards Atlanta. Grant crossed the Rapidan on May 4, and over the next six weeks he and Robert E. Lee clashed in an uninterrupted series of terrible battles – the Wilderness, Spotsylvania, Cold Harbor and Petersburg. "I propose to fight it on this line if it takes all summer," Grant wrote in a famous dispatch from Spotsylvania. His surprise crossing of the James River in June has been called one of the most brilliant operations of the war, for it forced Lee to adopt a static defense behind the lines at Petersburg. But Grant's army had been so

for the presidency and won an overwhelming election victory in November. His two terms were undistinguished and were marked by unprecedented graft and corruption, though scandal never touched Grant himself. He left office with a net worth of only a few thousand dollars. His final years were difficult. He tried business again – and failed again. He pledged his swords and other military memorabilia as credit and lost them. Then a painful throat cancer gradually weakened him. He died on July 23, 1885, not long after he finished his *Personal Memoirs*, one of the great classics of military literature. Grant's friend Mark Twain saw to publication of the manuscript. Royalties from the book left Grant's widow and children financially secure to the end of their lives.

Two Grant victories: Fort Donelson (top) and Lookout Mountain (right). Shown opposite are scenes of his life.

bled that it could not crack the Petersburg defenses. From his crossing of the Rapidan on May 4 to June 19, when Grant suspended the Petersburg offensive and settled down to a siege, the Potomac army had lost 66,000 men – fully half its strength at the start of the campaign.

Grant's last campaign opened on March 29, 1865, with the Union cavalry under Philip Sheridan ranging out beyond the Confederate flank. With strong infantry support, Sheridan turned Lee's right at Five Forks on April 1, forcing the abandonment of Petersburg and the evacuation of Richmond. Lee retreated westward along the Appomattox River, hoping to outrun the Federals and link up with J. E. Johnston's small army in North Carolina. But Sheridan forced the pursuit. "If the thing is pressed I think Lee will surrender," he wrote to Grant after the battle of Sayler's Creek on April 6. Grant passed the message on to Lincoln. "Let the thing be pressed," the president replied.

Grant offered Lee generous terms, including a proviso that Confederate officers and men would be paroled and could go home. Lee signed the surrender document at Appomattox Court House on the afternoon of April 9, and the Army of Northern Virginia passed out of existence.

Over the summer Grant supervised the dismantling of the vast Union war machine. As commander-in-chief of the army, he subsequently oversaw the military aspects of Reconstruction, often finding himself at odds with the martyred Lincoln's successor, Andrew Johnson. In 1868 Grant accepted the Republican nomination

Horace Greeley

Greeley, Horace
(1811-1872) Editor and politician

New Hampshire-born Greeley was a New York printer and newspaper editor after 1831. There he founded the Whig *Tribune* (1841, editor until 1872). The leading Northern newspaper, the New York *Tribune* was a forum for antislavery, anticompromise and emancipation views. Greeley was at first a powerful moral spokesman for the North, but he eroded his popular support by withholding support from Lincoln and opposing conciliatory policies for most of the war and then, towards its end, urging Lincoln to negotiate a peace treaty favorable to the South. As the Democratic presidential candidate in 1872, he was soundly defeated by Ulysses S. Grant. He died, apparently insane, two months later.

Green, Thomas
(1814-1864) Confederate general

Born in Virginia, Green served in the Texas army, as an Indian fighter and in the Mexican War. Commissioned a colonel in the Confederate army in August 1861, he fought in the New Mexico operations, at Galveston, Camp Bisland, LaFourche, Fordoche and Bayou Bourbeau. He was appointed a brigadier general in May 1863 and went to Texas when Union General Nathaniel Banks mounted some half-hearted operations along the Texas coast late in the year. He was killed leading a cavalry attack in Louisiana during the Red River Campaign.

Greene, George Sears
(1801-1899) Union general

Born into an old Rhode Island family, this West Point mathematics teacher and artilleryman had resigned from the army in 1836 to build railroads. On the outbreak of the Civil War he enlisted in the Union army and fought in the Shenandoah Valley Campaign of 1862 and at Cedar Mountain, Antietam, Chancellorsville and Gettysburg. Shot in the face at Wauhatchie, he recovered to participate in W. T. Sherman's North Carolina Campaign. He later engineered major railroad, water, and sewage systems in New York, Washington, D.C., Detroit and other cities.

Greenhow, Rose O'Neal
(*c.*1815-1864) Confederate spy

She was born in Maryland. Married in 1835 to a prominent physician and historian, Robert Greenhow (1800-1854), she was a well-connected Washington political hostess and proslavery activist. She relayed Union General Irvin McDowell's plans for First Bull Run to P. G. T. Beauregard, and her home remained an exchange for Confederate intelligence during her subsequent house arrest. Imprisoned in January 1862, she relayed yet more information to the Confederates from her Washington jail.

George Sears Greene

Tried and exiled to the South, she traveled to England as a Confederate agent but was accidentally drowned while returning home.

Gregg, David McMurtrie
(1833-1916) Union general

A Pennsylvanian, he was a West Point-trained cavalryman and veteran Indian fighter at the outbreak of the Civil War. Commanding various Potomac Army cavalry units, he had a distinguished war career, seeing almost constant action from the Peninsula until his resignation in February 1865. He published an account of the activities of the 2nd Cavalry Division at Gettysburg (1907), where he had been commended for repelling a Confederate attack led by J. E. B. Stuart on the third day of the great battle.

LEFT: The Confederate spy Rose O'Neal Greenhow, shown with her daughter, when she was being held in the Old Capitol Prison in Washington, D.C., in the early months of the grim year (for the North) 1862.

BELOW: David Gregg (seated right).

Benjamin Henry Grierson

Grierson, Benjamin Henry
(1826-1911) Union general

After settling in Illinois as a young man, he taught music for a time before taking up the selling of fresh produce. When the Civil war broke out he volunteered and became the aide-de-camp to Union General Benjamin Prentiss. Although he was reputed to dislike horses, he was commissioned a major in he cavalry in October 1861, and in command of what soon become known as Grierson's brigade he participated in

Charles Griffon

several operations in Tennessee and Mississippi. As a diverson in support of Ulysses Grant's Vicksburg Campaign, Grierson set off from La Grange, Tennessee, on April 17, 1863, riding and raiding through Mississippi until he and his force of 1700 men reached Baton Rouge, Louisiana, on May 2. Having gone some 600 miles, they had destroyed about 50 miles of railroad, captured 1000 mules and horses, taken 500 prisoners and inflicted some 100 Confederate casualties – all at the cost of only 24 Union casualties. Grierson continued to participate in numerous campaigns and battles till the end of the war and ended up a brevet major general. He remained in the regular army, and as a colonel he commanded the 10th Cavalry in campaigns against Indians on the western frontier. He retired from the army in 1890.

Griffin, Charles
(1825-1867) Union general

Ohio-born Griffin was a West Point graduate and veteran artilleryman. His Union artillery company was decimated at First Bull Run. He went on to fight in the Peninsula and at Antietam, Fredericksburg, Chancellorsville and Gettysburg, as well as in the Petersburg and Appomattox campaigns. He finished the war a major general commanding V Corps, and was a surrender commissioner at Appomattox.

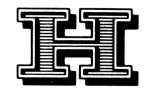

Hagood, Johnson
(1829-1898) Confederate general

A graduate of The Citadel, he was a South Carolina lawyer and planter. Hagood fought for the Confederacy at Fort Sumter and First Bull Run, participated in the defense of Charleston and returned to the field as a brigadier general for the Wilderness and Weldon Railroad battles and the Petersburg Campaign. Returning after the war to his plantation, he contributed much to the modernization of South Carolina's

Johnson Hagood

agriculture and educational system. He served as South Carolina's governor from 1880 to 1882.

Halleck, Henry Wager
(1815-1872) Union general

A farmer's son, he ran away from his Oneida County, New York, home to escape country life and to acquire an education. He earned a bachelor's degree from Union College, then went on to West Point, from which he was graduated, third in his class, in 1839.

Commissioned into the engineer corps, Halleck worked on harbor fortifications in New York and served in California during the Mexican War. A series of lectures he delivered in Boston was published in 1846 as *Elements of Military Art and Science*, and during the long sea passage to California he translated Jomini's *Vie de Napoléon*.

Known as "Old Brains" in the army for these scholarly contributions, he retired in 1854 to practice law in California. He turned down several political opportunities, including a seat on the state supreme court and the office of U.S. Senator, to concentrate on his business affairs; he managed

a quicksilver mine and was president of the Pacific & Atlantic Railroad.

When war broke out Winfield Scott, then commander-in-chief, urged President Lincoln to offer Halleck senior rank. Commissioned a major general in the Union army in August 1861, he took command of the Department of Missouri in St. Louis, where he restored honesty and order after the maladministration of John Frémont.

The success of Halleck's field commanders, Ulysses Grant and John Pope, brought command of the Department of the Mississippi to Halleck. Taking the field after the Battle of Shiloh in April 1862, he moved so cautiously on Corinth, Mississippi, that the outnumbered Confederate army under P. G. T. Beauregard managed to escape without serious harm.

This was Halleck's only field command. In July 1862 he went to Washington as military advisor to Lincoln, with the title of general-in-chief. Almost at once he showed himself ill-equipped for the task. He lacked strategic sense, hampered his field commanders by taking constant counsel of his fears for the safety of Washington and exasperated them with frequent, often offensive, advice.

ABOVE: Henry Wager Halleck.

BELOW: The Battle of Corinth.

Halleck was physically unattractive, with brusque and sometimes grating ways. The qualities that brought him success as lawyer and businessman made him an excellent army administrator, but his lack of charm and leadership ability greatly reduced his effectiveness as a commander and as an operator in Washington power circles. Halleck himself seemed to realize this; he once described his job as "political hell."

In March 1864, after Grant's promotion to lieutenant general, Halleck's job was downgraded to chief of staff. After the Confederate surrender Appomattox he briefly commanded the Military Division of the James, with his headquarters in Richmond. He headed the Military Division of the Pacific from 1865 to 1869, and the Division of the South, his last command, from 1869 to 1872. He died in Louisville, Kentucky, in January 1872.

Halpine, Charles Graham
(1829-1868) Union officer, author

Born in Ireland, he worked for the *New York Times* as their Washington correspondent. Enlisting as a Union private in April 1861, he fought in various battles until his resignation in July 1864, having been breveted to brigadier general for his service at Piedmont, Virginia. In contributing to newspapers about the Civil War, he wrote as "Pvt. Miles O'Reilly." In 1862 he wrote a poem entitled, "Sambo's Right to Be Kilt," referring to the first African-American troops mustered into the Federal forces. He later was active in the Democratic Party in New York City.

Charles Graham Halpine

Hamlin, Hannibal
(1809-1891)
Vice president of the United States

This Maine lawyer was an antislavery Democratic state and national legislator (U.S. Representative 1843-1847, Senator 1848-1861) who turned Republican in 1856 over slavery policy. He served as Abraham Lincoln's first-term vice president (1861-1865) and enjoyed good relations with Lincoln while promoting the Radical Republican emancipation agenda. After the war he represented Maine in the U.S. Senate (1869-1881) and was U.S. minister to Spain (1881-1882).

Hampton, Wade
(1818-1902) Confederate general

Born into the slaveholding aristocracy of upcountry South Carolina, the son and grandson of wealthy planters, Hampton

Hannibal Hamlin (left) and (below) cavalryman Wade Hampton

grew up on the family estate of Millwood, near Columbia, where he learned to ride and hunt in the cavalier tradition. He was graduated from South Carolina College in 1836.

Hampton studied law but decided not to practice, choosing instead to develop his family's Mississippi cotton plantations. He served in the South Carolina legislature from 1852-61. His experiences as a planter caused him to doubt the economic benefits of slavery, and he initially opposed secession. Nevertheless, when war came he raised the Hampton Legion, a mixed command of infantry, cavalry and artillery, and equipped it largely at his own expense.

He commanded the legion at First Bull Run and was wounded there. He recovered in time to lead an infantry brigade during the Peninsular Campaign in the spring of 1862. Wounded again at Seven Pines in May, he returned in late July to take charge of a brigade in J. E. B. Stuart's cavalry corps. Within two months, he had risen to become Stuart's second in command.

Hampton participated in the Antietam Campaign and the raid on Chambersburg, in the Gettysburg Campaign and in the Battle of Gettysburg itself, during which he received his third wound. He was promoted to major general in September 1863.

After Stuart's death in May 1864 he succeeded to the command of Robert E. Lee's cavalry corps. Hampton's troopers blocked Philip Sheridan's Trevilian Raid in June and fought at Sappony Church, Reams's Station and Burgess Mill during the Petersburg Campaign. Circumstances – especially the scarcity of fodder for his horses and the shortage of remounts – kept him largely on the defensive, and his chief responsibility turned out to be the protection of Richmond's lines of communication. In January 1865 he led a part of his command into the Carolinas in search of remounts. Ordered to cover Joseph E. Johnston's retreat, he did not return to the Virginia theater.

Hampton retired to his estates after the war and set about rebuilding his shrunken fortune. He re-entered politics in 1867 and 1868 to oppose Radical Republican Reconstruction policies in South Carolina. Elected governor in 1876 (over the protests of the "carpetbag" incumbent), he helped restore white supremacy to the state. He was re-elected in 1878 and sent to the U.S. Senate shortly thereafter.

Hampton represented a conservative political tradition, the old planter aristocracy. A populist movement developed in South Carolina during the 1880s under the leadership of Benjamin Tillman, whose supporters voted Hampton's conservatives out of office in 1890. Hampton was defeated in a bid for re-election to the Senate the following year.

He died at his home in Columbia in April 1902.

Hancock, Winfield Scott
(1824-1886) Union general

A Pennsylvania native, Hancock was graduated from West Point in 1844, fought in Mexico and was in California when the Civil War began. He returned east in August 1861 to help Union General George McClellan organize and train the Army of the Potomac. Hancock took charge of II Corps in June 1863 and became one of the best of the Potomac army's corps commanders. Seriously wounded at Gettysburg, where he played a major role, he returned to lead II Corps at the Wilderness, Spotsylvania, Cold Harbor and Petersburg. He saw postwar service on the frontier. Tall, dignified, known as "Hancock the Superb," he ran for president as a Democrat in 1880 and lost a close election to James Garfield.

Hardee, William Joseph
(1815-1873) Confederate general

This Georgian was graduated from West Point and fought in the Mexican War. He wrote *Hardee's Tactics* (1855), a definitive infantry manual later used by both sides in the Civil War. After 1956 he was commandant of cadets at West Point. As a Confederate officer he commanded Fort Morgan and, promoted to brigadier general, organized "Hardee's Brigade" in Arkansas. As a major general he led a Kentucky corps at Shiloh and Perryville and, promoted to lieutenant general, commanded the Confederate left wing at Stones River. Commanding the Department of South Carolina, Georgia and Florida, Hardee opposed W. T. Sherman during Sherman's Atlanta Campaign, March to the Sea and Carolinas Campaign. Forced to evacuate Savannah and Charleston, he retreated to North Carolina and surrendered. He was later an Alabama planter and businessman.

Winfield Scott Hancock (seated). With him, from the left: Francis Barlow, David B. Birney, and John Gibbon.

Harris, Eliza
Sanitary Commission volunteer

She distributed food and comforts and helped nurse the wounded from First Bull Run through Gettysburg. Her vivid newspaper accounts of life in the battle zone helped raise large sums for the Sanitary Commission. Mrs. Harris transferred her efforts to Tennessee in the autumn of 1863, returned to Virginia the following year and concluded her war service by nursing the survivors of the Andersonville prison camp.

Nathaniel Harrison Harris

Harris, Nathaniel Harrison
(1834-1900) Confederate general

He was born in Mississippi and was graduated from the University of Louisiana. In 1861 he organized the Warren Rifles in Vicksburg, where he had been practicing law. Joining the Confederate army's 19th Mississippi, he fought in he upper Shenandoah, at Williamsburg, in the Maryland Campaign, at Chancellorsville and Gettysburg and in every major engagement from Spotsylvania through Petersburg, later participating in the defense of Richmond and in the Appomattox Campaign. After the war he was a Vicksburg lawyer, a railroad president and, in later years, a California businessman.

Harrison, Benjamin
(1833-1901) Union officer and 23rd president of the United States

The grandson of President William Henry Harrison, he was an Indianapolis lawyer and Republican politician. He helped to raise the Union army's 70th Indiana and, despite his inexperience, held a series of commands in the Army of the Cumberland and was eventually breveted a brigadier general. He fought in Kentucky and Tennessee before joining W. T. Sherman for the Atlanta Campaign, March to the Sea and Carolinas Campaign. His unsuccessful Indiana gubernatorial race in 1876 brought him to national attention. After serving in the U.S. Senate (1881-1887), he was elected president of the U.S. (1888), failed in a re-election bid, and returned to his Indiana law practice.

Hatch, John Porter
(1822-1901) Union general

This New York-born West Point graduate, having served on the frontier and in the Mexican War, joined the U.S. cavalry at the outset of the war and was promoted to brigadier general by September 1861. He fought at Groveton and Second Bull Run and was so seriously wounded at South Mountain that he thereafter served only as a depot commander and on courts martial. He was given the Medal of Honor in 1893 for his service at South Mountain. He remained in the regular army until his retirement in 1866.

Haupt, Herman
(1817-1905) Union officer

Born in Pennsylvania, he was graduated from West Point in 1835 but soon resigned from the army to go into railroad engineering. He was famed for supervising the construction of the Hoosac Tunnel in western Massachusetts (1856) and for developing an improved pneumatic drill. Commissioned a colonel in the Union army in April 1862, he was placed in charge of the construction and operation of railroads for the Union forces. But he resigned in September 1863, objecting to what he regarded as bureaucratic interference, and went back to railroad building. He wrote several influential books on engineering and bridges.

Hawes, James Morrison
(c.1823-1889) Confederate general

This Kentucky-born West Point graduate served in the Mexican war, taught at West Point, spent two years at the French cavalry school and served on the frontier before resigning in May 1861 to join the Confederate forces as a captain. Promoted to brigadier general in 1862, he led cavalry brigades under A. S. Johnston and then in John Breckinridge's division. He fought at Shiloh, Vicksburg and Galveston Island. He was a hardware merchant after the war.

Hawley, Josph Roswell
(1826-1905) Union general

He was born into an old Connecticut family and there established a law practice. He helped to organize the state's Republican Party and in 1857 became the editor of

Herman Haupt (right) inspecting the construction of a Union railroad

the Republican Hartford *Evening Press* (later the *Courant*). He enlisted in the Union army in April 1861 and fought at First Bull Run, along the Confederacy's east coast and in Virginia, interrupting field service to recruit Northern volunteers. He led a peacekeeping force in New York during the 1864 election, and by the war's end he was Alfred Terry's chief of staff. Later he was Connecticut's governor (1866) and served as a U.S. Representative (1872-1875), (1879-1881) and Senator (1881-1905).

Hay, John Milton
(1838-1905) Author and statesman

He was born in Salem, Indiana, and was graduated from Brown University. Hay's Springfield, Illinois, law office was next to Abraham Lincoln's, and in 1861 he was

John Milton Hay (left), shown with President Abraham Lincoln

appointed Lincoln's private secretary, a job he performed with great ability and discretion throughout Lincoln's presidential years. Appointed an assistant adjutant general detailed to the White House (1864), he was formally the president's military aide during the last year of the war. He then held diplomatic posts in Paris, Madrid and Vienna (1865-1870; much later, he was ambassador to England, 1897). He served as assistant secretary of state (1879-1881), and, named secretary of state in 1898, sponsored the Open Door Policy toward China (1899-1900) and negotiated the peace after the Spanish-American War and the treaties that made possible the construction of the Panama Canal. In 1903 he settled the Alaskan boundary dispute with Canada. Alongside his diplomatic achievements he earned a reputation as one of the country's leading writers, publishing poems (*Pike Country Ballads*, 1871, and *Poems*, 1890), fiction (*The Bread-Winners*, 1884) and travel sketches (*Castilian Days*, 1871). With

John Nicolay, Hay also wrote the monumental 10-volume study, *Abraham Lincoln: A History* (1890).

Hayes, Rutherford Birchard
(1822-1893) Union general and 19th president of the United States

A Harvard Law School graduate, this Ohio lawyer and politician was commissioned a major in the Union army in 1861 and had an honorable, if modest, wartime career fighting in western Virginia and the Shenandoah Valley Campaigns of 1862 and 1864. He achieved national prominence as Ohio's governor (1868-1872, 1875-1877). As the price for winning the disputed presidential election of 1876, Republican Hayes kept his promise to the Democrats by withdrawing the last Union troops from the South on April 20, 1877, thus ending Reconstruction. He also campaigned to reform the treatment of both the inmates of prisons and the mentally ill.

Rutherford Birchard Hayes

Hazen, William Babcock
(1830-1887) Union general

This Vermont-born West Point graduate, an Indian fighter and teacher at West Point, was commissioned a colonel in the Union army in 1861. He fought at Shiloh, Perryville, Stones River,Chickamauga, Chattanooga, Missionary Ridge, Resaca, Pickett's Mills, Peach Tree Creek and Atlanta. He was promoted to major general in December 1864 and remained in the regular army after the war. He fought Indians on the frontier and went to France to observe the German forces during the Franco-Prussian War. In 1880 he became chief signal officer and head of the Weather Bureau.

Josiah Henson

slowed by his academic deficiencies in philosophy and chemistry, and he needed an extra year at the military academy, eventually being graduated in 1848, 15th in his class of 38.

Commissioned into the artillery, Hill fought in Mexico during the autumn of 1847. He later served in garrisons in Florida and Texas and took part in two Seminole campaigns (1849-50 and 1853-55) in Florida. From 1855 to 1860 he worked in the Washington, D.C., office of the U.S. Coast Survey. In 1859 he married a sister of John Hunt Morgan, soon to become famous as a Confederate cavalry commander.

Ambrose Powell Hill (left) and (below) James Butler Hickok

Henson, Josiah
(1789-1883)
Black leader and clergyman

Henson was born into slavery in Maryland. After escaping to Canada in 1830 he learned to read and write, worked for the Underground Railroad, preached and founded a community and industrial school at Dawn, Ontario (1842). He became an internationally renowned emancipation advocate. Having published his autobiography in 1849 and told his story to Harriet Beecher Stowe, Henson was widely regarded as the inspiration for the character Uncle Tom in *Uncle Tom's Cabin* (1852).

Hickok, James Butler
(1837-1876) **Union scout and spy**

"Wild Bill" Hickok moved from his native Illinois to Kansas in 1855 and became a stagecoach driver and free-state sympathizer. He served the Federals as a Missouri-based scout and spy in a war career characterized by dramatic adventures, arrests and escapes; in 1865 he publicly killed Dave Tutt, a fellow scout who had defected to the Confederates. He later became an American legend as a fast-drawing Kansas marshal. He was killed by Jack McCall in Deadwood, Dakota Territory.

Hill, Ambrose Powell
(1825-1865) **Confederate general**

The son of a soldier, born in Culpeper, Virginia, Hill received a standard local academy education before entering West Point in July 1842. His progress was

He resigned his U.S. commission during the secession crisis. Appointed colonel in the Confederate service in the spring of 1861, he commanded the 13th Virginia at the First Battle of Bull Run, where the regiment remained in reserve. He served in western Virginia later in 1861. In February 1862 he was promoted to brigadier general and given command of an infantry brigade.

Hill first achieved prominence as an infantry commander during the Peninsular Campaign of 1862. He fought at Williamsburg and, promoted to major general shortly thereafter, led his subsequently-legendary Light Division, so-called for its speed on the march, in the battles of the Seven Days. His division opened the Battle of Mechanicsville with an impetuous, probably ill-advised attack in the evening of June 26, 1862, and lost heavily. The Light Division fought later in the week at Gaines's Mill and Frayser's Farm.

After he quarrelled with James Longstreet, Hill's division was transferred to Thomas J. Jackson's command in July 1862. He fought with Jackson at Cedar Mountain on August 9 and anchored the left of Jackson's line at the Second Battle of Bull Run three weeks later, repulsing successive Federal attacks on August 29-30.

Hill took part in the capture of Harpers Ferry in September 1862, staying behind to supervise the details of the surrender while Jackson and the rest of the corps rejoined Robert E. Lee at Sharpsburg. On September 17, the day of the Battle of the Antietam, Hill rushed the Light Division from Harpers Ferry to Sharpsburg, reaching the battlefield just in time to stop a potential Federal breakthrough on the right of Lee's line.

He fought at Fredericksburg in December 1862 and participated in Jackson's decisive flank march at Chancellorsville in May 1863. He succeeded briefly to the corps command when Jackson was wounded the evening of May 2. Wounded himself shortly thereafter, he turned the corps over to J. E. B. Stuart for the concluding phases of Lee's great victory.

Promoted to lieutenant general in May 1863, he was given command of the newly-created Third Corps. He led the corps across the Potomac in the Gettysburg Campaign, made the initial contact with Federal forces around Gettysburg and

A.P. Hill fought with distinction in the Battle of the Wilderness.

attacked on July 1, 1863, touching off the great three-day battle. He directed the first day's fighting largely on his own – the only occasion during which he exercised independent command. His corps took part, with Longstreet's, in the indecisive echelon attacks of July 2, and 10 of his infantry brigades supported George Pickett's division during the debacle on Cemetery Ridge on the third day of the battle.

Hill fell ill after the Battle of the Wilderness in May 1864 and missed the Spotsylvania fighting entirely. He returned to command the Third Corps at Cold Harbor in June. He retained this command during the long Petersburg Campaign, taking part in most of the many actions on the Confederate right from 1864 to April 1865.

Hill had once said he did not wish to survive the wreck of the Confederacy. He returned from a brief sick leave on the morning of April 2, 1865, as Ulysses S. Grant was launching his final successful assault on Petersburg, and was shot dead as he rode to the front to rally his troops.

Daniel Harvey Hill (above) and (right) Jane Hoge

Hill, Daniel Harvey
(1821-1889) Confederate general

He was born in York district, South Carolina. After graduation from West Point he saw seven years of border, garrison and Mexican War service. For 10 years a college mathematics teacher, Hill was superintendent of the North Carolina Military Institute (1859-1861) when the Civil War erupted. After organizing North Carolina's first instruction camp, he led the Confederate army's 1st North Carolina at Big Bethel. Promoted to brigadier general (July 1861) and major general (March 1862), he led a division in the Peninsular Campaign (fighting at Seven Pines, in the Seven Days' Battles and at South Mountain) and at Antietam. At South Mountain he was accused (unfairly, he contended) of allowing Robert E. Lee's famous "lost dispatch" (detailing his Maryland Campaign) to fall into the hands of Union General George McClellan. He defended Richmond during the Gettysburg Campaign. As a lieutenant general (July 1863) he led the Second Corps in the Tennessee Army. He figured prominently in the Chickamauga and Chattanooga campaigns. After signing a petition recommending that Braxton Bragg be removed on the grounds of incompetence, he was himself relieved and sent to a minor command in North Carolina. He surrendered there with J. E. Johnston. Hill was a North Carolina newspaper and magazine publisher after the war and was president

both of the University of Arkansas (1877-1884) and of the forerunner of Georgia Military Academy (1885-1889). In these roles he did much to promote Southern revitalization through industrial and agricultural training.

Hoge, Jane (Mrs. A. H. Hoge)
(1811-1890)
Sanitary Commission worker

Born in Pennsylvania, she had given birth to 13 children and was a wealthy and socially conscious housewife when the Civil War broke out. She helped organize the Chicago branch of the Sanitary Fair in Chicago in October 1863. In addition to lecturing widely to raise money and supplies, she went to camps in the front lines and was tireless in trying to improve the sanitary conditions of the Union troops. After the war she devoted herself to religious and educational causes.

Holabird, Samuel Beckley
(1826-1907) **Union officer**

Born in Connecticut, Holabird was a West Point-trained career officer who had served in Texas and on scouting duty before the Civil War. He served the Union during the war as a quartermaster to Robert Paterson, Nathaniel Banks, Joseph Mansfield and A. S. Williams, and, after December 1862, he was chief quartermaster of the Department of the Gulf. He continued on active service, retiring as quartermaster general (1883-1890). He wrote a number of military works.

Hollins, George Nichols
(1799-1878) **Confederate commodore**

A Maryland native, Hollins became a midshipman in 1814 and resigned from the U.S. Navy as a captain in 1861 after distinguished service that included the War of

George Nichols Hollins

1812 and the bombardment of Nicaragua in 1854. He commanded the James River defenses for the Confederacy and, as a commodore in command of the New Orleans naval station, broke the Union Mississippi blockade (October 1861). He

Joseph Holt (seated left). R.S. Foster is standing to his left.

saw heavy fighting while leading the upper Mississippi naval forces until New Orleans fell (April 1862), then sat on naval boards. He worked in the Baltimore city court after the end of the war.

Holt, Joseph
(1807-1894)
Union judge advocate general

This Kentucky-born lawyer and Democratic orator served President James Buchanan as commissioner of patents, postmaster general and secretary of war. After Abraham Lincoln's inauguration he tried to sway Kentucky to stay with the Union and then became the Union army's first judge advocate general in 1862. Granted powers in both civil and military situations, he dealt harshly with many defendants, in particular with those charged with the conspiracy to assassinate President Lincoln. His brand of justice gradually lost favor, and he retired from the military in 1875.

Homer, Winslow
(1836-1910)
Painter, war correspondent

Born in Boston, he trained as a lithographer and was working for a New York publisher when *Harper's Weekly* sent him to Washington to sketch the inauguration of Lincoln in March 1861. He stayed on to

sketch the activities – both in camp and in battle – of the Union troops during the early months of the Peninsular Campaign in Virginia. Reproduced as lithographs in *Harper's*, they brought the war to the North with an unaccustomed immediacy and gave Homer a national reputation. Homer returned to New York and soon worked up a number of his sketches into full-fledged paintings, including such famous works as "The Briarwood Pipe" and "Prisoners from the Front" (1866). Homer would go on to gain a reputation as one of America's greatest artists.

John Bell Hood

Hood, John Bell
(1831-1879) **Confederate general**

Born in Owingsville, Kentucky, Hood was graduated near the bottom of his West Point class in 1853. He served on the California and Texas frontiers, and in Texas he became a favorite of his commander, Robert E. Lee. He joined the Confederate cavalry in April 1861. A "fighting general," he commanded John Magruder's cavalry at Yorktown and, as a brigadier general (March 1862), he led the "Texas Brigade" at Gaines's Mill, Second Bull Run and Antietam. Promoted to major general (October 1862), he led a division under James Longstreet at Fredericksburg and Gettysburg (where he led the assault on Round Top on the second day and lost the use of his left arm). He commanded Longstreet's corps at Chickamauga, where Hood lost his right leg and earned a promotion to lieutenant general. He assumed command of the Tennessee Army and, riding strapped to his hose, directed the

disastrous Atlanta and Franklin and Nashville campaigns. Relieved at his own request, he fought under P. G. T. Beauregard in Tennessee. He surrendered in Mississippi in May 1865. "The Gallant Hood," though no match for master tacticians like W. T. Sherman, was an unparalleled brigade and division commander: "Hood's Brigade" set a standard to which other troops aspired. After the war he was a New Orleans merchant. Financially ruined by the yellow fever epidemic of 1878, he himself succumbed to the disease the following year.

Hooker, Joseph
(1814-1879) Union general

Born in Hadley, Massachusetts, the grandson of an officer in George Washington's army, Hooker attended the local school and eventually decided he too would follow the drum. He was graduated from West Point in 1837 near the middle of a class that included the future Civil War generals Braxton bragg, Jubal Early and John Sedgwick.

Hooker served in Florida, on the Canadian border and as adjutant at West Point. He held staff positions during the Mexican War and won brevets for gallantry at Monterrey and Chapultepec. Resigning from the army in 1853, he took up farming in Sonoma, California.

Hooker volunteered to return to the Union service on the outbreak of war but was snubbed at first, possibly because he had feuded with senior officers in California. Obtaining a brigadier's commission finally, he served in the Washington defenses from May through October 1861. He commanded a division at Williamsburg on the Peninsula in May 1862, where he won the sobriquet "Fighting Joe," and performed capably during the Seven Days' Battles and at Second Bull Run.

Promoted to command of I Corps, he won a success at South Mountain on September 14, 1862, and had the lead role in the opening phase of the Battle of Antietam three days later. Hooker's corps appeared to be poised for important gains when he was wounded and carried from the field.

Tall, handsome, incautious, boastful, Hooker could not hold back his biting criticisms of Ambrose Burnside, George McClellan's successor as commander of

OPPOSITE TOP: Joseph Hooker was badly beaten at Chancellorsville.

OPPOSITE BOTTOM: Hooker (second from right, front row) and staff.

ABOVE: Joseph Hooker.

OVERLEAF: The Battle of Missionary Ridge.

the Army of the Potomac. He also spoke openly of the need for autocratic leadership in both the army and the government. After Burnside's debacle at Fredericksburg in December 1862, President Abraham Lincoln named Hooker to the command of the Army of the Potomac in spite of these views. "Only those general who gain success can set up dictators," Lincoln wrote him. "What I now ask of you is military success, and I will risk the dictatorship."

Hooker earned praise for reorganizing the army, improving conditions in the winter camps and building the troops' morale. In early spring he began to plan offensive operations against the Army of Northern Virginia. He set his 130,000-strong army in motion at the end of April 1863. "My plans are perfect," he said. "May God have mercy on General Lee, for I will have none." In a brilliant preliminary, he threw large forces across the Rappahannock and Rapidan rivers and moved up to Chancellorsville in Robert E. Lee's rear.

Then everything went wrong. Lee divided his far smaller army in thirds and defeated Hooker in detail in a masterly war of movement.

Rumor held that Hooker had been drunk at critical moments during the battle of the Chancellorsville. He denied it, saying simply that, "For once, I lost confidence in Joe Hooker." He recovered his nerve in time to maneuver skilfully in step with Lee during the Gettysburg Campaign, successfully screening Washington and Baltimore from attack. But Hooker resigned the Potomac command when the authorities in Washington refused his request for operational control of the garrison at Harpers Ferry. George Meade succeeded him on the eve of Gettysburg.

Staying on in the army just as Burnside had done, Hooker led XI and XII corps

from Virginia to Tennessee to reinforce Ulysses S. Grant in late 1863 and commanded XX Corps during the Chattanooga Campaign. In what became known as the Battle of the Clouds, he captured Lookout Mountain on November 24, 1863, and participated in the decisive victory at Missionary Ridge the following day.

In the spring of 1864 Hooker commanded XX Corps in the opening phases of the Atlanta Campaign: the battles of Mill Creek Gap, Resaca, Cassville, New Hope Church and Pine Mountain. He asked to be relieved of duty in July 1864 when Oliver O. Howard, who had served under him at Chancellorsville, was promoted over his head to the command of one of W. T. Sherman's armies.

Hooker remained in the service, though he did not return to the field, through the war's end. He retired from the regular army in 1868 after suffering a paralytic stroke.

Hough, Daniel
(d.1861) Union soldier

On April 14, 1861, Hough, a private in Battery E, 1st U.S. Artillery, was accidentally killed in an explosion during the Federal evacuation of Fort Sumter, making him the first fatality of the Civil War. He was buried in the grounds of the fort.

Howard, Joseph Jr.
(1833-1908) War correspondent

A businessman-turned-journalist, he earned one of the earliest bylines on the *New York Times* (1860). He sent vivid wartime dispatches from the front, but he is chiefly remembered for a journalistic hoax: in May 1864, as a disgruntled Brooklyn city editor, he helped to forge a presidential proclamation announcing the failure of Ulysses S. Grant's advance on Richmond and calling for 500,000 new Frederal recruits. Two newspapers printed the story: Howard was briefly imprisoned but went on to a successful career as a prolific New York journalist and popular lecturer.

Howard, Oliver Otis
(1830-1909) Union general

A Maine native, he was graduated from and taught mathematics at West Point (1857-1861). He fought for the Union at First Bull Run and in the Peninsular Campaign (losing an arm and earning a Congressional Medal of Honor at Fajr Oaks), as well as at Antietam, Fredericksburg and Chancellorsville, where, commanding XI Corps,

Oliver Otis Howard

his troopes were routed in T. J. Jackson's famous flank attack. He subsequently fought at Gettysburg (earning the Thanks of Congress), Lookout Mountain and Missionary Ride, then led IV Corps on W. T. Sherman's Atlanta Campaign, March to the Sea and Carolinas Campaign. He was eventually appointed commander of the Army and Department of the Tennessee. He presided over the Freedmen's Bureau (1865-1874), was superintendent of West Point (1880-1882) and commanded the Division of the East (1886-1894), retiring as a major general. From 1869 to 1874 he was founding president of Howard University (named for him).

Howe, Julia Ward
(1819-1910) Author, social reformer

Boston-born, she married Samuel, Gridley Howe and with him edited the abolitionist journal *The Commonwealth*. While visiting the Union army camps around Washington, D.C., she was moved to write a poem, and it was published in the *Atlantic Monthly* in the spring of 1862. The editor gave it the name "The Battle Hymn of the Republic." She seems to have written these words for a familiar melody, composed early in the nineteenth century by William Steffe and recently borrowed by Union soldiers for the rousing song "John Brown's body lies a moldering in the grave." In any case, that is the music that has been associated with the words ever since. A prolific writer of both prose and verse, she was the first woman ever to be elected to the prestigious American Academy of Arts and Letters.

Julia Ward Howe

Howe, Samuel Gridley
(1801-1876) Physician, social activist

After taking his medical degree from Harvard (1824), he went off to Greece to aid in the revolution against the Turks (1824-1829). On returning in Boston he devoted himself to the education of the blind, prison reform, aiding mental patients and public education. Inevitably, he took a stand against slavery and with his wife, Julia Ward Howe, co-edited the abolitionist newspaper, *The Commonwealth*. He was an early supporter of John Brown, but when Brown's Harpers Ferry raid occurred, Howe tried to disassociate himself from Brown – even fleeing briefly to Canada. During the Civil War he gave his medical talents to the Sanitary Commission, and he thereafter worked for getting the vote and better education for African-Americans.

Andrew Atkinson Humphreys

Huff, John A.
(c.1816-1864) Union soldier

He won a prize as the best shot in the 1st U.S. Sharpshooters before enlisting in the Union army. He was a private in the 5th Michigan Cavalry when he fatally wounded Jeb Stuart at Yellow Tavern on May 11, 1864. Huff himself died of wounds received at Haw's Shop, Virginia, 17 days later.

Humphreys, Andrew Atkinson
(1810-1883) Union general

Son and grandson of naval architects, this Pennylvania-born West Point graduate served as an engineer in the army; he wrote an important *Report upon the Physics and Hydraulics of the Mississippi River* (1861). Assigned to Union General George McClellan's staff in December 1861, he later became General George Meade's chief of staff. He participated in virtually all the major battles in the Eastern theater from the Peninsular Campaign through Antietam, Chancellorsville and Gettysburg to Cold Harbor, the Petersburg siege and the Appomattox Campaign. He was made a brigadier general, became chief of engineers in 1866 and retired in 1879.

Hunt, Henry Jackson
(1819-1889) Union general

In the 1850s Hunt, a West Point graduate and career officer, helped to create the light artillery tactics adopted in 1860 and used throughout the war. He trained and commanded Army of the Potomac artillery units, was chief of artillery at Fredericksburg (moving the infantry across the river in boats) and Gettysburg (where his guns stopped Pickett's Charge) and directed the siege at Petersburg for the last year of the war. He held territorial commands before retiring in 1883.

Hunter, David
(1802-1886) Union general

Born in Washington, D.C., this West Point graduate and Mexican War veteran was badly wounded at First Bull Run. As a Union major general he held various territorial commands and sat on courts martial and boards. As commander of the Southern Department, Hunter authorized the formation of the first black regiment (the 1st South Carolina). Lincoln annulled his unauthorized proclamation of May 1862 freeing all the slaves in that department. He presided over the trial of Lincoln's assassins. He lived in Washington, D.C., after his retirement in 1866.

Hunter, Robert Mercer Taliaferro
1809-1887)
Confederate secretary of state

This Virginian was graduated from his state university and began a long career in public service. He was a state legislator, a U.S. Representative (1839-1843, 1845-1847), a Senator (1847-1861) and was an ally of John C. Calhoun in promoting states' rights and slavery. He was a wartime Confederate secretary of state (July 1861-March 1862) and senator (1862-1865) and was a commissioner at the Hampton Roads Peace Conference. He was briefly imprisoned after the war, then returned to Virginia, where he helped to organise a conservative party in the state that served to blunt the worst effects of radical Reconstruction. He was state treasurer (1874-1880).

raid into West Virginia that became known as "Jones's and Imboden's Raid." He helped to cover the Confederates' retreat from Pennsylvania after Gettysburg and fought at Piedmont and New Market. After coming down with typhoid fever in autumn 1864, he helped to administer a Confederate prison at Aiken, South Carolina. He was a lawyer, developer and writer after the war.

Iverson, Alfred
1829-1911) Confederate general

This Georgian fought in the Mexican War and resigned to become a lawyer and railroad contractor. He re-enlisted in the cavalry in 1855 and served in Indian fighting and on the Utah Expedition (1858-1860). Joining the Confederate army, he fought in the Seven Days' Battles (wounded) and at South Mountain. He led brigades at Antietam, and, promoted to brigadier general, at Fredericksburg, Chancellorsville and Gettysburg, then organized troops in Georgia. During the Atlanta Campaign he captured George Stoneman at Hillsboro in July 1864. He surrendered after Appomattox and after the war was a businessman and farmer.

Imboden, John Daniel
(1823-1895) Confederate general

A Virginia-born lawyer and legislator, he participated in the arrest of John Brown at Harpers Ferry. After joining the Confederate army he fought at First Bull Run and, in April-May 1863, was joint commander with General William E. Jones of a daring

John Daniel Imboden

Jackson, John K.
(1828-1866) Confederate general

Born in Georgia, Jackson was a lawyer. Commissioned a colonel in a Georgian infantry regiment in May 1861, he fought for the Confederacy at Santa Rosa Island, was promoted to brigadier general in January 1862 and fought at Pensacola, Shiloh, Stones River, Chickamauga and in the Atlanta Campaign. He fought to the end in Florida and in the Carolinas. He returned to his law practice after the war.

John K. Jackson

Jackson, Thomas Jonathan "Stonewall"
(1824-1863) Confederate general

Thomas Jackson's parents died in poverty during his early childhood, and the orphan grew up with few amenities in the Clarksburg, Virginia, household of the uncle who raised him. Jackson's early schooling illprepared him for the rigors of West Point. He arrived there in 1842 awkward and behindhand. By dint of hard work he rose to 17th of 59 cadets in a 1846 graduating class that included George McClellan and A. P. Hill.

Jackson attracted the notice of his superiors in the Mexican War, serving with distinction at Vera Cruz, Cerro Gordo and Chapultepec. He found postwar life in garrison tedious, however, and resigned from the army early in 1852 to teach mathematics at the Virginia Military Institute in Lexington. His students graded him a poor teacher – they called him "Tom Fool Jackson" – but he seems to have found consolation in an obsessive Presbyterian piety and in a fulfilling domestic life. His first wife, Eleanor Junkin, died in 1854. He remarried three years later. Jackson and Mary Anna Morrison, like Eleanor the daughter of a Presbyterian minister, lived happily together, adequate compensation, perhaps, for his professional disappointments.

He took no part in secession quarrels, though by happenstance he commanded the cadet detachment at the hanging of abolition insurrectionist John Brown on December 2, 1859. He described war as "the sum of all evils," a view that did not discourage him from obtaining a Confederate commission shortly after the Fort Sumter attack. Soon promoted to brigadier, Jackson led Virginia troops at the First Battle of Bill Run/Manassas on July 21, 1861, so distinguishing himself in repulsing a Federal assault that he acquired the sobriquet "Stonewall."

His soldiers called him "Old Jack." Tall, thin and long-bearded, he looked commonplace except for his pale blue eyes, which – or so nearly everyone who knew him said – blazed up brilliantly in battle. His eccentricities were legendary. He did not smoke, drink or play cards and permitted himself only the sparest of meals. He sometimes refused to march or fight on the Sabbath and often rode about with one arm held above his head. He wore ragged uniforms with few symbols of rank and scorned all military pomp and display. He was a harsh disciplinarian and put tremendous demands on all who served under

Thomas Jonathan Jackson, greatest of Robert E. Lee's lieutenants

him. "I never saw one of Jackson's couriers without expecting an order to assault the North pole," one of his subordinates said. He may have thought war evil but he was a consummate practitioner of its arts.

In November 1861, promoted to major general, Jackson took command of Confederate forces in the Shenandoah Valley. His masterly Valley Campaign of 1862 was the first conclusive evidence of his military genius. He and Robert E. Lee then President's Davis's chief military adviser, had developed a plan to attack the Federal forces in the Valley under Nathaniel Banks as a strategic diversion to prevent reinforcements being sent to Union General George McClellan on the Virginia peninsula. Jackson at first suffered a tactical reverse at Kernstown on March 23 and, in the face of superior forces, retreated slowly up the Valley. But he repulsed a Federal attack on McDowell on May 8, then turned north

again and struck Banks at Front Royal on May 23, driving him back to Winchester. Following up closely, Jackson renewed the attack on the 25th, this time pushing the disorganized Federals all the way back across the Potomac. Alarmed, intent on destroying Jackson, the Federal high command suspended the southward march of a full army corps bound for McClellan and ordered all forces in the Valley to concentrate against Stonewall's little army. "Always mystify, mislead and surprise the enemy," Jackson said. Following his own maxim, he parried each enemy thrust and brought the campaign to a brilliant close with victories at Cross Keys and Port Republic on June 8 and 9.

Jackson's reputation suffered some damage during Lee's battles of the Seven

OPPOSITE TOP: Jackson is mortally wounded at Chancellorsville in a case of what would today be called "friendly fire".

OPPOSITE BOTTOM: Jackson's death on May 10, 1863. He was 39.

troops, mistaking Jackson's party for Yankees in the twilight, opened fire and brought Old Jack down, forcing him out of the battle.

Though he lost an arm to the surgeon's saw that night, his chances for recovery appeared excellent. But he contracted pneumonia, and on May 10, 1863, he died in a delirium of fever, calling out orders – "Pass the infantry to the front!" – as his life ebbed away. Lee never won another such victory as Chancellorsville, not least because he never found a second Stonewall Jackson. "I know not how to replace him," Lee wrote in a tribute that could also serve as Jackson's epitaph.

James Brothers Desperadoes

Frank (1843-1915) and Jesse (1847-1882) James were born and raised on a farm near Centralia, Missouri, without benefit of much education. Their mother and stepfather were Confederate sympathizers; this, along with the fact that Federal militia twice raided the James farm, helped turn the brothers into Confederate guerillas.

They received their criminal apprenticeship under the bushwhacker chief W. C. Quantrill, famous for the August 1863 sacking of Lawrence, Kansas, in which 150 men and boys were killed and $500,000 worth of property destroyed.

Quantrill did not survive the war, and Jesse James was wounded toward war's end and needed nearly a year of quiet life to recover. He, Frank and Coleman Younger embarked upon their career as brigands in 1866, specializing in bank robberies and, after 1873, train robberies. In April 1882, one of the gang members shot and killed Jesse. Frank James surrendered a few months later. Acquitted in two criminal trials, he lived on blamelessly until February 1915.

Johnson, Andrew
(1808-1875) Lincoln's vice president and 17th president of the United States

Born in Raleigh, North Carolina, he became a tailor's apprentice in 1822 and settled in Tennessee. At the age of 18 he married Eliza McCardle, who taught him to read. As a champion of local working men, he was elected mayor or Greeneville, Tennessee (1830-1833); he went on to serve

Jackson at the First Battle of Bull Run. It was here that he acquired his famous nickname, "Stonewall".

Days in late June and early July, when Jackson's chronic tardiness, partly the result of physical and nervous exhaustion after the stresses of the Valley, cost the Confederates an opportunity to inflict a serious·defeat on McClellan. But Jackson returned to form at the Second Battle of Bull Run/Manassas in August. Marching 51 miles in two days, his "foot cavalry" destroyed the Union depot at Manassas Junction, laid low for two days, then held off superior forces until Confederate General James Longstreet could bring up

his corps to deliver the blow that sent the Federals retreating back to the Washington lines. In September, commanding Lee's advance guard, Jackson captured the fortress of Harpers Ferry and reached Antietam/Sharpsburg in time to help Lee check McClellan and escape a serious, perhaps decisive defeat. In December his corps fought the Federals to a humiliating standstill on Lee's right at Fredericksburg.

Jackson's famous flank march of May 2, 1863, a daylong trek through the Wilderness swamps and thickets, made Lee's brilliant victory at Chancellorsville possible, for Jackson's late-afternoon assault routed the Union right wing. Jackson pressed the pursuit into the evening, but then Rebel

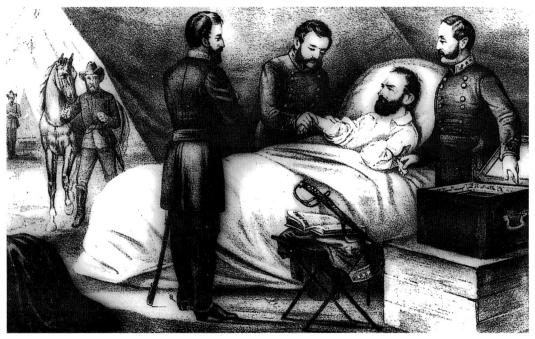

as U.S. Representative (1843-1853), governor of Tennessee (1853-1857), and U.S. Senator (1857-1862). An antislavery Democrat, he was the only Southern Senator to retain his seat after secession, and Lincoln rewarded him with the military governorship of Tennessee (1862-1865). He forged a loyal government there and was consequently nominated as vice president on the National Union-Republican Party ticket in 1864. Succeeding to the presidency after Lincoln's assassination, he issued a proclamation of amnesty, presided over the ratification of the 13th Amendment and succeeded in organizing loyal governments in the former Confederate states. His intention to continue Lincoln's moderate

Andrew Johnson

Southern reconstruction policies, however, was foiled by hostile Radical Republicans, who overrode a presidential veto to pass the Reconstruction Act of 1867 and generally impaired his effectiveness. After dismissing Secretary of war Edwin M. Stanton (a Radical Republican) in violation of the Tenure of Office Act, Johnson was impeached on charges of "high crimes and misdemeanors" and acquitted by only a single vote in May 1968. He failed thereafter to moderate the harshness of Congressional Radical Reconstruction policies. He was passed over in the 1868 presidential election and lost U.S. Senate and Congressional bids in 1869 and 1872. Finally elected to the Senate by Tennessee, he served from March to July 1875 before dying of a paralytic stroke.

Bushrod Rust Johnson

Johnson, Bushrod Rust
(1817-1880) Confederate general

Born in Ohio and a graduate of West Point, Johnson served on the frontier and in the Seminole and Mexican wars. He resigned in 1847 to teach, becoming the superintendent of a military college in Tennessee. Commissioned colonel in the Confederate army when the war broke out, he was promoted to brigadier general in January 1862. He escaped through the lines at Fort Donelson, was wounded at Shiloh and fought at Perryville, Stones River, Chickamauga and Knoxville, Drewry's Bluff and the Wilderness and was promoted to major general in May 1864. At Petersburg during the great mine explosion (July 1864), he commanded troops that captured 130 Union soldiers in the crater. He was chancellor of the University of Nashville after the war.

Johnson, Richard W.
(1827-1897) Union general

He was graduated from West Point in 1849 and fought in several Indian campaigns on the frontier. Johnson commanded a Union brigade and then a division at Corinth, Stones River, Chickamauga and Missionary Ridge in 1862 and 1863. Severely wounded at Resaca during W. T. Sherman's Atlanta Campaign, he returned to command XIV Corps and, later, the cavalry corps in the Army of the Cumber-

OVERLEAF: Albert Sidney Johnston was mortally wounded in the first day's fighting at Shiloh in 1862.

Texas seceded. He refused the Union's offer to serve as Winfield Scott's second in command, instead assuming command of the Confederate Western Department as a full general. A powerful personality, Johnston was regarded in 1861 by Jefferson Davis, among others, as "the greatest soldier . . . then living," an assessment not shared by later historians. He captured Bowling Green and began mustering and training an army, but after losses at Logan Cross Roads and forts Henry and Donelson, he withdrew to Nashville, and after D. C. Buell occupied Nashville, retreated to Corinth. He died of a leg wound sustained while leading the Confederates' east flank on the first day of fighting at Shiloh on April 6, 1862, a loss which Jefferson Davis called "irreparable."

Johnston, Joseph Eggleston
(1807-1891) Confederate general

Born in Prince Edward County, Virginia, son of a Revolutionary War veteran, he grew up in Abingdon and received his early schooling at an academy his father had helped to found. He was graduated 13th of 46 in the class of 1829 at West Point and entered the army as a second lieutenant of artillery.

Johnston served on the Black Hawk expedition and in garrison posts before resigning in 1837 to pursue a career as a civil engineer. On an expedition to Florida early in 1838 he took charge of the rear guard when a Seminole war party attacked. He conducted the retreat with such coolness and skill that he won a brevet and a new commission, as a first lieutenant in the elite corps of topographical engineers.

He fought in Mexico at Cerro Gordo and led the storming column at Chapultepec. Five times wounded, he won three brevets for his Mexican service. He later served as chief of topographical engineers in Texas and was lieutenant colonel of the 1st U.S. Cavalry in Kansas during the border disturbances of the late 1850s. He accompanied Albert Sidney Johnston's Utah expedition in 1858. By 1861 he was a brigadier general and chief quartermaster of the army.

Johnston resigned his U.S. commission in April 1861 and entered Confederate service as a major general the following month. Commanding at Harpers Ferry, he withdrew his small army from the enemy's front in time to make a decisive contribu-

Richard W. Johnson (above) and (right) Albert Sidney Johnston

land. Johnson retired in 1875 and later taught military science in Missouri and Minnesota.

Johnston, Albert Sidney
(1803-1862) Confederate general

Born in Washington, Kentucky, and graduated from West Point in 1826, Johnston fought in the Black Hawk War. He resigned from the U.S. Army in 1834 and became commander of the Texas army in 1837 (his appointment occasioning a duel with a disappointed rival officer) and was secretary of war for the Republic of Texas (1838-1840). A Texas farmer in between his military stints, he rejoined the U.S. Army after fighting in the Mexican War, later leading the Utah expedition against the Mormons (1858-1860) and commanding the Pacific Department. He resigned again when

ABOVE: The Battle of Fair Oaks.

OPPOSITE BOTTOM: William E. Jones.

tion to the Confederate victory at Bull Run on July 21, 1861, approving P. G. T. Beauregard's troop dispositions and overseeing the general direction of the battle.

Promoted to full general shortly after Bull Run, Johnston took command of the main Confederate army covering Richmond. Confederate President Jefferson Davis ranked him only fourth in seniority among general officers, however, precip-

itating a feud between the general and the president that would last the full course of the war.

When George McClellan shifted the Union Army of the Potomac to the Virginia peninsula in the spring of 1862, Johnston moved southeast to confront him. As in Florida, he proved himself a master of the fighting retreat, falling back to within a few miles of Richmond before launching a counterattack on May 31, 1862. The Battle of Seven Pines (Fair Oaks) checked McClellan's advance but achieved no decisive result. It did, however, cost Johnston

his command, for he was seriously wounded during the fighting. His successor was Robert E. Lee.

Davis assigned him in late 1862 to overall command in the west, with supervisory responsibility for the armies of Braxton Bragg in Tennessee and John Pemberton in Mississippi. Johnston exercised little operational control, however. Federal forces inflicted a series of defeats that culminated in the loss of the Mississippi River fortress of Vicksburg in July 1863 and the Confederate retreat from Tennessee after the Missionary Ridge debacle in November.

Hood had completely wrecked the army he had inherited.

Johnston returned to field command in February 1865 at the head of a small army opposing Sherman's advance through the Carolinas. Against Davis's wishes, he capitulated to Sherman in North Carolina on April 26, 17 days after Lee had surrendered the Army of Northern Virginia at Appomattox Court House, Virginia.

After the war Johnston served one term in the U.S. Congress and settled in Washington, D.C. His memoir, *Narrative of Military Operations*, appeared in 1874. Johnston's reputation rested on the fact that he never lost a battle, yet this skilled but cautious and pessimistic soldier never won a major victory either. He died of pneumonia in 1891, not long after he had stood bareheaded in the rain at the funeral of his old adversary, W. T. Sherman.

He took command of Bragg's beaten Army of Tennessee in December 1863 with orders to reorganize it and go over to the offensive. Instead, pleading lack of resources, he fought mainly defensively when W. T. Sherman opened the spring campaign in Georgia in May 1864. Sherman steadily forced Johnston back toward Atlanta, and Davis relieved Johnston of command on July 17 on the grounds he had not brought Sherman to battle. Johnston's successor, John Bell Hood, had no hesitancy about attacking, and within six months, in a series of ill-judged offensives,

Joseph Eggleston Johnston

1861, he fought at Cedar Mountain, Groveton and Second Bull Run. Promoted to brigadier general in 1862, he fought with J. E. B. Stuart at Gettysburg. He had a notable success in what became known as "Jones's and Imboden's West Virginia Raid" in April 1863. He was killed on June 5, 1864, at Piedmont, Virginia.

Jones, William Edmonson ("Grumble")
(1824-1864) Confederate general

This Virginia-born West Point graduate had served on the frontier before resigning from the army in 1857. Commissioned major in the Confederate army in May

Kearney, Philip
(1814-1862) **Union general**

Kearney was graduated from Columbia College, but, after inheriting a fortune in 1836, he opposed the wishes of his socially prominent New York family to fulfill a romantic dream of being a cavalry officer. He studied cavalry tactics in France and fought in Algiers: after 1844 he was aide-de-camp to commanders-in-chief Alexander Macomb and Winfield Scott. He lost an arm in the Mexican War. A dashing leader whose dragoons rode matched dapple-gray horses and whose troops wore distinctive scarlet, diamond-shaped "Kearney patches," he had an outstanding Civil War record, fighting for the Union at Williamsburg, Seven Pines and Second Bull Run. He was killed while reconnoitering at Chantilly in September 1862. Winfield Scott called him "a perfect soldier."

Philip Kearney sketched in action

Kemper, James Lawson
(1823-1895) **Confederate general**

Born in Virginia, Kemper was a lawyer who volunteered to serve in the Mexican War. He was the speaker of the House of Delegates in Virginia before he joined the Confederate army in May 1861. He fought at Fist Bull Run, Williamsburg, Seven

Erasmus Darwin Keyes

Pines, Frayer's Farm, Second Bull Run, South Mountain, Antietam, Fredericksburg and Gettysburg, where he was seriously wounded and captured. Exchanged three months later, he never returned to the field due to the severity of his injuries. Promoted to major general in September 1864, he ran the Conscript Bureau and was governor of Virginia, (1874-1878) after the war.

Keyes, Erasmus Darwin
(1810-1895) **Union general**

Keys, a Massachusetts-born West Point graduate and career officer, was a veteran of frontier and Indian fighting who also taught field artillery and cavalry at West Point. He was Winfield Scott's military secretary in 1860-1861. He commanded a Union brigade at First Bull Run and led IV Corps throughout the Peninsular Campaign. During the Battle of Gettysburg he conducted a feint toward Richmond. He resigned in May 1864. Later, his business interests in California included banking, mining and viniculture.

Kilpatrick, Hugh Judson
(1836-1881) Union general

The son of a New Jersey farmer, he was graduated from West Point in May 1861. Severely wounded at Big Bethel in June, Kilpatrick won appointment as lieutenant colonel of a New York cavalry regiment and embarked on a career as one of the most flamboyant Union cavalry commanders of the war. Known as Kill Cavalry, he led the infamous Kilpatrick-Dahlgren Raid on Richmond in 1864 and went west shortly thereafter at W. T. Sherman's request. "I know Kilpatrick is a hell of a damned fool," Sherman said, "but I want just that sort of man to command my cavalry." Kilpatrick led Sherman's mobile forces during the Atlanta Campaign, the March to the Sea and the Carolinas Campaign.

Kimball, Nathan
(1823-1898) Union general

Indiana-born, he had served as a young man in the Mexican War and subsequently became a doctor. Appointed a colonel in the Union army in 1861, he served at Cheat Mountain and Greenbrier. He became a division commander when General James Shields was wounded in the 1862 Shenandoah Valley Campaign, then went on to defeat Stonewall Jackson at Kernstown the following day. He fought at Antietam and Vicksburg and in the Atlanta and Franklin and Nashville campaigns. He was breveted a major general in 1865.

King, Rufus
(1814-1876) Union general

A West Point alumnus, he was an Albany newspaper editor and New York's adjutant general (1839-1843) before editing the influential *Milwaukee Sentinel* (c. 1845-1861). In 1861 he organized Wisconsin's famous "Iron Brigade." As a Union brigadier general King participated in Washington's defenses and led a division at Second Bull Run, where his retreat from Gainesville on August 28 was unfairly blamed for the Federal loss. He retired in ill-health in October 1863. He was U.S. minister to the Vatican when he arrested Lincoln assassination conspirator John Suratt in 1865.

ABOVE: Rufus King.

BELOW: H.J. Kilpatrick (right center).

U.S. and South America. Commissioned in the Texas Cavalry, he fought for the Confederacy at Wilson's Creek and Pea Ridge. He was wounded at Mansfield during the Red River Campaign (1864). Ultimately promoted to brigadier general, he became a merchant after the war. He wrote a well-received memoir, *Adventures and Recollections*.

Lawton, Alexander Robert
(1818-1896) Confederate general

A South Carolinian educated at West Point and Harvard Law School, he became a Georgia lawyer, railroad president and leading secessionist legislator. His seizure of Fort Pulaski in 1861 inaugurated hostilities in Georgia. As a Confederate brigadier

Walter Paye Lane (right) and (below) James Henry Lane

Lamar, Lucius Quintus Cincinnatus
(1825-1893) Confederate statesman

Georgia-born Lamar moved to Mississippi in 1849. A lawyer and antisecessionist U.S. Representative (1857-1860), he drafted his state's secession ordinance. Lamar led the 19th Mississippi until his health failed in 1862; later he represented the Confederacy in Europe (1862-1863) and served as a judge advocate in the Army of Northern Virginia (1864-1865). A leading Mississippi Democrat and national representative of the "New South," he was a U.S. Representative (1873-1877) and Senator (1877-1885), secretary of the interior (1885-1888) and Supreme Court justice (1888-1893).

Lane, James Henry
(1833-1907) Confederate general

This Virginian, a Virginia Military Institute alumnus and mathematics and tactics teacher, fought in every important engagement of the war with the Army of Northern Virginia, from scouting before Big Bethel in 1861 to the surrender at Appomattox in 1865. Three times wounded, he was a brigadier general at 29; his troops called him "The Little General." He ended his long career in education with a 25-year tenure teaching civil engineering at Alabama Polytechnic Institute.

Lane, Walter Paye
(1817-1892) Confederate general

Born in Ireland, Lane came to Ohio in 1821. He went off to aid Sam Houston in Texas and fought at San Jacinto in 1836. He led an exciting life – as a pirate of sorts in the Gulf of Mexico, an Indian fighter, a soldier in the Mexican War and a goldminer in the

general he commanded the Georgia coast and fought in the Shenandoah Valley Campaign of Jackson, in the Seven Days' Battles and at Second Bull Run and Antietam, Wounded and reassigned, he was an effective quartermaster general until the war's end. Returning to his Savannah law practice, he was an influential Democratic politician and was minister to Austria (1887-1889).

Lee, Fitzhugh
(1835-1905) Confederate general

The Virginia-born son of a naval officer and a nephew of Robert E. Lee, he was graduated from West Point in 1856 and served on the frontier. He led a Confederate cavalry brigade under J. E. B. Stuart during the Antietam, Gettysburg and Chancellorsville campaigns and commanded Robert E. Lee's cavalry during the war's last campaign, the retreat to Appomattox. Lee returned to the U.S. army in 1898 to command an infantry corps in Cuba during the Spanish-American War.

Lee, George Washington Custis
(1832-1913) Confederate general

Robert E. Lee's eldest son, he was graduated first in the West Point class of 1854 and saw service with the army's elite engineer corps. He resigned in May 1861 and obtained a Confederate army commission in July. Lee served for most of the war as Jefferson Davis's aide-de-camp. He taught engineering at the Virginia Military Institute after the war and succeeded his father as president of Washington (now Washington and Lee) College in 1871.

George Washington Custis Lee

Lee, Mary Commission worker

A native Briton, she began her war work in April 1861 offering food and drink to U.S. troops passing through Philadelphia. Her Union Refreshment Saloon soon grew to include dormitories, a medical center and other amenities and is said to have served more than 4 million soldiers. Lee volunteered as a Sanitary Commission nurse during the spring of 1862 and served almost continuously in Union field hospitals from the Peninsular Campaign to the Confederate surrender.

Lee, Robert Edward
(1807-1870) Confederate general

The fifth child and third son of Revolutionary War hero Light Horse Harry Lee, he grew up in modest circumstances in Alexandria, Virginia, where his father settled after nearly ruining himself with reckless financial speculations. When the improvident elder Lee died in 1818, care of his invalid widow fell to Robert. Despite such early responsibilities, he excelled in his studies, showing a particular aptitude for mathematics. West Point offered a free education and the prospect of a stable career as a soldier/engineer. After four distinguished years at the military academy, Lee was graduated second in his class in 1829.

He advanced slowly through the grades during 17 years of varied but routine garrison service. He saw combat and was wounded during the Mexican War of 1846-47. He served as superintendent of West Point from 1852 to 1855, a period when, among others, J. E. B. Stuart and the artist James McNeill Whistler were cadets

Robert Edward Lee in 1865.

At the Battle of Chancellorsville Robert E. Lee confers with Thomas J. (Stonewall) Jackson.

there. He commanded the detachment that captured John Brown and his raiders at Harpers Ferry, Virginia, in 1859. By the outbreak of Civil War his superiors and colleagues judged him the most promising officer in the U.S. Army.

Lee opposed secession in 1861, and his moderate political views encouraged President Lincoln to offer him field command of the Union army, but he resigned his commission when Virginia left the Union. His first field campaign, in western Virginia in the late summer of 1861, ended in failure. He afterward served as a military advisor to President Jefferson Davis. On July 1, 1862, at the age of 55, Lee succeeded General Joseph E. Johnston in command of the main Confederate field army in the East. He renamed it the Army of Northern Virginia and, with Union troops in sight of Richmond, launched the offensive known as the Seven Days' Battles. In a week of the bloodiest fighting of the war to date, Lee forced the Federals to retreat down the Vir-

ginia peninsula and, ultimately, to return to Washington.

He followed up with a victory at the Second Battle of Bull Run/Manassas (August 1862), the invasion of Maryland that ended in the drawn Battle of Antietam/Sharpsburg (September 1862) and the great defensive victory of Fredericksburg (December 1862). In May 1863, at Chancellorsville, he responded to a Federal offensive by boldly dividing his army to defeat a far larger enemy force in the battle of maneuver that became known as his masterpiece.

By then Lee's reputation had reached its zenith. But he had failed to destroy the Army of the Potomac at Chancellorsville, and the Federal blockade had begun to suffocate the Southern economy. As time passed, he recognized, the enemy would only grow stronger while the Confederacy expended its non-renewable resources of men and material. Lee thus resolved to try his greatest gamble, a second invasion of the North. A decisive victory on Union soil, he reasoned, would strengthen the Northern peace movement and encourage the European powers to recognize the

Confederacy – developments that might lead to a negotiated end to the war. The gamble failed. In early July 1863, after three days of savage fighting at Gettysburg, Pennsylvania, he led a defeated and badly damaged army back across the Potomac into Virginia.

By the spring of 1864 President Lincoln had at last found Lee's equal in Ulysses S. Grant. With diminishing resources, Lee fought Grant to a stalemate in a series of impressive but costly defensive struggles, from the Wilderness through Spotsylvania to Cold Harbor (where the Confederates claimed one of the most one-sided victories of the war). Then, in mid-June, Grant, in a brilliant tactical maneuver, gained a nearly decisive advantage when he surprised Lee by launching the Union army across the James River and attacking the vital communications center of Petersburg. Grant failed to capture the place, but he pinned Lee in Petersburg's fortifications, depriving him of all freedom of movement. Lee himself recognized the siege as the beginning of the end for his army.

The drain on the Confederacy continued through the winter of 1864-65, and by the time Grant launched his 1865 spring offensive, Lee commanded a doomed army. Grant forced Lee out of Petersburg in the opening phase of the battle. Then, in a swift and powerful drive, he caught and trapped the Army of Northern Virginia near Appo-

Robert E. Lee at the age of 38. He was at that time serving as a captain in the U.S. Army's corps of engineers.

mattox Court House, Virginia. "There is nothing left for me to do but go and see General Grant," Lee told his staff, "and I would rather die a thousand deaths." He surrendered in the front parlor of the Wilmer McLean house at Appomattox Court House on April 9, 1865.

Lee applied for parole in July, partly to set an example for recalcitrant Confederates. He was indicted for treason but not bought to trial, and the Union authorities never troubled him. He remained in Richmond until the autumn of 1865, when he accepted the presidency of Washington

The text of Robert E. Lee's farewell address to the men of his famous command, the Army of Northern Virginia

College (now Washington and Lee) in Lexington, Virginia.

Handsome and massively featured, patient and unfailingly courteous, legendary for his kindness to animals, Lee became many Americans' ideal of the gentleman Christian soldier. He was deeply religious, though formal affiliation had come late (he was not confirmed in the Episcopal Church until 1854). As a soldier, Lee's greatest gift was an ability to divine his adversary's intentions. Decisive, willing to run tremendous risks, a master at inspiring troops, he ranks among the greatest of battlefield commanders, though he has been faulted for a strategic short-sightedness that placed too much emphasis on defence of his native Virginia.

Lee died of a heart ailment in Lexington on October 12, 1870. He was the object even then, of his countrymens' veneration, and so he remains.

Lee, William Henry Fitzhugh
(1837-1891) Confederate general

Robert E. Lee's second son, he was graduated from Harvard, then entered the regular U.S. Army. Joining the Confederate service in May 1861, he led W. W. Loring's cavalry during the West Virginia Campaign and fought in J. E. B. Stuart's cavalry corps at Antietam and Chancellorsville. Taken captive after the Brandy Station cavalry action in June 1863, he remained in Union custody until the following March. He commanded the Confederate cavalry during the retreat to Appomattox.

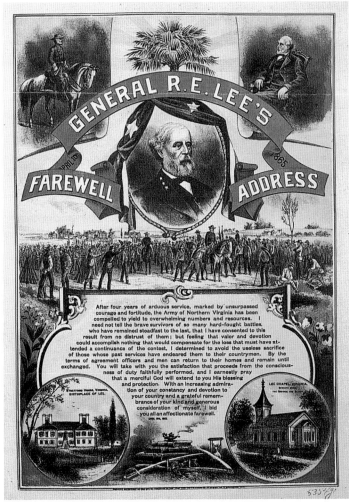

William Henry Fitzhugh Lee

Leggett, Mortimer Dormer
(1821-1896) Union general

This Ohio lawyer and school superintendent volunteered as his friend, Union General George McClellan's, unpaid aide-de-camp in 1861 and went on to raise the 78th Ohio, fighting at Fort Donelson, Shiloh, Corinth and Vicksburg, later participating in the Atlanta Campaign and the March to the Sea. The hill he captured and

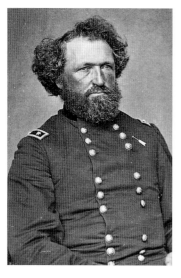

Mortimer Dormer Leggett

held at Atlanta was renamed Leggett's Hill. He reorganized the Patent Office as commissioner of patents (1871-1874), opened a Cleveland law practice and founded Brush Electric Company (1884).

Lincoln, Abraham
(1809-1865)
16th president of the United States

Born in a log cabin near Hodgenville, Kentucky, raised on a frontier farm in Indiana, he attended a "blab" school for a year and furthered his education with close readings of a handful of borrowed books, including The Bible, *Pilgrim's Progress* and Aesop's *Fables*. Lincoln moved to Illinois with his family in 1830 and began to read law in New Salem the following year. He clerked in a store there, managed a mill, split rails and sought other odd jobs to support himself during his long apprenticeship. He served in the militia during the brief Black Hawk War, won election to the state Legislature as a Whig in 1834 and finally received his license to practice as an attorney in september 1836.

Lincoln settled in Springfield, the state capital, established a modestly successful law practice and married the unstable, often-unhappy Mary Todd in 1842. The first of the couple's four children was born the following year. Lincoln left the legislature in 1841 but returned to politics six years later to wage a successful campaign for a seat in the U.S. Congress. After an undistinguished two years in Washington, he

decided not to seek re-election and returned to Springfield disillusioned with politics.

Hard-working, fair, honest and well-liked, he rose to top of the legal profession in Illinois. The slavery question finally prompted his return to public life. In the autumn of 1854 he spoke in opposition to the Kansas-Nebraska Act, fellow Illinoisan Stephen A. Douglas's effort to accommodate the pro-slavery forces, but failed to win the Senate nomination. He joined the new Republican Party in 1856 and challenged Douglas for a Senate seat in 1858. Though he lost that election as well, his brilliant performance in a series of debates with Douglas gave him national stature.

He was a striking figure, six feet, four inches tall, thin and bony, with rough unlovely features: coarse hair, deeply sunken eyes, hollow, wrinkled cheeks and a large nose. "On the whole, he is such a mixture of all sorts as only America brings forth," one observer said. "He is as much like a highly intellectual and benevolent satyr as anything I can think of." Lincoln's dress scarcely improve his appearance. He favored tall stovepipe hats and dark, ill-fitting ready-made suits. But he had developed tremendous powers of language, and his political skills were unmatched. The Republicans nominated him as their 1860 presidential candidate on the third ballot at the raucous "Wigwam" convention hall in Chicago. He did not campaign, nor did he try to reassure Southerners who viewed him as a militant abolitionist. "If slavery is not wrong, then nothing is wrong," he had said, and he left it at that. With the Democratic Party hopelessly split over slavery, Lincoln won election as a

BELOW: Abraham Lincoln.

OPPOSITE: The text of Lincoln's great Proclamation of Emancipation.

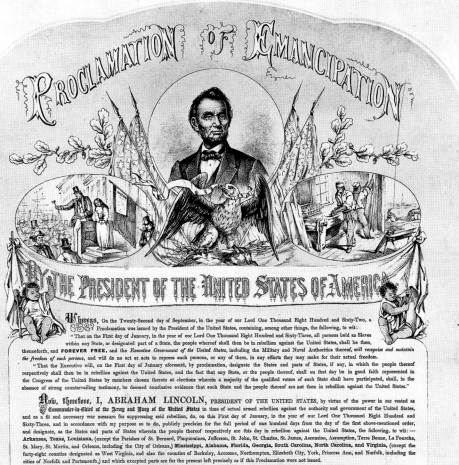

PROCLAMATION OF EMANCIPATION

BY THE PRESIDENT OF THE UNITED STATES OF AMERICA

Whereas, On the Twenty-Second day of September, in the year of our Lord One Thousand Eight Hundred and Sixty-Two, a Proclamation was issued by the President of the United States, containing, among other things, the following, to wit:

"That on the First day of January, in the year of our Lord One Thousand Eight Hundred and Sixty-Three, all persons held as Slaves within any State, or designated part of a State, the people whereof shall then be in rebellion against the United States, shall be then, thenceforth, and **FOREVER FREE**, and the *Executive Government of the United States, including the Military and Naval Authorities thereof, will recognise and maintain the freedom of such persons,* and will do no act or acts to repress such persons, or any of them, in any efforts they may make for their actual freedom.

"That the Executive will, on the First day of January aforesaid, by proclamation, designate the States and parts of States, if any, in which the people thereof respectively shall then be in rebellion against the United States, and the fact that any State, or the people thereof, shall on that day be in good faith represented in the Congress of the United States by members chosen thereto at elections wherein a majority of the qualified voters of such State shall have participated, shall, in the absence of strong countervailing testimony, be deemed conclusive evidence that such State and the people thereof are not then in rebellion against the United States."

Now, therefore, I, ABRAHAM LINCOLN, PRESIDENT OF THE UNITED STATES, by virtue of the power in me vested as Commander-in-Chief of the Army and Navy of the United States in time of actual armed rebellion against the authority and government of the United States, and as a fit and necessary war measure for suppressing said rebellion, do, on this First day of January, in the year of our Lord One Thousand Eight Hundred and Sixty-Three, and in accordance with my purpose so to do, publicly proclaim for the full period of one hundred days from the day of the first above-mentioned order, and designate, as the States and parts of States wherein the people thereof respectively are this day in rebellion against the United States, the following, to wit:— Arkansas, Texas, Louisiana, (except the Parishes of St. Bernard, Plaquemines, Jefferson, St. John, St. Charles, St. James, Ascension, Assumption, Terre Bonne, La Fourche, St. Mary, St. Martin, and Orleans, including the City of Orleans,) Mississippi, Alabama, Florida, Georgia, South Carolina, North Carolina, and Virginia, (except the forty-eight counties designated as West Virginia, and also the counties of Berkeley, Accomac, Northampton, Elizabeth City, York, Princess Ann, and Norfolk, including the cities of Norfolk and Portsmouth,) and which excepted parts are for the present left precisely as if this Proclamation were not issued.

And by virtue of the power and for the purpose aforesaid, I do order and declare that **ALL PERSONS HELD AS SLAVES** within said designated States and parts of States ARE, AND HENCEFORWARD **SHALL BE FREE!** and that the Executive Government of the United States, including the Military and Naval Authorities thereof, will recognize and maintain the freedom of said persons.

And I hereby enjoin upon the people so declared to be free to abstain from all violence, UNLESS IN NECESSARY SELF-DEFENCE; and I recommend to them that in all cases, when allowed, they LABOR FAITHFULLY FOR REASONABLE WAGES.

And I further declare and make known that such persons of suitable condition will be received into the armed service of the United States, to garrison forts, positions, stations, and other places, and to man vessels of all sorts in said service.

And upon this act, sincerely believed to be AN ACT OF JUSTICE, warranted by the Constitution, upon military necessity, I invoke the considerate judgment of mankind and the gracious favor of ALMIGHTY GOD!

In Testimony Whereof, I have hereunto set my name, and caused the seal of the United States to be affixed.

Done at the CITY OF WASHINGTON, this First day of January, in the Year of our Lord One Thousand Eight Hundred and Sixty-Three, and of the Independence of the United States the Eighty Seventh.

[L. S.]

By the President,   A. Lincoln.

William H. Seward

Secretary of State.

J. MAYER & CO. LITH 4 STATE ST. BOSTON.

PUBLISHED BY B.B. RUSSELL & CO. 55 CORNHILL BOSTON.

minority president on November 6, 1860.

South Carolina became the first Southern state to secede, in December; in early 1861 six other Deep South states followed. Given the oath as 16th president on March 4, 1861, Lincoln denounced secession in his inaugural address and appealed to "the mysic chords of memory" he hoped would bind the nation together and prevent war. Tensions continued to mount. Finally, on April 12, 1861, the Confederates opened fire on federal Fort Sumter in Charleston harbor, touching off four years of civil war.

Lincoln issued an immediate call for 75,000 militia and prepared to force the rebellious states to return to the Union. The first Richmond Campaign went awry at Bull Run in July, a portent of years of military disappointments and frustration to come. Lincoln assumed overall direction of the war effort, gradually extending his powers to near-dictatorial scope. He suspended *habeas corpus*, permitting the jailing of thousands of people on mere suspicion of disloyalty, and there were instances of newspaper suppression. For the first time, the government conscripted men into the armed forces.

At first, to build political support, Lincoln had maintained that the war was entirely about secession. His Emancipation Proclamation of Jan. 1, 1863, transformed the conflict into a crusade against slavery, giving high moral purpose to the Union effort. But it was a crusade that was still floundering militarily, for the Union at first seemed incapable of producing generals as able as their Southern counterparts. And Lincoln was beset by political challenges as well – even from members of his own cabinet, several of whom schemed to replace him in the White House. But Lincoln outmaneuvered all opponents, even the unruly and meddlesome Congress, and kept the Union war effort on a steady course.

He searched nearly three years for a general who could defeat Robert E. Lee, though for a time it looked as though his final choice, Ulysses S. Grant, might cost him the presidency. By the late summer of 1864 Grant's Virginia Campaign, with its unprecedented cost in blood and treasure, appeared to be a failure. The Democrats nominated one of Grant's unsuccessful predecessors, General George McClellan, still immensely popular with the Army of the Potomac, to oppose Lincoln. Then, in early September, Grant's lieutenant, W. T. Sherman, marched into Atlanta in one of the decisive victories of the war. Lincoln won re-election in November, gaining an overwhelming majority of the soldier vote.

He envisaged a generous peace. "With malice toward none, with charity for all . . . let is strive on to bind up the nation's wounds," Lincoln said at his second inaugural in March 1865. In early April, Grant trapped the Army of Northern Virginia near Appomattox Court House and forced Lee's surrender on April 9. Five days later an embittered Southerner, John Wilkes Booth, shot and mortally wounded Lincoln at Ford's Theatre in Washington.

He foretold his own end. In a dream the night before the assassination, Lincoln found himself aboard some "singular, indescribable vessel . . . floating, floating away on some indistinct expanse, toward an unknown shore." He died at 7:22 a.m. on April 15, 1865, in a seedy back room of a boarding house across the street from the theater. "Now he is for the ages," said his war secretary, Edwin Stanton.

Lincoln, Mary Todd
(1818-1882) Wife of Abraham Lincoln

Born into a genteel Kentucky family, she settled in Illinois in 1839 and married Abraham Lincoln in 1842. Her close Southern family ties, political interference, attempts to maintain social life in the capital during the war and unpredictable temperament attracted criticism during Abraham Lincoln's presidency, but his affection for her was apparently unwavering. She tended soldiers in Washington during the war. Her last years, which included much foreign travel, were clouded by mental instability.

Livermore, Mary Ashton Rice
(1820-1905)
Sanitary Commission organizer

This Boston-born teacher married a Universalist minister in 1845 and became active in antislavery and temperance causes. A Chicago writer and editor in 1861, she helped to organize the Sanitary Commission's northwestern branch. She was instrumental in assigning female nurses to the front and in fundraising, and as a national director of the Commission she inspected battlefields and lectured widely. She wrote a popular war memoir (1887). From 1870 to

Mary Todd Lincoln

Mary Ashton Rice Livermore

1895 she became known as "the Queen of the Platform" for her unstinting work as a professional lecturer working for temperance and women's suffrage.

Logan, John Alexander
(1826-1886) Union general

The son of an Illinois farmer, he was erratically educated and interrupted his study of law to fight in the Mexican War. Entering politics as an Illinois district prosecutor and Democratic state legislator in the 1850s, he was a staunch Unionist who opposed the proslavery Lecompton constitution in Kansas. He left his U.S. Congressional seat (1859-1862) to fight for the Union with a Michigan regiment at First Bull Run. He then raised and led the 31st Illinois, compiling a distinguished war record. He was twice wounded, the first

time at the capture of Fort Donelson. Promoted to brigadier general and major general in 1862, he fought in the Army of the Tennessee, leading XV Corps in the Vicksburg and Atlanta campaigns, the March to the Sea, and the Carolinas Campaign. An excellent fighter and field commander, despite his lack of formal military training, he twice briefly commanded the Tennessee Army, but his continuing political activity during the war and his impatience with detailed planning deterred his superiors from granting him a permanent major command. Joining the Republican Party after the war, he represented Illinois for two decades as a U.S. Representative (1867-1871) and Senator (1871-1877, 1879-1886). A vocal advocate for veterans, he helped to found the Grand Army of the Republic and the Society of the Army of the Tennessee and established Decoration (Memorial) Day as a national holiday (1868). He wrote *The Great Conspiracy* (1886) and *The Volunteer Soldier of America* (1887).

Logan, Thomas Muldrup
(1840-1914) Confederate general

The valedictorian of the South Carolina College class of 1860, he volunteered to serve the Confederacy at Fort Sumter in 1861, then joined the Hampton Legion as a first lieutenant. He fought at First Bull Run, Gaines's Mill, Second Bull Run and Antietam. Wounded twice and repeatedly promoted for gallantry, he was appointed the army's youngest brigadier general in February 1865 and led a brigade in the last charge of the war at Bentonville (March 1865). A Richmond lawyer after the war, he became a millionaire by organizing the Southern Railway.

Lunsford Lindsay Lomax

Lomax, Lunsford Lindsay
(1835-1913) Confederate general

This Rhode Island-born West Point graduate served as an Indian fighter on the frontier. His father was an army officer from Virginia, so Lunsford accepted a commission as a Confederate captain and then was appointed assistant adjutant general to General Joseph E. Johnston. Promoted to colonel, he fought at Gettysburg, the Wilderness and Petersburg. He was captured at Woodstock and escaped. After the Carolinas Campaign he surrendered with Johnston. He became president of a college in Virginia after the war. He also helped to compile *Official Records* and served as commissioner to Gettysburg National Park.

John Alexander Logan (fifth from the right) with his staff

Longstreet, James
(1821-1904) Confederate general

A farmer's son, South Carolina-born and raised in Georgia and Alabama, Longstreet was graduated from West Point in 1838 near the bottom of a large class that included such future distinguished soldiers as H. W. Halleck, W. T. Sherman and U. S. Grant.

Commissioned an infantry second lieutenant, he saw service in Missouri, Louisiana and Florida. He fought in Mexico with Zachary Taylor and accompanied Winfield Scott on the march to Mexico City. During the 1850s he served in garrison and on the frontier before changing into the paymaster corps; he told friends he had abandoned all dreams of military glory. Then the secession crisis flared. Longstreet resigned his paymaster commission and, in June 1861, obtained a brigadier's appointment in the Confederate army.

Longstreet commanded a brigade at the First Battle of Bull Run and stepped up to command a division under J. E. Johnston on the Virginia peninsula. He fought a tough rearguard action at Williamsburg on May 5, 1862, but reached his assigned position late and thus bore a share of the blame for Johnston's inability to convert opportunity into decisive victory at Seven Pines on May 31.

He came into his own as an infantry commander under Johnston's successor, Robert E. Lee, who called him his "Old War Horse." Lee's most reliable commander during the Seven Days' Battles, Longstreet in consequence had charge of more than half of Lee's infantry during the summer of 1862. Moving up on Stonewall Jackson's right near Manassas on August 29, he launched the powerful counterattack on the 30th that completed the rout John Pope's Union army at the Second Battle of Bull Run.

Promoted to lieutenant general and given charge of the newly-organized First Corps after Antietam, Longstreet's command bore the brunt of the fighting at Fredericksburg in December 1862. He failed to achieve success during a semi-independent assignment in southeastern Virginia during the winter of 1863, and the absence of his two divisions at Chancellorsville in May might have cost Lee a decisive follow-up success there.

Longstreet had strong convictions and a deep stubborn streak, and after Jackson's death he became ever more assertive in his views. He strongly opposed Lee's invasion of Pennsylvania in June 1863, arguing that the Army of Northern Virginia would be better employed in trying to deal with the military crisis developing in the west, at Vicksburg and in Tennessee. He tried to argue Lee out of attacking at Gettysburg on July 2 and bitterly opposed resuming the offensive with Pickett's division on the 3rd. The disastrous outcome of Pickett's Charge appeared to prove him correct.

The Confederate high command ordered Longstreet's corps to Tennessee in early September; his infantry reached the battlefield in time to make a decisive contribution to Braxton Bragg's victory at Chickamauga. He later sharply criticized Bragg for failing to follow up his gains. Again given independent command in November, Longstreet laid siege to Knoxville in eastern Tennessee but found it necessary to retreat after Ulysses S. Grant's decisive victory at Missionary Ridge.

Longstreet returned to Virginia for the spring campaign of 1864. Seriously wounded leading a successful counterattack at the Battle of the Wilderness in May, he missed the Spotsylvania and Cold Harbor fighting, as well as the first several months of the long siege at Petersburg. He returned to duty in the autumn of 1864, took part in the defense of Richmond over the winter and surrendered with Lee at Appomattox on April 9, 1865.

His postwar career fairly burned with controversy. He became an avowed Republican, and Southerners turned violently against him, unfairly blaming him for the Gettysburg defeat and, by implication, for the fall of the Confederacy. He held a series of federal patronage jobs from 1869 until the end of his life, including surveyor of customs in New Orleans, minister to Turkey, U.S. marshal for Georgia and U.S. railroad commissioner. His memoir, *From Manassas to Appomattox* (1896), made him still more enemies among adherents of the Lost Cause, for it dared to criticize the two holiest of Southern icons, Robert E. Lee and Stonewall Jackson.

Loring, William Wing
(1818-1886) Confederate general

He fought against the Seminole Indians while still a youth, became a lawyer and then served with distinction in the Mexican War. He stayed on in the regular army and participated in various actions. He resigned from the Union army in 1861 and accepted a commission as brigadier general in the Confederate army. In what is known as "the Loring-Jackson incident," in January 1862, Loring tried to avoid an order from Stonewall Jackson by appealing over his

James Longstreet

William Wing Loring

head to the Confederate secretary of war, but Jackson prevailed, and Loring was transferred to the west, where he was engaged in many major campaigns and battles. In 1869 he went to Egypt to serve in its army, and he returned in 1879, highly decorated for his services in battle and created a "pasha."

Lovejoy, Elijah Parish
(1802-1837) Abolitionist

A native of Maine, he studied for the ministry and then became editor of a Presbyterian weekly, the *St. Louis Observer* (1833-36), turning it into an outspoken opponent of slavery. Since St. Louis was hostile to his views, he moved to Alton, Illinois, in 1836 and started the *Alton Observer*. The locals there proved no more sympathetic to his abolitionist message, and he was killed by a mob in 1837.

Lovell, Mansfield
(1822-1884) Confederate general

An 1842 West Point graduate, he served on the frontier and in the Mexican War before resigning in 1849 to become an iron manufacturer. He later was deputy streets commissioner for the city of New York. Given charge of the Confederacy's New Orleans defenses after the outbreak of the war, he failed to stop the fleet from seizing the city in April 1862. Political pressures led to Lovell's removal after the fall of New Orleans; a court of inquiry cleared him, but the Confederacy offered him no further military employment.

Two of James Longstreet's many famous actions: below, The Second Battle of Bull Run (August 29–September 2, 1862) and, overleaf, the murderous Battle of Cold Harbor (May 31–June 3, 1864)

Lowe, Thaddeus Sobieski Coulincourt
(1832-1913)
Aeronaut, meteorologist and inventor

Born in New Hampshire, he made his first hot-air balloon ascent in 1858 and began preparing for a transatlantic flight. While investigating air currents on a flight from Cincinnati, he was arrested over the Carolinas on suspicion of spying for the Union in April 1861 (he claimed to have been the war's first prisoner). During the war years he pioneered the Union army aeronautics corps, a balloon fleet used for battlefield observation and communications. He later pioneered the manufacture of artificial ice, improved techniques for manufacturing gas and coke and built an inclined railway in California.

TOP: Thaddeus S. C. Lowe.

ABOVE: Thaddeus Lowe at the Battle of Fair Oaks in 1862 (right, with hand on one of his observation balloons).

Lyon, Nathaniel
(1818-1861) Union general

Born in Connecticut, this West Point-trained career soldier served in the Seminole and Mexican wars and on the frontier. He became a Republican polemicist while stationed in "Bleeding Kansas." Commanding the federal arsenal and troops in St. Louis, he saved the arsenal and captured the pro-secessionist militia gathering at Camp Jackson in May 1861, thereby probably saving Missouri for the Union. Appointed a brigadier general, he was killed at Wilson's Creek in August 1861.

MacArthur, Arthur
(1845-1912) Union officer

Raised in Milwaukee, he joined the Union's 24th Wisconsin Volunteers in August 1862 and fought at Perryville, Stones River, Missionary Ridge, (where he won a Medal of Honor) and in the Atlanta Campaign. Often breveted, he led his regiment in nine battles before he turned 20, making him one of the youngest regimental commanders of the war. He later served in the Spanish American War and was military governor of the Philippines (1900-1901). He retired as a lieutenant general in 1909. General Douglas MacArthur was his famous son.

Mackall, William Whann
(c. 1816-1891) Confederate general

Born in Washington, D.C., this West Point graduate fought in the Seminole and Mexican wars (wounded in both) and on the frontier. He resigned from the U.S. Army in 1861 and joined the Confederate army; he was promoted to brigadier general in 1862. He served at New Madrid and Island No. 10 and then became General Braxton Bragg's chief of staff, a post he left late in 1863 after the Battle of Chickamauga. He served as General Joseph E. Johnston's chief of staff during the unsuccessful campaign to save Atlanta from W. T. Sherman's attack in 1864. He surrendered at Macon, Georgia, in April 1865. He farmed in Virginia after the war.

Mackenzie, Ranald Slidell
(1840-1889) Union general

First in his class at West Point (1862), this New Yorker had a distinguished war record as an engineer officer. He fought for

Ranald Slidell Mackenzie

Magruder, John Bankhead
(1810-1871) Confederate general

He was born in Winchester, Virginia, and educated with a view to a West Point appointment. He was graduated from the academy in 1830, and over the next 15 years he saw service in a succession of garrisons and in the Seminole War.

Magruder commanded a light artillery unit during the Mexican War and was three times recognized for "gallant and meritorious conduct." Though he had a reputation for being restless and short-tempered, Thomas Jackson, for one, sought service with him, knowing that he would be likely to take his guns to wherever the action was hottest.

He earned the sobriquet "Prince John" while stationed in Newport, Rhode Island, where his lavish entertainments were much admired and discussed. He had a "brilliant ability to bring appearances up the necessity of the occasion," someone remarked of him.

Magruder resigned from the U.S. Army in March 1861 and accepted a colonelcy in the Confederate service. His victory at Big Bethel on June 10, which he reported as the first significant land engagement of the war, made him one of the South's first military celebrities. As a result, he was promoted to brigadier in June and to major general in October.

Commanding a force of about 12,000 infantry, Magruder drew on his Newport experiences in the spring of 1862 to bluff the Federals advancing up the Virginia

John Newland Maffitt

the Union in the Army of the Potomac from Kelly's Ford through Petersburg, helped to defend Washington against Jubal Early's 1864 raid and led a brigade in the Shenandoah Valley Campaign of Sheridan and an Army of the James cavalry division during the Appomattox Campaign, suffering three wounds in all. Ulysses S. Grant called him "the most promising young officer in the army." After the war he become one of the army's pre-eminent Indian fighters. He retired from service in 1884

Maffitt, John Newland
(1819-1886)
Confederate naval commander

Born at sea to emigrating Irish parents, Maffitt joined the U.S. Navy in 1832 and served at sea and on the coast survey before resigning to join the Confederate navy. Commanding the Confederate vessels *Savannah*, *Florida*, *Albemarle* and other ships, he was engaged in both combat and blockade-running. He became a commander in April 1863 after running the Federal blockade of Mobile against nearly insuperable odds, and he later captured dozens of Union ships. He retired to North Carolina in 1871.

Dennis Hart Mahan

Mahan, Dennis Hart
(1802-1871) **Military educator**

A New York native raised in Virginia, he was graduated first in his class from West Point in 1824, where he was to teach civil and military engineering for more than 40 years. Among his numerous textbooks, the seminal *Field Fortification* (1836) and *Advance-Guard, Out-Post . . .* (1847, several times revised) were standard military texts for officers in the Mexican War and on both sides throughout the Civil War. His son, Alfred Thayer Mahan (1840-1914), a junior Union naval officer during the war, later became one of the world's greatest naval historians.

Mahone, William
(1826-1895) **Confederate general**

Graduated from Virginia Military Academy, he was a Virginia railroad president when his state seceded. He was appointed state quartermaster general and helped to capture the Norfolk Navy Yard. As a Confederate brigadier general, "Little Billy" then commanded the Norfolk District until 1862. During his later field service he was promoted to major general for heroism at the Petersburg crater and led "Mahone's Brigade," famous for its *esprit de corps*, through Appomattox. He was later a railroad president, a U.S. Senator (1881-1887) and a Republican powerbroker.

John Bankhead Magruder

peninsula. His improvisations deceived George McClellan, the Union commander, and contributed materially to the success of Confederate operations. Among other ruses, "Prince John" ordered an infantry unit to march in a wide circle for several hours, convincing Federal observers, who saw a continuous line of troops passing their field of vision, that reinforcements were arriving in Magruder's front all the time.

His reputation suffered fatally during the subsequent Seven Days' Battles around Richmond. His bumbling and inefficiency helped deny Robert E. Lee a potentially decisive victory south of the Chickahominy. Magruder and Lee quarrelled, and

Lee, deciding he could not work with Magruder, caused him to be transferred to command the District of Texas in October.

Magruder worked to strengthen the Texas coastal defenses and could boast of at least one success. On January 1, 1863, with two cotton-clad gunboats, he took Galveston, captured the cutter *Harriet Lane* and drove off the Federal blockading squadron. His active operations ended in the spring of 1864, when he sent most of his troops to reinforce Richard Taylor in Louisiana.

He refused to ask for parole at war's end and went into exile in Mexico, where he obtained a major general's commission under Emperor Maxmilian. Forced to return to the U.S. after Maxmilian's fall, he settled in Houston, where he died in February 1871.

Stephen Russell Mallory

Mallory, Stephen Russell
(1813-1873)
Secretary of the Confederate navy

Raised in Key West, Florida, and early familiar with shipping and the sea, Mallory was a Key West attorney, county judge and customs collector. He fought in the Seminole War. As a U.S. Senator (1851-1861) he promoted naval reform and opposed secession and the war. When war broke out, however, he resigned to serve as secretary of the Confederate navy (1861-1865), a difficult job, since the Confederates had neither ships nor naval yards. With great resourcefulness he mobilized inventors and construction crews, organized English and French naval construction and advanced naval technology by using ironclads, torpedoes and submarines. Arrested in May 1865, he practiced law in Pensacola after his release.

Marmaduke, John Sappington
(1833-1887) Confederate general

The son of a Missouri governor, he was graduated from West Point in 1857 and participated in the Utah Expedition (1858-1860). He resigned to join the state militia and then the Confederate army. An extremely affective cavalry commander, Marmaduke fought in Arkansas and Missouri. His greatest achievements were his successes under A. S. Johnston at Shiloh (for which he was promoted to brigadier

general) and, as a major general in charge of the cavalry, in Sterling Price's 1864 Missouri Raid. He was captured in a rearguard action after Marais des Cygnes in October 1864. After his release in 1865 he became a St. Louis businessman and journal editor. He was governor of Missouri (1884-1887).

Marshall, Humphrey
(1812-1872) Confederate general

This Kentuckian, a West Point graduate and Mexican War cavalry veteran, was a lawyer, Whig U.S. Representative (1849-1852, 1855-1859) and minister to China (1852-1854). Failing to maintain peace in the border states, he became a Confederate brigadier general in 1861. He fought along Big Sandy River, successfully attacked J. D. Cox at Princeton, West Virginia, and participated in Braxton Bragg's invasion of Kentucky before resigning to sit in the Confederate congress (1864-1865). He was later a distinguished Louisville lawyer.

Mason, James Murray
(1798-1871) Confederate statesman

Trained at William and Mary Law School, this Virginia lawyer and member of Congress (U.S. Representative 1837-1839, Senator 1847-1861) was a states' rights Democrat and prominent secessionist; he drafted the Fugitive Slave Act (1850). As a Confederate diplomatic commissioner en route in a British ship to great Britain with John Slidell in 1861, he was captured at sea by the Federals in what became known as the *Trent* Affair, an incident that dangerously strained Anglo-U.S. relations. Despite years of diplomacy, he failed in the end to secure British recognition of the Confederacy.

Humphrey Marshall. His command in 1862, the so-called Army of Eastern Kentucky, a small militia force, was routed by Union troops under future president of the United States James A. Garfield.

Maury, Dabney Herndon
(1822-1900) Confederate general

A West Point graduate, Virginian Maury was a Mexican War and Texas frontier veteran and the author of a standard cavalry manual (1859). In 1861 he joined the Confederate cavalry; he fought at Pea Ridge and, promoted to brigadier general, at Iuka, Corinth and Hatchie Bridge. His command of the District of the Gulf after July 1863 (as a major general) was notable for the loss of Mobile – the use of its harbor to Admiral David Farragut in August 1864 and he city itself to General E. R. S. Canby in April 1865. In Richmond he later organized and chaired the Southern historical Society (1868-1886); he was U.S. minister to Colombia (1885-1889). Famed hydrographer Matthew Fontaine Maury (1806-1873) was his uncle.

Matthew Fontaine Maury

Maury, Matthew Fontaine
(1806-73) Hydrographer and Confederate naval commander

Born near Fredericksburg, Virginia, he was raised on a Tennessee frontier farm. Having joined the U.S. Navy in 1825, he established his reputation with *A New Theoretical and Practical Treatise on Navigation* (1836). After a crippling accident in 1839 ended his seagoing career, he devoted himself to naval administration and research. As superintendent of the navy's depot of charts and instruments (1842-1855, 1858-1861), he oversaw the U.S. naval observatory. He worked on the canal system, the Gulf Stream (which he was the first to describe), deep-sea sounding, the transatlantic cable and other important projects. He compiled his classic work, *Wind and Current Charts of the North Atlantic*, in 1847 and instituted a uniform international system of recording oceano-

Dabney Herndon Maury

graphical data that allowed the extension of these charts to other waters. (The sophisticated pilot charts published by today's Defense Mapping Agency still credit Maury's inspiration and follow his methodology.) This major contribution to international commerce earned him worldwide acclaim. His *Physical Geography of the Sea* (1855, published in numerous languages and many times revised) established oceanography as a major science. Maury resigned from the U.S. Navy in April 1861 and represented the Confederacy as a special agent in England (1862-1865). There he purchased foreign warships and invented a system of laying electric mines, but he returned to America too late for the Confederate navy to make use of his new technology. After a brief exile in Mexico and Europe, he joined the meteorology faculty at Virginia Military Institute (1868) and undertook a survey of Virginia.

Maximilian, Archduke
(1832-1867) Emperor of Mexico

Brother of the Austrian Emperor Franz Joseph, he was asked by Napoleon III of France to accept the "crown" of Mexico, which French troops had captured in 1862 while taking advantage of the unrest attending the Civil War in the United States. Maximilian, assured that he would be welcomed, went off to Mexico to become its Emperor in 1864, and Napoleon III provided French troops to protect him. During the Civil War, Union diplomatic pressure failed to dislodge him, but after the war the Union employed the threat of

military intervention until the French forces withdrew in 1866. Maximilian attempted to continue his reign in Mexico, and he was soon deposed, captured by troops of Benito Juarez and executed.

McCausland, John
(1836-1927) Confederate general

Born in Missouri, he was graduated first in his class from Virginia Military Institute and joined its mathematics faculty. He recruited Confederate troops in the Kanawha Valley, fought at Fort Donelson and defended the Virginia and Tennessee Railroad. As a brigadier general he led a cavalry brigade in the Shenandoah Valley and at Monocacy in 1864 and took part in the burning of Chambersburg, Pennsylvania, in retaliation for David Hunter's destruction in the Shenandoah Valley. He refused to surrender with Lee at Appomattox. He later farmed in West Virginia.

McClean, Wilmer
Virginia farmer

McClean would probably have remained an anonymous farmer in the Virginia countryside some 25 miles southwest of Washington, if, in July 1861, the battle known as First Bull Run had not destroyed his farmhouse. Wishing only to get away from the violence of the war, he moved to a new home at what he believed to be an obscure locale, Appomattox Court House, Virginia. It was in the parlor of McClean's house that, on April 9, 1865, Ulysses S. Grant chose to meet Robert E. Lee and accept the Confederate surrender.

McClellan, George Brinton
(1826-1885) Union general

The son of a distinguished Philadelphia surgeon, he attended preparatory schools and the University of Pennsylvania before entering West Point in 1842. McClellan was graduated second in his class in 1846, joined an engineer detachment and accompanied it to Mexico, where he served with notable competence throughout the war.

McClellan enjoyed a varied career during the next several years. He taught military engineering at West Point, took part in an expedition to the upper reaches of the Red River, worked on river and harbor engineering projects in Texas and surveyed a railroad route in the Pacific Northwest. In 1855-56 the army sent him abroad to study European military organizations. He returned to write a much-admired report on the siege of Sebastopol.

McClellan resigned from the service in 1857 to become chief engineer of the Illinois Central Railroad; three years later

Wilmer McClean's house in Appomattox Court House, Virginia, in 1865

he succeeded to the presidency of the Cincinnati-based Ohio & Mississippi line. He accepted a commission in the Union army as a major general of Ohio volunteers in April 1861, and took command of the Department of the Ohio in May.

His victory at Rich Mountain in early July cleared western Virginia of Confederate troops and made him one of the Union's first heroes, and President Abraham Lincoln soon turned to him to repair the damage caused by the Union defeat at First Bull Run. McClellan reached Washington on July 26, 1861, and set to work immediately to reorganize and train the army and strengthen the Washington defenses.

A brilliant organizer and administrator, McClellan transformed the beaten army almost overnight. But he seemed dilatory when the question of fighting arose. By autumn the president and key Congressmen were growing impatient with his lack of aggressiveness. "If General McClellan does not want to use the army," Lincoln said, "I would like to borrow it." Finally, early in the new year, the president ordered a general advance on Manassas. But McClellan argued for a move on Richmond from the Virginia peninsula, and Lincoln reluctantly approved. In March 1862 McClellan transported the Army of the

LEFT: George Brinton McClellan.

BELOW: McClellan and Lincoln confer in the field after Antietam.

Potomac by water to Fortress Monroe and advanced toward Yorktown. He proceeded up the peninsula at such a deliberate pace that his critics began calling him the "Virginia Creeper." Nevertheless, he had pushed the army to within sight of the spires of Richmond when J. E. Johnston counterattacked at Fair Oaks (Seven Pines) on May 31. Then, in the Seven Days' Battles of early June, Robert E. Lee checked McClellan's advance and forced him to withdraw to his base at Harrison's Landing on the James River, essentially ending the Peninsular Campaign.

Lincoln replaced McClellan with John Pope, then restored him to command after Pope's defeat at the Second Battle of Bull Run in August 1862. McClellan fought a drawn battle at Antietam Creek in Maryland on September 17 but failed to pursue the Confederates when they returned to Virginia. He finally marched in late October, but by then it was too late. Lincoln removed him for the last time on November 7, 1862. He never held another field command.

The troops loved McClellan, whom they dubbed "Little Mac," and many of the Army of the Potomac's senior offices remained devoted to him. His reputation is that of a brilliant failure, though his champions argue that the administration never gave him a fair chance. Lee, for one, thought him the ablest Union commander he faced. Yet the fact remains that McClellan never scored a significant battlefield success. He always wanted more men, more equipment, more time to plan. "He is an admirable engineer," Lincoln said of him, "but he seems to have a special talent for the stationary engine."

McClellan accepted the Democratic nomination for the presidency in 1864. The party platform called for an immediate cessation of the fighting, but McClellan, who supported vigorous prosecution of the war, simply ignored the platform. Even so, he carried only three states in November, and the soldier vote went overwhelmingly to Lincoln. His political ambitions were gratified to a small extent in 1878, when he was elected governor of New Jersey: he served until 1881. McClellan died at Orange, New Jersey, in 1885.

McClernand, John Alexander
(1812-1900) Union general

He was a lawyer, newspaper editor and Democratic politician in his native Illinois who, as a U.S. Representative (1843-1851, (1959-1961) helped to draft the Compromise of 1850. He proposed Congres-

John Alexander McClernand

sional war appropriations after First Bull Run, then left Congress to become a Union brigadier general. McClernand proved to be a politically ambitious, sometimes insubordinate and only occasionally effective officer. He commanded troops at forts Henry and Donelson and at Shiloh, and in January 1863 led 30,000 men in the unauthorized and controversial Arkansas Post expedition. Ulysses S. Grant subsequently disbanded McClernand's force and reassigned him to XIII Corps, which he led in the Vicksburg and Red River Campaigns. He resigned in ill health in November 1864 and resumed his legal and political career.

McCook Family of Ohio
("The Fighting McCooks")

The brothers Daniel (1798-1863) and John (1806-1865) McCook and their 13 sons ("the tribe of Dan" and "the tribe of John") all served the Union with distinction. The elder McCooks served respectively as an army paymaster and surgeon; of their sons, six became generals and three died in the war. The best known of their sons were General Alexander M. McCook (1831-1903, son of Dan), a career soldier who fought at First Bull Run, Shiloh,

Daniel McCook (above) and (above right) Alexander McCook.

RIGHT: Robert McCook

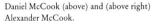

Perryville, Stones River and Chickamauga and General Edward M. McCook (1833-1909, son of John), a brilliant cavalry commander who cut Confederate communications and supply lines and prevented J. B. Hood's reinforcement during the Atlanta Campaign. Edward McCook was later governor of Colorado (1869-1875).

McCullagh, Joseph Burbridge
(1842-1896) War correspondent

Born in Ireland, McCullagh was working for the Cincinnati *Gazette* while reporting the Civil War. He volunteered to serve as Commodore Andrew Foote's secretary on the armored gunboat *St. Louis* when General Ulysses S. Grant mounted a combined attack on Fort Donelson in 1862. He later worked for various newspapers in the Midwest before starting the St. Louis *Mòrning Globe* (which later merged with the *Democrat*).

McDowell, Irvin
(1818-1885) Union general

Born in Ohio, McDowell received his early education in France, then returned home to enter West Point. He was graduated in the middle of his class in 1838 and joined the artillery. He taught tactics at the academy,

then served on the staff of General John Wool during the Mexican War.

McDowell held various staff assignments up to the outbreak of the Civil War. An early favorite of the Lincoln administration, particularly of treasury secretary Salmon P. Chase, he won promotion to brigadier general in May 1861, helped to organize troops assembling in Washington and took command of the forces south of the Potomac.

Although senior officers considered the army unfit for field operations, political pressures made an attack on the Confederates at Manassas Junction imperative. "You are green, it is true," President Lincoln told McDowell, "but they are green also; you are all green alike." Thus prodded, McDowell marched from Washington on July 16, 1861, to open the brief, disastrous Bull Run Campaign.

McDowell himself had never before held a field command, and he seems to have forgotten his own arguments about the inexperience of his troops when he planned the Bull Run offensive, since he called for a complicated turning operation that required a night march. The flanking column arrived in place hours behind schedule, and in any case, alert Confederates had discovered its presence. After a confused fight lasting several hours, McDowell's army was routed at Bull Run on July 21, the first major battle of the war.

"Both armies were defeated," said William T. Sherman, who commanded a brigade at Bull Run. "Whichever had stood fast, the other would have run."

Yet it was the Federals who ran, and McDowell took the blame: George McClellan superseded him a few days after the battle. McDowell became a division commander; he later led I Corps of the Army of the Potomac. His corps remained behind, covering Washington, when McClellan moved the army to Fortress Monroe in the spring of 1862 to open the Peninsular Campaign.

After the failure of the campaign and McClellan's removal. McDowell's command became III Corps of John Pope's Army of Virginia. His performance at the Second Battle of Bull Run drew heavy criticism, and he was relieved of his command. He called for an inquiry; the investigation exonerated him, but he never again held a command in the field.

McDowell served in California and in the departments of the East and South after the war. He returned to California in 1876 and retired there six years later. As a parks commissioner in San francisco, he is credited with laying out the roads in the Presidio overlooking the Golden Gate. He died in San francisco in May 1885 and was buried in the Presidio.

McKay, Charlotte Elizabeth
Union army nurse

Recently-widowed, McKay left her native Massachusetts to enlist as an army nurse in March 1862. Working in hospitals in Washington and in the field, she nursed men wounded in the Potomac Army campaigns from Winchester through Spotsylvania. She served in City Point hospital during the sieges of Petersburg and Richmond and earned the Kearny cross. After the war she worked with freed blacks in Virginia.

McLaws, Lafayette
(1821-1897) Confederate general

This Georgia-born West Point graduate served on the frontier, in the Mexican war, on the Utah expedition and as an Indian fighter. He resigned from the U.S. Army in 1861 and joined the Confederate army and was promoted to major general in 1862. He fought at Yorktown, helped to capture Harpers Ferry and also served at Antietam, Fredericksburg, Chancellorsville, Peach Orchard and Gettysburg. McLaws was charged by Confederate General James Longstreet of lack of cooperation at Knoxville in 1864, but, cleared of the charges, he went on to fight in the Carolinas Campaign in 1865. He worked for the Internal Revenue and Post Office departments in Savannah, Georgia, after the war.

Meade, George Gordon
(1815-1872) Union general

Meade was born in Cadiz, Spain, where his father served as the United States naval agent, but he was educated in the United States. Entering West Point in 1831, he was graduated four years later, 19th in his class

George Gordon Meade

ABOVE: The Battle of Gettysburg.

BELOW: George Meade's headquarters on Cemetery Ridge at Gettysburg.

of 56. He joined an artillery regiment, served for a year in Florida, where he was laid low with fever for much of the time, and resigned from the army in October 1836.

Meade found work immediately as assistant engineer of the Alabama, Florida & Georgia Railroad and later served as a civil engineer in a survey of the mouths of the Mississippi River. Re-entering the army in 1842, he had several engineering assignments and, during the Mexican War, saw action at Palo Alto, Monterey and Vera Cruz.

He held a succession of army engineering posts during the 1850s. On the outbreak of the Civil War he accepted a brigadier's commission in the Union army and took command of a brigade of Pennsylvania infantry. He fought in the battles of the Seven Days of June and July 1862 and was shot in the hip at Glendale, a wound that would trouble him for the remainder of his life.

Meade commanded a division at Antietam and Fredericksburg and led V Corps at Chancellorsville. On June 28, 1863, a messenger from President Lincoln informed him he had been chosen to replace Joseph Hooker as commander of the Army of the Potomac. When, three days later, advance elements of the armies met at Gettysburg, Meade decided to accept battle there. He has been praised for his masterly handling of the Union troops at Gettysburg, especially on July 2 and 3, but he has also been criticized for failing to counterattack and pursue the vulnerable Army of Northern Virginia in the aftermath of the battle.

He proved to be a solid if unspectacular commander. Tall, gaunt, hatchet-faced and irascible, his unruly temper became legendary in the army. "I don't know any thin old gentlemen with a hooked nose and cold blue eye who, when he is wrathy, exercises less of Christian charity than my well-beloved Chief," Theodore Lyman, one of his staff officers, wrote. In self-critical moods Meade recognized this failing, once describing himself as "an old snapping turtle."

Meade continued in independent command through the inconclusive Rapidan and Mine Run campaigns of late 1863, but he lost much of his authority when Ulysses S. Grant, appointed commander-in-chief, decided to make his headquarters with the army in the field. Meade retained nominal command through the surrender at Appomattox, though Grant apparently considered replacing him, in part because of his frequent quarrels with senior subordinates.

T.F. Meagher leads the Irish Brigade at the Battle of Fair Oaks (1862).

During the pursuit to Appomattox, Grant turned to Philip Sheridan as his chief tactical executive, leaving Meade with only a minor role in the campaign that closed out the war.

Meade commanded military departments in the East and South in the late 1860s. He died in Philadelphia in November 1872 while still on active duty, an indirect result of the wound he had received during the Seven Days' Battles a decade earlier.

Meagher, Thomas Francis
(1823-1867) Union general

A nationalist expelled from Ireland in 1849 for founding the Irish Confederation (1847), Meagher established himself after 1852 as a New York lawyer and newspaper editor, becoming the leader of the city's Irish community. He commanded a company of Union Zouaves, troops distinctive for their exotic costumes, at First Bull Run, and led the Irish Brigade through the Peninsula, Second Bull Run, Antietam, Fredericksburg and Chancellorsville. He later held territorial commands. He was the temporary governor of Montana when he died in a boat accident.

Meigs, John Rodgers
(1842-1864) Union officer

The son of General Montgomery Meigs and a graduate of West Point, he was a Union engineer on Philip Sheridan's staff. He was killed by one of Confederate General Williams Wickham's scouts, and, partly in retaliation, Sheridan ordered all houses within five-miles of Dayton, Virginia, to be burned.

Memminger, Christopher Gustavus
(1803-1888)
Confederate secretary of the treasury

This German immigrant was orphaned in South Carolina and fostered by a state governor. He became a Charleston lawyer and state legislator. A conservative Democrat, he opposed secession until late 1860, then attended the state and Montgomery secession conventions and helped to draft the provisional Confederate constitution.

Thomas Francis Meagher

Christopher Gustavus Memminger

prison guard that watched over Jefferson Davis at Fortress Monroe, Virginia. He later became a famous Indian fighter, saw extensive service on the frontier and led the force that captured Geronimo in 1886. Miles ended a long career as army commander-in-chief from 1895 to 1903.

Morgan, George Washington
(1820-1893) Union general

Morgan was born in Pennsylvania and attended West Point, but left it to study law. He served in the Mexican War and then entered the diplomatic service, serving as U.S. ambassador to Portugal (1858-1861). Upon the outbreak of the Civil War he was made a brigadier general in the Union army, served under Don Carlos Buell in Tennessee, led a division in the Yazoo expedition and led XIII Corps in the capture of Arkansas Post. In June 1863 he resigned due both to ill health and his objections to the Union's use of African-American troops. After the war he served Ohio in the U.S. House of Representatives.

Nelson Appleton Miles

As Confederate secretary of the treasury (1861-1864), he faced difficult choices in financing the war: inflation ballooned, making his treasury notes worthless; the Federal blockade halted cotton exports; all his bond and taxation schemes failed. The C.S.A. congress passed its own funding act in February 1864, and Memminger, held responsible for the collapse of the Confederacy's credit, resigned in June. He was afterward a lawyer and chemical manufacturer.

Merritt, Wesley
(1834-1910) Union general

A New Yorker, this young West Point graduate was aide-de-camp to Union generals Philip St. George Cooke and George Stoneman. Leading Shenandoah Army cavalry units, he saw nearly continuous action for the last two years of the war and ended his brilliant war career as a major general. He later served in Indian fighting and as superintendent of West Point (1882-1887) and held important territorial commands. He commanded the first Philippine expedition (1898) and accepted Manila's surrender with Admiral George Dewey before retiring from the army in 1900.

Miles, Nelson Appleton
(1839-1925) Union general

A Boston store clerk with dreams of military glory, he obtained a commission in the 22nd Massachusetts and advanced rapidly in the Union army, rising to colonel of the 61st New York after Antietam in September 1962. Miles fought at Chancellorsville, the Wilderness, Spotsylvania and Petersburg. At the war's end he commanded the

George Washington Morgan

John Hunt Morgan

Morgan, John Hunt
(1825-1864) Confederate general

Morgan was born in Alabama, the son of a merchant who moved his family to a farm near Lexington, Kentucky, in 1830. He was educated in local common schools, volunteered for service in the Mexican War in 1846 and saw action at Buena Vista.

Morgan went into business for himself on his return from Mexico, but the war had left him with a taste for soldiering, and in 1857 he organized a militia unit, the Lexington Rifles. When the Civil War broke out he enlisted in the Confederate army, became a scout and shortly was elected captain of a cavalry squadron.

Promoted to colonel, he commanded

Kentucky cavalry at Shiloh in April 1862 and began his career as a raider shortly thereafter, taking 400 prisoners in a raid into Mississippi and Tennessee before the Federals checked him at Lebanon, Tennessee, in early May. By June he had been given command of a brigade. He set out on July 4 on the first of his famous raids into Union-held territory.

Starting from outside Knoxville, Tennessee, with 800 troopers, Morgan advanced into Kentucky, wrecking the railroad, burning stores and harassing the movement of Don Carlos Buell's Federal army toward Chattanooga. He had a sharp fight with militia near Cynthiana on July 17, then began a slow withdrawal. His raiders covered 1,000 miles in 24 days, capturing 1,200 prisoners with a loss of fewer than 100 of their own men.

Morgan carried out two other substantial raids that summer and fall. On his last raid of the year, during the Stones River Campaign in late december 1862, he captured more than 1,800 prisoners and destroyed some $2 million-worth of property at a cost to himself of only two men killed and 24 wounded. This exploit, known as Morgan's Third Raid, won him promotion

John Hunt Morgan on his Second Raid in October 1862. On the 18th he defeated Union cavalrymen, entered Lexington, Kentucky, and seized 125 prisoners.

MORGAN'S GREAT RAID

to brigadier and command of a cavalry division.

In June 1863 he took his 1,800-strong division into Kentucky, crossed the Ohio River on July 2 and led a large force of pursuers on a wild chase, covering as many as 60 miles a day, through southern Ohio and Indiana. Federal troops finally captured him at New Lisbon, Ohio, on July 26. Though this raid has been called a reckless adventure, seemingly without purpose, it did draw substantial Federal troops out of East Tennessee, temporarily easing Union pressures on Confederate forces there.

Morgan escaped from the Ohio Penitentiary in late November, made his way home and resumed his raiding. Taking command of the Department of Southwest Virginia in April 1864, he reorganized his forces and in June launched yet another foray into Kentucky. His losses were heavy this time, and his troopers' plundering brought censure from higher authority. Nevertheless, he immediately began to plot another attack. But as luck would have it, there were to be no more raids. Morgan's whereabouts was known to the enemy. Federal troops infiltrating his lines surprised and killed him in Greenville, Tennessee, on September 4, 1864.

Thomas Jefferson Morgan

Morgan, Thomas Jefferson
(1839-1902) Union officer

Born in Indiana, he was commissioned a lieutenant in the Union's Indiana infantry at the outbreak of he Civil War; he would ultimately be breveted brigadier general for his war service. He was particularly known for his actions in enlisting and defending the rights of African-American troops. He became a Baptist minister after the war,

worked to provide education for ex-slaves and was U.S. commissioner of Indian Affairs from 1889 to 1893. He was also secretary of the American Baptist Home Mission Society for 10 years.

Mosby, John Singleton
(1833-1916) Confederate raider

While attending the university of his native state, Virginia, he was arrested and imprisoned for shooting a fellow student, but he was released when it was determined that the victim had provoked him. In jail he had begun to read law (with the help of his defense lawyer), and he eventually became a lawyer. When the Civil War broke out, he volunteered as a private in the Confederate army and fought at First Bull Run. He was commissioned a lieutenant in February 1862 and began to serve as a scout for Jeb Stuart's cavalry force, helping to guide it during Stuart's ride around George McClellan's forces in July 1862. In January 1863 Mosby was allowed to organize his own small cavalry force, known formally

John Singleton Mosby (center, with a plume in his hat) and some members of his "Partisan Rangers" troop

James Albert Myer strikes the colors of the U.S. Signal Corps at the end of the Civil War in 1865. Meyer would go on to found the U.S. Weather Bureau.

as the Partisan Rangers or Mosby's Irregulars. He would eventually have as many as 1,000 men in his unit, although he seldom took more than 300 on a single raid. He retained a loose association with Stuart's cavalry, doing advance scouting for him and sending him stolen supplies: Mosby's force usually managed to steal more than enough supplies for themselves from the enemy. Their main function was to impede and disrupt Federal operations, and their first major success came when they raided the Union camp at Fairfax Court House and captured Union General Edwin Stoughton and some 30 other prisoners, plus 58 horses. Eventually Mosby's men attained such control over eastern Virginia that the area was known as "Mosby's Confederacy." Mosby himself was so elusive that he became known as "The Grey Ghost." He simply disbanded his unit at the end of the war and went back to practicing law. He eventually became a friend and political supporter of Ulysses Grant, who had once ordered him hanged. Mosby served as U.S. consul in Hong Kong (1875-85) and later (1904-1910) as an attorney with the Department of Justice. He wrote *Mosby's War Reminiscences* (1887).

Mudd, Samuel
(1833-1883) **Physician**

Mudd was the doctor who set John Wilkes Booth's broken leg after the assassination of Abraham Lincoln. As a consequence, Mudd was brought to trial as a conspirator. Convicted and sentenced to life imprisonment in the Dry Tortugas off the Florida Keys, he cared for the garrison and prisoners during a severe yellow fever outbreak there. He returned to Maryland after being pardoned in 1869.

Mumford, William B.
(1820-1862) **Confederate patriot**

Mumford was a New Orleans gambler who removed a U.S. flag that was hanging over the U.S. Mint after Admiral David Farragut's capture of New Orleans in April 1862. The U.S. commandant in New Orleans, General Benjamin Butler, arrested Mumford and, finding him defiant, saw to it that he was convicted of treason and had him hanged in June.

Myer, Albert James
(1829-1880) **Union officer**

Trained at Buffalo Medical College, this New York-born army surgeon helped to develop the "wigwag" semaphore signal system in the 1850s: he wrote *A Manual of Signals* (1864). The Union army's first signal officer, he served on the staffs of Benjamin Butler, Irvin McDowell and George McClellan and organized and directed the Signal Corps before being reassigned to the Mississippi in late 1863. Still in active service, he founded, and was the first head of the U.S. Weather Bureau (1870-1880). Fort Myer, Virginia is named after him.

Nast, Thomas
(1840-1902) Cartoonist and illustrator

Born in Bavaria, he was brought to the U.S.
as a child. He studied at the National
Academy of Design in New York City,
and by the time he was 15 he was engaged as
a news illustrator for *Frank Leslie's Illustrated Magazine*. In 1859 he began contributing satirical drawings to *Harper's
Weekly*, and he joined its staff in 1862.
During the Civil War his drawings were so
strong and persuasive for the Union cause
that President Lincoln called him "our best
recruiting sergeant." Recognized now as
one of the true inventors of the modern
editorial cartoon, he invented the donkey
and elephant as emblems of the Democratic
and Republican parties, the tiger as the
symbol of Tammany Hall and an image of
Santa Claus that is the direct inspiration for
the one conventionally accepted today. He
was credited with having been instrumental in bringing down the corrupt Tweed
Ring in New York City. He was U.S. consul general to Ecuador when he died.

Nelson, William
(1824-1862) Union general

Born in Kentucky, Nelson served in the
navy during the Mexican war. A brother of
a friend of President Lincoln, he was asked
in 1861 to report to Lincoln on the situation
in Kentucky. He returned there, armed the
Kentucky Home Guard and later fought
with the Union army at Shiloh, Corinth
and Richmond, where he was wounded.
While organizing the defenses of Louisville, he was mortally shot by Union
General Jefferson C. Davis during a quar-
rel over Nelson's criticism of Davis.

RIGHT: William Nelson

Oliver, Paul Ambrose
(1830-1912) Union officer

Born on his father's ship in the English Channel, Oliver grew up in Germany, where he studied military science. He was a cotton exporter before the war. Commissioned a lieutenant in the Union army in October 1861, he received the Medal of Honor for his actions at Resaca, Georgia. The inventor of formulas and machinery for making explosives, he owned an explosives factory in Pennsylvania that was ultimately bought by E. I. Du Pont.

Paul Ambrose Oliver

Edward Asbury O'Neal (above) and (right) Emerson Opdycke

O'Neal, Edward Asbury
(1818-1890) Confederate general

This Alabama-born lawyer supported secession and became a Confederate major in 1861. He served in the Peninsular Campaign and was wounded at Seven Pines, Boonsboro and Chancellorsville. He fought at Gettysburg and in the Atlanta Campaign. He spent the end of the war arresting deserters in Alabama. As governor of that state after the war (1882-1886), he played an important role in providing stability during Reconstruction.

Opdycke, Emerson
(1830-1884) Union general

Born in Ohio, he entered the U.S. Army in 1861 and fought at Shiloh, Chattanooga, Chickamauga and Rocky Face Ridge. He was wounded at Resaca, Georgia, and was

credited with saving Union forces at Franklin in 1864 when he led his brigade to cover a gap in the Union line. Later in his life he wrote books about the Civil War and ran a wholesale drygoods business in New York City.

Ord, Edward Otho Cresap
(1818-1883) Union general

This Maryland native was a West Point graduate and 20-year veteran of the Seminole War and Indian fighting when he joined the Harpers Ferry expedition against John Brown (1859). In 1861 he commanded the Union defenses of Washington; he later fought at Dranesville, Iuka and Hatchie. Ord was a corps commander

OPPOSITE: Edward O.C. Ord and family.

BELOW: Peter Osterhaus.

at Vicksburg, Jackson and Fort Harrison, as well as in the Petersburg siege and the Appomattox Campaign. At the war's end he was commander of the Army of the James. Several times wounded, he was repeatedly breveted for bravery. He retired as a brigadier general in 1880.

Osterhaus, Peter
(1823-1917) Union general

Born in Prussia, he emigrated to the U.S. in 1848 and worked as a merchant and bookkeeper in Missouri. He fought for the Union at Wilson's Creek in August 1861 and commanded a brigade at Pea Ridge in March of the following year. Osterhaus led a division during the Vicksburg and Chattanooga campaigns and a corps in the Army of the Tennessee in 1864 and 1865. After the war, he held consular appointments in France and Germany.

Page, Charles Anderson
(1838-1873) War correspondent

A young Treasury official released for war reporting, Page became famous for fast, accurate and vivid dispatches to the New York *Tribune*, which awarded him the unusual distinction of a byline. He covered the Peninsula, Second Bull Run, the Wilderness, Spotsylvania and the Petersburg siege, and was one of the first reporters into Richmond in April 1865. During the temporary ban on reporters in the field he served as a hospital worker with John Pope's army.

Paine, Charles Jackson
(1833-1916) Union general

A Harvard-trained Boston lawyer, Paine recruited a company for the Union army in September 1861. He served on Benjamin

Charles Jackson Paine.

Butler's staff, commanded troops at Port Hudson and, after his promotion to brigadier general in July 1864, led divisions at New Market and Fort Fisher. He became wealthy developing railroads after the war. An internationally renowned yachtsman, he won the America's Cup in 1885, 1886 and 1887.

Halbert Eleazer Paine

Paine, Halbert Eleazer
(1826-1905) Union general

This Ohio-born lawyer and partner of Carl Shurz joined the Union army in 1861 and was commissioned a colonel. While taking his troops to the front he was offered the use of cattle cars; unwilling to allow his men to ride with cattle, he and his regiment stopped a passenger train and boarded it. He was promoted to brigadier general in 1863 and lost a leg at Port Hudson. Always an idealist, he was a Radical Republican in the House of Representatives after the war. Later, as U.S. commissioner of patents, he introduced such changes as the use of typewriters by the office clerks.

Palmer, John McAuley
(1817-1900) Union general

Palmer was a Kentucky and Illinois lawyer and Democratic legislator who was an early convert to the Republican Party and a delegate to the 1861 Peace Convention. Joining the Union Army's 14th Illinois, he was promoted to brigadier general in December 1861. He commanded troops in the Mississippi, Ohio and Cumberland

John McAuley Palmer

armies, fighting at New Madrid, Point Pleasant and Island No. 10 and distinguishing himself at Stones River and Chickamauga. He was governor of Illinois (1869-1873) and, after rejoining the Democrats, U.S. Senator (1891-1897). He ran for president as a National Democrat in 1896.

Parker, Ely Samuel
(1828-1895) Union officer

He was raised on a New York Seneca reservation and, after his education at local academies, represented Indian claims in Washington, D.C. He became a Seneca sachem, (his Indian name was Do-ne-ho-ga-wa) in 1852. Parker trained as a lawyer and then, refused admission to the bar, as an engineer. As superintendent of public works in Galena, Illinois (1857-1862), he befriended Ulysses S. Grant. Commissioned a captain of engineers in the Union

army in May 1863, he was J. E. Smith's division engineer, in September joining Ulysses S. Grant as staff officer and military secretary. Parker transcribed the official copies of Robert E. Lee's surrender. He was commissioner of Indian Affairs (1869-1871) and later a New York businessman.

Parsons, Lewis Baldwin
(1818-1907) Union general

A New York-born lawyer, Parsons went into railroading and, while still a civilian, served as an aide to Union General Francis P. Blair during the capture of Camp Jackson, Missouri. He was commissioned a captain afterward (October 1861) and ran river and rail transportation for the Federal Department of Mississippi. Later running

ABOVE: Lewis Baldwin Parsons.

BELOW: Ely Samuel Parker (far right).

river and rail transportation for the entire country, he was promoted to brigadier general in May 1865. He oversaw the transportation of discharged soldiers after the war and went into banking, railroading and Democratic politics.

Parsons, Mosby Munroe
(1819-1865) Confederate general

This Virginia-born lawyer and legislator who had served in the Mexican War, organized the Missouri State Guard at the outbreak of the Civil War. He was made a Confederate brigadier general in 1862 after fighting at Wilson's Creek and Pea Ridge. He fought in the 1864 Red River Campaign and in Arkansas. Escaping to Mexico after General Sterling Price's unsuccessful raid in Missouri (Price had invaded the state in September 1864 but had been defeated by Union troops by late October), he joined the Republicans in Mexico and was killed during the Mexican rebellion at Camargo on August 17, 1865.

Patrick, Marsena Rudolph
(1811-1888) Union general

A New Yorker, this West Point graduate resigned from the army in 1850 after service in the Seminole and Mexican wars. He left the presidency of New York State Agricultural College to re-enlist in the Union army as a brigadier general in May 1861. After serving on George McClellan's staff and in Washington's defenses, he fought at Second Bull Run, Chantilly, South Mountain and Antietam. He served capably as provost marshal general of the Union army after October 1862. After the war he promoted scientific farming and in his last years supervised an Ohio soldiers' home.

Payne, William Henry Fitzhugh
(1830-1904) Confederate general

This Virginian was graduated from Virginia Military Institute and became a lawyer. Joining the Confederate army as a captain

William Henry Fitzburgh Payne

in the Black Horse cavalry, he commanded cavalry at Williamsburg and Chancellorsville, in Jeb Stuart's 1863 Pennsylvania raid, in Jubal Early's 1864 Raid on Washington and at Richmond. He was repeatedly wounded and was captured three times: twice exchanged, he spent the last months of the war in detention on Johnson's Island. He was Washington-based counsel for the Southern Railroad after the 1880s.

John Pegram

Pegram, John
(1832-1865) Confederate general

The Virginian Pegram was graduated from West Point and served on the frontier and in Indian fighting. As a Confederate officer he fought a varied war. After surrendering to George McClellan at Rich Mountain in

1861, he was chief engineer under P. G. T. Beauregard and Braxton Bragg. He later fought under Kirby Smith, Richard Ewell and Jubal Early, participating at Chickamauga and leading divisions at the Wilderness, Cold Harbor, Winchester, Fisher's Hill and Cedar Creek and in the Petersburg siege. He was killed at Hatcher's Run in February 1865, three weeks after his wedding.

Pelham, John
(1838-1863) Confederate officer

Born in Alabama, Pelham left West Point in 1861 to return to the South and join the Confederate army. He fought at First and Second Bull Run, Williamsburg, Gaines's Mill, Antietam and Fredericksburg. He is famous for Robert E. Lee's description of him at Fredericksburg as "gallant" and courageous. Apparently quite handsome and a ladies man, it was said that three young ladies went into mourning after he was killed in March at Kelly's Ford. "The Gallant Pelham" was posthumously promoted to lieutenant colonel.

Pemberton, John Clifford
(1814-1881) Confederate general

Born into an old Pennsylvania Quaker family in Philadelphia, he was graduated from West Point, fought in the Seminole War and was breveted for bravery in numerous engagements in the Mexican War. He was serving on the northwest frontier at the outbreak of the Civil War. Married to a Virginian, Pemberton refused

John Clifford Pemberton (right) meets with Ulysses Grant outside Vicksburg.

a U.S. colonel's commission and joined the Confederate army in April 1861 as a lieutenant colonel. He organized Virginia's cavalry and artillery and was soon promoted to commands beyond his abilities. As a major general (February 1862) in command of the Department of South Carolina, Georgia and Florida, he built Fort Wagner and Battery "B" at Charleston. Promoted to lieutenant general (October 1862), he took command of the Department of Mississippi, Tennessee and East Louisiana, an assignment that was to cost the South dearly. Besieged at Vicksburg in a brilliant campaign conducted by Ulysses S. Grant, outnumbered, outgunned and under attack from land and water, Pemberton was, confusingly, instructed by Jefferson Davis to hold Vicksburg and by J. E. Johnston to surrender it. In a humiliating defeat for the Confederacy, he accepted Grant's terms of "unconditional surrender" on July 4, 1863; many Southerners, distrustful of his Northern origins, unfairly suspected him of treachery. He was exchanged and resigned his command in May 1864, serving out the war as a colonel and ordnance inspector. He retired to his Virginia farm, and spent his last years in Philadelphia.

Pender, William Dorsey
(1834-1863) Confederate general

This North Carolina-born West Point graduate (1854) served on the frontier until the Civil war began, resigning from the U.S. Army to accept a commission as a cap-

William Dorsey Pender

tain in the Confederate army. He fought in a whole series of battles – Seven Pines, the Seven Days' Battles, Second Bull Run, Antietam, Fredericksburg and Chancellorsville; he suffered three wounds at this last-named battle. A major general by the age of 29, he was mortally wounded on the second day of fighting at Gettysburg, dying on July 19. Pender was highly regarded in the Confederate army and some even compared him to Stonewall Jackson.

Pendleton, William Nelson
(1809-1883) Confederate general

This Virginia-born West Point graduate was a teacher and an Episcopal minister before the war. He was appointed Confederate General Joseph E. Johnston's chief of artillery in July 1861, was promoted to brigadier general in 1862 and then served as Robert E. Lee's chief of artillery (although the value of his contribution in this post has been questioned). He con-

tinued to serve as a minister during the war and was often mistaken for Lee because of their similar appearance. His daughter married Brigadier General Edwin G. Lee.

Perry, Edward Aylesworth
(1831-1889) Confederate general

Born in Massachusetts, Perry was a lawyer before accepting a commission in the Confederate army; he was promoted to colonel in May 1862. He was wounded at Frayer's Farm and was appointed a brigadier general after his recovery in August 1862. He led a brigade at Fredericksburg and Chancellorsville but missed Gettysburg due to illness. He was wounded again at the Wilderness in 1864 and spent the remainder of the war with reserve forces in Alabama. He was a lawyer and Democratic governor of Florida after the war.

Edward Aylesworth Perry was wounded in 1862 and again in 1864.

Pettigrew, James Johnston
(1828-1863) Confederate general

Born in North Carolina, Pettigrew was graduated with the highest marks ever from the University of North Carolina. He went on to become a lawyer and serve in his state's legislature. Although opposed to continuing the slave trade, he sided with the Confederacy from the moment the Federal forces took over Fort Sumter. He led a brigade in the Peninsular Campaign and was wounded and captured at Seven Pines. He was exchanged, and at Gettysburg he led one of the three divisions that made up "Pickett's Charge" on the third day of the battle. He was killed by Union cavalry during the Confederate retreat from Gettysburg.

Pettus, Edmund Winston
(1821-1907) Confederate general

This Alabama-born lawyer and judge had fought in the Mexican War. He was sent from Alabama to persuade his brother, the governor of Mississippi, to bring his state into the Confederacy. He fought for the Confederacy in Kentucky and at Vicksburg and was captured at Port Gibson; he

soon escaped but was recaptured. He was promoted to brigadier general in 1863 and went on to fight at Lookout Mountain and Missionary Ridge and in the Atlanta and Nashville campaigns. He surrendered with J. E. Johnston in he Carolinas. He was a Democratic U.S. Senator after the war.

Phillips, Wendell
(1811-1884) Abolitionist

Boston born, he attended Harvard Law School but soon abandoned a legal career, being drawn to the abolitionist movement by the inspiration of William Lloyd Garrison and Elijah Lovejoy. His impassioned speech at Boston's Funeuil Hall in 1837, protesting the murder of Elijah Lovejoy, launched him on a career as a lecturer against slavery. He took extremely radical positions – attacking the U.S. Constitution, refusing to seek public office and even advocating that the North secede from the flawed union that accommodated slavery. During the war he attacked Lincoln for compromising on slavery. After the war he succeeded Garrison as president of the American Anti-Slavery Society and continued to work for progressive social reforms of all kinds.

Pickett, George Edward
(1825-1875) Confederate general

Born in Richmond, Virginia, he absorbed the rudiments of an education there and in the Illinois law office of an uncle before obtaining a West Point appointment in 1842. He was graduated four years later at the very bottom of his class of 59 cadets.

Assigned to an infantry regiment, Pickett served in Mexico in 1846 and 1847, saw considerable fighting there and took part in the capture of Mexico City. He did duty in a Texas garrison from 1849 to 1856. Transferred to the Pacific northwest a latter year, he commanded an infantry detachment at San Juan Island in Puget Sound during the war scare with Britain in 1859.

He resigned his U.S. commission in 1861 and offered his services to the Confederacy. Commissioned a colonel, he was promoted to brigadier in February 1862. His

BELOW: Pickett's charge.

OPPOSITE: Pickett's charge, the climax.

OVERLEAF: Pickett's final defeat: the Battle of Five Forks, April 1865.

George Edward Pickett

"Game Cock Brigade" won a good fighting reputation at Williamsburg, Seven Pines and Gaines's Mill during the Peninsular Campaign; Pickett was wounded at Gaines's Mill. Promoted to major general after his recovery, he took command of a division of Virginia troops in October 1862.

Pickett fought at Fredericksburg and accompanied James Longstreet and most of the First Corps on the Suffolk expedition in the winter of 1862-63. Longstreet's corps missed the Battle of Chancellorsville, but rejoined the Army of Northern Virginia in time to cross the Potomac with Lee in his second invasion of the North.

Dapper, somewhat flashily dressed, his long hair worn in ringlets, Pickett thirsted for glory on the battlefield. His chance came at Gettysburg on July 3, 1863. He led one of the divisions that hot afternoon in what became known, inaccurately, as Pickett's Charge, an ill-judged frontal attack ordered by Robert E. Lee that cost the Confederates heavily. Pickett's division alone lost three-quarters of its

strength in the disastrous charge. In the aftermath, Lee sent Pickett's shattered division to recuperate in the comparative quiet of the Department of Virginia and North Carolina, but Pickett never wholly forgave Lee for having ordered the charge.

Pickett returned to Longstreet's corps for the Battle of Cold Harbor in June 1864. He served in the Petersburg lines during the siege of June 1864 to March 1865 and was in command on the extreme right of Lee's line when P. H. Sheridan's combined cavalry and infantry attacked at Five Forks on April 1, 1865. Pickett missed the earlier stages of this battle, as he and several of his officers were enjoying a shad bake at a secluded picnic spot several miles away. The rout of the Confederates there turned Lee's right and forced him to evacuate Petersburg and Richmond. Lee is alleged to have decided to remove Pickett from the army after Five Forks, but the surrender at Appomattox on April 9 made the issue moot.

Pickett declined a postwar offer of a generalship in the Egyptian army, went into the insurance business and died in Norfolk, Virginia, in July 1875.

Francis Harrison Pierpont

Pierpont, Francis Harrison
(1814-1899) Governor of Virginia

Raised in what would, in 1863, become West Virginia, this lawyer and businessman settled in Virginia in 1842. A Whig activist and Unionist, he supported Lincoln in 1860, and after Virginia's secession he organized the pro-Union forces that declared western Virginia's intention to seek independent statehood within the Union. He was wartime governor of the Federally-controlled Virginia counties (the "restored" Virginia), after the war serving as pre-Reconstruction governor of Virginia (1865-1868) before returning to a West Virginia law practice and public service.

Pike, Albert
(1809-1891) Confederate general

Born in Boston, Pike was educated in Massachusetts and taught school there before venturing west and settling Arkansas in the early 1830s. Pike bought a Little Rock newspaper in 1835 and by the outbreak of war in 1861 had become a wealthy and influential publisher and a writer and poet of national reputation. He entered Confederate service in August 1861 and commanded Indian troops at Pea Ridge in March 1862. After a brief military career marked by friction with his superiors, he resigned in July 1862. Pike had a distinguished postwar career as a lawyer and journalist. His voluminous writings on the rituals of Scottish Rite Masonry were widely read.

Pillow, Gideon Johnson
(1806-1878) Confederate general

This University of Nashville graduate became a well-known criminal lawyer in partnership with James K. Polk, later a close political ally. As president, Polk commissioned the inexperienced Pillow as a brigadier general during the Mexican War. While never holding elective office, Pillow exerted considerable Democratic influence in Tennessee, where he promoted compromise as the Civil War approached. He was the Confederate second-in-command at Fort Donelson, where he and his superior, John B. Floyd, relinquished their commands and fled, leaving Simon B. Buckner to surrender to Ulysses Grant. Pillow was reprimanded for "grave errors of judgment" and received no further significant commands.

Albert Pike in Masonic garb

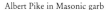

Allan Pinkerton (seated background, smoking pipe) when he was McClellan's chief of intelligence in 1862

Pinkerton, Allan
(1819-1884)
Detective and Union secret service chief

After emigrating to Illinois (1842), this Scot was a deputy sheriff and Underground Railroad foreman. He opened America's first private detective agency in Chicago (1850). He foiled a plot to assassinate President-elect Lincoln in February 1861. Subsequently recruited to set up the Union army's secret service, he worked under George McClellan in the field and in Washington, where he directed counter-espionage activities under the alias "Major E. J. Allen." The poor quality of the intelligence he supplied contributed to McClellan's lackluster performance in his unsuccessful Peninsular Campaign. After McClellan lost his command, Pinkerton investigated damage claims against the government (1862-1865). He later expanded his agency, won a controversial reputation as a "labor union buster," and wrote 18 popular volumes of detective stories.

Pleasonton, Alfred
(1824-1897) Union general

A native of Washington, D.C., and a graduate of West Point, Pleasonton was a career cavalryman who was breveted for gallantry in the Mexican War and served in Indian fighting and on the frontier. He performed

Alfred Pleasonton (right), with George
Custer, in April 1863. He would lead the
Union cavalry at Gettysburg in July.

brilliantly for the Union in the Peninsular
Campaign, fought at South Mountain,
Antietam and Fredericksburg, and earned
promotion to major general after helping
to stop T. J. Jackson's advance against
Joseph Hooker at Chancellorsville. He distinguished himself at Brandy Station and
commanded the Union cavalry at the Battle
of Gettysburg. He later routed Sterling
Price in Missouri at the battles of Westport
and Marais des Cygnes (October 1864). He
resigned from the army in 1868 and in his
last years lived on his army pension in
Washington, D.C.

Polignac, Prince Camille Armand Jules Marie de
(1832-1913) Confederate general

This French Crimean War veteran resigned
from the French army in 1859 to pursue
botanical studies. He was the only alien to
hold high rank in the Confederate army,
eventually becoming a major general in
June 1864. Polignac was P. G. T. Beauregard's chief of staff and fought at Corinth
and in the 1864 Red River Campaign. His
Texas brigade called him "Polecat." After
unsuccessfully seeking French aid for the
Confederacy, he retired to his French
estate in 1865 and became a noted mathe-
matician and civil engineer.

Polk, Leonidas
(1806-1864) Confederate general

His father had fought in the Revolution
and helped found the University of North
Carolina, where Polk studied for two years
before entering West Point. During his
fourth year at the academy he came under
the influence of a new chaplain, was converted and led what an early biographer
called a praying squad. Polk resigned his
army commission six months after he was
graduated in order to enter the Virginia
Theological Seminary.

Ordained a priest in the Episcopal
Church in May 1831, he served as assistant
rector of a Richmond parish before failing
health forced him to resign. After a sojourn
in Europe, he returned to the U.S. to accept
an appointment as missionary bishop of
the southwest, which at that time meant an
area which included Alabama, Mississippi,
Louisiana and Arkansas.

Polk became bishop of Louisiana in 1841
and settled on a large sugar plantation.
Through an inheritance of his wife's he
owned 400 slaves; the bishop is said to have
established a Sunday School for them. The
plantation enterprise proved a financial
failure, however, and Polk returned full
time to his pastoral duties.

He helped establish the University of the
South, which he hoped would educate a
Southern ruling class, laying the corner-
stone for the first building at Suwanee,
Tennessee, in October 1860. When war

broke out the following year Jefferson
Davis, who had been a cadet with Polk at
West Point, offered him a major general's
commission in the Confederate army.
Believing the South was fighting for a holy
cause, he accepted.

Polk's first military assignment involved
the defense of the Mississippi River. His
troops occupied Columbus, Kentucky, in
September 1861, violating that state's self-
declared neutrality and tilting it toward the

Leonidas Polk

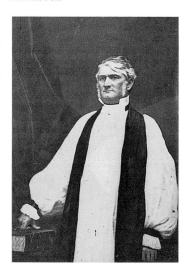

Union. He later became a corps commander under Albert Sidney Johnston (like Davis, a close friend) and fought with Johnston at Shiloh in April 1862.

He was Braxton Bragg's second in command at Perryville on October 8, 1862, and won promotion to lieutenant general later in the month. His performance at Stones River at the year's end and at Chickamauge in September 1863 left a great deal to be desired. His failure to attack at daybreak at Chickamauga prompted Bragg to remove him from command and recommend his court martial. Davis interceded and reinstated him.

Polk's reputation as a corps commander did not stand high with anyone (except, perhaps, Davis), though he probably did as well as could be expected, given his lack of military experience. He was killed near Marietta, Georgia, during the Atlanta Campaign, blown out of his saddle by the sharpshooting crew of a Parrott rifled cannon.

One of his kinsman, James Knox Polk, was the 11th president of the United States (1845-1849).

Pope, John
(1822-1892) union general

Born in Louisville, Kentucky, he was graduated from West Point in 1842 and performed survey work for the army's topographical engineers, first in Florida and later in the Northeast. He served with Zachary Taylor during the Mexican War, winning recognition for his contributions at Monterey and Buena Vista.

Pope served in New Mexico and elsewhere in the Southwest during the 1850s, surveying a potential route for a Pacific railroad. On the outbreak of the Civil War he became the Union army's mustering officer in Chicago. Appointed a brigadier at the end of July, he reported to John Frémont's command in St. Louis and took charge of a division of the Army of Southwest Missouri.

Assigned to command the Army of the Mississippi in the late winter of 1862, Pope scored his first important military successes at New Madrid, Missouri, and Island No. 10 in March (his forcing of the surrender of the island garrison opened the Mississippi River almost to Memphis). His army formed Henry Halleck's left wing on the slow, deliberate advance to Corinth, Mississippi, from April to June.

Lincoln chose him in the summer of 1862 to succeed George McClellan as the senior commander in the Virginia theater. He made himself instantly unpopular with all

ranks. In his famous address on taking command he alienated the troops by calling their courage into question. "Let us understand each other," he wrote. "I come to you from the west, where we have always seen the backs of our enemies; from an army whose business it has been to seek the adversary, and to beat him when he was found; whose policy has been attack and not defense." On the other side, Robert E. Lee conceived an unusually strong dislike for him.

Lee and his chief lieutenants, T. J. Jackson and James Longstreet, thoroughly outwitted and outfought Pope in the Second Battle of Bull Run, August 29-30, 1862. His badly beaten army retreated into the Washington defenses after the Battle of Chantilly on September 1, and Lincoln removed Pope from command the next day.

John Pope, whose defeat at the Second Battle of Bull Run ruined his career

Pope blamed his misfortunes on his subordinates, particularly Fitz-John Porter, a McClellan loyalist who was subsequently removed from command of V Corps and dismissed from the army for alleged failures during the Second Bull Run Campaign. (After a long fight, Porter won reinstatement in 1887). Pope never again had a field command.

Staying on in the regular army after Appomattox, he held a series of military district and department commands in the 1860s and 1870s. He retired from the service as commander of the Department of California in 1886. He died of "nervous prostration" in Sandusky, Ohio, in September 1892.

Porter, David Dixon
(1813-1891) Union admiral

He received a basic education in his native Chester, Pennsylvania, and joined the Mexican navy as a midshipman at age 13. Taken prisoner after an action with a Spanish frigate off the Cuban coast, he spent time in a Havana jail before being repatriated and entering the U.S. Navy in 1829. Midshipman Porter served in the Mediterranean aboard the sailing frigates *Constellation* and *United States* and worked on the U.S. coastal survey for six years. In 1841 he was promoted to lieutenant. Six years later, after a short, dull tour as a recruiting officer in New Orleans, he saw his first action in the Mexican War, taking part in an unsuccessful assault on Vera Cruz. He then commanded the landing party that stormed and captured a coastal fort at Tabasco. The Navy rewarded him with his first command, the steam vessel *Spitfire*.

He returned to coast survey duties after the war. From 1849 to 1855, on leave from the navy, he held several merchant commands. Returning to the navy, he made a cruise to the Black sea, where he had a glimpse of the Crimean War. He was second in command of the Portsmouth

Navy Yard in New Hampshire from 1857 to 1860. Frustrated by lack of opportunity, he was preparing to leave the navy for good when, with the Civil War on the horizon, he received command of the steamer USS *Powhatan* with orders to sail to the relief of Fort Pickens, Florida.

Porter participated in the blockade of Pensacola, Mobile and the Southwest Pass of the Mississippi River in 1861. Promoted to commander, he helped plan the New Orleans expedition in early 1862 and recommended David G. Farragut, his foster brother, to lead it. Farragut in turn chose him to command the mortar flotilla assembled to bombard the river forts guarding the city. After Farragut ran the water batteries at forts St. Philip and Jackson, defeated the defending Confederate naval squadron and sailed into New Orleans, Porter demanded the surrender of the garrisons. They capitulated on April 27, 1862.

He succeeded to the command of the Mississippi Squadron in October 1862, even though his name was far down on the seniority list. He had a powerful ally in G. V. Fox, the assistant navy secretary, and Gideon Welles, the secretary, thought him brave, energetic and full of dash. His gunboats helped W. T. Sherman capture

Arkansas Post in January 1863, and Porter himself received the surrender of the garrison. The river fleet also supported U. S. Grant's operations against Vicksburg; Porter was present when the river fortress capitulated on July 4, 1863. Both Grant and Sherman worked well with Porter and strongly commended his efforts. So did his Navy Department superiors; they promoted his two rungs to rear admiral that summer, skipping he ranks of captain and commodore.

In the spring of 1864 he commanded the naval forces in N. P. Banks's unsuccessful Red River Campaign. Later that year he came east to take command of the 120-vessel North Atlantic Blockading Squadron. His chief offensive assignment was to cooperate with the army in the capture of Fort Fisher, which protected the Confederacy's last important open port, Wilmington, North Carolina. The first attempt, in December, fizzled; Porter blamed the army for the failure. In January a more powerful force, 60 warships and 8,000 troops, succeeded in taking the fort and closing down Wilmington.

David Dixon Porter (opposite) and (below) Porter's squadron running past the guns of Vicksburg in April 1863

David Porter's ships at Baton Rouge in August 1862 (above) and (right) General Fitz-John Porter

Appointed superintendent of the Naval Academy in August 1865, Porter launched a four-year period of reform. He extended his influence navywide in 1869, when President Grant appointed him advisor to the navy secretary. Not all his reform schemes were sensible: among other things, he required steamships to be equipped with auxilary sails long after steam's reliability had been proven. He succeeded Farragut as full admiral in August 1870 and from 1877 until his death headed the Navy Board of Inspection,

Porter embarked on a literary career in his later years, producing his *Memoir of Commodore David Porter* in 1875 and the lively *Incidents and Anecdotes of the Civil War* a decade later. He also wrote several novels.

Porter, Fitz-John
(1822-1901) **Union general**

He was born in Portsmouth, New Hampshire, the son of a naval captain and the nephew of Admiral David Porter. As a recent West Point graduate, he was wounded

and breveted in the Mexican War. He later
taught artillery and cavalry at West Point
(1849-1855) and was chief of staff to A. S.
Johnston on the Utah Expedition. In 1860-
1861 Porter inspected Charleston's
defenses and restored rail lines north of
Washington, D.C., among other duties. As
a Union brigadier general, he commanded
the siege of Yorktown and fought against
Stonewall Jackson in the Shenandoah
Campaign of 1862. Promoted to major
general, he led V Corps on the Peninsula
(distinguishing himself at Malvern Hill)
and at Second Bull Run and Antietam.
John Pope blamed the Federal defeat at
Second Bull Run squarely on Porter's
failure to attack Jackson's right flank, and
Porter was relieved of his command in
November 1862 and cashiered in January
1863, convicted of disobeying battle
orders. He spent the next 23 years trying to
clear his record. In 1879 an army board
ruled in his favor; he received a presidential
remission of his lifetime disqualification in
1882 and finally won reappointment as a
colonel in the regular army in 1886. Historians still disagree on whether Porter was a
competent field commander or on whether
the order to attack was feasible, given prevailing battlefield conditions. Porter lived
in New Jersey after 1865, holding various
jobs there and in New York, where he
served variously as commissioner of public
works and of the police and fire services.

Powell, Lewis
(d. 1865) Conspirator

Under the alias Lewis Paine he helped John
Wilkes Booth plot the assassination of
Abraham Lincoln. Powell's assignment
was to kill Secretary of State William
Seward; he gravely wounded Seward on
the night of April 14, 1865. A military court
found him guilty of conspiracy and he was
hanged on July 7, 1865.

Preston, John Smith
(1809-1881) Confederate general

Born in Virginia, Preston was a planter, art
collector, legislator and advocate of states'
rights. Having settled in South Carolina, he
was sent to Virginia to urge the state to
secede in 1861. As a Confederate officer, he
aided P. G. T. beauregard at Fort Sumter
and First Bull Run. He commanded a
prison camp at Columbia, South Carolina,
in 1862 and was appointed head of the
Bureau of Conscription in July 1863. He
continued in that post until 1865. He went
to England after the fall of the Confederacy, finally returning in 1868.

Preston, William
(1816-1887) Confederate general

Born in Kentucky, Preston practiced law
and served in the Mexican War. A Whig in
the U.S. Congress, he then joined the
Democrats and became President James
Buchanan's ambassador to Spain. He returned to Kentucky to urge the state to
secede and was appointed brigadier general
in the Confederate army in 1862. He fought
at Corinth, Stones River, Vicksburg and
Chickamauga. Because of the Federal
blockade, he was forced to land in Mexico
when he attempted to assume a post as a
Confederate minister in Europe. After the
war he traveled and then served in the Kentucky legislature.

Price, Sterling
(1809-1867) Confederate general

Born and raised in Virginia, Price attended
Hampden-Sydney College there, studied
law and moved with his parents to Fayette,
Missouri, in 1831. He took up the successful practice of law and politics, serving
several terms in the Missouri legislature,
and commanded Missouri militia troops
during the Mexican War.

Price won election as governor of Missouri in 1852 and led the state capably for
four years. Though a conditional Union
supporter in 1860, he went with the Confederacy when war broke out in April 1861.
Forces under his command defeated a
Union army at Wilson's Creek in August,

Sterling Price

establishing him as one of the early Confederate military heroes.

Appointed a major general in the Confederate army in March 1862, Price, nick-
named "Pap," fought at Iuka, Corinth,
Helena and during the Red River Campaign of 1864, in which he inflicted a severe
defeat on a Union army under Fredrick
Steele.

He followed up this victory with an unsuccessful raid into Missouri in September
and October 1864. He retreated into Texas
in late 1864 and, after the Confederate surrender, went into exile in Mexico. He returned to Missouri after the collapse of
Maximilian's empire in 1866 and died in
September of the following year.

Pryor, Roger Atkinson
(1828-1919) Confederate general

Pryor was a newspaper publisher and influential Virginia secessionist who resigned
from his first term in Congress in March
1861 to join the Confederate army. As a brigadier general, he led brigades at Williamsburg and Seven Pines, succeeding to a division command at Antietam. Impatient with
the policies of the Confederate war department, he resigned his commission in
August 1863 to fight as a private in Fitzhugh Lee's cavalry. Pryor was captured
near Petersburg in November 1864 and was
exchanged several months later. A New
York lawyer and judge after the war, he
eventually served on the New York
supreme court (1894-1899).

Roger Atkinson Pryor

Quantrill, William Clarke
(1837-65) Confederate irregular

Quantrill was born in Canal Dover, Ohio. Within the space of a few years he was an Ohio and Illinois schoolteacher, a Kansas homesteader and a Utah gambler (alias

William Clarke Quantrill

"Charley Hart"). In 1859 he drifted back to Kansas and thence into petty thievery and border skirmishing. In December 1860 he betrayed five abolitionists, who were put to death for plotting to free the slaves of a Missouri farmer. He parlayed his involvement in murders, robberies and raids into a Confederate captaincy after taking Independence, Missouri, in August 1862, and continued operating as a guerrilla chief, despite being outlawed by the federal authorities. While his troops continued raiding and sacking pro-Union communities in Kansas and Missouri, Quantrill's own operations included the August 1863 pillaging of the free-state stronghold of Lawrence, Kansas, where he burned a substantial part of the town and murdered at least 150 people. A few months later he murdered 17 noncombatants after defeating Union cavalry at Baxter Springs, Kansas. His troops fractured by internal disagreement, he took 33 men into Kentucky early in 1865 on a fresh series of raids, robberies and killings and was killed there by Union troops at Taylorsville in May 1865. It is likely that he was the officer of whom the South was least proud.

Rains, Gabriel James
(1803-1881) Confederate general

This West Point graduate from North Carolina was a career soldier. A veteran of the Seminole and Mexican wars and a frontier fighting, he became a brigadier general in the Confederate army in September 1861. He directed the first-ever use of land mines and booby traps in the Peninsular Campaign. Superintending the torpedo bureau after June 1864, he sparked controversy by laying land mines in the South. He lived in Georgia and South Carolina after the war. His brother, George Washington Rains (1817-1898), was a leading Confederate munitions specialist.

Ramseur, Stephen Dodson
(1837-1864) Confederate general

This North Carolina-born West Point graduate resigned in 1861 and was commissioned a lieutenant in the Confederate army. He fought at the Seven Days' Battles and was gravely wounded at Malvern Hill. He was wounded again at Chancellorsville but went on to fight at Gettysburg and the Wilderness. He was wounded a third time at Spotsylvania. Promoted to major general in June 1864, he also fought at Cold Harbor and Winchester before he was mortally wounded at Cedar Creek.

Ransom, Robert Jr.
(1828-1892) Confederate general

Born in North Carolina, Ransom was a West Point-trained cavalryman who interrupted his frontier service to teach cavalry at the military academy. He organized the Confederate army's western cavalry and led troops at the Seven Days' Battles, Harpers Ferry, Antietam, Fredericksburg,

Reagan, John Henninger
(1818-1905) **Confederate politician**

He emigrated to Texas in 1839, received a license to practice law in 1848 and established himself as a leading lawyer/politician. Reagan served in the U.S. Congress from 1857 to 1861 and entered the Confederate congress after Texas seceded. Jefferson Davis appointed him postmaster general in 1861. He retained this post until late in the war, when he became treasury secretary and joined Jefferson Davis in his attempted flight south. The Federals held him prisoner for several months after his capture with Davis in Georgia. Returning to Texas after his release, Reagan practiced law and won re-election to the U.S. Congress, where he sat first as a Representative and later as a Senator.

LEFT: John Henninger Reagan.

BELOW: Thomas E.G. Ransom.

Robert Ransom, Jr.

the Bermuda Railroad defense and Jubel Early's Washington Raid. Ill-health ended his field service. He was later a farmer and civil engineer. His brother, Matt Whitaker Ransom (1826-1904), was also a Confederate general.

Ransom, Thomas Edward Greenfield
(1834-1864) **Union general**

Trained as a civil engineer, he left an Illinois business career to accept a captain's commission in the Union's 11th Illinois in April 1861. Wounded at Charleston, Fort Donelson and Shiloh, he also fought at Corinth and, after rapid promotions to brigadier general, in the Vicksburg, Red River and Atlanta campaigns. Wounded for the fourth time at Sabine Cross Roads, he finally died in the field of an illness in October 1864. Ulysses S. Grant called him "the best man I have ever had to send on expeditions."

Rawlins, John Aaron
(1831-1869) **Union general**

A Democratic Illinois politician, he joined the army in August 1861 and became Ulysses S. Grant's "most nearly indispensable" advisor. Trusted for his intelligence, honesty and sound judgment, Rawlins was promoted in tandem with Grant, eventually becoming chief of staff of the U.S. Army in March 1865.

out, he joined a Union infantry division and was made a brigadier general in August 1861. After helping to strengthen the defenses of Washington, D.C., he fought at such battles as Mechanicsville and Gaines's Mill. Captured in July 1862 at Glendale (White Oak Swamp) during the Seven Days' Battles, he was exchanged in time to lead a division at Second Bull Run. He fought at Fredericksburg and Chancellorsville as commander of the Army of the Potomac's I Corps. He was very highly regarded, and his partisans held that he, rather than George Meade, should have been chosen in June 1863 to replace Joseph Hooker as commander of the Army of the Potomac. He was killed by a sharpshooter on the first day of fighting at Gettysburg while directing the Union defense to the west of the town.

Alexander Reynolds (left) and (below) John Fulton Reynolds

Marcus Albert Reno

Reno, Marcus Albert
(1835-1889) Union officer

An Illinois native, he was graduated from West Point in 1857 and served in a Union cavalry regiment for most of the war. He commanded a Pennsylvania volunteer cavalry regiment from January to July 1865. He headed the Freedmen's Bureau in New Orleans in 1865 and 1866. A court of inquiry inconclusively investigated Reno's conduct during George A. Custer's ill-fated campaign against the Sioux in 1876. He was dismissed for unrelated reasons in 1880.

Reynolds, Alexander
(1817-1876) Confederate general

He was graduated from West Point in 1838, saw action in the Seminole War and was dismissed for discrepancies in his accounts in 1855. Reinstated, he was dismissed again after he went absent to join the Confederacy. Reynolds commanded a brigade at Vicksburg and Chattanooga and during the Atlanta Campaign. He joined the Egyptian army in 1869, rising to chief of staff in 1875.

Reynolds, John Fulton
(1820-1863) Union general

Born in Pennsylvania, this West Point graduate fought with distinction in the Mexican War, on the frontier, and in the Utah Expedition. Commandant of cadets at West Point when the Civil War broke

Reynolds, Joseph Jones
(1822-1899) Union general

Born in Kentucky, he was graduated from West Point, then taught there and served on the frontier before resigning from the army in 1857. An Indiana businessman when the war broke out, he was commissioned a Union brigadier general in May 1861 and secured West Virginia for the Union at Cheat Mountain. He led divisions at Hoover's Gap and Chickamauga, was chief of staff of the Cumberland Army at Chattanooga and, among other commands, led VII and XIX Corps and the Department of Arkansas. He remained in the regular army until 1877, then retiring to Washington, D.C.

Rhett, Robert Barnwell
(1800-1876) Confederate politician

This South Carolina planter, lawyer and legislator organized the radical separatist Bluffton movement (later suppressed) in 1844. A U.S Representative (1837-1849) and Senator (1850-1852), he was, after the 1850 Nashville Convention, an influential secessionist. He tirelessly agitated for secession in South Carolina, drafting the state's secession ordnance and calling for the Montgomery Convention; he chaired the committee that drafted the permanent Confederate constitution, over the years fairly earning the nickname, "Father of Secession." His extremist views cost him a Confederate political appointment, and he spent the war years promoting an anti-Jefferson Davis agenda in the *Charleston Mercury*. After the war he engaged in newspaper ventures with his son.

Rhodes, Elisha Hunt
(1842-1917) Union soldier

A sea captain's son, he quit his job as a clerk for a harness maker to enlist in the Union's 2nd Rhode Island Volunteers in 1861. He is remembered for the detailed and eloquent diary he kept of his war service, during which he fought at Bull Run, on the Virginia Peninsula and at Antietam, Fredericksburg, Gettysburg, Petersburg and Appomattox.

Richardson, Albert Deane
(1833-1869) War correspondent

He reported the Kansas troubles in 1857, accompanied an expedition to Pike's Peak, traveled incognito in the South during the secession crisis and covered the fighting in Virginia and the West. Captured with two

Robert Barnwell Rhett (above) and (left) Elisha Hunt Rhodes

other Northern newspapermen near Vicksburg in May 1863, he spent 18 months in a Confederate prison before breaking out and walking 400 miles to his freedom. A jealous husband sought him out in the newsroom of *The New York Tribune*, where he shot and mortally wounded him.

Ripley, Roswell Sabine
(1823-1887) Confederate general

This Ohio-born West Point graduate, after serving in the Mexican and Seminole wars, resigned from the U.S. Army in 1853 to enter business in South Carolina, where he joined the state militia. Entering the Confederate army in May 1861, he soon fell into disagreements with his superiors, generals John Pemberton and P. G. T. Beauregard. He led a brigade that fought at Antietam, where he was wounded. He was then

John Cleveland Robinson

assigned back to Charleston, South Carolina, where he finished out the war after briefly serving in the Army of the West. He went to England after the war and was for a time a manufacturer there. He later lived in Charleston and New York City.

Robertson, Jerome Bonaparte
(1815-1891) Confederate general

He was born in Kentucky and studied medicine at Transylvania University but settled in Texas after participating in the revolution there in 1836. In time he became a prominent doctor, legislator and Indian fighter. In the Confederate service, he led Texan troops in the Seven Days' Battles, Second Bull Run, Boonsboro Gap, Fredericksburg, Gettysburg and Chickamauga. In all, he fought in some 40 battles and was thrice wounded. Never a very successful field commander, he was eventually relegated to leading the Texas reserves. He continued practicing medicine until 1868, then promoted railroads in west Texas.

Robinson, John Cleveland
(1817-1897) union general

A New Yorker, he studied at West Point, fought in the Seminole and Mexican wars and joined the Utah Expedition of 1857-1858. As its commander in April 1861, he saved the Union's Fort McHenry from attack. He led Potomac Army troops continuously and gallantly in the Peninsular Campaign, at Fredericksburg, Chancel-

lorsville, Gettysburg and in the Wilderness. After losing a leg at Spotsylvania, he left field service. He was later active in veterans' organizations. He was awarded a Medal of Honor (1894), and his valiant stand at Gettysburg is commemorated by a statue on that battlefield.

Rosecrans, William Starke
(1819-1898) Union general

Born in Delaware County, Ohio, he was graduated from West Point (1842) and fortified Hampton Roads, Virginia, before returning to the military academy to teach natural and experimental philosophy and engineering. He resigned from the army in 1854 to pursue Cincinnati and Virginia business interests, including coal mining, oil refining and river navigation. He joined Union General George McClellan as a volunteer aide-de-camp in April 1861 and was commissioned in the 23rd Ohio Infantry in June. As a brigadier general he won an early victory at Rich Mountain: commencing the new Department of West Virginia, he expelled the Confederates from his territory, helping to bring West

Virginia to statehood. Succeeding John Pope in June 1862, "Old Rosy" took command of the Mississippi Army, occupied Iuka in September and attacked Corinth in October. Promoted to major general, he led the reorganized Cumberland Army through Stones River (for which he received the Thanks of Congress) and the Tullahoma Campaign. Rosecrans was a gifted strategist, but an error in one of his orders to the front at Chickamauga (September 1863) cost the Federals this crucial battle and Rosecrans his command. He saw no further significant action, commanding the Missouri Department until 1864 and awaiting orders for the duration of the war. After serving as U.S. minister to Mexico (1868, 1869), he pursued Mexican and Californian mining interests, represented California in Congress (1881-1885) and served as register of the U.S. treasury (1885-1893) before retiring to his California ranch.

William Starke Rosecrans (opposite and overleaf) at the Battle of Stones River, December 31, 1862–January 3, 1863.

BELOW: Jerome Bonaparte Robertson.

Rosser, Thomas Lafayette
(1836-1910) Confederate general

He resigned from West Point late in his final year to enter Confederate service. An artillerist at First Bull Run, he saw action with the cavalry during the Peninsular Campaign and led the Fifth Virginia Cavalry in the Second Bull Run, Chancellorsville and Gettysburg campaigns. As a brigade commander, Rosser met his West Point friend George Armstrong Custer in battle in the Shenandoah Valley and during the retreat to Appomattox. The three raids he led into West Virginia in 1864 and 1865 are remembered as "Rosser's Raids." He had a successful postwar career as a railway engineer and commanded a brigade of volunteers during the Spanish-American War of 1898.

Rousseau, Lovell Harrison
(1818-1869) Union general

This self-educated Indiana lawyer and Whig legislator returned to his native Kentucky after fighting in the Mexican War and became a leading Louisville lawyer and legislator. A strong Unionist, he is credited with keeping Kentucky in the Union. He enlisted in the Union army September 1861 and figured prominently in the fighting at Shiloh, Perryville and Chickamauga. From November 1863 to July 1865 Rousseau commanded the District of Nashville. Commissioned a brigadier general in the regular army in 1867, he was sent to receive Alaska from the Russians. He died on active duty.

Ruffin, Edmund
(1794-1865)
Secessionist, agriculturalist, publisher

This Virginian agriculturalist conducted early experiments with crop rotation, fertilizer and drainage. An influential reformer through his lectures and writing, he wrote a seminal *Essay on Calcareous Manures* (1832), founded the *Farmer's Register* (1833-1843) and, as state agricultural surveyor, published a landmark agricultural survey of South Carolina (1843). A committed secessionist, he wrote in defence of slavery and secession in the 1850s. He joined Charleston's Palmetto Guard before the attack on Fort Sumter (where some sources erroneously state he fired the first shot). He left field service soon after First Bull Run, however, and shuttled between his plantations and Charleston until June 1865, Distraught after the surrender, he committed suicide.

Ruggles, Daniel
(1810-1897) Confederate general

A career army officer, Massachusetts-born Ruggles was graduated from West Point in 1833, served on the frontier and in Texas and fought in the Mexican War. He joined the Confederate army as a brigadier general in 1861 and served along the Potomac and at New Orleans. He led a division at Shiloh and at Baton Rouge and, as a major general, commanded the Department of the Mississippi. In 1865 he was commissary general of prisoners. He lived on his Texas and Virginia estates after the war.

Russell, David Allen
(1820-1864) Union general

A West Point-trained career officer and frontier and Mexican War veteran, this New Yorker led the Union's 7th Massa-

Edmund Ruffin

David Allen Russell

chusetts in the Peninsular Campaign and at South Mountain and Antietam. As a brigadier general, he subsequently commanded troops at Fredericksburg, Gettysburg, Rappahannock Bridge (wounded), the Wilderness and Petersburg. After joining Philip Sheridan in the Shenandoah Valley Campaign, he was killed at the Battle of Winchester in September 1864.

Russell, Sir William Howard
(1820-1907) War correspondent

An Irish-born war correspondent famous for his Crimean War dispatches, he covered the Civil War for the pro-Confederate London *Times* in 1861-1862. His effectiveness was compromised by his unpopularity both in the South (because of his antislavery convictions) and in the North (for his unvarnished account of the Federal rout at First Bull Run). Regarded as the first modern special correspondent, he traveled widely covering wars and other world events. He was knighted in 1895.

Salm-Salm, Agnes Elisabeth Winona Leclerq Joy, Princess
(1840-1912) Union nurse.

Born in Vermont or Quebec, she went to Washington at the outbreak of the war and soon married Prussian Prince Felix Salm-Salm. She accompanied him in the field, promoting his career and earning for herself a captaincy for her hospital relief work. She later became famous for her futile but courageous intercession for Mexican Emperor Maximilian's life and for her relief work in Prussian army camps and field hospitals.

Salm-Salm, Felix Constantin Alexander Johann Nepomuk, Prince
(1828-1870) Union officer

A Prussian cavalryman, he fought in the Prussian-Danish War of 1848-49. He sailed to American in 1861 to fight for the North, serving first as aide-de-camp to Louis Blenker, commander of a German division. He later fought with the 8th and 68th New York. He became Emperor Maximilian's aide-de-camp in Mexico immediately after the war. He was killed fighting with the Prussian guards in the Franco-Prussian War of 1870.

Salomon Brothers
Union officers/state governor

These three brothers were Prussian refugees from the 1848 revolution. Carl Eberhard (1822-1881) and Frederick Sigel Salomon (1826-1897) became Union officers. A Wisconsin surveyor and railroad engineer, Frederick joined a Wisconsin infantry regiment and was promoted to brigadier general in June 1862. After the

Frederick Sigel Salomon

war he was surveyor general of Utah Territory. The third brother, Edward Selig Salomon (1836-1913), a prominent Wisconsin lawyer and Republican, was the wartime governor of Wisconsin (1862-1864, lieutenant governor 1861-1862) and a conspicuously successful military recruiter. He greatly improved the state university. After 1869 he practiced law in New York, where he was founding president of the legal aid society (1875-1889); he retired to Germany (1894).

Sanders, John Calhoun
(1840-1864) Confederate general

Born in Alabama, Sanders left college to join the Confederate army. He fought at Seven Pines, Gaines's Mill, Frayers's Farm, Antietam, Fredericksburg, Chancellorsville, Gettysburg, the Wilderness and Spotsylvania. (He was wounded at Frayser's Farm, Antietam and Gettysburg.) Promoted to brigadier general in May 1864, he was killed in August 1864 at Weldon Railroad.

Scammon, Eliakim Parker
(1816-1894) Union general

This West Point-trained Maine native fought in the Seminole and Mexican wars. He left the presidency of Cincinnati College to join the Union's 23rd Ohio in 1861. He fought in West Virginia and Maryland and was promoted to brigadier general in October 1862 for gallantry at South Mountain. His later commands in Missouri and the Carolinas were interrupted by his capture in 1864 and imprisonment at Libby Prison. He spent most of his later years as a college mathematics instructor.

Schenck, Robert Cumming
(1809-1890) Union general, politician

Born in Ohio, Schenck was a lawyer, U.S Congressman, ambassador to Brazil and railroad president before being named a Union brigadier general in 1861. He fought at Vienna and in T. J. Jackson's 1862 Valley Campaign. Wounded at Second Bull Run, he was promoted to major general. He resigned from the army in 1863 after he was elected to the U.S. House of Representatives, where he served until 1870, when he was named U.S. ambassador to England. He sat on the commission that made the treaty of Washington, the Geneva arbitration and the settlement of the *Alabama* claims. He wa forced to resign as ambassador when he was accused of involvement in a fraudulent mine in the American West, but he was never found guilty.

Robert Cumming Schenck (right) and (below) Robert Kingston Scott

Schofield, John McAlister
(1831-1906) Union general

A Baptist clergyman's son, he was graduated from West Point in 1853, taught there and was on a leave of absence teaching physics at Washington University in St Louis at he onset of war. He fought in the Union army at Wilson's Creek in August 1861 and subsequently commanded the Army of the Frontier in Missouri in 1862-63. Schofield led XXIII Corps in the Atlanta Campaign of 1864 and on W. T. Sherman's march through the Carolinas in early 1865. He served as secretary of war in 1868-69, was superintendent at West Point from 1876-81 and rose to commanding general of the army in 1888. Schofield retired in 1895 after 46 years in uniform.

Schurz, Carl
(1829-1906) Union general, social reformer, journalist

Having engaged in revolutionary actions as a young radical in his native Germany, he fled and emigrated to the United States in 1852. He took up farming in Wisconsin (one of the so-called "Latin farmers." highly educated European who took up farming in America), soon spoke out against slavery and became active in the new Republican Party. In 1861 he was sent as Abraham Lincoln's ambassador to Spain, but Schurz returned within months and soon was openly advocating the freeing of all slaves. He was appointed a brigadier general in the Union army in June 1862 and commanded a division at Second Bull Run. He subsequently commanded German-speaking units at Chancellorsville and Gettysburg but was criticized harshly for the unmilitary behavior of these units. He ultimately commanded XI Corps in the Army of the Cumberland. During the presidential campaign of 1864 he campaigned extensively for Lincoln (with whom he corresponded directly even while on active duty). After the war he gained a major reputation as a journalist and political philosopher, with time out to serve as U.S. Senator from Missouri (1869-1875) and secretary of the interior (1877-1881). He is most closely associated with calling for reform of the civil service.

Scott, Dred
(*c.* 1795-1858) Former slave

Born into slavery, he was purchased in 1832 by John Emerson, an army surgeon, who then took Scott to his military posts in Illinois and Minnesota. (Scott married a

Dred Scott

free black in Minnesota and they had a child born there.) After Emerson brought Scott and his family back to St. Louis, he died (1843) and Scott tried to gain his freedom on the grounds that he was legally a freedman because of his residence in non-slave states. The case was eventually brought up to the Supreme Court, and in 1857 Scott lost his appeal, 7-2, with Chief Justice Roger Taney giving his opinion that no Negro was a citizen under the U.S. Constitution and that slaveholders had the right to take their "property" wherever they went. Within a few weeks, however, Scott and his family were freed, but he lived only another 16 months, working as a doorman at a hotel in St. Louis.

Scott, Robert Kingston
(1826-1900) Union general

Born in Pennsylvania, he had served in the Mexican War. He was commissioned a lieutenant colonel in the Union army in 1861 and fought at Vicksburg, Thompson's Hill, Raymond, Jackson, Champion's Hill and in the Atlanta Campaign. He was promoted to major general in December 1865 and headed the South Carolina Freedman's Bureau until 1868. He was later a Republican governor of South Carolina.

Scott, Winfield
(1786-1866) Union general

Born on his family's estate near Petersburg, Virginia, the year after the Founding Fathers drew up the Constitution, he studied at home under tutors, attended William and Mary College and read law with a Petersburg attorney before entering the army in 1808. A brigade under his command bore the brunt of the fighting in the U.S. victory at Lundy's Lane in 1814.

Scott stayed on in the peacetime army and, among other things, campaigned for temperance; on an 1832 expedition, he decreed then any soldier found intoxicated must dig a grave his own size and study it with the knowledge that he soon would be laid down in it if he persisted in hard drinking. "Old Fuss and Feathers," as Scott was known, also had considerable success as a pacifier. He smoothed over the Nullification crisis in South Carolina in 1832 and settled a vexing boundary dispute between Maine and New Brunswick in 1838. He was mentioned as a possible Whig candidate for the presidency in 1840 and 1844.

Appointed general-in-chief of the army in 1841, Scott took command of U.S. forces in the field during the Mexican War. His army captured Vera Cruz in March 1847, and he then set out with 8,000 men for Mexico City in April. The Mexican capital fell after a series of battles on September 14, 1847. In 1852 Scott became the first officer since George Washington to hold the rank of lieutenant general. In the same year, he ran unsuccessfully for president on the Whig ticket.

Experienced in public as well as military affairs, Scott realized that winning a civil war for the Union would be an enormous undertaking, costly in lives and treasure. Too old, fat and ill to mount a horse, he could not take a field command; instead, he put forward his Anaconda Plan, which called for a complete blockade of the South and control of the Mississippi River, as the essential Union strategy for winning the

Winfield Scott

war. Derided at first, much of the plan eventually became Union policy. President Lincoln ordered the blockade of Southern ports in the early stages of hostilities, and, over time, the strategy contributed enormously to the Union victory.

Scott did not support the appointment of George McClellan to command the Army of the Potomac. McClellan resented this, and the two were unable ever to establish a good working partnership. Scott requested retirement on October 31, 1861, and Lincoln approved it the following day, ending Scott's public career of almost 50 years.

He lived to write a two-volume book of memoirs and to meet the all-conquering Ulysses S. Grant, who had been one of his junior officers in Mexico. In 1865 Scott presented Grant with a gift that bore the inscription, "from the oldest to the greatest general." He died at West Point two weeks before his 80th birthday.

Sedgwick, John
(1813-1864) Union general

This career officer was born in Connecticut and was educated at West Point. A veteran of the Seminole and Mexican wars and frontier service, he was affectionately called "Uncle John" by his men. Competent and hard-fighting, he early won recognition fighting for the Union in the Peninsular Campaign (wounded). He was twice wounded at Antietam but recovered in time to distinguish himself again at Fredericksburg. As a major general (July 1862) commanding VI Corps, he tried unsuccessfully to relieve Joseph Hooker at Chancellorsville. He commanded the Union left wing on the third day at Gettysburg and performed brilliantly in the Mine Run operations. Sedgwick was killed by a Rebel sharpshooter at Spotsylvania.

Semmes, Raphael
(1809-1877) Confederate naval officer

Maryland-born, orphaned at an early age and raised in Georgetown, D.C., by an uncle, he won an appointment as a naval midshipman in 1826. He served in the Mediterranean, read law, earned admission to the bar during leaves of absence and finally received a lieutenant's commission in 1837.

Semmes fought in Mexico in 1846 and 1847, both on blockade duty and ashore with the naval artillery; he marched with Winfield Scott's army to Mexico City. He published *Service Afloat and Ashore during the Mexican War* in 1851.

During the 1850s Semmes commanded

Raphael Semmes standing beside *Alabama's* massive 110-pounder

the storeship *Electra* and the schooner *Flirt*, but spent more than half his time ashore, during which he resumed the practice of law. He resigned from the U.S. Navy in February 1861 and went on a purchasing mission for the Confederacy, actually buying armaments from manufacturers in New England and New York. He took command of the commerce raider CSS *Sumter* in April.

Semmes took 18 prizes during a six-month cruise in *Sumter* before abandoning the ship in Gilbratar and making his way to England to take command of what became the screw sloop CSS *Alabama*. He set sail in *Alabama* in September 1862 on a commerce destroying cruise that would last nearly two years.

Raiding the whaling grounds in mid-Atlantic, he took and burned 10 whaling vessels, then moved on to the Gulf of Mexico, where he sank the paddlewheeler USS *Hatteras* after a running night action of a quarter-hour. Heading down the coast of Brazil, he preyed on the crossroads of shipping lanes to and from the Pacific, Europe and America.

Semmes called at Capetown, South Africa, in August 1863, then sailed into the Indian Ocean, raided there and in the Arabian Sea, and completed the long run to Cherbourg, France, in June 1864. Altogether, the *Alabama* took, burned, sank or destroyed 69 ships on its 23-month cruise.

He tried to arrange for an overhaul of the ship in the Cherbourg dockyards, but while he awaited permission to enter the harbor the Union screw sloop USS *Kearsarge* appeared. The two well-matched ships met in battle within sight of land on June 19, 1864. After an exchange of several broadsides the *Alabama* began to take on water. She sank stern first some two and-a-half hours after the action began.

Semmes did not surrender with his ship, escaping to England. He managed to return to the Confederacy before war's end and, promoted to rear admiral, commanded the James River squadron. He burned his ships with the evacuation of Richmond, armed his sailors as infantry and surrendered with Joseph E. Johnston at Greensboro, North Carolina.

Though paroled, Semmes was arrested in late 1865 and held for a time on what amounted to a charge of piracy. He later taught literature, edited a Memphis newspaper and praticed law in Mobile, Alabama. His *Memoirs of Service Afloat during the War between the States* appeared in 1869.

Seward, William Henry
(1801-1872) Union statesman

Son of an Orange County, New York, doctor, he entered Union College at age 15, was graduated four years later, read law and was admitted to the bar in 1822. He began his political career in Auburn, New York, with a successful run for the state senate in 1830, serving four years; he won

William Henry Seward

election to the governorship as a Whig in 1838 and 1840.

Seward's antislavery beliefs drew him into the Republican party in 1856 . In a famous 1858 speech he said that the slavery issue would bring about an "irrepressible conflict," though in fact many of his positions on the subject were relatively moderate. He unsuccessfully sought the Republican nomination in 1860.

Seward joined the Lincoln administration as secretary of state and, during the course of the war, proved to be an able diplomat. He smoothed over the *Trent* controversy with England in 1861, and his efforts helped keep Britain and France from overtly supporting the rebellion, though Britain did build warships and provide other aid to the Confederacy.

Gravely wounded in the Lincoln assassination plot in April 1865, Seward recovered and resumed his cabinet duties. His forward-looking purchase of Alaska from Russia for $6 million in 1867 was called at the time "Seward's Folly." His health failing, he returned to Auburn in 1871 and died there in October of the following year.

Truman Seymour

Seymour, Truman
(1824-1891) Union general

Vermont-born Seymour was a professional artilleryman trained at West Point and seasoned in the Seminole and Mexican wars. He was a captain of artillery at Fort Sumter and fought steadily throughout the war with the Union's Army of the Potomac and in the Department of the South. He was seriously wounded at Battery Wagner and was captured in the Battle of the Wilderness. Exchanged, he fought in the Shenandoah Valley in 1864 and at the siege of Petersburg and led a division at Sayler's Creek. In 1876 he retired to Italy.

Robert Gould Shaw

Shaw, Robert Gould
(1837-1863) Union army officer

This Boston reformer and abolitionist's son attended Harvard and was a New York merchant when the Civil War erupted. Enlisting in the Union army's 7th Massachusetts, he fought steadily in the Eastern theater. He organized and led the Union's first black regiment, the 54th Massachusetts Colored Infantry, which left Boston on May 28, 1863, and saw its first skirmish at James Island, South Carolina, on July 16. Shaw and half of his men were killed amid the heavy Federal losses at Battery Wagner on July 18. As a mark of contempt for this white officer's championing of blacks, Confederates threw his body into a common burial pit with the bodies of his black troops.

Shelby, Joseph Orville
(1830-1897) Confederate general

A wealthy Kentuckian, he joined the Confederate cavalry in 1861 and fought at Wilson's Creek, Lexington and Pea Ridge. He commanded a cavalry brigade on numerous raids in 1863 and 1864. Rather than surrender, "Jo" Shelby led his troopers across the Rio Grande to join Emperor Maxmilian's forces in Mexico. He later settled in Missouri.

Sheridan, Philip Henry
(1831-1888) Union general

The son of immigrants from County Cavan, Ireland, born in Albany, New York, Sheridan grew up in Ohio, where his father had gone in search of work on the canals and roads. Educated in the village school of Somerset, Ohio, he worked as a store clerk there before obtaining a West Point cadetship in 1848. Pugnacious and short-tempered, Sheridan soon found himself in trouble for threatening an older cadet with a bayonet. Suspended for a year, he returned, obeyed the rules (more or less) and was graduated with the class of 1853, 34th of 49.

Sheridan served in Texas and fought Indians in the Pacific Northwest, but his antebellum military career lacked distinction. When the Civil War began he was a quartermaster and commissary for Union General Samuel Curtis's Army of the Southwest. A poor bookkeeper and heedless of procedure, Sheridan was relieved and narrowly escaped court martial. He joined Henry Halleck's staff in Missouri and carried out a series of quartermaster odd jobs, including a roving assignment to buy remounts for Halleck's command.

In May 1862 Sheridan obtained a commission as colonel of the 2nd Michigan Cavalry, rising to the command of a brigade within two months. He defeated a Confederate cavalry force at Booneville, Mississippi, in July during Halleck's Cornith Campaign. At Perryville, Kentucky, in October he capably commanded an infantry division. Sheridan's stubborn defense at Stones River, Tennessee, in December helped save William Rosecrans's army from defeat. Shortly thereafter Sheridan won promotion to major general.

He saw action at Chickamauga in September 1863 and in November, under Ulysses S. Grant, led the infantry charge that carried Missionary Ridge and broke up Braxton Bragg's Confederate army at Chattanooga. When Grant went east as commander-in-chief in March 1864 he took Sheridan with him as commander-designate of the 10,000-strong Cavalry Corps of the Army of the Potomac. He quarreled with Grant's second-in-command, George Meade, over the use of cavalry during the Wilderness and Spotsylvania campaigns, but his first independent operation in Virginia, the Richmond Raid of May 9-24, proved to be a great success. On May 11 Sheridan's troopers clashed with pursuing Confederates at Yellow tavern near Richmond. J. E. B.

Philip Henry Sheridan (above, on left) and
(right) Sheridan's Ride.

PREVIOUS PAGES: The Battle of Winchester.

Stuart, Robert E. Lee's brilliant cavalry
commander, was mortally wounded in the
action. Sheridan went on to complete a circuit of Lee's army, destroying supplies,
tearing up railroad track and defeating the
Confederate cavalry in four separate engagements.

In August 1864 Grant sent him to the
Shenandoah Valley with orders to destroy
Jubal Early's small Confederate army, con-
fiscate livestock, burn crops and render the
region unfit as a supply center or base for
further Rebel operations. (In July, Early
had crossed the Potomac and approached
Washington, alarming the politicians and
distracting Grant.) When he finished with
Early, Sheridan was to turn the Shenandoah into "a barren waste," Grant said, "so
that crows flying over it for the balance of
this season will have to carry their proven-
der with them."

Sheridan pushed into the Valley and
defeated Early at Winchester on September
19 and at Fisher's Hill three days later. His
troops began stripping the countryside on
October 6. Thinking he had disposed of
Early, he made arrangements to return the
VI Corps infantry to Grant. But Early re-
grouped and surprised the Federals at

Cedar Creek on October 19, while Sheridan was absent. The Confederates were on the verge of victory when Sheridan arrived after his famous ride from Winchester and collected troops for a counterstroke that reversed the result. He then continued his work of destruction. In one report to Grant, he claimed to have burned 2,000 barns and 700 mills. In another report, one of his divisional commanders tabulated a precise 3,772 horses, 545 mules, 10,918 beef cattle and 435,802 bushels of wheat among the spoils of the operation.

Sheridan returned to Grant to take the leading part in the Appomattox Campaign of April 1865. His turning of Lee's flank at the Battle of Five Forks on April 1 forced the Confederate commander to begin a disorderly withdrawal to the west. Commanding a mobile force of cavalry and infantry, Sheridan pursued vigorously and blocked Lee's retreat beyond Appomattox Court House. Lee surrendered the Army of Northern Virginia there on April 9.

Hardly five feet tall, squat, with dark, close-cropped hair and a "sun-browned face and sailor air," Sheridan had a natural authority on the battlefield. His troops called him "Little Phil" and rarely failed to respond to his aggressive example. He could be brutal to subordinates whom he judged had failed him. At Five Forks he removed G. K. Warren from command of V Corps for lack of aggressiveness and cast aspersions on his personal bravery; the incident wrecked Warren's career and left him embittered to the end of his life.

In May 1865 Sheridan took command of a force of 50,000 veterans on the Rio Grande in a show of force meant to encourage the French to withdraw troops sent to Mexico to protect the regime of Emperor Maxmilian. He later served as postwar military governor of Texas and Louisiana, where he so rigorously enforced Reconstruction policies that President Andrew Johnson ordered his recall. In the 1870s Sheridan organized a series of punitive campaigns against the Plains Indians, forcing the tribes on to government reservation land. In 1884 he succeeded W. T. Sherman as commander-in-chief of the army. He completed his *Personal Memoirs* (1888) only a few days before his death.

Sherman, John
(1832-1900) **Northern legislator**

The younger brother of William Tecumseh Sherman, he became a lawyer and a member of the Whig Party, moving over to the new Republican Party only when it became clear that the Whigs had no political future.

He was, in fact, always more moderate than most Republicans. He served Ohio in the House of Representatives (1855-61) and then in the Senate (1861-77), trying vainly to take moderate positions on slavery and, later, on the treatment of the former Confederate states, but constantly being forced by his Republican constituency to vote for radical legislation. After serving as secretary of the treasury (1877-81), he returned to the Senate (1881-97) and put his name on a famous antitrust law (The Sherman Anti-Trust Act of 1890, the first regulatory legislation of its kind). He was secretary of state (1897-98), resigning to protest the decision to go to war against Spain.

Sherman, William Tecumseh
(1820-91) **Union general**

The son of an Ohio Supreme Court justice, Sherman was born at Lancaster, Ohio, orphaned at the age of nine and raised by a well-to-do connection of his father's, Thomas Ewing. He received his early education at a local academy – schooling sufficient to prepare him for West Point, from which he was graduated, sixth in his class, in 1840, an artillery second lieutenant.

"Cump" Sherman, as he was called, served in Florida and California and saw

William Tecumseh Sherman

limited action in the Mexican War. Bored with garrison life and frustrated by the glacial pace of advancement in the old army, he resigned in 1853 to become a banker in San Francisco. Like his friend Grant, he found the civilian world daunting. When the bank failed, Sherman turned to the practice of law. He lost his only case.

Appointed superintendent of the Louisiana Military Academy (forerunner of Louisiana State University) in 1859, he saw the secession movement close up, agonized over the potential breakup of the Union and viewed the prospect of war with undisguised horror. When it came, Sherman turned down the offer of a Confederate commission and accepted, in May 1861,

The Battle of Kennesaw Mountain (below and opposite top) and Sherman's March to the Sea (opposite bottom)

the colonecy of the 13th U.S. Infantry. In July he commanded a brigade at the First Battle of Bull Run.

Sent west to Kentucky as second-in-command to Robert Anderson in August, he experienced what amounted to a nervous breakdown growing out of his quarrels with his superiors and members of the press over his estimates of the resources of troops and material that would be required to meet the Confederate threat. The politicians responded to his request for 200,000 men to defend Kentucky with ridicule and soon caused him to be removed to a quiet post in Missouri. His forecasts proved, in the event, only too accurate.

After a short stop at Cairo, Illinois, where he forwarded troops and supplies for Ulysses S. Grant's river campaigns of early 1862, Sherman obtained command of a division in Grant's Army of the Ten-

nessee. There began one of the great partnerships of the war. Sherman's division, surprised early on the first day of Shiloh, recovered under his leadership and helped prevent a complete rout. Grant thereafter assigned him leading roles in what became two of the greatest campaigns of the war: Vicksburg in the spring and summer of 1863, and the breakout from besieged Chattanooga in October-November 1863.

When President Lincoln made Grant commander-in-chief of the Union land forces in March 1864, Sherman succeeded him as senior commander in the West. Around this time one of his officers characterized Sherman, with his red hair and beard, thin, sinewy frame and deeply lined face, as "the concentrated essence of Yankeedom." Brilliant, restless, expressive, "he perspired thought at every pore," another observer commented, "with a mood that shifted like a barometer in a tropic sea."

Sherman moved against Joseph E. Johnston in Georgia in May 1864 in a campaign of maneuver that ended with the capture of Atlanta four months later. There he began to articulate views on war that he long had been formulating. "War is cruelty and you cannot refine it," he told Atlantans. Sherman took it as an article of faith that the war could be ended only when its realities were brought home to the civilian population that supported the fighting fronts. He put the theory to the test in Atlanta, authorizing the destruction of all property of potential military value. The result was the near-destruction of the South's second city.

On November 15, 1864, he set out on his famous March to the Sea. "I can make Georgia howl," he told Grant, and his 60,000-man army, traveling light in two wings, cut a 60-mile-wide swath of destruction across interior Georgia. Here Sherman brought the war home to Georgians in the most uncompromising terms, proving as well that the Confederacy could no longer protect its citizens. Casualties, military and civilian, were, however, astonishingly light.

He reached Savannah before Christmas and, after resting his army for six weeks, struck out in February 1865 for the Carolinas and an eventual junction with Grant in Virginia. It was another brilliant success, more impressive – because more difficult – even than the George march. On April 26, 17 days after Lee's surrender at Appomattox, Sherman offered generous terms to large Confederate forces under Johnston in North Carolina. Johnston's acceptance effectively ended the war in the East.

Sherman and his generals: (l. to r.) Howard, Logan, Hazen, Sherman, Davis, Slocum and Mower

In the aftermath of Lincoln's assassination, Sherman's generosity to Johnston inspired much outrage, and leading government officials repudiated his terms. Johnston surrendered anyway, but Sherman never forgave War Secretary Edwin Stanton or the others. The controversy confirmed his contempt for politics and politicians.

He succeeded Grant as commander-in-chief of the army in 1869. His tenure of office saw the completion of the transcontinental railroad and the defeat and resettlement of many of the Plains Indian tribes. He published his excellent *Memoirs* in 1875. Retiring in 1883, he lived thereafter in St. Louis and New York City.

Sherman rebuffed all efforts to draw him into political life. "If nominated I will not accept. If elected I will not serve," he told Republicans who wanted to draft him for a presidential run in 1884. He remained active in veterans' affairs and enjoyed addressing encampments of the Grand Army of the Republic and other soldier organizations. At one such meeting he uttered his famous dictum: "War is all hell."

Some military historians rate Sherman the greatest Federal commander of the war. Certainly his campaigns of 1864-65 were masterworks of conception and execution. In 11 months they carried him from Chattanooga through Georgia and the Carolinas to the verges of Lee's domain and made his name an anathema in the South. Sherman died of pneumonia in his 71st year. His old adversary Joseph Johnston helped carry the casket at his funeral.

Shields, James
(1806-1879) Union general

Irish-born, Shields came to the U.S. about 1820 and became a lawyer in Illinois. He served in the Black Hawk War and the Mexican War and became a Democratic politician. He challenged Abraham Lincoln to a duel because of newspaper criticism, but they were able to resolve their differences and became friends. Shields was made governor of the Oregon Territory and then became a U.S. Senator, first from Illinois, then from Minnesota. Commis-

James Shields

sioned a Union brigadier general in 1861, he served in the Shenandoah Valley Campaign of 1862 and on the Rappahannock. He resigned from the army in March 1863 to become a railroad commissioner in California. Later he would briefly serve as a U.S. Senator from Missouri – thereby becoming the only person in all of U.S. history to serve three different states in the U.S. Senate.

brigadier general in the Confederate army in June 1861, he became commander of the Army of New Mexico and conducted operations in New Mexico and Arizona in 1861-1862 with no great success. He later led commands in Louisiana, south of the Red River. Courtmartialed on charges of refusing orders, he was acquitted – he apparently convinced the court that he was too sick to press an attack. At the end of the war he went to Egypt and served as an artillery general there (1865-1874). He is perhaps known best for his invention, the Sibley tent, which was a lightweight tent capable of holding 12 soldiers and their equipment.

ABOVE: Sickles with S.P. Heintzelman.

RIGHT: Henry Hopkins Sibley.

Sibley, Henry Hastings
(1811-1891) **Union general**

Born in Michigan, he was a fur trader in Minnesota and served as the latter state's first governor. Commissioned a Union brigadier in September 1862, he fought the Sioux in the Indian rebellion on 1862. Taking 2,000 prisoners, Sibley tried 400 Sioux by court material and executed 38 of them on December 26, 1862. He had postwar success as a banker and merchant.

Sibley, Henry Hopkins
(1816-1886) **Confederate general**

Born in Louisiana, Sibley was a West Point graduate who fought in the Seminole and Mexican wars and on the frontier. Named a

ABOVE: Daniel Edgar Sickles

Sickles, Daniel Edgar
(1825-1914) **Union general**

A New York City lawyer, legislator, and U.S. Representative (1857-1861), Sickles seemed to court notoriety. On trial for murder in 1859, he successfully used the first-ever temporary insanity defence. As a Union brigadier general he led New York's Excelsior Brigade in the Peninsular Campaign and at Antietam and Fredericksburg; he led III Corps at Chancellorsville. Without authorization he advanced his unit ahead of the Union line at Gettysburg, possibly helping to stop the Confederate advance but at the cost of half his men. In this action Sickles lost his leg, ending his field career. He won the Congressional Medal of Honor for his role Gettysburg. He was later instrumental in creating a national park at that battlefield. He was dismissed as chairman of the New York state monuments commission (1886-1912) for financial irregularities.

Franz Sigel

Sigel, Franz
(1824-1902) **Union general**

Forced to flee his native Germany after the 1848 revolution, he settled in New York City and then in St. Louis, where he was director of schools. He obtained a brigadier's commission in the Union army in May 1861 and fought at Wilson's Creek and Pea Ridge. Sigel held a series of senior commands in the Shenandoah Valley in 1864 and suffered a serious defeat at New Market in May. Though a mediocre general, Sigel materially assisted the Union cause by recruiting thousands of German-Americans. He returned to New York City after the war and became active in journalism and politics.

Slidell, John
(1793-1871) **Confederate diplomat**

A New York native and Columbia University graduate, he failed in business in New York and established a New Orleans law practice. As a Democratic Congressman (1843-1845) and Senator (1853-1861), he became an influential political power-broker. In 1861, in the so-called *Trent* affair, he was captured at sea by Union naval forces while he and James Mason were on a mission to seek Anglo-French recognition for the Confederacy, a goal he never achieved, despite his skilful diplo-

matic performance. He did, however, arrange for the French construction of ships and financing for the Confederacy. Union general Ranald Slidell MacKenzie (1840-1889) was his nephew.

Slocum, Henry Warner
(1827-1894) **Union general**

After graduation from West Point (1852), he became a Syracuse, New York, lawyer and state legislator. He was promoted to brigadier general in the Union army after First Bull Run, where he was badly wounded, and to major general during the Peninsular Campaign. He fought at South Mountain and Antietam and commanded a corps at Fredericksburg, Chancellorsville and Gettysburg, where he held the Union right wing. Toward the end of the Atlanta Campaign he took over XX Corps from Joseph Hooker; his troops were the first into the city. He led W. T. Sherman's left wing during the March to the Sea and in the Carolinas Campaign. He was a Brooklyn lawyer, Democratic politician and U.S. Congressman (1869-1873, 1883-1885) in later years.

Smalley, George Washburn
(1833-1916) **War correspondent**

Smalley was a Massachusetts-born lawyer and abolitionist who, between November 1861 and October 1862 served as the *New York Tribune*'s war correspondent. He

John Slidell

brought his report from Antietam to New York himself when he was unable to send it. Soon thereafter, Smalley became ill with "camp fever" and worked in the New York office until 1866, when he covered the Prussian-Austrian War. He opened the *Tribune* offices in Europe and then worked for the London *Times* (1895-1905).

Smalls, Robert
(1839-1915) Union sailor, legislator

Born a slave at Beaufort on the Sea Islands of South Carolina, he moved to Charleston, where he worked on the docks and as a sailmaker before becoming an expert boat pilot along the coasts of Georgia and South Carolina. Forced to pilot a Confederate ship, the *Planter*, transporting cotton, on May 13, 1862, he directed his fellow African-American crewmates to sail the ship out of Charleston harbor, past the Confederate guns, and delivered it to the Union fleet. In October of 1862 he went to New York to try to get Northern support for a colony of freed slaves at Port Royal, South Carolina. In June 1864 he was part of a delegation of free blacks who attended the Republican Party convention. After the war he was elected to the South Carolina legislature and then to the U.S. House of Representatives (1875-79, 1882-87), where he fought against many odds to gain fair treatment for his fellow African-Americans. He closed out his career as federal collector of the port of his native town of Beaufort, South Carolina (1889-1913).

Charles Ferguson Smith

Smith, Andrew Jackson
(1815-1897) Union general

He was graduated from West Point in 1838 and saw action on the frontier and in Mexico. Smith led a Union division during the Vicksburg Campaign and the right wing of XVI Corps during the Red River Campaign of 1864. He commanded large formations at Nashville later in 1864 and in operations around Mobile in 1865. He resigned from the regular army as colonel of the 7th Cavalry in 1869.

Smith, Charles Ferguson
(1807-1862) Union general

This Pennsylvania-born West Point graduate served in the Mexican War, on the Utah Expedition and as an instructor at West Point: Ulysses S. Grant had been a cadet under Smith. Serving under Grant in the Civil War, Smith won promotion to major general in March 1862 for a charge he led at Fort Donelson. He died on April 25, 1862, of a foot infection he received while leaping from a boat at the beginning of the Shiloh Campaign.

Smith, Edmund Kirby
(1824-1893) Confederate general

He was born in Florida, the son of a Connecticut lawyer and War of 1812 veteran, and by the age of 12 he had decided to become a soldier. He was graduated from West Point in 1845, joined the 5th Infantry and saw action during the Mexican War at

Edmond Kirby Smith

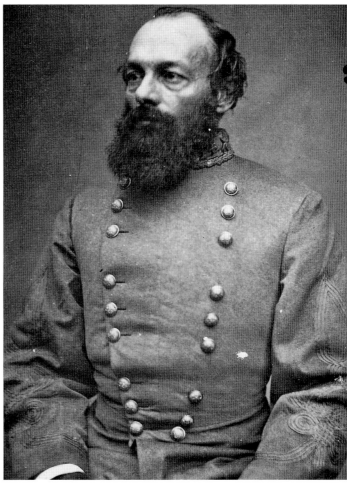

Palo Alto, Monterey, Vera Cruz, Cerro Gordo and Chapultepec.

Smith's peacetime career and assignments were typical: he served in garrison and on the frontier. He was a botanist on a Mexican boundary commission. He taught mathematics at West Point for three years. He fought Indians in Texas. A leave of absence in 1858 provided him the opportunity to tour Europe. When Florida seceded early in 1861, he resigned his U.S. commission to join the Confederacy.

Chief-of-staff to Joseph E. Johnston at Harpers Ferry, he helped organize the Shenandoah army in the spring of 1861, then took charge of an infantry brigade in Johnston's command. Seriously wounded at First Bull Run in July 1861, he recovered in time to accept a promotion to major general and command of a division in P. G. T. Beauregard's army.

Sent west in early 1862 to head the Department of East Tennessee, Smith launched an invasion of Kentucky in June. He defeated the Federals at Richmond, Kentucky, in August and cleared Cumberland Gap of enemy forces before joining Braxton Bragg for the battle of Perryville in October. He withdrew, along with Bragg, after the drawn battle there.

In February 1863 Smith took charge of he Transmississippi Department, a vast region including Texas, Louisiana and Arkansas, that became known after the fall of Vicksburg as Kirby Smithdom. His chief contribution was to ship cotton and other products through the blockade and to import machinery and other tools of war with the proceeds. Forces under his command deranged the Federal Red River Campaign of 1864 and later blunted a Union offensive in Arkansas.

Smith surrendered the last Confederate army to Edward Canby at Galveston, Texas, on June 2, 1865. He thought of settling in Mexico, but returned to the U.S., headed the Atlantic and Pacific Telegraph Co. for a time and considered entering the Episcopal ministry. From 1870 to 1875 he was president of the University of Nashville, then taught mathematics at the University of the South.

He and his wife, whom he met while recuperating from his Bull Run wound, raised 11 children.

Smith, Gustavus Woodson
(1822-1896) Confederate general

He was graduated from West Point in 1842, fought in Mexico and worked as a civil engineer, serving as New York City streets commissioner from 1858-61. Commis-

sioned a major general in the Confederate service, he briefly commanded the army after Joseph E. Johnston's wounding at Seven Pines on May 31, 1862, stepping aside next day in favor of Robert E. Lee. Smith later resigned in a seniority dispute in February 1863. He commanded a Georgia militia division during W. T. Sherman's March to the Sea in late 1864. After the war Smith became the first insurance commissioner of Kentucky.

Gustavus Woodson Smith

ABOVE: William (Extra Billy) Smith

Smith, William
(1796-1887) Confederate general

A lawyer, he served in Congress and as governor of Virginia (1846-49). He became known as "Extra Billy" on account of the large government subsidies he received for his mail-coach service from Washington to Milledgeville, Georgia. He commanded a Confederate regiment at First Bull Run, on the Peninsula and at Antietam and a brigade at Gettysburg. Smith carried out his duties as a Confederate congressman between campaigns. He took office a second time as the governor of the state of Virginia in January 1864.

Smith, William Farrar
(1824-1903) Union general

An 1845 West Point graduate, he fought for the Union at the First Battle of Bull Run and led a brigade, then a division, during the Peninsular Campaign. Sent west in 1863, he organized Ulysses S. Grant's defenses at Chattanooga and helped open the "Cracker Line" to supply the besieged city. Smith led XVIII Corps in the initial assault on Petersburg in June 1864, but the attack was dilatory and failed to carry the city. Had Smith succeeded, he might have shortened the war by a year. He was relieved in consequence and did not hold another field command.

Soulé, Pierre
(1802-1870) Confederate general

Born in France, educated in Jesuit schools there, he went into exile at the age of 15 after being accused of conspiring against the Bourbon monarchy. After many adventures he settled in New Orleans, read law and entered politics, serving in the U.S. Senate from 1847 to 1853. He was a clandestine Confederate operative early in the war. Commissioned brigadier in 1863, he served on the staff of P. G. T. Beauregard in Charleston. He resumed his New Orleans law practice after the war.

Sprague, Kate Chase
(1840-1899) Washington hostess

At the age of 15 she began serving as a precocious hostess for her widower-father, Salmon P. Chase, then governor of Ohio. When he became Abraham Lincoln's secretary of the treasury, she went with him to Washington and soon became known for her extravagant parties. In 1863 she married William Sprague, a Senator from Rhode Island. During the war they continued to be social leaders, although their marriage soon began to fall apart. Kate schemed to have her father replace Lincoln as the Republican candidate in 1864 and even had the bad grace to complain when Lincoln named Chase chief justice of the Supreme Court later that year. In 1868 she schemed again to get her father the Democratic presidential nomination. When her father died in 1873 she lost all control, drank heavily, carried on a scandalous friendship with N.Y. Senator Roscoe Conkling (whom William Sprague attacked with a shotgun in 1879) and finally divorced William in 1882. She lived in Europe for a while, returning to her father's estate near Washington later in life, an eccentric and disappointed woman.

Stanton, Edwin McMasters
(1814-1869) Union secretary of war

Ohio-born Stanton was a successful Northern lawyer before serving as U.S. attorney general for the last four months of James Buchanan's presidency. He was Abraham Lincoln's secretary of war after January 1862. An outstanding executive, he efficiently manned, equipped and reorganized the military, rooted out fraud and corruption and instituted harsh security measures such as press censorship and arbitary arrests. He was widely resented, however, for his abrasive personality and interference in field tactics.

Edwin McMasters Stanton (above) and (right) James Blair Steedman

Initially opposed to Lincoln, Stanton became one of his most ardent supporters. His dismissal by President Andrew Johnson in 1868 provided an opportunity for Stanton's Radical Republican Congressional colleagues to impeach the president, whose Reconstruction policies they had long opposed. Stanton died four days after his confirmation as a U.S. Supreme Court justice.

Steedman, James Blair
(1817-1873) Union general

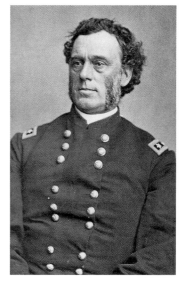

Steedman, a Toledo, Ohio, newspaper editor and Democratic state legislator, joined the Union army's 14th Ohio in 1861. He fought at Perryville, Stones River and in the Tullahoma Campaign and later, with great gallantry, at Chickamauga, where his division provided crucial aid to George

Thomas in his successful effort to prevent a Union rout. As a major general (April 1864), he commanded the post of Chattanooga, and during the Battle of Nashville he led the District of Etowah. He returned to Toledo journalism and public service after the war.

Steele, Frederick
(1819-1868) **Union general**

Born in New York, a West Point graduate and a veteran of fighting on the frontier and in the Mexican War, Steele was a major at the outbreak of the Civil war. He was promoted to major general in the Union army in 1862 and fought throughout Missouri and Arkansas. He served with distinction under Ulysses Grant in the Vicksburg Campaign. He led the Arkansas Campaign of 1864, a basically disastrous expedition, and ended the war by assisting in the final operations around Mobile, Alabama. Remaining in the army, he died when he fell from a horse-drawn vehicle after suffering an apoplectic attack.

Alexander Hamilton Stephens (above) and (left) Frederick Steele

Stephens, Alexander Hamilton
(1812-1883) **Confederate vice president**

This prominent lawyer and Congressman (1843-1859) helped to secure passage of the Kansas-Nebraska Act. He was a voice for moderation while serving as Jefferson Davis's vice president. Instrumental in drafting a moderate Confederate constitution, he worked for prisoner exchanges and opposed Davis's centralization of power and suspension of civil rights. He attended the Hampton Roads Peace Conference and wrote a constitutional study of the war. He again served in Congress (1873-1882) and then as Georgia's governor (1882).

Steuart, George H. ("Maryland Steuart")
(1828-1903) **Confederate general**

This Maryland-born West Point graduate served on the Utah Expedition and as an Indian fighter before resigning from the U.S. Army in 1861. Appointed a lieutenant colonel in the Confederate cavalry, he fought at First Bull Run and in the 1862 Shenandoah Valley Campaign, at Gettysburg, the Wilderness, Spotsylvania and Petersburg. A brigadier general since 1862, he was captured at Spotsylvania but exchanged in time to lead a brigade at Petersburg. He farmed in Maryland after the war.

Stevens, Thaddeus
(1792-1868) Radical Republican

This Dartmouth graduate settled in Pennsylvania in 1816. An uncompromising abolitionist lawyer and Congressman (Whig 1849-1853, Republican 1859-1868), Stevens was a formidable debater, famous for the ferocity of his oratory. He opposed the Compromise of 1850 and the Fugitive Slave Law. As wartime chairman of the House Ways and Means Committee, he controlled military appropriations, providing the government critical financial support. A founder and leader of the Radical Republicans, he advocated harsh treatment of the Confederates during and after the war. He was instrumental in securing passage of the Civil Rights, Freedmen's Bureau and radical Reconstruction Acts and in the impeachment of President Johnson.

Thaddeus Stevens (above) and (below) George H. Steuart

Carter Littlepage Stevenson

Stevenson, Carter Littlepage
(1817-1888) Confederate general

This Virginian career officer trained at West Point and served in the Seminole and Mexican wars and on the frontier. He joined the Confederate army, becoming a brigadier general in March 1862 and a major general the following October. After fighting with Braxton Bragg in Tennessee and Kentucky, he commanded Confederate troops in the Vicksburg Campaign, at Chickamauga and Missionary Ridge and in the Atlanta, Nashville and Carolinas campaigns. He was later a civil and mining engineer.

Stone, Charles Pomeroy
(1824-1887) Union general

This Massachusetts-born West Point graduate served in the Mexican War and then resigned from the army in 1856 to engage in business in Mexico. He was a banker in San Francisco when the Civil War began and accepted a U.S. commission as a colonel. He was promoted to brigadier general in May 1861 and led the capture of Alexandria, Virginia. His brigade and division became known by his name, but after the Union's disaster at Balls Bluff (October 1861), Stone was arrested and held in prison for over six months; although never charged, he was suspected of treason. He

returned to service but remained under suspicion and so resigned in 1864. From 1869 to 1883 he was in Egypt, serving as its army's chief of staff. Later he served as chief engineer for the building of the pedestal of the Statue of Liberty.

Stoneman, George
(1822-1894) **Union general**

He was graduated from West Point in 1846, fought in Mexico and served on several southwestern expeditions. Stoneman commanded the Union Army of the Potomac's cavalry division during the Peninsular Campaign and the newly established Cavalry Corps at Chancellorsville. Leading W. T. Sherman's cavalry during the Atlanta Campaign, he and 700 of his troopers were captured on what is known as Stoneman's Macon Raid.

Stowe, Harriet Elizabeth Beecher
(1811-1896) **Abolitionist author**

Born in Litchfield, Connecticut, she moved with her family to Cincinnati in 1832 and as a schoolteacher there began writing stories and sketches. Her antislavery novel *Uncle Tom's Cabin* (1851-1852) sold over a million copies in 10 years and was the subject of numerous dramatizations. Reviled by Southerners, it became a potent abolitionist weapon in the North and did much to define and solidify pro- and antislavery camps. The novel made Stowe an international celebrity, a position she used to raise large sums for the antislavery movement. Her later works include *Dred* (1856), another antislavery novel. A leading lecturer in later years, she lived after 1863 in Hartford, Connecticut.

Stuart, James Ewell Brown "Jeb"
(1833-1864) **Confederate general**

"Jeb" Stuart was born at Laurel Hill plantation, Patrick County, Virginia, the seventh of 10 children of a prosperous family. His father, Archibald Stuart, served a term in the U.S. Congress. Educated at home and at Emory and Henry College, young Jeb entered West Point in 1850. He proved to be a popular cadet, generally well-behaved and quietly religious, though prone to fighting (He seems to have been

beaten more often than he prevailed in his many brawls.) He was graduated in 1854, 13th of his class of 46.

Stuart served in Texas and Kansas, where he crossed paths with the radical abolitionist John Brown: during a leave of absence in 1859 he accompanied Robert E. Lee to Harpers Ferry as a volunteer aide and helped identify Brown as the leader of the raid on the U.S. armory there. In January 1861, as the secession crisis deepened, he wrote Jefferson Davis to request a commission in the "Army of the South."

He fought at First Manassas/Bull Run on July 21, 1861, as colonel of the 1st Virginia Cavalry, leading his troopers in a timely charge that contributed to the Confederate victory. Promoted to brigadier general in September, he brought his enlarged command to a peak of efficiency over the autumn and winter. His brigade effectively screened the army during the withdrawal up the Virginia peninsula in May 1862. On June 11, in an operation that began with a request from Robert E. Lee to report on Federal positions, Stuart set out on his first ride around the Army of the Potomac. He returned four days later with 165 prisoners and 260 captured horses and mules – a morale-building victory for the Confeder-

LEFT: Harriet Beecher Stowe.

BELOW: An 1862 Cavalry skirmish during "Stuart's First Ride Around McClellan."

ABOVE: James Ewell Brown Stuart.

RIGHT: Jeb Stuart's battlefield gravestone.

of effort into playing the part. He always rode a magnificent charger. He wore a fine gray cloak, trimmed in red, and a cavalier's cocked hat with a gilt star and a long peacock's plume. He enjoyed music and dancing and cutting a figure at parties and balls, though he discouraged drinking and his jollifications were nearly always temperate. He led a stolidly conventional private life, quite at odds with his romantic appearance.

Though his critics accused him of glory-hunting, Stuart's reputation rested on solid ground. He was Lee's best source of information on his adversarys' movements – the "eyes of the army," Lee called him. In December 1862 he carried out several strikes against Union General Ambrose Burnside's lines of communication, including the elaborate Dumfries Raid at year's end. In a six-day excursion, Stuart's troopers skirmished, stole horses and seized or burned supplies, and returned to the Confederate lines with some 200 prisoners. He skilfully held the Rappahannock outposts during the winter of 1862-63 and kept Lee fully informed of Union General Joseph Hooker's operations in the initial phases of the Chancellorsville Campaign in late April 1863. He handled the II Corps efficiently after Stonewall Jackson's fatal wounding on the night of May 2. But Lee did not retain Stuart in corps command, evidently because he found him irreplaceable as his chief of cavalry.

Stuart's troopers recovered from a surprise dawn strike from the much-improved

ates and an embarrassment for George McClellan's Union army.

Stuart was promoted to major general in July and given command of all the cavalry in the Army of Northern Virginia. During the preliminary phases of the Second Manassas/Bull Run Campaign he raided Federal commander John Pope's headquarters, making off with important documents and one of Pope's uniforms. His Chambersburg, Pennsylvania, raid of October 9-12, 1862, further embellished his popular reputation for brilliance and dash. In this second ride around the Union army, Stuart's 1,800 troopers covered 126 miles – the final 80 miles without a halt – and returned with another 500 captured horses.

These early exploits confirmed Jeb Stuart one of the great heroes of the Confederacy. A striking figure, with his flowing beard and powerful build, he put a lot

Federal cavalry at Brandy station on June 9, 1863, to fight a drawn battle in the largest cavalry action of the war. Though the Federals lost nearly 1,000 men – twice Stuart's toll – they did learn that Lee had begun the northward march that would take him to Gettysburg. After Brandy Station, Stuart threw an impenetrable screen over Lee's flank, holding off the hard-charging Federals in engagements at Aldie, Middleburg and Upperville in mid-June.

With what he interpreted as Lee's full approval, Stuart set off on June 24 on his Gettysburg Raid, an ill-advised operation that nearly became the ruin of his reputation. Passing Hooker's rear and right flank, he crossed the Potomac and harried Federal communications in Maryland and Pennsylvania. He captured 125 new wagons, took 400 prisoners and fought skirmishes at Fairfax, Westminster, Hanover and Carlisle. But he had strayed a long way from Lee, and meantime Hooker's (soon to be George Meade's) army had gotten between him and the Army of Northern Virginia. He thus left Lee in ignorance of the enemy's whereabouts for several critical days that culminated in the fateful Battle of Gettysburg. It is said that this was the only time Lee ever showed displeasure with him.

Stuart's cavalry covered Lee's movements during the Wilderness Campaign in May 1864. On May 9, Stuart led 4,500 troopers in pursuit of the 12,000-strong Federal Cavalry Corps under Philip Sheridan. Setting a furious pace, his command reached Yellow Tavern just ahead of Sheridan early on May 11 and took up a position astride the Richmond road. The Confederates turned Sheridan away from the direct route to the capital after an all-day fight, but at the cost of Stuart. He was shot in the abdomen late in the afternoon and died in Richmond the following day. "He never brought me a false piece of information," Lee said when he learned of Stuart's death.

Sturgis, Samuel Davis
(1822-1889) Union general

This Pennsylvania-born West Point alumnus and career officer served in the Mexican War, on the frontier and in Indian fighting. When his officers resigned to join the Confederate army in April 1861, he saved Fort Smith, Arkansas, for the Union. He commanded the defenses of Washington, D.C., and fought at Second Bull Run, South Mountain, Antietam, Fredericksburg and in Kansas, Tennessee and Mississippi. He attracted criticism for his actions at Wilson's Creek, and his disas-

Charles Sumner, Massachusetts Senator and staunch abolitionist

trous loss to Nathan B. Forrest at Brice's Cross Roads in June 1864 was the subject of an official investigation. After the war he was a cavalry commander and Indian fighter: he retired from the army in 1886.

Sumner, Charles
(1811-1874) U.S. Senator

Born in Massachusetts and educated at Harvard Law School, this Massachusetts lawyer and orator was first elected to the U.S. Senate (1851-1874) on the strength of his antislavery views. As a Radical Republican Senator, Sumner was an uncompromising abolitionist whose fiery oratory made him profoundly influential. Narrowly surviving a retaliatory beating on the Senate floor in 1856 after denouncing a South Carolina member, he maintained his staunch advocacy of emancipation and equal rights for blacks throughout and after the war.

Surratt, John and Mary
Confederate conspirators (?)

John Surratt served the Confederacy as a dispatch rider and spy in the early years of the war. His mother Mary ran a Washington boardinghouse that served as the meet-

ing place where John Wilkes Booth and his conspirators planned the murder of Abraham Lincoln. John Surratt fled to Canada after the assassination. His mother was arrested, accused of conspiracy, convicted by a military court and hanged on July 7, 1865, though she appears to have been innocent of any involvement in the plot. Her son returned to the U.S. in 1867; his trial ended in a hung jury. John Surratt later settled in Maryland and worked as a clerk. He died in 1916.

Swinton, William
(1833-1892) War correspondent

Born in Scotland, he emigrated with his family to Canada in 1843. As a young *New York Times* reporter he was sent to the front as a special war correspondent in 1862. His constant verbal attacks on generals and his underhanded methods of news-gathering – including eavesdropping on a Meade-Grant conference during the 1864 Virginia campaign – finally led the War Department to ban him from the field in July 1864. He later wrote several books about the war, as well as many textbooks.

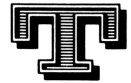

Taliaferro, William Booth
(1822-1898) Confederate general

He studied law at Harvard and fought in the Mexican War, returning home to sit in the Virginia legislature. In the Confederate army he served with distinction in 1862 under Stonewall Jackson in the Shenan-

Roger Brooke Taney

doah Valley and led the Stonewall Brigade at Cedar Mountain, Second Bull Run and Fredericksburg. He later commanded at Fort Wagner and James Island, ending the war a major general. He surrendered with J. E. Johnston (April 1865) and resumed his Virginia law and political career.

Taney, Roger Brooke
(1777-1864)
Chief justice of the Supreme Court

Born into a wealthy Maryland family, he became a lawyer and prominent Federalist in his home state. He was U.S. attorney general (1831-1833) and acting secretary of the treasury (1833-1834). He closely advised President Andrew Jackson during the "bank war" in these years. Taney became chief justice of the U.S. Supreme Court in 1836, and during his 28-year tenure ruled on cases that highlighted the growing North-South rift. The most explosive of these was *Dred Scott v. Sandford* (1857), in which the court held blacks to be unentitled to sue in the federal courts and Congress to be powerless to outlaw slavery in the territories. The case is generally regarded as one cause of the Civil War.

Tattnall, Josiah
(1795-1871) Confederate commodore

This Georgian began his long naval career in 1812. He fought West Indian pirates and was wounded in the Mexican War. Opposed to secession, he nevertheless accepted a Confederate naval captaincy and directed coastal defenses. As commander of CSS *Virginia* (formerly *Merrimac*) after her fight with USS *Monitor*, he ordered her destruction during the evacuation of Norfolk. He later challenged the Federal blockade and defended the Savannah River until Savannah fell (December 1864). He surrendered with J. E. Johnston. He was later port inspector of Savannah.

Taylor, Richard
(1826-1879) Confederate general

Zachary Taylor's son, he was born in Kentucky and educated in Edinburgh and France before graduation from Yale. He became a Louisiana planter, legislator and secessionist. As a Confederate brigadier general he led the Louisiana Brigade in the Shenandoah Valley Campaign of 1862 and in the Peninsular Campaign. As a major general (July 1862) he commanded the District of Western Louisiana, where he stopped Nathaniel Banks's Red River Campaign of 1864 with a victory at Sabine Cross Roads, earning a promotion to lieutenant general. Taylor commanded other Gulf departments before surrendering the last Confederate army east of the Mississippi to Edward Canby in May 1865. His *Destruction and Reconstruction* (1879) is a highly regarded military memoir.

Terry, Alfred Howe
(1827-1890) Union general

This Yale-educated lawyer was a New Haven, Connecticut, court clerk before the war. He served the Union at First Bull Run, led the 7th Connecticut in the Port Royal Expedition (November 1861), helped to capture Fort Pulaski (April 1862) and led a division in the attack on Fort Wagner (summer 1863). He later held James Army corps commands. He received the Thanks of Congress for his greatest wartime achievement, the taking of Fort Fisher in January 1865. Later a famous Indian fighter he directed the campaign against the Sioux in 1876 and himself led one of the three U.S. columns, that approaching from the east. Part of his command was George A. Custer's 7th Cavalry, soon to become famous for its part in the Battle of the Little Big Horn.

Thomas, George Henry
(1816-1870) Union general

The Virginia-born Thomas studied law briefly before obtaining an appointment to West Point, where he was graduated with W. T. Sherman and R. S. Ewell in the class of 1840. Commissioned into the artillery, he joined his unit in Florida and took part in the campaign against the Seminole Indians there. He later served in several garrisons in the South.

Thomas saw extensive action during the Mexican War, earning brevets for gallantry at Monterey and Buena Vista. He returned to Florida after the war, taught gunnery and cavalry tactics for three years at West Point and did garrison duty in California and Arizona. He later served in Texas with the 2nd Cavalry, whose officers' roll included many soon-to-be-famous names, A. S. Johnston, Robert E. Lee and Fitzhugh Lee among them. Wounded in an Indian skirmish, he was on convalescent leave when the Civil War began.

Though a Virginian, Thomas remained loyal to the Union. He commanded a brigade in the Shenandoah Valley in the early weeks of the war and went to Kentucky in August 1861 to organize new troops. He then took command of the 1st Division, Army of the Ohio, and led it to victory at Mill Springs (also known as Logan's Cross Roads) in January 1862. He commanded the division at Shiloh in April and during the advance on Corinth, Mississippi, later in the spring.

He returned to Kentucky for the campaign against Braxton Bragg. He declined an offer to succeed the army commander, Don Carlos Buell, who had fallen into disfavor; he was Buell's second in command at Perryville in October 1862. In late October, when William Rosecrans replaced Buell, Thomas took command of XIV Corps in what was now styled the Army of the Cumberland. He led the corps competently at Stones River at the year's end and in the 1863 Tullahoma Campaign.

A large, powerfully built man, he had a reputation for deliberateness that earned him the nickname "Slow Trot." His troops, who greatly admired him, also called him "Pap." He won his most famous nickname at Chickamauga Creek on September 20, 1863. There Thomas held out

ABOVE: George Henry Thomas.

BELOW: Chickamauga, the battle that made Thomas's name a household word.

for several hours against a violent Confederate attack, enabling the broken remnants of William Rosecran's other formations to retreat safely into Chattanooga. Henceforth, he was known as "the Rock of Chickamauga."

Ulysses S. Grant, newly appointed to the supreme command in the West, relieved Rosecrans and put Thomas in his place at the head of the Cumberland army. His first order to Thomas directed him to hold besieged Chattanooga at all hazards against the Confederate siege. "We will hold the town till we starve," Thomas answered. He did so until, with reinforcements, Grant managed to reopen a supply line and prepare for offensive operations. On November 25, 1863, Thomas's command stormed

Meriwether Jeff Thompson

Missionary Ridge, routing the Confederates under Bragg and forcing them out of Tennessee altogether.

Thomas marched with W. T. Sherman for Atlanta in the spring of 1864; elements of the Cumberland army received the surrender of the city on September 2. When Sherman set out on his March to the Sea, he left Thomas behind to oppose the Army of Tennessee, now under John B. Hood. Hood went off in the opposite direction to that of Sherman. Thomas's field force checked him at Franklin, Tennessee, on November 30, then retreated into the Nashville lines.

Grant ordered an immediate offensive against Hood. Thomas delayed, protesting he was not yet strong enough. Grant decided to relieve him. He stayed the order, then reissued it when Thomas still

failed to act. Grant actually ordered a replacement to Nashville, but before he could arrive, Thomas had fought the Battle of Nashville, one of the most crushing victories of the entire war: in two days of fighting, December 15 and 16, Hood's army was all but destroyed.

Thomas remained in command in Tennessee through the end of the war and into the early postwar period. He took charge of the Military Department of the Pacific in 1869 and died of apoplexy on active service in San Francisco in March 1870.

Thompson, Meriwether Jeff
(1826-1876) Confederate general

Virginia-born Thompson was the mayor of St. Joseph, Missouri, at the outbreak of the Civil War. After organizing a Confederate battalion in 1861, he inaugurated a notable war career leading his so-called "Swamp Rats" on border raids against J. C. Frémont's forces in southeastern Missouri. He later fought with Earl Van Dorn in the Transmississippi, and in 1864 he led Shelby's Brigade in Sterling Price's Missouri Raid. An eccentric but brilliant leader and a daring scout, he was a brigadier general by the end of the war. He surrendered in Arkansas in May 1865.

Tompkins, Sally Louisa
(1833-1916) Confederate nurse

Daughter of a wealthy Virginia family, even as a young woman she was noted for her care of the sick. As soon as the Civil

Sally Louisa Tompkins

War broke out she began a hospital in Richmond; so successful was she that she was made a captain by Jefferson Davis when the Confederate government took over medical services – the only woman ever given a regular commission by the Confederate army. After the war she continued to engage in charitable work and was always treated by Confederate veterans as one of them.

Toombs, Robert Augustus
(1810-1885) Confederate general

He studied law at the University of Virginia and returned to his native Georgia, where he was a planter, lawyer and politician. In the U.S. Congress (1845-1853) and Senate (1853-1861), Toombs consistently supported compromise measures, finally turning secessionist after the failure of the Crittenden Compromise in 1860. After losing the Southern presidency to Jefferson Davis, he was briefly and unhappily secre-

Robert Augustus Toombs

tary of state in the provisional Confederate government before joining the army in July 1861. Opposed to the South's defensive strategy and denied promotion after Malvern Hill and Antietam, he resigned in March 1863. He returned to his legal and political career after the war and opposed Radical Reconstruction in Georgia.

Townsend, George Alfred
(1841-1914) War correspondent

This Delaware native reported the Seven Days' Battles and Cedar Mountain for the *New York Herald*, then promoted the Union cause in articles and lectures in England (1862-1863). He became famous for his fine New York *World* coverage of the last battles of the war and of Lincoln's assassination. After 1867 he lived mostly in Washington, D.C., publishing political and social commentary under the pseudonym "Gath" in nearly 100 newspapers. In 1896 he erected a monument to 157 Civil War correspondents on the South Mountain battlefield.

Isaac Ridgeway Trimble

Trimble, Isaac Ridgeway
(1802-1888) Confederate general

This Kentuckian was graduated from West Point and spent 10 years as an army surveyor before resigning to become a railroad engineer. He disrupted Union supplies in 1861 by destroying railroad bridges north of Baltimore. As a Confederate army engineer, he constructed Potomac River batteries and fought in the Shenandoah Valley Campaign of Jackson, the Seven Days' Battles and at Second Bull Run (wounded). Leading a division in "Pickett's Charge" at Gettysburg, he lost a leg and was captured; he was imprisoned until February 1865. He was later a Baltimore engineer.

Tubman, Harriet
(1820?-1913) Abolitionist

She was born into slavery on a plantation in Dorchester County, Maryland, the granddaughter of Africans brought to America chained in the holds of slave ships. She worked as a house servant, nursing children and doing maid's chores, and as a fieldhand. She evidently was a refractory servant and was often punished: an overseer once struck her in the head with a heavy object, doing her an injury from whose ill effects she suffered intermittently for the rest of her long life.

She married a free black, John Tubman, in about 1844 and in the late 1840s worked in the household of a Methodist parson. She made her escape to free soil in 1849, leaving behind her husband, who declined

Harriet Tubman (far left), shown with some slaves she helped to escape

to accompany her. She soon discovered her true vocation: helping slaves escape to the free states. She made nearly 20 trips into Maryland in the 1850s. No exact accounting is possible, but estimates of the number of slaves she escorted north range from 60 to 300.

Tubman operated much as a secret agent would, setting out on trips south from her home base in St. Catharines, Ontario. She passed easily as an ordinary slavewoman traveling on her master's business. She carried a handgun for her own protection and – it was said – to encourage prospective runaways afflicted with 11th-hour doubts. She announced her coming with oracular messages: "Tell my brothers to be always watching unto prayer," ran one, "and when the good old ship of Zion comes along, to be ready to step on board." Her success caught the attention of Maryland slaveholders. Rewards of as much as $40,000 were offered for her capture.

She was plain-looking, uneducated, deeply religious. "Harriet was a woman of no pretensions, indeed, a more ordinary specimen of humanity could hardly be found among the most unfortunate-looking farm-hands of the South," an abolition colleague wrote of her. "Yet, in point of courage, shrewdness and disinterested

exertions to rescue her fellowmen, she was without her equal." She believed her actions were guided by a providential hand, and she remained always attentive to dreams and omens that might reveal the divine purpose.

Well known in abolition circles, Tubman became a regular speaker at anti-slavery conventions. In 1858 she advised John Brown as he planned his Harpers Ferry raid. (He afterwards referred to her as General Tubman.) At around this time William Seward, the Republican abolitionist leader, sold her the small farm near Auburn, New York, that would be her home for the rest of her life.

Tubman actively served the Union cause in the Civil War. In early 1862 she traveled to Beaufort, South Carolina, recently siezed by Federal forces, to volunteer as a spy and scout. She collected intelligence from slaves behind the Confederate lines and assisted newly freed slaves in Beaufort. Toward the war's end she worked as a nurse at a freedmen's hospital at Fortress Monroe, Virginia. The great abolition leader Frederick Douglass saluted her for her contributions. "Excepting John Brown," he wrote her in 1868, "I know of no one who has willingly encountered more perils and hardships to serve our enslaved people than you have."

Returning to her farm after the war, Tubman established the Harriet Tubman

Home for Indigent Aged Negroes, promoted educational opportunity for freedmen and proselytized for the African Methodist Episcopal Church. A short biography, *Harriet Tubman: The Moses of Her People*, appeared in 1869; the author, Sarah Bradford, donated the royalties to her. But she had barely a subsistence income, and in the late 1860s she began her long campaign for payment for her wartime services. She kept at the government for nearly three decades before Congress finally granted her a small monthly pension.

She died of pneumonia in March 1913.

Tucker, John Randolph
(1812-1883)
Confederate naval commander

The Virginian Tucker began his long naval career in 1826. During the Civil War, as a Confederate commander, he directed the James River defenses, commanding the gunboat *Patrick Henry* at Hampton Roads. He later attacked the Federal blockade and commanded a squadron at Charleston and the fleet off Drewry's Bluff. He destroyed his ships when Charleston was evacuated and created a naval brigade which fought at Sayler's Creek. He was later a rear admiral in the Peruvian navy and in 1873 led an Amazon surveying expedition.

Turchin, John Basil
(1822-1901) Union general

Born Ivan Vasilevitch Turchinoff in Russia, he fought in the Crimean War before emigrating in 1856 to Chicago, where he became a raildroad engineer. Joining the Union's 19th Illisnois in 1861, he served in Missouri, Kentucky and Alabama and fought at Stones River, Chickamauga and Missionary Ridge. Turchin's wife accompanied him as a nurse throughout his campaigns, once even leading his regiment into battle. He resigned in October 1864. He established the Polish farming community of Radom, Illinois (1873).

Turner, Nat
(1800-1831) Slave leader

Born into slavery on a plantation in Southampton County, Virginia, he found a vocation as a gospel preacher. Convincing slaves on his own and neighboring plantations that he was divinely inspired to lead them in revolt, he touched off a short, violent insurrection on August 21, 1831, in

The capture of Nat Turner

which more than 50 whites were murdered. Troops quickly restored order and killed or captured the rebellious slaves. Turner remained at large for several weeks but was taken, tried and condemned; he was hanged on November 11, 1831. Fifteen of his supporters were also put to death. The insurrection had widespread repercussions in the South, leading to a strengthening of the slave codes and the erosion of support for gradual emancipation.

Twiggs, David Emanuel
(1790-1862) Confederate general

The son of a Revolutionary War general, he entered the army in 1812 and saw service during the war with Britain. After a long period out of uniform, he returned in 1825. Twiggs fought in Mexico in 1846 and 1847 and served as a department commander, mainly in the South, during the 1850s. In February 1861, in command in Texas, Twiggs surrendered all Union troops and stores to the Confederates. Though he entered Confederate service, he never took the field for the Confederacy. He died near his birthplace outside Augusta, Georgia, in July 1862.

Upton, Emory
(1839-1881) Union general

This New Yorker was commissioned second lieutenant upon his 1861 West Point graduation. He saw continuous action with the Union's Army of the Potomac from 1861 to 1864, then joined the Army of the Shenandoah in fighting at Opequon and in Alabama and Georgia. Several times wounded and repeatedly cited for gallantry, he became one of the Federals' leading tacticians and most celebrated war heroes. He was West Point commandant of cadets (1870-1875). He committed suicide while commanding the Presidio, San Francisco. His military works include the outstanding *Military Policy of the United States* (posthumously published in 1904).

Emory Upton, one of the Union army's outstanding heroes

South after his conviction of treason in 1863 for speaking against the war in defiance of a military prohibition. Vallandigham re-entered the North via Canada and campaigned vigorously against Lincoln's re-election in 1864, while hurting the Democrats' chances by inserting an anti-war plank in their election platform. He opposed Reconstruction policies, but his influence on both political parties and on the public at large was waning and never revived.

Van Dorn, Earl
(1820-1863) Confederate general

An 1842 West Point graduate, he fought in Mexico and in many Indian campaigns. He took command of the Confederate Trans-mississippi Department early in 1862. Van Dorn's army was beaten at Pea Ridge, Arkansas, in March, and in October William Rosecrans inflicted a serious defeat on his forces at Corinth, Mississippi. A commission absolved Van Dorn of any blame in the Corinth defeat, and he led John Pemberton's cavalry at Holly Springs, Mississippi, in December. Van Dorn was shot and killed in May 1863 by a man who accused him of carrying on an affair with his wife.

Vallandigham, Clement Laird
(1820-1871) Democratic politician

He was an Ohio lawyer, journalist and Democratic politician who strenuously opposed the war. As a U.S. Congressman (1858-1863), he was prominent among the "Copperheads," or Peace Democrats, and tried to obstruct war-related legislation. Abraham Lincoln banished him to the

Clement Laird Vallandigham

Van Lew, Elizabeth L.
(1818-1900) Union spy

A Virginian educated in Philadelphia, she early opposed slavery. Ardently Unionist, Van Lew lived in Richmond throughout the war, and in addition to her relief work at Libby Prison she both gathered vital intelligence for the Union and helped Federal prisoners to escape. Disguising her spying with eccentric behavior, she earned the nickname "Crazy Bet." Her role became known after the war, and she was an outcast in Richmond society until her death.

Velazquez, Loreta Janeta
(1842?-1897)
Confederate officer and spy

Born in Cuba to an aristocratic Spanish family, she was educated in New Orleans. The wife of a U.S. Army officer (married 1856), she accompanied her husband into the Confederate army, raising and leading a volunteer battalion disguised as "Lieutenant Harry Buford." After her husband was killed early in the war, she fought at First Bull Run and Fort Donelson. She was unmasked in 1863 but continued to spy behind Federal lines. She later wrote *The Woman in Battle* (1876).

Villard, Henry
(1835-1900) War correspondent

Born in Bavaria, he emigrated Illinois and studied law before becoming a journalist. In an 1861 scoop he reported W. T. Sherman's views on the Union's lack of preparedness and the probable scope of the war, leading Union authorities to judge Sherman unbalanced and remove him from command of the Kentucky Department. Villard later reported for Horace Greely's *New York Tribune* and became one of the war's leading correspondents. He married a daughter of the famous abolitionist leader William Lloyd Garrison.

Von Steinwehr, Adolph
(1822-1877) Union general

Born into a Prussian military family, he came to America to fight in the Mexican War and later became a farmer in Connecticut. Chosen colonel of the Union's all-German 29th New York at the outbreak of war, Von Steinwehr led a brigade at the Second Battle of Bull Run and a division at Chancellorsville and Gettysburg. He briefly commanded XI Corps in Virginia and Tennessee. He taught military science at Yale after the war.

Mary Edwards Walker

Waddell, James Iredell
(1824-1886) **Confederate naval officer**

This North Carolinian, a career officer, became a midshipman in 1841. He returned from Asia at the outbreak of the Civil War and enlisted in the Confederate navy in March 1862. He helped to turn back a Union flotilla supporting the Peninsular Campaign, then joined the battery at Charleston. As commander of the raider *Shenandoah* after October 1864, he secured a number of prizes in the Pacific, some after the war ended (for he had not heard of the Confederate surrender). He became a civilian skipper after the war.

Wade, Benjamin Franklin
(1800-1878)
Radical Republican Senator

Born in Massachusetts, Wade practiced law in Ohio and became a strong abolitionist in the Republican party. As a U.S. Senator,

Benjamin Franklin Wade

Wade joined Representative Henry W. Davis in drafting a Reconstruction plan in 1864 that opposed Abraham Lincoln's policies, which they felt to be too moderate. After Lincoln vetoed the plan, Wade and Davis wrote a manifesto denouncing him. Not surprisingly, Wade later opposed President Andrew Johnson's moderate Reconstruction policies.

Walker, Leroy Page
(1817-1884) **Confederate general and secretary of war**

A lawyer, outspoken secessionist and Democratic power in Alabama, he was chosen for the sake of regional balance to be the first Confederate secretary of war (February-September 1861). Inexperienced and overwhelmed, he resigned in broken health and was commissioned brigadier general but, denied a field command, resigned in March 1862. He presided over an Alabama military court during the last year of the war, later returning to his Huntsville law practice and political deal-making.

Walker, Mary Edwards
(1831-1919) **Union surgeon**

This New Yorker was certified by Syracuse Medical College in 1855. For the first three years of the Civil War she was an army nurse and sometime spy. In 1864 she was commissioned as the first woman assistant surgeon in the U.S. Army: she dressed like her male colleagues in trousers and a greatcoat (she wore male dress throughout her life). After the war she was a Washington, D.C., physician, inventor and active suffragist.

Wallace, Lewis
(1827-1905) **Union general**

Indiana-born Wallace had a varied career in politics, journalism and the law before the war. He fought for the Union at Romney and Harpers Ferry, and, earning rapid promotions (brigadier general September 1861, major general March 1862), he led divisions

infantry regiment, and later a brigade, early in the war, then became chief engineer of the Army of the Potomac, playing a decisive role at Gettysburg in directing reinforcements to the Federeal left on Little Round Top. Warren commanded V Corps at the Wilderness, Spotsylvania, Cold Harbor and Petersburg. Philip Sheridan relieved him for lack of aggressiveness during the Appomattox Campaign; a court of inquiry cleared him of Sheridan's charges in 1881.

Lewis Wallace (above) and (right) Gouverneur Kemble Warren

ABOVE: Stand Watie

at Fort Donelson and Shiloh and saved Cincinnati from Edmund Kirby Smith. He led VIII Corps at Monocacy, where, although he lost the battle, he was commended by Ulysses Grant for saving Washington, D.C., from capture. His substantial administrative service included the courts martial of Abraham Lincoln's assassins and Andersonville Prison commandant Henry Wirz. A prolific novelist, "Lew" Wallace became famous for his *The Fair God* (1873) and more so for his *Ben Hur* (1880). He was governor of New Mexico (1878-1881) and minister to Turkey (1881-1885).

Warren, Gouverneur Kemble
(1830-1882) Union general

An 1850 West Point graduate, he joined the army engineer corps and later taught mathematics at the academy. He led a Union

B-4241

Watie, Stand
(1806-1871)
Cherokee leader, Confederate general

His father was a full-blooded Cherokee and his mother half-Indian. He attended mission schools in Georgia, where he grew up to become a fairly prosperous planter, as well as the publisher of a newspaper for the Cherokee. He was one of four Cherokee who signed a treaty in 1835 agreeing to give up their tribal lands in Georgia and to move to Oklahoma; some Cherokee who bitterly opposed this killed the three other signers (including Watie's brother), but he escaped and became the chief of the Cherokee who supported the treaty. When the Civil War broke out, a number of Cherokee formed an alliance with the Confederacy, and Watie was commissioned a captain and assigned command of a Cherokee unit in the Confederate army. As a colonel, he led his unit, the Cherokee Mounted

Rifles, through several battles, including Pea Ridge (Elkhorn Tavern), Arkansas. In 1863 most of the Cherokee repudiated the alliance with the Confederacy, but Watie still upheld it, thus becoming the effective chief of those Cherokee who stayed with the Confederacy. In May 1864 he was promoted to brigadier general, and he was one of the last Confederate generals to surrender (June 1865). After the war he went back to being a planter.

Waud, Alfred R.

(1818-1891) **War artist, correspondent**

Waud was the principal war artist for *Harper's Weekly* and produced hundreds of sketches from the frontlines, depicting some of the war's most important events. Because of the state of mid-nineteenth century printing technology, few of Waud's contemporaries ever saw his original sketches reproduced, but only hasty and often coarse wood-block prints made from them by *Harper's* engravers. Many of his sketches survive, however, and continue to provide an invaluable record of the Civil War. (His brother William was also a war artist.)

RIGHT: Alfred R. Waud.

BELOW: A Waud sketch of Fair Oaks.

Webb, Alexander Stewart
(1835-1911) Union general

This New York-born West Point graduate, having served in the Seminole War and taught at West Point, was commissioned a lieutenant in the Union artillery in April 1861. He served at First Bull Run, Yorktown, Mechanicsville, Gaines's Mill, Malvern Hill, Antietam, Chancellorsville, Gettysburg, and the Wilderness and Spotsylvania, where he was wounded. Due to his injuries, he was out of service until January 1865 but returned to duty for the end of the siege of Petersburg. He was breveted a major general and remained in the regular army until 1870. He received a Medal of Honor for his role at Gettysburg, and his statue stands at the Bloody Angle, Spotsylvania. He long served as president of City College of New York (1869-1902).

Alexander Stewart Webb (standing right of flagpole, center of tent entrance)

Weisiger, David Adams
(?-1899) Confederate general

Weisiger served in the Mexican War and then, while a merchant, in the Virginia militia. Assigned the rank of colonel, he led the Confederate forces that seized the Norfolk Navy Yard. He fought at Seven Pines, Charles City Cross Roads, the Seven Days' Battles, Second Bull Run, the Wilderness and Petersburg. He was wounded at Second Bull Run and was promoted to brigadier general in November 1864 for his service in Petersburg. He was wounded three times at Appomattox and lost two horses before finally surrendering there.

Welles, Gideon
(1802-1878)
Union secretary of the navy

A Connecticut native, he edited the *Hartford Times* (1826-1836) and brought much public service experience to Washington as

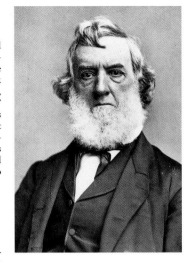

ABOVE: Gideon Welles

secretary of the navy (1861-1869). Welles served ably throughout the war. Despite a serious loss of personnel to the Confederates, Welles quickly established a Federal shipbuilding program and assembled a navy (during the war he increased Union naval strength from 90 to 670 ships and from 9000 to 57,000 men). He defined strategy, promoted new technology, including ironclad ships, and enforced the blockade of the South. The Union's naval successes made him influential in Lincoln's cabinet. His *Diary* (3 vols., 1911) is an important Civil War record. He later founded the *Hartford Evening Press*, one of New England's earliest Republican newspapers.

Wheat, Chatham Roberdeau
(1826-1862) Confederate officer

An Episcopal minister's son, he saw action in the Mexican War, practiced law and politics in New Orleans, fought in Nicaragua during the Walker filibuster in 1856 and served with Garibaldi's army in Italy. Wheat returned home in time to lead the Louisiana Tigers battalion at First Bull Run, where he was shot through both lungs. "I don't feel like dying yet," he said when told he had been mortally wounded. Wheat recovered, fought with Jackson in the Valley but was killed at Gaines's Mill in June.

Wheeler, Joseph
(1836-1906)
Confederate cavalry officer

This Georgian was graduated close to the bottom of his West Point class. He left frontier fighting when the war broke out. He fought for the Confederacy at Shiloh, Perryville and Stones River, reorganized and commanded the Army of the Mississippi's cavalry and led raids against Federal communications. One such raid on Union supply lines (October 1-9, 1863) nearly forced the besieged Federals in Chattanooga to evacuate th city. He wrote *Cavalry Tactics* (1863). By spring 1864 he was the senior Confederate cavalry officer. He participated in the Knoxville and Atlanta campaigns and fought W. T. Sherman during his March to the Sea. "Fightin' Joe" was said to have fought in 1000 engagements and skirmishes before his capture in May 1865. He represented Alabama in Congress (1880-1882, 1884-1899).

William Henry Chase Whiting

Whiting, William Henry Chase
(1824-1865) Confederate general

He was graduated at the head of his West Point class in 1845 and held engineering appointments in the old army. Joining the Confederate service, he planned the Charleston harbor defenses and led an infantry division during T. J. Jackson's Shenandoah Valley Campaign and on the Virginia peninsula in the spring and summer of 1862. Whiting later commanded the military district of Wilmington on the North Carolina coast. He was mortally wounded at Fort Fisher, North Carolina, in January 1865.

Whitman, Walt
(1819-1892) Poet

The second of nine children, born in West Hills, Long Island, New York, he moved with his family to Brooklyn, then a small city of 10,000 people, in 1823 and was educated in the public schools there. When he was about 13 years old he went to work,

Joseph Wheeler

Lincoln's funeral, inspiration for Walt Whitman's "When Lilacs in the Dooryard Bloom'd" and "Oh Captain! My Captain"

Walt Whitman

first as a lawyer's office boy and later as a printer's devil for the *Long Island Patriot*.

Whitman worked for newspapers as a compositor and sometime contributor during the first half of the 1830s and taught school in several Long Island communities in the latter years of the decade. He edited the *Long Islander* in Huntingdon in 1838-39 and began contributing verse to various other newspapers. People who knew him during these years described him variously as morose, lazy, untidy and rude to children. As one obsered, "He was a genius who lived, apparently, in a world of his own."

He moved restlessly from newspaper to newspaper during the 1840s. In 1841 the *Democratic Review*, a leading literary journal, began publishing his short stories: Nathaniel Hawthorne, Edgar Alen Poe and Henry David Thoreau were among the review's contributors. In January 1846 he became editor of the Brooklyn *Eagle*, and he used its editorial page to campaign for various reforms. His advocacy of the anti-slavery cause cost him his job early in 1848.

With his characteristic knack for finding jobs, Whitman landed a position as a writer on the New Orleans *Crescent* and journeyed south in the winter of 1848. He remained for only three months, however, returning to Brooklyn and a lonely, unstable freelancer's life. All the while he continued to write, and over the next few years he found his poetic voice. His *Leaves of Grass*, published in 1855, established him as

a leading poet. In an anonymous review of his own book, he described himself – as presented through the poems, one of which he later titled "Song of Myself" – as "of pure American breed, large and lusty, a naive, masculine, affectionate, contemplative, sensual, imperious person."

Though a critical success, *Leaves of Grass* was a commercial failure, and Whitman had to continue to support himself with newspaper work while producing more than a hundred new poems from 1856 to 1860. In them, he further developed the main themes of his work, love and death. The outbreak of Civil War gave both these themes a public dimension. The war had a tremendous imact on Whitman. In 1862 he published four articles on hospitals for a New York newspaper, and he wrote the first of the poems that would later appear in the *Drum Taps* collection. Then, late in the year, word came that his brother George had been wounded in Virginia, serving with the Union's 51st New York. Whitman found him in Falmouth, on the Rappahannock opposite Fredericksburg, where he had his first exposure to the immediate aftermath of the fighting.

He settled in Washington, D.C., and began to visit the wounded and sick in the city's military hospitals, distributing sweets, cool drinks and tobacco, reading to the convalescents and writing letters for them. "I can testify that friendship had literally cured a fever," he wrote, "and the medicine of daily effection, a bad wound."

Whitman's poem "A March in the Ranks Hard-Prest" is a poetic response to what he saw in a field hospital after the battle of Chancellorsville in May 1863:

Faces, varieties, postures beyond
  description, most in obscurity, some of
  them dead,
Surgeons operating, attendants holding
  lights, the smell of ether, the odor of
  blood,
The crowd, O the crowd of bloody
  forms, the yard outside also fill'd,
Some on the bare ground, some on
  planks or stretchers, some in the death-
  spasm sweating. . . .

Drum Taps appeared in 1865, with Whitman's most famous poem, "When Lilacs in the Dooryard Bloom'd," appended as a supplement. He brought out new editions of *Leaves of grass* in 1867 and 1871. Some of his collected prose, including wartime writings, appeared in *Specimen Days* (1882-83). By the 1870s Whitman had become a famous man of letters, though his critical reputation tended to fluctuate. He passed his last years quietly in Camden, New Jersey, where he died in March 1892.

Wickham, William Carter
(1820-1888) Confederate general

Born in Richmond, this Virginia planter, lawyer, and legislator opposed secession at his state's secession convention. At the outbreak of war he raised a Confederate cavalry company and fought steadily, participating at First Bull Run, on the Peninsula (wounded at Williamsburg) and under J. E. B. Stuart at Second Bull Run, Antietam, Fredericksburg, Chancellorsville and Gettysburg. Promoted to briga-

dier general (September 1863), he fought at the Wilderness, Spotsylvania and Cold Harbor, then joining Jubal Early for the fighting in the Shenandoah Valley. He resigned from the army in November 1864 to sit in the Confederate congress: he attended the Hampton Roads Peace Conference. After the war he was a Richmond lawyer and railroad president.

Wilcox, Cadmus Marcellus
(1824-1890) Confederate general

This North Carolina-born West Point graduate served in the Mexican and Seminole wars and taught at West Point; he was a member of Ulysses S. Grant's wedding party in 1848. He was stationed on the western frontier when he resigned to

William Carter Wickham (left) and (below) Cadmus Marcellus Wilcox

accept a commission in the Confederate army. He fought at First and Second Bull Run, on the Peninsula, at Fredericksburg, Chancellorsville, Bank's Ford, Gettysburg, the Wilderness, Spotsylvania and Petersburg, finally surrendering at Appomattox. He had been promoted to major general in 1863. After the war, he held government jobs in Washington and wrote and translated books on military subjects.

Wild, Edward Augustus
(1825-1891) Union general

Born in Massachusetts, he was a doctor who served as a medical officer in the Turkish army during the Crimean War. He was commissioned a U.S. Army captain in May 1861 and fought at First Bull Run. Wounded at Fair Oaks, he was mustered out in July 1862. He then helped to raise African-American forces in Massachusetts. Recommissioned as a brigadier general in April 1863, he led African-American units for the next year. He was arrested in 1864 when he refused to replace his quartermaster, but the charges were set aside and he continued to serve till the end of the war. He was with the Georgia Freedman's Bureau when mustered out in 1866. He went on to mine silver after the war.

Wilkes, Charles
(1798-1877) Union naval officer

He entered the U.S. Navy as a midshipman in 1818 and built a reputation as a surveyor and hydrographer. Wilkes led a six-ship scientific expedition to Antartica from 1838 to 1842. Commanding USS *San Jacinto*, his arrest of the Confederate envoys James Mason and John Slidell on board a British ship on the high seas on November 8, 1861, caused a serious diplomatic breach with England, though the *Trent* Affair, as it was known, made him a temporary hero. Assigned to command a squadron formed to hunt down Confederate raiders in the West Indies, he was recalled in June 1863 after several countries complained of violations of neutrality.

Wilmot, David
(1814-1868) Northern statesman

He was a lawyer and Democratic politician in his native Pennsylvania. As a U.S. Representative (1845-1851) he introduced the Wilmot Proviso (August 1846), a clause in a Mexican War appropriations bill that outlawed slavery in any territory acquired from Mexico. Passed 87-64 in the House, the measure failed in the Senate and failed again when reintroduced the following year. The acrimonious debate surrounding the bill deepened the growing rift between North and South and led to the foundation of the Free-Soil Party (1848) and later the Republican Party (1845). Wilmot joined both parties in his later career as a Pennsylvania and federal judge and U.S. Senator.

Wilson, James Harrison
(1837-1925) Union general

Graduated from West Point in 1860, this Illinois native was a Union major general by 1865, having served under W. T. Sherman, David Hunter and George McClellan; directed the Cavalry Bureau; and, in 1864-1865, led a cavalry corps. An outstanding commander, he led several spectacular raids: during the Petersburg siege Wilson and August V. Kautz destroyed many miles of vital railroad track, and, in May 1865, in a sensational finale to his bril-

liantly successful Selma Raid, Wilson's force captured Jefferson Davis. He built railroads and wrote military works in later life, and, following his re-enlistment for the Spanish-American War, he helped to suppress the Boxer Rebellion.

Winder, John Henry
(1800-1865)
Confederate provost marshal general

Born in Maryland, Winder was a West Point graduate and veteran of the frontier and the Seminole and Mexican wars. As a Confederate brigadier general his most significant commands were Libby, Belle Isle and Andersonville Prison: in November 1864 he became commissary general of all

OPPOSITE: James Harrison Wilson (sprawled on steps) and staff.

BELOW: John Henry Winder.

ABOVE: The execution of Henry Wirz, commandant of Andersonville Prison.

RIGHT: Henry Alexander Wise.

prisoners of war in the East. The degree of Winder's responsibility for the appalling conditions in prisons under his purview remains unresolved. His death was attributed to fatigue and strain.

Wirz, Henry
(1822-1865) Confederate officer

Swiss-born Wirz emigrated to the U.S. in 1849 and settled in Louisiana as a physician. During the Civil War he was a Confederate clerk in Libby Prison, fought at Seven Pines (wounded) and conducted a Confederate mission to Europe. He returned early in 1864 to become commandant of Andersonville Prison, Georgia, a prison camp notorious for its utter lack of shelter and sanitation, its overcrowding and its brutal guards: 13,000 Federal prisoners died there. The only person executed for war crimes after the war, he was hanged in November 1865 for conspiring to murder prisoners.

Wise, Henry Alexander
(1806-1876) Confederate general

A lawyer and politician, he served in Congress and was governor of Virginia (1856-1860). He opposed secession initially but volunteered for Confederate service and obtained a brigadier general's commission in May 1861. Wise served in western Virginia and at Roanoke Island, North Carolina, where one of his sons was mortally wounded. He later fought in the Petersburg and Richmond defenses and surrendered with Robert E. Lee's army at Appomattox. Wise returned to the practice of law after the war and died in Richmond in September 1876.

Wood, Thomas John
(1823-1906) Union general

Born in Kentucky, he was graduated from West Point in 1845 and participated in the Mexican War, frontier fighting and the Utah Expedition. He mustered 40,000 Indiana troops for the Union at the beginning of the Civil War. He commanded an Ohio Army division at Shiloh, Corinth and Perryville. He then fought in the Army of

Thomas John Wood (left) and (above) John Ellis Wool

the Cumberland at Stones River, in the Tullahoma Campaign, at Chickamauga, Missionary Ridge and Knoxville, and in the Atlanta Campaign. He commanded IV Corps at Nashville. He retired as a brigadier general in 1875.

Wool, John Ellis
(1784-1869) Union general

Wool raised a New York regiment for the War of 1812. As a brigadier general, he became a Mexican War hero by leading a superbly organized march through Chihuahua and securing victory at Buena Vista. He lived to become the fourth-ranking Union general in the Civil War. He saved Fort Monroe, occupied Norfolk and Portsmouth after the Confederate evacuation and commanded the Department of the East, the Middle Department and VIII Corps, retiring from active duty in August 1863 at the age of 79.

Worden, John Lorimer
(1818-1897) Union naval officer

This New Yorker was a 25-year navy veteran when the Civil War broke out. He earned national celebrity (and the Thanks of Congress) after commanding USS *Monitor* in the historic combat against CSS *Virginia* (ex-*Merrimac*) on March 9, 1862. Worden commanded the ironclad USS *Montauk* in the South Atlantic Blockading Squadron early in 1863 and spent the remainder of the war supervising the con-

struction of ironclad warships in New York. he retired as a rear admiral in 1886. He was also a superintendent of Annapolis (1869-1874).

Wright, Horatio Gouverneur
(1820-1899) **Union general**

Born in Connecticut, Wright was a West Point graduate. He became an army engineer who worked on harbors and fortifications. As chief engineer assigned to destroy the Union's Norfolk Navy Yard when the Civil War broke out, he was captured by the Confederates but was soon released. He served the Union at Fist Bull Run and on the Port Royal expedition, and fought in South Carolina and Florida, at Rappahannock Bridge and on the Bristoe Campaign. He led VI Corps from the Wilderness through the Petersburg assaults and on to Appomattox, then went to South Carolina to confront General Joseph Johnston's force. He was breveted a major general for his actions at Petersburg. He remained in the army until 1884.

Wright, Marcus Joseph
(1831-1922) **Confederate general**

A Tennessee court clerk, he joined the Confederacy's 154th Tennessee in 1861. He was wounded at Shiloh, and, promoted to brigadier general, led a brigade at Chickamauga and Chattanooga and participated in the defense of Atlanta. He surrendered as a Mississippi territorial commander. After the war he was a Memphis lawyer. Appointed to collect the C.S.A. archives (1878-1917), he made his major contribution to history by collecting, compiling, and editing the Southern records of the Civil War.

John Lorimer Worden (left) and (below) Horatio Gouverneur Wright

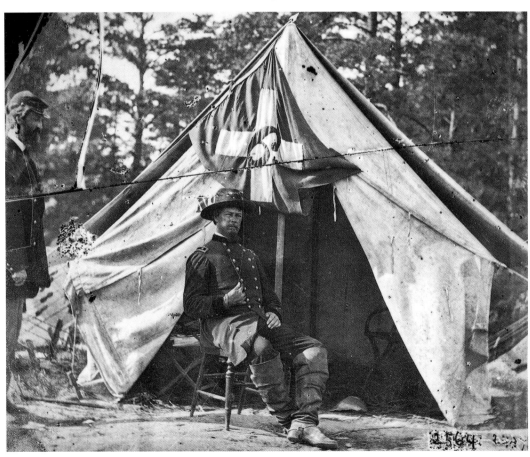

countered the Wilmot Proviso with the Alabama (or Yancey) Platform (1848) seeking the codification of slaveholders' rights. The Compromise of 1850 drove him to radical secessionism; he became a leader of the "Fire-Eaters," delivering hundreds of speeches and becoming a pivotal figure in the secessionist movement. He drafted Alabama's secession ordnance. In Europe (1861-1862) he sought diplomatic recognition of the Confederacy. He died in office in the Confederate senate.

Young, Pierce Manning Butler
(1836-1896) Confederate general

Born in South Carolina, Young resigned from West Point just before graduation to join the Confederate army. He was wounded at South Mountain and Fredericksburg, fought at Gettysburg, defended Augusta against W. T. Sherman and was promoted to major general in December 1864. After the war he became a planter, served in the U.S. House of Representatives, was a member of the West Point Board of Visitors and held various diplomatic posts.

Yancey, William Lowndes
(1814-1863) Confederate legislator

After graduation from Williams College, this Georgian returned south, where he was a newspaper editor, lawyer and legislator. He settled on an Alabama plantation. Yancey resigned his Congressional seat (1844-1846) to agitate for states' rights. He

Zollicoffer, Felix Kirk
(1812-1862) Confederate general

This Tennessee-born newspaper editor and Whig politician fought in the Seminole War, held various offices in Tennessee and served in the U.S. House of Representatives (1853-59). Although a staunch supporter of states' rights, he worked to avoid a confrontation between North and South and attended the 1861 peace conference in Washington. He was made a Confederate brigadier general in July 1861 and commanded a brigade in eastern Tennessee. He was killed in his first major battle, at Logan's Cross Roads (Mill Springs), Kentucky, in January 1862.

Felix Kirk Zollicoffer

William Lowndes Yancey

Pierce Manning Butler Young

The publisher would like to thank David Eldred, who designed this book as well as the following who supplied pictures.

The Bettmann Archive, New York, NY: pages 2 (bottom left), 18 (top), 22 (bottom right), 23 (bottom right, 26 (top right), 30 (top right), 31 (top), 33 (top right), 41 (bottom right), 64 (top right), 67 (top left), 71 (top left), 73 (bottom right), 77 (bottom), 83 (bottom), 102 (top left, bottom right), 114, 115 (bottom), 126 (bottom right), 141, 158 (bottom right), 160–61, 174 (bottom right), 175 (top), 183 (bottom center), 190, 191 (bottom), 201 (bottom), 202 (bottom right), 208, 209 (bottom left).
Boston Public Library, MA: page 185 (top center).
Brompton Picture Library: pages 35, 118–19, 188 (bottom right).
Brown University, Providence, RI/Anne S.K. Brown Military Collection: pages 2, (bottom center), 92 (top left), 93, 103, 142 (top left), 149 (bottom), 175 (bottom center), 182 (top center), 205 (top left).
John Hay Library: pages 18 (bottom), 85 (bottom right).
Chicago Historical Society, IL: pages 70 (top right), 82 (top center, bottom), 97 (top right), 202 (top left), 205 (bottom).
Library of Congress: pages 1, 2 (top, bottom right) 3, 6, 7, 8 (bottom left, top right), 9 (bottom right), 10 (top left), 11 (both), 12, 13 (bottom left), 16 (top left), 17 (both), 20 (bottom right), 21, 22 (top), 23 (top left), 24 (top left), 26 (top right), 27 (both), 28 (bottom left), 30 (top, bottom left), 32 (both), 34, 36 (top right), 37 (bottom left), 38 (both), 40 (both), 41 (top),

42 (bottom left), 43 (top left), 44 (bottom right), 45 (both), 46 (both), 48 (top right, bottom), 49 (both), 50, 51 (all three), 52 (both), 53 (top left), 54 (bottom left, right), 55 (both), 58 (top left, right), 61, 62–3, 64 (bottom left), 65 (all three), 67 (bottom right), 68–9, 70 (bottom left), 72 (all three), 73 (top left), 74 (right), 75, 76, 77 (top left, right), 78 (bottom left), 80–1, 82 (top left), 84, 85 (bottom left), 86 (bottom left, right) 87 (both), 88 (both), 89 (bottom left), 92 (bottom right), 94 (bottom right), 95 (both), 96 (top left, bottom right), 97 (bottom), 98 (all three), 99, 100 (both), 101 (bottom right), 102 (top center), 104 (top left), 105 (all three), 106 (bottom), 107, 108–11, 112 (both), 115 (top), 116 (both), 117 (top), 120–25, 126 (top left), 127 (both), 128 (top left), 129, 131 (top right, bottom), 132 (top right), 133 (bottom), 134–35, 137 (both), 138 (top left), 139 (top left), 140 (both), 142 (bottom), 143, 144 (all three), 145, 146–47, 148 (both), 149 (top), 151, 152, 153 (top right, bottom right), 154–57, 158 (top left), 162–63, 164 (both), 165 (bottom left), 166–73, 174 (top center), 176–77, 178–79, 181 (top left), 182 (bottom left), 183 (top left), 185 (left), 186–87, 191 (top), 192 (bottom right), 193 (right, bottom center), 194–200, 204, 207 (both), 210, 212 (top left, right), 213 (both), 214 (bottom), 215–17, 218 (left), 220 (bottom), 221–23.
Louis A. Warren Lincoln Library and Museum, Fort Wayne, IN: pages 29, 130.
The Museum of the Confederacy, Eleanor S. Brockenbrough Library, Richmond, VA: pages 19, 47 (right), 48 (top left), 106 (top).

National Archives: pages 4–5, 9 (top), 1. (bottom left), 16 (bottom right), 20 (top), 24 (bottom left), 31 (bottom), 37 (bottom right), 42 (top left), 47 (bottom left), 54 (top left), 56, 57 (all three), 58 (bottom center), 60 (both), 66 (bottom right), 70 (bottom left), 74 (bottom left), 78 (bottom right), 79 (both), 90, 94 (top left), 96 (bottom left), 113, 117 (bottom), 128 (bottom right), 136 (both), 139 (bottom right), 150 (bottom), 158 (bottom left), 159 (both), 165 (top right), 180, 184 (bottom right), 188 (top), 189, 192 (top), 193 (top left), 201 (top left), 203, 211 (both), 212 (bottom center), 214 (top right), 219.
National Portrait Gallery, Smithsonian Institution, Washington, D.C.: page 209 (bottom right).
U.S. Army Military History Institute, Carlisle Barracks, PA: pages 10 (center), 13 (bottom right), 14 (both), 15 (bottom right), 25, 28 (bottom right), 33 (bottom left), 36 (bottom center), 43 (bottom right), 44 (top right), 59, 66 (top right), 86 (top right), 89 (top right), 101 (bottom left), 104 (bottom right), 131 (top left), 138 (top right), 150 (bottom), 153 (bottom left), 174 (top left), 181 (top right), 206 (bottom left).
U.S. Military Academy Archives, West Point, NY: page 91.
U.S. Navy, Naval Photographic Center, Washington, D.C.: page 184 (top).
University of Maryland Baltimore County, Photographic Collections: page 220 (top).
The Valentine Museum, Cook Collection, Richmond, VA: pages 8 (center), 53 (top right), 133 (top left), 206 (bottom right).

TCP/IP
Protocol Suite

McGraw-Hill Forouzan Networking Series

Titles by Behrouz A. Forouzan:

Data Communications and Networking
TCP/IP Protocol Suite
Local Area Networks
Business Data Communications

TCP/IP

Protocol Suite

Third Edition

Behrouz A. Forouzan

with

Sophia Chung Fegan

Boston   Burr Ridge, IL   Dubuque, IA   Madison, WI   New York   San Francisco   St. Louis
Bangkok   Bogotá   Caracas   Kuala Lumpur   Lisbon   London   Madrid   Mexico City
Milan   Montreal   New Delhi   Santiago   Seoul   Singapore   Sydney   Taipei   Toronto

Higher Education

TCP/IP PROTOCOL SUITE, THIRD EDITION

Published by McGraw-Hill, a business unit of The McGraw-Hill Companies, Inc., 1221 Avenue of the Americas, New York, NY 10020. Copyright © 2006, 2003, 2000 by The McGraw-Hill Companies, Inc. All rights reserved. No part of this publication may be reproduced or distributed in any form or by any means, or stored in a database or retrieval system, without the prior written consent of The McGraw-Hill Companies, Inc., including, but not limited to, in any network or other electronic storage or transmission, or broadcast for distance learning.

Some ancillaries, including electronic and print components, may not be available to customers outside the United States.

This book is printed on acid-free paper.

2 3 4 5 6 7 8 9 0 DOC / DOC 0 9 8 7

ISBN: 978-0-07-296772-2
MHID: 0-07-296772-2

Publisher: *Elizabeth A. Jones*
Managing Developmental Editor: *Emily J. Lupash*
Marketing Manager: *Dawn R. Bercier*
Senior Project Manager: *Sheila M. Frank*
Senior Production Supervisor: *Sherry L. Kane*
Media Technology Producer: *Eric A. Weber*
Senior Designer: *David W. Hash*
Cover Designer: *Rokusek Design*
(USE) Cover Image: *©Digital Vision, Autograph Series: Global Interface/Steve Rawlings*
Compositor: *Interactive Composition Corporation*
Typeface: *10/12 Times Roman*
Printer: *R. R. Donnelley Crawfordsville, IN*

Library of Congress Cataloging-in-Publication Data

Forouzan, Behrouz A.
  TCP/IP protocol suite / Behrouz Forouzan. — 3rd ed.
    p. cm.
  Includes bibliographical references and index.
  ISBN 0–07–296772–2 (hardcopy : alk. paper)
    1. TCP/IP (Computer network protocol). I. Title.

TK5105.585.F67 2006
004.6'2—dc22   2004018240
                                         CIP

www.mhhe.com

To the memory of my father,
the source of my inspiration

—Behrouz Forouzan

BRIEF TABLE OF CONTENTS

Chapter 1   *Introduction*   *1*

Chapter 2   *The OSI Model and the TCP/IP Protocol Suite*   *17*

Chapter 3   *Underlying Technologies*   *43*

Chapter 4   *IP Addresses: Classful Addressing*   *81*

Chapter 5   *IP Addresses: Classless Addressing*   *115*

Chapter 6   *Delivery, Forwarding, and Routing of IP Packets*   *131*

Chapter 7   *ARP and RARP*   *159*

Chapter 8   *Internet Protocol (IP)*   *179*

Chapter 9   *Internet Control Message Protocol (ICMP)*   *211*

Chapter 10   *Internet Group Management Protocol (IGMP)*   *237*

Chapter 11   *User Datagram Protocol (UDP)*   *255*

Chapter 12   *Transmission Control Protocol (TCP)*   *275*

Chapter 13   *Stream Control Transmission Protocol (SCTP)*   *345*

Chapter 14   *Unicast Routing Protocols (RIP, OSPF, and BGP)*   *385*

Chapter 15   *Multicasting and Multicast Routing Protocols*   *437*

Chapter 16   *Host Configuration: BOOTP and DHCP*   *457*

Chapter 17   *Domain Name System (DNS)   471*

Chapter 18   *Remote Login: TELNET   499*

Chapter 19   *File Transfer: FTP and TFTP   519*

Chapter 20   *Electronic Mail: SMTP, POP, and IMAP   547*

Chapter 21   *Network Management: SNMP   575*

Chapter 22   *World Wide Web: HTTP   599*

Chapter 23   *IP over ATM   621*

Chapter 24   *Mobile IP   637*

Chapter 25   *Multimedia   651*

Chapter 26   *Private Networks, Virtual Private Networks, and Network Address Translation   679*

Chapter 27   *Next Generation: IPv6 and ICMPv6   689*

Chapter 28   *Network Security   727*

Appendix A   *ASCII Code   771*

Appendix B   *Numbering Systems   776*

Appendix C   *Checksum   783*

Appendix D   *Error Detection   790*

Appendix E   *Project 802   799*

Appendix F   *Contact Addresses   803*

Appendix G   *RFCs   805*

Appendix H   *UDP and TCP Ports   807*

Glossary   809

References   833

Index   835

TABLE OF CONTENTS

Preface   xxix

Chapter 1   Introduction   1

1.1   A BRIEF HISTORY   1
ARPANET   2
Birth of the Internet   2
Transmission Control Protocol/Internetworking Protocol (TCP/IP)   2
MILNET   3
CSNET   3
NSFNET   3
ANSNET   3
The Internet Today   4
Time Line   5
Growth of the Internet   6

1.2   PROTOCOLS AND STANDARDS   6
Protocols   6
Standards   7

1.3   STANDARDS ORGANIZATIONS   7
Standards Creation Committees   7
Forums   8
Regulatory Agencies   9

1.4   INTERNET STANDARDS   9
Maturity Levels   9
Requirement Levels   11

1.5   INTERNET ADMINISTRATION   12
Internet Society (ISOC)   12
Internet Architecture Board (IAB)   12
Internet Engineering Task Force (IETF)   13
Internet Research Task Force (IRTF)   13
Internet Assigned Numbers Authority (IANA) and Internet Corporation
for Assigned Names and Numbers (ICANN)   13
Network Information Center (NIC)   13

1.6   KEY TERMS   14
1.7   SUMMARY   15

1.8   PRACTICE SET   16
Exercises   16
Research Activities   16

Chapter 2   The OSI Model and the TCP/IP Protocol Suite   17

2.1   THE OSI MODEL   17
Layered Architecture   18
Peer-to-Peer Processes   18
Encapsulation   21

2.2   LAYERS IN THE OSI MODEL   21
Physical Layer   21
Data Link Layer   22
Network Layer   23
Transport Layer   24
Session Layer   26
Presentation Layer   27
Application Layer   28
Summary of Layers   29

2.3   TCP/IP PROTOCOL SUITE   30
Physical and Data Link Layers   31
Network Layer   31
Transport Layer   32
Application Layer   32

2.4   ADDRESSING   33
Physical Address   34
Logical Address   35
Port Address   36

2.5   IP VERSIONS   37
Version 4   37
Version 5   37
Version 6   38

2.6   KEY TERMS   38
2.7   SUMMARY   39
2.8   PRACTICE SET   40
Exercises   40
Research Activities   41

Chapter 3   Underlying Technologies   43

3.1   LOCAL AREA NETWORKS (LANS)   44
Wired LANs: Ethernet   44
Wireless LANs: IEEE 802.11   50

3.2   POINT-TO-POINT WANS   55
Physical Layer   55
Data Link Layer   61

3.3   SWITCHED WANS   63
X.25   63
Frame Relay   64
ATM   65

3.4   CONNECTING DEVICES   69
   Repeaters   70
   Hubs   71
   Bridges   71
   Routers   74
3.5   KEY TERMS   76
3.6   SUMMARY   77
3.7   PRACTICE SET   79
   Exercises   79
   Research Activities   79

Chapter 4   **IP Addresses: Classful Addressing   81**

4.1   INTRODUCTION   81
   Address Space   82
   Notation   82
4.2   CLASSFUL ADDRESSING   84
   Recognizing Classes   85
   Netid and Hostid   87
   Classes and Blocks   88
   Network Addresses   91
   Sufficient Information   92
   Mask   92
   CIDR Notation   94
   Address Depletion   95
4.3   OTHER ISSUES   95
   Multihomed Devices   95
   Location, Not Names   95
   Special Addresses   96
   Private Addresses   99
   Unicast, Multicast, and Broadcast Addresses   100
   An Example   101
4.4   SUBNETTING AND SUPERNETTING   102
   Subnetting   102
   Supernetting   107
   Supernet Mask   107
   Obsolescence   108
4.5   KEY TERMS   109
4.6   SUMMARY   109
4.7   PRACTICE SET   110
   Exercises   110
   Research Activities   113

Chapter 5   **IP Addresses: Classless Addressing   115**

5.1   VARIABLE-LENGTH BLOCKS   115
   Restrictions   116
   Finding the Block   118
   Granted Block   121

5.2   SUBNETTING   122
      Finding the Subnet Mask   122
      Finding the Subnet Addresses   123
      Variable-Length Subnets   124
5.3   ADDRESS ALLOCATION   126
5.4   KEY TERMS   127
5.5   SUMMARY   128
5.6   PRACTICE SET   128
      Exercises   128
      Research Activities   130

Chapter 6   **Delivery, Forwarding, and Routing
               of IP Packets   131**

6.1   DELIVERY   131
      Connection Types   131
      Direct Versus Indirect Delivery   132
6.2   FORWARDING   133
      Forwarding Techniques   134
      Forwarding with Classful Addressing   136
      Forwarding with Classless Addressing   141
      Combination   148
6.3   ROUTING   148
      Static Versus Dynamic Routing Tables   148
      Routing Table   149
6.4   STRUCTURE OF A ROUTER   151
      Components   151
6.5   KEY TERMS   154
6.6   SUMMARY   155
6.7   PRACTICE SET   156
      Exercises   156
      Research Activities   157

Chapter 7   **ARP and RARP   159**

7.1   ARP   160
      Packet Format   162
      Encapsulation   163
      Operation   163
      ARP over ATM   166
      Proxy ARP   166
7.2   ARP PACKAGE   166
      Cache Table   167
      Queues   168
      Output Module   168
      Input Module   169
      Cache-Control Module   170
      More Examples   171

7.3   RARP   173
Packet Format   174
Encapsulation   175
RARP Server   175
Alternative Solutions to RARP   175
7.4   KEY TERMS   175
7.5   SUMMARY   176
7.6   PRACTICE SET   176
Exercises   176
Research Activities   177

Chapter 8   Internet Protocol (IP)   179

8.1   DATAGRAM   180
8.2   FRAGMENTATION   186
Maximum Transfer Unit (MTU)   186
Fields Related to Fragmentation   188
8.3   OPTIONS   191
Format   191
Option Types 192
8.4   CHECKSUM   200
Checksum Calculation at the Sender   200
Checksum Calculation at the Receiver   200
Checksum in the IP Packet   201
8.5   IP PACKAGE   203
Header-Adding Module   204
Processing Module   204
Queues   205
Routing Table   205
Forwarding Module   205
MTU Table   205
Fragmentation Module   206
Reassembly Table   206
Reassembly Module   207
8.6   KEY TERMS   208
8.7   SUMMARY   208
8.8   PRACTICE SET   209
Exercises   209
Research Activities   210

Chapter 9   Internet Control Message Protocol (ICMP)   211

9.1   TYPES OF MESSAGES   212
9.2   MESSAGE FORMAT   213
9.3   ERROR REPORTING   213
Destination Unreachable   214
Source Quench   216
Time Exceeded   218

Parameter Problem   219
Redirection   219

9.4   QUERY   221
Echo Request and Reply   221
Timestamp Request and Reply   223
Address-Mask Request and Reply   224
Router Solicitation and Advertisement   225

9.5   CHECKSUM   226
Checksum Calculation   226
Checksum Testing   226

9.6   DEBUGGING TOOLS   227
Ping   227
Traceroute   229

9.7   ICMP PACKAGE   232
Input Module   232
Output Module   233

9.8   KEY TERMS   234
9.9   SUMMARY   234
9.10   PRACTICE SET   235
Exercises   235
Research Activities   236

Chapter 10   **Internet Group Management Protocol (IGMP)**   **237**

10.1   GROUP MANAGEMENT   237
10.2   IGMP MESSAGES   238
Message Format   238
10.3   IGMP OPERATION   239
Joining a Group   240
Leaving a Group   241
Monitoring Membership   241
10.4   ENCAPSULATION   244
IP Layer   244
Data Link Layer   245
Netstat Utility   247
10.5   IGMP PACKAGE   247
Group Table   248
Timers   249
Group-Joining Module   249
Group-Leaving Module   249
Input Module   250
Output Module   251
10.6   KEY TERMS   251
10.7   SUMMARY   251
10.8   PRACTICE SET   252
Exercises   252
Research Activities   254

Chapter 11   **User Datagram Protocol (UDP)**   **255**

11.1   PROCESS-TO-PROCESS COMMUNICATION   256
Port Numbers   256
Socket Addresses   260

11.2   USER DATAGRAM   260

11.3   CHECKSUM   262
Checksum Calculation at Sender   262
Checksum Calculation at Receiver   263
An Example   263
Optional Use of the Checksum   264

11.4   UDP OPERATION   264
Connectionless Services   264
Flow and Error Control   264
Encapsulation and Decapsulation   264
Queuing   265
Multiplexing and Demultiplexing   267

11.5   USE OF UDP   267

11.6   UDP PACKAGE   268
Control-Block Table   268
Input Queues   269
Control-Block Module   269
Input Module   269
Output Module   270
Examples   270

11.7   KEY TERMS   271

11.8   SUMMARY   272

11.9   PRACTICE SET   272
Exercises   272
Research Activities   274

Chapter 12   **Transmission Control Protocol (TCP)**   **275**

12.1   TCP SERVICES   276
Process-to-Process Communication   276
Stream Delivery Service   277
Full-Duplex Communication   278
Connection-Oriented Service   279
Reliable Service   279

12.2   TCP FEATURES   279
Numbering System   280
Flow Control   281
Error Control   281
Congestion Control   281

12.3   SEGMENT   281
Format   282
Encapsulation   284

12.4   A TCP CONNECTION   284
Connection Establishment   285
Data Transfer   287
Connection Termination   289
Connection Reset   291

12.5   STATE TRANSITION DIAGRAM   292
Scenarios   293

12.6   FLOW CONTROL   299
Sliding Window Protocol   300
Silly Window Syndrome   304

12.7   ERROR CONTROL   305
Checksum   305
Acknowledgment   306
Acknowledgment Type   307
Retransmission   307
Out-of-Order Segments   308
Some Scenarios   308

12.8   CONGESTION CONTROL   312
Network Performance   313
Congestion Control Mechanisms   315
Congestion Control in TCP   316

12.9   TCP TIMERS   320
Retransmission Timer   320
Persistence Timer   323
Keepalive Timer   324
TIME-WAIT Timer   325

12.10   OPTIONS   325

12.11   TCP PACKAGE   333
Transmission Control Blocks (TCBs)   333
Timers   334
Main Module   334
Input Processing Module   338
Output Processing Module   338

12.12   KEY TERMS   338
12.13   SUMMARY   339
12.14   PRACTICE SET   341
Exercises   341
Research Activities   343

Chapter 13   Stream Control Transmission Protocol (SCTP)   345

13.1   SCTP SERVICES   346
Process-to-Process Communication   346
Multiple Streams   347
Multihoming   347
Full-Duplex Communication   348
Connection-Oriented Service   348
Reliable Service   349

13.2   SCTP FEATURES   349
Transmission Sequence Number (TSN)   349
Stream Identifier (SI)   349
Stream Sequence Number (SSN)   349
Packets   350
Acknowledgment Number   352
Flow Control   352
Error Control   352
Congestion Control   352

13.3   PACKET FORMAT   353
General Header   353
Chunks   354

13.4   AN SCTP ASSOCIATION   362
Association Establishment   362
Data Transfer   365
Association Termination   368
Association Abortion   368

13.5   STATE TRANSITION DIAGRAM   369
Scenarios   370
Simultaneous Close   372

13.6   FLOW CONTROL   373
Receiver Site   373
Sender Site   374
A Scenario   375

13.7   ERROR CONTROL   376
Receiver Site   376
Sender Site   377
Sending Data Chunks   378
Generating SACK Chunks   379

13.8   CONGESTION CONTROL   380
Congestion Control and Multihoming   380
Explicit Congestion Notification   380

13.9   KEY TERMS   380
13.10   SUMMARY   381
13.11   PRACTICE SET   382
Exercises   382
Research Activities   384

Chapter 14   **Unicast Routing Protocols (RIP, OSPF, and BGP)**   **385**

14.1   INTRA- AND INTERDOMAIN ROUTING   386
14.2   DISTANCE VECTOR ROUTING   387
Initialization   387
Sharing   388
Updating   388
When to Share   389
Two-Node Loop Instability   390
Three-Node Instability   391

14.3   RIP   392
        RIP Message Format   394
        Requests and Responses   394
        Timers in RIP   396
        RIP Version 2   397
        Encapsulation   398
14.4   LINK STATE ROUTING   398
        Building Routing Tables   400
14.5   OSPF   404
        Areas   404
        Metric   404
        Types of Links   405
        Graphical Representation   407
        OSPF Packets   408
        Link State Update Packet   409
        Other Packets   418
        Encapsulation   421
14.6   PATH VECTOR ROUTING   421
        Initialization   422
        Sharing   422
        Updating   422
14.7   BGP   424
        Types of Autonomous Systems   424
        Path Attributes   424
        BGP Sessions   425
        External and Internal BGP   425
        Types of Packets   426
        Packet Format   426
        Encapsulation   430
14.8   KEY TERMS   430
14.9   SUMMARY   431
14.10   PRACTICE SET   432
        Exercises   432
        Research Activities   434

Chapter 15   **Multicasting and Multicast
              Routing Protocols   437**

15.1   UNICAST, MULTICAST, AND BROADCAST   437
        Unicasting   437
        Multicasting   438
        Broadcasting   439
        Multicasting versus Multiple Unicasting   439
15.2   MULTICAST APPLICATIONS   440
        Access to Distributed Databases   440
        Information Dissemination   440
        Dissemination of News   440
        Teleconferencing   441
        Distance Learning   441

15.3   MULTICAST ROUTING   441
    Optimal Routing: Shortest Path Trees   441
    Routing Protocols   444
15.4   MULTICAST LINK STATE ROUTING: MOSPF   444
    Multicast Link State Routing   444
    MOSPF   445
15.5   MULTICAST DISTANCE VECTOR: DVMRP   445
    Multicast Distance Vector Routing   445
    DVMRP   449
15.6   CBT   449
    Formation of the Tree   449
    Sending Multicast Packets   450
    Selecting the Rendezvous Router   450
    Summary   451
15.7   PIM   451
    PIM-DM   452
    PIM-SM   452
15.8   MBONE   452
15.9   KEY TERMS   454
15.10 SUMMARY   454
15.11 PRACTICE SET   455
    Exercises   455
    Research Activities   455

Chapter 16   **Host Configuration: BOOTP and DHCP**   **457**

16.1   BOOTP   457
    Operation   48
    Packet Format   461
16.2   DHCP   463
    Static Address Allocation   463
    Dynamic Address Allocation   464
    Manual and Automatic Configuration   464
    Packet Format   464
    Transition States   465
    Exchanging Messages   467
16.3   KEY TERMS   468
16.4   SUMMARY   468
16.5   PRACTICE SET   468
    Exercises   468
    Research Activities   469

Chapter 17   **Domain Name System (DNS)**   **471**

17.1   NAME SPACE   471
    Flat Name Space   472
    Hierarchical Name Space   472

17.2   DOMAIN NAME SPACE   472
       Label   472
       Domain Name   472
       Domain   474
17.3   DISTRIBUTION OF NAME SPACE   475
       Hierarchy of Name Servers   475
       Zone   475
       Root Server   476
       Primary and Secondary Servers   477
17.4   DNS IN THE INTERNET   477
       Generic Domains   478
       Country Domains   479
       Inverse Domain   480
       Registrar   481
17.5   RESOLUTION   481
       Resolver   481
       Mapping Names to Addresses   481
       Mapping Addresses to Names   481
       Recursive Resolution   481
       Iterative Resolution   482
       Caching   482
17.6   DNS MESSAGES   483
       Header   484
17.7   TYPES OF RECORDS   486
       Question Record   486
       Resource Record   488
17.8   COMPRESSION   489
17.9   DDNS   493
17.10   ENCAPSULATION   493
17.11   KEY TERMS   494
17.12   SUMMARY   495
17.13   PRACTICE SET   496
       Exercises   496
       Research Activities   497

Chapter 18   Remote Login: TELNET   499

18.1   CONCEPT   499
       Time-Sharing Environment   499
       Login   500
18.2   NETWORK VIRTUAL
       TERMINAL (NVT)   501
18.3   NVT CHARACTER SET   502
       Data Characters   502
       Remote Control Characters   502
18.4   EMBEDDING   503
18.5   OPTIONS   504

18.6   OPTION NEGOTIATION   505
       Enabling an Option   505
       Disabling an Option   506
       Symmetry   508
18.7   SUBOPTION NEGOTIATION   508
18.8   CONTROLLING THE SERVER   509
18.9   OUT-OF-BAND SIGNALING   510
18.10 ESCAPE CHARACTER   511
18.11 MODE OF OPERATION   512
       Default Mode   512
       Character Mode   512
       Line Mode   512
18.12 USER INTERFACE   513
18.13 SECURITY ISSUE   515
18.14 KEY TERMS   515
18.15 SUMMARY   515
18.16 PRACTICE SET   516
       Exercises   516
       Research Activities   517

Chapter 19   **File Transfer: FTP and TFTP   519**

19.1   FILE TRANSFER PROTOCOL (FTP)   519
       Connections   520
       Communication   521
       Command Processing   524
       File Transfer   529
       Anonymous FTP   532
19.2   TRIVIAL FILE TRANSFER PROTOCOL (TFTP)   533
       Messages   534
       Connection   536
       Data Transfer   537
       UDP Ports   539
       TFTP Example   540
       TFTP Options   541
       Security   542
       Applications   542
19.3   KEY TERMS   542
19.4   SUMMARY   543
19.5   PRACTICE SET   544
       Exercises   544
       Research Activities   545

Chapter 20   **Electronic Mail: SMTP, POP, and IMAP   547**

20.1   ARCHITECTURE   547
       First Scenario   547
       Second Scenario   548

Third Scenario   549
Fourth Scenario   550

20.2   USER AGENT   551
Services Provided by a User Agent   551
User Agent Types   552
Sending Mail   553
Receiving Mail   554
Addresses   554
Mailing List   555
MIME   555

20.3   MESSAGE TRANSFER AGENT: SMTP   561
Commands and Responses   561
Mail Transfer Phases   566

20.4   MESSAGE ACCESS AGENT: POP AND IMAP   569
POP3   569
IMAP4   570

20.5   WEB-BASED MAIL   571
20.6   KEY TERMS   571
20.7   SUMMARY   571
20.8   PRACTICE SET   571
Exercises   572
Research Activities   573

Chapter 21   Network Management: SNMP   575

21.1   CONCEPT   575
Managers and Agents   576

21.2   MANAGEMENT COMPONENTS   576
Role of SNMP   576
Role of SMI   577
Role of MIB   577
An Analogy   577
An Overview   578

21.3   SMI   579
Name   579
Type   580
Encoding Method   582

21.4   MIB   585
Accessing MIB Variables   585
Lexicographic Ordering   588

21.5   SNMP   589
PDUs   589
Format   591

21.6   MESSAGES   592
21.7   UDP PORTS   595
21.8   SECURITY   595
21.9   KEY TERMS   596
21.10 SUMMARY   596

21.11 PRACTICE SET   597
Exercises   597
Research Activities   597

Chapter 22   **World Wide Web: HTTP   599**

22.1 ARCHITECTURE   599
Client (Browser)   600
Server   600
Uniform Resource Locator (URL)   601
Cookies   601
22.2 WEB DOCUMENTS   602
Static Documents   603
Dynamic Documents   605
Active Documents   608
22.3 HTTP   609
HTTP Transaction   609
Persistent versus Nonpersistent Connection   616
Proxy Server   617
22.4 KEY TERMS   617
22.5 SUMMARY   617
22.6 PRACTICE SET   619
Exercises   619
Research Activities   620

Chapter 23   **IP over ATM   621**

23.1 ATM WANS   621
Layers   621
23.2 CARRYING A DATAGRAM IN CELLS   625
Why Use AAL5?   626
23.3 ROUTING THE CELLS   626
Addresses   627
Address Binding   627
23.4 ATMARP   627
Packet Format   628
ATMARP Operation   629
23.5 LOGICAL IP SUBNET (LIS)   632
23.6 KEY TERMS   633
23.7 SUMMARY   633
23.8 PRACTICE SET   634
Exercises   634
Research Activities   635

Chapter 24   **Mobile IP   637**

24.1 ADDRESSING   637
Stationary Hosts   637
Mobile Hosts   637

24.2   AGENTS   639
Home Agent   639
Foreign Agent   639

24.3   THREE PHASES   640
Agent Discovery   640
Registration   642
Data Transfer   644

24.4   INEFFICIENCY IN MOBILE IP   646
Double Crossing   646
Triangle Routing   646
Solution   647

24.5   KEY TERMS   647
24.6   SUMMARY   648
24.7   PRACTICE SET   648
Exercises   648
Research Activities   649

Chapter 25   **Multimedia**   **651**

25.1   DIGITIZING AUDIO AND VIDEO   652
Digitizing Audio   652
Digitizing Video   652

25.2   AUDIO AND VIDEO COMPRESSION   653
Audio Compression   653
Video Compression   654

25.3   STREAMING STORED AUDIO/VIDEO   659
First Approach: Using a Web Server   659
Second Approach: Using a Web Server with Metafile   659
Third Approach: Using a Media Server   660
Fourth Approach: Using a Media Server and RTSP   660

25.4   STREAMING LIVE AUDIO/VIDEO   662
25.5   REAL-TIME INTERACTIVE AUDIO/VIDEO   662
Characteristics   662

25.6   RTP   667
RTP Packet Format   667
UDP Port   669

25.7   RTCP   669
Sender Report   670
Receiver Report   670
Source Description Message   670
Bye Message   670
Application Specific Message   670
UDP Port   670

25.8   VOICE OVER IP   670
SIP   671
H.323   673

25.9   KEY TERMS   675
25.10 SUMMARY   676
25.11 PRACTICE SET   677
  Exercises   677
  Research Activities   677

Chapter 26   **Private Networks, Virtual Private Networks, and Network Address Translation   679**

26.1   PRIVATE NETWORKS   679
  Intranet   679
  Extranet   679
  Addressing   680
26.2   VIRTUAL PRIVATE NETWORKS (VPN)   680
  Achieving Privacy   680
  VPN Technology   682
26.3   NETWORK ADDRESS TRANSLATION (NAT)   684
  Address Translation   684
  Translation Table   684
  NAT and ISP   687
26.4   KEY TERMS   687
26.5   SUMMARY   687
26.6   PRACTICE SET   688
  Exercises   688
  Research Activities   688

Chapter 27   **Next Generation: IPv6 and ICMPv6   689**

27.1   IPv6   690
  IPv6 Addresses   690
  Address Space Assignment   692
  Packet Format   697
  Comparison between IPv4 and IPv6   709
27.2   ICMPv6   709
  Error Reporting   710
  Query   713
27.3   TRANSITION FROM IPv4 TO IPv6   718
  Dual Stack   718
  Tunneling   719
  Header Translation   720
27.4   KEY TERMS   722
27.5   SUMMARY   722
27.6   PRACTICE SET   723
  Exercises   723
  Research Activities   725

Chapter 28   Network Security   727

28.1   CRYPTOGRAPHY   727
Symmetric-Key Cryptography   728
Public-Key Cryptography   732
Comparison   734

28.2   PRIVACY   735
Privacy with Symmetric-Key Cryptography   735
Privacy with Asymmetric-Key Cryptography   736

28.3   DIGITAL SIGNATURE   736
Signing the Whole Document   737
Signing the Digest   738

28.4   ENTITY AUTHENTICATION   740
Entity Authentication with Symmetric-Key Cryptography   740
Entity Authentication with Public-Key Cryptography   741

28.5   KEY MANAGEMENT   742
Symmetric-Key Distribution   742
Public-Key Certification   749
Kerberos   751

28.6   SECURITY IN THE INTERNET   754
IP Level Security: IPSec   754
Transport Layer Security   758
Application Layer Security: PGP   762

28.7   FIREWALLS   763
Packet-Filter Firewall   763
Proxy Firewall   764

28.8   KEY TERMS   765
28.9   SUMMARY   766
28.10 PRACTICE SET   768
Exercises   768
Research Activities   769

Appendix A   ASCII Code   771

Appendix B   Numbering Systems   776

B.1   BASE 10: DECIMAL   776
Weights   777

B.2   BASE 2: BINARY   777
Weights   777
Binary to Decimal   777
Decimal to Binary   777

B.3   BASE 16: HEXADECIMAL   778
Weights   778
Hexadecimal to Decimal   778
Decimal to Hexadecimal   778

B.4   BASE 256: IP ADDRESSES   779
Weights   779
IP Addresses to Decimal   779
Decimal to IP Addresses   780

B.5   A COMPARISON   780
B.6   OTHER TRANSFORMATIONS   781
From Binary to Hexadecimal   781
From Hexadecimal to Binary   782
From Base 256 to Binary   782
From Binary to Base 256   782

Appendix C   Checksum   783

C.1   TRADITIONAL   784
Calculation in Binary   784
Calculation in Hexadecimal   785
Decimal Calculation   785
C.2   FLETCHER   786
Eight-Bit Fletcher   787
Sixteen-Bit Fletcher   788
C.3   ADLER   788

Appendix D   Error Detection   790

D.1   TYPES OF ERRORS   790
Single-Bit Error   790
Burst Error   791
D.2   DETECTION   792
Redundancy   792
Parity Check   793
Cyclic Redundancy Check (CRC)   794
Checksum   798

Appendix E   Project 802   799

E.1   PROJECT 802.1   800
E.2   PROJECT 802.2   800
LLC   800
MAC   801

Appendix F   Contact Addresses   803

Appendix G   RFCs   805

Appendix H   UDP and TCP Ports   807

Glossary   809

References   833

Index   835

Preface

Technologies related to networks and internetworking may be the fastest growing in our culture today. One of the ramifications of that growth is a dramatic increase in the number of professions where an understanding of these technologies is essential for success—and a proportionate increase in the number and types of students taking courses to learn about them.

This is a book about the TCP/IP protocol suite. It provides information necessary for students who seek a degree in data communications and networking. It is also a reference for professionals who are supporting or preparing to work with networks based on TCP/IP. In short, this book is for anyone who needs to understand the suite.

The book assumes the reader has no prior knowledge of the TCP/IP protocol suite, although a previous course in data communications is desirable.

Organization

This book is divided into five parts. The first part, comprising Chapters 1 to 3, reviews the basic concepts and underlying technologies that, although independent from the TCP/IP protocols, are needed to support them.

The second part of the text discusses the protocols in the network and transport layer. Chapters 4 to 10 emphasize the network layer protocols. Transport layer protocols are fully described in Chapters 11, 12, and 13. Chapters 14 and 15 are devoted to a detailed description of routing protocols.

The third part discusses the traditional application programs that use the network and transport layer protocols. Chapters 16 to 22 discuss these applications.

The fourth part (Chapters 23 to 27) covers issues and topics relatively new to the Internet. We discuss IP over ATM, mobile IP, multimedia, private and virtual private networks, network address translation, and IP next generation.

The fifth part of the book (Chapter 28) is devoted to network security. This chapter first discusses the concepts and issues related to security in general and then shows how they are applied in the Internet.

Features

Several features of this text are designed to make it particularly easy for students to understand TCP/IP.

Visual Approach

The book presents highly technical subject matter without complex formulas by using a balance of text and figures. More than 600 figures accompanying the text provide a visual and intuitive opportunity for understanding the material. Figures are particularly important in explaining networking concepts, which are based on connections and transmission. Often, these are more easily grasped visually rather than verbally.

Highlighted Points

We have repeated important concepts in boxes for quick reference and immediate attention.

Examples and Applications

Whenever appropriate, we have included examples that illustrate the concepts introduced in the text. Also, we have added real-life applications throughout each chapter to motivate students.

Protocol Packages

Although we have not tried to give the detailed code for implementing each protocol, many chapters contain a section that discusses the general idea behind the implementation of each protocol. These sections provide an understanding of the ideas and issues involved in each protocol, but may be considered optional material.

Key Terms

The new terms used in each chapter are listed at the end of the chapter with definitions included in the glossary.

Summary

Each chapter ends with a summary of the material covered by that chapter. The summary is a bulleted overview of all the key points in the chapter.

Practice Set

Each chapter includes a practice set designed to reinforce salient concepts and encourage students to apply them. It consists of two parts: exercises and research activities. Exercises require understanding of the material. Research activities challenge those who want to delve more deeply into the material.

Appendixes

The appendixes are intended to provide a quick reference or review of materials needed to understand the concepts discussed in the book.

Glossary and Acronyms

The book contains an extensive glossary and a list of acronyms.

New to the Third Edition

The following lists the changes in the third edition:

- ❏ Chapter 3 includes more underlying technologies.
- ❏ Chapters 4, 5, and 6 include a more detailed discussion of classless addressing.
- ❏ Chapter 12 was augmented to cover more features of TCP.
- ❏ Chapter 13 is totally new. It discusses SCTP, a new transport layer protocol.
- ❏ Chapters 14 and 15 were revised to make the routing protocols more understandable.
- ❏ FTP and TFTP are now in one chapter. WWW and HTTP are also combined into one chapter.
- ❏ The security chapter is augmented and revised to reflect more issues in security.
- ❏ More hands-on and real-life examples, using utilities such as *ping, grep,* and *netstat* were added to the appropriate chapters.
- ❏ Multiple-choice questions were removed from the practice set. They were revised and are posted online.
- ❏ Research activities to challenge the student were added to the practice set.

How to Use the Book

This book is written for both academic and professional audiences. The book can be used as a self-study guide for interested professionals. As a textbook, it can be used for a one-semester or one-quarter course. The chapters are organized to provide a great deal of flexibility. We suggest the following:

- ❏ Chapters 1 to 3 can be skipped if students have already taken a course in data communications and networking.
- ❏ Chapters 4 through 15 are essential for understanding TCP/IP.
- ❏ Chapters 16 to 22 can be covered in detail in a semester system and briefly in a quarter system.
- ❏ Chapters 23 to 27 can be skipped if there are time constraints.
- ❏ Chapter 28 can be used as a self-paced chapter.

Acknowledgments for the Third Edition

It is obvious that the development of a book of this scope needs the support of many people. We acknowledged the contribution of many people in the preface of the first and second editions. For the third edition, we would like to acknowledge the contributions from peer reviews to the development of the book. These reviewers are:

Paul D. Amer, *University of Delaware*

Edward Chlebus, *Illinois Institute of Technology*

Anthony Chung, *DePaul University*

Isaac Ghansah, *California State University, Sacramento*

Khalen Harfoush, *North Carolina State University*

Doug Jacobson, *Iowa State University*

Tulin Mangir, *California State University, Long Beach*

Xiao Su, *San Jose State University*

Mark Weiser, *Oklahoma State University*

We acknowledge the invaluable contributions of Paul Amer and Randall R. Stewart (designer of SCTP) for providing comments and feedbacks on the manuscript.

Special thanks go to the staff of McGraw-Hill. Betsy Jones, our publisher, proved how a proficient publisher can make the impossible, possible. Emily Lupash, the developmental editor, gave us help whenever we needed it. Sheila Frank, our project manager, guided us through the production process with enormous enthusiasm. We also thank Sherry Kane in production, David Hash in design, and George Watson, the copy editor.

Trademark Notices

Throughout the text we have used several trademarks. Rather than insert a trademark symbol with each mention of the trademarked name, we acknowledge the trademarks here and state that they are used with no intention of infringing upon them. Other product names, trademarks, and registered trademarks are the property of their respective owners.

- ❏ Apple, AppleTalk, EtherTalk, LocalTalk, TokenTalk, and Macintosh are registered trademarks of Apple Computer, Inc.
- ❏ Bell and StarLan are registered trademarks of AT&T.
- ❏ DEC, DECnet, VAX, and DNA are trademarks of Digital Equipment Corp.
- ❏ IBM, SDLC, SNA, and IBM PC are registered trademarks of International Business Machines Corp.
- ❏ Novell, Netware, IPX, and SPX are registered trademarks of Novell, Inc.
- ❏ Network File System and NFS are registered trademarks of Sun Microsystems, Inc.
- ❏ PostScript is a registered trademark of Adobe Systems, Inc.
- ❏ UNIX is a registered trademark of UNIX System Laboratories, Inc., a wholly owned subsidiary of Novell, Inc.
- ❏ Xerox is a trademark, and Ethernet is a registered trademark of Xerox Corp.

CHAPTER 1

Introduction

The Internet has revolutionized many aspects of our daily lives. It has affected the way we do business as well as the way we spend our leisure time. Count the ways you've used the Internet recently. Perhaps you've sent electronic mail (email) to a business associate, paid a utility bill, read a newspaper from a distant city, or looked up a local movie schedule—all by using the Internet. Or, maybe you researched a medical topic, booked a hotel reservation, chatted with a fellow Trekkie, or comparison-shopped for a car. The Internet is a communication system that has brought a wealth of information to our fingertips and organized it for our use.

The Internet is a structured, organized system. Before we discuss how it works and its relationship to TCP/IP, we first give a brief history of the Internet. We then define the concepts of protocols and standards and their relationships to each other. We discuss the various organizations that are involved in the development of Internet standards. These standards are not developed by any specific organization, but rather through a consensus of users. We discuss the mechanism through which these standards originated and matured. Also included in this introductory chapter is a section on Internet administrative groups.

1.1 A BRIEF HISTORY

A **network** is a group of connected, communicating devices such as computers and printers. An internet (note the lowercase *i*) is two or more networks that can communicate with each other. The most notable internet is called the **Internet** (uppercase *I*), composed of hundreds of thousands of interconnected networks. Private individuals as well as various organizations such as government agencies, schools, research facilities, corporations, and libraries in more than 100 countries use the Internet. Millions of people are users. Yet this extraordinary communication system only came into being in 1969.

ARPANET

In the mid-1960s, mainframe computers in research organizations were stand-alone devices. Computers from different manufacturers were unable to communicate with one another. The **Advanced Research Projects Agency (ARPA)** in the Department of Defense (DOD) was interested in finding a way to connect computers together so that the researchers they funded could share their findings, thereby reducing costs and eliminating duplication of effort.

In 1967, at an Association for Computing Machinery (ACM) meeting, ARPA presented its ideas for **ARPANET,** a small network of connected computers. The idea was that each host computer (not necessarily from the same manufacturer) would be attached to a specialized computer, called an *interface message processor* (IMP). The IMPs, in turn, would be connected to each other. Each IMP had to be able to communicate with other IMPs as well as with its own attached host.

By 1969, ARPANET was a reality. Four nodes, at the University of California at Los Angeles (UCLA), the University of California at Santa Barbara (UCSB), Stanford Research Institute (SRI), and the University of Utah, were connected via the IMPs to form a network. Software called the *Network Control Protocol* (NCP) provided communication between the hosts.

Birth of the Internet

In 1972, Vint Cerf and Bob Kahn, both of whom were part of the core ARPANET group, collaborated on what they called the *Internetting Project*. They wanted to link different networks together so that a host on one network could communicate with a host on a second, different network. There were many problems to overcome: diverse packet sizes, diverse interfaces, and diverse transmission rates, as well as differing reliability requirements. Cerf and Kahn devised the idea of a device called a *gateway* to serve as the intermediary hardware to transfer data from one network to another.

Transmission Control Protocol/Internetworking Protocol (TCP/IP)

Cerf and Kahn's landmark 1973 paper outlined the protocols to achieve end-to-end delivery of data. This was a new version of NCP. This paper on transmission control protocol (TCP) included concepts such as encapsulation, the datagram, and the functions of a gateway. A radical idea was the transfer of responsibility for error correction from the IMP to the host machine. This ARPA Internet now became the focus of the communication effort. Around this time responsibility for the ARPANET was handed over to the Defense Communication Agency (DCA).

In October 1977, an internet consisting of three different networks (ARPANET, packet radio, and packet satellite) was successfully demonstrated. Communication between networks was now possible.

Shortly thereafter, authorities made a decision to split TCP into two protocols: **Transmission Control Protocol (TCP)** and **Internetworking Protocol (IP).** IP would handle datagram routing while TCP would be responsible for higher level functions such as segmentation, reassembly, and error detection. The internetworking protocol became known as TCP/IP.

In 1981, under a DARPA contract, UC Berkeley modified the UNIX operating system to include TCP/IP. This inclusion of network software along with a popular operating system did much to further the popularity of networking. The open (non-manufacturer-specific) implementation on Berkeley UNIX gave every manufacturer a working code base on which they could build their products.

In 1983, authorities abolished the original ARPANET protocols, and TCP/IP became the official protocol for the ARPANET. Those who wanted to use the Internet to access a computer on a different network had to be running TCP/IP.

MILNET

In 1983, ARPANET split into two networks: **MILNET** for military users and ARPANET for nonmilitary users.

CSNET

Another milestone in Internet history was the creation of CSNET in 1981. **CSNET** was a network sponsored by the National Science Foundation (NSF). The network was conceived by universities that were ineligible to join ARPANET due to an absence of defense ties to DARPA. CSNET was a less expensive network; there were no redundant links and the transmission rate was slower. It featured connections to ARPANET and Telenet, the first commercial packet data service.

By the middle 1980s, most U.S. universities with computer science departments were part of CSNET. Other institutions and companies were also forming their own networks and using TCP/IP to interconnect. The term *Internet,* originally associated with government-funded connected networks, now referred to the connected networks using TCP/IP protocols.

NSFNET

With the success of CSNET, the NSF, in 1986, sponsored **NSFNET,** a backbone that connected five supercomputer centers located throughout the United States. Community networks were allowed access to this backbone, a T1 line with a 1.544 Mbps data rate, thus providing connectivity throughout the United States.

In 1990, ARPANET was officially retired and replaced by NSFNET. In 1995, NSFNET reverted back to its original concept of a research network.

ANSNET

In 1991, the U.S. government decided that NSFNET was not capable of supporting the rapidly increasing Internet traffic. Three companies, IBM, Merit, and MCI, filled the void by forming a nonprofit organization called Advanced Network and Services (ANS) to build a new, high-speed Internet backbone called **ANSNET.**

The Internet Today

The Internet today is not a simple hierarchical structure. It is made up of many wide and local area networks joined by connecting devices and switching stations. It is difficult to give an accurate representation of the Internet because it is continuously changing—new networks are being added, existing networks need more addresses, and networks of defunct companies need to be removed. Today most end users who want Internet connection use the services of Internet service providers (ISPs). There are international service providers, national service providers, regional service providers, and local service providers. The Internet today is run by private companies, not the government. Figure 1.1 shows a conceptual (not geographical) view of the Internet.

Figure 1.1   *Internet today*

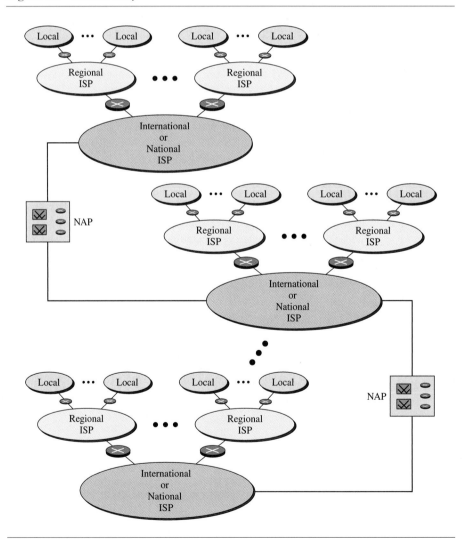

International ISPs

At the top of the hierarchy are the international ISPs that connect nations together.

National ISPs

National ISPs are backbone networks created and maintained by specialized companies. There are many national ISPs operating in North America; some of the most well-known are SprintLink, PSINet, UUNet Technology, AGIS, and internet MCI. To provide connectivity between the end users, these backbone networks are connected by complex switching stations (normally run by a third party) called **network access points (NAPs).** Some national ISP networks are also connected to each other by private switching stations called peering points. National ISPs normally operate at a high data rate (up to 600 Mbps).

Regional ISPs

Regional ISPs are small ISPs that are connected to one or more national ISPs. They are at the third level of hierarchy with a lesser data rate.

Local ISPs

Local ISPs provide direct service to the end users. The local ISPs can be connected to regional ISPs or directly to national ISPs. Most end users are connected to the local ISPs. Note that in this sense, a local ISP can be a company that just provides Internet services, a corporation with a network to supply services to its own employees, or a nonprofit organization, such as a college or a university, that runs its own network. Each of these can be connected to a regional or national service provider.

Time Line

The following is a list of important Internet events in chronological order:

- ❏ **1969.** Four-node ARPANET established.
- ❏ **1970.** ARPA hosts implement NCP.
- ❏ **1973.** Development of TCP/IP suite begins.
- ❏ **1977.** An internet tested using TCP/IP.
- ❏ **1978.** UNIX distributed to academic/research sites.
- ❏ **1981.** CSNET established.
- ❏ **1983.** TCP/IP becomes the official protocol for ARPANET.
- ❏ **1983.** MILNET was born.
- ❏ **1986.** NSFNET established.
- ❏ **1990.** ARPANET decommissioned and replaced by NSFNET.
- ❏ **1995.** NSFNET goes back to being a research network.
- ❏ **1995.** Companies known as **Internet Service Providers (ISPs)** started.

Growth of the Internet

The Internet has grown tremendously. In just a few decades, the number of networks has increased from tens to hundreds of thousands. Concurrently, the number of computers connected to the networks has grown from hundreds to hundreds of millions. The Internet is still growing. Factors that have an impact on this growth include the following:

❑ **New Protocols.** New protocols need to be added and obsolete ones need to be removed. For example, a protocol superior in many respects to IPv4 has been approved as a standard but is not yet fully implemented (see IPv6, Chapter 27).

❑ **New Technology.** New technologies are under development that will increase the capacity of networks and provide more bandwidth to the Internet's users.

❑ **Increasing Use of Multimedia.** It is predicted that the Internet, once just a vehicle to share data, will be used more and more for multimedia (audio and video).

1.2   PROTOCOLS AND STANDARDS

In this section, we define two widely used terms: protocols and standards. First, we define *protocol,* which is synonymous with "rule." Then we discuss *standards,* which are agreed-upon rules.

Protocols

In computer networks, communication occurs between entities in different systems. An entity is anything capable of sending or receiving information. However, two entities cannot simply send bit streams to each other and expect to be understood. For communication to occur, the entities must agree on a protocol. A **protocol** is a set of rules that governs data communication. A protocol defines what is communicated, how it is communicated, and when it is communicated. The key elements of a protocol are syntax, semantics, and timing.

❑ **Syntax.** Syntax refers to the structure or format of the data, meaning the order in which they are presented. For example, a simple protocol might expect the first 8 bits of data to be the address of the sender, the second 8 bits to be the address of the receiver, and the rest of the stream to be the message itself.

❑ **Semantics.** Semantics refers to the meaning of each section of bits. How is a particular pattern to be interpreted, and what action is to be taken based on that interpretation? For example, does an address identify the route to be taken or the final destination of the message?

❑ **Timing.** Timing refers to two characteristics: when data should be sent and how fast it can be sent. For example, if a sender produces data at 100 Megabits per second (Mbps) but the receiver can process data at only 1 Mbps, the transmission will overload the receiver and data will be largely lost.

Standards

Standards are essential in creating and maintaining an open and competitive market for equipment manufacturers and also in guaranteeing national and international interoperability of data and telecommunications technology and processes. They provide guidelines to manufacturers, vendors, government agencies, and other service providers to ensure the kind of interconnectivity necessary in today's marketplace and in international communications.

Data communication standards fall into two categories: *de facto* (meaning "by fact" or "by convention") and *de jure* (meaning "by law" or "by regulation").

❑ **De facto.** Standards that have not been approved by an organized body but have been adopted as standards through widespread use are **de facto standards.** De facto standards are often established originally by manufacturers that seek to define the functionality of a new product or technology.

❑ **De jure. De jure standards** are those that have been legislated by an officially recognized body.

1.3 STANDARDS ORGANIZATIONS

Standards are developed through the cooperation of standards creation committees, forums, and government regulatory agencies.

Standards Creation Committees

While many organizations are dedicated to the establishment of standards, data communications in North America rely primarily on those published by the following:

❑ **International Standards Organization (ISO).** The International Standards Organization (ISO; also referred to as the International Organization for Standardization) is a multinational body whose membership is drawn mainly from the standards creation committees of various governments throughout the world. Created in 1947, the ISO is an entirely voluntary organization dedicated to worldwide agreement on international standards. With a membership that currently includes representative bodies from many industrialized nations, it aims to facilitate the international exchange of goods and services by providing models for compatibility, improved quality, increased productivity, and decreased prices. The ISO is active in developing cooperation in the realms of scientific, technological, and economic activity. Of primary concern to this book are the ISO's efforts in the field of information technology, which have resulted in the creation of the Open Systems Interconnection (OSI) model for network communications. The United States is represented in the ISO by ANSI.

❑ **International Telecommunications Union–Telecommunications Standards Sector (ITU-T).** By the early 1970s, a number of countries were defining national standards for telecommunications, but there was still little international compatibility.

The United Nations responded by forming, as part of its International Telecommunications Union (ITU), a committee, the **Consultative Committee for International Telegraphy and Telephony (CCITT).** This committee was devoted to the research and establishment of standards for telecommunications in general and phone and data systems in particular. On March 1, 1993, the name of this committee was changed to the International Telecommunications Union–Telecommunications Standards Sector (ITU-T).

❏   **American National Standards Institute (ANSI).** Despite its name, the American National Standards Institute (ANSI) is a completely private, nonprofit corporation not affiliated with the U.S. federal government. However, all ANSI activities are undertaken with the welfare of the United States and its citizens occupying primary importance. ANSI's expressed aims include serving as the national coordinating institution for voluntary standardization in the United States, furthering the adoption of standards as a way of advancing the U.S. economy, and ensuring the participation and protection of the public interests. ANSI members include professional societies, industry associations, governmental and regulatory bodies, and consumer groups.

❏   **Institute of Electrical and Electronics Engineers (IEEE).** The Institute of Electrical and Electronics Engineers (IEEE) is the largest professional engineering society in the world. International in scope, it aims to advance theory, creativity, and product quality in the fields of electrical engineering, electronics, and radio as well as in all related branches of engineering. As one of its goals, the IEEE oversees the development and adoption of international standards for computing and communication.

❏   **Electronic Industries Association (EIA).** Aligned with ANSI, the Electronic Industries Association (EIA) is a nonprofit organization devoted to the promotion of electronics manufacturing concerns. Its activities include public awareness education and lobbying efforts in addition to standards development. In the field of information technology, the EIA has made significant contributions by defining physical connection interfaces and electronic signaling specifications for data communications.

Forums

Telecommunications technology development is moving faster than the ability of standards committees to ratify standards. Standards committees are procedural bodies and by nature slow moving. To accommodate the need for working models and agreements and to facilitate the standardization process, many special-interest groups have developed *forums* made up of representatives from interested corporations. The forums work with universities and users to test, evaluate, and standardize new technologies. By concentrating their efforts on a particular technology, the forums are able to speed acceptance and use of those technologies in the telecommunications community. The forums present their conclusions to the standards bodies. Some important forums for the telecommunications industry include the following:

❏   **Frame Relay Forum.** The Frame Relay Forum was formed by Digital Equipment Corporation, Northern Telecom, Cisco, and StrataCom to promote the acceptance and implementation of Frame Relay. Today, it has around 40 members representing North America, Europe, and the Pacific Rim. Issues under review include flow control, encapsulation, translation, and multicasting. The forum's results are submitted to the ISO.

❏ **ATM Forum.** The ATM Forum promotes the acceptance and use of Asynchronous Transfer Mode (ATM) technology. The ATM Forum is made up of Customer Premises Equipment (e.g., PBX systems) vendors and Central Office (e.g., telephone exchange) providers. It is concerned with the standardization of services to ensure interoperability.

Regulatory Agencies

All communications technology is subject to regulation by government agencies such as the Federal Communications Commission in the United States. The purpose of these agencies is to protect the public interest by regulating radio, television, and wire/cable communications.

❏ **Federal Communications Commission (FCC).** The Federal Communications Commission (FCC) has authority over interstate and international commerce as it relates to communications.

The websites for the above organizations are given in Appendix F.

1.4   INTERNET STANDARDS

An **Internet standard** is a thoroughly tested specification that is useful to and adhered to by those who work with the Internet. It is a formalized regulation that must be followed. There is a strict procedure by which a specification attains Internet standard status. A specification begins as an Internet draft. An **Internet draft** is a working document (a work in progress) with no official status and a six-month lifetime. Upon recommendation from the Internet authorities, a draft may be published as a **Request for Comment (RFC).** Each RFC is edited, assigned a number, and made available to all interested parties.

RFCs go through maturity levels and are categorized according to their requirement level.

Maturity Levels

An RFC, during its lifetime, falls into one of six **maturity levels:** proposed standard, draft standard, Internet standard, historic, experimental, and informational (see Figure 1.2).

Proposed Standard

A proposed standard is a specification that is stable, well understood, and of sufficient interest to the Internet community. At this level, the specification is usually tested and implemented by several different groups.

Figure 1.2   *Maturity levels of an RFC*

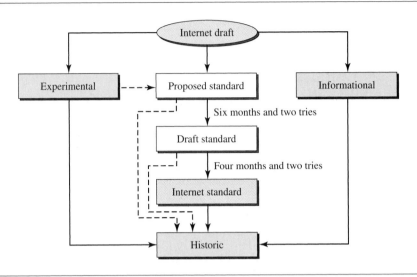

Draft Standard

A proposed standard is elevated to draft standard status after at least two successful independent and interoperable implementations. Barring difficulties, a draft standard, with modifications if specific problems are encountered, normally becomes an Internet standard.

Internet Standard

A draft standard reaches Internet standard status after demonstrations of successful implementation.

Historic

The historic RFCs are significant from a historical perspective. They either have been superseded by later specifications or have never passed the necessary maturity levels to become an Internet standard.

Experimental

An RFC classified as experimental describes work related to an experimental situation that does not affect the operation of the Internet. Such an RFC should not be implemented in any functional Internet service.

Informational

An RFC classified as informational contains general, historical, or tutorial information related to the Internet. It is usually written by someone in a non-Internet organization, such as a vendor.

Requirement Levels

RFCs are classified into five **requirement levels:** required, recommended, elective, limited use, and not recommended (see Figure 1.3).

Figure 1.3   *Requirement levels of an RFC*

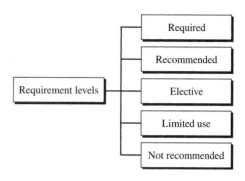

Required

An RFC is labeled *required* if it must be implemented by all Internet systems to achieve minimum conformance. For example, IP (Chapter 8) and ICMP (Chapter 9) are required protocols.

Recommended

An RFC labeled *recommended* is not required for minimum conformance; it is recommended because of its usefulness. For example, FTP (Chapter 19) and TELNET (Chapter 18) are recommended protocols.

Elective

An RFC labeled *elective* is not required and not recommended. However, a system can use it for its own benefit.

Limited Use

An RFC labeled *limited use* should be used only in limited situations. Most of the experimental RFCs fall under this category.

Not Recommended

An RFC labeled *not recommended* is inappropriate for general use. Normally a historic (obsolete) RFC may fall under this category.

RFCs can be found at www.faqs.org/rfcs

1.5   INTERNET ADMINISTRATION

The Internet, with its roots primarily in the research domain, has evolved and gained a broader user base with significant commercial activity. Various groups that coordinate Internet issues have guided this growth and development. Appendix F gives the addresses, email addresses, and telephone numbers for some of these groups. Figure 1.4 shows the general organization of Internet administration.

Figure 1.4   *Internet administration*

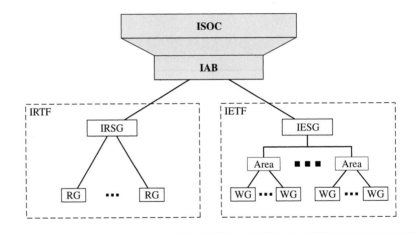

Internet Society (ISOC)

The **Internet Society (ISOC)** is an international, nonprofit organization formed in 1992 to provide support for the Internet standards process. ISOC accomplishes this through maintaining and supporting other Internet administrative bodies such as IAB, IETF, IRTF, and IANA (see the following sections). ISOC also promotes research and other scholarly activities relating to the Internet.

Internet Architecture Board (IAB)

The **Internet Architecture Board (IAB)** is the technical advisor to the ISOC. The main purposes of the IAB are to oversee the continuing development of the TCP/IP Protocol Suite and to serve in a technical advisory capacity to research members of the Internet community. IAB accomplishes this through its two primary components, the Internet Engineering Task Force (IETF) and the Internet Research Task Force (IRTF).

Another responsibility of the IAB is the editorial management of the RFCs, described earlier in this chapter. IAB is also the external liaison between the Internet and other standards organizations and forums.

Internet Engineering Task Force (IETF)

The **Internet Engineering Task Force (IETF)** is a forum of working groups managed by the Internet Engineering Steering Group (IESG). IETF is responsible for identifying operational problems and proposing solutions to these problems. IETF also develops and reviews specifications intended as Internet standards. The working groups are collected into areas, and each area concentrates on a specific topic. Currently nine areas have been defined, although this is by no means a hard and fast number. The areas are:

❑ Applications
❑ Internet protocols
❑ Routing
❑ Operations
❑ User services
❑ Network management
❑ Transport
❑ Internet protocol next generation (IPng)
❑ Security

Internet Research Task Force (IRTF)

The **Internet Research Task Force (IRTF)** is a forum of working groups managed by the Internet Research Steering Group (IRSG). IRTF focuses on long-term research topics related to Internet protocols, applications, architecture, and technology.

Internet Assigned Numbers Authority (IANA) and Internet Corporation for Assigned Names and Numbers (ICANN)

The **Internet Assigned Numbers Authority (IANA),** supported by the U.S. government, was responsible for the management of Internet domain names and addresses until October 1998. At that time the **Internet Corporation for Assigned Names and Numbers (ICANN),** a private nonprofit corporation managed by an international board, assumed IANA operations.

Network Information Center (NIC)

The **Network Information Center (NIC)** is responsible for collecting and distributing information about TCP/IP protocols.

The websites for Internet organizations can be found in Appendix F.

1.6   KEY TERMS

Advanced Research Projects
Agency (ARPA)

American National Standards
Institute (ANSI)

ANSNET

ARPANET

ATM Forum

Consultative Committee for
International Telegraphy and
Telephony (CCITT)

CSNET

de facto standards

de jure standards

Electronic Industries
Association (EIA)

Federal Communications
Commission (FCC)

Frame Relay Forum

Institute of Electrical and Electronics
Engineers (IEEE)

International Standards Organization
(ISO)

International Telecommunications
Union–Telecommunications
Standards Sector (ITU-T)

Internet

Internet Architecture Board (IAB)

Internet Assigned Numbers Authority
(IANA)

Internet Corporation for Assigned
Names and Numbers (ICANN)

Internet draft

Internet Engineering Task Force (IETF)

Internet Research Task Force (IRTF)

Internet Service Provider (ISP)

Internet Society (ISOC)

Internet standard

local Internet service providers

maturity levels

MILNET

network

network access points (NAPs)

Network Information Center (NIC)

NSFNET

protocol

Request for Comment (RFC)

requirement levels

semantics

syntax

timing

Transmission Control Protocol/
Internetworking Protocol (TCP/IP)

1.7   SUMMARY

- ❑   The Internet is a collection of hundreds of thousands of separate networks.
- ❑   ARPANET began as a network with four nodes.
- ❑   TCP/IP is the protocol suite for the Internet.
- ❑   CSNET provided communication between networks ineligible to join ARPANET.

❏ NSFNET provided communication between networks throughout the United States.

❏ Local ISPs connect individual users to the Internet.

❏ Regional ISPs connect local ISPs.

❏ National ISPs are backbone networks created and maintained by specialized companies.

❏ A protocol is a set of rules that governs data communication; the key elements of a protocol are syntax, semantics, and timing.

❏ Standards are necessary to ensure that products from different manufacturers can work together as expected.

❏ The ISO, ITU-T, ANSI, IEEE, and EIA are some of the organizations involved in standards creation.

❏ Forums are special-interest groups that quickly evaluate and standardize new technologies. Two important forums are the Frame Relay Forum and the ATM Forum.

❏ The FCC is a regulatory agency that regulates radio, television, and wire/cable communications.

❏ A Request for Comment (RFC) is an idea or concept that is a precursor to an Internet Standard.

❏ An RFC goes through the proposed standard level, then the draft standard level before it becomes an Internet standard.

❏ An RFC is categorized as required, recommended, elective, limited use, or not recommended.

❏ The Internet Society (ISOC) promotes research and other scholarly activities relating to the Internet.

❏ The Internet Architecture Board (IAB) is the technical advisor to the ISOC.

❏ The Internet Engineering Task Force (IETF) is a forum of working groups responsible for identifying operational problems and proposing solutions to these problems.

❏ The Internet Research Task Force (IRTF) is a forum of working groups focusing on long-term research topics related to Internet protocols, applications, architecture, and technology.

❏ The Internet Corporation for Assigned Names and Numbers (ICANN), formerly known as IANA, is responsible for the management of Internet domain names and addresses.

❏ The Network Information Center (NIC) is responsible for collecting and distributing information about TCP/IP protocols.

1.8   PRACTICE SET

Exercises

1. Use the Internet to find the number of RFCs.
2. Use the Internet to find the subject matter of RFCs 2418 and 1603.

3. Use the Internet to find the RFC that discusses the IRTF working group guidelines and procedures.
4. Use the Internet to find two examples of an historic RFC.
5. Use the Internet to find two examples of an experimental RFC.
6. Use the Internet to find two examples of an informational RFC.
7. Use the Internet to find the RFC that discusses the FTP application.
8. Use the Internet to find the RFC for the Internet Protocol (IP).
9. Use the Internet to find the RFC for the Transmission Control Protocol (TCP).
10. Use the Internet to find the RFC that details the Internet standards process.

Research Activities

11. Research and find three standards developed by ITU-T.
12. Research and find three standards developed by ANSI.
13. EIA has developed some standards for interfaces. Research and find two of these standards. What is EIA 232?
14. Research and find three regulations devised by FCC concerning AM and FM transmission.

CHAPTER 2

The OSI Model and the TCP/IP Protocol Suite

The layered model that dominated data communication and networking literature before 1990 was the **Open Systems Interconnection (OSI) model.** Everyone believed that the OSI model would become the ultimate standard for data communications—but this did not happen. The TCP/IP protocol suite became the dominant commercial architecture because it was used and tested extensively in the Internet; the OSI model was never fully implemented.

In this chapter, we first briefly discuss the OSI model and then we concentrate on TCP/IP as a protocol suite.

2.1 THE OSI MODEL

Established in 1947, the **International Standards Organization (ISO)** is a multinational body dedicated to worldwide agreement on international standards. An ISO standard that covers all aspects of network communications is the Open Systems Interconnection (OSI) model. It was first introduced in the late 1970s. An **open system** is a set of protocols that allows any two different systems to communicate regardless of their underlying architecture. The purpose of the OSI model is to show how to facilitate communication between different systems without requiring changes to the logic of the underlying hardware and software. The OSI model is not a protocol; it is a model for understanding and designing a network architecture that is flexible, robust, and interoperable.

> **ISO is the organization. OSI is the model.**

The OSI model is a layered framework for the design of network systems that allows communication between all types of computer systems. It consists of seven separate but related layers, each of which defines a part of the process of moving information across a network (see Figure 2.1). Understanding the fundamentals of the OSI model provides a solid basis for exploring data communications.

Figure 2.1   *The OSI model*

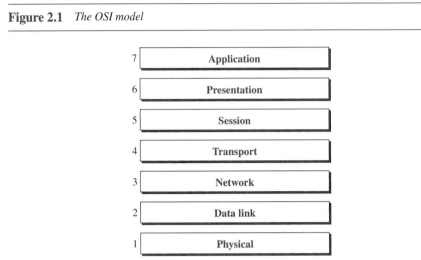

Layered Architecture

The OSI model is composed of seven ordered layers: physical (layer 1), data link (layer 2), network (layer 3), transport (layer 4), session (layer 5), presentation (layer 6), and application (layer 7). Figure 2.2 shows the layers involved when a message is sent from device A to device B. As the message travels from A to B, it may pass through many intermediate nodes. These intermediate nodes usually involve only the first three layers of the OSI model.

In developing the model, the designers distilled the process of transmitting data to its most fundamental elements. They identified which networking functions had related uses and collected those functions into discrete groups that became the layers. Each layer defines a family of functions distinct from those of the other layers. By defining and localizing functionality in this fashion, the designers created an architecture that is both comprehensive and flexible. Most important, the OSI model allows complete interoperability between otherwise incompatible systems.

Within a single machine, each layer calls upon the services of the layer just below it. Layer 3, for example, uses the services provided by layer 2 and provides services for layer 4. Between machines, layer *x* on one machine communicates with layer *x* on another machine. This communication is governed by an agreed-upon series of rules and conventions called protocols. The processes on each machine that communicate at a given layer are called **peer-to-peer processes.** Communication between machines is therefore a peer-to-peer process using the protocols appropriate to a given layer.

Peer-to-Peer Processes

At the physical layer, communication is direct: In Figure 2.2, device A sends a stream of bits to device B (through intermediate nodes). At the higher layers, however, communication must move down through the layers on device A, over to device B, and then

Figure 2.2 *OSI layers*

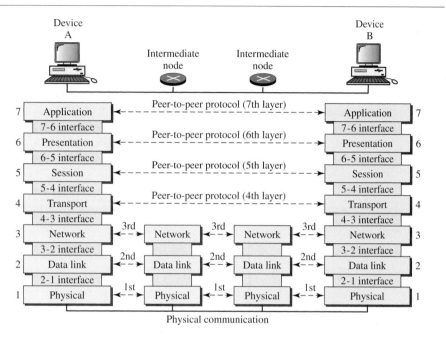

back up through the layers. Each layer in the sending device adds its own information to the message it receives from the layer just above it and passes the whole package to the layer just below it.

At layer 1 the entire package is converted to a form that can be transferred to the receiving device. At the receiving machine, the message is unwrapped layer by layer, with each process receiving and removing the data meant for it. For example, layer 2 removes the data meant for it, then passes the rest to layer 3. Layer 3 then removes the data meant for it and passes the rest to layer 4, and so on.

Interfaces between Layers

The passing of the data and network information down through the layers of the sending device and back up through the layers of the receiving device is made possible by an **interface** between each pair of adjacent layers. Each interface defines what information and services a layer must provide for the layer above it. Well-defined interfaces and layer functions provide modularity to a network. As long as a layer provides the expected services to the layer above it, the specific implementation of its functions can be modified or replaced without requiring changes to the surrounding layers.

Organization of the Layers

The seven layers can be thought of as belonging to three subgroups. Layers 1, 2, and 3—physical, data link, and network—are the network support layers; they deal with the physical aspects of moving data from one device to another (such as electrical specifications, physical connections, physical addressing, and transport timing and reliability). Layers 5, 6, and 7—session, presentation, and application—can be thought of as the user support layers; they allow interoperability among unrelated software systems. Layer 4, the transport layer, links the two subgroups and ensures that what the lower layers have transmitted is in a form that the upper layers can use. The upper OSI layers are almost always implemented in software; lower layers are a combination of hardware and software, except for the physical layer, which is mostly hardware.

In Figure 2.3, which gives an overall view of the OSI layers, D7 data means the data unit at layer 7, D6 data means the data unit at layer 6, and so on. The process starts at layer 7 (the application layer), then moves from layer to layer in descending, sequential order. At each layer, a header can be added to the data unit. At layer 2, a trailer may also be added. When the formatted data unit passes through the physical layer (layer 1), it is changed into an electromagnetic signal and transported along a physical link.

Figure 2.3 *An exchange using the OSI model*

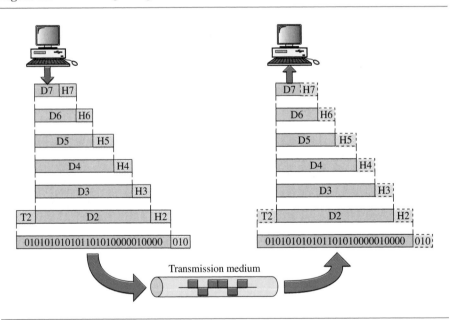

Upon reaching its destination, the signal passes into layer 1 and is transformed back into digital form. The data units then move back up through the OSI layers. As each block of data reaches the next higher layer, the headers and trailers attached to it at the corresponding sending layer are removed, and actions appropriate to that layer are taken. By the time it reaches layer 7, the message is again in a form appropriate to the application and is made available to the recipient.

Encapsulation

Figure 2.3 reveals another aspect of data communications in the OSI model: encapsulation. A packet at level 7 is encapsulated in the packet at level 6. The whole packet at level 6 is encapsulated in a packet at level 5, and so on.

In other words, the data part of a packet at level N is carrying the whole packet (data and overhead) from level $N - 1$. The concept is called encapsulation because level N is not aware what part of the encapsulated packet is data and what part is the header or trailer. For level N, the whole packet coming from level $N - 1$ is treated as one integral unit.

2.2   LAYERS IN THE OSI MODEL

In this section we briefly describe the functions of each layer in the OSI model.

Physical Layer

The **physical layer** coordinates the functions required to carry a bit stream over a physical medium. It deals with the mechanical and electrical specifications of the interface and transmission media. It also defines the procedures and functions that physical devices and interfaces have to perform for transmission to occur. Figure 2.4 shows the position of the physical layer with respect to the transmission media and the data link layer.

Figure 2.4   *Physical layer*

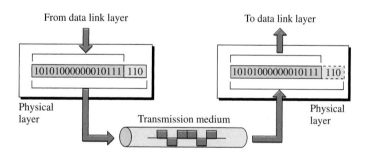

**The physical layer is responsible for movements of individual bits
from one hop (node) to the next.**

The physical layer is also concerned with the following:

❑ **Physical characteristics of interfaces and media.** The physical layer defines the characteristics of the interface between the devices and the transmission media. It also defines the type of transmission media (see Chapter 3).

❑ **Representation of bits.** The physical layer data consists of a stream of **bits** (sequence of 0s or 1s) with no interpretation. To be transmitted, bits must be encoded into signals—electrical or optical. The physical layer defines the type of **encoding** (how 0s and 1s are changed to signals).

❏ **Data rate.** The **transmission rate**—the number of bits sent each second—is also defined by the physical layer. In other words, the physical layer defines the duration of a bit, which is how long it lasts.

❏ **Synchronization of bits.** The sender and receiver must not only use the same bit rate but must also be synchronized at the bit level. In other words, the sender and the receiver clocks must be synchronized.

❏ **Line configuration.** The physical layer is concerned with the connection of devices to the media. In a **point-to-point configuration,** two devices are connected together through a dedicated link. In a **multipoint configuration,** a link is shared between several devices.

❏ **Physical topology.** The physical topology defines how devices are connected to make a network. Devices can be connected using a **mesh topology** (every device connected to every other device), a **star topology** (devices are connected through a central device), a **ring topology** (each device is connected to the next, forming a ring), or a **bus topology** (every device on a common link).

❏ **Transmission mode.** The physical layer also defines the direction of transmission between two devices: simplex, half-duplex, or full-duplex. In the **simplex mode,** only one device can send; the other can only receive. The simplex mode is a one-way communication. In the **half-duplex mode,** two devices can send and receive, but not at the same time. In a **full-duplex** (or simply duplex) **mode,** two devices can send and receive at the same time.

Data Link Layer

The **data link layer** transforms the physical layer, a raw transmission facility, to a reliable link. It makes the physical layer appear error free to the upper layer (network layer). Figure 2.5 shows the relationship of the data link layer to the network and physical layers.

Figure 2.5   *Data link layer*

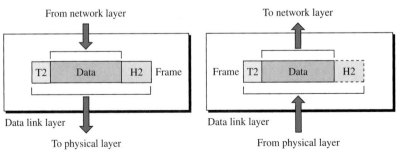

The data link layer is responsible for moving frames from one hop (node) to the next.

Other responsibilities of the data link layer include the following:

❑ **Framing.** The data link layer divides the stream of bits received from the network layer into manageable data units called **frames.**

❑ **Physical addressing.** If frames are to be distributed to different systems on the network, the data link layer adds a header to the frame to define the sender and/or receiver of the frame. If the frame is intended for a system outside the sender's network, the receiver address is the address of the connecting device that connects the network to the next one.

❑ **Flow control.** If the rate in which the data is absorbed by the receiver is less than the rate produced in the sender, the data link layer imposes a flow control mechanism to prevent overwhelming the receiver.

❑ **Error control.** The data link layer adds reliability to the physical layer by adding mechanisms to detect and retransmit damaged or lost frames. It also uses a mechanism to recognize duplicate frames. Error control is normally achieved through a trailer added to the end of the frame.

❑ **Access control.** When two or more devices are connected to the same link, data link layer protocols are necessary to determine which device has control over the link at any given time.

Figure 2.6 illustrates hop-to-hop (node-to-node) delivery by the data link layer.

Figure 2.6   *Hop-to-hop delivery*

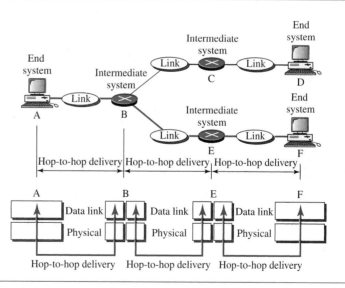

Network Layer

The **network layer** is responsible for the source-to-destination delivery of a packet, possibly across multiple networks (links). Whereas the data link layer oversees the delivery of the packet between two systems on the same network (links), the network layer ensures that each packet gets from its point of origin to its final destination.

If two systems are connected to the same link, there is usually no need for a network layer. However, if the two systems are attached to different networks (links) with connecting devices between the networks (links), there is often a need for the network layer to accomplish source-to-destination delivery. Figure 2.7 shows the relationship of the network layer to the data link and transport layers.

Figure 2.7 *Network layer*

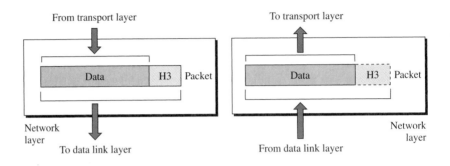

The network layer is responsible for the delivery of individual
packets from the source host to the destination host.

Other responsibilities of the network layer include the following:

❑ **Logical addressing.** The physical addressing implemented by the data link layer handles the addressing problem locally. If a packet passes the network boundary, we need another addressing system to help distinguish the source and destination systems. The network layer adds a header to the packet coming from the upper layer that, among other things, includes the logical addresses of the sender and receiver. We discuss logical addresses later in this chapter.

❑ **Routing.** When independent networks or links are connected together to create **internetworks** (network of networks) or a large network, the connecting devices (called *routers* or *switches*) route or switch the packets to their final destination. One of the functions of the network layer is to provide this mechanism.

Figure 2.8 illustrates end-to-end delivery by the network layer.

Transport Layer

The **transport layer** is responsible for **process-to-process delivery** of the entire message. A process is an application program running on the host. Whereas the network layer oversees **source-to-destination delivery** of individual packets, it does not recognize any relationship between those packets. It treats each one independently, as though each piece belonged to a separate message, whether or not it does. The transport layer, on the other hand, ensures that the whole message arrives intact and in order, overseeing both error control and flow control at the source-to-destination level. Figure 2.9 shows the relationship of the transport layer to the network and session layers.

Figure 2.8   *Source-to-destination delivery*

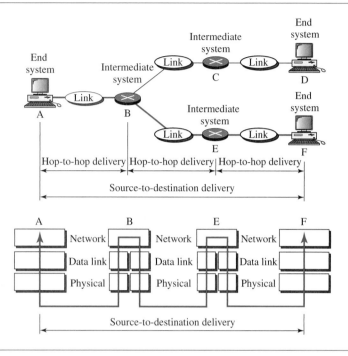

Figure 2.9   *Transport layer*

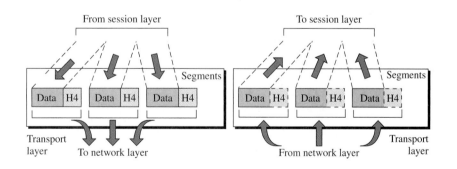

The transport layer is responsible for the delivery of a message from one process to another.

Other responsibilities of the transport layer include the following:

❏ **Service-point addressing.** Computers often run several programs at the same time. For this reason, source-to-destination delivery means delivery not only from one computer to the next but also from a specific process (running program) on one computer to a specific process (running program) on the other. The transport layer header must therefore include a type of address called a *service-point address* (or port address). The network layer gets each packet to the correct computer; the transport layer gets the entire message to the correct process on that computer.

❑ **Segmentation and reassembly.** A message is divided into transmittable segments, with each segment containing a sequence number. These numbers enable the transport layer to reassemble the message correctly upon arriving at the destination and to identify and replace packets that were lost in transmission.

❑ **Connection control.** The transport layer can be either connectionless or connection-oriented. A connectionless transport layer treats each segment as an independent packet and delivers it to the transport layer at the destination machine. A connection-oriented transport layer makes a connection with the transport layer at the destination machine first before delivering the packets. After all the data is transferred, the connection is terminated.

❑ **Flow control.** Like the data link layer, the transport layer is responsible for flow control. However, flow control at this layer is performed end to end rather than across a single link.

❑ **Error control.** Like the data link layer, the transport layer is responsible for error control. However, error control at this layer is performed process-to-process rather than across a single link. The sending transport layer makes sure that the entire message arrives at the receiving transport layer without *error* (damage, loss, or duplication). Error correction is usually achieved through retransmission.

Figure 2.10 illustrates process-to-process delivery by the transport layer.

Figure 2.10 *Reliable process-to-process delivery of a message*

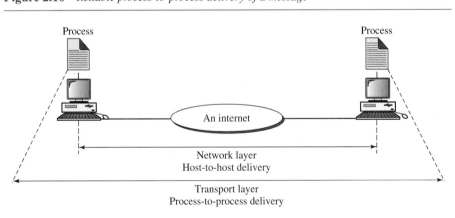

Session Layer

The services provided by the first three layers (physical, data link, and network) are not sufficient for some processes. The **session layer** is the network *dialog controller*. It establishes, maintains, and synchronizes the interaction between communicating systems.

Specific responsibilities of the session layer include the following:

❏ **Dialog control.** The session layer allows two systems to enter into a dialog. It allows the communication between two processes to take place either in half-duplex (one way at a time) or full-duplex (two ways at a time) mode.

❏ **Synchronization.** The session layer allows a process to add checkpoints (**synchronization points**) into a stream of data. For example, if a system is sending a file of 2,000 pages, it is advisable to insert checkpoints after every 100 pages to ensure that each 100-page unit is received and acknowledged independently. In this case, if a crash happens during the transmission of page 523, the only pages that need to be resent after system recovery are pages 501 to 523. Pages previous to 501 need not be resent. Figure 2.11 illustrates the relationship of the session layer to the transport and presentation layers.

> **The session layer is responsible for dialog control and synchronization.**

Figure 2.11   *Session layer*

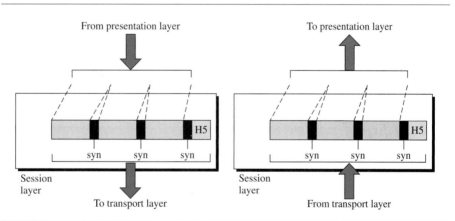

Presentation Layer

The **presentation layer** is concerned with the syntax and semantics of the information exchanged between two systems. Figure 2.12 shows the relationship between the presentation layer and the application and session layers.

Specific responsibilities of the presentation layer include the following:

❏ **Translation.** The processes (running programs) in two systems are usually exchanging information in the form of character strings, numbers, and so on. The information should be changed to bit streams before being transmitted. Because different computers use different encoding systems, the presentation layer is responsible for interoperability between these different encoding methods. The presentation layer at the sender changes the information from its sender-dependent format into a common format. The presentation layer at the receiving machine changes the common format into its receiver-dependent format.

Figure 2.12   *Presentation layer*

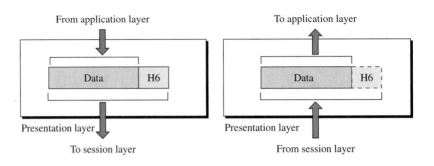

❏ **Encryption.** To carry sensitive information a system must be able to assure privacy. Encryption means that the sender transforms the original information to another form and sends the resulting message out over the network. Decryption reverses the original process to transform the message back to its original form.

❏ **Compression.** Data compression reduces the number of bits contained in the information. Data compression becomes particularly important in the transmission of multimedia such as text, audio, and video.

> **The presentation layer is responsible for translation, compression, and encryption.**

Application Layer

The **application layer** enables the user, whether human or software, to access the network. It provides user interfaces and support for services such as electronic mail, remote file access and transfer, shared database management, and other types of distributed information services.

Figure 2.13 shows the relationship of the application layer to the user and the presentation layer. Of the many application services available, the figure shows only three: X.400 (message-handling services), X.500 (directory services), and file transfer, access, and management (FTAM). The user in this example uses X.400 to send an email message.

Specific services provided by the application layer include the following:

❏ **Network virtual terminal.** A network virtual terminal is a software version of a physical terminal and allows a user to log on to a remote host. To do so, the application creates a software emulation of a terminal at the remote host. The user's computer talks to the software terminal, which, in turn, talks to the host, and vice versa. The remote host believes it is communicating with one of its own terminals and allows you to log on.

❏ **File transfer, access, and management (FTAM).** This application allows a user to access files in a remote host (to make changes or read data), to retrieve files from a remote computer for use in the local computer, and to manage or control files in a remote computer locally.

Figure 2.13   *Application layer*

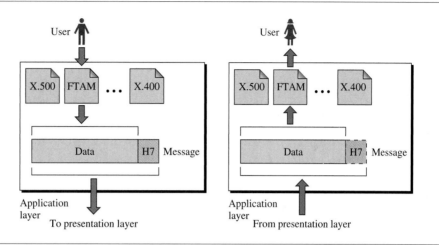

- ❏ **Mail services.** This application provides the basis for email forwarding and storage.
- ❏ **Directory services.** This application provides distributed database sources and access for global information about various objects and services.

The application layer is responsible for providing services to the user.

Summary of Layers

Figure 2.14 shows a summary of duties for each layer.

Figure 2.14   *Summary of layers*

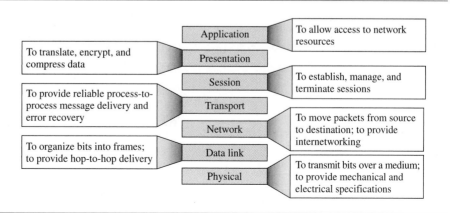

2.3 TCP/IP PROTOCOL SUITE

The **TCP/IP protocol suite** was developed prior to the OSI model. Therefore, the layers in the TCP/IP protocol suite do not match exactly with those in the OSI model. The TCP/IP protocol suite is made of five layers: physical, data link, network, transport, and application. The first four layers provide physical standards, network interface, internetworking, and transport functions that correspond to the first four layers of the OSI model. The three topmost layers in the OSI model, however, are represented in TCP/IP by a single layer called the *application layer* (see Figure 2.15).

Figure 2.15 *TCP/IP and OSI model*

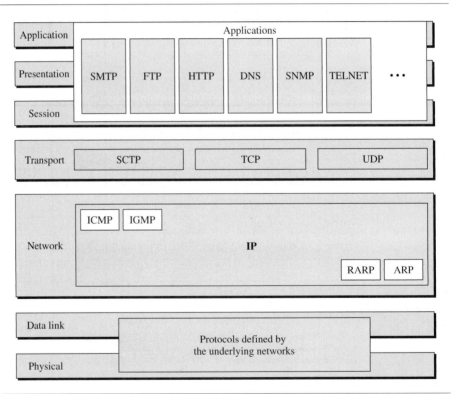

TCP/IP is a hierarchical protocol made up of interactive modules, each of which provides a specific functionality, but the modules are not necessarily interdependent. Whereas the OSI model specifies which functions belong to each of its layers, the layers of the TCP/IP protocol suite contain relatively independent protocols that can be mixed and matched depending on the needs of the system. The term *hierarchical* means that each upper level protocol is supported by one or more lower level protocols.

At the transport layer, TCP/IP defines three protocols: Transmission Control Protocol (TCP), User Datagram Protocol (UDP), and Stream Control Transmission

Protocol (SCTP). At the network layer, the main protocol defined by TCP/IP is the Internetworking Protocol (IP), although there are some other protocols that support data movement in this layer.

Physical and Data Link Layers

At the physical and data link layers, TCP/IP does not define any specific protocol. It supports all of the standard and proprietary protocols. A network in a TCP/IP internetwork can be a local area network (LAN) or a wide area network (WAN).

Network Layer

At the network layer (or, more accurately, the internetwork layer), TCP/IP supports the Internetworking Protocol (IP). IP, in turn, uses four supporting protocols: ARP, RARP, ICMP, and IGMP. Each of these protocols is described in more detail in later chapters.

Internetworking Protocol (IP)

The **Internetworking Protocol (IP)** is the transmission mechanism used by the TCP/IP protocols. It is an unreliable and connectionless protocol—a **best-effort delivery** service. The term *best-effort* means that IP provides no error checking or tracking. IP assumes the unreliability of the underlying layers and does its best to get a transmission through to its destination, but with no guarantees.

IP transports data in packets called *datagrams,* each of which is transported separately. Datagrams can travel along different routes and can arrive out of sequence or be duplicated. IP does not keep track of the routes and has no facility for reordering datagrams once they arrive at their destination.

The limited functionality of IP should not be considered a weakness, however. IP provides bare-bones transmission functions that free the user to add only those facilities necessary for a given application and thereby allows for maximum efficiency. IP will be discussed in Chapter 8.

Address Resolution Protocol (ARP)

The **Address Resolution Protocol (ARP)** is used to associate an IP address with the physical address. On a typical physical network, such as a LAN, each device on a link is identified by a physical or station address usually imprinted on the network interface card (NIC). ARP is used to find the physical address of the node when its Internet address is known. ARP will be discussed in Chapter 7.

Reverse Address Resolution Protocol (RARP)

The **Reverse Address Resolution Protocol (RARP)** allows a host to discover its Internet address when it knows only its physical address. It is used when a computer is connected to the network for the first time or when a diskless computer is booted. We will discuss RARP in Chapter 7.

Internet Control Message Protocol (ICMP)

The **Internet Control Message Protocol (ICMP)** is a mechanism used by hosts and gateways to send notification of datagram problems back to the sender. ICMP sends query and error reporting messages. We will thoroughly discuss ICMP in Chapter 9.

Internet Group Message Protocol (IGMP)

The **Internet Group Message Protocol (IGMP)** is used to facilitate the simultaneous transmission of a message to a group of recipients. We will thoroughly discuss IGMP in Chapter 10.

Transport Layer

Traditionally the transport layer was represented in TCP/IP by two protocols: TCP and UDP. The IP is a **host-to-host protocol,** meaning that it can deliver a packet from one physical device to another. UDP and TCP are **transport level protocols** responsible for delivery of a message from a process (running program) to another process. A new transport layer protocol, SCTP, has been devised to answer the needs of some new applications.

User Datagram Protocol (UDP)

The **User Datagram Protocol (UDP)** is the simpler of the two standard TCP/IP transport protocols. It is a process-to-process protocol that adds only port addresses, checksum error control, and length information to the data from the upper layer. UDP is discussed in Chapter 11.

Transmission Control Protocol (TCP)

The **Transmission Control Protocol (TCP)** provides full transport layer services to applications. TCP is a reliable stream transport protocol. The term *stream,* in this context, means connection-oriented: a connection must be established between both ends of a transmission before either can transmit data.

At the sending end of each transmission, TCP divides a stream of data into smaller units called *segments.* Each segment includes a sequence number for reordering after receipt, together with an acknowledgment number for the segments received. Segments are carried across the internet inside of IP datagrams. At the receiving end, TCP collects each datagram as it comes in and reorders the transmission based on sequence numbers. TCP is discussed in Chapter 12.

Stream Control Transmission Protocol (SCTP)

The new **Stream Control Transmission Protocol (SCTP)** provides support for new applications such as IP telephony. It is a transport layer protocol that combines the good features of UDP and TCP. We discuss SCTP in Chapter 13.

Application Layer

The *application layer* in TCP/IP is equivalent to the combined session, presentation, and application layers in the OSI model. Many protocols are defined at this layer. We cover most of the standard protocols in later chapters.

2.4   ADDRESSING

Three different levels of addresses are used in an internet using the TCP/IP protocols:
physical (link) **address, logical** (IP) **address,** and **port address** (see Figure 2.16).

Figure 2.16   *Addresses in TCP/IP*

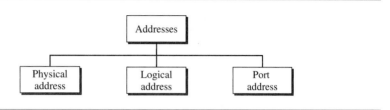

Each address belongs to a specific layer of TCP/IP architecture, as shown in
Figure 2.17.

Figure 2.17   *Relationship of layers and addresses in TCP/IP*

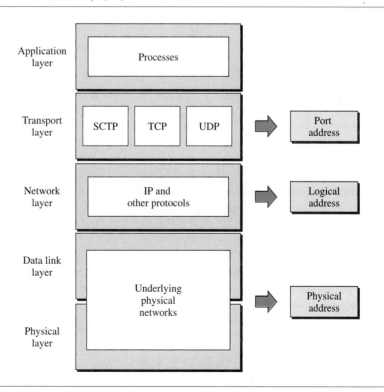

Physical Address

The **physical address,** also known as the link address, is the address of a node as defined by its LAN or WAN. It is included in the frame used by the data link layer. It is the lowest level address.

The physical addresses have authority over the network (LAN or WAN). The size and format of these addresses vary depending on the network. For example, Ethernet uses a 6-byte (48-bit) physical address that is imprinted on the network interface card (NIC). LocalTalk (Apple), however, has a 1-byte dynamic address that changes each time the station comes up.

Unicast, Multicast, and Broadcast Physical Addresses

Physical addresses can be either **unicast** (one single recipient), **multicast** (a group of recipients), or **broadcast** (to be received by all systems in the network). Some networks support all three addresses. For example, Ethernet (see Chapter 3) supports the unicast physical addresses (6 bytes), the multicast addresses, and the broadcast addresses. Some networks do not support the multicast or broadcast physical addresses. If a frame must be sent to a group of recipients or to all systems, the multicast or broadcast address must be simulated using unicast addresses. This means that multiple packets are sent out using unicast addresses.

Example 1

In Figure 2.18 a node with physical address 10 sends a frame to a node with physical address 87. The two nodes are connected by a link. At the data link level this frame contains physical (link) addresses in the header. These are the only addresses needed. The rest of the header contains other information needed at this level. The trailer usually contains extra bits needed for error detection.

Figure 2.18 *Physical addresses*

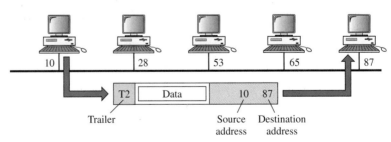

Example 2

As we will see in Chapter 3, most local area networks use a 48-bit (6 bytes) physical address written as 12 hexadecimal digits, with every 2 bytes separated by a colon as shown below:

07:01:02:01:2C:4B
A 6-byte (12 hexadecimal digits) physical address

Logical Address

Logical addresses are necessary for universal communication services that are independent of underlying physical networks. Physical addresses are not adequate in an internetwork environment where different networks can have different address formats. A
universal addressing system in which each host can be identified uniquely, regardless of
the underlying physical network, is needed.

The logical addresses are designed for this purpose. A logical address in the Internet
is currently a 32-bit address that can uniquely define a host connected to the Internet. No
two publicly addressed and visible hosts on the Internet can have the same IP address.

Unicast, Multicast, and Broadcast Addresses

The logical addresses can be either unicast (one single recipient), multicast (a group of
recipients), or broadcast (all systems in the network). There are limitations on broadcast addresses. We will discuss the three types of addresses in Chapter 4.

Example 3

In Figure 2.19 we want to send data from a node with network address A and physical address 10,
located on one LAN, to a node with a network address P and physical address 95, located on

Figure 2.19   *IP addresses*

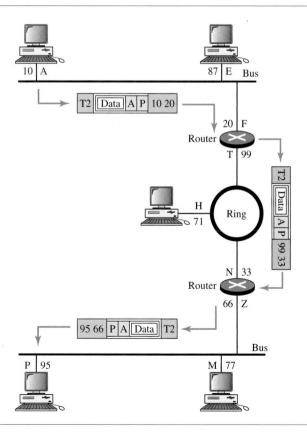

another LAN. Because the two devices are located on different networks, we cannot use link addresses only; the link addresses have only local jurisdiction. What we need here are universal addresses that can pass through the LAN boundaries. The network (logical) addresses have this characteristic. The packet at the network layer contains the logical addresses, which remain the same from the original source to the final destination (A and P, respectively, in the figure). They will not change when we go from network to network. However, the physical addresses will change as the packet moves from one network to another. The boxes labeled routers are internet-working devices, which we will discuss in Chapter 3.

Example 4

As we will see in Chapter 4, an Internet address (in IPv4) is 32 bits in length, normally written as four decimal numbers, with each number representing 1 byte. The numbers are separated by a dot. Below is an example of such an address.

> **132.24.75.9**
> **An internet address in IPv4 in decimal numbers**

Port Address

The IP address and the physical address are necessary for a quantity of data to travel from a source to the destination host. However, arrival at the destination host is not the final objective of data communication on the Internet. A system that sends nothing but data from one computer to another is not complete. Today, computers are devices that can run multiple processes at the same time. The end objective of Internet communication is a process communicating with another process. For example, computer A can communicate with computer C using TELNET. At the same time, computer A communicates with computer B using File Transfer Protocol (FTP). For these processes to occur simultaneously, we need a method to label different processes. In other words, they need addresses. In TCP/IP architecture, the label assigned to a process is called a port address. A port address in TCP/IP is 16 bits long.

Example 5

Figure 2.20 shows an example of transport layer communication. Data coming from the upper layers have port addresses j and k (j is the address of the sending process, and k is the address of the receiving process). Since the data size is larger than the network layer can handle, the data are split into two packets, each packet retaining the service-point addresses (j and k). Then in the network layer, network addresses (A and P) are added to each packet. The packets can travel on different paths and arrive at the destination either in order or out of order. The two packets are delivered to the destination transport layer, which is responsible for removing the network layer headers and combining the two pieces of data for delivery to the upper layers.

Example 6

As we will see in Chapters 11, 12, and 13, a port address is a 16-bit address represented by one decimal number as shown below.

753
A 16-bit port address represented as one single number

Figure 2.20   *Port addresses*

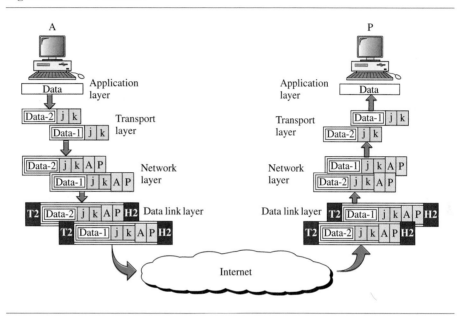

2.5   IP VERSIONS

IP became the official protocol for the Internet (then known as ARPANET; see Chapter 1) in 1983. As the Internet has evolved, so has IP. There have been six versions since its inception. We look at the latter three versions here.

Version 4

Most networks on the Internet are currently using version 4. However, this version has significant shortcomings. The primary problem is that the Internet address is only 32 bits in length with the address space divided into different classes. With the rapid growth of the Internet, this addressing scheme cannot handle the projected number of users.

Version 5

Version 5 was a proposal based on the OSI model. This version never went beyond the proposal stage due to extensive layer changes and the projected expense.

Version 6

IETF has designed a new version called version 6. In this version, the only protocols that are changed are the ones in the network layer. **IPv4** (IP version 4) becomes **IPv6** (IP version 6), ICMPv4 becomes ICMPv6, IGMP and ARP are merged into ICMPv6, and RARP is deleted.

IPv6, also known as IPng (IP *next generation*), uses 128-bit (16-byte) addresses, versus the 32-bit (4-byte) addresses currently used in version 4. IPv6 can thereby accommodate a larger number of users. In version 6, the packet format has been simplified, yet at the same time it is more flexible to allow for the future addition of features.

The new version supports authentication, data integrity, and confidentiality at the network layer. It is designed to handle the transmission of real-time data such as audio and video, and can carry data from other protocols. IPng can also handle congestion and route discovery better than the current version.

This book is based primarily on version 4, with Chapter 27 concentrating on version 6.

2.6   KEY TERMS

access control

Address Resolution Protocol (ARP)

application layer

best-effort delivery

bits

broadcast physical address

bus topology

compression

connection control

data link layer

dialog control

directory services

encoding

encryption

error control

file transfer, access, and management (FTAM)

flow control

frames

full-duplex mode

half-duplex mode

host-to-host protocol

interface

International Standards Organization (ISO)

Internet Control Message Protocol (ICMP)

Internet Group Message Protocol (IGMP)

Internetworking Protocol (IP)

internetworks

IPv4

IPv6

line configuration

logical address

logical addressing

mail services

mesh topology

multicast physical address

multipoint configuration

network layer

network virtual terminal

open system

Open Systems Interconnection (OSI)
   model

peer-to-peer processes

physical address

physical layer

physical topology

point-to-point configuration

port address

presentation layer

process-to-process delivery

Reverse Address Resolution Protocol
   (RARP)

ring topology

routing

segmentation

service-point addressing

session layer

simplex mode

source-to-destination delivery

star topology

Stream Control Transmission Protocol (SCTP)

synchronization points

TCP/IP protocol suite

translation

Transmission Control Protocol (TCP)

transmission mode

transmission rate

transport layer

transport level protocol

unicast physical address

User Datagram Protocol (UDP)

2.7   SUMMARY

❑ The International Standards Organization (ISO) created a model called the Open Systems Interconnection (OSI), which allows diverse systems to communicate.

❑ The seven-layer OSI model provides guidelines for the development of universally compatible networking protocols.

❑ The physical, data link, and network layers are the network support layers.

❑ The session, presentation, and application layers are the user support layers.

❑ The transport layer links the network support layers and the user support layers.

❑ The physical layer coordinates the functions required to transmit a bit stream over a physical medium.

❑ The data link layer is responsible for delivering data units from one station to the next without errors.

❑ The network layer is responsible for the source-to-destination delivery of a packet across multiple network links.

❑ The transport layer is responsible for the process-to-process delivery of the entire message.

❑ The session layer establishes, maintains, and synchronizes the interactions between communicating devices.

❏ The presentation layer ensures interoperability between communicating devices through transformation of data into a mutually agreed-upon format.

❏ The application layer enables the users to access the network.

❏ TCP/IP is a five-layer hierarchical protocol suite developed before the OSI model.

❏ The TCP/IP application layer is equivalent to the combined session, presentation, and application layers of the OSI model.

❏ Three types of addresses are used by systems using the TCP/IP protocol: the physical address, the internetwork address (IP address), and the port address.

❏ The physical address, also known as the link address, is the address of a node as defined by its LAN or WAN.

❏ The IP address uniquely defines a host on the Internet.

❏ The port address identifies a process on a host.

❏ Most networks use IPv4.

❏ IPv6 is supposed to replace IPv4 in the near future.

2.8   PRACTICE SET

Exercises

1. How are OSI and ISO related to each other?
2. Match the following to one or more layers of the OSI model:
   a. route determination
   b. flow control
   c. interface to transmission media
   d. provides access for the end user
3. Match the following to one or more layers of the OSI model:
   a. reliable process-to-process message delivery
   b. route selection
   c. defines frames
   d. provides user services such as email and file transfer
   e. transmission of bit stream across physical medium
4. Match the following to one or more layers of the OSI model:
   a. communicates directly with user's application program
   b. error correction and retransmission
   c. mechanical, electrical, and functional interface
   d. responsibility for carrying frames between adjacent nodes
5. Match the following to one or more layers of the OSI model:
   a. format and code conversion services
   b. establishes, manages, and terminates sessions

c. ensures reliable transmission of data

d. log-in and log-out procedures

e. provides independence from differences in data representation

Research Activities

6. Domain Name System or DNS (see Chapter 17) is an application program in the TCP/IP protocol suite. Research and find the equivalent of this protocol (if any) in the OSI model. Compare and contrast the two.

7. File Transfer Protocol or FTP (see Chapter 19) is an application program in the TCP/IP protocol suite. Research and find the equivalent of this protocol (if any) in the OSI model. Compare and contrast the two.

8. Trivial File Transfer Protocol or TFTP (see Chapter 19) is an application program in the TCP/IP protocol suite. Research and find the equivalent of this protocol (if any) in the OSI model. Compare and contrast the two.

9. There are several transport layer models proposed in the OSI model. Research and find all of them. Explain the differences between them.

10. There are several network layer models proposed in the OSI model. Research and find all of them. Explain the differences between them.

CHAPTER 3

Underlying Technologies

We can think of the Internet as a series of backbone networks that are run by international, national, and regional ISPs. The backbones are joined together by connecting devices such as routers or by switching stations. The end-users are either part of the local ISP LAN or connected via point-to-point networks to the LANs. Conceptually, the Internet is a set of switched WANs (backbones), LANs, point-to-point WANs, and connecting or switching devices as shown in Figure 3.1.

Figure 3.1 *Internet*

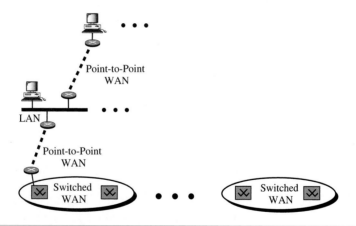

Although the TCP/IP protocol suite is normally shown as a five-layer stack, it only defines the three upper layers; TCP/IP is only concerned with the network, transport, and application layers. This means that TCP/IP assumes the existence of these WANs, LANs, and the connecting devices that join them.

We do the same. We assume that the reader is already familiar with the underlying technology of data communications, telecommunications, LANs, WANs, and connecting devices.

However, as a brief review, we touch upon these underlying technologies in this chapter. Note that we do not cover any of these topics in detail. For more in-depth coverage, see Forouzan, *Data Communications and Networking,* 3 ed., McGraw-Hill, 2004.

3.1   LOCAL AREA NETWORKS (LANS)

A **local area network (LAN)** is a data communication system that allows a number of independent devices to communicate directly with each other in a limited geographic area such as a single department, a single building, or a campus. A large organization may need several connected LANs.

The most popular LANs are Ethernet and wireless LANs. We briefly review these technologies in this section. For further discussion of LANs, see Forouzan, *Local Area Networks,* McGraw-Hill, 2003.

Wired LANs: Ethernet

Ethernet is the most widely used local area network protocol. The protocol was designed in 1973 by Xerox with a data rate of 10 Mbps and a bus topology. Today it has a data rate of 100 Mbps and 1000 Mbps (1 gigabit per second). Ethernet is formally defined by the IEEE 802.3 standard (see Appendix E).

Traditional Ethernet (10 Mbps)

The original Ethernet, usually referred to as traditional Ethernet, has a 10-Mbps data rate. We discuss this Ethernet version first.

Access Method: CSMA/CD   The IEEE 802.3 standard defines **carrier sense multiple access with collision detection (CSMA/CD)** as the access method for traditional Ethernet. Stations on a traditional Ethernet can be connected together using a physical bus or star topology, but the logical topology is always a bus. By this, we mean that the medium (channel) is shared between stations and only one station at a time can use it. It also implies that all stations receive a frame sent by a station (broadcasting). The real destination keeps the frame while the rest drop it. In this situation, how can we be sure that two stations are not using the medium at the same time? If they do, their frames will collide with each other. CSMA/CD is designed to solve the problem according to the following principles:

1. Every station has an equal right to the medium (multiple access).
2. Every station with a frame to send first listens to (senses) the medium. If there is no data on the medium, the station can start sending (carrier sense).
3. It may happen that two stations both sense the medium, find it idle, and start sending. In this case, a collision occurs. The protocol forces the station to continue to listen to the line after sending has begun. If there is a collision, all stations sense the collision; each sending station sends a jam signal to destroy the data on the line and, after each waits a different random amount of time, try again. The random times prevent the simultaneous re-sending of data. Figure 3.2 shows CSMA/CD.

Figure 3.2   *CSMA/CD*

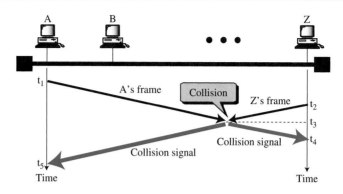

Three factors are related in the CSMA/CD standard: the minimum frame length, the data transmission rate, and the collision domain. The time the station needs to wait to be sure that there is no data on the line is the minimum frame length divided by the transmission rate (the time required to send out the minimum frame length). This time is proportional to the time needed for the first bit to travel the maximum network distance (collision domain). In other words, we have

> **Minimum frame length / Transmission rate**
> **is proportional to**
> **Collision domain / Propagation speed**

For traditional Ethernet, the minimum frame length is 520 bits, the transmission rate is 10 Mbps, the propagation speed is almost two-third the speed of light, and the collision domain is almost 2500 meters.

Layers   Figure 3.3 shows the 10-Mbps Ethernet layers. The data link layer has two sublayers: the logical link control (LLC) sublayer and the media access control (MAC)

Figure 3.3   *Ethernet layers*

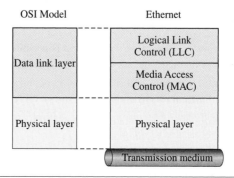

sublayer. The LLC layer is responsible for flow and error control at the data link layer. The MAC sublayer is responsible for the operation of the CSMA/CD access method. The MAC sublayer also frames data received from the LLC layer and passes the frames to the physical layer for encoding. The physical layer transfers data into electrical signals and sends them to the next station via the transmission medium. This bottom layer also detects and reports collisions to the data link layer.

Frame   IEEE 802.3 specifies one frame type containing seven fields: preamble, SFD, DA, SA, length/type, 802.2 frame, and the CRC. Ethernet does not provide any mechanism for acknowledging received frames, making it what is known as an unreliable medium. Acknowledgments must be implemented at the higher layers. The format of the CSMA/CD MAC frame is shown in Figure 3.4.

Figure 3.4   *Ethernet frame*

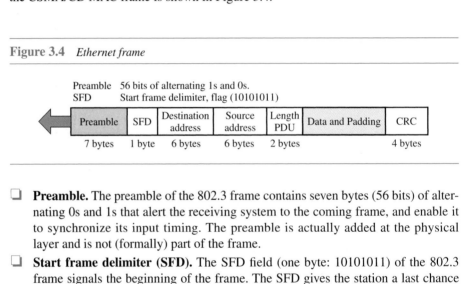

☐ **Preamble.** The preamble of the 802.3 frame contains seven bytes (56 bits) of alternating 0s and 1s that alert the receiving system to the coming frame, and enable it to synchronize its input timing. The preamble is actually added at the physical layer and is not (formally) part of the frame.

☐ **Start frame delimiter (SFD).** The SFD field (one byte: 10101011) of the 802.3 frame signals the beginning of the frame. The SFD gives the station a last chance for synchronization. The last two bits are 11 to signal that the next field is the destination address.

☐ **Destination address (DA).** The DA field is six bytes and contains the physical address of the next station.

☐ **Source address (SA).** The SA field is also six bytes and contains the physical address of the previous station.

☐ **Length/type.** The length/type field has one of two meanings. If the value of the field is less than 1518, it is a length field and defines the length of the data field that follows. If the value of this field is greater than 1536, it defines the upper layer protocol that uses the services of the Internet.

☐ **Data.** The data field carries data encapsulated from the upper layer protocols. It is a minimum of 46 and a maximum 1500 bytes.

☐ **CRC.** The last field in the 802.3 frame contains the error detection information, in this case a CRC-32 (See Appendix D).

Addressing   Each station such as a PC, workstation, or printer on an Ethernet network has its own network interface card (NIC). The NIC fits inside the station and provides the station with a six-byte physical address. The Ethernet address is 6 bytes (48 bits) that is normally written in hexadecimal notation with a colon to separate bytes as shown below:

07:01:02:01:2C:4B

The addresses in Ethernet are sent byte by byte, left-to-right; however, for each byte, the least significant bit is sent first and the most significant bit is sent last.

There are three types of addresses in Ethernet: unicast, multicast, and broadcast. In a unicast address, the least significant bit of the first byte is 0; in the multicast address, the least significant bit is 1. A broadcast address is forty-eight 1s. A source address is always unicast. The destination address can be unicast (one single recipient), multicast (a group of recipients), or multicast (all stations connected to the LAN).

Implementations   The IEEE standard defines four implementations for traditional Ethernet. A simple representation of these four implementations is shown in Figure 3.5. The transceiver, which can be external or internal, is responsible for encoding, collision detection, and transmitting/receiving signals.

Figure 3.5   *Ethernet implementations*

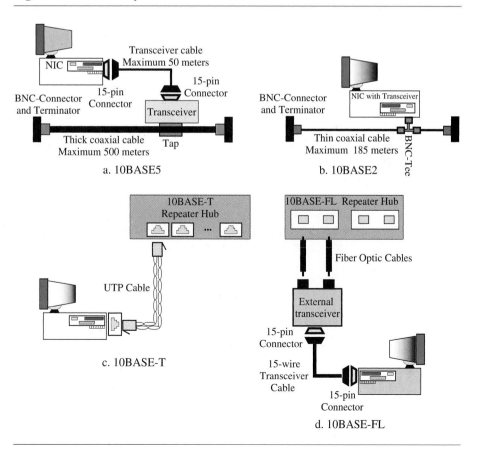

❑ **10BASE5** (thick Ethernet) uses a bus topology with a thick coaxial cable as the transmission medium.

❑ **10BASE2** (thin Ethernet or Cheapernet) uses a bus topology with a thin coaxial cable as the transmission medium.

❑ **10BASE-T** (twisted-pair Ethernet) uses a physical star topology (the logical topology is still a bus) with stations connected by two pairs of twisted-pair cable to the hub.

❑ **10BASE-FL** (fiber link Ethernet) uses a star topology (the logical topology is still a bus) with stations connected by a pair of fiber-optic cables to the hub.

Fast Ethernet

The need for a higher data rate resulted in the **Fast Ethernet** protocol (100 Mbps). In the MAC layer, Fast Ethernet uses the same principles as traditional Ethernet (CSMA/CD) except that the transmission rate has been increased from 10 Mbps to 100 Mbps. When the data rate is increased, it takes less time for a frame to leave the sending station. This means the sending station has less time to hear the collision. With a fixed propagation speed, this means a shorter collision domain.

For CSMA/CD to work, we have two choices: either increase the minimum frame length or decrease the collision domain (the speed of light cannot be changed). Increasing the minimum length of the frame involves additional overhead. If the data to be sent is not long enough, we must add extra bytes, which means more overhead and loss of efficiency. Fast Ethernet has chosen the other option; the collision domain has been decreased by a factor of 10 (from 2500 meters to 250 meters). With a star topology, 250 meters is acceptable in many cases. In the physical layer, Fast Ethernet uses different signaling methods and different media to achieve a data rate of 100 Mbps.

Fast Ethernet Implementation   Fast Ethernet can be categorized as either a two-wire or four-wire implementation. The two-wire implementation is called 100BASE-X, with either twisted-pair cable (100BASE-TX) or fiber-optic cable (100BASE-FX). The four wire implementation is designed only for twisted-pair cable (100BASE-T4). In other words, we have three implementations: 100BASE-TX, 100BASE-FX, and 100BASE-T4 (see Figure 3.6).

Gigabit Ethernet

The need for a data rate higher than 100 Mbps resulted in the **Gigabit Ethernet** protocol (1000 Mbps). To achieve this data rate the MAC layer has two options: keeping CSMA/CD or dropping it. For the former, the two choices are, once again, to decrease the collision domain or increase the minimum frame length. Since a collision domain of 25 meters is unacceptable, the minimum length of the frame is increased in a very elegant way.

In the second option, dropping CSMA/CD, every station is connected by two separate paths to the central hub. This is called full-duplex Ethernet with no collision and no need for CSMA/CD.

Figure 3.6 *Fast Ethernet implementations*

100BASE-TX Repeater Hub
Twisted-pair Cable
NIC with
internal transceiver
a. 100BASE-TX
100Base-FX Repeater Hub
Fiber Optic
Cables
NIC with
internal transceiver
b. 100BASE-FX
100BASE-T4
Repeater Hub
External
transceiver
40-wire
Cable
40-pin
Connector
40-pin
Connector
NIC
c. 100BASE-T4

At the physical level, many changes have been made to allow the transmission of data at this rate.

Gigabit Ethernet Implementation Gigabit Ethernet can be classified as either a two-wire or four-wire implementation. The two common two-wire implementation are called 1000BASE-X, with optical fibers transmitting short-wave laser signals (1000BASE-SX) and optical fibers transmitting long-wave laser signals (1000BASE-LX). The four wire version uses twisted-pair cables (1000BASE-T). These implementations are shown in Figure 3.7.

Figure 3.7 *Gigabit Ethernet implementations*

1000BASE-SX/LX
Repeater Hub
2 Pairs of fiber-optic
cable
NIC with
internal transceiver
a. 1000BASE-SX/LX
1000BASE-T
Repeater Hub
4 Pairs of UTP cable
NIC with
internal transceiver
b. 1000BASE-T

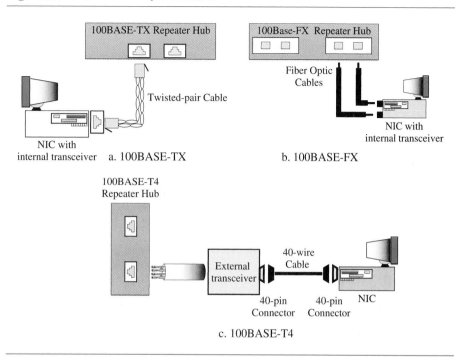

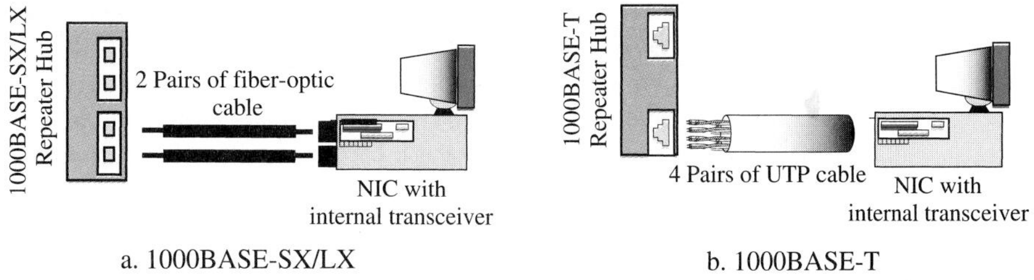

Wireless LANs: IEEE 802.11

In this section, we concentrate on one wireless technology for LANs: IEEE 802.11 wireless LANs, sometimes called wireless Ethernet. We study this technology as wireless links, links that can connect us to the Internet. How the connection is made and how end-to-end communication is accomplished are the subjects of future chapters.

IEEE has defined the specification for a wireless LAN, called **IEEE 802.11,** which covers the physical and data link layers. But before discussing these layers, we describe the architecture of the protocol in general.

Architecture

The standard defines two kinds of services: the basic service set (BSS) and the extended service set (ESS). The **basic service set (BSS)** is the building block of a wireless LAN. A basic service set is made of stationary or mobile wireless stations and a possible central base station, known as the **access point (AP).** Figure 3.8 shows two sets in this standard.

Figure 3.8   *BSSs*

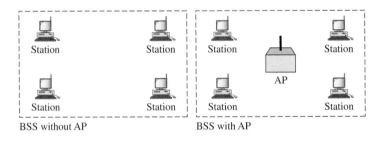

| Station | Station | Station | AP | Station |

BSS without AP   BSS with AP

The BSS without an AP is a stand-alone network and cannot send data to other BSSs. It is what is called an *ad hoc architecture.* In this architecture, stations can form a network without the need of an AP; they can locate each other and agree to be part of a BSS.

An **extended service set (ESS)** is made up of two or more BSSs with APs. In this case, the BSSs are connected through a *distribution system,* which is usually a wired LAN. The distribution system connects the APs in the BSSs. IEEE 802.11 does not restrict the distribution system; it can be any IEEE LAN such as an Ethernet. Note that the extended service set uses two types of stations: mobile and stationary. The mobile stations are normal stations inside a BSS. The stationary stations are AP stations that are part of a wired LAN. Figure 3.9 shows an ESS.

When BSSs are connected, we have what is called an *infrastructure network.* In this network, the stations within reach of one another can communicate without the use of an AP. However, communication between two stations in two different BSSs usually occurs via two APs. The idea is similar to communication in a cellular network if we consider each BSS to be a cell and each AP to be a base station. Note that a mobile station can belong to more than one BSS at the same time.

Figure 3.9   *ESS*

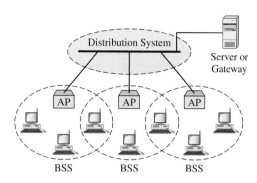

Physical Layer

IEEE 802.11 defines specifications for the conversion of bits to a signal in the physical layer; one specification is in the infrared frequencies and is not discussed here. The other five specifications are in the radio frequency range as shown in Figure 3.10.

Figure 3.10   *Physical layer*

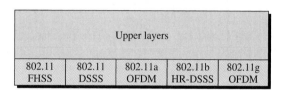

❑ **IEEE 802.11 FHSS.** This standard describes the **frequency hopping spread spectrum (FHSS)** method for signal generation in a 2.40–2.48-GHz band with a data rate of 1 or 2 Mbps. FHSS is a method in which the sender sends on one carrier frequency for a short amount of time, then hops to another carrier frequency for the same amount of time, hops again to still another for the same amount of time, and so on. After N hops, the cycle is repeated (see Figure 3.11). If the bandwidth of the original signal is B, the allocated spread spectrum bandwidth is $N \times B$.

❑ **IEEE 802.11 DSSS.** This standard describes the **direct sequence spread spectrum (DSSS)** method for signal generation in a 2.40–2.48-GHz band with a data rate of 1 or 2 Mbps. In DSSS, each bit sent by the sender is replaced by a sequence of bits called a chip code. To avoid buffering, however, the time needed to send one chip code must be the same as the time needed to send one original bit. If N is the number of bits in each chip code, then the data rate for sending chip codes is N times the data rate of the original bit stream. Figure 3.12 shows an example of DSSS.

[etc.]

Figure 3.11   *FHSS*

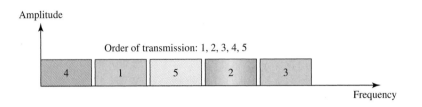

Figure 3.12   *DSSS*

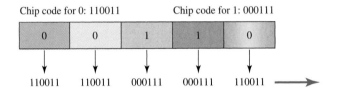

❑ **IEEE 802.11a OFDM.** This standard describes **orthogonal frequency-division multiplexing (OFDM)** for data rates of 18 Mbps and 54 Mbps. For more information about OFDM, see Forouzan, *Data Communications and Networking,* 3 ed., McGraw-Hill, 2004.

❑ **IEEE 802.11b HR-DSSS.** This standard describes the **high-rate DSSS (HR-DSSS)** method for signal generation in a 2.40–2.48 GHz band with a data rate of 1 or 2, 5.5 and 11 Mbps. It is backward compatible with DSSS.

❑ **IEEE 802.11g OFDM.** This relatively new specification uses OFDM for signal generation in a 2.40–2.48-GHz band with a data rate of 54 Mbps. The high data rate is achieved using a complex modulation technique.

MAC Layer

IEEE 802.11 defines two MAC sublayers: the **distributed coordination function (DCF)** and **point coordination function (PCF)** as shown in Figure 3.13.

Figure 3.13   *MAC layers in IEEE 802.11 standard*

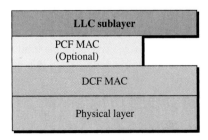

PCF is an optional and complex access method that can be implemented in an infrastructure network (not in an ad hoc network). We do not discuss this here; for more information refer to Forouzan, *Local Area Networks,* McGraw-Hill, 2003.

DCF uses an access method called **carrier sense multiple access with collision avoidance (CSMA/CA).** The first two principles of CSMA/CD also apply to CSMA/CA; each station has equal access to the medium (multiple access) and each station senses the medium before sending. However, collision detection is not applicable for several reasons, the dominant one being the **hidden terminal problem.**

To understand the hidden terminal problem, imagine we have three stations (1, 2, and 3). Station 1 sends a frame to station 2 at the same time that station 3 sends a frame to station 2. It may happen that stations 1 and 3 cannot hear each other (perhaps because of some obstruction like a mountain or a wall). In this case, collision may occur, with stations 1 and 3 unable to detect it: they think their packets have arrived safely.

To prevent this situation, collision must be avoided. Each station defines how long it needs the medium and tells other stations to refrain from sending data during this period. Figure 3.14 shows the procedure.

Figure 3.14   *CSMA/CA*

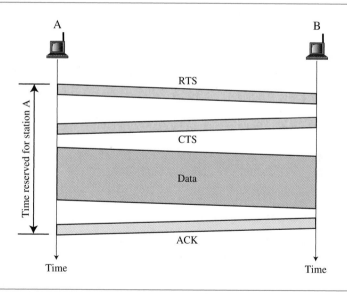

The procedure is as follows:

1. The sending station, after sensing that the medium is idle, sends a special small frame called request to send (RTS). In this message, the sender defines the total time it needs the medium.

2. The receiver acknowledges the request (broadcast to all stations) by sending a small packet called clear to send (CTS).

3. The sender sends the data frame.

4. The receiver acknowledges the receipt of data.

Frame   The MAC layer frame consists of nine fields, as shown in Figure 3.15.

Figure 3.15 *Frame*

2 bytes	2 bytes	6 bytes	6 bytes	6 bytes	2 bytes	6 bytes	0 to 2312 bytes	4 bytes
FC	D	Address 1	Address 2	Address 3	SC	Address 4	**Frame body**	FCS

❏ **Frame control (FC).** The FC field is 2 bytes long and defines the type of the frame and some control information.

❏ **D.** In all frame types except one, this field defines the duration of the transmission. In one control frame, this field defines the ID of the frame.

❏ **Addresses.** There are four address fields, each 6 bytes long. The meaning of each address field depends on the value of the *To DS* and the *From DS* subfields and will be discussed later.

❏ **Sequence control.** This field defines the sequence number of the frame used in flow control.

❏ **Frame body.** This field, which can be between 0 and 2312 bytes, contains information based on the type and the subtype defined in the FC field.

❏ **FCS.** The FCS field is 4 bytes long and contains a CRC-32 error detection sequence.

Addressing Mechanism   The IEEE 802.11 addressing mechanism is complicated. The complexity stems from the fact that there may be intermediate stations (APs). There are four cases, defined by the value of the two flags in the FC field, *To DS* and *From DS*. Each flag can be either 0 or 1, thus defining four different situations. The interpretation of the four addresses (address 1 to address 4) in the MAC frame depends on the value of these flags, as shown in Table 3.1.

Table 3.1 *Addresses in IEEE 802.11*

To DS	From DS	Address 1	Address 2	Address 3	Address 4
0	0	Destination station	Source station	BSS ID	N/A
0	1	Destination station	Sending AP	Source station	N/A
1	0	Receiving AP	Source station	Destination station	N/A
1	1	Receiving AP	Sending AP	Destination station	Source station

Note that address 1 is always the address of the next device. Address 2 is always the address of the previous device. Address 3 is the address of the final destination station if it is not defined by address 1. Address 4 is the address of the original source station if it is not the same as address 2.

3.2 POINT-TO-POINT WANS

A second type of network we encounter in the Internet is the point-to-point wide area network. A point-to-point WAN connects two remote devices using a line available from a public network such as a telephone network. We discuss the physical and data link layers of these technologies here.

Physical Layer

At the physical layer, the point-to-point connection between two devices can be accomplished using one of the services available today such as traditional modem technology, a DSL line, cable modem, a T-line, or SONET.

56K Modems

We still use traditional modems to upload data to the Internet and download data from the Internet, as shown in Figure 3.16.

Figure 3.16 *56K modem*

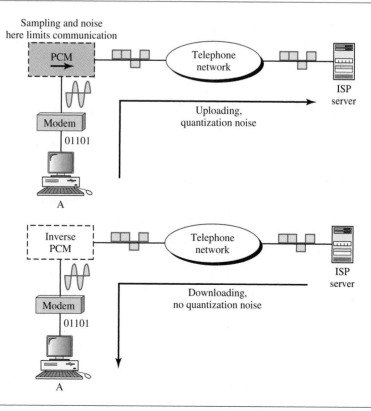

In **uploading,** the analog signal must be sampled at the switching station, which means the data rate in uploading is limited to 33.6 kbps. However, there is no sampling in **downloading.** The signal is not affected by quantization noise and not subject to the Shannon capacity limitation. The maximum data rate in the uploading direction is 33.6 kbps, but the data rate in the downloading direction is 56 kbps.

One may wonder why 56 kbps. The telephone companies sample voice 8000 times per second with 8 bits per sample. One of the bits in each sample is used for control purposes, which means each sample is 7 bits. The rate is therefore 8000×7, or 56,000 bps or 56 kbps.

The **V.90** and **V.92** standard modems operate at 56 kbps to connect a host to the Internet.

DSL Technology

After traditional modems reached their peak data rate, telephone companies developed another technology, DSL, to provide higher-speed access to the Internet. **Digital subscriber line (DSL)** technology is one of the most promising for supporting high-speed digital communication over the existing local loops (telephone line). DSL technology is a set of technologies, each differing in the first letter (ADSL, VDSL, HDSL, and SDSL). The set is often referred to as *x*DSL, where *x* can be replaced by A, V, H, or S.

ADSL   The first technology in the set is **asymmetric DSL (ADSL).** ADSL, like a 56K modem, provides higher speed (bit rate) in the downstream direction (from the Internet to the resident) than in the upstream direction (from the resident to the Internet). That is the reason it is called asymmetric. Unlike the asymmetry in 56K modems, the designers of ADSL specifically divided the available bandwidth of the local loop unevenly for the residential customer. The service is not suitable for business customers who need a large bandwidth in both directions.

ADSL is an asymmetric communication technology designed for residential users; it is not suitable for businesses.

Figure 3.17 shows how the bandwidth is divided:

- ❏ **Voice.** Channel 0 is reserved for voice communication.
- ❏ **Idle.** Channels 1 to 5 are not used, to allow a gap between voice and data communication.
- ❏ **Upstream data and control.** Channels 6 to 30 (25 channels) are used for upstream data transfer and control. One channel is for control, and 24 channels are for data transfer. If there are 24 channels, each using 4 kHz (out of 4.312 kHz available) with 15 bits per Hz, we have $24 \times 4000 \times 15$, or a 1.44-Mbps bandwidth, in the upstream direction.
- ❏ **Downstream data and control.** Channels 31 to 255 (225 channels) are used for downstream data transfer and control. One channel is for control, and 224 channels are for data. If there are 224 channels, we can achieve up to $224 \times 4000 \times 15$, or 13.4 Mbps.

Figure 3.17   *Bandwidth division*

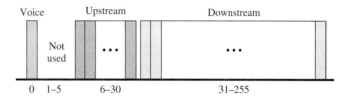

Because of the high signal/noise ratio, the actual bit rate is much lower than the above-mentioned rates. The bit rates are as follows:

Upstream: 64 kbps to 1 Mbps
Downstream: 500 kbps to 8 Mbps

Figure 3.18 shows an ADSL modem installed at a customer's site. The local loop connects to the filter which separates voice and data communication. The ADSL modem modulates the data and creates downstream and upstream channels.

Figure 3.18   *ADSL and DSLAM*

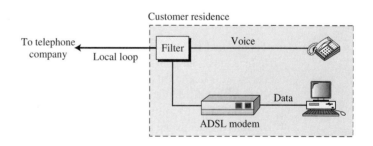

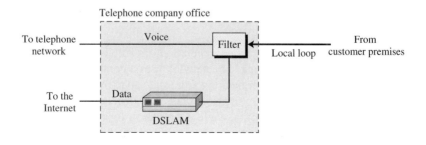

At the telephone company site, the situation is different. Instead of an ADSL modem, a device called a **digital subscriber line access multiplexer (DSLAM)** is installed that functions similarly to an ADSL modem. In addition, it packetizes the data to be sent to the Internet. Figure 3.18 shows the configuration.

Other DSL Technologies   ADSL provides asymmetric communication. The downstream bit rate is much higher than the upstream bit rate. Although this feature meets the needs of most residential subscribers, it is not suitable for businesses that send and receive data in large volumes in both directions. The **symmetric digital subscriber line (SDSL)** is designed for these types of businesses. It divides the available bandwidth equally between the downstream and upstream directions.

The **high bit rate digital subscriber line (HDSL)** was designed as an alternative to the T-1 line (1.544 Mbps). The T-1 line (discussed later) uses alternate mark inversion (AMI) encoding, which is very susceptible to attenuation at high frequencies. This limits the length of a T-1 line to 1 km. For longer distances, a repeater is necessary, which means increased costs.

The **very high bit rate digital subscriber line (VDSL),** an alternative approach that is similar to ADSL, uses coaxial, fiber-optic, or twisted-pair cable for short distances (300 to 1800 m). The modulating technique is discrete multitone technique (DMT) with a bit rate of 50 to 55 Mbps downstream and 1.5 to 2.5 Mbps upstream.

Cable Modem

Cable companies are now competing with telephone companies for the residential customer who wants high-speed access to the Internet. DSL technology provides high-data-rate connections for residential subscribers over the local loop. However, DSL uses the existing unshielded twisted-pair cable, which is very susceptible to interference. This imposes an upper limit on the data rate. Another solution is the use of the cable TV network.

Traditional Cable Networks   **Cable TV** started to distribute broadcast video signals to locations with poor or no reception. It was called **community antenna TV (CATV)** because an antenna at the top of a high hill or building received the signals from the TV stations and distributed them, via coaxial cables, to the community.

The cable TV office, called the **head end,** receives video signals from broadcasting stations and feeds the signals into coaxial cables. The traditional cable TV system used coaxial cable end to end. Because of attenuation of the signals and the use of a large number of amplifiers, communication in the traditional network was unidirectional (one-way). Video signals were transmitted downstream, from the head end to the subscriber premises.

HFC Network   The second generation of cable networks is called a **hybrid fiber-coaxial (HFC) network.** The network uses a combination of fiber-optic and coaxial cable. The transmission medium from the cable TV office to a box, called the **fiber node,** is optical fiber; from the fiber node through the neighborhood and into the house, the medium is still coaxial cable. One reason for moving from traditional to hybrid infrastructure is to make the cable network bidirectional (two-way).

Bandwidth   Even in an HFC system, the last part of the network, from the fiber node to the subscriber premises, is still a coaxial cable. This coaxial cable has a bandwidth that ranges from 5 to 750 MHz (approximately). The cable company has divided this bandwidth into three bands: video, downstream data, and upstream data, as shown in Figure 3.19.

Figure 3.19   *Cable bandwidth*

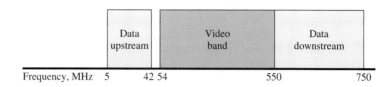

- ❏ **Video Band.** The downstream-only **video band** occupies frequencies from 54 to 550 MHz. Since each TV channel occupies 6 MHz, this can accommodate more than 80 channels.
- ❏ **Downstream Data Band.** The downstream data (from the Internet to the subscriber premises) occupies the upper band, from 550 to 750 MHz. This band is also divided into 6-MHz channels. The downstream data can be received at 30 Mbps. The standard specifies only 27 Mbps. However, since the cable modem is connected to the computer through a 10BASE-T cable, this limits the data rate to 10 Mbps.
- ❏ **Upstream Data Band.** The upstream data (from the subscriber premises to the Internet) occupies the lower band, from 5 to 42 MHz. This band is also divided into 6-MHz channels. The **upstream data band** uses lower frequencies that are more susceptible to noise and interference. Theoretically, downstream data can be sent at 12 Mbps (2 bits/Hz × 6 MHz). However, the data rate is usually less than 12 Mbps.

Sharing   Both upstream and downstream bands are shared by the subscribers. The upstream data bandwidth is only 37 MHz. This means that there are only six 6-MHz channels available in the upstream direction. A subscriber needs to use one channel to send data in the upstream direction. The question is, How can six channels be shared in an area with 1000, 2000, or even 100,000 subscribers? The solution is time-sharing. The band is divided into channels; these channels must be shared between subscribers in the same neighborhood. The cable provider allocates one channel, statically or dynamically, for a group of subscribers. If one subscriber wants to send data, she or he contends for the channel with others who want access; the subscriber must wait until the channel is available. The situation is similar to CSMA discussed for Ethernet LANs.

We have a similar situation in the downstream direction. The downstream band has 33 channels of 6 MHz. A cable provider probably has more than 33 subscribers; therefore, each channel must be shared between a group of subscribers. However, the situation is different for the downstream direction; here we have a multicasting situation. If there are data for any of the subscribers in the group, the data are sent to that channel. Each subscriber is sent the data. But since each subscriber also has an address registered with the provider, the cable modem for the group matches the address carried with the data to the address assigned by the provider. If the address matches, the data are kept; otherwise, they are discarded.

Devices   To use a cable network for data transmission, we need two key devices: a CM and a CMTS. The **cable modem (CM)** is installed on the subscriber premises. It is similar to an ADSL modem. Figure 3.20 shows its location. The **cable modem transmission system (CMTS)** is installed inside the distribution hub by the cable company.

It receives data from the Internet and passes them to the combiner, which sends them to the subscriber. The CMTS also receives data from the subscriber and passes them to the Internet. Figure 3.20 shows the location of the CMTS.

Figure 3.20 *Cable modem configurations*

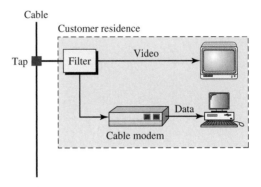

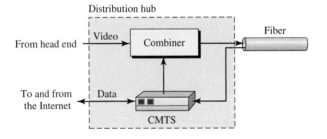

T Lines

T lines are standard digital telephone carriers originally designed to multiplex voice channels (after being digitized). Today, however, T lines can be used to carry data from a residence or an organization to the Internet. They can also be used to provide a physical link between nodes in a switched wide area network. T lines are commercially available in two data rates: T-1 and T-3 (see Table 3.2).

Table 3.2 *T line rates*

Line	Rate (Mbps)
T-1	1.544
T-3	44.736

T-1 Line   The data rate of a T-1 line is 1.544 Mbps. Twenty-four voice channels are sampled, with each sample digitized to 8 bits. An extra bit is added to provide synchronization. This makes the frame 193 bits in length. By sending 8000 frames per second, we get a data rate of 1.544 Mbps. When we use a T-1 line to connect to the Internet, we can use all or part of the capacity of the line to send digital data.

T-3 Line   A T-3 line has a data rate of 44.736 Mbps. It is equivalent to 28 T-1 lines. Many subscribers may not need the entire capacity of a T line. To accommodate these customers, the telephone companies have developed fractional T line services, which allow several subscribers to share one line by multiplexing their transmissions.

SONET

The high bandwidths of fiber-optic cable are suitable for today's highest data rate technologies (such as video conferencing) and for carrying large numbers of lower-rate technologies at the same time. ANSI created a set of standards called **Synchronous Optical Network (SONET)** to handle the use of fiber-optic cables. It defines a high-speed data carrier.

SONET first defines a set of electrical signals called **synchronous transport signals (STSs).** It then converts these signals to optical signals called **optical carriers (OCs).** The optical signals are transmitted at 8000 frames per second.

Table 3.3 shows the data rates for STSs and OCs. Note that the lowest level in this hierarchy has a data rate of 51.840 Mbps, which is greater than that of a T-3 line (44.736 Mbps).

Table 3.3 *SONET rates*

STS	OC	Rate (Mbps)
STS-1	OC-1	51.840
STS-3	OC-3	155.520
STS-9	OC-9	466.560
STS-12	OC-12	622.080
STS-18	OC-18	933.120
STS-24	OC-24	1244.160
STS-36	OC-36	1866.230
STS-48	OC-48	2488.320
STS-96	OC-96	4976.640
STS-192	OC-192	9953.280

Data Link Layer

To have a reliable point-to-point connection, a user needs a protocol at the data link layer. The most common protocol for this purpose is **Point-to-Point Protocol (PPP).**

PPP

The telephone line or cable companies provide a physical link, but to control and manage the transfer of data, there is a need for a special protocol. The Point-to-Point Protocol (PPP) was designed to respond to this need.

PPP Layers PPP has only physical and data link layers. No specific protocol is defined for the physical layer by PPP. Instead, it is left to the implementer to use whatever is available. PPP supports any of the protocols recognized by ANSI. At the data link layer, PPP defines the format of a frame and the protocol that are used for controlling the link and transporting user data. The format of a PPP frame is shown in Figure 3.21.

Figure 3.21 *PPP frame*

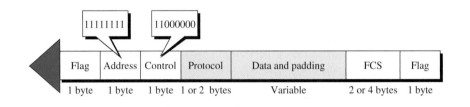

The descriptions of the fields are as follows:

1. **Flag field.** The flag field identifies the boundaries of a PPP frame. Its value is 01111110.
2. **Address field.** Because PPP is used for a point-to-point connection, it uses the broadcast address used in most LANs, 11111111, to avoid a data link address in the protocol.
3. **Control field.** The control field is assigned the value 11000000 to show that, as in most LANs, the frame has no sequence number; each frame is independent.
4. **Protocol field.** The protocol field defines the type of data being carried in the data field: user data or other information.
5. **Data field.** This field carries either user data or other information.
6. **FCS.** The frame check sequence field is simply a 2-byte or 4-byte CRC used for error detection.

Link Control Protocol (LCP)

The **Link Control Protocol (LCP)** is responsible for establishment, maintenance, and termination of the link. When the data field of a frame is carrying data related to this protocol, it means that PPP is handling the link; it does not carry data.

Network Control Protocol (NCP)

The **Network Control Protocol (NCP)** has been defined to give flexibility to PPP. PPP can carry data from different network protocols, including IP. After establishment of the link, PPP can carry IP packets in its data field.

PPPoE

PPP was designed to connect a single user to the Internet via a conventional modem and a telephone line. Today, DSL, cable modem, and wireless technology allow a group of users, on an Ethernet LAN, to access the Internet through a single physical line. In other words, the hosts connected to the LAN can share one single physical line to access the Internet. **PPP over Ethernet (PPPoE)** is a new protocol that uses a discovery technique to find the Ethernet address of the host to be connected to the Internet. After address discovery, a regular PPP session can be used to provide the connection.

3.3 SWITCHED WANS

The backbone networks in the Internet are usually switched WANs. A switched WAN is a wide area network that covers a large area (a state or a country) and provides access at several points to the users. Inside the network, there is a mesh of point-to-point networks that connects switches. The switches, multiple port connectors, allow the connection of several inputs and outputs.

Switched WAN technology differs from LAN technology in many ways. First, instead of a bus or star topology, switches are used to create multiple paths. LAN technology is considered a connectionless technology; there is no relationship between packets sent by a sender to a receiver. Switched WAN technology, on the other hand, is a connection-oriented technology. Before a sender can send a packet, a connection must be established between the sender and the receiver. After the connection is established, it is assigned an identifier used during the transmission. The connection is formally terminated when the transmission is over. The connection identifier is used instead of the source and destination addresses in LAN technology.

We discuss three common switched WANs in this section. The first, X.25, is almost obsolete. The second, Frame Relay, will still be in use for a few more years to come. The third, ATM, is the prevailing technology. Our discussion for the first two will be short; we devote more time to the third.

X.25

X.25, introduced in the 1970s, was the first switched WAN to become popular both in Europe and the United States. Although still used in Europe, it is disappearing from the United States. It was mostly used as a public network to connect individual computers or LANs. It provides an end-to-end service.

Although X.25 was (and still is, to some extent) used as the WAN to carry IP packets from one part of the world to another, there was always a conflict between IP and X.25. IP is a third- (network) layer protocol. An IP packet is supposed to be carried by a frame at the second (data link) layer. X.25, which was designed before the Internet, is a three-layer protocol; it has its own network layer. IP packets had to be encapsulated in an X.25 network-layer packet to be carried from one side of the network to another. This is analogous to a person who has a car but has to load it in a truck to go from one point to another.

Another problem with X.25 is that it was designed at a time when transmission media were not very reliable (no use of optical fibers). For this reason, X.25 performs extensive error control. This makes transmission very slow and is not popular given the ever increasing demand for speed.

For the above reasons, X.25 will most likely soon disappear from the Internet.

Frame Relay

Frame Relay, a switched technology that provides low-level (physical and data link layers) service, was designed to replace X.25. Frame Relay has some advantages over X.25:

1. **High Data Rate.** Although Frame Relay was originally designed to provide a 1.544-Mbps data rate (equivalent to a T-1 line), today most implementations can handle up to 44.736 Mbps (equivalent to a T-3 line).

2. **Bursty Data.** Some services offered by wide area network providers assume that the user has a fixed-rate need. For example, a T-1 line is designed for a user who wants to use the line at a consistent 1.544 Mbps. This type of service is not suitable for the many users today who need to send **bursty data** (nonfixed-rate data). For example, a user may want to send data at 6 Mbps for 2 seconds, 0 Mbps (nothing) for 7 seconds, and 3.44 Mbps for 1 second for a total of 15.44 Mb during a period of 10 seconds. Although the average data rate is still 1.544 Mbps, the T-1 line cannot fulfill this type of demand because it is designed for fixed-rate data, not bursty data. Bursty data requires what is called **bandwidth on demand.** The user needs different bandwidth allocations at different times. Frame Relay accepts bursty data. A user is granted an average data rate that can be exceeded when needed.

3. **Less Overhead Due to Improved Transmission Media.** The quality of transmission media has improved tremendously since the last decade. They are more reliable and less error prone. There is no need to have a WAN that spends time and resources checking and double-checking potential errors. X.25 provides extensive error checking and flow control. Frame Relay does not provide error checking or require acknowledgment in the data link layer. Instead, all error checking is left to the protocols at the network and transport layers that use the services of Frame Relay.

Frame Relay Architecture

The devices that connect a user to the network are called data terminating equipment or DTE. The switches that route the frames through the network are called data circuit equipment or DCE (see Figure 3.22). Frame Relay is normally used as a WAN to connect LANs or mainframe computers. In the first case, a router or a bridge can serve as the DTE and connects, through a leased line, the LAN to the Frame Relay switch, which is considered a DCE. In the second case, the mainframe itself can be used as a DTE with the installation of appropriate software.

Virtual Circuits

Frame Relay, like other switched LANs, uses a virtual circuit and virtual circuit identifiers called DLCIs.

Frame Relay Layers

Frame Relay has only physical and data link layers. No specific protocol is defined for the physical layer in Frame Relay. Instead, it is left to the implementer to use whatever is available. Frame Relay supports any of the protocols recognized by ANSI.

Figure 3.22   *Frame Relay network*

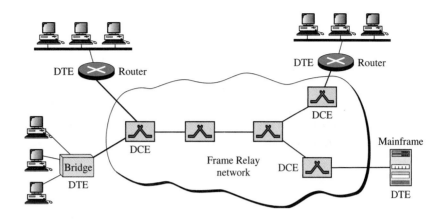

At the data link layer, Frame Relay employs a simple protocol responsible for delivering data from one DTE to another.

ATM

Asynchronous Transfer Mode (ATM) is the *cell relay* protocol designed by the ATM Forum and adopted by the ITU-T.

Design Goals

Among the challenges faced by the designers of ATM, six stand out. First and foremost is the need for a transmission system to optimize the use of high-data-rate transmission media, in particular optical fiber. Second is the need for a system that can interface with existing systems, such as the various packet networks, and provide wide area inter-connectivity between them without lowering their effectiveness or requiring their replacement. Third is the need for a design that can be implemented inexpensively so that cost would not be a barrier to adoption. If ATM is to become the backbone of inter-national communications, as intended, it must be available at low cost to every user who wants it. Fourth, the new system must be able to work with and support the exist-ing telecommunications hierarchies (local loops, local providers, long-distance carriers, and so on). Fifth, the new system must be connection-oriented to ensure accurate and predictable delivery. And last but not least, one objective is to move as many of the functions to hardware as possible (for speed) and eliminate as many software functions as possible (again for speed).

Cell Networks

ATM is a *cell network*. A **cell** is a small data unit of fixed size that is the basic unit of data exchange in a cell network. In this type of network, all data are loaded into identical cells that can be transmitted with complete predictability and uniformity. Cells are multiplexed with other cells and routed through a cell network. Because each cell is the same size and all are small, any problems associated with multiplexing different-sized packets are avoided.

> **A cell network uses the cell as the basic unit of data exchange. A cell is defined as a small, fixed-size block of information.**

Asynchronous TDM

ATM uses **asynchronous time-division multiplexing**—that is why it is called Asynchronous Transfer Mode—to multiplex cells coming from different channels. It uses fixed-size slots the size of a cell. ATM multiplexers fill a slot with a cell from any input channel that has a cell; the slot is empty if none of the channels has a cell to send.

Figure 3.23 shows how cells from three inputs are multiplexed. At the first tick of the clock, channel 2 has no cell (empty input slot), so the multiplexer fills the slot with a cell from the third channel. When all the cells from all the channels are multiplexed, the output slots are empty.

Figure 3.23   *ATM multiplexing*

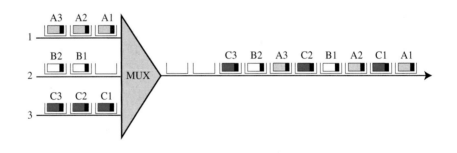

ATM Architecture

ATM is a switched network. The user access devices, called the end points, are connected through a **user-to-network interface (UNI)** to the switches inside the network. The switches are connected through **network-to-network interfaces (NNIs).** Figure 3.24 shows an example of an ATM network.

Virtual Connection   Connection between two end points is accomplished through transmission paths (TPs), virtual paths (VPs), and virtual circuits (VCs). A **transmission path (TP)** is the physical connection (wire, cable, satellite, and so on) between an end point and a switch or between two switches. Think of two switches as two cities. A transmission path is the set of all highways that directly connects the two cities.

A transmission path is divided into several virtual paths. A **virtual path (VP)** provides a connection or a set of connections between two switches. Think of a virtual path as a highway that connects two cities. Each highway is a virtual path; the set of all highways is the transmission path.

Figure 3.24   *Architecture of an ATM network*

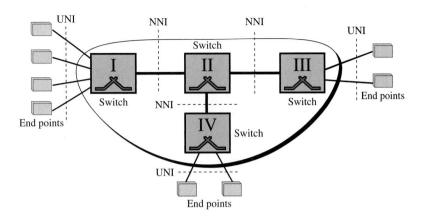

Cell networks are based on **virtual circuits (VCs).** All cells belonging to a single message follow the same virtual circuit and remain in their original order until they reach their destination. Think of a virtual circuit as the lanes of a highway (virtual path) as shown in Figure 3.25.

Figure 3.25   *Virtual circuits*

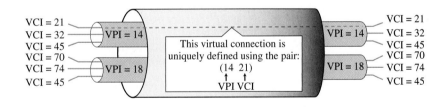

The figure also shows the relationship between a transmission path (a physical connection), virtual paths (a combination of virtual circuits that are bundled together because parts of their paths are the same), and virtual circuits that logically connect two points together.

In a virtual circuit network, to route data from one end point to another, the virtual connections need to be identified. For this purpose, the designers of ATM created a hierarchical identifier with two levels: a **virtual path identifier (VPI)** and a **virtual circuit identifier (VCI).** The VPI defines the specific VP and the VCI defines a particular VC inside the VP. The VPI is the same for all virtual connections that are bundled (logically) into one VP.

Note that a virtual connection is defined by a pair of numbers: the VPI and the VCI.

Cells   A cell is 53 bytes in length with 5 bytes allocated to header and 48 bytes carrying payload (user data may be less than 48 bytes). Most of the header is occupied by the VPI and VCI. Figure 3.26 shows the cell structure.

Figure 3.26   *An ATM cell*

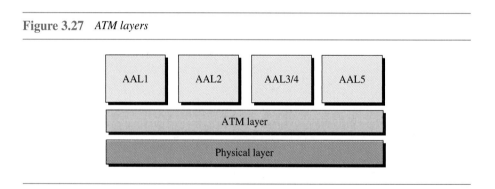

ATM Layers

The ATM standard defines three layers. They are, from top to bottom, the application adaptation layer, the ATM layer, and the physical layer as shown in Figure 3.27.

Figure 3.27   *ATM layers*

AAL1	AAL2	AAL3/4	AAL5
ATM layer				
Physical layer				

Application Adaptation Layer (AAL)   The **application adaptation layer (AAL)** allows existing networks (such as packet networks) to connect to ATM facilities. AAL protocols accept transmissions from upper-layer services (e.g., packet data) and map them into fixed-sized ATM cells. These transmissions can be of any type (voice, data, audio, video) and can be of variable or fixed rates. At the receiver, this process is reversed—segments are reassembled into their original formats and passed to the receiving service.

❏   **AAL1.** AAL1 supports applications that transfer information at constant bit rates, such as video and voice. It allows ATM to connect existing digital telephone networks such as voice channels and T lines.

❏   **AAL2.** AAL2 was originally intended to support a variable-data-rate bit stream, but it has been redesigned. It is now used for low-bit-rate traffic and short-frame traffic such as audio (compressed or uncompressed), video, and fax. A good example of AAL2 use is in mobile telephony. AAL2 allows the multiplexing of short frames into one cell.

❏ **AAL3/4.** Initially, AAL3 was intended to support connection-oriented data services and AAL4 to support connectionless services. As they evolved, however, it became evident that the fundamental issues of the two protocols were the same. They have therefore been combined into a single format called AAL3/4.

❏ **AAL5.** AAL3/4 provides comprehensive sequencing and error control mechanisms that are not necessary for every application. For these applications, the designers of ATM have provided a fifth AAL sublayer, called the **simple and efficient adaptation layer (SEAL).** AAL5 assumes that all cells belonging to a single message travel sequentially and that control functions are included in the upper layers of the sending application. AAL5 is designed for connectionless packet protocols that use a datagram approach to routing (such as the IP protocol in TCP/IP).

The IP protocol uses the AAL5 sublayer.

ATM Layer   The ATM layer provides routing, traffic management, switching, and multiplexing services. It processes outgoing traffic by accepting 48-byte segments from the AAL sublayers and transforming them into 53-byte cells by the addition of a 5-byte header.

Physical Layer   The physical layer defines the transmission medium, bit transmission, encoding, and electrical to optical transformation. It provides convergence with physical transport protocols, such as SONET and T-3, as well as the mechanisms for transforming the flow of cells into a flow of bits.

We will discuss IP over ATM in Chapter 23.

3.4   CONNECTING DEVICES

LANs or WANs do not normally operate in isolation. They are connected to one another or to the Internet. To connect LANs or WANs, we use connecting devices. Connecting devices can operate in different layers of the Internet model. We discuss three kinds of **connecting devices:** repeaters (or hubs), bridges (or two-layer switches), and routers (or three-layer switches). Repeaters and hubs operate in the first layer of the Internet model. Bridges and two-layer switches operate in the first two layers. Routers and three-layer switches operate in the first three layers. Figure 3.28 shows the layers in which each device operates.

Figure 3.28   *Connecting devices*

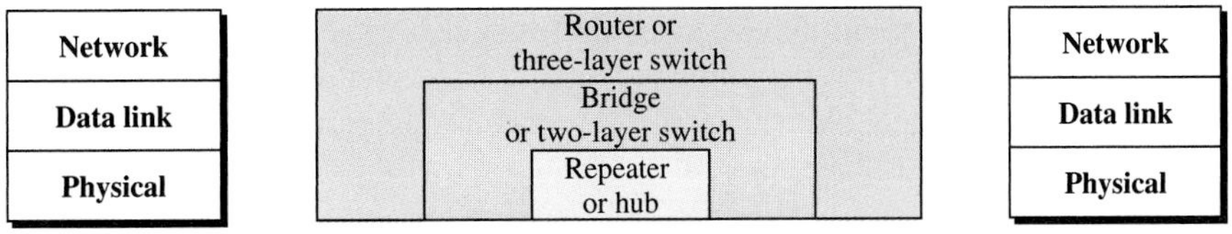

Network	Router or three-layer switch	Network
Data link	Bridge or two-layer switch	Data link
Physical	Repeater or hub	Physical

Repeaters

A **repeater** is a device that operates only in the physical layer. Signals that carry information within a network can travel a fixed distance before attenuation endangers the integrity of the data. A repeater receives a signal and, before it becomes too weak or corrupted, regenerates the original bit pattern. The repeater then sends the refreshed signal. A repeater can extend the physical length of a LAN, as shown in Figure 3.29.

Figure 3.29   *Repeater*

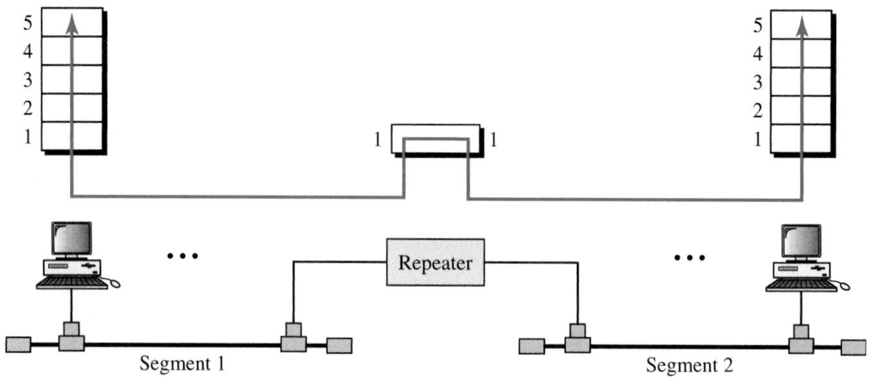

A repeater does not actually connect two LANs; it connects two segments of the same LAN. The segments connected are still part of one single LAN.

A repeater connects segments of a LAN.

A repeater can overcome the 10BASE5 Ethernet length restriction. In this standard, the length of the cable is limited to 500 m. To extend this length, we divide the cable into segments and install repeaters between segments. Note that the whole network is still considered one LAN, but the portions of the network separated by repeaters are called **segments.** The repeater acts as a two-port node, but operates only in the physical layer. When it receives a frame from any of the ports, it regenerates and forwards it to the other port.

A repeater forwards every bit; it has no filtering capability.

It is tempting to compare a repeater to an amplifier, but the comparison is inaccurate. An **amplifier** cannot discriminate between the intended signal and noise; it amplifies equally everything fed into it. A repeater does not amplify the signal; it regenerates the signal. When it receives a weakened or corrupted signal, it creates a copy, bit for bit, at the original strength.

A repeater is a regenerator, not an amplifier.

The location of a repeater on a link is vital. A repeater must be placed so that a signal reaches it before any noise changes the meaning of any of its bits. A little noise can alter the precision of a bit's voltage without destroying its identity (see Figure 3.30). If the corrupted bit travels much farther, however, accumulated noise can change its meaning completely. At that point, the original voltage is not recoverable, and the error needs to be corrected. A repeater placed on the line before the legibility of the signal becomes lost can still read the signal well enough to determine the intended voltages and replicate them in their original form.

Figure 3.30   *Function of a repeater*

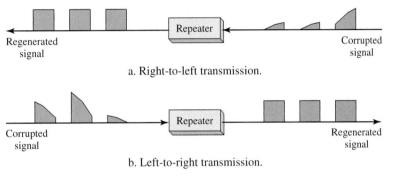

a. Right-to-left transmission.

b. Left-to-right transmission.

Hubs

Although, in a general sense, the word *hub* can refer to any connecting device, it does have a specific meaning. A **hub** is actually a multiport repeater. It is normally used to create connections between stations in a physical star topology.

Bridges

A **bridge** operates in both the physical and the data link layers. As a physical-layer device, it regenerates the signal it receives. As a data link layer device, the bridge can check the physical (MAC) addresses (source and destination) contained in the frame. Note that with properly spaced repeaters, all bits could be carried any distance. However the collision domain does not allow for this. Bridges are needed to overcome the collision domain restriction.

Filtering

One may ask what is the difference in functionality between a bridge and a repeater. A bridge has **filtering** capability. It can check the destination address of a frame and decide if the frame should be forwarded or dropped. If the frame is to be forwarded, the decision must specify the port. A bridge has a table that maps addresses to ports.

A bridge has a table used in filtering decisions.

Let us give an example. In Figure 3.31, two LANs are connected by a bridge. If a frame destined for station 712B1345642 arrives at port 1, the bridge consults its table to find the departing port. According to its table, frames for 712B1345642 leave through port 1; therefore, there is no need for forwarding; the frame is dropped. On the other hand, if a frame for 712B1345641 arrives at port 2, the departing port is port 1 and the frame is forwarded. In the first case, LAN 2 remains free of traffic; in the second case, both LANs have traffic. In our example, we show a two-port bridge; in reality a bridge usually has more ports. Note also that a bridge does not change the physical addresses contained in the frame.

Figure 3.31 *Bridge*

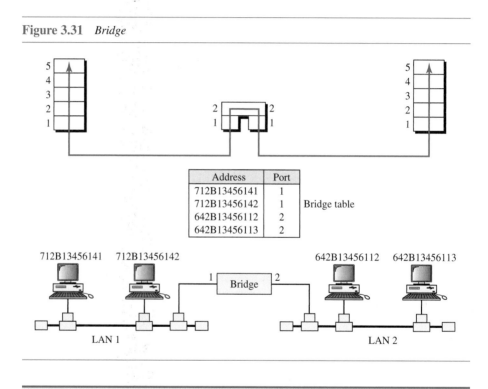

Address	Port
712B13456141	1
712B13456142	1
642B13456112	2
642B13456113	2

Bridge table

A bridge does not change the physical (MAC) addresses in a frame.

Transparent Bridges

A **transparent bridge** is a bridge in which the stations are completely unaware of the bridge's existence. If a bridge is added or deleted from the system, reconfiguration of the stations is unnecessary. According to the IEEE 802.1d specification, a system equipped with transparent bridges must meet three criteria:

1. Frames must be forwarded from one station to another.
2. The forwarding table is automatically made by learning frame movements in the network.
3. Loops in the system must be prevented.

Forwarding   A transparent bridge must correctly forward the frames, as discussed in the previous section.

Learning   The earliest bridges had forwarding tables that were static. The system administrator would manually enter each table entry during bridge setup. Although the process was simple, it was not practical. If a station was added or deleted, the table had to be modified manually. The same was true if a station's MAC address changed, which is not a rare event. For example, putting in a new network card means a new MAC address.

A better solution to the static table is a dynamic table that maps addresses to ports automatically. To make a table dynamic, we need a bridge that gradually learns from the frame movements. To do this, the bridge inspects both the destination and the source addresses. The destination address is used for the forwarding decision (table lookup); the source address is used for adding entries to the table and for updating purposes. Let us elaborate on this process using Figure 3.32.

Figure 3.32   *Learning bridge*

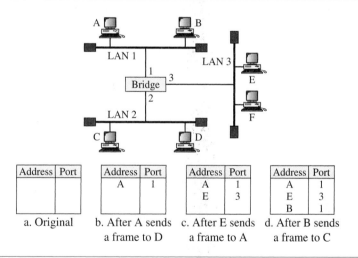

a. Original

b. After A sends a frame to D

c. After E sends a frame to A

d. After B sends a frame to C

1. When station A sends a frame to station D, the bridge does not have an entry for either D or A. The frame goes out from all three ports; the frame floods the network. However, by looking at the source address, the bridge learns that station A must be located on the LAN connected to port 1. This means that frames destined for A, in the future, must be sent out through port 1. The bridge adds this entry to its table. The table has its first entry now.

2. When station E sends a frame to station A, the bridge has an entry for A, so it forwards the frame only to port 1. There is no flooding. In addition, it uses the source address of the frame, E, to add a second entry to the table.

3. When station B sends a frame to C, the bridge has no entry for C, so once again it floods the network and adds one more entry to the table.

4. The process of learning continues as the bridge forwards frames.

Two-Layer Switch

When we use the term *switch,* we must be careful because a switch can mean two different things. We must clarify the term by adding the level at which the device operates. We can have a two-layer switch or a three-layer switch. A **three-layer switch** is used at the network layer; it is a kind of router. The **two-layer switch** performs at the physical and data link layer.

A two-layer switch is a bridge, a bridge with many ports and a design that allows better (faster) performance. A bridge with a few ports can connect a few LANs together. A bridge with many ports may be able to allocate a unique port to each station, with each station on its own independent entity. This means no competing traffic (no collision as we saw in Ethernet). In this book, to avoid confusion, we use the term *bridge* for a two-layer switch.

Routers

A **router** is a three-layer device; it operates in the physical, data link, and network layers. As a physical layer device, it regenerates the signal it receives. As a data link layer device, the router checks the physical addresses (source and destination) contained in the packet. As a network layer device, a router checks the network layer addresses (addresses in the IP layer). Note that bridges change collision domains, but routers limit broadcast domains.

A router is a three-layer (physical, data link, and network) device.

A router can connect LANs together; a router can connect WANs together; and a router can connect LANs and WANs together. In other words, a router is an internetworking device; it connects independent networks together to form an internetwork. According to this definition, two networks (LANs or WANs) connected by a router become an internetwork or an internet.

There are three major differences between a router and a repeater or a bridge.

1. A router has a physical and logical (IP) address for each of its interfaces.

A repeater or a bridge connects segments of a LAN.
A router connects independent LANs or WANs to create an internetwork (internet).

---

2. A router acts only on those packets in which the physical destination address matches the address of the interface at which the packet arrives.
3. A router changes the physical address of the packet (both source and destination) when it forwards the packet.

Let us give an example. In Figure 3.33, we show two LANs separated by a router. The left LAN has two segments separated by a bridge. The router changes the source and destination physical addresses of the packet. When the packet travels in the left LAN, its source physical address is the address of the sending station; its destination physical address is the address of the router. When the same packet travels in the second LAN, its source physical address is the address of the router and its destination physical address is the address of the final destination.

Figure 3.33 *Routing example*

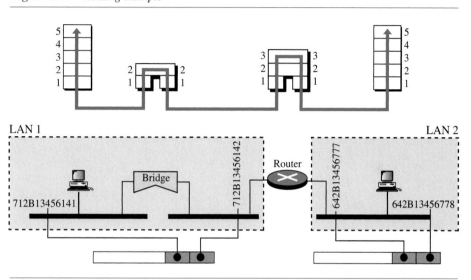

Routers route packets among multiple interconnected networks. They route packets from one network to any of a number of potential destination networks on an internet. Routers act like stations on a network. But unlike most stations, which are members of only one network, routers have addresses on, and links to, two or more networks.

A router changes the physical addresses in a packet.

We will learn more about routers and routing in future chapters after we have discussed IP addressing.

Three-Layer Switch

A three-layer switch is a router, a router with an improved design to allow better performance. A three-layer switch can receive, process, and dispatch a packet much faster than a traditional router even though the functionality is the same. In this book, to avoid confusion, we use the term router for a three-layer switch.

3.5 KEY TERMS

1000BASE-CX

1000BASE-LX

1000BASE-SX

1000BASE-T

100BASE-FX

100BASE-T4

100BASE-TX

100BASE-X

10BASE2

10BASE5

10BASE-FL

10BASE-T

access point (AP)

amplifier

application adaptation layer (AAL)

asymmetric digital subscriber line (ADSL)

asynchronous time-division multiplexing

Asynchronous Transfer Mode (ATM)

ATM switch

bandwidth on demand

basic service set (BSS)

bridge

bursty data

cable modem (CM)

cable modem transmission system (CMTS)

cable TV

carrier sense multiple access with collision avoidance (CSMA/CA)

carrier sense multiple access with collision detection (CSMA/CD)

cell

collision

community antenna TV (CATV)

connecting device

destination address (DA)

digital subscriber line (DSL)

digital subscriber line access multiplexer (DSLAM)

direct sequence spread spectrum (DSSS)

distributed coordination function (DCF)

downloading

Ethernet

extended service set (ESS)

Fast Ethernet

filtering

frame

frame check sequence (FCS)

Frame Relay

frequency hopping spread spectrum (FHSS)

full-duplex Ethernet

Gigabit Ethernet

hidden terminal problem

high bit rate digital subscriber line (HDSL)

high-rate DSSS (HR-DSSS)

hub

hybrid fiber-coaxial (HFC) network

Link Control Protocol (LCP)

local area network (LAN)

local loop

Network Control Protocol (NCP)

network interface card (NIC)

network-to-network interface (NNI)

optical carrier (OC)

orthogonal frequency-division multiplexing (OFDM)

point coordination function (PCF)

Point-to-Point Protocol (PPP)

PPP over Ethernet (PPPoE)

preamble

rate adaptive asymmetrical digital subscriber line (RADSL)

repeater

router

segment

simple and efficient adaptation layer (SEAL)

source address (SA)

spread spectrum

start frame delimiter (SFD)

switch

switched Ethernet

symmetric digital subscriber line (SDSL)

Synchronous Digital Hierarchy (SDH)

Synchronous Optical Network (SONET)

synchronous transport module (STM)

synchronous transport signal (STS)

T lines

three-layer switch

transmission path (TP)

transparent bridge

two-layer switch

T-1 line

T-3 line

uploading

upstream data band

user-to-network interface (UNI)

very high bit rate digital subscriber line (VDSL)

virtual circuit (VC)

virtual circuit identifier (VCI)

virtual connection identifier (VCI)

virtual path (VP)

virtual path identifier (VPI)

V.90

V.92

wide area network (WAN)

X.25

3.6 SUMMARY

❏ Ethernet is the most widely used local area network protocol.

❏ Traditional Ethernet uses CSMA/CD with a data rate of 10 Mbps and a collision domain of 2500 meters.

❏ The data link layer of Ethernet consists of the LLC sublayer and the MAC sublayer.

❏ The MAC sublayer is responsible for the operation of the CSMA/CD access method.

❏ Each station on an Ethernet network has a unique 48-bit address imprinted on its network interface card (NIC).

❏ The common implementations of 10-Mbps Ethernet are 10BASE5, 10BASE2, 10BASE-T, and 10BASE-FL.

❏ Fast Ethernet uses CSMA/CD with a data rate of 100 Mbps and a collision domain of 250 meters.

❏ The common Fast Ethernet implementations are 100BASE-TX, 100BASE-FX, and 100BASE-T4.

❏ Gigabit Ethernet has a data rate of 1000 Mbps. Common implementations are 1000BASE-SX, 1000BASE-LX, and 1000BASE-T.

❏ The IEEE 802.11 standard for wireless LANs defines two service sets: basic service set (BSS) and extended service set (ESS). An ESS consists of two or more BSSs; each BSS must have an access point (AP).

❏ The physical layer methods used by wireless LANs include frequency hopping spread spectrum (FHSS), direct sequence spread spectrum (DSSS), orthogonal frequency-division multiplexing (OFDM), and high-rate direct sequence spread spectrum (HR-DSSS).

❏ FHSS is a signal generation method in which repeated sequences of carrier frequencies are used for protection against hackers.

❏ One bit is replaced by a chip code in DSSS.

❏ OFDM specifies that one source must use all the channels of the bandwidth.

❏ HR-DSSS is DSSS with an encoding method called complementary code keying (CCK).

❏ The wireless LAN access method is CSMA/CA.

❏ A point-to-point connection to the Internet is possible using regular telephone lines and traditional modems, DSL lines, cable modems, T-lines, or SONET networks.

❏ The Point-to-Point Protocol (PPP) was designed for users who need a reliable point-to-point connection to the Internet.

❏ PPP operates at the physical and data link layers of the OSI model.

❏ X.25 is a switched WAN that is being replaced by other technologies.

❏ Frame Relay eliminates the extensive error checking necessary in X.25 protocol. Frame Relay operates in the physical and data link layers of the OSI model.

❏ Asynchronous Transfer Mode (ATM) is the cell relay protocol designed to support the transmission of data, voice, and video through high data-rate transmission media such as fiber-optic cable.

❏ The ATM data packet is called a cell and is composed of 53 bytes (5 bytes of header and 48 bytes of payload).

❏ The ATM standard defines three layers: the application adaptation layer (AAL), the ATM layer, and the physical layer.

❏ There are four different AALs, each specific for a data type. TCP/IP uses AAL5, which converts data coming from a connectionless packet switching network.

❏ Connecting devices can connect segments of a network together; they can also connect networks together to create an internet.

❏ There are three types of connecting devices: repeaters (and hubs), bridges (and two-layer switches), and routers (and three-layer switches).

❏ Repeaters regenerate a signal at the physical layer. A hub is a multiport repeater.

❏ Bridges have access to station addresses and can forward or filter a packet in a network. They operate at the physical and data link layers. A two-layer switch is a sophisticated bridge.

❏ Routers determine the path a packet should take. They operate at the physical, data link, and network layers. A three-layer switch is a sophisticated router.

3.7 PRACTICE SET

Exercises

1. Why do you think that an Ethernet frame should have a minimum data size?

2. Imagine the length of a 10BASE5 cable is 2500 meters. If the speed of propagation in a thick coaxial cable is 200,000,000 meters/second, how long does it take for a bit to travel from the beginning to the end of the network? Ignore any propagation delay in the equipment.

3. Using the data in Exercise 2, find the maximum time it takes to sense a collision. The worst case occurs when data are sent from one end of the cable and the collision happens at the other end. Remember that the signal needs to make a round-trip.

4. The data rate of 10BASE5 is 10 Mbps. How long does it take to create the smallest frame? Show your calculation.

5. Using the data in Exercises 3 and 4, find the minimum size of an Ethernet frame for collision detection to work properly.

6. An Ethernet MAC sublayer receives 42 bytes of data from the LLC sublayer. How many bytes of padding must be added to the data?

7. An Ethernet MAC sublayer receives 1510 bytes of data from the LLC layer. Can the data be encapsulated in one frame? If not, how many frames need to be sent? What is the size of the data in each frame?

8. Compare and contrast CSMA/CD with CSMA/CA.

9. Use Table 3.4 to compare and contrast the fields in IEEE 802.3 and 802.11.

Research Activities

10. Traditional Ethernet uses a version of the CSMA/CD access method. It is called CSMA/CD with 1-persistent. Find some information about this method.

11. Another wireless LAN today is Bluetooth. Find some information about this LAN and how it can be used in the Internet.

12. DSL uses a modulation technique called DMT. Find some information about this modulation technique and how it can be used in DSL.

Table 3.4   *Exercise 9*

Fields	IEEE 802.3 Field Size	IEEE 802.11 Field Size
Destination address		
Source address		
Address 1		
Address 2		
Address 3		
Address 4		
FC		
D/ID		
SC		
PDU length		
Data and padding		
Frame body		
FCS (CRC)		

13. PPP goes through different phases, which can be shown in a transition state diagram. Find the transition diagram for a PPP connection.

14. Find the format of an LCP packet (encapsulated in a PPP frame). Include all fields, their codes, and their purposes.

15. Find the format of an NCP packet (encapsulated in a PPP frame). Include all fields, their codes, and their purposes.

16. Find the format of an ICP packet (encapsulated in a PPP frame). Include all fields, their codes, and their purposes.

17. PPP uses two authentication protocols, PAP and CHAP. Find some information about these two protocols and how they are used in PPP.

18. Find the format of a PPPoE packet. Include all fields and their purposes.

19. Find how an IP packet can be encapsulated in ATM cells using AAL5 layer.

20. To prevent loops in a network using transparent bridges, one uses the spanning tree algorithm. Find some information about this algorithm and how it can prevent loops.

CHAPTER 4

IP Addresses: Classful Addressing

At the network (or IP) layer, we need to uniquely identify each device on the Internet to allow global communication between all devices. This is analogous to the telephone system, where each telephone subscriber has a unique telephone number with the country code and the area code as part of the identifying scheme.

In this chapter, we discuss the general idea behind IP addressing and classful addressing, the addressing mechanisms of the early Internet. In Chapter 5, we introduce **classless addressing,** the prevailing addressing mechanism in the current Internet.

4.1 INTRODUCTION

The identifier used in the IP layer of the TCP/IP protocol suite to identify each device connected to the Internet is called the Internet address or **IP address.** An IP address is a 32-bit address that *uniquely* and *universally* defines the connection of a host or a router to the Internet.

An IP address is a 32-bit address.

IP addresses are unique. They are unique in the sense that each address defines one, and only one, connection to the Internet. Two devices on the Internet can never have the same address. However, if a device has two connections to the Internet, via two networks, it has two IP addresses.

The IP addresses are unique.

The IP addresses are universal in the sense that the addressing system must be accepted by any host that wants to be connected to the Internet.

Address Space

A protocol like IP that defines addresses has an **address space.** An address space is the total number of addresses used by the protocol. If a protocol uses N bits to define an address, the address space is 2^N because each bit can have two different values (0 or 1) and N bits can have 2^N values.

IPv4 uses 32-bit addresses, which means that the address space is 2^{32} or 4,294,967,296 (more than four billion). This means that, theoretically, if there were no restrictions, more than 4 billion devices could be connected to the Internet. We will see shortly that the actual number is much less.

> The address space of IPv4 is 2^{32} or 4,294,967,296.

Notation

There are three common notations to show an IP address: **binary notation, dotted-decimal notation,** and **hexadecimal notation.**

Binary Notation

In binary notation, the IP address is displayed as 32 bits. To make the address more readable, one or more spaces is usually inserted between each octet (8 bits). Each octet is often referred to as a byte. So it is common to hear an IP address referred to as a 32-bit address, a 4-octet address, or a 4-byte address. The following is an example of an IP address in binary notation:

> 01110101   10010101   00011101   11101010

Dotted-Decimal Notation

To make the IP address more compact and easier to read, Internet addresses are usually written in decimal form with a decimal point (dot) separating the bytes. Figure 4.1 shows an IP address in dotted-decimal notation. Note that because each byte (octet) is only 8 bits, each number in the dotted-decimal notation is between 0 and 255.

Figure 4.1   *Dotted-decimal notation*

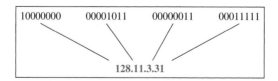

> The binary, decimal, and hexadecimal number systems are reviewed in Appendix B.

Example 1

Change the following IP addresses from binary notation to dotted-decimal notation.

    a. 10000001 00001011 00001011 11101111

    b. 11000001 10000011 00011011 11111111

    c. 11100111 11011011 10001011 01101111

    d. 11111001 10011011 11111011 00001111

Solution

We replace each group of 8 bits with its equivalent decimal number (see Appendix B) and add dots for separation:

    a. 129.11.11.239

    b. 193.131.27.255

    c. 231.219.139.111

    d. 249.155.251.15

Example 2

Change the following IP addresses from dotted-decimal notation to binary notation.

    a. 111.56.45.78

    b. 221.34.7.82

    c. 241.8.56.12

    d. 75.45.34.78

Solution

We replace each decimal number with its binary equivalent (see Appendix B):

    a. 01101111 00111000 00101101 01001110

    b. 11011101 00100010 00000111 01010010

    c. 11110001 00001000 00111000 00001100

    d. 01001011 00101101 00100010 01001110

Example 3

Find the error, if any, in the following IP addresses:

    a. 111.56.045.78

    b. 221.34.7.8.20

    c. 75.45.301.14

    d. 11100010.23.14.67

Solution

    a. There are no leading zeroes in dotted-decimal notation (045).

    b. We may not have more than four numbers in an IP address.

    c. In dotted-decimal notation, each number is less than or equal to 255; 301 is outside this range.

    d. A mixture of binary notation and dotted-decimal notation is not allowed.

Hexadecimal Notation

We sometimes see an IP address in hexadecimal notation. Each hexadecimal digit is equivalent to four bits. This means that a 32-bit address has 8 hexadecimal digits. This notation is often used in network programming.

Example 4

Change the following IP addresses from binary notation to hexadecimal notation.

  a. 10000001 00001011   00001011 11101111
  b. 11000001 10000011   00011011 11111111

Solution

We replace each group of 4 bits with its hexadecimal equivalent (see Appendix B). Note that hexadecimal notation normally has no added spaces or dots; however, 0X (or 0x) is added at the beginning or the subscript 16 at the end to show that the number is in hexadecimal.

  a. 0X810B0BEF   or   810B0BEF$_{16}$
  b. 0XC1831BFF   or   C1831BFF$_{16}$

4.2   CLASSFUL ADDRESSING

IP addresses, when started a few decades ago, used the concept of classes. This architecture is called **classful addressing.** In the mid-1990s, a new architecture, called **classless addressing,** was introduced and will eventually supersede the original architecture. However, although part of the Internet is still using classful addressing, the migration is proceeding very fast. In this chapter, we introduce the concept of classful addressing; in the next chapter, we discuss classless addressing. The concept of "classful" is needed to understand the concept of "classless."

In classful addressing, the IP address space is divided into five classes: A, B, C, D, and E. Each class occupies some part of the whole address space. Figure 4.2 shows the class occupation of the address space (approximation).

Figure 4.2   *Occupation of the address space*

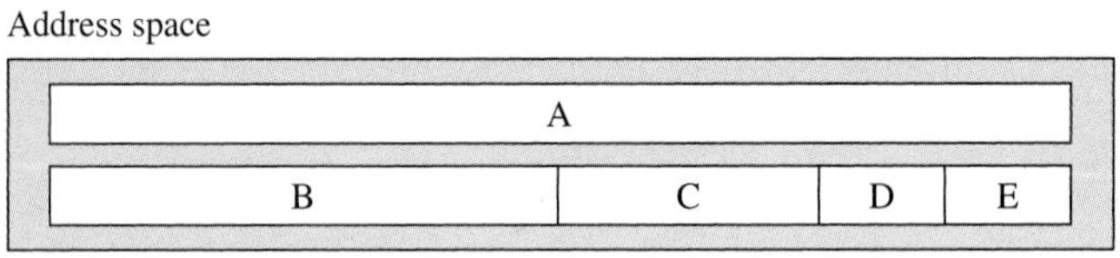

We can see from the figure that class A covers half of the address space, a serious design flaw. Class B covers 1/4 of the whole address space, another design flaw. Class C covers 1/8 of the address space, and classes D and E each cover 1/16 of the address space. Table 4.1 shows the number of addresses in each class.

Table 4.1   *Addresses per class*

Class	Number of Addresses	Percentage
A	$2^{31} = 2,147,483,648$	50%
B	$2^{30} = 1,073,741,824$	25%
C	$2^{29} = 536,870,912$	12.5%
D	$2^{28} = 268,435,456$	6.25%
E	$2^{28} = 268,435,456$	6.25%

In classful addressing, the address space is divided into five classes: A, B, C, D, and E.

Recognizing Classes

We can find the class of an address when the address is given in binary notation or dotted-decimal notation.

Finding the Class in Binary Notation

If the address is given in binary notation, the first few bits can immediately tell us the class of the address as shown in Figure 4.3.

Figure 4.3   *Finding the class in binary notation*

	First byte	Second byte	Third byte	Fourth byte
Class A	0			
Class B	10			
Class C	110			
Class D	1110			
Class E	1111			

One can follow the procedure shown in Figure 4.4 to systematically check the bits and find the class. The procedure can be easily programmed in any language.

Figure 4.4   *Finding the address class*

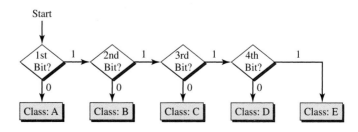

Note that some special addresses fall in class A or E. We emphasize that these special addresses are exceptions to the classification; they are discussed later in this chapter.

Example 5

How can we prove that we have 2,147,483,648 addresses in class A?

Solution

In class A, only 1 bit defines the class. The remaining 31 bits are available for the address. With 31 bits, we can have 2^{31} or 2,147,483,648 addresses.

Example 6

Find the class of each address:

    a. **00000001** 00001011 00001011 11101111
    b. **11000001** 10000011 00011011 11111111
    c. **10100111** 11011011 10001011 01101111
    d. **11110011** 10011011 11111011 00001111

Solution

See the procedure in Figure 4.4.

    a. The first bit is 0. This is a **class A address.**
    b. The first 2 bits are 1; the third bit is 0. This is a **class C address.**
    c. The first bit is 0; the second bit is 1. This is a **class B address.**
    d. The first 4 bits are 1s. This is a **class E address.**

Finding the Class in Dotted-Decimal Notation

When the address is given in dotted-decimal notation, then we need to look only at the first byte (number) to determine the class of the address. Each class has a specific range of numbers. Figure 4.5 shows the idea.

Figure 4.5   *Finding the class in decimal notation*

	First byte	Second byte	Third byte	Fourth byte
Class A	0 to 127			
Class B	128 to 191			
Class C	192 to 223			
Class D	224 to 239			
Class E	240 to 255			

This means that if the first byte (in decimal) is between 0 and 127, the class is A. If the first byte is between 128 and 191, the class is B. And so on.

Example 7

Find the class of each address:

    a. **227**.12.14.87
    b. **193**.14.56.22
    c. **14**.23.120.8
    d. **252**.5.15.111
    e. **134**.11.78.56

Solution

    a. The first byte is 227 (between 224 and 239); the class is D.
    b. The first byte is 193 (between 192 and 223); the class is C.
    c. The first byte is 14 (between 0 and 127); the class is A.
    d. The first byte is 252 (between 240 and 255); the class is E.
    e. The first byte is 134 (between 128 and 191); the class is B.

Example 8

In Example 5 we showed that class A has 2^{31} (2,147,483,648) addresses. How can we prove this same fact using dotted-decimal notation?

Solution

The addresses in class A range from 0.0.0.0 to 127.255.255.255. We need to show that the difference between these two numbers is 2,147,483,648. This is a good exercise because it shows us how to define the range of addresses between two addresses. We notice that we are dealing with base 256 numbers here. Each byte in the notation has a weight. The weights are as follows (see Appendix B):

$$256^3, 256^2, 256^1, 256^0$$

Now to find the integer value of each number, we multiply each byte by its weight:

$$\text{Last address:}\ \ 127 \times 256^3 + 255 \times 256^2 + 255 \times 256^1 + 255 \times 256^0 = 2{,}147{,}483{,}647$$

$$\text{First address:}\ \ = 0$$

If we subtract the first from the last and add 1 to the result (remember we always add 1 to get the range), we get 2,147,483,648 or 2^{31}.

Netid and Hostid

In classful addressing, an IP address in classes A, B, and C is divided into **netid** and **hostid.** These parts are of varying lengths, depending on the class of the address. Figure 4.6 shows the netid and hostid bytes. Note that classes D and E are not divided into netid and hostid for reasons that we will discuss later.

    In class A, 1 byte defines the netid and 3 bytes define the hostid. In class B, 2 bytes define the netid and 2 bytes define the hostid. In class C, 3 bytes define the netid and 1 byte defines the hostid.

Figure 4.6   *Netid and hostid*

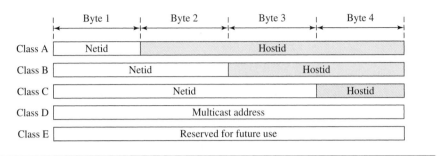

Classes and Blocks

One problem with classful addressing is that each class is divided into a fixed number of blocks with each block having a fixed size. Let us look at each class.

Class A

Class A is divided into 128 blocks with each block having a different netid. The first block covers addresses from **0**.0.0.0 to **0**.255.255.255 (netid **0**). The second block covers addresses from **1**.0.0.0 to **1**.255.255.255 (netid **1**). The last block covers addresses from **127**.0.0.0 to **127**.255.255.255 (netid **127**). Note that for each **block of addresses** the first byte (netid) is the same, but the other 3 bytes (hostid) can take any value in the given range.

   The first and the last blocks in this class are reserved for special purposes as we will discuss shortly. In addition, one block (netid 10) is used for private addresses. The remaining 125 blocks can be assigned to organizations. This means that the total number of organizations that can have class A addresses is only 125. However, each block in this class contains 16,777,216 addresses, which means the organization should be a really large one to use all these addresses. Figure 4.7 shows the blocks in class A.

   Figure 4.7 also shows how an organization that is granted a block with netid 73 uses its addresses. The first address in the block is used to identify the organization to the rest of the Internet. This address is called the **network address;** it defines the network of the organization, not individual hosts. The organization is not allowed to use the last address; it is reserved for a special purpose as we will see shortly.

   Class A addresses were designed for large organizations with a large number of hosts or routers attached to their network. However, the number of addresses in each block, 16,777,216, is probably larger than the needs of almost all organizations. Many addresses are wasted in this class.

Millions of class A addresses are wasted.

Class B

Class B is divided into 16,384 blocks with each block having a different netid. Sixteen blocks are reserved for private addresses, leaving 16,368 blocks for assignment to organizations. The first block covers addresses from **128.0**.0.0 to **128.0**.255.255 (netid

Figure 4.7   *Blocks in class A*

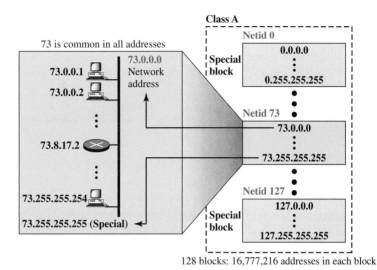

128 blocks: 16,777,216 addresses in each block

128.0). The last block covers addresses from **191.255**.0.0 to **191.255**.255.255 (netid **191.255**). Note that for each block of addresses the first 2 bytes (netid) are the same, but the other 2 bytes (hostid) can take any value in the given range.

There are 16,368 blocks that can be assigned. This means that the total number of organizations that can have a class B address is 16,368. However, since each block in this class contains 65,536 addresses, the organization should be large enough to use all of these addresses. Figure 4.8 shows the blocks in class B.

Figure 4.8   *Blocks in class B*

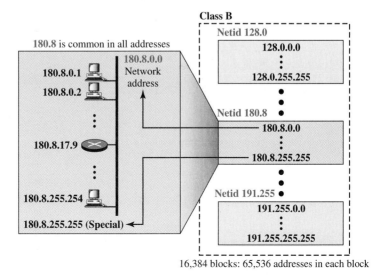

16,384 blocks: 65,536 addresses in each block

Figure 4.8 also shows how an organization that is granted a block with netid 180.8 uses its addresses. The first address is the network address; the last address is reserved for a special purpose as we will see shortly.

Class B addresses were designed for mid-size organizations that may have tens of thousands of hosts or routers attached to their networks. However, the number of addresses in each block, 65,536, is larger than the needs of most mid-size organizations. Many addresses are also wasted in this class.

> **Many class B addresses are wasted.**

Class C

Class C is divided into 2,097,152 blocks with each block having a different netid. Two hundred fifty-six blocks are used for private addresses, leaving 2,096,896 blocks for assignment to organizations. The first block covers addresses from **192.0.0.0** to **192.0.0.255** (netid **192.0.0**). The last block covers addresses from **223.255.255.0.** to **223.255.255.255** (netid **223.255.255**). Note that for each block of addresses the first 3 bytes (netid) are the same, but the remaining byte (hostid) can take any value in the given range.

There are 2,096,896 blocks that can be assigned. This means that the total number of organizations that can have a class C address is 2,096,896. However, each block in this class contains 256 addresses, which means the organization should be small enough to need less than 256 addresses. Figure 4.9 shows the blocks in class C.

Figure 4.9 *Blocks in class C*

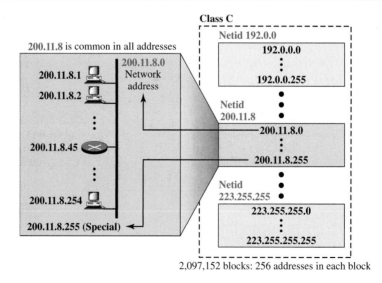

Figure 4.9 also shows how an organization that is granted a block with netid 200.11.8 uses the addresses. The first address is the network address; the last address is reserved for a special purpose as we will see shortly.

Class C addresses were designed for small organizations with a small number of hosts or routers attached to their networks. The number of addresses in each block is so limited that most organizations do not want a block in this class.

The number of addresses in class C is smaller than the needs of most organizations.

Class D

There is just one block of class D addresses. It is designed for multicasting as we will see in a later section. Each address in this class is used to define one group of hosts on the Internet. When a group is assigned an address in this class, every host that is a member of this group will have a multicast address in addition to its normal (unicast) address.

Class D addresses are used for multicasting; there is only one block in this class.

Class E

There is just one block of class E addresses. It was designed for use as reserved addresses.

Class E addresses are reserved for future purposes; most of the block is wasted.

Network Addresses

Network addresses play a very important role in classful addressing. A network address has several properties:

1. The network address is the first address in the block.
2. The network address defines the network to the rest of the Internet. In later chapters, we learn that routers route a packet based on the network address.
3. Given the network address, we can find the class of the address, the block, and the range of the addresses in the block.

In classful addressing, the network address (the first address in the block) is the one that is assigned to the organization. The range of addresses can automatically be inferred from the network address.

Example 9

Given the network address 17.0.0.0, find the class, the block, and the range of the addresses.

Solution

The class is A because the first byte is between 0 and 127. The block has a netid of 17. The addresses range from 17.0.0.0 to 17.255.255.255.

Example 10

Given the network address 132.21.0.0, find the class, the block, and the range of the addresses.

Solution

The class is B because the first byte is between 128 and 191. The block has a netid of 132.21. The addresses range from 132.21.0.0 to 132.21.255.255.

Example 11

Given the network address 220.34.76.0, find the class, the block, and the range of the addresses.

Solution

The class is C because the first byte is between 192 and 223. The block has a netid of 220.34.76. The addresses range from 220.34.76.0 to 220.34.76.255.

Sufficient Information

The reader may have noticed that in classful addressing, the network address gives sufficient information about the network. Given the network address, we can find the number of addresses in the block. The reason is that the number of addresses in each block is predetermined. All blocks in class A have the same range, all blocks in class B have the same range, and all blocks in class C have the same range.

Mask

In the previous section, we said that if the network address is given, we can find the block and the range of addresses in the block. What about the reverse? If an address is given, can we find the network address (the beginning address in the block)? This is important because to route a packet to the correct network, a router needs to extract a network address from the destination address (a host address) in the packet header.

One way we can find the network address is to first find the class of the address and the netid. We then set the hostid to zero to find the network address. For example, if the address 134.45.78.2 is given, we can immediately say that the address belongs to class B. The netid is 134.45 (2 bytes) and the network address is 134.45.0.0.

The above method is feasible if we have not subnetted the network; that is, if we have not divided the network into subnetworks. A general procedure that can be used involves a **mask** to find the network address from a given address.

Concept

A mask is a 32-bit number that gives the first address in the block (the network address) when bitwise ANDed with an address in the block. Figure 4.10 shows the concept of masking.

AND Operation

Masking uses the bitwise **AND operation** defined in computer science. The operation is applied bit by bit to the address and the mask. For our purpose, it is enough to know that the AND operation does the following:

1. If the bit in the mask is 1, the corresponding bit in the address is retained in the output (no change).
2. If the bit in the mask is 0, a 0 bit in the output is the result.

Figure 4.10   *Masking concept*

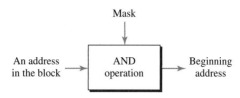

In other words, the bits in the address corresponding to the 1s in the mask are preserved (remain 0 or 1, as they were) and the bits corresponding to the 0s in the mask change to 0. Figure 4.11 shows the two cases.

Figure 4.11   *AND operation*

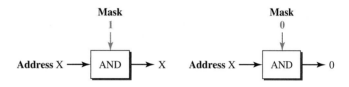

Default Masks

In the AND operation for classful addressing, there are three masks, one for each class. Table 4.2 shows the mask for each class. For class A, the mask is eight 1s and twenty-four 0s. For class B, the mask is sixteen 1s and sixteen 0s. For class C, the mask is twenty-four 1s and eight 0s. The 1s preserve the netid; the 0s set the hostid to 0. Remember that the network address in any class is the netid with the hostid all 0s. Table 4.2 shows the **default mask** for each class.

Table 4.2   *Default masks*

Class	Mask in binary	Mask in dotted-decimal
A	11111111 00000000 00000000 00000000	255.0.0.0
B	11111111 11111111 00000000 00000000	255.255.0.0
C	11111111 111111111 11111111 00000000	255.255.255.0

Note that the number of 1s in each class matches the number of bits in the netid and the number of 0s matches the number of bits in the hostid. In other words, when a mask is ANDed with an address, the netid is retained and the hostid is set to 0s.

> The network address is the beginning address of each block. It can be found by applying the default mask to any of the addresses in the block (including itself). It retains the netid of the block and sets the hostid to zero.

Applying the Masks

Applying the mask to an unsubnetted network is simple. Two rules can help find the network address without applying the AND operation to each bit.

1. If the mask byte is 255, retain the corresponding byte in the address.
2. If the mask byte is 0, set the corresponding byte to 0.

Example 12

Given the address 23.56.7.91, find the beginning address (network address).

Solution

The default mask is 255.0.0.0, which means that only the first byte is preserved and the other 3 bytes are set to 0s. The network address is 23.0.0.0.

Example 13

Given the address 132.6.17.85, find the beginning address (network address).

Solution

The default mask is 255.255.0.0, which means that the first 2 bytes are preserved and the other 2 bytes are set to 0s. The network address is 132.6.0.0.

Example 14

Given the address 201.180.56.5, find the beginning address (network address).

Solution

The default mask is 255.255.255.0, which means that the first 3 bytes are preserved and the last byte is set to 0. The network address is 201.180.56.0.

Note that we must not apply the default mask of one class to an address belonging to another class.

CIDR Notation

Although in classful addressing each address has a default mask, it is sometimes convenient (and compatible with classless addressing, see the next chapter) to explicitly indicate the default mask. The CIDR (pronounced cider), or **classless interdomain routing,** notation is used for this purpose. In this notation, the number of 1s in the mask is added after a slash at the end of the address. For example, the address 18.46.74.10, which is a class A address with the mask 255.0.0.0, is written as 18.46.74.10/8 to show that there are eight 1s in the mask. Similarly, the address 141.24.74.69 is written as 141.24.74.69/16 to show that it is a class B address and the mask has sixteen 1s. In the same way, the address 200.14.70.22 is written as 200.14.70.22/24. In the next chapter, we will see that CIDR is particularly useful in classless addressing.

Address Depletion

Due to the classful addressing scheme and due to the fast growth of the Internet, the available addresses are almost depleted. Despite this, the number of devices on the Internet is much less than the 2^{32} address space. We have run out of class A and B addresses, and a class C block is too small for most middle-size organizations. Later, we discuss some remedies to this problem.

4.3   OTHER ISSUES

In this section, we discuss some other issues that are related to addressing in general and classful addressing in particular.

Multihomed Devices

An Internet address defines the node's connection to its network. It follows, therefore, that any device connected to more than one network must have more than one Internet address. In fact, a device has a different address for each network connected to it. A computer that is connected to different networks is called a **multihomed** computer and will have more than one address, each possibly belonging to a different class. A router must be connected to more than one network, otherwise it cannot route. Therefore, a router definitely has more than one IP address, one for each interface. In Figure 4.12 we have one multihomed computer and one router. The computer is connected to two networks and its two IP addresses reflect this. Likewise, the router is connected to three networks and therefore has three IP addresses.

Figure 4.12   *Multihomed devices*

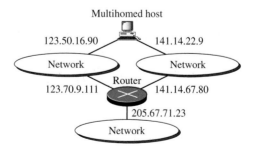

Location, Not Names

An Internet address defines the network location of a device, not its identity. In other words, because an Internet address is made of two parts (netid and hostid), it can only define the connection of a device to a specific network. One of the ramifications of this is that the movement of a computer from one network to another means that its IP address must be changed.

Special Addresses

Some parts of the address space are used for special addresses (see Table 4.3).

Table 4.3   *Special addresses*

Special Address	Netid	Hostid	Source or Destination
Network address	Specific	All 0s	None
Direct broadcast address	Specific	All 1s	Destination
Limited broadcast address	All 1s	All 1s	Destination
This host on this network	All 0s	All 0s	Source
Specific host on this network	All 0s	Specific	Destination
Loopback address	127	Any	Destination

Network Address

We have already covered the topic of network addresses. The first address in a block (in classes A, B, and C) defines the network address. Figure 4.13 shows three examples of network address, one for each class.

Figure 4.13   *Network address*

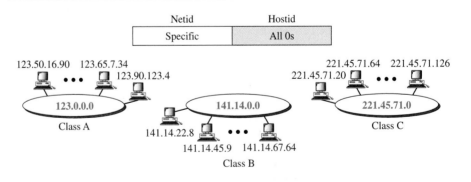

Direct Broadcast Address

In classes A, B, and C, if the hostid is all 1s, the address is called a **direct broadcast address.** It is used by a router to send a packet to all hosts in a specific network. All hosts will accept a packet having this type of destination address. Note that this address can be used only as a destination address in an IP packet. Note also that this special address also reduces the number of available hostids for each netid in classes A, B, and C.

In Figure 4.14, the router sends a datagram using a destination IP address with a hostid of all 1s. All devices on this network receive and process the datagram.

Figure 4.14   *Example of direct broadcast address*

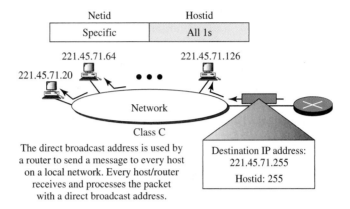

The direct broadcast address is used by a router to send a message to every host on a local network. Every host/router receives and processes the packet with a direct broadcast address.

Destination IP address: 221.45.71.255

Hostid: 255

Limited Broadcast Address

In classes A, B, and C, an address with all 1s for the netid and hostid (32 bits) defines a broadcast address in the current network. A host that wants to send a message to every other host can use this address as a destination address in an IP packet. However, a router will block a packet having this type of address to confine the broadcasting to the local network. Note that this address belongs to class E. In Figure 4.15, a host sends a datagram using a destination IP address consisting of all 1s. All devices on this network receive and process this datagram.

Figure 4.15   *Example of limited broadcast address*

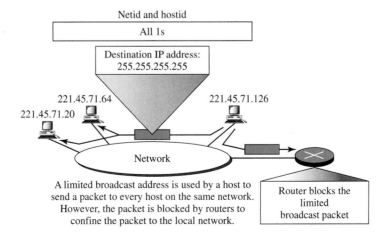

A limited broadcast address is used by a host to send a packet to every host on the same network. However, the packet is blocked by routers to confine the packet to the local network.

Router blocks the limited broadcast packet

This Host on This Network

If an IP address is composed of all zeros, it means *this host on this network*. This is used by a host at bootstrap time when it does not know its IP address. The host sends an IP packet to a bootstrap server using this address as the source address and a limited broadcast address as the destination address to find its own address. Note that this address can be used only as a source address. Note also that this address is always a class A address regardless of the network. It reduces the number of blocks in class A by one (see Figure 4.16).

Figure 4.16   *Examples of "this host on this network"*

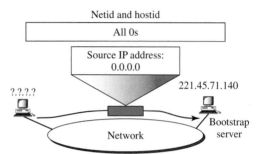

A host that does not know its IP address uses the
IP address 0.0.0.0 as the source address and
255.255.255.255 as the destination address to send
a message to a bootstrap server.

Specific Host on This Network

An IP address with a netid of all zeros means a specific host on this network. It is used by a host to send a message to another host on the same network. Because the packet is blocked by the router, it is a way of confining the packet to the local network. Note that it can be used only for a destination address. Note also it is actually a class A address regardless of the network (see Figure 4.17).

Figure 4.17   *Example of "specific host on this network"*

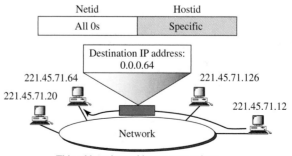

This address is used by a router or host
to send a message to a specific host on the same network.

Loopback Address

The IP address with the first byte equal to 127 is used for the **loopback address,** which is an address used to test the software on a machine. When this address is used, a packet never leaves the machine; it simply returns to the protocol software. It can be used to test the IP software. For example, an application such as "ping" can send a packet with a loopback address as the destination address to see if the IP software is capable of receiving and processing a packet. As another example, the loopback address can be used by a **client process** (a running application program) to send a message to a server process on the same machine. Note that this can be used only as a destination address in an IP packet. Note also that this is actually a class A address. It reduces the number of blocks in class A by 1 (see Figure 4.18).

Figure 4.18   *Example of loopback address*

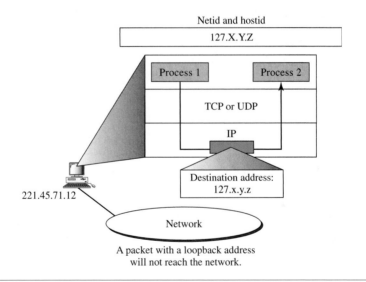

A packet with a loopback address
will not reach the network.

Private Addresses

A number of blocks in each class are assigned for private use. They are not recognized globally. These blocks are depicted in Table 4.4. These addresses are used either in isolation or in connection with network address translation techniques (see Chapter 26).

Table 4.4   *Addresses for private networks*

Class	Netids	Blocks
A	10.0.0	1
B	172.16 to 172.31	16
C	192.168.0 to 192.168.255	256

Unicast, Multicast, and Broadcast Addresses

Communication on the Internet can be achieved using unicast, multicast, or broadcast addresses.

Unicast Addresses

Unicast communication is *one-to-one*. When a packet is sent from an individual source to an individual destination, a unicast communication takes place. All systems directly connected to the Internet have at least one unique unicast address. Unicast addresses belong to classes A, B, or C.

Multicast Addresses

Multicast communication is *one-to-many*. When a packet is sent from an individual source to a group of destinations, a multicast communication takes place. A multicast address is a **class D address.** The entire address defines a groupid. A system on the Internet can have one or more class D multicast addresses (in addition to its unicast address or addresses). If a system (usually a host) has seven multicast addresses, it means that it belongs to seven different groups. Note that a class D address can be used only as a destination address, not as a source address.

Multicasting on the Internet can be at the local level or at the global level. At the local level, hosts on a LAN can form a group and be assigned a multicast address. At the global level, hosts on different networks can form a group and be assigned a multicast address.

Multicast delivery will be discussed in depth in Chapter 15.

Assigned Multicast Addresses   The Internet authorities have designated some multicast addresses to specific groups. We mention two here.

❑ **Category.** Some multicast addresses are assigned for some special use. These multicast addresses start with a 224.0.0 prefix. Table 4.5 shows some of these addresses.

Table 4.5   *Category addresses*

Address	Group
224.0.0.0	Reserved
224.0.0.1	All SYSTEMS on this SUBNET
224.0.0.2	All ROUTERS on this SUBNET
224.0.0.4	DVMRP ROUTERS
224.0.0.5	OSPFIGP All ROUTERS
224.0.0.6	OSPFIGP Designated ROUTERS
224.0.0.7	ST Routers
224.0.0.8	ST Hosts
224.0.0.9	RIP2 Routers
224.0.0.10	IGRP Routers
224.0.0.11	Mobile-Agents

❏ **Conferencing.** Some multicast addresses are used for conferencing and teleconferencing. These multicast addresses start with the 224.0.1 prefix. Table 4.6 shows some of these addresses.

Table 4.6   *Addresses for conferencing*

Address	Group
224.0.1.7	AUDIONEWS
224.0.1.10	IETF-1-LOW-AUDIO
224.0.1.11	IETF-1-AUDIO
224.0.1.12	IETF-1-VIDEO
224.0.1.13	IETF-2-LOW-AUDIO
224.0.1.14	IETF-2-AUDIO
224.0.1.15	IETF-2-VIDEO
224.0.1.16	MUSIC-SERVICE
224.0.1.17	SEANET-TELEMETRY
224.0.1.18	SEANET-IMAGE

Broadcast Addresses

Broadcast communication is *one-to-all*. The Internet allows broadcasting only at the local level. We have already discussed two broadcast addresses used at the local level: the limited broadcast address (all 1s) and the direct broadcast address (netid: specific, hostid: all 1s).

No broadcasting is allowed at the global level. This means that a system (host or router) cannot send a message to all hosts and routers in the Internet. You can imagine the traffic that would result without this restriction.

An Example

Figure 4.19 shows a part of an internet with five networks.

1. A LAN with network address 220.3.6.0 (class C).
2. A LAN with network address 134.18.0.0 (class B).
3. A LAN with network address 124.0.0.0 (class A).
4. A point-to-point WAN (broken line). This network (a T-1 line, for example) just connects two routers; there are no hosts. In this case, to save addresses, no network address is assigned to this type of WAN.
5. A switched WAN (such as Frame Relay or ATM) that can be connected to many routers. We have shown three. One router connects the WAN to the left LAN, one connects the WAN to the right LAN, and one connects the WAN to the rest of the Internet.

Figure 4.19 *Sample internet*

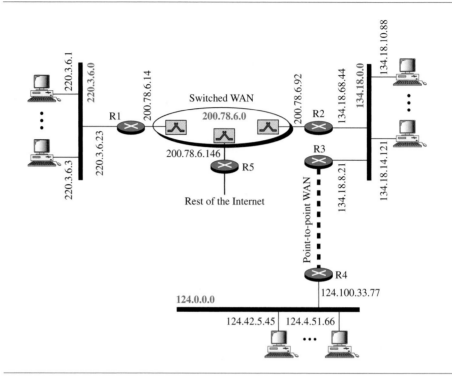

4.4   SUBNETTING AND SUPERNETTING

In the previous sections we discussed the problems associated with classful addressing. Specifically, the network addresses available for assignment to organizations are close to depletion. This is coupled with the ever-increasing demand for addresses from organizations that want connection to the Internet. In this section we briefly discuss two solutions: subnetting and supernetting.

Subnetting

In **subnetting,** a network is divided into several smaller subnetworks with each subnetwork (or subnet) having its own subnetwork address.

Two Levels of Hierarchy

As we learned before, an IP address is 32 bits long. A portion of the address indicates the network (netid), and a portion indicates the host (hostid) on the network. This means that there is a sense of hierarchy in IP addressing. To reach a host on the Internet, we must first reach the network using the first portion of the address (netid).

Then we must reach the host itself using the second portion (hostid). In other words, IP addresses are designed with two levels of hierarchy.

IP addresses are designed with two levels of hierarchy.

However, in many cases, these two levels of hierarchy are not enough. For example, imagine an organization with the network address 141.14.0.0 (a class B block). The organization has two-level hierarchical addressing, but, as shown in Figure 4.20, it cannot have more than one physical network. Note that the default mask (255.255.0.0) means that all addresses have 16 common bits. The remaining bits define the different addresses on the network. Note also that the network address is the first address in the block; the hostid part is all 0s in the network address.

Figure 4.20   *A network with two levels of hierarchy (not subnetted)*

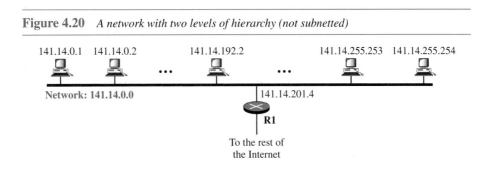

With this scheme, the organization is limited to two levels of hierarchy. The hosts cannot be organized into groups; all of the hosts are at the same level. The organization has one network with many hosts.

One solution to this problem is subnetting, the further division of a network into smaller networks called *subnetworks* (or *subnets*). For example, Figure 4.21 shows the network in Figure 4.20 divided into four subnetworks.

In this example, the rest of the Internet is not aware that the network is divided into physical subnetworks: The subnetworks still appear as a single network to the rest of the Internet. A packet destined for host 141.14.192.2 still reaches router R1. However, when the datagram arrives at router R1, the interpretation of the IP address changes. Router R1 knows that network 141.14.0.0 is physically divided into subnetworks. It knows that the packet must be delivered to subnetwork (subnet) 141.14.192.0.

Three Levels of Hierarchy

Adding subnetworks creates an intermediate level of hierarchy in the IP addressing system. Now we have three levels: site, subnet, and host. The site is the first level. The second level is the **subnet.** The host is the third level; it defines the connection of the host to the subnetwork. See Figure 4.22.

Figure 4.21   *A network with three levels of hierarchy (subnetted)*

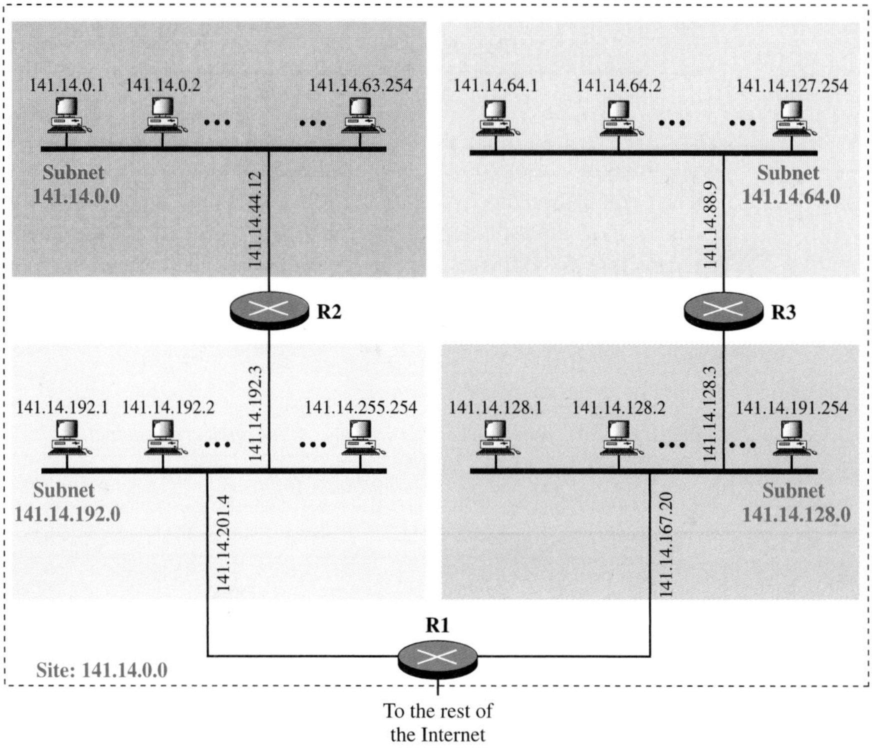

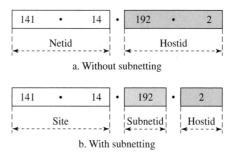

141.14.0.1   141.14.0.2   141.14.63.254

Subnet 141.14.0.0

141.14.44.12

141.14.64.1   141.14.64.2   141.14.127.254

Subnet 141.14.64.0

141.14.88.9

R2

R3

141.14.192.3

141.14.192.1   141.14.192.2   141.14.255.254

Subnet 141.14.192.0

141.14.201.4

141.14.128.1   141.14.128.2   141.14.191.254

141.14.128.3

Subnet 141.14.128.0

141.14.167.20

R1

Site: 141.14.0.0

To the rest of
the Internet

Figure 4.22   *Addresses in a network with and without subnetting*

141	•	14	•	192	•	2

Netid   Hostid

a. Without subnetting

141	•	14	•	192	•	2

Site   Subnetid   Hostid

b. With subnetting

The routing of an IP datagram now involves three steps: delivery to the site, delivery to the subnetwork, and delivery to the host.

This is analogous to the 10-digit telephone number in the United States. As Figure 4.23 shows, a telephone number is divided into three levels: area code, exchange number, and connection number.

Figure 4.23   *Hierarchy concept in a telephone number*

Area code   Exchange   Connection

Subnet Mask

We discussed the default mask before. The default mask is used when a network is not subnetted. The default mask is used to find the first address in the block or the network address. However, when a network is subnetted, the situation is different. We must have a subnet mask. The subnet mask has more 1s. Figure 4.24 shows the situations in two previous networks (see Figure 4.20 and Figure 4.21). The default mask creates the network address; the subnet mask creates the subnetwork address.

Figure 4.24   *Default mask and subnet mask*

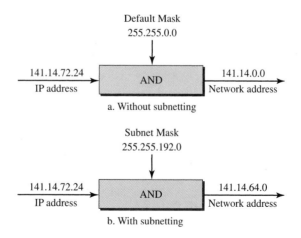

Contiguous versus Noncontiguous Subnet Mask   In the early days of subnetting, a noncontiguous subnet mask might have been used. By noncontiguous we mean a series of bits that is not a string of 1s followed by a string of 0s, but a mixture of 0s and 1s. Today, however, only contiguous masks (a run of 1s followed by a run of 0s) are used.

Finding the Subnet Address   Given an IP address, we can find the subnet address the same way we found the network address in the previous chapter. We apply the mask to the address.

Example 15

What is the subnetwork address if the destination address is 200.45.34.56 and the subnet mask is 255.255.240.0?

Solution
We apply the AND operation on the address and the subnet mask.

Address	➡	**11001000 00101101 00100010 00111000**
Subnet Mask	➡	**11111111 11111111 11110000 00000000**
Subnetwork Address	➡	**11001000 00101101 00100000 00000000**

The subnetwork address is 200.45.32.0.

Default Mask and Subnet Mask   The number of 1s in a default mask is predetermined (8, 16, or 24). In a subnet mask the number of 1s is more than the number of 1s in the corresponding default mask. In other words, for a subnet mask, we change some of the leftmost 0s in the default mask to 1s to make a subnet mask. Figure 4.25 shows the difference between a class B default mask and a subnet mask for the same block.

Figure 4.25   *Comparison of a default mask and a subnet mask*

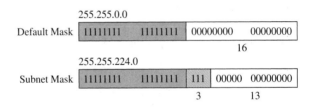

Number of Subnetworks   The number of subnetworks can be found by counting the extra 1s that are added to the default mask to make the subnet mask. For example, in Figure 4.25 the number of extra 1s is 3; therefore, the number of subnets is 2^3 or 8.

Number of Addresses per Subnet   The number of addresses per subnetwork can be found by counting the number of 0s in the subnet mask. For example, in Figure 4.25 the number of 0s is 13; therefore, the number of possible addresses in each subnet is $2^{13} = 8192$.

Special Addresses in Subnetting

With subnetting, two addresses in each subnet are added to the list of special addresses we discussed before. The first address in each subnet (with hostid all 0s) is the subnetwork address. The last address in each subnet (with hostid all 1s) is reserved for limited broadcast inside the subnet. Some other addresses were originally reserved as special addresses, but with the advent of classless addressing, as we will see shortly, this idea is obsolete.

CIDR Notation

CIDR notation can also be used when we have subnets. An address in a subnet can be easily defined using this notation. For example, the notation 141.14.92.3/16 shows a class B address, but the address 141.14.192.3/18 shows that the address belongs to the subnet with the mask 255.255.192.0. We will develop on this concept when we discuss classless addressing in the next chapter.

Supernetting

Although class A and B addresses are almost depleted, class C addresses are still available. However, the size of a class C block with a maximum number of 256 addresses may not satisfy the needs of an organization. Even a mid-size organization may need more addresses.

One solution is **supernetting.** In supernetting, an organization can combine several class C blocks to create a larger range of addresses. In other words, several networks are combined to create a supernetwork. By doing this, an organization can apply for a set of class C blocks instead of just one. For example, an organization that needs 1000 addresses can be granted four class C blocks. The organization can then use these addresses in one supernetwork as shown in Figure 4.26.

Figure 4.26   *A supernetwork*

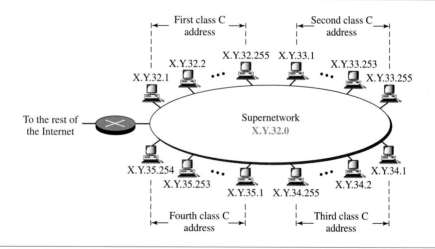

Supernet Mask

When an organization is granted one block of addresses (class A, B, or C), the first address in the block and the mask define the block (the range of addresses). We always know this range of addresses since the mask is always known (default mask).

When an organization divides its block into subnets, the first address in the subblock and the subnet mask completely define the subblock (the range of addresses). In this case, however, the first address alone is not enough; we must have the subnet mask.

Similarly, when an organization combines several blocks into a superblock, we need to know the first address in the block and the supernet mask. Here also, the first address alone cannot define the range; we need a supernet mask to find how many blocks are combined to make a superblock.

> In subnetting, we need the first address of the subnet and the subnet mask to define the range of addresses.
>
> In supernetting, we need the first address of the supernet and the supernet mask to define the range of addresses.

A supernet mask is the reverse of a subnet mask. A subnet mask for class C has more 1s than the default mask for this class. A supernet mask for class C has less 1s than the default mask for this class.

Figure 4.27 shows the difference between a subnet mask and a supernet mask. A subnet mask that divides a block into eight subblocks has three more 1s ($2^3 = 8$) than the default mask; a supernet mask that combines eight blocks into one superblock has three less 1s than the default mask.

Figure 4.27   *Comparison of subnet, default, and supernet masks*

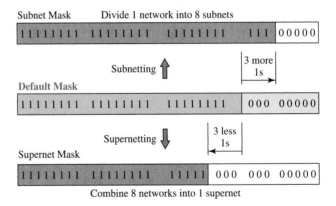

Subnet Mask   Divide 1 network into 8 subnets

Combine 8 networks into 1 supernet

CIDR Notation

CIDR notation can also be used when we have supernets. An address in a supernet can be easily defined using this notation. For example, the notation 141.14.192.3/24 shows a class C address, but the address 141.14.192.3/21 shows that the address belongs to the a supernet with the mask 255.255.248.0.

Obsolescence

With the advent of classless addressing, the idea of subnetting and supernetting of classful addresses is almost obsolete. We briefly discussed the concept here from a historical point of view and to prepare the reader for classless addressing in the next chapter.

The idea of subnetting and supernetting of classful addresses is almost obsolete.

4.5   KEY TERMS

address space	hostid
AND operation	IP address
binary notation	limited broadcast address
block of addresses	loopback address
class A address	mask
class B address	multihomed device
class C address	netid
class D address	network address
class E address	noncontiguous mask
classful addressing	specific host on this network
classless addressing	subnet
classless interdomain routing (CIDR)	subnet mask
contiguous mask	subnetting
default mask	subnetwork
direct broadcast address	supernet mask
dotted-decimal notation	supernetting
hexadecimal notation	this host on this network

4.6   SUMMARY

❏ At the network layer, a global identification system that uniquely identifies every host and router is necessary for delivery of a packet from host to host.

❏ The Internet address (or IP address) is 32 bits (for IPv4) that uniquely and universally defines a host or router on the Internet.

❏ The portion of the IP address that identifies the network is called the netid.

❏ The portion of the IP address that identifies the host or router on the network is called the hostid.

❏ An IP address defines a device's connection to a network.

❏ There are five classes of IP addresses. Classes A, B, and C differ in the number of hosts allowed per network. Class D is for multicasting and Class E is reserved.

❏ The class of a network is easily determined by examination of the first byte.

❏ A multihomed device is connected to multiple networks and has an IP address for each network to which it is connected.

❏ For Classes A, B, and C, a direct broadcast address (hostid all 1s) is used by a router to send a packet to all hosts on a specific network.

❏ A limited broadcast address (all 1s) is used by a host to send a packet to all hosts on its network.

❏ A source IP address of all 0s is used by a host at bootstrap if it does not know its IP address.

❏ A destination IP address with a netid of all 0s is used by a host to send a packet to another host on the same network.

❏ A loopback address with the first byte equal to 127 is used by a host to test its internal software.

❏ Addresses in Classes A, B, or C are mostly used for unicast communication.

❏ Addresses in Class D are used for multicast communication.

❏ The Internet does not support broadcast communication at the global level.

❏ Subnetting divides one large network into several smaller ones.

❏ Subnetting adds an intermediate level of hierarchy in IP addressing.

❏ Classes A, B, and C addresses can be subnetted.

❏ Subnet masking is a process that extracts the subnetwork address from an IP address.

❏ A network or subnet address is obtained from applying the bit-wise AND operation on the IP address and the mask.

❏ The concept of special addresses in IP addressing carries over to subnetting.

❏ A contiguous mask (a string of 1s followed by a string of 0s) is highly recommended.

❏ Supernetting combines several networks into one large one.

4.7   PRACTICE SET

Exercises

1. What is the address space in each of the following systems?

    a. a system with 8-bit addresses

    b. a system with 16-bit addresses

    c. a system with 64-bit addresses

2. An address space has a total of 1,024 addresses. How many bits are needed to represent an address?

3. An address space uses three symbols: 0, 1, and 2 represent addresses. If each address is made of 10 symbols, how many addresses are available in this system?

4. Change the following IP addresses from dotted-decimal notation to binary notation:
   a. 114.34.2.8
   b. 129.14.6.8
   c. 208.34.54.12
   d. 238.34.2.1
   e. 241.34.2.8

5. Change the following IP addresses from dotted-decimal notation to hexadecimal notation:
   a. 114.34.2.8
   b. 129.14.6.8
   c. 208.34.54.12
   d. 238.34.2.1
   e. 241.34.2.8

6. Change the following IP addresses from hexadecimal notation to binary notation:
   a. 0x1347FEAB
   b. 0xAB234102
   c. 0x0123A2BE
   d. 0x00001111

7. How many digits are needed to define the netid in hexadecimal notation in each of the following classes?
   a. Class A
   b. Class B
   c. Class C

8. Change the following IP addresses from binary notation to dotted-decimal notation:
   a. 01111111 11110000 01100111 01111101
   b. 10101111 11000000 11111000 00011101
   c. 11011111 10110000 00011111 01011101
   d. 11101111 11110111 11000111 00011101
   e. 11110111 11110011 10000111 11011101

9. Find the class of the following IP addresses:
   a. 208.34.54.12
   b. 238.34.2.1
   c. 114.34.2.8
   d. 129.14.6.8
   e. 241.34.2.8

10. Find the class of the following IP addresses:
    a. 11110111 11110011 10000111 11011101
    b. 10101111 11000000 11110000 00011101
    c. 11011111 10110000 00011111 01011101
    d. 11101111 11110111 11000111 00011101
    e. 01111111 11110000 01100111 01111101

11. Find the netid and the hostid of the following IP addresses:
    a. 114.34.2.8
    b. 132.56.8.6
    c. 208.34.54.12

12. A host with IP address 128.23.67.3 sends a message to a host with IP address 193.45.23.7. Does the message travel through any router? Assume no subnetting.

13. A host with IP address 128.23.67.3 sends a message to a host with IP address 128.45.23.7. Does the message travel through any router? Assume no subnetting.

14. A host with IP address 128.23.67.3 sends a message to a host with IP address 128.23.23.7. Does the message travel through any router? Assume no subnetting.

15. Draw a diagram of a network with address 8.0.0.0 that is connected through a router to a network with IP address 131.45.0.0. Choose IP addresses for each interface of the router. Show also some hosts on each network with their IP addresses. What is the class of each network?

16. A router has an IP address of 108.5.18.22. It sends a direct broadcast packet to all hosts in this network. What are the source and destination IP addresses used in this packet?

17. A host with IP address 108.67.18.70 sends a limited broadcast packet to all hosts in the same network. What are the source and destination IP addresses used in this packet?

18. A host with IP address 185.67.89.34 needs loopback testing. What are the source and destination addresses?

19. A host with IP address 123.27.19.24 sends a message to a host with IP address 123.67.89.56 using the "Specific Host on This Network" special address. What are the source and destination addresses?

20. A host in class C that does not know its IP address wants to send a message to a bootstrap server to find its address. What are the source and destination addresses?

21. Can we have an address such as x.y.z.t/32? Explain.

22. In class A, the first address in a network (network address) is 20.0.0.0. What is the 220000th address? Hint: use the base 256 numbering system discussed in Appendix B.

23. In a network, the address of one computer is 201.78.24.56 and the address of another computer is 201.78.120.202. How many addresses are in between? Hint: use the base 256 numbering system in Appendix B.

24. In a class A subnet, we know the IP address of one of the hosts and the mask as given below:

    IP Address: 25.34.12.56
    Mask: 255.255.0.0

    What is the first address (subnet address)?

25. In a class B subnet, we know the IP address of one of the hosts and the mask as given below:

    IP Address: 125.134.112.66
    Mask: 255.255.224.0

    What is the first address (subnet address)?

26. In a class C subnet, we know the IP address of one of the hosts and the mask as given below:

    IP Address: 182.44.82.16
    Mask: 255.255.255.192

    What is the first address (subnet address)?

27. Find the contiguous mask in each case
    a. 1024 subnets in class A
    b. 256 subnets in class B
    c. 32 subnets in class C
    d. 4 subnets in class C

28. What is the maximum number of subnets in each case?
    a. Class A; mask 255.255.192.0
    b. Class B; mask 255.255.192.0
    c. Class C; mask 255.255.255.192
    d. Class C; mask 255.255.255.240

Research Activities

29. Is your school or organization using a classful address? If so, find out the class of the address.

30. Find all RFCs dealing with IP addresses.

31. Find all RFCs dealing with a loopback address.

32. Find all RFCs dealing with private addresses.

33. Find all RFCs dealing with a direct broadcast address.

34. Find all RFCs dealing with multicast addresses.

CHAPTER 5

IP Addresses:
Classless Addressing

The use of classful addressing has created many problems. Until the mid 1990s, a range of addresses meant a block of addresses in class A, B, or C. The minimum number of addresses granted to an organization was 256 (class C); the maximum was 16,777,216 (class A). In between these limits an organization could have a class B block or several class C blocks. These address assignments were always in multiples of 256. However, what about a small business that needed only 16 addresses? Or a household that needed only two addresses?

During the 1990s, Internet service providers (ISPs) came into prominence. An ISP is an organization that provides Internet access for individuals, small businesses, and midsize organizations that do not want to create an Internet site and become involved in providing Internet services (such as email services) for their employees. An ISP can provide these services. An ISP is granted a large range of addresses and then subdivides the addresses (in groups of 2, 4, 8, 16, and so on), giving a range to a household or a small business. The customers are connected via a dial-up modem, DSL, or cable modem to the ISP. However, each customer needs an IP address (we will see other solutions such as private addresses and networks address transformation in Chapter 26).

To facilitate this evolution and to resolve the problems of classful addressing, in 1996, the Internet authorities announced a new architecture called **classless addressing** that will eventually render classful addressing obsolete.

5.1 VARIABLE-LENGTH BLOCKS

In classless addressing variable-length blocks are assigned that belong to no class. We can have a block of 2 addresses, 4 addresses, 128 addresses, and so on. There are some restrictions that we will discuss shortly, but in general a block can range from very small to very large.

In this architecture, the entire address space (2^{32} addresses) is divided into blocks of different sizes. An organization is granted a block suitable for its purposes. Figure 5.1 shows the architecture of classless addressing. Compare this figure with Figure 4.2 in Chapter 4.

Figure 5.1   *Variable-length blocks*

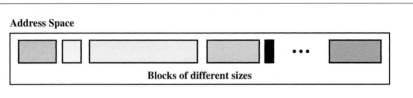

Restrictions

Classless addressing, as we will see, solves many problems. However, restrictions are necessary to make this architecture work.

Number of Addresses in a Block

There is only one restriction on the number of addresses in a block; it must be a power of two (2, 4, 8, . . .). For example, a household may be given a block of 2 (2^1) addresses. A small business may be given a block of 16 (2^4) addresses. A large organization may be given a block of 1024 (2^{10}) addresses.

First Address

The first address must be evenly divisible by the number of addresses. For example, if a block contains 4 addresses, the first address must be divisible by 4. If the block contains 16 addresses, the first address must be divisible by 16.

   If the block has 256 addresses or less, we need to check only the right-most byte. If it has 65536 addresses or less, we need to check only the two right-most bytes, and so on.

Example 1

Which of the following can be the beginning address of a block that contains 16 addresses?

   a. 205.16.37.32
   b. 190.16.42.44
   c. 17.17.33.80
   d. 123.45.24.52

Solution

Only two are eligible (a and c). The address 205.16.37.32 is eligible because 32 is divisible by 16. The address 17.17.33.80 is eligible because 80 is divisible by 16.

Example 2

Which of the following can be the beginning address of a block that contains 256 addresses?

   a. 205.16.37.32
   b. 190.16.42.0
   c. 17.17.32.0
   d. 123.45.24.52

Solution
In this case, the right-most byte must be 0. As we mentioned in Chapter 4, the IP addresses use base 256 arithmetic. When the right-most byte is 0, the total address is divisible by 256. Only two addresses are eligible (b and c).

Example 3

Which of the following can be the beginning address of a block that contains 1024 addresses?
    a. 205.16.37.32
    b. 190.16.42.0
    c. 17.17.32.0
    d. 123.45.24.52

Solution
In this case, we need to check two bytes because $1024 = 4 \times 256$. The right-most byte must be divisible by 256. The second byte (from the right) must be divisible by 4. Only one address is eligible (c).

Mask

In classful addressing, the mask for each block is implicit. The mask for a class A block is 255.0.0.0 (/8). The mask for a class B block is 255.255.0.0 (/16). The mask for a class C block is 255.255.255.0 (/24). When an address is given, we can first find the class of the address (using the first byte); we can then apply the mask to find the beginning address and the range of addresses.

In classless addressing, on the other hand, when an address is given, the block the address belongs to cannot be found unless we have the mask. In other words, in classless addressing, the address must be accompanied by the mask. The mask is given in CIDR notation with the number of 1s in the mask. An address in classless addressing architecture is usually given as shown in Figure 5.2.

Figure 5.2   *Format of classless addressing address*

$$\textbf{x.y.z.t/}\boldsymbol{n}$$

The *n* after the slash defines the number of bits that are the same in every address in the block. So if *n* is 20, it means the twenty leftmost bits are identical in each address with 12 bits not the same. We can easily find the number of addresses in the block and the last address from this information.

Prefix and Prefix Length   Two terms that are often used in classless addressing are **prefix** and **prefix length.** The prefix is another name for the common part of the address range (similar to the netid). The prefix length is the length of the prefix (*n* in the CIDR notation). There is a one-to-one relationship between a mask and a prefix length as shown in Table 5.1.

Table 5.1   *Prefix lengths*

/n	Mask	/n	Mask	/n	Mask	/n	Mask
/1	128.0.0.0	/9	255.128.0.0	/17	255.255.128.0	/25	255.255.255.128
/2	192.0.0.0	/10	255.192.0.0	/18	255.255.192.0	/26	255.255.255.192
/3	224.0.0.0	/11	255.224.0.0	/19	255.255.224.0	/27	255.255.255.224
/4	240.0.0.0	/12	255.240.0.0	/20	255.255.240.0	/28	255.255.255.240
/5	248.0.0.0	/13	255.248.0.0	/21	255.255.248.0	/29	255.255.255.248
/6	252.0.0.0	/14	255.252.0.0	/22	255.255.252.0	/30	255.255.255.252
/7	254.0.0.0	/15	255.254.0.0	/23	255.255.254.0	/31	255.255.255.254
/8	255.0.0.0	/16	255.255.0.0	/24	255.255.255.0	/32	255.255.255.255

Note that the entries in color are the default masks for classes A, B, and C. This means that classful addressing is a special case of classless addressing in CIDR notation.

> **Classful addressing is a special case of classless addressing.**

Suffix and Suffix Length   Two terms that are occasionally used in classless addressing are **suffix** and **suffix length.** The suffix is the varying part (similar to the hostid). The suffix length is the length of the suffix $(32 - n)$ in CIDR notation.

Finding the Block

In classless addressing, an organization is assigned a block of addresses. The size of the block is not fixed; it varies according to the needs of the organization. However, when a classless address is given, we can find the block. We can find the first address, the number of addresses, and the last address.

Finding the First Address

In classless addressing, the prefix length is the mask. Because the addresses in classless addressing are guaranteed to be contiguous and the prefix determines the number of 1s, we can AND the mask and the address to find the first address. Just keep the first n bits and change the rest of the bits to 0s.

Example 4

What is the first address in the block if one of the addresses is 167.199.170.82/27?

Solution

The prefix length is 27, which means that we must keep the first 27 bits as is and change the remaining bits (5) to 0s. The following shows the process:

```
Address in binary:        10100111  11000111  10101010  01010010
Keep the left 27 bits:    10100111  11000111  10101010  01000000
Result in CIDR notation: 167.199.170.64/27
```

First Short Cut We can use the following short cut to find the first address:

1. Divide the prefix length into four groups (corresponding to the four bytes in an address) and find the number of 1s in each group.
2. If the number of 1s in a group is 8, the corresponding byte in the first address is the same (no change).
3. If the number of 1s in the group is zero (no 1s), the corresponding byte in the first address is 0.
4. If the number of 1s in a group is between zero and eight, we keep the corresponding bits in that group.

Example 5

What is the first address in the block if one of the addresses is 140.120.84.24/20?

Solution

Figure 5.3 shows the solution. The first, second, and fourth bytes are easy; for the third byte we keep the bits corresponding to the number of 1s in that group. The first address is 140.120.80.0/20.

Figure 5.3 *Example 5*

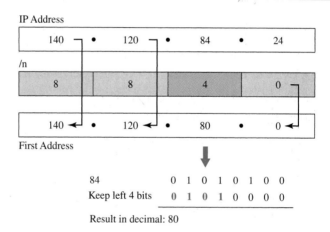

Second Short Cut To avoid using binary numbers, we give an alternative method for a byte that is neither all 1s nor all 0s. We write the byte in the address as a sum of powers of 2 (128, 64, 32, 16, 8, 4, 2, 1). If a power is missing we insert a 0 as a placeholder. We then choose the m highest powers, where m is the corresponding number in the prefix length.

Example 6

Find the first address in the block if one of the addresses is 140.120.84.24/20.

Solution

The first, second, and fourth bytes are as defined in the previous example. To find the third byte, we write 84 as the sum of powers of 2 and select only the leftmost 4 (m is 4) as shown in Figure 5.4. The first address is 140.120.80.0/20.

Figure 5.4   *Example 6*

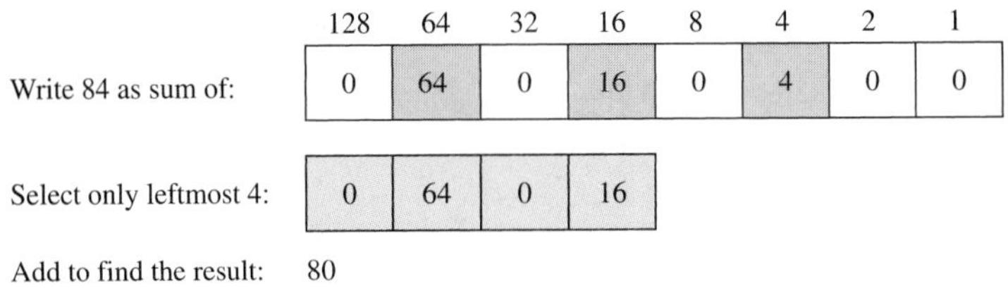

128	64	32	16	8	4	2	1

Write 84 as sum of:

0	64	0	16	0	4	0	0

Select only leftmost 4:

0	64	0	16

Add to find the result: 80

Finding the Number of Addresses in the Block

Finding the number of addresses in the block is very simple. The total number of addresses in the block is 2^{32-n}.

Example 7

Find the number of addresses in the block if one of the addresses is 140.120.84.24/20.

Solution
The prefix length is 20. The number of addresses in the block is 2^{32-20} or 2^{12} or 4096. Note that this is a large block with 4096 addresses.

Finding the Last Address in the Block

We give two methods that find the last address in the block. In the first method, we add the number of addresses in the block minus 1 to the first address to find the last address. Note that we subtract 1 because the first and the last addresses are included in the number of addresses. In the second method, we add the first address to the complement of the mask. The complement of the mask is found by changing all 0s to 1s and all 1s to 0s.

Example 8

Using the first method, find the last address in the block if one of the addresses is 140.120.84.24/20.

Solution
We found in the previous examples that the first address is 140.120.80.0/20 and the number of addresses is 4096. To find the last address, we need to add 4095 (4096−1) to the first address. To keep the format in dotted-decimal notation, we need to represent 4095 in base 256 (see Appendix B) and do the calculation in base 256. We write 4095 as 15.255. We then add the first address to this number (in base 255) to obtain the last address as shown below:

```
140 . 120 . 80 .   0
            15 . 255
----------------------------
140 . 120 . 95 . 255
```

The last address is 140.120.95.255/20.

Example 9

Using the second method, find the last address in the block if one of the addresses is 140.120.84.24/20.

Solution

The mask has twenty 1s and twelve 0s. The complement of the mask has twenty 0s and twelve 1s. In other words, the mask complement is 00000000 00000000 00001111 11111111 or 0.0.15.255. We add the mask complement to the beginning address to find the last address.

```
140 . 120 . 80 .  0
  0 .   0 . 15 . 255
-----------------------------
140 . 120 . 95 . 255
```

The last address is 140.120.95.255/20.

Example 10

Find the block if one of the addresses is 190.87.140.202/29.

Solution

We follow the procedure in the previous examples to find the first address, the number of addresses, and the last address. To find the first address, we notice that the mask (/29) has five 1s in the last byte. So we write the last byte as powers of 2 and retain only the leftmost five as shown below:

```
202                        ➡  128 + 64 + 0 + 0 + 8 + 0 + 2 + 0
The leftmost 5 numbers are  ➡  128 + 64 + 0 + 0 + 8
The first address is  190.87.140.200/29
```

The number of addresses is 2^{32-29} or 8. To find the last address, we use the complement of the mask. The mask has twenty-nine 1s; the complement has three 1s. The complement is 0.0.0.7. If we add this to the first address, we get 190.87.140.207/29. In other words, the first address is 190.87.140.200/29, the last address is 190.87.140.207/20. There are only 8 addresses in this block.

Example 11

Show a network configuration for the block in the previous example.

Solution

The organization that is granted the block in the previous example can assign the addresses in the block to the hosts in its network. However, the first address needs to be used as the network address and the last address is kept as a special address (limited broadcast address). Figure 5.5 shows how the block can be used by an organization. Note that the last address ends with 207, which is different from the 255 seen in classful addressing.

In classless addressing, the last address in the block does not necessarily end in 255.

Granted Block

The block of addresses, as we will see shortly, is granted by an ISP. The granted block is defined by the first address and the prefix length. This CIDR notation, as we have seen, totally determines the block. For instance, in our previous example, the block is defined as 190.87.140.200/29.

In CIDR notation, the block granted is defined by the first address and the prefix length.

Figure 5.5   *Example 11*

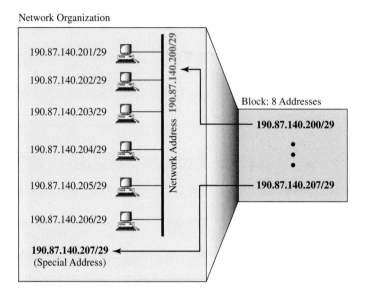

5.2   SUBNETTING

We can, of course, have subnetting with classless addressing. When an organization is granted a block of addresses, it can create subnets to meet its needs. The network administrator can design a subnet mask for each subnet. The prefix length (*n*) increases to define the subnet prefix length.

Finding the Subnet Mask

The number of desired subnets defines the subnet prefix. If the number of subnets is s, the number of extra 1s in the prefix length is $\log_2 s$, where $s = 2^{\text{number of extra 1s}}$. Note that if we want fixed-length subnets (each subnet has the same number of addresses), the number of subnets needs to be a power of 2.

In fixed-length subnetting, the number of subnets is a power of 2.

Example 12

An organization is granted the block 130.34.12.64/26. The organization needs 4 subnets. What is the subnet prefix length?

Solution

We need 4 subnets, which means we need to add two more 1s ($\log_2 4 = 2$) to the site prefix. The subnet prefix is then /28.

Finding the Subnet Addresses

After finding the subnet mask, it is easy to find the range of addresses in each subnet.

Example 13

What are the subnet addresses and the range of addresses for each subnet in the previous example?

Solution
Figure 5.6 shows one configuration.

Figure 5.6 *Example 13*

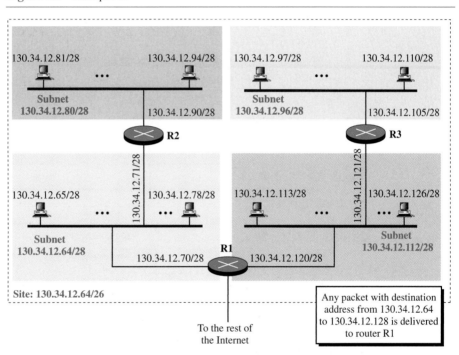

The site has $2^{32-26} = 64$ addresses. Each subnet has $2^{32-28} = 16$ addresses. Now let us find the first and last address in each subnet.

1. The first address in the first subnet is 130.34.12.64/28, using the procedure we showed in the previous examples. Note that the first address of the first subnet is the first address of the block. The last address of the subnet can be found by adding 15 (16 − 1) to the first address. The last address is 130.34.12.79/28.

2. The first address in the second subnet is 130.34.12.80/28; it is found by adding 1 to the last address of the previous subnet. Again adding 15 to the first address, we obtain the last address, 130.34.12.95/28.

3. Similarly, we find the first address of the third subnet to be 130.34.12.96/28 and the last to be 130.34.12.111/28.

4. Similarly, we find the first address of the fourth subnet to be 130.34.12.112/28 and the last to be 130.34.12.127/28.

Variable-Length Subnets

In the previous section, all of our subnets had the same mask (same *n*). We can also design subnets having variable-length masks. In other words, we can design subnets of different sizes. This allows an organization to assign addresses based on the needs of the subnet. The procedure is the same as discussed previously. We show the concept with an example.

Example 14

An organization is granted a block of addresses with the beginning address 14.24.74.0/24. There are $2^{32-24} = 256$ addresses in this block. The organization needs to have 11 subnets as shown below:

    a. two subnets, each with 64 addresses.

    b. two subnets, each with 32 addresses.

    c. three subnets, each with 16 addresses.

    d. four subnets, each with 4 addresses.

Design the subnets.

Solution

Figure 5.7 shows one configuration.

Figure 5.7 *Example 14*

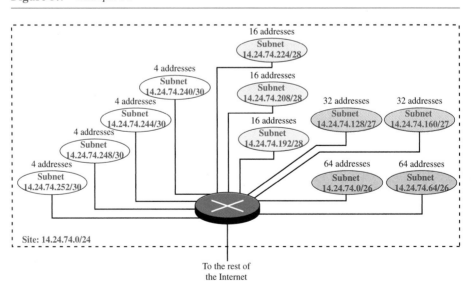

1. We use the first 128 addresses for the first two subnets, each with 64 addresses. Note that the mask for each network is /26. The subnet address for each subnet is given in the figure.

2. We use the next 64 addresses for the next two subnets, each with 32 addresses. Note that the mask for each network is /27. The subnet address for each subnet is given in the figure.

3. We use the next 48 addresses for the next three subnets, each with 16 addresses. Note that the mask for each network is /28. The subnet address for each subnet is given in the figure.

4. We use the last 16 addresses for the last four subnets, each with 4 addresses. Note that the mask for each network is /30. The subnet address for each subnet is given in the figure.

Example 15

As another example, assume a company has three offices: Central, East, and West. The Central office is connected to the East and West offices via private, point-to-point WAN lines. The company is granted a block of 64 addresses with the beginning address 70.12.100.128/26. The management has decided to allocate 32 addresses for the Central office and divides the rest of addresses between the two offices. Figure 5.8 shows the configuration designed by the management.

Figure 5.8 *Example 15*

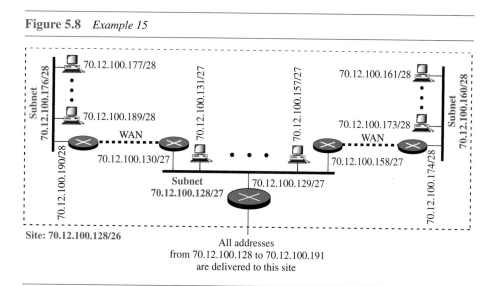

Site: 70.12.100.128/26

All addresses
from 70.12.100.128 to 70.12.100.191
are delivered to this site

The company will have three subnets, one at Central, one at East, and one at West. The following lists the subblocks allocated for each network:

a. The Central office uses the network address 70.12.100.128/27. This is the first address, and the mask /27 shows that there are 32 addresses in this network. Note that three of these addresses are used for the routers and the company has reserved the last address in the sub-block. The addresses in this subnet are 70.12.100.128/27 to 70.12.100.159/27. Note that the interface of the router that connects the Central subnet to the WAN needs no address because it is a point-to-point connection.

b. The West office uses the network address 70.12.100.160/28. The mask /28 shows that there are only 16 addresses in this network. Note that one of these addresses is used for the router and the company has reserved the last address in the sub-block. The addresses in this subnet are 70.12.100.160/28 to 70.12.100.175/28. Note also that the interface of the router that connects the West subnet to the WAN needs no address because it is a point-to-point connection.

c. The East office uses the network address 70.12.100.176/28. The mask /28 shows that there are only 16 addresses in this network. Note that one of these addresses is used for the router and the company has reserved the last address in the sub-block. The addresses in this subnet are 70.12.100.176/28 to 70.12.100.191/28. Note also that the interface of the router that connects the East subnet to the WAN needs no address because it is a point-to-point connection.

5.3   ADDRESS ALLOCATION

The next issue in classless addressing is address allocation. How are the blocks allocated? The ultimate responsibility of address allocation is given to a global authority called the Internet Corporation for Assigned Names and Addresses (ICANN). However, ICANN does not normally allocate addresses to individual organizations. It assigns a large block of addresses to an ISP. Each ISP, in turn, divides its assigned block into smaller subblocks and grants the subblocks to its customers. In other words, an ISP receives one large block to be distributed to its Internet users. This is called **address aggregation**: many blocks of addresses are aggregated in one block and granted to one ISP.

Example 16

An ISP is granted a block of addresses starting with 190.100.0.0/16 (65,536 addresses). The ISP needs to distribute these addresses to three groups of customers as follows:

a. The first group has 64 customers; each needs 256 addresses.
b. The second group has 128 customers; each needs 128 addresses.
c. The third group has 128 customers; each needs 64 addresses.

Design the subblocks and find out how many addresses are still available after these allocations.

Solution
Figure 5.9 shows the situation.

Figure 5.9   *Example 16*

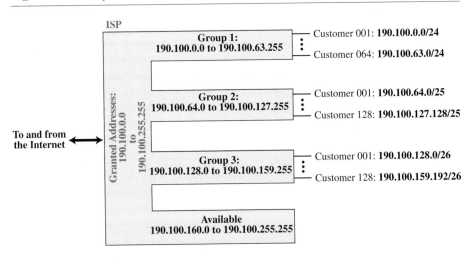

1. **Group 1**

   For this group, each customer needs 256 addresses. This means the suffix length is 8 ($2^8 =$ 256). The prefix length is then $32 - 8 = 24$. The addresses are:

1st Customer 190.100.0.0/24	190.100.0.255/24
2nd Customer 190.100.1.0/24	190.100.1.255/24
	.
	.
	.
64th Customer 190.100.63.0/24	190.100.63.255/24

   Total = $64 \times 256 = 16{,}384$

2. **Group 2**

   For this group, each customer needs 128 addresses. This means the suffix length is 7 ($2^7 =$ 128). The prefix length is then $32 - 7 = 25$. The addresses are:

1st Customer 190.100.64.0/25	190.100.64.127/25
2nd Customer 190.100.64.128/25	190.100.64.255/25
	.
	.
	.
128th Customer 190.100.127.128/25	190.100.127.255/25

   Total = $128 \times 128 = 16{,}384$

3. **Group 3**

   For this group, each customer needs 64 addresses. This means the suffix length is 6 ($2^6 =$ 64). The prefix length is then $32 - 6 = 26$. The addresses are:

1st Customer 190.100.128.0/26	190.100.128.63/26
2nd Customer 190.100.128.64/26	190.100.128.127/26
	.
	.
	.
128th Customer 190.100.159.192/26	190.100.159.255/26

   Total = $128 \times 64 = 8{,}192$

Number of granted addresses to the ISP: 65,536
Number of allocated addresses by the ISP: 40,960
Number of available addresses: 24,576

5.4   KEY TERMS

address aggregation	subnet mask
classless addressing	suffix
prefix	suffix length
prefix length	variable-length subnetting

5.5   SUMMARY

❏ In classless addressing, we can divide the address space into variable-length blocks.

❏ There are three restrictions in classless addressing:

a. The number of addresses needs to be a power of 2.

b. The mask needs to be included in the address to define the block.

c. The starting address must be divisible by the number of addresses in the block.

❏ The mask in classless addressing is expressed as the prefix length (/n) in CIDR notation.

❏ To find the first address in a block, we need to apply the mask to one of the addresses.

❏ To find the number of addresses in the block, we calculate 2^{32-n}, where n is the prefix length.

❏ To find the last address in the block, we add the first address to the number of addresses and subtract one.

❏ We can have both fixed-length and variable-length subnetting. In fixed-length subnetting, the number of addresses in each subnet is the same. In variable-length subnetting, the number of addresses in each subnet can be different.

❏ In fixed-length subnetting, the number of subnets needs to be a power of 2. There is no such restriction in variable-length subnetting.

❏ Subnetting increases the value of n.

❏ The global authority for address allocation is ICANN. ICANN normally grants large blocks of addresses to ISPs, which in turn, grant small subblocks to individual customers.

5.6   PRACTICE SET

Exercises

1. In a block of addresses, we know the IP address of one host is 25.34.12.56/16. What is the first address (network address) and the last address (limited broadcast address) in this block?

2. In a block of addresses, we know the IP address of one host is 182.44.82.16/26. What is the first address (network address) and the last address (limited broadcast address) in this block?

3. In fixed-length subnetting, find the number of 1s that must be added to the mask if the number of desired subnets is _____.

a. 2

b. 62

c. 122

d. 250

4. What is the maximum number of subnets if the prefix length of a block is?

   a. 18

   b. 10

   c. 27

   d. 31

5. An organization is granted the block 16.0.0.0/8. The administrator wants to create 500 fixed-length subnets.

   a. Find the subnet mask.

   b. Find the number of addresses in each subnet.

   c. Find the first and the last address in the first subnet.

   d. Find the first and the last address in the last subnet (subnet 500).

6. An organization is granted the block 130.56.0.0/16. The administrator wants to create 1024 subnets.

   a. Find the subnet mask.

   b. Find the number of addresses in each subnet.

   c. Find the first and the last address in the first subnet.

   d. Find the first and the last address in the last subnet (subnet 1024).

7. An organization is granted the block 211.17.180.0/24. The administrator wants to create 32 subnets.

   a. Find the subnet mask.

   b. Find the number of addresses in each subnet.

   c. Find the first and the last address in the first subnet.

   d. Find the first and the last address in the last subnet (subnet 32).

8. Write the following mask in slash notation ($/n$):

   a. 255.255.255.0

   b. 255.0.0.0

   c. 255.255.224.0

   d. 255.255.240.0

9. Find the range of addresses in the following blocks:

   a. 123.56.77.32/29

   b. 200.17.21.128/27

   c. 17.34.16.0/23

   d. 180.34.64.64/30

10. An ISP is granted a block of addresses starting with 150.80.0.0/16. The ISP wants to distribute these blocks to 1000 customers as follows:

    a. The first group has 200 medium-size businesses; each needs 128 addresses.

    b. The second group has 400 small businesses; each needs 16 addresses.

    c. The third group has 2000 households; each needs 4 addresses.

    Design the subblocks and give the slash notation for each subblock. Find out how many addresses are still available after these allocations.

11. An ISP is granted a block of addresses starting with 120.60.4.0/20. The ISP wants to distribute these blocks to 100 organizations with each organization receiving 8 addresses only. Design the subblocks and give the slash notation for each sub-block. Find out how many addresses are still available after these allocations.

12. An ISP has a block of 1024 addresses. It needs to divide the addresses to 1024 cus-tomers, does it need subnetting? Explain your answer.

Research Activities

13. Find the RFCs that define classless addressing.

14. Find the block of addresses assigned to your organization or institution.

15. If you are using an ISP to connect from your home to the Internet, find the name of the ISP and the block of addresses assigned to it.

16. Some people argue that we can consider the whole address space as one single block in which each range of addresses is a subblock to this single block. Elaborate on this idea. What happens to subnetting if we accept this concept?

CHAPTER 6

Delivery, Forwarding, and Routing of IP Packets

This chapter describes the delivery, forwarding, and routing of IP packets to their final destinations. **Delivery** refers to the way a packet is handled by the underlying networks under the control of the network layer. Concepts such as connectionless and connection-oriented services and direct and indirect delivery are discussed. **Forwarding** refers to the way a packet is delivered to the next station or stations. We discuss several forwarding methods. **Routing** refers to the way routing tables are created to help in forwarding. We discuss two types of routing: static and dynamic.

6.1 DELIVERY

The network layer supervises the handling of the packets by the underlying physical networks.We define this handling as the delivery of a packet. Two important concepts here are the type of connection and direct versus indirect delivery.

Connection Types

Delivery of a packet in the network layer is accomplished using either a connection-oriented service or a connectionless service.

Connection-Oriented Service

In a **connection-oriented service,** the local network layer protocol first makes a connection with the network layer protocol at the remote site before sending a data packet. When the connection is established, a sequence of packets from the source to the destination can be sent one after another. In this case, there is a relationship between the packets. They are sent on the same path in sequential order. A packet is logically connected to the packet traveling before it and to the packet traveling after it. When all packets of a message have been delivered, the connection is terminated.

In a connection-oriented service, the decision about the route for a sequence of packets with the same source and destination addresses can be made only once, when the connection is established. Routers do not recalculate the route for each individual packet.

Connectionless Service

In a **connectionless service**, the network layer protocol treats each packet independently, with each packet having no relationship to any other packet. The packets in a message may or may not travel the same path to their destination. In a connectionless service, the decision about the route of a packet is made individually by each router. The IP protocol is a **connectionless protocol**; it provides a connectionless service.

> **IP is a connectionless protocol.**

Direct Versus Indirect Delivery

The delivery of a packet to its final destination is accomplished using two different methods of delivery: direct and indirect.

Direct Delivery

In a **direct delivery,** the final destination of the packet is a host connected to the same physical network as the deliverer. Direct delivery occurs when the source and destination of the packet are located on the same physical network or if the delivery is between the last router and the destination host (see Figure 6.1).

Figure 6.1   *Direct delivery*

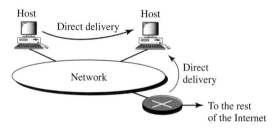

The sender can easily determine if the delivery is direct. It can extract the network address of the destination (using the mask) and compare this address with the addresses of the networks to which it is connected. If a match is found, the delivery is direct.

In direct delivery, the sender uses the destination IP address to find the destination physical address. The IP software then gives the destination IP address with the destination physical address to the data link layer for actual delivery. This process is called *mapping the IP address to the physical address*. Although this mapping can be done by finding a match in a table, we will see in Chapter 7 that a protocol called Address Resolution Protocol (ARP) dynamically maps an IP address to the corresponding physical address.

Indirect Delivery

If the destination host is not on the same network as the deliverer, the packet is delivered indirectly. In an **indirect delivery,** the packet goes from router to router until it reaches the one connected to the same physical network as its final destination (see Figure 6.2).

Figure 6.2 *Indirect delivery*

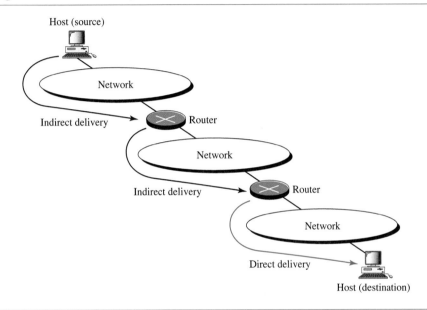

Note that a delivery always involves one direct delivery but zero or more indirect deliveries. Note also that the last delivery is always a direct delivery.

In an indirect delivery, the sender uses the destination IP address and a routing table to find the IP address of the next router to which the packet should be delivered. The sender then uses ARP to find the physical address of the next router. Note that in direct delivery, the address mapping is between the IP address of the final destination and the physical address of the final destination. In an indirect delivery, the address mapping is between the IP address of the next router and the physical address of the next router.

6.2   FORWARDING

Forwarding means to place the packet in its route to its destination. Forwarding requires a host or a router to have a routing table. When a host has a packet to send or when a router has received a packet to be forwarded, it looks at this table to find the route to the final destination. However, this simple solution is impossible today in an internetwork such as the Internet because the number of entries needed in the routing table would make table lookups inefficient.

Forwarding Techniques

Several techniques can make the size of the routing table manageable and also handle issues such as security. We briefly discuss these methods here.

Next-Hop Method

One technique to reduce the contents of a routing table is called the **next-hop method.** In this technique, the routing table holds only the address of the next hop instead of information about the complete route. The entries of a routing table must be consistent with each other. Figure 6.3 shows how routing tables can be simplified using this technique.

Figure 6.3   *Next-hop method*

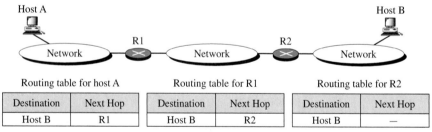

Routing table for host A

Destination	Route
Host B	R1, R2, Host B

Routing table for R1

Destination	Route
Host B	R2, Host B

Routing table for R2

Destination	Route
Host B	Host B

a. Routing tables based on route

Routing table for host A

Destination	Next Hop
Host B	R1

Routing table for R1

Destination	Next Hop
Host B	R2

Routing table for R2

Destination	Next Hop
Host B	—

b. Routing tables based on next hop

Network-Specific Method

A second technique to reduce the routing table and simplify the searching process is called the **network-specific method.** Here, instead of having an entry for every destination host connected to the same physical network, we have only one entry that defines the address of the destination network itself. In other words, we treat all hosts connected to the same network as one single entity. For example, if 1000 hosts are attached to the same network, only one entry exists in the routing table instead of 1000. Figure 6.4 shows the concept.

Host-Specific Method

In the **host-specific method,** the destination host address is given in the routing table. The rationale behind this method is the inverse of the network-specific method. Here

Figure 6.4 *Network-specific method*

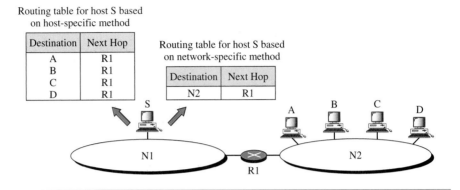

Routing table for host S based on host-specific method

Destination	Next Hop
A	R1
B	R1
C	R1
D	R1

Routing table for host S based on network-specific method

Destination	Next Hop
N2	R1

efficiency is sacrificed for other advantages: Although it is not efficient to put the host address in the routing table, there are occasions in which the administrator wants to have more control over routing. For example, in Figure 6.5 if the administrator wants all packets arriving for host B delivered to router R3 instead of R1, one single entry in the routing table of host A can explicitly define the route.

Figure 6.5 *Host-specific routing*

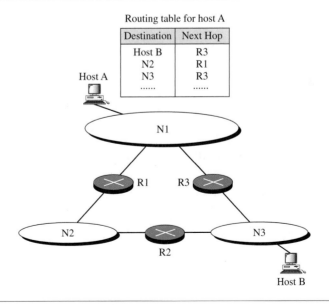

Routing table for host A

Destination	Next Hop
Host B	R3
N2	R1
N3	R3
......	......

Host-specific routing is used for purposes such as checking the route or providing security measures.

Default Method

Another technique to simplify routing is called the **default method.** In Figure 6.6 host A is connected to a network with two routers. Router R1 routes the packets to hosts connected to network N2. However, for the rest of the Internet, router R2 is used. So instead of listing all networks in the entire Internet, host A can just have one entry called the *default* (normally defined as network address 0.0.0.0).

Figure 6.6   *Default routing*

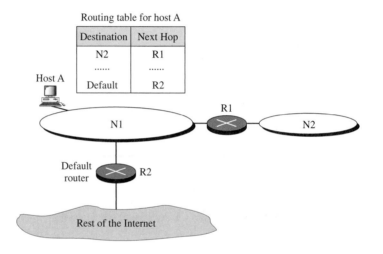

Forwarding with Classful Addressing

As we mentioned in the previous chapter, classful addressing has several disadvantages. However, the existence of a default mask in a classful address makes the forwarding process simple. In this section, we first show the contents of a routing table and forwarding module for the situation in which there is no subnetting. We then show how the module changes if subnetting is involved.

Forwarding without Subnetting

In classful addressing, most of the routers in the global Internet are not involved in subnetting. Subnetting happens inside the organization. A typical forwarding module in this case can be designed using three tables, one for each unicast class (A, B, C). If the router supports multicasting, another table can be added to handle class D addresses. Having three different tables makes searching more efficient. Each routing table has a minimum of three columns:

1. The network address of the destination network tells us where the destination host is located. Note that we use network-specific forwarding and not the rarely-used host-specific forwarding.

2. The next-hop address tells us to which router the packet must be delivered for an indirect delivery. This column is empty for a direct delivery.

3. The interface number defines the outgoing port from which the packet is sent out. A router is normally connected to several networks. Each connection has a different numbered port or interface. We show them as m0, m1, and so on.

Figure 6.7 shows a simplified module.

Figure 6.7   *Simplified forwarding module in classful address without subnetting*

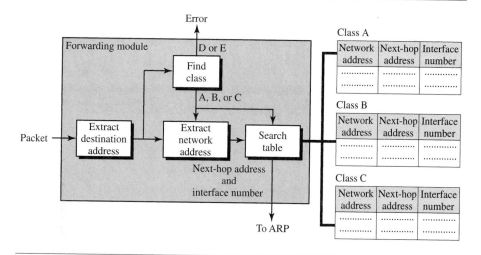

In its simplest form, the forwarding module follows these steps:

1. The destination address of the packet is extracted.

2. A copy of the destination address is used to find the class of the address. This is done by shifting the copy of the address 28 bits to the right. The result is a 4-bit number between 0 and 15. If the result is

   a. 0 to 7, the class is A.

   b. 8 to 11, the class is B.

   c. 12 or 13, the class is C

   d. 14, the class is D.

   e. 15, the class is E.

3. The result of Step 2 for class A, B, or C and the destination address are used to extract the network address. This is done by masking off (changing to 0s) the rightmost 8, 16, or 24 bits based on the class.

4. The class of the address and the network address are used to find next-hop information. The class determines the table to be searched. The module searches this table for the network address. If a match is found, the **next-hop address** and the interface number of the output port are extracted from the table. If no match is found, the default is used.

5. The ARP module (Chapter 7) uses the next-hop address and the interface number to find the physical address of the next router. It then asks the data link layer to deliver the packet to the next hop.

Example 1

Figure 6.8 shows an imaginary part of the Internet. Show the routing tables for router R1.

Figure 6.8   *Configuration for routing, Example 1*

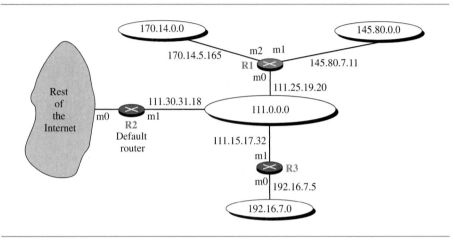

Solution

Figure 6.9 shows the three tables used by router R1. Note that some entries in the next-hop address column are empty because in these cases, the destination is in the same network to which the router is connected (direct delivery). In these cases, the next-hop address used by ARP is simply the destination address of the packet as we will see in Chapter 7.

Figure 6.9   *Tables for Example 1*

Class A

Network address	Next-hop address	Interface
111.0.0.0	------------	m0

Class C

Network address	Next-hop address	Interface
192.16.7.0	111.15.17.32	m0

Class B

Network address	Next-hop address	Interface
145.80.0.0	------------	m1
170.14.0.0	------------	m2

Default: 111.30.31.18, m0

Example 2

Router R1 in Figure 6.8 receives a packet with destination address 192.16.7.14. Show how the packet is forwarded.

Solution

The destination address in binary is 11000000 00010000 00000111 00001110. A copy of the address is shifted 28 bits to the right. The result is 00000000 00000000 00000000 0000**1100** or 12. The destination network is class C. The network address is extracted by masking off the left-most 24 bits of the destination address; the result is 192.16.7.0. The table for Class C is searched. The network address is found in the first row. The next-hop address 111.15.17.32. and the interface m0 are passed to ARP.

Example 3

Router R1 in Figure 6.8 receives a packet with destination address 167.24.160.5. Show how the packet is forwarded.

Solution

The destination address in binary is 10100111 00011000 10100000 00000101. A copy of the address is shifted 28 bits to the right. The result is 00000000 00000000 00000000 0000**1010** or 10. The class is B. The network address can be found by masking off 16 bits of the destination address, the result is 167.24.0.0. The table for Class B is searched. No matching network address is found. The packet needs to be forwarded to the default router (the network is somewhere else in the Internet). The next-hop address 111.30.31.18 and the interface number m0 are passed to ARP.

Forwarding with Subnetting

In classful addressing, subnetting happens inside the organization. The routers that handle subnetting are either at the border of the organization site or inside the site boundary. If the organization is using variable-length subnetting, we need several tables; otherwise, we need only one table. Figure 6.10 shows a simplified module for fixed-length subnetting.

Figure 6.10   *Simplified forwarding module in classful address with subnetting*

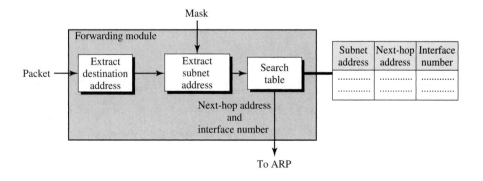

1. The module extracts the destination address of the packet.
2. The destination address and the mask are used to extract the subnet address.
3. The table is searched using the subnet address to find the next-hop address and the interface number. If no match is found, the default is used.
4. The next-hop address and the interface number are given to ARP.

Example 4

Figure 6.11 shows a router connected to four subnets.

Figure 6.11   *Configuration for Example 4*

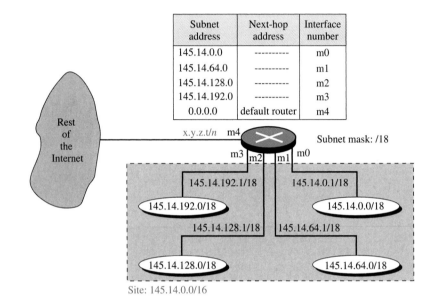

Site: 145.14.0.0/16

Note several points. First, the site address is 145.14.0.0/16 (a class B address). Every packet with destination address in the range 145.14.0.0 to 145.14.255.255 is delivered to the interface m4 and distributed to the final destination subnet by the router. Second, we have used the address x.y.z.t/n for the interface m4 because we do not know to which network this router is connected. Third, the table has a default entry for packets that are to be sent out of the site. The router is configured to apply the subnet mask /18 to any destination address.

Example 5

The router in Figure 6.11 receives a packet with destination address 145.14.32.78. Show how the packet is forwarded.

Solution

The mask is /18. After applying the mask, the subnet address is 145.14.0.0. The packet is delivered to ARP with the next-hop address 145.14.32.78 and the outgoing interface m0.

Example 6

A host in network 145.14.0.0 in Figure 6.11 has a packet to send to the host with address 7.22.67.91. Show how the packet is routed.

Solution

The router receives the packet and applies the mask (/18). The network address is 7.22.64.0. The table is searched and the address is not found. The router uses the address of the default router (not shown in figure) and sends the packet to that router.

Forwarding with Classless Addressing

In classless addressing, the whole address space is one entity; there are no classes. This means that forwarding requires one row of information for each block involved. The table needs to be searched based on the network address (first address in the block). Unfortunately, the destination address in the packet gives no clue about the network address (as it does in classful addressing).

To solve the problem, we need to include the mask (/n) in the table; we need to have an extra column that includes the mask for the corresponding block. In other words, although a classful routing table can be designed with three columns, a classless routing table needs at least four columns.

> **In classful addressing we can have a routing table with three columns;**
> **in classless addressing, we need at least four columns.**

Figure 6.12 shows a simple forwarding module for classless addressing. Note that network address extraction is done at the same time as table searching because there is no inherent information in the destination address that can be used for network address extraction.

Figure 6.12 *Simplified forwarding module in classless address*

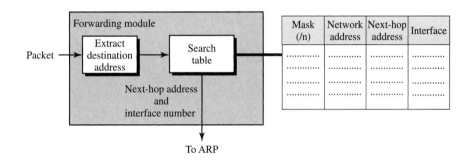

Example 7

Make a routing table for router R1 using the configuration in Figure 6.13.

Solution
Table 6.1 shows the corresponding table.

Example 8

Show the forwarding process if a packet arrives at R1 in Figure 6.13 with the destination address 180.70.65.140.

Solution
The router performs the following steps:

1. The first mask (/26) is applied to the destination address. The result is 180.70.65.128, which does not match the corresponding network address.

Figure 6.13   *Configuration for Example 7*

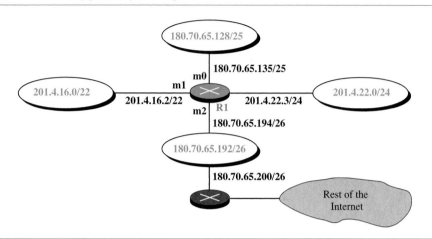

Table 6.1   *Routing table for router R1 in Figure 6.13*

Mask	Network Address	Next Hop	Interface
/26	180.70.65.192	-	m2
/25	180.70.65.128	-	m0
/24	201.4.22.0	-	m3
/22	201.4.16.0	....	m1
Default	Default	180.70.65.200	m2

2. The second mask (/25) is applied to the destination address. The result is 180.70.65.128, which matches the corresponding network address. The next-hop address (the destination address of the packet in this case) and the interface number m0 are passed to ARP for further processing.

Example 9

Show the forwarding process if a packet arrives at R1 in Figure 6.13 with the destination address 201.4.22.35.

Solution

The router performs the following steps:

1. The first mask (/26) is applied to the destination address. The result is 201.4.22.0, which does not match the corresponding network address (row 1).

2. The second mask (/25) is applied to the destination address. The result is 201.4.22.0, which does not match the corresponding network address (row 2).

3. The third mask (/24) is applied to the destination address. The result is 201.4.22.0, which matches the corresponding network address. The destination address of the packet and the interface number m3 are passed to ARP.

Example 10

Show the forwarding process if a packet arrives at R1 in Figure 6.13 with the destination address 18.24.32.78.

Solution

This time all masks are applied to the destination address, but no matching network address is found. When it reaches the end of the table, the module gives the next-hop address 180.70.65.200 and interface number m2 to ARP. This is probably an outgoing package that needs to be sent, via the default router, to someplace else in the Internet.

Example 11

Now let us give a different type of example. Can we find the configuration of a router, if we know only its routing table? The routing table for router R1 is given in Table 6.2. Can we draw its topology?

Table 6.2   *Routing table for Example 11*

Mask	Network Address	Next-Hop Address	Interface Number
/26	140.6.12.64	180.14.2.5	m2
/24	130.4.8.0	190.17.6.2.0	m1
/16	110.70.0.0	-----------------	m0
/16	180.14.0.0	-----------------	m2
/16	190.17.0.0	-----------------	m1
Default	Default	110.70.4.6	m0

Solution

We know some facts but we don't have all for a definite topology. We know that router R1 has three interfaces: m0, m1, and m2. We know that there are three networks directly connected to router R1. We know that there are two networks indirectly connected to R1. There must be at least three other routers involved (see next-hop column). We know to which networks these routers are connected by looking at their IP addresses. So we can put them at their appropriate place. We know that one router, the default router, is connected to the rest of the Internet. But there is some missing information. We do not know if network 130.4.8.0 is directly connected to router R2 or through a point-to-point network (WAN) and another router. We do not know if network 140.6.12.64 is connected to router R3 directly or through a point-to-point network (WAN) and another router. Point-to-point networks normally do not have an entry in the routing table because no hosts are connected to them. Figure 6.14 shows our guessed topology.

Address Aggregation

When we use classful addressing, there is only one entry in the routing table for each site outside the organization. The entry defines the site even if that site is subnetted. When a packet arrives at the router, the router checks the corresponding entry and forwards the packet accordingly.

When we use classless addressing, it is likely that the number of routing table entries will increase. This is because the intent of classless addressing is to divide up

Figure 6.14   *Guessed topology for Example 6*

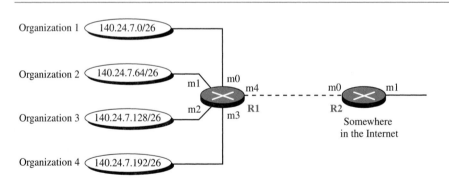

the whole address space into manageable blocks. The increased size of the table results in an increase in the amount of time needed to search the table.

To alleviate the problem, the idea of **address aggregation** was designed. In Figure 6.15 we have two routers.

Figure 6.15   *Address aggregation*

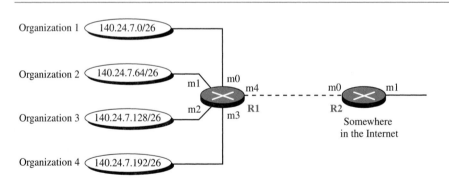

Mask	Network address	Next-hop address	Interface
/26	140.24.7.0	----------	m0
/26	140.24.7.64	----------	m1
/26	140.24.7.128	----------	m2
/26	140.24.7.192	----------	m3
/0	0.0.0.0	default router	m4

Routing table for R1

Mask	Network address	Next-hop address	Interface
/24	140.24.7.0	----------	m0
/0	0.0.0.0	default router	m1

Routing table for R2

R1 is connected to networks of four organizations that each use 64 addresses. R2 is somewhere far from R1. R1 has a longer routing table because each packet must be correctly routed to the appropriate organization. R2, on the other hand, can have a very small routing table. For R2, any packet with destination 140.24.7.0 to 140.24.7.255 is sent out from interface m0 regardless of the organization number. This is called address aggregation because the blocks of addresses for four organizations are aggregated into one larger block. R2 would have a longer routing table if each organization had addresses that could not be aggregated into one block.

Note that although the idea of address aggregation is similar to the idea of subnetting, we do not have a common site here; the network for each organization is independent. In addition, we can have several levels of aggregation.

Longest Mask Matching

What happens if one of the organizations in the previous figure is not geographically close to the other three? For example, if organization 4 cannot be connected to router R1 for some reason, can we still use the idea of address aggregation and still assign block 140.24.7.192/26 to organization 4? The answer is yes because routing in classless addressing uses another principle, **longest mask matching.** This principle states that the routing table is sorted from the longest mask to the shortest mask. In other words, if there are three masks, /27, /26, and /24, the mask /27 must be the first entry and /24 must be last. Let us see if this principle solves the situation in which organization 4 is separated from the other three organizations. Figure 6.16 shows the situation.

Figure 6.16   *Longest mask matching*

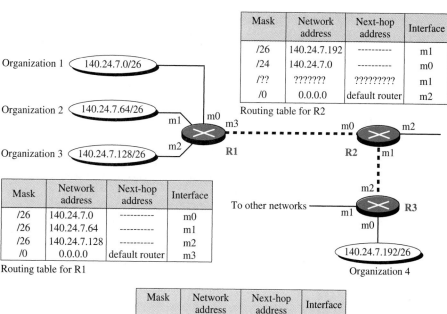

Mask	Network address	Next-hop address	Interface
/26	140.24.7.192	----------	m1
/24	140.24.7.0	----------	m0
/??	???????	?????????	m1
/0	0.0.0.0	default router	m2

Routing table for R2

Mask	Network address	Next-hop address	Interface
/26	140.24.7.0	----------	m0
/26	140.24.7.64	----------	m1
/26	140.24.7.128	----------	m2
/0	0.0.0.0	default router	m3

Routing table for R1

Mask	Network address	Next-hop address	Interface
/26	140.24.7.192	----------	m0
/??	???????	?????????	m1
/0	0.0.0.0	default router	m2

Routing table for R3

Suppose a packet arrives for organization 4 with destination address 140.24.7.200. The first mask at router R2 is applied, which gives the network address 140.24.7.192. The packet is routed correctly from interface m1 and reaches organization 4. If, however, the routing table was not stored with the longest prefix first, applying the /24 mask would result in the incorrect routing of the packet to router R1.

Hierarchical Routing

To solve the problem of gigantic routing tables, we can create a sense of hierarchy in the routing tables. In Chapter 1, we mentioned that the Internet today has a sense of hierarchy. We said that the Internet is divided into international and national ISPs. National ISPs are divided into regional ISPs, and regional ISPs are divided into local ISPs. If the routing table has a sense of hierarchy like the Internet architecture, the routing table can decrease in size.

Let us take the case of a local ISP. A local ISP can be assigned a single, but large block of addresses with a certain prefix length. The local ISP can divide this block into smaller blocks of different sizes, and assign these to individual users and organizations, both large and small. If the block assigned to the local ISP starts with a.b.c.d/n, the ISP can create blocks starting with e.f.g.h/m, where m may vary for each customer and is greater than n.

How does this reduce the size of the routing table? The rest of the Internet does not have to be aware of this division. All customers of the local ISP are defined as a.b.c.d/n to the rest of the Internet. Every packet destined for one of the addresses in this large block is routed to the local ISP. There is only one entry in every router in the world for all of these customers. They all belong to the same group. Of course, inside the local ISP, the router must recognize the subblocks and route the packet to the destined customer. If one of the customers is a large organization, it also can create another level of hierarchy by subnetting and dividing its subblock into smaller subblocks (or sub-subblocks). In classless routing, the levels of hierarchy are unlimited so long as we follow the rules of classless addressing.

Example 12

As an example of **hierarchical routing,** let us consider Figure 6.17. A regional ISP is granted 16384 addresses starting from 120.14.64.0. The regional ISP has decided to divide this block into four subblocks, each with 4096 addresses. Three of these subblocks are assigned to three local ISPs, the second subblock is reserved for future use. Note that the mask for each block is /20 because the original block with mask /18 is divided into 4 blocks.

The first local ISP has divided its assigned subblock into 8 smaller blocks and assigned each to a small ISP. Each small ISP provides services to 128 households (H001 to H128), each using four addresses. Note that the mask for each small ISP is now /23 because the block is further divided into 8 blocks. Each household has a mask of /30, because a household has only 4 addresses (2^{32-30} is 4).

The second local ISP has divided its block into 4 blocks and has assigned the addresses to 4 large organizations (LOrg01 to LOrg04). Note that each large organization has 1024 addresses and the mask is /22.

The third local ISP has divided its block into 16 blocks and assigned each block to a small organization (SOrg01 to SOrg15). Each small organization has 256 addresses and the mask is /24.

There is a sense of hierarchy in this configuration. All routers in the Internet send a packet with destination address 120.14.64.0 to 120.14.127.255 to the regional ISP. The regional ISP

Figure 6.17   *Hierarchical routing with ISPs*

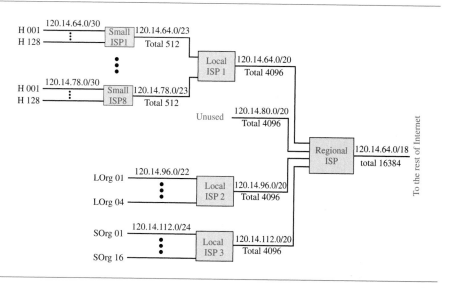

sends every packet with destination address 120.14.64.0 to 120.14.79.255 to Local ISP1. Local ISP1 sends every packet with destination address 120.14.64.0 to 120.14.64.3 to H001.

Geographical Routing

To decrease the size of the routing table even further, we need to extend hierarchical routing to include geographical routing. We must divide the entire address space into a few large blocks. We assign a block to North America, a block to Europe, a block to Asia, a block to Africa, and so on. The routers of ISPs outside of Europe will have only one entry for packets to Europe in their routing tables. The routers of ISPs outside of North America will have only one entry for packets to North America in their routing tables. And so on.

Routing Table Search Algorithms

The algorithms in classful addressing that search the routing tables must be changed to make classless routing more efficient. This includes the algorithms that update routing tables. We will discuss this updating issue in Chapter 14.

Searching in Classful Addressing   In classful addressing, the routing table is organized as a list. However, to make searching more efficient, the routing table can be divided into three tables (sometimes called buckets), one for each class. When the packet arrives, the router applies the default mask (which is inherent in the address itself) to find the corresponding bucket (A, B, or C). The router then searches the corresponding bucket instead of the whole table. Some routers even assign 8 buckets for class A, 4 buckets for class B, and 2 buckets for class C based on the outcome of the class finding process.

Searching in Classless Addressing   In classless addressing, there is no network information in the destination address. The simplest, but not the most efficient search method, is called the **longest match** (as we discussed before). The routing table can be divided into buckets, one for each prefix. The router first tries the longest prefix. If the destination address is found in this bucket, the search is complete. If the address is not found, the next prefix is searched. And so on. It is obvious that this type of search takes a long time.

One solution is to change the data structure used for searching. Instead of a list, other data structures (such as a tree or a binary tree) can be used. One candidate is a trie (a special kind of tree). However, this discussion is beyond the scope of this book.

Combination

We must mention here that modern routers are all based on classless addressing. They all include the mask in the routing table. Until classful addressing is totally eliminated from the Internet, it is treated as a special case of classless addressing using the masks /24, /16, and /8.

6.3   ROUTING

Routing deals with the issues of creating and maintaining routing tables.

Static Versus Dynamic Routing Tables

A host or a router has a routing table with an entry for each destination or a combination of destinations, to route IP packets. The routing table can be either static or dynamic.

Static Routing Table

A **static routing table** contains information entered manually. The administrator enters the route for each destination into the table. When a table is created, it cannot update automatically when there is a change in the Internet. The table must be manually altered by the administrator.

A static routing table can be used in a small internet that does not change very often, or in an experimental internet for troubleshooting. It is not good strategy to use a static routing table in a big internet such as the Internet.

Dynamic Routing Table

A **dynamic routing table** is updated periodically using one of the dynamic routing protocols such as RIP, OSPF, or BGP (see Chapter 14). Whenever there is a change in the Internet, such as a shutdown of a router or breaking of a link, the dynamic routing protocols update all of the tables in the routers (and eventually in the host) automatically.

The routers in a big internet such as the Internet need to be updated dynamically for efficient delivery of the IP packets. We will discuss in detail the three dynamic routing protocols in Chapter 14.

Routing Table

As mentioned previously, a routing table for classless addressing has a minimum of four columns. However, some of today's routers have even more columns. We should be aware that the number of columns are vendor dependent and not all columns can be found in all routers. Figure 6.18 shows some common columns in today's routers.

Figure 6.18 *Common fields in a routing table*

Mask	Network address	Next-hop address	Interface	Flags	Reference count	Use
....	....	....	....	....	....	....

❏ **Mask.** This field defines the mask applied for the entry.

❏ **Network address.** This field defines the network address to which the packet is finally delivered. In the case of host-specific routing, this field defines the address of the destination host.

❏ **Next-hop address.** This field defines the address of the next-hop router to which the packet is delivered.

❏ **Interface.** This field shows the name of the interface.

❏ **Flags.** This field defines up to five flags. Flags are on/off switches that signify either presence or absence. The five flags are U (up), G (gateway), H (host-specific), D (added by redirection), and M (modified by redirection).

   a. **U (up).** The U flag indicates the router is up and running. If this flag is not present, it means that the router is down. The packet cannot be forwarded and is discarded.

   b. **G (gateway).** The G flag means that the destination is in another network. The packet is delivered to the next-hop router for delivery (indirect delivery). When this flag is missing, it means the destination is in this network (direct delivery).

   c. **H (host-specific).** The H flag indicates that the entry in the network address field is a host-specific address. When it is missing, it means that the address is only the network address of the destination.

   d. **D (added by redirection).** The D flag indicates that routing information for this destination has been added to the host routing table by a redirection message from ICMP. We will discuss redirection and the ICMP protocol in Chapter 9.

   e. **M (modified by redirection).** The M flag indicates that the routing information for this destination has been modified by a redirection message from ICMP. We will discuss redirection and the ICMP protocol in Chapter 9.

❏ **Reference count.** This field gives the number of users that are using this route at the moment. For example, if five people at the same time are connecting to the same host from this router, the value of this column is 5.

❏ **Use.** This field shows the number of packets transmitted through this router for the corresponding destination.

Example 13

One utility that can be used to find the contents of a routing table for a host or router is *netstat* in UNIX or LINUX. The following shows the listing of the contents of the default server. We have used two options, r and n. The option *r* indicates that we are interested in the routing table and the option *n* indicates that we are looking for numeric addresses. Note that this is a routing table for a host, not a router. Although we discussed the routing table for a router throughout the chapter, a host also needs a routing table.

```
$ netstat -rn
Kernel IP routing table
```

Destination	Gateway	Mask	Flags	Iface
153.18.16.0	0.0.0.0	255.255.240.0	U	eth0
127.0.0.0	0.0.0.0	255.0.0.0	U	lo
0.0.0.0	153.18.31.254	0.0.0.0	UG	eth0

Note also that the order of columns is different from what we showed. The destination column here defines the network address. The term **gateway** used by UNIX is synonymous with *router*. This column actually defines the address of the next hop. The value 0.0.0.0 shows that the delivery is direct. The last entry has a flag of G, which means that the destination can be reached through a router (default router). The *Iface* defines the interface. The host has only one real interface, eth0, which means interface 0 connected to an Ethernet network. The second interface, lo, is actually a virtual loopback interface indicating that the host accepts packets with loopback address 127.0.0.0.

More information about the IP address and physical address of the server can be found using the *ifconfig* command on the given interface (eth0).

```
$ ifconfig eth0
eth0   Link encap:Ethernet  HWaddr 00:B0:D0:DF:09:5D
inet addr:153.18.17.11  Bcast:153.18.31.255  Mask:255.255.240.0
...
```

From the above information, we can deduce the configuration of the server as shown in Figure 6.19.

Figure 6.19   *Configuration of the server for Example 13*

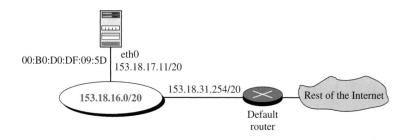

Note that the *ifconfig* command gives us the IP address and the physical (hardware) address of the interface.

6.4   STRUCTURE OF A ROUTER

In our discussion of forwarding and routing, we represented a router as a black box that accepts incoming packets from one of the input ports (interfaces), uses a routing table to find the output port from which the packet departs, and sends the packet from this output port. In this section we open the black box and look inside. However, our discussion won't be very detailed; entire books have been written about routers. We just give an overview to the reader.

Components

We can say that a router has four components: **input ports, output ports,** the **routing processor,** and the **switching fabric,** as shown in Figure 6.20.

Figure 6.20   *Router components*

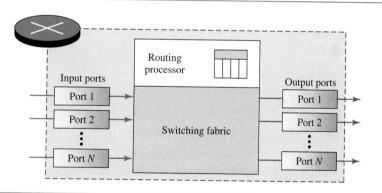

Input Ports

An input port performs the physical and data link layer functions of the router. The bits are constructed from the received signal. The packet is decapsulated from the frame. Errors are detected and corrected. The packet is ready to be forwarded by the network layer. In addition to a physical layer processor and a data link processor, the input port has buffers (queues) to hold the packets before they are directed to the switching fabric. Figure 6.21 shows a schematic diagram of an input port.

Output Ports

An output port performs the same functions as the input port, but in the reverse order. First the outgoing packets are queued, then the packet is encapsulated in a frame, and

Figure 6.21 *Input port*

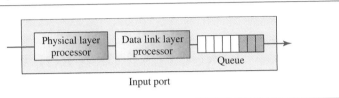

Input port

finally the physical layer functions are applied to the frame to create the signal to be sent on the line. Figure 6.22 shows a schematic diagram of an output port.

Figure 6.22 *Output port*

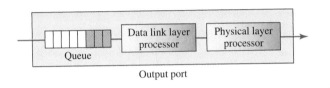

Output port

Routing Processor

The routing processor performs the functions of the network layer. The destination address is used to find the address of the next hop and, at the same time, the output port number from which the packet is sent out. This activity is sometimes referred to as *table lookup* because the routing processor searches the routing table. In the newer routers, this function of the routing processor is being moved to the input ports to facilitate and expedite the process.

Switching Fabrics

The most difficult task in a router is to move the packet from the input queue to the output queue. The speed with which this is done affects the size of the input/output queue and the overall delay in packet delivery. In the past, when a router was actually a dedicated computer, the memory of the computer or a bus was used as the switching fabric. The input port stored the packet in memory; the output port got the packet from the memory. Today, routers are specialized mechanisms that use a variety of switching fabrics. We briefly discuss some of these fabrics here.

Crossbar Switch   The simplest type of switching fabric is the crossbar switch shown in Figure 6.23. A **crossbar switch** connects *n* inputs to *n* outputs in a grid, using electronic microswitches at each **crosspoint.**

Banyan Switch   More realistic than the crossbar switch is the **banyan switch** (named after the banyan tree). A banyan switch is a multistage switch with microswitches at each stage that route the packets based on the output port represented as a binary string. For *n* inputs and *n* outputs, we have $\log_2(n)$ stages with $n/2$ microswitches at each stage. The first stage routes the packet based on the highest order bit of the binary string. The second stage routes the packets based on the second highest

Figure 6.23 *Crossbar switch*

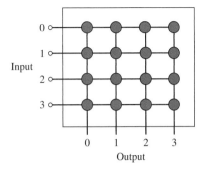

order bit, and so on. Figure 6.24 shows a banyan switch with eight inputs and eight outputs. The number of stages is $\log_2(8) = 3$.

Figure 6.24 *A banyan switch*

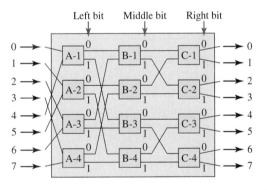

Figure 6.25 shows the operation. In part a, a packet has arrived at input port 1 and must go to output port 6 (110 in binary). The first microswitch (A-2) routes the packet based on the first bit (1), the second microswitch (B-4) routes the packet based on the second bit (1), and the third microswitch (C-4) routes the packet based on the third bit (0). In part b, a packet has arrived at input port 5 and must go to output port 2 (010 in binary). The first microswitch (A-2) routes the packet based on the first bit (0), the second microswitch (B-2) routes the packet based on the second bit (1), and the third microswitch (C-2) routes the packet based on the third bit (0).

Batcher-Banyan Switch   The problem with the banyan switch is the possibility of internal collision even when two packets are not heading for the same output port. We can solve this problem by sorting the arriving packets based on their destination port.

K. E. Batcher designed a switch that comes before the banyan switch and sorts the incoming packets according to their final destination. The combination is called the

Figure 6.25   *Examples of routing in a banyan switch*

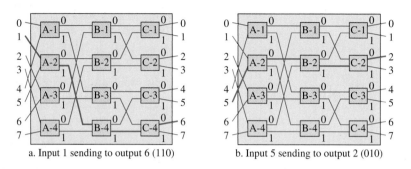

a. Input 1 sending to output 6 (110)   b. Input 5 sending to output 2 (010)

Batcher-banyan switch. The sorting switch uses hardware merging techniques, but we will not discuss the details here. Normally, another hardware module called a trap is added between the Batcher switch and the banyan switch (see Figure 6.26) The trap module prevents duplicate packets (packets with the same output destination) from passing to the banyan switch simultaneously. Only one packet for each destination is allowed at each tick; if there is more than one, they wait for the next tick.

Figure 6.26   *Batcher-banyan switch*

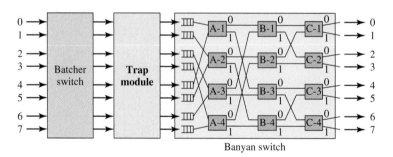

Banyan switch

6.5   KEY TERMS

address aggregation	default method
banyan switch	delivery
Batcher-banyan switch	direct delivery
connectionless service	dynamic routing method
connection-oriented service	dynamic routing table
crossbar switch	forwarding
crosspoint	hierarchical routing

host-specific method

ifconfig command

indirect delivery

input ports

longest mask matching

netstat command

network-specific method

next-hop method

output ports

routing

routing processor

static routing table

switching fabric

6.6   SUMMARY

❑ In a connection-oriented service, the local network layer protocol first makes a con-nection with the network layer protocol at the remote site before sending a packet.

❑ In a connectionless service, the network layer protocol treats each packet indepen-dently, with each packet having no relationship to any other packet. The packets in a message may or may not travel the same path to their destination. The IP proto-col is a connectionless protocol.

❑ The delivery of a packet is called direct if the deliverer (host or router) and the des-tination are on the same network.

❑ The delivery of a packet is called indirect if the deliverer (host or router) and the destination are on different networks.

❑ In the next-hop method, instead of a complete list of the stops the packet must make, only the address of the next hop is listed in the routing table.

❑ In the network-specific method, all hosts on a network share one entry in the rout-ing table.

❑ In the host-specific method, the full IP address of a host is given in the routing table.

❑ In the default method, a router is assigned to receive all packets with no match in the routing table.

❑ The routing table for classful forwarding can have three columns.

❑ The routing table for classless addressing needs at least four columns.

❑ The number of columns in a routing table is vendor dependent.

❑ Address aggregation simplifies the forwarding process in classless addressing.

❑ Longest mask matching is required in classless addressing.

❑ Classless addressing requires hierarchical and geographical routing to prevent immense routing tables.

❑ Search algorithms for classful addressing are not efficient for classless addressing.

❑ A static routing table's entries are updated manually by an administrator.

❑ A dynamic routing table's entries are updated automatically by a routing protocol.

❑ A router is normally made of four components: input ports, output ports, the rout-ing processor, and the switching fabric.

6.7   PRACTICE SET

Exercises

1. A host with IP address 137.23.56.23/16 sends a packet to a host with IP address 137.23.67.9/16. Is the delivery direct or indirect? Assume no subnetting.

2. A host with IP address 137.23.56.23/16 sends a packet to a host with IP address 142.3.6.9/24. Is the delivery direct or indirect? Assume no subnetting.

3. In Figure 6.8, find the routing table for router R2.

4. In Figure 6.8, find the routing table for router R3.

5. A packet arrives at router R1 in Figure 6.8 with destination address 192.16.7.42. Show how it is forwarded.

6. A packet arrives at router R1 in Figure 6.8 with destination address 145.80.14.26. Show how it is forwarded.

7. A packet arrives at router R1 in Figure 6.8 with destination address 147.26.50.30. Show how it is forwarded.

8. A packet arrives at the router in Figure 6.11 with destination address 145.14.192.71. Show how it is forwarded.

9. A packet arrives at the router in Figure 6.11 with destination address 135.11.80.21. Show how it is forwarded.

10. A packet arrives at router R1 in Figure 6.13 with destination address 201.4.16.70. Show how it is forwarded.

11. A packet arrives at router R1 in Figure 6.13 with destination address 202.70.20.30. Show how it is forwarded.

12. Show a routing table for a host that is totally isolated.

13. Show a routing table for a host that is connected to a LAN without being connected to the Internet.

14. Find the topology of the network if Table 6.3 is the routing table for router R1.

Table 6.3   *Routing table for Exercise 14*

Mask	Network Address	Next-Hop Address	Interface
/27	202.14.17.224	----	m1
/18	145.23.192.0	----	m0
default	default	130.56.12.4	m2

15. Can router R1 in Figure 6.16 receive a packet with destination address 140.24.7.194? Explain your answer.

16. Can router R1 in Figure 6.16 receive a packet with destination address 140.24.7.42? Explain your answer.

17. Show the routing table for regional ISP in Figure 6.17.

18. Show the routing table for local ISP 1 in Figure 6.17.

19. Show the routing table for local ISP 2 in Figure 6.17.

20. Show the routing table for local ISP 3 in Figure 6.17.

21. Show the routing table for small ISP 1 in Figure 6.17.

Research Activities

22. If you have access to UNIX (or LINUX), use *netstat* to find the routing table for the server to which you are connected.

23. If you have access to UNIX (or LINUX), use *ifconfig* to find specifications for the interface of the server to which you are connected.

24. Find how your ISP uses address aggregation and longest mask match principles.

25. Find whether or not your IP address is part of the geographical address allocation.

26. Find the RFCs for address aggregation.

27. Find the RFCs for the longest prefix match.

28. If you are using a router, find the number and names of the columns in the routing table.

29. CISCO is one of the dominant manufacturers of routers. Find information about the different types of routers manufactured by this company.

CHAPTER 7

ARP and RARP

An internet is made of a combination of physical networks connected together by internetworking devices such as routers. A packet starting from a source host may pass through several different physical networks before finally reaching the destination host.

The hosts and routers are recognized at the network level by their logical addresses. A **logical address** is an internetwork address. Its jurisdiction is universal. A logical address is unique universally. It is called a *logical* address because it is usually implemented in software. Every protocol that deals with interconnecting networks requires logical addresses. The logical addresses in the TCP/IP protocol suite are called **IP addresses** and are 32 bits long.

However, packets pass through physical networks to reach these hosts and routers. At the physical level, the hosts and routers are recognized by their physical addresses. A **physical address** is a local address. Its jurisdiction is a local network. It should be unique locally, but not necessarily universally. It is called a *physical* address because it is usually (but not always) implemented in hardware. Examples of physical addresses are 48-bit MAC addresses in the Ethernet protocol, which are imprinted on the NIC installed in the host or router.

The physical address and the logical address are two different identifiers. We need both of them because a physical network such as Ethernet can have two different protocols at the network layer such as IP and IPX (Novell) at the same time. Likewise, a packet at a network layer such as IP may pass through different physical networks such as Ethernet and LocalTalk (Apple).

This means that delivery of a packet to a host or a router requires two levels of addressing: logical and physical. We need to be able to map a logical address to its corresponding physical address and vice versa. These can be done using either static or dynamic mapping.

Static mapping means creating a table that associates a logical address with a physical address. This table is stored in each machine on the network. Each machine that knows, for example, the IP address of another machine but not its physical address can look it up in the table. This has some limitations because physical addresses may change in the following ways:

1. A machine could change its NIC, resulting in a new physical address.

2. In some LANs, such as LocalTalk, the physical address changes every time the computer is turned on.

3. A mobile computer can move from one physical network to another, resulting in a change in its physical address.

To implement these changes, a static mapping table must be updated periodically. This overhead could affect network performance.

In **dynamic mapping** each time a machine knows one of the two addresses (logical or physical), it can use a protocol to find the other one.

Two protocols have been designed to perform dynamic mapping: **address resolution protocol (ARP)** and **reverse address resolution protocol (RARP).** The first maps a logical address to a physical address; the second maps a physical address to a logical address. Figure 7.1 shows the idea.

Figure 7.1   *ARP and RARP*

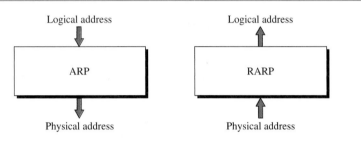

ARP and RARP use unicast and broadcast physical addresses. We discussed unicast and broadcast physical addresses in Chapter 3. We mentioned that, for example, Ethernet uses the all 1s address (FF:FF:FF:FF:FF:FF) as the broadcast address.

Figure 7.2 shows the position of the ARP and RARP protocols in the TCP/IP protocol suite.

Figure 7.2   *Position of ARP and RARP in TCP/IP protocol suite*

7.1   ARP

Anytime a host or a router has an IP datagram to send to another host or router, it has the logical (IP) address of the receiver. But the IP datagram must be encapsulated in a frame to be able to pass through the physical network. This means that the sender needs the physical address of the receiver. A mapping corresponds a logical address to a physical address.

As we said before, this can be done either statically or dynamically. The association between logical and physical addresses can be statically stored in a table. The sender can look in the table and find the physical address corresponding to a logical address. But as we discussed before, this is not a good solution. Every time a physical address is changed, the table must be updated. Updating tables on all machines at frequent intervals is a very demanding task.

The mapping, however, can be done dynamically, which means that the sender asks the receiver to announce its physical address when needed. ARP is designed for this purpose.

ARP associates an IP address with its physical address. On a typical physical network, such as a LAN, each device on a link is identified by a physical or station address that is usually imprinted on the NIC.

Anytime a host, or a router, needs to find the physical address of another host or router on its network, it sends an ARP query packet. The packet includes the physical and IP addresses of the sender and the IP address of the receiver. Because the sender does not know the physical address of the receiver, the query is broadcast over the network (see Figure 7.3).

Figure 7.3   *ARP operation*

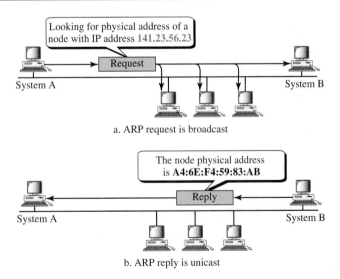

a. ARP request is broadcast

b. ARP reply is unicast

Every host or router on the network receives and processes the ARP query packet, but only the intended recipient recognizes its IP address and sends back an ARP response packet. The response packet contains the recipient's IP and physical addresses. The packet is unicast directly to the inquirer using the physical address received in the query packet.

In Figure 7.3a, the system on the left (A) has a packet that needs to be delivered to another system (B) with IP address 141.23.56.23. System A needs to pass the packet to its data link layer for the actual delivery, but it does not know the physical address of the recipient. It uses the services of ARP by asking the ARP protocol to send a broadcast ARP request packet to ask for the physical address of a system with an IP address of 141.23.56.23.

This packet is received by every system on the physical network, but only system B will answer it, as shown in Figure 7.3b. System B sends an ARP reply packet that includes its physical address. Now system A can send all the packets it has for this destination using the physical address it received.

Packet Format

Figure 7.4 shows the format of an ARP packet.

Figure 7.4   *ARP packet*

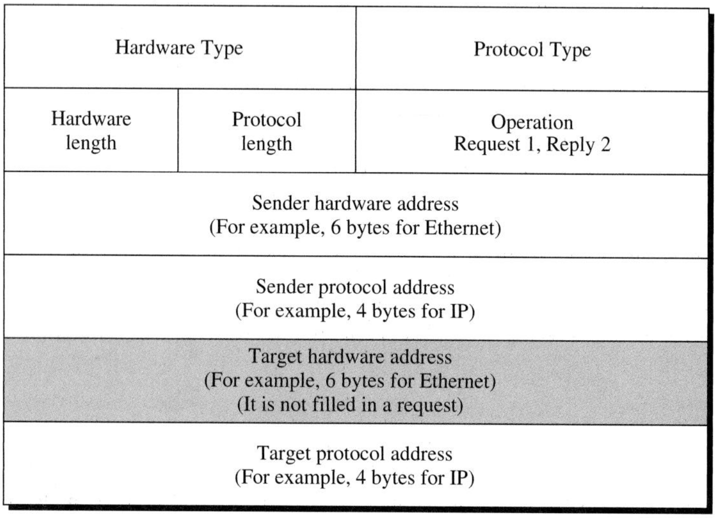

The fields are as follows:

❏ **Hardware type.** This is a 16-bit field defining the type of the network on which ARP is running. Each LAN has been assigned an integer based on its type. For example, Ethernet is given the type 1. ARP can be used on any physical network.

❏ **Protocol type.** This is a 16-bit field defining the protocol. For example, the value of this field for the IPv4 protocol is 0800_{16}. ARP can be used with any higher-level protocol.

❏ **Hardware length.** This is an 8-bit field defining the length of the physical address in bytes. For example, for Ethernet the value is 6.

❏ **Protocol length.** This is an 8-bit field defining the length of the logical address in bytes. For example, for the IPv4 protocol the value is 4.

❑ **Operation.** This is a 16-bit field defining the type of packet. Two packet types are defined: ARP request (1), ARP reply (2).

❑ **Sender hardware address.** This is a variable-length field defining the physical address of the sender. For example, for Ethernet this field is 6 bytes long.

❑ **Sender protocol address.** This is a variable-length field defining the logical (for example, IP) address of the sender. For the IP protocol, this field is 4 bytes long.

❑ **Target hardware address.** This is a variable-length field defining the physical address of the target. For example, for Ethernet this field is 6 bytes long. For an ARP request message, this field is all 0s because the sender does not know the physical address of the target.

❑ **Target protocol address.** This is a variable-length field defining the logical (for example, IP) address of the target. For the IPv4 protocol, this field is 4 bytes long.

Encapsulation

An ARP packet is encapsulated directly into a data link frame. For example, in Figure 7.5 an ARP packet is encapsulated in an Ethernet frame. Note that the type field indicates that the data carried by the frame is an ARP packet.

Figure 7.5   *Encapsulation of ARP packet*

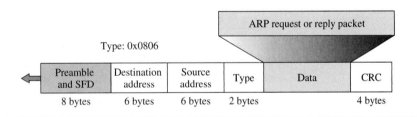

Operation

Let us see how ARP functions on a typical internet. First we describe the steps involved. Then we discuss the four cases in which a host or router needs to use ARP.

Steps Involved

These are the steps involved in an ARP process:

1. The sender knows the IP address of the target. We will see how the sender obtains this shortly.

2. IP asks ARP to create an ARP request message, filling in the sender physical address, the sender IP address, and the target IP address. The target physical address field is filled with 0s.

3. The message is passed to the data link layer where it is encapsulated in a frame using the physical address of the sender as the source address and the physical broadcast address as the destination address.

4. Every host or router receives the frame. Because the frame contains a broadcast destination address, all stations remove the message and pass it to ARP. All

machines except the one targeted drop the packet. The target machine recognizes the IP address.

5. The target machine replies with an ARP reply message that contains its physical address. The message is unicast.

6. The sender receives the reply message. It now knows the physical address of the target machine.

7. The IP datagram, which carries data for the target machine, is now encapsulated in a frame and is unicast to the destination.

Four Different Cases

The following are four different cases in which the services of ARP can be used (see Figure 7.6).

Figure 7.6   *Four cases using ARP*

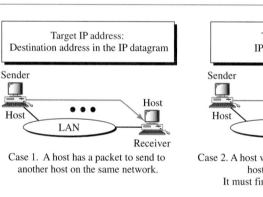

Target IP address:
Destination address in the IP datagram

Sender

Host

Host

LAN

Receiver

Case 1. A host has a packet to send to another host on the same network.

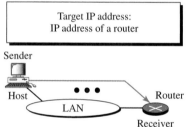

Target IP address:
IP address of a router

Sender

Host

LAN

Router

Receiver

Case 2. A host wants to send a packet to another host on another network. It must first be delivered to a router.

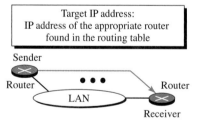

Target IP address:
IP address of the appropriate router found in the routing table

Sender

Router

LAN

Router

Receiver

Case 3. A router receives a packet to be sent to a host on another network. It must first be delivered to the appropriate router.

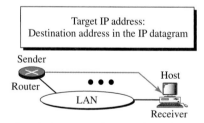

Target IP address:
Destination address in the IP datagram

Sender

Router

LAN

Host

Receiver

Case 4. A router receives a packet to be sent to a host on the same network.

1. The sender is a host and wants to send a packet to another host on the same network. In this case, the logical address that must be mapped to a physical address is the destination IP address in the datagram header.

2. The sender is a host and wants to send a packet to another host on another network. In this case, the host looks at its routing table and finds the IP address of the next hop (router) for this destination. If it does not have a routing table, it looks for the IP address of the default router. The IP address of the router becomes the logical address that must be mapped to a physical address.

3. The sender is a router that has received a datagram destined for a host on another network. It checks its routing table and finds the IP address of the next router. The IP address of the next router becomes the logical address that must be mapped to a physical address.

4. The sender is a router that has received a datagram destined for a host in the same network. The destination IP address of the datagram becomes the logical address that must be mapped to a physical address.

An ARP request is broadcast; an ARP reply is unicast.

Example 1

A host with IP address 130.23.43.20 and physical address B2:34:55:10:22:10 has a packet to send to another host with IP address 130.23.43.25 and physical address A4:6E:F4:59:83:AB (which is unknown to the first host). The two hosts are on the same Ethernet network. Show the ARP request and reply packets encapsulated in Ethernet frames.

Solution
Figure 7.7 shows the ARP request and reply packets. Note that the ARP data field in this case is 28 bytes, and that the individual addresses do not fit in the 4-byte boundary. That is why we do

---

Figure 7.7   *Example 1*

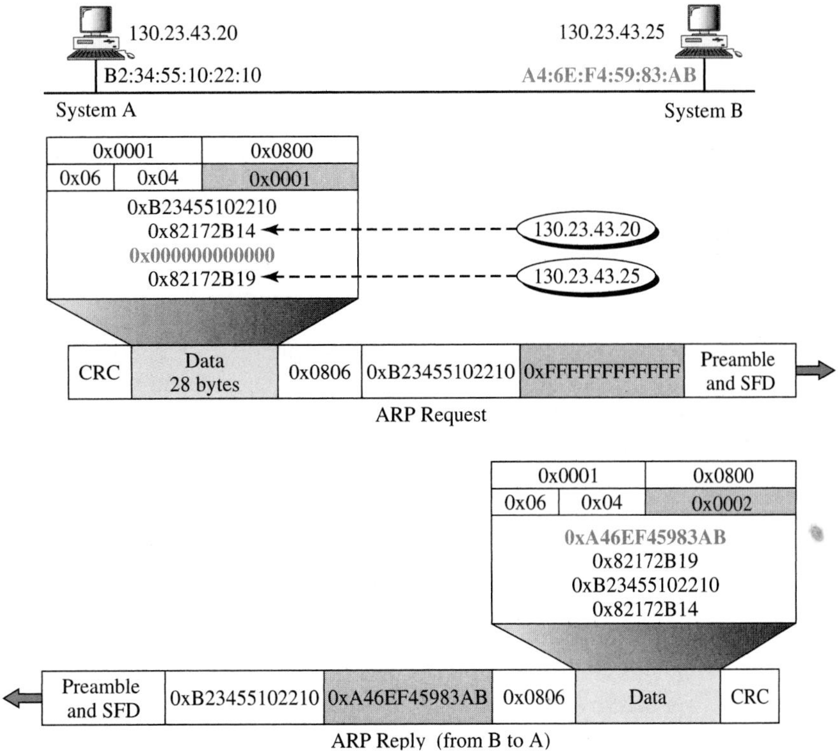

ARP Request

ARP Reply (from B to A)

not show the regular 4-byte boundaries for these addresses. Also note that the IP addresses are shown in hexadecimal. For information on binary or hexadecimal notation see Appendix B.

ARP over ATM

ARP is also used when an IP packet wants to pass over an ATM network. We will talk about this aspect of ARP when we discuss IP over ATM in Chapter 23.

Proxy ARP

A technique called *proxy* ARP is used to create a subnetting effect. A **proxy ARP** is an ARP that acts on behalf of a set of hosts. Whenever a router running a proxy ARP receives an ARP request looking for the IP address of one of these hosts, the router sends an ARP reply announcing its own hardware (physical) address. After the router receives the actual IP packet, it sends the packet to the appropriate host or router.

Let us give an example. In Figure 7.8 the ARP installed on the right-hand host will answer only to an ARP request with a target IP address of 141.23.56.23.

Figure 7.8   *Proxy ARP*

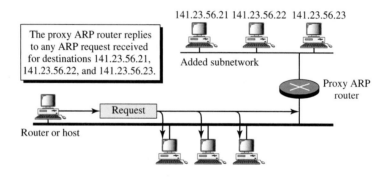

However, the administrator may need to create a subnet without changing the whole system to recognize subnetted addresses. One solution is to add a router running a proxy ARP. In this case, the router acts on behalf of all of the hosts installed on the subnet. When it receives an ARP request with a target IP address that matches the address of one of its protégés (141.23.56.21, 141.23.56.22, and 141.23.56.23), it sends an ARP reply and announces its hardware address as the target hardware address. When the router receives the IP packet, it sends the packet to the appropriate host.

7.2   ARP PACKAGE

In this section, we give an example of a simplified ARP software package. The purpose is to show the components of a hypothetical ARP package and the relationships between the components.

We can say that this ARP package involves five components: a **cache table,** queues, an output module, an input module, and a cache-control module. Figure 7.9 shows these five components and their interactions. The package receives an IP datagram that needs to be encapsulated in a frame that needs the destination physical (hardware) address. If the ARP package finds this address, it delivers the IP packet and the physical address to the data link layer for transmission.

Figure 7.9   *ARP components*

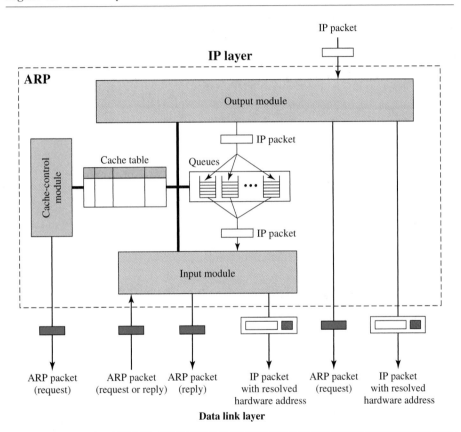

Cache Table

A sender usually has more than one IP datagram to send to the same destination. It is inefficient to use the ARP protocol for each datagram destined for the same host or router. The solution is the cache table. When a host or router receives the corresponding physical address for an IP datagram, the address can be saved in the cache table. This address can be used for the datagrams destined for the same receiver within the next few minutes. However, as space in the cache table is very limited, mappings in the cache are not retained for an unlimited time.

The cache table is implemented as an array of entries. In our package, each entry contains the following fields:

❑ **State.** This column shows the state of the entry. It can have one of three values: *FREE, PENDING,* or *RESOLVED.* The FREE state means that the time-to-live for this entry has expired. The space can be used for a new entry. The PENDING state means a request for this entry has been sent, but the reply has not yet been received. The RESOLVED state means that the entry is complete. The entry now has the physical (hardware) address of the destination. The packets waiting to be sent to this destination can use the information in this entry.

❑ **Hardware type.** This field is the same as the corresponding field in the ARP packet.

❑ **Protocol type.** This field is the same as the corresponding field in the ARP packet.

❑ **Hardware length.** This field is the same as the corresponding field in the ARP packet.

❑ **Protocol length.** This field is the same as the corresponding field in the ARP packet.

❑ **Interface number.** A router (or a multihomed host) can be connected to different networks, each with a different interface number. Each network can have different hardware and protocol types.

❑ **Queue number.** ARP uses numbered queues to enqueue the packets waiting for address resolution. Packets for the same destination are usually enqueued in the same queue.

❑ **Attempts.** This column shows the number of times an ARP request is sent out for this entry.

❑ **Time-out.** This column shows the lifetime of an entry in seconds.

❑ **Hardware address.** This column shows the destination hardware address. It remains empty until resolved by an ARP reply.

❑ **Protocol address.** This column shows the destination IP address.

Queues

Our ARP package maintains a set of queues, one for each destination, to hold the IP packets while ARP tries to resolve the hardware address. The output module sends unresolved packets into the corresponding **queue.** The input module removes a packet from a queue and sends it, with the resolved physical address, to the data link layer for transmission.

Output Module

The **output module** waits for an IP packet from the IP software. The output module checks the cache table to find an entry corresponding to the destination IP address of this packet. The destination IP address of the IP packet must match the protocol address of the entry.

If the entry is found and the state of the entry is RESOLVED, the packet along with the destination hardware address is passed to the data link layer for transmission.

If the entry is found and the state of the entry is PENDING, the packet waits until the destination hardware address is found. Because the state is PENDING, there is a queue already created for this destination. The module sends the packet to this queue.

If no entry is found, the module creates a queue and enqueues the packet. A new entry with the state of PENDING is created for this destination and the value of the ATTEMPTS field is set to 1. An ARP request packet is then broadcast.

Output Module
1. Sleep until an IP packet is received from IP software.
2. Check cache table for an entry corresponding to the destination of this IP packet.
3. If (found)
1. If (the state is RESOLVED)
1. Extract the value of the hardware address from the entry.
2. Send the packet and the hardware address to data link layer.
3. Return.
2. If (the state is PENDING)
1. Enqueue the packet to the corresponding queue.
2. Return.
4. If (not found)
1. Create a cache entry with state set to PENDING and ATTEMPTS set to 1.
2. Create a queue.
3. Enqueue the packet.
4. Send an ARP request.
5. Return.

Input Module

The **input module** waits until an ARP packet (request or reply) arrives. The input module checks the cache table to find an entry corresponding to this ARP packet. The target protocol address should match the protocol address of the entry.

If the entry is found and the state of the entry is PENDING, the module updates the entry by copying the target hardware address in the packet to the hardware address field of the entry and changing the state to RESOLVED. The module also sets the value of the TIME-OUT for this entry. It then dequeues the packets from the corresponding queue, one by one, and delivers them along with the hardware address to the data link layer for transmission.

If the entry is found and the state is RESOLVED, the module still updates the entry. This is because the target hardware address could have been changed. The value of the TIME-OUT field is also reset.

If the entry is not found, the module creates a new entry and adds it to the table. The protocol requires that any information received is added to the table for future use. The state is set to RESOLVED and TIME-OUT is set.

Now the module checks to see if the arrived ARP packet is a request. If it is, the module immediately creates an ARP reply message and sends it to the sender. The ARP reply packet is created by changing the value of the operation field from request to reply and filling in the target hardware address.

Input Module
1. Sleep until an ARP packet (request or reply) arrives.
2. Check the cache table to find an entry corresponding to this ARP packet.
3. If (found)
1. Update the entry.
2. If (the state is PENDING)
1. While the queue is not empty
1. Dequeue one packet.
2. Send the packet and the hardware address to data link.
4. If (not found)
1. Create an entry.
2. Add the entry to the table.
5. If (the packet is a request)
1. Send an ARP reply.
6. Return.

Cache-Control Module

The **cache-control module** is responsible for maintaining the cache table. It periodically (for example, every 5 s) checks the cache table, entry by entry.

If the state of the entry is FREE, it continues to the next entry. If the state is PENDING, the module increments the value of the attempts field by 1. It then checks the value of the attempts field. If this value is greater than the maximum number of attempts allowed, the state is changed to FREE and the corresponding queue is destroyed. However, if the number of attempts is less than the maximum, the module creates and sends another ARP request.

If the state of the entry is RESOLVED, the module decrements the value of the time-out field by the amount of time elapsed since the last check. If this value is less than or equal to zero, the state is changed to FREE and the queue is destroyed.

Cache-Control Module
1. Sleep until the periodic timer matures.
2. For every entry in the cache table
1. If (the state is FREE)
1. Continue.
2. If (the state is PENDING)
1. Increment the value of attempts by 1.

Cache-Control Module (continued)
2. If (attempts greater than maximum)
1. Change the state to FREE.
2. Destroy the corresponding queue.
3. Else
1. Send an ARP request.
4. Continue.
3. If (the state is RESOLVED)
1. Decrement the value of time-out by the value of elapsed time.
2. If (time-out less than or equal to zero)
1. Change the state to FREE.
2. Destroy the corresponding queue.
3. Return.

More Examples

In this section we show some examples of the ARP operation and the changes in the cache table. Table 7.1 shows some of the cache table fields at the start of our examples.

Table 7.1   *Original cache table used for examples*

State	Queue	Attempt	Time-Out	Protocol Addr.	Hardware Addr.
R	5		900	180.3.6.1	ACAE32457342
P	2	2		129.34.4.8	
P	14	5		201.11.56.7	
R	8		450	114.5.7.89	457342ACAE32
P	12	1		220.55.5.7	
F					
R	9		60	19.1.7.82	4573E3242ACA
P	18	3		188.11.8.71	

Example 2

The ARP output module receives an IP datagram (from the IP layer) with the destination address 114.5.7.89. It checks the cache table and finds that an entry exists for this destination with the RESOLVED state (R in the table). It extracts the hardware address, which is 457342ACAE32, and sends the packet and the address to the data link layer for transmission. The cache table remains the same.

Example 3

Twenty seconds later, the ARP output module receives an IP datagram (from the IP layer) with the destination address 116.1.7.22. It checks the cache table and does not find this destination in the table. The module adds an entry to the table with the state PENDING and the Attempt value 1. It creates a new queue for this destination and enqueues the packet. It then sends an ARP request to the data link layer for this destination. The new cache table is shown in Table 7.2.

Table 7.2   *Updated cache table for Example 3*

State	Queue	Attempt	Time-Out	Protocol Addr.	Hardware Addr.
R	5		900	180.3.6.1	ACAE32457342
P	2	2		129.34.4.8	
P	14	5		201.11.56.7	
R	8		450	114.5.7.89	457342ACAE32
P	12	1		220.55.5.7	
P	23	1		116.1.7.22	
R	9		60	19.1.7.82	4573E3242ACA
P	18	3		188.11.8.71	

Example 4

Fifteen seconds later, the ARP input module receives an ARP packet with target protocol (IP) address 188.11.8.71. The module checks the table and finds this address. It changes the state of the entry to RESOLVED and sets the time-out value to 900. The module then adds the target hardware address (E34573242ACA) to the entry. Now it accesses queue 18 and sends all the packets in this queue, one by one, to the data link layer. The new cache table is shown in Table 7.3.

Table 7.3   *Updated cache table for Example 4*

State	Queue	Attempt	Time-Out	Protocol Addr.	Hardware Addr.
R	5		900	180.3.6.1	ACAE32457342
P	2	2		129.34.4.8	
P	14	5		201.11.56.7	
R	8		450	114.5.7.89	457342ACAE32
P	12	1		220.55.5.7	
P	23	1		116.1.7.22	
R	9		60	19.1.7.82	4573E3242ACA
R	18		900	188.11.8.71	E34573242ACA

Example 5

Twenty-five seconds later, the cache-control module updates every entry. The time-out values for the first three resolved entries are decremented by 60. The time-out value for the last resolved entry is decremented by 25. The state of the next-to-the last entry is changed to FREE because the time-out is zero. For each of the three pending entries, the value of the attempts field is incremented by one. After incrementing, the attempts value for one entry (the one with IP address 201.11.56.7) is more than the maximum; the state is changed to FREE, the queue is deleted, and an ICMP message is sent to the original destination (see Chapter 9). See Table 7.4.

Table 7.4   *Updated cache table for Example 5*

State	Queue	Attempt	Time-Out	Protocol Addr.	Hardware Addr.
R	5		840	180.3.6.1	ACAE32457342
P	2	3		129.34.4.8	
F					
R	8		390	114.5.7.89	457342ACAE32
P	12	2		220.55.5.7	
P	23	2		116.1.7.22	
F					
R	18		875	188.11.8.71	E34573242ACA

7.3   RARP

RARP finds the logical address for a machine that only knows its physical address. Each host or router is assigned one or more logical (IP) addresses, which are unique and independent of the physical (hardware) address of the machine. To create an IP datagram, a host or a router needs to know its own IP address or addresses. The IP address of a machine is usually read from its configuration file stored on a disk file.

However, a diskless machine is usually booted from ROM, which has minimum booting information. The ROM is installed by the manufacturer. It cannot include the IP address because the IP addresses on a network are assigned by the network administrator.

The machine can get its physical address (by reading its NIC, for example), which is unique locally. It can then use the physical address to get the logical address using the RARP protocol. A RARP request is created and broadcast on the local network. Another machine on the local network that knows all the IP addresses will respond with a RARP reply. The requesting machine must be running a RARP client program; the responding machine must be running a RARP server program (see Figure 7.10).

The RARP request packets are broadcast; the RARP reply packets are unicast.

In Figure 7.10a, the diskless host on the left is booted. To get its IP address, it broadcasts a RARP request to all systems on the network.

This packet is received by every host (or router) on the physical network, but only the RARP server on the right will answer it as shown in Figure 7.10b. The server sends a RARP reply packet that includes the IP address of the requestor.

Figure 7.10   *RARP operation*

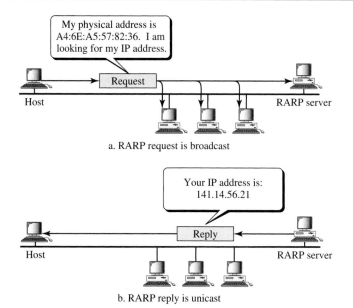

a. RARP request is broadcast

b. RARP reply is unicast

Packet Format

The format of the RARP packet is exactly the same as the ARP packet except that values of the operation field is either three (RARP request) or four (RARP reply). See Figure 7.11.

Figure 7.11   *RARP packet*

Hardware type		Protocol type
Hardware length	Protocol length	Operation Request 3, Reply 4
Sender hardware address (For example, 6 bytes for Ethernet)		
Sender protocol address (For example, 4 bytes for IP) (It is not filled for request)		
Target hardware address (For example, 6 bytes for Ethernet) (It is not filled for request)		
Target protocol address (For example, 4 bytes for IP) (It is not filled for request)		

Encapsulation

A RARP packet is encapsulated directly into a data link frame. For example, Figure 7.12 shows a RARP packet encapsulated in an Ethernet frame. Note that the type field shows that the data carried by the frame is a RARP packet.

Figure 7.12   *Encapsulation of RARP packet*

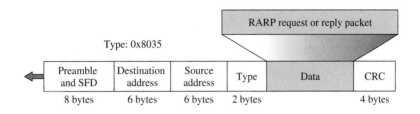

RARP Server

The RARP server provides mapping from a physical address to a logical address. The mapping is stored in a disk file. The interesting, and somehow complicated, point is that a server is normally implemented at the application layer and the files used by a server are accessed at that level. The RARP server is implemented at the data link layer. To access a file, a RARP server needs the help of the underlying operating system such as UNIX.

Another problem with a RARP server is that the server can sometimes be down. To provide a RARP reply to diskless computers, an administrator normally will install more than one RARP server. If all servers are running, several RARP replies will be travelling on the network at the same time, and that may create heavy traffic.

Alternative Solutions to RARP

When a diskless computer is booted, it needs more information in addition to its IP address. It normally needs to know its subnet mask, the IP address of a router, and the IP address of a name server. RARP cannot provide this extra information. New protocols have been developed to provide this information. In Chapter 16 we discuss two protocols, BOOTP and DHCP, that can be used instead of RARP.

7.4   KEY TERMS

address resolution protocol (ARP)	logical address
cache-control module	output module
cache table	physical address
dynamic mapping	proxy ARP
encapsulation	queue
input module	reverse address resolution protocol (RARP)
IP address	static mapping

7.5   SUMMARY

❏ Delivery of a packet to a host or router requires two levels of addresses: logical and physical.

❏ A logical address identifies a host or router at the network level. TCP/IP calls this logical address an IP address.

❏ A physical address identifies a host or router at the physical level.

❏ Mapping of a logical address to a physical address can be static or dynamic.

❏ Static mapping involves a list of logical and physical address correspondences; maintenance of the list requires high overhead.

❏ The address resolution protocol (ARP) is a dynamic mapping method that finds a physical address given a logical address.

❏ An ARP request is broadcast to all devices on the network.

❏ An ARP reply is unicast to the host requesting the mapping.

❏ In proxy ARP, a router represents a set of hosts. When an ARP request seeks the physical address of any host in this set, the router sends its own physical address. This creates a subnetting effect.

❏ The ARP software package consists of five components: a cache table, queues, an output module, an input module, and a cache-control module.

❏ The cache table has an array of entries used and updated by ARP messages.

❏ A queue contains packets going to the same destination.

❏ The output module takes a packet from the IP layer and sends it either to the data link layer or to a queue.

❏ The input module uses an ARP packet to update the cache table. The input module can also send an ARP reply.

❏ The cache-control module maintains the cache table by updating entry fields.

❏ Reverse address resolution protocol (RARP) is a form of dynamic mapping in which a given physical address is associated with a logical address.

7.6   PRACTICE SET

Exercises

1. Is the size of the ARP packet fixed? Explain.
2. Is the size of the RARP packet fixed? Explain.
3. What is the size of an ARP packet when the protocol is IP and the hardware is Ethernet?
4. What is the size of a RARP packet when the protocol is IP and the hardware is Ethernet?
5. What is the size of an Ethernet frame carrying an ARP packet?
6. What is the size of an Ethernet frame carrying a RARP packet?

7. What is the broadcast address for Ethernet?

8. A router with IP address 125.45.23.12 and Ethernet physical address 23:45:AB:4F:67:CD has received a packet for a host destination with IP address 125.11.78.10 and Ethernet physical address AA:BB:A2:4F:67:CD. Show the entries in the ARP request packet sent by the router. Assume no subnetting.

9. Show the entries in the ARP packet sent in response to Exercise 8.

10. Encapsulate the result of Exercise 8 in a data link frame. Fill in all the fields.

11. Encapsulate the result of Exercise 9 in a data link frame. Fill in all the fields.

12. A router with IP address 195.5.2.12 and Ethernet physical address AA:25:AB:1F:67:CD has received a packet for a destination with IP address 185.11.78.10. When the router checks its routing table, it finds out the packet should be delivered to a router with IP address 195.5.2.6 and Ethernet physical address AD:34:5D:4F:67:CD. Show the entries in the ARP request packet sent by the router. Assume no subnetting.

13. Show the entries in the ARP packet sent in response to Exercise 12.

14. Encapsulate the result of Exercise 12 in a data link frame. Fill in all the fields.

15. Encapsulate the result of Exercise 13 in a data link frame. Fill in all the fields.

16. A diskless host with an Ethernet physical address 98:45:23:4F:67:CD has been booted. Show the entries in the RARP packet sent by this host.

17. Show the entries in the RARP packet sent in response to Exercise 16. Assume that the IP address of the requesting host is 200.67.89.33. Choose appropriate physical and logical addresses for the server. Assume the server is on the same network as the requesting host.

18. Encapsulate the result of Exercise 16 in a data link frame. Fill in all the fields.

19. Encapsulate the result of Exercise 17 in a data link frame. Fill in all the fields.

Research Activities

20. Find the RFCs describing ARP.

21. Find the RFCs describing RARP.

22. Find the name of the file storing physical-logical address mapping for the RARP server in UNIX.

CHAPTER 8

Internet Protocol (IP)

The **Internet Protocol (IP)** is the transmission mechanism used by the TCP/IP protocols. Figure 8.1 shows the position of IP in the suite.

Figure 8.1 *Position of IP in TCP/IP protocol suite*

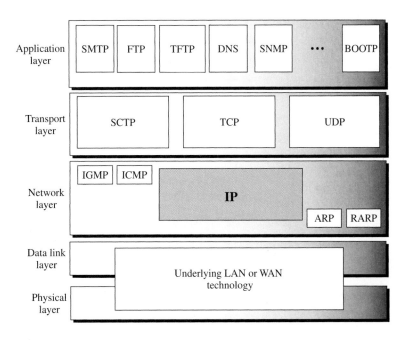

IP is an unreliable and connectionless datagram protocol—a **best-effort delivery** service. The term *best-effort* means that IP provides no error checking or tracking. IP assumes the unreliability of the underlying layers and does its best to get a transmission through to its destination, but with no guarantees.

If reliability is important, IP must be paired with a reliable protocol such as TCP. An example of a more commonly understood best-effort delivery service is the post office. The post office does its best to deliver the mail but does not always succeed. If an unregistered letter is lost, it is up to the sender or would-be recipient to discover the loss and rectify the problem. The post office itself does not keep track of every letter and cannot notify a sender of loss or damage.

IP is also a connectionless protocol for a packet switching network that uses the datagram approach (see Chapter 6). This means that each datagram is handled independently, and each datagram can follow a different route to the destination. This implies that datagrams sent by the same source to the same destination could arrive out of order. Also, some could be lost or corrupted during transmission. Again, IP relies on a higher level protocol to take care of all these problems.

8.1 DATAGRAM

Packets in the IP layer are called **datagrams.** Figure 8.2 shows the IP datagram format. A datagram is a variable-length packet consisting of two parts: header and data. The header is 20 to 60 bytes in length and contains information essential to routing and delivery. It is customary in TCP/IP to show the header in 4-byte sections. A brief description of each field is in order.

Figure 8.2 *IP datagram*

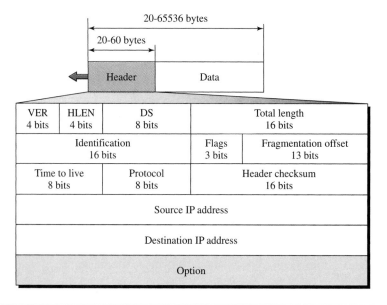

❑ **Version (VER).** This 4-bit field defines the version of the IP protocol. Currently the version is 4. However, version 6 (or IPng) may totally replace version 4 in the future. This field tells the IP software running in the processing machine that the datagram has the format of version 4. All fields must be interpreted as specified in the fourth version of the protocol. If the machine is using some other version of IP, the datagram is discarded rather than interpreted incorrectly.

❑ **Header length (HLEN).** This 4-bit field defines the total length of the datagram header in 4-byte words. This field is needed because the length of the header is variable (between 20 and 60 bytes). When there are no options, the header length is 20 bytes, and the value of this field is 5 ($5 \times 4 = 20$). When the option field is at its maximum size, the value of this field is 15 ($15 \times 4 = 60$).

❑ **Differentiated services (DS).** IETF has changed the interpretation and name of this 8-bit field. This field, previously called **service type,** is now called **differentiated services.** We show both interpretations in Figure 8.3.

Figure 8.3   *Service type or differentiated services*

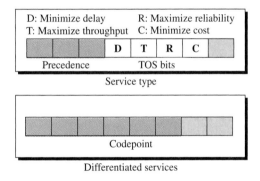

Service type

Differentiated services

1. **Service Type**

   In this interpretation, the first 3 bits are called precedence bits. The next 4 bits are called TOS bits and the last bit is not used.

   a. **Precedence** is a 3-bit subfield ranging from 0 (000 in binary) to 7 (111 in binary). The precedence defines the priority of the datagram in issues such as congestion. If a router is congested and needs to discard some datagrams, those datagrams with lowest precedence are discarded first. Some datagrams in the Internet are more important than others. For example, a datagram used for network management is much more urgent and important than a datagram containing optional information for a group.

The precedence subfield was part of version 4, but never used.

b. **TOS bits** is a 4-bit subfield with each bit having a special meaning. Although a bit can be either 0 or 1, one and only one of the bits can have the value of 1 in each datagram. The bit patterns and their interpretations are given in Table 8.1. With only one bit set at a time, we can have five different types of services.

Table 8.1   *Types of service*

TOS Bits	Description
0000	Normal (default)
0001	Minimize cost
0010	Maximize reliability
0100	Maximize throughput
1000	Minimize delay

Application programs can request a specific type of service. The defaults for some applications are shown in Table 8.2.

Table 8.2   *Default types of service*

Protocol	TOS Bits	Description
ICMP	0000	Normal
BOOTP	0000	Normal
NNTP	0001	Minimize cost
IGP	0010	Maximize reliability
SNMP	0010	Maximize reliability
TELNET	1000	Minimize delay
FTP (data)	0100	Maximize throughput
FTP (control)	1000	Minimize delay
TFTP	1000	Minimize delay
SMTP (command)	1000	Minimize delay
SMTP (data)	0100	Maximize throughput
DNS (UDP query)	1000	Minimize delay
DNS (TCP query)	0000	Normal
DNS (zone)	0100	Maximize throughput

It is clear from the above table that interactive activities, activities requiring immediate attention, and activities requiring immediate response need minimum delay. Those activities that send bulk data require maximum throughput. Management activities need maximum reliability. Background activities need minimum cost.

2. **Differentiated Services**

   In this interpretation, the first 6 bits make up the **codepoint** subfield and the last two bits are not used. The codepoint subfield can be used in two different ways.

   a. When the 3 right-most bits are 0s, the 3 left-most bits are interpreted the same as the precedence bits in the service type interpretation. In other words, it is compatible with the old interpretation.

   b. When the 3 right-most bits are not all 0s, the 6 bits define 64 services based on the priority assignment by the Internet or local authorities according to Table 8.3. The first category contains 32 service types; the second and the third each contain 16. The first category (numbers 0, 2, 4, . . . , 62) is assigned by the Internet authorities (IETF). The second category (3, 7, 11, 15, . . . , 63) can be used by local authorities (organizations). The third category (1, 5, 9, . . . , 61) is temporary and can be used for experimental purposes. Note that the numbers are not contiguous. If they were, the first category would range from 0 to 31, the second 32 to 47, and the third 48 to 63. This would be incompatible with the TOS interpretation because XXX000 (which includes 0, 8, 16, 24, 32, 40, 48, and 56) would fall into all three categories. Instead, in this assignment method all these services belong to category 1. Note that these assignments have not yet been finalized.

   Table 8.3 *Values for codepoints*

Category	Codepoint	Assigning Authority
1	XXXXX0	Internet
2	XXXX11	Local
3	XXXX01	Temporary or experimental

❏ **Total length.** This is a 16-bit field that defines the total length (header plus data) of the IP datagram in bytes. To find the length of the data coming from the upper layer, subtract the header length from the total length. The header length can be found by multiplying the value in the HLEN field by four.

length of data = total length − header length

Since the field length is 16 bits, the total length of the IP datagram is limited to 65,535 (2^{16} − 1) bytes, of which 20 to 60 bytes are the header and the rest is data from the upper layer.

The total length field defines the total length of the datagram including the header.

Though a size of 65,535 bytes might seem large, the size of the IP datagram may increase in the near future as the underlying technologies allow even more throughput (more bandwidth).

When we discuss fragmentation in the next section, we will see that some physical networks are not able to encapsulate a datagram of 65,535 bytes in their frames. The datagram must be fragmented to be able to pass through those networks.

One may ask why we need this field anyway. When a machine (router or host) receives a frame, it drops the header and the trailer leaving the datagram. Why include an extra field that is not needed? The answer is that in many cases we really do not need the value in this field. However, there are occasions in which the datagram is not the only thing encapsulated in a frame; it may be that padding has been added. For example, the Ethernet protocol has a minimum and maximum restriction on the size of data that can be encapsulated in a frame (46 to 1500 bytes). If the size of an IP datagram is less than 46 bytes, some padding will be added to meet this requirement. In this case, when a machine decapsulates the datagram, it needs to check the total length field to determine how much is really data and how much is padding (see Figure 8.4).

Figure 8.4 *Encapsulation of a small datagram in an Ethernet frame*

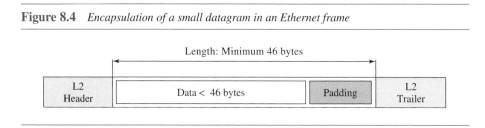

- ❏ **Identification.** This field is used in fragmentation (discussed in the next section).
- ❏ **Flags.** This field is used in fragmentation (discussed in the next section).
- ❏ **Fragmentation offset.** This field is used in fragmentation (discussed in the next section).
- ❏ **Time to live.** A datagram has a limited lifetime in its travel through an internet. This field was originally designed to hold a timestamp, which was decremented by each visited router. The datagram was discarded when the value became zero. However, for this scheme, all the machines must have synchronized clocks and must know how long it takes for a datagram to go from one machine to another. Today, this field is mostly used to control the maximum number of hops (routers) visited by the datagram. When a source host sends the datagram, it stores a number in this field. This value is approximately two times the maximum number of routes between any two hosts. Each router that processes the datagram decrements this number by one. If this value, after being decremented, is zero, the router discards the datagram.

  This field is needed because routing tables in the Internet can become corrupted. A datagram may travel between two or more routers for a long time without ever getting delivered to the destination host. This field limits the lifetime of a datagram.

  Another use of this field is to intentionally limit the journey of the packet. For example, if the source wants to confine the packet to the local network, it can store 1 in this field. When the packet arrives at the first router, this value is decremented to 0, and the datagram is discarded.

❏ **Protocol.** This 8-bit field defines the higher-level protocol that uses the services of the IP layer. An IP datagram can encapsulate data from several higher level protocols such as TCP, UDP, ICMP, and IGMP. This field specifies the final destination protocol to which the IP datagram should be delivered. In other words, since the IP protocol multiplexes and demultiplexes data from different higher-level protocols, the value of this field helps in the demultiplexing process when the datagram arrives at its final destination (see Figure 8.5).

Figure 8.5   *Multiplexing*

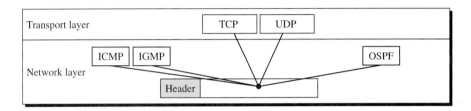

The value of this field for different higher-level protocols is shown in Table 8.4.

Table 8.4   *Protocols*

Value	Protocol
1	ICMP
2	IGMP
6	TCP
17	UDP
89	OSPF

❏ **Checksum.** The checksum concept and its calculation are discussed later in this chapter.

❏ **Source address.** This 32-bit field defines the IP address of the source. This field must remain unchanged during the time the IP datagram travels from the source host to the destination host.

❏ **Destination address.** This 32-bit field defines the IP address of the destination. This field must remain unchanged during the time the IP datagram travels from the source host to the destination host.

Example 1

An IP packet has arrived with the first 8 bits as shown:

◄━━ 01000010

The receiver discards the packet. Why?

Solution

There is an error in this packet. The 4 left-most bits (0100) show the version, which is correct. The next 4 bits (0010) show the wrong header length ($2 \times 4 = 8$). The minimum number of bytes in the header must be 20. The packet has been corrupted in transmission.

Example 2

In an IP packet, the value of HLEN is 1000 in binary. How many bytes of options are being carried by this packet?

Solution

The HLEN value is 8, which means the total number of bytes in the header is 8×4 or 32 bytes. The first 20 bytes are the base header, the next 12 bytes are the options.

Example 3

In an IP packet, the value of HLEN is 5_{16} and the value of the total length field is 0028_{16}. How many bytes of data are being carried by this packet?

Solution

The HLEN value is 5, which means the total number of bytes in the header is 5×4 or 20 bytes (no options). The total length is 40 bytes, which means the packet is carrying 20 bytes of data ($40 - 20$).

Example 4

An IP packet has arrived with the first few hexadecimal digits as shown below:

$$\longleftarrow \quad 45000028000100000102 \ldots$$

How many hops can this packet travel before being dropped? The data belong to what upper layer protocol?

Solution

To find the time-to-live field, we skip 8 bytes (16 hexadecimal digits). The time-to-live field is the ninth byte, which is 01. This means the packet can travel only one hop. The protocol field is the next byte (02), which means that the upper layer protocol is IGMP (see Table 8.4).

8.2   FRAGMENTATION

A datagram can travel through different networks. Each router decapsulates the IP datagram from the frame it receives, processes it, and then encapsulates it in another frame. The format and size of the received frame depend on the protocol used by the physical network through which the frame has just traveled. The format and size of the sent frame depend on the protocol used by the physical network through which the frame is going to travel. For example, if a router connects a LAN to a WAN, it receives a frame in the LAN format and sends a frame in the WAN format.

Maximum Transfer Unit (MTU)

Each data link layer protocol has its own frame format in most protocols. One of the fields defined in the format is the maximum size of the data field. In other words, when a datagram is encapsulated in a frame, the total size of the datagram must be less than this maximum size, which is defined by the restrictions imposed by the hardware and software used in the network (see Figure 8.6).

Figure 8.6 *MTU*

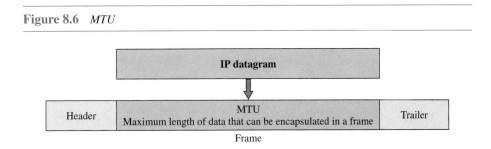

The value of the MTU differs from one physical network protocol to another. Table 8.5 shows the values for some protocols.

Table 8.5 *MTUs for some networks*

Protocol	MTU
Hyperchannel	65,535
Token Ring (16 Mbps)	17,914
Token Ring (4 Mbps)	4,464
FDDI	4,352
Ethernet	1,500
X.25	576
PPP	296

In order to make the IP protocol independent of the physical network, the designers decided to make the maximum length of the IP datagram equal to 65,535 bytes. This makes transmission more efficient if we use a protocol with an MTU of this size. However, for other physical networks, we must divide the datagram to make it possible to pass through these networks. This is called **fragmentation.**

The source usually does not fragment the IP packet. The transport layer will instead segment the data into a size that can be accomodated by IP and the data link layer in use.

When a datagram is fragmented, each fragment has its own header with most of the fields repeated, but some changed. A fragmented datagram may itself be fragmented if it encounters a network with an even smaller MTU. In other words, a datagram can be fragmented several times before it reaches the final destination.

A datagram can be fragmented by the source host or any router in the path. The reassembly of the datagram, however, is done only by the destination host because each fragment becomes an independent datagram. Whereas the fragmented datagram can travel through different routes, and we can never control or guarantee which route a fragmented datagram may take, all of the fragments belonging to the same datagram should finally arrive at the destination host. So it is logical to do the reassembly at the final destination. An even stronger objection for reassembling packets during the transmission is the loss of efficiency it incurs.

When a datagram is fragmented, required parts of the header must be copied by all fragments. The option field may or may not be copied as we will see in the next section. The host or router that fragments a datagram must change the values of three fields: flags, fragmentation offset, and total length. The rest of the fields must be copied. Of course, the value of the checksum must be recalculated regardless of fragmentation.

Fields Related to Fragmentation

The fields that are related to fragmentation and reassembly of an IP datagram are the identification, flags, and fragmentation offset fields.

❏ **Identification.** This 16-bit field identifies a datagram originating from the source host. The combination of the identification and source IP address must uniquely define a datagram as it leaves the source host. To guarantee uniqueness, the IP protocol uses a counter to label the datagrams. The counter is initialized to a positive number. When the IP protocol sends a datagram, it copies the current value of the counter to the identification field and increments the counter by one. As long as the counter is kept in the main memory, uniqueness is guaranteed. When a datagram is fragmented, the value in the identification field is copied into all fragments. In other words, all fragments have the same identification number, which is also the same as the original datagram. The identification number helps the destination in reassembling the datagram. It knows that all fragments having the same identification value should be assembled into one datagram.

❏ **Flags.** This is a three-bit field. The first bit is reserved. The second bit is called the *do not fragment* bit. If its value is 1, the machine must not fragment the datagram. If it cannot pass the datagram through any available physical network, it discards the datagram and sends an ICMP error message to the source host (see Chapter 9). If its value is 0, the datagram can be fragmented if necessary. The third bit is called the *more fragment* bit. If its value is 1, it means the datagram is not the last fragment; there are more fragments after this one. If its value is 0, it means this is the last or only fragment (see Figure 8.7).

Figure 8.7 *Flags field*

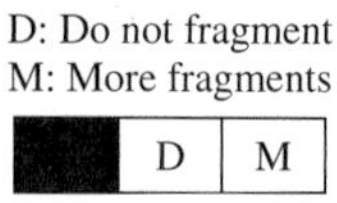

D: Do not fragment
M: More fragments

❏ **Fragmentation offset.** This 13-bit field shows the relative position of this fragment with respect to the whole datagram. It is the offset of the data in the original datagram measured in units of 8 bytes. Figure 8.8 shows a datagram with a data size of 4000 bytes fragmented into three fragments. The bytes in the original datagram are numbered 0 to 3999. The first fragment carries bytes 0 to 1399. The offset

Figure 8.8   *Fragmentation example*

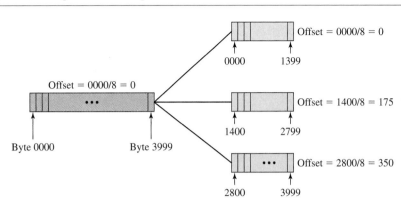

for this datagram is 0/8 = 0. The second fragment carries bytes 1400 to 2799; the offset value for this fragment is 1400/8 = 175. Finally, the third fragment carries bytes 2800 to 3999. The offset value for this fragment is 2800/8 = 350.

Remember that the value of the offset is measured in units of 8 bytes. This is done because the length of the offset field is only 13 bits long and cannot represent a sequence of bytes greater than 8191. This forces hosts or routers that fragment datagrams to choose the size of each fragment so that the first byte number is divisible by 8.

Figure 8.9 shows an expanded view of the fragments in the previous figure. Notice the value of the identification field is the same in all fragments. Notice the value of the flags field with the *more* bit set for all fragments except the last. Also, the value of the offset field for each fragment is shown.

The figure also shows what happens if a fragment itself is fragmented. In this case the value of the offset field is always relative to the original datagram. For example, in the figure, the second fragment is itself fragmented later to two fragments of 800 bytes and 600 bytes, but the offset shows the relative position of the fragments to the original data.

It is obvious that even if each fragment follows a different path and arrives out of order, the final destination host can reassemble the original datagram from the fragments received (if none of them is lost) using the following strategy:

a. The first fragment has an offset field value of zero.

b. Divide the length of the first fragment by 8. The second fragment has an offset value equal to that result.

c. Divide the total length of the first and second fragment by 8. The third fragment has an offset value equal to that result.

d. Continue the process. The last fragment has a *more* bit value of 0.

Example 5

A packet has arrived with an *M* bit value of 0. Is this the first fragment, the last fragment, or a middle fragment? Do we know if the packet was fragmented?

Figure 8.9 *Detailed fragmentation example*

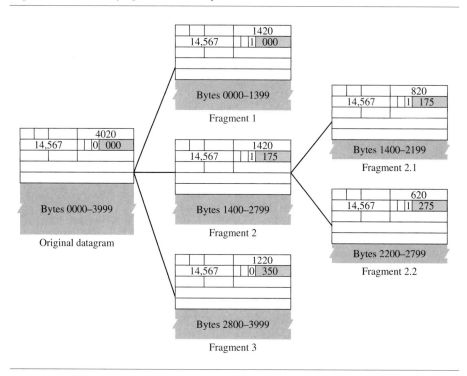

Solution

If the *M* bit is 0, it means that there are no more fragments; the fragment is the last one. However, we cannot say if the original packet was fragmented or not. A nonfragmented packet is considered the last fragment.

Example 6

A packet has arrived with an *M* bit value of 1. Is this the first fragment, the last fragment, or a middle fragment? Do we know if the packet was fragmented?

Solution

If the *M* bit is 1, it means that there is at least one more fragment. This fragment can be the first one or a middle one, but not the last one. We don't know if it is the first one or a middle one; we need more information (the value of the fragmentation offset). See also the next example.

Example 7

A packet has arrived with an *M* bit value of 1 and a fragmentation offset value of zero. Is this the first fragment, the last fragment, or a middle fragment?

Solution

Because the *M* bit is 1, it is either the first fragment or a middle one. Because the offset value is 0, it is the first fragment.

Example 8

A packet has arrived in which the offset value is 100. What is the number of the first byte? Do we know the number of the last byte?

Solution

To find the number of the first byte, we multiply the offset value by 8. This means that the first byte number is 800. We cannot determine the number of the last byte unless we know the length of the data.

Example 9

A packet has arrived in which the offset value is 100, the value of HLEN is 5 and the value of the total length field is 100. What is the number of the first byte and the last byte?

Solution

The first byte number is $100 \times 8 = 800$. The total length is 100 bytes and the header length is 20 bytes (5×4), which means that there are 80 bytes in this datagram. If the first byte number is 800, the last byte number must be 879.

8.3 OPTIONS

The header of the IP datagram is made of two parts: a fixed part and a variable part. The fixed part is 20 bytes long and was discussed in the previous section. The variable part comprises the options that can be a maximum of 40 bytes.

Options, as the name implies, are not required for a datagram. They can be used for network testing and debugging. Although options are not a required part of the IP header, option processing is required of the IP software. This means that all implementations must be able to handle options if they are present in the header.

Format

Figure 8.10 shows the format of an option. It is composed of a 1-byte code field, a 1-byte length field, and a variable-sized data field.

Code

The **code field** is 8 bits long and contains three subfields: copy, class, and number.

❏ **Copy.** This 1-bit subfield controls the presence of the option in fragmentation. When its value is 0, it means that the option must be copied only to the first fragment. If its value is 1, it means the option must be copied to all fragments.

❏ **Class.** This 2-bit subfield defines the general purpose of the option. When its value is 00, it means that the option is used for datagram control. When its value is 10, it means that the option is used for debugging and management. The other two possible values (01 and 11) have not yet been defined.

❏ **Number.** This 5-bit subfield defines the type of option. Although 5 bits can define up to 32 different types, currently only 6 types are in use. These will be discussed in a later section.

Figure 8.10   *Option format*

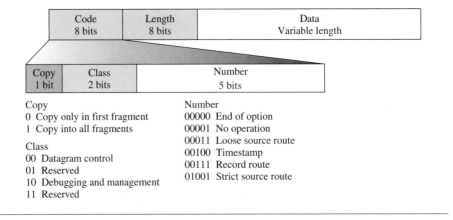

Copy
0 Copy only in first fragment
1 Copy into all fragments

Class
00 Datagram control
01 Reserved
10 Debugging and management
11 Reserved

Number
00000 End of option
00001 No operation
00011 Loose source route
00100 Timestamp
00111 Record route
01001 Strict source route

Length

The **length field** defines the total length of the option including the code field and the length field itself. This field is not present in all of the option types.

Data

The **data field** contains the data that specific options require. Like the length field, this field is also not present in all option types.

Option Types

As mentioned previously, only six options are currently being used. Two of these are 1-byte options, and they do not require the length or the data fields. Four of them are multiple-byte options; they require the length and the data fields (see Figure 8.11).

Figure 8.11   *Categories of options*

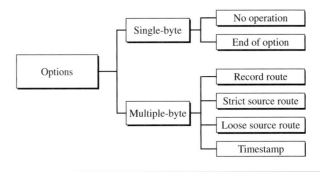

No Operation

A **no operation option** is a 1-byte option used as a filler between options. For example, it can be used to align the next option on a 16-bit or 32-bit boundary (see Figure 8.12).

Figure 8.12   *No operation option*

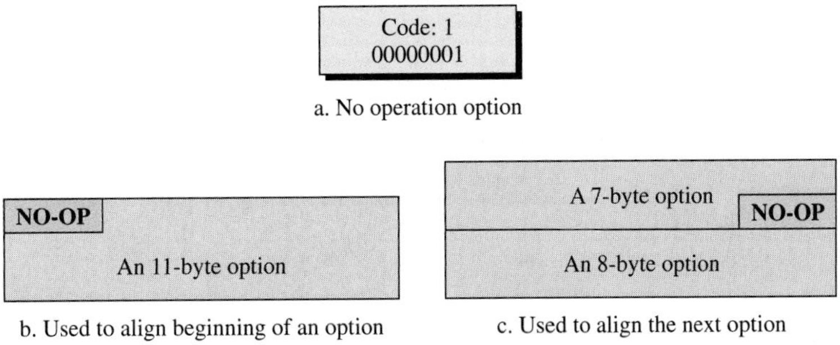

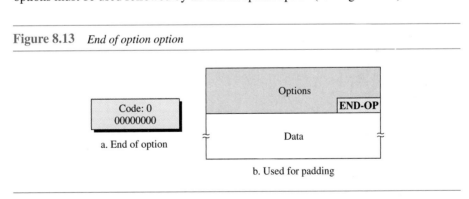

a. No operation option

b. Used to align beginning of an option

c. Used to align the next option

End of Option

An **end of option option** is also a 1-byte option used for padding at the end of the option field. It, however, can only be used as the last option. Only one *end of option* option can be used. After this option, the receiver looks for the payload data. This means that if more than 1 byte is needed to align the option field, some no operation options must be used followed by an end of option option (see Figure 8.13).

Figure 8.13   *End of option option*

Code: 0
00000000

a. End of option

Options
END-OP

Data

b. Used for padding

Record Route

A **record route option** is used to record the internet routers that handle the datagram. It can list up to nine router IP addresses since the maximum size of the header is 60 bytes, which must include 20 bytes for the base header. This implies that only 40 bytes are left over for the option part. The source creates placeholder fields in the option to be filled by the visited routers. Figure 8.14 shows the format of the record route option.

Figure 8.14   *Record route option*

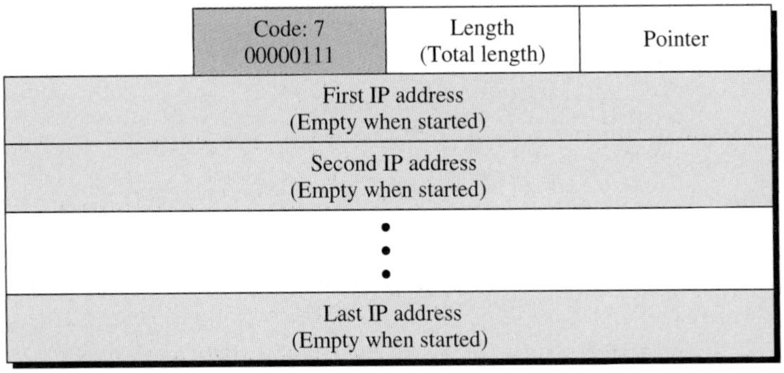

Code: 7 00000111	Length (Total length)	Pointer
First IP address (Empty when started)		
Second IP address (Empty when started)		
• • •		
Last IP address (Empty when started)		

Both the code and length fields have been described above. The **pointer field** is an offset integer field containing the byte number of the first empty entry. In other words, it points to the first available entry.

The source creates empty fields for the IP addresses in the data field of the option. When the datagram leaves the source, all of the fields are empty. The pointer field has a value of 4, pointing to the first empty field.

When the datagram is traveling, each router that processes the datagram compares the value of the pointer with the value of the length. If the value of the pointer is greater than the value of the length, the option is full and no changes are made. However, if the value of the pointer is not greater than the value of the length, the router inserts its outgoing IP address in the next empty field (remember that a router has more than one IP address). In this case, the router adds the IP address of its interface from which the datagram is leaving. The router then increments the value of the pointer by 4. Figure 8.15 shows the entries as the datagram travels left to right from router to router.

Figure 8.15   *Record route concept*

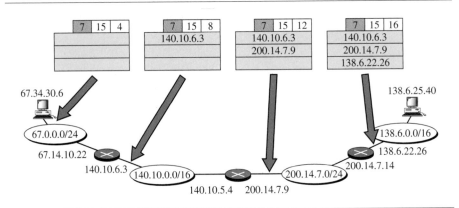

Strict Source Route

A **strict source route option** is used by the source to predetermine a route for the datagram as it travels through the Internet. Dictation of a route by the source can be useful for several purposes. The sender can choose a route with a specific type of service, such as minimum delay or maximum throughput. Alternatively, it may choose a route that is safer or more reliable for the sender's purpose. For example, a sender can choose a route so that its datagram does not travel through a competitor's network.

If a datagram specifies a strict source route, all of the routers defined in the option must be visited by the datagram. A router must not be visited if its IP address is not listed in the datagram. If the datagram visits a router that is not on the list, the datagram is discarded and an error message is issued. If the datagram arrives at the destination and some of the entries were not visited, it will also be discarded and an error message issued.

Regular users of the Internet, however, are not usually aware of the physical topology of the Internet. Consequently, strict source routing is not the choice of most users. Figure 8.16 shows the format of the strict source route option.

Figure 8.16   *Strict source route option*

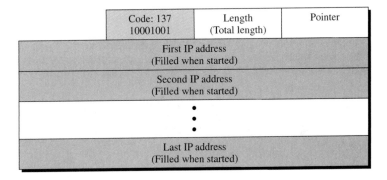

The format is similar to the record route option with the exception that all of the IP addresses are entered by the sender.

When the datagram is traveling, each router that processes the datagram compares the value of the pointer with the value of the length. If the value of the pointer is greater than the value of the length, the datagram has visited all of the predefined routers. The datagram cannot travel anymore; it is discarded and an error message is created. If the value of the pointer is not greater than the value of the length, the router compares the destination IP address with its incoming IP address: If they are equal, it processes the datagram, swaps the IP address pointed by the pointer with the destination address, increments the pointer value by 4, and forwards the datagram. If they are not equal, it discards the datagram and issues an error message. Figure 8.17 shows the actions taken by each router as a datagram travels from source to destination.

Figure 8.17   *Strict source route concept*

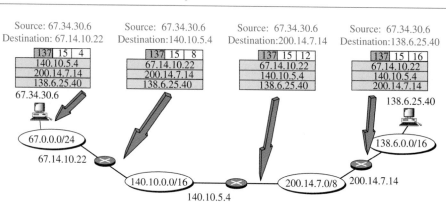

Loose Source Route

A **loose source route option** is similar to the strict source route, but it is more relaxed. Each router in the list must be visited, but the datagram can visit other routers as well. Figure 8.18 shows the format of the loose source route option.

Figure 8.18   *Loose source route option*

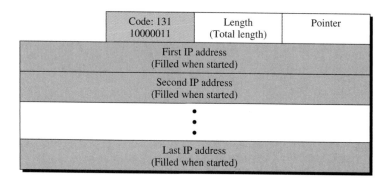

Timestamp

A **timestamp option** is used to record the time of datagram processing by a router. The time is expressed in milliseconds from midnight, Universal Time. Knowing the time a datagram is processed can help users and managers track the behavior of the routers in the Internet. We can estimate the time it takes for a datagram to go from one router to another. We say *estimate* because, although all routers may use Universal Time, their local clocks may not be synchronized.

However, nonprivileged users of the Internet are not usually aware of the physical topology of the Internet. Consequently, a timestamp option is not a choice for most users. Figure 8.19 shows the format of the timestamp option.

Figure 8.19 *Timestamp option*

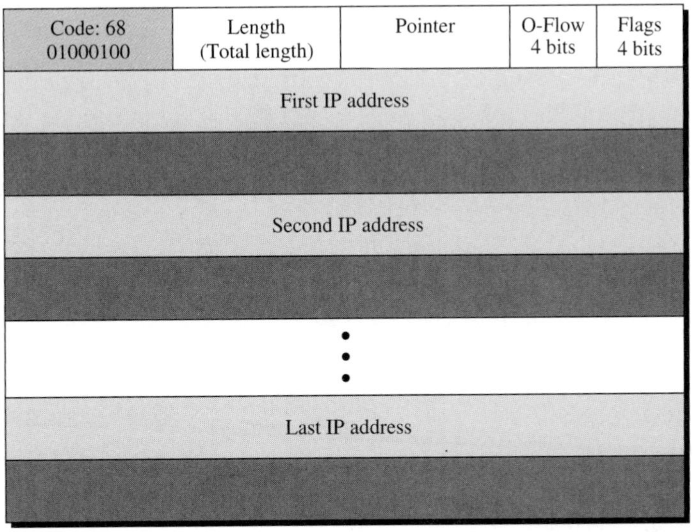

Code: 68 01000100	Length (Total length)	Pointer	O-Flow 4 bits	Flags 4 bits
First IP address				
Second IP address				
• • •				
Last IP address				

In this figure, the definition of the code and length fields are the same as before. The overflow field records the number of routers that could not add their timestamp because no more fields were available. The flags field specifies the visited router responsibilities. If the flag value is 0, each router adds only the timestamp in the provided field. If the flag value is 1, each router must add its outgoing IP address and the timestamp. If the value is 3, the IP addresses are given, and each router must check the given IP address with its own incoming IP address. If there is a match, the router overwrites the IP address with its outgoing IP address and adds the timestamp (see Figure 8.20).

Figure 8.20 *Use of flag in timestamp*

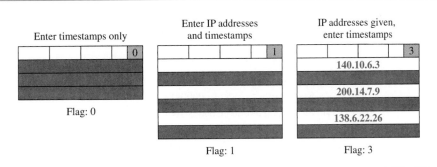

Figure 8.21 shows the actions taken by each router when a datagram travels from source to destination. The figure assumes a flag value of 1.

Figure 8.21   *Timestamp concept*

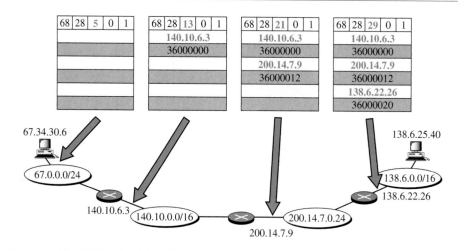

Example 10

Which of the six options must be copied to each fragment?

Solution

We look at the first (left-most) bit of the code for each option.

    a. No operation: Code is **0**0000001; not copied.

    b. End of option: Code is **0**0000000; not copied.

    c. Record route: Code is **0**0000111; not copied.

    d. Strict source route: Code is **1**0001001; copied.

    e. Loose source route: Code is **1**0000011; copied.

    f. Timestamp: Code is **0**1000100; not copied.

Example 11

Which of the six options are used for datagram control and which are used for debugging and management?

Solution

We look at the second and third (left-most) bits of the code.

    a. No operation: Code is 0**00**00001; datagram control.

    b. End of option: Code is 0**00**00000; datagram control.

    c. Record route: Code is 0**00**00111; datagram control.

    d. Strict source route: Code is 1**00**01001; datagram control.

    e. Loose source route: Code is 1**00**00011; datagram control.

    f. Time stamp: Code is 0**10**00100; debugging and management control.

Example 12

One of the utilities available in UNIX to check the travelling of the IP packets is **ping**. In the next chapter, we talk about the *ping* program in more detail. In this example, we want to show how to use the program to see if a host is available. We ping a server at De Anza College named *fhda.edu*. The result shows that the IP address of the host is 153.18.8.1.

```
$ ping fhda.edu
PING fhda.edu (153.18.8.1) 56(84) bytes of data.
64 bytes from tiptoe.fhda.edu (153.18.8.1): icmp_seq = 0 ttl=62 time=1.87 ms
...
```

The result also shows the number of bytes used.

Example 13

We can also use the *ping* utility with the -R option to implement the record route option.

```
$ ping -R fhda.edu
PING fhda.edu (153.18.8.1) 56(124) bytes of data.
64 bytes from tiptoe.fhda.edu (153.18.8.1): icmp_seq=0 ttl=62 time=2.70 ms
RR:  voyager.deanza.fhda.edu (153.18.17.11)
     Dcore_G0_3-69.fhda.edu (153.18.251.3)
     Dbackup_V13.fhda.edu (153.18.191.249)
     tiptoe.fhda.edu (153.18.8.1)
     Dbackup_V62.fhda.edu (153.18.251.34)
     Dcore_G0_1-6.fhda.edu (153.18.31.254)
     voyager.deanza.fhda.edu (153.18.17.11)
```

The result shows the interfaces and IP addresses.

Example 14

The **traceroute** utility can also be used to keep track of the route of a packet.

```
$ traceroute fhda.edu
traceroute to fhda.edu (153.18.8.1), 30 hops max, 38 byte packets
 1 Dcore_G0_1-6.fhda.edu (153.18.31.254) 0.972 ms 0.902 ms 0.881 ms
 2 Dbackup_V69.fhda.edu (153.18.251.4) 2.113 ms 1.996 ms 2.059 ms
 3 tiptoe.fhda.edu (153.18.8.1) 1.791 ms 1.741 ms 1.751 ms
```

The result shows the three routers visited.

Example 15

The *traceroute* program can be used to implement loose source routing. The -g option allows us to define the routers to be visited, from the source to destination. The following shows how we can send a packet to the fhda.edu server with the requirement that the packet visit the router 153.18.251.4.

```
$ traceroute -g 153.18.251.4 fhda.edu.
traceroute to fhda.edu (153.18.8.1), 30 hops max, 46 byte packets
 1 Dcore_G0_1-6.fhda.edu (153.18.31.254) 0.976 ms 0.906 ms 0.889 ms
 2 Dbackup_V69.fhda.edu (153.18.251.4) 2.168 ms 2.148 ms 2.037 ms
```

Example 16

The *traceroute* program can also be used to implement strict source routing. The -G option forces the packet to visit the routers defined in the command line. The following shows how we can send a packet to the *fhda.edu* server and force the packet to visit only the router 153.18.251.4.

```
$ traceroute -G  153.18.251.4 fhda.edu.
traceroute to fhda.edu (153.18.8.1), 30 hops max, 46 byte packets
 1  Dbackup_V69.fhda.edu (153.18.251.4) 2.168 ms  2.148 ms  2.037 ms
```

8.4   CHECKSUM

The error detection method used by most TCP/IP protocols is called the **checksum.** The checksum protects against the corruption that may occur during the transmission of a packet. It is redundant information added to the packet.

The checksum is calculated at the sender and the value obtained is sent with the packet. The receiver repeats the same calculation on the whole packet including the checksum. If the result is satisfactory (see below), the packet is accepted; otherwise, it is rejected.

Checksum Calculation at the Sender

At the sender, the packet is divided into n-bit sections (n is usually 16). These sections are added together using one's complement arithmetic (see Appendix C), resulting in a sum that is also n bits long. The sum is then complemented (all 0s changed to 1s and all 1s to 0s) to produce the checksum.

To create the checksum the sender does the following:

❏   The packet is divided into k sections, each of n bits.
❏   All sections are added together using one's complement arithmetic.
❏   The final result is complemented to make the checksum.

Checksum Calculation at the Receiver

The receiver divides the received packet into k sections and adds all sections. It then complements the result. If the final result is 0, the packet is accepted; otherwise, it is rejected.

Figure 8.22 shows graphically what happens at the sender and the receiver.

We said when the receiver adds all of the sections and complements the result, it should get zero if there is no error in the data during transmission or processing. This is true because of the rules in one's complement arithmetic.

Assume that we get a number called T when we add all the sections in the sender. When we complement the number in one's complement arithmetic, we get the negative of the number. This means that if the sum of all sections is T, the checksum is $-T$.

When the receiver receives the packet, it adds all the sections. It adds T and $-T$ which, in one's complement, is -0 (minus zero). When the result is complemented, -0 becomes 0. Thus if the final result is 0, the packet is accepted; otherwise, it is rejected (see Figure 8.23).

Figure 8.22 *Checksum concept*

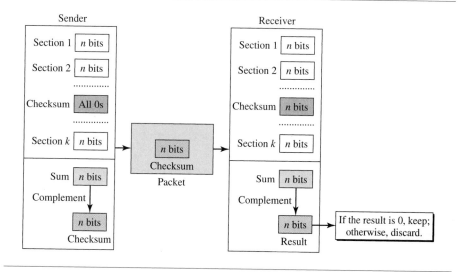

Figure 8.23 *Checksum in one's complement arithmetic*

Checksum in the IP Packet

The implementation of the checksum in the IP packet follows the same principles discussed above. First, the value of the checksum field is set to 0. Then, the entire header is divided into 16-bit sections and added together. The result (sum) is complemented and inserted into the checksum field.

The checksum in the IP packet covers only the header, not the data. There are two good reasons for this. First, all higher-level protocols that encapsulate data in the IP datagram have a checksum field that covers the whole packet. Therefore, the checksum for the IP datagram does not have to check the encapsulated data. Second, the header of the IP packet changes with each visited router, but the data does not. So the checksum includes only the part that has changed. If the data were included, each router must recalculate the checksum for the whole packet, which means an increase in processing time.

Example 17

Figure 8.24 shows an example of a checksum calculation for an IP header without options. The header is divided into 16-bit sections. All the sections are added and the sum is complemented. The result is inserted in the checksum field.

Figure 8.24   *Example of checksum calculation in binary*

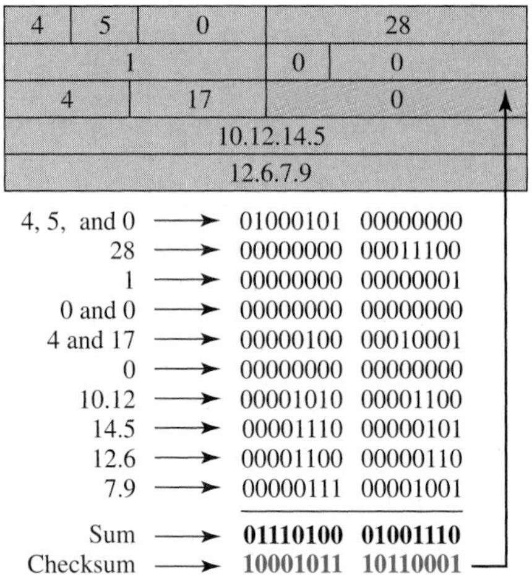

4	5	0	28
	1	0	0
4	17		0
		10.12.14.5	
		12.6.7.9	

4, 5, and 0	→	01000101 00000000
28	→	00000000 00011100
1	→	00000000 00000001
0 and 0	→	00000000 00000000
4 and 17	→	00000100 00010001
0	→	00000000 00000000
10.12	→	00001010 00001100
14.5	→	00001110 00000101
12.6	→	00001100 00000110
7.9	→	00000111 00001001
Sum	→	**01110100 01001110**
Checksum	→	**10001011 10110001**

Example 18

Let us do the same example in hexadecimal. Each row has four hexadecimal digits. We calculate the sum first. Note that if an addition results in more than one hexadecimal digit, the right-most digit becomes the current-column digit and the rest are carried to other columns. From the sum, we make the checksum by complementing the sum. However, note that we subtract each digit from 15 in hexadecimal arithmetic (just as we subtract from 1 in binary arithmetic). This means the complement of E (14) is 1 and the complement of 4 is B (11). Figure 8.25 shows the calculation. Note that the result (8BB1) is exactly the same as in Example 17.

Figure 8.25   *Example of checksum calculation in hexadecimal*

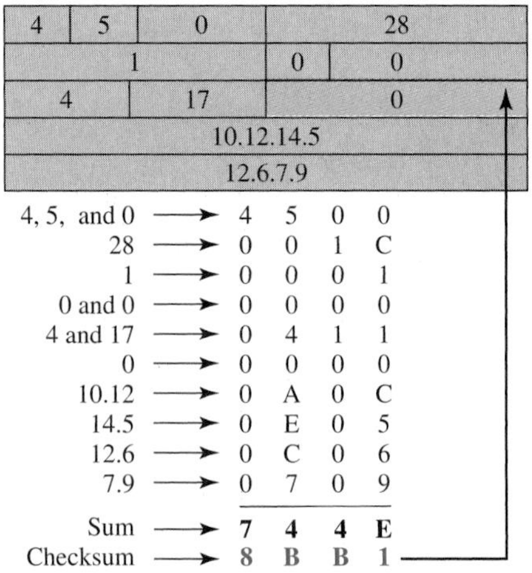

4	5	0	28
	1	0	0
4	17		0
		10.12.14.5	
		12.6.7.9	

4, 5, and 0	→	4	5	0	0
28	→	0	0	1	C
1	→	0	0	0	1
0 and 0	→	0	0	0	0
4 and 17	→	0	4	1	1
0	→	0	0	0	0
10.12	→	0	A	0	C
14.5	→	0	E	0	5
12.6	→	0	C	0	6
7.9	→	0	7	0	9
Sum	→	**7**	**4**	**4**	**E**
Checksum	→	**8**	**B**	**B**	**1**

> **Check Appendix C for a detailed description of checksum calculation and the handling of carries.**

8.5   IP PACKAGE

In this section, we present a simplified example of a hypothetical IP package. Our purpose is to show the relationships between the different concepts discussed in this chapter. Figure 8.26 shows eight components and their interactions.

Figure 8.26   *IP components*

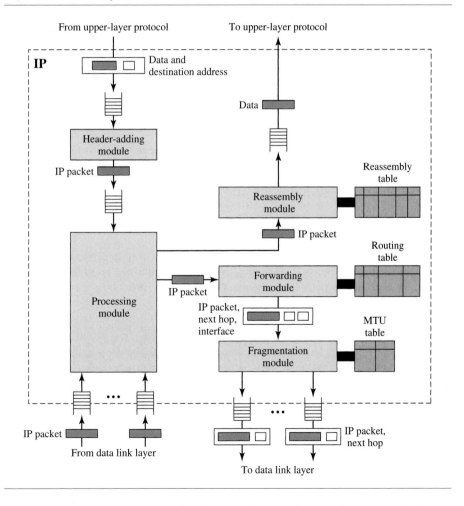

Although IP supports several options, we have omitted option processing in our package to make it easier to understand at this level. In addition, we have sacrificed efficiency for the sake of simplicity.

We can say that the IP package involves eight components: a header-adding module, a processing module, a forwarding module, a fragmentation module, a reassembly module, a routing table, an MTU table, and a reassembly table. In addition, the package includes input and output queues.

The package receives a packet, either from the data link layer or from a higher-level protocol. If the packet comes from an upper-layer protocol, it is delivered to the data link layer for transmission (unless it has a loopback address of 127.X.Y.Z). If the packet comes from the data link layer, it is either delivered to the data link layer for forwarding (in a router) or it is delivered to a higher-layer protocol if the destination IP address of the packet is the same as the station IP address. Note that we used multiple queues to and from data link layer because a router is multihomed.

Header-Adding Module

The **header-adding module** receives data from an upper-layer protocol along with the destination IP address. It encapsulates the data in an IP datagram by adding the IP header.

Header-Adding Module
Receive: data, destination address
1. Encapsulate the data in an IP datagram.
2. Calculate the checksum and insert it in the checksum field.
3. Send the data to the corresponding queue.
4. Return.

Processing Module

The **processing module** is the heart of the IP package. In our package, the processing module receives a datagram from an interface or from the header-adding module. It treats both cases the same. A datagram must be processed and routed regardless of where it comes from.

The processing module first checks to see if the datagram is a loopback packet (with the destination address of 127.X.Y.Z) or a packet that has reached its final destination. In either case, the packet is sent to the reassembly module.

If the node is a router, it decrements the time-to-live (TTL) field by one. If this value is less than or equal to zero, the datagram is discarded and an ICMP message (see Chapter 9) is sent to the original sender. If the value of TTL is greater than zero after decrement, the processing module sends the datagram to the forwarding module (see Figure 8.26).

Processing Module
1. Remove one datagram from one of the input queues.
2. If (destination address is 127.X.Y.Z or matches one of the local addresses)
1. Send the datagram to the reassembly module.
2. Return.

Processing Module (continued)
3. If (machine is a router)
1. Decrement TTL.
4. If (TTL less than or equal to zero)
1. Discard the datagram.
2. Send an ICMP error message.
3. Return.
5. Send the datagram to the forwarding module.
6. Return.

Queues

Our package uses two types of queues: input queues and output queues. The **input queues** store the datagrams coming from the data link layer or the upper-layer protocols. The **output queues** store the datagrams going to the data link layer or the upper-layer protocols. The processing module dequeues (removes) the datagrams from the input queues. The fragmentation and reassembly modules enqueue (add) the datagrams into the output queues.

Routing Table

We discussed the routing table in Chapter 6. The routing table is used by the forwarding module to determine the next-hop address of the packet.

Forwarding Module

We discussed the forwarding module in Chapter 6. The forwarding module receives an IP packet from the processing module. If the packet is to be forwarded, it is passed to this module. The module finds the IP address of the next station along with the interface number to which the packet should be sent. It then sends the packet with this information to the fragmentation module.

MTU Table

The MTU table is used by the fragmentation module to find the maximum transfer unit of a particular interface. Figure 8.27 shows the format of an MTU table.

Figure 8.27   *MTU table*

Interface Number	MTU
....	....
....	....
....	....

Fragmentation Module

In our package, the **fragmentation module** receives an IP datagram from the forwarding module. The forwarding module gives the IP datagram, the IP address of the next station (either the final destination in a direct delivery or the next router in an indirect delivery), and the interface number through which the datagram is sent out.

The fragmentation module consults the MTU table to find the MTU for the specific interface number. If the length of the datagram is larger than the MTU, the fragmentation module fragments the datagram, adds a header to each fragment, and sends them to the ARP package (see Chapter 7) for address resolution and delivery.

Fragmentation Module

Receive: an IP packet from routing module

1. Extract the size of the datagram.

2. If (size > MTU of the corresponding network)

    1. If [D (*do not fragment*) bit is set]

        1. Discard the datagram.

        2. Send an ICMP error message (see Chapter 9).

        3. Return.

    2. Else

        1. Calculate the maximum size.

        2. Divide the datagram into fragments.

        3. Add header to each fragment.

        4. Add required options to each fragment.

        5. Send the datagrams.

        6. Return.

3. Else

    1. Send the datagram.

4. Return.

Reassembly Table

The **reassembly table** is used by the reassembly module. In our package, the reassembly table has five fields: state, source IP address, datagram ID, time-out, and fragments (see Figure 8.28).

The value of the state field can be either FREE or IN-USE. The IP address field defines the source IP address of the datagram. The datagram ID is a number that uniquely defines a datagram and all of the fragments belonging to that datagram. The time-out is a predetermined amount of time in which all fragments must arrive. Finally, the fragments field is a pointer to a linked list of fragments.

Figure 8.28 *Reassembly table*

St.: State
S. A.: Source address   T. O.: Time-out
D. I.: Datagram ID   F.: Fragments

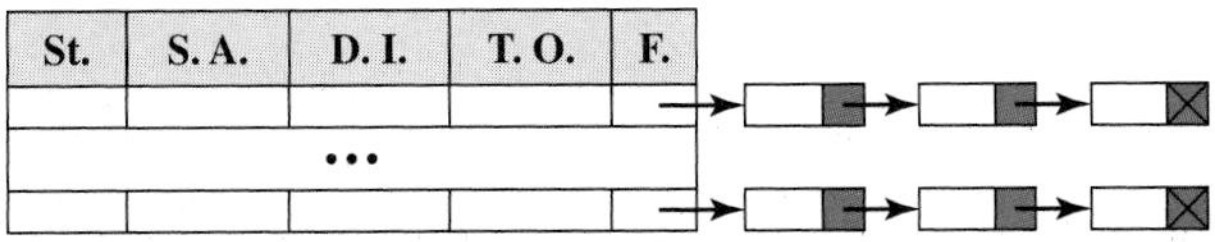

Reassembly Module

The **reassembly module** receives, from the processing module, those datagram fragments that have arrived at their final destinations. In our package, the reassembly module treats an unfragmented datagram as a fragment belonging to a datagram with only one fragment.

Because the IP protocol is a connectionless protocol, there is no guarantee that the fragments arrive in order. Besides, the fragments from one datagram can be intermixed with fragments from another datagram. To keep track of these situations, the module uses a reassembly table with associated linked lists, as we described earlier.

The job of the reassembly module is to find the datagram to which a fragment belongs, to order the fragments belonging to the same datagram, and reassemble all fragments of a datagram when all have arrived. If the established time-out has expired and any fragment is missing, the module discards the fragments.

Reassembly Module
Receive: an IP datagram from the processing module
1. If (offset value is zero and the *M* bit is 0)
1. Send the datagram to the appropriate queue.
2. Return.
2. Search the reassembly table for the corresponding entry.
3. If (not found)
1. Create a new entry.
4. Insert the fragment at the appropriate place in the linked list.
1. If (all fragments have arrived)
1. Reassemble the fragments.
2. Deliver the datagram to the corresponding upper layer protocol.
3. Return.
2. Else
1. Check the time-out.
2. If (time-out expired)
1. Discard all fragments.
2. Send an ICMP error message (see Chapter 9).
5. Return.

8.6   KEY TERMS

best-effort delivery	loose source route option
checksum	maximum transfer unit (MTU)
code field	no operation option
codepoint	output queue
data field	ping
datagram	pointer field
destination address	precedence
differentiated services	processing module
end of option option	reassembly module
forwarding module	reassembly table
fragmentation	record route option
fragmentation module	service type
fragmentation offset	source address
header-adding module	strict source route option
header length	time to live
input queue	timestamp option
Internet Protocol (IP)	traceroute
length field	type of service (TOS)

8.7   SUMMARY

❑   IP is an unreliable connectionless protocol responsible for source-to-destination delivery.

❑   Packets in the IP layer are called datagrams.

❑   A datagram consists of a header (20 to 60 bytes) and data.

❑   The IP header contains the following information: version number, header length, differentiated services, datagram length, identification number, fragmentation flags, fragmentation offset, time to live, protocol, checksum, source address, destination address, and options.

❑   The maximum length of a datagram is 65,535 bytes.

❑   The MTU is the maximum number of bytes that a data link protocol can encapsulate. MTUs vary from protocol to protocol.

❑   Fragmentation is the division of a datagram into smaller units to accommodate the MTU of a data link protocol.

❏ The fields in the IP header that relate to fragmentation are the identification number, the fragmentation flags, and the fragmentation offset.

❏ The IP datagram header consists of a fixed, 20-byte section and a variable options section with a maximum of 40 bytes.

❏ The options section of the IP header is used for network testing and debugging.

❏ The options header contains the following information: a code field that identifies the option, option length, and the specific data.

❏ The six IP options each have a specific function. They are as follows: filler between options for alignment purposes, padding, recording the route the datagram takes, selection of a mandatory route by the sender, selection of certain routers that must be visited, and recording of processing times at routers.

❏ The ping and traceroute utilities in UNIX can be used to implement some of the IP options.

❏ The error detection method used by IP is the checksum.

❏ The checksum uses one's complement arithmetic to add equal-size sections of the IP header. The complemented result is stored in the checksum field. The receiver also uses one's complement arithmetic to check the header.

❏ An IP package can consist of the following: a header-adding module, a processing module, a forwarding module, a fragmentation module, a reassembly module, a routing table, an MTU table, and a reassembly table.

8.8   PRACTICE SET

Exercises

1. Which fields of the IP header change from router to router?

2. Calculate the HLEN value if the total length is 1200 bytes, 1176 of which is data from the upper layer.

3. Table 8.5 lists the MTUs for many different protocols. The MTUs range from 296 to 65,535. What would be the advantages of having a large MTU? What would be the advantages of having a small MTU?

4. Given a fragmented datagram with an offset of 120, how can you determine the first and last byte number?

5. An IP datagram must go through router 128.46.10.5. There are no other restrictions on the routers to be visited. Draw the IP options with their values.

6. What is the maximum number of routers that can be recorded if the timestamp option has a flag value of 1? Why?

7. Can the value of the header length in an IP packet be less than 5? When is it exactly 5?

8. The value of HLEN in an IP datagram is 7. How many option bytes are present?

9. The size of the option field of an IP datagram is 20 bytes. What is the value of HLEN? What is the value in binary?

10. The value of the total length field in an IP datagram is 36 and the value of the header length field is 5. How many bytes of data is the packet carrying?

11. A datagram is carrying 1024 bytes of data. If there is no option information, what is the value of the header length field? What is the value of the total length field?

12. A host is sending 100 datagrams to another host. If the identification number of the first datagram is 1024, what is the identification number of the last?

13. An IP datagram arrives with fragmentation offset of 0 and an *M* bit (more fragment bit) of 0. Is this a first fragment, middle fragment, or last fragment?

14. An IP fragment has arrived with an offset value of 100. How many bytes of data were originally sent by the source before the data in this fragment?

15. An IP datagram has arrived with the following information in the header (in hexa-decimal):

> 45 00 00 54 00 03 00 00 20 06 00 00 7C 4E 03 02 B4 0E 0F 02

   a. Are there any options?

   b. Is the packet fragmented?

   c. What is the size of the data?

   d. Is a checksum used?

   e. How many more routers can the packet travel to?

   f. What is the identification number of the packet?

   g. What is the type of service?

16. In a datagram, the *M* bit is zero, the value of HLEN is 5, the value of total length is 200, and the offset value is 200. What is the number of the first byte and number of the last byte in this datagram? Is this the last fragment, the first fragment, or a middle fragment?

Research Activities

17. Use the *ping* utility with the -R option to check the routing of a packet to a destination. Interpret the result.

18. Use the *traceroute* utility with the -g option to implement the loose source route option. Choose some routers between the source and destination. Interpret the result and find if all defined routers have been visited.

19. Use the *traceroute* utility with the -G option to implement the strict source route option. Choose some routers between the source and destination. Interpret the result and find if all defined routers have been visited and no undefined router visited.

20. Do research and find the RFCs related to the IP protocols. Which one defines fragmentation?

21. Find the RFCs related to the IP options. Which one defines the record route option? Which one defines the loose source route option? Which one defines the strict source route option?

CHAPTER 9

Internet Control Message Protocol (ICMP)

As discussed in Chapter 8, the IP provides unreliable and connectionless datagram delivery. It was designed this way to make efficient use of network resources. The IP protocol is a best-effort delivery service that delivers a datagram from its original source to its final destination. However, it has two deficiencies: lack of error control and lack of assistance mechanisms.

The IP protocol has no error-reporting or error-correcting mechanism. What happens if something goes wrong? What happens if a router must discard a datagram because it cannot find a router to the final destination, or because the time-to-live field has a zero value? What happens if the final destination host must discard all fragments of a datagram because it has not received all fragments within a predetermined time limit? These are examples of situations where an error has occurred and the IP protocol has no built-in mechanism to notify the original host.

The IP protocol also lacks a mechanism for host and management queries. A host sometimes needs to determine if a router or another host is alive. And sometimes a network manager needs information from another host or router.

The **Internet Control Message Protocol (ICMP)** has been designed to compensate for the above two deficiencies. It is a companion to the IP protocol. Figure 9.1 shows the position of ICMP in relation to IP and other protocols in the network layer.

Figure 9.1 *Position of ICMP in the network layer*

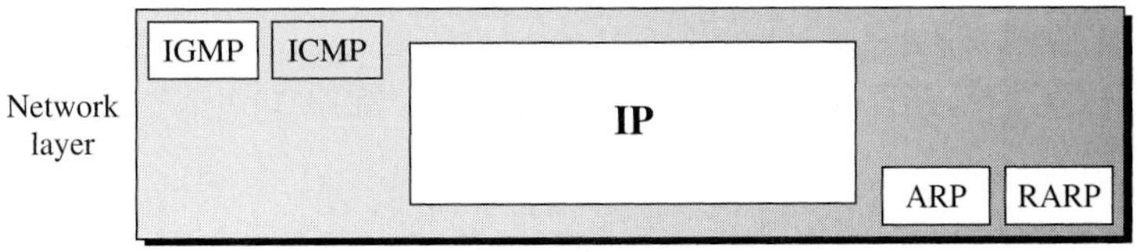

ICMP itself is a network layer protocol. However, its messages are not passed directly to the data link layer as would be expected. Instead, the messages are first encapsulated inside IP datagrams before going to the lower layer (see Figure 9.2).

Figure 9.2   *ICMP encapsulation*

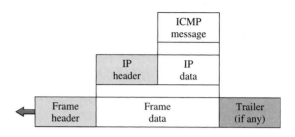

The value of the protocol field in the IP datagram is 1 to indicate that the IP data is an ICMP message.

9.1   TYPES OF MESSAGES

ICMP messages are divided into two broad categories: **error-reporting messages** and **query messages** as shown in Figure 9.3.

Figure 9.3   *ICMP messages*

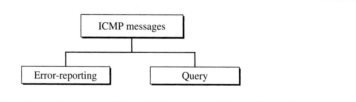

The error-reporting messages report problems that a router or a host (destination) may encounter when it processes an IP packet.

The query messages, which occur in pairs, help a host or a network manager get specific information from a router or another host. For example, nodes can discover their neighbors. Also, hosts can discover and learn about routers on their network and routers can help a node redirect its messages. Table 9.1 lists the ICMP messages in each category.

Table 9.1   *ICMP messages*

Category	Type	Message
Error-reporting messages	3	Destination unreachable
	4	Source quench
	11	Time exceeded
	12	Parameter problem
	5	Redirection

Table 9.1   *ICMP messages (continued)*

Category	Type	Message
Query messages	8 or 0	Echo request or reply
	13 or 14	Timestamp request or reply
	17 or 18	Address mask request or reply
	10 or 9	Router solicitation or advertisement

9.2   MESSAGE FORMAT

An ICMP message has an 8-byte header and a variable-size data section. Although the general format of the header is different for each message type, the first 4 bytes are common to all. As Figure 9.4 shows, the first field, ICMP type, defines the type of the message. The code field specifies the reason for the particular message type. The last common field is the checksum field (to be discussed later in the chapter). The rest of the header is specific for each message type.

The data section in error messages carries information for finding the original packet that had the error. In query messages, the data section carries extra information based on the type of the query.

Figure 9.4   *General format of ICMP messages*

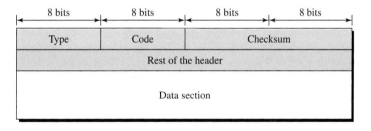

9.3   ERROR REPORTING

One of the main responsibilities of ICMP is to report errors. Although technology has produced increasingly reliable transmission media, errors still exist and must be handled. IP, as discussed in Chapter 8, is an unreliable protocol. This means that error checking and error control are not a concern of IP. ICMP was designed, in part, to compensate for this shortcoming. However, ICMP does not correct errors, it simply reports them. Error correction is left to the higher-level protocols. Error messages are always sent to the original source because the only information available in the datagram about the route is the source and destination IP addresses. ICMP uses the source IP address to send the error message to the source (originator) of the datagram.

ICMP always reports error messages to the original source.

Five types of errors are handled: destination unreachable, source quench, time exceeded, parameter problems, and redirection (see Figure 9.5).

Figure 9.5   *Error-reporting messages*

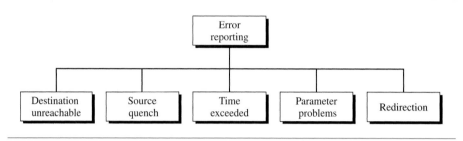

The following are important points about ICMP error messages:

❑ **No ICMP error message will be generated in response to a datagram carrying an ICMP error message.**

❑ **No ICMP error message will be generated for a fragmented datagram that is not the first fragment.**

❑ **No ICMP error message will be generated for a datagram having a multicast address.**

❑ **No ICMP error message will be generated for a datagram having a special address such as 127.0.0.0 or 0.0.0.0.**

Note that all error messages contain a data section that includes the IP header of the original datagram plus the first 8 bytes of data in that datagram. The original datagram header is added to give the original source, which receives the error message, information about the datagram itself. The 8 bytes of data are included because, as we will see in Chapters 11 and 12 on UDP and TCP protocols, the first 8 bytes provide information about the port numbers (UDP and TCP) and sequence number (TCP). This information is needed so the source can inform the protocols (TCP or UDP) about the error. ICMP forms an error packet, which is then encapsulated in an IP datagram (see Figure 9.6).

Destination Unreachable

When a router cannot route a datagram or a host cannot deliver a datagram, the datagram is discarded and the router or the host sends a **destination-unreachable message** back to the source host that initiated the datagram. Figure 9.7 shows the format of the destination-unreachable message. The code field for this type specifies the reason for discarding the datagram:

❑ **Code 0.** The network is unreachable, possibly due to hardware failure. This type of message can only be generated by a router.

Figure 9.6 *Contents of data field for the error messages*

Received datagram
IP header
8 bytes
IP data
ICMP header
IP header
8 bytes
ICMP packet
IP header
ICMP header
IP header
8 bytes
Sent IP datagram

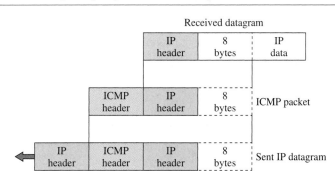

Figure 9.7 *Destination-unreachable format*

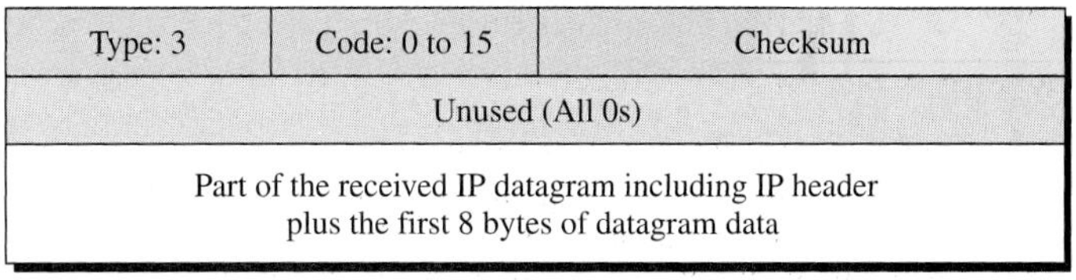

Type: 3
Code: 0 to 15
Checksum
Unused (All 0s)
Part of the received IP datagram including IP header
plus the first 8 bytes of datagram data

- **Code 1.** The host is unreachable. This can also be due to hardware failure. This type of message can only be generated by a router.
- **Code 2.** The protocol is unreachable. An IP datagram can carry data belonging to higher-level protocols such as UDP, TCP, and OSPF. If the destination host receives a datagram that must be delivered, for example, to the TCP protocol, but the TCP protocol is not running at the moment, a code 2 message is sent. This type of message is generated only by the destination host.
- **Code 3.** The port is unreachable. The application program (process) that the datagram is destined for is not running at the moment.
- **Code 4.** Fragmentation is required, but the DF (do not fragment) field of the datagram has been set. In other words, the sender of the datagram has specified that the datagram not be fragmented, but routing is impossible without fragmentation.
- **Code 5.** Source routing cannot be accomplished. In other words, one or more routers defined in the source routing option cannot be visited.
- **Code 6.** The destination network is unknown. This is different from code 0. In code 0, the router knows that the destination network exists, but it is unreachable at the moment. For code 6, the router has no information about the destination network.
- **Code 7.** The destination host is unknown. This is different from code 1. In code 1, the router knows that the destination host exists, but it is unreachable

at the moment. For code 7, the router is unaware of the existence of the destination host.

❏ **Code 8.** The source host is isolated.

❏ **Code 9.** Communication with the destination network is administratively prohibited.

❏ **Code 10.** Communication with the destination host is administratively prohibited.

❏ **Code 11.** The network is unreachable for the specified type of service. This is different from code 0. Here the router can route the datagram if the source had requested an available type of service.

❏ **Code 12.** The host is unreachable for the specified type of service. This is different from code 1. Here the router can route the datagram if the source had requested an available type of service.

❏ **Code 13.** The host is unreachable because the administrator has put a filter on it.

❏ **Code 14.** The host is unreachable because the host precedence is violated. The message is sent by a router to indicate that the requested precedence is not permitted for the destination.

❏ **Code 15.** The host is unreachable because its precedence was cut off. This message is generated when the network operators have imposed a minimum level of precedence for the operation of the network, but the datagram was sent with a precedence below this level.

Note that destination-unreachable messages can be created either by a router or the destination host. Code 2 and code 3 messages can only be created by the destination host; the messages of the remaining codes can only be created by routers.

> **Destination-unreachable messages with codes 2 or 3 can be created only by the destination host.**
> **Other destination-unreachable messages can be created only by routers.**

Note that even if a router does not report a destination-unreachable message, it does not necessarily mean that the datagram has been delivered. For example, if a datagram is traveling through an Ethernet network, there is no way that a router knows that the datagram has been delivered to the destination host or the next router because Ethernet does not provide any acknowledgment mechanism.

> **A router cannot detect all problems that prevent the delivery of a packet.**

Source Quench

The IP protocol is a connectionless protocol. There is no communication between the source host, which produces the datagram, the routers, which forward it, and the destination host, which processes it. One of the ramifications of this absence of communication is the lack of *flow control*. IP does not have a flow-control mechanism embedded in the protocol. The lack of flow control can create a major problem in the operation of IP: congestion. The source host never knows if the routers or the destination host have been overwhelmed with datagrams. The source host never knows if it is producing datagrams faster than can be forwarded by routers or processed by the destination host.

There is no flow-control mechanism in the IP protocol.

The lack of flow control can create congestion in routers or the destination host. A router or a host has a limited-size queue (buffer) for incoming datagrams waiting to be forwarded (in the case of a router) or to be processed (in the case of a host). If the datagrams are received much faster than they can be forwarded or processed, the queue may overflow. In this case, the router or the host has no choice but to discard some of the datagrams.

The **source-quench message** in ICMP was designed to add a kind of flow control to the IP. When a router or host discards a datagram due to congestion, it sends a source-quench message to the sender of the datagram. This message has two purposes. First, it informs the source that the datagram has been discarded. Second, it warns the source that there is congestion somewhere in the path and that the source should slow down (quench) the sending process. The source-quench format is shown in Figure 9.8.

Figure 9.8   *Source-quench format*

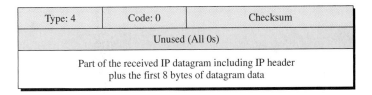

Type: 4	Code: 0	Checksum
Unused (All 0s)		
Part of the received IP datagram including IP header plus the first 8 bytes of datagram data		

A source-quench message informs the source that a datagram has been discarded due to congestion in a router or the destination host.
The source must slow down the sending of datagrams until the congestion is relieved.

There are some points that deserve more explanation. First, the router or destination host that has experienced the congestion sends one source-quench message for each discarded datagram to the source host. Second, there is no mechanism to tell the source that the congestion has been relieved and the source can resume sending datagrams at its previous rate. The source continues to lower the rate until no more source-quench messages are received. Third, the congestion can be created either by a one-to-one or many-to-one communication. In a one-to-one communication, a single high-speed host could create datagrams faster than a router or the destination host can handle. In this case, source-quench messages can be helpful. They tell the source to slow down. In a many-to-one communication, many sources create datagrams that must be handled by a router or the destination host. In this case, each source can be sending datagrams at different speeds, some of them at a low rate, others at a high rate. In this case, the source-quench message may not be very useful. The router or the destination host has no clue which source is responsible for the congestion. It may drop a datagram from a very slow source instead of dropping the datagram from the source that has actually created the congestion.

> **One source-quench message is sent for each datagram that is discarded due to congestion.**

Time Exceeded

The **time-exceeded message** is generated in two cases:

❏ As we saw in Chapter 6, routers use routing tables to find the next hop (next router) that must receive the packet. If there are errors in one or more routing tables, a packet can travel in a loop or a cycle, going from one router to the next or visiting a series of routers endlessly. As we saw in Chapter 8, each datagram contains a field called *time to live* that controls this situation. When a datagram visits a router, the value of this field is decremented by 1. When the time-to-live value reaches 0, after decrementing, the router discards the datagram. However, when the datagram is discarded, a time-exceeded message must be sent by the router to the original source.

> **Whenever a router decrements a datagram with a time-to-live value to zero, it discards the datagram and sends a time-exceeded message to the original source.**

❏ Second, a time-exceeded message is also generated when all fragments that make up a message do not arrive at the destination host within a certain time limit. When the first fragment arrives, the destination host starts a timer. If all the fragments have not arrived when the time expires, the destination discards all the fragments and sends a time-exceeded message to the original sender.

> **When the final destination does not receive all of the fragments in a set time, it discards the received fragments and sends a time-exceeded message to the original source.**

Figure 9.9 shows the format of the time-exceeded message. Code 0 is used when the datagram is discarded by the router due to a time-to-live field value of zero. Code 1 is used when arrived fragments of a datagram are discarded because some fragments have not arrived within the time limit.

> **In a time-exceeded message, code 0 is used only by routers to show that the value of the time-to-live field is zero. Code 1 is used only by the destination host to show that not all of the fragments have arrived within a set time.**

Figure 9.9   *Time-exceeded message format*

Type: 11	Code: 0 or 1	Checksum
Unused (All 0s)		
Part of the received IP datagram including IP header plus the first 8 bytes of datagram data		

Parameter Problem

Any ambiguity in the header part of a datagram can create serious problems as the datagram travels through the Internet. If a router or the destination host discovers an ambiguous or missing value in any field of the datagram, it discards the datagram and sends a parameter-problem message back to the source.

> **A parameter-problem message can be created by a router or the destination host.**

Figure 9.10 shows the format of the **parameter-problem message.** The code field in this case specifies the reason for discarding the datagram:

❏ **Code 0.** There is an error or ambiguity in one of the header fields. In this case, the value in the pointer field points to the byte with the problem. For example, if the value is zero, then the first byte is not a valid field.

❏ **Code 1.** The required part of an option is missing. In this case, the pointer is not used.

Figure 9.10   *Parameter-problem message format*

Type: 12	Code: 0 or 1	Checksum
Pointer	Unused (All 0s)	
Part of the received IP datagram including IP header plus the first 8 bytes of datagram data		

Redirection

When a router needs to send a packet destined for another network, it must know the IP address of the next appropriate router. The same is true if the sender is a host. Both routers and hosts then must have a routing table to find the address of the router or the next router. Routers take part in the routing update process as we will see in Chapter 14 and are supposed to be updated constantly. Routing is dynamic.

However, for efficiency, hosts do not take part in the routing update process because there are many more hosts in an internet than routers. Updating the routing tables of hosts dynamically produces unacceptable traffic. The hosts usually use static routing. When a host comes up, its routing table has a limited number of entries. It usually knows only the IP address of one router, the default router. For this reason, the host may send a datagram, which is destined for another network, to the wrong router. In this case, the router that receives the datagram will forward the datagram to the correct router. However, to update the routing table of the host, it sends a redirection message to the host. This concept of redirection is shown in Figure 9.11. Host A wants to send a datagram to host B. Router R2 is obviously the most efficient routing choice, but host A did not choose router R2. The datagram goes to R1 instead. R1, after consulting its table, finds that the packet should have gone to R2. It sends the packet to R2 and, at the same time, sends a redirection message to host A. Host A's routing table can now be updated.

Figure 9.11   *Redirection concept*

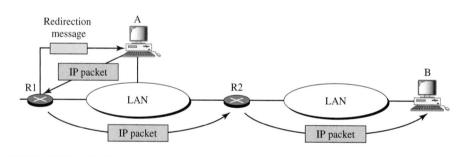

A host usually starts with a small routing table that is gradually augmented and updated. One of the tools to accomplish this is the redirection message.

The format of the redirection message is shown in Figure 9.12. Note that the IP address of the appropriate target is given in the second row.

Figure 9.12   *Redirection message format*

Type: 5	Code: 0 to 3	Checksum
IP address of the target router		
Part of the received IP datagram including IP header plus the first 8 bytes of datagram data		

Although the redirection message is considered an error-reporting message, it is different from other error messages. The router does not discard the datagram in this case; it is sent to the appropriate router. The code field for the redirection message narrows down the redirection:

❏ **Code 0.** Redirection for a network-specific route.

❏ **Code 1.** Redirection for a host-specific route.

❏ **Code 2.** Redirection for a network-specific route based on a specified type of service.

❏ **Code 3.** Redirection for a host-specific route based on a specified type of service.

> **A redirection message is sent from a router to a host on the same local network.**

9.4   QUERY

In addition to error reporting, ICMP can also diagnose some network problems. This is accomplished through the query messages, a group of four different pairs of messages, as shown in Figure 9.13. In this type of ICMP message, a node sends a message that is answered in a specific format by the destination node. Note that originally two other types of messages (information request and information reply) were defined, but they are now obsolete. They were designed to allow a host to get its Internet address at start-up; this function is now performed by RARP (see Chapter 7) and BOOTP (see Chapter 16).

Figure 9.13   *Query messages*

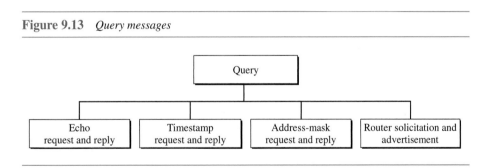

Echo Request and Reply

The **echo-request and echo-reply messages** are designed for diagnostic purposes. Network managers and users utilize this pair of messages to identify network problems. The combination of echo-request and echo-reply messages determines whether two systems (hosts or routers) can communicate with each other.

A host or router can send an echo-request message to another host or router. The host or router that receives an echo-request message creates an echo-reply message and returns it to the original sender.

> **An echo-request message can be sent by a host or router. An echo-reply message is sent by the host or router which receives an echo-request message.**

The echo-request and echo-reply messages can be used to determine if there is communication at the IP level. Because ICMP messages are encapsulated in IP datagrams, the receipt of an echo-reply message by the machine that sent the echo request is proof that the IP protocols in the sender and receiver are communicating with each other using the IP datagram. Also, it is proof that the intermediate routers are receiving, processing, and forwarding IP datagrams.

> **Echo-request and echo-reply messages can be used by network managers to check the operation of the IP protocol.**

The echo-request and echo-reply messages can also be used by a host to see if another host is reachable. At the user level, this is done by invoking the packet Internet groper (ping) command. Today, most systems provide a version of the *ping* command that can create a series (instead of just one) of echo-request and echo-reply messages, providing statistical information. We will see the use of this program at the end of the chapter.

> **Echo-request and echo-reply messages can test the reachability of a host. This is usually done by invoking the ping command.**

Echo request, together with echo reply, can determine whether or not a node is functioning properly. The node to be tested is sent an echo-request message. The optional data field contains a message that must be repeated exactly by the responding node in its echo-reply message. Figure 9.14 shows the format of the echo-reply and echo-request message. The identifier and sequence number fields are not formally defined by the protocol and can be used arbitrarily by the sender. The identifier is often the same as the process ID.

Figure 9.14   *Echo-request and echo-reply messages*

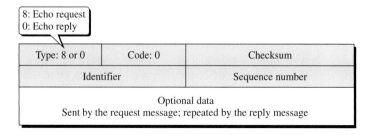

Timestamp Request and Reply

Two machines (hosts or routers) can use the **timestamp-request and timestamp-reply messages** to determine the round-trip time needed for an IP datagram to travel between them. It can also be used to synchronize the clocks in two machines. The format of these two messages is shown in Figure 9.15.

Figure 9.15   *Timestamp-request and timestamp-reply message format*

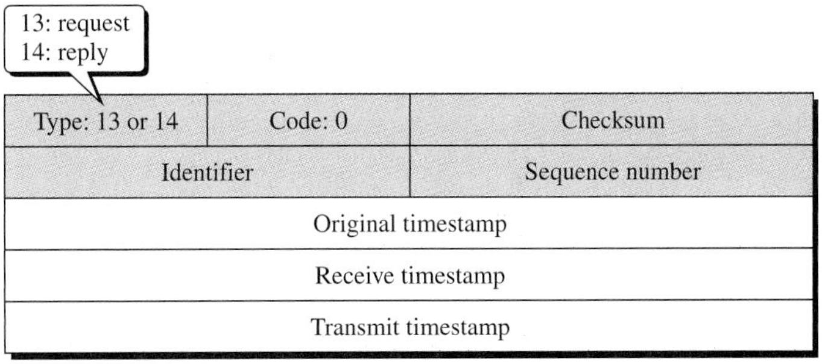

The three timestamp fields are each 32 bits long. Each field can hold a number representing time measured in milliseconds from midnight in Universal Time (formerly called Greenwich Mean Time). (Note that 32 bits can represent a number between 0 and 4,294,967,295, but a timestamp in this case cannot exceed $86,400,000 = 24 \times 60 \times 60 \times 1000$.)

The source creates a timestamp-request message. The source fills the *original timestamp* field with the Universal Time shown by its clock at departure time. The other two timestamp fields are filled with zeros.

The destination creates the timestamp-reply message. The destination copies the original timestamp value from the request message into the same field in its reply message. It then fills the *receive timestamp* field with the Universal Time shown by its clock at the time the request was received. Finally, it fills the *transmit timestamp* field with the Universal Time shown by its clock at the time the reply message departs.

The timestamp-request and timestamp-reply messages can be used to compute the one-way or round-trip time required for a datagram to go from a source to a destination and then back again. The formulas are

sending time = receive timestamp − original timestamp
receiving time = returned time − transmit timestamp
round-trip time = sending time + receiving time

Note that the sending and receiving time calculations are accurate only if the two clocks in the source and destination machines are synchronized. However, the round-trip calculation is correct even if the two clocks are not synchronized because each clock contributes twice to the round-trip calculation, thus canceling any difference in synchronization.

Timestamp-request and timestamp-reply messages can be used to calculate the round-trip time between a source and a destination machine even if their clocks are not synchronized.

For example, given the following information:

original timestamp: 46
receive timestamp: 59
transmit timestamp: 60
return time: 67

We can calculate the round-trip time to be 20 milliseconds:

sending time = 59 − 46 = 13 milliseconds
receiving time = 67 − 60 = 7 milliseconds
round-trip time = 13 + 7 = 20 milliseconds

Given the actual one-way time, the timestamp-request and timestamp-reply messages can also be used to synchronize the clocks in two machines using the following formula:

Time difference = receive timestamp −
      (original timestamp field + one-way time duration)

The one-way time duration can be obtained either by dividing the round-trip time duration by two (if we are sure that the sending time is the same as the receiving time) or by other means. For example, we can tell that the two clocks in the previous example are 3 milliseconds out of synchronization because

Time difference = 59 − (46 + 10) = 3

The timestamp-request and timestamp-reply messages can be used to synchronize two clocks in two machines if the exact one-way time duration is known.

Address-Mask Request and Reply

A host may know its IP address, but it may not know the corresponding mask. For example, a host may know its IP address as 159.31.17.24, but it may not know that the corresponding mask is /24.

To obtain its mask, a host sends an **address-mask-request message** to a router on the LAN. If the host knows the address of the router, it sends the request directly to the router. If it does not know, it broadcasts the message. The router receiving the address-mask-request message responds with an **address-mask-reply message,** providing the necessary mask for the host. This can be applied to its full IP address to get its subnet address.

The format of the address-mask request and address-mask reply is shown in Figure 9.16. The address-mask field is filled with zeros in the request message. When the router sends the address-mask reply back to the host, this field contains the actual mask (1s for the netid and subnetid and 0s for the hostid).

Figure 9.16 *Mask-request and mask-reply message format*

17: Request
18: Reply
Type: 17 or 18
Code: 0
Checksum
Identifier
Sequence number
Address mask

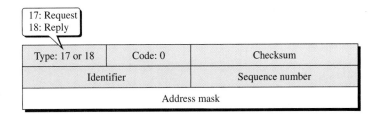

Masking is needed for diskless stations at start-up time. When a diskless station comes up for the first time, it may ask for its full IP address using the RARP protocol (see Chapter 7); after receiving its IP address, it may use the address-mask request and reply to find out which part of the address defines the subnet.

Another way to get subnet mask information is through the use of the BOOTP protocol, as we will see in Chapter 16.

Router Solicitation and Advertisement

As we discussed in the redirection message section, a host that wants to send data to a host on another network needs to know the address of routers connected to its own network. Also, the host must know if the routers are alive and functioning. The **router-solicitation and router-advertisement messages** can help in this situation. A host can broadcast (or multicast) a router-solicitation message. The router or routers that receive the solicitation message broadcast their routing information using the router-advertisement message. A router can also periodically send router-advertisement messages even if no host has solicited. Note that when a router sends out an advertisement, it announces not only its own presence but also the presence of all routers on the network of which it is aware. Figure 9.17 shows the format of the router-solicitation message.

Figure 9.17 *Router-solicitation message format*

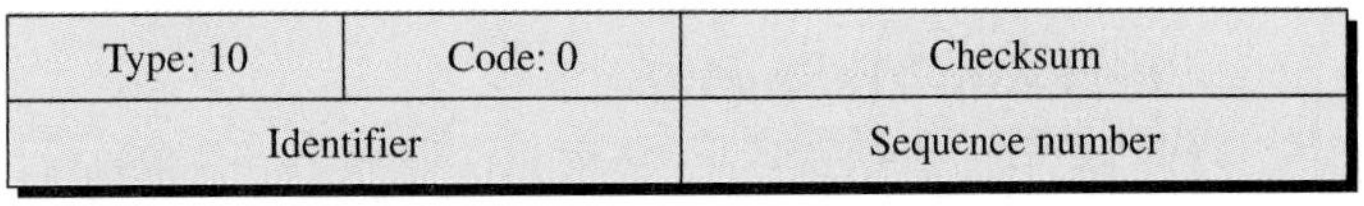

Type: 10
Code: 0
Checksum
Identifier
Sequence number

Figure 9.18 shows the format of the router-advertisement message. The lifetime field shows the number of seconds that the entries are considered to be valid. Each router entry in the advertisement contains at least two fields: the router address and the address preference level. The address preference level defines the ranking of the router. The preference level is used to select a router as the default router. If the address preference level is zero, that router is considered the default router. If the address preference level is 80000000_{16}, the router should never be selected as the default router.

Figure 9.18   *Router-advertisement message format*

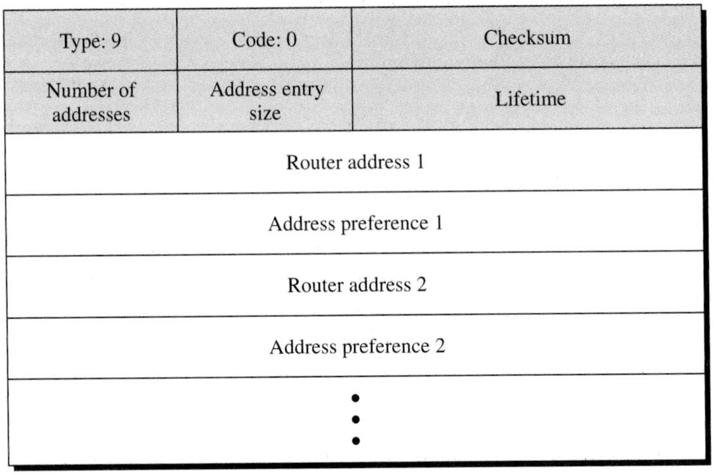

Type: 9	Code: 0	Checksum
Number of addresses	Address entry size	Lifetime
Router address 1		
Address preference 1		
Router address 2		
Address preference 2		
⋮		

9.5   CHECKSUM

In Chapter 8, we learned the concept and idea of the checksum. In ICMP the checksum is calculated over the entire message (header and data).

Checksum Calculation

The sender follows these steps using one's complement arithmetic:

1. The checksum field is set to zero.
2. The sum of all the 16-bit words (header and data) is calculated.
3. The sum is complemented to get the checksum.
4. The checksum is stored in the checksum field.

Checksum Testing

The receiver follows these steps using one's complement arithmetic:

1. The sum of all words (header and data) is calculated.
2. The sum is complemented.
3. If the result obtained in step 2 is 16 0s, the message is accepted; otherwise, it is rejected.

Example 1

Figure 9.19 shows an example of checksum calculation for a simple echo-request message (see Figure 9.14). We randomly chose the identifier to be 1 and the sequence number to be 9. The message is divided into 16-bit (2-byte) words. The words are added together and the sum is complemented. Now the sender can put this value in the checksum field.

Figure 9.19   *Example of checksum calculation*

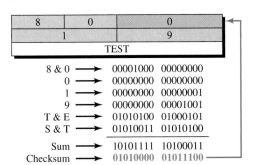

8	0	0
1		9
TEST		

```
    8 & 0  ──▶   00001000  00000000
        0  ──▶   00000000  00000000
        1  ──▶   00000000  00000001
        9  ──▶   00000000  00001001
    T & E  ──▶   01010100  01000101
    S & T  ──▶   01010011  01010100
                 ─────────────────────
     Sum   ──▶   10101111  10100011
Checksum  ──▶   01010000  01011100
```

9.6   DEBUGGING TOOLS

There are several tools that can be used in the Internet for debugging. We can find if a host or router is alive and running. We can trace the route of a packet. We introduce two tools that use ICMP for debugging: *ping* and *traceroute*. We will introduce more tools in future chapters after we have discussed the corresponding protocols.

Ping

We can use the *ping* program to find if a host is alive and responding. We used the *ping* program in Chapter 8 to simulate the record route option. We discuss *ping* in more detail to see how it uses ICMP packets.

The source host sends ICMP echo request messages (type: 8, code: 0); the destination, if alive, responds with ICMP echo reply messages. The *ping* program sets the identifier field in the echo request and reply message and starts the sequence number from 0; this number is incremented by one each time a new message is sent. Note that *ping* can calculate the round trip time. It inserts the sending time in the data section of the message. When the packet arrives it subtracts the arrival time from the departure time to get the round-trip time (RTT).

Example 2

We use the *ping* program to test the server fhda.edu. The result is shown below:

```
$ ping fhda.edu
PING fhda.edu (153.18.8.1)   56 (84)  bytes of data.
64 bytes from tiptoe.fhda.edu (153.18.8.1): icmp_seq=0   ttl=62   time=1.91 ms
64 bytes from tiptoe.fhda.edu (153.18.8.1): icmp_seq=1   ttl=62   time=2.04 ms
64 bytes from tiptoe.fhda.edu (153.18.8.1): icmp_seq=2   ttl=62   time=1.90 ms
64 bytes from tiptoe.fhda.edu (153.18.8.1): icmp_seq=3   ttl=62   time=1.97 ms
64 bytes from tiptoe.fhda.edu (153.18.8.1): icmp_seq=4   ttl=62   time=1.93 ms
```

```
64 bytes from tiptoe.fhda.edu (153.18.8.1): icmp_seq=5    ttl=62    time=2.00 ms
64 bytes from tiptoe.fhda.edu (153.18.8.1): icmp_seq=6    ttl=62    time=1.94 ms
64 bytes from tiptoe.fhda.edu (153.18.8.1): icmp_seq=7    ttl=62    time=1.94 ms
64 bytes from tiptoe.fhda.edu (153.18.8.1): icmp_seq=8    ttl=62    time=1.97 ms
64 bytes from tiptoe.fhda.edu (153.18.8.1): icmp_seq=9    ttl=62    time=1.89 ms
64 bytes from tiptoe.fhda.edu (153.18.8.1): icmp_seq=10   ttl=62    time=1.98 ms

--- fhda.edu ping statistics ---
11 packets transmitted, 11 received, 0% packet loss, time 10103ms
rtt min/avg/max = 1.899/1.955/2.041 ms
```

The *ping* program sends messages with sequence numbers starting from 0. For each probe it gives us the RTT time. The TTL (time to live) field in the IP datagram that encapsulates an ICMP message has been set to 62, which means the packet cannot travel more than 62 hops. At the beginning, *ping* defines the number of data bytes as 56 and the total number of bytes as 84. It is obvious that if we add 8 bytes of ICMP header and 20 bytes of IP header to 56, the result is 84. However, note that in each probe *ping* defines the number of bytes as 64. This is the total number of bytes in the ICMP packet (56 + 8).

The *ping* program continues to send messages if we do not stop it using the interrupt key (ctrl + c, for example). After it is interrupted, it prints the statistics of the probes. It tells us the number of packets sent, the number of packets received, the total time, and the RTT minimum, maximum, and average. Some systems may print more information.

Example 3

For the second example, we want to know if the adelphia.net mail server is alive and running. The result is shown below:

```
$ ping mail.adelphia.net
PING mail.adelphia.net (68.168.78.100) 56(84) bytes of data.
64 bytes from mail.adelphia.net (68.168.78.100): icmp_seq=0    ttl=48    time=85.4 ms
64 bytes from mail.adelphia.net (68.168.78.100): icmp_seq=1    ttl=48    time=84.6 ms
64 bytes from mail.adelphia.net (68.168.78.100): icmp_seq=2    ttl=48    time=84.9 ms
64 bytes from mail.adelphia.net (68.168.78.100): icmp_seq=3    ttl=48    time=84.3 ms
64 bytes from mail.adelphia.net (68.168.78.100): icmp_seq=4    ttl=48    time=84.5 ms
64 bytes from mail.adelphia.net (68.168.78.100): icmp_seq=5    ttl=48    time=84.7 ms
64 bytes from mail.adelphia.net (68.168.78.100): icmp_seq=6    ttl=48    time=84.6 ms
64 bytes from mail.adelphia.net (68.168.78.100): icmp_seq=7    ttl=48    time=84.7 ms
64 bytes from mail.adelphia.net (68.168.78.100): icmp_seq=8    ttl=48    time=84.4 ms
64 bytes from mail.adelphia.net (68.168.78.100): icmp_seq=9    ttl=48    time=84.2 ms
64 bytes from mail.adelphia.net (68.168.78.100): icmp_seq=10   ttl=48    time=84.9 ms
64 bytes from mail.adelphia.net (68.168.78.100): icmp_seq=11   ttl=48    time=84.6 ms
64 bytes from mail.adelphia.net (68.168.78.100): icmp_seq=12   ttl=48    time=84.5 ms

--- mail.adelphia.net ping statistics ---
14 packets transmitted, 13 received, 7% packet loss, time 13129ms
rtt min/avg/max/mdev = 84.207/84.694/85.469
```

Note that in this case, we sent 14 packets, but only 13 have been returned. We may have interrupted the program before the last packet, with sequence number 13, was returned.

Traceroute

The **traceroute** program in UNIX or **tracert** in Windows can be used to trace the route of a packet from the source to the destination. We have seen an application of the *traceroute* program to simulate the loose source route and strict source route options of an IP datagram in the previous chapter. We use this program in conjunction with ICMP packets in this chapter.

The program elegantly uses two ICMP messages, time exceeded and destination unreachable, to find the route of a packet. This is a program at the application level that uses the services of UDP (see Chapter 11).

Let us show the idea of the *traceroute* program using Figure 9.20.

Figure 9.20   *The traceroute program operation*

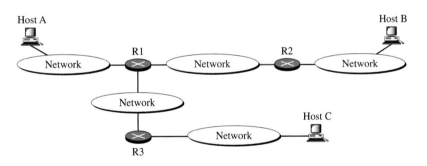

Given the topology, we know that a packet from host A to host B travels through routers R1 and R2. However, most of the time, we are not aware of this topology. There could be several routes from A to B. The *traceroute* program uses the ICMP messages and the TTL (time to live) field in the IP packet to find the route.

1. The *traceroute* program uses the following steps to find the address of the router R1 and the round trip time between host A and router R1.

   a. The *traceroute* application at host A sends a packet to destination B using UDP; the message is encapsulated in an IP packet with a TTL value of 1. The program notes the time the packet is sent.

   b. Router R1 receives the packet and decrements the value of TTL to 0. It then discards the packet (because TTL is 0). The router, however, sends a time-exceeded ICMP message (type: 11, code: 0) to show that the TTL value is 0 and the packet was discarded.

   c. The *traceroute* program receives the ICMP messages and uses the destination address of the IP packet encapsulating ICMP to find the IP address of router R1.

The program also makes note of the time the packet has arrived. The difference between this time and the time at step a is the round trip time.

The *traceroute* program repeats steps a to c three times to get a better average round trip time. The first trip time may be much longer than the second or third because it takes time for the ARP program to find the physical address of router R1. For the second and third trip, ARP has the address in its cache.

2. The *traceroute* program repeats the previous steps to find the address of router R2 and the round trip time between host A and router R2. However, in this step, the value of TTL is set to 2. So router R1 forwards the message, while router R2 discards it and sends a time-exceeded ICMP message.

3. The *traceroute* program repeats the previous step to find the address of host B and the round trip time between host A and host B. When host B receives the packet, it decrements the value of TTL, but it does not discard the message since it has reached its final destination. How can an ICMP message be sent back to host A? The *traceroute* program uses a different strategy here. The destination port of the UDP packet is set to one that is not supported by the UDP protocol. When host B receives the packet, it cannot find an application program to accept the delivery. It discards the packet and sends an ICMP destination-unreachable message (type: 3, code: 3) to host A. Note that this situation does not happen at router R1 or R2 because a router does not check the UDP header. The *traceroute* program records the destination address of the arrived IP datagram and makes note of the round trip time. Receiving the destination-unreachable message with a code value 3 is an indication that the whole route has been found and there is no need to send more packets.

Example 4

We use the *traceroute* program to find the route from the computer voyager.deanza.edu to the server fhda.edu. The following shows the result:

$ traceroute fhda.edu				
traceroute to fhda.edu	(153.18.8.1), 30 hops max, 38 byte packets			
1 Dcore.fhda.edu	(153.18.31.254)	0.995 ms	0.899 ms	0.878 ms
2 Dbackup.fhda.edu	(153.18.251.4)	1.039 ms	1.064 ms	1.083 ms
3 tiptoe.fhda.edu	(153.18.8.1)	1.797 ms	1.642 ms	1.757 ms

The un-numbered line after the command shows that the destination is 153.18.8.1. The TTL value is 30 hops. The packet contains 38 bytes: 20 bytes of IP header, 8 bytes of UDP header, and 10 bytes of application data. The application data is used by *traceroute* to keep track of the packets.

The first line shows the first router visited. The router is named Dcore.fhda.edu with IP address 153.18.31.254. The first round trip time was 0.995 milliseconds, the second was 0.899 milliseconds, and the third was 0.878 milliseconds.

The second line shows the second router visited. The router is named Dbackup.fhda.edu with IP address 153.18.251.4. The three round trip times are also shown.

The third line shows the destination host. We know that this is the destination host because there are no more lines. The destination host is the server fhda.edu, but it is named tiptoe.fhda.edu with the IP address 153.18.8.1. The three round trip times are also shown.

Example 5

In this example, we trace a longer route, the route to xerox.com

```
$ traceroute xerox.com
traceroute to xerox.com (13.1.64.93), 30 hops max, 38 byte packets
  1 Dcore.fhda.edu    (153.18.31.254)    0.622 ms    0.891 ms    0.875 ms
  2 Ddmz.fhda.edu     (153.18.251.40)    2.132 ms    2.266 ms    2.094 ms
  3 Cinic.fhda.edu    (153.18.253.126)   2.110 ms    2.145 ms    1.763 ms
  4 cenic.net         (137.164.32.140)   3.069 ms    2.875 ms    2.930 ms
  5 cenic.net         (137.164.22.31)    4.205 ms    4.870 ms    4.197 ms
  6 cenic.net         (137.164.22.167)   4.250 ms    4.159 ms    4.078 ms
  7 cogentco.com      (38.112.6.225)     5.062 ms    4.825 ms    5.020 ms
  8 cogentco.com      (66.28.4.69)       6.070 ms    6.207 ms    5.653 ms
  9 cogentco.com      (66.28.4.94)       6.070 ms    5.928 ms    5.499 ms
 10 cogentco.com      (154.54.2.226)     6.545 ms    6.399 ms    6.535 ms
 11 sbcglobal.net     (151.164.89.241)   6.379 ms    6.370 ms    6.210 ms
 12 sbcglobal.net     (64.161.1.45)      6.908 ms    6.748 ms    7.359 ms
 13 sbcglobal.net     (64.161.1.29)      7.023 ms    7.040 ms    6.734 ms
 14 snfc21.pbi.net    (151.164.191.49)   7.656 ms    7.129 ms    6.866 ms
 15 sbcglobal.net     (151.164.243.58)   7.844 ms    7.545 ms    7.353 ms
 16 pacbell.net       (209.232.138.114)  9.857 ms    9.535 ms    9.603 ms
 17 209.233.48.223    (209.233.48.223)  10.634 ms   10.771 ms   10.592 ms
 18 alpha.Xerox.COM   (13.1.64.93)      11.172 ms   11.048 ms   10.922 ms
```

Here there are 17 hops between source and destination. Note that some round trip times look unusual. It could be that a router is too busy to process the packet immediately.

Example 6

An interesting point is that a host can send a *traceroute* packet to itself. This can be done by specifying the host as the destination. The packet goes to the loopback address as we expect.

```
$ traceroute voyager.deanza.edu
traceroute to voyager.deanza.edu  (127.0.0.1), 30 hops max, 38 byte packets
  1 voyager        (127.0.0.1)     0.178 ms      0.086 ms      0.055 ms
```

Example 7

Finally, we use the *traceroute* program to find the route between fhda.edu and mhhe.com (McGraw-Hill server). We notice that we cannot find the whole route. When *traceroute* does not receive a response within 5 seconds, it prints an asterisk to signify a problem, and then tries the next hop.

```
$ traceroute mhhe.com
traceroute to mhhe.com (198.45.24.104), 30 hops max, 38 byte packets
 1  Dcore.fhda.edu       (153.18.31.254)    1.025 ms     0.892 ms     0.880 ms
 2  Ddmz.fhda.edu        (153.18.251.40)    2.141 ms     2.159 ms     2.103 ms
 3  Cinic.fhda.edu       (153.18.253.126)   2.159 ms     2.050 ms     1.992 ms
 4  cenic.net            (137.164.32.140)   3.220 ms     2.929 ms     2.943 ms
 5  cenic.net            (137.164.22.59)    3.217 ms     2.998 ms     2.755 ms
 6  SanJose1.net         (209.247.159.109)  10.653 ms   10.639 ms    10.618 ms
 7  SanJose2.net         (64.159.2.1)       10.804 ms   10.798 ms    10.634 ms
 8  Denver1.Level3.net   (64.159.1.114)     43.404 ms   43.367 ms    43.414 ms
 9  Denver2.Level3.net   (4.68.112.162)     43.533 ms   43.290 ms    43.347 ms
10  unknown              (64.156.40.134)    55.509 ms   55.462 ms    55.647 ms
11  mcleodusa1.net       (64.198.100.2)     60.961 ms   55.681 ms    55.461 ms
12  mcleodusa2.net       (64.198.101.202)   55.692 ms   55.617 ms    55.505 ms
13  mcleodusa3.net       (64.198.101.142)   56.059 ms   55.623 ms    56.333 ms
14  mcleodusa4.net       (209.253.101.178)  297.199 ms  192.790 ms  250.594 ms
15  eppg.com             (198.45.24.246)    71.213 ms   70.536 ms    70.663 ms
16  * * *
17  * * *
..............
```

9.7   ICMP PACKAGE

To give an idea of how ICMP can handle the sending and receiving of ICMP messages, we present our version of an ICMP package made of two modules: an input module and an output module. Figure 9.21 shows these two modules.

Figure 9.21   *ICMP package*

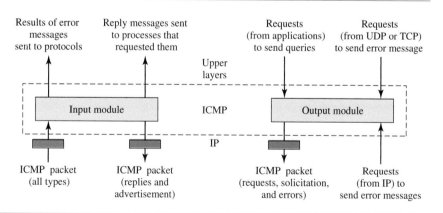

Input Module

The input module handles all received ICMP messages. It is invoked when an ICMP packet is delivered to it from the IP layer. If the received packet is a request or solicitation, the module creates a reply or an advertisement and sends it out.

If the received packet is a redirection message, the module uses the information to update the routing table. If the received packet is an error message, the module informs the protocol about the situation that caused the error. The pseudocode is shown below:

Input Module
Receive: an ICMP packet from the IP layer
1. If (the type is any of the three request types)
1. Create a reply.
2. Send the reply.
2. If (the type is a router solicitation)
1. If (station is a router)
1. Create a router advertisement.
2. Send the advertisement.
3. If (the type is one of the three reply messages or router advertisement)
1. Extract information in the data section of the packet.
2. Deliver extracted information to the process that requested it.
4. If (the type defines a redirection)
1. Modify the routing table.
5. If (the type defines an error message other than a redirection)
1. Inform the appropriate source protocol about the situation.
6. Return.

Output Module

The output module is responsible for creating request, solicitation, or error messages requested by a higher level or the IP protocol. The module receives a demand from IP, UDP, or TCP to send one of the ICMP error messages. If the demand is from IP, the output module must first check that the request is allowed. Remember, an ICMP message cannot be created for four situations: an IP packet carrying an ICMP error message, a fragmented IP packet, a multicast IP packet, or an IP packet having IP address 0.0.0.0 or 127.X.Y. Z.

The output module may also receive a demand from an application program to send one of the ICMP request or solicitation messages. The pseudocode is shown below:

Output Module
Receive: a demand
1. If (the demand defines an error message)
1. If (the demand is from IP)
1. If (the demand is forbidden)
1. Return.

Output Module (continued)
2. If (the type defines a redirection message)
1. If (the station is not a router)
1. Return.
3. Create the error message using the type, the code, and the IP packet.
2. If (the demand defines a request or solicitation)
1. Create a request or solicitation message.
3. Send the message.
4. Return.

9.8 KEY TERMS

address-mask-reply message	redirection
address-mask-request message	round-trip time (RTT)
destination-unreachable message	router-solicitation and router-advertisement messages
echo-request and echo-reply messages	
error-reporting message	source-quench message
Internet Control Message Protocol (ICMP)	time-exceeded message
parameter-problem message	timestamp-request and timestamp reply messages
query message	traceroute

9.9 SUMMARY

❏ The Internet Control Message Protocol (ICMP) sends five types of error reporting messages and four pairs of query messages to support the unreliable and connectionless Internet Protocol (IP).

❏ ICMP messages are encapsulated in IP datagrams.

❏ The destination-unreachable error message is sent to the source host when a datagram is undeliverable.

❏ The source-quench error message is sent in an effort to alleviate congestion.

❏ The time-exceeded message notifies a source host that (1) the time-to-live field has reached zero, or (2) fragments of a message have not arrived in a set amount of time.

❏ The parameter-problem message notifies a host that there is a problem in the header field of a datagram.

❏ The redirection message is sent to make the routing table of a host more efficient.

❏ The echo-request and echo-reply messages test the connectivity between two systems.

❏ The timestamp-request and timestamp-reply messages can determine the round-trip time between two systems or the difference in time between two systems.

❏ The address-mask-request and address-mask-reply messages are used to obtain the subnet mask.

❏ The router-solicitation and router-advertisement messages allow hosts to update their routing tables.

❏ The checksum for ICMP is calculated using both the header and the data fields of the ICMP message.

❏ Packet InterNet Groper (ping) is an application program that uses the services of ICMP to test the reachability of a host.

❏ A simple ICMP design can consist of an input module that handles incoming ICMP packets and an output module that handles demands for ICMP services.

9.10   PRACTICE SET

Exercises

1. Host A sends a timestamp-request message to host B and never receives a reply. Discuss three possible causes and the corresponding course of action.

2. Why is there a restriction on the generation of an ICMP message in response to a failed ICMP error message?

3. Host A sends a datagram to host B. Host B never receives the datagram and host A never receives notification of failure. Give two different explanations of what might have happened.

4. What is the purpose of including the IP header and the first 8 bytes of datagram data in the error reporting ICMP messages?

5. What is the maximum value of the pointer field in a parameter-problem message?

6. Give an example of a situation in which a host would never receive a redirection message.

7. Make a table showing which ICMP messages are sent by routers, which are sent by the nondestination hosts, and which are sent by the destination hosts.

8. Can the calculated sending time, receiving time, or round-trip time have a negative value? Why or why not? Give examples.

9. Why isn't the one-way time for a packet simply the round-trip time divided by two?

10. What is the minimum size of an ICMP packet? What is the maximum size of an ICMP packet?

11. What is the minimum size of an IP packet that carries an ICMP packet? What is the maximum size?

12. What is the minimum size of an Ethernet frame that carries an IP packet which in turn carries an ICMP packet? What is the maximum size?

13. How can we determine if an IP packet is carrying an ICMP packet?

14. Calculate the checksum for the following ICMP packet:
    Type: Echo Request   Identifier: 123   Sequence Number: 25   Message: Hello

15. A router receives an IP packet with source IP address 130.45.3.3 and destination IP address 201.23.4.6. The router cannot find the destination IP address in its routing table. Fill in the fields (as much as you can) for the ICMP message sent.

16. TCP receives a segment with destination port address 234. TCP checks and cannot find an open port for this destination. Fill in the fields for the ICMP message sent.

17. An ICMP message has arrived with the header (in hexadecimal):

> 03 0310 20 00 00 00 00

What is the type of the message? What is the code? What is the purpose of the message?

18. An ICMP message has arrived with the header (in hexadecimal):

> 05 00 11 12 11 0B 03 02

What is the type of the message? What is the code? What is the purpose of the message? What is the value of the last 4 bytes? What do the last bytes signify?

19. A computer sends a timestamp request. If its clock shows 5:20:30 A.M. (Universal Time), show the entries for the message.

20. Repeat Exercise 19 for the time of 3:40:30 P.M. (Universal Time).

21. A computer receives a timestamp request from another computer at 2:34:20 P.M. The value of the original timestamp is 52,453,000. If the sender clock is 5 ms slow, what is the one-way time?

22. A computer sends a timestamp request to another computer. It receives the corresponding timestamp reply at 3:46:07 A.M. The values of the original timestamp, receive timestamp, and transmit timestamp are 13,560,000, 13,562,000, and 13,564,300, respectively. What is the sending trip time? What is the receiving trip time? What is the round-trip time? What is the difference between the sender clock and the receiver clock?

23. If two computers are 5000 miles apart, what is the minimum time for a message to go from one to the other?

Research Activities

24. Use the ping program to test your own computer (loopback).

25. Use the ping program to test a host inside the United States.

26. Use the ping program to test a host outside the United States.

27. Use traceroute (or tracert) to find the route from your computer to a computer in a college or university.

28. Show how you can find the RTT between two routers using Exercise 27.

29. Find the RFCs related to the ICMP protocol. Is there an RFC for each particular message type?

CHAPTER 10

Internet Group Management Protocol (IGMP)

The IP protocol can be involved in two types of communication: unicasting and multi-casting. Unicasting is the communication between one sender and one receiver. It is a one-to-one communication. However, some processes sometimes need to send the same message to a large number of receivers simultaneously. This is called **multicasting,** which is a one-to-many communication. Multicasting has many applications. For example, multiple stockbrokers can simultaneously be informed of changes in a stock price, or travel agents can be informed of a trip cancellation. Some other applications include distance learning and video-on-demand.

The **Internet Group Management Protocol (IGMP)** is one of the necessary, but not sufficient (as we will see), protocols that is involved in multicasting. IGMP is a companion to the IP protocol. Figure 10.1 shows the position of the IGMP protocol in relation to other protocols in the network layer.

Figure 10.1 *Position of IGMP in the network layer*

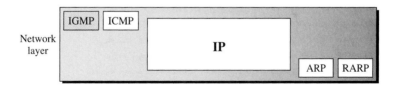

10.1 GROUP MANAGEMENT

For multicasting in the Internet we need routers that are able to route multicast packets. The routing tables of these routers must be updated using one of the multicasting rout-ing protocols that we will discuss in Chapter 15.

IGMP is not a multicasting routing protocol; it is a protocol that manages **group membership.** In any network, there are one or more multicast routers that distribute multicast packets to hosts or other routers. The IGMP protocol gives the **multicast routers** information about the membership status of hosts (routers) connected to the network.

A multicast router may receive thousands of multicast packets every day for different groups. If a router has no knowledge about the membership status of the hosts, it must broadcast all of these packets. This creates a lot of traffic and consumes bandwidth. A better solution is to keep a list of groups in the network for which there is at least one loyal member. IGMP helps the multicast router create and update this list.

> **IGMP is a group management protocol. It helps a multicast router create and update a list of loyal members related to each router interface.**

10.2   IGMP MESSAGES

IGMP has gone through two versions. We discuss IGMPv2, the current version. IGMPv2 has three types of **messages:** the **query,** the **membership report,** and the **leave report.** There are two types of **query messages, general** and **special** (see Figure 10.2).

Figure 10.2   *IGMP message types*

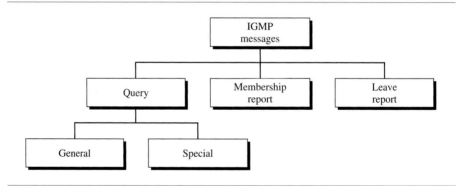

Message Format

Figure 10.3 shows the format of an IGMP (version 2) message.

Figure 10.3   *IGMP message format*

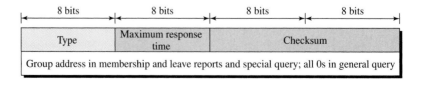

❏ **Type.** This 8-bit field defines the type of message as shown in Table 10.1. The value of the type is shown in both hexadecimal and binary notation.

Table 10.1   *IGMP type field*

Type	Value
General or Special Query	0x11 or 00010001
Membership Report	0x16 or 00010110
Leave Report	0x17 or 00010111

❏ **Maximum Response Time.** This 8-bit field defines the amount of time in which a query must be answered. The value is in tenths of a second; for example, if the value is 100, it means 10 s. The value is nonzero in the query message, it is set to zero in the other two message types. We will see its use shortly.

❏ **Checksum.** This is a 16-bit field carrying the checksum. The checksum is calculated over the 8-byte message.

❏ **Group address.** The value of this field is 0 for a general query message. The value defines the groupid (multicast address of the group) in the special query, the membership report, and the leave report messages.

10.3   IGMP OPERATION

IGMP operates locally. A multicast router connected to a network has a list of multicast addresses of the groups with at least one loyal member in that network (see Figure 10.4).

Figure 10.4   *IGMP operation*

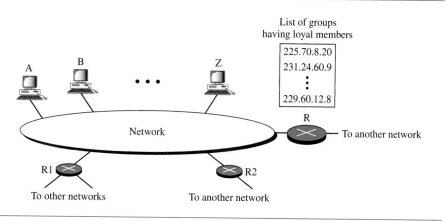

For each group, there is one router that has the duty of distributing the multicast packets destined for that group. This means that if there are three multicast routers connected to a network, their lists of **groupids** are mutually exclusive. For example, in the figure only router R distributes packets with the multicast address of 225.70.8.20.

A host or multicast router can have membership in a group. When a host has membership, it means that one of its processes (an application program) receives multicast packets from some group. When a router has membership, it means that a network connected to one of its other interfaces receives these multicast packets. We say that the host or the router has an *interest* in the group. In both cases, the host and the router keep a list of groupids and relay their interest to the distributing router.

For example, in Figure 10.4, router R is the distributing router. There are two other multicast routers (R1 and R2) that, depending on the group list maintained by router R, could be the recipients of router R in this network. R1 and R2 may be distributors for some of these groups in other networks, but not on this network.

Joining a Group

A host or a router can join a group. A host maintains a list of processes that have membership in a group. When a process wants to join a new group, it sends its request to the host. The host adds the name of the process and the name of the requested group to its list. If this is the first entry for this particular group, the host sends a membership report message. If this is not the first entry, there is no need to send the membership report since the host is already a member of the group; it already receives multicast packets for this group.

A router also maintains a list of groupids that shows membership for the networks connected to each interface. When there is new interest in a group for any of these interfaces, the router sends out a membership report. In other words, a router here acts like a host, but its group list is much broader because it is the accumulation of all loyal members that are connected to its interfaces. Note that the membership report is sent out of all interfaces except the one from which the new interest comes.

Figure 10.5 shows a membership report sent by a host or a router.

Figure 10.5   *Membership report*

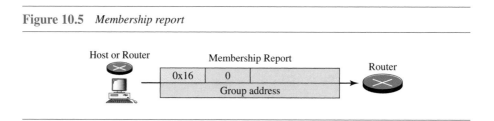

The protocol requires that the membership report be sent twice, one after the other within a few moments. In this way, if the first one is lost or damaged, the second one replaces it.

In IGMP, a membership report is sent twice, one after the other.

Leaving a Group

When a host sees that no process is interested in a specific group, it sends a leave report. Similarly, when a router sees that none of the networks connected to its interfaces is interested in a specific group, it sends a leave report about that group.

However, when a multicast router receives a leave report, it cannot immediately purge that group from its list because the report comes from just one host or router; there may be other hosts or routers that are still interested in that group. To make sure, the router sends a special query message and inserts the groupid (**multicast address**) related to the group. The router allows a specified time for any host or router to respond. If, during this time, no interest (membership report) is received, the router assumes that there are no loyal members in the network and it purges the group from its list. Figure 10.6 shows the mechanism for leaving a group.

Figure 10.6   *Leave report*

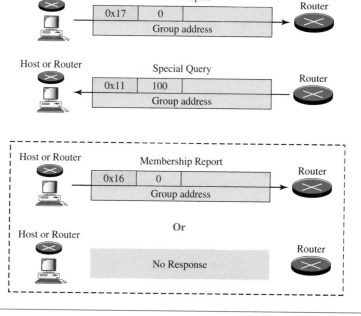

Monitoring Membership

A host or router can join a group by sending a membership report message. They can leave a group by sending a leave report message. However, sending these two types of reports is not enough. Consider the situation in which there is only one host interested in a group, but the host is shut down or removed from the system. The multicast router will never receive a leave report. How is this handled? The multicast router is responsible for monitoring all of the hosts or routers in a LAN to see if they want to continue their membership in a group.

The router periodically (by default, every 125 s) sends a general query message. In this message, the group address field is set to 0.0.0.0. This means the query for membership continuation is for all groups in which a host is involved, not just one.

The general query message does not define a particular group.

The router expects an answer for each group in its group list; even new groups may respond. The query message has a maximum response time of 10 s (the value of the field is actually 100, but this is in tenths of a second). When a host or router receives the general query message, it responds with a membership report if it is interested in a group. However, if there is a common interest (two hosts, for example, are interested in the same group), only one response is sent for that group to prevent unnecessary traffic. This is called a delayed response and will be discussed in the next section. Note that the query message must be sent by only one router (normally called the query router), also to prevent unnecessary traffic. We discuss this issue shortly. Figure 10.7 shows the query mechanism.

Figure 10.7   *General query message*

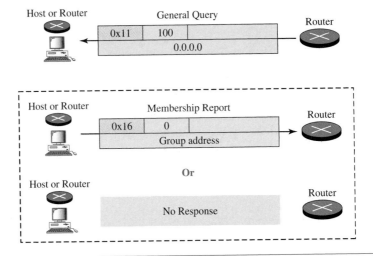

Delayed Response

To prevent unnecessary traffic, IGMP uses a **delayed response strategy.** When a host or router receives a query message, it does not respond immediately; it delays the response. Each host or router uses a random number to create a timer, which expires between 1 and 10 seconds. The expiration time can be in steps of 1 second or less. A timer is set for each group in the list. For example, the timer for the first group may expire in 2 seconds, but the timer for the third group may expire in 5 seconds. Each host or router waits until its timer has expired before sending a membership report message. During this waiting time, if the timer of another host or router, for the same group, expires earlier, that host or router sends a membership report. Because, as we will see shortly, the report is broadcast, the waiting host or router receives the report and knows that there is no need to send a duplicate report for this group; thus, the waiting station cancels its corresponding timer.

Example 1

Imagine there are three hosts in a network as shown in Figure 10.8.

Figure 10.8   *Example 1*

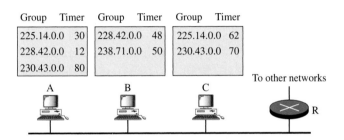

A query message was received at time 0; the random delay time (in tenths of seconds) for each group is shown next to the group address. Show the sequence of report messages.

Solution

The events occur in this sequence:

a. **Time 12:** The timer for 228.42.0.0 in host A expires and a membership report is sent, which is received by the router and every host including host B which cancels its timer for 228.42.0.0.

b. **Time 30:** The timer for 225.14.0.0 in host A expires and a membership report is sent, which is received by the router and every host including host C which cancels its timer for 225.14.0.0.

c. **Time 50:** The timer for 238.71.0.0 in host B expires and a membership report is sent, which is received by the router and every host.

d. **Time 70:** The timer for 230.43.0.0 in host C expires and a membership report is sent, which is received by the router and every host including host A which cancels its timer for 230.43.0.0.

Note that if each host had sent a report for every group in its list, there would have been seven reports; with this strategy only four reports are sent.

Query Router

Query messages may create a lot of responses. To prevent unnecessary traffic, IGMP designates one router as the **query router** for each network. Only this designated router sends the query message and the other routers are passive (they receive responses and update their lists).

10.4   ENCAPSULATION

The IGMP message is encapsulated in an IP datagram, which is itself encapsulated in a frame. See Figure 10.9.

Figure 10.9   *Encapsulation of IGMP packet*

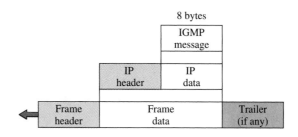

There are several issues related to **encapsulation** that we need to discuss here. We first discuss the issue at the IP level and then at the data link layer.

IP Layer

At the IP layer, three fields are of concern to us: the protocol field, the TTL field, and the destination IP address.

Protocol Field

The value of the protocol field is 2 for the IGMP protocol. Every IP packet carrying this value in its protocol field has data delivered to the IGMP protocol.

> **The IP packet that carries an IGMP packet has a value of 2 in its protocol field.**

TTL Field

When the message is encapsulated in the IP datagram, the value of TTL must be one. This is required because the domain of IGMP is the LAN. No IGMP message should travel beyond the LAN. A TTL value of 1 guarantees that the message does not leave the LAN since this value is decremented to zero by the next router and, consequently, the packet is discarded.

> **The IP packet that carries an IGMP packet has a value of 1 in its TTL field.**

Destination IP Addresses

Table 10.2 shows the destination IP address for each type of message.

Table 10.2 *Destination IP addresses*

Type	IP Destination Address
Query	224.0.0.1 All systems on this subnet
Membership Report	The multicast address of the group
Leave Report	224.0.0.2 All routers on this subnet

A query message is multicast using the multicast address 224.0.0.1 (all systems on this subnet; see Table 4.5 in Chapter 4). All hosts and all routers will receive the message.

A membership report is multicast using a destination address equal to the multicast address being reported (groupid). Every station (host or router) that receives the packet can immediately determine (from the header) the group for which a report has been sent. As discussed previously, the timers for the corresponding unsent reports can then be cancelled. Stations do not need to open the packet to find the groupid. This address is duplicated in a packet; it's part of the message itself and also a field in the IP header. The duplication prevents errors.

A leave report message is multicast using the multicast address 224.0.0.2 (all routers on this subnet) so that routers receive this type of message. Hosts receive this message too, but disregard it.

Data Link Layer

At the network layer, the IGMP message is encapsulated in an IP packet and is treated as an IP packet. However, because the IP packet has a multicast IP address, the ARP protocol cannot find the corresponding MAC (physical) address to forward the packet at the data link layer. What happens next depends on whether or not the underlying data link layer supports physical multicast addresses.

Physical Multicast Support

Most LANs support physical multicast addressing. Ethernet is one of them. An Ethernet physical address (MAC address) is six octets (48 bits) long. If the first 25 bits in an Ethernet address are 0000000100000000010111100, this identifies a physical multicast address for the TCP/IP protocol. The remaining 23 bits can be used to define a group. To convert an IP multicast address into an Ethernet address, the multicast router extracts the least significant 23 bits of a class D IP address and inserts them into a multicast Ethernet physical address (see Figure 10.10).

However, the group identifier of a class D IP address is 28 bits long, which implies that 5 bits are not used. This means that 32 (2^5) multicast addresses at the IP level are mapped to a single multicast address. In other words, the mapping is many-to-one instead of one-to-one. If the 5 left-most bits of the group identifier of a class D address are not all zeros, a host may receive packets that do not really belong to the group in

Figure 10.10 *Mapping class D to Ethernet physical address*

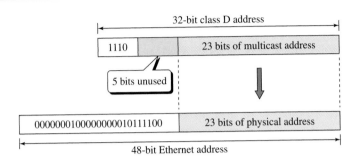

which it is involved. For this reason, the host must check the IP address and discard any packets that do not belong to it.

Other LANs support the same concept but have different methods of mapping.

> **An Ethernet multicast physical address is in the range**
> **01:00:5E:00:00:00   to   01:00:5E:7F:FF:FF.**

Example 2

Change the multicast IP address 230.43.14.7 to an Ethernet multicast physical address.

Solution

We can do this in two steps:

   a. We write the rightmost 23 bits of the IP address in hexadecimal. This can be done by changing the rightmost 3 bytes to hexadecimal and then subtracting 8 from the leftmost digit if it is greater than or equal to 8. In our example, the result is 2B:0E:07.

   b. We add the result of part a to the starting Ethernet multicast address, which is 01:00:5E:00:00:00. The result is

> **01:00:5E:2B:0E:07**

Example 3

Change the multicast IP address 238.212.24.9 to an Ethernet multicast address.

Solution

   a. The rightmost three bytes in hexadecimal are D4:18:09. We need to subtract 8 from the leftmost digit, resulting in 54:18:09.

   b. We add the result of part a to the Ethernet multicast starting address. The result is

> **01:00:5E:54:18:09**

No Physical Multicast Support

Most WANs do not support physical multicast addressing. To send a multicast packet through these networks, a process called *tunneling* is used. In **tunneling,** the multicast packet is encapsulated in a unicast packet and sent through the network, where it emerges from the other side as a multicast packet (see Figure 10.11).

Figure 10.11   *Tunneling*

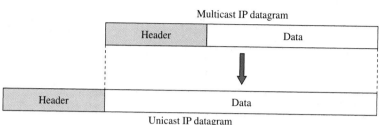

Multicast IP datagram

Unicast IP datagram

Netstat Utility

We used the *netstat* utility in previous chapters. In this section, we use it to find the multicast addresses supported by an interface.

Example 4

We use *netstat* with three options, -n, -r, and -a. The -n option gives the numeric versions of IP addresses, the -r option gives the routing table, and the -a option gives all addresses (unicast and multicast). Note that we show only the fields relative to our discussion.

```
$ netstat -nra
Kernel IP routing table
```

Destination	Gateway	Mask	Flags	Iface
153.18.16.0	0.0.0.0	255.255.240.0	U	eth0
169.254.0.0	0.0.0.0	255.255.0.0	U	eth0
127.0.0.0	0.0.0.0	255.0.0.0	U	lo
224.0.0.0	**0.0.0.0**	**224.0.0.0**	**U**	**eth0**
0.0.0.0	153.18.31.254	0.0.0.0	UG	eth0

Note that the multicast address is shown in color. Any packet with a multicast address from 224.0.0.0 to 239.255.255.255 is masked and delivered to the Ethernet interface.

10.5   IGMP PACKAGE

We can show how IGMP can handle the sending and receiving of IGMP packets through our simplified version of an IGMP package.

The package shows only the modules used in an IGMP host. The IGMP router is left as an exercise. In our design an IGMP package involves a group table, a set of timers, and four software modules: a group-joining module, a group-leaving module, an input module, and an output module. Figure 10.12 shows these six components and their interactions.

Figure 10.12   *IGMP package*

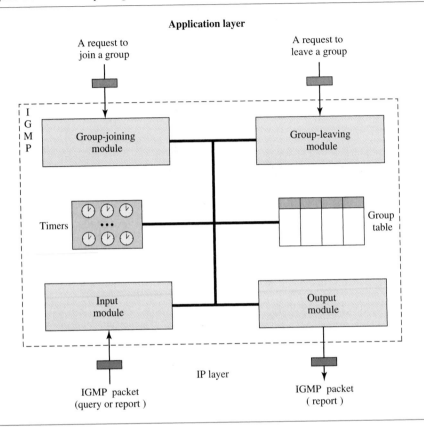

Group Table

The group table gives information about a multicast address that has at least one process as a member. The table has four fields: state, interface number, group address, and reference count (see Figure 10.13).

Figure 10.13   *Group table*

State	Interface No.	Group Address	Reference Count
....	....	....	....
....	....	....	....
....	....	....	....

❑   **State.** This field defines the state of the entry. It can have one of the following values: FREE, DELAYING, or IDLE. If the state is FREE, there are no processes left in the group. If the state is DELAYING, a report must be sent for this entry when the timer matures. If the state is IDLE, there is no timer running for this entry.

❑ **Interface number.** This field defines the interface through which the multicast packet is sent and received.

❑ **Group address.** This is the multicast address that defines the group.

❑ **Reference count.** This is the number of processes still interested in the group. Every time a process joins the group, the reference count is incremented. Every time a process leaves the group, the reference count is decremented. When this value is zero, the state is changed to FREE.

Timers

Each entry in the table in the DELAYING state has a timer to govern the sending of reports. Each timer has a randomly selected expiration time to prevent a burst of report generation. When an expiration time matures, a signal goes to the output module which then generates a report.

Group-Joining Module

A process that wants to join a group invokes this module. The module searches the group table to find an entry with the same multicast address. If found, the module increments the reference count to show that one more process has joined this group. If the multicast address is not found, the module creates a new entry and sets the reference count to one. In this case the module communicates to both the output module and the data link layer. It tells the output module to send a membership report. It tells the data link layer to update its configuration table so that this type of multicast packet can be received.

Group-Joining Module
Receive: a request from a process to join a group
1. Look for the corresponding entry in the table.
2. If (found)
1. Increment the reference count.
3. If (not found)
1. Create an entry with reference count set to one.
2. Add the entry to the table.
3. Request a membership report from the output module.
4. Inform the data link layer to update its configuration table.
4. Return.

Group-Leaving Module

A process that wants to leave a group invokes this module. The module searches the group table to find an entry with the same multicast address. If found, the module decrements the reference count. If the count is zero, the state is changed to FREE and a leave report is sent.

Group-Leaving Module

Receive: a request from a process to leave a group

1. Look for the corresponding entry in the table.
2. If (found)
    1. Decrement the reference count.
    2. If (reference count is zero)
        1. If (any timer for this entry)
            1. Cancel the timer.
        2. Change the state to FREE.
        3. Request a leave report from the output module.
3. Return.

Input Module

The input module is invoked by an IGMP message. If the message is a query, the module starts a timer for each entry in the group table with an IDLE state and changes the state to DELAYING. To do this, the module generates a random number between zero and the maximum delay time and creates a timer with the maturation time equal to this random number. The random number generation is required so that reports will be sent by the output module at different times to prevent congestion.

If the message received is a membership report, the module checks for a corresponding entry in its table. If it is found and the state is DELAYING, it means another host on the network has sent a membership report for this group and there is no need for this host to send another report. The module cancels the timer and changes the state to IDLE. Remember that hosts do not receive leave reports.

Input Module

Receive: an IGMP message

1. Check the message type.
2. If (query)
    1. Start a timer for each entry in the table with the state IDLE.
    2. Change each IDLE state to DELAYING state.
    3. Return.
3. If (membership report)
    1. Look for the corresponding entry in the table.
    2. If (found and state is DELAYING)
        1. Cancel the timer for this entry.
        2. Change the state to IDLE.
4. Return.

Output Module

The output module is invoked by a matured timer or a request from a joining group or a leaving group. It then looks for the corresponding entry and, if the state is DELAYING, the module creates a report and sends it. It then resets the state to IDLE.

Output Module
Receive: a signal from a timer or a request from joining or leaving module
1. If the message comes from a timer.
1. If (found and state is DELAYING)
1. Create a membership report.
2. Reset the state to IDLE.
2. If the message comes from the group-joining module.
1. Create a membership report.
3. If the message comes from the group-leaving module.
1. Create a leave report.
4. Send the message.
5. Return.

10.6   KEY TERMS

delayed response strategy	multicast address
general query message	multicast router
group membership	multicasting
groupid	query message
Internet Group Management Protocol (IGMP)	query router
leave report	special query message
membership report	tunneling

10.7   SUMMARY

❑ Multicasting is the sending of the same message to more than one receiver simultaneously.

❑ The Internet Group Management Protocol (IGMP) helps multicast routers create and update a list of loyal members related to a router interface.

❑ The three IGMP message types are the query message, the membership report, and the leave report.

❑ IGMP operates locally.

❑ A host or router can have membership in a group.

❑ A host maintains a list of processes that have membership in a group.

❑ A router maintains a list of groupids that shows group membership for each interface.

❑ A router or host sends a membership report to join a group.

❑ A router or host sends a leave report to leave a group.

❑ A router sends a general query message to monitor group membership.

❑ A delayed response strategy prevents unnecessary traffic on a LAN.

❑ The IGMP message is encapsulated in an IP datagram.

❑ Most LANs, including Ethernet, support physical multicast addressing.

❑ WANs that do not support physical multicast addressing can use a process called tunneling to send multicast packets.

❑ An IGMP package can consist of a host group table, a set of timers, and four software modules: an input module, an output module, a group-joining module, and a group-leaving module.

10.8   PRACTICE SET

Exercises

1. Why is there no need for the IGMP message to travel outside its own network?

2. A multicast router list contains four groups (W, X, Y, and Z). There are three hosts on the LAN. Host A has three loyal members belonging to group W and one loyal member belonging to group X. Host B has two loyal members belonging to group W and one loyal member belonging to group Y. Host C has no processes belonging to any group. Show the IGMP messages involved in monitoring.

3. A multicast address for a group is 231.24.60.9. What is its 48-bit Ethernet address for a LAN using TCP/IP?

4. If a router has 20 entries in its group table, should it send 20 different queries periodically or just one? Explain your answer.

5. If a host wants to continue membership in five groups, should it send five different membership report messages or just one?

6. A router with IP address 202.45.33.21 and physical Ethernet address 23:4A:45:12:EC:D1 sends an IGMP general query message. Show all of the entries in the message.

7. Encapsulate the message of Exercise 6 in an IP packet. Fill in all the fields.

8. Encapsulate the message of Exercise 7 in an Ethernet frame. Fill in all the fields.

9. A host with IP address 124.15.13.1 and physical Ethernet address 4A:22:45:12:E1:E2 sends an IGMP membership report message about groupid 228.45.23.11. Show all of the entries in the message.

10. Encapsulate the message of Exercise 9 in an IP packet. Fill in all the fields.

11. Encapsulate the message of Exercise 10 in an Ethernet frame. Fill in all the fields.

12. A router on an Ethernet network has received a multicast IP packet with groupid 226.17.18.4. When the host checks its multicast group table, it finds this address.

Show how the router sends this packet to the recipients by encapsulating the IP packet in an Ethernet frame. Show all of the entries of the Ethernet frame. The outgoing IP address of the router is 185.23.5.6 and its outgoing physical address is 4A224512E1E2. Does the router need the services of ARP?

13. What if the router in Exercise 12 cannot find the groupid in its table?

14. Redo Exercise 12 with a physical network that does not support physical multicast addressing.

15. A host with IP address 114.45.7.9 receives an IGMP query. When it checks its group table, it finds no entries. What action should the host take? Should it send any messages? If so, show the packet fields.

16. A host with IP address 222.5.7.19 receives an IGMP query. When it checks its routing table, it finds two entries in its table: 227.4.3.7 and 229.45.6.23. What action should the host take? Should it send any messages? If so, what type and how many? Show the fields.

17. A host with IP address 186.4.77.9 receives a request from a process to join a group with groupid 230.44.101.34. When the host checks its group table, it does not find an entry for this groupid. What action should the host take? Should it send any messages? If so, show the packet field.

18. Redo Exercise 17 with the host finding an entry in its table.

19. A router with IP address 184.4.7.9 receives a report from a host that wants to join a group with groupid 232.54.10.34. When the router checks its group table, it does not find an entry for this groupid. What action should the router take? Should it send any messages? If so, show the packet fields.

20. Redo Exercise 19 with the router finding an entry in its table.

21. A router sends a query and receives only three reports about groupids 225.4.6.7, 225.32.56.8, and 226.34.12.9. When it checks its routing table, it finds five entries: 225.4.6.7, 225.11.6.8, 226.34.12.9, 226.23.22.67, and 229.12.4.89. What action should be taken?

22. The contents of an IGMP message in hexadecimal notation are:

> 11 00 EE FF 00 00 00 00

Answer the following questions:
a. What is the type?
b. What is the checksum?
c. What is the groupid?

23. The contents of an IGMP message in hexadecimal notation are:

> 16 00 F9 C0 E1 2A 13 14

Answer the following questions:
a. What is the type?
b. What is the checksum?
c. What is the groupid?

24. Is there an error in the following hexadecimal representation of an IGMP message?

11 00 A0 11 E1 2A 13 14

25. Is there an error in the following hexadecimal representation of an IGMP message?

17 00 A0 11 00 00 00 00

26. How many multicast addresses can be supported for the IP protocol in Ethernet?
27. How many multicast addresses can be supported by the IP protocol?
28. What is the size of address space lost when we transform a multicast IP address to an Ethernet multicast address?
29. Change the following IP multicast addresses to Ethernet multicast addresses. How many of them specify the same Ethernet address?
   a. 224.18.72.8
   b. 235.18.72.8
   c. 237.18.6.88
   d. 224.88.12.8

Research Activities

30. Modify the IGMP package in the text to be also applicable to a router.
31. Do some research on IGMPv1. What is the size of the type field? Is there any field in the first version that is not in the second? Are versions 1 and 2 compatible? If a router supporting version 2 receives a message in version 1, what can the router do? If a router supporting version 1 receives a message in version 2, what can the router do?
32. Use *netstat* to find if your server supports multicast addressing.
33. Find the RFCs related to IGMP protocols.

CHAPTER 11

User Datagram Protocol (UDP)

The original TCP/IP protocol suite specifies two protocols for the transport layer: UDP and TCP. We first focus on UDP, the simpler of the two, before discussing TCP in Chapter 12. A new transport-layer protocol, SCTP, has been designed, which we will discuss in Chapter 13.

Figure 11.1 shows the relationship of UDP to the other protocols and layers of the TCP/IP protocol suite: UDP lies between the application layer and the IP layer and, like TCP, serves as the intermediary between the application programs and the network operations.

Figure 11.1 *Position of UDP in the TCP/IP protocol suite*

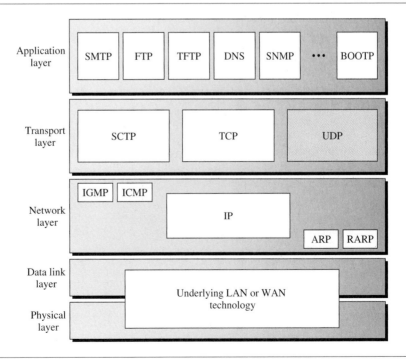

A transport layer protocol usually has several responsibilities. One is to create a process-to-process (a **process** is a running application program) communication; UDP uses port numbers to accomplish this. Another responsibility is to provide control mechanisms at the transport level. UDP does this task at a very minimal level. There is no flow control mechanism and there is no acknowledgment for received packets. UDP, however, does provide error control to some extent. If UDP detects an error in the received packet, it silently drops it.

The **transport layer** also provides a connection mechanism for the processes. The processes must be able to send streams of data to the transport layer. It is the responsibility of the transport layer at the sending station to make the connection with the receiver, chop the stream into transportable units, number them, and send them one by one. It is the responsibility of the transport layer at the receiving end to wait until all the different units belonging to the same process have arrived, check and pass those that are error free, and deliver them to the receiving process as a stream. After the entire stream has been sent, the transport layer closes the connection. UDP does not do any of the above. It can only receive a data unit from the processes and deliver it, unreliably, to the receiver. The data unit must be small enough to fit in a UDP packet.

UDP is called a *connectionless, unreliable* transport protocol. It does not add anything to the services of IP except for providing process-to-process communication instead of host-to-host communication. Also, it performs very limited error checking.

If UDP is so powerless, why would a process want to use it? With the disadvantages come some advantages. UDP is a very simple protocol using a minimum of overhead. If a process wants to send a small message and does not care much about reliability, it can use UDP. Sending a small message using UDP takes much less interaction between the sender and receiver than using TCP.

11.1 PROCESS-TO-PROCESS COMMUNICATION

Before we examine UDP, we must first understand host-to-host communication and **process-to-process communication** and the difference between them.

The IP is responsible for communication at the computer level (host-to-host communication). As a network-layer protocol, IP can deliver the message only to the destination computer. However, this is an incomplete delivery. The message still needs to be handed to the correct process. This is where a transport layer protocol such as UDP takes over. UDP is responsible for delivery of the message to the appropriate process. Figure 11.2 shows the domains of IP and UDP.

Port Numbers

Although there are several ways to achieve process-to-process communication, the most common is through the **client-server** paradigm. A process on the local host, called a *client*, needs services from a process usually on the remote host, called a *server*.

Both processes (client and server) have the same name. For example, to get the day and time from a remote machine, we need a Daytime client process running on the local host and a Daytime server process running on a remote machine.

Figure 11.2   *UDP versus IP*

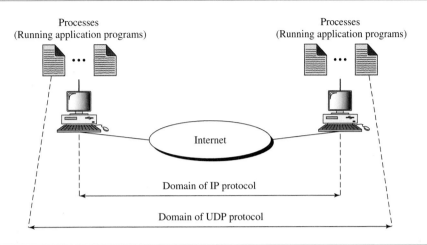

However, operating systems today support both multiuser and multiprogramming environments. A remote computer can run several server programs at the same time, just as several local computers can run one or more client programs at the same time. For communication, we must define the

❏ Local host
❏ Local process
❏ Remote host
❏ Remote process

The local host and the remote host are defined using IP addresses. To define the processes, we need second identifiers called **port numbers.** In the TCP/IP protocol suite, the port numbers are integers between 0 and 65,535.

The client program defines itself with a port number, called the **ephemeral port number.** The word ephemeral means *short lived* and is used because the life of a client is normally short. An ephemeral port number is recommended to be greater than 1023 for some client/server programs to work properly (see Chapter 16).

The server process must also define itself with a port number. This port number, however, cannot be chosen randomly. If the computer at the server site runs a server process and assigns a random number as the port number, the process at the client site that wants to access that server and use its services will not know the port number. Of course, one solution would be to send a special packet and request the port number of a specific server, but this creates more overhead. TCP/IP has decided to use universal port numbers for servers; these are called **well-known port numbers.** There are some exceptions to this rule; for example, there are clients that are assigned well-known port numbers. Every client process knows the well-known port number of the corresponding server process. For example, while the Daytime client process, discussed above, can use an ephemeral (temporary) port number 52,000 to identify itself, the Daytime server process must use the well-known (permanent) port number 13. Figure 11.3 shows this concept.

Figure 11.3   *Port numbers*

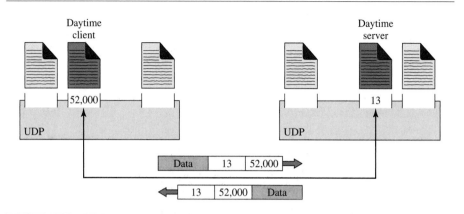

It should be clear by now that the IP addresses and port numbers play different roles in selecting the final destination of data. The destination IP address defines the host among the different hosts in the world. After the host has been selected, the port number defines one of the processes on this particular host (see Figure 11.4).

Figure 11.4   *IP addresses versus port numbers*

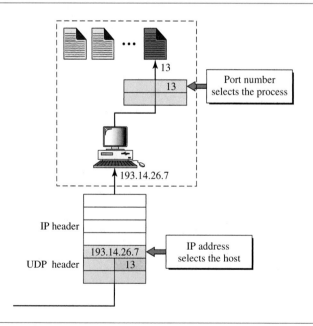

ICANN Ranges

ICANN has divided the port numbers into three ranges: well-known, registered, and dynamic (or private) as shown in Figure 11.5.

Figure 11.5   *ICANN ranges*

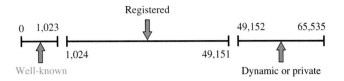

❑ **Well-known ports.** The ports ranging from 0 to 1,023 are assigned and controlled by ICANN. These are the well-known ports.

❑ **Registered ports.** The ports ranging from 1,024 to 49,151 are not assigned or controlled by ICANN. They can only be registered with ICANN to prevent duplication.

❑ **Dynamic ports.** The ports ranging from 49,152 to 65,535 are neither controlled nor registered. They can be used as temporary or private port numbers. The original recommendation was that the ephemeral port numbers for clients to be chosen from this range. However, most systems do not follow this recommendation.

> **The well-known port numbers are less than 1024.**

Well-Known Ports for UDP

Table 11.1 shows some well-known port numbers used by UDP. Some port numbers can be used by both UDP and TCP. We will discuss them when we talk about TCP in Chapter 12.

Table 11.1   *Well-known ports used with UDP*

Port	Protocol	Description
7	Echo	Echoes a received datagram back to the sender
9	Discard	Discards any datagram that is received
11	Users	Active users
13	Daytime	Returns the date and the time
17	Quote	Returns a quote of the day
19	Chargen	Returns a string of characters
53	Nameserver	Domain Name Service
67	Bootps	Server port to download bootstrap information
68	Bootpc	Client port to download bootstrap information
69	TFTP	Trivial File Transfer Protocol
111	RPC	Remote Procedure Call
123	NTP	Network Time Protocol
161	SNMP	Simple Network Management Protocol
162	SNMP	Simple Network Management Protocol (trap)

Example 1

In UNIX, the well-known ports are stored in a file called /etc/services. Each line in this file gives the name of the server and the well-known port number. We can use the grep utility to extract the line corresponding to the desired application. The following shows the port for TFTP. Note TFTP can use port 69 on either UDP or TCP.

$grep	tftp	/etc/services
tftp	69/tcp	
tftp	69/udp	

SNMP uses two port numbers (161 and 162), each for a different purpose, as we will see in Chapter 21.

$grep	snmp /etc/services	
snmp	161/tcp	#Simple Net Mgmt Proto
snmp	161/udp	#Simple Net Mgmt Proto
snmptrap	162/udp	#Traps for SNMP

Socket Addresses

As we have seen, UDP needs two identifiers, the IP address and the port number, at each end to make a connection. The combination of an IP address and a port number is called a **socket address.** The client socket address defines the client process uniquely just as the server socket address defines the server process uniquely (see Figure 11.6).

Figure 11.6   *Socket address*

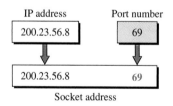

To use the services of UDP, we need a pair of socket addresses: the client socket address and the server socket address. These four pieces of information are part of the IP header and the UDP header. The IP header contains the IP addresses; the UDP header contains the port numbers.

11.2   USER DATAGRAM

UDP packets, called **user datagrams,** have a fixed-size header of 8 bytes. Figure 11.7 shows the format of a user datagram.

Figure 11.7   *User datagram format*

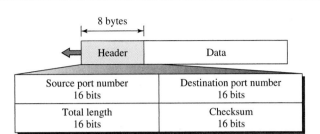

The fields are as follows:

❑ **Source port number.** This is the port number used by the process running on the source host. It is 16 bits long, which means that the port number can range from 0 to 65,535. If the source host is the client (a client sending a request), the port number, in most cases, is an ephemeral port number requested by the process and chosen by the UDP software running on the source host. If the source host is the server (a server sending a response), the port number, in most cases, is a well-known port number.

❑ **Destination port number.** This is the port number used by the process running on the destination host. It is also 16 bits long. If the destination host is the server (a client sending a request), the port number, in most cases, is a well-known port number. If the destination host is the client (a server sending a response), the port number, in most cases, is an ephemeral port number. In this case, the server copies the ephemeral port number it has received in the request packet.

❑ **Length.** This is a 16-bit field that defines the total length of the user datagram, header plus data. The 16 bits can define a total length of 0 to 65,535 bytes. However, the total length needs to be much less because an UDP user datagram is stored in an IP datagram with the total length of 65535 bytes.

The length field in a UDP user datagram is actually not necessary. A user datagram is encapsulated in an IP datagram. There is a field in the IP datagram that defines the total length. There is another field in the IP datagram that defines the length of the header. So if we subtract the value of the second field from the first, we can deduce the length of the UDP datagram that is encapsulated in an IP datagram.

UDP length = IP length − IP header's length

However, the designers of the UDP protocol felt that it was more efficient for the destination UDP to calculate the length of the data from the information provided in the UDP user datagram rather than asking the IP software to supply this information. We should remember that when the IP software delivers the UDP user datagram to the UDP layer, it has already dropped the IP header.

❑ **Checksum.** This field is used to detect errors over the entire user datagram (header plus data). The checksum is discussed in the next section.

11.3   CHECKSUM

We have already talked about the concept of the **checksum** and the way it is calculated in Chapter 8. We have also shown how to calculate the checksum for the IP and ICMP packet. We now show how this is done for UDP.

UDP checksum calculation is different from the one for IP and ICMP. Here the checksum includes three sections: a pseudoheader, the UDP header, and the data coming from the application layer.

The **pseudoheader** is the part of the header of the IP packet in which the user datagram is to be encapsulated with some fields filled with 0s (see Figure 11.8).

Figure 11.8   *Pseudoheader for checksum calculation*

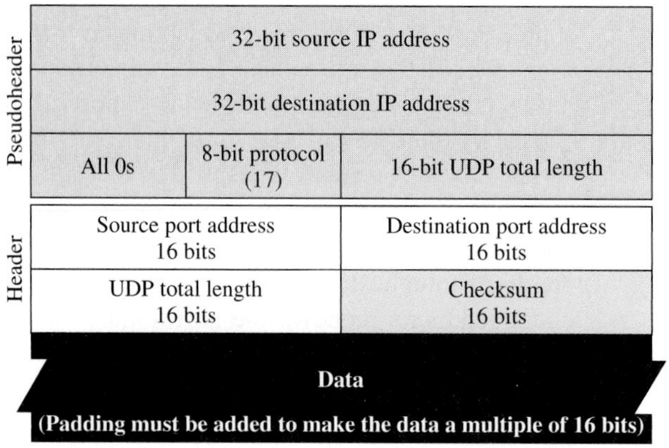

If the checksum does not include the pseudoheader, a user datagram may arrive safe and sound. However, if the IP header is corrupted, it may be delivered to the wrong host.

The protocol field is added to ensure that the packet belongs to UDP, and not to TCP. We will see later that if a process can use either UDP or TCP, the destination port number can be the same. The value of the protocol field for UDP is 17. If this value is changed during transmission, the checksum calculation at the receiver will detect it and UDP drops the packet. It is not delivered to the wrong protocol.

Note the similarities between the pseudoheader fields and the last 12 bytes of the IP header.

Checksum Calculation at Sender

The sender follows these eight steps to calculate the checksum:

1. Add the pseudoheader to the UDP user datagram.
2. Fill the checksum field with zeros.
3. Divide the total bits into 16-bit (2-byte) words.
4. If the total number of bytes is not even, add 1 byte of padding (all 0s). The padding is only for the purpose of calculating the checksum and will be discarded afterwards.

5. Add all 16-bit sections using one's complement arithmetic.
6. Complement the result (change all 0s to 1s and all 1s to 0s), which is a 16-bit number, and insert it in the checksum field.
7. Drop the pseudoheader and any added padding.
8. Deliver the UDP user datagram to the IP software for encapsulation.

Note that the order of the rows in the pseudoheader does not make any difference in checksum calculation. Also, adding 0s does not change the result. For this reason, the software that calculates the checksum can easily add the whole IP header (20 bytes) to the UDP datagram, set the first bytes to zero, set the TTL field to zero, replace the IP checksum with UDP length, and calculate the checksum. The result would be the same.

Checksum Calculation at Receiver

The receiver follows these six steps to calculate the checksum:

1. Add the pseudoheader to the UDP user datagram.
2. Add padding if needed.
3. Divide the total bits into 16-bit sections.
4. Add all 16-bit sections using one's complement arithmetic.
5. Complement the result.
6. If the result is all 0s, drop the pseudoheader and any added padding and accept the user datagram. If the result is anything else, discard the user datagram.

An Example

Figure 11.9 shows the checksum calculation for a very small user datagram with only 7 bytes of data. Because the number of bytes of data is odd, padding is added for checksum calculation. The pseudoheader as well as the padding will be dropped when the user datagram is delivered to IP.

Figure 11.9   *Checksum calculation of a simple UDP user datagram*

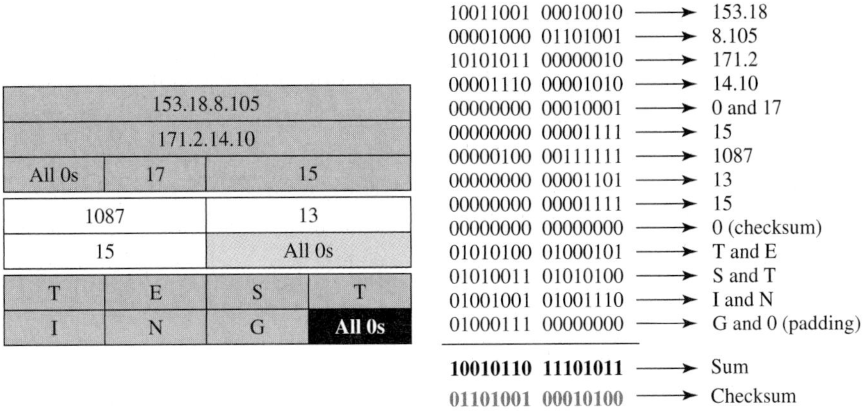

10011001 00010010	⟶	153.18	
00001000 01101001	⟶	8.105	
10101011 00000010	⟶	171.2	
00001110 00001010	⟶	14.10	
00000000 00010001	⟶	0 and 17	
00000000 00001111	⟶	15	
00000100 00111111	⟶	1087	
00000000 00001101	⟶	13	
00000000 00001111	⟶	15	
00000000 00000000	⟶	0 (checksum)	
01010100 01000101	⟶	T and E	
01010011 01010100	⟶	S and T	
01001001 01001110	⟶	I and N	
01000111 00000000	⟶	G and 0 (padding)	
10010110 11101011	⟶	Sum	
01101001 00010100	⟶	Checksum	

Pseudoheader box (left):
153.18.8.105
171.2.14.10
All 0s | 17 | 15
1087 | 13
15 | All 0s
T | E | S | T
I | N | G | All 0s

Optional Use of the Checksum

The calculation of the checksum and its inclusion in a user datagram is optional. If the checksum is not calculated, the field is filled with 0s. One might ask, when the UDP software on the destination computer receives a user datagram with a checksum value of zero, how can it determine if the checksum was not used or if it was used and the result happened to be all 0s? The answer is very simple. If the source does calculate the checksum and the result happens to be all 0s, it must be complemented. So what is sent is all 1s. Note that a calculated checksum can never be all 0s because this implies that the sum is all 1s which is impossible in two's complement arithmetic (see Appendix C).

11.4   UDP OPERATION

UDP uses concepts common to the transport layer. These concepts will be discussed here briefly, and then expanded in the next chapter on the TCP protocol.

Connectionless Services

As mentioned previously, UDP provides a **connectionless service.** This means that each user datagram sent by UDP is an independent datagram. There is no relationship between the different user datagrams even if they are coming from the same source process and going to the same destination program. The user datagrams are not numbered. Also, there is no connection establishment and no connection termination as is the case for TCP. This means that each user datagram can travel on a different path.

One of the ramifications of being connectionless is that the process that uses UDP cannot send a stream of data to UDP and expect UDP to chop them into different related user datagrams. Instead each request must be small enough to fit into one user datagram. Only those processes sending short messages should use UDP.

Flow and Error Control

UDP is a very simple, unreliable transport protocol. There is no flow control, and hence no window mechanism. The receiver may overflow with incoming messages.

There is no error control mechanism in UDP except for the checksum. This means that the sender does not know if a message has been lost or duplicated. When the receiver detects an error through the checksum, the user datagram is silently discarded.

The lack of **flow control** and **error control** means that the process using UDP should provide for these mechanisms.

Encapsulation and Decapsulation

To send a message from one process to another, the UDP protocol encapsulates and decapsulates messages (see Figure 11.10).

Encapsulation

When a process has a message to send through UDP, it passes the message to UDP along with a pair of socket addresses and the length of data. UDP receives the data and

Figure 11.10   *Encapsulation and decapsulation*

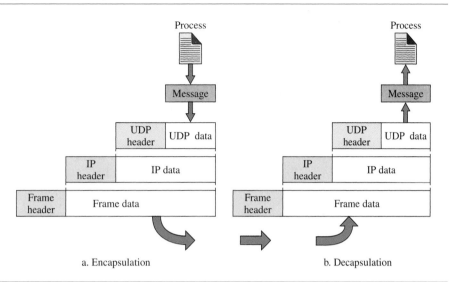

a. Encapsulation   b. Decapsulation

adds the UDP header. UDP then passes the user datagram to IP with the socket addresses. IP adds its own header, using the value 17 in the protocol field, indicating that the data has come from the UDP protocol. The IP datagram is then passed to the data link layer. The data link layer receives the IP datagram, adds its own header (and possibly a trailer), and passes it to the physical layer. The physical layer encodes the bits into electrical or optical signals and sends it to the remote machine.

Decapsulation

When the message arrives at the destination host, the physical layer decodes the signals into bits and passes it to the data link layer. The data link layer uses the header (and the trailer) to check the data. If there is no error, the header and trailer are dropped and the datagram is passed to IP. The IP software does its own checking. If there is no error, the header is dropped and the user datagram is passed to UDP with the sender and receiver IP addresses. UDP uses the checksum to check the entire user datagram. If there is no error, the header is dropped and the application data along with the sender socket address is passed to the process. The sender socket address is passed to the process in case it needs to respond to the message received.

Queuing

We have talked about ports without discussing the actual implementation of them. In UDP, queues are associated with ports (see Figure 11.11).

At the client site, when a process starts, it requests a port number from the operating system. Some implementations create both an incoming and an outgoing queue associated with each process. Other implementations create only an incoming queue associated with each process.

Figure 11.11 *Queues in UDP*

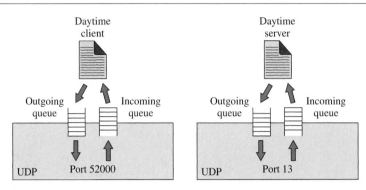

Note that even if a process wants to communicate with multiple processes, it obtains only one port number and eventually one outgoing and one incoming **queue.** The queues opened by the client are, in most cases, identified by ephemeral port numbers. The queues function as long as the process is running. When the process terminates, the queues are destroyed.

The client process can send messages to the outgoing queue by using the source port number specified in the request. UDP removes the messages one by one, and, after adding the UDP header, delivers them to IP. An outgoing queue can overflow. If this happens, the operating system can ask the client process to wait before sending any more messages.

When a message arrives for a client, UDP checks to see if an incoming queue has been created for the port number specified in the destination port number field of the user datagram. If there is such a queue, UDP sends the received user datagram to the end of the queue. If there is no such queue, UDP discards the user datagram and asks the ICMP protocol to send a *port unreachable* message to the server. All of the incoming messages for one particular client program, whether coming from the same or a different server, are sent to the same queue. An incoming queue can overflow. If this happens, UDP drops the user datagram and asks for a port unreachable message to be sent to the server.

At the server site, the mechanism of creating queues is different. In its simplest form, a server asks for incoming and outgoing queues using its well-known port when it starts running. The queues remain open as long as the server is running.

When a message arrives for a server, UDP checks to see if an incoming queue has been created for the port number specified in the destination port number field of the user datagram. If there is such a queue, UDP sends the received user datagram to the end of the queue. If there is no such queue, UDP discards the user datagram and asks the ICMP protocol to send a port unreachable message to the client. All of the incoming messages for one particular server, whether coming from the same or a different client, are sent to the same queue. An incoming queue can overflow. If this happens, UDP drops the user datagram and asks for a port unreachable message to be sent to the client.

When a server wants to respond to a client, it sends messages to the outgoing queue using the source port number specified in the request. UDP removes the messages one by one, and, after adding the UDP header, delivers them to IP. An outgoing queue can overflow. If this happens, the operating system asks the server to wait before sending any more messages.

Multiplexing and Demultiplexing

In a host running a TCP/IP protocol suite, there is only one UDP but possibly several processes that may want to use the services of UDP. To handle this situation, UDP multiplexes and demultiplexes (see Figure 11.12).

Figure 11.12   *Multiplexing and demultiplexing*

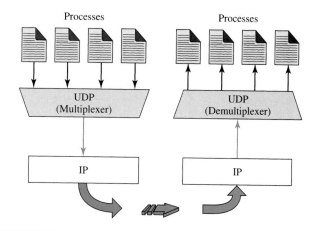

Multiplexing

At the sender site, there may be several processes that need to send user datagrams. However, there is only one UDP. This is a many-to-one relationship and requires multiplexing. UDP accepts messages from different processes, differentiated by their assigned port numbers. After adding the header, UDP passes the user datagram to the IP.

Demultiplexing

At the receiver site, there is only one UDP. However, we may have many processes that can receive user datagrams. This is a one-to-many relationship and requires demultiplexing. UDP receives user datagrams from IP. After error checking and dropping of the header, UDP delivers each message to the appropriate process based on the port numbers.

11.5   USE OF UDP

The following lists some uses of the UDP protocol:

❏   UDP is suitable for a process that requires simple request-response communication with little concern for flow and error control. It is not usually used for a process such as FTP that needs to send bulk data (see Chapter 19).

❏ UDP is suitable for a process with internal flow and error-control mechanisms. For example, the Trivial File Transfer Protocol (TFTP) (see Chapter 19) process includes flow and error control. It can easily use UDP.

❏ UDP is a suitable transport protocol for multicasting. Multicasting capability is embedded in the UDP software but not in the TCP software.

❏ UDP is used for management processes such as SNMP (see Chapter 21).

❏ UDP is used for some route updating protocols such as Routing Information Protocol (RIP) (see Chapter 14).

11.6   UDP PACKAGE

To show how UDP handles the sending and receiving of UDP packets, we present a simple version of the UDP package.

We can say that the UDP package involves five components: a control-block table, input queues, a control-block module, an input module, and an output module. Figure 11.13 shows these five components and their interactions.

Figure 11.13   *UDP design*

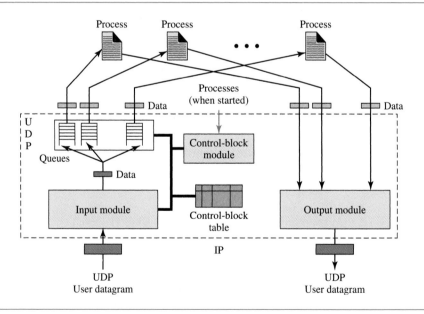

Control-Block Table

In our package, UDP has a control-block table to keep track of the open ports. Each entry in this table has a minimum of four fields: the state, which can be FREE or IN-USE, the process ID, the port number, and the corresponding queue number.

Input Queues

Our UDP package uses a set of input queues, one for each process. In this design, we do not use output queues.

Control-Block Module

The control-block module is responsible for the management of the control-block table. When a process starts, it asks for a port number from the operating system. The operating system assigns well-known port numbers to servers and ephemeral port numbers to clients. The process passes the process ID and the port number to the control-block module to create an entry in the table for the process. The module does not create the queues. The field for queue number has a value of zero. Note that we have not included a strategy to deal with a table that is full.

Control-Block Module
Receive: a process ID and a port number
1. Search the control block table for a FREE entry.
1. If (not found)
1. Delete an entry using a predefined strategy.
2. Create a new entry with the state IN-USE.
3. Enter the process ID and the port number.
2. Return.

Input Module

The input module receives a user datagram from the IP. It searches the control-block table to find an entry having the same port number as this user datagram. If the entry is found, the module uses the information in the entry to enqueue the data. If the entry is not found, it generates an ICMP message.

Input Module
Receive: a user datagram from IP
1. Look for the corresponding entry in the control-block table.
1. If (found)
1. Check the queue field to see if a queue is allocated.
1. If (no)
1. Allocate a queue.
2. Enqueue the data in the corresponding queue.
2. If (not found)
1. Ask the ICMP module to send an "unreachable port" message.
2. Discard the user datagram.
2. Return.

Output Module

The output module is responsible for creating and sending user datagrams.

Output Module
Receive: data and information from a process
1. Create a UDP user datagram.
2. Send the user datagram.
3. Return.

Examples

In this section we show some examples of how our package responds to input and output. The control-block table at the start of our examples is shown in Table 11.2.

Table 11.2   *The control-block table at the beginning of examples*

State	Process ID	Port Number	Queue Number
IN-USE	2,345	52,010	34
IN-USE	3,422	52,011	
FREE			
IN-USE	4,652	52,012	38
FREE			

Example 2

The first activity is the arrival of a user datagram with destination port number 52,012. The input module searches for this port number and finds it. Queue number 38 has been assigned to this port, which means that the port has been previously used. The input module sends the data to queue 38. The control-block table does not change.

Example 3

After a few seconds, a process starts. It asks the operating system for a port number and is granted port number 52,014. Now the process sends its ID (4,978) and the port number to the control-block module to create an entry in the table. The module takes the first FREE entry and inserts the information received. The module does not allocate a queue at this moment because no user datagrams have arrived for this destination (see Table 11.3).

Table 11.3   *Control-block table after Example 3*

State	Process ID	Port Number	Queue Number
IN-USE	2,345	52,010	34
IN-USE	3,422	52,011	
IN-USE	**4,978**	**52,014**	
IN-USE	4,652	52,012	38
FREE			

Example 4

A user datagram now arrives for port 52,011. The input module checks the table and finds that no queue has been allocated for this destination since this is the first time a user datagram has arrived for this destination. The module creates a queue and gives it a number (43). See Table 11.4.

Table 11.4   *Control-block after Example 4*

State	Process ID	Port Number	Queue Number
IN-USE	2,345	52,010	34
IN-USE	3,422	52,011	**43**
IN-USE	4,978	52,014	
IN-USE	4,652	52,012	38
FREE			

Example 5

After a few seconds, a user datagram arrives for port 52,222. The input module checks the table and cannot find an entry for this destination. The user datagram is dropped and a request is made to ICMP to send an "unreachable port" message to the source.

11.7   KEY TERMS

application program

checksum

client

connectionless service

connectionless, unreliable transport
    protocol

decapsulation

dynamic port

encapsulation

ephemeral port number

error control

flow control

ICANN

multiplexing

port number

process

process-to-process communication

pseudoheader

queue

registered port

server

socket address

transport layer

user datagram

User Datagram Protocol (UDP)

well-known port number

11.8   SUMMARY

❑   UDP is a transport protocol that creates a process-to-process communication.

❑   UDP is a (mostly) unreliable and connectionless protocol that requires little overhead and offers fast delivery.

❑   In the client-server paradigm, an application program on the local host, called the client, needs services from an application program on the remote host, called a server.

❑   Each application program has a unique port number that distinguishes it from other programs running at the same time on the same machine.

❑   The client program is assigned a random port number called an ephemeral port number.

❑   The server program is assigned a universal port number called a well-known port number.

❑   The ICANN has specified ranges for the different types of port numbers.

❑   The combination of the IP address and the port number, called the socket address, uniquely defines a process and a host.

❑   UDP requires a pair of socket addresses: the client socket address and the server socket address.

❑   The UDP packet is called a user datagram.

❑   UDP's only attempt at error control is the checksum.

❑   Inclusion of a pseudoheader in the checksum calculation allows source and destination IP address errors to be detected.

❑   UDP has no flow-control mechanism.

❑   A user datagram is encapsulated in the data field of an IP datagram.

❑   Incoming and outgoing queues hold messages going to and from UDP.

❑   UDP uses multiplexing to handle outgoing user datagrams from multiple processes on one host.

❑   UDP uses demultiplexing to handle incoming user datagrams that go to different processes on the same host.

❑   A UDP package can involve five components: a control-block table, a control-block module, input queues, an input module, and an output module.

❑   The input queues hold incoming user datagrams.

❑   The control-block module is responsible for maintenance of entries in the control-block table.

❑   The input module creates input queues; the output module sends out user datagrams.

11.9   PRACTICE SET

Exercises

1. In cases where reliability is not of primary importance, UDP would make a good transport protocol. Give examples of specific cases.

2. Are both UDP and IP unreliable to the same degree? Why or why not?

3. Do port addresses need to be unique? Why or why not? Why are port addresses shorter than IP addresses?

4. What is the dictionary definition of the word *ephemeral?* How does it apply to the concept of the ephemeral port number?

5. Show the entries for the header of a UDP user datagram that carries a message from a TFTP client to a TFTP server. Fill the checksum field with 0s. Choose an appropriate ephemeral port number and the correct well-known port number. The length of data is 40 bytes. Show the UDP packet using the format in Figure 11.7.

6. An SNMP client residing on a host with IP address 122.45.12.7 sends a message to an SNMP server residing on a host with IP address 200.112.45.90. What is the pair of sockets used in this communication?

7. A TFTP server residing on a host with IP address 130.45.12.7 sends a message to a TFTP client residing on a host with IP address 14.90.90.33. What is the pair of sockets used in this communication?

8. What is the minimum size of a UDP datagram?

9. What is the maximum size of a UDP datagram?

10. What is the minimum size of the process data that can be encapsulated in a UDP datagram?

11. What is the maximum size of the process data that can be encapsulated in a UDP datagram?

12. A client has a packet of 68,000 bytes. Show how this packet can be transferred using only one UDP user datagram.

13. A client uses UDP to send data to a server. The data is 16 bytes. Calculate the efficiency of this transmission at the UDP level (ratio of useful bytes to total bytes).

14. Redo the Exercise 13 calculating the efficiency of transmission at the IP level. Assume no options for the IP header.

15. Redo the previous Exercise 13 calculating the efficiency of transmission at the data link layer. Assume no options for the IP header and use Ethernet at the data link layer.

16. The following is a dump of a UDP header in hexadecimal format.

06 32|00 0D|00 1C|E2 17

a. What is the source port number?
b. What is the destination port number?
c. What is the total length of the user datagram?
d. What is the length of the data?
e. Is the packet directed from a client to a server or vice versa?
f. What is the client process?

Research Activities

17. Use the grep utility to find more well-known ports.
18. Find the RFCs related to the UDP protocol.
19. Find the RFCs related to port numbers. Is there any specific RFC related to well-known or ephemeral ports?
20. Find more information about ICANN. What was it called before its name changed?
21. Prove that a calculated checksum in UDP is never all 0s. *Hint:* Use modular arithmetic.

CHAPTER 12

Transmission Control Protocol (TCP)

Traditionally, the TCP/IP protocol suite has specified two protocols for the transport layer: UDP and TCP. We studied UDP in Chapter 11; we will study TCP in this chapter. A new transport-layer protocol called SCTP is now in use by some implementations and will be discussed in Chapter 13.

Figure 12.1 shows the relationship of TCP to the other protocols in the TCP/IP protocol suite. TCP lies between the application layer and the network layer and serves as the intermediary between the application programs and the network operations.

Figure 12.1 *TCP/IP protocol suite*

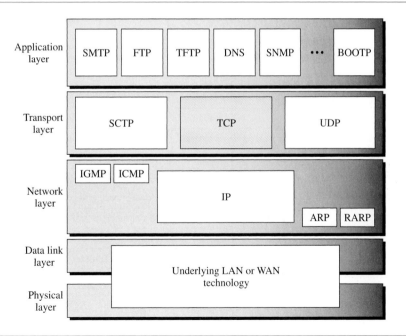

TCP, like UDP, is a process-to-process (program-to-program) protocol. TCP, there-fore, like UDP, uses port numbers. Unlike UDP, TCP is a connection-oriented protocol; it creates a virtual connection between two TCPs to send data. In addition, TCP uses flow- and error-control mechanisms at the transport level.

In brief, TCP is called a *connection-oriented, reliable* transport protocol. It adds connection-oriented and reliability features to the services of IP.

12.1   TCP SERVICES

Before discussing TCP in detail, let us explain the services offered by TCP to the pro-cesses at the application layer.

Process-to-Process Communication

Like UDP, TCP provides process-to-process communication using port numbers (see Chapter 11). Table 12.1 lists some well-known port numbers used by TCP.

Table 12.1   *Well-known ports used by TCP*

Port	Protocol	Description
7	Echo	Echoes a received datagram back to the sender
9	Discard	Discards any datagram that is received
11	Users	Active users
13	Daytime	Returns the date and the time
17	Quote	Returns a quote of the day
19	Chargen	Returns a string of characters
20	FTP, Data	File Transfer Protocol (data connection)
21	FTP, Control	File Transfer Protocol (control connection)
23	TELNET	Terminal Network
25	SMTP	Simple Mail Transfer Protocol
53	DNS	Domain Name Server
67	BOOTP	Bootstrap Protocol
79	Finger	Finger
80	HTTP	Hypertext Transfer Protocol
111	RPC	Remote Procedure Call

Example 1

As we said in Chapter 11, in UNIX, the well-known ports are stored in a file called */etc/services*. Each line in this file gives the name of the server and the well-known port number. We can use the *grep* utility to extract the line corresponding to the desired application. The following shows the ports for FTP.

> **$ grep   ftp   /etc/services**
> ftp-data   20/tcp
> ftp-control   21/tcp

Stream Delivery Service

TCP, unlike UDP, is a stream-oriented protocol. In UDP, a process (an application program) sends messages, with predefined boundaries, to UDP for delivery. UDP adds its own header to each of these messages and delivers it to IP for transmission. Each message from the process is called a user datagram, and becomes, eventually, one IP datagram. Neither IP nor UDP recognizes any relationship between the datagrams.

TCP, on the other hand, allows the sending process to deliver data as a stream of bytes and allows the receiving process to obtain data as a stream of bytes. TCP creates an environment in which the two processes seem to be connected by an imaginary "tube" that carries their data across the Internet. This imaginary environment is depicted in Figure 12.2. The sending process produces (writes to) the stream of bytes and the receiving process consumes (reads from) them.

Figure 12.2   *Stream delivery*

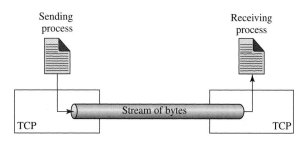

Sending and Receiving Buffers

Because the sending and the receiving processes may not write or read data at the same speed, TCP needs buffers for storage. There are two buffers, the sending buffer and the receiving buffer, one for each direction. (We will see later that these buffers are also necessary for flow- and error-control mechanisms used by TCP.) One way to implement a buffer is to use a circular array of 1-byte locations as shown in Figure 12.3. For simplicity, we have shown two buffers of 20 bytes each; normally the buffers are hundreds or thousands of bytes, depending on the implementation. We also show the buffers as the same size, which is not always the case.

The figure shows the movement of the data in one direction. At the sending site, the buffer has three types of chambers. The white section contains empty chambers that can be filled by the sending process (producer). The gray area holds bytes that have been sent but not yet acknowledged. TCP keeps these bytes in the buffer until it receives an acknowledgment. The colored area contains bytes to be sent by the sending TCP. However, as we will see later in this chapter, TCP may be able to send only part of this colored section. This could be due to the slowness of the receiving process or

Figure 12.3 *Sending and receiving buffers*

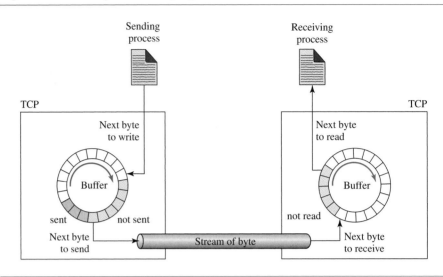

perhaps to congestion in the network. Also note that after the bytes in the gray chambers are acknowledged, the chambers are recycled and available for use by the sending process. This is why we show a circular buffer.

The operation of the buffer at the receiver site is simpler. The circular buffer is divided into two areas (shown as white and colored). The white area contains empty chambers to be filled by bytes received from the network. The colored sections contain received bytes that can be read by the receiving process. When a byte is read by the receiving process, the chamber is recycled and added to the pool of empty chambers.

Segments

Although buffering handles the disparity between the speed of the producing and consuming processes, we need one more step before we can send data. The IP layer, as a service provider for TCP, needs to send data in packets, not as a stream of bytes. At the transport layer, TCP groups a number of bytes together into a packet called a *segment*. TCP adds a header to each segment (for control purposes) and delivers the segment to the IP layer for transmission. The segments are encapsulated in an IP datagram and transmitted. This entire operation is transparent to the receiving process. Later we will see that segments may be received out of order, lost, or corrupted and resent. All of these are handled by TCP with the receiving process unaware of any activities. Figure 12.4 shows how segments are created from the bytes in the buffers.

Note that the segments are not necessarily the same size. In the figure, for simplicity, we show one segment carrying 3 bytes and the other carrying 5 bytes. In reality segments carry hundreds if not thousands of bytes.

Full-Duplex Communication

TCP offers **full-duplex service,** where data can flow in both directions at the same time. Each TCP then has a sending and receiving buffer and segments move in both directions.

Figure 12.4 *TCP segments*

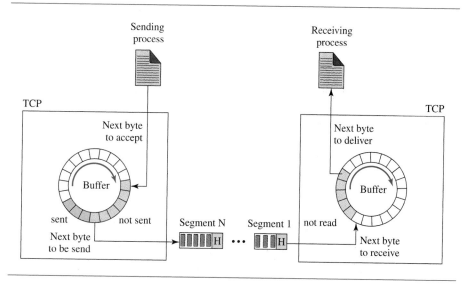

Connection-Oriented Service

TCP, unlike UDP, is a connection-oriented protocol. When a process at site A wants to send and receive data from another process at site B, the following occurs:

1. The two TCPs establish a connection between them.
2. Data are exchanged in both directions.
3. The connection is terminated.

Note that this is a virtual connection, not a physical connection. The TCP segment is encapsulated in an IP datagram and can be sent out of order, or lost, or corrupted, and then resent. Each may use a different path to reach the destination. There is no physical connection. TCP creates a stream-oriented environment in which it accepts the responsibility of delivering the bytes in order to the other site. The situation is similar to creating a bridge that spans multiple islands and passing all of the bytes from one island to another in one single connection. We will discuss this feature later in the chapter.

Reliable Service

TCP is a reliable transport protocol. It uses an acknowledgment mechanism to check the safe and sound arrival of data. We will discuss this feature further in the section on error control.

12.2   TCP FEATURES

To provide the services mentioned in the previous section, TCP has several features that are briefly summarized in this section and discussed later in detail.

Numbering System

Although the TCP software keeps track of the segments being transmitted or received, there is no field for a segment number value in the segment header. Instead, there are two fields called the *sequence number* and the *acknowledgment number*. These two fields refer to the byte number and not the segment number.

Byte Number

TCP numbers all data bytes that are transmitted in a connection. Numbering is independent in each direction. When TCP receives bytes of data from a process it stores them in the sending buffer and numbers them. The numbering does not necessarily start from 0. Instead, TCP generates a random number between 0 and $2^{32} - 1$ for the number of the first byte. For example, if the random number happens to be 1,057 and the total data to be sent is 6,000 bytes, the bytes are numbered from 1,057 to 7,056. We will see that byte numbering is used for flow and error control.

The bytes of data being transferred in each connection are numbered by TCP. The numbering starts with a randomly generated number.

Sequence Number

After the bytes have been numbered, TCP assigns a sequence number to each segment that is being sent. The sequence number for each segment is the number of the first byte carried in that segment.

Example 2

Suppose a TCP connection is transferring a file of 5000 bytes. The first byte is numbered 10001. What are the sequence numbers for each segment if data is sent in five segments, each carrying 1000 bytes?

Solution

The following shows the sequence number for each segment:

Segment 1 ➡ Sequence Number: 10,001 (range: 10,001 to 11,000)
Segment 2 ➡ Sequence Number: 11,001 (range: 11,001 to 12,000)
Segment 3 ➡ Sequence Number: 12,001 (range: 12,001 to 13,000)
Segment 4 ➡ Sequence Number: 13,001 (range: 13,001 to 14,000)
Segment 5 ➡ Sequence Number: 14,001 (range: 14,001 to 15,000)

The value in the sequence number field of a segment defines the number of the first data byte contained in that segment.

When a segment carries a combination of data and control information (piggybacking), it uses a sequence number. If a segment does not carry user data, it does not logically define a sequence number. The field is there, but the value is not valid. However, some segments, when carrying only control information need a sequence number to allow an acknowledgment from the receiver. These segments are used for connection establishment, termination, or abortion. Each of these segments consume one sequence number as though it carries one byte, but there is no actual data. If the randomly generated sequence number is x, the first data byte is numbered $x + 1$. The byte x is considered a phony byte that is used for a control segment to open a connection, as we will see shortly.

Acknowledgment Number

As we discussed previously, communication in TCP is full duplex; when a connection is established, both parties can send and receive data at the same time. Each party numbers the bytes, usually with a different starting byte number. The sequence number in each direction shows the number of the first byte carried by the segment. Each party also uses an acknowledgment number to confirm the bytes it has received. However, the acknowledgment number defines the number of the next byte that the party expects to receive. In addition, the acknowledgment number is cumulative, which means that the party takes the number of the last byte that it has received, safe and sound, adds 1 to it, and announces this sum as the acknowledgment number. The term *cumulative* here means that if a party uses 5,643 as an acknowledgment number, it has received all bytes from the beginning up to 5,642. Note that this does not mean that the party has received 5,642 bytes because the first byte number does not have to start from 0.

> **The value of the acknowledgment field in a segment defines the number of the next byte a party expects to receive.**
> **The acknowledgment number is cumulative.**

Flow Control

TCP, unlike UDP, provides **flow control.** The receiver of the data controls how much data are to be sent by the sender. This is done to prevent the receiver from being overwhelmed with data. The numbering system allows TCP to use a byte-oriented flow control.

Error Control

To provide reliable service, TCP implements an error control mechanism. Although error control considers a segment as the unit of data for error detection (loss or corrupted segments), error control is byte-oriented, as we will see later.

Congestion Control

TCP, unlike UDP, takes into account congestion in the network. The amount of data sent by a sender is not only controlled by the receiver (flow control), but is also determined by the level of congestion in the network.

12.3   SEGMENT

Before discussing TCP in more detail, let us discuss the TCP packets themselves. A packet in TCP is called a **segment.**

Format

The format of a segment is shown in Figure 12.5.

Figure 12.5 *TCP segment format*

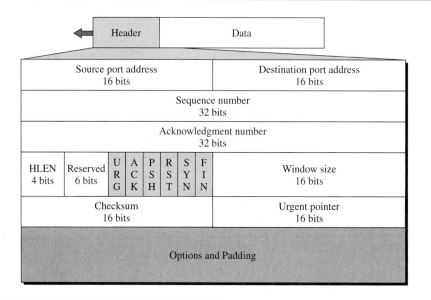

The segment consists of a 20- to 60-byte header, followed by data from the application program. The header is 20 bytes if there are no options and up to 60 bytes if it contains options. We will discuss some of the header fields in this section. The meaning and purpose of these will become clearer as we proceed through the chapter.

❑ **Source port address.** This is a 16-bit field that defines the port number of the application program in the host that is sending the segment. This serves the same purpose as the source port address in the UDP header discussed in Chapter 11.

❑ **Destination port address.** This is a 16-bit field that defines the port number of the application program in the host that is receiving the segment. This serves the same purpose as the destination port address in the UDP header discussed in Chapter 11.

❑ **Sequence number.** This 32-bit field defines the number assigned to the first byte of data contained in this segment. As we said before, TCP is a stream transport protocol. To ensure connectivity, each byte to be transmitted is numbered. The sequence number tells the destination which byte in this sequence comprises the first byte in the segment. During connection establishment (see Section 12.12) each party uses a random number generator to create an **initial sequence number** (ISN), which is usually different in each direction.

❑ **Acknowledgment number.** This 32-bit field defines the byte number that the receiver of the segment is expecting to receive from the other party. If the receiver of the segment has successfully received byte number x from the other party, it defines $x + 1$ as the acknowledgment number. Acknowledgment and data can be piggybacked together.

❑ **Header length.** This 4-bit field indicates the number of 4-byte words in the TCP header. The length of the header can be between 20 and 60 bytes. Therefore, the value of this field can be between 5 ($5 \times 4 = 20$) and 15 ($15 \times 4 = 60$).

❑ **Reserved.** This is a 6-bit field reserved for future use.

❑ **Control.** This field defines 6 different control bits or flags as shown in Figure 12.6. One or more of these bits can be set at a time.

Figure 12.6 *Control field*

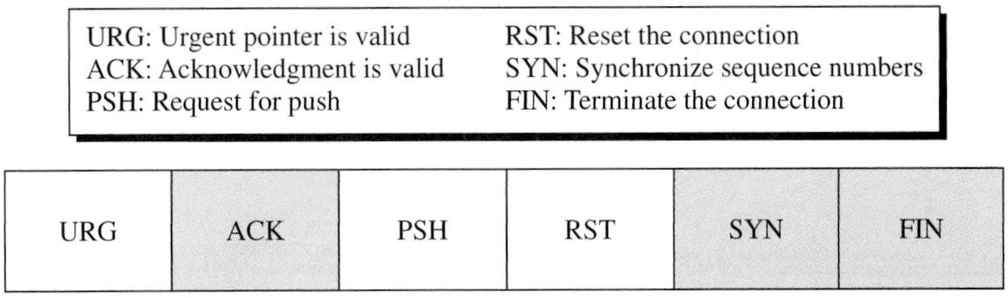

These bits enable flow control, connection establishment and termination, connection abortion, and the mode of data transfer in TCP. A brief description of each bit is shown in Table 12.2. We will discuss them further when we study the detailed operation of TCP later in the chapter.

Table 12.2 *Description of flags in the control field*

Flag	Description
URG	The value of the urgent pointer field is valid
ACK	The value of the acknowledgment field is valid
PSH	Push the data
RST	The connection must be reset
SYN	Synchronize sequence numbers during connection
FIN	Terminate the connection

❑ **Window size.** This field defines the size of the window, in bytes, that the other party must maintain. Note that the length of this field is 16 bits, which means that the maximum size of the window is 65,535 bytes. This value is normally referred to as the receiving window (rwnd) and is determined by the receiver. The sender must obey the dictation of the receiver in this case.

❑ **Checksum.** This 16-bit field contains the checksum. The calculation of the checksum for TCP follows the same procedure as the one described for UDP in Chapter 11. However, the inclusion of the checksum in the UDP datagram is optional, whereas the inclusion of the checksum for TCP is mandatory. The same pseudoheader, serving the same purpose, is added to the segment. For the TCP pseudoheader, the value for the protocol field is six. See Figure 12.7.

❑ **Urgent pointer.** This 16-bit field, which is valid only if the urgent flag is set, is used when the segment contains urgent data. It defines the number that must be added to the sequence number to obtain the number of the l ast urgent byte in the data section of the segment. This will be discussed later in this chapter.

❏ **Options.** There can be up to 40 bytes of optional information in the TCP header. We will discuss the different options currently used in the TCP header later in the chapter.

Figure 12.7   *Pseudoheader added to the TCP datagram*

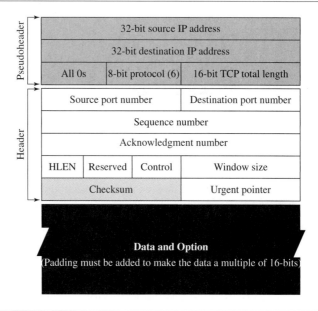

> **The inclusion of the checksum in TCP is mandatory.**

Encapsulation

A TCP segment is encapsulated in an IP datagram, which in turn is encapsulated in a frame at the data-link layer as shown in Figure 12.8.

Figure 12.8   *Encapsulation and decapsulation*

Frame header	IP header	TCP Segment

12.4   A TCP CONNECTION

TCP is connection-oriented. A connection-oriented transport protocol establishes a virtual path between the source and destination. All of the segments belonging to a message are then sent over this virtual path. Using a single virtual pathway for the entire message facilitates the acknowledgment process as well as retransmission of damaged or lost frames. You may wonder how TCP, which uses the services of IP, a connectionless protocol, can be connection-oriented. The point is that a TCP connection is virtual, not physical. TCP operates at a higher level. TCP uses the services of IP to deliver individual segments to the receiver, but it controls the connection itself. If a segment is lost or corrupted, it is retransmitted. Unlike TCP, IP is unaware of this retransmission. If a segment arrives out of order, TCP holds it until the missing segments arrive; IP is unaware of this reordering.

In TCP, connection-oriented transmission requires three phases: connection establishment, data transfer, and connection termination.

Connection Establishment

TCP transmits data in full-duplex mode. When two TCPs in two machines are connected, they are able to send segments to each other simultaneously. This implies that each party must initialize communication and get approval from the other party before any data is transferred.

Three-Way Handshaking

The connection establishment in TCP is called **three-way handshaking.** In our example, an application program, called the client, wants to make a connection with another application program, called the server, using TCP as the transport layer protocol.

The process starts with the server. The server program tells its TCP that it is ready to accept a connection. This is called a request for a *passive open*. Although the server TCP is ready to accept any connection from any machine in the world it cannot make the connection itself.

The client program issues a request for an *active open*. A client that wishes to connect to an open server tells its TCP that it needs to be connected to that particular server. TCP can now start the three-way handshaking process as shown in Figure 12.9. To show the process we use two time lines: one at each site. Each segment has values for all its header fields and perhaps for some of its option fields too. However, we show only the few fields necessary to understand each phase. We show the sequence number, the acknowledgment number, the control flags (only those that are set) and window size if not empty. The three steps in this phase are as follows.

1. The client sends the first segment, a SYN segment, in which only the SYN flag is set. This segment is for synchronization of sequence numbers. The client in our example chooses a random number as the first sequence number and sends this to the server. This sequence number is called the initial sequence number (ISN). Note that this segment does not contain an acknowledgment number. It does not define the window size either; a window size definition makes sense only when a segment includes an acknowledgment. The segment can also include some options that we discuss later in the chapter. Note that the SYN segment is a control segment and does not carry any data. However, it consumes one sequence number. When the data transfer starts, the sequence number is incremented by 1. We can say that the SYN segment carries no real data, but we can think of it as containing one imaginary byte.

Figure 12.9 *Connection establishment using three-way handshaking*

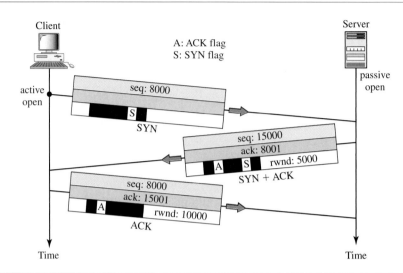

A SYN segment cannot carry data, but it consumes one sequence number.

---

2. The server sends the second segment, a SYN + ACK segment with two flag bits set: SYN and ACK. This segment has a dual purpose. First, it is a SYN segment for communication in the other direction. The server uses this segment to initialize a sequence number for numbering the bytes sent from the server to the client. The server also acknowledges the receipt of the SYN segment from the client by setting the ACK flag and displaying the next sequence number it expects to receive from the client. Because it contains an acknowledgment, it also needs to define the receiver window size, *rwnd* (to be used by the client) as we will see in the flow control section.

**A SYN + ACK segment cannot carry data, but does consume one
sequence number.**

---

3. The client sends the third segment. This is just an ACK segment. It acknowledges the receipt of the second segment with the ACK flag and acknowledgment number field. Note that the sequence number in this segment is the same as the one in the SYN segment; the ACK segment does not consume any sequence numbers. The client must also define the server window size. Some implementations allow this third segment in the connection phase to carry the first chunk of data from the client. In this case, the third segment must have a new sequence number showing the byte number of the first byte in the data. In general, the third segment usually does not carry data and consumes no sequence numbers.

An ACK segment, if carrying no data, consumes no sequence number.

Simultaneous Open

A rare situation may occur when both processes issue an active open. In this case, both TCPs transmit a SYN + ACK segment to each other and one single connection is established between them. We will show this case when we discuss the transition diagram in the next section.

SYN Flooding Attack

The connection establishment procedure in TCP is susceptible to a serious security problem called **SYN flooding attack.** This happens when a malicious attacker sends a large number of SYN segments to a server pretending that each of them is coming from a different client by faking the source IP addresses in the datagrams. The server, assuming that the clients are issuing an active open, allocates the necessary resources, such as creating TCB tables (explained later in the chapter) and setting timers. The TCP server then sends the SYN+ACK segments to the fake clients, which are lost. During this time, however, a lot of resources are occupied without being used. If, during this short period of time, the number of SYN segments is large, the server eventually runs out of resources and may crash. This SYN flooding attack belongs to a group of security attacks known as a **denial of service attack,** in which an attacker monopolizes a system with so many service requests that the system collapses and denies service to every request.

Some implementations of TCP have strategies to alleviate the effect of a SYN attack. Some have imposed a limit of connection requests during a specified period of time. Others filter out datagrams coming from unwanted source addresses. One recent strategy is to postpone resource allocation until the entire connection is set up using what is called a **cookie.** SCTP, the new transport-layer protocol that we discuss in the next chapter, uses this strategy.

Data Transfer

After connection is established, bidirectional **data transfer** can take place. The client and server can send data and acknowledgments in both directions. We will study the rules of acknowledgment later in the chapter; for the moment, it is enough to know that data traveling in the same direction as an acknowledgment are carried on the same segment. The acknowledgment is piggybacked with the data. Figure 12.10 shows an example. In this example, after connection is established (not shown in the figure) the client sends 2000 bytes of data in two segments. The server then sends 2000 byes in one segment. The client sends one more segment. The first three segments carry both data and acknowledgment, but the last segment carries only an acknowledgment because there is no more data to be sent. Note the values of the sequence and acknowledgment numbers. The data segments sent by the client have the PSH (push) flag set so that the server TCP knows to deliver data to the server process as soon as they are received. We discuss the use of this flag in more detail later. The segment from the server, on the other hand, does not set the push flag. Most TCP implementations have the option to set or not set this flag.

Figure 12.10 *Data transfer*

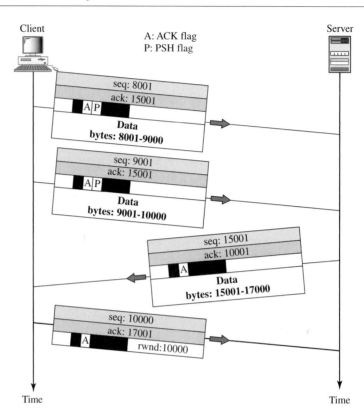

Pushing Data

We saw that the sending TCP uses a buffer to store the stream of data coming from the sending application program. The sending TCP can select the segment size. The receiving TCP also buffers the data when they arrive and delivers them to the application program when the application program is ready or when it is convenient for the receiving TCP. This type of flexibility increases the efficiency of TCP.

However, there are occasions in which the application program has no need for this flexibility. For example, consider an application program that communicates interactively with another application program on the other end. The application program on one site wants to send a keystroke to the application at the other site and receive an immediate response. Delayed transmission and delayed delivery of data may not be acceptable by the application program.

TCP can handle such a situation. The application program at the sending site can request a *push* operation. This means that the sending TCP must not wait for the window to be filled. It must create a segment and send it immediately. The sending TCP must also set the push bit (PSH) to let the receiving TCP know that the segment includes data that must be delivered to the receiving application program as soon as possible and not to wait for more data to come.

Although the push operation can be requested by the application program, most current implementations ignore such requests. TCP can choose whether or not to use this feature.

Urgent Data

TCP is a stream-oriented protocol. This means that the data is presented from the application program to TCP as a stream of bytes. Each byte of data has a position in the stream. However, there are occasions in which an application program needs to send *urgent* bytes. This means that the sending application program wants a piece of data to be read out of order by the receiving application program. As an example, suppose that the sending application program is sending data to be processed by the receiving application program. When the result of processing comes back, the sending application program finds that everything is wrong. It wants to abort the process, but it has already sent a huge amount of data. If it issues an abort command (control + C), these two characters will be stored at the end of the receiving TCP buffer. It will be delivered to the receiving application program after all the data has been processed.

The solution is to send a segment with the URG bit set. The sending application program tells the sending TCP that the piece of data is urgent. The sending TCP creates a segment and inserts the urgent data at the beginning of the segment. The rest of the segment can contain normal data from the buffer. The urgent pointer field in the header defines the end of the urgent data and the start of normal data.

When the receiving TCP receives a segment with the URG bit set, it extracts the urgent data from the segment, using the value of the urgent pointer, and delivers it, out of order, to the receiving application program.

Connection Termination

Any of the two parties involved in exchanging data (client or server) can close the connection, although it is usually initiated by the client. Most implementations today allow two options for connection termination: three-way handshaking and four-way handshaking with a half-close option.

Three-Way Handshaking

Most implementations today allow *three-way handshaking* for connection termination as shown in Figure 12.11.

1. In a normal situation, the client TCP, after receiving a close command from the client process, sends the first segment, a FIN segment in which the FIN flag is set. Note that a FIN segment can include the last chunk of data sent by the client or it can be just a control segment as shown in the figure. If it is only a control segment, it consumes only one sequence number.

The FIN segment consumes one sequence number if it does not carry data.

---

2. The server TCP after receiving the FIN segment, informs its process of the situation and sends the second segment, a FIN+ACK segment, to confirm the receipt of

Figure 12.11   *Connection termination using three-way handshaking*

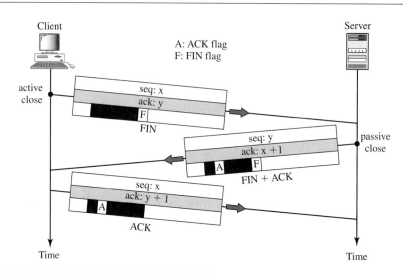

the FIN segment from the client and at the same time to announce the closing of the connection in the other direction. This segment can also contain the last chunk of data from the server. If it does not carry data, it consumes only one sequence number.

> **The FIN + ACK segment consumes one sequence
> number if it does not carry data.**

3. The client TCP sends the last segment, an ACK segment, to confirm the receipt of the FIN segment from the TCP server. This segment contains the acknowledgment number, which is one plus the sequence number received in the FIN segment from the server. This segment cannot carry data and consumes no sequence numbers.

Half-Close

In TCP, one end can stop sending data while still receiving data. This is called a **half-close.** Although either end can issue a half-close, it is normally initiated by the client. It can occur when the server needs all the data before processing can begin. A good example is sorting. When the client sends data to the server to be sorted, the server needs to receive all the data before sorting can start. This means the client, after sending all data, can close the connection in the outbound direction. However, the inbound direction must remain open to receive the sorted data. The server, after receiving the data still needs time for sorting; its outbound direction must remain open.

Figure 12.12 shows an example of a half-close. The client half-closes the connection by sending a FIN segment. The server accepts the half-close by sending the ACK segment. The data transfer from the client to the server stops. The server, however, can still send data. When the server has sent all of the processed data, it sends a FIN segment, which is acknowledged by an ACK from the client.

Figure 12.12 *Half-close*

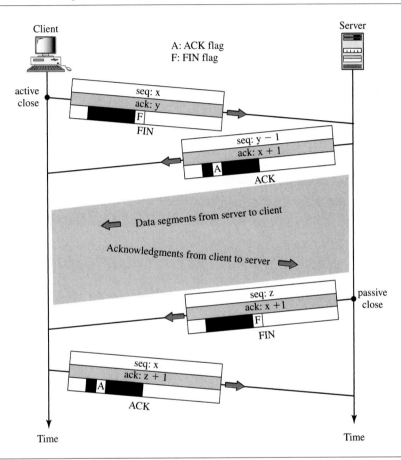

After half closing the connection, data can travel from the server to the client and acknowledgments can travel from the client to the server. The client cannot send any more data to the server. Note the sequence numbers we have used. The second segment (ACK) consumes no sequence number. Although the client has received sequence number $y - 1$ and is expecting y, the server sequence number is still $y - 1$. When the connection finally closes, the sequence number of the last ACK segment is still x, because no sequence numbers are consumed during data transfer in that direction.

Connection Reset

The TCP at one end may deny a connection request, may abort a connection, or may terminate an idle connection. All of these are done with the RST (reset) flag.

Denying a Connection

Suppose the TCP on one side has requested a connection to a nonexistent port. The TCP on the other side may send a segment with its RST bit set to annul the request. We will show an example of this case in the next section.

Aborting a Connection

One TCP may want to abort a connection due to an abnormal situation. It can send an RST segment to close the connection. We also show an example of this case in the next section.

Terminating an Idle Connection

The TCP on one side may discover that the TCP on the other side has been idle for a long time. It may send an RST segment to destroy the connection. The process is the same as aborting a connection.

12.5   STATE TRANSITION DIAGRAM

To keep track of all the different events happening during connection establishment, connection termination, and data transfer, the TCP software is implemented as a finite state machine. A **finite state machine** is a machine that goes through a limited number of states. At any moment, the machine is in one of the states. It remains in that state until an event happens. The event can take the machine to a new state. At the same time, the event can also make the machine perform some actions. In other words, the event is an input applied to a state. It can change the state and can also create an output. Table 12.3 shows the states for TCP.

Table 12.3   *States for TCP*

State	Description
CLOSED	There is no connection
LISTEN	Passive open received; waiting for SYN
SYN-SENT	SYN sent; waiting for ACK
SYN-RCVD	SYN+ACK sent; waiting for ACK
ESTABLISHED	Connection established; data transfer in progress
FIN-WAIT-1	First FIN sent; waiting for ACK
FIN-WAIT-2	ACK to first FIN received; waiting for second FIN
CLOSE-WAIT	First FIN received, ACK sent; waiting for application to close
TIME-WAIT	Second FIN received, ACK sent; waiting for 2MSL time-out
LAST-ACK	Second FIN sent; waiting for ACK
CLOSING	Both sides have decided to close simultaneously

Figure 12.13 shows the finite state machine as a transition diagram.

Figure 12.13   *State transition diagram*

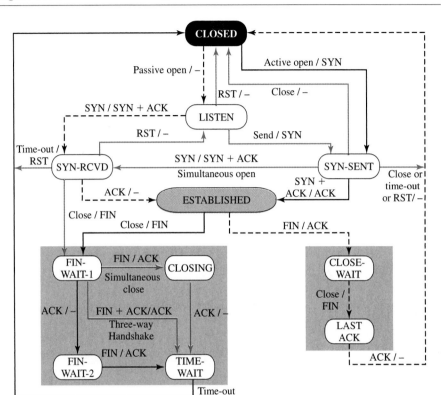

The ovals represent the states. The transition from one state to another is shown using directed lines. Each line has two strings separated by a slash. The first string is the input, what TCP receives. The second is the output, what TCP sends. Figure 12.13 shows the **state transition diagram** for both client and server. The dotted black lines in the figure represent the transition that a server normally goes through; the solid black lines shows the transitions that a client normally goes through. However, in some situations, a server transitions through a solid line or a client transitions through a dotted line. The colored lines show special situations.

Scenarios

To understand the TCP state machines and the transition diagrams, we go through some scenarios in this section.

Connection Establishment and Termination

Figure 12.14 shows a scenario where the server process issues a passive open and passive close, and the client process issues an active open and active close. The half-close termination allows us to show more states. The states and their relative durations are shown on the time line.

Figure 12.14 *Connection establishment and termination*

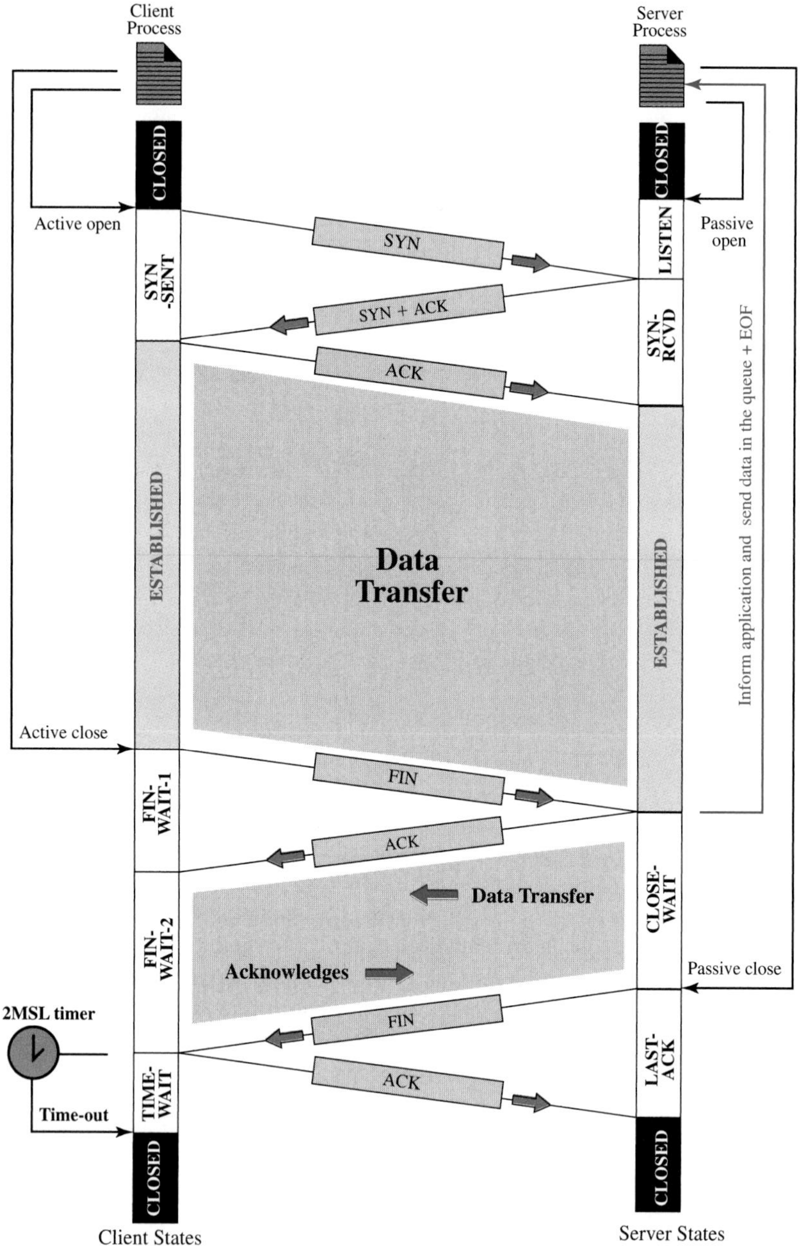

Client
Process

Server
Process

CLOSED

LISTEN | CLOSED

Active open

Passive
open

SYN
-SENT

SYN

LISTEN

SYN + ACK

SYN-
RCVD

ACK

ESTABLISHED

**Data
Transfer**

ESTABLISHED

Inform application and send data in the queue + EOF

Active close

FIN-
WAIT-1

FIN

ACK

CLOSE-
WAIT

FIN-
WAIT-2

← **Data Transfer**

Acknowledges ⟹

Passive close

2MSL timer

FIN

LAST-
ACK

Time-out

TIME-
WAIT

ACK

CLOSED

CLOSED

Client States

Server States

The common value for MSL is between 30 seconds and 1 minute.

Client States The client process issues a command to its TCP to request a connection to a specific socket address. This called an *active open*. TCP sends a SYN segment and moves to the **SYN-SENT** state. After receiving the SYN+ACK segment, TCP sends an ACK segment and goes to the **ESTABLISHED** state. Data is transferred, possibly in both directions, and acknowledged.

When the client process has no more data to send, it issues a command called an *active close*. The client TCP sends a FIN segment and goes to the **FIN-WAIT-1** state. When it receives the ACK for the sent FIN, it goes to **FIN-WAIT-2** state and remains there until it receives a FIN segment from the server. When the FIN segment is received, the client sends an ACK segment and goes to the **TIME-WAIT** state and sets a timer for a time-out value of twice the maximum segment lifetime (MSL). The MSL is the maximum time a segment can exist in the Internet before it is dropped. Remember that a TCP segment is encapsulated in a IP datagram which has a limited life time (TTL). When the IP datagram is dropped, the encapsulated TCP segment is also dropped. The common value for MSL is between 30 seconds and 1 minutes. There are two reasons for the existence of the **TIME-WAIT** state and the 2SML timer:

1. If the last ACK segment is lost, the server TCP, which sets a timer for the last FIN, assumes that its FIN is lost and resends it. If the client goes to the **CLOSED** state and closes the connection before the 2MSL timer expires, it never receives this resent FIN segment, and consequently, the server never receives the final ACK. The server cannot close the connection. The 2MSL timer makes the client wait for a duration that is enough time for an ACK to be lost (one SML) and a FIN to arrive (another SML). If during the **TIME-WAIT** state, a new FIN arrives, the client sends a new ACK and restarts the 2SML timer.

2. A duplicate segment from one connection might appear in the next one. Assume a client and a server have closed a connection. After a short period of time, they open a connection with the same socket addresses (same source and destination IP addresses and same source and destination port numbers). This new connection is called the *incarnation* of the old one. A duplicated segment from the previous connection may arrive in this new connection and be interpreted as belonging to the new connection if there is not enough time between the two connections. To prevent this problem, TCP requires that incarnation cannot take place unless 2MSL amount of time has elapsed. Some implementations however, ignore this rule if the initial sequence number of the incarnation is greater than the last sequence number used in the previous connection.

Server States In our scenario, the server process issues an *open* command. This must happen before the client issues an *open* command. The server TCP goes to the **LISTEN** state and remains there, passively, until it receives a SYN segment. When the server TCP receives a SYN segment, it sends a SYN+ACK segment and goes to **SYN-RCVD** state, waiting for the client to send an ACK segment. After receiving the ACK segment, it goes to **ESTABLISHED** state, where data transfer can take place.

TCP remains in this state until it receives a FIN segment from the client TCP signifying that there are no more data to be sent and that the connection can be closed. At this moment, the server sends an ACK to the client, delivers outstanding data in its queue to the application, and goes to the **CLOSE-WAIT** state. In our scenario, we assume a half-close connection. The server TCP can still send data to the client and receive acknowledgments, but no data can flow in the other direction. The server TCP remains in this state until the application actually issues a *close* command. It then sends a FIN to the client to show that it is closing the connection too, and goes to **LAST-ACK** state. It remains in this state until it receives the final ACK, when it then goes to the **CLOSED** state. The termination phase beginning with the first FIN is called a four-way handshake.

Connection Termination Using Three-Way Handshake

As mentioned before, a three-way handshake in the connection termination phase is common. In this case, the site that receives the first FIN segment, sends a FIN+ACK segment, combining the FIN and ACK segments used in four-way handshaking. The client eliminates the **FIN-WAIT-2** state and goes directly to the **TIME-WAIT** state. Figure 12.15 shows that the client issues a *close* after the data transfer phase. The client TCP sends a FIN segment and goes to **FIN-WAIT-1** state. The server TCP, upon receiving the FIN segment, sends all queued data to the server with the EOF marker, which means that the connection must be closed. It goes to the **CLOSE-WAIT** state, but postpones acknowledging the FIN segment received from the client until it receives a passive close from its process. After receiving the passive close command, it sends a FIN+ACK segment to the client and goes to the **LAST-ACK** state waiting for the final ACK. The rest is the same as four-way handshaking.

Figure 12.15   *Connection termination using three-way handshake*

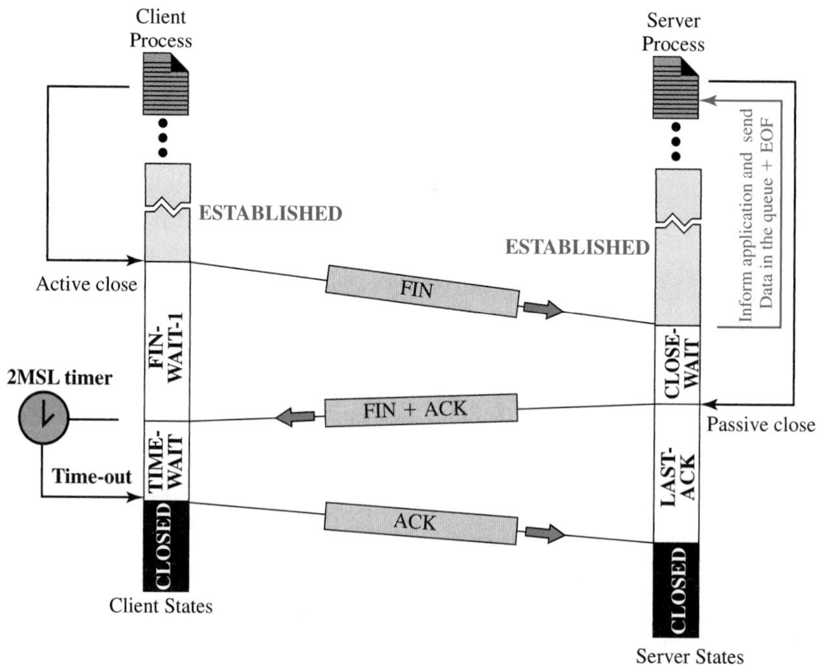

Simultaneous Open

In a **simultaneous open,** both applications issue active opens. This is a very rare situation in which there is no client or server; communication is between two peers that know their local port numbers. This case is allowed by TCP, but is unlikely to happen because both ends need to send SYN segments to each other and the segments are in transit simultaneously. This means that the two applications must issue active opens almost at the same time. Figure 12.16 shows the connection establishment phase for this scenario. Both TCPs go through **SYN-SENT** and **SYN-RCVD** states before going to the **ESTABLISHED** state. A close look shows that both processes act as client and server at the same time. The two SYN+ACK segments acknowledge the SYN segments and open the connection. Note that connection establishment involves a four-way hand-shake.The data transfer and the connection termination phases are the same as previous examples and are not shown in the figure.

Figure 12.16   *Simultaneous open*

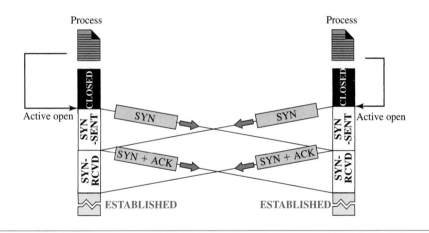

Simultaneous Close

Another uncommon, but possible scenario is the **simultaneous close** shown in Figure 12.17. In this situation, both ends issue an active close. Both TCPs go to the **FIN-WAIT-1** state and send a FIN segment that are in transit simultaneously. After receiving the FIN segment, each end goes to the **CLOSING** state and sends an ACK segment. The **CLOSING** state takes the place of **FIN-WAIT-2** or **CLOSE-WAIT** in a common scenario. After receiving the ACK segment, each end moves to the **TIME-WAIT** state. Note that this duration is required for both ends because each end has sent an ACK that may get lost. We have eliminated the connection establishment and the data transfer phases in the figure.

Denying a Connection

One common situation occurs when a server TCP denies the connection because the destination port number in the SYN segment defines a server that is not in the **LISTEN** state at the moment. The server TCP, after receiving the SYN segment sends an RST+ACK

Figure 12.17 *Simultaneous close*

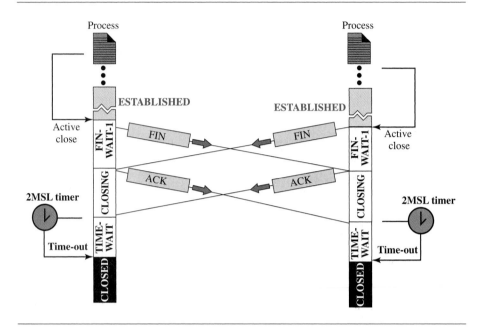

segment that acknowledges the SYN segment, and, at the same time, resets (denies) the connection. It goes to the **LISTEN** state to wait for another connection. The client, after receiving the RST+ACK, goes to the **CLOSED** state. Figure 12.18 shows this situation.

Figure 12.18 *Denying a connection*

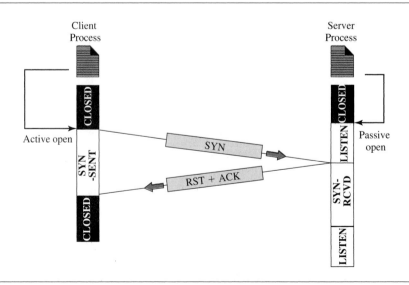

Aborting a Connection

A process can abort a connection instead of closing it. This can happen if the process has failed (perhaps locked up in an infinite loop) or does not want the data in the queue to be sent (due to some discrepancy in the data). TCP may also want to abort the connection. This can happen if it receives a segment belonging to the previous connection. In all of these cases the TCP can send an RST segment to abort the connection. Figure 12.19 shows a situation in which the client process has issued an abort. Its TCP sends an RST+ACK segment and throws away all data in the queue. The server TCP also throws away all queued data and informs the server process via an error message. Both TCPs go to the **CLOSED** state immediately. Note that no ACK segment is generated in response to the RST segment.

Figure 12.19 *Aborting a connection*

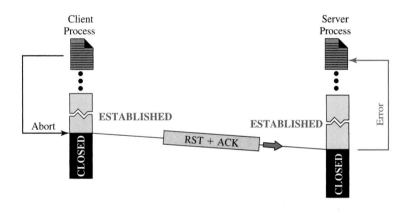

12.6 FLOW CONTROL

Flow control regulates the amount of data a source can send before receiving an acknowledgment from the destination. In the extreme case, a transport layer protocol could send 1 byte of data and wait for an acknowledgment before sending the next byte. This would be an extremely slow process. If the data are traveling a long distance, the source is idle while it waits for an acknowledgment.

At the other extreme, a transport layer protocol can send all of the data without worrying about acknowledgments. This speeds up the process, but it may overwhelm the receiver. Besides, if some part of the data is lost, duplicated, received out of order, or corrupted, the source will not know until all has been checked by the destination.

TCP offers a solution in between these two extremes. It defines a window that is imposed on the buffer of data delivered from the application program and ready to be sent. TCP sends an amount of data defined by the sliding window protocol.

Sliding Window Protocol

To accomplish flow control, TCP uses a **sliding window protocol.** In this method, a host uses a window for outbound communication (sending data). The window spans a portion of the buffer containing bytes received from the process. The bytes inside the window are the bytes that can be in transit; they can be sent without worrying about acknowledgment. The imaginary window has two walls: one left and one right. The window is called a **sliding window** because the right and left walls can slide as shown in Figure 12.20. The numbers shows the bytes inside and outside the window.

Figure 12.20   *Sliding window*

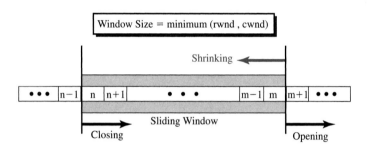

The window is *opened, closed,* or *shrunk.* These three activities, as we will see, are in the control of the receiver (and depend on congestion in the network), not the sender. The sender must obey the commands of the receiver in this matter.

Opening a window means moving the right wall to the right. This allows more new bytes in the buffer that are eligible for sending. Closing the window means moving the left wall to the right. This means that some bytes have been acknowledged and the sender needs not worry about them anymore. Shrinking the window means moving the right wall to the left. This is strongly discouraged and not allowed in some implementations because it means revoking the eligibility of some bytes for sending. This is a problem if the sender has already sent these bytes. Note that the left wall cannot move to the left because this would revoke some of the previously sent acknowledgments.

> **A sliding window is used to make transmission more efficient as well as to control the flow of data so that the destination does not become overwhelmed with data. TCP's sliding windows are byte oriented.**

The size of the window at one end, is determined by the lesser of two values: *receiver window* (*rwnd*) or *congestion window* (*cwnd*). The *receiver window* is the value advertised by the opposite end in a segment containing acknowledgment. It is the number of bytes the other end can accept before its buffer overflows and data is discarded. The congestion window is a value determined by the network to avoid congestion. We will discuss congestion later in the chapter.

Example 3

What is the value of the receiver window (rwnd) for host A if the receiver, host B, has a buffer size of 5,000 bytes and 1,000 bytes of received and unprocessed data?

Solution

The value of rwnd = 5,000 − 1,000 = 4,000. Host B can receive only 4,000 bytes of data before overflowing its buffer. Host B advertises this value in its next segment to A.

Example 4

What is the size of the window for host A if the value of rwnd is 3,000 bytes and the value of cwnd is 3,500 bytes?

Solution

The size of the window is the smaller of rwnd and cwnd, which is 3,000 bytes.

Example 5

Figure 12.21 shows an unrealistic example of a sliding window. The sender has sent bytes up to 202. We assume that cwnd is 20 (in reality this value is thousands of bytes). The receiver has sent an acknowledgment number of 200 with an rwnd of 9 bytes (in reality this value is thousands of bytes). The size of the sender window is the minimum of rwnd and cwnd or 9 bytes. Bytes 200 to 202 are sent, but not acknowledged. Bytes 203 to 208 can be sent without worrying about acknowledgment. Bytes 209 and above cannot be sent.

Figure 12.21   *Example 5*

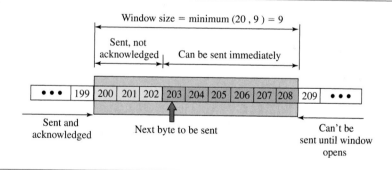

Example 6

In Figure 12.21 the server receives a packet with an acknowledgment value of 202 and an rwnd of 9. The host has already sent bytes 203, 204, and 205. The value of cwnd is still 20. Show the new window.

Solution

Figure 12.22 shows the new window. Note that this is a case in which the window closes from the left and opens from the right by an equal number of bytes; the size of the window has not been changed. The acknowledgment value, 202, declares that bytes 200 and 201 have been received and the sender needs not worry about them; the window can slide over them.

Figure 12.22   *Example 6*

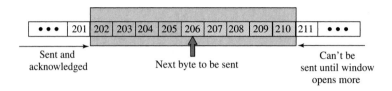

Example 7

In Figure 12.22 the sender receives a packet with an acknowledgment value of 206 and an rwnd of 12. The host has not sent any new bytes. The value of cwnd is still 20. Show the new window.

Solution

The value of rwnd is less than cwnd, so the size of the window is 12. Figure 12.23 shows the new window. Note that the window has been opened from the right by 7 and closed from the left by 4; the size of the window has increased.

Figure 12.23   *Example 7*

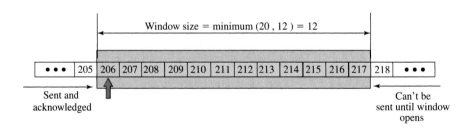

Example 8

In Figure 12.23 the host receives a packet with an acknowledgment value of 210 and an rwnd of 5. The host has sent bytes 206, 207, 208, and 209. The value of cwnd is still 20. Show the new window.

Solution

The value of rwnd is less than cwnd, so the size of the window is 5. Figure 12.24 shows the situation. Note that this is a case not allowed by most implementations. Although the sender has not sent bytes 215 to 217, the receiver does not know this.

Example 9

How can the receiver avoid shrinking the window in the previous example?

Solution

The receiver needs to keep track of the last acknowledgment number and the last rwnd. If we add the acknowledgment number to rwnd we get the byte number following the right wall. If we want

Figure 12.24   *Example 8*

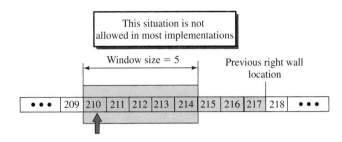

to prevent the right wall from moving to the left (shrinking), we must always have the following relationship.

> **new ack + new rwnd $\geq$ last ack + last rwnd**
>
> **or**
>
> **new rwnd $\geq$ (last ack + last rwnd) − new ack**

In Example 8 the new ack is 210 and the new rwnd is 5. The last ack was 206 and the last rwnd was 12. The relationship does not hold because $5 < (206 + 12) - 210$. The receiver needs to wait until more buffer space is free before sending an acknowledgment.

> **To avoid shrinking the sender window, the receiver must wait until more space is available in its buffer.**

Window Shutdown

We said that shrinking the window is strongly discouraged. However, there is one exception: the receiver can temporarily shut down the window by sending an rwnd of 0. This can happen if for some reason the receiver does not want to receive any data from the sender for a while. In this case, the sender does not actually shrink the size of the window, but stops sending data until a new advertisement has arrived. As we will see later, even when the window is shut down by an order from the receiver, the sender can always send a segment with one byte of data. This is called probing and is used to prevent a deadlock (see the section on TCP timers).

> **Some points about TCP's sliding windows:**
>
> ❏ **The size of the window is the lesser of rwnd and cwnd.**
> ❏ **The source does not have to send a full window's worth of data.**
> ❏ **The window can be opened or closed by the receiver, but should not be shrunk.**
> ❏ **The destination can send an acknowledgment at any time as long as it does not result in a shrinking window.**
> ❏ **The receiver can temporarily shut down the window; the sender, however, can always send a segment of one byte after the window is shut down.**

Silly Window Syndrome

A serious problem can arise in the sliding window operation when either the sending application program creates data slowly or the receiving application program consumes data slowly, or both. Any of these situations results in the sending of data in very small segments, which reduces the efficiency of the operation. For example, if TCP sends segments containing only 1 byte of data, it means that a 41-byte datagram (20 bytes of TCP header and 20 bytes of IP header) transfers only 1 byte of user data. Here the overhead is 41/1, which indicates that we are using the capacity of the network very inefficiently. This problem is called the **silly window syndrome.** For each site, we first describe how the problem is created and then give a proposed solution.

Syndrome Created by the Sender

The sending TCP may create a silly window syndrome if it is serving an application program that creates data slowly, for example, 1 byte at a time. The application program writes 1 byte at a time into the buffer of the sending TCP. If the sending TCP does not have any specific instructions, it may create segments containing 1 byte of data. The result is a lot of 41-byte segments that are traveling through an internet.

The solution is to prevent the sending TCP from sending the data byte by byte. The sending TCP must be forced to wait and collect data to send in a larger block. How long should the sending TCP wait? If it waits too long, it may delay the process. If it does not wait long enough, it may end up sending small segments. Nagle found an elegant solution.

Nagle's Algorithm   Nagle's algorithm is very simple:

1. The sending TCP sends the first piece of data it receives from the sending application program even if it is only 1 byte.
2. After sending the first segment, the sending TCP accumulates data in the output buffer and waits until either the receiving TCP sends an acknowledgment or until enough data has accumulated to fill a maximum-size segment. At this time, the sending TCP can send the segment.
3. Step 2 is repeated for the rest of the transmission. Segment 3 must be sent if an acknowledgment is received for segment 2 or if enough data have accumulated to fill a maximum-size segment.

The elegance of Nagle's algorithm is in its simplicity and in the fact that it takes into account the speed of the application program that creates the data and the speed of the network that transports the data. If the application program is faster than the network, the segments are larger (maximum-size segments). If the application program is slower than the network, the segments are smaller (less than the maximum segment size).

Syndrome Created by the Receiver

The receiving TCP may create a silly window syndrome if it is serving an application program that consumes data slowly, for example, 1 byte at a time. Suppose that the sending application program creates data in blocks of 1 kbyte, but the receiving application program consumes data 1 byte at a time. Also suppose that the input buffer of the receiving TCP is 4 kbytes. The sender sends the first 4 kbytes of data. The receiver stores it in its buffer. Now its buffer is full. It advertises a window size of zero, which means the sender should stop sending data. The receiving application reads the first byte of data from the input buffer of the receiving TCP. Now there is 1 byte of space in the incoming buffer. The receiving TCP announces a window size of 1 byte, which means that the sending TCP, which is eagerly waiting to send data, takes this advertisement as good news and sends a segment carrying only 1 byte of data. The procedure will continue. One byte of data is consumed and a segment carrying 1 byte of data is sent. Again we have an efficiency problem and a silly window syndrome.

Two solutions have been proposed to prevent the silly window syndrome created by an application program that consumes data slower than they arrive.

Clark's Solution   Clark's solution is to send an acknowledgment as soon as the data arrives, but to announce a window size of zero until either there is enough space to accommodate a segment of maximum size or until half of the buffer is empty.

Delayed Acknowledgment   The second solution is to delay sending the acknowledgment. This means that when a segment arrives, it is not acknowledged immediately. The receiver waits until there is a decent amount of space in its incoming buffer before acknowledging the arrived segments. The delayed acknowledgment prevents the sending TCP from sliding its window. After it has sent the data in the window, it stops. This kills the syndrome.

Delayed acknowledgment also has another advantage: It reduces traffic. The receiver does not have to acknowledge each segment. However, there also is a disadvantage in that the delayed acknowledgment may force the sender to retransmit the unacknowledged segments.

The protocol balances the advantages and disadvantages. It now defines that the acknowledgment should not be delayed by more than 500 ms.

12.7   ERROR CONTROL

TCP is a reliable transport layer protocol. This means that an application program that delivers a stream of data to TCP relies on TCP to deliver the entire stream to the application program on the other end in order, without error, and without any part lost or duplicated.

TCP provides reliability using **error control.** Error control includes mechanisms for detecting corrupted segments, lost segments, out-of-order segments, and duplicated segments. Error control also includes a mechanism for correcting errors after they are detected. Error detection and correction in TCP is achieved through the use of three simple tools: checksum, acknowledgment, and time-out.

Checksum

Each segment includes a checksum field which is used to check for a corrupted segment. If the segment is corrupted, it is discarded by the destination TCP and is considered as lost. TCP uses a 16-bit checksum that is mandatory in every segment. We will see, in the next chapter, that the 16-bit checksum is considered inadequate for the new transport layer, SCTP. However, it can not be changed for TCP because this would involve reconfiguration of the entire header format.

Acknowledgment

TCP uses acknowledgments to confirm the receipt of data segments. Control segments that carry no data, but consume a sequence number are also acknowledged. ACK segments are never acknowledged.

> **ACK segments do not consume sequence numbers and are not acknowledged.**

Generating Acknowledgments

When does a receiver generate acknowledgments? During the evolution of TCP, several rules have been defined and used by several implementations. We give the most common rules here. The order of a rule does not necessarily define its importance.

1. When one end sends a data segment to the other end, it must include (piggyback) an acknowledgment that gives the next sequence number it expects to receive. This rule decreases the number of segments needed and therefore reduces traffic.

2. When the receiver has no data to send and it receives an in-order segment (with expected sequence number) and the previous segment has already been acknowledged, the receiver delays sending an ACK segment until another segment arrives or until a period of time (normally 500 ms) has passed. In other words, the receiver needs to delay sending an ACK segment if there is only one outstanding in-order segment. This rule again prevents ACK segments from creating extra traffic.

3. When a segment arrives with a sequence number that is expected by the receiver, and the previous in-order segment has not been acknowledged, the receiver immediately sends an ACK segment. In other words, there should not be more than two in-order unacknowledged segments at any time. This prevents the unnecessary retransmission of segments that may create congestion in the network.

4. When a segment arrives with an out-of-order sequence number that is higher than expected, the receiver immediately sends an ACK segment announcing the sequence number of the next expected segment. This leads to the fast retransmission of any missing segments as we will see in one of our scenarios.

5. When a missing segment arrives, the receiver sends an ACK segment to announce the next sequence number expected. This informs the receiver that segments reported missing have been received.

6. If a duplicate segment arrives, the receiver immediately sends an acknowledgment. This solves some problems when an ACK segment itself is lost.

Acknowledgment Type

In the past, TCP used only one type of acknowledgment: accumulative acknowledgment. Today, some TCP implementations also use selective acknowledgments.

Accumulative Acknowledgment (ACK)   TCP was originally designed to acknowledge receipt of segments accumulatively. The receiver advertises the next byte it expects to receive, ignoring all segments received out-of-order. This is sometimes referred to as positive accumulative acknowledgment or ACK. The word "positive" indicates that discarded, lost, or duplicate segments are not reported. The 32-bit ACK field in the TCP header is used for accumulative acknowledgments and its value is valid only when the ACK flag bit is set to 1.

Selective Acknowledgment (SACK)   More and more implementations are adding another type of acknowledgment called **selective acknowledgment** or **SACK.** A SACK does not replace ACK, but reports additional information to the sender. A SACK reports the block of data that is out-of-order and the block of segments that is duplicated. However, since there is no provision in the TCP header for adding this type of information, SACK is implemented as an option at the end of the TCP header. We discuss this new feature when we discuss options in TCP.

Retransmission

The heart of the error control mechanism is the retransmission of segments. When a segment is corrupted, lost, or delayed, it is retransmitted. In modern implementations, a segment is retransmitted on two occasions: when a retransmission timer expires or when the sender receives three duplicate ACKs.

> **In modern implementations, a retransmission occurs if the retransmission timer expires or three duplicate ACK segments have arrived.**

Note that no retransmission occurs for segments that do not consume sequence numbers. In particular, there is no transmission for an ACK segment.

> **No retransmission timer is set for an ACK segment.**

Retransmission after RTO

The source TCP starts one **retransmission time-out (RTO)** timer for each segment sent. When the timer matures, the corresponding segment is considered to be either corrupted or lost, and the segment is retransmitted even though lack of a received ACK can be due to a delayed segment, a delayed ACK, or a lost acknowledgment. Note that no time-out timer is set for a segment that carries only an acknowledgment, which means that no such segment is resent. We will see later that the value of RTO is dynamic in TCP and is updated based on the round trip time (RTT) of segments. An RTT is the time needed for a segment to reach a destination and for an acknowledgment to be received.

Retransmission after Three Duplicate ACK Segments

The previous rule about retransmission of a segment is sufficient if the value of RTO is not very large. Sometimes, however, one segment is lost and the receiver receives so many out of order segments that they cannot be saved (limited buffer size). To alleviate this situation, most implementations today follow the three duplicate ACKs rule and retransmit the missing segment immediately. This feature is referred to as **fast retransmission,** which we will see in an example shortly.

Out-of-Order Segments

When a segment is delayed, lost, or discarded, the segments following that segment arrive out of order. Originally, TCP was designed to discard all out-of-order segments, resulting in the retransmission of the missing segment and the following segments. Most implementations today do not discard the out-of-order segments. They store them temporarily, and flag them as out-of-order segments until the missing segment arrives. Note however, that the out-of-order segments are not delivered to the process. TCP guarantees that data are delivered to the process in order.

> Data may arrive out of order and be temporarily stored by the receiving TCP, but TCP guarantees that no out-of-order segment is delivered to the process.

Some Scenarios

In this section we give some examples of scenarios that occur during the operation of TCP. In these scenarios, we show a segment by a rectangle. If the segment carries data we show the range of byte numbers and the value of the acknowledgment field. If it carries only an acknowledgment, we show only the acknowledgment number in a smaller box.

Normal Operation

The first scenario shows bidirectional data transfer between two systems as shown in Figure 12.25. The client TCP sends one segment; the server TCP sends three. The figure shows which rule applies to each acknowledgment. For the client's first segment and all three server segments, rule 1 applies. There are data to be sent so the segment displays the next byte expected. When the client receives the first segment from the server, it does not have any more data to send; it sends only an ACK segment. However, according to rule 2, the acknowledgment needs to be delayed for 500 ms to see if any more segments arrive. When the timer matures, it triggers an acknowledgment. This is because the client has no knowledge if other segments are coming; it cannot delay the acknowledgment forever. When the next segment arrives another acknowledgment timer is set. However, before it matures, the third segment arrives. The arrival of the third segment triggers another acknowledgment based on rule 3.

Figure 12.25 *Normal operation*

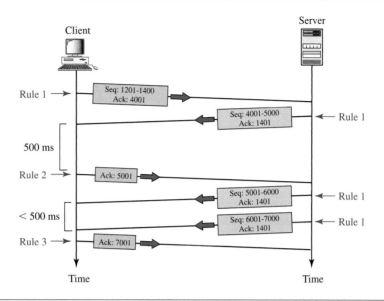

Lost Segment

In this scenario, we show what happens when a segment is lost or corrupted. A lost or corrupted segment is treated the same way by the receiver. A lost segment is discarded somewhere in the network; a corrupted segment is discarded by the receiver itself. Both are considered lost. Figure 12.26 shows a situation in which a segment is lost and discarded by some router in the network, perhaps due to congestion.

Figure 12.26 *Lost segment*

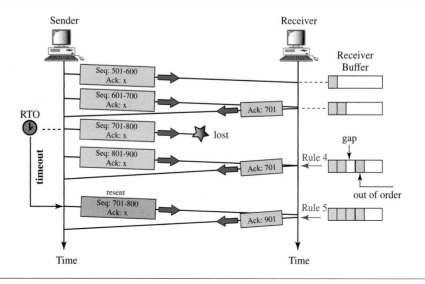

We are assuming that data transfer is unidirectional: one site is sending, the other receiving. In our scenario, the sender sends segments 1 and 2, which are acknowledged immediately by an ACK (rule 3). Segment 3, however, is lost. The receiver receives segment 4, which is out of order. The receiver stores the data in the segment in its buffer but leaves a gap to indicate that there is no continuity in the data. The receiver immediately sends an acknowledgment to the sender displaying the next byte it expects (rule 4). Note that the receiver stores bytes 801 to 900, but never delivers these bytes to the application until the gap is filled.

The receiver TCP delivers only ordered data to the process.

Although the sender TCP keeps an RTO timer for each sent segment, we have shown it only for segment 3, which is lost. The timer for this definitely runs out because the receiver never sends an acknowledgment for lost or out-of-order segments. When the timer matures, the sending TCP resends segment 3, which arrives this time and is acknowledged properly (rule 5). Note that the value in the second and third acknowledgment differs according to the corresponding rule.

Fast Retransmission

In this scenario, we want to show the idea of **fast retransmission.** Our scenario is the same as the second except that the RTO has a higher value (see Figure 12.27).

Figure 12.27   *Fast retransmission*

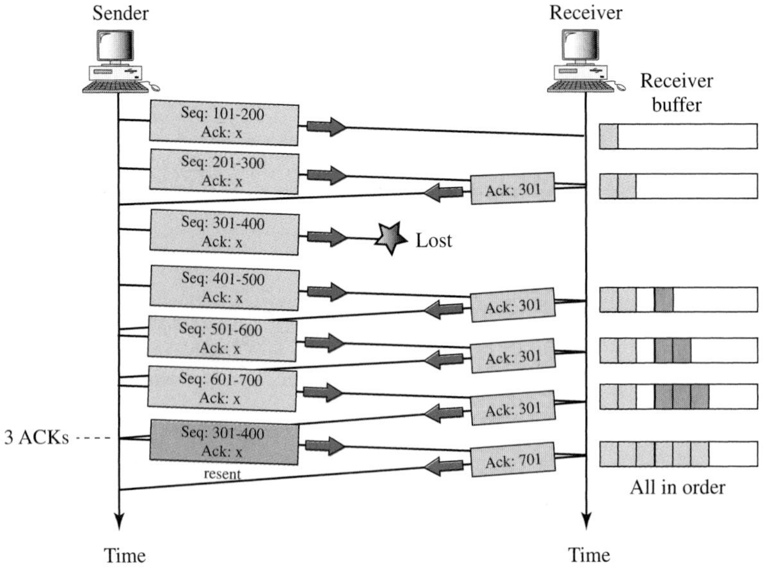

When the receiver receives the fourth, fifth, and sixth segments, it triggers an acknowledgment. The sender receives four acknowledgments with the same value (three duplicates). Although the timer for segment 3 has not matured yet, the rule for fast transmission requires that segment 3, the segment that is expected by all of these acknowledgments, be resent immediately.

Delayed Segment

The fourth scenario features a delayed segment. TCP uses the services of IP, which is a connectionless protocol. Each IP datagram encapsulating a TCP segment may reach the final destination through a different route with a different delay. TCP segments may be delayed. Delayed segments are treated the same way as lost or corrupted segments by the receiver. The delayed segment may arrive after it has been resent (a duplicate segment).

Duplicate Segment

A duplicate segment can be created, for example, by a sending TCP when a segment is delayed and treated as lost by the receiver. Handling the duplicated segment is a simple process for the destination TCP. The destination TCP expects a continuous stream of bytes. When a segment arrives that contains a sequence number less than the previously acknowledged bytes, it is discarded.

Automatically Corrected Lost ACK

This scenario shows a situation in which a lost acknowledgment is automatically replaced by the next. Figure 12.28 shows a lost acknowledgment sent by the receiver of data. In the TCP acknowledgment mechanism, a lost acknowledgment may not even be noticed by the source TCP. TCP uses an accumulative acknowledgment system. We can say that the next acknowledgment automatically corrects the loss of the acknowledgment.

Figure 12.28 *Lost acknowledgment*

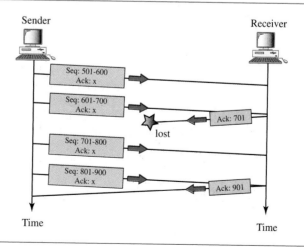

Lost Acknowledgment Corrected by Resending a Segment

If the next acknowledgment is delayed for a long time or there is no next acknowledgment (the lost acknowledgment is the last one sent), the correction is triggered by the

RTO timer at the end that is supposed to receive the acknowledgment. A duplicate segment is the result. When the receiver receives a duplicate segment, it discards it, but it does resend the last ACK immediately to inform the sender that the segment or segments are safe and sound. Figure 12.29 shows this scenario.

Figure 12.29   *Lost acknowledgment corrected by resending a segment*

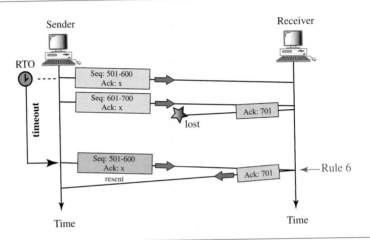

Note that only one segment is retransmitted although two segments are not acknowledged. When the sender receives the retransmitted ACK, it knows that both segments are safe and sound because acknowledgment is accumulative.

Deadlock Created by Lost Acknowledgment

There is one situation in which loss of an acknowledgment may result in system deadlock. This is the case in which a receiver sends an acknowledgment with *rwnd* set to 0 and requests that the sender shut down its window temporarily. After a while, the receiver wants to remove the restriction; however, if it has no data to send, it sends an ACK segment and removes the restriction with a nonzero value for *rwnd*. The problem arises if this acknowledgment is lost. The sender is waiting for an acknowledgment that announces the nonzero *rwnd*. The receiver thinks that the sender has received this and is waiting for data. This situation is called a **deadlock;** each end is waiting for a response from the other end and nothing is happening. A retransmission timer is not set. To prevent deadlock, a persistence timer was designed that we will study later in the chapter.

> **Lost acknowledgments may create deadlock if they are not properly handled.**

12.8   CONGESTION CONTROL

An important issue in a network is **congestion.** Congestion in a network may occur if the load on the network—the number of packets sent to the network—is greater than the *capacity* of the network—the number of packets a network can handle. **Congestion control** refers to the mechanisms and techniques to control the congestion and keep the load below the capacity.

We may ask why there is congestion on a network. Congestion happens in any system that involves waiting. For example, congestion happens on a freeway because any abnormality in the flow, such as an accident during rush hour, creates blockage.

Congestion in a network or internetwork occurs because routers and switches have queues—buffers that hold the packets before and after processing. A router, for example, has an input queue and an output queue for each interface. When a packet arrives at the incoming interface, it undergoes three steps before departing, as shown in Figure 12.30.

Figure 12.30 *Router queues*

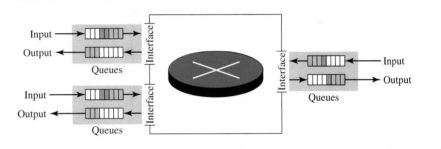

1. The packet is placed at the end of the input queue while waiting to be checked.
2. The processing module of the router removes the packet from the input queue once it reaches the front of the queue and uses its routing table and the destination address to find the route.
3. The packet is put in the appropriate output queue and waits its turn to be sent.

We need to be aware of two issues. First, if the rate of packet arrival is higher than the packet processing rate, the input queues become longer and longer. Second, if the packet departure rate is less than the packet processing rate, the output queues become longer and longer.

Network Performance

Congestion control involves two factors that measure the performance of a network: **delay** and **throughput.**

Delay versus Load

Figure 12.31 shows the relationship between packet delay and network load. Note that when the load is much less than the capacity of the network, the delay is at a minimum. This minimum delay is composed of propagation delay and processing delay, both of which are negligible. However, when the load reaches the network capacity, the delay increases sharply because we now need to add the waiting time in the queues (for all routers in the path) to the total delay. Note that the delay becomes infinite when the

Figure 12.31 *Packet delay and network load*

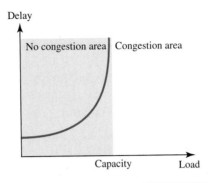

load is greater than the capacity. If this is not obvious, consider the size of the queues when almost no packets reach the destination, or reach the destination with infinite delay; the queues become longer and longer. Delay has a negative effect on the load and consequently the congestion. When a packet is delayed, the source, not receiving an acknowledgment, retransmits the packet, which makes the delay, and the congestion, worse.

Throughput versus Load

We can define *throughput* in a network as the number of packets passing through the network in a unit of time. We can then plot the throughput versus the network load, as shown in Figure 12.32.

Figure 12.32 *Throughput versus network load*

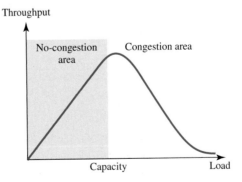

Notice that when the load is below the capacity of the network, the throughput increases proportionally with the load. We expect the throughput to remain constant after the load reaches the capacity, but instead the throughput declines sharply. The reason is the discarding of packets by the routers. When the load exceeds the capacity, the queues become full and the routers have to discard some packets. Discarding packets does not reduce the number of packets in the network because the sources retransmit the packets, using time-out mechanisms when the packets do not reach the destinations.

Congestion Control Mechanisms

Congestion control refers to techniques and mechanisms that can either prevent congestion, before it happens, or remove congestion, after it has happened. In general, we can divide congestion control mechanisms into two broad categories: open-loop congestion control (prevention) and closed-loop congestion control (removal).

Open-Loop Congestion Control

In **open-loop congestion control,** policies are applied to prevent congestion before it happens. In these mechanisms, congestion control is handled by either the source or the destination. We give a brief list of policies that can prevent congestion.

Retransmission Policy   A good retransmission policy can prevent congestion. The retransmission policy and the retransmission timers must be designed to optimize efficiency and at the same time prevent congestion.

Acknowledgment Policy   The acknowledgment policy imposed by the receiver may also affect congestion. If the receiver does not acknowledge every packet it receives, it may slow down the sender and help prevent congestion.

Discard Policy   A good discard policy possessed by the routers may prevent congestion and at the same time will not harm the integrity of the transmission. For example, in audio transmission, if the policy is to discard less sensitive packets when congestion is likely, the quality of sound is still preserved and congestion is prevented.

Closed-Loop Congestion Control

Closed-loop congestion control mechanisms try to alleviate congestion after it happens. Several mechanisms have been used by different protocols. We describe a few of them here.

Back Pressure   When a router is congested, it can inform the previous upstream router to reduce the rate of outgoing packets. The action can be recursive all the way to the router just prior to the source. This mechanism is called *back pressure.*

Choke Point   A **choke point** is a packet sent by a router to the source to inform it of congestion. This type of control is similar to ICMP's source quench packet.

Implicit Signaling   The source can detect an implicit signal warning of congestion and slow down its sending rate. For example, the mere delay in receiving an acknowledgment can be a signal that the network is congested. We will see this type of signaling when we discuss TCP congestion control.

Explicit Signaling   The routers that experience congestion can send an explicit signal, the setting of a bit in a packet, for example, to inform the sender or the receiver of congestion.

Congestion Control in TCP

Congestion Window

Previously, we talked about flow control and tried to discuss solutions when the receiver is overwhelmed with data. We said that the sender window size is determined by the available buffer space in the receiver (rwnd). In other words, we assumed that it is only the receiver that can dictate to the sender the size of the sender's window. We totally ignored another entity here, the network. If the network cannot deliver the data as fast as it is created by the sender, it must tell the sender to slow down. In other words, in addition to the receiver, the network is a second entity that determines the size of the sender's window.

Today, the sender's window size is determined not only by the receiver but also by congestion in the network.

The sender has two pieces of information: the receiver-advertised window size and the congestion window size. The actual size of the window is the minimum of these two.

> **Actual window size = minimum (rwnd , cwnd)**

We show shortly how the size of the congestion window (cwnd) is determined.

Congestion Policy

TCP's general policy for handling congestion is based on three phases: slow start, congestion avoidance, and congestion detection. In the slow start phase, the sender starts with a very slow rate of transmission, but increases the rate rapidly to reach a threshold. When the threshold is reached, the data rate is reduced to avoid congestion. Finally if congestion is detected, the sender goes back to the slow start or congestion avoidance phase based on how the congestion is detected.

Slow Start: Exponential Increase One of the algorithms used in TCP congestion control is called **slow start.** This algorithm is based on the idea that the size of the congestion window (cwnd) starts with one maximum segment size (MSS). The MSS is determined during connection establishment using an option of the same name. The size of the window increases one MSS each time one segment is acknowledged. As the name implies, the algorithm starts slowly, but grows exponentially. To show the idea let us look at Figure 12.33. Note that we have used three simplifications to make the discussion more understandable and the figure much smaller. We have used segment numbers instead of byte numbers (as though each segment contains only one byte). We have assumed that *rwnd* is much higher than *cwnd,* so that the sender window size always equals *cwnd*. We have shown only the acknowledgments after receipt of window-size segments, which means that we have ignored the rules for generating acknowledgments.

The sender starts with cwnd = 1 MSS. This means that the sender can send only one segment. After receiving the acknowledgment for segment 1, the size of the congestion window is increased by 1, which means that cwnd is now 2. Now two more segments can be sent. When the two segments are acknowledged, the size of the window is increased by 1 MSS for each acknowledged segment, which means cwnd is 4. Now four more segments can be sent. When all four segments are acknowledged, the size of

Figure 12.33 *Slow start, exponential increase*

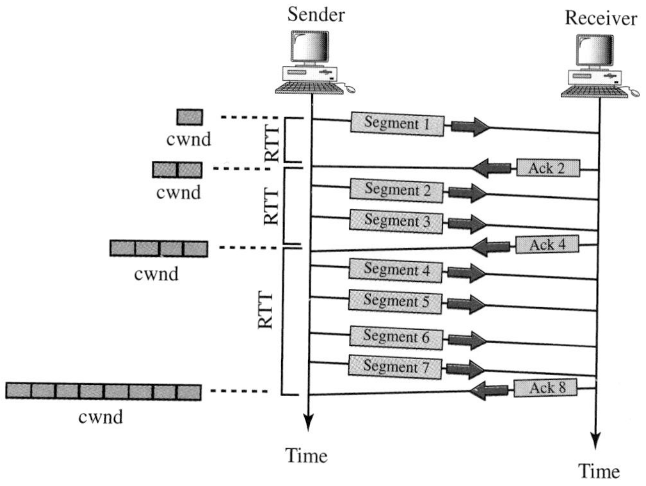

the window increases by 4, which means that cwnd = 8. Note that it does not matter if the segments are acknowledged one by one, two by two, or so on. The result is the same.

If we look at the size of the cwnd in terms of round trip time (RTT), we find that the rate is exponential as shown below:

Start	➡	cwnd = 1
After 1 RTT	➡	cwnd = $1 \times 2 = 2$ ➡ 2^1
After 2 RTT	➡	cwnd = $2 \times 2 = 4$ ➡ 2^2
After 3 RTT	➡	cwnd = $4 \times 2 = 8$ ➡ 2^3

Slow start cannot continue indefinitely. There must be a threshold to stop this phase. The sender keeps track of a variable named *ssthresh* (slow start threshold). When the size of window in bytes reaches this threshold, slow start stops and the next phase starts. In most implementations the value of ssthresh is 65535 bytes.

> **In the slow start algorithm the size of the congestion window increases exponentially until it reaches a threshold.**

Congestion Avoidance: Additive Increase   If we start with the slow start algorithm, the size of the congestion window increases exponentially. To avoid congestion before it happens, one must slow down this exponential growth. TCP defines another algorithm called **congestion avoidance,** which increases additively instead of exponentially. When the size of the congestion window reaches the slow start threshold, the slow start phase stops and the additive phase begins. In this algorithm, each time the whole window of segments is acknowledged, the size of the congestion window is increased by one. To show the idea, we apply this algorithm to the same scenario as slow start although as we will see that the congestion avoidance algorithm usually starts when the size of the window is much greater than 1. Figure 12.34 shows the idea.

Figure 12.34 *Congestion avoidance, additive increase*

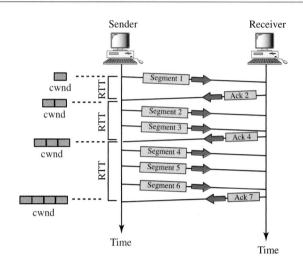

In this case, after the sender has received acknowledgments for a complete window-size of segments, the size of the window is increased one segment.

If we look at the size of cwnd in terms of round trip time (RTT), we find that the rate is additive as shown below:

Start	➡	**cwnd = 1**
After 1 RTT	➡	**cwnd = 1 + 1 = 2**
After 2 RTT	➡	**cwnd = 2 + 1 = 3**
After 3 RTT	➡	**cwnd = 3 + 1 = 4**

> **In the congestion avoidance algorithm the size of the congestion window increases additively until congestion is detected.**

Congestion Detection: Multiplicative Decrease   If congestion occurs, the congestion window size must be decreased. The only way the sender can guess that congestion has occurred is the need to retransmit a segment. However, retransmission can occur in one of two cases: when an RTO timer times out or when three ACKs are received. In both cases, the size of the threshold is dropped to half (**multiplicative decrease**). Most TCP implementations have two reactions:

1. If a time-out occurs, there is a stronger possibility of congestion; a segment has probably been dropped in the network and there is no news about the following sent segments. In this case TCP reacts strongly:

   a. It sets the value of the threshold to half of the current window size.

   b. It sets cwnd to the size of one segment.

   c. It starts the slow start phase again.

2. If three ACKs are received, there is a weaker possibility of congestion; a segment may have been dropped but some segments after that may have arrived safely since

three ACKs are received. This is called fast transmission and fast recovery. In this case, TCP has a weaker reaction as shown below:

a. It sets the value of the threshold to half of the current window size.

b. It sets cwnd to the value of the threshold (some implementations add three segment sizes to the threshold).

c. It starts the congestion avoidance phase.

Most implementations react differently to congestion detection:

❑ **If detection is by time-out, a new *slow start* phase starts.**
❑ **If detection is by three ACKs, a new *congestion avoidance* phase starts.**

Summary   In Figure 12.35, we summarize the congestion policy of TCP and the relationships between the three phases.

Figure 12.35   *TCP congestion policy summary*

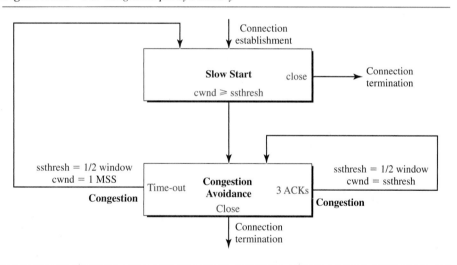

We give an example in Figure 12.36. We assume that the maximum window size is 32 segments. The threshold is set to 16 segments (half of the maximum window size). In the *slow start* phase the window size starts from 1 and grows exponentially until it reaches the threshold. After reaching the threshold, the *congestion avoidance (additive increase)* procedure allows the window size to increase linearly until a time-out occurs or the maximum window size is reached. In the figure, the time-out occurs when the window size is 20. At this moment, the *multiplicative decrease* procedure takes over and reduces the threshold to half of the previous window size. The previous window size was 20 when the time-out happened so the new threshold is now 10.

TCP moves to slow start again and starts with a window size of 1, and moves to additive increase when the new threshold is reached. When the window size is 12, a three-ACKs event happens. The multiplicative decrease procedure takes over again.

The threshold is set to 6 and TCP goes to the additive increase phase this time. It remains in this phase until another time-out or another three-ACKs happens.

Figure 12.36   *Congestion example*

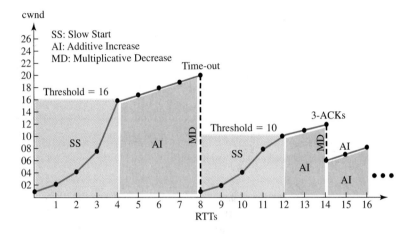

12.9   TCP TIMERS

To perform its operation smoothly, most TCP implementations use at least four timers as shown in Figure 12.37.

Figure 12.37   *TCP timers*

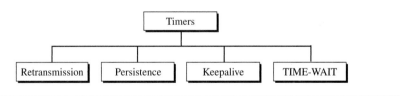

Retransmission Timer

To retransmit a lost segment, TCP employs a retransmission timer that handles the retransmission time-out (RTO), the waiting time for an acknowledgment of a segment. When TCP sends a segment, it creates a retransmission timer for that particular segment. Two situations may occur:

1. If an acknowledgment is received for this particular segment before the timer goes off, the timer is destroyed.

2. If the timer goes off before the acknowledgment arrives, the segment is retransmitted and the timer is reset.

Round Trip Time (RTT)

To calculate the retransmission time-out (RTO), we first need to calculate the round-trip time (RTT). However, calculating RTT in TCP is an involved process that we explain step by step with some examples.

Measured RTT   We need to find how long it takes to send a segment and receive an acknowledgment for it. This is the measured RTT. We need to remember that the segments and their acknowledgments do not have a one-to-one relationship; several segments may be acknowledged together. The measured round trip time for a segment is the time required for the segment to reach the destination and be acknowledged, although the acknowledgment may include other segments. Note that in TCP, only one RTT measurement can be in progress at any time. This means that if an RTT measurement is started, no other measurement starts until the value of this RTT is finalized. We use the notation RTT_M to stand for measured RTT.

> **In TCP, there can be only be one RTT measurement in progress at any time.**

Smoothed RTT   The measured RTT, RTT_M, changes for round trip. The fluctuation is so high in today's Internet that it cannot be used for retransmission time-out purposes. Most implementations use a smoothed RTT, called RTT_S, which is a weighted average of RTT_M and the previous RTT_S as shown below:

Original	⟹ No value
After first measurement	⟹ $RTT_S = RTT_M$
After any other measurement	⟹ $RTT_S = (1 - \alpha) RTT_S + \alpha \cdot RTT_M$

The value of α is implementation-dependent, but it is normally set to 1/8. In other words, the new RTT_S is calculated as 7/8 of the old RTT_S and 1/8 of the current RTT_M.

RTT Deviation   Most implementations do not just use RTT_S; they also calculate the RTT deviation, called RTT_D, based on the RTT_S and RTT_M using the following formulas:

Original	⟹ No value
After first measurement	⟹ $RTT_D = RTT_M / 2$
After any other measurement	⟹ $RTT_D = (1 - \beta) RTT_D + \beta \cdot \lvert RTT_S - RTT_M \rvert$

The value of β is also implementation-dependent, but is usually is set to 1/4.

Retransmission Timeout (RTO)

The value of RTO is based on the smoothed round trip time and its deviation. Most implementations use the following formula to calculate the RTO:

Original	⟹ Initial value
After any measurement	⟹ $RTO = RTT_S + 4 \cdot RTT_D$

In other words, take the most recent value of RTT_S, and add four times the value of RTT_D (normally a small value) for balance.

Example 10

Let us give a hypothetical example. Figure 12.38 shows part of a connection. The figure shows the connection establishment and part of the data transfer phases.

Figure 12.38   *Example 10*

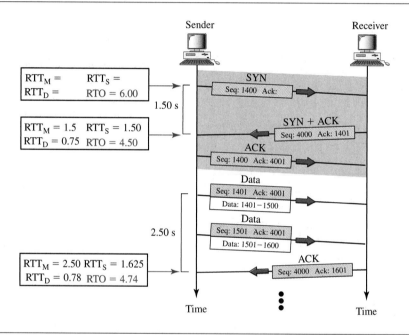

1. When the SYN segment is sent, there is no value for RTT_M, RTT_S, or RTT_D. The value of RTO is set to 6.00 seconds. The following shows the value of these variables at this moment:

$$RTO = 6$$

2. When the SYN+ACK segment arrives, RTT_M is measured and is equal to 1.5 seconds. The following shows the values of these variables:

RTT_M = 1.5
RTT_S = 1.5
RTT_D = 1.5 / 2 = 0.75
RTO = 1.5 + 4 . 0.75 = 4.5

3. When the first data segment is sent, a new RTT measurement starts. Note that the sender does not start an RTT measurement when it sends the ACK segment, because it does not

consume a sequence number and there is no time-out. No RTT measurement starts for the second data segment because a measurement is already in progress. The arrival of the last ACK segment is used to calculate the next value of RTT_M. Although the last ACK segment acknowledges both data segments (accumulative), its arrival finalizes the value of RTT_M for the first segment. The values of these variables are now as shown below.

$$RTT_M = 2.5$$
$$RTT_S = 7/8 \ (1.5) + 1/8 \ (2.5) = 1.625$$
$$RTT_D = 3/4 \ (7.5) + 1/4 \ |1.625 - 2.5| = 0.78$$
$$RTO = 1.625 + 4 \ (0.78) = 4.74$$

Karn's Algorithm

Suppose that a segment is not acknowledged during the retransmission period and is therefore retransmitted. When the sending TCP receives an acknowledgment for this segment, it does not know if the acknowledgment is for the original segment or for the retransmitted one. The value of the new RTT is based on the departure of the segment. However, if the original segment was lost and the acknowledgment is for the retransmitted one, the value of the current RTT must be calculated from the time the segment was retransmitted. This is a dilemma that was solved by Karn. Karn's solution is very simple. Do not consider the round trip time of a retransmitted segment in the calculation of the new RTT. Do not update the value of RTT until you send a segment and receive an acknowledgment without the need for retransmission.

> **TCP does not consider the RTT of a retransmitted segment in its calculation of a new RTO.**

Exponential Backoff

What is the value of RTO if a retransmission occurs? Most TCP implementations use an exponential backoff strategy. The value of RTO is doubled for each retransmission. So if the segment is retransmitted once, the value is two times the RTO. if it transmitted twice, the value is four times the RTO, and so on.

Example 11

Figure 12.39 is a continuation of the previous example. There is retransmission and Karn's algorithm is applied.

The first segment in the figure is sent, but lost. The RTO timer expires after 4.74 seconds. The segment is retransmitted and the timer is set to 9.48, twice the previous value of RTO. This time an ACK is received before the time-out. We wait until we send a new segment and receive the ACK for it before recalculating the RTO (Karn's algorithm).

Persistence Timer

To deal with a zero-window-size advertisement, TCP needs another timer. If the receiving TCP announces a window size of zero, the sending TCP stops transmitting segments until the receiving TCP sends an ACK segment announcing a non-zero window size. This ACK segment can be lost. Remember that ACK segments are not acknowledged in TCP. If this

---

Figure 12.39 *Example 11*

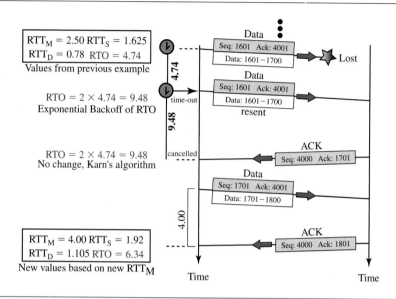

acknowledgment is lost, the receiving TCP thinks that it has done its job and waits for the sending TCP to send more segments. There is no retransmission timer for a segment containing only an acknowledgment. The sending TCP has not received an acknowledgment and waits for the other TCP to send an acknowledgment advertising the size of the window. Both TCPs can continue to wait for each other forever (a deadlock).

To correct this deadlock, TCP uses a **persistence timer** for each connection. When the sending TCP receives an acknowledgment with a window size of zero, it starts a persistence timer. When the persistence timer goes off, the sending TCP sends a special segment called a *probe*. This segment contains only 1 byte of data. It has a sequence number, but its sequence number is never acknowledged; it is even ignored in calculating the sequence number for the rest of the data. The probe alerts the receiving TCP that the acknowledgment was lost and must be resent.

The value of the persistence timer is set to the value of the retransmission time. However, if a response is not received from the receiver, another probe segment is sent and the value of the persistence timer is doubled and reset. The sender continues sending the probe segments and doubling and resetting the value of the persistence timer until the value reaches a threshold (usually 60 s). After that the sender sends one probe segment every 60 s until the window is reopened.

Keepalive Timer

A **keepalive timer** is used in some implementations to prevent a long idle connection between two TCPs. Suppose that a client opens a TCP connection to a server, transfers some data, and becomes silent. Perhaps the client has crashed. In this case, the connection remains open forever.

To remedy this situation, most implementations equip a server with a keepalive timer. Each time the server hears from a client, it resets this timer. The time-out is usually two hours. If the server does not hear from the client after two hours, it sends a probe segment. If there is no response after 10 probes, each of which is 75 s apart, it assumes that the client is down and terminates the connection.

TIME-WAIT Timer

The TIME-WAIT (2MSL) timer is used during connection termination. We discussed the reasons for this timer in Section 12.5 (State Transition Diagram).

12.10   OPTIONS

The TCP header can have up to 40 bytes of optional information. Options convey additional information to the destination or align other options. We can define two categories of options: 1-byte options and multiple-byte options. The first category contains two types of options: end of option list and no operation. The second category, in most implementations, contains five types of options: maximum segment size, window scale factor, timestamp, SACK-permitted, and SACK (see Figure 12.40).

Figure 12.40   *Options*

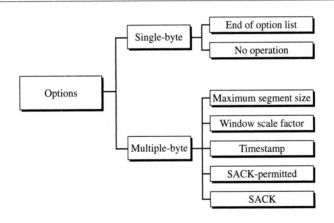

End of Option (EOP)

The **end-of-option (EOP) option** is a 1-byte option used for padding at the end of the option section. It can only be used as the last option. Only one occurrence of this option is allowed. After this option, the receiver looks for the payload data. Figure 12.41 shows an example. A 3-byte option is used after the header; the data section follows this option. One EOP option is inserted to align the data with the boundary of the next word.

The EOP option imparts two pieces of information to the destination:

1. There are no more options in the header.

2. Data from the application program starts at the beginning of the next 32-bit word.

Figure 12.41 *End-of-option option*

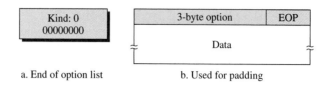

a. End of option list   b. Used for padding

EOP can be used only once.

No Operation (NOP)

The **no-operation (NOP) option** is also a 1-byte option used as a filler. However, it normally comes before another option to make an option fit in a four-word slot. For example, in Figure 12.42 it is used to align one 3-byte option such as the window scale factor and one 10-byte option such as the timestamp.

Figure 12.42 *No-operation option*

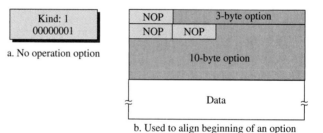

a. No operation option

b. Used to align beginning of an option

NOP can be used more than once.

Maximum Segment Size (MSS)

The **maximum-segment-size option** defines the size of the biggest unit of data that can be received by the destination of the TCP segment. In spite of its name, it defines the maximum size of the data, not the maximum size of the segment. Since the field is 16 bits long, the value can be 0 to 65,535 bytes. Figure 12.43 shows the format of this option.

Figure 12.43 *Maximum-segment-size option*

Kind: 2 00000010	Length: 4 00000100	Maximum segment size
1 byte	1 byte	2 bytes

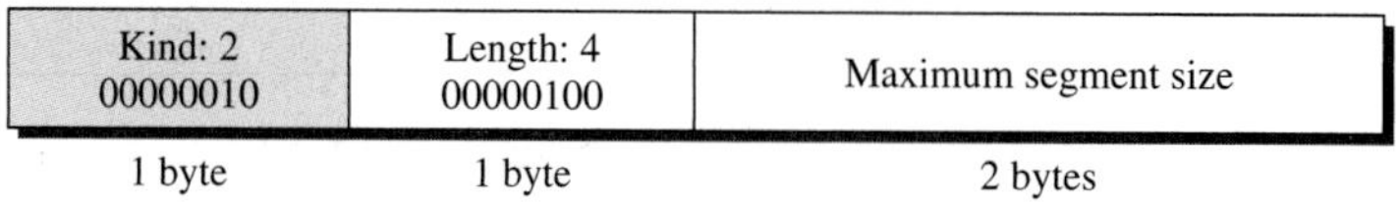

MSS is determined during connection establishment. Each party defines the MSS for the segments it will receive during the connection. If a party does not define this, the default values is 536 bytes.

> **The value of MSS is determined during connection establishment and does not change during the connection.**

Window Scale Factor

The window size field in the header defines the size of the sliding window. This field is 16 bits long, which means that the window can range from 0 to 65,535 bytes. Although this seems like a very large window size, it still may not be sufficient, especially if the data is traveling through a *long fat pipe,* a long channel with a wide bandwidth.

To increase the window size, a **window scale factor** is used. The new window size is found by first raising 2 to the number specified in the window scale factor. Then this result is multiplied by the value of the window size in the header.

> **new window size = window size defined in the header × 2** ^{window scale factor}

Figure 12.44 shows the format of the window-scale-factor option.

Figure 12.44   *Window-scale-factor option*

The scale factor is sometimes called the *shift count* because multiplying a number by a power of 2 is the same as a left shift in a bitwise operation. In other words, the actual value of the window size can be determined by taking the value of the window size advertisement in the packet and shifting it to the left in the amount of the window scale factor.

For example, suppose the value of the window scale factor is 3. An end point receives a acknowledgment in which the window size is advertised as 32768. The size of window this end can use is $32,768 \times 2^3$ or 262,144 bytes. The same value can be obtained if we shift the number 32,768 three bits to the left.

Although the scale factor could be as large as 255, the largest value allowed by TCP/IP is 14, which means that the maximum window size is $2^{16} \times 2^{14} = 2^{30}$, which is less than the maximum value for the sequence number. Note that the size of the window cannot be greater than the maximum value of the sequence number.

The window scale factor can also be determined only during the connection establishment phase. During data transfer, the size of the window (specified in the header) may be changed, but it must be multiplied by the same window scale factor.

> **The value of the window scale factor can be determined only during connection establishment; it does not change during the connection.**

Note that one end may set the value of the window scale factor to 0, which means that although it supports this option, it does not want to use it for this connection.

Timestamp

This is a 10-byte option with the format shown in Figure 12.45. Note that the end with the active open announces a timestamp in the connection request segment (SYN segment). If it receives a timestamp in the next segment (SYN + ACK) from the other end, it is allowed to use the timestamp; otherwise, it does not use it any more. The **timestamp option** has two applications: it measures the round trip time and prevents wraparound sequence numbers.

Figure 12.45 *Timestamp option*

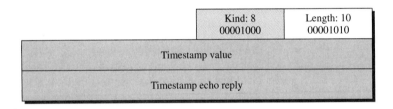

Measuring RTT   Timestamp can be used to measure the round-trip time (RTT). TCP, when is ready to send a segment, reads the value of the system clock and inserts this value, a 32-bit number, in the timestamp value field. The receiver, when sending an acknowledgment for this segment or an accumulative acknowledgment that covers the bytes in this segment, copies the timestamp received in the timestamp echo reply. The sender, upon receiving the acknowledgment, subtracts the value of the timestamp echo reply from the time shown by the clock to find RTT.

Note that there is no need for the sender's and receiver's clocks to be synchronized because all calculations are based on the sender clock. Also note that the sender does not have to remember or store the time a segment left because this value is carried by the segment itself.

The receiver needs to keep track of two variables. The first, *lastack,* is the value of the last acknowledgment sent. The second, *tsrecent,* is the value of the recent timestamp that has not yet echoed. When the receiver receives a segment that contains the byte matching the value of lastack, it inserts the value of the timestamp field in the *tsrecent* variable. When it sends an acknowledgment, it inserts the value of tsrecent in the echo reply field.

> **One application of the timestamp option is the calculation of round trip time (RTT).**

Example 12

Figure 12.46 shows an example that calculates the round-trip time for one end. Everything must be flipped if we want to calculate the RTT for the other end.

Figure 12.46 *Example 12*

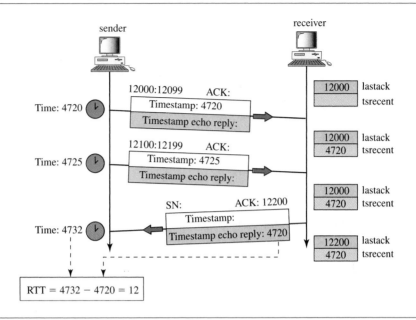

The sender simply inserts the value of the clock (for example, the number of seconds past from midnight) in the timestamp field for the first and second segment. When an acknowledgment comes (the third segment), the value of the clock is checked and the value of the echo reply field is subtracted from the current time. RTT is 12 s in this scenario.

The receiver's function is more involved. It keeps track of the last acknowledgment sent (12000). When the first segment arrives, it contains the bytes 12000 to 12099. The first byte is the same as the value of *lastack*. It then copies the timestamp value (4720) into the *tsrecent* variable. The value of lastack is still 12000 (no new acknowledgment has been sent). When the second segment arrives, since none of the byte numbers in this segment include the value of *lastack,* the value of the timestamp field is ignored. When the receiver decides to send an accumulative acknowledgment with acknowledgment 12200, it changes the value of *lastack* to 12200 and inserts the value of tsrecent in the echo reply field. The value of tsrecent will not change until it is replaced by a new segment that carries byte 12200 (next segment).

Note that as the example shows, the RTT calculated is the time difference between sending the first segment and receiving the third segment. This is actually the meaning of RTT: the time difference between a packet sent and the acknowledgment received. The third segment carries the acknowledgment for the first and second segments.

PAWS The timestamp option has another application, **protection against wrapped sequence numbers (PAWS).** The sequence number defined in the TCP protocol is only 32 bits long. Although this is a large number, it could be wrapped around in a high-speed connection. This implies that if a sequence number is *n* at one time, it could be *n* again during the lifetime of the same connection. Now if the first segment is duplicated and arrives during the second round of the sequence numbers, the segment belonging to the past is wrongly taken as the segment belonging to the new round.

One solution to this problem is to increase the size of the sequence number, but this involves increasing the size of the window as well as the format of the segment and more. The easiest solution is to include the timestamp in the identification of a segment. In other words, the identity of a segment can be defined as the combination of timestamp and sequence number. This means increasing the size of the identification. Two segments 400:12001 and 700:12001 definitely belong to different incarnations. The first was sent at time 400, the second at time 700.

The timestamp option can also be used for PAWS.

SACK-Permitted and SACK Options

As we discussed before, the acknowledgment field in the TCP segment is designed as an accumulative acknowledgment, which means it reports the receipt of the last consecutive byte: it does not report the bytes that have arrived out of order. It is also silent about duplicate segments. This may have a negative effect on TCP's performance. If some packets are lost or dropped, the sender must wait until a time-out and then send all packets that have not been acknowledged. The receiver may receive duplicate packets. To improve performance, selective acknowledgment (SACK) was proposed. Selective acknowledgment allows the sender to have a better idea of which segments are actually lost and which have arrived out of order. The new proposal even includes a list for duplicate packets. The sender can then send only those segments that are really lost. The list of duplicate segments can help the sender find the segments which have been retransmitted by a short time-out.

The proposal defines two new options: SACK-permitted and SACK as shown in Figure 12.47.

Figure 12.47   *SACK*

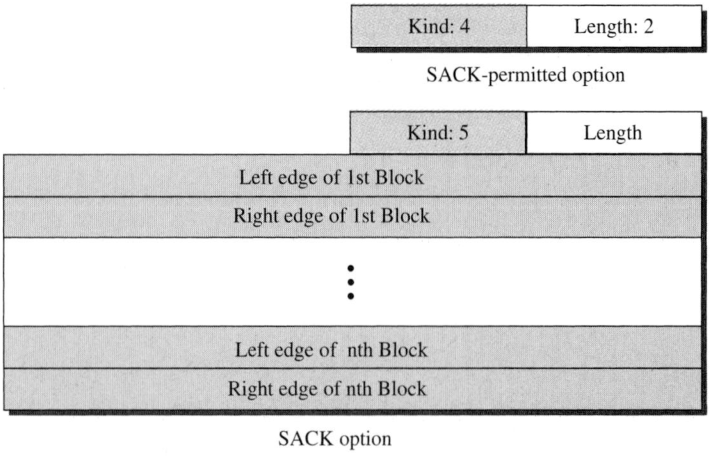

SACK-permitted option

SACK option

The *SACK-permitted* **option** of two bytes is used only during connection establishment. The host that sends the SYN segment adds this option to show that it can support the SACK option. If the other end, in its SYN + ACK segment, also includes this option, then the two ends can use the SACK option during data transfer. Note that the SACK-permitted option is not allowed during the data transfer phase.

The **SACK option,** of variable length, is used during data transfer only if both ends agree (if they have exchanged SACK-Permitted options during connection establishment). The option includes a list for blocks arriving out-of-order. Each block occupies two 32-bit numbers that define the beginning and the end of the blocks. We will show the use of this option in examples; for the moment, remember that the allowed size of an option in TCP is only 40 bytes. This means that a SACK option cannot define more than 4 blocks. The information for 5 blocks occupies $(5 \times 2) \times 4 + 2$ or 42 bytes which is beyond the available size for the option section in a segment. If the SACK option is used with other options, then the number of blocks may be reduced.

The first block of the SACK option can be used to report the duplicates. This is used only if the implementation allows this feature.

Example 13

Let us see how the SACK option is used to list out-of-order blocks. In Figure 12.48 an end has received five segments of data.

Figure 12.48 *Example 13*

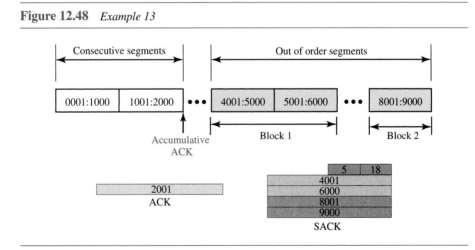

The first and second segments are in consecutive order. An accumulative acknowledgment can be sent to report the reception of these two segments. Segments 3, 4, and 5, however, are out of order with a gap between the second and third and a gap between the fourth and the fifth. An ACK and a SACK together can easily clear the situation for the sender. The value of ACK is 2001, which means that the sender need not worry about bytes 1 to 2000. The SACK has two blocks. The first block announces that bytes 4001 to 6000 have arrived out of order. The second block shows that bytes 8001 to 9000 have also arrived out of order. This means that bytes 2001 to 4000 and bytes 6001 to 8000 are lost or discarded. The sender can resend only these bytes.

Example 14

The example in Figure 12.49 shows how a duplicate segment can be detected with a combination of ACK and SACK. In this case, we have some out-of-order segments (in one block) and one duplicate segment. To show both out-of-order and duplicate data, SACK uses the first block, in this case, to show the duplicate data and other blocks to show out-of-order data. Note that only the first block can be used for duplicate data. The natural question is how the sender, when it receives these ACK and SACK values knows that the first block is for duplicate data (compare this example with the previous example). The answer is that the bytes in the first block are already acknowledged in the ACK field; therefore, this block must be a duplicate.

Figure 12.49 *Example 14*

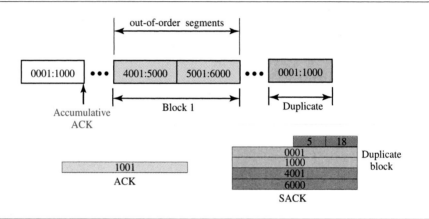

Example 15

The example in Figure 12.50 shows what happens if one of the segments in the out-of-order section is also duplicated. In this example, one of the segments (4001:5000) is duplicated. The SACK

Figure 12.50 *Example 15*

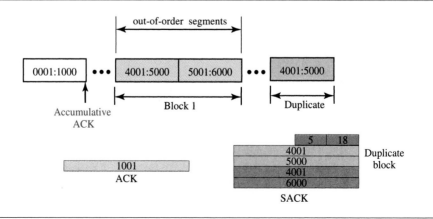

option announces this duplicate data first and then the out-of-order block. This time, however, the duplicated block is not yet acknowledged by ACK, but because it is part of the out-of-order block (4001:5000 is part of 4001:6000), it is understood by the sender that it defines the duplicate data.

12.11   TCP PACKAGE

TCP is a very complex protocol. It is a stream-service, connection-oriented protocol with an involved state transition diagram. It uses flow and error control. It is so complex that the actual code is tens of thousands of lines.

In this section, we present a simplified, bare-bones TCP package. Our purpose is to show how we can simulate the heart of TCP, as represented by the state transition diagram.

The package involves tables called transmission control blocks, a set of timers, and three software modules: a main module, an input processing module, and an output processing module. Figure 12.51 shows these five components and their interactions.

Figure 12.51   *TCP package*

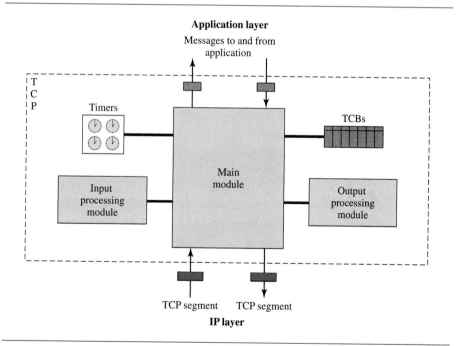

Transmission Control Blocks (TCBs)

TCP is a connection-oriented transport protocol. A connection may be open for a long period of time. To control the connection, TCP uses a structure to hold information about each connection. This is called a *transmission control block* (TCB). Because at any time there can be several connections, TCP keeps an array of TCBs in the form of a table. The table is usually referred to as the TCB (see Figure 12.52).

Figure 12.52   *TCBs*

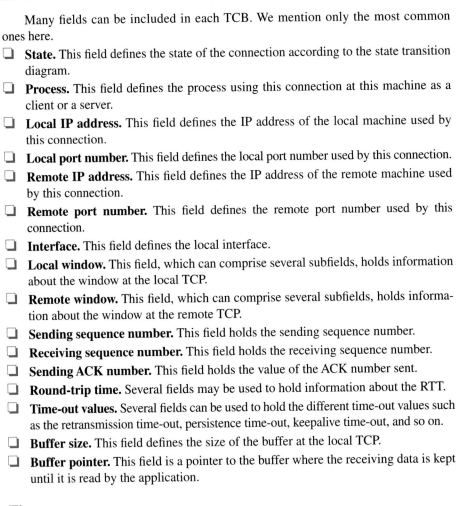

Many fields can be included in each TCB. We mention only the most common ones here.

❏ **State.** This field defines the state of the connection according to the state transition diagram.

❏ **Process.** This field defines the process using this connection at this machine as a client or a server.

❏ **Local IP address.** This field defines the IP address of the local machine used by this connection.

❏ **Local port number.** This field defines the local port number used by this connection.

❏ **Remote IP address.** This field defines the IP address of the remote machine used by this connection.

❏ **Remote port number.** This field defines the remote port number used by this connection.

❏ **Interface.** This field defines the local interface.

❏ **Local window.** This field, which can comprise several subfields, holds information about the window at the local TCP.

❏ **Remote window.** This field, which can comprise several subfields, holds information about the window at the remote TCP.

❏ **Sending sequence number.** This field holds the sending sequence number.

❏ **Receiving sequence number.** This field holds the receiving sequence number.

❏ **Sending ACK number.** This field holds the value of the ACK number sent.

❏ **Round-trip time.** Several fields may be used to hold information about the RTT.

❏ **Time-out values.** Several fields can be used to hold the different time-out values such as the retransmission time-out, persistence time-out, keepalive time-out, and so on.

❏ **Buffer size.** This field defines the size of the buffer at the local TCP.

❏ **Buffer pointer.** This field is a pointer to the buffer where the receiving data is kept until it is read by the application.

Timers

We have previously discussed the several timers TCP needs to keep track of its operations.

Main Module

The main module is invoked by an arriving TCP segment, a time-out event, or a message from an application program. This is a very complicated module because the action to be taken depends on the current state of the TCP. Several approaches have been used to implement the state transition diagram including using a process for each state, using a table (two-dimensional array), and so on. To keep our discussion simple, we use cases to handle the state. We have 11 states; we use 11 different cases. Each state is implemented as defined in the state transition diagram. The ESTABLISHED state needs further explanation. When TCP is in this state and data or an acknowledgment segment arrives, another module, the input processing module, is called to handle the situation. Also, when TCP is in this state and a "send data" message is issued by an application program, another module, the output processing module, is called to handle the situation.

Main Module
Receive: a TCP segment, a message from an application, or a time-out event
1. Search the TCB table.
2. If (corresponding TCB is not found)
1. Create a TCB with the state **CLOSED**.
3. Find the state of the entry in the TCB table.
4. Case (state)
CLOSED:
1. If ("passive open" message from application received)
1. Change the state to **LISTEN**.
2. If ("active open" message from application received)
1. Send a SYN segment.
2. Change the state to **SYN-SENT**.
3. If (any segment received)
1. Send an RST segment.
4. If (any other message received)
1. Issue an error message.
5. Return.
LISTEN:
1. If ("send data" message from application received)
1. Send a SYN segment.
2. Change the state to **SYN-SENT**.
2. If (SYN segment received)
1. Send a SYN + ACK segment.
2. Change the state to SYN + RCVD.
3. If (any other segment or message received)
1. Issue an error message.
4. Return.
SYN-SENT:
1. If (time-out)
1. Change the state to **CLOSED**.

Main Module (continued)

2. If (SYN segment received)

    1. Send a SYN + ACK segment.

    2. Change the state to **SYN-RCVD**.

3. If (SYN + ACK segment received)

    1. Send an ACK segment.

    2. Change the state to **ESTABLISHED**.

4. If (any other segment or message received)

    1. Issue an error message.

5. Return.

SYN-RCVD:

1. If (ACK segment received)

    1. Change the state to **ESTABLISHED**.

2. If (time-out)

    1. Send an RST segment.

    2. Change the state to **CLOSED**.

3. If ("close" message from application received)

    1. Send a FIN segment.

    2. Change the state to **FIN-WAIT-1**.

4. If (RST segment received)

    1. Change the state to **LISTEN**.

5. If (any other segment or message received)

    1. Issue an error message.

6. Return.

ESTABLISHED:

1. If (FIN segment received)

    1. Send an ACK segment.

    2. Change the state to **CLOSE-WAIT**.

2. If ("close" message from application received)

    1. Send a FIN segment.

    2. Change the state to **FIN-WAIT-1**.

3. If (RST or SYN segment received)

    1. Issue an error message.

4. If (data or ACK segment is received)

    1. Call the input module.

5. If ("send" message from application received)

    1. Call the output module.

6. Return.

Main Module (continued)

FIN-WAIT-1:

    1. If (FIN segment received)

        1. Send an ACK segment.

        2. Change the state to **CLOSING**.

    2. If (FIN + ACK segment received)

        1. Send an ACK segment.

        2. Change the state to **TIME-WAIT**.

    3. If (ACK segment received)

        1. Change the state to **FIN-WAIT-2**.

    4. If (any other segment or message received)

        1. Issue an error message.

    5. Return.

FIN-WAIT-2:

    1. If (FIN segment received)

        1. Send an ACK segment.

        2. Change the state to **TIME-WAIT**.

    2. Return.

CLOSING:

    1. If (ACK segment received)

        1. Change the state to **TIME-WAIT**.

    2. If (any other segment or message received)

        1. Issue an error message.

    3. Return.

TIME-WAIT:

    1. If (time-out)

        1. Change the state to **CLOSED**.

    2. If (any other segment or message received)

        1. Issue an error message.

    3. Return.

CLOSE-WAIT:

    1. If ("close" message from application received)

        1. Send a FIN segment.

        2. Change the state to **LAST-ACK**.

    2. If (any other segment or message received)

        1. Issue an error message.

    3. Return.

Main Module (continued)

LAST-ACK:
   1. If (ACK segment received)
      1. Change the state to **CLOSED**.
   2. If (any other segment or message received)
      1. Issue an error message.
   3. Return.

Input Processing Module

In our design, the input processing module handles all the details needed to process data or an acknowledgment received when TCP is in the ESTABLISHED state. This module sends an ACK if needed, takes care of the window size announcement, does error checking, and so on. The details of this module are not needed for an introductory textbook.

Output Processing Module

In our design, the output processing module handles all the details needed to send out data received from application program when TCP is in the ESTABLISHED state. This module handles retransmission time-outs, persistent time-outs, and so on. One of the ways to implement this module is to use a small transition diagram to handle different output conditions. Again, the details of this module are not needed for an introductory textbook.

12.12   KEY TERMS

additive increase	data transfer
choke point	deadlock
Clark's solution	delay
congestion	denial-of-service attack
congestion avoidance	end-of-option (EOP) option
congestion control	error control
congestion detection	exponential increase
connection	fast retransmission
connection abortion	finite state machine
connection establishment	flow control
connection resetting	four-way handshaking
connection termination	full-duplex service
cookie	half-close

initial sequence number

Karn's algorithm

keepalive timer

maximum segment size (MSL)

maximum-segment-size (MSS) option

multiplicative decrease

Nagle's algorithm

no-operation (NOP) option

persistence timer

piggybacking

protection against wrapped sequence
    numbers (PAWS)

retransmission timeout (RTO)

retransmission timer

round-trip time (RTT)

SACK option

SACK-permitted option

segment

sequence number

silly window syndrome

simultaneous close

simultaneous open

sliding window

sliding window protocol

slow start

state transition diagram

SYN flooding attack

three-way handshaking

throughput

timestamp option

TIME-WAIT timer

Transmission Control Protocol (TCP)

window scale factor

12.13   SUMMARY

❑ Transmission Control Protocol (TCP) is one of the transport layer protocols in the TCP/IP protocol suite.

❑ TCP provides process-to-process, full-duplex, and connection-oriented service.

❑ The unit of data transfer between two devices using TCP software is called a segment; it has 20 to 60 bytes of header, followed by data from the application program.

❑ A TCP connection normally consists of three phases: connection establishment, data transfer, and connection termination.

❑ Connection establishment requires three-way handshaking; connection termination requires three- or four-way handshaking.

❑ TCP software is implemented as a finite state machine.

❑ TCP uses flow control, implement as a sliding window mechanism, to avoid overwhelming a receiver with data.

❑ The TCP window size is determined by the receiver-advertised window size (rwnd) or the congestion window size (cwnd), whichever is smaller. The window can be opened or closed by the receiver, but should not be shrunk.

❏ The bytes of data being transferred in each connection are numbered by TCP. The numbering starts with a randomly generated number.

❏ TCP uses error control to provide a reliable service. Error control is handled by the checksum, acknowledgment, and time-out. Corrupted and lost segments are retransmitted and duplicate segments are discarded. Data may arrive out of order and temporarily stored by the receiving TCP, but TCP guarantees that no out-of-order segment is delivered to the process.

❏ In modern implementations, a retransmission occurs if the retransmission timer expires or three duplicate ACK segments have arrived.

❏ TCP uses congestion control to avoid and detect congestion in the network.

❏ The slow start (exponential increase), congestion avoidance (additive increase), and congestion detection (multiplicative decrease) strategies are used for congestion control.

❏ In the slow start algorithm the size of the congestion window increases exponentially until it reaches a threshold.

❏ In the congestion avoidance algorithm the size of the congestion window increases additively until congestion is detected.

❏ Most implementations react differently to congestion detection: If detection is by time-out, a new slow start phase starts. If detection is by three ACKs, a new congestion avoidance phase starts.

❏ TCP uses four timers (retransmission, persistence, keepalive, and time-waited) in its operation.

❏ In TCP, there can be only be one RTT measurement in progress at any time.

❏ TCP does not consider the RTT of a retransmitted segment in its calculation of a new RTO.

❏ TCP uses several options to provide more services.

❏ The end-of-option (EOP) option is used for alignment and indicates there are no more options in the header. EOP can be used only once.

❏ The no-operation (NOP) option is used for filler and alignment purposes. NOP can be used more than once.

❏ The maximum segment size option is used in connection setup to define the largest allowable data segment. The value of MSS is determined during connection establishment and does not change during the connection.

❏ The window scale factor is a multiplier that increases the window size.

❏ The timestamp option shows how much time it takes for data to travel from sender to receiver. One application of timestamp option is in the calculation of round trip time (RTT). Another application is for PAWS.

❏ Recent implementations of TCP use two more options, SACK-permitted option and SACK option. These two options allow the selective acknowledgment of the received segments by the receiver.

❏ Transmission control blocks (TCBs) hold information about each TCP connection.

❏ A TCP package can contain TCBs, timers, a main module, an input processing module, and an output processing module.

12.14 PRACTICE SET

Exercises

1. Compare the TCP header and the UDP header. List the fields in the TCP header that are missing from UDP header. Give the reason for their absence.

2. An IP datagram is carrying a TCP segment destined for address 130.14.16.17/16. The destination port address is corrupted and it arrives at destination 130.14.16.19/16. How does the receiving TCP react to this error?

3. One ICMP message, discussed in Chapter 9, reports a destination port unreachable error. How can TCP detect the error in the destination port?

4. UDP is a message-oriented protocol. TCP is a byte-oriented protocol. If an application needs to protect the boundaries of its message, which protocol should be used, UDP or TCP?

5. What is the maximum size of the TCP header? What is the minimum size of the TCP header?

6. If the value of HLEN is 0111, how many bytes of option are included in the segment?

7. Show the entries for the header of a TCP segment that carries a message from an FTP client to an FTP server. Fill the checksum field with 0s. Choose an appropriate ephemeral port number and the correct well-known port number. The length of data is 40 bytes.

8. What can you say about the TCP segment in which the value of the control field is one of the following:
   a. 000000
   b. 000001
   c. 010001
   d. 000100
   e. 000010
   f. 010010

9. The following is a dump of a TCP header in hexadecimal format.

   05320017 00000001 00000000 500207FF 00000000

   a. What is the source port number?
   b. What is the destination port number?
   c. What the sequence number?
   d. What is the acknowledgment number?
   e. What is the length of the header?
   f. What is the type of the segment?
   g. What is the window size?

10. The control field in a TCP segment is 6 bits. We can have 64 different combinations of bits. List some combinations that are valid.

11. To make the initial sequence number a random number, most systems start the counter at 1 during bootstrap and increment the counter by 64,000 every half second. How long does it take for the counter to wrap around?

12. Using a state diagram, show what happens if a server process issues an active close instead of the client.

13. In a TCP connection, the initial sequence number at client site is 2171. The client opens the connection, sends only one segment carrying 1000 bytes of data, and closes the connection. What is the value of the sequence number in each of the following segments sent by the client?

    a. The SYN segment?

    b. The data segment?

    c. The FIN segment?

14. In a connection, the value of cwnd is 3000 and the value of rwnd is 5000. The host has sent 2000 bytes which have not been acknowledged. How many more bytes can be sent?

15. TCP opens a connection using an initial sequence number (ISN) of 14,534. The other party opens the connection with an ISN of 21,732. Show the three TCP segments during the connection establishment.

16. Using Exercise 15, show the contents of the segments during the data transmission if the initiator sends a segment containing the message "Hello dear customer" and the other party answers with a segment containing "Hi there seller."

17. Using Exercises 15 and 16, show the contents of the segments during the connection termination.

18. A client uses TCP to send data to a server. The data is 16 bytes. Calculate the efficiency of this transmission at the TCP level (ratio of useful bytes to total bytes). Calculate the efficiency of transmission at the IP level. Assume no options for the IP header. Calculate the efficiency of transmission at the data link layer. Assume no options for the IP header and use Ethernet at the data link layer.

19. TCP is sending data at 1 megabyte per second. If the sequence number starts with 7,000, how long does it take before the sequence number goes back to zero?

20. A TCP connection is using a window size of 10,000 bytes and the previous acknowledgment number was 22,001. It receives a segment with acknowledgment number 24,001 and window size advertisement of 12, 000. Draw a diagram to show the situation of the window before and after.

21. A window holds bytes 2001 to 5000. The next byte to be sent is 3001. Draw a figure to show the situation of the window after the following two events.

    a. An ACK segment with the acknowledgment number 2500 and window size advertisement 4000 is received.

    b. A segment carrying 1000 bytes is sent.

22. A TCP connection is in the **ESTABLISHED** state. The following events occur one after another:

    a. A FIN segment is received.

    b. The application sends a "close" message.

    What is the state of the connection after each event? What is the action after each event?

23. A TCP connection is in the **ESTABLISHED** state. The following events occur one after another:

   a. The application sends a "close" message.

   b. An ACK segment is received.

   What is the state of the connection after each event? What is the action after each event?

24. A host has no data to send. It receives the following segments at the times shown (hour:minute:second:milliseconds after midnight). Show the acknowledgments sent by the host.

   a. Segment 1 received at 0:0:0:000.

   b. Segment 2 received at 0:0:0:027.

   c. Segment 3 received at 0:0:0:400.

   d. Segment 4 received at 0:0:1:200.

   e. Segment 5 received at 0:0:1:208.

25. A host sends five packets and receives three acknowledgments. The time is shown as hour:minute:seconds.

   a. Segment 1 was sent at 0:0:00.

   b. Segment 2 was sent at 0:0:05.

   c. ACK for segments 1 and 2 received at 0:0:07.

   d. Segment 3 was sent at 0:0:20.

   e. Segment 4 was sent at 0:0:22.

   f. Segment 5 was sent at 0:0:27.

   g. ACK for segments 1 and 2 received at 0:0:45.

   h. ACK for segment 3 received at 0:0:65.

   Calculate the values of RTT_M, RTT_S, RTT_D, and RTO if the original RTO is 6 seconds. Did the sender miss the retransmission of any segment? Show which segments should have been retransmitted and when. Rewrite the events including the retransmission time.

26. Show the contents of a SACK option to be sent if a host has received bytes 2001 to 3000 in order. Bytes 4001 to 6000 are out-of-order, and bytes 3501 to 4000 are duplicate.

27. Show a congestion control diagram like Figure 12.36 using the following scenario. Assume a maximum window size of 64 segments.

   a. Three duplicate ACKs are received after the fourth RTT.

   b. A timeout occurs after the sixth RTT.

Research Activities

28. Find some RFCs about the TCP protocol.

29. Find RFCs about the SACK option.

30. Find RFCs about Karn's algorithm.

31. We have not given all the rules about the transition diagram and TCP states. To be complete, we should show the next state for any state with the arrival of any type of

segment. TCP should know what action to take if any of the segment types arrive when it is in any of the states. What are some of these rules?

32. What is the "half-open" case in TCP?

33. What is the "half-duplex close" case in TCP?

34. The *tcpdump* command in UNIX or LINUX can be used to print the headers of packets of a network interface. Use *tcpdump* to see the segments sent and received.

CHAPTER 13

Stream Control Transmission Protocol (SCTP)

Stream Control Transmission Protocol (SCTP) is a new reliable, message-oriented transport-layer protocol. Figure 13.1 shows the relationship of SCTP to the other protocols in the Internet protocol suite. SCTP lies between the application layer and the network layer and serves as the intermediary between the application programs and the network operations.

Figure 13.1 *TCP/IP protocol suite*

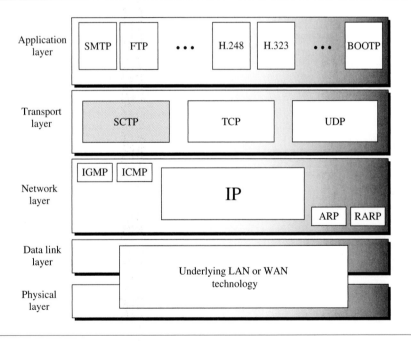

SCTP, however, is mostly designed for Internet applications that have recently been introduced. These new applications, such as IUA (ISDN over IP), M2UA and

M3UA (telephony signalling), H.248 (media gateway control), H.323 (IP telephony), and SIP (IP telephony), need a more sophisticated service than TCP can provide. SCTP provides this enhanced performance and reliability. We briefly compare UDP, TCP, and SCTP:

❏ UDP is a **message-oriented** protocol. A process delivers a message to UDP, which is encapsulated in a user datagram and sent over the network. UDP *conserves the message boundaries;* each message is independent from any other message. This is a desirable feature when we are dealing with applications such as IP telephony and transmission of real-time data as we will see later in the text. However, UDP is unreliable; the sender cannot know the destiny of messages sent. A message can be lost, duplicated, or received out of order. UDP also lacks some other features, such as congestion control and flow control, needed for a friendly transport-layer protocol.

❏ TCP is a **byte-oriented** protocol. It receives a message or messages from a process, stores them as a stream of bytes, and sends them in segments. There is no preservation of the message boundaries. However, TCP is a reliable protocol. The duplicate segments are detected, the lost segments are resent, the bytes are delivered to the end process in order. TCP also has congestion control and flow control mechanisms.

❏ SCTP combines the best features of UDP and TCP. SCTP is a reliable message-oriented protocol. It preserves the message boundaries and at the same time detects lost data, duplicate data, and out-of-order data. It also has congestion control and flow control mechanisms. Later we will see that SCTP has other innovative features unavailable in UDP and TCP.

> **SCTP is a *message-oriented, reliable* protocol that combines the good features of UDP and TCP.**

13.1   SCTP SERVICES

Before discussing the operation of SCTP, let us explain the services offered by SCTP to the application layer processes.

Process-to-Process Communication

SCTP uses all well-known ports in the TCP space. Table 13.1 lists some extra port numbers used by SCTP.

Table 13.1   *Some SCTP applications*

Protocol	Port Number	Description
IUA	9990	ISDN over IP
M2UA	2904	SS7 telephony signalling

Table 13.1   *Some SCTP applications (continued)*

Protocol	Port Number	Description
M3UA	2905	SS7 telephony signalling
H.248	2945	Media gateway control
H.323	1718, 1719, 1720, 11720	IP telephony
SIP	5060	IP telephony

Multiple Streams

We learned in Chapter 12 that TCP is a stream-oriented protocol. Each connection between a TCP client and a TCP server involves one single stream. The problem with this approach is that a loss at any point in the stream blocks the delivery of the rest of the data. This can be acceptable when we are transferring text; it is not when we are sending real-time data such as audio or video. SCTP allows **multistream service** in each connection, which is called **association** in SCTP terminology. If one of the streams is blocked, the other streams can still deliver their data.The idea is similar to multiple lanes on a highway. Each lane can be used for a different type of traffic. For example, one lane can be used for regular traffic, another for car pools. If the traffic is blocked for regular vehicles, car pool vehicles can still reach their destinations. Figure 13.2 shows the idea of multiple-stream delivery.

Figure 13.2   *Multiple-stream concept*

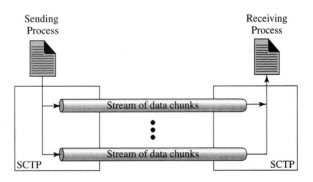

An association in SCTP can involve multiple streams.

Multihoming

A TCP connection involves one source and one destination IP address. This means that even if the sender or receiver is a multihomed host (connected to more than one physical address with multiple IP addresses), only one of these IP addresses per end can be utilized during the connection. An SCTP association, on the other hand, supports **multihoming service.** The sending and receiving host can define multiple IP addresses in each end for an association. In this fault-tolerant approach, when one path fails, another interface can be used for data delivery without interruption. This fault-tolerant feature is very helpful when we are sending and receiving a real-time payload such as Internet telephony. Figure 13.3 shows the idea of multihoming.

Figure 13.3 *Multihoming concept*

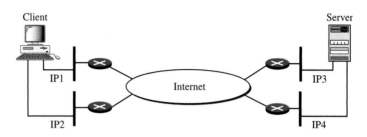

In the figure, the client is connected to two local networks with two IP addresses. The server is also connected to two networks with two IP addresses. The client and the server can make an association using four different pairs of IP addresses. However, note that in the current implementations of SCTP, only one pair of IP addresses can be chosen for normal communication; the alternative is used if the main choice fails. In other words, at present, SCTP does not allow load sharing between different paths.

> **SCTP association allows multiple IP addresses for each end.**

Full-Duplex Communication

Like TCP, SCTP offers **full-duplex service,** where data can flow in both directions at the same time. Each SCTP then has a sending and receiving buffer and packets are sent in both directions.

Connection-Oriented Service

Like TCP, SCTP is a connection-oriented protocol. However, in SCTP, a connection is called an **association.** When a process at site A wants to send and receive data from another process at site B, the following occurs:

1. The two SCTPs establish an association between each other.
2. Data are exchanged in both directions.
3. The association is terminated.

Reliable Service

SCTP, like TCP, is a reliable transport protocol. It uses an acknowledgment mechanism to check the safe and sound arrival of data. We will discuss this feature further in the section on error control.

13.2   SCTP FEATURES

Let us first discuss the general features of SCTP and then compare them with those of TCP.

Transmission Sequence Number (TSN)

The unit of data in TCP is a byte. Data transfer in TCP is controlled by numbering bytes using a sequence number. On the other hand, the unit of data in SCTP is a data chunk which may or may not have a one-to-one relationship with the message coming from the process because of fragmentation (discussed later). Data transfer in SCTP is controlled by numbering the data chunks. SCTP uses a **transmission sequence number (TSN)** to number the data chunks. In other words, the TSN in SCTP plays the analogous role as the sequence number in TCP. TSNs are 32-bits long and randomly initialized between 0 and $2^{32} - 1$. Each data chunk must carry the corresponding TSN in its header.

> **In SCTP, a data chunk is numbered using a TSN.**

Stream Identifier (SI)

In TCP, there is only one stream in each connection. In SCTP, there may be several streams in each association. Each stream in SCTP needs to be identified using a **stream identifier (SI)**. Each data chunk must carry the SI in its header so that when it arrives at the destination, it can be properly placed in its stream. The SI is a 16-bit number starting from 0.

> **To distinguish between different streams, SCTP uses a SI.**

Stream Sequence Number (SSN)

When a data chunk arrives at the destination SCTP, it is delivered to the appropriate stream and in the proper order. This means that, in addition to an SI, SCTP defines each data chunk in each stream with a **stream sequence number (SSN)**.

> **To distinguish between different data chunks belonging to the same stream, SCTP uses SSNs.**

Packets

In TCP, a segment carries data and control information. Data are carried as a collection of bytes; control information is defined by six control flags in the header. The design of SCTP is totally different: data are carried as data chunks, control information as control chunks. Several control chunks and data chunks can be packed together in a packet. A packet in SCTP plays the same role as a segment in TCP. Figure 13.4 compares a segment in TCP and a packet in SCTP.

Figure 13.4   *Comparison between a TCP segment and an SCTP packet*

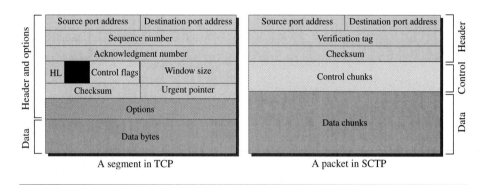

TCP has segments; SCTP has packets.

We will discuss the format of the SCTP packet in the next section. For the moment, let us briefly list the differences between an SCTP packet and a TCP segment:

1. The control information in TCP is part of the header; the control information in SCTP is included in the control chunks. There are several types of control chunks; each is used for a different purpose.

2. The data in a TCP segment treated as one entity; an SCTP packet can carry several data chunks; each can belong to a different stream.

3. The options section, which can be part of a TCP segment, does not exist in an SCTP packet. Options in SCTP are handled by defining new chunk types.

4. The mandatory part of the TCP header is 20 bytes, while the general header in SCTP is only 12 bytes. The SCTP header is shorter due to the following:

   a. An SCTP sequence number (TSN) belongs to each data chunk, and hence is located in the chunk's header.

   b. The acknowledgment number and window size are part of each control chunk.

   c. There is no need for a header length field (shown as HL in the TCP segment) because there are no options to make the length of the header variable; the SCTP header length is fixed (12 bytes).

   d. There is no need for an urgent pointer in SCTP as we will see later.

5. The checksum in TCP is 16 bits; in SCTP, it is 32 bits.

6. The verification tag in SCTP is an association identifier, which does not exist in TCP. In TCP, the combination of IP and port addresses define a connection; in SCTP we may have multihoming using different IP addresses. A unique verification tag is needed to define each association.

7. TCP includes one sequence number in the header, which defines the number of the first byte in the data section. An SCTP packet can include several different data chunks. TSNs, ISs, and SSNs define each data chunk.

8. Some segments in TCP that carry control information (such as SYN and FIN), need to consume one sequence number; control chunks in SCTP never use a TSN, IS, or SSN number. These three identifiers belong only to data chunks, not to the whole packet.

> **In SCTP, control information and data information are carried in separate chunks.**

In SCTP, we have data chunks, streams, and packets. An association may send many packets, a packet may contain several chunks, and chunks may belong to different streams. To make the definitions of these terms clear, let us suppose that process A needs to send 11 messages to process B in three streams. The first four messages are in the first stream, the second three messages are in the second stream, and the last four messages are in the third stream.

Although a message, if long, can be carried by several data chunks, we assume that each message fits into one data chunk. Therefore, we have 11 data chunks in three streams.

The application process delivers 11 messages to SCTP, where each message is earmarked for the appropriate stream. Although the process could deliver one message from the first stream and then another from the second, we assume that it delivers all messages belonging to the first stream first, all messages belonging to the second stream next, and finally, all messages belonging to the last stream.

We also assume that the network allows only 3 data chunks per packet, which means that we need 4 packets as shown in Figure 13.5. Data chunks in stream 0 are carried in

Figure 13.5   *Packet, data chunks, and streams*

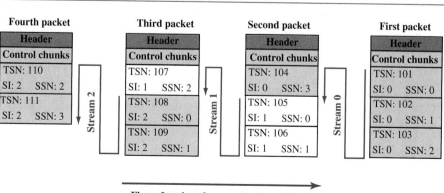

Flow of packets from sender to receiver

the first and part of the second packet; those in stream 1 are carried in the second and the third packet; those in stream 3 are carried in third and fourth packet.

Note that each data chunk needs three identifiers: TSN, SI, and SSN. TSN is a cumulative number and used, as we will see later, for flow control and error control. SI defines the stream to which the chunk belongs. SSN defines the chunk's order in a particular stream. In our example, SSN starts from 0 for each stream.

> **Data chunks are identified by three identifiers: TSN, SI, and SSN.**
> **TSN is a cumulative number identifying the association; SI defines the stream;**
> **SSN defines the chunk in a stream.**

Acknowledgment Number

TCP acknowledgment numbers are byte-oriented and refer to the sequence numbers. SCTP acknowledgment numbers are chunk-oriented. They refer to the TSN. A second difference between TCP and SCTP acknowledgments is the control information. Recall that this information is part of the segment header in TCP. To acknowledge segments that carry only control information, TCP uses a sequence number and acknowledgment number (for example, a SYN segment needs to be acknowledged by an ACK segment). In SCTP, however, the control information is carried by control chunks, which do not need a TSN. These control chunks are acknowledged by another control chunk of the appropriate type (some need no acknowledgment). For example, an INIT control chunk is acknowledged by an INIT-ACK chunk. There is no need for a sequence number or an acknowledgment number.

> **In SCTP, acknowledgment numbers are used to acknowledge only data chunks;**
> **control chunks are acknowledged by other control chunks if necessary.**

Flow Control

Like TCP, SCTP implements flow control to avoid overwhelming the receiver. We will discuss SCTP flow control later in the chapter.

Error Control

Like TCP, SCTP implements error control to provide reliability. TSN numbers and acknowledgment numbers are used for error control. We will discuss error control later in the chapter.

Congestion Control

Like TCP, SCTP implements congestion control to determine how many data chunks can be injected into the network. We will discuss congestion control later in the chapter.

13.3   PACKET FORMAT

In this section, we show the format of a packet and different types of chunks. Most of the information presented in this section will become clear later; this section can be skipped in the first reading or used only as the reference. An SCTP packet has a mandatory general header and a set of blocks called chunks. There are two types of chunks: control chunks and data chunks. A control chunk controls and maintains the association; a data chunk carries user data. In a packet, the control chunks come before the data chunks. Figure 13.6 shows the general format of an SCTP packet.

Figure 13.6 *SCTP packet format*

General header
(12 bytes)

Chunk 1
(variable length)

•
•
•

Chunk N
(variable length)

In an SCTP packet, control chunks come before data chunks.

General Header

The **general header** (packet header) defines the end points of each association to which the packet belongs, guarantees that the packet belongs to a particular association, and preserves the integrity of the contents of the packet including the header itself. The format of the general header is shown in Figure 13.7.

Figure 13.7 *General header*

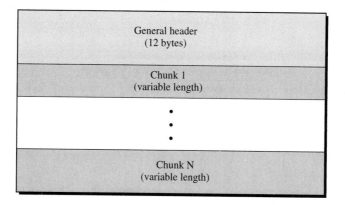

Source port address 16 bits	Destination port address 16 bits
Verification tag 32 bits	
Checksum 32 bits	

There are four fields in the general header:

❏ **Source port address.** This is a 16-bit field that defines the port number of the process sending the packet.

❏ **Destination port address.** This is a 16-bit field that defines the port number of the process receiving the packet.

❏ **Verification tag.** This is a number that matches a packet to an association. This prevents a packet from a previous association from being mistaken as a packet in this association. It serves as an identifier for the association; it is repeated in every packet during the association. There is a separate verification used for each direction in the association.

❏ **Checksum.** This 32-bit field contains a CRC-32 checksum (see Appendix D). Note that the size of the checksum is increased from 16 to 32 bits (in UDP, TCP, and IP) to allow the use of the CRC-32 checksum. It can also contain a CRC-32 (see Appendix D).

Chunks

Control information or user data are carried in chunks. Chunks have a common layout as shown in Figure 13.8.

Figure 13.8 *Common layout of a chunk*

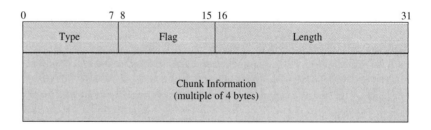

The first three fields are common to all chunks; the information field depends on the type of chunk. The important point to remember is that SCTP requires the information section to be a multiple of 4 bytes; if not, padding bytes (eight 0s) are added at the end of the section.

Chunks need to terminate on a 32-bit (4 byte) boundary.

The description of the common fields are as follows:

❏ **Type.** This 8-bit field can define up to 256 types of chunks. Only a few have been defined so far; the rest are reserved for future use. See Table 13.2 for a list of chunks and their descriptions.

❏ **Flag.** This 8-bit field defines special flags that a particular chunk may need. Each bit has a different meaning depending on the type of chunk.

Table 13.2   *Chunks*

Type	Chunk	Description
0	**DATA**	User data
1	**INIT**	Sets up an association
2	**INIT ACK**	Acknowledges INIT chunk
3	**SACK**	Selective acknowledgment
4	**HEARTBEAT**	Probes the peer for liveliness
5	**HEARTBEAT ACK**	Acknowledges HEARTBEAT chunk
6	**ABORT**	Abort an association
7	**SHUTDOWN**	Terminates an association
8	**SHUTDOWN ACK**	Acknowledges SHUTDOWN chunk
9	**ERROR**	Reports errors without shutting down
10	**COOKIE ECHO**	Third packet in association establishment
11	**COOKIE ACK**	Acknowledges COOKIE ECHO chunk
14	**SHUTDOWN COMPLETE**	Third packet in association termination
192	**FORWARD TSN**	For adjusting cummulating TSN

❏ **Length.** Since the size of the information section is dependent on the type of chunk, we need to define the chunk boundaries. This 16-bit field defines the total size of the chunk, in bytes, including the type, flag, and length fields. If a chunk carries no information the value of the length field is 4 (4 bytes). Note that the length of the padding, if any, is not included in the calculation of the length field. This helps the receiver find out how many useful bytes a chunk carries. If the value is not a multiple of 4, the receiver knows there is padding. For example, when the receiver sees a length of 17, it knows the next number that is a multiple of 4 is 20, so there are 3 bytes of padding that must be discarded. But if the receiver sees a length of 16, it knows that there is no padding.

The number of padding bytes are not included in the value of the length field.

DATA

The **DATA chunk** carries the user data. A packet may contain zero or more data chunks. Figure 13.9 shows the format of a DATA chunk.

The description of the common fields are the same. The type field has a value of 0. The flag field has 5 reserved bits and 3 defined bits: U, B, and E. The U (unordered) field, when set to 1, signals unordered data (explained later). In this case, the value of the stream sequence number is ignored. The B (beginning) and E (end) bits together define the position of a chunk in a message that is fragmented. When B = 1 and E = 1, there is no fragmentation (first and last); the whole message is carried in one chunk. When B = 1 and E = 0, it is the first fragment. When B = 0 and E = 1, it is the last

Figure 13.9   *DATA chunk*

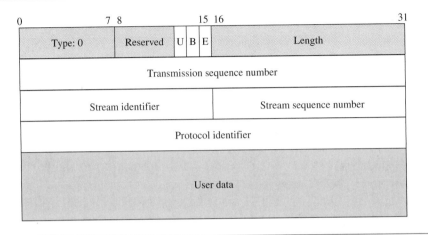

fragment. When B = 0 and E = 0, it is a middle fragment (neither the first, nor the last). Note that the value of the length field does not include padding. This value cannot be less than 17 because a DATA chunk must always carry at least one byte of data.

❑ **Transmission sequence number (TSN).** This 32-bit field defines the transmission sequence number. It is a sequence number that is initialized in an INIT chunk for one direction and in the INIT ACK chunk for the opposite direction.

❑ **Stream identifier (SI).** This 16-bit field defines each stream in an association. All chunks belonging to the same stream in one direction carry the same stream identifier.

❑ **Stream sequence number (SSN).** This 16-bit field defines a chunk in a particular stream in one direction.

❑ **Protocol identifier.** This 32-bit field can be used by the application program to define the type of data. It is ignored by the SCTP layer.

❑ **User data.** This field carries the actual user data. SCTP has some specific rules about the user data field. First, no chunk can carry data belonging to more than one message, but a message can be spread over several data chunks. Second, this field cannot be empty; it must have at least one byte of user data. Third, if the data cannot end at a 32-bit boundary, padding must be added. These padding bytes are not included in the value of the length field.

> A DATA chunk cannot carry data belonging to more than one message, but a message can be split into several chunks. The data field of the DATA chunk must carry at least one byte of data, which means the value of length field cannot be less than 17.

INIT

The **INIT chunk** (initiation chunk) is the first chunk sent by an end point to establish an association. The packet that carries this chunk cannot carry any other control or data chunks. The value of the verification tag for this packet is 0, which means no tag has yet been defined. The format is shown in Figure 13.10.

Figure 13.10 *INIT chunk*

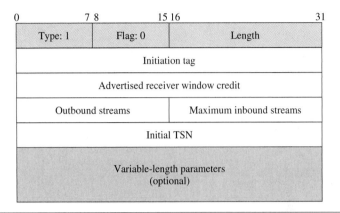

The three common fields (type, flag, and length) are as before. The value of the type field is 1. The value of the flag field is zero (no flags); and the value of the length field is a minimum of 20 (more if there are optional parameters). The other fields are explained below:

❏ **Initiation tag.** This 32-bit field defines the value of the verification tag for packets traveling in the opposite direction. As we mentioned before, all packets have a verification tag in the general header; this tag is the same for all packets traveling in one direction in an association. The value of this tag is determined during association establishment. The end point that initiates the association defines the value of this tag in the initiation tag field. This value is used as the verification tag in the rest of the packets sent from the other direction. For example, when end point A starts an association with end point B, A defines an initiation tag value, say x, which is used as the verification tag for all packets sent from B to A. The initiation tag is a random number between 1 and $2^{32} - 1$. The value of 0 defines no association and is permitted only by the general header of the INIT chunk.

❏ **Advertised receiver window credit.** This 32-bit field is used in flow control and defines the initial amount of data in bytes that the sender of the INIT chunk can allow. It is the rwnd value that will be used by the receiver to know how much data to send. Note that, in SCTP, sequence numbers are in terms of chunks.

❏ **Outbound stream.** This 16-bit field defines the number of streams that the initiator of the association suggests for streams in the outbound direction. It may be reduced by the other end point.

❏ **Maximum inbound stream.** This 16-bit field defines the maximum number of streams that the initiator of the association can support in the inbound direction. Note that this is a maximum number and cannot be increased by the other end point.

❏ **Initial TSN.** This 32-bit field initializes the transmission sequence number (TSN) in the outbound direction. Note that each data chunk in an association has to have one TSN. The value of this field is also a random number less than 2^{32}.

❏ **Variable-length parameters.** These optional parameters may be added to the INIT chunk to define the IP address of sending end point, the number of IP addresses the end point can support (multihome), the preservation of the cookie state, the type of addresses, and support of explicit congestion notification (ECN).

> **No other chunk can be carried in a packet that carries an INIT chunk.**

INIT ACK

The **INIT ACK chunk** (initiation acknowledgment chunk) is the second chunk sent during association establishment. The packet that carries this chunk cannot carry any other control or data chunks. The value of the verification tag for this packet (located in the general header) is the value of the initiation tag defined in the received INIT chunk. The format is shown in Figure 13.11.

Figure 13.11 *INIT ACK chunk*

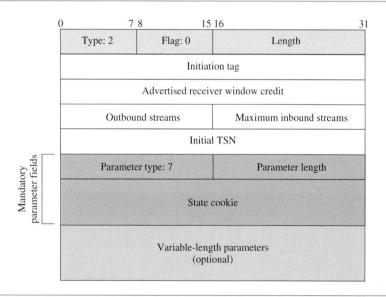

Note that the fields in the main part of the chunk are the same as those defined in the INIT chunk. However, a mandatory parameter is required for this chunk. The parameter of type 7 defines the state cookie sent by the sender of this chunk. We discuss the use of cookies later in the chapter. The chunk can also have optional parameters. Note that the initiation tag field in this chunk initiates the value of the verification tag for future packets traveling from the opposite direction.

> **No other chunk can be carried in a packet that carries an INIT ACK chunk.**

COOKIE ECHO

The **COOKIE ECHO chunk** is the third chunk sent during association establishment. It is sent by the end point that receives an INIT ACK chunk (normally the sender of the INIT chunk). The packet that carries this chunk can also carry user data. The format is shown in Figure 13.12.

Figure 13.12   *COOKIE ECHO chunk*

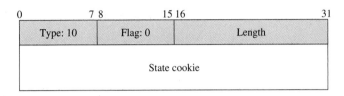

Note that this is a very simple chunk of type 10. In the information section it echoes the state cookie that the end point has previously received in the INIT ACK. The receiver of the INIT ACK cannot open the cookie.

COOKIE ACK

The **COOKIE ACK chunk** is the fourth and last chunk sent during association establishment. It is sent by an end point that receives a COOKIE ECHO chunk. The packet that carries this chunk can also carry user data. The format is shown in Figure 13.13.

Figure 13.13   *COOKIE ACK*

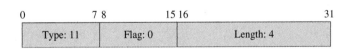

Note that this is a very simple chunk of type 11. The length of the chunk is exactly 4 bytes.

SACK

The **SACK chunk** (selective ACK chunk) acknowledges the receipt of data packets. Figure 13.14 shows the format of the SACK chunk.

The common fields are the same as discussed previously. The type field has a value of 3. The flag bits are all set to 0s.

❏ **Cumulative TSN acknowledgment.** This 32-bit field defines the TSN of the last data chunk received in sequence.

❏ **Advertised receiver window credit.** This 32-bit field is the updated value for the receiver window size.

❏ **Number of gap ACK blocks.** This 16-bit field defines the number of gaps in the data chunk received after the cumulative TSN. Note that the term *gap* is misleading here: the gap defines the sequence of received chunks, not the missing chunks.

Figure 13.14   *SACK chunk*

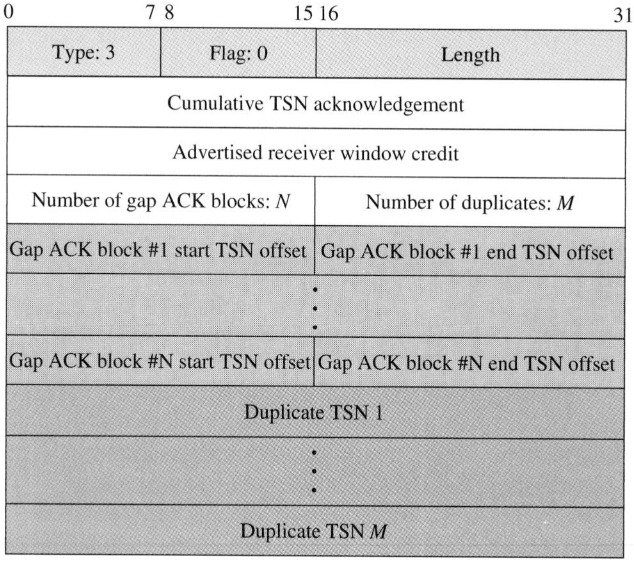

0	7 8	15 16	31
Type: 3	Flag: 0	Length	
Cumulative TSN acknowledgement			
Advertised receiver window credit			
Number of gap ACK blocks: *N*		Number of duplicates: *M*	
Gap ACK block #1 start TSN offset		Gap ACK block #1 end TSN offset	
• • •			
Gap ACK block #N start TSN offset		Gap ACK block #N end TSN offset	
Duplicate TSN 1			
• • •			
Duplicate TSN *M*			

❑ **Number of duplicates.** This 16-bit field defines the number of duplicate chunks following the cumulative TSN.

❑ **Gap ACK block start offset.** For each gap block, this 16-bit field gives the starting TSN relative to the cumulative TSN.

❑ **Gap ACK block end offset.** For each gap block, this 16-bit field gives the ending TSN relative to the cumulative TSN.

❑ **Duplicate TSN.** For each duplicate chunk, this 32-bit field gives the TSN of the chunk relative to the cumulative TSN.

HEARTBEAT and HEARTBEAT ACK

The **HEARTBEAT chunk** and **HEARTBEAT ACK chunk** are similar except for the type field. The first has a type of 4 and the second a type of 5. Figure 13.15 shows the format of these chunks. These two chunks are used to periodically probe the condition

Figure 13.15   *HEARTBEAT and HEARTBEAT ACK chunks*

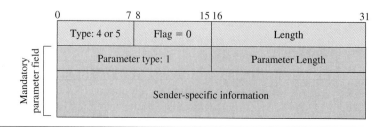

of an association. An end point sends a HEARTBEAT chunk; the peer responds with a HEARTBEAT ACK if it is alive. The format has the common three fields and mandatory parameter fields that provide sender specific information. This information in the HEARTBEAT chunk includes the local time and the address of the sender. It is copied without change into the HEARTBEAT ACK chunk.

SHUTDOWN, SHUTDOWN ACK, and SHUTDOWN COMPLETE

These three chunks (used for closing an association) are similar. The **SHUTDOWN chunk,** type 7, is eight bytes in length; the second four bytes define the cumulative TSN. The **SHUTDOWN ACK chunk,** type 8, is four bytes in length. The **SHUTDOWN COMPLETE chunk,** type 14, is also 4 bytes long, and has a one bit flag, the T flag. The T flag shows that the sender does not have a TCB table (see Chapter 12). Figure 13.16 shows the formats.

Figure 13.16   *SHUTDOWN, SHUTDOWN ACK, and SHUTDOWN COMPLETE chunks*

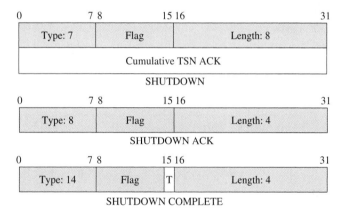

ERROR

The **ERROR chunk** is sent when an end point finds some error in a received packet. Note that the sending of an ERROR chunk does not imply the aborting of the association. (This would require an ABORT chunk.) Figure 13.17 shows the format of the ERROR chunk.

Figure 13.17   *ERROR chunk*

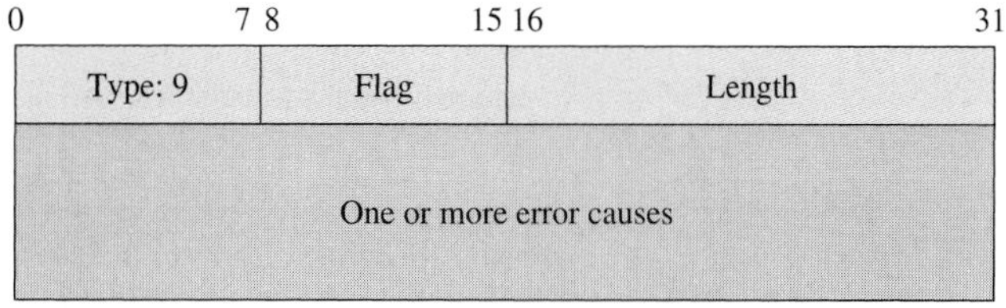

The errors are defined in Table 13.3.

Table 13.3   *Errors*

Code	Description
1	Invalid stream identifier
2	Missing mandatory parameter
3	State cookie error
4	Out of resource
5	Unresolvable address
6	Unrecognized chunk type
7	Invalid mandatory parameters
8	Unrecognized parameter
9	No user data
10	Cookie received while shutting down

ABORT

The **ABORT chunk** is sent when an end point finds a fatal error and needs to abort the association. The error types are the same as those for the ERROR chunk (see Table 13.3). Figure 13.18 shows the format of an ABORT chunk.

Figure 13.18   *ABORT chunk*

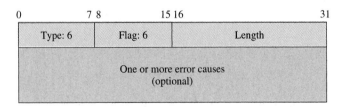

FORWARD TSN

This is a chunk recently added to the standard (see RFC 3758) to inform the receiver to adjust its cummulative TSN. It provides partial reliable service.

13.4   AN SCTP ASSOCIATION

SCTP, like TCP, is a connection-oriented protocol. However, a connection in SCTP is called an *association* to emphasize multihoming.

A connection in SCTP is called an association.

Association Establishment

Association establishment in SCTP requires a *four-way handshake*. In this procedure, a process, normally a client, wants to establish an association with another process, normally a server, using SCTP as the transport layer protocol. Similar to TCP, the SCTP server needs to be prepared to receive any association (passive open). Association establishment, however, is initiated by the client (active open). SCTP association establishment is shown in Figure 13.19.

Figure 13.19   *Four-way handshaking*

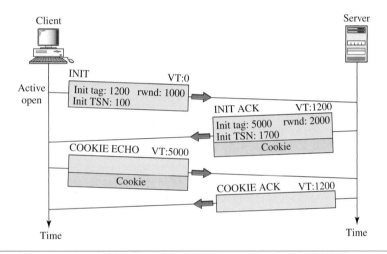

The steps, in a normal situation, are as follows:

1. The client sends the first packet, which contains an INIT chunk. The **verification tag** (VT) of this packet (defined in the general header) is 0 because no verification tag has yet been defined for this direction (client to server).The INIT tag includes an initiation tag to be used for packets from the other direction (server to client). The chunk also defines the initial TSN for this direction and advertises a value for rwnd. The value of rwnd is normally advertised in a SACK chunk; it is done here because SCTP allows the inclusion of a DATA chunk in the third and fourth packets; the server must be aware of the available client buffer size. Note that no other chunks can be sent with the first packet.

2. The server sends the second packet, which contains an INIT ACK chunk. The verification tag is the value of the initial tag field in the INIT chunk. This chunk initiates the tag to be used in the other direction, defines the initial TSN, for data flow from server to client, and sets the servers' rwnd. The value of rwnd is defined to allow the client to send a DATA chunk with the third packet. The INIT ACK also sends a cookie that defines the state of the server at this moment. We will discuss the use of the cookie shortly.

3. The client sends the third packet, which includes a COOKIE ECHO chunk. This is a very simple chunk that echoes, without change, the cookie sent by the server. SCTP allows the inclusion of data chunks in this packet.

4. The server sends the fourth packet, which includes the COOKIE ACK chunk that acknowledges the receipt of the COOKIE ECHO chunk. SCTP allows the inclusion of data chunks with this packet.

> **No other chunk is allowed in a packet carrying**
> **an INIT or INIT ACK chunk.**
> **A COOKIE ECHO or a COOKIE ACK chunk can carry data chunks.**

Number of Packets Exchanged

The number of packets exchanged is three in a TCP connection establishment, and four in an SCTP association establishment. It might seem that SCTP is less efficient than TCP, but we need to consider that SCTP allows the exchange of data in the third and fourth packets and, as we shall see, provides better security against SYN denial-of-service attacks. After two packets are exchanged, data can be transferred.

Verification Tag

When we compare TCP and SCTP, we find that the verification tag in SCTP does not exist in TCP. In TCP, a connection is identified by a combination of IP addresses and port numbers which is part of each segment. This has created two problems:

1. A blind attacker (not an interceptor) can send segments to a TCP server using randomly chosen source and destination port numbers such as those we discussed in a SYN flooding attack.

2. A delayed segment from a previous connection can show up in a new connection that uses the same source and destination port addresses (incarnation). This was one of the reasons that TCP needs a TIME-WAIT timer when terminating a connection.

SCTP solves these two problems by using a verification tag, a common value that is carried in all packets traveling in one direction in an association. A blind attacker cannot inject a random packet into an association because the packet would most likely not carry the appropriate tag (odds are 1 out of 2^{32}). A packet from an old association cannot show up in an incarnation because, even if the source and destination port addresses are the same, the verification tag would surely be different. Two verification tags, one for each direction, identify an association.

Cookie

We discussed a SYN flooding attack in Chapter 12. With TCP, a malicious attacker can flood a TCP server with a huge number of phony SYN segments using different forged IP addresses. Each time the server receives a SYN segment, it sets up a TCB and allocates other resources while waiting for the next segment to arrive. After a while, however, the server may collapse due to the exhaustion of resources.

The designers of SCTP have a strategy to prevent this type of attack. The strategy is to postpone the allocation of resources until the reception of the third packet, when the IP address of the sender is verified. The information received in the first packet must somehow be saved until the third packet arrives. But if the server saves the information, that would require the allocation of resources (memory); this is the dilemma. The solution is to pack the information and send it back to the client. This is called generating a **cookie.** The cookie is sent with the second packet to the address received in the first packet. There are two potential situations.

1. If the sender of the first packet is an attacker, the server never receives the third packet; the cookie is lost and no resources are allocated. The only effort for the server is "baking" the cookie.

2. If the sender of the first packet is an honest client that needs to make a connection, it receives the second packet, with the cookie. It sends a packet (third in the series) with the cookie, with no changes. The server receives the third packet and knows that it has come from an honest client because the cookie that the sender has sent is there. The server can now allocate resources.

The above strategy works if no entity can "eat" a cookie "baked" by the server. To guarantee this, the server creates a digest (see Chapter 28) from the information using its own secret key. The information and the digest, together make the cookie, which is sent to the client in the second packet. When the cookie is returned in the third packet, the server calculates the digest from the information. If the digest matches the one that is sent, the cookie has not been changed by any other entity.

Data Transfer

The whole purpose of an association is to transfer data between two ends. After the association is established, bidirectional data transfer can take place. The client and the server can both send data. Like TCP, SCTP supports piggybacking.

There is a major difference, however, between data transfer in TCP and SCTP. TCP receives messages from a process as a stream of bytes without recognizing any boundary between them. The process may insert some boundaries for its peer use, but TCP treats that mark as part of the text. In other words, TCP takes each message and appends it to its buffer. A segment can carry parts of two different messages. The only ordering system imposed by TCP is the byte numbers.

SCTP, on the other hand, recognizes and maintains boundaries. Each message coming from the process is treated as one unit and inserted into a DATA chunk unless it is fragmented (discussed later). In this sense, SCTP is like UDP, with one big advantage: data chunks are related to each other.

A message received from a process becomes a DATA chunk, or chunks if fragmented, by adding a DATA chunk header to the message. Each DATA chunk formed by a message or a fragment of a message has one TSN. We need to remember that only DATA chunks use TSNs and only DATA chunks are acknowledged by SACK chunks.

**In SCTP, only data chunks consume TSNs;
data chunks are the only chunks that are acknowledged.**

Let us show a simple scenario in Figure 13.20. In this figure a client sends four DATA chunks and receives two DATA chunks from the server. Later, we will discuss, in more detail, the use of flow and error control in SCTP. For the moment, we assume that everything goes well in this scenario. The client uses the verification tag 85, the server 700. The packets sent are described below:

1. The client sends the first packet carrying two DATA chunks with TSNs 7105 and 7106.

Figure 13.20   *Simple data transfer*

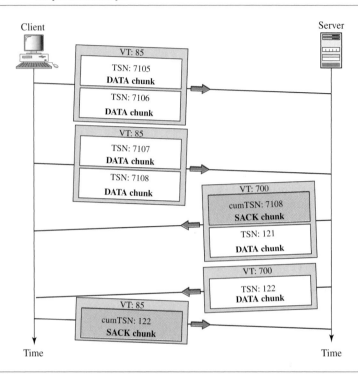

2. The client sends the second packet carrying two DATA chunks with TSNs 7107 and 7108.

3. The third packet is from the server. It contains the SACK chunk needed to acknowledge the receipt of DATA chunks from the client. Contrary to TCP, SCTP acknowledges the last in-order TSN received, not the next expected. The third packet also includes the first DATA chunk from the server with TSN 121.

4. After a while, the server sends another packet carrying the last DATA chunk with TSN 122, but it does not include a SACK chunk in the packet because the last DATA chunk received from the client was already acknowledged.

5. Finally, the client sends a packet that contains a SACK chunk acknowledging the receipt of the last two DATA chunks from the server.

**The acknowledgment in SCTP defines the cumulative TSN,
the TSN of the last data chunk received in order.**

Multihoming Data Transfer

We discussed the multihoming capability of SCTP, a feature that distinguishes SCTP from UDP and TCP. Multihoming allows both ends to define multiple IP addresses for communication. However, only one of these addresses can be defined as the **primary address;** the rest are alternative addresses. The primary address is defined during association establishment. The interesting point is that the primary address of an end is determined by the other end. In other words, a source defines the primary address for a destination.

Data transfer, by default, uses the primary address of the destination. If the primary is not available, one of the alternative addresses is used. The process, however, can always override the primary address and explicitly request that a message be sent to one of the alternative addresses. A process can also explicitly change the primary address of the current association.

A logical question that arises is where to send a SACK. SCTP dictates that a SACK be sent to the address from which the corresponding SCTP packet originated.

Multistream Delivery

One interesting feature of SCTP is the distinction between data transfer and data delivery. SCTP uses TSN numbers to handle data transfer, movement of data chunks between the source and destination. The delivery of the data chunks are controlled by SIs and SSNs. SCTP can support multiple streams, which means that the sender process can define different streams and a message can belong to one of these streams. Each stream is assigned a stream identifier (SI) which uniquely defines that stream. However, SCTP supports two types of data delivery in each stream: **ordered** (default) and **unordered.** In ordered data delivery, data chunks in a stream use stream sequence numbers (SSNs) to define their order in the stream. When the chunks arrive at the destination, SCTP is responsible for message delivery according to the SSN defined in the chunk. This may delay the delivery because some chunks may arrive out of order. In unordered data delivery, the data chunks in a stream have the U flag set, but their SSN field value is ignored. They do not consume SSNs. When an unordered data chunk arrives at the destination SCTP, it delivers the message carrying the chunk to the application without waiting for the other messages. Most of the time, applications use the ordered-delivery service, but occasionally some applications need to send urgent data that must be delivered out of order (recall the urgent data and urgent pointer facility of TCP). In these cases, the application can define the delivery as unordered.

Fragmentation

Another issue in data transfer is **fragmentation.** Although, SCTP shares this term with IP, fragmentation in IP and SCTP belong to different levels: the former at the network layer, the latter at the transport layer.

SCTP preserves the boundaries of the message from process to process when creating a DATA chunk from a message if the size of the message (when encapsulated in an IP datagram) does not exceed the MTU of the path. The size of an IP datagram carrying a message can be determined by adding the size of the message, in bytes, to the four overheads: data chunk header, necessary SACK chunks, SCTP general header, and IP header. If the total size exceeds the MTU, the message needs to be fragmented.

Fragmentation at the source SCTP takes place using the following steps:

1. The message is broken into smaller fragments to meet the size requirement.

2. A DATA chunk header is added to each fragment that carries a different TSN. The TSN needs to be in sequence.

3. All header chunks carry the same stream identifier (SI), the same stream sequence number (SSN), the same payload protocol identifier, and the same U flag.

4. The combination of B and E are assigned as follows:

    a. First fragment: 10

    b. Middle fragments: 00

    c. Last fragment: 01.

The fragments are reassembled at the destination. If a DATA chunk arrives with its B/E bits not equal to 11, it is not fragmented. The receiver knows how to reassemble all chunks with the same SIs and SSNs. The number of fragments is determined by the TSN number of the first and the last fragments.

Association Termination

In SCTP, like TCP, either of the two parties involved in exchanging data (client or server) can close the connection. However, unlike TCP, SCTP does not allow a "half-closed" association. If one end closes the association, the other end must stop sending new data. If any data are left over in the queue of the recipient of the termination request, it is sent and the association is closed. Association termination uses three packets as shown in Figure 13.21. Note that although the figure shows the case in which termination is initiated by the client, it can also be initiated by the server.

Figure 13.21 *Association termination*

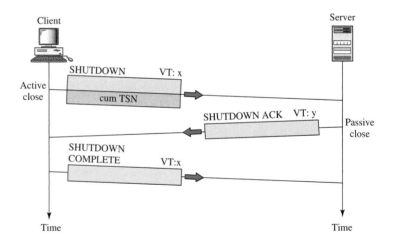

There can be several scenarios of association termination. We discuss some of them later.

Association Abortion

The termination of association discussed in the previous section is sometimes referred to as "graceful termination." An association in SCTP can also be aborted. The abortion may be requested by the process at either end or by SCTP. A process may wish to abort the association if there is a problem in the process itself (receiving wrong data from the other end, going into an infinite loop, and so on). The server may wish to abort the association because it has received an INIT chunk with wrong parameters, the requested resources are not available after receiving the cookie, the operating system needs to shut down, and so on.

The abortion process in SCTP is very simple. Either end can send an ABORT chunk and abort the association as shown in Figure 13.22. No further chunks are needed.

Figure 13.22 *Association abortion*

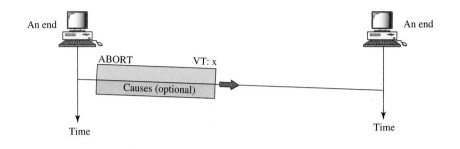

13.5 STATE TRANSITION DIAGRAM

To keep track of all the different events happening during association establishment, association termination, and data transfer, the SCTP software, like TCP, is implemented as a finite state machine. Figure 13.23 shows the state transition diagram for both client and server.

Figure 13.23 *State transition diagram*

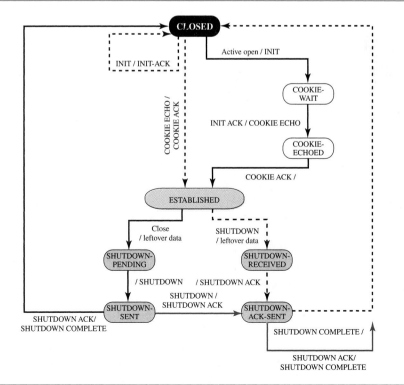

The dotted black lines of the figure represent the normal transitions for the server; the solid black lines represent the normal transitions for the client, and the colored lines represent unusual situations. In special situations, a server can go through a transition shown by a solid line; a client can go through a transition shown by a broken line. Table 13.4 shows the states for SCTP.

Table 13.4   *States for SCTP*

State	Description
CLOSED	No connection
COOKIE-WAIT	Waiting for a cookie
COOKIE-ECHOED	Waiting for cookie acknowledgment
ESTABLISHED	Connection is established; data are being transferred
SHUTDOWN-PENDING	Sending data after receiving *close*.
SHUTDOWN-SENT	Waiting for SHUTDOWN acknowledgment
SHUTDOWN-RECEIVED	Sending data after receiving SHUTDOWN
SHUTDOWN-ACK-SENT	Waiting for termination completion.

Scenarios

To understand the SCTP state machines and the transition diagrams, we go through some scenarios in this section.

A Common Scenario

Figure 13.24 shows a typical scenario. This is a routine situation in which the open and close commands come from the client. We have shown the states as we did for the corresponding TCP scenario. The figure specifically shows association establishment (the first four packets) and association termination (the last three packets) and the states the client and server go through. Note that the server remains in the **CLOSED** state during association establishment, but the client goes through two states (**COOKIE-WAIT** and **COOKIE-ECHOED**).

When the client SCTP receives an active close, it goes to the **SHUTDOWN-PENDING** state. It remains in this state until all leftover data is sent. It then sends a SHUTDOWN chunk and goes to **SHUTDOWN-SENT** state. The server, after receiving the SHUTDOWN chunk, informs its process that no more data will be accepted. It then goes to **SHUTDOWN-RECEIVED** state. While in this state, it sends all leftover data to the client and then sends a SHUTDOWN ACK chunk. It then goes to **SHUTDOWN-ACK-SENT** state. After receiving the last chunk, the client sends a SHUTDOWN COMPLETE chunk and closes the association. The server closes the association after receiving the last chunk.

Simultaneous Open

The cookie has created some complexity in association establishment. When an end receives an INIT chunk and sends an INIT-ACK chunk, it is still in the **CLOSED** state; it does not remember what it has received or sent. This creates a problem if an end

Figure 13.24 *A common scenario of states*

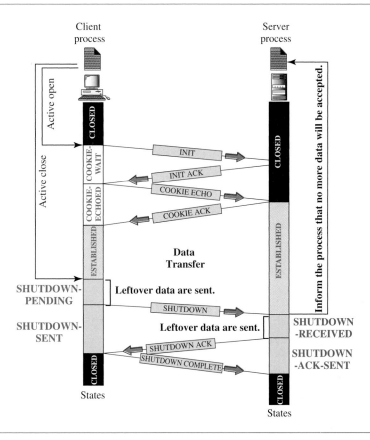

process issues an active open, and, before the association is established, the other end process also issues an active open. Figure 13.25 shows a scenario.

The process at site A issues an active open and sends an INIT chunk. Site B receives the INIT chunk and sends an INIT-ACK chunk. Before site B receives a COOKIE-ECHO chunk from site A, the process at site B issues an active open. SCTP at site B, not remembering that an association has started, sends an INIT chunk to site A and starts a new association. The two associations collide.

To handle this type of problem, SCTP requires that each site, when sending an INIT or an INIT-ACT chunk, also send an initiation tag. This tag is saved in a variable, say *local tag*. At any time, only one local tag value is held in this variable. Each time a packet arrives with a verification tag that does not match the value of the local tag, it is discarded. SCTP can also start a new association when it is in the middle of association setup and a new INIT chunk arrives.

Our scenario shows the use of these tags. Site A starts with an INIT chunk and initiation tag of 2000; the value of local tag is now 2000. Site B sends an INIT-ACK with an initialization tag of 500; the value of local tag for this site is 500. When site B sends an INIT chunk, the initialization tag and the local tag change to 600. Site B discards the

Figure 13.25 *Simultaneous open*

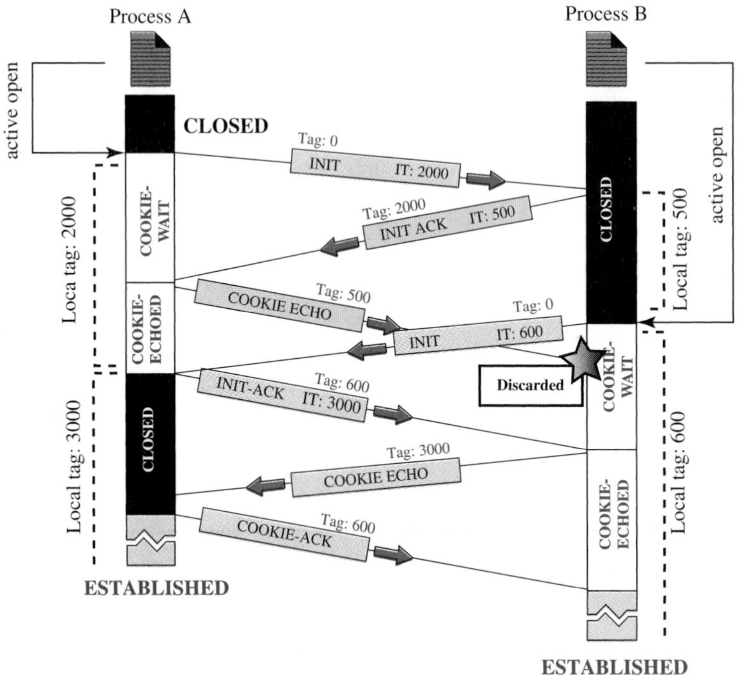

COOKIE-ECHO received because the tag on the packet is 500, which does not match the local tag of 600. The unfinished first association is aborted here. The new association, however, continues with site B as the initiator.

Simultaneous Close

Two end points can close the association simultaneously. This happens when a client's SHUTDOWN chunk reaches the server that has already sent a SHUTDOWN chunk itself. In this case both the client and the server can go to different states to terminate the association as shown in Figure 13.26.

The figure shows that both the client and the server issue an active close. We assume that none of the SCTPs has leftover data to send. So the **SHUTDOWN PENDING** state is skipped. Both SCTPs go to the **SHUTDOWN-SENT** state after receiving the SHUTDOWN chunks. Both send a SHUTDOWN ACK chunk and go to **SHUTDOWN-ACK-SENT** state. Both remain in this state until they receive the SHUTDOWN ACK chunk from the other party. They then send SHUTDOWN COMPLETE chunks and go to the closed state. Note that when they receive the last chunks, both SCTPs are already in the **CLOSED** state. If we look at the state transition diagram of Figure 13.23, we see that both the client and server follow the same path after the **ESTABLISHED** state. This is the path the client follows. However, after reaching the **SHUTDOWN-SENT** state, both turn to the right, instead of the left. When each of them reach the **SHUTDOWN-ACK-SENT** state, they go downward instead of straight.

Figure 13.26   *Simultaneous close*

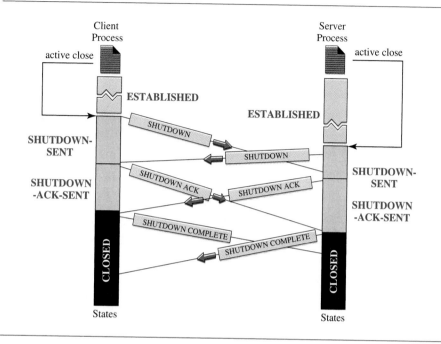

Other Scenarios

There are many scenarios that neither space nor time allows us to discuss. We would need to present information about timers as well as the procedures for the receipt of unexpected chunks. We would need additional information on SCTP including appropriate RFCs. We leave these scenarios as exercises or research activities.

13.6   FLOW CONTROL

Flow control in SCTP is similar to that in TCP. In TCP, we need to deal with only one unit of data, the byte. In SCTP, we need to handle two units of data, the byte and the chunk. The values of rwnd and cwnd are expressed in bytes; the values of TSN and acknowledgments are expressed in chunks. To show the concept, we make some unrealistic assumptions. We assume that there is never congestion in the network and that the network is error free. In other words, we assume that cwnd is infinite and no packet is lost, delayed, or arrives out of order. We also assume that data transfer is unidirectional. We correct our unrealistic assumptions in later sections. Current SCTP implementations still use a byte-oriented window for flow control. We, however, shows buffer in terms of chunk to make the concept easier to understand.

Receiver Site

The receiver has one buffer (queue) and three variables. The queue holds the received data chunks that have not yet been read by the process. The first variable holds the last TSN received, *cumTSN*. The second variable holds the available buffer size, *winsize*. The third variable holds the last accumulative acknowledgment, *lastACK*. Figure 13.27 shows the queue and variables at the receiver site.

Figure 13.27   *Flow control, receiver site*

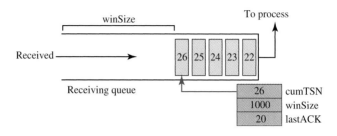

1. When the site receives a data chunk, it stores it at the end of the buffer (queue) and subtracts the size of the chunk from winSize. The TSN number of the chunk is stored in the cumTSN variable.
2. When the process reads a chunk, it removes it from the queue and adds the size of the removed chunk to winSize (recycling).
3. When the receiver decides to send a SACK, it checks the value of lastAck; if it is less than cumTSN, it sends a SACK with a cumulative TSN number equal to the cumTSN. It also includes the value of winSize as the advertised window size.

Sender Site

The sender has one buffer (queue) and three variables: *curTSN*, *rwnd*, and *inTransit*, as shown in Figure 13.28. We assume each chunk is 100 bytes long.

Figure 13.28   *Flow control, sender site*

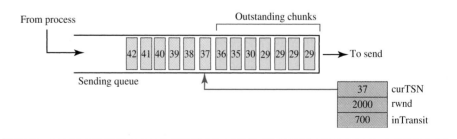

The buffer holds the chunks produced by the process that have either been sent or are ready to be sent. The first variable, curTSN, refers to the next chunk to be sent. All chunks in the queue with a TSN less than this value have been sent, but not acknowledged; they are outstanding. The second variable, rwnd, holds the last value advertised by the receiver (in bytes). The third variable, inTransit, holds the number of bytes in transit, bytes sent but not yet acknowledged. The following is the procedure used by the sender.

1. A chunk pointed to by curTSN can be sent if the size of the data is less than or equal to the quantity (rwnd − inTransit). After sending the chunk, the value of curTSN is incremented by one and now points to the next chunk to be sent. The value of inTransit is incremented by the size of the data in the transmitted chunk.

2. When a SACK is received, the chunks with a TSN less than or equal to the cumulative TSN in the SACK are removed from the queue and discarded. The sender does not have to worry about them any more. The value of inTransit is reduced by the total size of the discarded chunks. The value of rwnd is updated with the value of the advertised window in the SACK.

A Scenario

Let us give a simple scenario as shown in Figure 13.29. At the start the value of rwnd at the sender site and the value of winSize at the receiver site is 2000 (advertised during association establishment). Originally, there are four messages in the sender queue. The sender sends one data chunk and adds the number of bytes (1000) to the inTransit variable. After awhile, the sender checks the difference between the rwnd and inTransit, which is 1000 bytes, so it can send another data chunk. Now the difference between the two variables is 0 and no more data chunks can be sent. After awhile, a SACK arrives that acknowledges data chunks 1 and 2. The two chunks are removed from the queue. The value of inTransit is now 0. The SACK however, advertised a receiver window of value 0, which makes the sender update rwnd to 0. Now the sender is blocked; it cannot send any data chunks (with one exception explained later).

At the receiver site, the queue is empty at the beginning. After the first data chunk is received, there is one message in the queue and the value of cumTSN is 1. The value of

Figure 13.29 *Flow control scenario*

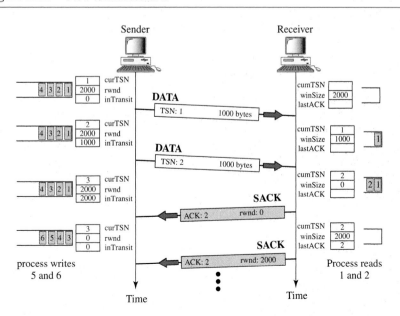

winSize is reduced to 1000 because the first message occupies 1000 bytes. After the second data chunk is received, the value of window size is 0 and the cumTSN is 2. Now, as we will see, the receiver is required to send a SACK with cumulative TSN of 2. After the first SACK was sent, the process reads the two messages, which means that there is now room in the queue; the receiver advertises the situation with a SACK to allow the sender to send more data chunks. The remaining events are not shown in the figure.

13.7 ERROR CONTROL

SCTP, like TCP, is a reliable transport-layer protocol. It uses a SACK chunk to report the state of the receiver buffer to the sender. Each implementation uses a different set of entities and timers for the receiver and sender sites. We use a very simple design to convey the concept to the reader.

Receiver Site

In our design, the receiver stores all chunks that have arrived in its queue including the out-of-order ones. However, it leaves spaces for any missing chunks. It discards duplicate messages, but keeps track of them for reports to the sender. Figure 13.30 shows a

Figure 13.30 *Error control, receiver site*

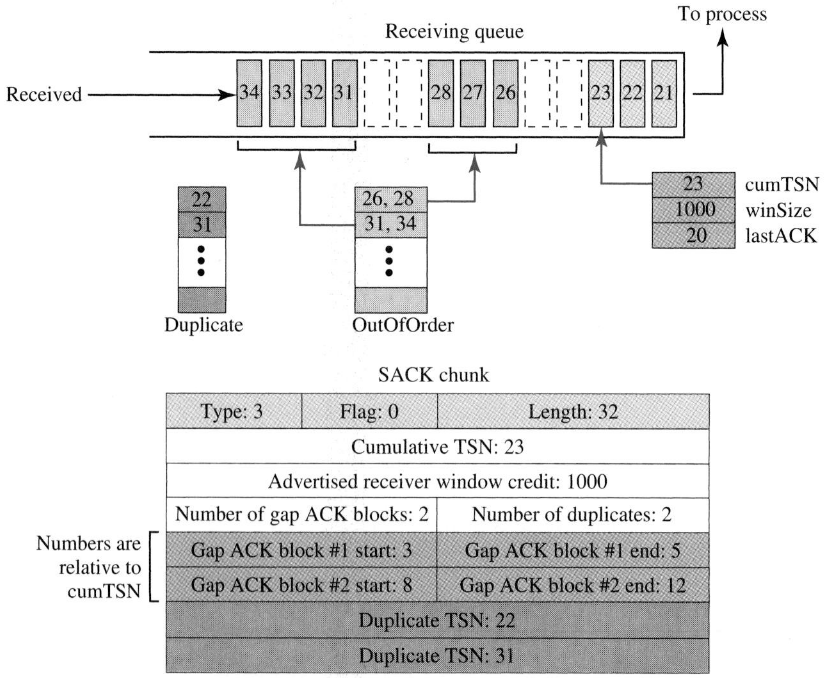

typical design for the receiver site and the state of the receiving queue at a particular point in time.

The last acknowledgment sent was for data chunk 20. The available window size is 1000 bytes. Chunks 21 to 23 have been received in order. The first out-of-order block contains chunks 26 to 28. The second out-of-order block contains chunks 31 to 34. A variable holds the value of cumTSN. An array of variables keeps track of the beginning and the end of each block that is out of order. An array of variables holds the duplicate chunks received. Note that there is no need for storing duplicate chunks in the queue, they will be discarded. The figure also shows the SACK chunk that will be sent to report the state of the receiver to the sender. The TSN numbers for out of order chunks are relative (offsets) to the cummulative TSN.

Sender Site

At the sender site, our design demands two buffers (queues): a sending queue and a retransmission queue. We also use three variables: rwnd, inTransit, and curTSN as described in the previous section. Figure 13.31 shows a typical design.

Figure 13.31   *Error control, sender site*

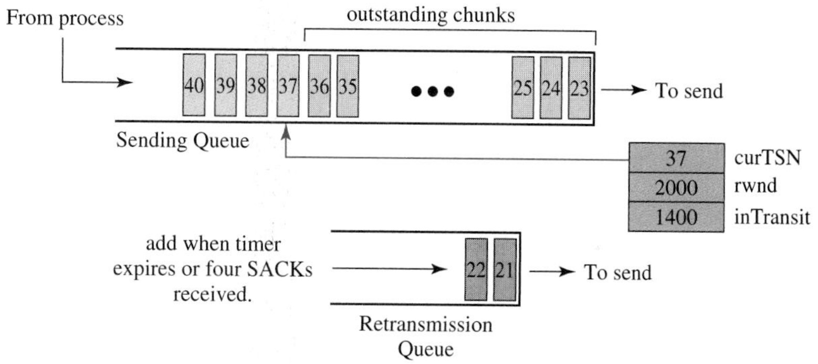

The sending queue holds chunks 23 to 40. The chunks 23 to 36 have already been sent, but not acknowledged; they are outstanding chunks. The curTSN points to the next chunk to be sent (37). We assume that each chunk is 100 bytes, which means that 1400 bytes of data (chunks 23 to 36) are in transit. The sender at this moment has a retransmission queue. When a packet is sent, a retransmission timer starts for that packet (all data chunks in that packet). Some implementations use one single timer for the entire association, but we continue with our tradition of one timer for each packet for simplification. When the retransmission timer for a packet expires, or four duplicate SACKs arrive that declare a packet as missing (fast retransmission was discussed in Chapter 12), the chunks in that packet are moved to the retransmission queue to be resent. These chunks are considered lost, rather than outstanding. The chunks in the retransmission queue have priority. In other words, the next time the sender sends a chunk, it would be chunk 21 from the retransmission queue.

To see how the state of the sender changes, assume that the SACK in Figure 13.30 arrives at the sender site in Figure 13.31. Figure 13.32 shows the new state.

Figure 13.32 *New state at the sender site after receiving a SACK chunk*

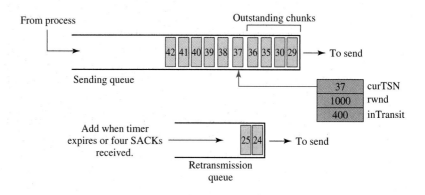

1. All chunks having a TSN equal to or less than the cumTSN in the SACK are removed from the sending or retransmission queue. They are no longer outstanding or marked for retransmission. Chunks 21 and 22 are removed from the retransmission queue and 23 is removed from the sending queue.
2. Our design also removes all chunks from the sending queue that are declared in the gap blocks; some conservative implementations, however, save these chunks until a cumTSN arrives that includes them. This precaution is needed for the rare occasion when the receiver finds some problem with these out-of-order chunks. We ignore these rare occasions. Chunks 26 to 28 and chunks 31 to 34, therefore, are removed from the sending queue.
3. The list of duplicate chunks does not have any effect.
4. The value of rwnd is changed to 1000 as advertised in the SACK chunk.
5. We also assume that the transmission timer for the packet that carried chunks 24 and 25 has expired. These move to the retransmission queue and a new retransmission timer is set according to the exponential backoff rule discussed in Chapter 12.
6. The value of inTransit becomes 400 because only 4 chunks are now in transit. The chunks in the retransmission queue are not counted because they are assumed lost, not in transit.

Sending Data Chunks

An end can send a data packet whenever there are data chunks in the sending queue with a TSN greater than or equal to curTSN or if there are data chunks in the retransmission queue. The retransmission queue has priority. However, the total size of the data chunk or chunks included in the packet must not exceed the (rwnd − inTransit) value and the total size of the frame must not exceed the MTU size as we discussed in previous sections. If we assume in our previous scenario, that our packet can take 3 chunks (due to the MTU restriction), then chunks 24 and 25 from the retransmission queue and chunk 37, the next chunk ready to be sent in the sending queue, can be sent. Note that the outstanding chunks in the sending queue cannot be sent; they are assumed to be in transit. Note also that any chunk sent from the retransmission queue is also timed for retransmission again. The new timer affects chunks 24, 25, and 37. We need to mention here that some implementations may not allow mixing chunks from the retransmission queue and the sending queue. In this case, only chunks 24 and 25 can be sent in the packet.

Retransmission

To control a lost or discarded chunk, SCTP, like TCP, employs two strategies: using retransmission timers and receiving four SACKs with the same missing chunks.

Retransmission Timer   SCTP uses a retransmission timer, which handles the retransmission time, the waiting time for an acknowledgment of a segment. The procedures for calculating RTO and RTT in SCTP are the same as we described for TCP. SCTP uses a measured RTT (RTT_M), a smoothed RTT (RTT_S), and an RTT deviation (RTT_D) to calculate the RTO. SCTP also uses Karn's algorithm to avoid acknowledgment ambiguity. Note that if a host is using more than one IP address (multihoming), separate RTOs must be calculated and kept for each path.

Three SACKs   Whenever a sender receives four consecutive duplicate SACKs whose gap ack information indicate some missing chunks, the sender needs to consider those chunks as lost and immediately move them to the retransmission queue.

Generating SACK Chunks

Another issue in error control is the generation of SACK chunks. The rules for generating SCTP SACK chunks are similar to the rules used for acknowledgment with the TCP ACK flag. We summarize the rules as listed below.

1. When an end sends a DATA chunk to the other end, it must include a SACK chunk advertising the receipt of unacknowledged DATA chunks.
2. When an end receives a packet containing data, but has no data to send, it needs to acknowledge the receipt of the packet within a specified time (usually 500 ms).
3. An end must send at least one SACK for every other packet it receives. This rule overrides the second rule.
4. When a packet arrives with out-of-order data chunks, the receiver needs to immediately send a SACK chunk reporting the situation to the sender.
5. When an end receives a packet with duplicate DATA chunks and no new DATA chunks, the duplicate data chunks must be reported immediately with a SACK chunk.

13.8   CONGESTION CONTROL

SCTP, like TCP, is a transport layer protocol with packets subject to congestion in the network. The SCTP designers have used the same strategies we described for congestion control in Chapter 12 for TCP. SCTP has slow start (exponential increase), congestion avoidance (additive increase), and congestion detection (multiplicative decrease) phases. Like TCP, SCTP also uses fast retransmission and fast recovery.

Congestion Control and Multihoming

Congestion control in SCTP is more complicated since the host may have more than one IP address. In this case, there can be more than one path for the data in the network. Each of these paths may encounter different levels of congestion. This implies that the site needs to have different values of cwnd for each IP address.

Explicit Congestion Notification

Explicit congestion notification (ECN), as defined for other wide area networks, is a process that enables a receiver to explicitly inform the sender of any congestion experienced in the network. If a receiver encounters many delayed or lost packets, it is an indication of probable congestion. SCTP can use an ECN option in the INIT and INIT ACK chunks to allow both ends to negotiate the use of ECN. If both parties agree, the receiver can inform the sender of congestion by sending an ECNE (explicit congestion notification echo) chunk with each packet until it receives a CWR (congestion window reduce) chunk to show that the sender has reduced its cwnd. We have not discussed these two chunks because they are not yet part of the standard and because the discussion of explicit congestion notification is beyond the scope of this book.

13.9   KEY TERMS

ABORT chunk	COOKIE-ECHOED state
association	COOKIE-WAIT state
association abortion	cumulative TSN
association establishment	DATA chunk
association termination	ERROR chunk
byte-oriented	ESTABLISHED state
chunk	FORWARD TSN chunk
CLOSED state	fragmentation
cookie	HEARTBEAT ACK chunk
COOKIE ACK chunk	HEARTBEAT chunk
COOKIE ECHO chunk	inbound stream

INIT ACK chunk	SHUTDOWN chunk
INIT chunk	SHUTDOWN COMPLETE chunk
initial TSN	SHUTDOWN-ACT-SENT state
initiation tag	SHUTDOWN-PENDING state
message-oriented	SHUTDOWN-RECEIVED state
multihoming service	SHUTDOWN-SENT state
multistream service	stream identifier (SI)
ordered delivery	stream sequence number (SSN)
outbound stream	transmission sequence number (TSN)
primary address	unordered delivery
SACK chunk	verification tag
SHUTDOWN ACK chunk	

13.10   SUMMARY

❏ SCTP is a message-oriented, reliable protocol that combines the good features of UDP and TCP.

❏ SCTP provides additional services not provided by UDP or TCP, such as multiple-stream and multihoming services.

❏ SCTP is a connection-oriented protocol. An SCTP connection is called an association.

❏ SCTP uses the term *packet* to define a transportation unit.

❏ In SCTP, control information and data information are carried in separate chunks.

❏ An SCTP packet can contain control chunks and data chunks with control chunks coming before data chunks.

❏ The control chunks defined in this text are INIT, INIT ACK, SACK, HEART-BEAT, HEARTBEAT ACK, ABORT, SHUTDOWN, SHUTDOWN ACK, SHUT-DOWN COMPLETE, ERROR, COOKIE ECHO, COOKIE ACK, and FORWARD TSN.

❏ In SCTP, each data chunk is numbered using a transmission sequence number (TSN).

❏ To distinguish between different streams, SCTP uses the sequence identifier (SI).

❏ To distinguish between different data chunks belonging to the same stream, SCTP uses the stream sequence number (SSN).

❏ Data chunks are identified by three identifiers: TSN, SI, and SSN. TSN is a cumulative number recognized by the whole association; SSN starts from 0 in each stream.

❏ SCTP acknowledgment numbers are used only to acknowledge data chunks; control chunks are acknowledged, if needed, by another control chunk.

❑ SCTP has states within a transition diagram. The states defined for SCTP are **CLOSED, COOKIE-WAIT, COOKIE-ECHOED, ESTABLISHED, SHUTDOWN-PENDING, SHUTDOWN-SENT, SHUTDOWN-RECEIVED,** and **SHUTDOWN-ACK-SENT.**

❑ A DATA chunk cannot carry data belonging to more than one message, but a message can be split into several chunks (fragmentation).

❑ An SCTP association is normally established using four packets (four-way handshaking). An association is normally terminated using three packets (three-way handshaking).

❑ An SCTP association uses a cookie to prevent blind flooding attacks and a verification tag to avoid insertion attacks.

❑ SCTP provides flow control, error control, and congestion control.

❑ The SCTP acknowledgment SACK reports the cumulative TSN, the TSN of the last data chunk received in order, and selective TSN that have been received.

13.11   PRACTICE SET

Exercises

1. A packet is carrying two DATA chunks, each containing 22 bytes of user data. What is the size of each DATA chunk? What is the total size of the packet?

2. A SACK chunk reports the receipt of three out-of-order data chunks and five duplicate data chunks. What is the total size of the chunk in bytes?

3. A packet is carrying a COOKIE ECHO message and a DATA chunk. If the size of the cookie is 200 bytes and that of the user data is 20 bytes, what is the size of the packet?

4. A packet is carrying a COOKIE ACK message and a DATA chunk. If the user data is 20 bytes, what is the size of the packet?

5. Four DATA chunks have arrived carrying the following information:

   TSN:27 SI:2 SSN:14 BE:00
   TSN:33 SI:2 SSN:15 BE:11
   TSN:26 SI:2 SSN:14 BE:00
   TSN:24 SI:2 SSN:14 BE:00
   TSN:21 SI:2 SSN:14 BE:10

   a. Which data chunk is a fragment?

   b. Which data chunk is the first fragment?

   c. Which data chunk is the last fragment?

   d. How many middle fragments are missing?

6. The value of the cumulative TSN in a SACK is 23. The value of the previous cumulative TSN in the SACK was 29. What is the problem?

7. An SCTP association is in the **ESTABLISHED** state. It receives a SHUTDOWN chunk. If the host does not have any outstanding or pending data, what does it need to do?

8. An SCTP association is in the **COOKIE-WAIT** state. It receives an INIT chunk; what does it need to do?

9. The following is a dump of a DATA chunk in hexadecimal format.

   00000015 00000005 0003000A 00000000 48656C6C 6F000000

   a. Is this an ordered or unordered chunk?
   b. Is this the first, the last, the middle, or the only fragment?
   c. How many bytes of padding are carried by the chunk?
   d. What is the TSN?
   e. What is the SI?
   f. What is the SSN?
   g. What is the message?

10. The following is a dump of an SCTP general header in hexadecimal format.

    04320017 00000001 00000000

    a. What is the source port number?
    b. What is the destination port number?
    c. What is the value of the verification tag?
    d. What is the value of the checksum?

11. The state of a receiver is as follows:

    a. The receiving queue has chunks 1 to 8, 11 to 14, and 16 to 20.
    b. There are 1800 bytes of space in the queue.
    c. The value of lastAck is 4.
    d. No duplicate chunk has been received.
    e. The value of cumTSN is 5.

    Show the contents of the receiving queue and the variables.

12. Show the contents of the SACK message sent by the receiver in Exercise 11.

13. The state of a sender is as follows:

    a. The sending queue has chunks 18 to 23.
    b. The value of curTSN is 20.
    c. The value of the window size is 2000 bytes.
    d. The value of inTransit is 200.

    If each data chunk contains 100 bytes of data, how many DATA chunks can be sent now? What is the next data chunk to be sent?

14. An SCTP client opens an association using an initial tag of 806, an initial TSN of 14534, and a window size of 20000. The server responds with an initial tag of 2000, an initial TSN of 670, and a window size of 14000. Show the contents of all four packets exchanged during association establishment. Ignore the value of the cookie.

15. If the client in the previous exercise sends 7600 data chunks and the server sends 570 data chunks, show the contents of the three packets exchanged during association termination.

Research Activities

16. Find the RFCs related to SCTP.

17. We have defined only a few scenarios related to the transition diagram. Show these other scenarios including, but not limited to, the following cases:

    a. The loss, delay, or duplication of any of the four packets during association establishment.

    b. The loss, delay, or duplication of any of the three packets during association termination.

18. What happens if a SACK chunk is delayed or lost?

19. Find the steps a server takes to validate a cookie.

20. We discussed two timers in TCP: persistence and keepalive. Find out the functionality of these timers in SCTP.

21. Find out more about ECN in SCTP. Find the format of these two chunks.

22. Find out more about the parameters used in some SCTP control chunks.

23. Some application programs, such as FTP, need more than one connection when using TCP. Find how the multistream service of SCTP can help these applications establish only one association with several streams.

CHAPTER 14

Unicast Routing Protocols
(RIP, OSPF, and BGP)

An internet is a combination of networks connected by routers. When a datagram goes from a source to a destination, it will probably pass through many routers until it reaches the router attached to the destination network.

A router receives a packet from a network and passes it to another network. A router is usually attached to several networks. When it receives a packet, to which network should it pass the packet? The decision is based on optimization: Which of the available pathways is the optimum pathway? What is the definition of the term *optimum*?

One approach is to assign a cost for passing through a network. We call this cost a **metric.** However, the metric assigned to each network depends on the type of protocol. Some simple protocols, like the Routing Information Protocol (RIP), treat all networks as equals. The cost of passing through a network is the same; it is one hop count. So if a packet passes through 10 networks to reach the destination, the total cost is 10 hop counts.

Other protocols, such as Open Shortest Path First (OSPF), allow the administrator to assign a cost for passing through a network based on the type of service required. A route through a network can have different costs (metrics). For example, if maximum throughput is the desired type of service, a satellite link has a lower metric than a fiber-optic line. On the other hand, if minimum delay is the desired type of service, a fiber-optic line has a lower metric than a satellite line. Routers use routing tables to help decide the best route. OSPF allows each router to have several routing tables based on the required type of service.

Other protocols define the metric in a totally different way. In the Border Gateway Protocol (BGP), the criterion is the policy, which can be set by the administrator. The policy defines what paths should be chosen.

A routing table can be either static or dynamic. A *static table* is one with manual entries. A *dynamic table,* on the other hand, is one that is updated automatically when there is a change somewhere in the internet. Today, an internet needs dynamic routing tables. The tables need to be updated as soon as there is a change in the internet. For instance, they need to be updated when a router is down, and they need to be updated whenever a better route has been found.

Routing protocols have been created in response to the demand for dynamic routing tables. A routing protocol is a combination of rules and procedures that lets routers in the internet inform each other of changes. It allows routers to share whatever they know about the internet or their neighborhood. The sharing of information allows a router in San Francisco to know about the failure of a network in Texas. The routing protocols also include procedures for combining information received from other routers.

14.1   INTRA- AND INTERDOMAIN ROUTING

Today, an internet can be so large that one routing protocol cannot handle the task of updating the routing tables of all routers. For this reason, an internet is divided into autonomous systems. An **autonomous system (AS)** is a group of networks and routers under the authority of a single administration. Routing inside an autonomous system is referred to as *intradomain routing*. Routing between autonomous systems is referred to as *interdomain routing*. Each autonomous system can choose one or more intradomain routing protocols to handle routing inside the autonomous system. However, only one interdomain routing protocol handles routing between autonomous systems. See Figure 14.1.

Figure 14.1   *Autonomous systems*

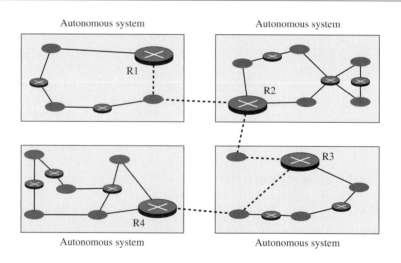

Several intradomain and interdomain routing protocols are in use. In this chapter, we cover only the most popular ones. We discuss two intradomain routing protocols: distance vector and link state. We also introduce one interdomain routing protocol: path vector (see Figure 14.2).

Routing Information Protocol (RIP) is the implementation of the distance vector protocol. **Open Shortest Path First (OSPF)** is the implementation of the link state protocol. **Border Gateway Protocol (BGP)** is the implementation of the path vector protocol.

Figure 14.2   *Popular routing protocols*

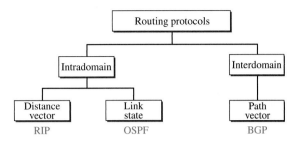

14.2   DISTANCE VECTOR ROUTING

In **distance vector routing,** the least cost route between any two nodes is the route with minimum distance. In this protocol, as the name implies, each node maintains a vector (table) of minimum distances to every node. The table at each node also guides the packets to the desired node by showing the next stop in the route (next-hop routing).

We can think of nodes as the cities in an area and the lines as the roads connecting them. A table can show a tourist the minimum distance between cities.

In Figure 14.3, we show a system of five nodes with their corresponding tables.

Figure 14.3   *Distance vector routing tables*

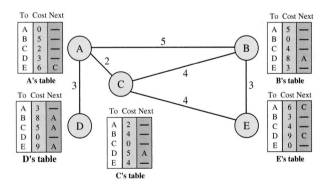

The table for node A shows how we can reach any node from this node. For example, our least cost to reach node E is 6. The route passes through C.

Initialization

The tables in Figure 14.3 are stable; each node knows how to reach any other node and the cost. At the beginning, however, this is not the case. Each node can know only the distance between itself and its **immediate neighbors,** those directly connected to it. So for the moment, we assume that each node can send a message to the immediate neighbors and find the distance between itself and these neighbors. Figure 14.4 shows the initial tables for each node. The distance for any entry that is not a neighbor is marked as infinite (unreachable).

Figure 14.4   *Initialization of tables in distance vector routing*

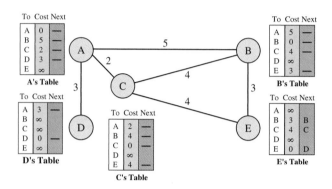

Sharing

The whole idea of distance vector routing is the sharing of information between neighbors. Although node A does not know about node E, node C does. So if node C shares its routing table with A, node A can also know how to reach node E. On the other hand, node C does not know how to reach node D, but node A does. If node A shares its routing table with node C, node C also knows how to reach node D. In other words, nodes A and C, as immediate neighbors, can improve their routing tables if they help each other.

There is only one problem. How much of the table must be shared with each neighbor? A node is not aware of a neighbor's table. The best solution for each node is to send its entire table to the neighbor and let the neighbor decide what part to use and what part to discard. However, the third column of a table (next stop) is not useful for the neighbor. When the neighbor receives a table, this column needs to be replaced with the sender's name. If any of the rows can be used, the next node is the sender of the table. A node therefore can send only the first two columns of its table to any neighbor. In other words, sharing here means only sharing the first two columns.

> In distance vector routing, each node shares its routing table with its immediate neighbors periodically and when there is a change.

Updating

When a node receives a two-column table from a neighbor, it needs to update its routing table. Updating takes three steps:

1. The receiving node needs to add the cost between itself and the sending node to each value in the second column. The logic is clear. If node C claims that its

distance to a destination is x miles, and the distance between A and C is y miles, then the distance between A and that destination, via C, is $x + y$ miles.

2. The receiving node needs to add the name of the sending node to each row as the third column if the receiving node uses information from any row. The sending node is the next node in the route.

3. The receiving node needs to compare each row of its old table with the corresponding row of the modified version of the received table.

    a. If the next-node entry is different, the receiving node chooses the row with the smaller cost. If there is a tie, the old one is kept.

    b. If the next-node entry is the same, the receiving node chooses the new row. For example, if node C has previously advertised a route to node X with distance 3. Suppose that now there is no path between C and X; node C now advertises this route with a distance of infinity. Node A must not ignore this value even though its old entry is smaller. The old route does not exist any more. The new route has a distance of infinity.

Figure 14.5 shows how node A updates its routing table after receiving the partial table from node C.

Figure 14.5 *Updating in distance vector routing*

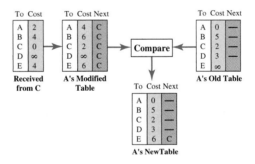

There are several points we need to emphasize here. First, as we know from mathematics, when we add any number to infinity, the result is still infinity. Second, the modified table shows how to reach A from A via C. If A needs to reach itself via C, it needs to go to C and come back, a distance of 4. Third, the only benefit from this updating of node A is the last entry, how to reach E. Previously, node A did not know how to reach E (distance of infinity); now it knows that the cost is 6 via C.

Each node can update its table using the tables received from other nodes. In a short period of time, if there is no change in the network itself, such as a failure in a link, all nodes reach a stable condition in which the contents of the table remain the same.

When to Share

The question now is when does a node send its partial routing table (only two columns) to all its immediate neighbors? The table is sent both periodically and when there is a change in the table.

Periodic Update

A node sends its routing table, normally every 30 seconds, in a periodic update. The period depends on the protocol that is using distance vector routing.

Triggered Update

A node sends its 2-column routing table to its neighbors any time there is a change in its routing table. This is called a triggered update. The change can result from the following.

1. A node receives a table from a neighbor resulting in changes in its own table after updating.
2. A node detects some failure in the neighboring links which results in a distance change to infinity.

Two-Node Loop Instability

A problem with distance vector routing is instability, which means that a network using this protocol can become unstable. To understand the problem, let us look at the scenario depicted in Figure 14.6.

Figure 14.6 *Two-node instability*

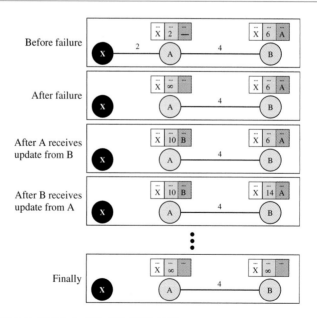

The figure shows a system with three nodes. We have shown only the portions of the routing table needed for our discussion. At the beginning, both nodes A and B know how to reach node X. But suddenly, the link between A and X fails. Node A changes its table. If A can send its table to B immediately, everything is fine. However, the system becomes unstable if B sends its routing table to A before receiving A's routing table.

Node A receives the update and, assuming that B has found a way to reach X, immediately updates its routing table. Based on the triggered update strategy, A sends its new update to B. Now B thinks that something has been changed around A and updates its routing table. The cost of reaching X increases gradually until it reaches infinity. At this moment, both A and B know that X cannot be reached. However, during this time the system is not stable. Node A thinks that the route to X is via B; node B thinks that the route to X is via A. If A receives a packet destined for X, it goes to B and then comes back to A. Similarly, if B receives a packet destined for X, it goes to A and comes back to B. Packets bounce between A and B, creating a two-node loop problem. A few solutions have been proposed for instability of this kind.

Defining Infinity

The first obvious solution is to re-define infinity to a smaller number, such as 100. For our previous scenario, the system will be stable in less than 20 updates. As a matter of fact, most implementations of the distance vector protocol define the distance between each node to be 1 and define 16 as infinity. However, this means that distance vector cannot be used in large systems. The size of the network, in each direction, can not exceed 15 hops.

Split Horizon

Another solution is called **split horizon.** In this strategy, instead of flooding the table through each interface, each node sends only part of its table through each interface. If, according to its table, node B thinks that the optimum route to reach X is via A, it does not need to advertise this piece of information to A; the information has come from A (A already knows). Taking information from node A, modifying it, and sending it back to node A is what creates the confusion. In our scenario, node B eliminates the last line of its routing table before it sends it to A. In this case, node A keeps the value of infinity as the distance to X. Later when node A sends its routing table to B, node B also corrects its routing table. The system becomes stable after the first update: both node A and B know that X is not reachable.

Split Horizon and Poison Reverse

Using the split horizon strategy has one drawback. Normally, the distance vector protocol uses a timer and if there is no news about a route, the node deletes the route from its table. When node B in the previous scenario eliminates the route to X from its advertisement to A, node A cannot guess that this is due to the split horizon strategy (the source of information was A) or because B has not received any news about X recently. The split horizon strategy can be combined with the **poison reverse** strategy. Node B can still advertise the value for X, but if the source of information is A, it can replace the distance with infinity as a warning: "Do not use this value; what I know about this route comes from you."

Three-Node Instability

The two-node instability can be avoided using split horizon combined with poison reverse. However, if the instability is between three nodes, stability cannot be guaranteed. Figure 14.7 shows the scenario.

Figure 14.7 *Three-node instability*

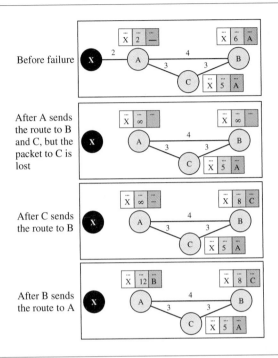

Suppose, after finding that X is not reachable, node A sends a packet to B and C to inform them of the situation. Node B immediately updates its table, but the packet to C is lost in the network and never reaches C. Node C remains in the dark and still thinks that there is a route to X via A with a distance of 5. After a while, node C sends to B its routing table, which includes the route to X. Node B is totally fooled here. It receives information on the route to X from C, and according to the algorithm, it updates its table showing the route to X via C with a cost of 8. This information has come from C, not from A, so after awhile node B may advertise this route to A. Now A is fooled and updates its table to show that A can reach X via B with a cost of 12. Of course, the loop continues; now A advertises the route to X to C, with increased cost, but not to B. C then advertises the route to B with an increased cost. B does the same to A. And so on. The loop stops when the cost in each node reaches infinity.

14.3 RIP

The **Routing Information Protocol (RIP)** is an intradomain routing protocol used inside an autonomous system. It is a very simple protocol based on distance vector routing. RIP implements distance vector routing directly with some considerations:

1. In an autonomous system, we are dealing with routers and networks (links). The routers have routing tables, networks don't.

2. The destination in a routing table is a network, which means the first column defines a network address.

3. The metric used by RIP is very simple; the distance is defined as the number of links (networks) that have to be used to reach the destination. For this reason, the metric in RIP is called a **hop count.**

4. Infinity is defined as 16, which means that any route in an autonomous system using RIP cannot have more than 15 hops.

5. The next node column defines the address of the router to which the packet is to be sent to reach its destination.

Figure 14.8 shows an autonomous system with seven networks and four routers. The table of each router is also shown. Let us look at the routing table for R1. The table has seven entries to show how to reach each network in the autonomous system. Router R1 is directly connect to networks 130.10.0.0 and 130.11.0.0, which means that there are no next hop entries for these two networks. To send a packet to one of the three networks at the far left, router R1 needs to deliver the packet to R2. The next node entry for these three networks is the interface of router R2 with IP address 130.10.0.1. To send a packet to the two networks at the far right, router R1 needs to send the packet to the interface of router R4 with IP address 130.11.0.1. The other tables can be explained similarly.

Figure 14.8   *Example of a domain using RIP*

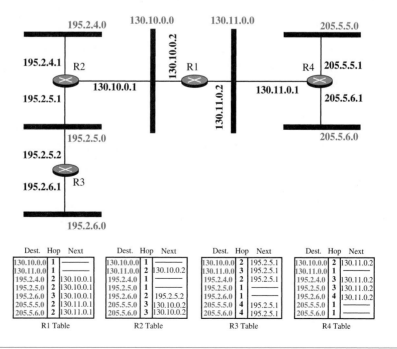

Dest.	Hop	Next
130.10.0.0	1	———
130.11.0.0	1	———
195.2.4.0	2	130.10.0.1
195.2.5.0	2	130.10.0.1
195.2.6.0	3	130.10.0.1
205.5.5.0	2	130.11.0.1
205.5.6.0	2	130.11.0.1

R1 Table

Dest.	Hop	Next
130.10.0.0	1	———
130.11.0.0	2	130.10.0.2
195.2.4.0	1	———
195.2.5.0	1	———
195.2.6.0	2	195.2.5.2
205.5.5.0	3	130.10.0.2
205.5.6.0	3	130.10.0.2

R2 Table

Dest.	Hop	Next
130.10.0.0	2	195.2.5.1
130.11.0.0	3	195.2.5.1
195.2.4.0	2	195.2.5.1
195.2.5.0	1	———
195.2.6.0	1	———
205.5.5.0	4	195.2.5.1
205.5.6.0	4	195.2.5.1

R3 Table

Dest.	Hop	Next
130.10.0.0	2	130.11.0.2
130.11.0.0	1	———
195.2.4.0	3	130.11.0.2
195.2.5.0	3	130.11.0.2
195.2.6.0	4	130.11.0.2
205.5.5.0	1	———
205.5.6.0	1	———

R4 Table

RIP Message Format

The format of the RIP message is shown in Figure 14.9.

Figure 14.9 *RIP message format*

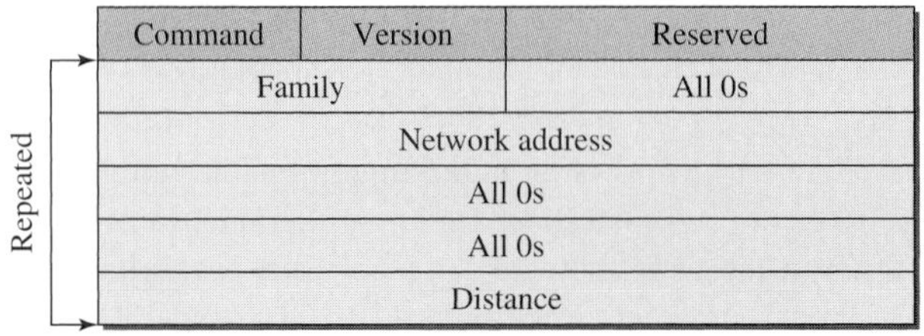

❏ **Command.** This 8-bit field specifies the type of message: request (1) or response (2).
❏ **Version.** This 8-bit field defines the version. In this book we use version 1, but at the end of this section, we give some new features of version 2.
❏ **Family.** This 16-bit field defines the family of the protocol used. For TCP/IP the value is 2.
❏ **Network address.** The address field defines the address of the destination network. RIP has allocated 14 bytes for this field to be applicable to any protocol. However, IP currently uses only 4 bytes. The rest of the address is filled with 0s.
❏ **Distance.** This 32-bit field defines the hop count from the advertising router to the destination network.

Note that part of the message is repeated for each destination network. We refer to this as an *entry.*

Requests and Responses

RIP has two types of messages: request and response.

Request

A request message is sent by a router that has just come up or by a router that has some time-out entries. A request can ask about specific entries or all entries (see Figure 14.10).

Response

A response can be either solicited or unsolicited. A *solicited response* is sent only in answer to a request. It contains information about the destination specified in the corresponding request. An *unsolicited response,* on the other hand, is sent periodically, every 30 s or when there is a change in the routing table. The response is sometimes called an update packet. Figure 14.9 shows the response message format.

Figure 14.10   *Request messages*

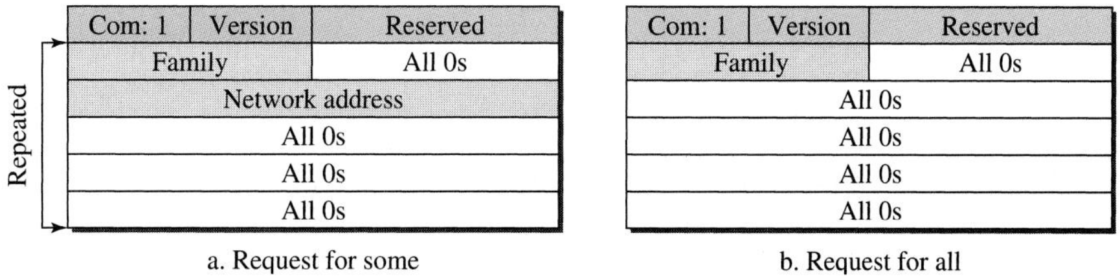

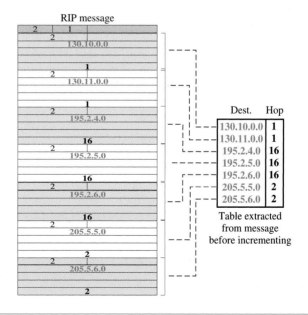

a. Request for some   b. Request for all

Example 1

Figure 14.11 shows the update message sent from router R1 to router R2 in Figure 14.8. The
message is sent out of interface 130.10.0.2.

Figure 14.11   *Solution to Example 1*

The message is prepared with the combination of split horizon and poison reverse strategy
in mind. Router R1 has obtained information about networks 195.2.4.0, 195.2.5.0, and
195.2.6.0 from router R2. When R1 sends an update message to R2, it replaces the actual value
of the hop counts for these three networks with 16 (infinity) to prevent any confusion for R2.
The figure also shows the table extracted from the message. Router R2 uses the source address
of the IP datagram carrying the RIP message from R1 (130.10.02) as the next hop address.
Router R2 also increments each hop count by 1 because the values in the message are relative
to R1, not R2.

Timers in RIP

RIP uses three timers to support its operation (see Figure 14.12). The periodic timer controls the sending of messages, the expiration timer governs the validity of a route, and the garbage collection timer advertises the failure of a route.

Figure 14.12   *RIP timers*

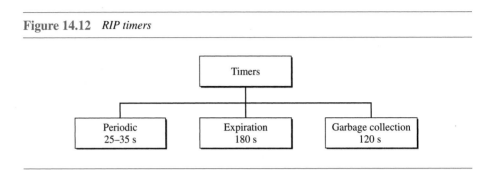

Periodic Timer

The **periodic timer** controls the advertising of regular update messages. Although the protocol specifies that this timer must be set to 30 s, the working model uses a random number between 25 and 35 s. This is to prevent any possible synchronization and therefore overload on an internet if routers update simultaneously.

Each router has one periodic timer that is randomly set to a number between 25 and 35. It counts down; when zero is reached, the update message is sent, and the timer is randomly set once again.

Expiration Timer

The **expiration timer** governs the validity of a route. When a router receives update information for a route, the expiration timer is set to 180 s for that particular route. Every time a new update for the route is received, the timer is reset. In normal situations this occurs every 30 s. However, if there is a problem on an internet and no update is received within the allotted 180 s, the route is considered expired and the hop count of the route is set to 16, which means the destination is unreachable. Every route has its own expiration timer.

Garbage Collection Timer

When the information about a route becomes invalid, the router does not immediately purge that route from its table. Instead, it continues to advertise the route with a metric value of 16. At the same time, a timer called the **garbage collection timer** is set to 120 s for that route. When the count reaches zero, the route is purged from the table. This timer allows neighbors to become aware of the invalidity of a route prior to purging.

Example 2

A routing table has 20 entries. It does not receive information about five routes for 200 s. How many timers are running at this time?

Solution

The 21 timers are listed below:

 Periodic timer: 1

 Expiration timer: $20 - 5 = 15$

 Garbage collection timer: 5

RIP Version 2

RIP version 2 was designed to overcome some of the shortcomings of version 1. The designers of version 2 have not augmented the length of the message for each entry. They have only replaced those fields in version 1 that were filled with 0s for the TCP/IP protocol with some new fields.

Message Format

Figure 14.13 shows the format of a RIP version 2 message. The new fields of this message are as follows:

- ❏ **Route tag.** This field carries information such as the autonomous system number. It can be used to enable RIP to receive information from an interdomain routing protocol.

- ❏ **Subnet mask.** This is a 4-byte field that carries the subnet mask (or prefix). This means that RIP2 supports classless addressing and CIDR.

- ❏ **Next-hop address.** This field shows the address of the next hop. This is particularly useful if two autonomous systems share a network (a backbone, for example). Then the message can define the router, in the same autonomous system or another autonomous system, to which the packet next goes.

Figure 14.13   *RIP version 2 format*

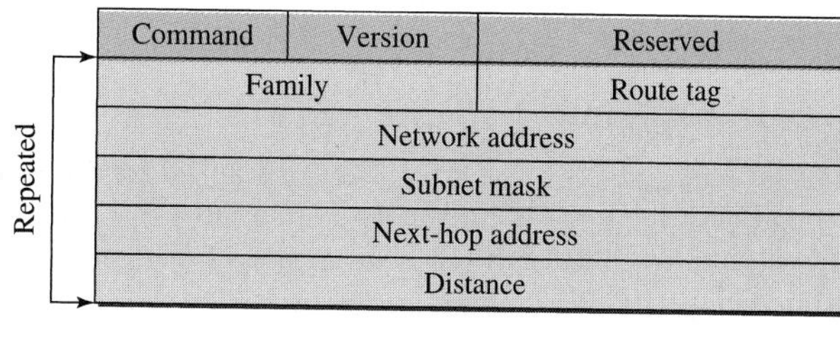

Classless Addressing

Probably the most important difference between the two versions of RIP is classful versus classless addressing. RIPv1 uses classful addressing. The only entry in the message format is the network address (with a default mask). RIPv2 adds one field for the subnet mask, which can be used to define a network prefix length. This means that in this version, we can use classless addressing. A group of networks can be combined into one prefix and advertised collectively as we saw in Chapters 5 and 6.

Authentication

Authentication is added to protect the message against unauthorized advertisement. No new fields are added to the packet; instead, the first entry of the message is set aside for authentication information. To indicate that the entry is authentication information and not routing information, the value of $FFFF_{16}$ is entered in the family field (see Figure 14.14). The second field, the authentication type, defines the protocol used for authentication, and the third field contains the actual authentication data.

Figure 14.14   *Authentication*

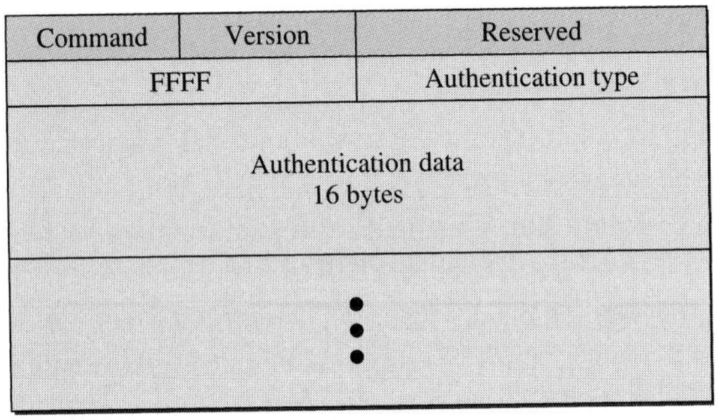

Command	Version	Reserved
FFFF		Authentication type
Authentication data 16 bytes		
⋮		

Multicasting

Version 1 of RIP uses broadcasting to send RIP messages to every neighbor. In this way, all the routers on the network receive the packets, as well as the hosts. RIP version 2, on the other hand, uses the all-router multicast address to send the RIP messages only to RIP routers in the network.

Encapsulation

RIP messages are encapsulated in UDP user datagrams. A RIP message does not include a field that indicates the length of the message. This can be determined from the UDP packet. The well-known port assigned to RIP in UDP is port 520.

RIP uses the services of UDP on well-known port 520.

14.4   LINK STATE ROUTING

Link state routing has a different philosophy from that of distance vector routing. In link state routing, if each node in the domain has the entire topology of the domain—the list of nodes and links, how they are connected including the type, cost (metric), and the condition of the links (up or down)—the node can use the **Dijkstra's algorithm,** to build a routing table. Figure 14.15 shows the concept.

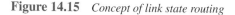

Figure 14.15   *Concept of link state routing*

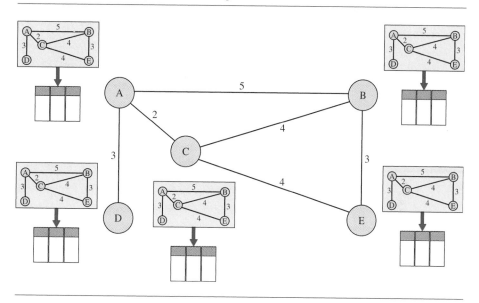

The figure shows a simple domain with five nodes. Each node uses the same topology to create a routing table, but the routing table for each node is unique because the calculations are based on different interpretations of the topology. This is analogous to a city map. Different persons may have the same map, but each needs to take a different route to reach his destination.

The topology must be dynamic, representing the latest situation of each node and each link. If there are changes in any point in the network (a link is down, for example), the topology must be updated for each node.

How can a common topology be dynamic and stored in each node? No node can know the topology at the beginning or after a change somewhere in the network. Link state routing is based on the assumption that, although the global knowledge about the topology is not clear, each node has partial knowledge: it knows the state (type, condition, and cost) of its links. In other words, the whole topology can be compiled from the partial knowledge of each node. Figure 14.16 shows the same domain as in the previous figure indicating the part of the knowledge belonging to each node.

Node A knows that it is connected to node B with metric 5, to node C with metric 2, and to node D with metric 3. Node C knows that it is connected to node A with metric 2, to node B with metric 4, and node E with metric 4. Node D knows that it is connected only to node A with metric 3. And so on. Although there is an overlap in the knowledge, the overlap guarantees the creation of a common topology: a picture of the whole domain for each node.

Figure 14.16 *Link state knowledge*

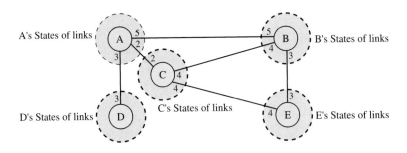

Building Routing Tables

In **link state routing,** four sets of actions are required to ensure that each node has the routing table showing the least-cost node to every other node.

1. Creation of the states of the links by each node, called the link state packet or LSP.
2. Dissemination of LSPs to every other router, called **flooding,** in an efficient and reliable way.
3. Formation of a shortest path tree for each node.
4. Calculation of a routing table based on the shortest path tree.

Creation of Link State Packet (LSP)

A link state packet (LSP) can carry a large amount of information. For the moment, however, we assume that it carries a minimum amount of data: the node identity, the list of links, a sequence number, and age. The first two, node identity and the list of links, are needed to make the topology. The third, sequence number, facilitates flooding and distinguishes new LSPs from old ones. The fourth, age, prevents old LSPs from remaining in the domain for a long time. LSPs are generated on two occasions:

1. *When there is a change in the topology of the domain.* Triggering of LSP dissemination is the main way of quickly informing any node in the domain to update its topology.
2. *On a periodic basis.* The period in this case is much longer compared to distance vector routing. As a matter of fact, there is no actual need for this type of LSP dissemination. It is done to ensure that old information is removed from the domain. The timer set for periodic dissemination is normally in the range of 60 minutes or 2 hours based on the implementation. A longer period ensures that flooding does not create too much traffic on the network.

Flooding of LSPs

After a node has prepared an LSP, it must be disseminated to all other nodes, not only to its neighbors. The process is called flooding and based on the following:

1. The creating node sends a copy of the LSP out of each interface.

2. A node that receives an LSP compares it with the copy it may already have. If the newly arrived LSP is older than the one it has (found by checking the sequence number), it discards the LSP. If it is newer, the node does the following:

   a. It discards the old LSP and keeps the new one.

   b. It sends a copy of it out of each interface except the one from which the packet arrived. This guarantees that flooding stops somewhere in the domain (where a node has only one interface).

Formation of Shortest Path Tree: Dijkstra Algorithm

After receiving all LSPs, each node will have a copy of the whole topology. However, the topology is not sufficient to find the shortest path to every other node; a **shortest path tree** is needed.

A tree is a graph of nodes and links; one node is called the root. All other nodes can be reached from the root through only one single route. A shortest path tree is a tree in which the path between the root and every other node is the shortest. What we need for each node is a shortest path tree with that node as the root.

The **Dijkstra algorithm** creates a shortest path tree from a graph. The algorithm divides the nodes into two sets: tentative and permanent. It finds the neighbors of a current node, makes them tentative, examines them, and if they pass the criteria, makes them permanent. We can informally define the algorithm using the flowchart in Figure 14.17.

Figure 14.17   *Dijkstra algorithm*

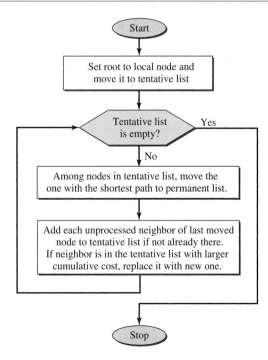

Let us apply the algorithm to node A of our sample graph in Figure 14.18. To find the shortest path in each step, we need the cumulative cost from the root to each node, which is shown next to the node.

Figure 14.18 *Example of formation of shortest path tree*

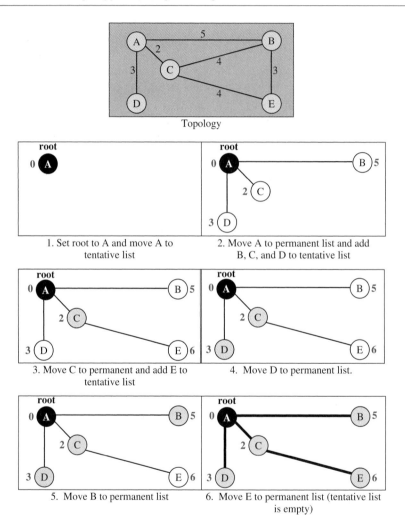

The following shows the steps. At the end of each step, we show the permanent (filled circles) and the tentative (open circles) nodes and lists with the cumulative costs.

1. We make node A the root of the tree and move it to the tentative list. Our two lists are

Permanent list: empty   Tentative list: A (0)

2. Node A has the shortest cumulative cost from all nodes in the tentative list. We move A to the permanent list and add all neighbors of A to the tentative list. Our new lists are

> Permanent list: A (0)   Tentative list: B (5), C (2), D (3)

3. Node C has the shortest cumulative cost from all nodes in the tentative list. We move C to the permanent list. Node C has three neighbors, but node A is already processed, which makes the unprocessed neighbors just B and E. However, B is already in the tentative list with a cumulative cost of 5. Node A could also reach node B through C with a cumulative cost of 6. Since 5 is less than 6, we keep node B with a cumulative cost of 5 in the tentative list and do not replace it. Our new lists are

> Permanent list: A (0), C (2)   Tentative list: B (5), D (3), E (6)

4. Node D has the shortest cumulative cost out of all the nodes in the tentative list. We move D to the permanent list. Node D has no unprocessed neighbor to be added to the tentative list. Our new lists are

> Permanent list: A (0), C (2), D (3)   Tentative list: B (5), E (6)

5. Node B has the shortest cumulative cost out of all the nodes in the tentative list. We move B to the permanent list. We need to add all unprocessed neighbors of B to the tentative list (this is just node E). However, E (6) is already in the list with a smaller cumulative cost. The cumulative cost to node E, as the neighbor of B, is 8. We keep node E(6) in the tentative list. Our new lists are

> Permanent list: A (0), B (5), C (2), D (3)   Tentative list: E (6)

6. Node E has the shortest cumulative cost from all nodes in the tentative list. We move E to the permanent list. Node E has no neighbor. Now the tentative list is empty. We stop; our shortest path tree is ready. The final lists are

> Permanent list: A (0), B (5), C (2), D (3), E (6)   Tentative list: empty

Calculation of Routing Table from Shortest Path Tree

Each node uses the shortest path tree protocol to construct its routing table. The routing table shows the cost of reaching each node from the root. Table 14.1 shows the routing table for node A.

Table 14.1   *Routing table for node A*

Node	Cost	Next Router
A	0	—
B	5	—
C	2	—
D	3	—
E	6	C

Compare the above routing table with the one in Figure 14.3. Both distance vector routing and link state routing end up with the same routing table for node A.

14.5 OSPF

The **Open Shortest Path First (OSPF) protocol** is an intradomain routing protocol based on link state routing. Its domain is also an autonomous system.

Areas

To handle routing efficiently and in a timely manner, OSPF divides an autonomous system into areas. An **area** is a collection of networks, hosts, and routers all contained within an autonomous system. An autonomous system can be divided into many different areas. All networks inside an area must be connected.

Routers inside an area flood the area with routing information. At the border of an area, special routers called **area border routers** summarize the information about the area and send it to other areas. Among the areas inside an autonomous system is a special area called the *backbone;* all of the areas inside an autonomous system must be connected to the backbone. In other words, the backbone serves as a primary area and the other areas as secondary areas. This does not mean that the routers within areas cannot be connected to each other, however. The routers inside the backbone are called the *backbone routers*. Note that a backbone router can also be an area border router.

If, because of some problem, the connectivity between a backbone and an area is broken, a **virtual link** between routers must be created by the administration to allow continuity of the functions of the backbone as the primary area.

Each area has an area identification. The area identification of the backbone is zero. Figure 14.19 shows an autonomous system and its areas.

Figure 14.19 *Areas in an autonomous system*

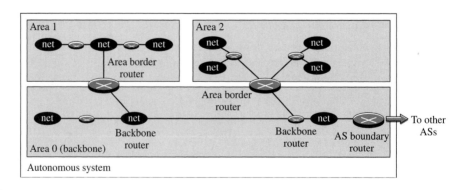

Metric

The OSPF protocol allows the administrator to assign a cost, called the **metric,** to each route. The metric can be based on a type of service (minimum delay, maximum throughput, and so on). As a matter of fact, a router can have multiple routing tables, each based on a different type of service.

Types of Links

In OSPF terminology, a connection is called a *link*. Four types of links have been defined: point-to-point, transient, stub, and virtual (see Figure 14.20).

Figure 14.20   *Types of links*

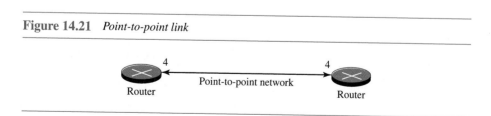

Point-to-Point Link

A **point-to-point link** connects two routers without any other host or router in between. In other words, the purpose of the link (network) is just to connect the two routers. An example of this type of link is two routers connected by a telephone line or a T-line. There is no need to assign a network address to this type of link. Graphically, the routers are represented by nodes, and the link is represented by a bidirectional edge connecting the nodes. The metrics, which are usually the same, are shown at the two ends, one for each direction. In other words, each router has only one neighbor at the other side of the link (see Figure 14.21).

Figure 14.21   *Point-to-point link*

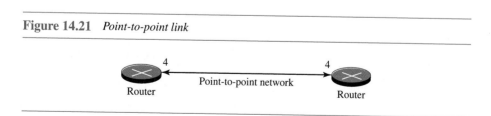

Transient Link

A **transient link** is a network with several routers attached to it. The data can enter through any of the routers and leave through any router. All LANs and some WANs with two or more routers are of this type. In this case, each router has many neighbors. For example, consider the Ethernet in Figure 14.22a. Router A has routers B, C, D, and E as neighbors. Router B has routers A, C, D, and E as neighbors. If we want to show the neighborhood relationship in this situation, we have the graph shown in Figure 14.22b.

Figure 14.22   *Transient link*

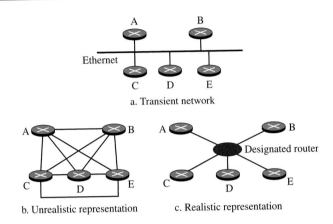

a. Transient network

b. Unrealistic representation   c. Realistic representation

This is neither efficient nor realistic. It is not efficient because each router needs to advertise the neighborhood to four other routers, for a total of 20 advertisements. It is not realistic, because there is no single network (link) between each pair of routers; there is only one network that serves as a crossroad between all five routers.

To show that each router is connected to every other router through one single network, the network itself is represented by a node. However, because a network is not a machine, it cannot function as a router. One of the routers in the network takes this responsibility. It is assigned a dual purpose; it is a true router and a designated router. We can use the topology shown in Figure 14.22c to show the connections of a transient network.

Now each router has only one neighbor, the designated router (network). On the other hand, the designated router (the network) has five neighbors. We see that the number of neighbor announcements is reduced from 20 to 10. Still, the link is represented as a bidirectional edge between the nodes. However, while there is a metric from each node to the designated router, there is no metric from the designated router to any other node. The reason is that the designated router represents the network. We can only assign a cost to a packet that is passing through the network. We cannot charge for this twice. When a packet enters a network, we assign a cost; when a packet leaves the network to go to the router, there is no charge.

Stub Link

A **stub link** is a network that is connected to only one router. The data packets enter the network through this single router and leave the network through this same router. This is a special case of the transient network. We can show this situation using the router as a node and using the designated router for the network. However, the link is only one-directional, from the router to the network (see Figure 14.23).

Figure 14.23   *Stub link*

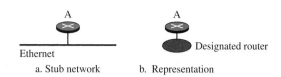

Ethernet

a. Stub network   b. Representation

Designated router

Virtual Link

When the link between two routers is broken, the administration may create a **virtual link** between them using a longer path that probably goes through several routers.

Graphical Representation

Let us now examine how an AS can be represented graphically. Figure 14.24 shows a small AS with seven networks and six routers. Two of the networks are point-to-point networks. We use symbols such as N1 and N2 for transient and stub networks. There is no need to assign an identity to a point-to-point network. The figure also shows the graphical representation of the AS as seen by OSPF.

Figure 14.24   *Example of an AS and its graphical representation in OSPF*

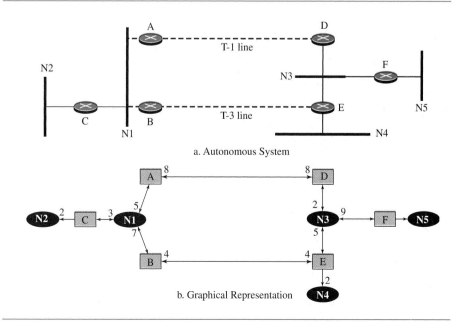

We have used square nodes for the routers and ovals for the networks (represented by designated routers). However, OSPF sees both as nodes. Note that we have three stub networks.

OSPF Packets

OSPF uses five different types of packets: *hello, database description, link state request, link state update,* and *link state acknowledgment* (see Figure 14.25). The most important one is the link state update that itself has five different kinds.

Figure 14.25 *Types of OSPF packets*

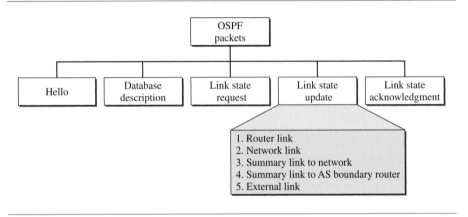

Common Header

All OSPF packets have the same common header (see Figure 14.26). Before studying the different types of packets, let us talk about this common header.

Figure 14.26 *OSPF common header*

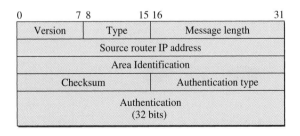

❏ **Version.** This 8-bit field defines the version of the OSPF protocol. It is currently version 2.

❏ **Type.** This 8-bit field defines the type of the packet. As we said before, we have five types, with values 1 to 5 defining the types.

❏ **Message length.** This 16-bit field defines the length of the total message including the header.

❏ **Source router IP address.** This 32-bit field defines the IP address of the router that sends the packet.

❏ **Area identification.** This 32-bit field defines the area within which the routing takes place.

❏ **Checksum.** This field is used for error detection on the entire packet excluding the authentication type and authentication data field.

❏ **Authentication type.** This 16-bit field defines the authentication protocol used in this area. At this time, two types of authentication are defined: 0 for none and 1 for password.

❏ **Authentication.** This 64-bit field is the actual value of the authentication data. In the future, when more authentication types are defined, this field will contain the result of the authentication calculation. For now, if the authentication type is 0, this field is filled with 0s. If the type is 1, this field carries an eight-character password.

Link State Update Packet

We first discuss the **link state update packet,** the heart of the OSPF operation. It is used by a router to advertise the states of its links. The general format of the link state update packet is shown in Figure 14.27.

Figure 14.27 *Link state update packet*

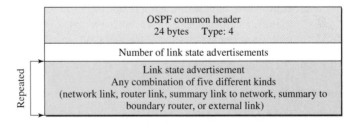

Each update packet may contain several different LSAs. All five kinds have the same general header. This general header is shown in Figure 14.28 and described below:

❏ **Link state age.** This field indicates the number of seconds elapsed since this message was first generated. Recall that this type of message goes from router to router (flooding). When a router creates the message, the value of this field is 0. When each successive router forwards this message, it estimates the transit time and adds it to the cumulative value of this field.

Figure 14.28 *LSA general header*

Link state age	Reserved	E	T	Link state type
Link state ID				
Advertising router				
Link state sequence number				
Link state checksum		Length		

❑ **E flag.** If this 1-bit flag is set to 1, it means that the area is a stub area. A stub area is an area that is connected to the backbone area by only one path.

❑ **T flag.** If this 1-bit flag is set to 1, it means that the router can handle multiple types of service.

❑ **Link state type.** This field defines the LSA type. As we discussed before, there are five different advertisement types: router link (1), network link (2), summary link to network (3), summary link to AS boundary router (4), and external link (5).

❑ **Link state ID.** The value of this field depends on the type of link. For type 1 (router link), it is the IP address of the router. For type 2 (network link), it is the IP address of the designated router. For type 3 (summary link to network), it is the address of the network. For type 4 (summary link to AS boundary router), it is the IP address of the AS boundary router. For type 5 (external link), it is the address of the external network.

❑ **Advertising router.** This is the IP address of the router advertising this message.

❑ **Link state sequence number.** This is a sequence number assigned to each link state update message.

❑ **Link state checksum.** This is not the usual checksum. Instead, the value of this field is calculated using *Fletcher's checksum* (see Appendix C), which is based on the whole packet except for the age field.

❑ **Length.** This defines the length of the whole packet in bytes.

Router Link LSA

A router link defines the links of a true router. A true router uses this advertisement to announce information about all of its links and what is at the other side of the link (neighbors). See Figure 14.29 for a depiction of a router link.

The router link LSA advertises all of the links of a router (true router). The format of the router link packet is shown in Figure 14.30.

The fields of the router link LSA are as follows:

❑ **Link ID.** The value of this field depends on the type of link. Table 14.2 shows the different link identifications based on link type.

❑ **Link data.** This field gives additional information about the link. Again, the value depends on the type of the link (see Table 14.2).

Figure 14.29   *Router link*

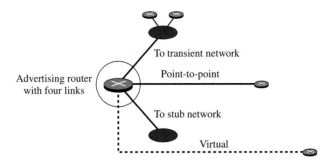

Figure 14.30   *Router link LSA*

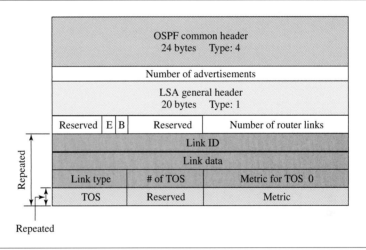

❏ **Link type.** Four different types of links are defined based on the type of network to which the router is connected (see Table 14.2).

Table 14.2   *Link types, link identification, and link data*

Link Type	Link Identification	Link Data
Type 1: Point-to-point	Address of neighbor router	Interface number
Type 2: Transient	Address of designated router	Router address
Type 3: Stub	Network address	Network mask
Type 4: Virtual	Address of neighbor router	Router address

❏ **Number of types of service (TOS).** This field defines the number of types of services announced for each link.

❏ **Metric for TOS 0.** This field defines the metric for the default type of service (TOS 0).

❏ **TOS.** This field defines the type of service.

❏ **Metric.** This field defines the metric for the corresponding TOS.

Example 3

Give the router link LSA sent by router 10.24.7.9 in Figure 14.31.

Figure 14.31   *Example 3*

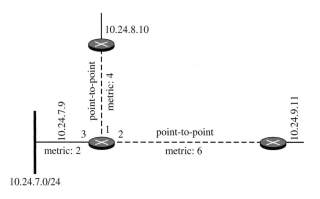

10.24.8.10

10.24.7.0/24

Solution

This router has three links: two of type 1 (point-to-point) and one of type 3 (stub network). Figure 14.32 shows the router link LSA.

Network Link LSA

A network link defines the links of a network. A designated router, on behalf of the transient network, distributes this type of LSP packet. The packet announces the existence of all of the routers connected to the network (see Figure 14.33). The format of the network link advertisement is shown in Figure 14.34. The fields of the network link LSA are as follows:

❏ **Network mask.** This field defines the network mask.

❏ **Attached router.** This repeated field defines the IP addresses of all attached routers.

Figure 14.32 *Solution to Example 3*

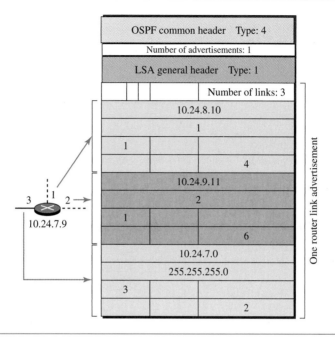

Figure 14.33 *Network link*

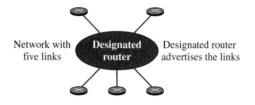

Network with
five links

**Designated
router**

Designated router
advertises the links

Figure 14.34 *Network link advertisement format*

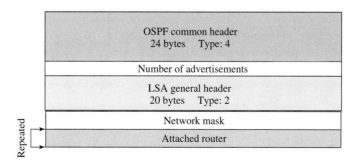

Example 4

Give the network link LSA in Figure 14.35.

Figure 14.35 *Example 4*

Solution

The network for which the network link advertises has three routers attached. The LSA shows the mask and the router addresses. Figure 14.36 shows the network link LSA.

Figure 14.36 *Solution to Example 4*

OSPF common header   Type: 4
Number of advertisements: 1
LSA general header   Type: 2
255.255.255.0
10.24.7.14
10.24.7.15
10.24.7.16

Example 5

In Figure 14.37, which router(s) sends out router link LSAs?

Figure 14.37 *Example 5 and Example 6*

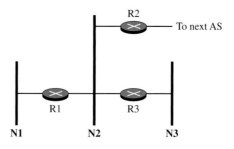

Solution

All routers advertise router link LSAs.

   a. R1 has two links, N1 and N2.

b. R2 has one link, N1.

c. R3 has two links, N2 and N3.

Example 6

In Figure 14.37, which router(s) sends out the network link LSAs?

Solution

All three networks must advertise network links:

a. Advertisement for N1 is done by R1 because it is the only attached router and therefore the designated router.

b. Advertisement for N2 can be done by either R1, R2, or R3, depending on which one is chosen as the designated router.

c. Advertisement for N3 is done by R3 because it is the only attached router and therefore the designated router.

Summary Link to Network LSA

Router link and network link advertisements flood the area with information about the router links and network links inside an area. But a router must also know about the networks outside its area; the area border routers can provide this information. An area border router is active in more than one area. It receives router link and network link advertisements, and, as we will see, creates a routing table for each area. For example, in Figure 14.38, router R1 is an area border router. It has two routing tables, one for area 1 and one for area 0. R1 floods area 1 with information about how to reach a network located in area 0. In the same way, router R2 floods area 2 with information about how to reach the same network in area 0.

Figure 14.38   *Summary link to network*

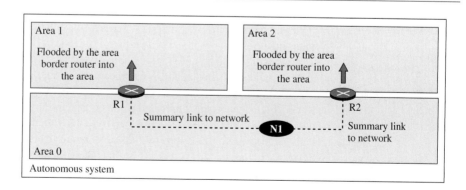

The summary link to network LSA is used by the area border router to announce the existence of other networks outside the area. The summary link to network advertisement is very simple. It consists of the network mask and the metric for each type of service. Note that each advertisement announces only one single network. If there is more than one network, a separate advertisement must be issued for each. The reader may ask why only the mask of the network is advertised. What about the network address itself? The IP address of the advertising router is announced in the header of the link state advertisement. From this information and the mask, one can deduce the network address. The format of this advertisement is shown in Figure 14.39. The fields of the summary link to network LSA are as follows:

Figure 14.39   *Summary link to network LSA*

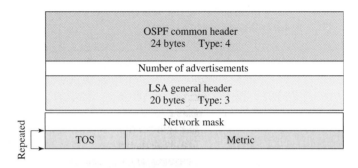

❏ **Network mask.** This field defines the network mask.
❏ **TOS.** This field defines the type of service.
❏ **Metric.** This field defines the metric for the type of service defined in the TOS field.

Summary Link to AS Boundary Router LSA

The previous advertisement lets every router know the cost to reach all of the networks inside the autonomous system. But what about a network outside the autonomous system? If a router inside an area wants to send a packet outside the autonomous system, it should first know the route to an autonomous boundary router; the summary link to AS boundary router provides this information. The area border routers flood their areas with this information (see Figure 14.40). This packet is used to announce the route to an AS boundary router. Its format is the same as the previous summary link. The packet just defines the network to which the AS boundary router is attached. If a message can reach the network, it can be picked up by the AS boundary router. The format of the packet is shown in Figure 14.41. The fields are the same as the fields in the summary link to network advertisement message.

External Link LSA

Although the previous advertisement lets each router know the route to an AS boundary router, this information is not enough. A router inside an autonomous system wants to know which networks are available outside the autonomous system; the external link advertisement provides this information. The AS boundary router floods

Figure 14.40   *Summary link to AS boundary router*

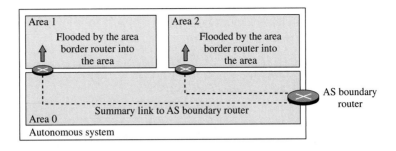

Figure 14.41   *Summary link to AS boundary router LSA*

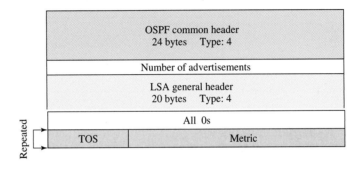

the autonomous system with the cost of each network outside the autonomous system using a routing table created by an interdomain routing protocol. Each advertisement announces one single network. If there is more than one network, separate announcements are made. Figure 14.42 depicts an external link. This is used to announce all the

Figure 14.42   *External link*

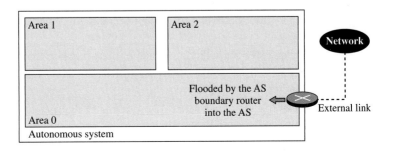

networks outside the AS. The format of the LSA is similar to the summary link to AS boundary router LSA, with the addition of two fields. The AS boundary router may define a forwarding router that can provide a better route to the destination. The packet also can include an external route tag, used by other protocols, but not by OSPF. The format of the packet is shown in Figure 14.43.

Figure 14.43 *External link LSA*

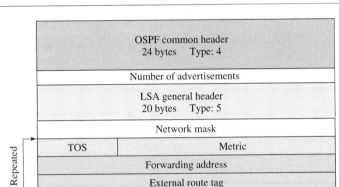

Other Packets

Now we discuss four other packet types (See Figure 14.25). They are not used as LSAs, but are essential to the operation of OSPF.

Hello Message

OSPF uses the **hello message** to create neighborhood relationships and to test the reachability of neighbors. This is the first step in link state routing. Before a router can flood all of the other routers with information about its neighbors, it must first greet its neighbors. It must know if they are alive, and it must know if they are reachable (see Figure 14.44).

❑ **Network mask.** This 32-bit field defines the network mask of the network over which the hello message is sent.

❑ **Hello interval.** This 16-bit field defines the number of seconds between hello messages.

❑ **E flag.** This is a 1-bit flag. When it is set, it means that the area is a stub area.

❑ **T flag.** This is a 1-bit flag. When it is set, it means that the router supports multiple metrics.

❑ **Priority.** This field defines the priority of the router. The priority determines the selection of the designated router. After all neighbors declare their priorities, the router with the highest priority is chosen as the designated router. The one with the second highest priority is chosen as the backup designated router. If the value

Figure 14.44 *Hello packet*

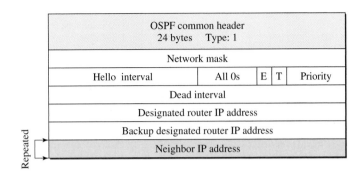

of this field is 0, it means that the router never wants to be a designated or a backup designated router.

❑ **Dead interval.** This 32-bit field defines the number of seconds that must pass before a router assumes that a neighbor is dead.

❑ **Designated router IP address.** This 32-bit field is the IP address of the designated router for the network over which the message is sent.

❑ **Backup designated router IP address.** This 32-bit field is the IP address of the backup designated router for the network over which the message is sent.

❑ **Neighbor IP address.** This is a repeated 32-bit field that defines the routers that have agreed to be the neighbors of the sending router. In other words, it is a current list of all the neighbors from which the sending router has received the hello message.

Database Description Message

When a router is connected to the system for the first time or after a failure, it needs the complete link state database immediately. It cannot wait for all link state update packets to come from every other router before making its own database and calculating its routing table. Therefore, after a router is connected to the system, it sends hello packets to greet its neighbors. If this is the first time that the neighbors hear from the router, they send a database description message. The database description packet does not contain complete database information; it only gives an outline, the title of each line in the database. The newly connected router examines the outline and finds out which lines of information it does not have. It then sends one or more link state request packets to get full information about that particular link. When two routers want to exchange database description packets, one of them takes the role of master and the other the role of slave. Because the message can be very long, the contents of the database can be divided into several messages. The format of the database description packet is shown in Figure 14.45. The fields are as follows:

❑ **E flag.** This 1-bit flag is set to 1 if the advertising router is an autonomous boundary router (*E* stands for external).

Figure 14.45 *Database description packet*

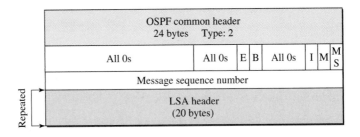

❏ **B flag.** This 1-bit flag is set to 1 if the advertising router is an area border router.

❏ **I flag.** This 1-bit field, the *initialization* flag, is set to 1 if the message is the first message.

❏ **M flag.** This 1-bit field, the *more* flag, is set to 1 if this is not the last message.

❏ **M/S flag.** This 1-bit field, the *master/slave* bit, indicates the origin of the packet: master (M/S = 1) or slave (M/S = 0).

❏ **Message sequence number.** This 32-bit field contains the sequence number of the message. It is used to match a request with the response.

❏ **LSA header.** This 20-byte field is used in each LSA. The format of this header is discussed in the link state update message section. This header gives the outline of each link, without details. It is repeated for each link in the link state database.

Link State Request Packet

The format of the **link state request packet** is shown in Figure 14.46. This is a packet that is sent by a router that needs information about a specific route or routes. It is answered with a link state update packet. It can be used by a newly connected router to request more information about some routes after receiving the database description packet. The three fields here are part of the LSA header which have already been discussed. Each set of the three fields is a request for one single LSA. The set is repeated if more than one advertisement is desired.

Figure 14.46 *Link state request packet*

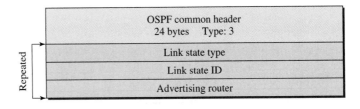

Link State Acknowledgment Packet

OSPF makes routing more reliable by forcing every router to acknowledge the receipt of every link state update packet. The format of the **link state acknowledgment packet** is shown in Figure 14.47. It has the common OSPF header and the general LSA header. These two sections are sufficient to acknowledge a packet.

Figure 14.47   *Link state acknowledgment packet*

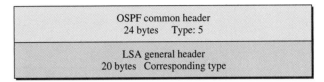

Encapsulation

OSPF packets are encapsulated in IP datagrams. They contain the acknowledgment mechanism for flow and error control. They do not need a transport layer protocol to provide these services.

OSPF packets are encapsulated in IP datagrams.

14.6   PATH VECTOR ROUTING

Distance vector and link state routing are both intradomain routing protocols. They can be used inside an autonomous system, but not between autonomous systems. These two protocols are not suitable for interdomain routing mostly because of scalability. Both of these routing protocols become intractable when the domain of operation becomes large. Distance vector routing is subject to instability if there is more than a few hops in the domain of operation. Link state routing needs a huge amount of resources to calculate routing tables. It also creates heavy traffic because of flooding. There is a need for a third routing protocol which we call **path vector routing.**

Path vector routing proved to be useful for interdomain routing. The principle of path vector routing is similar to distance vector routing. In path vector routing, we assume that there is one node (there can be more, but one is enough for our conceptual discussion) in each autonomous system that acts on behalf of the entire autonomous system. Let us call it the **speaker node.** The speaker node in an AS creates a routing table and advertises it to speaker nodes in the neighboring ASs. The idea is the same as for distance vector routing except that only speaker nodes in each AS can communicate with each other. However, what is advertised is different. A speaker node advertises the path, not the metric of the nodes, in its autonomous system or other autonomous systems.

Initialization

At the beginning, each speaker node can know only the reachability of nodes inside its autonomous system. Figure 14.48 shows the initial tables for each speaker node in a system made of four ASs.

Figure 14.48   *Initial routing tables in path vector routing*

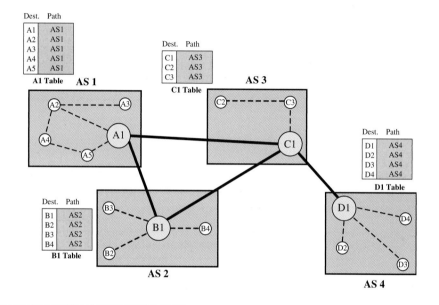

A1 is the speaker node for AS1, B1 for AS2, C1 for AS3 and D1 for AS4. A1 creates an initial table that shows A1 to A5 are located in AS1 and can be reached through it. B1 advertises that B1 to B4 are located in AS2 and can be reached through B1. And so on.

Sharing

Just like distance vector routing, in path vector routing, a speaker in an autonomous system shares its table with immediate neighbors. In Figure 14.48, node A1 shares its table with nodes B1 and C1. Node C1 shares its table with nodes D1, B1, and A1. Node B1 shares its table with C1 and A1. Node D1 shares its table with C1.

Updating

When a speaker node receives a two-column table from a neighbor, it updates its own table by adding the nodes that are not in its routing table and adding its own autonomous system and the autonomous system that sent the table. After a while each speaker has a table and knows how to reach each node in other ASs. Figure 14.49 shows the tables for each speaker node after the system is stabilized.

Figure 14.49   *Stabilized tables for four autonomous systems*

Dest.	Path
A1	AS1
...	...
A5	AS1
B1	AS1-AS2
...	...
B4	AS1-AS2
C1	AS1-AS3
...	...
C3	AS1-AS3
D1	AS1-AS2-AS4
...	...
D4	AS1-AS2-AS4

A1 Table

Dest.	Path
A1	AS2-AS1
...	...
A5	AS2-AS1
B1	AS2
...	...
B4	AS2
C1	AS2-AS3
...	...
C3	AS2-AS3
D1	AS2-AS3-AS4
...	...
D4	AS2-AS3-AS4

B1 Table

Dest.	Path
A1	AS3-AS1
...	...
A5	AS3-AS1
B1	AS3-AS2
...	...
B4	AS3-AS2
C1	AS3
...	...
C3	AS3
D1	AS3-AS4
...	...
D4	AS3-AS4

C1 Table

Dest.	Path
A1	AS4-AS3-AS1
...	...
A5	AS4-AS3-AS1
B1	AS4-AS3-AS2
...	...
B4	AS4-AS3-AS2
C1	AS4-AS3
...	...
C3	AS4-AS3
D1	AS4
...	...
D4	AS4

D1 Table

According to the figure, if router A1 receives a packet for nodes A3, it knows that the path is in AS1 (the packet is at home), but if it receives a packet for D1, it knows that the packet should go from AS1, to AS2, and then to AS3. The routing table shows the path completely. On the other hand, if node D1 in AS4 receives a packet for node A2, it knows it should go through AS4, AS3, and AS1.

Loop Prevention

The instability of distance vector routing and the creation of loops can be avoided in path vector routing. When a router receives a message, it checks to see if its autonomous system is in the path list to the destination. If it is, looping is involved and the message is ignored.

Policy Routing

Policy routing can be easily implemented through path vector routing. When a router receives a message, it can check the path. If one of the autonomous systems listed in the path is against its policy, it can ignore that path and that destination. It does not update its routing table with this path, and it does not send this message to its neighbors.

Optimum Path

What is the optimum path in path vector routing? We are looking for a path to a destination that is the best for the organization that runs the autonomous system. We definitely cannot include metrics in this route because each autonomous system that is included in the path may use a different criteria for the metric. One system may use, internally, RIP, which defines hop count as the metric; another may use OSPF with minimum delay defined as the metric. The optimum path is the path that fits the organization. In our previous figure, each autonomous system may have more than one path to a destination. For example, a path from AS4 to AS1 can be AS4-AS3-AS2-AS1 or it can be AS4-AS3-AS1. For the tables, we chose the one that had the smaller number of autonomous systems, but this is not always the case. Other criteria such as security and safety, and reliability can also be applied.

14.7   BGP

Border Gateway Protocol (BGP) is an interdomain routing protocol using path vector routing. It first appeared in 1989 and has gone through four versions.

Types of Autonomous Systems

As we said before, the Internet is divided into hierarchical domains called autonomous systems (ASs). For example, a large corporation that manages its own network and has full control over it is an autonomous system. A local ISP that provides services to local customers is an autonomous system. We can divide autonomous systems into three categories: stub, multihomed, and transit.

Stub AS

A stub AS has only one connection to another AS. The interdomain data traffic in a stub AS can be either created or terminated in the AS. The hosts in the AS can send data traffic to other ASs. The hosts in the AS can receive data coming from hosts in other ASs. Data traffic, however, cannot pass through a stub AS. A stub AS is either a source or a sink. A good example of a stub AS is a small corporation or a small local ISP.

Multihomed AS

A multihomed AS has more than one connection to other ASs, but it is still only a source or sink for data traffic. It can receive data traffic from more than one AS. It can send data traffic to more than AS, but there is no transient traffic. It does not allow data coming from one AS and going to another AS to pass through. A good example of a multihomed AS is a large corporation that is connected to more than one regional or national AS that does not allow transient traffic.

Transit AS

A transit AS is a multihomed AS that also allows transient traffic. Good examples of transit ASs are national and international ISPs (Internet backbones).

CIDR

BGP uses Classless Interdomain Routing addresses. In other words, BGP uses a prefix, as discussed in Chapter 5, to define a destination address. The address and the number of bits (prefix length) are used in updating messages.

Path Attributes

In our previous example, we discussed a path for a destination network. The path was presented as a list of autonomous systems, but is, in fact, a list of attributes. Each attribute gives some information about the path. The list of attributes helps the receiving router make a better decision when applying its policy.

Attributes are divided into two broad categories: well-known and optional. A **well-known attribute** is one that every BGP router must recognize. An *optional attribute* is one that needs not be recognized by every router.

Well-known attributes are themselves divided into two categories: mandatory and discretionary. A *well-known mandatory attribute* is one that must appear in the description of a route. A *well-known discretionary attribute* is one that must be recognized by each router, but is not required to be included in every update message. One well-known mandatory attribute is ORIGIN. This defines the source of the routing information (RIP, OSPF, and so on). Another well-known mandatory attribute is AS_PATH. This defines the list of autonomous systems through which the destination can be reached. Still another well-known mandatory attribute is NEXT-HOP, which defines the next router to which the data packet should be sent.

The optional attributes can also be subdivided into two categories: transitive and nontransitive. An *optional transitive attribute* is one that must be passed to the next router by the router that has not implemented this attribute. An *optional nontransitive attribute* is one that must be discarded if the receiving router has not implemented it.

BGP Sessions

The exchange of routing information between two routers using BGP takes place in a session. A session is a connection that is established between two BGP routers only for the sake of exchanging routing information. To create a reliable environment, BGP uses the services of TCP. In other words, a session at the BGP level, as an application program, is a connection at the TCP level. However, there is a subtle difference between a connection in TCP made for BGP and other application programs. When a TCP connection is created for BGP, it can last for a long time, until something unusual happens. For this reason, BGP sessions are sometimes referred to as *semi-permanent connections*.

External and Internal BGP

If we want to be precise, BGP can have two types of sessions: external BGP (E-BGP) and internal BGP (I-BGP) sessions. The E-BGP session is used to exchange information between two speaker nodes belonging to two different autonomous systems. The I-BGP session, on the other hand, is used to exchange routing information between two routers inside an autonomous system. Figure 14.50 shows the idea.

Figure 14.50   *Internal and external BGP sessions*

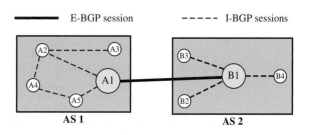

AS 1

AS 2

The session established between AS1 and AS2 is an E-BGP session. The two speaker routers exchange information they know about networks in the Internet. However, these two routers need to collect information from other routers in the autonomous systems. This is done using I-BGP sessions.

Types of Packets

BGP uses four different types of messages: **open, update, keepalive,** and **notification** (see Figure 14.51).

Figure 14.51 *Types of BGP messages*

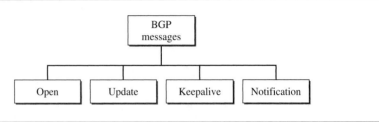

Packet Format

All BGP packets share the same common header. Before studying the different types of packets, let us talk about this common header (see Figure 14.52). The fields of this header are as follows:

❑ **Marker.** The 16-byte marker field is reserved for authentication.

❑ **Length.** This 2-byte field defines the length of the total message including the header.

Figure 14.52 *BGP packet header*

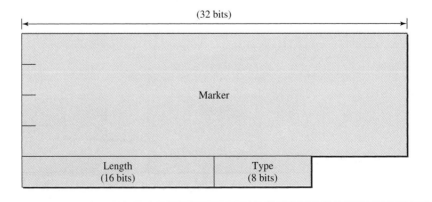

❑ **Type.** This 1-byte field defines the type of the packet. As we said before, we have four types, and the values 1 to 4 define those types.

Open Message

To create a neighborhood relationship, a router running BGP opens a TCP connection with a neighbor and sends an **open message.** If the neighbor accepts the neighborhood relationship, it responds with a **keepalive message,** which means that a relationship has been established between the two routers. See Figure 14.53 for a depiction of the open message format.

Figure 14.53   *Open message*

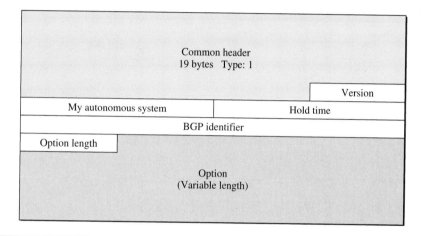

The fields of the open message are as follows:
❑ **Version.** This 1-byte field defines the version of BGP. The current version is 4.
❑ **My autonomous system.** This 2-byte field defines the autonomous system number.
❑ **Hold time.** This 2-byte field defines the maximum number of seconds that can elapse until one of the parties receives a keepalive or update message from the other. If a router does not receive one of these messages during the hold time period, it considers the other party dead.
❑ **BGP identifier.** This 4-byte field defines the router that sends the open message. The router usually uses one of its IP addresses (because it is unique) for this purpose.
❑ **Option length.** The open message may contain some option parameters. In this case, this 1-byte field defines the length of the total option parameters. If there are no option parameters, the value of this field is zero.

❑ **Option parameters.** If the value of the option parameter length is not zero, it means that there are some option parameters. Each option parameter itself has two subfields: the length of the parameter and the parameter value. The only option parameter defined so far is authentication.

Update Message

The update message is the heart of the BGP protocol. It is used by a router to withdraw destinations that have been advertised previously, announce a route to a new destination, or both. Note that BGP can withdraw several destinations that were advertised before, but it can only advertise one new destination in a single update message. The format of the update message is shown in Figure 14.54.

Figure 14.54   *Update message*

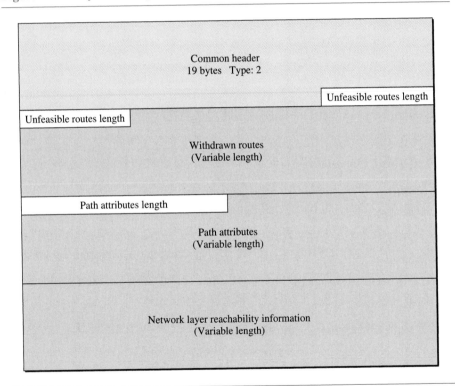

The update message fields are listed below:

❑ **Unfeasible routes length.** This 2-byte field defines the length of the next field.

❑ **Withdrawn routes.** This field lists all the routes that must be deleted from the previously advertised list.

❑ **Path attributes length.** This 2-byte field defines the length of the next field.

❑ **Path attributes.** This field defines the attributes of the path (route) to the network whose reachability is being announced in this message.

❑ **Network layer reachability information (NLRI).** This field defines the network that is actually advertised by this message. It has a length field and an IP address prefix. The length defines the number of bits in the prefix. The prefix defines the common part of the network address. For example, if the network is 153.18.7.0/24, the length of the prefix is 24 and the prefix is 153.18.7. BGP4 supports classless addressing and CIDR.

BGP supports classless addressing and CIDR.

Keepalive Message

The routers (called *peers* in BGP parlance) running the BGP protocols exchange keepalive messages regularly (before their hold time expires) to tell each other that they are alive. The keepalive message consists of only the common header shown in Figure 14.55.

Figure 14.55 *Keepalive message*

Common header
19 bytes Type: 3

Notification Message

A notification message is sent by a router whenever an error condition is detected or a router wants to close the connection. The format of the message is shown in Figure 14.56.

Figure 14.56 *Notification message*

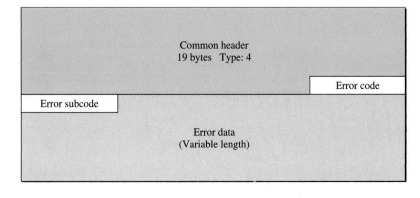

Common header
19 bytes Type: 4

Error code

Error subcode

Error data
(Variable length)

The fields making up the notification message follow:

❑ **Error code.** This 1-byte field defines the category of the error. See Table 14.3.

❑ **Error subcode.** This 1-byte field further defines the type of error in each category.

❑ **Error data.** This field can be used to give more diagnostic information about the error.

Table 14.3   *Error codes*

Error Code	Error Code Description	Error Subcode Description
1	Message header error	Three different subcodes are defined for this type of error: synchronization problem (1), bad message length (2), and bad message type (3).
2	Open message error	Six different subcodes are defined for this type of error: unsupported version number (1), bad peer AS (2), bad BGP identifier (3), unsupported optional parameter (4), authentication failure (5), and unacceptable hold time (6).
3	Update message error	Eleven different subcodes are defined for this type of error: malformed attribute list (1), unrecognized well-known attribute (2), missing well-known attribute (3), attribute flag error (4), attribute length error (5), invalid origin attribute (6), AS routing loop (7), invalid next hop attribute (8), optional attribute error (9), invalid network field (10), malformed AS_PATH (11).
4	Hold timer expired	No subcode defined.
5	Finite state machine error	This defines the procedural error. No subcode defined.
6	Cease	No subcode defined.

Encapsulation

BGP messages are encapsulated in TCP segments using the well-known port 179. This means that there is no need for error control and flow control. When a TCP connection is opened, the exchange of update, keepalive, and notification messages is continued until a notification message of type cease is sent.

BGP uses the services of TCP on port 179.

14.8   KEY TERMS

area

area border router

area identification

autonomous system (AS)

autonomous system boundary router

backbone router

Border Gateway Protocol (BGP)

database description message

Dijkstra algorithm	Open Shortest Path First (OSPF)
distance vector routing	optional attribute
expiration timer	packet
external link	path vector routing
external link LSA	periodic timer
flooding	point-to-point link
garbage collection timer	poison reverse
hello interval	policy routing
hello message	router
hop count	router link LSA
immediate neighbors	Routing Information Protocol (RIP)
interdomain routing	slow convergence
intradomain routing	solicited response
keepalive message	split horizon
link state acknowledgment packet	static routing table
link state advertisement (LSA)	stub link
link state database	subnet mask
link state request packet	summary link to AS boundary router LSA
link state routing	summary link to network LSA
link state update packet	transient link
metric	triggered update process
network link LSA	unsolicited response
next-hop address	update message
notification message	virtual link
open message	well-known attribute

14.9   SUMMARY

❑   A metric is the cost assigned for passage of a packet through a network.

❑   A router consults its routing table to determine the best path for a packet.

❑   An autonomous system (AS) is a group of networks and routers under the authority of a single administration.

❏ RIP and OSPF are popular intradomain routing protocols used to update routing tables in an AS.

❏ RIP is based on distance vector routing, in which each router shares, at regular intervals, its knowledge about the entire AS with its neighbors.

❏ A RIP routing table entry consists of a destination network address, the hop count to that destination, and the IP address of the next router.

❏ RIP uses three timers: the periodic timer controls the advertising of the update message, the expiration timer governs the validity of a route, and the garbage collection timer advertises the failure of a route.

❏ Two shortcomings associated with the RIP protocol are slow convergence and instability.

❏ Procedures to remedy RIP instability include triggered update, split horizons, and poison reverse.

❏ The RIP version 2 packet format contains fields carrying AS information and authentication information.

❏ OSPF divides an AS into areas, defined as collections of networks, hosts, and routers.

❏ OSPF is based on link state routing, in which each router sends the state of its neighborhood to every other router in the area. A packet is sent only if there is a change in the neighborhood.

❏ OSPF defines four types of links (networks): point-to-point, transient, stub, and virtual.

❏ Five types of link state advertisements (LSAs) disperse information in OSPF: router link, network link, summary link to network, summary link to AS boundary router, and external link.

❏ A router compiles all the information from the LSAs it receives into a link state database. This database is common to all routers in an area.

❏ OSPF routing tables are calculated using Dijkstra's algorithm.

❏ There are five types of OSPF packets: hello, database description, link state request, link state update, and link state acknowledgment.

❏ An LSA is a multifield entry in a link state update packet.

❏ BGP is an interautonomous system routing protocol used to update routing tables.

❏ BGP is based on a routing protocol called path vector routing. In this protocol, the ASs through which a packet must pass are explicitly listed.

❏ Path vector routing does not have the instability nor looping problems of distance vector routing.

❏ There are four types of BGP messages: open, update, keepalive, and notification.

14.10   PRACTICE SET

Exercises

1. What is the purpose of RIP?
2. What are the functions of a RIP message?

3. Why is the expiration timer value six times that of the periodic timer value?

4. How does the hop count limit alleviate RIP's problems?

5. List RIP shortcomings and their corresponding fixes.

6. What is the basis of classification for the four types of links defined by OSPF?

7. Contrast and compare distance vector routing with link state routing.

8. Draw a flowchart of the steps involved when a router receives a distance vector message from a neighbor.

9. Why do OSPF messages propagate faster than RIP messages?

10. What is the size of a RIP message that advertises only one network? What is the size of a RIP message that advertises N packets? Devise a formula that shows the relationship between the number of networks advertised and the size of a RIP message.

11. A router running RIP has a routing table with 20 entries. How many periodic timers are needed to handle this table?

12. A router running RIP has a routing table with 20 entries. How many expiration timers are needed to handle this table?

13. A router running RIP has a routing table with 20 entries. How many garbage collection timers are needed to handle this table if five routes are invalid?

14. A router has the following RIP routing table:

Net1	4	B
Net2	2	C
Net3	1	F
Net4	5	G

    What would be the contents of the table if the router receives the following RIP message from router C:

Net1	2
Net2	1
Net3	3
Net4	7

15. How many bytes are empty in a RIP message that advertises N networks?

16. A router has the following RIP routing table:

Net1	4	B
Net2	2	C
Net3	1	F
Net4	5	G

    Show the response message sent by this router.

17. Using Figure 14.24, show the link state update/router link advertisement for router A.

18. Using Figure 14.24, show the link state update/router link advertisement for router D.

19. Using Figure 14.24, show the link state update/router link advertisement for router E.

20. Show the link state update/network link advertisement for network N2 in Figure 14.24.

21. Show the link state update/network link advertisement for network N4 in Figure 14.24.

22. Show the link state update/network link advertisement for network N5 in Figure 14.24.

23. In Figure 14.24 assume that the designated router for network N1 is router A. Show the link state update/network link advertisement for this network.

24. In Figure 14.24 assume that the designated router for network N3 is router D. Show the link state update/network link advertisement for this network.

25. Assign IP addresses to networks and routers in Figure 14.24.

26. Using the result of Exercise 25, show the OSPF hello message sent by router C.

27. Using the result of Exercise 25, show the OSPF database description message sent by router C.

28. Using the result of Exercise 25, show the OSPF link state request message sent by router C.

29. Show the autonomous system with the following specifications:
    a. There are eight networks (N1 to N8)
    b. There are eight routers (R1 to R8)
    c. N1, N2, N3, N4, N5, and N6 are Ethernet LANs
    d. N7 and N8 are point-to-point WANs
    e. R1 connects N1 and N2
    f. R2 connects N1 and N7
    g. R3 connects N2 and N8
    h. R4 connects N7 and N6
    i. R5 connects N6 and N3
    j. R6 connects N6 and N4
    k. R7 connects N6 and N5
    l. R8 connects N8 and N5

30. Draw the graphical representation of the autonomous system of Exercise 29 as seen by OSPF.

31. Which of the networks in exercise 29 is a transient network? Which is a stub network?

32. Show the BGP open message for router A1 in Figure 14.50.

33. Show the BGP update message for router A1 in Figure 14.50.

34. Show the BGP keepalive message for router A1 in Figure 14.50.

35. Show the BGP notification message for router A1 in Figure 14.50.

Research Activities

36. Find the RFCs related to RIP.

37. Find the RFCs related to OSPF.

38. Find the RFCs related to BGP

39. Before BGP, there was a protocol called EGP. Find some information about this protocol. Find out why this protocol has not survived.

40. In UNIX, there are some programs under the general name *daemon*. Find the daemons that can handle routing protocols.

41. If you have access to a UNIX system, find some information about the *routed* program. How can this program help to trace the messages exchanged in RIP? Does *routed* support the other routing protocols we discussed in the chapter?

42. If you have access to a UNIX system, find some information about the *gated* program. Which routing protocols discussed in this chapter can be supported by *gated*?

43. There is a routing protocol called HELLO, which we did not discuss in this chapter. Find some information about this protocol.

CHAPTER 15

Multicasting and Multicast Routing Protocols

In this chapter, we discuss multicasting and multicast routing protocols. We first define the term multicasting and compare it to unicasting and broadcasting. We also briefly discuss the applications of multicasting. Finally, we move on to multicast routing and the general ideas and goals related to it. We also discuss some common multicast routing protocols used in the Internet today.

15.1   UNICAST, MULTICAST, AND BROADCAST

A message can be unicast, multicast, or broadcast. Let us clarify these terms as they relate to the Internet.

Unicasting

In unicast communication, there is one source and one destination. The relationship between the source and the destination is one-to-one. In this type of communication, both the source and destination addresses, in the IP datagram, are the unicast addresses assigned to the hosts (or host interfaces, to be more exact). In Figure 15.1, a unicast packet starts from the source S1 and passes through routers to reach the destination D1. We have shown the networks as a link between the routers to simplify the figure.

Figure 15.1   *Unicasting*

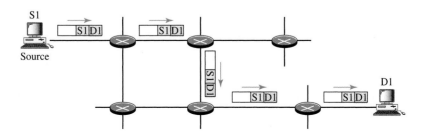

Note that in **unicasting,** when a router receives a packet, it forwards the packet through only one of its interfaces (the one belonging to the optimum path) as defined in the routing table. The router may discard the packet if it cannot find the destination address in its routing table.

> **In unicasting, the router forwards the received packet through only one of its interfaces.**

Multicasting

In multicast communication, there is one source and a group of destinations. The relationship is one-to-many. In this type of communication, the source address is a unicast address, but the destination address is a group address, a group of one or more destinations. The group address defines the members of the group. Figure 15.2 shows the idea behind **multicasting.**

Figure 15.2 *Multicasting*

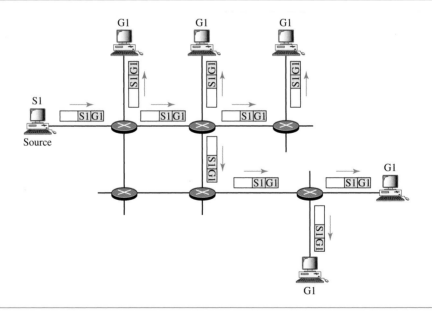

A multicast packet starts from the source S1 and goes to all destinations that belong to group G1. In **multicasting,** when a router receives a packet, it may forward it through several of its interfaces.

> **In multicasting, the router may forward the received packet through several of its interfaces.**

Broadcasting

In broadcast communication, the relationship between the source and the destination is one-to-all. There is only one source, but all of the other hosts are the destinations. The Internet does not explicitly support **broadcasting** because of the huge amount of traffic it would create and because of the bandwidth it would need. Imagine the traffic generated in the Internet if one person wanted to send a message to everyone else connected to the Internet.

Multicasting versus Multiple Unicasting

Before we finish this section we need to distinguish between multicasting and multiple unicasting. Figure 15.3 illustrates both concepts.

Figure 15.3   *Multicasting versus multiple unicasting*

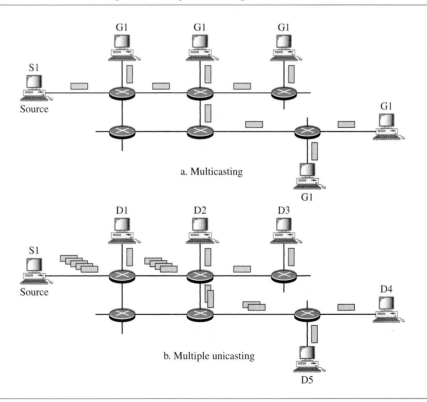

Multicasting starts with one single packet from the source that is duplicated by the routers. The destination address in each packet is the same for all duplicates. Note that only one single copy of the packet travels between any two routers.

In **multiple unicasting,** several packets start from the source. If there are five destinations, for example, the source sends five packets, each with a different unicast destination address. Note that there may be multiple copies traveling between two routers. For example, when a person sends an email message to a group of people, this is multiple unicasting. The email software creates replicas of the message, each with a different destination address and sends them one by one. This is not multicasting; it is multiple unicasting.

Emulation of Multicasting with Unicasting

You might wonder why we have a separate mechanism for multicasting, when it can be emulated with unicasting. There are several reasons for this; two are obvious:

1. Multicasting is more efficient than multiple unicasting. In Figure 15.3, we can see how multicasting requires less bandwidth than multiple unicasting. In multiple unicasting, some of the links must handle several copies.

2. In multiple unicasting, the packets are created by the source with a relative delay between packets. If there are 1,000 destinations, the delay between the first and the last packet may be unacceptable. In multicasting, there is no delay because only one packet is created by the source.

> Emulation of multicasting through multiple unicasting is not efficient and may create long delays, particularly with a large group.

15.2   MULTICAST APPLICATIONS

Multicasting has many applications today such as access to distributed databases, information dissemination, teleconferencing, and distance learning.

Access to Distributed Databases

Most of the large databases today are distributed. That is, the information is stored in more than one location, usually at the time of production. The user who needs to access the database does not know the location of the information. A user's request is multicast to all the database locations, and the location that has the information responds.

Information Dissemination

Businesses often need to send information to their customers. If the nature of the information is the same for each customer, it can be multicast. In this way a business can send one message that can reach many customers. For example, a software update can be sent to all purchasers of a particular software package.

Dissemination of News

In a similar manner news can be easily disseminated through multicasting. One single message can be sent to those interested in a particular topic. For example, the statistics of the championship high school basketball tournament can be sent to the sports editors of many newspapers.

Teleconferencing

Teleconferencing involves multicasting. The individuals attending a teleconference all need to receive the same information at the same time. Temporary or permanent groups can be formed for this purpose. For example, an engineering group that holds meetings every Monday morning could have a permanent group while the group that plans the holiday party could form a temporary group.

Distance Learning

One growing area in the use of multicasting is **distance learning.** Lessons taught by one single professor can be received by a specific group of students. This is especially convenient for those students who find it difficult to attend classes on campus.

15.3 MULTICAST ROUTING

In this section, we first discuss the idea of optimal routing, common in all multicast protocols. We then give an overview of multicast routing protocols.

Optimal Routing: Shortest Path Trees

The process of optimal interdomain routing eventually results in the finding of the **shortest path tree.** The root of the tree is the source and the leaves are the potential destinations. The path from the root to each destination is the shortest path. However, the number of trees and the formation of the trees in unicast and multicast routing are different. Let us discuss each separately.

Unicast Routing

In unicast routing, when a router receives a packet to forward, it needs to find the shortest path to the destination of the packet. The router consults its routing table for that particular destination. The next-hop entry corresponding to the destination is the start of the shortest path. The router knows the shortest path for each destination, which means that the router has a shortest path tree to optimally reach all destinations. In other words, each line of the routing table is a shortest path; the whole routing table is a shortest path tree. In unicast routing, each router needs only one shortest path tree to forward a packet; however, each router has its own shortest path tree. Figure 15.4 shows the situation.

The figure shows the details of the routing table and the shortest path tree for router R1. Each line in the routing table corresponds to one path from the root to the corresponding network. The whole table represents the shortest path tree.

> **In unicast routing, each router in the domain has a table that defines a shortest path tree to possible destinations.**

Multicast Routing

When a router receives a multicast packet, the situation is different. A multicast packet may have destinations in more than one network. Forwarding of a single packet to

Figure 15.4 *Shortest path tree in unicast routing*

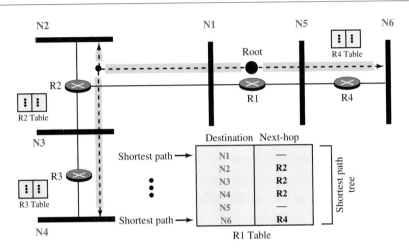

members of a group requires a shortest path tree. If we have *n* groups, we may need *n* shortest path trees. We can imagine the complexity of multicast routing. Two approaches have been used to solve the problem: source-based trees and group-shared trees.

> **In multicast routing, each involved router needs to construct a shortest path tree for each group.**

Source-Based Tree In the **source-based tree** approach, each router needs to have one shortest path tree for each group. The shortest path tree for a group defines the next hop for each network that has loyal member(s) for that group. In Figure 15.5, we assume that we have only five groups in the domain: G1, G2, G3, G4, and G5. At the moment G1 has loyal members in four networks, G2 in three, G3 in two, G4 in two, and G5 in two. We have shown the names of the groups with loyal members on each network. The figure also shows the multicast routing table for router R1. There is one shortest path tree for each group; therefore there are five shortest path trees for five groups. If router R1 receives a packet with destination address G1, it needs to send a copy of the packet to the attached network, a copy to router R2, and a copy to router R4 so that all members of G1 can receive a copy.

In this approach, if the number of groups is *m*, each router needs to have *m* shortest path trees, one for each group. We can imagine the complexity of the routing table if we have hundreds or thousands of groups. However, we will show how different protocols manage to alleviate the situation.

> **In the source-based tree approach, each router needs to have one shortest path tree for each group.**

Figure 15.5   *Source-based tree approach*

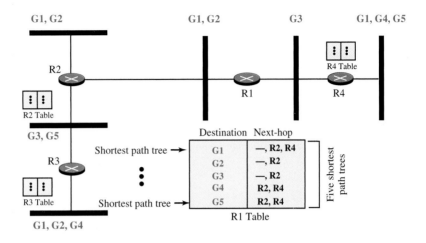

Group-Shared Tree   In the **group-shared tree** approach, instead of each router having *m* shortest path trees, only one designated router, called the center core, or rendezvous router, takes the responsibility of distributing multicast traffic. The core has *m* shortest path trees in its routing table. The rest of the routers in the domain have none. If a router receives a multicast packet, it encapsulates the packet in a unicast packet and sends it to the core router. The core router removes the multicast packet from its capsule, and consults its routing table to route the packet. Figure 15.6 shows the idea.

Figure 15.6   *Group-shared tree approach*

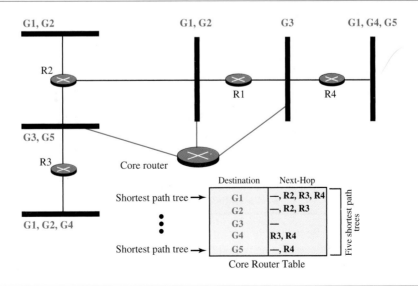

> In the group-shared tree approach, only the core router, which has a shortest path tree for each group, is involved in multicasting.

Routing Protocols

During the last few decades, several multicast routing protocols have emerged. Some of these protocols are extensions of unicast routing protocols; some are totally new. We discuss these protocols in the remainder of this chapter. Figure 15.7 shows the taxonomy of these protocols.

Figure 15.7   *Taxonomy of common multicast protocols*

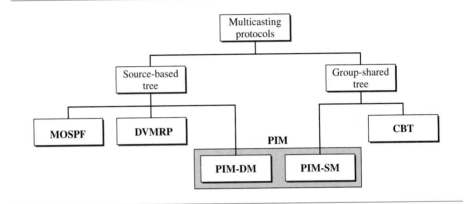

15.4   MULTICAST LINK STATE ROUTING: MOSPF

In this section, we briefly discuss multicast link state routing and its implementation in the Internet, MOSPF.

Multicast Link State Routing

We discussed unicast link state routing in Chapter 14. We said that each router creates a shortest path tree using Dijkstra's algorithm. The routing table is a translation of the shortest path tree. Multicast link state routing is a direct extension of unicast routing and uses a source-based tree approach. Although unicast routing is quite involved, the extension to multicast routing is very simple and straightforward.

> Multicast link state routing uses the source-based tree approach.

Recall that in unicast routing, each node needs to advertise the state of its links. For multicast routing, a node needs to revise the interpretation of *state*. A node advertises every group which has any loyal member on the link. Here the meaning of state is "what groups are active on this link." The information about the group comes from

IGMP (see Chapter 10). Each router running IGMP solicits the hosts on the link to find out the membership status.

When a router receives all these LSPs, it creates *n* (n is the number of groups) topologies, from which *n* shortest path trees are made using Dijkstra's algorithm. So each router has a routing table that represents as many shortest path trees as there are groups.

The only problem with this protocol is the time and space needed to create and save the many shortest path trees. The solution is to create the trees only when needed. When a router receives a packet with a multicast destination address, it runs the Dijkstra algorithm to calculate the shortest path tree for that group. The result can be cached in case there are additional packets for that destination.

MOSPF

Multicast Open Shortest Path First (MOSPF) protocol is an extension of the OSPF protocol that uses multicast link state routing to create source-based trees. The protocol requires a new link state update packet to associate the unicast address of a host with the group address or addresses the host is sponsoring. This packet is called the group-membership LSA. In this way, we can include in the tree only the hosts (using their unicast addresses) that belong to a particular group. In other words, we make a tree that contains all the hosts belonging to a group, but we use the unicast address of the host in the calculation. For efficiency, the router calculates the shortest path trees on demand (when it receives the first multicast packet). In addition, the tree can be saved in cache memory for future use by the same source/group pair. MOSPF is a **data-driven** protocol; the first time an MOSPF router sees a datagram with a given source and group address, the router constructs the Dijkstra shortest path tree.

15.5   MULTICAST DISTANCE VECTOR: DVMRP

In this section, we briefly discuss multicast distance vector routing and its implementation in the Internet, DVMRP.

Multicast Distance Vector Routing

Unicast distance vector routing is very simple; extending it to support multicast routing is complicated. Multicast routing does not allow a router to send its routing table to its neighbors. The idea is to create a table from scratch using the information from the unicast distance vector tables.

Multicast distance vector routing uses source-based trees, but the router never actually makes a routing table. When a router receives a multicast packet, it forwards the packet as though it is consulting a routing table. We can say that the shortest path tree is evanescent. After its use (after a packet is forwarded) the table is destroyed.

To accomplish this, the multicast distance vector algorithm uses a process based on four decision-making strategies. Each strategy is built on its predecessor. We explain them one by one and see how each strategy can improve the shortcomings of the previous one.

Flooding

Flooding is the first strategy that comes to mind. A router receives a packet and without even looking at the destination group address, sends it out from every interface except the one from which it was received. **Flooding** accomplishes the first goal of multicasting: every network with active members receives the packet. However, so will networks without active members. This is a broadcast, not a multicast. There is another problem: it creates loops. A packet that has left the router may come back again from another interface or the same interface and be forwarded again. Some flooding protocols keep a copy of the packet for a while and discard any duplicates to avoid loops. The next strategy, reverse path forwarding, corrects this defect.

Flooding broadcasts packets, but creates loops in the systems.

Reverse Path Forwarding (RPF)

Reverse path forwarding (RPF) is a modified flooding strategy. To prevent loops, only one copy is forwarded; the other copies are dropped. In RPF, a router forwards only the copy that has traveled the shortest path from the source to the router. To find this copy, RPF uses the unicast routing table. The router receives a packet and extracts the source address (a unicast address). It consults its unicast routing table as though it wants to send a packet to the source address. The routing table tells the router the next hop. If the multicast packet has just come from the hop defined in the table, the packet has traveled the shortest path from the source to the router because the shortest path is reciprocal in unicast distance vector routing protocols. If the path from A to B is the shortest, then it is also the shortest from B to A. The router forwards the packet if it has traveled from the shortest path; it discards it otherwise.

This strategy prevents loops because there is always one shortest path from the source to the router. If a packet leaves the router and comes back again, it has not traveled the shortest path. To make the point clear, let us look at Figure 15.8.

The figure shows part of a domain and a source. The shortest path tree as calculated by routers R1, R2, and R3 is shown by a thick line. When R1 receives a packet from the source through the interface m1, it consults its routing table and finds that the shortest path from R1 to the source is through interface m1. The packet is forwarded. However, if a copy of the packet has arrived through interface m2, it is discarded because m2 does not define the shortest path from R1 to the source. The story is the same with R2 and R3. You may wonder what happens if a copy of a packet that arrives at the m1 interface of R3, travels through R6, R5, R2, and then enters R3 through interface m1. This interface is the correct interface for R3. Is the copy of the packet forwarded? The answer is that this scenario never happens because when the packet goes from R5 to R2, it will be discarded by R2 and never reaches R3. The upstream routers toward the source always discard a packet that has not gone through the shortest path, thus preventing confusion for the downstream routers.

RPF eliminates the loop in the flooding process.

Figure 15.8 *RPF*

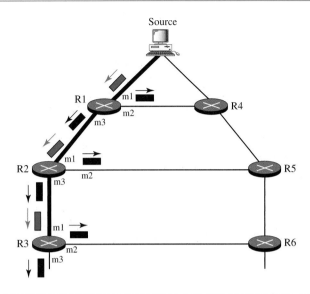

Reverse Path Broadcasting (RPB)

RPF guarantees that each network receives a copy of the multicast packet without formation of loops. However, RPF does not guarantee that each network receives only one copy; a network may receive two or more copies. The reason is that RPF is not based on the destination address (a group address); forwarding is based on the source address. To visualize the problem, let us look at Figure 15.9.

Figure 15.9 *Problem with RPF*

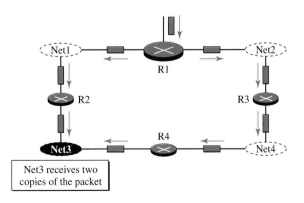

Net3 in this figure receives two copies of the packet even though each router just sends out one copy from each interface. There is duplication because a tree has not been made; instead of a tree we have a graph. Net3 has two parents: routers R2 and R4.

To eliminate duplication, we must define only one parent router for each network. We must have this restriction: A network can receive a multicast packet from a particular source only through a designated parent router.

Now the policy is clear. For each source, the router sends the packet only out of those interfaces for which it is the designated parent. This policy is called **reverse path broadcasting (RPB)**. RPB guarantees that the packet reaches every network and that every network receives only one copy. Figure 15.10 shows the difference between RPF and RPB.

Figure 15.10   *RPF versus RPB*

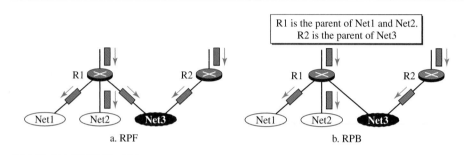

a. RPF   b. RPB

R1 is the parent of Net1 and Net2.
R2 is the parent of Net3

The reader may ask how the designated parent is determined. The designated parent router can be the router with the shortest path to the source. Because routers periodically send updating packets to each other (in RIP), they can easily determine which router in the neighborhood has the shortest path to the source (when interpreting the source as the destination). If more than one router qualifies, the router with the smallest IP address is selected.

> **RPB creates a shortest path broadcast tree from the source to each destination. It guarantees that each destination receives one and only one copy of the packet.**

Reverse Path Multicasting (RPM)

As you may have noticed, RPB does not multicast the packet, it broadcasts it. This is not efficient. To increase efficiency, the multicast packet must reach only those networks that have active members for that particular group. This is called **reverse path multicasting (RPM).** To convert broadcasting to multicasting, the protocol uses two procedures, pruning and grafting. Figure 15.11 shows the idea of pruning and grafting.

Pruning   The designated parent router of each network is responsible for holding the membership information. This is done through the IGMP protocol described in Chapter 10. The process starts when a router connected to a network finds that there is no interest in a multicast packet. The router sends a **prune message** to the upstream router so that it can prune the corresponding interface. That is, the upstream router can stop sending multicast messages for this group through that interface. Now if this router receives prune messages from all downstream routers, it, in turn, sends a prune message to its upstream router.

Figure 15.11   *RPF, RPB, and RPM*

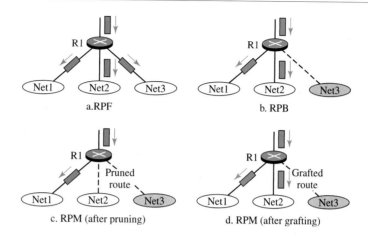

a.RPF

b. RPB

c. RPM (after pruning)

d. RPM (after grafting)

Grafting   What if a leaf router (a router at the bottom of the tree) has sent a prune message but suddenly realizes, through IGMP, that one of its networks is again interested in receiving the multicast packet? It can send a **graft message.** The graft message forces the upstream router to resume sending the multicast messages.

> **RPM adds pruning and grafting to RPB to create a multicast shortest path tree that supports dynamic membership changes.**

DVMRP

The **Distance Vector Multicast Routing Protocol (DVMRP)** is an implementation of multicast distance vector routing. It is a source-based routing protocol, based on RIP.

15.6   CBT

The **Core-Based Tree (CBT) protocol** is a group-shared protocol that uses a core as the root of the tree. The autonomous system is divided into regions and a core (center router or rendezvous router) is chosen for each region.

Formation of the Tree

After the rendezvous point is selected, every router is informed of the unicast address of the selected router. Each router then sends a unicast join message (similar to a grafting message) to show that it wants to join the group. This message passes through all routers that are located between the sender and the rendezvous router. Each intermediate router extracts the necessary information from the message, such as the unicast address of the sender and the interface through which the packet has arrived, and forwards the message to the next router in the path. When the rendezvous router has received all join messages from every member of the group, the tree is formed. Now every router knows its upstream router (the router that leads to the root) and the downstream router (the router that leads to the leaf).

If a router wants to leave the group, it sends a leave message to its upstream router. The upstream router removes the link to that router from the tree and forwards the message to its upstream router, and so on. Figure 15.12 shows a group-shared tree with its rendezvous router.

Figure 15.12 *Group-shared tree with rendezvous router*

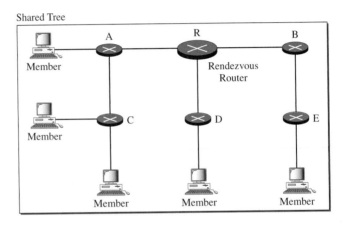

The reader may have noticed two differences between DVMRP and MOSPF, on one hand, and CBT, on the other. First, the tree for the first two is made from the root up; the tree for CBT is formed from the leaves down. Second, in DVMRP, the tree is first made (broadcasting) and then pruned; in CBT, there is no tree at the beginning; the joining (grafting) gradually makes the tree.

Sending Multicast Packets

After formation of the tree, any source (belonging to the group or not) can send a multicast packet to all members of the group. It simply sends the packet to the rendezvous router, using the unicast address of the rendezvous router; the rendezvous router distributes the packet to all members of the group. Figure 15.13 shows how a host can send a multicast packet to all members of the group. Note that the source host can be any of the hosts inside the shared tree or any host outside the shared tree. In the figure we show one located outside the shared tree.

Selecting the Rendezvous Router

This approach is simple except for one point. How do we select a rendezvous router to optimize the process and multicasting as well? Several methods have been implemented.

Figure 15.13 *Sending a multicast packet to the rendezvous router*

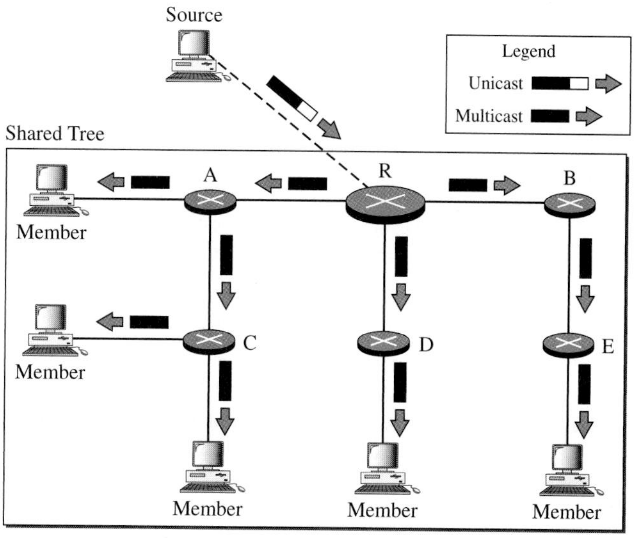

However, this topic is beyond the scope of this book and we leave it to more advanced books.

Summary

In summary, the Core-Based Tree (CBT) is a group-shared tree, center-based protocol using one tree per group. One of the routers in the tree is called the core. A packet is sent from the source to members of the group following this procedure:

1. The source, which may or may not be part of the tree, encapsulates the multicast packet inside a unicast packet with the unicast destination address of the core and sends it to the core. This part of delivery is done using a unicast address; the only recipient is the core router.
2. The core decapsulates the unicast packet and forwards it to all interested interfaces.
3. Each router that receives the multicast packet, in turn, forwards it to all interested interfaces.

> In CBT, the source sends the multicast packet (encapsulated in a unicast packet) to the core router. The core router decapsulates the packet and forwards it to all interested interfaces.

15.7 PIM

Protocol Independent Multicast (PIM) is the name given to two independent multicast routing protocols: **Protocol Independent Multicast, Dense Mode (PIM-DM)** and

Protocol Independent Multicast, Sparse Mode (PIM-SM). Both protocols are unicast-protocol dependent, but the similarity ends here. We discuss each separately.

PIM-DM

PIM-DM is used when there is a possibility that each router is involved in multicasting (dense mode). In this environment, the use of a protocol that broadcasts the packet is justified because almost all routers are involved in the process.

> **PIM-DM is used in a dense multicast environment, such as a LAN.**

PIM-DM is a source-based tree routing protocol that uses RPF and pruning/grafting strategies for multicasting. Its operation is like DVMRP; however, unlike DVMRP, it does not depend on a specific unicasting protocol. It assumes that the autonomous system is using a unicast protocol and each router has a table that can find the outgoing interface that has an optimal path to a destination. This unicast protocol can be a distance vector protocol (RIP) or link state protocol (OSPF).

> **PIM-DM uses RPF and pruning/grafting strategies to handle multicasting. However, it is independent from the underlying unicast protocol.**

PIM-SM

PIM-SM is used when there is a slight possibility that each router is involved in multicasting (sparse mode). In this environment, the use of a protocol that broadcasts the packet is not justified; a protocol such as CBT that uses a group-shared tree is more appropriate.

> **PIM-SM is used in a sparse multicast environment such as a WAN.**

PIM-SM is a group-shared tree routing protocol that has a rendezvous point (RP) as the source of the tree. Its operation is like CBT; however, it is simpler because it does not require acknowledgment from a join message. In addition, it creates a backup set of RPs for each region to cover RP failures.

One of the characteristics of PIM-SM is that it can switch from a group-shared tree strategy to a source-based tree strategy when necessary. This can happen if there is a dense area of activity far from the RP. That area can be more efficiently handled with a source-based tree strategy instead of a group-shared tree strategy.

> **PIM-SM is similar to CBT but uses a simpler procedure.**

15.8   MBONE

Multimedia and real-time communication have increased the need for multicasting in the Internet. However, only a small fraction of Internet routers are multicast routers. In other words, a multicast router may not find another multicast router in the neighborhood to forward the multicast packet. Although this problem may be solved in the next few years by adding more and more multicast routers, there is another solution for this problem. The solution is tunneling. The multicast routers are seen as a group of routers on top of unicast routers. The multicast routers may not be connected directly, but they are connected logically. Figure 15.14 shows the idea. In this figure, only the routers enclosed in the shaded circles are capable of multicasting. Without tunneling, these routers are isolated islands. To enable multicasting, we make a **multicast backbone (MBONE)** out of these isolated routers using the concept of tunneling.

Figure 15.14   *Logical tunneling*

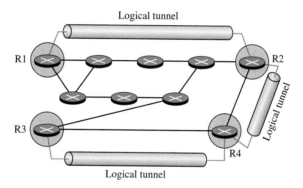

A logical tunnel is established by encapsulating the multicast packet inside a unicast packet. The multicast packet becomes the payload (data) of the unicast packet. The intermediate (non multicast) routers forward the packet as unicast routers and deliver the packet from one island to another. It's as if the unicast routers do not exist and the two multicast routers are neighbors. Figure 15.15 shows the concept. So far the only protocol that supports MBONE and tunneling is DVMRP.

Figure 15.15   *MBONE*

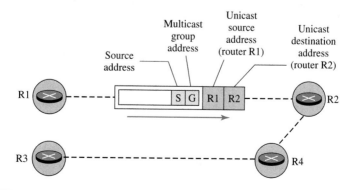

15.9 KEY TERMS

broadcasting

Core-Based Tree (CBT) protocol

designated parent router

Distance Vector Multicast Routing Protocol (DVMRP)

distributed database

flooding

grafting

group-shared tree

least-cost tree

logical tunnel

multicast backbone (MBONE)

multicasting

Multicast Open Shortest Path First (MOSPF)

multicast router

multicast routing

multiple unicasting

Protocol Independent Multicast (PIM)

Protocol Independent Multicast, Dense Mode (PIM-DM)

Protocol Independent Multicast, Sparse Mode (PIM-SM)

pruning

rendezvous-point tree

rendezvous router

reverse path broadcasting (RPB)

reverse path forwarding (RPF)

reverse path multicasting (RPM)

shortest path

source-based tree

tunneling

unicasting

15.10 SUMMARY

❏ In multicasting there is one source and a group of destinations.

❏ In multiple unicasting, multiple copies of a message, each with a different unicast destination address, are sent from a source.

❏ Multicasting applications include distributed databases, information dissemination, teleconferencing, and distance learning.

❏ For efficient multicasting we use a shortest path tree to represent the communication path.

❏ In a source-based tree approach to multicast routing, the source/group combination determines the tree.

❏ In a group-shared tree approach to multicast routing, the group determines the tree.

❏ MOSPF is a multicast routing protocol that uses multicast link state routing to create a source-based least-cost tree.

❏ In reverse path forwarding (RPF), the router forwards only the packets that have traveled the shortest path from the source to the router.

❏ Reverse path broadcasting (RPB) creates a shortest path broadcast tree from the source to each destination. It guarantees that each destination receives one and only one copy of the packet.

❏ Reverse path multicasting (RPM) adds pruning and grafting to RPB to create a multicast shortest path tree that supports dynamic membership changes.

❏ DVMRP is a multicast routing protocol that uses the distance routing protocol to create a source-based tree.

❏ The Core-Based Tree (CBT) protocol is a multicast routing protocol that uses a router as the root of the tree.

❏ PIM-DM is a source-based tree routing protocol that uses RPF and pruning/grafting strategies to handle multicasting.

❏ PIM-SM is a group-shared tree routing protocol that is similar to CBT and uses a rendezvous router as the source of the tree.

❏ For multicasting between two noncontiguous multicast routers, we make a multicast backbone (MBONE) to enable tunneling.

15.11   PRACTICE SET

Exercises

1. In Figure 15.4, find the unicast routing tables for routers R2, R3, and R4. Show the shortest path trees.

2. In Figure 15.5, find the multicast routing tables for routers R2, R3, and R4.

3. A router using DVMRP receives a packet with source address 10.14.17.2 from interface 2. If the router forwards the packet, what are the contents of the entry related to this address in the unicast routing table?

4. Router A sends a unicast RIP update packet to router B that says 134.23.0.0/16 is 7 hops away. Network B sends an update packet to router A that says 13.23.0.0/16 is 4 hops away. If these two routers are connected to the same network, which one is the designated parent router?

5. Does RPF actually create a shortest path tree? Explain.

6. Does RPB actually create a shortest path tree? Explain. What are the leaves of the tree?

7. Does RPM actually create a shortest path tree? Explain. What are the leaves of the tree?

Research Activities

8. Find the format of the DVMRP prune message. What is the format of the graft message?

9. For MOSPF find the format of the group-membership-LSA packet that associates a network with a group.

10. CBT uses nine types of packets. Use the Internet to find the purpose and format of each packet.

11. Use the Internet to find how CBT messages are encapsulated.

12. Use the Internet to find information regarding the scalability of each multicast routing protocol we discussed. Make a table and compare them.

13. Use the Internet to find information about the interautonomous multicast protocols.

CHAPTER 16

Host Configuration: BOOTP and DHCP

Each computer that uses the TCP/IP protocol suite needs to know its IP address. If the computer uses classless addressing or is a member of a subnet, it also needs to know its subnet mask. Most computers today need two other pieces of information: the address of a default router to be able to communicate with other networks and the address of a name server to be able to use names instead of addresses as we will see in the next chapter. In other words, four pieces of information are normally needed:

❑ The IP address of the computer
❑ The subnet mask of the computer
❑ The IP address of a router
❑ The IP address of a name server

This information is usually stored in a configuration file and accessed by the computer during the bootstrap process. But what about a diskless workstation or a computer with a disk that is booted for the first time?

In the case of a diskless computer, the operating system and the networking software could be stored in read-only memory (ROM). However, the above information is not known to the manufacturer and thus cannot be stored in ROM. The information is dependent on the individual configuration of the machine and defines the network to which the machine is connected.

16.1 BOOTP

The **Bootstrap Protocol (BOOTP)** is a client/server protocol designed to provide the four pieces of information for a diskless computer or a computer that is booted for the first time. We have already studied one protocol, RARP, that provides the IP address for a diskless computer. Why do we need yet another protocol? The answer is that RARP provides only the IP address. Another reason is that RARP uses a data-link layer service, not a network-layer service. The RARP client and server must be on the same network. BOOTP has none of the above limitations. It can provide all four pieces of information. It is an application-layer program, which means that the client and server can be on different networks.

Operation

The BOOTP client and server can either be on the same network or on different networks. Let us discuss each situation separately.

Same Network

Although the practice is not very common, the administrator may put the client and the server on the same network as shown in Figure 16.1.

Figure 16.1   *Client and server on the same network*

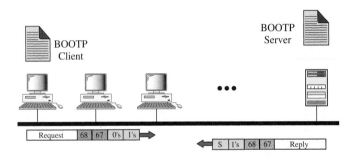

In this case, the operation can be described as follows:

1. The BOOTP server issues a passive open command on UDP port number 67 and waits for a client.

2. A booted client issues an active open command on port number 68 (this number will be explained later). The message is encapsulated in a UDP user datagram, using the destination port number 67 and the source port number 68. The UDP user datagram, in turn, is encapsulated in an IP datagram. The reader may ask how a client can send an IP datagram when it knows neither its own IP address (the source address) nor the server's IP address (the destination address). The client uses all 0s as the source address and all 1s as the destination address.

3. The server responds with either a broadcast or a unicast message using UDP source port number 67 and destination port number 68. The response can be unicast because the server knows the IP address of the client. It also knows the physical address of the client, which means it does not need the services of ARP for logical to physical address mapping. However, some systems do not allow the bypassing of ARP, resulting in the use of the broadcast address.

Different Networks

One of the advantages of BOOTP over RARP is that the client and server are application-layer processes. As in other application-layer processes, a client can be in one network and the server in another, separated by several other networks. However, there is one problem that must be solved. The BOOTP request is broadcast because the client does not know the IP address of the server. A broadcast IP datagram cannot pass through any router. A router receiving such a packet discards it. Recall that an IP address of all 1s is a limited broadcast address.

To solve the problem, there is a need for an intermediary. One of the hosts (or a router that can be configured to operate at the application layer) can be used as a relay. The host in this case is called a **relay agent.** The relay agent knows the unicast address of a BOOTP server and listens for broadcast messages on port 67. When it receives this type of packet, it encapsulates the message in a unicast datagram and sends the request to the BOOTP server. The packet, carrying a unicast destination address, is routed by any router and reaches the BOOTP server. The BOOTP server knows the message comes from a relay agent because one of the fields in the request message defines the IP address of the relay agent. The relay agent, after receiving the reply, sends it to the BOOTP client. Figure 16.2 shows the situation.

Figure 16.2   *Client and server on two different networks*

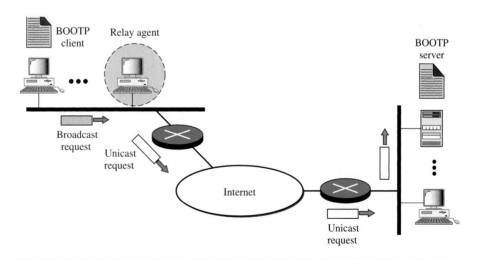

UDP Ports

Figure 16.3 shows the interaction between a client and a BOOTP server. The server uses the well-known port 67, which is normal. The client uses the well-known port 68, which is unusual. The reason for choosing the well-known port 68 instead of an ephemeral port is to prevent a problem when the reply, from the server to the client, is broadcast. To understand the problem, let us look at a situation where an ephemeral port is

Figure 16.3   *Use of UDP ports*

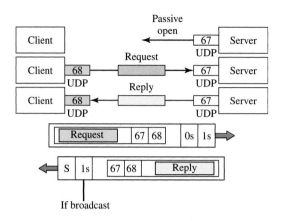

used. Suppose host A on a network is using a BOOTP client on ephemeral port 2017 (randomly chosen). Host B, on the same network, is using a DAYTIME client on ephemeral port 2017 (accidentally the same). Now the BOOTP server sends a broadcast reply message with the destination port number 2017 and broadcast IP address $FFFFFFFF_{16}$. Every host needs to open a packet carrying this destination IP address. Host A finds a message from an application program on ephemeral port 2017. A correct message is delivered to the BOOTP client. An incorrect message is delivered to the DAYTIME client. The confusion is due to the demultiplexing of packets based on the socket address (see Chapter 11), which is a combination of IP address and port number. In this case, both are the same.

The use of a well-known port (less than 1024) prevents the use of the same two destination port numbers. Host B cannot select 68 as the ephemeral port because ephemeral port numbers are greater than 1023.

The curious reader may ask what happens if host B is also running the BOOTP client. In this case, the socket address is the same and both clients will receive the message. In this situation, a third identification number differentiates the clients. BOOTP uses another number, called the transaction ID, which is randomly chosen for each connection involving BOOTP. It is highly improbable that two hosts will choose the same ID at the same time.

Using TFTP

The server does not send all of the information that a client may need for booting. In the reply message, the server defines the pathname of a file in which the client can find complete booting information. The client can then use a TFTP (see Chapter 19) message, which is encapsulated in a UDP user datagram, to obtain the rest of the needed information.

Error Control

What if a request is lost or damaged? What if the response is damaged? There is a need for error control when using BOOTP. BOOTP uses UDP, which does not provide error control. Therefore, BOOTP must provide error control. Error control is accomplished through two strategies:

1. BOOTP requires that UDP uses the checksum. Remember that the use of the checksum in UDP is optional.

2. The BOOTP client uses timers and a retransmission policy if it does not receive the BOOTP reply to a request. However, to prevent a traffic jam when several hosts need to retransmit a request (for example, after a power failure), BOOTP forces the client to use a random number to set its timers.

Packet Format

Figure 16.4 shows the format of a BOOTP packet.

Figure 16.4   *BOOTP packet format*

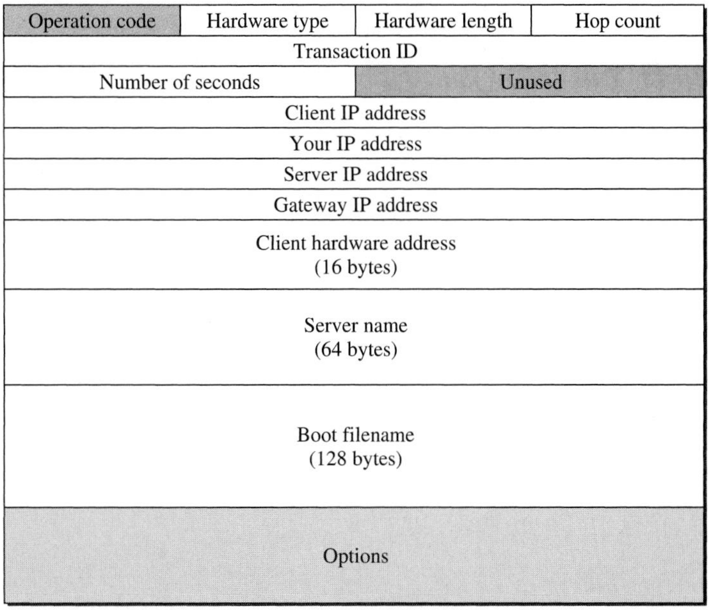

❏ **Operation code.** This 8-bit field defines the type of BOOTP packet: request (1) or reply (2).

❏ **Hardware type.** This is an 8-bit field defining the type of physical network. Each type of network has been assigned an integer. For example, for Ethernet the value is 1.

❏ **Hardware length.** This is an 8-bit field defining the length of the physical address in bytes. For example, for Ethernet the value is 6.

❏ **Hop count.** This is an 8-bit field defining the maximum number of hops the packet can travel.

❏ **Transaction ID.** This is a 4-byte field carrying an integer. The transaction identification is set by the client and is used to match a reply with the request. The server returns the same value in its reply.

❏ **Number of seconds.** This is a 16-bit field that indicates the number of seconds elapsed since the time the client started to boot.

❏ **Client IP address.** This is a 4-byte field that contains the client IP address. If the client does not have this information, this field has a value of 0.

❏ **Your IP address.** This is a 4-byte field that contains the client IP address. It is filled by the server (in the reply message) at the request of the client.

❏ **Server IP address.** This is a 4-byte field containing the server IP address. It is filled by the server in a reply message.

❏ **Gateway IP address.** This is a 4-byte field containing the IP address of a router. It is filled by the server in a reply message.

❏ **Client hardware address.** This is the physical address of the client. Although the server can retrieve this address from the frame sent by the client, it is more efficient if the address is supplied explicitly by the client in the request message.

❏ **Server name.** This is an optional 64-byte field filled by the server in a reply packet. It contains a null-terminated string consisting of the domain name of the server.

❏ **Boot filename.** This is an optional 128-byte field that can be filled by the server in a reply packet. It contains a null-terminated string consisting of the full pathname of the boot file. The client can use this path to retrieve other booting information.

❏ **Options.** This is a 64-byte field with a dual purpose. It can carry either additional information (such as the network mask or default router address) or some specific vendor information. The field is used only in a reply message. The server uses a number, called a **magic cookie,** in the format of an IP address with the value of 99.130.83.99. When the client finishes reading the message, it looks for this magic cookie. If present, the next 60 bytes are options. An option is composed of three fields: a 1-byte tag field, a 1-byte length field, and a variable-length value field. The length field defines the length of the value field, not the whole option. See Figure 16.5.

Figure 16.5   *Option format*

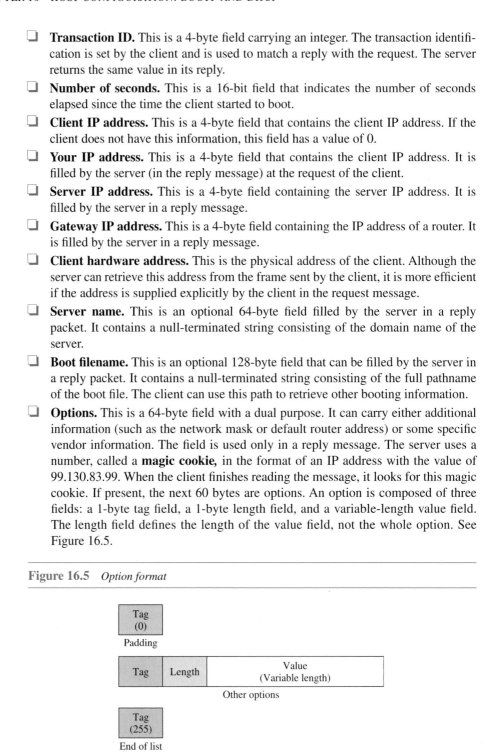

The list of options is shown in Table 16.1.

Table 16.1   *Options for BOOTP*

Description	Tag	Length	Value
Padding	0		
Subnet mask	1	4	Subnet mask
Time offset	2	4	Time of the day
Default routers	3	Variable	IP addresses
Time servers	4	Variable	IP addresses
DNS servers	6	Variable	IP addresses
Print servers	9	Variable	IP addresses
Host name	12	Variable	DNS name
Boot file size	13	2	Integer
Vendor specific	128–254	Variable	Specific information
End of list	255		

The length of the fields that contain IP addresses are multiples of 4 bytes. The padding option, which is only 1 byte long, is used only for alignment. The end-of-list option, which is also only 1 byte long, indicates the end of the option field. Vendors can use option tags 128 to 254 to supply extra information in a reply message.

16.2   DHCP

BOOTP is not a **dynamic configuration protocol.** When a client requests its IP address, the BOOTP server consults a table that matches the physical address of the client with its IP address. This implies that the binding between the physical address and the IP address of the client already exists. The binding is predetermined.

However, what if a host moves from one physical network to another? What if a host wants a temporary IP address? BOOTP cannot handle these situations because the binding between the physical and IP addresses is static and fixed in a table until changed by the administrator. BOOTP is a static configuration protocol.

The **Dynamic Host Configuration Protocol (DHCP)** has been devised to provide static and dynamic address allocation that can be manual or automatic.

> **DHCP provides static and dynamic address allocation
> that can be manual or automatic.**

Static Address Allocation

In this capacity DHCP acts like BOOTP. It is backward compatible with BOOTP, which means a host running the BOOTP client can request a static address from a DHCP server. A DHCP server has a database that statically binds physical addresses to IP addresses.

Dynamic Address Allocation

DHCP has a second database with a pool of available IP addresses. This second database makes DHCP dynamic. When a DHCP client requests a temporary IP address, the DHCP server goes to the pool of available (unused) IP addresses and assigns an IP address for a negotiable period of time.

When a DHCP client sends a request to a DHCP server, the server first checks its static database. If an entry with the requested physical address exists in the static database, the permanent IP address of the client is returned. On the other hand, if the entry does not exist in the static database, the server selects an IP address from the available pool, assigns the address to the client, and adds the entry to the dynamic database.

The dynamic aspect of DHCP is needed when a host moves from network to network or is connected and disconnected from a network (like a subscriber to a service provider). DHCP provides temporary IP addresses for a limited period of time.

The addresses assigned from the pool are temporary addresses. The DHCP server issues a **lease** for a specific period of time. When the lease expires, the client must either stop using the IP address or renew the lease. The server has the choice to agree or disagree with the renewal. If the server disagrees, the client stops using the address.

Manual and Automatic Configuration

One major problem with BOOTP protocol is that the table mapping the IP addresses to physical addresses needs to be manually configured. This means that every time there is a change in a physical or IP address, the administrator needs to manually enter the changes. DHCP, on the other hand, allows both manual and automatic configurations. Static addresses are created manually; dynamic addresses are created automatically.

Packet Format

To make DHCP backward compatible with BOOTP, the designers of DHCP have decided to use almost the same packet format. They have only added a 1-bit flag to the packet. However, to allow different interactions with the server, extra options have been added to the option field. Figure 16.6 shows the format of a DHCP message.

The new fields are as follows:

❏ **Flag.** A 1-bit flag has been added to the packet (the first bit of the unused field) to let the client specify a forced broadcast reply (instead of unicast) from the server. If the reply were to be unicast to the client, the destination IP address of the IP packet is the address assigned to the client. Since the client does not know its IP address, it may discard the packet. However, if the IP datagram is broadcast, every host will receive and process the broadcast message.

❏ **Options.** Several options have been added to the list of options. One option, with the value 53 for the tag subfield (see Figure 16.5), is used to define the type of interaction between the client and the server (see Table 16.2). Other options define parameters such as lease time and so on. The options field in DHCP can be up to 312 bytes.

Figure 16.6 *DHCP packet*

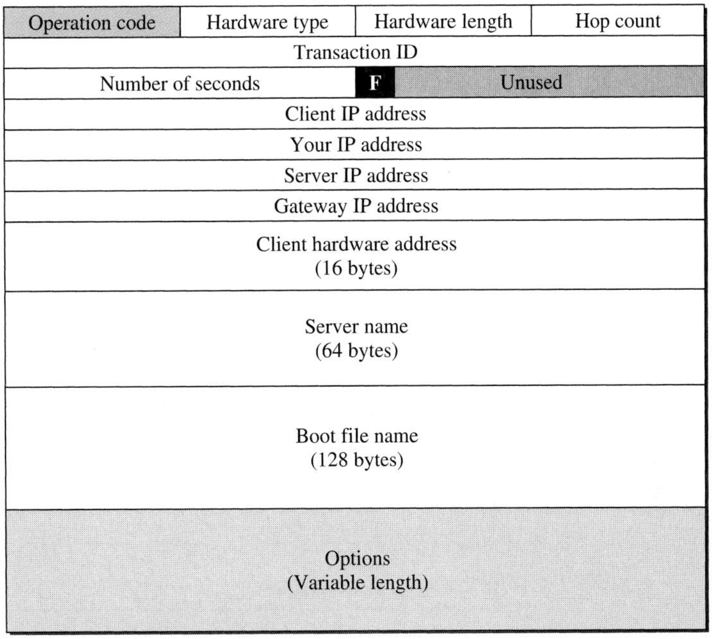

Operation code	Hardware type	Hardware length	Hop count
Transaction ID			
Number of seconds	F	Unused	

Client IP address
Your IP address
Server IP address
Gateway IP address

Client hardware address
(16 bytes)

Server name
(64 bytes)

Boot file name
(128 bytes)

Options
(Variable length)

Table 16.2 *Options for DHCP*

Value	Value
1 DHCPDISCOVER	5 DHCPACK
2 DHCPOFFER	6 DHCPNACK
3 DHCPREQUEST	7 DHCPRELEASE
4 DHCPDECLINE	

We will see the use of these options in the next section.

Transition States

The DHCP client transitions from one state to another depending on the messages it receives or sends. See Figure 16.7.

Initializing State

When the DHCP client first starts, it is in the initializing state. The client broadcasts a DHCPDISCOVER message (a request message with the DHCPDISCOVER option) using port 67.

Figure 16.7   *DHCP transition diagram*

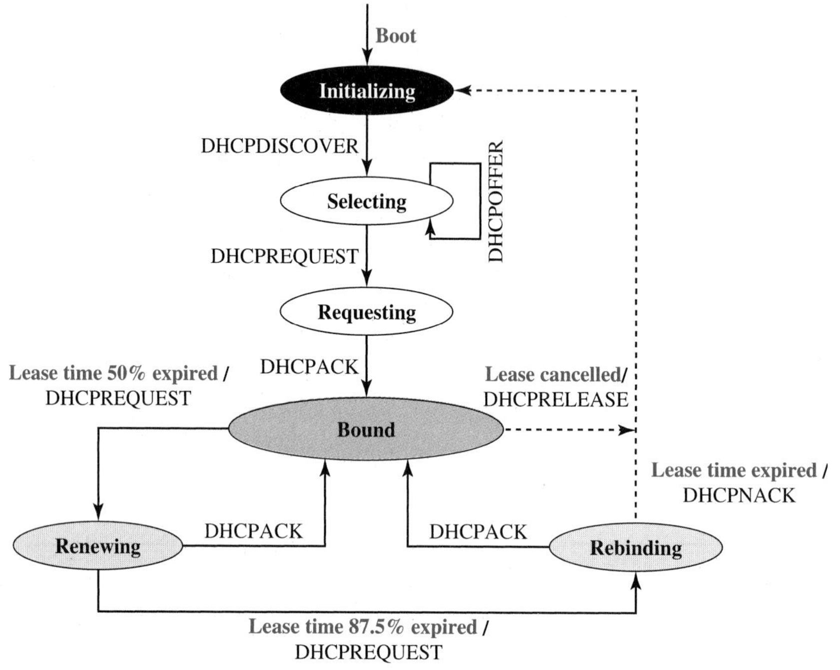

Selecting State

After sending the DHCPDISCOVER message, the client goes to the selecting state. Those servers that can provide this type of service respond with a DHCPOFFER message. In these messages, the servers offer an IP address. They can also offer the lease duration. The default is 1 h. The server that sends a DHCPOFFER locks the offered IP address so that it is not available to any other clients. The client chooses one of the offers and sends a DHCPREQUEST message to the selected server. It then goes to the requesting state. However, if the client receives no DHCPOFFER message, it tries four more times, each with a span of 2 s. If there is no reply to any of these DHCPDISCOVERs, the client sleeps for 5 minutes before trying again.

Requesting State

The client remains in the requesting state until it receives a DHCPACK message from the server which creates the binding between the client physical address and its IP address. After receipt of the DHCPACK, the client goes to the bound state.

Bound State

In this state, the client can use the IP address until the lease expires. When 50 percent of the lease period is reached, the client sends another DHCPREQUEST to ask for renewal. It then goes to the renewing state. When in the bound state, the client can also cancel the lease and go to the initializing state.

Renewing State

The client remains in the renewing state until one of two events happens. It can receive a DHCPACK, which renews the lease agreement. In this case, the client resets its timer and goes back to the bound state. Or, if a DHCPACK is not received, and 87.5% of the lease time expires, the client goes to the rebinding state.

Rebinding State

The client remains in the rebinding state until one of three events happens. If the client receives a DHCPNACK or the lease expires, it goes back to the initializing state and tries to get another IP address. If the client receives a DHCPACK it goes to the bound state and resets the timer.

Exchanging Messages

Figure 16.8 shows the exchange of messages related to the transition diagram.

Figure 16.8   *Exchanging messages*

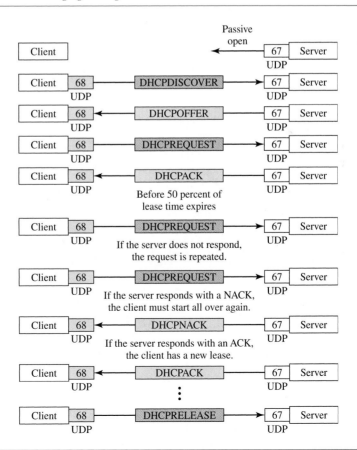

16.3   KEY TERMS

bootstrap process

Bootstrap Protocol (BOOTP)

configuration file

dynamic configuration protocol

Dynamic Host Configuration Protocol
  (DHCP)

gateway

lease

magic cookie

name server

read-only memory (ROM)

relay agent

static configuration protocol

16.4   SUMMARY

❏ Every computer attached to a TCP/IP internet must know its IP address, the IP address of a router, the IP address of a name server, and its subnet mask.

❏ BOOTP and Dynamic Host Configuration Protocol (DHCP) are client-server applications that deliver vital network information to either diskless computers or computers at first boot.

❏ One BOOTP packet format is used for both the client request and the server reply.

❏ The BOOTP server waits passively for a client request.

❏ A server reply can be broadcast or unicast.

❏ A BOOTP request is encapsulated in a UDP user datagram.

❏ BOOTP, a static configuration protocol, uses a table that maps IP addresses to physical addresses.

❏ A relay agent is a router that helps send local BOOTP requests to remote servers.

❏ DHCP is a dynamic configuration protocol with two databases: one is similar to BOOTP and the other is a pool of IP addresses available for temporary assignment.

❏ The DHCP server issues a lease for an IP address to a client for a specific period of time.

❏ The DHCP packet format is similar to that of BOOTP. DHCP has extra options.

❏ DHCP is backward compatible with BOOTP.

16.5   PRACTICE SET

Exercises

1. What is the minimum length of a BOOTP packet? What is the maximum length?

2. A BOOTP packet is encapsulated in a UDP packet, which is encapsulated in an IP packet, which is encapsulated in a frame. A RARP packet, on the other hand, is

encapsulated only in a frame. Find the efficiency of a BOOTP packet versus a RARP packet.

3. Show an example of a BOOTP packet with a padding option.

4. Show an example of a BOOTP packet with an end-of-list option.

5. What is the maximum number of seconds that can be stored in the Number of Seconds field of a BOOTP packet?

6. Show the contents of all fields for a BOOTP request packet sent from a client with physical address 00:11:21:15:EA:21.

7. Show the contents of all fields for a BOOTP reply sent in response to the request in Exercise 6.

8. Encapsulate the packet in Exercise 6 in a UDP user datagram. Fill all the fields.

9. Encapsulate the packet in Exercise 7 in a UDP user datagram. Fill all the fields.

10. Encapsulate the packet in Exercise 8 in an IP datagram. Fill all the fields.

11. Encapsulate the packet in Exercise 9 in an IP datagram. Fill all the fields.

12. Why does a newly added host need to know its subnet mask?

13. Why does a newly added host need to know the IP address of a router?

14. Why does a newly added host need to know the IP address of a name server?

15. Why do you think BOOTP needs to use TFTP to get additional information? Why can't all the information be retrieved using BOOTP?

16. A diskless client on a Class C Ethernet network uses BOOTP. The BOOTP server is on a Class B Ethernet network. Draw a figure of the networks with appropriate IP addresses for the client, server, and relay agent. Fill out a BOOTP request and reply packet.

Research Activities

17. Show the format and contents of a DHCPDISCOVER message.

18. Show the format and contents of a DHCPOFFER message.

19. Show the format and contents of a DHCPREQUEST message.

20. Show the format and contents of a DHCPDECLINE message.

21. Show the format and contents of a DHCPACK message.

22. Show the format and contents of a DHCPNACK message.

23. Show the format and contents of a DHCPRELEASE message.

24. Find the RFCs related to BOOTP.

25. Find the RFCs related to DHCP.

CHAPTER 17

Domain Name System (DNS)

To identify an entity, TCP/IP protocols use the IP address, which uniquely identifies the connection of a host to the Internet. However, people prefer to use names instead of numeric addresses. Therefore, we need a system that can map a name to an address or an address to a name.

When the Internet was small, mapping was done using a *host file*. The host file had only two columns: name and address. Every host could store the host file on its disk and update it periodically from a master host file. When a program or a user wanted to map a name to an address, the host consulted the host file and found the mapping.

Today, however, it is impossible to have one single host file to relate every address with a name and vice versa. The host file would be too large to store in every host. In addition, it would be impossible to update all the host files every time there is a change.

One solution would be to store the entire host file in a single computer and allow access to this centralized information to every computer that needs mapping. But we know that this would create a huge amount of traffic on the Internet.

Another solution, the one used today, is to divide this huge amount of information into smaller parts and store each part on a different computer. In this method, the host that needs mapping can contact the closest computer holding the needed information. This method is used by the **Domain Name System (DNS).** In this chapter, we first discuss the concepts and ideas behind the DNS. We then describe the DNS protocol itself.

17.1 NAME SPACE

To be unambiguous, the names assigned to machines must be carefully selected from a name space with complete control over the binding between the names and IP addresses. In other words, the names must be unique because the addresses are unique. A **name space** that maps each address to a unique name can be organized in two ways: flat or hierarchical.

Flat Name Space

In a **flat name space,** a name is assigned to an address. A name in this space is a sequence of characters without structure. The names may or may not have a common section; if they do, it has no meaning. The main disadvantage of a flat name space is that it cannot be used in a large system such as the Internet because it must be centrally controlled to avoid ambiguity and duplication.

Hierarchical Name Space

In a **hierarchical name space,** each name is made of several parts. The first part can define the nature of the organization, the second part can define the name of an organization, the third part can define departments in the organization, and so on. In this case, the authority to assign and control the name spaces can be decentralized. A central authority can assign the part of the name that defines the nature of the organization and the name of the organization. The responsibility of the rest of the name can be given to the organization itself. The organization can add suffixes (or prefixes) to the name to define its host or resources. The management of the organization need not worry that the prefix chosen for a host is taken by another organization because, even if part of an address is the same, the whole address is different. For example, assume two colleges and a company call one of their computers *challenger*. The first college is given a name by the central authority such as *fhda.edu,* the second college is given the name *berkeley.edu,* and the company is given the name *smart.com.* When each of these organizations adds the name *challenger* to the name they have already been given, the end result is three distinguishable names: *challenger.fhda.edu, challenger.berkeley.edu,* and *challenger.smart.com.* The names are unique without the need for assignment by a central authority. The central authority controls only part of the name, not the whole.

17.2   DOMAIN NAME SPACE

To have a hierarchical name space, a **domain name space** was designed. In this design the names are defined in an inverted-tree structure with the root at the top. The tree can have only 128 levels: level 0 (root) to level 127 (see Figure 17.1).

Label

Each node in the tree has a **label,** which is a string with a maximum of 63 characters. The root label is a null string (empty string). DNS requires that children of a node (nodes that branch from the same node) have different labels, which guarantees the uniqueness of the domain names.

Domain Name

Each node in the tree has a domain name. A full **domain name** is a sequence of labels separated by dots (.). The domain names are always read from the node up to the root.

Figure 17.1 *Domain name space*

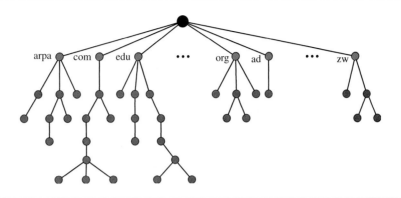

The last label is the label of the root (null). This means that a full domain name always ends in a null label, which means the last character is a dot because the null string is nothing. Figure 17.2 shows some domain names.

Figure 17.2 *Domain names and labels*

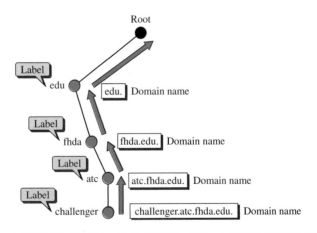

Fully Qualified Domain Name (FQDN)

If a label is terminated by a null string, it is called a **fully qualified domain name (FQDN).** An FQDN is a domain name that contains the full name of a host. It contains all labels, from the most specific to the most general, that uniquely define the name of the host. For example, the domain name

challenger.atc.fhda.edu.

is the FQDN of a computer named *challenger* installed at the Advanced Technology Center (ATC) at De Anza College. A DNS server can only match an FQDN to an address. Note that the name must end with a null label, but because null means nothing, the label ends with a dot (.).

Partially Qualified Domain Name (PQDN)

If a label is not terminated by a null string, it is called a **partially qualified domain name (PQDN).** A PQDN starts from a node, but it does not reach the root. It is used when the name to be resolved belongs to the same site as the client. Here the resolver can supply the missing part, called the *suffix,* to create an FQDN. For example, if a user at the *fhda.edu.* site wants to get the IP address of the challenger computer, he or she can define the partial name

> challenger

The DNS client adds the suffix *atc.fhda.edu.* before passing the address to the DNS server.

The DNS client normally holds a list of suffixes. The following can be the list of suffixes at De Anza College. The null suffix defines nothing. This suffix is added when the user defines an FQDN.

> atc.fhda.edu
> fhda.edu
> *null*

Figure 17.3 shows some FQDNs and PQDNs.

Figure 17.3 *FQDN and PQDN*

Domain

A **domain** is a subtree of the domain name space. The name of the domain is the domain name of the node at the top of the subtree. Figure 17.4 shows some domains. Note that a domain may itself be divided into domains (or **subdomains** as they are sometimes called).

Figure 17.4 *Domains*

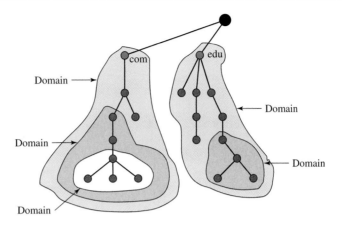

17.3 DISTRIBUTION OF NAME SPACE

The information contained in the domain name space must be stored. However, it is very inefficient and also not reliable to have just one computer store such a huge amount of information. It is inefficient because responding to requests from all over the world places a heavy load on the system. It is not reliable because any failure makes the data inaccessible.

Hierarchy of Name Servers

The solution to these problems is to distribute the information among many computers called **DNS servers.** One way to do this is to divide the whole space into many domains based on the first level. In other words, we let the root stand alone and create as many domains (subtrees) as there are first-level nodes. Because a domain created this way could be very large, DNS allows domains to be divided further into smaller domains (subdomains). Each server can be responsible (authoritative) for either a large or small domain. In other words, we have a hierarchy of servers in the same way that we have a hierarchy of names (see Figure 17.5).

Zone

Since the complete domain name hierarchy cannot be stored on a single server, it is divided among many servers. What a server is responsible for or has authority over is called a **zone.** We can define a zone as a contiguous part of the entire tree. If a server accepts responsibility for a domain and does not divide the domain into smaller domains, the "domain" and the "zone" refer to the same thing. The server makes a database called a *zone file* and keeps all the information for every node under that domain. However, if a server divides its domain into subdomains and delegates part of its

Figure 17.5   *Hierarchy of name servers*

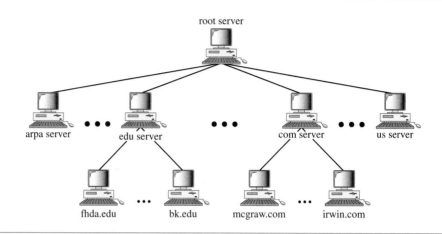

authority to other servers, "domain" and "zone" refer to different things. The information about the nodes in the subdomains is stored in the servers at the lower levels, with the original server keeping some sort of reference to these lower-level servers. Of course the original server does not free itself from responsibility totally: It still has a zone, but the detailed information is kept by the lower-level servers (see Figure 17.6).

Figure 17.6   *Zones and domains*

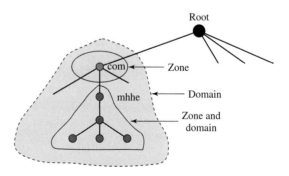

A server can also divide part of its domain and delegate responsibility but still keep part of the domain for itself. In this case, its zone is made of detailed information for the part of the domain that is not delegated and references to those parts that are delegated.

Root Server

A **root server** is a server whose zone consists of the whole tree. A root server usually does not store any information about domains but delegates its authority to other servers, keeping references to those servers. There are several root servers, each covering the whole domain name space. The servers are distributed all around the world.

Primary and Secondary Servers

DNS defines two types of servers: primary and secondary. A **primary server** is a server that stores a file about the zone for which it is an authority. It is responsible for creating, maintaining, and updating the zone file. It stores the zone file on a local disk.

A **secondary server** is a server that transfers the complete information about a zone from another server (primary or secondary) and stores the file on its local disk. The secondary server neither creates nor updates the zone files. If updating is required, it must be done by the primary server, which sends the updated version to the secondary.

The primary and secondary servers are both authoritative for the zones they serve. The idea is not to put the secondary server at a lower level of authority but to create redundancy for the data so that if one server fails, the other can continue serving clients. Note also that a server can be a primary server for a specific zone and a secondary server for another zone. Therefore, when we refer to a server as a primary or secondary server, we should be careful to which zone we refer.

> **A primary server loads all information from the disk file; the secondary server loads all information from the primary server. When the secondary downloads information from the primary, it is called zone transfer.**

17.4   DNS IN THE INTERNET

DNS is a protocol that can be used in different platforms. In the Internet, the domain name space (tree) is divided into three different sections: generic domains, country domains, and the inverse domain (see Figure 17.7).

Figure 17.7 *DNS used in the Internet*

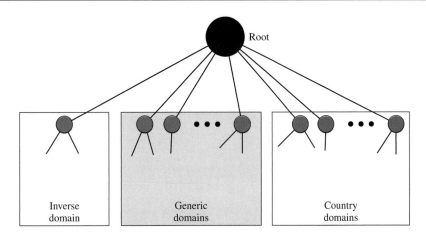

Generic Domains

The **generic domains** define registered hosts according to their generic behavior. Each node in the tree defines a domain, which is an index to the domain name space database (see Figure 17.8).

Figure 17.8 *Generic domains*

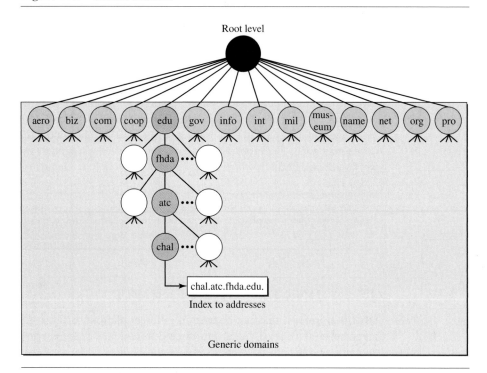

Generic domains

Looking at the tree, we see that the first level in the generic domains section allows 14 possible labels. These labels describe the organization types as listed in Table 17.1.

Table 17.1 *Generic domain labels*

Label	Description
aero	Airlines and aerospace companies
biz	Businesses or firms (similar to "com")
com	Commercial organizations
coop	Cooperative business organizations
edu	Educational institutions
gov	Government institutions
info	Information service providers

Table 17.1 *Generic domain labels (continued)*

Label	Description
int	International organizations
mil	Military groups
museum	Museums and other non-profit organizations
name	Personal names (individuals)
net	Network support centers
org	Nonprofit organizations
pro	Professional individual organizations

Country Domains

The **country domains** section uses two-character country abbreviations (e.g., us for United States). Second-labels can be organizational, or they can be more specific, national designations. The United States, for example, uses state abbreviations as a sub-division of us (e.g., ca.us.).

Figure 17.9 shows the country domains section. The address *anza.cup.ca.us* can be translated to De Anza College in Cupertino in California in the United States.

Figure 17.9 *Country domains*

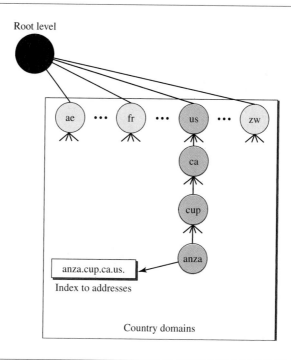

Inverse Domain

The **inverse domain** is used to map an address to a name. This may happen, for example, when a server has received a request from a client to do a task. Although the server has a file that contains a list of authorized clients, only the IP address of the client (extracted from the received IP packet) is listed. The server asks its resolver to send a query to the DNS server to map an address to a name to determine if the client is on the authorized list.

This type of query is called an inverse or pointer (PTR) query. To handle a pointer query, the inverse domain is added to the domain name space with the first-level node called *arpa* (for historical reasons). The second level is also one single node named *in-addr* (for inverse address). The rest of the domain defines IP addresses.

The servers that handle the inverse domain are also hierarchical. This means the netid part of the address should be at a higher level than the subnetid part, and the subnetid part higher than the hostid part. In this way, a server serving the whole site is at a higher level than the servers serving each subnet. This configuration makes the domain look inverted when compared to a generic or country domain. To follow the convention of reading the domain labels from the bottom to the top, an IP address such as 132.34.45.121 (a class B address with netid 132.34) is read as 121.45.34.132.in-addr. arpa. See Figure 17.10 for an illustration of the inverse domain configuration.

Figure 17.10 *Inverse domain*

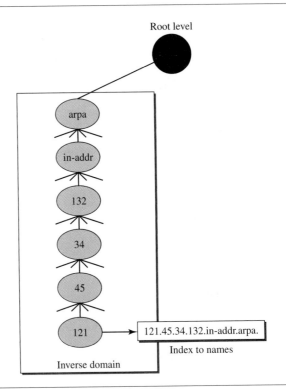

Registrar

How are the new domains added to DNS? This is done through a **registrar,** a commercial entity accredited by ICANN. A registrar first verifies that the requested domain name is unique and then enters it into the DNS database. A fee is charged.

17.5 RESOLUTION

Mapping a name to an address or an address to a name is called *name-address resolution.*

Resolver

DNS is designed as a client-server application. A host that needs to map an address to a name or a name to an address calls a DNS client called a **resolver.** The resolver accesses the closest DNS server with a mapping request. If the server has the information, it satisfies the resolver; otherwise, it either refers the resolver to other servers or asks other servers to provide the information.

After the resolver receives the mapping, it interprets the response to see if it is a real resolution or an error, and finally delivers the result to the process that requested it.

Mapping Names to Addresses

Most of the time, the resolver gives a domain name to the server and asks for the corresponding address. In this case, the server checks the generic domains or the country domains to find the mapping.

If the domain name is from the generic domains section, the resolver receives a domain name such as "*chal.atc.fhda.edu.*". The query is sent by the resolver to the local DNS server for resolution. If the local server cannot resolve the query, it either refers the resolver to other servers or asks other servers directly.

If the domain name is from the country domains section, the resolver receives a domain name such as "*ch.fhda.cu.ca.us.*". The procedure is the same.

Mapping Addresses to Names

A client can send an IP address to a server to be mapped to a domain name. As mentioned before, this is called a PTR query. To answer queries of this kind, DNS uses the inverse domain. However, in the request, the IP address is reversed and two labels, *in-addr* and *arpa,* are appended to create a domain acceptable by the inverse domain section. For example, if the resolver receives the IP address 132.34.45.121, the resolver first inverts the address and then adds the two labels before sending. The domain name sent is "*121.45.34.132.in-addr.arpa.*", which is received by the local DNS and resolved.

Recursive Resolution

The client (resolver) can ask for a recursive answer from a name server. This means that the resolver expects the server to supply the final answer. If the server is the authority for the domain name, it checks its database and responds. If the server is not the authority, it sends the request to another server (the parent usually) and waits for the response. If the parent is the authority, it responds; otherwise, it sends the query to yet another server. When the query is finally resolved, the response travels back until it finally reaches the requesting client. This is shown in Figure 17.11.

Figure 17.11   *Recursive resolution*

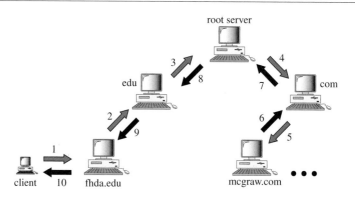

Iterative Resolution

If the client does not ask for a recursive answer, the mapping can be done iteratively. If the server is an authority for the name, it sends the answer. If it is not, it returns (to the client) the IP address of the server that it thinks can resolve the query. The client is responsible for repeating the query to this second server. If the newly addressed server can resolve the problem, it answers the query with the IP address; otherwise, it returns the IP address of a new server to the client. Now the client must repeat the query to the third server. This process is called *iterative* because the client repeats the same query to multiple servers. In Figure 17.12 the client queries four servers before it gets an answer from the mcgraw.com server.

Caching

Each time a server receives a query for a name that is not in its domain, it needs to search its database for a server IP address. Reduction of this search time would increase efficiency. DNS handles this with a mechanism called **caching.** When a server asks for a mapping from another server and receives the response, it stores this information in its cache memory before sending it to the client. If the same or another client asks for the same mapping, it can check its cache memory and resolve the problem. However, to inform the client that the response is coming from the cache memory and not from an authoritative source, the server marks the response as *unauthoritative.*

Caching speeds up resolution, but it can also be problematic. If a server caches a mapping for a long time, it may send an outdated mapping to the client. To counter this,

Figure 17.12 *Iterative resolution*

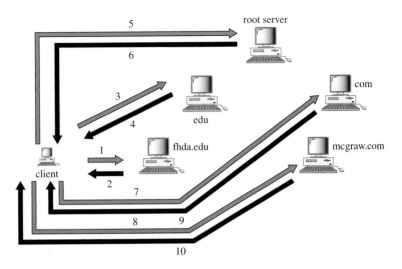

two techniques are used. First, the authoritative server always adds information to the mapping called *time-to-live* (TTL). It defines the time in seconds that the receiving server can cache the information. After that time, the mapping is invalid and any query must be sent again to the authoritative server. Second, DNS requires that each server keep a TTL counter for each mapping it caches. The cache memory must be searched periodically and those mappings with an expired TTL must be purged.

17.6   DNS MESSAGES

DNS has two types of messages: query and response (see Figure 17.13). Both types have the same format. The query message consists of a header and question records; the response message consists of a header, question records, answer records, authoritative records, and additional records (see Figure 17.14).

Figure 17.13 *DNS messages*

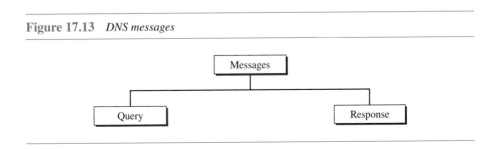

Figure 17.14   *Query and response messages*

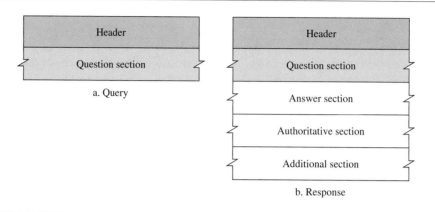

Header

Both query and response messages have the same header format with some fields set to zero for the query messages. The header is 12 bytes and its format is shown in Figure 17.15.

Figure 17.15   *Header format*

Identification	Flags
Number of question records	Number of answer records (All 0s in query message)
Number of authoritative records (All 0s in query message)	Number of additional records (All 0s in query message)

The header fields are as follows:

❏ **Identification.** This is a 16-bit field used by the client to match the response with the query. The client uses a different identification number each time it sends a query. The server duplicates this number in the corresponding response.

❏ **Flags.** This is a 16-bit field consisting of the subfields shown in Figure 17.16.

Figure 17.16   *Flags field*

QR		OpCode		AA	TC	RD	RA	Three 0s		rCode	

A brief description of each flag subfield follows.

a. **QR (query/response).** This is a 1-bit subfield that defines the type of message. If it is 0, the message is a query. If it is 1, the message is a response.

b. **OpCode.** This is a 4-bit subfield that defines the type of query or response (0 if standard, 1 if inverse, and 2 if a server status request).

c. **AA (authoritative answer).** This is a 1-bit subfield. When it is set (value of 1) it means that the name server is an authoritative server. It is used only in a response message.

d. **TC (truncated).** This is a 1-bit subfield. When it is set (value of 1), it means that the response was more than 512 bytes and truncated to 512. It is used when DNS uses the services of UDP (see Section 17.10 on Encapsulation).

e. **RD (recursion desired).** This is a 1-bit subfield. When it is set (value of 1) it means the client desires a recursive answer. It is set in the query message and repeated in the response message.

f. **RA (recursion available).** This is a 1-bit subfield. When it is set in the response, it means that a recursive response is available. It is set only in the response message.

g. **Reserved.** This is a 3-bit subfield set to 000.

h. **rCode.** This is a 4-bit field that shows the status of the error in the response. Of course, only an authoritative server can make such a judgment. Table 17.2 shows the possible values for this field.

Table 17.2   *Values of rCode*

Value	Meaning
0	No error
1	Format error
2	Problem at name server
3	Domain reference problem
4	Query type not supported
5	Administratively prohibited
6–15	Reserved

❏ **Number of question records.** This is a 16-bit field containing the number of queries in the question section of the message.

❏ **Number of answer records.** This is a 16-bit field containing the number of answer records in the answer section of the response message. Its value is zero in the query message.

❏ **Number of authoritative records.** This is a 16-bit field containing the number of authoritative records in the authoritative section of a response message. Its value is zero in the query message.

❏ **Number of additional records.** This is a 16-bit field containing the number of additional records in the additional section of a response message. Its value is zero in the query message.

Question Section

This is a section consisting of one or more question records. It is present on both query and response messages. We will discuss the question records in a following section.

Answer Section

This is a section consisting of one or more resource records. It is present only on response messages. This section includes the answer from the server to the client (resolver). We will discuss resource records in a following section.

Authoritative Section

This is a section consisting of one or more resource records. It is present only on response messages. This section gives information (domain name) about one or more authoritative servers for the query.

Additional Information Section

This is a section consisting of one or more resource records. It is present only on response messages. This section provides additional information that may help the resolver. For example, a server may give the domain name of an authoritative server to the resolver in the authoritative section, and include the IP address of the same authoritative server in the additional information section.

17.7   TYPES OF RECORDS

As we saw in the previous section, two types of records are used in DNS. The question records are used in the question section of the query and response messages. The resource records are used in the answer, authoritative, and additional information sections of the response message.

Question Record

A **question record** is used by the client to get information from a server. This contains the domain name. Figure 17.17 shows the format of a question record. The list below describes question record fields.

Figure 17.17   *Question record format*

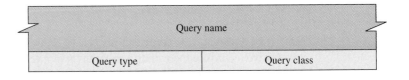

❑   **Query name.** This is a variable-length field containing a domain name (see Figure 17.18).

Figure 17.18 *Query name format*

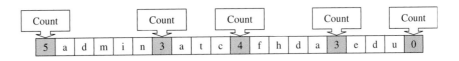

- ❏ **Query type.** This is a 16-bit field defining the type of query. Table 17.3 shows some of the types commonly used. The last two can only be used in a query.

Table 17.3 *Types*

Type	Mnemonic	Description
1	A	Address. A 32-bit IPv4 address. It is used to convert a domain name to an IPv4 address.
2	NS	Name server. It identifies the authoritative servers for a zone.
5	CNAME	Canonical name. It defines an alias for the official name of a host.
6	SOA	Start of authority. It marks the beginning of a zone. It is usually the first record in a zone file.
11	WKS	Well-known services. It defines the network services that a host provides.
12	PTR	Pointer. It is used to convert an IP address to a domain name.
13	HINFO	Host information. It gives the description of the hardware and the operating system used by a host.
15	MX	Mail exchange. It redirects mail to a mail server.
28	AAAA	Address. An IPv6 address (see Chapter 27).
252	AXFR	A request for the transfer of the entire zone.
255	ANY	A request for all records.

- ❏ **Query class.** This is a 16-bit field defining the specific protocol using DNS. Table 17.4 shows the current values. In this text we are interested only in class 1 (the Internet).

Table 17.4 *Classes*

Class	Mnemonic	Description
1	IN	Internet
2	CSNET	CSNET network (obsolete)
3	CS	The COAS network
4	HS	The Hesiod server developed by MIT

Resource Record

Each domain name (each node on the tree) is associated with a record called the **resource record.** The server database consists of resource records. Resource records are also what is returned by the server to the client. Figure 17.19 shows the format of a resource record.

Figure 17.19   *Resource record format*

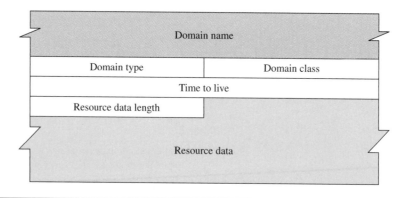

❏ **Domain name.** This is a variable-length field containing the domain name. It is a duplication of the domain name in the question record. Since DNS requires the use of compression everywhere a name is repeated, this field is a pointer offset to the corresponding domain name field in the question record. See Section 17.8 on Compression.

❏ **Domain type.** This field is the same as the query type field in the question record except the last two types are not allowed. Refer to Table 17.3 for more information.

❏ **Domain class.** This field is the same as the query class field in the question record (see Table 17.4).

❏ **Time to live.** This is a 32-bit field that defines the number of seconds the answer is valid. The receiver can cache the answer for this period of time. A zero value means that the resource record is used only in a single transaction and is not cached.

❏ **Resource data length.** This is a 16-bit field defining the length of the resource data.

❏ **Resource data.** This is a variable-length field containing the answer to the query (in the answer section) or the domain name of the authoritative server (in the authoritative section) or additional information (in the additional information section). The format and contents of this field depend on the value of the type field. It can be one of the following:

    a. **A number.** This is written in octets. For example, an IPv4 address is a 4-octet integer and an IPv6 address is a 16-octet integer.

b. **A domain name.** Domain names are expressed as a sequence of labels. Each label is preceded by a 1-byte length field that defines the number of characters in the label. Since every domain name ends with the null label, the last byte of every domain name is the length field with the value of 0. To distinguish between a length field and an offset pointer (as we will discuss later), the two high-order bits of a length field are always zero (00). This will not create a problem because the length of a label cannot be more than 63, which is a maximum of 6 bits (111111).

c. **An offset pointer.** Domain names can be replaced with an offset pointer. An offset pointer is a 2-byte field with each of the 2 high-order bits set to 1 (11).

d. **A character string.** A character string is represented by a 1-byte length field followed by the number of characters defined in the length field. The length field is not restricted like the domain name length field. The character string can be as long as 255 characters (including the length field).

17.8   COMPRESSION

DNS requires that a domain name be replaced by an offset pointer if it is repeated. For example, in a resource record the domain name is usually a repetition of the domain name in the question record. For efficiency, DNS defines a 2-byte offset pointer that points to a previous occurrence of the domain or part of it. The format of the field is shown in Figure 17.20.

Figure 17.20   *Format of an offset pointer*

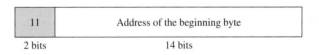

The first 2 high-order bits are two 1s to distinguish an offset pointer from a length field. The other 14 bits represent a number that points to the corresponding byte number in the message. The bytes in a message are counted from the beginning of the message with the first byte counted as byte 0. For example, if an offset pointer refers to byte 12 (the thirteenth byte) of the message, the value should be 1100000000001100. Here the 2 leftmost bits define the field as an offset pointer and the other bits define the decimal number 12. We will show the use of the offset pointers in the following examples.

Example 1

A resolver sends a query message to a local server to find the IP address for the host "*chal. fhda.edu.*". We discuss the query and response messages separately.

Figure 17.21 shows the query message sent by the resolver. The first 2 bytes show the identifier (1333). It is used as a sequence number and relates a response to a query. Because a resolver may even send many queries to the same server, the identifier helps to sort responses that arrive out of order. The next bytes contain the flags with the value of 0x0100 in hexadecimal. In binary it is 0000000100000000, but it is more meaningful to divide it into the fields as shown below:

QR	OpCode	AA	TC	RD	RA	Reserved	rCode
0	0000	0	0	1	0	000	0000

Figure 17.21   *Example 1: Query message*

0x1333		0x0100	
1		0	
0		0	
4	'c'	'h'	'a'
'l'	4	'f'	'h'
'd'	'a'	3	'e'
'd'	'u'	0	Continued on next line
1		1	

The QR bit defines the message as a query. The OpCode is 0000, which defines a standard query. The recursion desired (RD) bit is set. (Refer back to Figure 17.16 for the flags field descriptions.) The message contains only one question record. The domain name is *4chal4fhda3edu0*. The next 2 bytes define the query type as an IP address; the last 2 bytes define the class as the Internet.

Figure 17.22 shows the response of the server. The response is similar to the query except that the flags are different and the number of answer records is one. The flags value is 0x8180 in hexadecimal. In binary it is 1000000110000000, but again we divide it into fields as shown below:

QR	OpCode	AA	TC	RD	RA	Reserved	rCode
1	0000	0	0	1	1	000	0000

The QR bit defines the message as a response. The OpCode is 0000, which defines a standard response. The recursion available (RA) and RD bits are set. The message contains one question record and one answer record. The question record is repeated from the query message. The answer record has a value of 0xC00C (split in two lines), which points to the question record instead of repeating the domain name. The next field defines the domain type (address). The field after that defines the class (Internet). The field with the value 12,000 is the TTL (12,000 s). The next field is the length of the resource data, which is an IP address (153.18.8.105).

Figure 17.22   *Example 1: Response message*

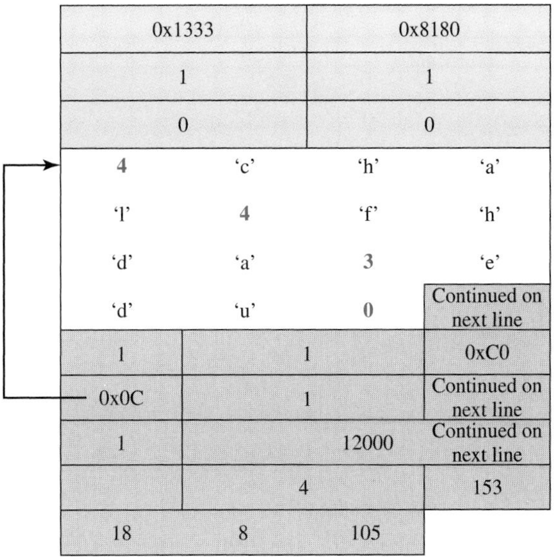

0x1333		0x8180	
1		1	
0		0	
4	'c'	'h'	'a'
'l'	4	'f'	'h'
'd'	'a'	3	'e'
'd'	'u'	0	Continued on next line
1		1	0xC0
0x0C		1	Continued on next line
1		12000	Continued on next line
		4	153
18	8	105	

Example 2

An FTP server has received a packet from an FTP client with IP address 153.2.7.9. The FTP server wants to verify that the FTP client is an authorized client. The FTP server can consult a file containing the list of authorized clients. However, the file consists only of domain names. The FTP server has only the IP address of the requesting client, which was the source IP address in the received IP datagram. The FTP server asks the resolver (DNS client) to send an inverse query to a DNS server to ask for the name of the FTP client. We discuss the query and response messages separately.

Figure 17.23 shows the query message sent from the resolver to the server. The first 2 bytes show the identifier (0x1200). The flags value is 0x0900 in hexadecimal. In binary it is 0000100100000000, and we divide it into fields as shown below:

QR	OpCode	AA	TC	RD	RA	Reserved	rCode
0	0001	0	0	1	0	000	0000

The OpCode is 0001, which defines an inverse query. The message contains only one question record. The domain name is *19171231537in-addr4arpa*. The next 2 bytes define the query type as PTR, and the last 2 bytes define the class as the Internet.

Figure 17.24 shows the response. The flags value is 0x8D80 in hexadecimal. In binary it is 1000110110000000, and we divide it into fields as shown below:

QR	OpCode	AA	TC	RD	RA	Reserved	rCode
1	0001	1	0	1	1	000	0000

Figure 17.23   *Example 2: Inverse query message*

0x1200		0x0900	
1		0	
0		0	
1	'9'	1	'7'
1	'2'	3	'l'
'5'	'3'	7	'i'
'n'	'-'	'a'	'd'
'd'	'r'	4	'a'
'r'	'p'	'a'	0
12		1	

Figure 17.24   *Example 2: Inverse response message*

0x1200		0x8D80	
1		1	
0		0	
1	'9'	1	'7'
1	'2'	3	'l'
'5'	'3'	7	'i'
'n'	'-'	'a'	'd'
'd'	'r'	4	'a'
'r'	'p'	'a'	0
12		1	
0xC00C		12	
1		Continued on next line	
24000		10	
4	'm'	'h'	'h'
'e'	3	'c'	'o'
'm'	0		

The message contains one question record and one answer record. The question record is repeated from the query message. The answer record has a value of 0xC00C, which points to the question record instead of repeating the domain name. The next field defines the domain type (PTR). The field after that defines the class (Internet), and the field after that defines the TTL (24,000 s). The next field is the length of the resource data (10). The last field is the domain name *4mhhe3com0,* which means "mhhe.com.".

Example 3

In UNIX and Windows, the *nslookup* utility can be used to retrieve address/name mapping. The following shows how we can retrieve an address when the domain name is given.

```
$ nslookup  fhda.edu
Name:  fhda.edu
Address: 153.18.8.1
```

The *nslookup* utility can also be used to retrieve the domain name when the address is given as shown below:

```
$ nslookup 153.18.8.1
1.8.18.153.in-addr.arpa name = tiptoe.fhda.edu.
```

17.9   DDNS

When the DNS was designed, no one predicted that there would be so many address changes. In DNS, when there is a change, such as adding a new host, removing a host, or changing an IP address, the change must be made to the DNS master file. These types of changes involve a lot of manual updating. The size of today's Internet does not allow for this kind of manual operation.

The DNS master file must be updated dynamically. The **Dynamic Domain Name System (DDNS)** therefore was devised to respond to this need. In DDNS, when a binding between a name and an address is determined, the information is sent, usually by DHCP (see Chapter 16) to a primary DNS server. The primary server updates the zone. The secondary servers are notified either actively or passively. In active notification, the primary server sends a message to the secondary servers about the change in the zone, whereas in passive notification, the secondary servers periodically check for any changes. In either case, after being notified about the change, the secondary requests information about the entire zone (zone transfer).

To provide security and prevent unauthorized changes in the DNS records, DDNS can use an authentication mechanism.

17.10   ENCAPSULATION

DNS can use either UDP or TCP. In both cases the well-known port used by the server is port 53. UDP is used when the size of the response message is less than 512 bytes because most UDP packages have a 512-byte packet size limit. If the size of the response message is more than 512 bytes, a TCP connection is used. In that case, one of two scenarios can occur:

❏   If the resolver has prior knowledge that the size of the response message is more than 512 bytes, it uses the TCP connection. For example, if a secondary name server (acting as a client) needs a zone transfer from a primary server, it uses the TCP connection because the size of the information being transferred usually exceeds 512 bytes.

❏   If the resolver does not know the size of the response message, it can use the UDP port. However, if the size of the response message is more than 512 bytes, the server truncates the message and turns on the TC bit. The resolver now opens a TCP connection and repeats the request to get a full response from the server.

DNS can use the services of UDP or TCP using the well-known port 53.

17.11   KEY TERMS

caching	name space
compression	name-address resolution
country domain	partially qualified domain name (PQDN)
DNS server	primary server
domain	query message
domain name	question record
domain name space	recursive resolution
Domain Name System (DNS)	registrar
Dynamic Domain Name System (DDNS)	resolver
flat name space	resource record
fully qualified domain name (FQDN)	response message
generic domain	root label
hierarchical name space	root server
host file	secondary server
inverse domain	subdomain
iterative resolution	suffix
label	zone

17.12   SUMMARY

❑ The Domain Name System (DNS) is a client-server application that identifies each host on the Internet with a unique user-friendly name.

❑ DNS organizes the name space in a hierarchical structure to decentralize the responsibilities involved in naming.

❑ DNS can be pictured as an inverted hierarchical tree structure with one root node at the top and a maximum of 128 levels.

❑ Each node in the tree has a domain name.

❑ A domain is defined as any subtree of the domain name space.

❑ The name space information is distributed among DNS servers. Each server has jurisdiction over its zone.

❑ A root server's zone is the entire DNS tree.

❑ A primary server creates, maintains, and updates information about its zone.

❑ A secondary server gets its information from a primary server.

❑ The domain name space is divided into three sections: generic domains, country domains, and inverse domain.

❑ There are fourteen generic domains, each specifying an organization type.

❑ Each country domain specifies a country.

❑ The inverse domain finds a domain name for a given IP address. This is called address-to-name resolution.

❑ Name servers, computers that run the DNS server program, are organized in a hierarchy.

❑ The DNS client, called a resolver, maps a name to an address or an address to a name.

❑ In recursive resolution, the client sends its request to a server that eventually returns a response.

❑ In iterative resolution, the client may send its request to multiple servers before getting an answer.

❑ Caching is a method whereby an answer to a query is stored in memory (for a limited time) for easy access to future requests.

❑ A fully qualified domain name (FQDN) is a domain name consisting of labels beginning with the host and going back through each level to the root node.

❑ A partially qualified domain name (PQDN) is a domain name that does not include all the levels between the host and the root node.

❑ There are two types of DNS messages: queries and responses.

❑ There are two types of DNS records: question records and resource records.

❑ DNS uses an offset pointer for duplicated domain name information in its messages.

❑ Dynamic DNS (DDNS) automatically updates the DNS master file.

❑ DNS uses the services of UDP for messages of less than 512 bytes; otherwise, TCP is used.

17.13   PRACTICE SET

Exercises

1. Determine which of the following is an FQDN and which is a PQDN:
   a. xxx
   b. xxx.yyy.
   c. xxx.yyy.net
   d. zzz.yyy.xxx.edu.

2. Determine which of the following is an FQDN and which is a PQDN:
   a. mil.
   b. edu.
   c. xxx.yyy.net
   d. zzz.yyy.xxx.edu

3. Find the value of the flags field (in hexadecimal) for a query message requesting an address and demanding a recursive answer.

4. Find the value of the flags field (in hexadecimal) for an unauthoritative message carrying an inverse response. The resolver had asked for a recursive response, but the recursive answer was not available.

5. Analyze the flag 0x8F80.

6. Analyze the flag 0x0503. Is it valid?

7. Is the size of a question record fixed?

8. Is the size of a resource record fixed?

9. What is the size of a question record containing the domain name fhda.edu?

10. What is the size of a question record containing an IP address?

11. What is the size of a resource record containing the domain name fhda.edu?

12. What is the size of a resource record containing an IP address?

13. What is the size of a query message requesting the IP address for challenger. atc.fhda.edu?

14. What is the size of a query message requesting the domain name for 185.34.23.12?

15. What is the size of the response message responding to the query message in Exercise 13?

16. What is the size of the response message responding to the query message in Exercise 14?

17. Redo Example 1 using a response message with one answer record and one authoritative record which defines "fhda.edu." as the authoritative server.

18. Redo Exercise 17, but add one additional record that defines the address of the authoritative server as 153.18.9.0.

19. A DNS client is looking for the IP address of xxx.yyy.com. Show the query message with values for each field.

20. Show the response message of a DNS server to Exercise 19. Assume the IP address is 201.34.23.12.

21. A DNS client is looking for the IP addresses corresponding to xxx.yyy.com and aaa.bbb.edu. Show the query message.

22. Show the response message of a DNS server to the query in Exercise 21 if the addresses are 14.23.45.12 and 131.34.67.89.

23. Show the response message of Exercise 22 if the DNS server can resolve the first enquiry but not the second.

24. A DNS client is looking for the name of the computer with IP address 132.1.17.8. Show the query message.

25. Show the response message sent by the server to the query in Exercise 24.

26. Encapsulate the query message of Exercise 19 in a UDP user datagram.

27. Encapsulate the response message of Exercise 20 in a UDP user datagram.

Research Activities

28. Compare and contrast the DNS structure with the UNIX directory structure.

29. What is the equivalent of dots in the DNS structure for the UNIX directory structure?

30. A DNS domain name starts with a node and goes up to the root of the tree. Do the pathnames in UNIX do the same?

31. Can we say that the FQDNs in DNS are the same as absolute pathnames in UNIX and PQDNs are the same as relative pathnames in UNIX?

32. Find the RFCs related to DNS.

33. Find how to use the *nslookup* utility in Windows.

34. Find all the options of the *nslookup* utility.

35. Try the *nslookup* utility on some domain name you are familiar with.

36. Use the *nslookup* utility to find the address of some commercial web servers.

CHAPTER 18

Remote Login: TELNET

The main task of the Internet and its TCP/IP protocol suite is to provide services for users. For example, users may want to run application programs at a remote site and create results that can be transferred to their local site. One way to satisfy that demand and others is to create a client-server application program for each desired service. Programs such as file transfer programs (FTP and TFTP), email (SMTP), and so on are currently available. However, it would be impossible to write a specific client-server program for each demand.

The better solution is a general-purpose client-server program that lets a user access any application program on a remote computer; in other words, allow the user to log on to a remote computer. After logging on, a user can use the services available on the remote computer and transfer the results back to the local computer.

In this chapter, we discuss such a client-server application program: TELNET. **TELNET** is an abbreviation for *TErminaL NETwork*. It is the standard TCP/IP protocol for virtual terminal service as proposed by ISO. TELNET enables the establishment of a connection to a remote system in such a way that the local terminal appears to be a terminal at the remote system.

> **TELNET is a general-purpose client-server application program.**

18.1   CONCEPT

TELNET is related to several concepts that we briefly describe here.

Time-Sharing Environment

TELNET was designed at a time when most operating systems, such as UNIX, were operating in a **time-sharing** environment. In such an environment, a large computer supports multiple users. The interaction between a user and the computer occurs through a terminal, which is usually a combination of keyboard, monitor, and mouse. Even a microcomputer can simulate a terminal with a terminal emulator.

In a time-sharing environment, all of the processing must be done by the central computer. When a user types a character on the keyboard, the character is usually sent to the computer and echoed to the monitor. Time-sharing creates an environment in which each user has the illusion of a dedicated computer. The user can run a program, access the system resources, switch from one program to another, and so on.

Login

In a time-sharing environment, users are part of the system with some right to access resources. Each authorized user has an identification and probably a password. The user identification defines the user as part of the system. To access the system, the user logs into the system with a user id or login name. The system also includes password checking to prevent an unauthorized user from accessing the resources.

Local Login

When a user logs into a local time-sharing system, it is called **local login.** As a user types at a terminal or at a workstation running a terminal emulator, the keystrokes are accepted by the terminal driver. The terminal driver passes the characters to the operating system. The operating system, in turn, interprets the combination of characters and invokes the desired application program or utility (see Figure 18.1).

Figure 18.1   *Local login*

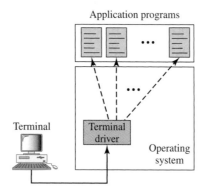

The mechanism, however, is not as simple as it seems because the operating system may assign special meanings to special characters. For example, in UNIX some combinations of characters have special meanings, such as the combination of the control character with the character "z," which means suspend; the combination of the control character with the character "c," which means abort; and so on. Whereas these special situations do not create any problem in local login because the terminal emulator and the terminal driver know the exact meaning of each character or combination of characters, they may create problems in remote login. Which process should interpret special characters? The client or the server? We will clarify this situation later in the chapter.

Remote Login

When a user wants to access an application program or utility located on a remote machine, he or she performs **remote login.** Here the TELNET client and server programs come into use. The user sends the keystrokes to the terminal driver where the local operating system accepts the characters but does not interpret them. The characters are sent to the TELNET client, which transforms the characters to a universal character set called *Network Virtual Terminal characters* and delivers them to the local TCP/IP stack (see Figure 18.2).

Figure 18.2   *Remote login*

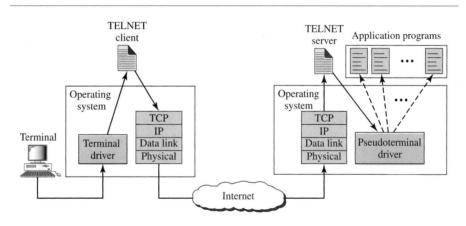

The commands or text, in NVT form, travel through the Internet and arrive at the TCP/IP stack at the remote machine. Here the characters are delivered to the operating system and passed to the TELNET server, which changes the characters to the corresponding characters understandable by the remote computer. However, the characters cannot be passed directly to the operating system because the remote operating system is not designed to receive characters from a TELNET server: It is designed to receive characters from a terminal driver. The solution is to add a piece of software called a *pseudoterminal driver* which pretends that the characters are coming from a terminal. The operating system then passes the characters to the appropriate application program.

18.2   NETWORK VIRTUAL TERMINAL (NVT)

The mechanism to access a remote computer is complex. This is because every computer and its operating system accepts a special combination of characters as tokens. For example, the end-of-file token in a computer running the DOS operating system is Ctrl+z, while the UNIX operating system recognizes Ctrl+d.

We are dealing with heterogeneous systems. If we want to access any remote computer in the world, we must first know what type of computer we will be connected to, and we must also install the specific terminal emulator used by that computer. TELNET solves this problem by defining a universal interface called the **Network Virtual Terminal (NVT)** character set. Via this interface, the client TELNET translates characters (data or commands) that come from the local terminal into NVT form and delivers them to the network. The server TELNET, on the other hand, translates data and commands from NVT form into the form acceptable by the remote computer. For an illustration of this concept, see Figure 18.3.

Figure 18.3   *Concept of NVT*

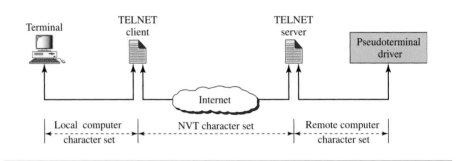

18.3   NVT CHARACTER SET

NVT uses two sets of characters, one for data and one for control. Both are 8-bit bytes.

Data Characters

For data, NVT normally uses what is called NVT ASCII. This is an 8-bit character set in which the seven lowest order bits are the same as US ASCII and the highest order bit is 0 (see Figure 18.4). Although it is possible to send an 8-bit ASCII (with the highest order bit set to be 0 or 1), this must first be agreed upon between the client and the server using option negotiation.

Figure 18.4   *Format of data characters*

Control Characters

To send **control characters** between computers (from client to server or vice versa), NVT uses an 8-bit character set in which the highest order bit is set (see Figure 18.5).

Figure 18.5   *Format of control characters*

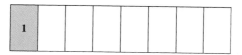

Table 18.1 lists some of the control characters and their meanings. Later we will categorize these control characters on the basis of their functionalities.

Table 18.1   *Some NVT control characters*

Character	Decimal	Binary	Meaning
EOF	236	11101100	End of file
EOR	239	11101111	End of record
SE	240	11110000	Suboption end
NOP	241	11110001	No operation
DM	242	11110010	Data mark
BRK	243	11110011	Break
IP	244	11110100	Interrupt process
AO	245	11110101	Abort output
AYT	246	11110110	Are you there?
EC	247	11110111	Erase character
EL	248	11111000	Erase line
GA	249	11111001	Go ahead
SB	250	11111010	Suboption begin
WILL	251	11111011	Agreement to enable option
WONT	252	11111100	Refusal to enable option
DO	253	11111101	Approval to option request
DONT	254	11111110	Denial of option request
IAC	255	11111111	Interpret (the next character) as control

18.4   EMBEDDING

TELNET uses only one TCP connection. The server uses the well-known port 23 and the client uses an ephemeral port. The same connection is used for sending both data and control characters. TELNET accomplishes this by embedding the control characters in the data stream. However, to distinguish data from control characters, each sequence of control characters is preceded by a special control character called *interpret as control* (IAC).

For example, imagine a user wants a server to display a file (*file1*) on a remote server. She can type:

> *cat file1*

However, the name of the file has been mistyped (*filea* instead of *file1*). The user uses the backspace key to correct this situation.

> *cat filea<backspace>1*

However, in the default implementation of TELNET, the user cannot edit locally; the editing is done at the remote server. The backspace character is translated into two remote characters (IAC EC), which is embedded in the data and sent to the remote server. What is sent to the server is shown in Figure 18.6.

Figure 18.6   *An example of embedding*

18.5   OPTIONS

TELNET lets the client and server negotiate options before or during the use of the service. Options are extra features available to a user with a more sophisticated terminal. Users with simpler terminals can use default features. Some control characters discussed previously are used to define options. Table 18.2 shows some common options.

Table 18.2   *Options*

Code	Option	Meaning
0	Binary	Interpret as 8-bit binary transmission
1	Echo	Echo the data received on one side to the other
3	Suppress go ahead	Suppress go-ahead signals after data
5	Status	Request the status of TELNET
6	Timing mark	Define the timing marks
24	Terminal type	Set the terminal type
32	Terminal speed	Set the terminal speed
34	Line mode	Change to line mode

The option descriptions are as follows:

❏ **Binary.** This option allows the receiver to interpret every 8-bit character received, except IAC, as binary data. When IAC is received, the next character or characters are interpreted as commands. However, if two consecutive IAC characters are received, the first is discarded and the second is interpreted as data.

❏ **Echo.** This option allows the server to echo data received from the client. This means that every character sent by the client to the sender will be echoed back to the screen of the client terminal. In this case, the user terminal usually does not echo characters when they are typed but waits until it receives them from the server.

❏ **Suppress go-ahead.** This option suppresses the go-ahead (GA) character (see section on TELNET modes).

❏ **Status.** This option allows the user or the process running on the client machine to get the status of the options being enabled at the server site.

❏ **Timing mark.** This option allows one party to issue a timing mark that indicates all previously received data has been processed.

❏ **Terminal type.** This option allows the client to send its terminal type.

❏ **Terminal speed.** This option allows the client to send its terminal speed.

❏ **Line mode.** This option allows the client to switch to the line mode. We will discuss the line mode later.

18.6   OPTION NEGOTIATION

To use any of the options mentioned in the previous section first requires **option negotiation** between the client and the server. Four control characters are used for this purpose; these are shown in Table 18.3.

Table 18.3   *NVT character set for option negotiation*

Character	*Decimal*	*Binary*	*Meaning*
WILL	251	11111011	1. Offering to enable 2. Accepting a request to enable
WONT	252	11111100	1. Rejecting a request to enable 2. Offering to disable 3. Accepting a request to disable
DO	253	11111101	1. Approving an offer to enable 2. Requesting to enable
DONT	254	11111110	1. Disapproving an offer to enable 2. Approving an offer to disable 3. Requesting to disable

Enabling an Option

Some options can only be enabled by the server, some only by the client, and some by both. An option is enabled either through an *offer* or a *request*.

Offer to Enable

A party can offer to enable an option if it has the right to do so. The offering can be approved or disapproved by the other party. The offering party sends the *WILL* command, which means "Will I enable the option?" The other party sends either the *DO* command, which means "Please Do," or the *DONT* command, which means "Please Don't." See Figure 18.7.

Figure 18.7   *Offer to enable an option*

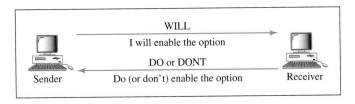

Request to Enable

A party can request from the other party the enabling of an option. The request can be accepted or refused by the other party. The requesting party sends the *DO* command, which means "Please do enable the option." The other party sends either the *WILL* command, which means "I will," or the *WONT* command, which means "I won't." See Figure 18.8.

Figure 18.8   *Request to enable an option*

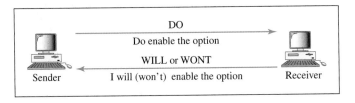

Disabling an Option

An option that has been enabled can be disabled by one of the parties. An option is disabled either through an *offer* or a *request*.

Offer to Disable

A party can offer to disable an option. The other party must approve the offering; it cannot be disapproved. The offering party sends the *WONT* command, which means "I won't use this option any more." The answer must be the *DONT* command, which means "Don't use it anymore." Figure 18.9 shows an offer to disable an option.

Figure 18.9   *Offer to disable an option*

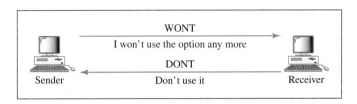

Request to Disable

A party can request from another party the disabling of an option. The other party must accept the request; it cannot be rejected. The requesting party sends the *DONT* command, which means "Please don't use this option anymore." The answer must be the *WONT* command, which means "I won't use it anymore." Figure 18.10 shows a request to disable an option.

Figure 18.10   *Request to disable an option*

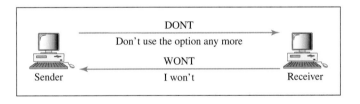

Example 1

Figure 18.11 shows an example of option negotiation. In this example, the client wants the server to echo each character sent to the server. In other words, when a character is typed at the user keyboard terminal, it goes to the server and is sent back to the screen of the user before being processed. The echo option is enabled by the server because it is the server that sends the

Figure 18.11   *Example 1: Echo option*

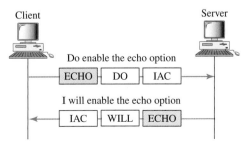

characters back to the user terminal. Therefore, the client should *request* from the server the enabling of the option using DO. The request consists of three characters: IAC, DO, and ECHO. The server accepts the request and enables the option. It informs the client by sending the three-character approval: IAC, WILL, and ECHO.

Symmetry

One interesting feature of TELNET is its symmetric option negotiation in which the client and server are given equal opportunity. This means that, at the beginning of connection, it is assumed that both sides are using a default TELNET implementation with no options enabled. If one party wants an option enabled, it can offer or request. The other party has the right to approve the offer or reject the request if the party is not capable of using the option or does not want to use the option. This allows for the expansion of TELNET. A client or server can install a more sophisticated version of TELNET with more options. When it is connected to a party, it can offer or request these new options. If the other party also supports these options, the options can be enabled; otherwise, they are rejected.

18.7 SUBOPTION NEGOTIATION

Some options require additional information. For example, to define the type or speed of a terminal, the negotiation includes a string or a number to define the type or speed. In either case, the two suboption characters indicated in Table 18.4 are needed for **suboption negotiation.**

Table 18.4 *NVT character set for suboption negotiation*

Character	Decimal	Binary	Meaning
SE	240	11110000	Suboption end
SB	250	11111010	Suboption begin

For example, the type of the terminal is set by the client, as is shown in Figure 18.12.

Figure 18.12 *Example of suboption negotiation*

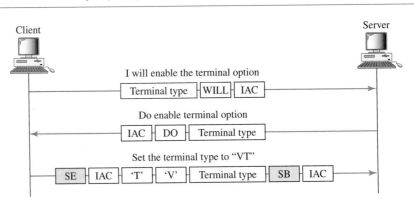

18.8   CONTROLLING THE SERVER

Some control characters can be used to control the remote server. When an application program is running on the local computer, special characters are used to interrupt (abort) the program (for example, Ctrl+c), or erase the last character typed (for example, delete key or backspace key), and so on. However, when a program is running on a remote computer, these control characters are sent to the remote machine. The user still types the same sequences, but they are changed to special characters and sent to the server. Table 18.5 shows some of the characters that can be sent to the server to control the application program that is running there.

Table 18.5   *Characters used to control the application program running on remote server*

Character	Decimal	Binary	Meaning
IP	244	11110100	Interrupt process
AO	245	11110101	Abort output
AYT	246	11110110	Are you there?
EC	247	11110111	Erase the last character
EL	248	11111000	Erase line

Let's look at these characters in more detail:

❏ **IP (interrupt process).** When a program is being run locally, the user can interrupt (abort) the program if, for example, the program has gone into an infinite loop. The user can type the Ctrl+c combination, the operating system calls a function, and the function aborts the program. However, if the program is running on a remote machine, the appropriate function should be called by the operating system of the remote machine. TELNET defines the IP (interrupt process) control character that is read and interpreted as the appropriate command for invoking the interrupting function in the remote machine.

❏ **AO (abort output).** This is the same as IP, but it allows the process to continue without creating output. This is useful if the process has another effect in addition to creating output. The user wants this effect but not the output. For example, most commands in UNIX generate output and have an exit status. The user may want the exit status for future use but is not interested in the output data.

❏ **AYT (are you there?).** This control character is used to determine if the remote machine is still up and running, especially after a long silence from the server. When this character is received, the server usually sends an audible or visual signal to confirm that it is running.

❏ **EC (erase character).** When a user sends data from the keyboard to the local machine, the delete or backspace character can erase the last character typed. To do the same in a remote machine, TELNET defines the EC control character.

❏ **EL (erase line).** This is used to erase the current line in the remote host.

For example, Figure 18.13 shows how to interrupt a runaway application program at the server site. The user types Ctrl+c, but the TELNET client sends the combination of IAC and IP to the server.

Figure 18.13   *Example of interrupting an application program*

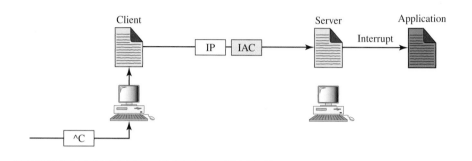

18.9   OUT-OF-BAND SIGNALING

To make control characters effective in special situations, TELNET uses **out-of-band signaling.** In out-of-band signaling, the control characters are preceded by IAC and are sent to the remote process out of order.

Imagine a situation in which an application program running at the server site has gone into an infinite loop and does not accept any more input data. The user wants to interrupt the application program, but the program does not read data from the buffer. The TCP at the server site has found that the buffer is full and has sent a segment specifying that the client window size should be zero. In other words, the TCP at the server site is announcing that no more regular traffic is accepted. To remedy such a situation, an urgent TCP segment should be sent from the client to the server. The urgent segment overrides the regular flow-control mechanism. Although TCP is not accepting normal segments, it must accept an urgent segment.

When a TELNET process (client or server) wants to send an out-of-band sequence of characters to the other process (client or server), it embeds the sequence in the data stream and inserts a special character called a DM (data mark). However, to force the other party to handle the sequence out of order, it creates a TCP segment with the urgent bit set and the urgent pointer pointing to the DM character. When the receiving TCP receives the segment, it reads the data and discards any data preceding the control characters (IAC and IP, for example). When it reaches the DM character, the remaining data are handled normally. In other words, the DM character is used as a *synchronization* character that switches the receiving TCP from the urgent mode to the normal mode and *resynchronizes* the two ends (see Figure 18.14).

In this way, the control character (IP) is delivered out of band to the operating system, which uses the appropriate function to interrupt the running application program.

Figure 18.14   *Out-of-band signaling*

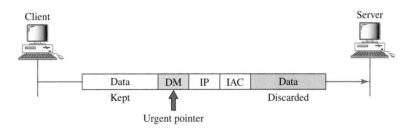

18.10   ESCAPE CHARACTER

A character typed by the user is normally sent to the server. However, sometimes the user wants characters interpreted by the client instead of the server. In this case, the user can use an *escape* character, normally Ctrl+] (shown as ^]). Figure 18.15 compares the interruption of an application program at the remote site with the interruption of the client process at the local site using the escape character. The TELNET prompt is displayed after this escape character.

Figure 18.15   *Two different interruptions*

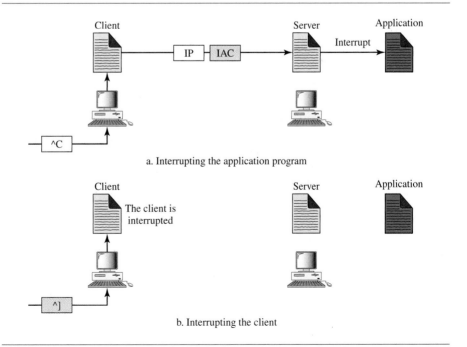

18.11   MODE OF OPERATION

Most TELNET implementations operate in one of three modes: default mode, character mode, or line mode.

Default Mode

The default mode is used if no other modes are invoked through option negotiation. In this mode, the echoing is done by the client. The user types a character and the client echoes the character on the screen (or printer) but does not send it until a whole line is completed. After sending the whole line to the server, the client waits for the GA (go ahead) command from the server before accepting a new line from the user. The operation is half-duplex. Half-duplex operation is not efficient when the TCP connection itself is full-duplex, and so this mode is becoming obsolete.

Character Mode

In the character mode, each character typed is sent by the client to the server. The server normally echoes the character back to be displayed on the client screen. In this mode the echoing of the character can be delayed if the transmission time is long (such as in a satellite connection). It also creates overhead (traffic) for the network because three TCP segments must be sent for each character of data:

1. The user enters a character that is sent to the server.
2. The server acknowledges the received character and echos the character back (in one segment).
3. The client acknowledges the receipt of the echoed character.

Line Mode

A new mode has been proposed to compensate for the deficiencies of the default mode and the character mode. In this mode, called the line mode, line editing (echoing, character erasing, line erasing, and so on) is done by the client. The client then sends the whole line to the server.

Although the line mode looks like the default mode, it is not. The default mode operates in the half-duplex mode; the line mode is full-duplex with the client sending one line after another, without the need for an intervening GA (go ahead) character from the server.

Example 2

In this example, we use the default mode to show the concept and its deficiencies even though it is almost obsolete today. The client and the server negotiate the terminal type and terminal speed and then the server checks the login and password of the user (see Figure 18.16).

Figure 18.16   *Example 2*

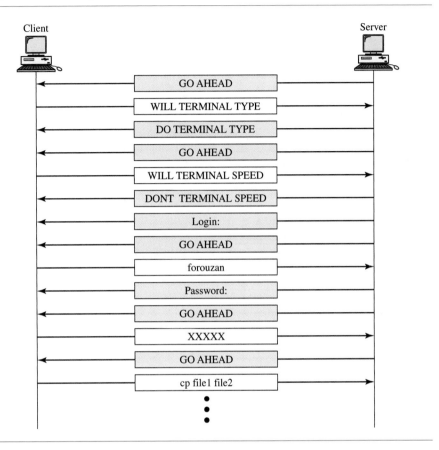

Example 3

In this example, we show how the client switches to the character mode. This requires that the client request the server to enable the SUPPRESS GO AHEAD and ECHO options (see Figure 18.17).

18.12   USER INTERFACE

The normal user does not use TELNET commands as defined above. Usually, the operating system (UNIX, for example) defines an interface with user-friendly commands. An example of such a set of commands can be found in Table 18.6. Note that the interface is responsible for translating the user-friendly commands to the previously defined commands in the protocol.

Figure 18.17   *Example 3*

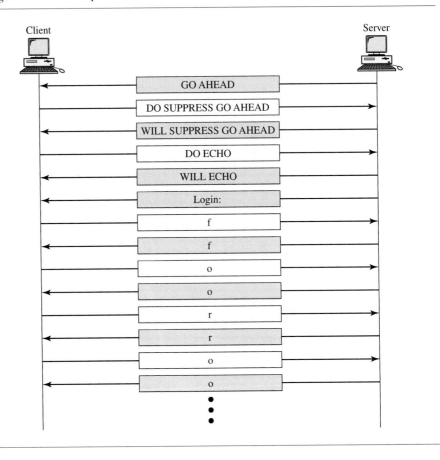

Table 18.6   *Examples of interface commands*

Command	Meaning
open	Connect to a remote computer
close	Close the connection
display	Show the operating parameters
mode	Change to line mode or character mode
set	Set the operating parameters
status	Display the status information
send	Send special characters
quit	Exit TELNET

18.13 SECURITY ISSUE

TELNET suffers from security problems. Although TELNET requires a login name and password (when exchanging text), often this is not enough. A microcomputer connected to a broadcast LAN can easily eavesdrop using snooper software and capture a login name and the corresponding password (even if it is encrypted). In Chapter 28, we will learn more about authentication and security.

18.14 KEY TERMS

character mode

control character

default mode

line mode

local login

network virtual terminal (NVT)

option negotiation

out-of-band signaling

remote login

remote server

suboption negotiation

terminal network (TELNET)

time-sharing

18.15 SUMMARY

❏ TELNET is a client-server application that allows a user to log on to a remote machine, giving the user access to the remote system.

❏ When a user accesses a remote system via the TELNET process, this is comparable to a time-sharing environment.

❏ A terminal driver correctly interprets the keystrokes on the local terminal or terminal emulator. This may not occur between a terminal and a remote terminal driver.

❏ TELNET uses the Network Virtual Terminal (NVT) system to encode characters on the local system. On the server machine, NVT decodes the characters to a form acceptable to the remote machine.

❏ NVT uses a set of characters for data and a set of characters for control.

❏ In TELNET, control characters are embedded in the data stream and preceded by the *interpret as control* (IAC) control character.

❏ Options are features that enhance the TELNET process.

❏ TELNET allows negotiation to set transfer conditions between the client and server before and during the use of the service.

❏ Some options can only be enabled by the server, some only by the client, and some by both.

❏ An option is enabled or disabled through an offer or a request.

❏ An option that needs additional information requires the use of suboption characters.

❏ Control characters can be used to handle the remote server.

❏ In out-of-band signaling, commands are sent out of order.

❏ A TELNET implementation operates in the default, character, or line mode.

❏ In the default mode, the client sends one line at a time to the server and waits for the go ahead (GA) character before a new line from the user can be accepted.

❏ In the character mode, the client sends one character at a time to the server.

❏ In the line mode, the client sends one line at a time to the server, one after the other, without the need for an intervening GA character.

❏ TELNET is usually not accessed directly by the user. User-friendly software acts as an interface between TELNET and the user.

❏ Security is an issue with TELNET.

18.16   PRACTICE SET

Exercises

1. Show the sequence of bits sent from a client TELNET for the binary transmission of 11110011 00111100 11111111.

2. If TELNET is using the character mode, how many characters are sent back and forth between the client and server to copy a file named file1 to another file named file2 in UNIX (*cp file1 file2*)?

3. What is the minimum number of bits sent at the TCP level to accomplish the task in Exercise 1?

4. What is the minimum number of bits sent at the data link layer level (using Ethernet) to accomplish the task in Exercise 1?

5. What is the ratio of the useful bits to the total bits in Exercise 4?

6. Show the sequence of characters exchanged between the TELNET client and the server to switch from the default mode to the character mode.

7. Show the sequence of characters exchanged between the TELNET client and the server to switch from the character mode to the default mode.

8. Show the sequence of characters exchanged between the TELNET client and the server to switch from the default mode to line mode.

9. Show the sequence of characters exchanged between the TELNET client and the server to switch from the character mode to the line mode.

10. Show the sequence of characters exchanged between the TELNET client and the server to switch from the line mode to the character mode.

11. Show the sequence of characters exchanged between the TELNET client and the server to switch from the line mode to the default mode.

12. Interpret the following sequence of characters (in hexadecimal) received by a TELNET client or server:

    a. FF FB 01
    b. FF FE 01
    c. FF F4
    d. FF F9

Research Activities

13. Find the extended options proposed for TELNET.

14. Another login protocol is called Rlogin. Find some information about Rlogin and compare it with TELNET.

15. A more secured login protocol in UNIX is called Secure Shell (SSH). Find some information about this protocol.

CHAPTER 19

File Transfer: FTP and TFTP

Transferring files from one computer to another is one of the most common tasks expected from a networking or internetworking environment. As a matter of fact, the greatest volume of data exchange in the Internet today is due to file transfer. In this chapter, we discuss two protocols involved in transferring files: File Transfer Protocol (FTP) and Trivial File Transfer Protocol (TFTP).

19.1   FILE TRANSFER PROTOCOL (FTP)

File Transfer Protocol (FTP) is the standard mechanism provided by TCP/IP for copying a file from one host to another. Although transferring files from one system to another seems simple and straightforward, some problems must be dealt with first. For example, two systems may use different file name conventions. Two systems may have different ways to represent text and data. Two systems may have different directory structures. All of these problems have been solved by FTP in a very simple and elegant approach.

FTP differs from other client-server applications in that it establishes two connections between the hosts. One connection is used for data transfer, the other for control information (commands and responses). Separation of commands and data transfer makes FTP more efficient. The control connection uses very simple rules of communication. We need to transfer only a line of command or a line of response at a time. The data connection, on the other hand, needs more complex rules due to the variety of data types transferred.

FTP uses two well-known TCP ports: Port 21 is used for the control connection, and port 20 is used for the data connection.

> **FTP uses the services of TCP. It needs two TCP connections.**
> **The well-known port 21 is used for the control connection and the well-known port 20 for the data connection.**

Figure 19.1 shows the basic model of FTP. The client has three components: user interface, client control process, and the client data transfer process. The server has two components: the server control process and the server data transfer process. The control connection is made between the control processes. The data connection is made between the data transfer processes.

Figure 19.1   *FTP*

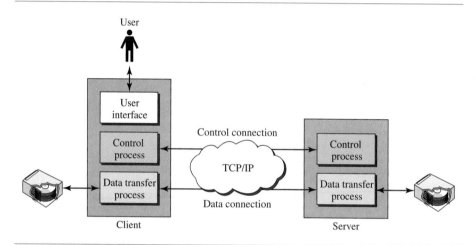

The **control connection** remains connected during the entire interactive FTP session. The data connection is opened and then closed for each file transferred. It opens each time commands that involve transferring files are used, and it closes when the file is transferred. In other words, when a user starts an FTP session, the control connection opens. While the control connection is open, the data connection can be opened and closed multiple times if several files are transferred.

Connections

The two FTP connections, control and data, use different strategies and different port numbers.

Control Connection

The control connection is created in the same way as other application programs described so far. There are two steps:

1. The server issues a passive open on the well-known port 21 and waits for a client.
2. The client uses an ephemeral port and issues an active open.

The connection remains open during the entire process. The service type, used by the IP protocol, is *minimize delay* because this is an interactive connection between a user (human) and a server. The user types commands and expects to receive responses without significant delay. Figure 19.2 shows the initial connection between the server and the client.

Figure 19.2   *Opening the control connection*

a. Passive open by server

b. Active open by client

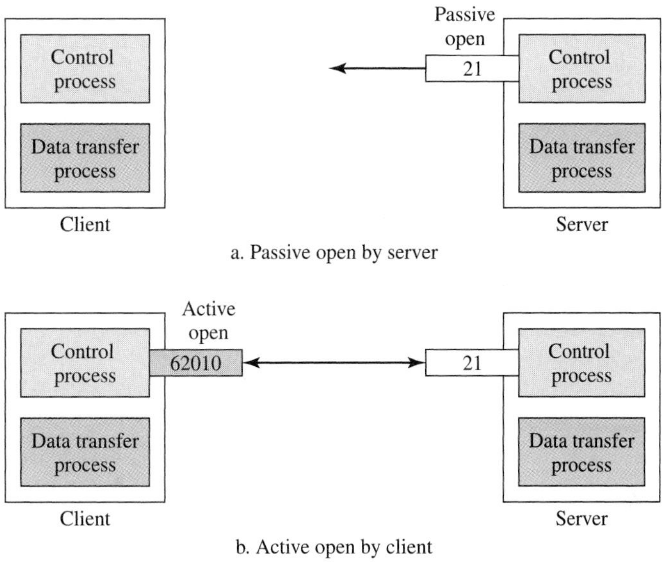

Data Connection

The **data connection** uses the well-known port 20 at the server site. However, the creation of a data connection is different from what we have seen so far. The following shows how FTP creates a data connection:

1. The client, not the server, issues a passive open using an ephemeral port. This must be done by the client because it is the client that issues the commands for transferring files.

2. The client sends this port number to the server using the PORT command (we will discuss this command shortly).

3. The server receives the port number and issues an active open using the well-known port 20 and the received ephemeral port number.

The steps for creating the initial data connection are shown in Figure 19.3. Later we will see that these steps are changed if the PASV command is used.

Communication

The FTP client and server, which run on different computers, must communicate with each other. These two computers may use different operating systems, different character sets, different file structures, and different file formats. FTP must make this heterogeneity compatible.

FTP has two different approaches, one for the control connection and one for the data connection. We will study each approach separately.

Figure 19.3   *Creating the data connection*

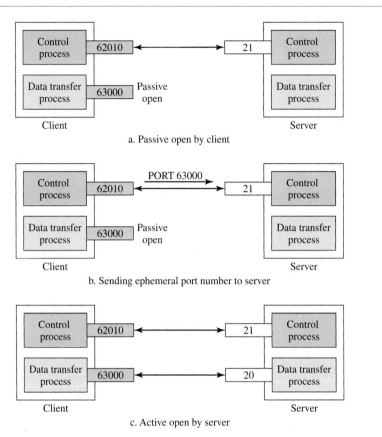

a. Passive open by client

b. Sending ephemeral port number to server

c. Active open by server

Communication over Control Connection

FTP uses the same approach as TELNET or SMTP to communicate across the control connection. It uses the NVT ASCII character set (see Figure 19.4). Communication is

Figure 19.4   *Using the control connection*

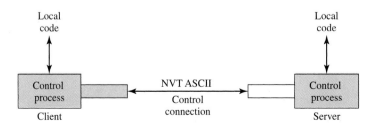

achieved through commands and responses. This simple method is adequate for the control connection because we send one command (or response) at a time. Each command or response is only one short line so we need not worry about file format or file structure. Each line is terminated with a two-character (carriage return and line feed) end-of-line token.

Communication over Data Connection

The purpose and implementation of the data connection are different from that of the control connection. We want to transfer files through the data connection. The client must define the type of file to be transferred, the structure of the data, and the transmission mode. Before sending the file through the data connection, we prepare for transmission through the control connection. The heterogeneity problem is resolved by defining three attributes of communication: file type, data structure, and transmission mode (see Figure 19.5).

Figure 19.5 *Using the data connection*

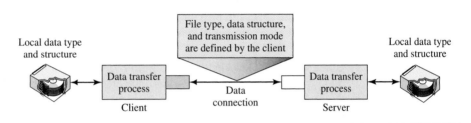

File Type   FTP can transfer one of the following file types across the data connection:

❏ **ASCII file.** This is the default format for transferring text files. Each character is encoded using NVT ASCII. The sender transforms the file from its own representation into NVT ASCII characters and the receiver transforms the NVT ASCII characters to its own representation.

❏ **EBCDIC file.** If one or both ends of the connection use EBCDIC encoding, the file can be transferred using EBCDIC encoding.

❏ **Image file.** This is the default format for transferring binary files. The file is sent as continuous streams of bits without any interpretation or encoding. This is mostly used to transfer binary files such as compiled programs.

If the file is encoded in ASCII or EBCDIC, another attribute must be added to define the printability of the file.

a. **Nonprint.** This is the default format for transferring a text file. The file contains no vertical specifications for printing. This means that the file cannot be printed without further processing because there are no characters to be interpreted for vertical movement of the print head. This format is used for files that will be stored and processed later.

b. **TELNET.** In this format the file contains NVT ASCII vertical characters such as CR (carriage return), LF (line feed), NL (new line), and VT (vertical tab). The file is printable after transfer.

Data Structure FTP can transfer a file across the data connection using one of the following interpretations about the structure of the data:

❏ **File structure (default).** The file has no structure. It is a continuous stream of bytes.

❏ **Record structure.** The file is divided into records. This can be used only with text files.

❏ **Page structure.** The file is divided into pages, with each page having a page number and a page header. The pages can be stored and accessed randomly or sequentially.

Transmission Mode FTP can transfer a file across the data connection using one of the following three transmission modes:

❏ **Stream mode.** This is the default mode. Data are delivered from FTP to TCP as a continuous stream of bytes. TCP is responsible for chopping data into segments of appropriate size. If the data is simply a stream of bytes (file structure), no end-of-file is needed. End-of-file in this case is the closing of the data connection by the sender. If the data is divided into records (record structure), each record will have a 1-byte end-of-record (EOR) character and the end of the file will have a 1-byte end-of-file (EOF) character.

❏ **Block mode.** Data can be delivered from FTP to TCP in blocks. In this case, each block is preceded by a 3-byte header. The first byte is called the *block descriptor;* the next two bytes define the size of the block in bytes.

❏ **Compressed mode.** If the file is big, the data can be compressed. The compression method normally used is run-length encoding. In this method, consecutive appearances of a data unit are replaced by one occurrence and the number of repetitions. In a text file, this is usually spaces (blanks). In a binary file, null characters are usually compressed.

Command Processing

FTP uses the control connection to establish a communication between the client control process and the server control process. During this communication, the commands are sent from the client to the server and the responses are sent from the server to the client (see Figure 19.6).

Figure 19.6 *Command processing*

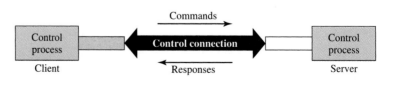

Commands

Commands, which are sent from the FTP client control process, are in the form of ASCII uppercase, which may or may not be followed by an argument. We can roughly divide the commands into six groups: access commands, file management commands, data formatting commands, port defining commands, file transferring commands, and miscellaneous commands.

❑   **Access commands.** These commands let the user access the remote system. Table 19.1 lists common commands in this group.

Table 19.1   *Access commands*

Command	*Argument(s)*	*Description*
USER	User id	User information
PASS	User password	Password
ACCT	Account to be charged	Account information
REIN		Reinitialize
QUIT		Log out of the system
ABOR		Abort the previous command

❑   **File management commands.** These commands let the user access the file system on the remote computer. They allow the user to navigate through the directory structure, create new directories, delete files, and so on. Table 19.2 gives common commands in this group.

Table 19.2   *File management commands*

Command	*Argument(s)*	*Description*
CWD	Directory name	Change to another directory
CDUP		Change to the parent directory
DELE	File name	Delete a file
LIST	Directory name	List subdirectories or files
NLIST	Directory name	List the names of subdirectories or files without other attributes
MKD	Directory name	Create a new directory
PWD		Display name of current directory
RMD	Directory name	Delete a directory
RNFR	File name (old file name)	Identify a file to be renamed
RNTO	File name (new file name)	Rename the file
SMNT	File system name	Mount a file system

❏ **Data formatting commands.** These commands let the user define the data structure, file type, and transmission mode. The defined format is then used by the file transfer commands. Table 19.3 shows common commands in this group.

Table 19.3   *Data formatting commands*

Command	Argument(s)	Description
TYPE	A (ASCII), E (EBCDIC), I (Image), N (Nonprint), or T (TELNET)	Define the file type and if necessary the print format
STRU	F (File), R (Record), or P (Page)	Define the organization of the data
MODE	S (Stream), B (Block), or C (Compressed)	Define the transmission mode

❏ **Port defining commands.** These commands define the port number for the data connection on the client site. There are two methods to do this. In the first method, using the PORT command, the client can choose an ephemeral port number and send it to the server using a passive open. The server uses that port number and creates an active open. In the second method, using the PASV command, the client just asks the server to first choose a port number. The server does a passive open on that port and sends the port number in the response (see response numbered 227 in Table 19.7). The client issues an active open using that port number. Table 19.4 shows the port defining commands.

Table 19.4   *Port defining commands*

Command	Argument(s)	Description
PORT	6-digit identifier	Client chooses a port
PASV		Server chooses a port

❏ **File transfer commands.** These commands actually let the user transfer files. Table 19.5 lists common commands in this group.

Table 19.5   *File transfer commands*

Command	Argument(s)	Description
RETR	File name(s)	Retrieve files; file(s) are transferred from server to the client
STOR	File name(s)	Store files; file(s) are transferred from the client to the server
APPE	File name(s)	Similar to STOR except if the file exists, data must be appended to it
STOU	File name(s)	Same as STOR except that the file name will be unique in the directory; however, the existing file should not be overwritten

Table 19.5   *File transfer commands (continued)*

Command	Argument(s)	Description
ALLO	File name(s)	Allocate storage space for the files at the server
REST	File name(s)	Position the file marker at a specified data point
STAT	File name(s)	Return the status of files

❏ **Miscellaneous commands.** These commands deliver information to the FTP user at the client site. Table 19.6 shows common commands in this group.

Table 19.6   *Miscellaneous commands*

Command	Argument(s)	Description
HELP		Ask information about the server
NOOP		Check if server is alive
SITE	Commands	Specify the site-specific commands
SYST		Ask about operating system used by the server

Responses

Every FTP command generates at least one response. A response has two parts: a three-digit number followed by text. The numeric part defines the code; the text part defines needed parameters or extra explanations. We represent the three digits as *xyz*. The meaning of each digit is described below.

First Digit   The first digit defines the status of the command. One of five digits can be used in this position:

❏ **1yz (positive preliminary reply).** The action has started. The server will send another reply before accepting another command.

❏ **2yz (positive completion reply).** The action has been completed. The server will accept another command.

❏ **3yz (positive intermediate reply).** The command has been accepted, but further information is needed.

❏ **4yz (transient negative completion reply).** The action did not take place, but the error is temporary. The same command can be sent later.

❏ **5yz (permanent negative completion reply).** The command was not accepted and should not be retried again.

Second Digit   The second digit also defines the status of the command. One of six digits can be used in this position:

❏ **x0z (syntax).**

❏ **x1z (information).**

❏ **x2z (connections).**

❏ **x3z (authentication and accounting).**

❏   **x4z (unspecified).**

❏   **x5z (file system).**

Third Digit   The third digit provides additional information.

Table 19.7 shows a brief list of possible responses (using all three digits).

Table 19.7   *Responses*

Code	Description
Positive Preliminary Reply	
120	Service will be ready shortly
125	Data connection open; data transfer will start shortly
150	File status is OK; data connection will be open shortly
Positive Completion Reply	
200	Command OK
211	System status or help reply
212	Directory status
213	File status
214	Help message
215	Naming the system type (operating system)
220	Service ready
221	Service closing
225	Data connection open
226	Closing data connection
227	Entering passive mode; server sends its IP address and port number
230	User login OK
250	Request file action OK
Positive Intermediate Reply	
331	User name OK; password is needed
332	Need account for logging
350	The file action is pending; more information needed
Transient Negative Completion Reply	
425	Cannot open data connection
426	Connection closed; transfer aborted
450	File action not taken; file not available
451	Action aborted; local error
452	Action aborted; insufficient storage
Permanent Negative Completion Reply	
500	Syntax error; unrecognized command

Table 19.7   *Responses (continued)*

Code	Description
501	Syntax error in parameters or arguments
502	Command not implemented
503	Bad sequence of commands
504	Command parameter not implemented
530	User not logged in
532	Need account for storing file
550	Action is not done; file unavailable
552	Requested action aborted; exceeded storage allocation
553	Requested action not taken; file name not allowed

File Transfer

File transfer occurs over the data connection under the control of the commands sent over the control connection. However, we should remember that file transfer in FTP means one of three things (see Figure 19.7).

❑ A file is to be copied from the server to the client. This is called *retrieving a file*. It is done under the supervision of the RETR command.

❑ A file is to be copied from the client to the server. This is called *storing a file*. It is done under the supervision of the STOR command.

❑ A list of directory or file names is to be sent from the server to the client. This is done under the supervision of the LIST command. Note that FTP treats a list of directory or file names as a file. It is sent over the data connection.

Figure 19.7   *File transfer*

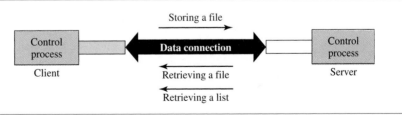

Example 1

Figure 19.8 shows an example of using FTP for retrieving a list of items in a directory.

1. After the control connection to port 21 is created, the FTP server sends the 220 (service ready) response on the control connection.

2. The client sends the USER command.

3. The server responds with 331 (user name is OK, password is required).

4. The client sends the PASS command.

Figure 19.8   *Example 1*

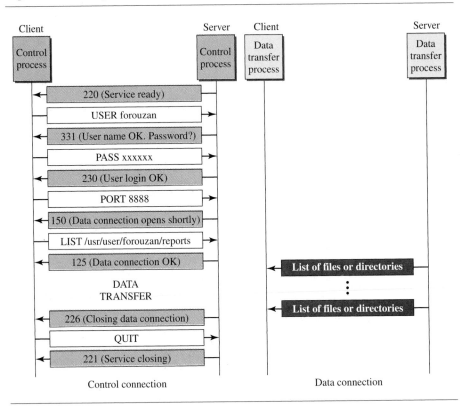

5. The server responds with 230 (user login is OK)
6. The client issues a passive open on an ephemeral port for the data connection and sends the PORT command (over the control connection) to give this port number to the server.
7. The server does not open the connection at this time, but it prepares itself for issuing an active open on the data connection between port 20 (server side) and the ephemeral port received from the client. It sends response 150 (data connection will open shortly).
8. The client sends the LIST message.
9. Now the server responds with 125 and opens the data connection.
10. The server then sends the list of the files or directories (as a file) on the data connection. When the whole list (file) is sent, the server responds with 226 (closing data connection) over the control connection.
11. The client now has two choices. It can use the QUIT command to request the closing of the control connection or it can send another command to start another activity (and eventually open another data connection). In our example, the client sends a QUIT command.
12. After receiving the QUIT command, the server responds with 221 (service closing) and then closes the control connection.

Example 2

The following shows an actual FTP session that parallels Example 1. The colored lines show the responses from the server control connection; the black lines show the commands sent by the client. The lines in white with black background shows data transfer.

```
$ ftp voyager.deanza.fhda.edu
Connected to voyager.deanza.fhda.edu.
220 (vsFTPd 1.2.1)
530 Please login with USER and PASS.
Name (voyager.deanza.fhda.edu:forouzan): forouzan
331 Please specify the password.
Password:
230 Login successful.
Remote system type is UNIX.
Using binary mode to transfer files.
ftp> ls reports
227 Entering Passive Mode (153,18,17,11,238,169)
150 Here comes the directory listing.
drwxr-xr-x   2 3027   411      4096 Sep 24  2002 business
drwxr-xr-x   2 3027   411      4096 Sep 24  2002 personal
drwxr-xr-x   2 3027   411      4096 Sep 24  2002 school
226 Directory send OK.
ftp> quit
221 Goodbye.
```

Example 3

Figure 19.9 shows an example of how an image (binary) file is stored.

1. After the control connection to port 21 is created, the FTP server sends the 220 (service ready) response on the control connection.
2. The client sends the USER command.
3. The server responds with 331 (user name is OK, a password is required).
4. The client sends the PASS command.
5. The server responds with 230 (user login is OK).
6. The client issues a passive open on an ephemeral port for the data connection and sends the PORT command (over the control connection) to give this port number to the server.
7. The server does not open the connection at this time, but prepares itself for issuing an active open on the data connection between port 20 (server side) and the ephemeral port received from the client. It sends the response 150 (data connection will open shortly).
8. The client sends the TYPE command.
9. The server responds with the response 200 (command OK).
10. The client sends the STRU command.
11. The server responds with 200 (command OK).
12. The client sends the STOR command.
13. The server opens the data connection and sends the response 250.

Figure 19.9   *Example 3*

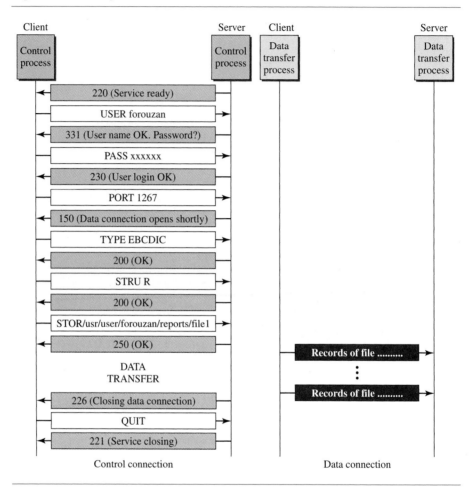

14. The client sends the file on the data connection. After the entire file is sent, the data connection is closed. Closing the data connection means end-of-file.

15. The server sends the response 226 on the control connection.

16. The client sends the QUIT command or uses other commands to open another data connection for transferring another file. In our example, the QUIT command is sent.

17. The server responds with 221 (service closing) and it closes the control connection.

Anonymous FTP

To use FTP, a user needs an account (user name) and a password on the remote server. Some sites have a set of files available for public access. To access these files, a user does not need to have an account or password. Instead, the user can use *anonymous* as the user name and *guest* as the password.

User access to the system is very limited. Some sites allow anonymous users only a subset of commands. For example, most sites allow the user to copy some files, but do not allow navigation through the directories.

Example 4

We show an example of anonymous FTP. We assume that some public data are available at internic.net.

```
$ ftp internic.net
Connected to internic.net
220 Server ready
Name: anonymous
331 Guest login OK, send "guest" as password
Password: guest
ftp > pwd
257 '/' is current directory
ftp > ls
200 OK
150 Opening ASCII mode
bin
. . .
. . .
. . .
ftp > close
221 Goodbye
ftp > quit
```

19.2   TRIVIAL FILE TRANSFER PROTOCOL (TFTP)

There are occasions when we need to simply copy a file without the need for all of the features of the FTP protocol. For example, when a diskless workstation or a router is booted, we need to download the bootstrap and configuration files. Here we do not need all of the sophistication provided in FTP. We just need a protocol that quickly copies the files.

Trivial File Transfer Protocol (TFTP) is designed for these types of file transfer. It is so simple that the software package can fit into the read-only memory of a diskless workstation. It can be used at bootstrap time. The reason that it fits on ROM is that it requires only basic IP and UDP. However, there is no security for TFTP. TFTP can read or write a file for the client. *Reading* means copying a file from the server site to the client site. *Writing* means copying a file from the client site to the server site.

TFTP uses the services of UDP on the well-known port 69.

Messages

There are five types of TFTP messages, RRQ, WRQ, DATA, ACK, and ERROR, as shown in Figure 19.10.

Figure 19.10   *Message categories*

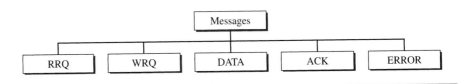

RRQ

The read request (RRQ) message is used by the client to establish a connection for reading data from the server. Its format is shown in Figure 19.11.

Figure 19.11   *RRQ format*

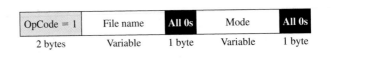

The RRQ message fields are as follows:

- ❏ **OpCode.** The first field is a 2-byte operation code. The value is 1 for the RRQ message.
- ❏ **File name.** The next field is a variable-size string (encoded in ASCII) that defines the name of the file. Since the file name varies in length, termination is signaled by a 1-byte field of 0s.
- ❏ **Mode.** The next field is another variable-size string defining the transfer mode. The mode field is terminated by another 1-byte field of 0s. The mode can be one of two strings: "netascii" (for an ASCII file) or "octet" (for a binary file). The file name and mode fields can be in upper- or lowercase, or a combination of both.

WRQ

The write request (WRQ) message is used by the client to establish a connection for writing data to the server. The format is the same as RRQ except that the OpCode is 2 (see Figure 19.12).

Figure 19.12   *WRQ format*

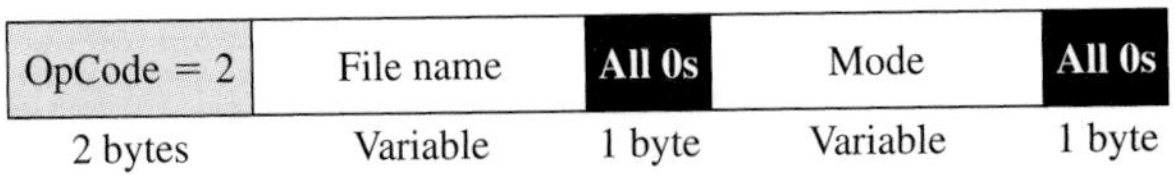

OpCode = 2	File name	All 0s	Mode	All 0s
2 bytes	Variable	1 byte	Variable	1 byte

DATA

The data (DATA) message is used by the client or the server to send blocks of data. Its format is shown in Figure 19.13. The DATA message fields are as follows:

❏ **OpCode.** The first field is a 2-byte operation code. The value is 3 for the DATA message.

Figure 19.13   *DATA format*

OpCode = 3	Block number	Data
2 bytes	2 bytes	0–512 bytes

❏ **Block number.** This is a 2-byte field containing the block number. The sender of the data (client or server) uses this field for sequencing. All blocks are numbered sequentially starting with 1. The block number is necessary for acknowledgment as we will see shortly.

❏ **Data.** This block must be exactly 512 bytes in all DATA messages except the last block which must be between 0 and 511 bytes. A non-512 byte block is used as a signal that the sender has sent all the data. In other words, it is used as an end-of-file indicator. If the data in the file happens to be an exact multiple of 512 bytes, the sender must send one extra block of zero bytes to show the end of transmission. Data can be transferred in either NVT ASCII (netascii) or binary octet (octet).

ACK

The acknowledge (ACK) message is used by the client or server to acknowledge the receipt of a data block. The message is only 4 bytes long. Its format is shown in Figure 19.14.

Figure 19.14   *ACK format*

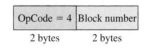

OpCode = 4	Block number
2 bytes	2 bytes

The ACK message fields are as follows:

❏ **OpCode.** The first field is a 2-byte operation code. The value is 4 for the ACK message.

❏ **Block number.** The next field is a 2-byte field containing the number of the block received.

The ACK message can also be a response to a WRQ. It is sent by the server to indicate that it is ready to receive data from the client. In this case the value of the block number field is 0. An example of an ACK message is given in a later section.

ERROR

The ERROR message is used by the client or the server when a connection cannot be established or when there is a problem during data transmission. It can be sent as a negative response to RRQ or WRQ. It can also be used if the next block cannot be transferred during the actual data transfer phase. The error message is not used to declare a damaged or duplicated message. These problems are resolved by error-control mechanisms discussed later in this chapter. The format of the ERROR message is shown in Figure 19.15.

Figure 19.15   *ERROR format*

OpCode = 5	Error number	Error data	**All 0s**
2 bytes	2 bytes	Variable	1 byte

The ERROR message fields are as follows:

❏ **OpCode.** The first field is a 2-byte operation code. The value is 5 for the ERROR message.

❏ **Error number.** This 2-byte field defines the type of error. Table 19.8 shows the error numbers and their corresponding meanings.

Table 19.8   *Error numbers and their meanings*

Number	Meaning
0	Not defined
1	File not found
2	Access violation
3	Disk full or quota on disk exceeded
4	Illegal operation
5	Unknown port number
6	File already exists
7	No such user

❏ **Error data.** This variable-byte field contains the textual error data and is terminated by a 1-byte field of 0s.

Connection

TFTP uses UDP services. Because there is no provision for connection establishment and termination in UDP, UDP transfers each block of data encapsulated in an independent user datagram. In TFTP, however, we do not want to transfer only one block of data; we do not want to transfer the file as independent blocks either. We need connections for the blocks of data being transferred if they all belong to the same file. TFTP uses RRQ, WRQ, ACK, and ERROR messages to establish connection. It uses the DATA message with a block of data of fewer than 512 bytes (0–511) to terminate connection.

Connection Establishment

Connection establishment for reading files is different from connection establishment for writing files (see Figure 19.16).

Figure 19.16   *Connection establishment*

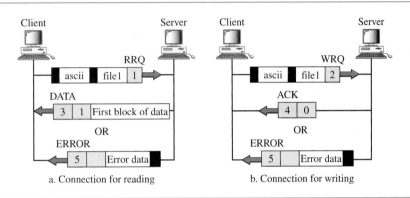

a. Connection for reading   b. Connection for writing

❏ **Reading.** To establish a connection for **reading,** the TFTP client sends the RRQ message. The name of the file and the transmission mode is defined in this message. If the server can transfer the file, it responds positively with a DATA message containing the first block of data. If there is a problem, such as difficulty in opening the file or permission restriction, the server responds negatively by sending an ERROR message.

❏ **Writing.** To establish a connection for **writing,** the TFTP client uses the WRQ message. The name of the file and the transmission mode is defined in this message. If the server can accept a copy of the file, it responds positively with an ACK message using a value of 0 for the block number. If there is any problem, the server responds negatively by sending an ERROR message.

Connection Termination

After the entire file is transferred, the connection must be terminated. As mentioned previously, TFTP does not have a special message for termination. Termination is accomplished by sending the last block of data, which is less than 512 bytes.

Data Transfer

The data transfer phase occurs between connection establishment and termination. TFTP uses the services of UDP, which is unreliable.

The file is divided into blocks of data, in which each block except the last one is exactly 512 bytes. The last block must be between 0 and 511 bytes. TFTP can transfer data in ASCII or binary format.

UDP does not have any mechanism for flow and error control. TFTP has to create a flow- and error-control mechanism to transfer a file made of continuous blocks of data.

Flow Control

TFTP sends a block of data using the DATA message and waits for an ACK message. If the sender receives an acknowledgment before the time-out, it sends the next block. Thus, **flow control** is achieved by numbering the data blocks and waiting for an ACK before the next data block is sent.

Retrieve a File   When the client wants to retrieve (read) a file, it sends the RRQ message. The server responds with a DATA message sending the first block of data (if there is no problem) with a block number of 1.

Store a File   When the client wants to store (write) a file, it sends the WRQ message. The server responds with an ACK message (if there is no problem) using 0 for the block number. After receiving this acknowledgment, the client sends the first data block with a block number of 1.

Error Control

The TFTP error-control mechanism is different from those of other protocols. It is *symmetric,* which means that the sender and the receiver both use time-outs. The sender uses a time-out for data messages; the receiver uses a time-out for acknowledgment messages. If a data message is lost, the sender retransmits it after time-out expiration. If an acknowledgment is lost, the receiver retransmits it after time-out expiration. This guarantees a smooth operation.

Error control is needed in four situations: a damaged message, a lost message, a lost acknowledgment, or a duplicated message.

Damaged Message   There is no negative acknowledgment. If a block of data is damaged, it is detected by the receiver and the block is discarded. The sender waits for the acknowledgment and does not receive it within the time-out period. The block is then sent again. Note that there is no checksum field in the DATA message of TFTP. The only way the receiver can detect data corruption is through the checksum field of the UDP user datagram.

Lost Message   If a block is lost, it never reaches the receiver and no acknowledgment is sent. The sender resends the block after the time-out.

Lost Acknowledgment   If an acknowledgment is lost, we can have two situations. If the timer of the receiver matures before the timer of the sender, the receiver retransmits the acknowledgment; otherwise, the sender retransmits the data.

Duplicate Message   Duplication of blocks can be detected by the receiver through block number. If a block is duplicated, it is simply discarded by the receiver.

Sorcerer's Apprentice Bug

Although the flow- and error-control mechanism is symmetric in TFTP, it can lead to a problem known as the **sorcerer's apprentice bug,** named for the cartoon character who inadvertently conjures up a mop that continuously replicates itself. This will happen if the ACK message for a packet is not lost but delayed. In this situation, every succeeding block is sent twice and every succeeding acknowledgment is received twice.

Figure 19.17 shows this situation. The acknowledgment for the fifth block is delayed. After the time-out expiration, the sender retransmits the fifth block, which will be acknowledged by the receiver again. The sender receives two acknowledgments for the fifth block, which triggers it to send the sixth block twice. The receiver receives the sixth block twice and again sends two acknowledgments, which results in sending the seventh block twice. And so on.

Figure 19.17 *Sorcerer's apprentice bug*

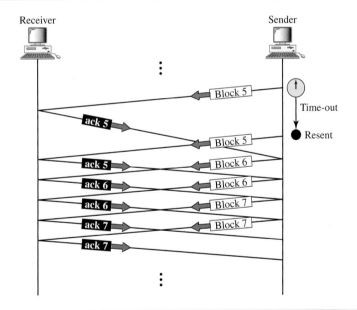

UDP Ports

When a process uses the services of UDP, the server process issues a passive open on the well-known port and waits for the client process to issue an active open on an ephemeral port. After the connection is established, the client and server communicate using these two ports.

TFTP follows a different set of steps because the communication between a client TFTP and a server TFTP can be quite lengthy (seconds or even minutes). If a TFTP server uses the well-known port 69 to communicate with a single client, no other clients can use these services during that time. The solution to this problem, as shown in Figure 19.18, is to use the well-known port for the initial connection and an ephemeral port for the remaining communication.

Figure 19.18   *UDP port numbers used by TFTP*

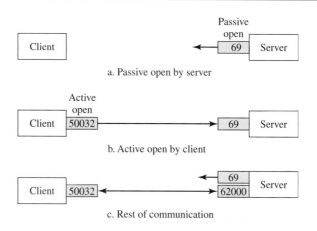

a. Passive open by server

b. Active open by client

c. Rest of communication

The steps are as follows:

1. The server passively opens the connection using the well-known port 69.

2. A client actively opens a connection using an ephemeral port for the source port and the well-known port 69 for the destination port. This is done through the RRQ message or the WRQ message.

3. The server actively opens a connection using a new ephemeral port for the source port and uses the ephemeral port received from the client as the destination port. It sends the DATA or ACK or ERROR message using these ports. This frees the well-known port (69) for use by other clients. When the client receives the first message from the server, it uses its own ephemeral port and the ephemeral port sent by the server for future communication.

TFTP Example

Figure 19.19 shows an example of a TFTP transmission. The client wants to retrieve a copy of the contents of a 2,000-byte file called *file1*. The client sends an RRQ message. The server sends the first block, carrying the first 512 bytes, which is received intact and acknowledged. These two messages are the connection establishment. The second block, carrying the second 512 bytes, is lost. After the time-out, the server retransmits the block, which is received. The third block, carrying the third 512 bytes, is received intact, but the acknowledgment is lost. After the time-out, the receiver retransmits the acknowledgment. The last block, carrying the remaining 464 bytes, is received damaged, so the client simply discards it. After the time-out, the server retransmits the block. This message is considered the connection termination because the block carries fewer than 512 bytes.

Figure 19.19   *TFTP example*

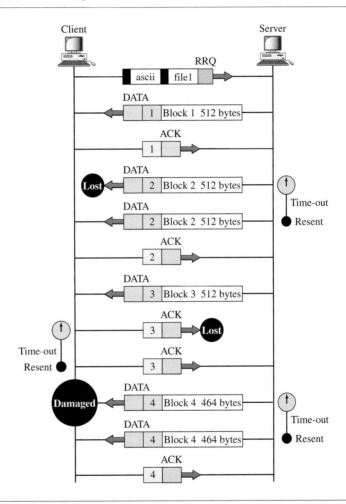

TFTP Options

An extension to the TFTP protocol that allows the appending of options to the RRQ and WRQ messages has been proposed. The options are mainly used to negotiate the size of the block and possibly the initial sequence number. Without the options the size of a block is 512 bytes except for the last block. The negotiation can define a size of block to be any number of bytes so long as the message can be encapsulated in a UDP user datagram.

A new type of message, option acknowledgment (OACK), to let the other party accept or reject the options, has also been proposed.

Security

One important point about TFTP is that there is no provision for security: There is no user identification or password. Today, however, precautions must be taken to prevent hackers from accessing files. One security measure is to limit the access of TFTP to non-critical files. One way to achieve minimal security is to implement security in the router close to a TFTP server, which would allow only certain hosts to access the server.

Applications

TFTP is very useful for basic file transfer where security is not a big issue. It can be used to initialize devices such as bridges or routers. Its main application is in conjunction with the BOOTP or DHCP protocols. TFTP requires only a small amount of memory and uses only the services of UDP and IP. It can easily be configured in ROM (or PROM). When the station is powered on, TFTP will be connected to a server and can download the configuration files from there. Figure 19.20 shows the idea. The powered-on station uses the BOOTP (or DHCP) client to get the name of the configuration file from the BOOTP server. The station then passes the name of the file to the TFTP client to get the contents of the configuration file from the TFTP server.

Figure 19.20 *Use of TFTP with BOOTP*

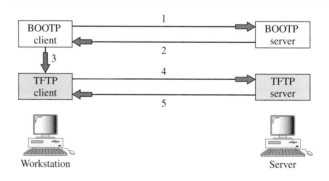

19.3   KEY TERMS

anonymous FTP	data connection
ASCII file	DHCP
block mode	EBCDIC file
BOOTP	file structure
compressed mode	File Transfer Protocol (FTP)
control connection	image file

reading

record structure

sorcerer's apprentice bug

stream mode

Trivial File Transfer Protocol (TFTP)

UDP

user interface

writing

19.4 SUMMARY

❏ File Transfer Protocol (FTP) is a TCP/IP client-server application for copying files from one host to another.

❏ FTP requires two connections for data transfer: a control connection and a data connection.

❏ FTP employs NVT ASCII for communication between dissimilar systems.

❏ Prior to the actual transfer of files, the file type, data structure, and transmission mode are defined by the client through the control connection.

❏ There are six classes of commands sent by the client to establish communication with the server. They are:

    a. access commands

    b. file management commands

    c. data formatting commands

    d. port defining commands

    e. file transferring commands

    f. miscellaneous commands

❏ Responses are sent from the server to the client during connection establishment.

❏ There are three types of file transfer:

    a. a file is copied from the server to the client

    b. a file is copied from the client to the server

    c. a list of directories or filenames is sent from the server to the client

❏ Most operating systems provide a user-friendly interface between FTP and the user.

❏ Anonymous FTP provides a method for the general public to access files on remote sites.

❏ Trivial File Transfer Protocol (TFTP) is a simple file transfer protocol without the complexities and sophistication of FTP.

❏ A client uses the services of TFTP to retrieve a copy of a file or send a copy of a file to a server.

❏ There are five types of TFTP messages:

    a. RRQ is a client message that establishes a connection for reading data from the server.

    b. WRQ is a client message that establishes a connection for writing data to the server.

❏   c. DATA is a client or server message that sends blocks of data.

       d. ACK acknowledges the receipt of a data block.

       e. ERROR is a message to convey a connection or transmission problem.

❏ TFTP is an application that uses UDP for its transport mechanism.

❏ TFTP uses RRQ, WRQ, ACK, and ERROR to establish connection. A DATA message with a block of data less than 512 bytes terminates connection.

❏ Each DATA message, except the last, carries 512 bytes of data from the file.

❏ Error control is needed in four situations: a damaged message, a lost message, a lost acknowledgment, or a duplicated message.

❏ TFTP employs symmetric transmission whereby both sender and receiver use time-outs for error handling.

❏ The sorcerer's apprentice bug is the duplication of both acknowledgments and data messages caused by TFTP's flow- and error-control mechanism.

❏ An extension to the TFTP protocol to allow options regarding the data block size has been proposed.

❏ TFTP can be used in conjunction with BOOTP or DHCP to initialize devices by downloading configuration files.

19.5   PRACTICE SET

Exercises

1. What do you think would happen if the control connection is accidentally severed during an FTP transfer?

2. Explain why the client issues an active open for the control connection and a passive open for the data connection.

3. Why should there be limitations on anonymous FTP? What could an unscrupulous user do?

4. Explain why FTP does not have a message format.

5. Show a TCP segment carrying one of the FTP commands.

6. Show a TCP segment carrying one of the FTP responses.

7. Show a TCP segment carrying FTP data.

8. Explain what will happen if the file in Example 3 already exists.

9. Redo Example 1 using the PASV command instead of the PORT command.

10. Redo Example 3 using the STOU command instead of the STOR command to store a file with a unique name. What happens if a file already exists with the same name?

11. Redo Example 3 using the RETR command instead of the STOR command to retrieve a file.

12. Give an example of the use of the HELP command. Follow the format of Example 1.

13. Give an example of the use of the NOOP command. Follow the format of Example 1.

14. Give an example of the use of the SYST command. Follow the format of Example 1.

15. A user wants to make a directory called *Jan* under the directory */usr/usrs/letters*. The host is called "*mcGraw.com.*". Show all of the commands and responses using Examples 1 and 2 as a guide.

16. A user wants to move to the parent of its current directory. The host is called "*mcGraw.com.*". Show all of the commands and responses using Examples 1 and 3 as a guide.

17. A user wants to move a file named *file1* from */usr/usrs/report* directory to */usr/usrs/letters* directory. The host is called "*mcGraw.com.*". Show all the commands and responses using Examples 1 and 2 as a guide.

18. A user wants to retrieve an EBCDIC file named *file1* from */usr/usrs/report* directory. The host is called "*mcGraw.com.*". The file is so large that the user wants to compress it before transferring. Show all the commands and responses using Examples 1 and 2 as a guide.

19. Why do we need an RRQ or WRQ message in TFTP but not in FTP?

20. Show the encapsulation of an RRQ message in a UDP user datagram. Assume the file name is "Report" and the mode is ASCII. What is the size of the UDP datagram?

21. Show the encapsulation of a WRQ message in a UDP user datagram. Assume the file name is "Report" and the mode is ASCII. What is the size of the UDP datagram?

22. Show the encapsulation of a TFTP data message, carrying block number 7, in a UDP user datagram. What is the total size of the user datagram?

23. Host A uses TFTP to read 2,150 bytes of data from host B. Show all the TFTP commands including commands needed for connection establishment and termination. Assume no error.

24. Show all the user datagrams exchanged between the two hosts in Exercise 23.

25. Redo Exercise 23 but assume the second block is in error.

26. Show all the user datagrams exchanged between the two hosts in Exercise 25.

Research Activities

27. Find the RFCs for FTP.

28. Find the RFCs for TFTP.

29. Find how routers can use security for TFTP.

30. Use UNIX or Windows to find all commands used in FTP.

31. Use UNIX or Windows to find all commands used in TFTP.

32. Find the format of the proposed OACK message.

33. Find the types of options proposed to be appended to the RRQ and WRQ messages.

CHAPTER 20

Electronic Mail:
SMTP, POP, and IMAP

One of the most popular Internet services is electronic mail (email). The designers of the Internet probably never imagined the popularity of this application program. Its architecture consists of several components that we will discuss in this chapter.

At the beginning of the Internet era, the messages sent by electronic mail were short and consisted of text only; they let people exchange quick memos. Today, electronic mail is much more complex. It allows a message to include text, audio, and video. It also allows one message to be sent to one or more recipients.

In this chapter, we first study the general architecture of an email system including the three main components: user agent, message transfer agent, and message access agent. We then describe the protocols that implement these components.

20.1 ARCHITECTURE

To explain the architecture of email, we give four scenarios. We begin with the simplest situation and add complexity as we proceed. The fourth scenario is the most common in the exchange of email.

First Scenario

In the first scenario, the sender and the receiver of the email are users (or application programs) on the same system; they are directly connected to a shared system. The administrator has created one mailbox for each user where the received messages are stored. A *mailbox* is part of a local hard drive, a special file with permission restrictions. Only the owner of the mailbox has access to it. When Alice needs to send a message to Bob, she runs a *user agent (UA)* program to prepare the message and store it in Bob's mailbox. The message has the sender and recipient mailbox addresses (names of files). Bob can retrieve and read the contents of his mailbox at his convenience using a user agent. Figure 20.1 shows the concept.

Figure 20.1   *First scenario*

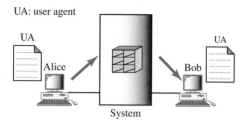

This is similar to the traditional memo exchange between employees in an office. There is a mail room where each employee has a mailbox with his or her name on it. When Alice needs to send a memo to Bob, she writes the memo and inserts it into Bob's mailbox. When Bob checks his mailbox, he finds Alice's memo and reads it.

When the sender and the receiver of an email are on the same system, we need only two user agents.

Second Scenario

In the second scenario, the sender and the receiver of the email are users (or application programs) on two different systems. The message needs to be sent over the Internet. Here we need **user agents (UAs)** and **message transfer agents (MTAs)** as shown in Figure 20.2.

Figure 20.2   *Second scenario*

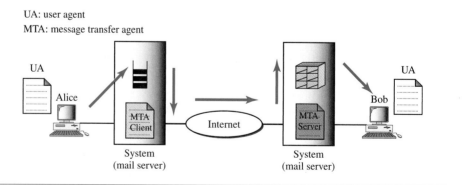

Alice needs to use a user agent program to send her message to the system at her own site. The system (sometimes called the mail server) at her site uses a queue to store messages waiting to be sent. Bob also needs a user agent program to retrieve messages stored in the mailbox of the system at his site. The message, however, needs to be sent through the Internet from Alice's site to Bob's site. Here two message transfer agents are needed: one client and one server. Like most client-server programs on the Internet, the server needs to run all of the time because it does not know when a client will ask for a connection. The client, on the other hand, can be triggered by the system when there is message in the queue to be sent.

> **When the sender and the receiver of an email are on different systems,**
> **we need two UAs and a pair of MTAs (client and server).**

Third Scenario

In the third scenario, Bob, as in the second scenario, is directly connected to his system. Alice, however, is separated from her system. Alice is either connected to the system via a point-to-point WAN—such as a dial-up modem, a DSL, or a cable modem—or she is connected to a LAN in an organization that uses one mail server for handling emails; all users need to send their messages to this mail server. Figure 20.3 shows the situation.

Figure 20.3   *Third scenario*

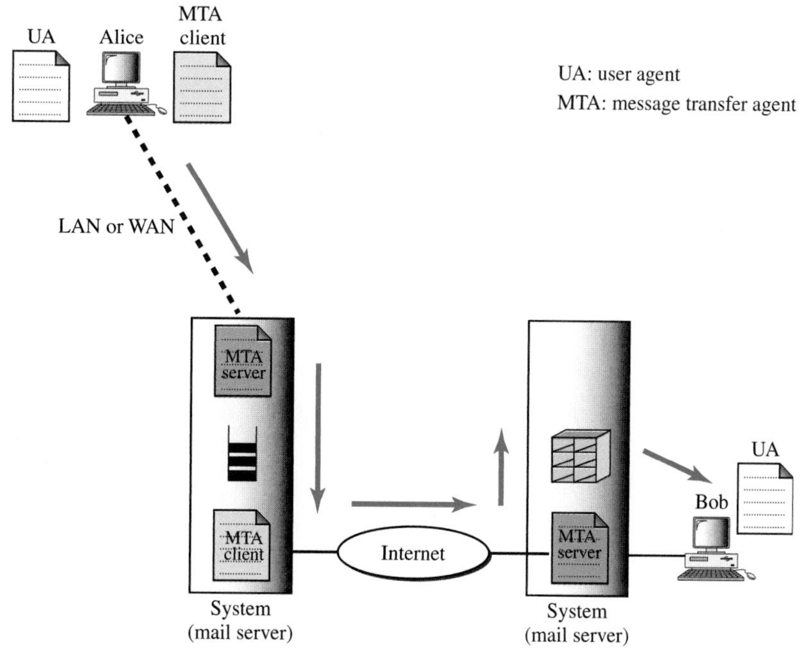

Alice still needs a user agent to prepare her message. She then needs to send the message through the LAN or WAN. This can be done through a pair of message transfer agents (client and server). Whenever Alice has a message to send, she calls the user agent which, in turn, calls the MTA client. The MTA client establishes a connection with the MTA server on the system, which is running all the time. The system at Alice's site queues all messages received. It then uses an MTA client to send the messages to the system at Bob's site; the system receives the message and stores it in Bob's mailbox. At his convenience, Bob uses his user agent to retrieve the message and reads it. Note that we need two pairs of MTA client-server programs.

> **When the sender is connected to the mail server via a LAN or a WAN,**
> **we need two UAs and two pairs of MTAs (client and server).**

Fourth Scenario

In the fourth and most common scenario, Bob is also connected to his mail server by a WAN or a LAN. After the message has arrived at Bob's mail server, Bob needs to retrieve it. Here, we need another set of client-server agents, which we call **message access agents (MAAs).** Bob uses an MAA client to retrieve his messages. The client sends a request to the MAA server, which is running all the time, and requests the transfer of the messages. The situation is shown in Figure 20.4.

Figure 20.4 *Fourth scenario*

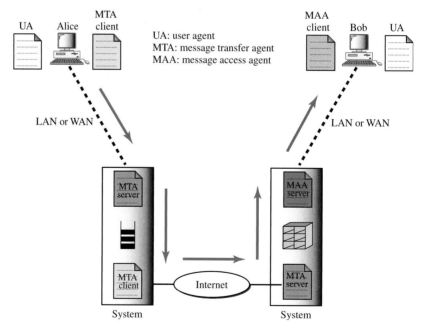

There are two important points we need to emphasize here. First, Bob cannot bypass the mail server and use the MTA server directly. To use MTA server directly, Bob would need to run the MTA server all the time because he does not know when a message will arrive. This implies that Bob must keep his computer on all the time if he is connected to his system through a LAN. If he is connected through a WAN, he must keep the connection up all the time. Neither of these situations is feasible today.

Second, note that Bob needs another pair of client-server programs: message access programs. This is because an MTA client-server program is a *push* program: the client pushes the message to the server. Bob needs a *pull* program. The client needs to pull the message from the server. Figure 20.5 shows the difference.

Figure 20.5   *Push vs. pull*

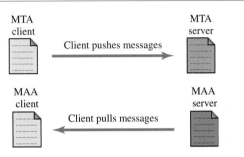

> When both sender and receiver are connected to the mail server via a LAN or a WAN, we need two UAs, two pairs of MTAs (client and server), and a pair of MAAs (client and server). This is the most common situation today.

20.2   USER AGENT

The first component of an electronic mail system is the **user agent (UA).** It provides service to the user to make the process of sending and receiving a message easier.

Services Provided by a User Agent

A user agent is a software package (program) that composes, reads, replies to, and forwards messages. It also handles mailboxes. Figure 20.6 shows the services of a typical user agent.

Figure 20.6   *User agent*

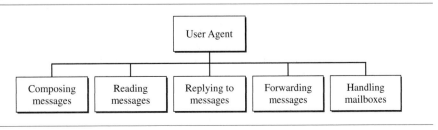

Composing Messages

A user agent helps the user compose the email message to be sent out. Most user agents provide a template on the screen to be filled in by the user. Some even have a built-in editor that can do spell checking, grammar checking, and other tasks expected from a sophisticated word processor. A user, of course, could alternatively use his or her favorite text editor or word processor to create the message and import it, or cut and paste it, into the user agent template.

Reading Messages

The second duty of the user agent is to read the incoming messages. When a user invokes a user agent, it first checks the mail in the incoming mailbox. Most user agents show a one-line summary of each received mail. Each email contains the following fields.

1. A number field.
2. A flag field that shows the status of the mail such as new, already read but not replied to, or read and replied to.
3. The size of the message.
4. The sender.
5. The optional subject field.

Replying to Messages

After reading a message, a user can use the user agent to reply to a message. A user agent usually allows the user to reply to the original sender or to reply to all recipients of the message. The reply message usually contains the original message (for quick reference) and the new message.

Forwarding Messages

Replying is defined as sending a message to the sender or recipients of the copy. Forwarding is defined as sending the message to a third party. A user agent allows the receiver to forward the message, with or without extra comments, to a third party.

Handling Mailboxes

A user agent normally creates two mailboxes: inbox and outbox. Each box is a file with a special format that can be handled by the user agent. The inbox keeps all the received email until they are deleted by the user. The outbox keeps all the sent email until the user deletes them. Most user agents today are capable of creating customized mailboxes.

User Agent Types

There are two types of user agents: command-driven and GUI-based.

Command-Driven

Command-driven user agents belong to the early days of electronic mail. They are still present as the underlying user agents in servers. A command-driven user agent normally accepts a one-character command from the keyboard to perform its task. For example, a user can type the character *r*, at the command prompt, to reply to the sender of the message, or type the character *R* to reply to the sender and all recipients. Some examples of command-driven user agents are *mail, pine,* and *elm.*

> **Some examples of command-driven user agents are *mail, pine,* and *elm.***

GUI-Based

Modern user agents are GUI-based. They contain graphical user interface (GUI) components that allow the user to interact with the software by using both the keyboard and the mouse. They have graphical components such as icons, menu bars, and windows that make the services easy to access. Some examples of GUI-based user agents are Eudora, Microsoft's Outlook, and Netscape.

> **Some examples of GUI-based user agents are *Eudora, Outlook,* and *Netscape.***

Sending Mail

To send mail, the user, through the UA, creates mail that looks very similar to postal mail. It has an *envelope* and a *message* (see Figure 20.7).

Figure 20.7   *Format of an email*

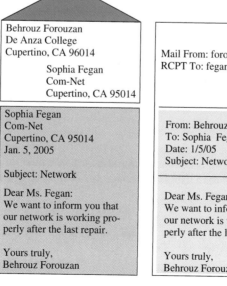
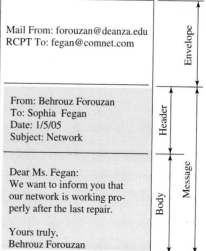

Envelope

The **envelope** usually contains the sender address, the receiver address, and other information.

Message

The message contains the **header** and the **body.** The header of the message defines the sender, the receiver, the subject of the message, and some other information. The body of the message contains the actual information to be read by the recipient.

Receiving Mail

The user agent is triggered by the user (or a timer). If a user has mail, the UA informs the user with a notice. If the user is ready to read the mail, a list is displayed in which each line contains a summary of the information about a particular message in the mailbox. The summary usually includes the sender mail address, the subject, and the time the mail was sent or received. The user can select any of the messages and display its contents on the screen.

Addresses

To deliver mail, a mail handling system must use an addressing system with unique addresses. In the Internet, the address consists of two parts: a **local part** and a **domain name,** separated by an @ sign (see Figure 20.8).

Figure 20.8   *Email address*

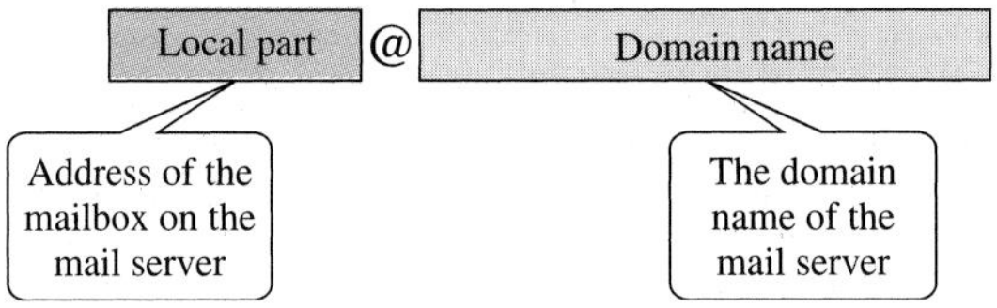

Local Part

The local part defines the name of a special file, called the user mailbox, where all of the mail received for a user is stored for retrieval by the message access agent.

Domain Name

The second part of the address is the domain name. An organization usually selects one or more hosts to receive and send email; they are sometimes called *mail servers* or *exchangers.* The domain name assigned to each mail exchanger either comes from the DNS database or is a logical name (for example, the name of the organization).

Mailing List

Electronic mail allows one name, an **alias,** to represent several different email addresses; this is called a mailing list. Every time a message is to be sent, the system checks the recipient's name against the alias database; if there is a mailing list for the defined alias, separate messages, one for each entry in the list, must be prepared and handed to the MTA. If there is no mailing list for the alias, the name itself is the receiving address and a single message is delivered to the mail transfer entity.

MIME

Electronic mail has a simple structure. Its simplicity, however, comes with a price. It can send messages only in NVT 7-bit ASCII format. In other words, it has some limitations. For example, it cannot be used for languages that are not supported by 7-bit ASCII characters (such as French, German, Hebrew, Russian, Chinese, and Japanese). Also, it cannot be used to send binary files or video or audio data.

Multipurpose Internet Mail Extensions (MIME) is a supplementary protocol that allows non-ASCII data to be sent through email. MIME transforms non-ASCII data at the sender site to NVT ASCII data and delivers it to the client MTA to be sent through the Internet. The message at the receiving side is transformed back to the original data.

We can think of MIME as a set of software functions that transforms non-ASCII data to ASCII data and vice versa, as shown in Figure 20.9.

Figure 20.9   *MIME*

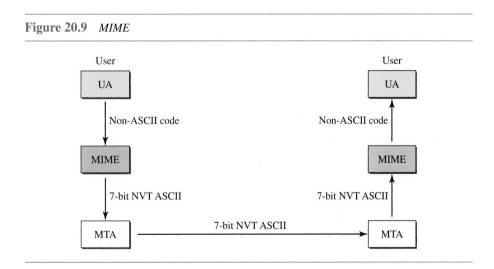

MIME defines five headers that can be added to the original email header section to define the transformation parameters:

1. MIME-Version
2. Content-Type
3. Content-Transfer-Encoding

4. Content-Id

5. Content-Description

Figure 20.10 shows the MIME headers. We will describe each header in detail.

Figure 20.10   *MIME header*

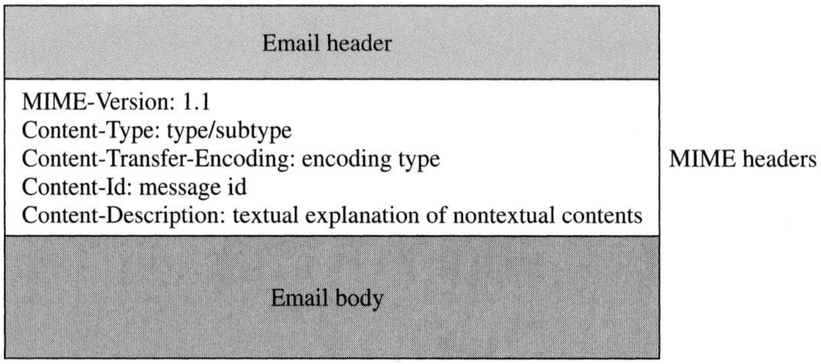

Email header
MIME-Version: 1.1 Content-Type: type/subtype Content-Transfer-Encoding: encoding type Content-Id: message id Content-Description: textual explanation of nontextual contents
Email body

MIME headers

MIME-Version

This header defines the version of MIME used. The current version is 1.1.

MIME-Version: 1.1

Content-Type

This header defines the type of data used in the body of the message. The content type and the content subtype are separated by a slash. Depending on the subtype, the header may contain other parameters.

Content-Type: <type / subtype; parameters>

MIME allows seven different types of data. These are listed in Table 20.1 and described in more detail below.

Table 20.1   *Data types and subtypes in MIME*

Type	Subtype	Description
Text	Plain	Unformatted
	HTML	HTML format (see Chapter 22)
Multipart	Mixed	Body contains ordered parts of different data types
	Parallel	Same as above, but no order
	Digest	Similar to Mixed, but the default is message/RFC822
	Alternative	Parts are different versions of the same message

Table 20.1 *Data types and subtypes in MIME (continued)*

Type	Subtype	Description
Message	RFC822	Body is an encapsulated message
	Partial	Body is a fragment of a bigger message
	External-Body	Body is a reference to another message
Image	JPEG	Image is in JPEG format
	GIF	Image is in GIF format
Video	MPEG	Video is in MPEG format
Audio	Basic	Single channel encoding of voice at 8 KHz
Application	PostScript	Adobe PostScript
	Octet-stream	General binary data (eight-bit bytes)

❏ **Text.** The original message is in 7-bit ASCII format and no transformation by MIME is needed. There are two subtypes currently used, *plain* and *HTML*.

❏ **Multipart.** The body contains multiple, independent parts. The multipart header needs to define the boundary between each part. A parameter is used for this purpose. The parameter is a string token that comes before each part; it is on a separate line by itself and is preceded by two hyphens. The body is terminated using the boundary token, again preceded by two hyphen and then terminated with two hyphens.

Four subtypes are defined for this type: *mixed, parallel, digest,* and *alternative.* In the mixed subtype, the parts must be presented to the recipient in the exact order as in the message. Each part has a different type and is defined at the boundary. The parallel subtype is similar to the mixed subtype, except that the order of the parts is unimportant. The digest subtype is also similar to the mixed subtype except that the default type/subtype is message/RFC822 as defined below. In the alternative subtype, the same message is repeated using different formats. The following is an example of a multipart message using a mixed subtype:

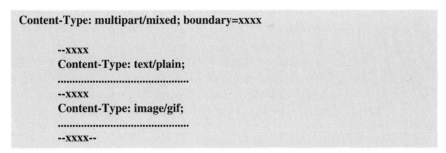

```
Content-Type: multipart/mixed; boundary=xxxx


--xxxx
Content-Type: text/plain;

....................................
--xxxx
Content-Type: image/gif;

....................................
--xxxx--
```

❏ **Message.** In the message type, the body is itself an entire mail message, a part of a mail message, or a pointer to a message. Three subtypes are currently used: *RFC822, partial,* and *external-body.* The subtype RFC822 is used if the body is encapsulating another message (including header and the body). The partial subtype is used if the original message has been fragmented into different mail messages and this mail message is one of the fragments. The fragments must be

reassembled at the destination by MIME. Three parameters must be added: *id,*
number, and the *total.* The id identifies the message and is present in all the fragments. The number defines the sequence order of the fragment. The total defines
the number of fragments that comprise the original message. The following is an
example of a message with three fragments:

Content-Type: message/partial;
id="forouzan@challenger.atc.fhda.edu";
number=1;
total=3;

....
....

The subtype external-body indicates that the body does not contain the actual message
but is only a reference (pointer) to the original message. The parameters following the
subtype define how to access the original message. The following is an example:

Content-Type: message/external-body;
name="report.txt";
site="fhda.edu";
access-type="ftp";

....
....

❑ **Image.** The original message is a stationary image, indicating that there is no animation. The two currently used subtypes are *Joint Photographic Experts Group*
(JPEG), which uses image compression, and *Graphics Interchange Format (GIF).*

❑ **Video.** The original message is a time-varying image (animation). The only subtype is Moving Picture Experts Group (*MPEG*). If the animated image contains
sounds, it must be sent separately using the audio content type.

❑ **Audio.** The original message is sound. The only subtype is basic, which uses 8 kHz
standard audio data.

❑ **Application.** The original message is a type of data not previously defined. There
are only two subtypes used currently: *PostScript* and *octet-stream.* PostScript is
used when the data are in Adobe PostScript format. Octet-stream is used when the
data must be interpreted as a sequence of 8-bit bytes (binary file).

Content-Transfer-Encoding

This header defines the method used to encode the messages into 0s and 1s for
transport:

Content-Transfer-Encoding: <type>

The five types of encoding methods are listed in Table 20.2.

Table 20.2   *Content-transfer-encoding*

Type	Description
7bit	NVT ASCII characters and short lines
8bit	Non-ASCII characters and short lines
Binary	Non-ASCII characters with unlimited-length lines
Base64	6-bit blocks of data are encoded into 8-bit ASCII characters
Quoted-printable	Non-ASCII characters are encoded as an equal sign followed by an ASCII code

❏ **7bit.** This is 7-bit NVT ASCII encoding. Although no special transformation is needed, the length of the line should not exceed 1,000 characters.

❏ **8bit.** This is 8-bit encoding. Non-ASCII characters can be sent, but the length of the line still should not exceed 1,000 characters. MIME does not do any encoding here; the underlying SMTP protocol must be able to transfer 8-bit non-ASCII characters. It is, therefore, not recommended. Base64 and quoted-printable types are preferable.

❏ **Binary.** This is 8-bit encoding. Non-ASCII characters can be sent, and the length of the line can exceed 1,000 characters. MIME does not do any encoding here; the underlying SMTP protocol must be able to transfer binary data. It is, therefore, not recommended. Base64 and quoted-printable types are preferable.

❏ **Base64.** This is a solution for sending data made of bytes when the highest bit is not necessarily zero. Base64 transforms this type of data to printable characters, which can then be sent as ASCII characters or any type of character set supported by the underlying mail transfer mechanism.

Base64 divides the binary data (made of streams of bits) into 24-bit blocks. Each block is then divided into four sections, each made of 6 bits (see Figure 20.11).

Figure 20.11   *Base64*

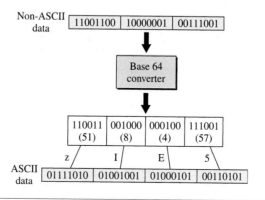

Each 6-bit section is interpreted as one character according to Table 20.3.

Table 20.3   *Base64 encoding table*

Value	Code	Value	Code	Value	Code	Value	Code	Value	Code	Value	Code
0	A	11	L	22	W	33	h	44	s	55	3
1	B	12	M	23	X	34	i	45	t	56	4
2	C	13	N	24	Y	35	j	46	u	57	5
3	D	14	O	25	Z	36	k	47	v	58	6
4	E	15	P	26	a	37	l	48	w	59	7
5	F	16	Q	27	b	38	m	49	x	60	8
6	G	17	R	28	c	39	n	50	y	61	9
7	H	18	S	29	d	40	o	51	z	62	+
8	I	19	T	30	e	41	p	52	0	63	/
9	J	20	U	31	f	42	q	53	1		
10	K	21	V	32	g	43	r	54	2		

❏ **Quoted-printable.** Base64 is a redundant encoding scheme; that is, 24 bits become four characters, and eventually are sent as 32 bits. We have an overhead of 25 percent. If the data consist mostly of ASCII characters with a small non-ASCII portion, we can use quoted-printable encoding. If a character is ASCII, it is sent as is. If a character is not ASCII, it is sent as three characters. The first character is the equal sign (=). The next two characters are the hexadecimal representations of the byte. Figure 20.12 shows an example.

Figure 20.12   *Quoted-printable*

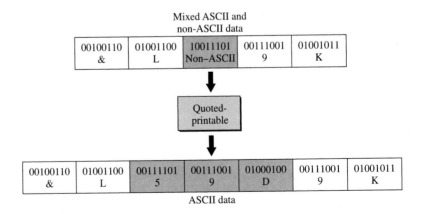

Content-Id

This header uniquely identifies the whole message in a multiple message environment.

> **Content-Id:** id=<content-id>

Content-Description

This header defines whether the body is image, audio, or video.

> **Content-Description:** <description>

20.3   MESSAGE TRANSFER AGENT: SMTP

The actual mail transfer is done through message transfer agents (MTAs). To send mail, a system must have the client MTA, and to receive mail, a system must have a server MTA. The formal protocol that defines the MTA client and server in the Internet is called **Simple Mail Transfer Protocol (SMTP).** As we said before, two pairs of MTA client-server programs are used in the most common situation (fourth scenario). Figure 20.13 shows the range of the SMTP protocol in this scenario.

Figure 20.13   *SMTP range*

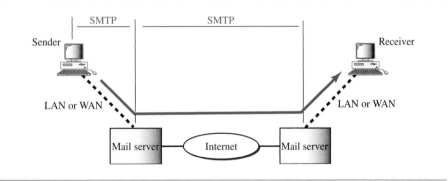

SMTP is used two times, between the sender and the sender's mail server and between the two mail servers. As we will see shortly, another protocol is needed between the mail server and the receiver.

SMTP simply defines how commands and responses must be sent back and forth. Each network is free to choose a software package for implementation. We will discuss the mechanism of mail transfer by SMTP in the remainder of the section.

Commands and Responses

SMTP uses commands and responses to transfer messages between an MTA client and an MTA server (see Figure 20.14).

Each command or reply is terminated by a two-character (carriage return and line feed) end-of-line token.

Figure 20.14   *Commands and responses*

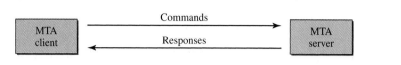

Commands

Commands are sent from the client to the server. The format of a command is shown in Figure 20.15. It consists of a keyword followed by zero or more arguments. SMTP defines 14 commands. The first five are mandatory; every implementation must support these five commands. The next three are often used and highly recommended. The last six are seldom used. The commands are listed in Table 20.4 and described in more detail below.

Figure 20.15   *Command format*

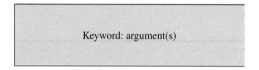

Keyword: argument(s)

Table 20.4   *Commands*

Keyword	Argument(s)
HELO	Sender's host name
MAIL FROM	Sender of the message
RCPT TO	Intended recipient of the message
DATA	Body of the mail
QUIT	
RSET	
VRFY	Name of recipient to be verified
NOOP	
TURN	
EXPN	Mailing list to be expanded
HELP	Command name
SEND FROM	Intended recipient of the message
SMOL FROM	Intended recipient of the message
SMAL FROM	Intended recipient of the message

❑   **HELO.** This command is used by the client to identify itself. The argument is the domain name of the client host. The format is

> **HELO:** challenger.atc.fhda.edu

❑ **MAIL FROM.** This command is used by the client to identify the sender of the message. The argument is the email address of the sender (local part plus the domain name). The format is

> **MAIL FROM:** forouzan@challenger.atc.fhda.edu

❑ **RCPT TO.** This command is used by the client to identify the intended recipient of the message. The argument is the email address of the recipient. If there are multiple recipients, the command is repeated. The format is

> **RCPT TO:** betsy@mcgraw-hill.com

❑ **DATA.** This command is used to send the actual message. All lines that follow the DATA command are treated as the mail message. The message is terminated by a line containing just one period. The format is

> **DATA**
>
> **This is the message
> to be sent to the McGraw-Hill
> Company.**
>
> **.**

❑ **QUIT.** This command terminates the message. The format is

> **QUIT**

❑ **RSET.** This command aborts the current mail transaction. The stored information about the sender and recipient is deleted. The connection will be reset.

> **RSET**

❑ **VRFY.** This command is used to verify the address of the recipient, which is sent as the argument. The sender can ask the receiver to confirm that a name identifies a valid recipient. Its format is

> **VRFY:** betsy@mcgraw-hill.com

❑ **NOOP.** This command is used by the client to check the status of the recipient. It requires an answer from the recipient. Its format is

> **NOOP**

❑ **TURN.** This command lets the sender and the recipient switch positions, whereby the sender becomes the recipient and vice versa. However, most SMTP implementations today do not support this feature. The format is

> **TURN**

❑ **EXPN.** This command asks the receiving host to expand the mailing list sent as the arguments and to return the mailbox addresses of the recipients that comprise the list. The format is

> **EXPN:** x   y   z

❑ **HELP.** This command asks the recipient to send information about the command sent as the argument. The format is

> **HELP:** mail

❑ **SEND FROM.** This command specifies that the mail is to be delivered to the terminal of the recipient, and not the mailbox. If the recipient is not logged in, the mail is bounced back. The argument is the address of the sender. The format is

> **SEND FROM:** forouzan@fhda.atc.edu

❑ **SMOL FROM.** This command specifies that the mail is to be delivered to the terminal or the mailbox of the recipient. This means that if the recipient is logged in, the mail is delivered only to the terminal. If the recipient is not logged in, the mail is delivered to the mailbox. The argument is the address of the sender. The format is

> **SMOL FROM:** forouzan@fhda.atc.edu

❑ **SMAL FROM.** This command specifies that the mail is to be delivered to the terminal and the mailbox of the recipient. This means that if the recipient is logged in, the mail is delivered to the terminal and the mailbox. If the recipient is not logged in, the mail is delivered only to the mailbox. The argument is the address of the sender. The format is

> **SMAL FROM:** forouzan@fhda.atc.edu

Responses

Responses are sent from the server to the client. A response is a three-digit code that may be followed by additional textual information. The meanings of the first digit are as follows:

❑ **2yz (positive completion reply).** If the first digit is 2 (digit 1 is not in use today), it means that the requested command has been successfully completed and a new command can be started.

❑ **3yz (positive intermediate reply).** If the first digit is 3, it means that the requested command has been accepted, but the recipient needs some more information before completion can occur.

❑ **4yz (transient negative completion reply).** If the first digit is 4, it means the requested command has been rejected, but the error condition is temporary. The command can be sent again.

❑ **5yz (permanent negative completion reply).** If the first digit is 5, it means the requested command has been rejected. The command cannot be sent again.

The second and the third digits provide further details about the responses. Table 20.5 lists some of the responses.

Table 20.5   *Responses*

Code	Description
Positive Completion Reply	
211	System status or help reply
214	Help message
220	Service ready
221	Service closing transmission channel
250	Request command completed
251	User not local; the message will be forwarded
Positive Intermediate Reply	
354	Start mail input
Transient Negative Completion Reply	
421	Service not available
450	Mailbox not available
451	Command aborted: local error
452	Command aborted; insufficient storage
Permanent Negative Completion Reply	
500	Syntax error; unrecognized command
501	Syntax error in parameters or arguments
502	Command not implemented
503	Bad sequence of commands
504	Command temporarily not implemented
550	Command is not executed; mailbox unavailable
551	User not local
552	Requested action aborted; exceeded storage location
553	Requested action not taken; mailbox name not allowed
554	Transaction failed

Mail Transfer Phases

The process of transferring a mail message occurs in three phases: connection establishment, mail transfer, and connection termination.

Connection Establishment

After a client has made a TCP connection to the well-known port 25, the SMTP server starts the connection phase. This phase involves the following three steps, which are illustrated in Figure 20.16.

Figure 20.16 *Connection establishment*

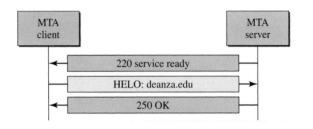

1. The server sends code 220 (service ready) to tell the client that it is ready to receive mail. If the server is not ready, it sends code 421 (service not available).
2. The client sends the HELO message to identify itself using its domain name address. This step is necessary to inform the server of the domain name of the client. Remember that during TCP connection establishment, the sender and receiver know each other through their IP addresses.
3. The server responds with code 250 (request command completed) or some other code depending on the situation.

Message Transfer

After connection has been established between the SMTP client and server, a single message between a sender and one or more recipients can be exchanged. This phase involves eight steps. Steps 3 and 4 are repeated if there is more than one recipient (see Figure 20.17).

1. The client sends the MAIL FROM message to introduce the sender of the message. It includes the mail address of the sender (mailbox and the domain name). This step is needed to give the server the return mail address for returning errors and reporting messages.
2. The server responds with code 250 or some other appropriate code.
3. The client sends the RCPT TO (recipient) message, which includes the mail address of the recipient.
4. The server responds with code 250 or some other appropriate code.
5. The client sends the DATA message to initialize the message transfer.

Figure 20.17 *Message transfer*

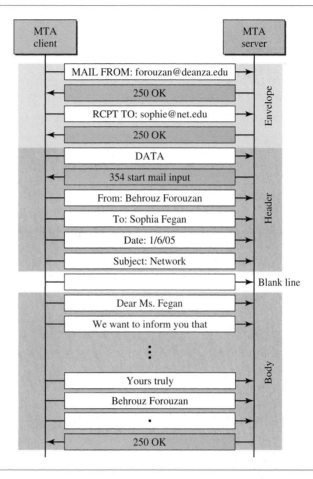

6. The server responds with code 354 (start mail input) or some other appropriate message.

7. The client sends the contents of the message in consecutive lines. Each line is terminated by a two-character end-of-line token (carriage return and line feed). The message is terminated by a line containing just one period.

8. The server responds with code 250 (OK) or some other appropriate code.

Connection Termination

After the message is transferred successfully, the client terminates the connection. This phase involves two steps (see Figure 20.18).

1. The client sends the QUIT command.

2. The server responds with code 221 or some other appropriate code.

After the connection termination phase, the TCP connection must be closed.

Figure 20.18 *Connection termination*

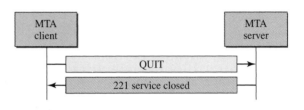

Example 1

Let us see how we can directly use SMTP to send an email and simulate the commands and responses we described in this section. We use TELNET to log into port 25 (the well-known port for SMTP). We then use the commands directly to send an email. In this example, forouzanb@adelphia.net is sending an email to himself. The first few lines show TELNET trying to connect to the adelphia mail server.

```
$ telnet mail.adelphia.net 25
Trying 68.168.78.100...
Connected to mail.adelphia.net (68.168.78.100).
```

After connection, we can type the SMTP commands and then receive the responses as shown below. We have shown the commands in black and the responses in color. Note that we have added for clarification some comment lines, designated by the "=" sign. These lines are not part of the email procedure.

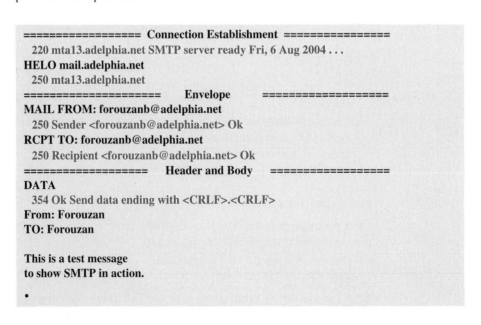

```
===================== Connection Termination ================
    250 Message received: adelphia.net@mail.adelphia.net
QUIT
    221 mta13.adelphia.net SMTP server closing connection
Connection closed by foreign host.
```

20.4   MESSAGE ACCESS AGENT: POP AND IMAP

The first and the second stages of mail delivery use SMTP. However, SMTP is not involved in the third stage because SMTP is a *push* protocol; it pushes the message from the client to the server. In other words, the direction of the bulk data (messages) is from the client to the server. On the other hand, the third stage needs a *pull* protocol; the client must pull messages from the server. The direction of the bulk data are from the server to the client. The third stage uses a message access agent.

Currently two message access protocols are available: Post Office Protocol, version 3 (POP3) and Internet Mail Access Protocol, version 4 (IMAP4). Figure 20.19 shows the position of these two protocols in the most common situation (fourth scenario).

Figure 20.19   *POP3 and IMAP4*

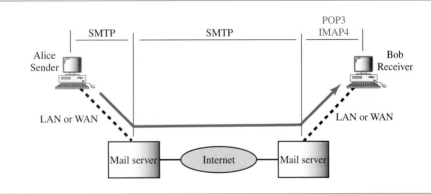

POP3

Post Office Protocol, version 3 (POP3) is simple and limited in functionality. The client POP3 software is installed on the recipient computer; the server POP3 software is installed on the mail server.

Mail access starts with the client when the user needs to download its email from the mailbox on the mail server. The client opens a connection to the server on TCP port 110. It then sends its user name and password to access the mailbox. The user can then list and retrieve the mail messages, one by one. Figure 20.20 shows an example of downloading using POP3.

Figure 20.20   *POP3*

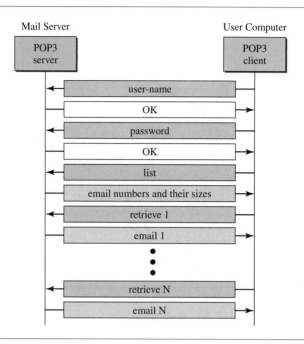

POP3 has two modes: the delete mode and the keep mode. In the delete mode, the mail is deleted from the mailbox after each retrieval. In the keep mode, the mail remains in the mailbox after retrieval. The delete mode is normally used when the user is working at her permanent computer and can save and organize the received mail after reading or replying. The keep mode is normally used when the user accesses her mail away from her primary computer (e.g., a laptop). The mail is read but kept in the system for later retrieval and organizing.

IMAP4

Another mail access protocol is **Internet Mail Access Protocol, version 4 (IMAP4).** IMAP4 is similar to POP3, but it has more features; IMAP4 is more powerful and more complex.

POP3 is deficient in several ways. It does not allow the user to organize her mail on the server; the user cannot have different folders on the server. (Of course, the user can create folders on her own computer.) In addition, POP3 does not allow the user to partially check the contents of the mail before downloading.

IMAP4 provides the following extra functions:

❏ A user can check the email header prior to downloading.

❏ A user can search the contents of the email for a specific string of characters prior to downloading.

❏ A user can partially download email. This is especially useful if bandwidth is limited and the email contains multimedia with high bandwidth requirements.

❏ A user can create, delete, or rename mailboxes on the mail server.

❏ A user can create a hierarchy of mailboxes in a folder for email storage.

20.5 WEB-BASED MAIL

Email is such a common application that some websites today provide this service to anyone who accesses the site. Two common sites are Hotmail and Yahoo. The idea is very simple. Mail transfer from Alice's browser to her mail server is done through HTTP (see Chapter 22). The transfer of the message from the sending mail server to the receiving mail server is still through SMTP. Finally, the message from the receiving server (the web server) to Bob's browser is done through HTTP.

The last phase is very interesting. Instead of POP3 or IMAP4, HTTP is normally used. When Bob needs to retrieve his emails, he sends a message to the website (Hotmail, for example). The website sends a form to be filled in by Bob, which includes the log-in name and the password. If the log-in name and password match, the email is transferred from the web server to Bob's browser in HTML format.

20.6 KEY TERMS

alias	local part
body	message access agent (MAA)
connection establishment	message transfer agent (MTA)
connection termination	Multipurpose Internet Mail Extensions (MIME)
domain name	
envelope	Post Office Protocol, version 3 (POP3)
header	Simple Mail Transfer Protocol (SMTP)
Internet Mail Access Protocol, version 4 (IMAP4)	user agent (UA)

20.7 SUMMARY

❏ The UA prepares the message, creates the envelope, and puts the message in the envelope.

❏ The mail address consists of two parts: a local part (user mailbox) and a domain name. The form is localpart@domainname.

❏ An alias allows the use of a mailing list.

❏ Multipurpose Internet Mail Extension (MIME) allows the transfer of multimedia messages.

❏ The MTA transfers the mail across the Internet, a LAN, or a WAN.

❏ SMTP uses commands and responses to transfer messages between an MTA client and an MTA server.

❏ The steps in transferring a mail message are:

    a. connection establishment

    b. mail transfer

    c. connection termination

❏ Post Office Protocol, version 3 (POP3) and Internet Mail Access Protocol, version 4 (IMAP4) are protocols used for pulling messages from a mail server.

20.8 PRACTICE SET

Exercises

1. A sender sends unformatted text. Show the MIME header.

2. A sender sends a JPEG message. Show the MIME header.

3. A non-ASCII message of 1,000 bytes is encoded using base64. How many bytes are in the encoded message? How many bytes are redundant? What is the ratio of redundant bytes to the total message?

4. A message of 1,000 bytes is encoded using quoted-printable. The message consists of 90 percent ASCII and 10 percent non-ASCII characters. How many bytes are in the encoded message? How many bytes are redundant? What is the ratio of redundant bytes to the total message?

5. Compare the results of Exercises 3 and 4. How much is the efficiency improved if the message is a combination of ASCII and non-ASCII characters?

6. Encode the following message in base64:

```
01010111  00001111 11110000 10101111  01110001  01010100
```

7. Encode the following message in quoted-printable:

```
01010111  00001111 11110000  10101111 01110001  01010100
```

8. Encode the following message in base64:

```
01010111  00001111 11110000  10101111 01110001
```

9. Encode the following message in quoted-printable:

```
01010111  00001111 11110000  10101111 01110001
```

10. Are the HELO and MAIL FROM commands both necessary? Why or why not?

11. In Figure 20.17 what is the difference between MAIL FROM in the envelope and the FROM in the header?

12. Why is a connection establishment for mail transfer needed if TCP has already established a connection?

13. Show the connection establishment phase from aaa@xxx.com to bbb@yyy.com.

14. Show the message transfer phase from aaa@xxx.com to bbb@yyy.com. The message is "Good morning my friend."

15. Show the connection termination phase from aaa@xxx.com to bbb@yyy.com.

16. User aaa@xxx.com sends a message to user bbb@yyy.com, which is forwarded to user ccc@zzz.com. Show all SMTP commands and responses.

17. User aaa@xxx.com sends a message to user bbb@yyy.com. The latter replies. Show all SMTP commands and responses.

18. In SMTP, if we send a one-line message between two users, how many lines of commands and responses are exchanged?

Research Activities

19. Find the RFCs related to SMTP.

20. Find the RFCs related to POP3.

21. Find the RFCs related to IMAP4.

22. Find any RFCs related to the message format.

23. A new version of SMTP, called ESMTP, is in use today. Find the differences between the two.

24. Find information about the *smileys* used to express a user's emotions.

CHAPTER 21

Network Management: SNMP

The **Simple Network Management Protocol (SNMP)** is a framework for managing devices in an internet using the TCP/IP protocol suite. It provides a set of fundamental operations for monitoring and maintaining an internet.

21.1 CONCEPT

SNMP uses the concept of manager and agent. That is, a manager, usually a host, controls and monitors a set of agents, usually routers (see Figure 21.1).

Figure 21.1 *SNMP concept*

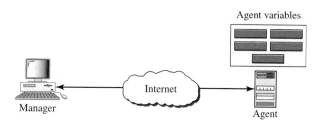

SNMP is an application-level protocol in which a few manager stations control a set of agents. The protocol is designed at the application level so that it can monitor devices made by different manufacturers and installed on different physical networks. In other words, SNMP frees management tasks from both the physical characteristics of the managed devices and the underlying networking technology. It can be used in a heterogeneous internet made of different LANs and WANs connected by routers made by different manufacturers.

Managers and Agents

A management station, called a **manager,** is a host that runs the SNMP client program. A managed station, called an **agent,** is a router (or a host) that runs the SNMP server program. Management is achieved through simple interaction between a manager and an agent.

The agent keeps performance information in a database. The manager has access to the values in the database. For example, a router can store in appropriate variables the number of packets received and forwarded. The manager can fetch and compare the values of these two variables to see if the router is congested or not.

The manager can also make the router perform certain actions. For example, a router periodically checks the value of a reboot counter to see when it should reboot itself. It reboots itself, for example, if the value of the counter is 0. The manager can use this feature to reboot the agent remotely at any time. It simply sends a packet to force a 0 value in the counter.

Agents can also contribute to the management process. The server program running on the agent can check the environment and, if it notices something unusual, it can send a warning message (called a **trap**) to the manager.

In other words, management with SNMP is based on three basic ideas:

1. A manager checks an agent by requesting information that reflects the behavior of the agent.

2. A manager forces an agent to perform a task by resetting values in the agent database.

3. An agent contributes to the management process by warning the manager of an unusual situation.

21.2   MANAGEMENT COMPONENTS

To do management tasks, SNMP uses two other protocols: **Structure of Management Information (SMI)** and **Management Information Base (MIB).** In other words, management on the Internet is done through the cooperation of three protocols: SNMP, SMI, and MIB as shown in Figure 21.2.

Figure 21.2   *Components of network management on the Internet*

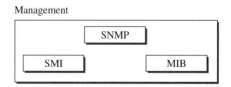

Let us elaborate on the interactions between these protocols.

Role of SNMP

SNMP has some very specific roles in network management. It defines the format of the packet to be sent from a manager to an agent and vice versa. It also interprets the result and creates statistics (often with the help of other management software). The packets exchanged contain the object (variable) names and their status (values). SNMP is responsible for reading and changing these values.

> **SNMP defines the format of packets exchanged between a manager and an agent.**
> **It reads and changes the status (values) of objects (variables) in SNMP packets.**

Role of SMI

To use SNMP, we need rules. We need rules for naming objects. This is particularly important because the objects in SNMP form a hierarchical structure (an object may have a parent object and some children objects). Part of a name can be inherited from the parent. We also need rules to define the type of the objects. What types of objects are handled by SNMP? Can SNMP handle simple types or structured types? How many simple types are available? What are the sizes of these types? What is the range of these types? In addition, how are each of these types encoded?

We need these universal rules because we do not know the architecture of the computers that send, receive, or store these values. The sender may be a powerful computer in which an integer is stored as 8-byte data; the receiver may be a small computer that stores an integer as 4-byte data.

SMI is a protocol that defines these rules. However, we must understand that SMI only defines the rules; it does not define how many objects are managed in an entity or which object uses which type. SMI is a collection of general rules to name objects and to list their types. The association of an object with the type is not done by SMI.

> **SMI defines the general rules for naming objects, defining object types (including range and length), and showing how to encode objects and values.**
> **SMI defines neither the number of objects an entity should manage, nor names the objects to be managed nor defines the association between the objects and their values.**

Role of MIB

We hope it is clear that we need another protocol. For each entity to be managed, this protocol must define the number of objects, name them according to the rules defined by SMI, and associate a type to each named object. This protocol is MIB. MIB creates a set of objects defined for each entity similar to a database (mostly meta data in a database, names and types without values).

> **MIB creates a collection of named objects, their types, and their relationships to each other in an entity to be managed.**

An Analogy

Before discussing each of these protocols in more detail, let us give an analogy. The three network management components are similar to what we need when we write a program in a computer language to solve a problem.

Before we write a program, the syntax of the language (such as C or Java) must be predefined. The language also defines the structure of variables (simple, structured, pointer, and so on) and how the variables must be named. For example, a variable name must be 1 to N characters in length and start with a letter followed by alphanumeric characters. The language also defines the type of data to be used (integer, float, char, etc.). In programming the rules are defined by the language. In network management the rules are defined by SMI.

Most computer languages require that variables be declared in each specific program. The declaration names each variable and defines the predefined type. For example, if a program has two variables (an integer named *counter* and an array named *grades* of type char), they must be declared at the beginning of the program:

> **int** *counter* ;
> **char** *grades* **[40]** ;

Note that the declarations name the variables (counter and grades) and define the type of each variable. Because the types are predefined in the language, the program knows the range and size of each variable.

MIB does this task in network management. MIB names each object and defines the type of the objects. Because the type is defined by SMI, SNMP knows the range and size.

After declaration in programming, the program needs to write statements to store values in the variables and change them if needed. SNMP does this task in network management. SNMP stores, changes, and interprets the values of objects already declared by MIB according to the rules defined by SMI.

We can compare the task of network management to the task of writing a program.

❏ **Both tasks need rules. In network management this is handled by SMI.**
❏ **Both tasks need variable declarations. In network management this is handled by MIB.**
❏ **Both tasks have actions performed by statements. In network management this is handled by SNMP.**

An Overview

Before discussing each component in detail, let us show how each of them is involved in a simple scenario. This is an overview that will be developed later at the end of the chapter. A manager station (SNMP client) wants to send a message to an agent station (SNMP server) to find the number of UDP user datagrams received by the agent. Figure 21.3 shows an overview of steps involved.

MIB is responsible for finding the object that holds the number of UDP user datagram received. SMI, with the help of another embedded protocol, is responsible for encoding the name of the object. SNMP is responsible for creating a message, called a GetRequest message, and encapsulating the encoded message. Of course, things are more complicated than this simple overview, but we first need more details of each protocol.

Figure 21.3   *Management overview*

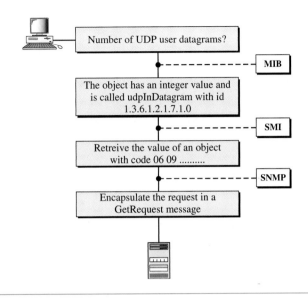

21.3 SMI

The Structure of Management Information, version 2 (SMIv2) is a component for network management. Its functions are:

1. To name objects.
2. To define the type of data that can be stored in an object.
3. To show how to encode data for transmission over the network.

SMI is a guideline for SNMP. It emphasizes three attributes to handle an object: name, data type, and encoding method (see Figure 21.4).

Figure 21.4   *Object attributes*

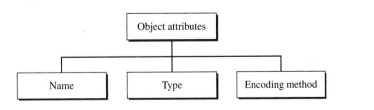

Name

SMI requires that each managed object (such as a router, a variable in a router, a value, etc.) have a unique name. To name objects globally, SMI uses an **object identifier,** which is a hierarchical identifier based on a tree structure (see Figure 21.5).

Figure 21.5   *Object identifier*

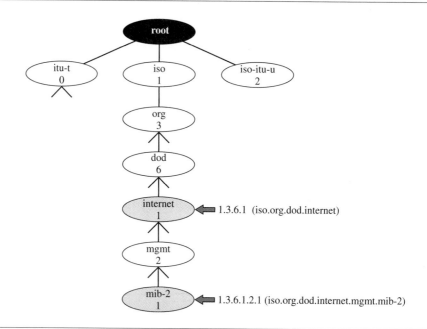

The tree structure starts with an unnamed root. Each object can be defined using a sequence of integers separated by dots. The tree structure can also define an object using a sequence of textual names separated by dots. The integer-dot representation is used in SNMP. The name-dot notation is used by people. For example, the following shows the same object in two different notations:

iso.org.dod.internet.mgmt.mib-2 ←——→ 1.3.6.1.2.1

The objects that are used in SNMP are located under the *mib-2* object, so their identifiers always start with 1.3.6.1.2.1.

> **All objects managed by SNMP are given an object identifier.**
> **The object identifier always starts with 1.3.6.1.2.1.**

Type

The second attribute of an object is the type of data stored in it. To define the data type, SMI uses fundamental **Abstract Syntax Notation 1 (ASN.1)** definitions and adds some new definitions. In other words, SMI is both a subset and a superset of ASN.1.

SMI has two broad categories of data type: *simple* and *structured*. We first define the simple types and then show how the structured types can be constructed from the simple ones (see Figure 21.6).

Figure 21.6   *Data type*

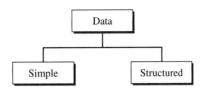

Simple Type

The **simple data types** are atomic data types. Some of them are taken directly from ASN.1; some are added by SMI. The most important ones are given in Table 21.1. The first five are from ASN.1; the next seven are defined by SMI.

Table 21.1   *Data types*

Type	Size	Description
INTEGER	4 bytes	An integer with a value between -2^{31} and $2^{31}-1$
Integer32	4 bytes	Same as INTEGER
Unsigned32	4 bytes	Unsigned with a value between 0 and $2^{32}-1$
OCTET STRING	Variable	Byte-string up to 65,535 bytes long
OBJECT IDENTIFIER	Variable	An object identifier
IPAddress	4 bytes	An IP address made of four integers
Counter32	4 bytes	An integer whose value can be incremented from zero to 2^{32}; when it reaches its maximum value it wraps back to zero
Counter64	8 bytes	64-bit counter
Gauge32	4 bytes	Same as Counter32, but when it reaches its maximum value, it does not wrap; it remains there until it is reset
TimeTicks	4 bytes	A counting value that records time in 1/100ths of a second
BITS		A string of bits
Opaque	Variable	Uninterpreted string

Structured Type

By combining simple and structured data types, we can make new structured data types. SMI defines two **structured data types:** *sequence* and *sequence of.*

❑   **Sequence.** A *sequence* data type is a combination of simple data types, not necessarily of the same type. It is analogous to the concept of a *struct* or a *record* used in programming languages such as C.

❑ **Sequence of.** A *sequence of* data type is a combination of simple data types all of the same type or a combination of sequence data types all of the same type. It is analogous to the concept of an *array* used in programming languages such as C.

Figure 21.7 shows a conceptual view of data types.

Figure 21.7   *Conceptual data types*

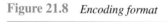

a. Simple variable

c. Sequence

b. Sequence of
(simple variables)

d. Sequence of
(sequences)

Encoding Method

SMI uses another standard, **Basic Encoding Rules (BER),** to encode data to be transmitted over the network. BER specifies that each piece of data be encoded in triplet format: tag, length, and value, as illustrated in Figure 21.8.

Figure 21.8   *Encoding format*

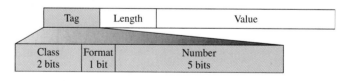

❑ **Tag.** The tag is a 1-byte field that defines the type of data. It is composed of three subfields: *class* (2 bits), *format* (1 bit), and *number* (5 bits). The class subfield defines the scope of the data. Four classes are defined: universal (00), application-wide (01), context-specific (10), and private (11). The universal data types are those taken from ASN.1 (INTEGER, OCTET STRING, and ObjectIdentifier). The application-wide data types are those added by SMI (IPAddress, Counter, Gauge, and TimeTicks). The five context-specific data types have meanings that may change from one protocol to another. The private data types are vendor-specific.

The format subfield indicates whether the data is simple (0) or structured (1). The number subfield further divides simple or structured data into subgroups. For example, in the universal class, with simple format, INTEGER has a value of 2, OCTET STRING has a value of 4, and so on. Table 21.2 shows the data types we use in this chapter and their tags in binary and hexadecimal numbers.

Table 21.2   *Codes for data types*

Data Type	Class	Format	Number	Tag (Binary)	Tag (Hex)
INTEGER	00	0	00010	**00000010**	**02**
OCTET STRING	00	0	00100	**00000100**	**04**
OBJECT IDENTIFIER	00	0	00110	**00000110**	**06**
NULL	00	0	00101	**00000101**	**05**
Sequence, sequence of	00	1	10000	**00110000**	**30**
IPAddress	01	0	00000	**01000000**	**40**
Counter	01	0	00001	**01000001**	**41**
Gauge	01	0	00010	**01000010**	**42**
TimeTicks	01	0	00011	**01000011**	**43**
Opaque	01	0	00100	**01000100**	**44**

❏ **Length.** The length field is 1 or more bytes. If it is 1 byte, the most significant bit must be 0. The other 7 bits define the length of the data. If it is more than 1 byte, the most significant bit of the first byte must be 1. The other 7 bits of the first byte define the number of bytes needed to define the length. See Figure 21.9 for a depiction of the length field.

Figure 21.9   *Length format*

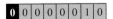

a. The colored part defines the length (2)

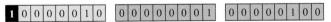

b. The shaded part defines the length of the length (2 bytes);
the colored bytes define the length (260 bytes)

❏ **Value.** The value field codes the value of the data according to the rules defined in BER.

To show how these three fields—tag, length, and value—can define objects, we give some examples.

Example 1

Figure 21.10 shows how to define INTEGER 14.

Figure 21.10   *Example 1, INTEGER 14*

02	04	00	00	00	0E
00000010	00000100	00000000	00000000	00000000	00001110
Tag (integer)	Length (4 bytes)	| Value (14)			

Example 2

Figure 21.11 shows how to define the OCTET STRING "HI."

Figure 21.11   *Example 2, OCTET STRING "HI"*

04	02	48	49
00000100	00000010	01001000	01001001
Tag (String)	Length (2 bytes)	Value (H)	Value (I)

Example 3

Figure 21.12 shows how to define ObjectIdentifier 1.3.6.1 (iso.org.dod.internet).

Figure 21.12   *Example 3, ObjectIdentifier 1.3.6.1*

06	04	01	03	06	01
00000110	00000100	00000001	00000011	00000110	00000001
Tag (ObjectId)	Length (4 bytes)	Value (1)	Value (3)	Value (6)	Value (1)

|← 1.3.6.1 (iso.org.dod.internet) →|

Example 4

Figure 21.13 shows how to define IPAddress 131.21.14.8.

Figure 21.13   *Example 4, IPAddress 131.21.14.8*

40	04	83	15	0E	08
01000000	00000100	10000011	00010101	00001110	00001000
Tag (IPAddress)	Length (4 bytes)	Value (131)	Value (21)	Value (14)	Value (8)

|← 131.21.14.8 →|

21.4   MIB

The Management Information Base, version 2 (MIB2) is the second component used in network management. Each agent has its own MIB2, which is a collection of all the objects that the manager can manage. The objects in MIB2 are categorized under ten different groups: system, interface, address translation, ip, icmp, tcp, udp, egp, transmission, and snmp. These groups are under the mib-2 object in the object identifier tree (see Figure 21.14). Each group has defined variables and/or tables.

Figure 21.14   *mib-2*

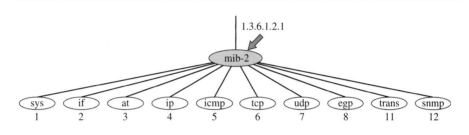

The following is a brief description of some of the objects:

❏   **sys**   This object (*system*) defines general information about the node (system), such as the name, location, and lifetime.

❏   **if**   This object (*interface*) defines information about all of the interfaces of the node including interface number, physical address, and IP address.

❏   **at**   This object (*address translation*) defines the information about the ARP table.

❏   **ip**   This object defines information related to IP, such as the routing table and the IP address.

❏   **icmp**   This object defines information related to ICMP, such as the number of packets sent and received and total errors created.

❏   **tcp**   This object defines general information related to TCP, such as the connection table, time-out value, number of ports, and number of packets sent and received.

❏   **udp**   This object defines general information related to UDP, such as the number of ports and number of packets sent and received.

❏   **snmp**   This object defines general information related to SNMP itself.

Accessing MIB Variables

To show how to access different variables, we use the udp group as an example. There are four simple variables in the udp group and one sequence of (table of) records. Figure 21.15 shows the variables and the table.

We will show how to access each entity.

Figure 21.15 *udp group*

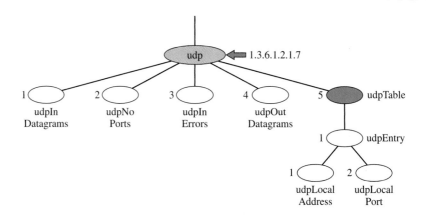

Simple Variables

To access any of the simple variables, we use the id of the group (1.3.6.1.2.1.7) followed by the id of the variable. The following shows how to access each variable.

udpInDatagrams	➡ 1.3.6.1.2.1.7.1
udpNoPorts	➡ 1.3.6.1.2.1.7.2
udpInErrors	➡ 1.3.6.1.2.1.7.3
udpOutDatagrams	➡ 1.3.6.1.2.1.7.4

However, these object identifiers define the variable, not the instance (contents). To show the instance or the contents of each variable, we must add an instance suffix. The instance suffix for a simple variable is simply a zero. In other words, to show an instance of the above variables, we use the following:

udpInDatagrams.0	➡ 1.3.6.1.2.1.7.1.**0**
udpNoPorts.0	➡ 1.3.6.1.2.1.7.2.**0**
udpInErrors.0	➡ 1.3.6.1.2.1.7.3.**0**
udpOutDatagrams.0	➡ 1.3.6.1.2.1.7.4.**0**

Tables

To identify a table, we first use the table id. The udp group has only one table (with id 5) as illustrated in Figure 21.16.

So to access the table, we use the following:

udpTable	➡ 1.3.6.1.2.1.7.5

Figure 21.16 *udp variables and tables*

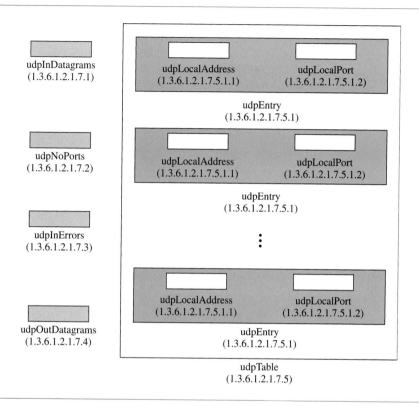

However, the table is not at the leaf level in the tree structure. We cannot access the table; we define the entry (sequence) in the table (with id of 1), as follows:

$$udpEntry \implies 1.3.6.1.2.1.7.5.\mathbf{1}$$

This entry is also not a leaf and we cannot access it. We need to define each entity (field) in the entry.

$$udpLocalAddress \implies 1.3.6.1.2.1.7.5.\mathbf{1.1}$$
$$udpLocalPort \implies 1.3.6.1.2.1.7.5.\mathbf{1.2}$$

These two variables are at the leaf of the tree. Although we can access their instances, we need to define *which* instance. At any moment, the table can have several values for each local address/local port pair. To access a specific instance (row) of the table, we add the index to the above ids. In MIB, the indexes of arrays are not integers (like most programming languages). The indexes are based on the value of one or more fields in the entries. In our example, the udpTable is indexed based on both the local address and the local port number. For example, Figure 21.17 shows a table with four rows and values for each field. The index of each row is a combination of two values.

Figure 21.17   *Indexes for udpTable*

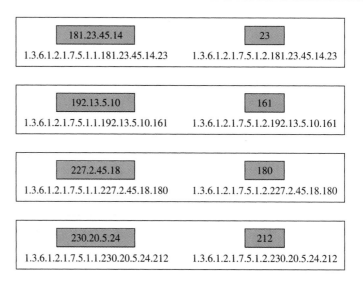

To access the instance of the local address for the first row, we use the identifier augmented with the instance index:

udpLocalAddress.181.23.45.14.23 ➡ 1.3.6.1.2.7.5.1.1.181.23.45.14.23

Note that not all tables are indexed the same way. Some tables are indexed using the value of one field, some using the value of two fields, and so on.

Lexicographic Ordering

One interesting point about the MIB variables is that the object identifiers (including the instance identifiers) follow in lexicographic order. Tables are ordered according to column-row rules, which means one should go column by column. In each column, one should go from the top to the bottom, as shown in Figure 21.18.

The **lexicographic ordering** enables a manager to access a set of variables one after another by defining the first variable, as we will see in the GetNextRequest command in the next section.

Figure 21.18   *Lexicographic ordering*

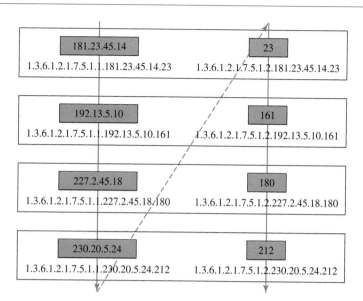

21.5   SNMP

SNMP uses both SMI and MIB in Internet network management. It is an application program that allows:

1. A manager to retrieve the value of an object defined in an agent.
2. A manager to store a value in an object defined in an agent.
3. An agent to send an alarm message about an abnormal situation to the manager.

PDUs

SNMPv3 defines eight types of packets (or PDUs): GetRequest, GetNextRequest, GetBulkRequest, SetRequest, Response, Trap, InformRequest, and Report (see Figure 21.19).

GetRequest

The GetRequest PDU is sent from the manager (client) to the agent (server) to retrieve the value of a variable or a set of variables.

GetNextRequest

The GetNextRequest PDU is sent from the manager to the agent to retrieve the value of a variable. The retrieved value is the value of the object following the defined ObjectId in the PDU. It is mostly used to retrieve the values of the entries in a table. If the manager

Figure 21.19   *SNMP PDUs*

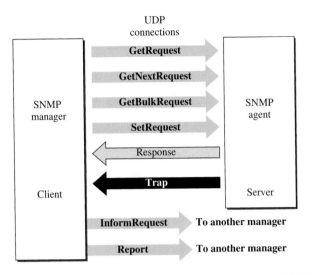

does not know the indexes of the entries, it cannot retrieve the values. However, it can use GetNextRequest and define the ObjectId of the table. Because the first entry has the ObjectId immediately after the ObjectId of the table, the value of the first entry is returned. The manager can use this ObjectId to get the value of the next one, and so on.

GetBulkRequest

The GetBulkRequest PDU is sent from the manager to the agent to retrieve a large amount of data. It can be used instead of multiple GetRequest and GetNextRequest PDUs.

SetRequest

The SetRequest PDU is sent from the manager to the agent to set (store) a value in a variable.

Response

The Response PDU is sent from an agent to a manager in response to GetRequest or GetNextRequest. It contains the value(s) of the variable(s) requested by the manager.

Trap

The **Trap** (also called SNMPv2 Trap to distinguish it from SNMPv1 Trap) PDU is sent from the agent to the manager to report an event. For example, if the agent is rebooted, it informs the manager and reports the time of rebooting.

InformRequest

The InformRequest PDU is sent from one manager to another remote manager to get the value of some variables from agents under the control of the remote manager. The remote manager responds with a Response PDU.

Report

The Report PDU is designed to report some types of errors between managers. It is not yet in use.

Format

The format for the eight SNMP PDUs is shown in Figure 21.20. The GetBulkRequest PDU differs from the others in two areas as shown in the figure.

Figure 21.20 *SNMP PDU format*

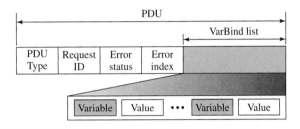

The fields are listed below:

❏ **PDU type.** This field defines the type of the PDU (see Table 21.4).

❏ **Request ID.** This field is a sequence number used by the manager in a request PDU and repeated by the agent in a response. It is used to match a request to a response.

❏ **Error status.** This is an integer that is used only in response PDUs to show the types of errors reported by the agent. Its value is 0 in request PDUs. Table 21.3 lists the types of errors that can occur.

❏ **Non-repeaters.** This field is used only in GetBulkRequest and replaces the error status field, which is empty in request PDUs.

Table 21.3 *Types of errors*

Status	Name	Meaning
0	noError	No error
1	tooBig	Response too big to fit in one message
2	noSuchName	Variable does not exist
3	badValue	The value to be stored is invalid
4	readOnly	The value cannot be modified
5	genErr	Other errors

❑ **Error index.** The error index is an offset that tells the manager which variable caused the error.

❑ **Max-repetition.** This field is also used only in GetBulkRequest and replaces the error index field, which is empty in request PDUs.

❑ **VarBind list.** This is a set of variables with the corresponding values the manager wants to retrieve or set. The values are null in GetRequest and GetNextRequest. In a Trap PDU, it shows the variables and values related to a specific PDU.

21.6   MESSAGES

SNMP does not send only a PDU, it embeds the PDU in a message. A message in SNMPv3 is made of four elements: version, header, security parameters, and data (which includes the encoded PDU) as shown in Figure 21.21.

Figure 21.21   *SNMP message*

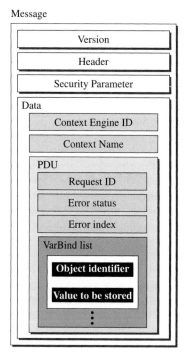

Because the length of these elements is different from message to message, SNMP uses BER to encode each element. Remember that BER uses the tag and the length to define a value. The *version* defines the current version (3). The *header* contains values for message identification, maximum message size (the maximum size of the reply), message flag (one octet of data type OCTET STRING where each bit defines security type, such as privacy or authentication, or other information), and a message security model (defining the security protocol). The message *security parameter* is used to create a message digest (see Chapter 28). The data contains the PDU. If the data are encrypted, there is information about the encrypting engine (the manager program that did the encryption) and the encrypting context (the type of encryption) followed by the encrypted PDU. If the data are not encrypted, the data consists of just the PDU.

To define the type of PDU, SNMP uses a tag. The class is context-sensitive (10), the format is structured (1), and the numbers are 0, 1, 2, 3, 5, 6, 7, and 8 (see Table 21.4). Note that SNMPv1 defined A4 for Trap, which is obsolete today.

Table 21.4   *Codes for SNMP messages*

Data	Class	Format	Number	Whole Tag (Binary)	Whole Tag (Hex)
GetRequest	10	1	00000	**10100000**	**A0**
GetNextRequest	10	1	00001	**10100001**	**A1**
Response	10	1	00010	**10100010**	**A2**
SetRequest	10	1	00011	**10100011**	**A3**
GetBulkRequest	10	1	00101	**10100101**	**A5**
InformRequest	10	1	00110	**10100110**	**A6**
Trap (SNMPv2)	10	1	00111	**10100111**	**A7**
Report	10	1	01000	**10101000**	**A8**

Example 5

In this example, a manager station (SNMP client) uses the GetRequest message to retrieve the number of UDP datagrams that a router has received.

There is only one VarBind entity. The corresponding MIB variable related to this information is udpInDatagrams with the object identifier 1.3.6.1.2.1.7.1.0 The manager wants to retrieve a value (not to store a value), so the value defines a null entity. Figure 21.22 shows the conceptual view of the packet showing the hierarchical nature of sequences. We have used white and color boxes for the sequence and a gray one for the PDU.

The VarBind list has only one VarBind. The variable is of type 06 and length 09. The value is of type 05 and length 00. The whole VarBind is a sequence of length 0D (13). The VarBind list is also a sequence of length 0F (15). The GetRequest PDU is of length ID (29).

Now we have three OCTET STRINGs related to security parameter, security model, and flags. Then we have two integers defining maximum size (1024) and message ID (64). The header is a sequence of length 12, which we left blank for simplicity. There is one integer, version (version 3). The whole message is a sequence of 52 bytes.

Figure 21.23 shows the actual message sent by the manager station (client) to the agent (server).

Figure 21.22 *Example 5*

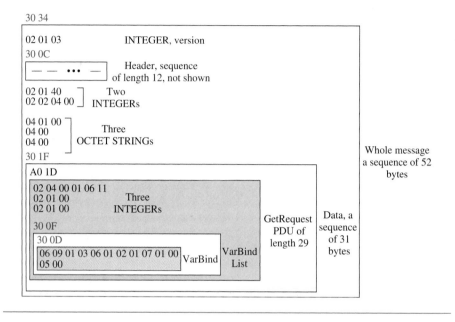

Figure 21.23 *GetRequest message*

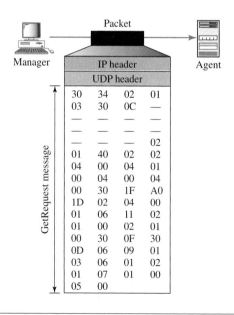

21.7   UDP PORTS

SNMP uses the services of UDP on two well-known ports, 161 and 162. The well-known port 161 is used by the server (agent), and the well-known port 162 is used by the client (manager).

The agent (server) issues a passive open on port 161. It then waits for a connection from a manager (client). A manager (client) issues an active open using an ephemeral port. The request messages are sent from the client to the server using the ephemeral port as the source port and the well-known port 161 as the destination port. The response messages are sent from the server to the client using the well-known port 161 as the source port and the ephemeral port as the destination port.

The manager (client) issues a passive open on port 162. It then waits for a connection from an agent (server). Whenever it has a Trap message to send, an agent (server) issues an active open, using an ephemeral port. This connection is only one-way, from the server to the client (see Figure 21.24).

Figure 21.24   *Port numbers for SNMP*

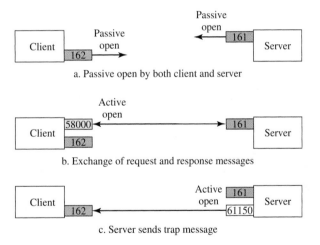

a. Passive open by both client and server

b. Exchange of request and response messages

c. Server sends trap message

The client-server mechanism in SNMP is different from other protocols. Here both the client and the server use well-known ports. In addition, both the client and the server are running infinitely. The reason is that request messages are initiated by a manager (client), but Trap messages are initiated by an agent (server).

21.8   SECURITY

The main difference between SNMPv3 and SNMPv2 is the enhanced security. SNMPv3 provides two types of security: general and specific. SNMPv3 provides message authentication, privacy, and manager authorization. We discuss these three aspects in Chapter 28. In addition, SNMPv3 allows a manager to remotely change the security configuration, which means that the manager does not have to be physically present at the manager station.

21.9 KEY TERMS

Abstract Syntax Notation 1 (ASN.1)	object identifier
agent	simple data type
Basic Encoding Rules (BER)	Simple Network Management Protocol (SNMP)
lexicographic ordering	
Management Information Base (MIB)	Structure of Management Information (SMI)
manager	structured data type
object	trap

21.10 SUMMARY

❑ Simple Network Management Protocol (SNMP) is a framework for managing devices in an internet using the TCP/IP protocol suite.

❑ A manager, usually a host, controls and monitors a set of agents, usually routers.

❑ The manager is a host that runs the SNMP client program.

❑ The agent is a router or host that runs the SNMP server program.

❑ SNMP frees management tasks from both the physical characteristics of the managed devices and the underlying networking technology.

❑ SNMP uses the services of two other protocols: Structure of Management Information (SMI) and Management Information Base (MIB).

❑ SMI names objects, defines the type of data that can be stored in an object, and encodes the data.

❑ SMI objects are named according to a hierarchical tree structure.

❑ SMI data types are defined according to Abstract Syntax Notation 1 (ASN.1).

❑ SMI uses Basic Encoding Rules (BER) to encode data.

❑ MIB is a collection of groups of objects that can be managed by SNMP.

❑ MIB uses lexicographic ordering to manage its variables.

❑ SNMP functions in three ways:

    a. A manager can retrieve the value of an object defined in an agent.

    b. A manager can store a value in an object defined in an agent.

    c. An agent can send an alarm message to the manager.

❑ SNMP defines eight types of packets: GetRequest, GetNextRequest, SetRequest, GetBulkRequest, Trap, InformRequest, Response, and Report.

❏ SNMP uses the services of UDP on two well-known ports, 161 and 162.

❏ SNMPv3 has enhanced security features over previous versions.

21.11   PRACTICE SET

Exercises

1. Show the encoding for the INTEGER 1456.

2. Show the encoding for the OCTET STRING "Hello World."

3. Show the encoding for an arbitrary OCTET STRING of length 1,000.

4. Show how the following record (sequence) is encoded.

INTEGER	OCTET STRING	IP Address
2345	"COMPUTER"	185.32.1.5

5. Show how the following record (sequence) is encoded.

Time Tick	INTEGER	Object Id
12000	14564	1.3.6.1.2.1.7

6. Show how the following array (sequence of) is encoded. Each element is an integer.

2345
1236
122
1236

7. Show how the following array of records (sequence of sequence) is encoded.

INTEGER	OCTET STRING	Counter
2345	"COMPUTER"	345
1123	"DISK"	1430
3456	"MONITOR"	2313

8. Decode the following:

   a. 02 04 01 02 14 32

   b. 30 06 02 01 11 02 01 14

   c. 30 09 04 03 41 43 42 02 02 14 14

   d. 30 0A 40 04 23 51 62 71 02 02 14 12

Research Activities

9. Find RFCs related to SNMP.

10. Find RFCs related to MIB.

11. Find more information about ASN.1.

CHAPTER 22

World Wide Web: HTTP

The **World Wide Web (WWW)** is a repository of information linked together from points all over the world. The WWW has a unique combination of flexibility, portability, and user-friendly features that distinguish it from other services provided by the Internet. The WWW project was initiated by CERN (European Laboratory for Particle Physics) to create a system to handle distributed resources necessary for scientific research. In this chapter we first discuss issues related to the Web. We then discuss a protocol, HTTP, that is used to retrieve information from the Web.

22.1 ARCHITECTURE

The WWW today is a distributed client-server service, in which a client using a browser can access a service using a server. However, the service provided is distributed over many locations called *sites* as shown in Figure 22.1.

Figure 22.1 *Architecture of WWW*

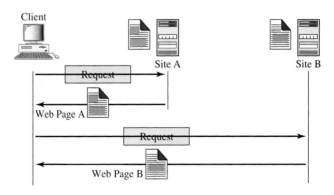

Each site holds one or more documents, referred to as *Web pages*. Each Web page can contain a link to other pages in the same or other sites. The pages can be retrieved and viewed using browsers. Let us go through the scenario shown in the figure. The client needs to see some information that it knows belong to site A. It sends a request, through its browser, a program that is designed to fetch **Web** documents. The request, among other information, includes the address of the site and the Web page, called the URL, which we will discuss shortly. The server at site A finds the document and sends it to the client. When the user views the document, it finds some references to other documents, including a Web page at site B. The reference has the URL for the new site. The user is also interested in seeing this document. The client sends another request to the new site and the new page is retrieved.

Client (Browser)

A variety of vendors offer commercial browsers that interpret and display a Web document, and all of them use nearly the same architecture. Each browser usually consists of three parts: a controller, client protocol, and interpreters. The controller receives input from the keyboard or the mouse and uses the client programs to access the document. After the document has been accessed, the controller uses one of the interpreters to display the document on the screen. The client protocol can be one of the protocols described previously such as FTP, or TELNET, or HTTP (described later in the chapter). The interpreter can be HTML, Java, or JavaScript, depending on the type of document. We discuss the use of these interpreters based on the document type later in the chapter (see Figure 22.2).

Figure 22.2 *Browser*

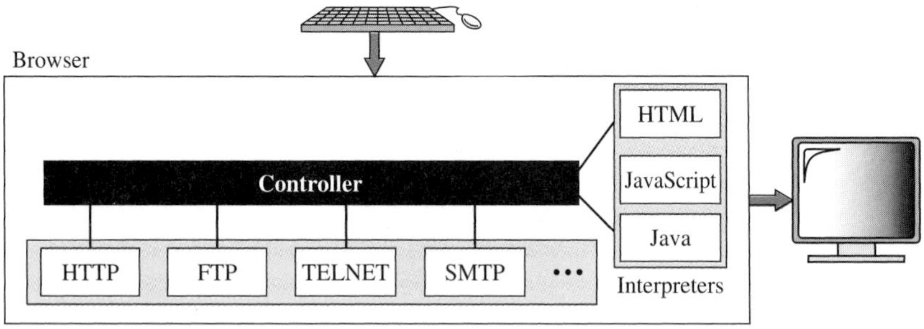

Server

The Web page is stored at the server. Each time a client request arrives, the corresponding document is sent to the client. To improve efficiency, servers normally store requested files in a cache in memory; memory is faster to access than disk. A server can also become more efficient through multithreading or multiprocessing. In this case, a server can answer more than one request at a time.

Uniform Resource Locator (URL)

A client that wants to access a Web page needs the address. To facilitate the access of documents distributed throughout the world, HTTP uses locators. The **uniform resource locator (URL)** is a standard for specifying any kind of information on the Internet. The URL defines four things: protocol, host computer, port, and path (see Figure 22.3).

Figure 22.3   *URL*

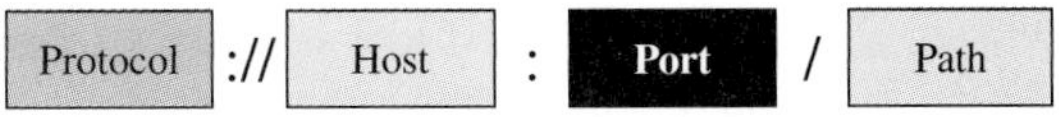

| Protocol | :// | Host | : | **Port** | / | Path |

The *protocol* is the client-server program used to retrieve the document. Many different protocols can retrieve a document; among them are Gopher, FTP, HTTP, News, and TELNET. The most common today is HTTP.

The **host** is the computer on which the information is located, although the name of the computer can be an alias. Web pages are usually stored in computers, and computers are given alias names that usually begin with the characters "www". This is not mandatory, however, as the host can be any name given to the computer that hosts the Web page.

The URL can optionally contain the port number of the server. If the *port* is included, it is inserted between the host and the path, and it is separated from the host by a colon.

Path is the pathname of the file where the information is located. Note that the path can itself contain slashes that, in the UNIX operating system, separate the directories from the subdirectories and files.

Cookies

The World Wide Web was originally designed as a stateless entity. A client sends a request; a server responds. Their relationship is over. The original design of WWW, retrieving publicly available documents, exactly fits this purpose. Today the Web has other functions; some are listed below:

a. Some websites need to allow access to registered clients only.

b. Websites are being used as electronic stores that allow users to browse through the store, select wanted items, put them in an electronic cart, and pay at the end with a credit card.

c. Some websites are used as portals: the user selects the Web pages he wants to see.

d. Some websites are just advertising.

For these purposes, the cookie mechanism was devised. We discussed the use of cookies at the transport layer in Chapter 13; we now discuss their use in Web pages.

Creating and Storing of Cookies

The creation and storing of cookies depend on the implementation; however, the principle is the same.

1. When a server receives a request from a client, it stores information about the client in a file or a string. The information may include the domain name of the client,

the contents of the cookie (information the server has gathered about the client such as name, registration number, and so on), a timestamp, and other information depending on the implementation.

2. The server includes the cookie in the response that it sends to the client.

3. When the client receives the response, the browser stores the cookie in the cookie directory, which is sorted by the domain server name.

Using Cookies

When a client sends a request to a server, the browser looks in the cookie directory to see if it can find a cookie sent by that server. If found, the cookie is included in the request. When the server receives the request, it knows that this is an old client, not a new one. Note that the contents of the cookie are never read by the browser or disclosed to the user. It is a cookie *made* by the server and *eaten* by the server. Now let us see how a cookie is used for the four previously mentioned purposes:

a. The site that restricts access to registered clients only sends a cookie to the client when the client registers for the first time. For any repeated access, only those clients that send the appropriate cookie are allowed.

b. An electronic store (e-commerce) can use a cookie for its client shoppers. When a client selects an item and inserts it into a cart, a cookie that contains information about the item, such as its number and unit price, is sent to the browser. If the client selects a second item, the cookie is updated with the new selection information. And so on. When the client finishes shopping and wants to check out, the last cookie is retrieved and the total charge is calculated.

c. A Web portal uses the cookie in a similar way. When a user selects her favorite pages, a cookie is made and sent. If the site is accessed again, the cookie is sent to the server to show what the client is looking for.

d. A cookie is also used by advertising agencies. An advertising agency can place banner ads on some main website that is often visited by users. The advertising agency supplies only a URL that gives the banner address instead of the banner itself. When a user visits the main website and clicks the icon of an advertised corporation, a request is sent to the advertising agency. The advertising agency sends the banner, a GIF file for example, but it also includes a cookie with the ID of the user. Any future use of the banners adds to the database that profiles the Web behavior of the user. The advertising agency has compiled the interests of the user and can sell this information to other parties. This use of cookies has made them very controversial. Hopefully, some new regulations will be devised to preserve the privacy of users.

22.2   WEB DOCUMENTS

The documents in the WWW can be grouped into three broad categories: static, dynamic, and active. The category is based on the time the contents of the document are determined.

Static Documents

Static documents are fixed-content documents that are created and stored in a server. The client can get a copy of the document only. In other words, the contents of the file are determined when the file is created, not when it is used. Of course, the contents in the server can be changed, but the user cannot change them. When a client accesses the document, a copy of the document is sent. The user can then use a browsing program to display the document (see Figure 22.4).

Figure 22.4   *Static document*

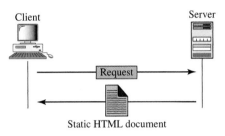

Client

Server

Request

Static HTML document

HTML

Hypertext Markup Language (HTML) is a language for creating Web pages. The term *markup language* comes from the book publishing industry. Before a book is typeset and printed, a copy editor reads the manuscript and puts marks on it. These marks tell the compositor how to format the text. For example, if the copy editor wants part of a line to be printed in boldface, he or she draws a wavy line under that part. In the same way, data for a Web page are formatted for interpretation by a browser.

Let us clarify the idea with an example. To make part of a text displayed in boldface with HTML, we put beginning and ending boldface tags (marks) in the text as shown in Figure 22.5.

Figure 22.5   *Boldface tags*

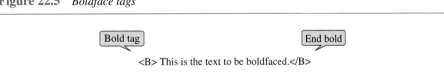

Bold tag   End bold

<B> This is the text to be boldfaced.</B>

The two tags <B> and </B> are instructions for the browser. When the browser sees these two marks, it knows that the text must be boldfaced (see Figure 22.6).

A markup language such as HTML allows us to embed formatting instructions in the file itself. The instructions are included with the text. In this way, any browser can read the instructions and format the text according to the specific workstation. One might ask why we do not use the formatting capabilities of word processors to create

Figure 22.6 *Effect of boldface tags*

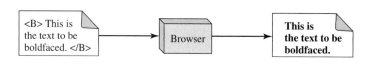

and save formatted text. The answer is that different word processors use different techniques or procedures for formatting text. For example, imagine that a user creates formatted text on a Macintosh computer and stores it in a Web page. Another user who is on an IBM computer would not be able to receive the Web page because the two computers use different formatting procedures.

HTML lets us use only ASCII characters for both the main text and formatting instructions. In this way, every computer can receive the whole document as an ASCII document. The main text is the data, and the formatting instructions can be used by the browser to format the data.

A Web page is made up of two parts: the head and the body. The head is the first part of a Web page. The head contains the title of the page and other parameters that the browser will use. The actual contents of a page are in the body, which includes the text and the tags. Whereas the text is the actual information contained in a page, the tags define the appearance of the document. Every HTML tag is a name followed by an optional list of attributes, all enclosed between less-than and greater-than brackets (< and >).

An attribute, if present, is followed by an equal sign and the value of the attribute. Some tags can be used alone; some must be used in pairs. Those that are used in pairs are called *beginning* and *ending* tags. The beginning tag can have attributes and values and starts with the name of the tag. The ending tag cannot have attributes or values but must have a slash before the name of the tag. The browser makes a decision about the structure of the text based on the tags, which are embedded into the text. Figure 22.7 shows the format of a tag.

Figure 22.7 *Beginning and ending tags*

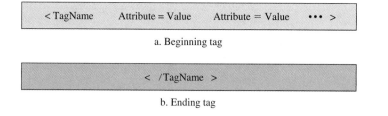

One commonly used tag category is the text formatting tags such as <B> and </B>, which make the text bold; <I> and </I>, which make the text italic; and <U> and </U>, which underline the text.

Another interesting tag category is the image tag. Nontextual information such as digitized photos or graphic images are not a physical part of an HTML document. But we can use an image tag to point to the file of a photo or image. The image tag defines the address (URL) of the image to be retrieved. It also specifies how the image can be inserted after retrieval. We can choose from among several attributes. The most common are SRC (source), which defines the source (address), and ALIGN, which defines the alignment of the image. The SRC attribute is required. Most browsers accept images in the GIF or JPEG formats. For example, the following tag can retrieve an image stored as image1.gif in the directory /bin/images:

<IMG   SRC= "/bin/images/image1.gif"   ALIGN=MIDDLE >

A third interesting category is the hyperlink tag, which is needed to link documents together. Any item (word, phrase, paragraph, or image) can refer to another document through a mechanism called an *anchor*. The anchor is defined by <A.....> and </A> tags, and the anchored item uses the URL to refer to another document. When the document is displayed, the anchored item is underlined, blinking, or boldfaced. The user can click on the anchored item to go to another document, which may or may not be stored on the same server as the original document. The reference phrase is embedded between the beginning and ending tags. The beginning tag can have several attributes, but the one required is HREF (hyperlink reference), which defines the address (URL) of the linked document. For example, the link to the author of a book can be:

<A   HREF= "http://www.deanza.edu/forouzan"> Author   </A>

What appears in the text is the word "Author," on which the user can click to go to the author's Web page.

Dynamic Documents

A **dynamic document** is created by a Web server whenever a browser requests the document. When a request arrives, the Web server runs an application program or a script that creates the dynamic document. The server returns the output of the program or script as a response to the browser that requested the document. Because a fresh document is created for each request, the contents of a dynamic document can vary from one request to another. A very simple example of a dynamic document is the retrieval of the time and date from a server. Time and date are kinds of information that are dynamic in that they change from moment to moment. The client can ask the server to run a program such as the *date* program in UNIX and send the result of the program to the client.

Common Gateway Interface (CGI)

The **Common Gateway Interface (CGI)** is a technology that creates and handles dynamic documents. CGI is a set of standards that defines how a dynamic document is written, how data are input to the program, and how the output result is used.

CGI is not a new language; instead, it allows programmers to use any of several languages such as C, C++, Bourne Shell, Korn Shell, C Shell, Tcl, or Perl. The only thing that CGI defines is a set of rules and terms that the programmer must follow.

The term *common* in CGI indicates that the standard defines a set of rules that is common to any language or platform. The term *gateway* here means that a CGI program can be used to access other resources such as databases, graphic packages, and so on. The term *interface* here means that there is a set of predefined terms, variables, calls, and so on that can be used in any CGI program. A CGI program in its simplest form is code written in one of the languages supporting CGI. Any programmer who can encode a sequence of thoughts in a program and knows the syntax of one of the above-mentioned languages can write a simple CGI program. Figure 22.8 illustrates the steps in creating a dynamic program using CGI technology.

Figure 22.8   *Dynamic document using CGI*

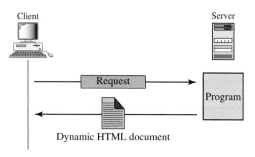

Input   In traditional programming, when a program is executed, parameters can be passed to the program. Parameter passing allows the programmer to write a generic program that can be used in different situations. For example, a generic copy program can be written to copy any file to another. A user can use the program to copy a file named x to another file named y by passing x and y as parameters.

The input from a browser to a server is sent using a *form*. If the information in a form is small (such as a word), it can be appended to the URL after a question mark. For example, the following URL is carrying form information (23, a value):

http://www.deanza/cgi-bin/prog.pl?23

When the server receives the URL, it uses the part of the URL before the question mark to access the program to be run, and it interprets the part after the question mark (23) as the input sent by the client. It stores this string in a variable. When the CGI program is executed, it can access this value.

If the input from a browser is too long to fit in the query string, the browser can ask the server to send a form. The browser can then fill the form with the input data and send it to the server. The information in the form can be used as the input to the CGI program.

Output   The whole idea of CGI is to execute a CGI program at the server site and send the output to the client (browser). The output is usually plain text or a text with HTML structures; however, the output can be a variety of other things. It can be graphics or binary data, a status code, instructions to the browser to cache the result, or instructions to the server to send an existing document instead of the actual output.

To let the client know about the type of document sent, a CGI program creates headers. As a matter of fact, the output of the CGI program always consists of two parts: a header and a body. The header is separated by a blank line from the body. This means any CGI program first creates the header, then a blank line, and then the body. Although the header and the blank line are not shown on the browser screen, the header is used by the browser to interpret the body.

Scripting Technologies for Dynamic Documents

The problem with CGI technology is the inefficiency that results if part of the dynamic document that is to be created is fixed and not changing from request to request. For example, assume that we need to retrieve a list of spare parts, their availability, and prices for a specific car brand. Although the availability and prices vary from time to time, the name, description, and the picture of the parts are fixed. If we use CGI, the program must create an entire document each time a request is made. The solution is to create a file containing the fixed part of the document using HTML and embed a script, a source code, that can be run by the server to provide the varying availability and price section. Figure 22.9 shows the idea.

Figure 22.9   *Dynamic document using server-site script*

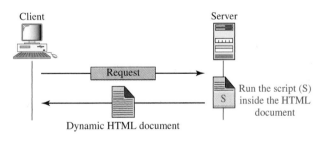

A few technologies have been involved in creating dynamic documents using scripts. Among the most common are **Hypertext Preprocessor (PHP),** which uses the Perl language; **Java Server Pages (JSP),** which uses the Java language for scripting; **Active Server Pages (ASP)** a Microsoft product, which uses Visual Basic language for scripting; and **ColdFusion,** which embeds SQL database queries in the HTML document.

**Dynamic documents are sometimes referred to as
server-site dynamic documents.**

Active Documents

For many applications, we need a program or a script to be run at the client site. These are called **active documents.** For example, suppose we want to run a program that creates animated graphics on the screen or a program that interacts with the user. The program definitely needs to be run at the client site where the animation or interaction takes place. When a browser requests an active document, the server sends a copy of the document or a script. The document is then run at the client (browser) site.

Java Applets

One way to create an active document is to use **Java applets. Java** is a combination of a high-level programming language, a run-time environment, and a class library that allows a programmer to write an active document (an applet) and a browser to run it. It can also be a stand-alone program that doesn't use a browser.

An applet is a program written in Java on the server. It is compiled and ready to be run. The document is in bytecode (binary) format. The client process (browser) creates an instance of this applet and runs it. A Java applet can be run by the browser in two ways. In the first method, the browser can directly request the Java applet program in the URL and receive the applet in binary form. In the second method, the browser can retrieve and run an HTML file that has embedded the address of the applet as a tag. Figure 22.10 shows how Java applets are used in the first method; the second is similar but needs two transactions.

Figure 22.10   *Active document using Java applet*

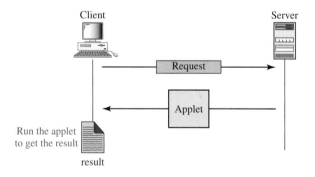

JavaScript

The idea of scripts in dynamic documents can also be used for active documents. If the active part of the document is small, it can be written in a scripting language; then it can be interpreted and run by the client at the same time. The script is in source code (text) and not in binary form. The scripting technology used in this case is usually JavaScript. JavaScript, which bears a small resemblance to Java, is a very high level scripting language developed for this purpose. Figure 22.11 shows how JavaScript is used to create an active document.

Figure 22.11 *Active document using client-site script*

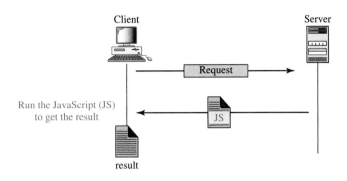

22.3 HTTP

The **Hypertext Transfer Protocol (HTTP)** is a protocol used mainly to access data on
the World Wide Web. HTTP functions like a combination of FTP and SMTP. It is similar to FTP because it transfers files and uses the services of TCP. However, it is much
simpler than FTP because it uses only one TCP connection. There is no separate control
connection; only data are transferred between the client and the server.

HTTP is like SMTP because the data transferred between the client and the server
look like SMTP messages. In addition, the format of the messages is controlled by
MIME-like headers. Unlike SMTP, the HTTP messages are not destined to be read by
humans; they are read and interpreted by the HTTP server and HTTP client (browser).
SMTP messages are stored and forwarded, but HTTP messages are delivered immediately. The commands from the client to the server are embedded in a request message.
The contents of the requested file or other information are embedded in a response
message. HTTP uses the services of TCP on well-known port 80.

HTTP uses the services of TCP on well-known port 80.

HTTP Transaction

Figure 22.12 illustrates the HTTP transaction between the client and server. Although
HTTP uses the services of TCP, HTTP itself is a stateless protocol. The client initializes the transaction by sending a request message. The server replies by sending a
response.

Figure 22.12   *HTTP transaction*

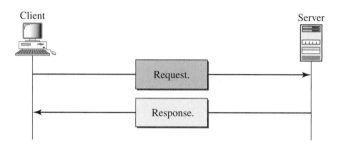

Messages

The format of the request and response message are similar; both are shown in Figure 22.13. A request message consists of a request line, a header, and sometimes a body. A response message consists of a status line, a header, and sometimes a body.

Figure 22.13   *Request and response messages*

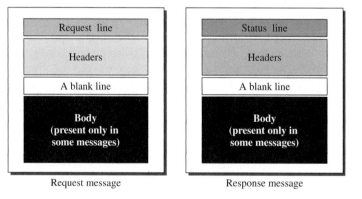

Request and Status Lines   The first line in a request message is called a **request line;** the first line in the response message is called the **status line.** There is one common field as shown in Figure 22.14.

❏ **Request type.** This field is used in the request message. In version 1.1 of HTTP, several request types are defined. The request type is categorized into **methods** as defined in Table 22.1.

❏ **URL.** We discussed the URL earlier in the chapter.

❏ **Version.** The most current version of HTTP is 1.1.

Figure 22.14 *Request and status lines*

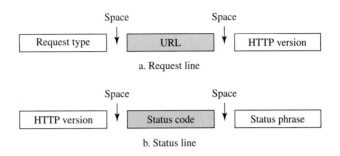

a. Request line

b. Status line

Table 22.1 *Methods*

Method	Action
GET	Requests a document from the server
HEAD	Requests information about a document but not the document itself
POST	Sends some information from the client to the server
PUT	Sends a document from the server to the client
TRACE	Echoes the incoming request
CONNECT	Reserved
OPTION	Enquires about available options

❑ **Status code.** This field is used in the response message. The status code field is similar to those in the FTP and the SMTP protocols. It consists of three digits. Whereas the codes in the 100 range are only informational, the codes in the 200 range indicate a successful request. The codes in the 300 range redirect the client to another URL, and the codes in the 400 range indicate an error at the client site. Finally, the codes in the 500 range indicate an error at the server site. We list the most common codes in Table 22.2.

❑ **Status phrase.** This field is used in the response message. It explains the status code in text form. Table 22.2 also gives the status phrase.

Table 22.2 *Status codes*

Code	Phrase	Description
Informational		
100	Continue	The initial part of the request has been received and the client may continue with its request.
101	Switching	The server is complying with a client request to switch protocols defined in the upgrade header.

Table 22.2   *Status codes (continued)*

Code	Phrase	Description
Success		
200	OK	The request is successful.
201	Created	A new URL is created.
202	Accepted	The request is accepted, but it is not immediately acted upon.
204	No content	There is no content in the body.
Redirection		
301	Moved permanently	The requested URL is no longer used by the server.
302	Moved temporarily	The requested URL has moved temporarily.
304	Not modified	The document has not modified.
Client Error		
400	Bad request	There is a syntax error in the request.
401	Unauthorized	The request lacks proper authorization.
403	Forbidden	Service is denied.
404	Not found	The document is not found.
405	Method not allowed	The method is not supported in this URL.
406	Not acceptable	The format requested is not acceptable.
Server Error		
500	Internal server error	There is an error, such as a crash, at the server site.
501	Not implemented	The action requested cannot be performed.
503	Service unavailable	The service is temporarily unavailable, but may be requested in the future.

Header   The header exchanges additional information between the client and the server. For example, the client can request that the document be sent in a special format or the server can send extra information about the document. The header can consist of one or more header lines. Each header line has a header name, a colon, a space, and a header value (see Figure 22.15). We will show some header lines in the examples at the end of this chapter. A header line belongs to one of four categories: **general header, request header, response header,** and **entity header.** A request message can contain

Figure 22.15   *Header format*

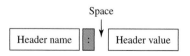

only general, request, and entity headers. A response message, on the other hand, can contain only general, response, and entity headers.

❏ **General Header** The general header gives general information about the message and can be present in both a request and a response. Table 22.3 lists some general headers with their descriptions.

Table 22.3 *General headers*

Header	Description
Cache-control	Specifies information about caching
Connection	Shows whether the connection should be closed or not
Date	Shows the current date
MIME-version	Shows the MIME version used
Upgrade	Specifies the preferred communication protocol

❏ **Request Header** The request header can be present only in a request message. It specifies the client's configuration and the client's preferred document format. See Table 22.4 for a list of some request headers and their descriptions.

Table 22.4 *Request headers*

Header	Description
Accept	Shows the media format the client can accept
Accept-charset	Shows the character set the client can handle
Accept-encoding	Shows the encoding scheme the client can handle
Accept-language	Shows the language the client can accept
Authorization	Shows what permissions the client has
From	Shows the e-mail address of the user
Host	Shows the host and port number of the client
If-modified-since	Send the document if newer than specified date
If-match	Send the document only if it matches given tag
If-non-match	Send the document only if it does not match given tag
If-range	Send only the portion of the document that is missing
If-unmodified-since	Send the document if not changed since specified date
Referrer	Specifies the URL of the linked document
User-agent	Identifies the client program

❏ **Response Header** The response header can be present only in a response message. It specifies the server's configuration and special information about the request. See Table 22.5 for a list of some response headers with their descriptions.

Table 22.5   *Response headers*

Header	Description
Accept-range	Shows if server accepts the range requested by client
Age	Shows the age of the document
Public	Shows the supported list of methods
Retry-after	Specifies the date after which the server is available
Server	Shows the server name and version number

❑ **Entity Header** The entity header gives information about the body of the document. Although it is mostly present in response messages, some request messages, such as POST or PUT methods, that contain a body, also use this type of header. See Table 22.6 for a list of some entity headers and their descriptions.

Table 22.6   *Entity headers*

Header	Description
Allow	Lists valid methods that can be used with a URL
Content-encoding	Specifies the encoding scheme
Content-language	Specifies the language
Content-length	Shows the length of the document
Content-range	Specifies the range of the document
Content-type	Specifies the media type
Etag	Gives an entity tag
Expires	Gives the date and time when contents may change
Last-modified	Gives the date and time of the last change
Location	Specifies the location of the created or moved document

Body   The body can be present in a request or response message. Usually, it contains the document to be sent or received.

Example 1

This example retrieves a document. We use the GET method to retrieve an image with the path /usr/bin/image1. The request line shows the method (GET), the URL, and the HTTP version (1.1). The header has two lines that show that the client can accept images in the GIF or JPEG format. The request does not have a body. The response message contains the status line and four lines of header. The header lines define the date, server, MIME version, and length of the document. The body of the document follows the header (see Figure 22.16).

Example 2

In this example, the client wants to send data to the server. We use the POST method. The request line shows the method (POST), URL, and HTTP version (1.1). There are four lines of headers. The request body contains the input information. The response message contains the status line and four lines of headers. The created document, which is a CGI document, is included as the body (see Figure 22.17).

Figure 22.16   *Example 1*

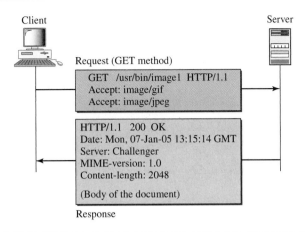

Figure 22.17   *Example 2*

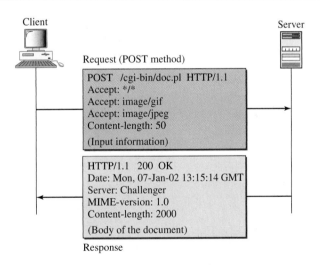

Example 3

HTTP uses ASCII characters. A client can directly connect to a server using TELNET, which logs into port 80. The next three lines shows that the connection is successful.

We then type three lines. The first shows the request line (GET method), the second is the header (defining the host), the third is a blank terminating the request.

The server response is seven lines starting with the status line. The blank line at the end terminates the server response. The file of 14230 lines is received after the blank line (not shown here). The last line is the output by the client.

$ telnet www.mhhe.com 80
Trying 198.45.24.104...
Connected to www.mhhe.com (198.45.24.104).
Escape character is '^]'.
GET /engcs/compsci/forouzan HTTP/1.1
From: forouzanbehrouz@fhda.edu

HTTP/1.1 200 OK
Date: Thu, 28 Oct 2004 16:27:46 GMT
Server: Apache/1.3.9 (Unix) ApacheJServ/1.1.2 PHP/4.1.2 PHP/3.0.18
MIME-version:1.0
Content-Type: text/html
Last-modified: Friday, 15-Oct-04 02:11:31 GMT
Content-length: 14230

Connection closed by foreign host.

Persistent versus Nonpersistent Connection

HTTP prior to version 1.1 specified a nonpersistent connection, while a persistent connection is the default in version 1.1.

Nonpersistent Connection

In a **nonpersistent connection,** one TCP connection is made for each request/response. The following lists the steps in this strategy:

1. The client opens a TCP connection and sends a request.
2. The server sends the response and closes the connection.
3. The client reads the data until it encounters an end-of-file marker; it then closes the connection.

In this strategy, for *N* different pictures in different files, the connection must be opened and closed *N* times. The nonpersistent strategy imposes high overhead on the server because the server needs *N* different buffers and requires a slow start procedure each time a connection is opened.

Persistent Connection

HTTP version 1.1 specifies a **persistent connection** by default. In a persistent connection, the server leaves the connection open for more requests after sending a response. The server can close the connection at the request of a client or if a time-out has been reached. The sender usually sends the length of the data with each response. However, there are some occasions when the sender does not know the length of the data. This is the case when a document is created dynamically or actively. In these cases, the server informs the client that the length is not known and closes the connection after sending the data so the client knows that the end of the data has been reached.

HTTP version 1.1 specifies a persistent connection by default.

Proxy Server

HTTP supports **proxy servers.** A proxy server is a computer that keeps copies of responses to recent requests. The HTTP client sends a request to the proxy server. The proxy server checks its cache. If the response is not stored in the cache, the proxy server sends the request to the corresponding server. Incoming responses are sent to the proxy server and stored for future requests from other clients.

The proxy server reduces the load on the original server, decreases traffic, and improves latency. However, to use the proxy server, the client must be configured to access the proxy instead of the target server.

22.4   KEY TERMS

active document	Java Server Pages (JSP)
Active Server Pages (ASP)	nonpersistent connection
applet	persistent connection
browser	proxy server
ColdFusion	request header
Common Gateway Interface (CGI)	request line
dynamic document	request type
entity header	response header
general header	static document
hypertext	status code
Hypertext Markup Language (HTML)	status line
Hypertext Preprocessor (PHP)	tag
Hypertext Transfer Protocol (HTTP)	uniform resource locator (URL)
Java	Web
JavaScript	World Wide Web (WWW)

22.5   SUMMARY

❏ The World Wide Web (WWW) is a repository of information linked together from points all over the world.

❏ Hypertexts are documents linked to one another through the concept of pointers.

❏ Browsers interpret and display a Web document.

❏ A browser consists of a controller, client programs, and interpreters.

❏ A Web document can be classified as static, dynamic, or active.

❏ A static document is one in which the contents are fixed and stored in a server. The client can make no changes in the server document.

❏ Hypertext Markup Language (HTML) is a language used to create static Web pages.

❏ Any browser can read formatting instructions (tags) embedded in an HTML document.

❏ Tags provide structure to a document, define titles and headers, format text, control the data flow, insert figures, link different documents together, and define executable code.

❏ A dynamic Web document is created by a server only at a browser request.

❏ The Common Gateway Interface (CGI) is a standard for creating and handling dynamic Web documents.

❏ A CGI program with its embedded CGI interface tags can be written in a language such as C, C++, shell script, or Perl.

❏ An active document is a copy of a program retrieved by the client and run at the client site.

❏ Java is a combination of a high-level programming language, a run-time environment, and a class library that allows a programmer to write an active document and a browser to run it.

❏ Java is used to create applets (small application programs).

❏ The Hypertext Transfer Protocol (HTTP) is the main protocol used to access data on the World Wide Web (WWW).

❏ HTTP uses a TCP connection to transfer files.

❏ An HTTP message is similar in form to an SMTP message.

❏ The HTTP request line consists of a request type, a URL, and the HTTP version number.

❏ The uniform resource locator (URL) consists of a method, host computer, optional port number, and pathname to locate information on the WWW.

❏ The HTTP request type or method is the actual command or request issued by the client to the server.

❏ The status line consists of the HTTP version number, a status code, and a status phrase.

❏ The HTTP status code relays general information, information related to a successful request, redirection information, or error information.

❏ The HTTP header relays additional information between the client and server.

❏ An HTTP header consists of a header name and a header value.

❏ An HTTP general header gives general information about the request or response message.

❏ An HTTP request header specifies a client's configuration and preferred document format.

❏ A response header specifies a server's configuration and special information about the request.

❑   An HTTP entity header provides information about the body of a document.

❑   HTTP, version 1.1 specifies a persistent connection.

❑   A proxy server keeps copies of responses to recent requests.

22.6   PRACTICE SET

Exercises

1. Where will each figure be shown on the screen?

    Look at the following picture:
    then tell me what you feel:
    <IMG SRC="Pictures/Funny1.gif" ALIGN=middle>
    <IMG SRC="Pictures/Funny2.gif" ALIGN=bottom>
    <B>What is your feeling? </B>

2. Show the effect of the following HTML segment.

    The publisher of this book is <A HREF="www.mhhe">
    McGraw-Hill Publisher </A>

3. Show a request that retrieves the document /usr/users/doc/doc1. Use at least two general headers, two request headers, and one entity header.

4. Show the response to Exercise 3 for a successful request.

5. Show the response to Exercise 3 for a document that has permanently moved to /usr/deads/doc1.

6. Show the response to Exercise 3 if there is a syntax error in the request.

7. Show the response to Exercise 3 if the client is unauthorized to access the document.

8. Show a request that asks for information about a document at /bin/users/file. Use at least two general headers and one request header.

9. Show the response to Exercise 8 for a successful request.

10. Show the request to copy the file at location /bin/usr/bin/file1 to /bin/file1.

11. Show the response to Exercise 10.

12. Show the request to delete the file at location /bin/file1.

13. Show the response to Exercise 12.

14. Show a request to retrieve the file at location /bin/etc/file1. The client needs the document only if it was modified after January 23, 1999.

15. Show the response to Exercise 14.

16. Show a request to retrieve the file at location /bin/etc/file1. The client should identify itself.

17. Show the response to Exercise 16.

18. Show a request to store a file at location /bin/letter. The client identifies the types of documents it can accept.

19. Show the response to exercise 18. The response shows the age of the document as well as the date and time when the contents may change.

Research Activities

20. Find the RFCs related to HTTP.
21. Find the RFCs related to cookies.
22. Find out why IP addresses cannot replace cookies.
23. What is XHTML?
24. What is XML?
25. What is XSL?

CHAPTER 23

IP over ATM

Throughout this book, we have defined an internet (and the Internet) as a combination of LANs and WANs connected together by routers. This means that an IP datagram, from its source to its destination, may travel through several of these networks.

We have shown how a datagram is encapsulated in a frame to pass through a LAN. The frame uses the physical address defined by the LAN protocol and the binding between the IP address and the physical address attained through ARP. If the size of the IP packet is larger than the MTU of the LAN, the IP layer fragments the IP packet; the LAN has no responsibility here.

In this chapter we show how an IP datagram can pass through an ATM WAN. We will see that there are similarities as well as differences. The IP packet is encapsulated in cells (not just one). An ATM network has its own definition for the physical address of a device. Binding between an IP address and a physical address is attained through a protocol called ATMARP. Fragmentation occurs at two levels: at the IP layer to break the packet into a default size, and at the AAL level to divide a packet into even smaller chunks.

23.1 ATM WANS

Let us review some features of the ATM WAN needed to understand IP over ATM. We discussed ATM WANs in Chapter 3. ATM, a cell-switched network, can be a highway for an IP datagram. Figure 23.1 shows how an ATM network can be used in the Internet.

Layers

We discussed ATM layers in Chapter 3 (see Figure 3.23). Routers connected to an ATM network use all three layers (AAL, ATM, and physical), but the switches inside the network use only the bottom two layers (ATM and physical) as shown in Figure 23.2.

Figure 23.1   *An ATM WAN in the Internet*

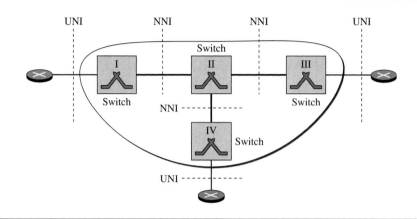

Figure 23.2   *ATM layers in routers and switches*

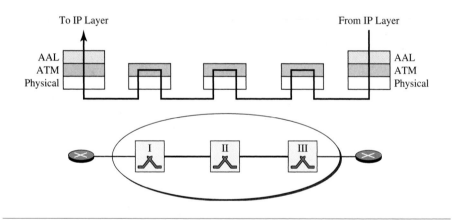

> **End devices such as routers use all three layers, while switches use only the bottom two layers.**

AAL5 Layer

In Chapter 3, we discussed different AALs and their applications. The only AAL used by the Internet is AAL5. It is sometimes called the *simple and efficient adaptation layer* (SEAL). AAL5 assumes that all cells created from one IP datagram belong to a single message. AAL5 therefore provides no addressing, sequencing, or other header information. Instead, only padding and a four-field trailer are added to the IP packet.

AAL5 accepts an IP packet of no more than 65,536 bytes and adds an 8-byte trailer as well as any padding required to ensure that the position of the trailer falls where the receiving equipment expects it (at the last 8 bytes of the last cell). See Figure 23.3.

Figure 23.3 *AAL5*

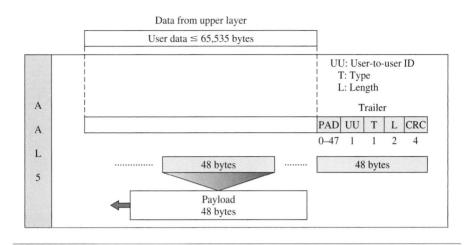

Once the padding and trailer are in place, AAL5 passes the message in 48-byte segments to the ATM layer.

Fields added at the end of the message include the following:

❏ **Pad (PAD).** The total padding for a packet is between 0 and 47 bytes.

❏ **User-to-user ID (UU).** Use of the 1-byte UU field is left to the discretion of the user.

❏ **Type (T).** The 1-byte T field is reserved but not yet defined.

❏ **Length (L).** The 2-byte L field indicates how much of the message is data.

❏ **CRC.** The last 4 bytes are an error check for the entire data unit.

The AAL layer used by the IP protocol is AAL5.

ATM Layer

The ATM layer provides routing, traffic management, switching, and multiplexing services. It processes outgoing traffic by accepting 48-byte segments from the AAL sublayer. The addition of a 5-byte header transforms the segment into a 53-byte cell (see Figure 23.4).

Header Format

ATM has two formats for this header, one for **user-to-network interface (UNI)** cells and another for **network-to-network interface (NNI)** cells. Figure 23.5 shows these headers in the byte-by-byte format preferred by the ITU-T (each row represents a byte).

❏ **Generic flow control (GFC).** The 4-bit GFC field provides flow control at the UNI level. The ITU-T has determined that this level of flow control is not necessary at the NNI level. In the NNI header, therefore, these bits are added to the VPI.

Figure 23.4   *ATM layer*

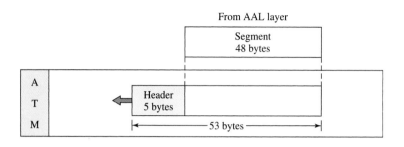

Figure 23.5   *ATM headers*

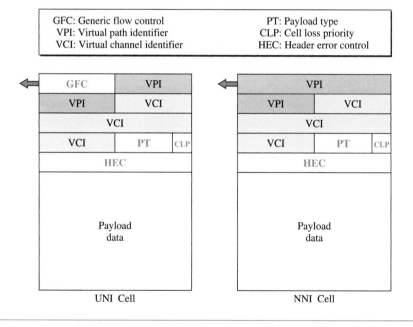

The longer VPI allows more virtual paths to be defined at the NNI level. The format for this additional VPI has not yet been determined. Currently, it is not used.

❏ **Virtual path identifier (VPI).** The VPI is an 8-bit field in a UNI cell and a 12-bit field in an NNI cell (see Chapter 3).

❏ **Virtual channel identifier (VCI).** The VCI is a 16-bit field in both frames (see Chapter 3).

❏ **Payload type (PT).** This 3-bit field is used to define the type of the payload. When the cell is carrying part of an IP packet, the value of this field is 000 if the cell is not the last cell and 001 if the cell is the last cell.

❑ **Cell loss priority (CLP).** The 1-bit CLP field is provided for congestion control. When links become congested, low-priority cells may be discarded to protect the quality of service for higher priority cells. This bit indicates to a switch which cells may be dropped and which must be retained. A cell with its CLP bit set to 1 must be retained as long as there are cells with a CLP of 0.

❑ **Header error correction (HEC).** The HEC is an error correction method computed over the first four bytes of the header. It is a CRC with the divisor $x^8 + x^2 + x + 1$ that can correct single-bit errors as well as a large class of multiple-bit errors.

Physical Layer

The physical layer defines the transmission medium, bit transmission, encoding, and electrical to optical transformation. It provides convergence with physical transport protocols, such as SONET (described in Chapter 3) and T-3, as well as the mechanisms for transforming the flow of cells into a flow of bits.

23.2   CARRYING A DATAGRAM IN CELLS

As an example, let us show how a datagram of 140 bytes is encapsulated in four cells and transmitted through an ATM network. Before encapsulation, an 8-byte trailer is added to the datagram. However, the size of the packet is now 148, which is not divisible by 48. We must add 44 bytes of padding, which makes the total length 192 bytes. The packet is then divided into four chunks of 48 bytes each as shown in Figure 23.6.

Figure 23.6   *Fragmentation*

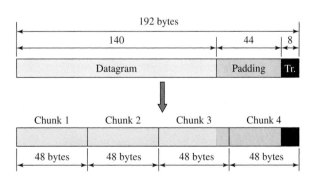

> **Only the last cell carries the 8-byte trailer added to the IP datagram. Padding can be added only to the last cell or the last two cells.**

At the ATM layer, each chunk of data is encapsulated into a cell as shown in Figure 23.7. Note that the last cell carries no data. Also note that the value of the PT field in the last cell is 001 to show that this is the last cell.

> **The value of the PT field is 000 in all cells carrying an IP datagram fragment except for the last cell; the value is 001 in the last cell.**

Figure 23.7   *ATM cells*

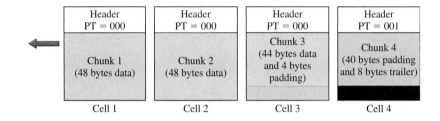

Header PT = 000	Header PT = 000	Header PT = 000	Header PT = 001
Chunk 1 (48 bytes data)	Chunk 2 (48 bytes data)	Chunk 3 (44 bytes data and 4 bytes padding)	Chunk 4 (40 bytes padding and 8 bytes trailer)
Cell 1	Cell 2	Cell 3	Cell 4

Why Use AAL5?

A question that frequently comes up is why do we use AAL5. Why can't we just encapsulate an IP packet in a cell? The answer is that it is more efficient to use AAL5. If an IP datagram is to be encapsulated in a cell, the data at the IP level must be $53 - 5 - 20 = 27$ bytes because a minimum of 20 bytes is needed for the IP header and 5 bytes is needed for the ATM header. The efficiency is 27/53, or almost 51%. By letting an IP datagram span over several cells, we are dividing the IP overhead (20 bytes) among those cells and increasing efficiency.

23.3   ROUTING THE CELLS

The ATM network creates a route between two routers. We call these routers entering-point and exiting-point routers. The cells start from the entering-point router and end at the exiting-point router as shown in Figure 23.8.

Figure 23.8   *Entering-point and exiting-point routers*

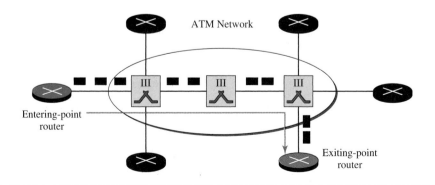

Addresses

Routing the cells from one specific entering-point router to one specific exiting-point router requires three types of addressing: IP addresses, physical addresses, and virtual circuit identifiers.

IP Addresses

Each router connected to the ATM network has an IP address. Later we will see that the addresses may or may not have the same prefix. The IP address defines the router at the IP layer. It does not have anything to do with the ATM network.

Physical Addresses

Each router (or any other device) connected to the ATM network has also a physical address. The physical address is associated with the ATM network and does not have anything to do with the Internet. The ATM Forum defines 20-byte addresses for ATM networks. Each address must be unique in a network and is defined by the network administrator. The physical addresses in an ATM network play the same role as the MAC addresses in a LAN. The physical addresses are used during connection establishment.

Virtual Circuit Identifiers

The switches inside the ATM network route the cells based on the virtual circuit identifiers (VPIs and VCIs), as we discussed in Chapter 3. The virtual circuit identifiers are used during data transfer.

Address Binding

An ATM network needs virtual circuit identifiers to route the cells. The IP datagram contains only source and destination IP addresses. Virtual circuit identifiers must be determined from the destination IP address. These are the steps:

1. The **entering-point router** receives an IP datagram. It uses the destination address and its routing table to find the IP address of the next router, the **exiting-point router.** This is exactly the same step followed when a datagram passes through a LAN.

2. The entering-point router uses the services of a protocol called ATMARP to find the physical address of the exiting-point router. ATMARP is similar to ARP (discussed in Chapter 7). We discuss ATMARP in the next section.

3. The virtual circuit identifiers are bound to the physical addresses.

23.4 ATMARP

A protocol is needed to find (map) the physical address of the exiting-point router given the IP address of the exiting-point router. This is the same task performed by ARP on a LAN. However, there is a difference between a LAN and an ATM network. A LAN is a broadcast network (at the data link layer); ARP uses the broadcasting capability of a LAN to send (broadcast) an ARP request. An ATM network is not a broadcast network; some other solution is needed to handle the task.

Packet Format

The format of an **ATMARP** packet, which is similar to the ARP packet, is shown in Figure 23.9.

Figure 23.9   *ATMARP packet*

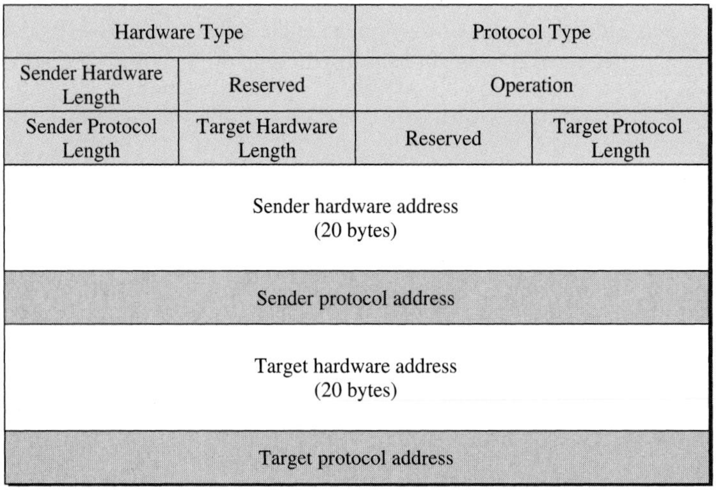

Hardware Type		Protocol Type	
Sender Hardware Length	Reserved	Operation	
Sender Protocol Length	Target Hardware Length	Reserved	Target Protocol Length
Sender hardware address (20 bytes)			
Sender protocol address			
Target hardware address (20 bytes)			
Target protocol address			

The fields are as follows:

❏ **Hardware type (HTYPE).** The 16-bit HTYPE field defines the type of the physical network. Its value is 0013_{16} for an ATM network.

❏ **Protocol type (PTYPE).** The 16-bit PTYPE field defines the type of the protocol. For IPv4 protocol the value is 0800_{16}.

❏ **Sender hardware length (SHLEN).** The 8-bit SHLEN field defines the length of the sender's physical address in bytes. For an ATM network the value is 20. Note that if the binding is done across an ATM network and two levels of hardware addressing are necessary, the neighboring 8-bit **reserved** field is used to define the length of the second address.

❏ **Operation (OPER).** The 16-bit OPER field defines the type of the packet. Five packet types are defined as shown in Table 23.1.

Table 23.1   *OPER field*

Message	OPER value
Request	1
Reply	2
Inverse Request	8
Inverse Reply	9
NACK	10

❏ **Sender protocol length (SPLEN).** The 8-bit SPLEN field defines the length of the address in bytes. For IPv4 the value is 4 bytes.

❏ **Target hardware length (TLEN).** The 8-bit TLEN field defines the length of the receiver's physical address in bytes. For an ATM network the value is 20. Note that if the binding is done across an ATM network and two levels of hardware addressing are necessary, the neighboring 8-bit **reserved field** is used to define the length of the second address.

❏ **Target protocol length (TPLEN).** The 8-bit TPLEN field defines the length of the address in bytes. For IPv4 the value is 4 bytes.

❏ **Sender hardware address (SHA).** The variable-length SHA field defines the physical address of the sender. For ATM networks defined by the ATM Forum, the length is 20 bytes.

❏ **Sender protocol address (SPA).** The variable-length SPA field defines the address of the sender. For IPv4 the length is 4 bytes.

❏ **Target hardware address (THA).** The variable-length THA field defines the physical address of the receiver. For ATM networks defined by the ATM Forum, the length is 20 bytes. This field is left empty for request messages and filled in for reply and NACK messages.

❏ **Target protocol address (TPA).** The variable-length TPA field defines the address of the receiver. For IPv4 the length is 4 bytes.

ATMARP Operation

There are two methods to connect two routers on an ATM network: through a permanent virtual circuit (PVC) or through a switched virtual circuit (SVC). The operation of ATMARP depends on the connection method.

PVC

A **permanent virtual circuit (PVC)** connection is established between two end points by the network provider. The VPIs and VCIs are defined for the permanent connections and the values are entered in a table for each switch.

If a permanent virtual circuit is established between two routers, there is no need for an ATMARP server. However, the routers must be able to bind a physical address to an IP address. The **inverse request message** and **inverse reply message** can be used for the binding. When a PVC is established for a router, the router sends an inverse request message. The router at the other end of the connection receives the message (which contains the physical and IP address of the sender) and sends back a reply (which contains its own physical and IP address).

After the exchange, both routers add a table entry that maps the physical addresses to the PVC. Now, when a router receives an IP datagram, the table provides information so that the router can encapsulate the datagram using the virtual circuit identifier. Figure 23.10 shows the exchange of messages between two routers.

> The inverse request and inverse reply messages can bind the physical address to an IP address in a PVC situation.

Figure 23.10   *Binding with PVC*

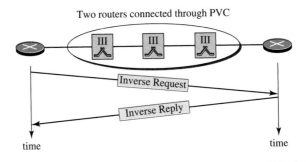

SVC

In a **switched virtual circuit (SVC)** connection, each time a router wants to make a connection with another router (or any computer), a new virtual circuit must be established. However, the virtual circuit can be created only if the entering-point router knows the physical address of the exiting-point router (ATM does not recognize IP addresses).

To map the IP addresses to physical addresses, each router runs a client ATMARP program, but only one computer runs an ATMARP server program. To understand the difference between ARP and ATMARP, remember that ARP operates on a LAN, which is a broadcast network. An ARP client can broadcast an ARP request message and each router on the network will receive it; only the target router will respond. ATM is a nonbroadcast network; an ATMARP request cannot reach all routers connected to the network.

The process of establishing a virtual connection requires three steps: connecting to the server, receiving the physical address, and establishing the connection. Figure 23.11 shows the steps.

Connecting to the Server   Normally, there is a permanent virtual circuit established between each router and the server. If there is no PVC connection between the router and the server, the server must at least know the physical address of the router to create an SVC connection just for exchanging ATMARP request and reply messages.

Receiving the Physical Address   When there is a connection between the entering-point router and the server, the router sends an *ATMARP request* to the server. The server sends back an *ATMARP reply* if the physical address can be found or an *ATMARP NACK* otherwise. If the entering-point router receives a NACK, the datagram is dropped.

Establishing Virtual Circuits   After the entering-point router receives the physical address of the exiting-point router, it can request an SVC between itself and the exiting-point router. The ATM network uses the two physical addresses to set up a virtual circuit which lasts until the entering-point router asks for disconnection. In this step, each switch inside the network adds an entry to their tables to enable them to route the cells carrying the IP datagram.

Figure 23.11 *Binding with ATMARP*

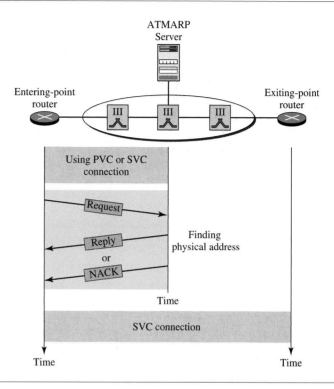

The request and reply message can be used to bind a physical address to an IP address in an SVC situation.

Building the Table

How does the ATM server build its mapping table? This is also done through the use of ATMARP and the two inverse messages (inverse request and inverse reply). When a router is connected to an ATM network for the first time and a permanent virtual connection is established between the router and the server, the server sends an inverse request message to the router. The router sends back an inverse reply message which includes its IP address and physical address. Using these two addresses, the server creates an entry in its routing table to be used if the router becomes an exiting-point router in the future. Figure 23.12 shows the inverse operation of ATMARP.

The inverse request and inverse reply can also be used to build the server's mapping table.

Figure 23.12   *Building a table*

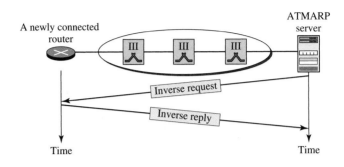

23.5   LOGICAL IP SUBNET (LIS)

Before we leave the subject of IP over ATM, we need to discuss a concept called **logical IP subnet (LIS).** For the same reason that a large LAN can be divided into several subnets, an ATM network can be divided into logical (not physical) subnetworks. This facilitates the operation of ATMARP and other protocols (such as IGMP) that need to simulate broadcasting on an ATM network.

Routers connected to an ATM network can belong to one or more logical subnets. as shown in Figure 23.13. In the figure, routers B, C, and D belong to one logical subnet (shown by broken-line boxes); routers F, G, and H belong to another logical subnet (shown by shaded boxes). Routers A and E belong to both logical subnets. A router can communicate and send IP packets directly to a router in the same subnet; however,

Figure 23.13   *LIS*

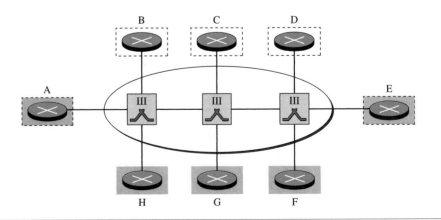

if it needs to send a packet to a router that belongs to another subnet, the packet must first go to a router that belongs to both subnets. For example, router B can send a packet directly to routers C and D. But a packet from B to F must first pass through A or E.

Note that routers belonging to the same logical subnet share the same prefix and subnet mask. The prefix for routers in different subnets is different.

To use ATMARP, there must be a different ATMARP server in each subnet. For example, in the above figure, we need two ATMARP servers, one for each subnet.

LIS allows an ATM network to be divided into several logical subnets. To use ATMARP, we need a separate server for each subnet.

23.6 KEY TERMS

AAL5 layer	inverse request message
application adaptation layer (AAL)	logical IP subnet (LIS)
asynchronous transfer mode (ATM)	permanent virtual circuit (PVC)
ATMARP	reply message
entering-point router	request message
exiting-point router	switched virtual circuit (SVC)
inverse reply message	

23.7 SUMMARY

❏ The AAL layer used by the IP protocol is AAL5.

❏ The ATM layer accepts 48-byte segments from the AAL and transforms them into 53-byte cells through the addition of a 5-byte header.

❏ An ATM network creates a route between an entering-point router and an exiting-point router.

❏ ATM can use a permanent virtual circuit (PVC) or a switched virtual circuit (SVC).

❏ If there is a PVC between an entering-point router and an exiting-point router, inverse request and inverse reply messages are exchanged to bind IP addresses to physical addresses. Then physical addresses can be bound to the PVC.

❏ ATMARP is a protocol used on ATM networks that binds a physical address to an IP address.

❏ To establish a SVC between an entering-point router and an exiting-point router, the services of an ATMARP server are needed to find the physical address of the exiting-point router.

❏ The ATMARP server's mapping table is built through the use of the inverse request and the inverse reply messages.

❏ An ATM network can be divided into logical subnetworks to facilitate ATMARP and other protocol operations.

23.8   PRACTICE SET

Exercises

1. What is the minimum number of cells resulting from an IP datagram? What is the maximum number of cells resulting from an IP datagram?

2. Explain why padding is necessary in AAL5.

3. Using AAL5, show a situation where we need _____ of padding.
   a. zero bytes (no padding)
   b. 40 bytes
   c. 47 bytes

4. In a 53-byte cell (not the last cell), how many bytes belong to the IP packet if there is no padding? How many bytes belong to the IP packet in the last cell if there is no padding?

5. How many cells are created from an IP packet of 42 bytes? Show the contents of each cell.

6. Explain why no more than two cells can carry padding.

7. Show the contents of ATMARP inverse packets exchanged between two routers that have a PVC connection. The IP addresses are 172.14.20.16/16 and 180.25.23.14/24. Choose two arbitrary 20-byte physical addresses. Use hexadecimal values in filling the fields.

8. Show the contents of ATMARP packets (request and reply) exchanged between a router and a server. The IP address of the router is 14.56.12.8/16 and the IP address of the server is 200.23.54.8/24. Choose two arbitrary 20-byte physical addresses. Use hexadecimal values in filling the fields.

9. Add IP addresses for the routers in Figure 23.13. Note that the prefix in each LIS must be the same, but it must be different for the two LISs. Note also that the routers that belong to two LISs must have two IP addresses.

10. An ATMARP packet must also be carried in cells. How many cells are needed to carry an ATMARP packet discussed in this chapter?

11. A datagram is sent through an ATM network. What happens if the network is congested and one of the cells is discarded by one of the switches?

12. A datagram is sent through an ATM network. The last cell carries only padding and a trailer. What happens if the network is congested and the last cell is discarded by one of the switches? Can the IP datagram be recovered? Explain your answer.

13. Calculate the efficiency of transmission at the IP level for a packet of 1024 bytes in two cases:

   a. The datagram is fragmented so that each independent fragment (with its own header) can be carried in a cell.

   b. The whole datagram is carried by cells using AAL5 (Figure 23.3).

Research Activities

14. Find the RFCs related to AAL.

15. Find the RFCs related to ATMARP.

16. Compare ARP and ATMARP.

17. Find why there is no need for ATMRARP.

CHAPTER 24

Mobile IP

Mobile communication has received a lot of attention in the last decade. The interest in mobile communication on the Internet means that the IP protocol, originally designed for stationary devices, must be enhanced to allow the use of mobile computers, computers that move from one network to another.

24.1 ADDRESSING

The main problem that must be solved in providing mobile communication using the IP protocol is addressing.

Stationary Hosts

The original IP addressing was based on the assumption that a host is stationary, attached to one specific network. A router uses an IP address to route an IP datagram. As we learned in Chapter 4 and 5, an IP address has two parts: a prefix and a suffix. The prefix associates a host to a network. For example, the IP address 10.3.4.24/8 defines a host attached to the network 10.0.0.0/8. This implies that a host in the Internet does not have an address that it can carry with itself from one place to another. The address is valid only when the host is attached to the network. If the network changes, the address is no longer valid. Routers use this association to route a packet; they use the prefix to deliver the packet to the network to which the host is attached. This scheme works perfectly with **stationary hosts.**

> **The IP addresses are designed to work with stationary hosts because part of the address defines the network to which the host is attached.**

Mobile Hosts

When a host moves from one network to another, the IP addressing structure needs to be modified. Several solutions have been proposed.

Changing the Address

One simple solution is to let the **mobile host** change its address as it goes to the new network. The host can use DHCP to obtain a new address to associate it with the new network. This approach has several drawbacks. First, the configuration files would need to be changed. Second, each time the computer moves from one network to another, it must be rebooted. Third, the DNS tables need to be revised so that every other host in the Internet is aware of the change. Fourth, if the host roams from one network to another during a transmission, the data exchange will be interrupted. This is because the ports and IP addresses of the client and the server must remain constant for the duration of the connection.

Two Addresses

The approach that is more feasible is the use of two addresses. The host has its original address, called the **home address** and a temporary address, called the **care-of address.** The home address is permanent; it associates the host to its **home network,** the network that is the permanent home of the host. The care-of address is temporary. When a host moves from one network to another, the care-of address changes; it is associated with the **foreign network,** the network to which the host moves. Figure 24.1 shows the concept.

Figure 24.1   *Home address and care-of address*

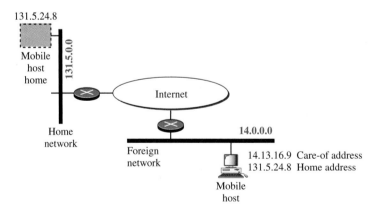

Mobile IP has two addresses for a mobile host: one home address and one care-of address. The home address is permanent; the care-of address changes as the mobile host moves from one network to another.

When a mobile host visits a foreign network, it receives its care-of address during the agent discovery and registration phase.

24.2   AGENTS

To make the change of address transparent to the rest of the Internet requires a **home agent** and a **foreign agent.** Figure 24.2 shows the position of a home agent relative to the home network and a foreign agent relative to the foreign network. We have shown the home and the foreign agents as computers, not routers, to emphasize that their specific function as an agent is performed in the application layer. In other words, they are both routers and hosts.

Figure 24.2   *Home agent and foreign agent*

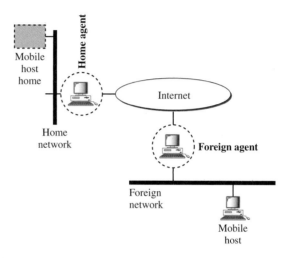

Home Agent

The home agent is usually a router attached to the home network of the mobile host. The home agent acts on behalf of the mobile host when a remote host sends a packet to the mobile host. The home agent receives the packet and sends it to the foreign agent.

Foreign Agent

The foreign agent is usually a router attached to the foreign network. The foreign agent receives and delivers packets sent by the home agent to the mobile host.

The mobile host can also act as a foreign agent. In other words, the mobile host and the foreign agent can be the same. However, to do this, a mobile host must be able to receive a care-of address by itself, which can be done through the use of DHCP. In addition, the mobile host needs the necessary software to allow it to communicate with the home agent and to have two addresses: its home address and its care-of address. This dual addressing must be transparent to the application programs.

When the mobile host acts as a foreign agent, the care-of address is called a **co-located care-of address.**

> **When the mobile host and the foreign agent are the same, the care-of address is called a co-located care-of address.**

The advantage of using a co-located care-of address is that the mobile host can move to any network without worrying about the availability of a foreign agent. The disadvantage is that the mobile host needs extra software to act as its own foreign agent.

24.3 THREE PHASES

To communicate with a remote host, a mobile host goes through three phases: agent discovery, registration, and data transfer as shown in Figure 24.3.

Figure 24.3 *Remote host and mobile host communication*

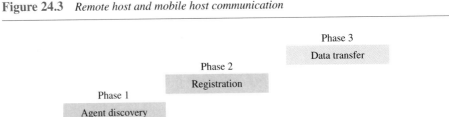

The first phase, agent discovery, involves the mobile host, the foreign agent, and the home agent. The second phase, registration, also involves the mobile host and the two agents. Finally, in the third phase, the remote host is also involved. We discuss each phase separately.

Agent Discovery

The first phase in mobile communication, **agent discovery,** consists of two subphases. A mobile host must discover (learn the address of) a home agent before it leaves its home network. A mobile host must also discover a foreign agent after it has moved to a foreign network. This discovery consists of learning the care-of address as well as the foreign agent's address. The discovery involves two types of messages: advertisement and solicitation.

Agent Advertisement

When a router advertises its presence on a network using an ICMP router advertisement, it can append an **agent advertisement** to the packet if it acts as an agent. Figure 24.4 shows how an agent advertisement is piggybacked to the router advertisement packet.

> **Mobile IP does not use a new packet type for agent advertisement; it uses the router advertisement packet of ICMP, and appends an agent advertisement message.**

Figure 24.4   *Agent advertisement*

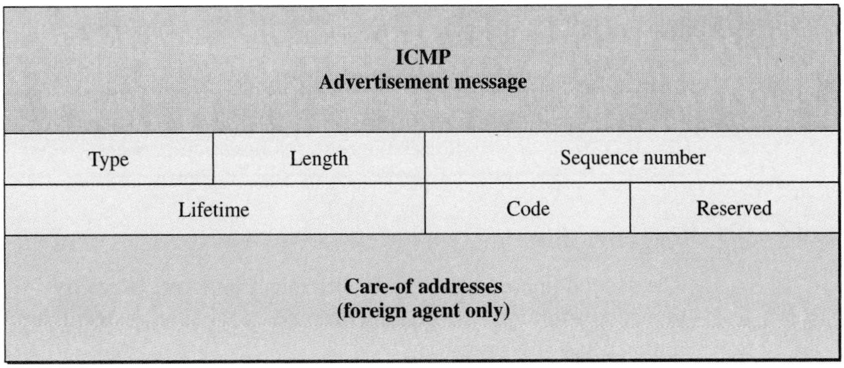

ICMP **Advertisement message**		

Type	Length	Sequence number	
Lifetime		Code	Reserved

Care-of addresses **(foreign agent only)**

The field descriptions are as follows:

❏ **Type.** The 8-bit type field is set to 16.

❏ **Length.** The 8-bit length field defines the total length of the extension message (not the length of the ICMP advertisement message).

❏ **Sequence number.** The 16-bit sequence number field holds the message number. The recipient can use the sequence number to determine if a message is lost.

❏ **Lifetime.** The lifetime field defines the number of seconds that the agent will accept requests. If the value is a string of 1s, the lifetime is infinite.

❏ **Code.** The code field is an 8-bit flag in which each bit is set (1) or unset (0). The meanings of the bits are shown in Table 24.1.

Table 24.1   *Code bits*

Bit	Meaning
0	Registration required. No co-located care-of address.
1	Agent is busy and does not accept registration at this moment.
2	Agent acts as a home agent.
3	Agent acts as a foreign agent.
4	Agent uses minimal encapsulation.
5	Agent uses generic routing encapsulation (GRE).
6	Agent supports header compression.
7	Unused (0).

❏ **Care-of Addresses.** This field contains a list of addresses available for use as care-of addresses. The mobile host can choose one of these addresses. The selection of this care-of address is announced in the registration request. Note that this field is used only by a foreign agent.

Agent Solicitation

When a mobile host has moved to a new network and has not received agent advertisements, it can initiate an **agent solicitation.** It can use the ICMP solicitation message to inform an agent that it needs assistance.

> **Mobile IP does not use a new packet type for agent solicitation;
> it uses the router solicitation packet of ICMP.**

Registration

The second phase in mobile communication is **registration.** After a mobile host has moved to a foreign network and discovered the foreign agent, it must register. There are four aspects of registration:

1. The mobile host must register itself with the foreign agent.
2. The mobile host must register itself with its home agent. This is normally done by the foreign agent on behalf of the mobile host.
3. The mobile host must renew registration if it has expired.
4. The mobile host must cancel its registration (deregistration) when it returns home.

Request and Reply

To register with the foreign agent and the home agent, the mobile host uses a **registration request** and a **registration reply** as shown in Figure 24.5.

Figure 24.5   *Registration request and reply*

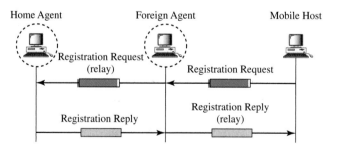

Registration Request   A registration request is sent from the mobile host to the foreign agent to register its care-of address and also to announce its home address and home agent address. The foreign agent, after receiving and registering the request, relays the message to the home agent. Note that the home agent now knows the address of the foreign agent because the IP packet that is used for relaying has the IP address of the foreign agent as the source address. Figure 24.6 shows the format of the registration request.

Figure 24.6   *Registration request format*

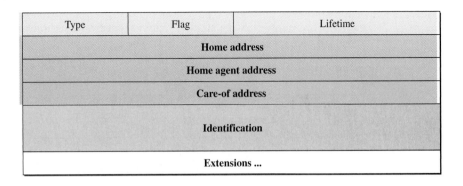

Type	Flag	Lifetime
Home address		
Home agent address		
Care-of address		
Identification		
Extensions ...		

The field descriptions are as follows:

❏ **Type.** The 8-bit type field defines the type of the message. For a request message the value of this field is 1.

❏ **Flag.** The 8-bit flag field defines forwarding information. The value of each bit can be set or unset. The meaning of each bit is given in Table 24.2.

Table 24.2   *Registration request flag field bits*

Bit	Meaning
0	Mobile host requests that home agent retain its prior care-of address.
1	Mobile host requests that home agent tunnel any broadcast message.
2	Mobile host is using co-located care-of address.
3	Mobile host requests that home agent use minimal encapsulation.
4	Mobile host requests generic routing encapsulation (GRE).
5	Mobile host requests header compression.
6–7	Reserved bits.

❏ **Lifetime.** This field defines the number of seconds the registration is valid. If the field is a string of 0s, the request message is asking for deregistration. If the field is a string of 1s, the lifetime is infinite.

❏ **Home address.** This field contains the permanent (first) address of the mobile host.

❏ **Home agent address.** This field contains the address of the home agent.

❏ **Care-of address.** This field is the temporary (second) address of the mobile host.

❏ **Identification.** This field contains a 64-bit number that is inserted into the request by the mobile host and repeated in the reply message. It matches a request with a reply.

❏ **Extensions.** Variable length extensions are used for authentication. They allow a home agent to authenticate the mobile agent. We discuss authentication in Chapter 28.

Registration Reply   A registration reply is sent from the home agent to the foreign agent and then relayed to the mobile host. The reply confirms or denies the registration request. Figure 24.7 shows the format of the registration reply.

Figure 24.7   *Registration reply format*

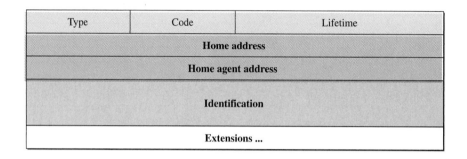

The fields are similar to those of the registration request with the following exceptions. The value of the type field is 3. The code field replaces the flag field and shows the result of the registration request (acceptance or denial). The care-of address field is not needed.

Encapsulation

Registration messages are encapsulated in a UDP user datagram. An agent uses the well-known port 434; a mobile host uses an ephemeral port.

> **A registration request or reply is sent by UDP using the well-known port 434.**

Data Transfer

After agent discovery and registration, a mobile host can communicate with a remote host. Figure 24.8 shows the idea.

From Remote Host to Home Agent

When a remote host wants to send a packet to the mobile host, it uses its address as the source address and the home address of the mobile host as the destination address. In other words, the remote host sends a packet as though the mobile host is at its home network. The packet, however, is intercepted by the home agent, which pretends it is

Figure 24.8   *Data transfer*

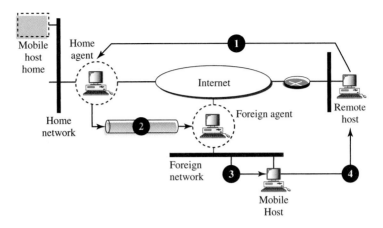

the mobile host. This is done using the proxy ARP technique discussed in Chapter 7. Path 1 of Figure 24.8 shows this step.

From Home Agent to Foreign Agent

After receiving the packet, the home agent sends the packet to the foreign agent using the tunneling concept discussed in Chapter 15. The home agent encapsulates the whole IP packet inside another IP packet using its address as the source and the foreign agent's address as the destination. Path 2 of Figure 24.8 shows this step.

From Foreign Agent to Mobile Host

When the foreign agent receives the packet, it removes the original packet. However, since the destination address is the home address of the mobile host, the foreign agent consults a registry table to find the care-of address of the mobile host. (Otherwise, the packet would just be sent back to the home network.) The packet is then sent to the care-of address. Path 3 of Figure 24.8 shows this step.

From Mobile Host to Remote Host

When a mobile host wants to send a packet to a remote host (for example, a response to the packet it has received), it sends as it does normally. The mobile host prepares a packet with its home address as the source, and the address of the remote host as the destination. Although the packet comes from the foreign network, it has the home address of the mobile host. Path 4 of Figure 24.8 shows this step.

Transparency

In this data transfer process, the remote host is unaware of any movement by the mobile host. The remote host sends packets using the home address of the mobile host as the destination address; it receives packets that have the home address of the mobile host as the source address. The movement is totally transparent. The rest of the Internet is not aware of the mobility of the moving host.

The movement of the mobile host is transparent to the rest of the Internet.

24.4   INEFFICIENCY IN MOBILE IP

Communication involving mobile IP can be inefficient. The inefficiency can be severe or moderate. The severe case is called *double crossing* or *2X*. The moderate case is called *triangle routing* or *dog-leg routing*.

Double Crossing

Double crossing occurs when a remote host communicates with a mobile host that has moved to the same network (or site) as the remote host. When the mobile host sends a packet to the remote host, there is no inefficiency; the communication is local. However, when the remote host sends a packet to the mobile host, the packet crosses the Internet twice (see Figure 24.9).

Figure 24.9   *Double crossing*

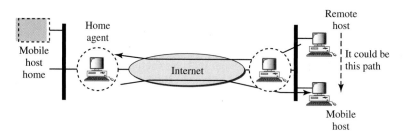

Since a computer usually communicates with other local computers (principle of locality), the inefficiency from double crossing is significant.

Triangle Routing

Triangle routing, the less severe case, occurs when the remote host communicates with a mobile host that is not attached to the same network (or site) as the mobile host. When the mobile host sends a packet to the remote host, there is no inefficiency. However, when the remote host sends a packet to the mobile host, the packet goes from the remote host to the home agent and then to the mobile host. The packet travels the two sides of a triangle, instead of just one side (see Figure 24.10).

Figure 24.10 *Triangle routing*

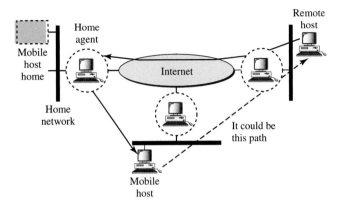

Solution

One solution to inefficiency is for the remote host to bind the care-of address to the home address of a mobile host. For example, when a home agent receives the first packet for a mobile host, it forwards the packet to the foreign agent; it could also send an **update binding packet** to the remote host so that future packets to this host could be sent to the care-of address. The remote host can keep this information in a cache.

The problem with this strategy is that the cache entry becomes outdated once the mobile host moves. In this case the home agent needs to send a **warning packet** to the remote host to inform it of the change.

24.5 KEY TERMS

agent advertisement

agent discovery

agent solicitation

care-of address

co-located care-of address

double crossing

foreign agent

foreign network

home address

home agent

home network

mobile host

registration

registration reply

registration request

stationary host

triangle routing

update binding packet

warning packet

24.6   SUMMARY

❏ Mobile IP, designed for mobile communication, is an enhanced version of the Internetworking Protocol (IP).

❏ A mobile host has a home address on its home network and a care-of address on its foreign network.

❏ When the mobile host is on a foreign network, a home agent relays messages (for the mobile host) to a foreign agent.

❏ A foreign agent sends relayed messages to a mobile host.

❏ A mobile host on its home network learns the address of a home agent through a process called agent discovery. A mobile host on a foreign network learns the address of a foreign agent through agent discovery or agent solicitation.

❏ A mobile host on a foreign network must register itself with both the home and foreign agents.

❏ A message from a remote host goes from the remote host to the home agent, to the foreign agent, and then to the mobile host.

❏ Mobile communication can be inefficient due to the extra distance a message must travel. Double crossing and triangle routing are two instances of inefficient routing.

24.7   PRACTICE SET

Exercises

1. Is registration required if the mobile host acts as a foreign agent? Explain your answer.

2. Redraw Figure 24.5 if the mobile host acts as a foreign agent.

3. Create a home agent advertisement message using 1456 as the sequence number and a lifetime of 3 hours. Select your own values for the bits in the code field. Calculate and insert the value for the length field.

4. Create a foreign agent advertisement message using 1672 as the sequence number and a lifetime of 4 hours. Select your own values for the bits in the code field. Use at least three care-of addresses of your choice. Calculate and insert the value for the length field.

5. Discuss how the ICMP router solicitation message can also be used for agent solicitation. Why are there no extra fields?

6. Which protocol is the carrier of the agent advertisement and solicitation messages?

7. Show the encapsulation of the advertisement message in Exercise 3 in an IP datagram. What is the value for the protocol field?

8. Explain why the registration request and reply are not directly encapsulated in an IP datagram. Why is there a need for the UDP user datagram?

9. We have the following information:

Mobile host home address: 130.45.6.7/16
Mobile host care-of address: 14.56.8.9/8
Remote host address: 200.4.7.14/24
Home agent address: 130.45.10.20/16
Foreign agent address: 14.67.34.6/8

Show the contents of the IP datagram header sent from the remote host to the home agent.

10. Using the information in Exercise 9, show the contents of the IP datagram sent by the home agent to the foreign agent. Use tunneling.

11. Using the information in Exercise 9, show the contents of the IP datagram sent by the foreign agent to the mobile host.

12. Using the information in Exercise 9, show the contents of the IP datagram sent by the mobile host to the remote host.

13. What type of inefficiency do we have in Exercise 9? Explain your answer.

Research Activities

14. Find the RFCs related to mobile IP.

15. We mentioned that registration messages are encapsulated in UDP. Find why UDP is chosen instead of TCP.

16. Find how frequently an agent advertisement is sent.

17. Find the different types of authentication needed in mobile IP.

18. Find the role of multicasting in mobile IP.

CHAPTER 25

Multimedia

Recent advances in technology have changed our use of audio and video. In the past, we listened to an audio broadcast through a radio and watched a video program broadcast through a TV. We used the telephone network to interactively communicate with another party. But times have changed. People want to use the Internet not only for text and image communications, but also for audio and video services. In this chapter, we concentrate on applications that use the Internet for audio and video services.

We can divide audio and video services into three broad categories: **streaming stored audio/video, streaming live audio/video,** and **interactive audio/video,** as shown in Figure 25.1. Streaming means a user can listen (or watch) the file after the downloading has started.

Figure 25.1 *Internet audio/video*

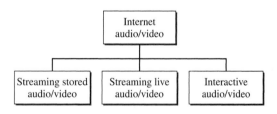

In the first category, streaming stored audio/video, the files are compressed and stored on a server. A client downloads the files through the Internet. This is sometimes referred to as **on-demand audio/video.** Examples of stored audio files are songs, symphonies, books on tape, and famous lectures. Examples of stored video files are movies, TV shows, and music video clips.

> **Streaming stored audio/video refers to on-demand requests for compressed audio/video files.**

In the second category, streaming live audio/video, a user listens to broadcast audio and video through the Internet. A good example of this type of application is the Internet radio. Some radio stations broadcast their programs only on the Internet; many broadcast them both on the Internet and on the air. Internet TV is not popular yet, but many people believe that TV stations will broadcast their programs on the Internet in the future.

> **Streaming live audio/video refers to the broadcasting of radio and TV programs through the Internet.**

In the third category, interactive audio/video, people use the Internet to interactively communicate with one another. A good example of this application is Internet telephony and Internet teleconferencing.

> **Interactive audio/video refers to the use of the Internet for interactive audio/video applications.**

We will discuss these three applications in this chapter, but first we need to discuss some other issues related to audio/video: digitizing audio and video and compressing audio and video.

25.1 DIGITIZING AUDIO AND VIDEO

Before audio or video signals can be sent on the Internet, they need to be digitized. We discuss audio and video separately.

Digitizing Audio

When sound is fed into a microphone, an electronic analog signal is generated which represents the sound amplitude as a function of time. The signal is called an *analog audio signal*. An analog signal, such as audio, can be digitized to produce a digital signal. According to the Nyquist theorem, if the highest frequency of the signal is f, we need to sample the signal $2f$ times per second. There are other methods for digitizing an audio signal, but the principle is the same.

Voice is sampled at 8000 samples per second with 8 bits per sample. This results in a digital signal of 64 kbps. Music is sampled at 44,100 samples per second with 16 bits per sample. This results in a digital signal of 705.6 kbps for monaural and 1.411 Mbps for stereo.

Digitizing Video

A video consists of a sequence of frames. If the frames are displayed on the screen fast enough, we get an impression of motion. The reason is that our eyes cannot distinguish the rapidly flashing frames as individual ones. There is no standard number of frames per second; in North America 25 frames per second is common. However, to avoid a condition known as flickering, a frame needs to be refreshed. The TV industry repaints each frame twice. This means 50 frames need to be sent, or if there is memory at the sender site, 25 frames with each frame repainted from the memory.

Each frame is divided into small grids, called picture elements or **pixels.** For black-and-white TV, each 8-bit pixel represents one of 256 different gray levels. For a color TV, each pixel is 24 bits, with 8 bits for each primary color (red, green, and blue).

We can calculate the number of bits in a second for a specific resolution. In the lowest resolution a color frame is made of 1024×768 pixels. This means that we need

$$2 \times 25 \times 1024 \times 768 \times 24 = 944 \text{ Mbps}$$

This data rate needs a very high data rate technology such as SONET. To send video using lower-rate technologies, we need to compress the video.

Compression **is needed to send video over the Internet.**

25.2   AUDIO AND VIDEO COMPRESSION

To send audio or video over the Internet requires **compression.** In this section, we first discuss audio compression and then video compression.

Audio Compression

Audio compression can be used for speech or music. For speech, we need to compress a 64-kHz digitized signal; for music, we need to compress a 1.411-MHz signal. Two categories of techniques are used for audio compression: predictive encoding and perceptual encoding.

Predictive Encoding

In **predictive encoding,** the differences between the samples are encoded instead of encoding all the sampled values. This type of compression is normally used for speech. Several standards have been defined such as GSM (13 kbps), G.729 (8 kbps), and G.723.3 (6.4 or 5.3 kbps). Detailed discussions of these techniques are beyond the scope of this book.

Perceptual Encoding: MP3

The most common compression technique that is used to create CD-quality audio is based on the **perceptual encoding** technique. As we mentioned before, this type of audio needs at least 1.411 Mbps; this cannot be sent over the Internet without compression. **MP3** (MPEG audio layer 3), a part of the MPEG standard (discussed in the video compression section), uses this technique.

Perceptual encoding is based on the science of psychoacoustics, which is the study of how people perceive sound. The idea is based on some flaws in our auditory system: Some sounds can mask other sounds. Masking can happen in frequency and time. In **frequency masking,** a loud sound in a frequency range can partially or totally mask a softer sound in another frequency range. For example, we cannot hear what our dance partner says in a room where a loud heavy metal band is performing. In **temporal masking,** a loud sound can numb our ears for a short time even after the sound has stopped.

MP3 uses these two phenomena, frequency and temporal masking, to compress audio signals. The technique analyzes and divides the spectrum into several groups. Zero bits are allocated to the frequency ranges that are totally masked. A small number of bits are allocated to the frequency ranges that are partially masked. A larger number of bits are allocated to the frequency ranges that are not masked.

MP3 produces three data rates: 96 kbps, 128 kbps, and 160 kbps. The rate is based on the range of the frequencies in the original analog audio.

Video Compression

As we mentioned before, video is composed of multiple frames. Each frame is one image. We can compress video by first compressing images. Two standards are prevalent in the market. **Joint Photographic Experts Group (JPEG)** is used to compress images. **Moving Picture Experts Group (MPEG)** is used to compress video. We briefly discuss JPEG and then MPEG.

Image Compression: JPEG

As we discussed previously, if the picture is not in color (gray scale), each pixel can be represented by an 8-bit integer (256 levels). If the picture is in color, each pixel can be represented by 24 bits (3 × 8 bits), with each 8 bits representing red, blue, or green (RBG). To simplify the discussion, we concentrate on a gray scale picture.

In JPEG, a gray scale picture is divided into blocks of 8 × 8 pixels (see Figure 25.2).

Figure 25.2 *JPEG gray scale*

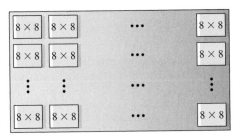

The purpose of dividing the picture into blocks is to decrease the number of calculations because, as you will see shortly, the number of mathematical operations for each picture is the square of the number of units.

The whole idea of JPEG is to change the picture into a linear (vector) set of numbers that reveals the redundancies. The redundancies (lack of changes) can then be removed by using one of the text compression methods. A simplified scheme of the process is shown in Figure 25.3.

Figure 25.3 *JPEG process*

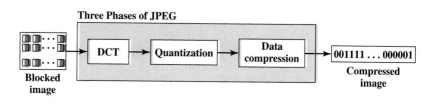

Discrete Cosine Transform (DCT)   In this step, each block of 64 pixels goes through a transformation called the **discrete cosine transform (DCT).** The transformation changes the 64 values so that the relative relationships between pixels are kept but the redundancies are revealed. We do not give the formula here, but we do show the results of the transformation for three cases.

Case 1   In this case, we have a block of uniform gray, and the value of each pixel is 20. When we do the transformations, we get a nonzero value for the first element (upper left corner); the rest of the pixels have a value of 0. The value of $T(0,0)$ is the average (multiplied by a constant) of the $P(x,y)$ values and is called the *dc value* (direct current, borrowed from electrical engineering). The rest of the values, called *ac values,* in $T(m,n)$ represent changes in the pixel values. But because there are no changes, the rest of the values are 0s (see Figure 25.4).

Figure 25.4 *Case 1: uniform gray scale*

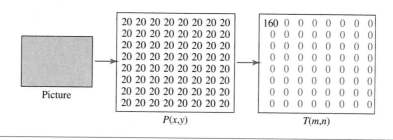

Case 2   In the second case, we have a block with two different uniform gray scale sections. There is a sharp change in the values of the pixels (from 20 to 50). When we do the transformations, we get a dc value as well as nonzero ac values. However, there are only a few nonzero values clustered around the dc value. Most of the values are 0 (see Figure 25.5).

Figure 25.5   *Case 2: two sections*

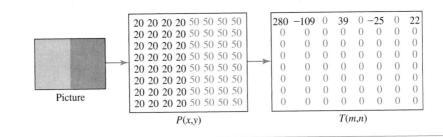

Case 3   In the third case, we have a block that changes gradually. That is, there is no sharp change between the values of neighboring pixels. When we do the transformations, we get a dc value, with many nonzero ac values also (Figure 25.6).

Figure 25.6   *Case 3: gradient gray scale*

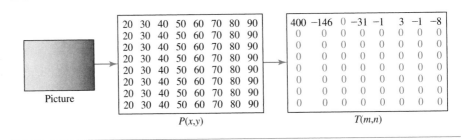

From Figures 25.4, 25.5, and 25.6, we can state the following:

❏ The transformation creates table T from table P.

❏ The dc value is the average value (multiplied by a constant) of the pixels.

❏ The ac values are the changes.

❏ Lack of changes in neighboring pixels creates 0s.

Quantization   After the T table is created, the values are quantized to reduce the number of bits needed for encoding. Previously in **quantization,** we dropped the fraction from each value and kept the integer part. Here, we divide the number by a constant and then drop the fraction. This reduces the required number of bits even more. In most implementations, a quantizing table (8 by 8) defines how to quantize each value. The divisor depends on the position of the value in the T table. This is done to optimize the number of bits and the number of 0s for each particular application. Note that the only phase in the process that is not reversible is the quantizing phase. We lose some information here that is not recoverable. As a matter of fact, the only reason that JPEG is called *lossy compression* is because of this quantization phase.

Compression After quantization, the values are read from the table, and redundant 0s are removed. However, to cluster the 0s together, the table is read diagonally in a zigzag fashion rather than row by row or column by column. The reason is that if the picture changes smoothly, the bottom right corner of the *T* table is all 0s. Figure 25.7 shows the process.

Figure 25.7 *Reading the table*

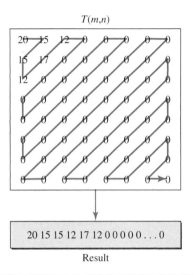

$T(m,n)$

Result

20 15 15 12 17 12 0 0 0 0 0 ... 0

Video Compression: MPEG

The Moving Picture Experts Group (MPEG) method is used to compress video. In principle, a motion picture is a rapid flow of a set of frames, where each frame is an image. In other words, a frame is a spatial combination of pixels, and a video is a temporal combination of frames that are sent one after another. Compressing video, then, means spatially compressing each frame and temporally compressing a set of frames.

Spatial Compression The **spatial compression** of each frame is done with JPEG (or a modification of it). Each frame is a picture that can be independently compressed.

Temporal Compression In **temporal compression,** redundant frames are removed. When we watch television, we receive 50 frames per second. However, most of the consecutive frames are almost the same. For example, when someone is talking, most of the frame is the same as the previous one except for the segment of the frame around the lips, which changes from one frame to another.

To temporally compress data, the MPEG method first divides frames into three categories: I-frames, P-frames, and B-frames.

❏ **I-frames.** An **intracoded frame (I-frame)** is an independent frame that is not related to any other frame (not to the frame sent before or to the frame sent after). They are present at regular intervals (e.g., every ninth frame is an I-frame). An

I-frame must appear periodically to handle some sudden change in the frame that the previous and following frames cannot show. Also, when a video is broadcast, a viewer may tune at any time. If there is only one I-frame at the beginning of the broadcast, the viewer who tunes in late will not receive a complete picture. I-frames are independent of other frames and cannot be constructed from other frames.

❑ **P-frames.** A **predicted frame (P-frame)** is related to the preceding I-frame or P-frame. In other words, each P-frame contains only the changes from the preceding frame. The changes, however, cannot cover a big segment. For example, for a fast-moving object, the new changes may not be recorded in a P-frame. P-frames can be constructed only from previous I- or P-frames. P-frames carry much less information than other frame types and carry even fewer bits after compression.

❑ **B-frames.** A **bidirectional frame (B-frame)** is related to the preceding and following I-frame or P-frame. In other words, each B-frame is relative to the past and the future. Note that a B-frame is never related to another B-frame.

Figure 25.8 shows a sample sequence of frames.

Figure 25.8 *MPEG frames*

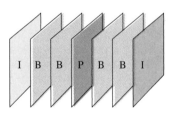

Figure 25.9 shows how I-, P-, and B-frames are constructed from a series of seven frames.

Figure 25.9 *MPEG frame construction*

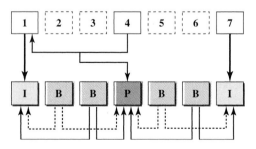

MPEG has gone through two versions. MPEG1 was designed for a CD-ROM with a data rate of 1.5 Mbps. MPEG2 was designed for high-quality DVD with a data rate of 3 to 6 Mbps.

25.3   STREAMING STORED AUDIO/VIDEO

Now that we have discussed digitizing and compressing audio/video, we turn our attention to specific applications. The first is streaming stored audio and video. Downloading these types of files from a Web server can be different from downloading other types of files. To understand the concept, let us discuss four approaches, each with a different complexity.

First Approach: Using a Web Server

A compressed audio/video file can be downloaded as a text file. The client (browser) can use the services of HTTP and send a GET message to download the file. The Web server can send the compressed file to the browser. The browser can then use a help application, normally called a **media player,** to play the file. Figure 25.10 shows this approach.

Figure 25.10   *Using a Web server*

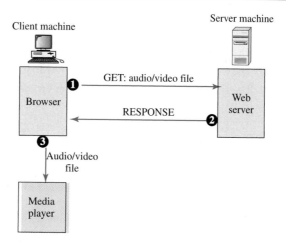

This approach is very simple and does not involve *streaming*. However, it has a drawback. An audio/video file is usually large even after compression. An audio file may contain tens of megabits, and a video file may contain hundreds of megabits. In this approach, the file needs to download completely before it can be played. Using contemporary data rates, the user needs some seconds or tens of seconds before the file can be played.

Second Approach: Using a Web Server with Metafile

In another approach, the media player is directly connected to the Web server for downloading the audio/video file. The Web server stores two files: the actual audio/video file and a **metafile** that holds information about the audio/video file. Figure 25.11 shows the steps in this approach.

Figure 25.11 *Using a Web server with a metafile*

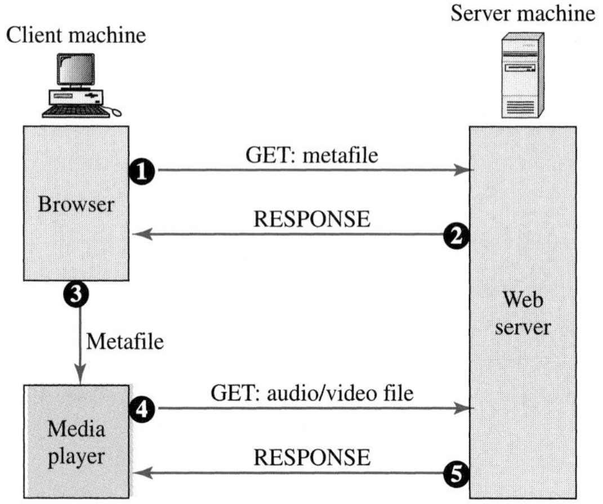

1. The HTTP client accesses the Web server using the GET message.
2. The information about the metafile comes in the response.
3. The metafile is passed to the media player.
4. The media player uses the URL in the metafile to access the audio/video file.
5. The Web server responds.

Third Approach: Using a Media Server

The problem with the second approach is that the browser and the media player both use the services of HTTP. HTTP is designed to run over TCP. This is appropriate for retrieving the metafile, but not for retrieving the audio/video file. The reason is that TCP retransmits a lost or damaged segment, which is counter to the philosophy of streaming. We need to dismiss TCP and its error control; we need to use UDP. However, HTTP, which accesses the Web server, and the Web server itself are designed for TCP; we need another server, a **media server.** Figure 25.12 shows the concept.

1. The HTTP client accesses the Web server using a GET message.
2. The information about the metafile comes in the response.
3. The metafile is passed to the media player.
4. The media player uses the URL in the metafile to access the media server to download the file. Downloading can take place by any protocol that uses UDP.
5. The media server responds.

Fourth Approach: Using a Media Server and RTSP

The **Real-Time Streaming Protocol (RTSP)** is a control protocol designed to add more functionalities to the streaming process. Using RTSP, we can control the playing

Figure 25.12   *Using a media server*

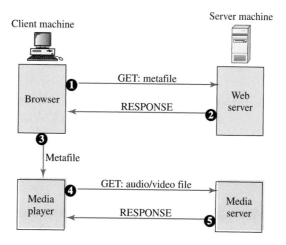

of audio/video. RTSP is an out-of-band control protocol that is similar to the second connection in FTP. Figure 25.13 shows a media server and RTSP.

Figure 25.13   *Using a media server and RTSP*

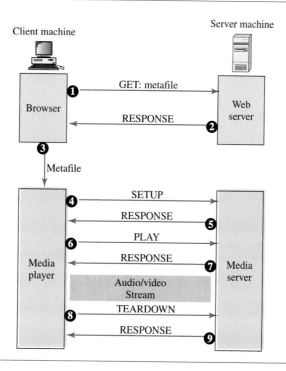

1. The HTTP client accesses the Web server using a GET message.
2. The information about the metafile comes in the response.
3. The metafile is passed to the media player.
4. The media player sends a SETUP message to create a connection with the media server.
5. The media server responds.
6. The media player sends a PLAY message to start playing (downloading).
7. The audio/video file is downloaded using another protocol that runs over UDP.
8. The connection is broken using the TEARDOWN message.
9. The media server responds.

The media player can send other types of messages. For example, a PAUSE message temporarily stops the downloading; downloading can be resumed with a PLAY message.

25.4   STREAMING LIVE AUDIO/VIDEO

Streaming live audio/video is similar to the broadcasting of audio and video by radio and TV stations. Instead of broadcasting to the air, the stations broadcast through the Internet. There are several similarities between streaming stored audio/video and streaming live audio/video. They are both sensitive to delay; neither can accept retransmission. However, there is a difference. In the first application, the communication is unicast and on-demand. In the second, the communication is multicast and live. Live streaming is better suited to the multicast services of IP and the use of protocols such as UDP and RTP (discussed later). However, presently, live streaming is still using TCP and multiple unicasting instead of multicasting. There is still much progress to be made in this area.

25.5   REAL-TIME INTERACTIVE AUDIO/VIDEO

In real-time interactive audio/video, people communicate with one another in real time. The Internet phone or voice over IP is an example of this type of application. Video conferencing is another example that allows people to communicate visually and orally.

Characteristics

Before discussing the protocols used in this class of applications, we discuss some characteristics of real-time audio/video communication.

Time Relationship

Real-time data on a packet-switched network require the preservation of the time relationship between packets of a session. For example, let us assume that a real-time video server creates live video images and sends them online. The video is digitized and packetized. There are only three packets, and each packet holds 10 s of video information.

The first packet starts at 00:00:00, the second packet starts at 00:00:10, and the third packet starts at 00:00:20. Also imagine that it takes 1 s (an exaggeration for simplicity) for each packet to reach the destination (equal delay). The receiver can play back the first packet at 00:00:01, the second packet at 00:00:11, and the third packet at 00:00:21. Although there is a 1-s time difference between what the server sends and what the client sees on the computer screen, the action is happening in real time. The time relationship between the packets is preserved. The 1-s delay is not important. Figure 25.14 shows the idea.

Figure 25.14   *Time relationship*

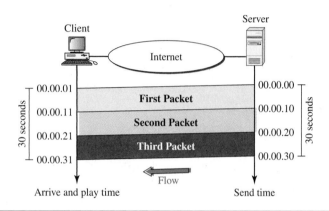

But what happens if the packets arrive with different delays? For example, the first packet arrives at 00:00:01 (1-s delay), the second arrives at 00:00:15 (5-s delay), and the third arrives at 00:00:27 (7-s delay). If the receiver starts playing the first packet at 00:00:01, it will finish at 00:00:11. However, the next packet has not yet arrived; it arrives 4 s later. There is a gap between the first and second packets and between the second and the third as the video is viewed at the remote site. This phenomenon is called **jitter.** Figure 25.15 shows the situation.

Jitter is introduced in real-time data by the delay between packets.

Timestamp

One solution to jitter is the use of a **timestamp.** If each packet has a timestamp that shows the time it was produced relative to the first (or previous) packet, then the receiver can add this time to the time at which it starts the playback. In other words, the receiver knows when each packet is to be played. Imagine the first packet in the previous example has a timestamp of 0, the second has a timestamp of 10, and the third a timestamp of 20. If the receiver starts playing back the first packet at 00:00:08, the second will be played at 00:00:18, and the third at 00:00:28. There are no gaps between the packets. Figure 25.16 shows the situation.

Figure 25.15 *Jitter*

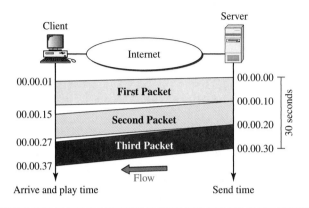

Figure 25.16 *Timestamp*

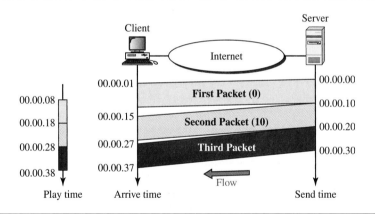

> **To prevent jitter, we can timestamp the packets and separate the arrival time from the playback time.**

Playback Buffer

To be able to separate the arrival time from the playback time, we need a buffer to store the data until they are played back. The buffer is referred to as a **playback buffer.** When a session begins (the first bit of the first packet arrives), the receiver delays playing the data until a threshold is reached. In the previous example, the first bit of the first packet arrives at 00:00:01; the threshold is 7 s, and the playback time is 00:00:08. The threshold is measured in time units of data. The replay does not start until the time units of data are equal to the threshold value.

Data are stored in the buffer at a possibly variable rate, but they are extracted and played back at a fixed rate. Note that the amount of data in the buffer shrinks or expands, but as long as the delay is less than the time to play back the threshold amount of data, there is no jitter. Figure 25.17 shows the buffer at different times for our example.

Figure 25.17 *Playback buffer*

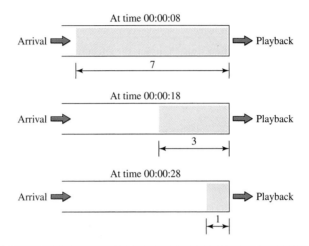

> **A playback buffer is required for real-time traffic.**

Ordering

In addition to time relationship information and timestamps for real-time traffic, one more feature is needed. We need a *sequence number* for each packet. The timestamp alone cannot inform the receiver if a packet is lost. For example, suppose the timestamps are 0, 10, and 20. If the second packet is lost, the receiver receives just two packets with timestamps 0 and 20. The receiver assumes that the packet with timestamp 20 is the second packet, produced 20 s after the first. The receiver has no way of knowing that the second packet has actually been lost. A sequence number to order the packets is needed to handle this situation.

> **A sequence number on each packet is required for real-time traffic.**

Multicasting

Multimedia play a primary role in audio and video conferencing. The traffic can be heavy, and the data are distributed using **multicasting** methods. Conferencing requires two-way communication between receivers and senders.

> **Real-time traffic needs the support of multicasting.**

Translation

Sometimes real-time traffic needs **translation.** A translator is a computer that can change the format of a high-bandwidth video signal to a lower-quality narrow-bandwidth signal. This is needed, for example, for a source creating a high-quality video signal at 5 Mbps and sending to a recipient having a bandwidth of less than 1 Mbps. To receive the signal, a translator is needed to decode the signal and encode it again at a lower quality that needs less bandwidth.

> **Translation means changing the encoding of a payload to a lower quality to match the bandwidth of the receiving network.**

Mixing

If there is more than one source that can send data at the same time (as in a video or audio conference), the traffic is made of multiple streams. To converge the traffic to one stream, data from different sources can be mixed. A **mixer** mathematically adds signals coming from different sources to create one single signal.

> **Mixing means combining several streams of traffic into one stream.**

Support from Transport Layer Protocol

The procedures mentioned in the previous sections can be implemented in the application layer. However, they are so common in real-time applications that implementation in the transport layer protocol is preferable. Let's see which of the existing transport layers is suitable for this type of traffic.

TCP is not suitable for interactive traffic. It has no provision for timestamping, and it does not support multicasting. However, it does provide ordering (sequence numbers). One feature of TCP that makes it particularly unsuitable for interactive traffic is its error control mechanism. In interactive traffic, we cannot allow the retransmission of a lost or corrupted packet. If a packet is lost or corrupted in interactive traffic, it must just be ignored. Retransmission upsets the whole idea of timestamping and playback. Today there is so much redundancy in audio and video signals (even with compression) that we can simply ignore a lost packet. The listener or viewer at the remote site may not even notice it.

> **TCP, with all its sophistication, is not suitable for interactive multimedia traffic because we cannot allow retransmission of packets.**

UDP is more suitable for interactive multimedia traffic. UDP supports multicasting and has no retransmission strategy. However, UDP has no provision for timestamping, sequencing, or mixing. A new transport protocol, Real-Time Transport Protocol (RTP), provides these missing features.

> **UDP is more suitable than TCP for interactive traffic. However, we need the services of RTP, another transport layer protocol, to make up for the deficiencies of UDP.**

25.6   RTP

Real-time Transport Protocol (RTP) is the protocol designed to handle real-time traffic on the Internet. RTP does not have a delivery mechanism (multicasting, port numbers, and so on); it must be used with UDP. RTP stands between UDP and the application program. The main contributions of RTP are timestamping, sequencing, and mixing facilities. Figure 25.18 shows the position of RTP in the protocol suite.

Figure 25.18   *RTP*

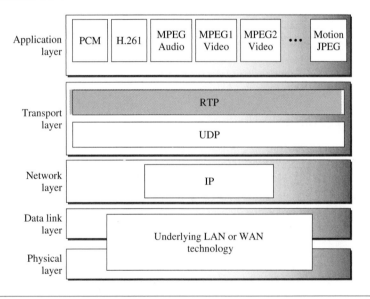

RTP Packet Format

Figure 25.19 shows the format of the RTP packet header. The format is very simple and general enough to cover all real-time applications. An application that needs more information adds it to the beginning of its payload. A description of each field follows.

- ❑   **Ver.** This 2-bit field defines the version number. The current version is 2.
- ❑   **P.** This 1-bit field, if set to 1, indicates the presence of padding at the end of the packet. In this case, the value of the last byte in the padding defines the length of the padding. Padding is the norm if a packet is encrypted. There is no padding if the value of the P field is 0.

Figure 25.19   *RTP packet header format*

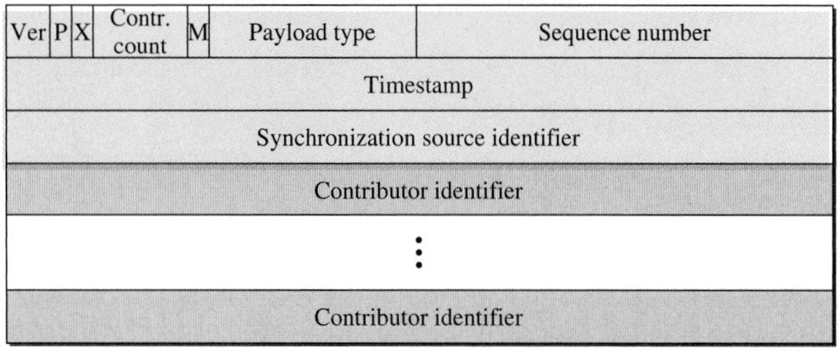

- ❑ **X.** This 1-bit field, if set to 1, indicates an extra extension header between the basic header and the data. There is no extra extension header if the value of this field is 0.

- ❑ **Contributor count.** This 4-bit field indicates the number of contributors. Note that we can have a maximum of 15 contributors because a 4-bit field only allows a number between 0 and 15.

- ❑ **M.** This 1-bit field is a marker used by the application to indicate, for example, the end of its data.

- ❑ **Payload type.** This 7-bit field indicates the type of the payload. Several payload types have been defined so far. We list some common applications in Table 25.1. A discussion of the types is beyond the scope of this book.

Table 25.1   *Payload types*

Type	Application	Type	Application	Type	Application
0	PCMμ Audio	7	LPC audio	15	G728 audio
1	1016	8	PCMA audio	26	Motion JPEG
2	G721 audio	9	G722 audio	31	H.261
3	GSM audio	10-11	L16 audio	32	MPEG1 video
5-6	DV14 audio	14	MPEG audio	33	MPEG2 video

- ❑ **Sequence number.** This field is 16 bits in length. It is used to number the RTP packets. The sequence number of the first packet is chosen randomly; it is incremented by 1 for each subsequent packet. The sequence number is used by the receiver to detect lost or out of order packets.

- ❑ **Timestamp.** This is a 32-bit field that indicates the time relationship between packets. The timestamp for the first packet is a random number. For each succeeding packet, the value is the sum of the preceding timestamp plus the time the first byte is produced (sampled). The value of the clock tick depends on the application. For example, audio applications normally generate chunks of 160 bytes; the clock tick for this application is 160. The timestamp for this application increases 160 for each RTP packet.

❏ **Synchronization source identifier.** If there is only one source, this 32-bit field defines the source. However, if there are several sources, the mixer is the synchronization source and the other sources are contributors. The value of the source identifier is a random number chosen by the source. The protocol provides a strategy in case of conflict (two sources start with the same sequence number).

❏ **Contributor identifier.** Each of these 32-bit identifiers (a maximum of 15) defines a source. When there is more than one source in a session, the mixer is the synchronization source and the remaining sources are the contributors.

UDP Port

Although RTP is itself a transport layer protocol, the RTP packet is not encapsulated directly in an IP datagram. Instead, RTP is treated like an application program and is encapsulated in a UDP user datagram. However, unlike other application programs, no well-known port is assigned to RTP. The port can be selected on demand with only one restriction: The port number must be an even number. The next number (an odd number) is used by the companion of RTP, Real-time Transport Control Protocol (RTCP).

RTP uses a temporary even-numbered UDP port.

25.7   RTCP

RTP allows only one type of message, one that carries data from the source to the destination. In many cases, there is a need for other messages in a session. These messages control the flow and quality of data and allow the recipient to send feedback to the source or sources. **Real-time Transport Control Protocol (RTCP)** is a protocol designed for this purpose. RTCP has five types of messages as shown in Figure 25.20. The number next to each box defines the type of the message.

Figure 25.20   *RTCP message types*

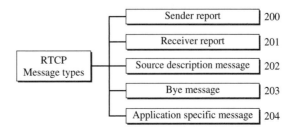

Sender Report

The sender report is sent periodically by the active senders in a conference to report transmission and reception statistics for all RTP packets sent during the interval. The sender report includes an absolute timestamp, which is the number of seconds elapsed since midnight January 1, 1970. The absolute timestamp allows the receiver to synchronize different RTP messages. It is particularly important when both audio and video are transmitted (audio and video transmissions use separate relative timestamps).

Receiver Report

The receiver report is for passive participants, those that do not send RTP packets. The report informs the sender and other receivers about the quality of service.

Source Description Message

The source periodically sends a source description message to give additional information about itself. This information can be the name, email address, telephone number, and address of the owner or controller of the source.

Bye Message

A source sends a bye message to shut down a stream. It allows the source to announce that it is leaving the conference. Although other sources can detect the absence of a source, this message is a direct announcement. It is also very useful to a mixer.

Application Specific Message

The application specific message is a packet for an application that wants to use new applications (not defined in the standard). It allows the definition of a new message type.

UDP Port

RTCP, like RTP, does not use a well-known UDP port. It uses a temporary port. The UDP port chosen must be the number immediately following the UDP port selected for RTP. It must be an odd-numbered port.

RTCP uses an odd-numbered UDP port number that follows the port number selected for RTP.

25.8   VOICE OVER IP

Let us concentrate on one real-time interactive audio/video application: **voice over IP,** or Internet telephony. The idea is to use the Internet as a telephone network with some additional capabilities. Instead of communicating over a circuit-switched network, this application allows communication between two parties over the packet-switched Internet. Two protocols have been designed to handle this type of communication: SIP and H.323. We briefly discuss both.

SIP

The **Session Initiation Protocol (SIP)** was designed by IETF. It is an application layer protocol that establishes, manages, and terminates a multimedia session (call). It can be used to create two-party, multiparty, or multicast sessions. SIP is designed to be independent of the underlying transport layer; it can run on either UDP, TCP, or SCTP.

Messages

SIP is a text-based protocol like HTTP. SIP, like HTTP, uses messages. Six messages are defined as shown in Figure 25.21.

Figure 25.21   *SIP messages*

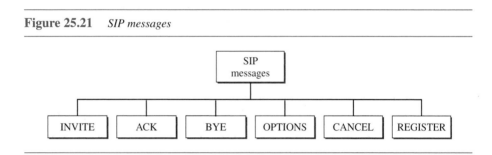

Each message has a header and a body. The header consists of several lines that describe the structure of the message, caller's capability, media type, and so on. We give a brief description of each message. Then we show their applications in a simple session.

The caller initializes a session with the INVITE message. After the callee answers the call, the caller sends an ACK message for confirmation. The BYE message terminates a session. The OPTIONS message queries a machine about its capabilities. The CANCEL message cancels an already started initialization process. The REGISTER message makes a connection when the callee is not available.

Addresses

In a regular telephone communication a telephone number identifies the sender, and another telephone number identifies the receiver. SIP is very flexible. In SIP, an email address, an IP address, a telephone number, and other types of addresses can be used to identify the sender and receiver. However, the address needs to be in SIP format (also called scheme). Figure 25.22 shows some common formats.

Simple Session

A simple session using SIP consists of three modules: establishing, communicating, and terminating. Figure 25.23 shows a simple session using SIP.

Figure 25.22   *SIP formats*

sip:bob@201.23.45.78	sip:bob@fhda.edu	sip:bob@408-864-8900
IPv4 address	Email address	Phone number

Figure 25.23   *SIP simple session*

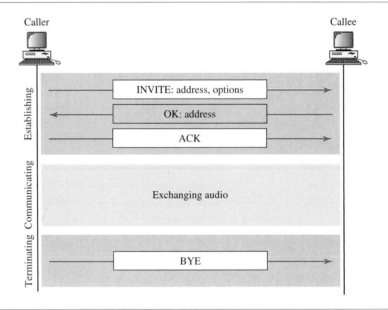

Establishing a Session   Establishing a session in SIP requires a three-way handshake. The caller sends an INVITE message, using UDP, TCP, or SCTP to begin the communication. If the callee is willing to start the session, she sends a reply message. To confirm that a reply code has been received, the caller sends an ACK message.

Communicating   After the session has been established, the caller and the callee can communicate using two temporary ports.

Terminating the Session   The session can be terminated with a BYE message sent by either party.

Tracking the Callee

What happens if the callee is not sitting at her terminal? She may be away from her system or at another terminal. She may not even have a fixed IP address if DHCP is being used. SIP has a mechanism (similar to one in DNS) that finds the IP address of the terminal at which the callee is sitting. To perform this tracking, SIP uses the concept of registration. SIP defines some servers as registrars. At any moment a user is registered with at least one **registrar server;** this server knows the IP address of the callee.

When a caller needs to communicate with the callee, the caller can use the email address instead of the IP address in the INVITE message. The message goes to a proxy server. The proxy server sends a lookup message (not part of SIP) to some registrar server that has registered the callee. When the proxy server receives a reply message from the registrar server, the proxy server takes the caller's INVITE message and inserts the newly discovered IP address of the callee. This message is then sent to the callee. Figure 25.24 shows the process.

Figure 25.24   *Tracking the callee*

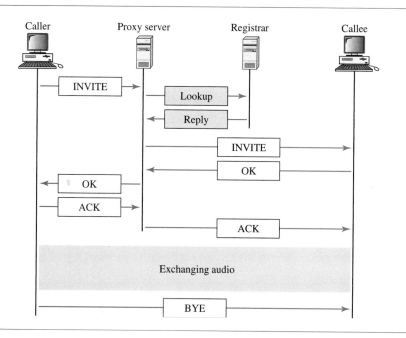

H.323

H.323 is a standard designed by ITU to allow telephones on the public telephone network to talk to computers (called *terminals* in H.323) connected to the Internet. Figure 25.25 shows the general architecture of H.323.

A **gateway** connects the Internet to the telephone network. In general, a gateway is a five-layer device that can translate a message from one protocol stack to another. The gateway here does exactly the same thing. It transforms a telephone network message to an Internet message. The **gatekeeper** server on the local area network plays the role of the registrar server, as we discussed in the SIP protocol.

Protocols

H.323 uses a number of protocols to establish and maintain voice (or video) communication. Figure 25.26 shows these protocols.

Figure 25.25   *H.323 architecture*

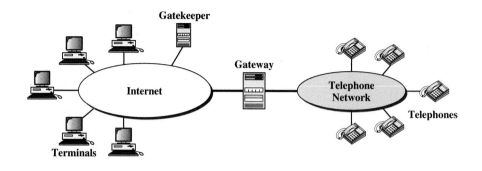

Figure 25.26   *H.323 protocols*

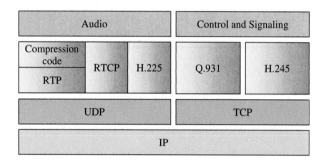

H.323 uses G.71 or G.723.1 for compression. It uses a protocol named H.245 which allows the parties to negotiate the compression method. Protocol Q.931 is used for establishing and terminating connections. Another protocol called H.225, or RAS (Registration/Administration/Status), is used for registration with the gatekeeper.

Operation

Let us show the operation of a telephone communication using H.323 with a simple example. Figure 25.27 shows the steps used by a terminal to communicate with a telephone.

1. The terminal sends a broadcast message to the gatekeeper. The gatekeeper responds with its IP address.
2. The terminal and gatekeeper communicate, using H.225 to negotiate bandwidth.
3. The terminal, the gatekeeper, gateway, and the telephone communicate using Q.931 to set up a connection.
4. The terminal, the gatekeeper, gateway, and the telephone communicate using H.245 to negotiate the compression method.

Figure 25.27   *H.323 example*

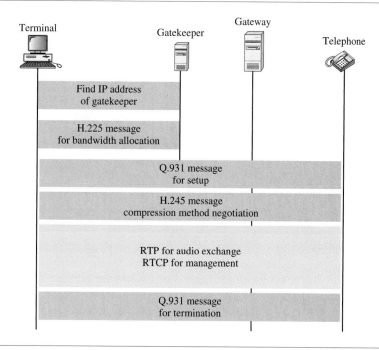

5. The terminal, gateway, and the telephone exchange audio using RTP under the management of RTCP.
6. The terminal, the gatekeeper, gateway, and the telephone communicate using Q.931 to terminate the communication.

25.9   KEY TERMS

bidirectional frame (B-frame)	Joint Photographic Experts Group (JPEG)
discrete cosine transform (DCT)	media player
frequency masking	media server
gatekeeper	metafile
gateway	mixer
H.323	Moving Picture Experts Group (MPEG)
interactive audio/video	MP3
intracoded frame (I-frame)	on-demand audio/video
jitter	perceptual encoding

pixel	registrar server
playback buffer	Session Initiation Protocol (SIP)
predicted frame (P-frame)	spatial compression
predictive encoding	streaming live audio/video
quantization	streaming stored audio/video
Real-Time Streaming Protocol (RTSP)	temporal compression
real-time traffic	temporal masking
Real-Time Transport Control Protocol (RTCP)	translation
Real-Time Transport Protocol (RTP)	voice over IP

25.10   SUMMARY

❑ Audio/video files can be downloaded for future use (streaming stored audio/video) or broadcast to clients over the Internet (streaming live audio/video). The Internet can also be used for live audio/video interaction.

❑ Audio and video need to be digitized before being sent over the Internet.

❑ Audio files are compressed through predictive encoding or perceptual encoding.

❑ Joint Photographic Experts Group (JPEG) is a method to compress pictures and graphics.

❑ The JPEG process involves blocking, the discrete cosine transform, quantization, and lossless compression.

❑ Moving Pictures Experts Group (MPEG) is a method to compress video.

❑ MPEG involves both spatial compression and temporal compression. The former is similar to JPEG, and the latter removes redundant frames.

❑ We can use a Web server, or a Web server with a metafile, or a media server, or a media server and RTSP to download a streaming audio/video file.

❑ Real-time data on a packet-switched network require the preservation of the time relationship between packets of a session.

❑ Gaps between consecutive packets at the receiver cause a phenomenon called jitter.

❑ Jitter can be controlled through the use of timestamps and a judicious choice of the playback time.

❑ A playback buffer holds data until they can be played back.

❑ A receiver delays playing back real-time data held in the playback buffer until a threshold level is reached.

❑ Sequence numbers on real-time data packets provide a form of error control.

❑ Real-time data are multicast to receivers.

❑ Real-time traffic sometimes requires a translator to change a high-bandwidth signal to a lower-quality narrow-bandwidth signal.

❏ A mixer combines signals from different sources into one signal.

❏ Real-time multimedia traffic requires both UDP and Real-Time Transport Protocol (RTP).

❏ RTP handles timestamping, sequencing, and mixing.

❏ Real-Time Transport Control Protocol (RTCP) provides flow control, quality of data control, and feedback to the sources.

❏ Voice over IP is a real-time interactive audio/video application.

❏ The Session Initiation Protocol (SIP) is an application layer protocol that establishes, manages, and terminates multimedia sessions.

❏ H.323 is an ITU standard that allows a telephone connected to a public telephone network to talk to a computer connected to the Internet.

25.11   PRACTICE SET

Exercises

1. In Figure 25.17 what is the amount of data in the playback buffer at each of the following times?
   a. 00:00:17
   b. 00:00:20
   c. 00:00:25
   d. 00:00:30

2. Compare and contrast TCP with RTP. Are both doing the same thing?

3. Can we say UDP plus RTP is the same as TCP?

4. Why does RTP need the service of another protocol, RTCP, but TCP does not?

5. In Figure 25.12, can the Web server and media server run on different machines?

6. We discuss the use of SIP in this chapter for audio. Is there any drawback to prevent using it for video?

7. Do you think H.323 is actually the same as SIP? What are the differences? Make a comparison between the two.

8. What are the problems for full implementation of voice over IP? Do you think we will stop using the telephone network very soon?

9. Can H.323 also be used for video?

Research Activities

10. Find the format of an RTCP sender report. Pay particular attention to the packet length and the parts repeated for each source. Describe each field.

11. Find the format of an RTCP receiver report. Pay particular attention to the packet length and the parts repeated for each source. Describe each field.

12. Find the format of an RTCP source description. Pay particular attention to the packet length and the parts repeated for each source. Describe each field.

13. Find the meaning of the source description items used in the RTCP source description packet. Specifically, find the meaning of CNAME, NAME, EMAIL, PHONE, LOC, TOOL, NOTE, and PRIV.

14. Find the format of an RTCP bye message. Pay particular attention to the packet length and the parts repeated for each source. Describe each field.

15. Find the format for the RTCP application-specific packet.

CHAPTER 26

Private Networks,
Virtual Private Networks, and
Network Address Translation

In this chapter, we discuss three related topics that are becoming increasingly important as the Internet grows. We first discuss the idea of private networks—networks that are isolated from the Internet but use the TCP/IP protocol suite. We then discuss virtual private networks—networks that use the Internet and at the same time require privacy like a private network. Finally, we discuss network address translation—a technology that allows a private network to use two sets of addresses: one private and one global.

26.1 PRIVATE NETWORKS

A **private network** is designed to be used only inside an organization. It allows access to shared resources and, at the same time, provides privacy. Before we discuss some aspects of these networks, let us define two commonly used related terms: intranet and extranet.

Intranet

An **intranet** is a private network (LAN) that uses the TCP/IP protocol suite. However, access to the network is limited to only the users inside the organization. The network uses application programs defined for the global Internet, such as HTTP, and may have Web servers, print servers, file servers, and so on.

Extranet

An **extranet** is the same as an intranet with one major difference. Some resources may be accessed by specific groups of users outside the organization under the control of the network administrator. For example, an organization may allow authorized customers access to product specifications, availability, and on-line ordering. A university or a college can allow distance learning students access to the computer lab after passwords have been checked.

Addressing

A private network that uses the TCP/IP protocol suite must use IP addresses. Three choices are available:

1. The network can apply for a set of addresses from the Internet authorities and use them without being connected to the Internet. This strategy has an advantage. If in the future the organization desires Internet connection, it can do so with relative ease. However, there is also a disadvantage: The address space is wasted.

2. The network can use any set of addresses without registering with the Internet authorities. Because the network is isolated, the addresses do not have to be unique. However, this strategy has a serious drawback: Users might mistakenly confuse the addresses as part of the global Internet.

3. To overcome the problems associated with the first and second strategies, the Internet authorities have reserved three sets of addresses, shown in Table 26.1.

Table 26.1   *Addresses for private networks*

Range	Total
10.0.0.0 to 10.255.255.255	2^{24}
172.16.0.0 to 172.31.255.255	2^{20}
192.168.0.0 to 192.168.255.255	2^{16}

Any organization can use an address out of this set without permission from the Internet authorities. Everybody knows that these **reserved addresses** are for private networks. They are unique inside the organization, but they are not unique globally. No router will forward a packet that has one of these addresses as the destination address.

26.2   VIRTUAL PRIVATE NETWORKS (VPN)

Virtual private network (VPN) is a technology that is gaining popularity among large organizations that use the global Internet for both intra- and interorganization communication, but require privacy in their intraorganization communication.

Achieving Privacy

To achieve privacy, organizations can use one of three strategies: private networks, hybrid networks, and virtual private networks.

Private Networks

An organization that needs privacy when routing information inside the organization can use a private network as discussed previously. A small organization with one single site can use an isolated LAN. People inside the organization can send data to one another that totally remain inside the organization, secure from outsiders. A larger organization with several sites can create a private internet. The LANs at different sites can be connected to each other using routers and leased lines. In other words, an internet can be made out of private LANs and private WANs. Figure 26.1 shows such a situation for an organization with two sites. The LANs are connected to each other using routers and one leased line.

Figure 26.1   *Private network*

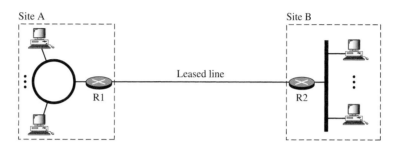

In this situation, the organization has created a private internet that is totally isolated from the global Internet. For end-to-end communication between stations at different sites, the organization can use the TCP/IP protocol suite. However, there is no need for the organization to apply for IP addresses with the Internet authorities. It can use private IP addresses. The organization can use any IP class and assign network and host addresses internally. Because the internet is private, duplication of addresses by another organization in the global Internet is not a problem.

Hybrid Networks

Today, most organizations need to have privacy in intraorganization data exchange, but, at the same time, they need to be connected to the global Internet for data exchange with other organizations. One solution is the use of a **hybrid network.** A hybrid network allows an organization to have its own private internet and, at the same time, access to the global Internet. Intraorganization data is routed through the private internet; interorganization data is routed through the global Internet. Figure 26.2 shows an example of this situation.

An organization with two sites uses routers R1 and R2 to connect the two sites privately through a leased line; it uses routers R3 and R4 to connect the two sites to the rest of the world. The organization uses global IP addresses for both types of communication. However, packets destined for internal recipients are routed only through routers R1 and R2. Routers R3 and R4 route the packets destined for outsiders.

Virtual Private Networks

Both private and hybrid networks have a major drawback: cost. Private wide area networks are expensive. To connect several sites, an organization needs several leased lines, which can lead to a high monthly cost. One solution is to use the global Internet for both private and public communication. A technology called virtual private network (VPN) allows organizations to use the global Internet for both purposes.

Figure 26.2   *Hybrid network*

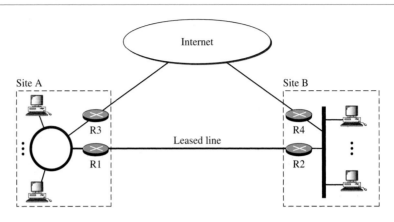

VPN is a network that is private but virtual. It is private because it guarantees privacy inside the organization. It is virtual because it does not use real private WANs; the network is physically public but virtually private.

Figure 26.3 shows the idea of a virtual private network. Routers R1 and R2 use VPN technology to guarantee privacy for the organization.

Figure 26.3   *Virtual private network*

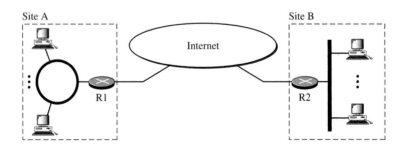

VPN Technology

VPN technology uses two simultaneous techniques to guarantee privacy for an organization: IPSec and tunneling.

IPSec

We will discuss IPSec in Chapter 28.

Tunneling

To guarantee privacy for an organization, VPN specifies that each IP datagram destined for private use in the organization must be encapsulated in another datagram as shown in Figure 26.4.

Figure 26.4   *Tunneling*

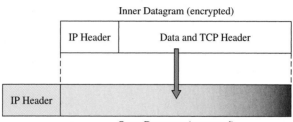

Inner Datagram (encrypted)

| IP Header | Data and TCP Header |

IP Header

Outer Datagram (encrypted)

This is called **tunneling** because the original datagram is hidden inside the outer datagram after exiting R1 in Figure 26.5 and is invisible until it reaches R2. It appears that the original datagram has gone through a tunnel spanning R1 and R2.

As the figure shows, the entire IP datagram (including the header) is first encrypted and then encapsulated in another datagram with a new header. The inner datagram here carries the actual source and destination address of the packet (two stations inside the organization). The outer datagram header carries the source and destination of the two routers at the boundary of the private and public networks as shown in Figure 26.5.

Figure 26.5   *Addressing in a VPN*

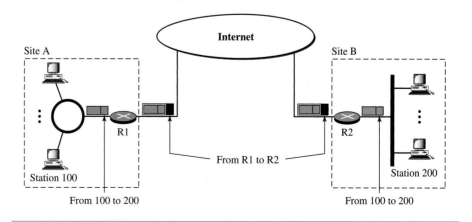

The public network (Internet) is responsible for carrying the packet from R1 to R2. Outsiders cannot decipher the contents of the packet or the source and destination addresses. Deciphering takes place at R2, which finds the destination address of the packet and delivers it.

26.3   NETWORK ADDRESS TRANSLATION (NAT)

A technology that is related to private networks and virtual private networks is **network address translation (NAT).** The technology allows a site to use a set of private addresses for internal communication and a set of **global Internet** addresses (at least one) for communication with another site. The site must have only one single connection to the global Internet through a router that runs NAT software. Figure 26.6 shows a simple implementation of NAT.

Figure 26.6   *NAT*

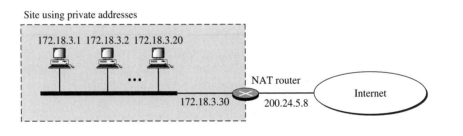

As the figure shows, the private network uses private addresses. The router that connects the network to the global address uses one private address and one global address. The private network is transparent to the rest of the Internet; the rest of the Internet sees only the NAT router with the address 200.24.5.8.

Address Translation

All of the outgoing packets go through the NAT router, which replaces the *source address* in the packet with the global NAT address. All incoming packets also pass through the NAT router, which replaces the *destination address* in the packet (the NAT router global address) with the appropriate private address. Figure 26.7 shows an example of address translation.

Translation Table

The reader may have noticed that translating the source addresses for an outgoing packets is straightforward. But how does the NAT router know the destination address for a packet coming from the Internet? There may be tens or hundreds of private IP

Figure 26.7 *Address translation*

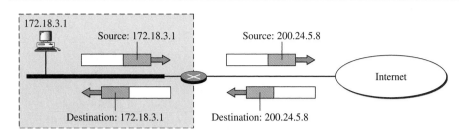

addresses, each belonging to one specific host. The problem is solved if the NAT router has a **translation table.**

Using One IP Address

In its simplest form, a translation table has only two columns: the private address and the external address (destination address of the packet). When the router translates the source address of the outgoing packet, it also makes note of the destination address—where the packet is going. When the response comes back from the destination, the router uses the source address of the packet (as the external address) to find the private address of the packet. Figure 26.8 shows the idea. Note that the addresses that are changed (translated) are shown in color.

Figure 26.8 *Translation*

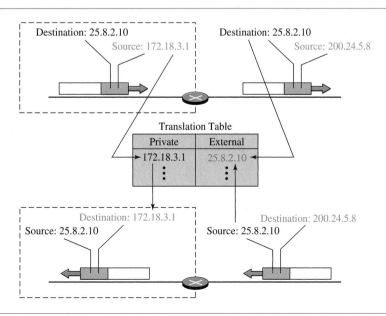

In this strategy, communication must always be initiated by the private network. The NAT mechanism described requires that the private network start the communication. As we will see, NAT is used mostly by ISPs which assign one single address to a customer. The customer, however, may be a member of a private network that has many private addresses. In this case, communication with the Internet is always initiated from the customer site, using a client program such as HTTP, TELNET, or FTP to access the corresponding server program. For example, when email that originates from a noncustomer site is received by the ISP email server it is stored in the mailbox of the customer until retrieved with a protocol such as POP.

A private network cannot run a server program for clients outside of its network if it is using NAT technology.

Using a Pool of IP Addresses

Using only one global address by the NAT router allows only one private-network host to access the same external host. To remove this restriction, the NAT router can use a pool of global addresses. For example, instead of using only one global address (200.24.5.8), the NAT router can use four addresses (200.24.5.8, 200.24.5.9, 200.24.5.10, and 200.24.5.11). In this case, four private-network hosts can communicate with the same external host at the same time because each pair of addresses defines a connection. However, there are still some drawbacks. No more than four connections can be made to the same destination. No private-network host can access two external server programs (e.g., HTTP and TELNET) at the same time. And, likewise, two private-network hosts cannot access the same external server program (e.g., HTTP or TELNET) at the same time.

Using Both IP Addresses and Port Addresses

To allow a many-to-many relationship between private-network hosts and external server programs, we need more information in the translation table. For example, suppose two hosts inside a private network with addresses 172.18.3.1 and 172.18.3.2 need to access the HTTP server on external host 25.8.3.2. If the translation table has five columns, instead of two, that include the source and destination port addresses and the transport layer protocol, the ambiguity is eliminated. Table 26.2 shows an example of such a table.

Table 26.2   *Five-column translation table*

Private Address	Private Port	External Address	External Port	Transport Protocol
172.18.3.1	1400	25.8.3.2	80	TCP
172.18.3.2	1401	25.8.3.2	80	TCP
. . .	. . .	. . .	. . .	. . .

Note that when the response from HTTP comes back, the combination of source address (25.8.3.2) and destination port address (1400) defines the private network host to which the response should be directed. Note also that for this translation to work, the ephemeral port addresses (1400 and 1401) must be unique.

NAT and ISP

An ISP that serves dial-up customers can use NAT technology to conserve addresses. For example, imagine an ISP is granted 1000 addresses, but has 100,000 customers. Each of the customers is assigned a private network address. The ISP translates each of the 100,000 source addresses in outgoing packets to one of the 1000 global addresses; it translates the global destination address in incoming packets to the corresponding private address. Figure 26.9 shows this concept.

Figure 26.9 *An ISP and NAT*

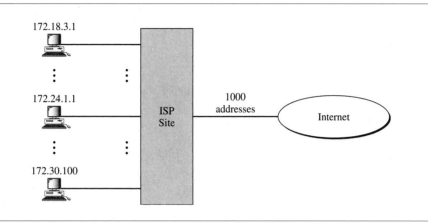

26.4 KEY TERMS

extranet	private network
global Internet	reserved addresses
hybrid network	translation table
intranet	tunneling
network address translation (NAT)	virtual private network (VPN)

26.5 SUMMARY

- ❏ A private network is used inside an organization.
- ❏ An intranet is a private network that uses the TCP/IP protocol suite.
- ❏ An extranet is an intranet that allows authorized access from outside users.
- ❏ The Internet authorities have reserved addresses for private networks.
- ❏ A virtual private network (VPN) provides privacy for LANs that must communicate through the global Internet.

❏ VPN technology involves the simultaneous use of encryption/authentication and tunneling to guarantee privacy.

❏ A common technique to encrypt and authenticate in VPNs is IP security (IPSec).

❏ Tunneling involves the encapsulation of an encrypted IP datagram in a second outer datagram.

❏ Network address translation allows a private network to use a set of private addresses for internal communication and a set of global Internet addresses for external communication.

❏ NAT uses translation tables to route messages.

26.6   PRACTICE SET

Exercises

1. Explain how a personal computer using a dial-up connection to the Internet can access a private network using VPN technology.

2. How can one prevent a translation table from constantly expanding? When can an entry be deleted from the table? What strategy can you propose?

Research Activities

3. Find out how Point-to-Point Tunneling Protocol (PPTP) can be used in VPN technology.

4. Find out how Layer 2 Forwarding (L2F) can be used in VPN technology.

5. Find out how Layer 2 Tunneling Protocol (L2TP) can be used in VPN technology.

6. Find out how Multiprotocol Label Switching (MPLS) can be used in VPN technology.

7. Find out if there is a way for communication to be initiated from the external host on a network using NAT.

8. Find out how DNS can be used in NAT.

9. Find out how Security Association (SA) in IPSec is used in VPN technology.

10. Find out how Internet Key Exchange (IKE) in IPSec is used in VPN technology.

CHAPTER 27

Next Generation: IPv6 and ICMPv6

The network layer protocol in the TCP/IP protocol suite is currently IPv4 (Internet-working Protocol, version 4). IPv4 provides the host-to-host communication between systems in the Internet. Although IPv4 is well designed, data communication has evolved since the inception of IPv4 in the 1970s. IPv4 has some deficiencies that make it unsuitable for the fast-growing Internet, including the following:

❏ Despite all short-term solutions, such as subnetting, classless addressing, and NAT, address depletion is still a long term problem in the Internet.

❏ The Internet must accommodate real-time audio and video transmission. This type of transmission requires minimum delay strategies and reservation of resources not provided in the IPv4 design.

❏ The Internet must accommodate encryption and authentication of data for some applications. No encryption or authentication is provided by IPv4.

To overcome these deficiencies, **IPv6 (Internetworking Protocol, version 6),** also known as **IPng (Internetworking Protocol, next generation)** was proposed and is now a standard. In IPv6, the Internet protocol was extensively modified to accommodate the unforeseen growth of the Internet. The format and the length of the IP addresses were changed along with the packet format. Related protocols, such as ICMP, were also modified. Other protocols in the network layer, such as ARP, RARP, and IGMP, were either deleted or included in the ICMPv6 protocol. Routing protocols, such as RIP and OSPF, were also slightly modified to accommodate these changes. Communication experts predict that IPv6 and its related protocols will soon replace the current IP version. In this chapter we talk first about IPv6. Then we discuss ICMPv6. Finally we explore the strategies used for the transition from version 4 to version 6.

The adoption of IPv6 has been slow. The reason is that the original reason for its development, depletion of IPv4 addresses, has been slowed down because of three short-term remedies: classless addressing, use of DHCP for dynamic address alloca-tion, and NAT. However, the fast-spreading use of the Internet, and new services, such as mobile IP, IP telephony, and IP-capable mobile telephony, may require the total replacement of IPv4 with IPv6.

27.1   IPv6

The next-generation IP, or IPv6, has some advantages over IPv4 that can be summarized as follows:

❑ **Larger address space.** An IPv6 address is 128 bits long. Compared with the 32-bit address of IPv4, this is a huge (2^{96}) increase in the address space.

❑ **Better header format.** IPv6 uses a new header format in which options are separated from the base header and inserted, when needed, between the base header and the upper-layer data. This simplifies and speeds up the routing process because most of the options do not need to be checked by routers.

❑ **New options.** IPv6 has new options to allow for additional functionalities.

❑ **Allowance for extension.** IPv6 is designed to allow the extension of the protocol if required by new technologies or applications.

❑ **Support for resource allocation.** In IPv6, the type-of-service field has been removed, but a mechanism (called *flow label*) has been added to enable the source to request special handling of the packet. This mechanism can be used to support traffic such as real-time audio and video.

❑ **Support for more security.** The encryption and authentication options in IPv6 provide confidentiality and integrity of the packet.

IPv6 Addresses

An IPv6 address consists of 16 bytes (octets); it is 128 bits long (see Figure 27.1).

Figure 27.1   *IPv6 address*

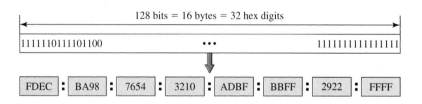

Hexadecimal Colon Notation

To make addresses more readable, IPv6 specifies **hexadecimal colon notation.** In this notation, 128 bits are divided into eight sections, each 2 bytes in length. Two bytes in hexadecimal notation require four hexadecimal digits. Therefore, the address consists of 32 hexadecimal digits, with every four digits separated by a colon.

Abbreviation   Although the IP address, even in hexadecimal format, is very long, many of the digits are zeros. In this case, we can abbreviate the address. The leading zeros of a section (four digits between two colons) can be omitted. Only the leading zeros can be dropped, not the trailing zeros. For an example, see Figure 27.2.

Figure 27.2 *Abbreviated address*

Unabbreviated

FDEC ⋮ BA98 ⋮ 0074 ⋮ 3210 ⋮ 000F ⋮ BBFF ⋮ 0000 ⋮ FFFF

FDEC ⋮ BA98 ⋮ 74 ⋮ 3210 ⋮ F ⋮ BBFF ⋮ 0 ⋮ FFFF

Abbreviated

Using this form of **abbreviation,** 0074 can be written as 74, 000F as F, and 0000 as 0. Note that 3210 cannot be abbreviated. Further abbreviations are possible if there are consecutive sections consisting of zeros only. We can remove the zeros altogether and replace them with a double semicolon. Figure 27.3 shows the concept.

Figure 27.3 *Abbreviated address with consecutive zeros*

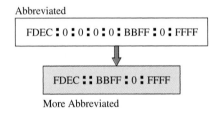

Abbreviated

FDEC ⋮ 0 ⋮ 0 ⋮ 0 ⋮ 0 ⋮ BBFF ⋮ 0 ⋮ FFFF

FDEC ⋮⋮ BBFF ⋮ 0 ⋮ FFFF

More Abbreviated

Note that this type of abbreviation is allowed only once per address. If there are two runs of zero sections, only one of them can be abbreviated. Reexpansion of the abbreviated address is very simple: Align the unabbreviated portions and insert zeros to get the original expanded address.

CIDR Notation IPv6 allows classless addressing and CIDR notation. For example, Figure 27.4 shows how we can define a prefix of 60 bits using CIDR.

Figure 27.4 *CIDR address*

FDEC ⋮⋮ BBFF ⋮ 0 ⋮ FFFF/60

Categories of Addresses

IPv6 defines three types of addresses: unicast, anycast, and multicast.

A **unicast address** defines a single computer. The packet sent to a unicast address must be delivered to that specific computer.

An **anycast address** defines a group of computers with addresses that have the same prefix. For example, all computers connected to the same physical network share the same prefix address. A packet sent to an anycast address must be delivered to exactly one of the members of the group—the closest or the most easily accessible.

A **multicast address** defines a group of computers. A packet sent to a multicast address must be delivered to each member of the group.

Address Space Assignment

The **address space** has many different purposes. The designers of the IP addresses divided the address space into two parts, with the first part called the *type prefix*. This variable-length prefix defines the purpose of the address. The codes are designed such that no code is identical to the first part of any other code. In this way, there is no ambiguity; when an address is given, the type prefix can easily be determined. Figure 27.5 shows the IPv6 address format.

Figure 27.5   *Address structure*

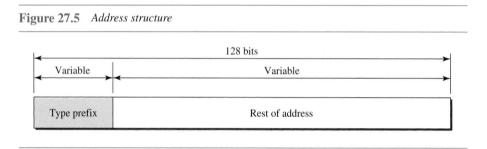

Table 27.1 shows the prefix for each type of address. The third column shows the fraction of each type of address relative to the whole address space.

Table 27.1   *Type prefixes for IPv6 addresses*

Type Prefix	Type	Fraction
0000 0000	Reserved	1/256
0000 0001	Reserved	1/256
0000 001	NSAP (Network Service Access Point)	1/128
0000 010	IPX (Novell)	1/128
0000 011	Reserved	1/128
0000 100	Reserved	1/128
0000 101	Reserved	1/128
0000 110	Reserved	1/128
0000 111	Reserved	1/128
0001	Reserved	1/16
001	Reserved	1/8

Table 27.1 *Type prefixes for IPv6 addresses (continued)*

Type Prefix	Type	Fraction
010	**Provider-based unicast addresses**	**1/8**
011	Reserved	1/8
100	Geographic unicast addresses	1/8
101	Reserved	1/8
110	Reserved	1/8
1110	Reserved	1/16
1111 0	Reserved	1/32
1111 10	Reserved	1/64
1111 110	Reserved	1/128
1111 1110 0	Reserved	1/512
1111 1110 10	Link local addresses	1/1024
1111 1110 11	Site local addresses	1/1024
1111 1111	Multicast addresses	1/256

Provider-Based Unicast Addresses

The provider-based address is generally used by a normal host as a unicast address. The address format is shown in Figure 27.6.

Figure 27.6 *Provider-based address*

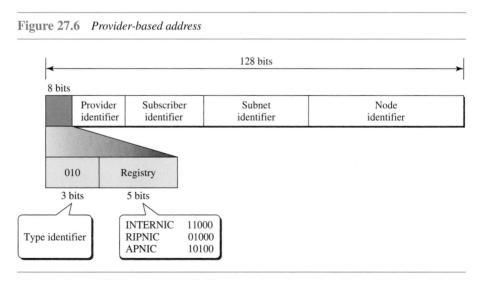

Fields for the provider-based addresses are as follows:

❏ **Type identifier.** This 3-bit field defines the address as a provider-based address.

❏ **Registry identifier.** This 5-bit field indicates the agency that has registered the address. Currently three registry centers have been defined. INTERNIC (code 11000) is the center for North America; RIPNIC (code 01000) is the center for European registration; and APNIC (code 10100) is for Asian and Pacific countries.

❏ **Provider identifier.** This variable-length field identifies the provider for Internet access (such as an ISP). A 16-bit length is recommended for this field.

❏ **Subscriber identifier.** When an organization subscribes to the Internet through a provider, it is assigned a subscriber identification. A 24-bit length is recommended for this field.

❏ **Subnet identifier.** Each subscriber can have many different subnetworks and each network can have different identifiers. The subnet identifier defines a specific network under the territory of the subscriber. A 32-bit length is recommended for this field.

❏ **Node identifier.** The last field defines the identity of the node connected to a subnet. A length of 48 bits is recommended for this field to make it compatible with the 48-bit link (physical) address used by Ethernet. In the future, this link address will probably be the same as the node physical address.

We can think of a provider-based address as a hierarchical identity having several prefixes. As shown in Figure 27.7, each prefix defines a level of hierarchy. The type prefix defines the type, the registry prefix uniquely defines the registry level, the provider prefix uniquely defines a provider, the subscriber prefix uniquely defines a subscriber, and the subnet prefix uniquely defines a subnet.

Figure 27.7   *Address hierarchy*

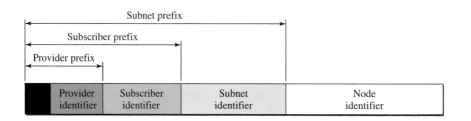

Reserved Addresses

Addresses that use the reserved prefix (00000000) will be discussed here briefly.

Unspecified address   This is an address in which the nonprefix part is also zero. In other words, the entire address consists of zeros. This address is used when a host does not know its own address and sends an inquiry to find its address. However, in the inquiry it must define a source address. The **unspecified address** can be used for this purpose. Note that the unspecified address cannot be used as a destination address. The unspecified address format is shown in Figure 27.8.

Loopback address   This is an address used by a host to test itself without going into the network. In this case, a message is created in the application layer, sent to the transport layer, and passed to the network layer. However, instead of going to the physical network, it returns to the transport layer and then passes to the application layer. This is

Figure 27.8 *Unspecified address*

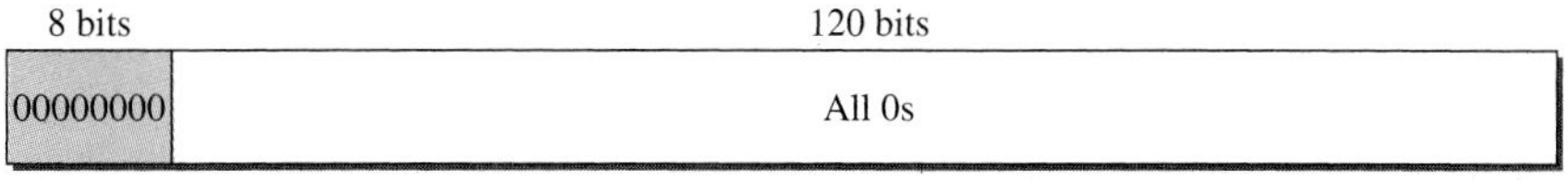

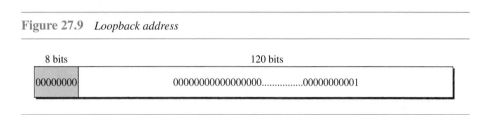

very useful for testing the functions of software packages in these layers before even connecting the computer to the network. The **loopback address** as shown in Figure 27.9 consists of the prefix 00000000 followed by 119 zero bits and 1 one bit.

Figure 27.9 *Loopback address*

8 bits	120 bits
00000000	0000000000000000...............00000000001

IPv4 addresses   As we will see later in this chapter, during transition from IPv4 to IPv6, hosts can use their IPv4 addresses embedded in IPv6 addresses. Two formats have been designed for this purpose: compatible and mapped. A **compatible address** is an address of 96 bits of zero followed by 32 bits of IPv4 address. It is used when a computer using IPv6 wants to send a message to another computer using IPv6. However, suppose the packet passes through a region where the networks are still using IPv4. The sender then must use the IPv4-compatible address to facilitate the passage of the packet through the IPv4 region (see Section 27.3 on Transition from IPv4 to IPv6). For example, the IPv4 address 2.13.17.14 (in dotted decimal format) becomes 0::020D:110E (in hexadecimal colon format). The IPv4 address is prepended with 96 zeros to create a 128-bit IPv6 address (see Figure 27.10).

A **mapped address** comprises 80 bits of zero, followed by 16 bits of one, followed by the 32-bit IPv4 address. It is used when a computer that has migrated

Figure 27.10 *Compatible address*

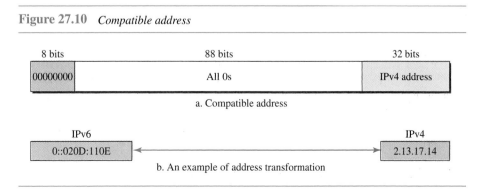

a. Compatible address

b. An example of address transformation

to IPv6 wants to send a packet to a computer still using IPv4. The packet travels mostly through IPv6 networks but is finally delivered to a host that uses IPv4. For example, the IPv4 address 2.13.17.14 (in dotted decimal format) becomes 0::FFFF:020D:110E (in hexadecimal colon format). The IPv4 address is prepended with 16 ones and 80 zeros to create a 128-bit IPv6 address (see Section 27.3 on Transition Strategies). Figure 27.11 shows a mapped address.

Figure 27.11   *Mapped address*

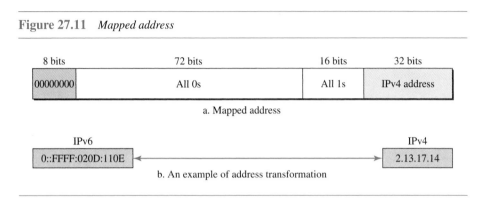

a. Mapped address

b. An example of address transformation

A very interesting point about mapped and compatible addresses is that they are designed such that, when calculating the checksum, one can use either the embedded address or the total address because extra 0s or 1s in multiples of 16 do not have any effect in checksum calculation. This is important because the checksum calculation is not affected if the address of the packet is changed from IPv6 to IPv4 by a router.

Local Addresses

Addresses that use the reserved prefix (11111110) are discussed here briefly.

Link local address   These addresses are used if a LAN uses the Internet protocols but is not connected to the Internet for security reasons. This type of addressing uses the prefix 1111 1110 10. The **link local address** is used in an isolated network and does not have a global effect. Nobody outside an isolated network can send a message to the computers attached to a network using these addresses (see Figure 27.12).

Figure 27.12   *Link local address*

10 bits	70 bits	48 bits
1111111010	All 0s	Node address

Site local address   These addresses are used if a site with several networks uses the Internet protocols but is not connected to the Internet, also for security reasons. This type of addressing uses the prefix 1111 1110 11. The **site local address** is used in isolated networks and does not have a global effect. Nobody outside the isolated networks can send a message to any of the computers attached to a network using these addresses (see Figure 27.13).

Figure 27.13 *Site local address*

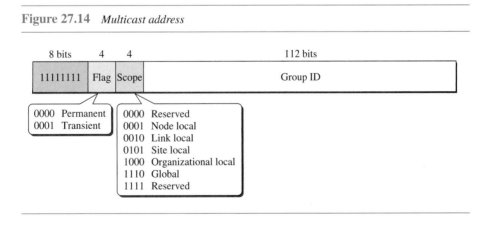

Multicast Addresses

Multicast addresses are used to define a group of hosts instead of just one. All use the prefix 11111111 in the first field. The second field is a flag that defines the group address as either permanent or transient. A permanent group address is defined by the Internet authorities and can be accessed at all times. A transient group address, on the other hand, is used only temporarily. Systems engaged in a teleconference, for example, can use a transient group address. The third field defines the scope of the group address. Many different scopes have been defined, as shown in Figure 27.14.

Figure 27.14 *Multicast address*

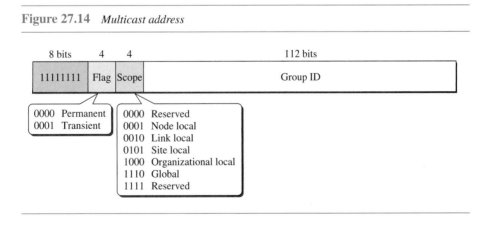

Packet Format

The IPv6 packet is shown in Figure 27.15. Each packet is composed of a mandatory base header followed by the payload. The payload consists of two parts: optional extension headers and data from an upper layer. The base header occupies 40 bytes, whereas the extension headers and data from the upper layer contain up to 65,535 bytes of information.

Figure 27.15 *IPv6 datagram*

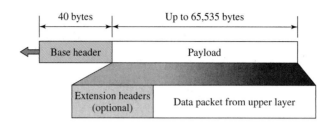

Base Header

Figure 27.16 shows the **base header** with its eight fields.

Figure 27.16 *Format of an IPv6 datagram*

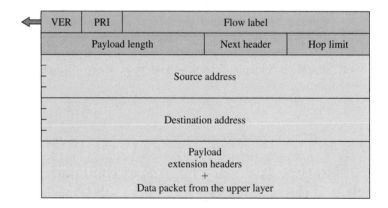

These fields are as follows:

❑ **Version.** This 4-bit field defines the version number of the IP. For IPv6, the value is 6.

❑ **Priority.** The 4-bit priority field defines the priority of the packet with respect to traffic congestion. We will discuss this field later.

❑ **Flow label.** The **flow label** is a 3-byte (24-bit) field that is designed to provide special handling for a particular flow of data. We will discuss this field later.

❑ **Payload length.** The 2-byte payload length field defines the length of the IP datagram excluding the base header.

❑ **Next header.** The **next header** is an 8-bit field defining the header that follows the base header in the datagram. The next header is either one of the optional extension headers used by IP or the header of an encapsulated packet such as UDP or TCP. Each extension header also contains this field. Table 27.2 shows the values of next headers. Note that this field in version 4 is called the *protocol.*

Table 27.2 *Next header codes*

Code	Next Header
0	Hop-by-hop option
2	ICMP
6	TCP
17	UDP
43	Source routing
44	Fragmentation
50	Encrypted security payload
51	Authentication
59	Null (No next header)
60	Destination option

❑ **Hop limit.** This 8-bit **hop limit** field serves the same purpose as the TTL field in IPv4.

❑ **Source address.** The source address field is a 16-byte (128-bit) Internet address that identifies the original source of the datagram.

❑ **Destination address.** The destination address field is a 16-byte (128-bit) Internet address that usually identifies the final destination of the datagram. However, if source routing is used, this field contains the address of the next router.

Priority

The priority field of the IPv6 packet defines the priority of each packet with respect to other packets from the same source. For example, if one of two consecutive datagrams must be discarded due to congestion, the datagram with the lower **packet priority** will be discarded. IPv6 divides traffic into two broad categories: congestion-controlled and noncongestion-controlled.

Congestion-Controlled Traffic   If a source adapts itself to traffic slowdown when there is congestion, the traffic is referred to as **congestion-controlled traffic.** For example, TCP, which uses the sliding window protocol, can easily respond to the traffic. In congestion-controlled traffic, it is understood that packets may arrive delayed or even lost or received out of order. Congestion-controlled data are assigned priorities from 0 to 7, as listed in Table 27.3. A priority of 0 is the lowest; a priority of 7 is the highest.

The priority descriptions are as follows:

❑ **No specific traffic.** The priority 0 is assigned to a packet when the process does not define a priority.

❑ **Background data.** This group (priority 1) defines data that is usually delivered in the background. Delivery of the news is a good example.

❑ **Unattended data traffic.** If the user is not waiting (attending) for the data to be received, the packet will be given a priority 2. Email belongs to this group. The recipient of an email does not know when a message has arrived. In addition, an

Table 27.3   *Priorities for congestion-controlled traffic*

Priority	Meaning
0	No specific traffic
1	Background data
2	Unattended data traffic
3	Reserved
4	Attended bulk data traffic
5	Reserved
6	Interactive traffic
7	Control traffic

email is usually stored before it is forwarded. A little bit of delay is of little consequence.

❑ **Attended bulk data traffic.** A protocol that transfers data while the user is waiting (attending) to receive the data (possibly with delay) is given a priority 4. FTP and HTTP belong to this group.

❑ **Interactive traffic.** Protocols such as TELNET that need user interaction are assigned the second highest priority (6) in this group.

❑ **Control traffic.** Control traffic is given the highest priority (7). Routing protocols such as OSPF and RIP and management protocols such as SNMP have this priority.

Noncongestion-Controlled Traffic   This refers to a type of traffic that expects minimum delay. Discarding of packets is not desirable. Retransmission in most cases is impossible. In other words, the source does not adapt itself to congestion. Real-time audio and video are examples of this type of traffic.

Priority numbers from 8 to 15 are assigned to **noncongestion-controlled traffic.** Although there are not yet any particular standard assignments for this type of data, the priorities are usually assigned based on how much the quality of received data is affected by discarding some packets. Data containing less redundancy (such as low-fidelity audio or video) can be given a higher priority (15). Data containing more redundancy (such as high-fidelity audio or video) are given a lower priority (8). See Table 27.4.

Table 27.4   *Priorities for noncongestion-controlled traffic*

Priority	Meaning
8	Data with most redundancy
.	.
.	.
.	.
15	Data with least redundancy

Flow Label

A sequence of packets, sent from a particular source to a particular destination, that needs special handling by routers is called a *flow* of packets. The combination of the source address and the value of the *flow label* uniquely defines a flow of packets.

To a router, a flow is a sequence of packets that share the same characteristics, such as traveling the same path, using the same resources, having the same kind of security, and so on. A router that supports the handling of flow labels has a flow label table. The table has an entry for each active flow label; each entry defines the services required by the corresponding flow label. When the router receives a packet, it consults its flow label table to find the corresponding entry for the flow label value defined in the packet. It then provides the packet with the services mentioned in the entry. However, note that the flow label itself does not provide the information for the entries of the flow label table; the information is provided by other means such as the hop-by-hop options or other protocols.

In its simplest form, a flow label can be used to speed up the processing of a packet by a router. When a router receives a packet, instead of consulting the routing table and going through a routing algorithm to define the address of the next hop, it can easily look in a flow label table for the next hop.

In its more sophisticated form, a flow label can be used to support the transmission of real-time audio and video. Real-time audio or video, particularly in digital form, requires resources such as high bandwidth, large buffers, long processing time, and so on. A process can make a reservation for these resources beforehand to guarantee that real-time data will not be delayed due to a lack of resources. The use of real-time data and the reservation of these resources require other protocols such as Real-Time Protocol (RTP) and Resource Reservation Protocol (RSVP) in addition to IPv6.

To allow the effective use of flow labels, three rules have been defined:

1. The flow label is assigned to a packet by the source host. The label is a random number between 1 and $2^{24} - 1$. A source must not reuse a flow label for a new flow while the existing flow is still alive.

2. If a host does not support the flow label, it sets this field to zero. If a router does not support the flow label, it simply ignores it.

3. All packets belonging to the same flow have the same source, same destination, same priority, and same options.

Comparison between IPv4 and IPv6 Headers

Table 27.5 compares IPv4 and IPv6 headers.

Table 27.5 *Comparison between IPv4 and IPv6 packet header*

Comparison
1. The header length field is eliminated in IPv6 because the length of the header is fixed in this version.
2. The service type field is eliminated in IPv6. The priority and flow label fields together take over the function of the service type field.
3. The total length field is eliminated in IPv6 and replaced by the payload length field.

(continued)

Table 27.5   *Comparison between IPv4 and IPv6 packet header (continued)*

Comparison
4. The identification, flag, and offset fields are eliminated from the base header in IPv6. They are included in the fragmentation extension header.
5. The TTL field is called hop limit in IPv6.
6. The protocol field is replaced by the next header field.
7. The header checksum is eliminated because the checksum is provided by upper layer protocols; it is therefore not needed at this level.
8. The option fields in IPv4 are implemented as extension headers in IPv6.

Extension Headers

The length of the base header is fixed at 40 bytes. However, to give more functionality to the IP datagram, the base header can be followed by up to six **extension headers.** Many of these headers are options in IPv4. Figure 27.17 shows the extension header format.

Figure 27.17   *Extension header format*

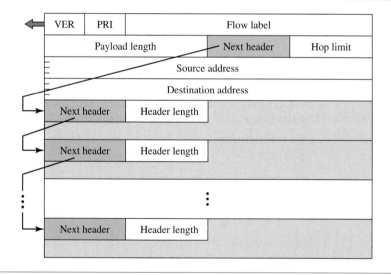

Six types of extension headers have been defined. These are hop-by-hop option, source routing, fragmentation, authentication, encrypted security payload, and destination option (see Figure 27.18).

Hop-by-Hop Option   The **hop-by-hop option** is used when the source needs to pass information to all routers visited by the datagram. For example, perhaps routers must be informed about certain management, debugging, or control functions. Or, if the length of the datagram is more than the usual 65,535 bytes, routers must have this

Figure 27.18 *Extension header types*

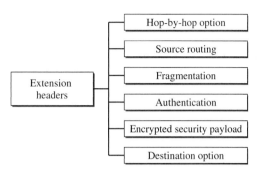

information. Figure 27.19 shows the format of the hop-by-hop option header. The first field defines the next header in the chain of headers. The header length defines the number of bytes in the header (including the next header field). The rest of the header contains different options.

Figure 27.19 *Hop-by-hop option header format*

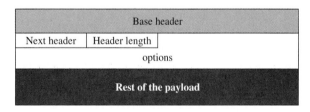

So far, only three options have been defined: **Pad1, PadN,** and **jumbo payload.** Figure 27.20 shows the general format of the option.

❏ **Pad1.** This option is 1 byte long and is designed for alignment purposes. Some options need to start at a specific bit of the 32-bit word (see the jumbo payload description to come). If an option falls short of this requirement by exactly one byte, Pad1 is added to make up the difference. Pad1 contains neither the option length field nor the option data field. It consists solely of the option code field with all bits set to 0 (action is 00, the change bit is 0, and type is 00000). Pad1 can be inserted anywhere in the hop-by-hop option header (see Figure 27.21).

❏ **PadN.** PadN is similar in concept to Pad1. The difference is that PadN is used when 2 or more bytes are needed for alignment. This option consists of 1 byte of option code, 1 byte of the option length, and a variable number of zero padding bytes. The value of the option code is 1 (action is 00, the change bit is 0, and type is 00001). The option length contains the number of padding bytes. See Figure 27.22.

Figure 27.20   *The format of options in a hop-by-hop option header*

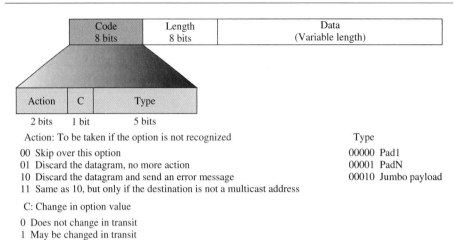

| Code
8 bits | Length
8 bits | Data
(Variable length) |

| Action | C | Type |
| 2 bits | 1 bit | 5 bits |

Action: To be taken if the option is not recognized

00 Skip over this option
01 Discard the datagram, no more action
10 Discard the datagram and send an error message
11 Same as 10, but only if the destination is not a multicast address

C: Change in option value

0 Does not change in transit
1 May be changed in transit

Type

00000 Pad1
00001 PadN
00010 Jumbo payload

Figure 27.21   *Pad1*

| Code
00000000 |

a. Pad1

Options

Pad1

Rest of the payload

b. Used for padding

Figure 27.22   *PadN*

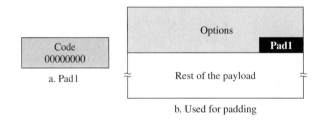

| Code
00000001 | Length | Data
All 0s |
| 1 byte | 1 byte | Variable |

❑ **Jumbo payload.** Recall that the length of the payload in the IP datagram can be a maximum of 65,535 bytes. However, if for any reason a longer payload is required, we can use the jumbo payload option to define this longer length. The 1-byte option code has a value of 194 (11 for action, 0 for the change bit, and 00010 for type). The 1-byte option length defines the size in bytes of the next field and has a fixed value of 4. This means that the maximum length of the jumbo payload is $2^{32} - 1$ (4,294,967,295) bytes.

This option has an alignment restriction. The jumbo payload option must always start at a multiple of 4 bytes plus 2 from the beginning of the extension headers. The jumbo payload option starts at the $(4n + 2)$ byte, where n is a small integer. See Figure 27.23.

Figure 27.23   *Jumbo payload*

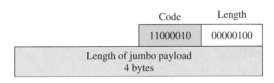

Source Routing   The source routing extension header combines the concepts of the strict source route and the loose source route options of IPv4. The source routing header contains a minimum of seven fields (see Figure 27.24). The first two fields, next header and header length, are identical to that of the hop-by-hop extension header. The type field defines loose or strict routing. The addresses left field indicates the number of hops still needed to reach the destination. The strict/loose mask field determines the rigidity of routing. If set to strict, routing must follow exactly as indicated by the source. If, instead, the mask is loose, other routers may be visited in addition to those in the header.

Figure 27.24   *Source routing*

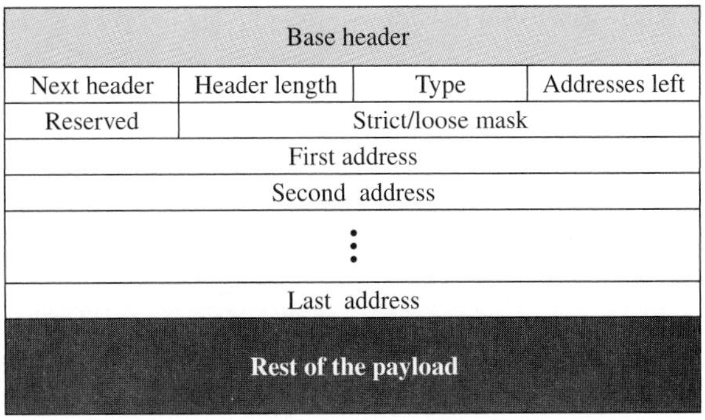

Base header			
Next header	Header length	Type	Addresses left
Reserved	Strict/loose mask		
First address			
Second address			
⋮			
Last address			
Rest of the payload			

The destination address in source routing does not conform to our previous definition (the final destination of the datagram). Instead, it changes from router to router. For example, in Figure 27.25, Host A wants to send a datagram to Host B using a specific route: A to R1 to R2 to R3 to B. Notice the destination address in the base headers. It is not constant as you might expect. Instead, it changes at each router. The addresses in the extension headers also change from router to router.

Figure 27.25   *Source routing example*

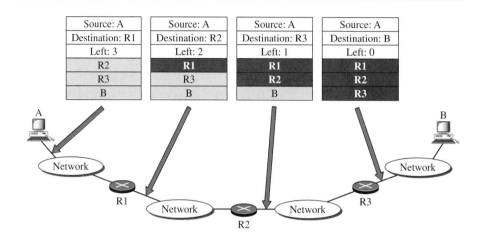

Fragmentation   The concept of **fragmentation** is the same as that in IPv4. However, the place where fragmentation occurs differs. In IPv4, the source or a router is required to fragment if the size of the datagram is larger than the MTU of the network over which the datagram travels. In IPv6, only the original source can fragment. A source must use a **Path MTU Discovery technique** to find the smallest MTU supported by any network on the path. The source then fragments using this knowledge.

If the source does not use a Path MTU Discovery technique, it fragments the datagram to a size of 576 bytes or smaller. This is the minimum size of MTU required for each network connected to the Internet. Figure 27.26 shows the format of the fragmentation extension header.

Figure 27.26   *Fragmentation*

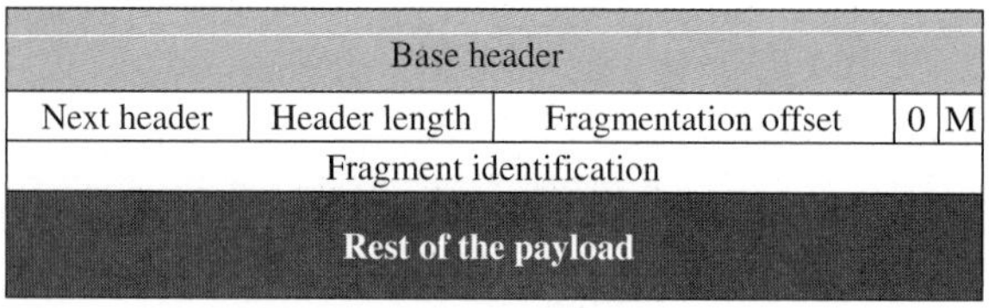

Base header				
Next header	Header length	Fragmentation offset	0	M
Fragment identification				
Rest of the payload				

Authentication   The **authentication** extension header has a dual purpose: it validates the message sender and ensures the integrity of data. The former is needed so the receiver can be sure that a message is from the genuine sender and not from an imposter. The latter is needed to check that the data is not altered in transition by some hacker.

The format of the authentication extension header is shown in Figure 27.27. The security parameter index field defines the algorithm used for authentication. The

Figure 27.27   *Authentication*

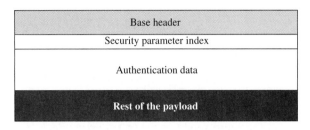

Base header
Security parameter index
Authentication data
Rest of the payload

authentication data field contains the actual data generated by the algorithm. We will discuss authentication in Chapter 28.

Many different algorithms can be used for authentication. Figure 27.28 outlines the method for calculating the authentication data field. The sender passes a 128-bit security key, the entire IP datagram, and the 128-bit security key again to the algorithm. Those fields in the datagram with values that change during transmission (for example, hop count) are set to zero. The datagram passed to the algorithm includes the authentication header extension, with the authentication data field set to zero. The algorithm creates authentication data which is inserted into the extension header prior to datagram transmission.

Figure 27.28   *Calculation of authentication data*

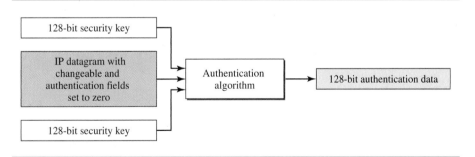

The receiver functions in a similar manner. It takes the secret key and the received datagram (again, with changeable fields set to zero) and passes them to the authentication algorithm. If the result matches that in the authentication data field, the IP datagram is authentic; otherwise, the datagram is discarded.

Encrypted Security Payload   The **encrypted security payload (ESP)** is an extension that provides confidentiality and guards against eavesdropping. Figure 27.29 shows the format. The security parameter index field is a 32-bit word that defines the type of encryption/decryption used. The other field contains the encrypted data along with any extra parameters needed by the algorithm. **Encryption** can be implemented in two ways: transport mode or tunnel mode.

Figure 27.29   *Encrypted security payload*

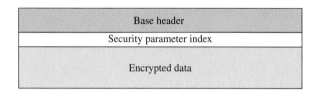

☐ **Transport mode.** In the **transport mode,** a TCP segment or a UDP user datagram is first encrypted and then encapsulated in an IPv6 packet. The transport mode of encryption is used mostly to encrypt data from host to host (see Figure 27.30).

Figure 27.30   *Transport mode encryption*

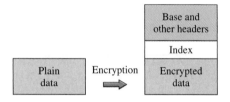

☐ **Tunnel mode.** In the **tunnel mode,** the entire IP datagram with its base header and extension headers is encrypted and then encapsulated in a new IP packet using the ESP extension header. In other words, you have two base headers: one encrypted, one not. The tunnel mode of encryption is mostly used by security gateways to encrypt data. Figure 27.31 shows the idea.

Figure 27.31   *Tunnel-mode encryption*

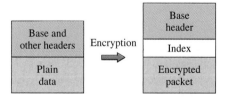

Destination Option   The **destination option** is used when the source needs to pass information to the destination only. Intermediate routers are not permitted access to this information. The format of the destination option is the same as the hop-by-hop option (refer back to Figure 27.19). So far, only the Pad1 and PadN options have been defined.

Comparison between IPv4 and IPv6

Table 27.6 compares the options in IPv4 with the extension headers in IPv6.

Table 27.6   *Comparison between IPv4 options and IPv6 extension headers*

Comparison
1. The no-operation and end-of-option options in IPv4 are replaced by Pad1 and PadN options in IPv6.
2. The record route option is not implemented in IPv6 because it was not used.
3. The timestamp option is not implemented because it was not used.
4. The source route option is called the source route extension header in IPv6.
5. The fragmentation fields in the base header section of IPv4 have moved to the fragmentation extension header in IPv6.
6. The authentication extension header is new in IPv6.
7. The encrypted security payload extension header is new in IPv6.

27.2   ICMPv6

Another protocol that has been modified in version 6 of the TCP/IP protocol suite is ICMP (ICMPv6). This new version follows the same strategy and purposes of version 4. ICMPv4 has been modified to make it more suitable for IPv6. In addition, some protocols that were independent in version 4 are now part of Internetworking Control Message Protocol (ICMPv6). Figure 27.32 compares the network layer of version 4 to version 6.

Figure 27.32   *Comparison of network layers in version 4 and version 6*

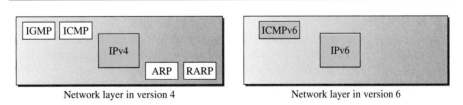

Network layer in version 4   Network layer in version 6

The ARP and IGMP protocols in version 4 are combined in ICMPv6. The RARP protocol is dropped from the suite because it was rarely used and BOOTP has the same functionality.

Just as in ICMPv4, we divide the ICMP messages into two categories. However, each category has more types of messages than before (see Figure 27.33). Although the general format of an ICMP message is different for each message type, the first 4 bytes are common to all, as is shown in Figure 27.34. The first field, the ICMP type, defines the broad category of the message. The code field specifies the reason for the particular message type. The last common field is the checksum field, calculated in the same manner as was described for ICMP version 4.

Figure 27.33   *Categories of ICMPv6 messages*

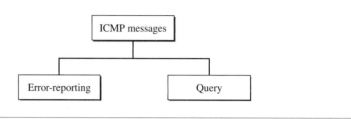

Figure 27.34   *General format of ICMP messages*

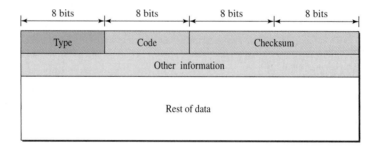

Error Reporting

As we saw in our discussion of version 4, one of the main responsibilities of ICMP is to report errors. Five types of errors are handled: destination unreachable, packet too big, time exceeded, parameter problems, and redirection (see Figure 27.35). ICMPv6 forms an error packet, which is then encapsulated in an IP datagram. This is delivered to the original source of the failed datagram.

Figure 27.35   *Error-reporting messages*

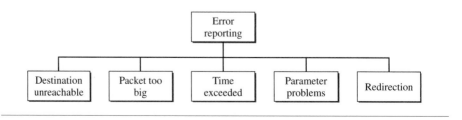

Table 27.7 compares the **error-reporting messages** of ICMPv4 with ICMPv6. The source-quench message is eliminated in version 6 because the priority and the flow label fields allow the router to control congestion and discard the least important messages. In this version, there is no need to inform the sender to slow down. The packet-too-big message is added because fragmentation is the responsibility of the sender in IPv6. If the sender does not make the right packet size decision, the router has no choice but to drop the packet and send an error message to the sender.

Table 27.7   *Comparison of error-reporting messages in ICMPv4 and ICMPv6*

Type of Message	Version 4	Version 6
Destination unreachable	Yes	Yes
Source quench	Yes	No
Packet too big	No	Yes
Time exceeded	Yes	Yes
Parameter problem	Yes	Yes
Redirection	Yes	Yes

Destination Unreachable

The concept of the **destination unreachable message** is exactly the same as described for ICMP version 4. Figure 27.36 shows the format of the destination-unreachable message. It is similar to the one defined for version 4, with the type value equal to 1.

Figure 27.36   *Destination-unreachable message format*

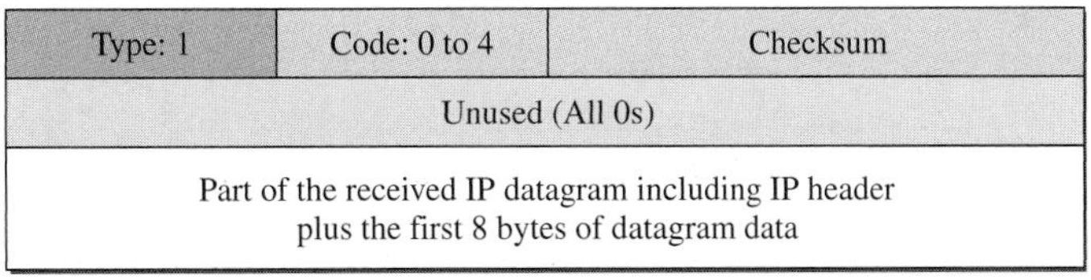

The code field for this type specifies the reason for discarding the datagram and explains exactly what has failed:

❑ **Code 0.** No path to destination.

❑ **Code 1.** Communication is prohibited.

❑ **Code 2.** Strict source routing is impossible.

❑ **Code 3.** Destination address is unreachable.

❑ **Code 4.** Port is not available.

Packet Too Big

This is a new type of message added to version 6. If a router receives a datagram that is larger than the maximum transmission unit (MTU) size of the network through which the datagram should pass, two things happen. First, the router discards the datagram and then an ICMP error packet—a **packet-too-big message**—is sent to the source. Figure 27.37 shows the format of the packet. Note that there is only one code (0) and that the MTU field informs the sender of the maximum size packet accepted by the network.

Figure 27.37 *Packet-too-big message format*

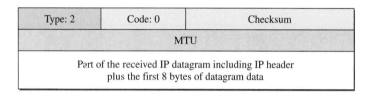

Time Exceeded

This message is similar to the one in version 4. The only difference is that the type value has changed to 3. Figure 27.38 shows the format of the **time-exceeded message.**

Figure 27.38 *Time-exceeded message format*

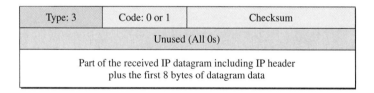

As in version 4, code 0 is used when the datagram is discarded by the router due to a hop-limit field value of zero. Code 1 is used when fragments of a datagram are discarded because other fragments have not arrived within the time limit.

Parameter Problem

This message is similar to its version 4 counterpart. However, the type value has been changed to 4 and the size of the offset pointer field has been increased to 4 bytes. There are also three different codes instead of two. The code field specifies the reason for discarding the datagram and the cause of failure:

❑ **Code 0.** There is error or ambiguity in one of the header fields. In this case the value in the pointer field points to the byte with the problem. For example, if the value is zero, then the first byte is not a valid field.

❏ **Code 1.** This defines an unrecognizable extension header.

❏ **Code 2.** This defines an unrecognizable option.

Figure 27.39 shows the format of the **parameter problem message.**

Figure 27.39 *Parameter-problem message format*

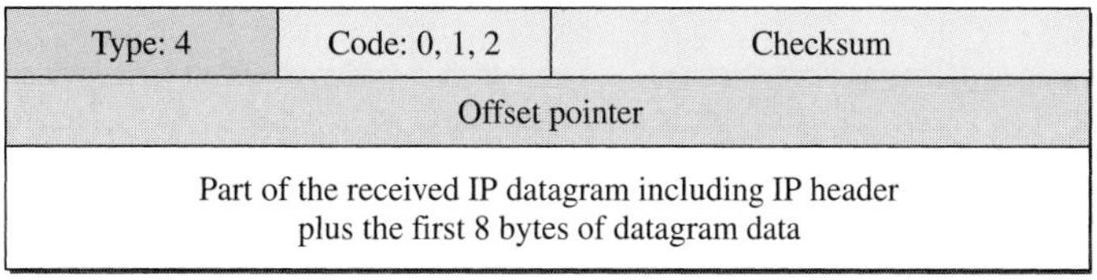

Type: 4	Code: 0, 1, 2	Checksum
Offset pointer		
Part of the received IP datagram including IP header plus the first 8 bytes of datagram data		

Redirection

The purpose of the **redirection message** is the same as described for version 4. However, the format of the packet now accommodates the size of the IP address in version 6. Also, an option is added to let the host know the physical address of the target router (see Figure 27.40).

Figure 27.40 *Redirection message format*

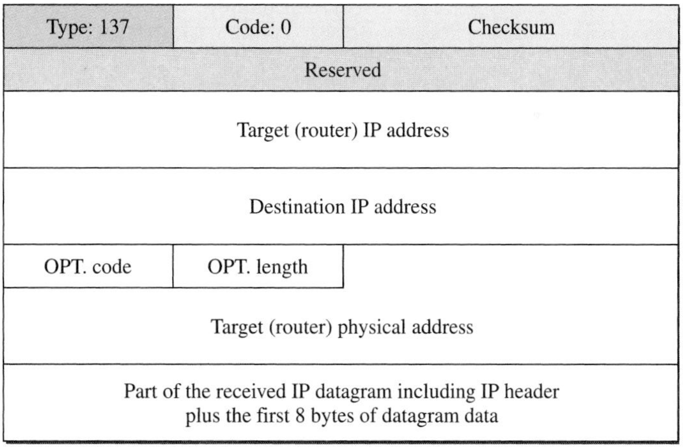

Type: 137	Code: 0	Checksum
Reserved		
Target (router) IP address		
Destination IP address		
OPT. code	OPT. length	
Target (router) physical address		
Part of the received IP datagram including IP header plus the first 8 bytes of datagram data		

Query

In addition to error reporting, ICMP can also diagnose some network problems. This is accomplished through the **query messages.** Four different groups of messages have been defined: echo request and reply, router solicitation and advertisement, neighbor solicitation and advertisement, and group membership (see Figure 27.41).

Figure 27.41   *Query messages*

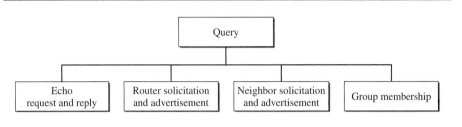

Table 27.8 shows a comparison between the query messages in versions 4 and 6. Two sets of query messages are eliminated from ICMPv6: timestamp request and reply and address mask request and reply. The timestamp request and reply messages are eliminated because they are implemented in other protocols such as TCP and because they were rarely used in the past. The address-mask request and reply messages are eliminated in IPv6 because the subnet section of an address allows the subscriber to use up to $2^{32} - 1$ subnets. Therefore, subnet masking, as defined in IPv4, is not needed here.

Table 27.8   *Comparison of query messages in ICMPv4 and ICMPv6*

Type of Message	Version 4	Version 6
Echo request and reply	Yes	Yes
Timestamp request and reply	Yes	No
Address mask request and reply	Yes	No
Router solicitation and advertisement	Yes	Yes
Neighbor solicitation and advertisement	ARP	Yes
Group membership	IGMP	Yes

Echo Request and Reply

The idea and format of the echo request and reply messages are the same as those in version 4. The only difference is the value for the type as shown in Figure 27.42.

Figure 27.42   *Echo request and reply messages*

Type: 128 or 129	Code: 0	Checksum	
Identifier		Sequence number	
Optional data Sent by the request message; repeated by the reply message			

Router Solicitation and Advertisement

The idea behind the router-solicitation and advertisement messages is the same as in version 4. The router-solicitation format is similar to the one in ICMPv4. However, an option is added to allow the host to announce its physical address to make it easier for the router to respond. The router-advertisement format is different from the one in ICMPv4; here the router announces just itself and not any other router. Options can be added to the packet. One option announces the router physical address for the convenience of the host. Another option lets the router announce the MTU size. A third option allows the router to define the valid and preferred lifetime. Figure 27.43 shows the format of the router-solicitation and advertisement messages.

Figure 27.43   *Router-solicitation and advertisement message formats*

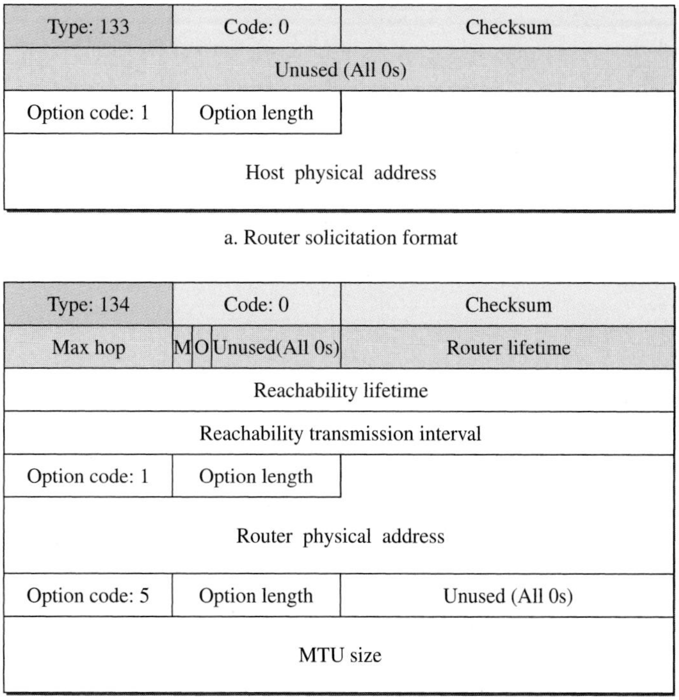

a. Router solicitation format

b. Router advertisement format

Neighbor Solicitation and Advertisement

As previously mentioned, the network layer in version 4 contains an independent protocol called Address Resolution Protocol (ARP). In version 6, this protocol is eliminated, and its duties are included in ICMPv6. The idea is exactly the same, but the format of the message has changed. Figure 27.44 shows the format of **neighbor-solicitation and**

advertisement messages. The only option announces the sender physical address for the convenience of the receiver.

Figure 27.44   *Neighbor-solicitation and advertisement message formats*

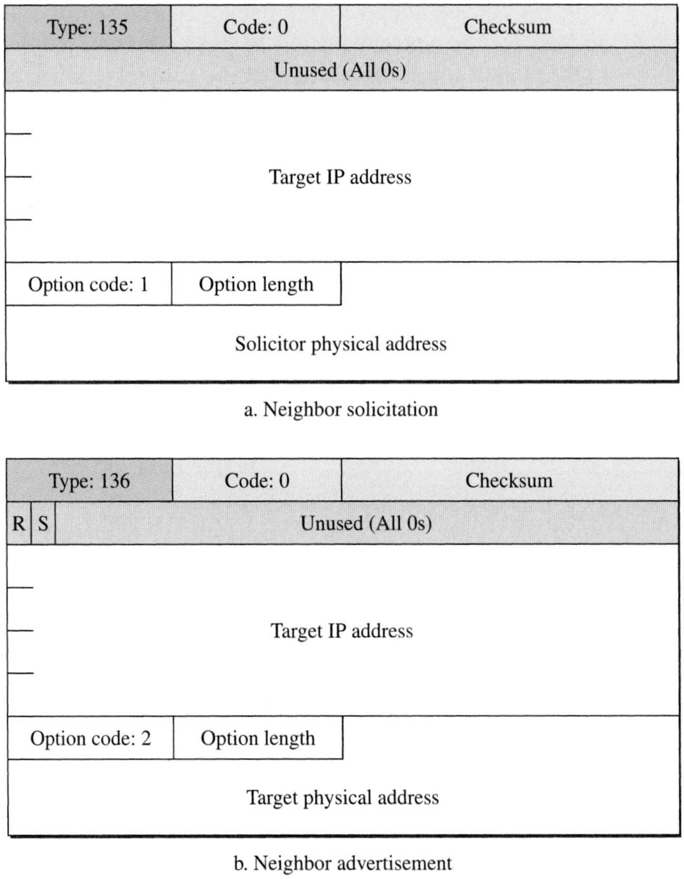

Type: 135	Code: 0	Checksum
Unused (All 0s)		
Target IP address		
Option code: 1	Option length	
Solicitor physical address		

a. Neighbor solicitation

Type: 136	Code: 0	Checksum
R S Unused (All 0s)		
Target IP address		
Option code: 2	Option length	
Target physical address		

b. Neighbor advertisement

Group Membership

As previously mentioned, the network layer in version 4 contains an independent protocol called IGMP. In version 6, this protocol is eliminated, and its duties are included in ICMPv6. The purpose is exactly the same.

There are three types of **group-membership messages:** report, query, and termination (see Figure 27.45). The report and termination messages are sent from the host to the router. The query message is sent from the router to the host. Figure 27.46 shows the formats of group-membership messages.

Figure 27.45 *Group-membership messages*

Host
Report
Router
Query
Termination
R

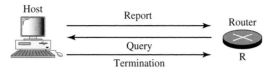

Figure 27.46 *Group-membership message formats*

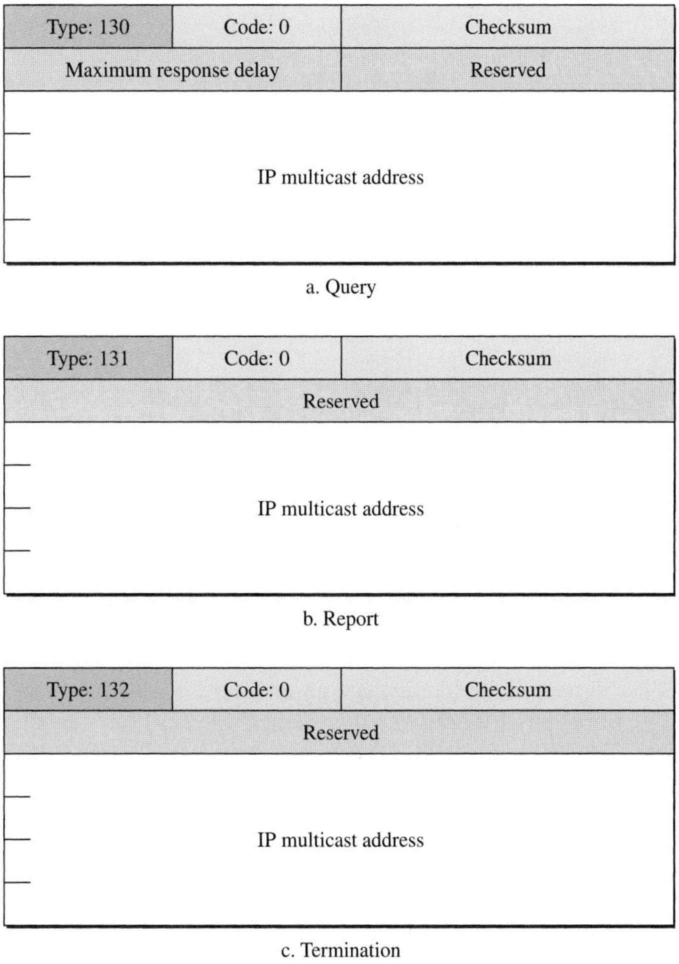

Type: 130
Code: 0
Checksum
Maximum response delay
Reserved
IP multicast address
a. Query
Type: 131
Code: 0
Checksum
Reserved
IP multicast address
b. Report
Type: 132
Code: 0
Checksum
Reserved
IP multicast address
c. Termination

As we noted in our discussion of version 4, four different situations involve group-membership messages; these are shown in Figure 27.47.

Figure 27.47 *Four situations of group-membership operation*

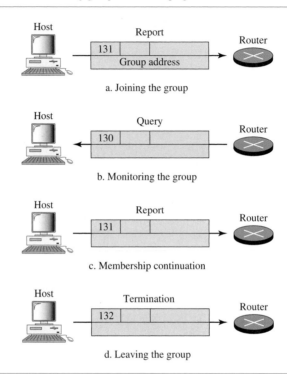

a. Joining the group

b. Monitoring the group

c. Membership continuation

d. Leaving the group

27.3 TRANSITION FROM IPv4 TO IPv6

Because of the huge number of systems on the Internet, the transition from IPv4 to IPv6 cannot happen suddenly. It takes a considerable amount of time before every system in the Internet can move from IPv4 to IPv6. The transition must be smooth to prevent any problems between IPv4 and IPv6 systems. Three strategies have been devised by the IETF to help the transition (see Figure 27.48).

Dual Stack

It is recommended that all hosts, before migrating completely to version 6, have a **dual stack** of protocols. In other words, a station should run IPv4 and IPv6 simultaneously until all of the Internet uses IPv6. See Figure 27.49 for the layout of a dual-stack configuration.

To determine which version to use when sending a packet to a destination, the source host queries the DNS. If the DNS returns an IPv4 address, the source host sends an IPv4 packet. If the DNS returns an IPv6 address, the source host sends an IPv6 packet.

Figure 27.48   *Three transition strategies*

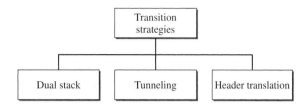

Figure 27.49   *Dual stack*

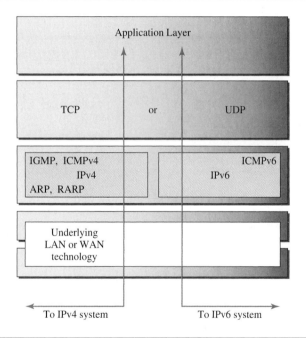

Tunneling

Tunneling is a strategy used when two computers using IPv6 want to communicate with each other and the packet must pass through a region that uses IPv4. To pass through this region, the packet must have an IPv4 address. So the IPv6 packet is encapsulated in an IPv4 packet when it enters the region, and it leaves its capsule when it exits the region. It seems as if the IPv6 packet goes through a tunnel at one end and emerges at the other end. To make it clear that the IPv4 packet is carrying an IPv6 packet as data, the protocol value is set to 41. Tunneling uses the compatible addresses discussed in Section 27.1 under "IPv6 Addresses."

Automatic Tunneling

If the receiving host uses a compatible IPv6 address, tunneling occurs automatically without any reconfiguration. In **automatic tunneling,** the sender sends the receiver an IPv6 packet using the IPv6 compatible address as the destination address. When the packet reaches the boundary of the IPv4 network, the router encapsulates it in an IPv4 packet, which should have an IPv4 address. To get this address, the router extracts the IPv4 address embedded in the IPv6 address. The packet then travels the rest of its journey as an IPv4 packet. The destination host, which is using a dual stack, now receives an IPv4 packet. Recognizing its IPv4 address, it reads the header, and finds (through the protocol field value) that the packet is carrying an IPv6 packet. It then passes the packet to the IPv6 software for processing (see Figure 27.50).

Figure 27.50   *Automatic tunneling*

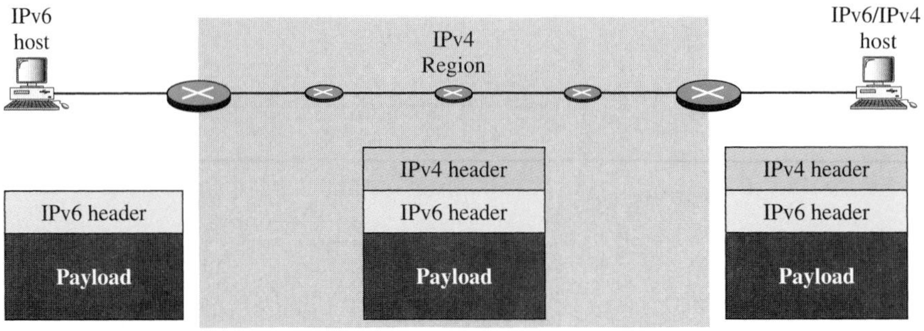

Configured Tunneling

If the receiving host does not support an IPv6-compatible address, the sender receives a noncompatible IPv6 address from the DNS. In this case, **configured tunneling** is used. The sender sends the IPv6 packet with the receiver's noncompatible IPv6 address. However, the packet cannot pass through the IPv4 region without first being encapsulated in an IPv4 packet. The two routers at the boundary of the IPv4 region are configured to pass the packet encapsulated in an IPv4 packet. The router at one end sends the IPv4 packet with its own IPv4 address as the source and the other router's IPv4 address as the destination. The other router receives the packet, decapsulates the IPv6 packet, and sends it to the destination host. The destination host then receives the packet in IPv6 format and processes it (see Figure 27.51).

Header Translation

Header translation is necessary when the majority of the Internet has moved to IPv6 but some systems still use IPv4. The sender wants to use IPv6, but the receiver does not understand IPv6. Tunneling does not work in this situation because the packet must be in the IPv4 format to be understood by the receiver. In this case, the header format must be changed totally through header translation. The header of the IPv6 packet is converted to an IPv4 header (see Figure 27.52).

Figure 27.51   *Configured tunneling*

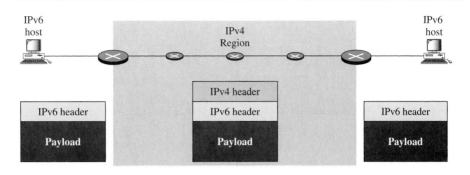

Figure 27.52   *Header translation*

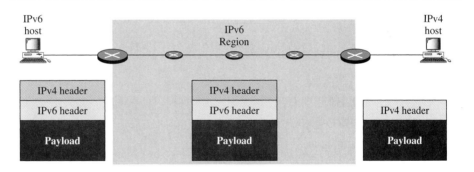

Header translation uses the mapped address to translate an IPv6 address to an IPv4 address. Table 27.9 lists some rules used in transforming an IPv6 packet header to an IPv4 packet header.

Table 27.9   *Header translation*

Header Translation Procedure
1. The IPv6 mapped address is changed to an IPv4 address by extracting the rightmost 32 bits.
2. The value of the IPv6 priority field is discarded.
3. Set the type of service field in IPv4 to zero.
4. The checksum for IPv4 is calculated and inserted in the corresponding field.
5. The IPv6 flow label is ignored.
6. Compatible extension headers are converted to options and inserted in the IPv4 header.
7. The length of IPv4 header is calculated and inserted into the corresponding field.
8. The total length of the IPv4 packet is calculated and inserted in the corresponding field.

27.4   KEY TERMS

abbreviation

anycast address

attended bulk data traffic

automatic tunneling

background data

base header

compatible address

configured tunneling

control traffic

destination option

dual stack

encrypted security payload (ESP)

extension header

flow label

header translation

hexadecimal colon notation

hop limit

hop-by-hop option

interactive traffic

Internetworking Control Message Protocol, version 6 (ICMPv6)

Internetworking Protocol, next generation (IPng)

Internetworking Protocol, version 6 (Ipv6)

jumbo payload

link local address

mapped address

neighbor-solicitation and advertisement message

next header

noncongestion-controlled traffic

packet priority

packet-too-big message

Pad1

PadN

Path MTU Discovery technique

reserved address

resource allocation

site local address

transport mode

tunnel mode

tunneling

unattended data traffic

unspecified address

27.5   SUMMARY

❑   IPv6, the latest version of the Internet Protocol, has a 128-bit address space, a revised header format, new options, an allowance for extension, support for resource allocation, and increased security measures.

❑   IPv6 uses hexadecimal colon notation with abbreviation methods available.

❑   There are three types of addresses: unicast, anycast, and multicast.

❑   The variable type prefix field defines the address type or purpose.

❑ An IPv6 datagram is composed of a base header and a payload.

❑ The 40-byte base header consists of the version, priority, flow label, payload length, next header, hop limit, source address, and destination address fields.

❑ The priority field is a measure of the importance of a datagram.

❑ The flow label identifies the special-handling needs of a sequence of packets.

❑ A payload consists of optional extension headers and data from an upper layer.

❑ Extension headers add functionality to the IPv6 datagram.

❑ The hop-by-hop option is used to pass information to all routers in the path.

❑ The source routing extension is used when the source wants to specify the transmission path.

❑ The fragmentation extension is used if the payload is a fragment of a message.

❑ The authentication extension validates the sender of the message and protects the data from hackers.

❑ The encrypted security payload extension provides confidentiality between sender and receiver.

❑ The destination extension passes information from the source to the destination exclusively.

❑ ICMPv6, like version 4, reports errors, handles group memberships, updates specific router and host tables, and checks the viability of a host.

❑ The five error-reporting messages deal with unreachable destinations, packets that are too big, expired timers for fragments and hop counts, header problems, and inefficient routing.

❑ Query messages are in the form of a response and a reply.

❑ The echo request and reply query messages test the connectivity between two systems.

❑ The router-solicitation and advertisement messages allow routers to update their routing tables.

❑ The group-membership messages can add a host to a group, terminate a group membership, monitor a group, or maintain group membership.

❑ Three strategies used to handle the transition from version 4 to version 6 are dual stack, tunneling, and header translation.

27.6 PRACTICE SET

Exercises

1. Show the shortest form of the following addresses:

   a. 2340:1ABC:119A:A000:0000:0000:0000:0000

   b. 0000:00AA:0000:0000:0000:0000:119A:A231

   c. 2340:0000:0000:0000:0000:119A:A001:0000

   d. 0000:0000:0000:2340:0000:0000:0000:0000

2. Show the original (unabbreviated) form of the following addresses:
   a. 0::0
   b. 0:AA::0
   c. 0:1234::3
   d. 123::1:2

3. What is the type of each of the following addresses:
   a. FE80::12
   b. FEC0::24A2
   c. FF02::0
   d. 0::01

4. What is the type of each of the following addresses:
   a. 0::0
   b. 0::FFFF:0:0
   c. 582F:1234::2222
   d. 4821::14:22
   e. 54EF::A234:2

5. Show the provider prefix (in hexadecimal colon notation) of an address assigned to a subscriber if it is registered in the USA with the provider identification ABC1.

6. Show in hexadecimal colon notation the IPv6 address compatible to the IPv4 address 129.6.12.34.

7. Show in hexadecimal colon notation the IPv6 address mapped to the IPv4 address 129.6.12.34.

8. Show in hexadecimal colon notation the IPv6 loopback address.

9. Show in hexadecimal colon notation the link local address in which the node identifier is 0::123/48.

10. Show in hexadecimal colon notation the site local address in which the node identifier is 0::123/48.

11. Show in hexadecimal colon notation the permanent multicast address used in a link local scope.

12. What are the possible first two bytes for a multicast address?

13. A host has the address 581E:1456:2314:ABCD::1211. If the node identification is 48 bits, find the address of the subnet to which the host is attached.

14. A host has the address 581E:1456:2314:ABCD::1211. If the node identification is 48 bits, and the subnet identification is 32 bits, find the provider prefix.

15. A site with 200 subnets has the class B address of 132.45.0.0. The site recently migrated to IPv6 with the subscriber prefix 581E:1456:2314::ABCD/80. Design the subnets and define the subnet address using a subnet identifier of 32 bits.

16. An IPv6 packet consists of the base header and a TCP segment. The length of data is 320 bytes. Show the packet and enter a value for each field.

17. An IPv6 packet consists of a base header and a TCP segment. The length of data is 128,000 bytes (jumbo payload). Show the packet and enter a value for each field.

18. What types of ICMP messages contain part of the IP datagram? Why is this included?

19. Compare and contrast, field by field, the destination-unreachable message format in ICMPv4 and ICMPv6.

20. Compare and contrast, field by field, the time-exceeded message format in ICMPv4 and ICMPv6.

21. Compare and contrast, field by field, the parameter-problem message format in ICMPv4 and ICMPv6.

22. Compare and contrast, field by field, the redirection-message format in ICMPv4 and ICMPv6.

23. Compare and contrast, field by field, the echo-request and reply messages format in ICMPv4 and ICMPv6.

24. Compare and contrast, field by field, the router-solicitation and advertisement messages format in ICMPv4 and ICMPv6.

25. Compare and contrast, field by field, the neighbor-solicitation and advertisement messages format in ICMPv6 with the query and reply messages in ARP.

26. Compare and contrast, field by field, the group-membership messages in IPv6 with the corresponding messages in IGMP.

27. Why are the IPv4-compatible addresses and the IPv4-mapped addresses different?

28. What is the IPv4-compatible address for 119.254.254.254?

29. What is the IPv4-mapped address for 119.254.254.254?

30. How many more addresses are available with IPv6 than IPv4?

31. In designing the IPv4-mapped address, why didn't the designers just prepend 96 1s to the IPv4 address?

Research Activities

32. Find the RFCs related to IPv6.

33. Find the RFCs related to ICMPv6.

34. Find out how transition from ICMPv4 and IGMPv4 to ICMPv6 will occur.

35. Show a comparison between the use of CIDR in version 4 and version 6.

36. Find out why there are two security protocols (AH and ESP) in IPv6.

CHAPTER 28

Network Security

Security is a very broad subject that encompasses many aspects. However, in this chapter, we want to discuss network security as related to the Internet. To do so, we first need to review some topics that are normally discussed in an introductory data communications or security course. We start with cryptography, without going into abstract mathematical topics such as number theory. We then show how four aspects of security, namely privacy, integrity, authentication, and nonrepudiation, are applied to a message. We continue with entity authentication and key management. We follow that with security in the Internet. Finally, we discuss firewalls as applied to system access by the user.

28.1 CRYPTOGRAPHY

We begin our discussion of network security with an introduction to cryptography. The science of cryptography is very complex; there are entire books devoted to the subject. A cryptography expert needs to be knowledgeable in areas such as mathematics, electronics, and programming. In this section, we consider the concepts needed to understand the security issues and network security discussed in the rest of the chapter.

The word **cryptography** in Greek means "secret writing." However, the term today refers to the science and art of transforming messages to make them secure and immune to attacks. Figure 28.1 shows the components involved in cryptography.

Figure 28.1 *Cryptography components*

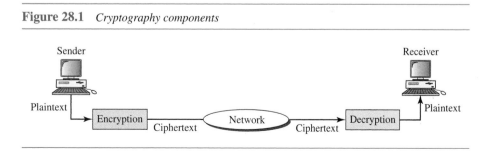

The original message, before being transformed, is called **plaintext.** After the message is transformed, it is called **ciphertext.** An **encryption** algorithm transforms the plaintext to ciphertext; a **decryption** algorithm transforms the ciphertext back to plaintext. The sender uses an encryption algorithm, and the receiver uses a decryption algorithm.

Throughout this chapter, we refer to encryption/decryption algorithms as **ciphers.** The term *cipher* is also used to refer to different categories of algorithms in cryptography. We should remember that not every sender-receiver pair needs its very own unique cipher for a secure communication. Instead, through the use of keys, one cipher can serve millions of communicating pairs. A **key** is a number (value) that the cipher, as an algorithm, operates on. To encrypt a message, we need an encryption algorithm, an encryption key, and the plaintext. These create the ciphertext. To decrypt a message, we need a decryption algorithm, a decryption key, and the ciphertext. These reveal the original plaintext.

The encryption and decryption algorithms are public; anyone can access them. The keys are secret; they need to be protected.

In cryptography, the encryption/decryption algorithms are public; the keys are secret.

It is customary to introduce three characters in cryptography; we use Alice, Bob, and Eve. Alice is the person who needs to send secure data. Bob is the recipient of the data. Eve is the person who somehow disturbs the communication between Alice and Bob by intercepting messages or sending her own disguised messages. These three names represent computers or processes that actually send or receive data, or intercept or change data.

We can divide all the cryptography algorithms in the world into two groups: symmetric-key (sometimes called secret-key) cryptography algorithms and asymmetric-key (often called public-key) cryptography algorithms.

Symmetric-Key Cryptography

In **symmetric-key cryptography,** the same key is used by both parties. The sender uses this key and an encryption algorithm to encrypt data; the receiver uses the same key and the corresponding decryption algorithm to decrypt the data (see Figure 28.2).

In symmetric-key cryptography, the same key is used by the sender (for encryption) and the receiver (for decryption). The key is shared.

In symmetric-key cryptography, the algorithm used for decryption is the inverse of the algorithm used for encryption. This means that if the encryption algorithm uses a combination of addition and multiplication, the decryption algorithm uses a combination of division and subtraction.

Note that the symmetric-key cryptography algorithms are so named because the same key can be used in both directions.

Figure 28.2   *Symmetric-key cryptography*

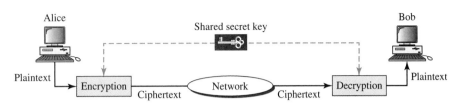

> **In symmetric-key cryptography, the same key is used in both directions.**

Traditional Ciphers

In the earliest and simplest ciphers, a character was the unit of data to be encrypted. These traditional ciphers involved either substitution or transposition.

Substitution Cipher   A cipher using the **substitution** method substitutes one symbol with another. If the symbols in the plaintext are alphabetic characters, we replace one character with another. For example, we can replace character A with D and character T with Z. If the symbols are digits (0 to 9), we can replace 3 with 7 and 2 with 6. We will concentrate on alphabetic characters.

The first recorded ciphertext was used by Julius Caesar and is still called the *Caesar cipher*. The cipher shifts each character down by three. Figure 28.3 shows idea of the Caesar cipher.

Figure 28.3   *Caesar cipher*

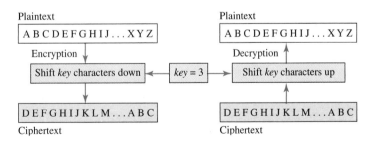

Before we go further, let us analyze the Caesar cipher which has an encryption algorithm, a decryption algorithm, and a symmetric key. As the figure shows, the encryption algorithm is "shift *key* characters down." The decryption algorithm is "shift *key* characters up." The key is 3. Note that the encryption and decryption algorithms are the inverses of each other; the key is the same in encryption and decryption.

We can think of substitution cipher in another way. We can assign numbers to the alphabet characters (A = 0, B = 1, C = 3, . . . , Z = 25). We can think of the encryption algorithm as simply "add the key to the plaintext number to get the ciphertext number."

Decryption is the same, but we replace *add* with *subtract* and switch *plaintext* with *ciphertext*. Of course adding and subtracting are modulo 26, which means that 24 + 3 is 1, not 27; Y (24) is substituted with B (1).

Transpositional Cipher In a **transpositional cipher,** the characters retain their plaintext form but change their positions to create the ciphertext. The text is organized into a two-dimensional table, and the columns are interchanged according to a key. For example, we can organize the plaintext into an 8-column table and then reorganize the columns according to a key that indicates the interchange rule. Figure 28.4 shows an example of transpositional cryptography. The key defines which columns should be swapped.

Figure 28.4 *Transpositional cipher*

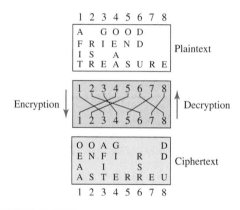

Data Encryption Standard (DES)

Traditional ciphers used a character or symbol as the unit of encryption/decryption. Modern ciphers, on the other hand, use a block of bits as the unit of encryption/decryption. One example of a complex block cipher is the **Data Encryption Standard (DES).** DES was designed by IBM and adopted by the U.S. government as the standard encryption method for nonmilitary and nonclassified use. The algorithm encrypts a 64-bit plaintext using a 56-bit key. The text is put through 19 different and complex procedures to create a 64-bit ciphertext, as shown in Figure 28.5. DES has two transposition blocks, one swapping block, and 16 complex blocks called iteration blocks.

Although the 16 iteration blocks are conceptually the same, each uses a different key derived from the original key. Figure 28.6 shows the schematics of an iteration block.

In each block, the previous right 32 bits become the next left 32 bits (swapping). The next right 32 bits, however, come from first applying an operation (a function) on the previous right 32 bits and then XORing the result with the left 32 bits.

Note that the whole DES cipher block is a substitution block that changes a 64-bit plaintext to a 64-bit ciphertext. In other words, instead of substituting one character at a time, it substitutes 8 characters (bytes) at a time, using complex encryption and decryption algorithms.

Figure 28.5 *DES*

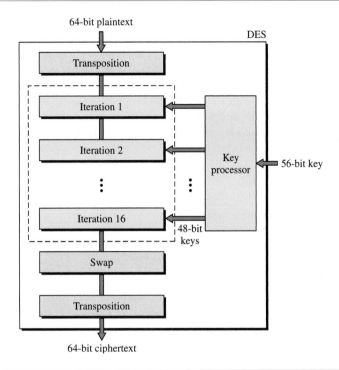

Figure 28.6 *Iteration block*

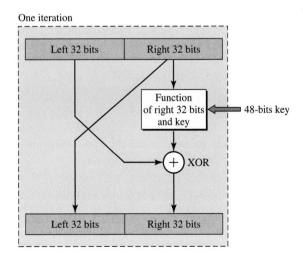

DES takes the data and chops them into 8-byte segments. However, the encryption algorithm and the key are the same for each segment. So if the data are four equal segments, the result is also four equal segments.

Triple DES   Critics of DES contend that the key is too short. To lengthen the key and at the same time keep the new block compatible with that of the original DES, **triple DES** was designed. This uses three DES blocks and two 56-bit keys, as shown in Figure 28.7. Note that the encrypting block uses an encryption-decryption-encryption combination of DESs, while the decryption block uses a decryption-encryption-decryption combination. It was designed this way to provide compatibility between triple DES and the original DES when K1 and K2 are the same.

Figure 28.7   *Triple DES*

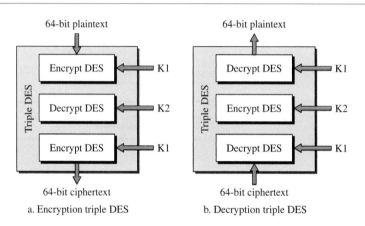

a. Encryption triple DES

b. Decryption triple DES

> **The DES cipher uses the same concept as the Caesar cipher, but the encryption/ decryption algorithm is much more complex.**

Public-Key Cryptography

In **public-key cryptography,** there are two keys: a **private key** and a **public key.** The private key is kept by the receiver. The public key is announced to the public.

Imagine Alice, as shown in Figure 28.8, wants to send a message to Bob. Alice uses the public key to encrypt the message. When the message is received by Bob, the private key is used to decrypt the message.

In public-key encryption/decryption, the public key that is used for encryption is different from the private key that is used for decryption. The public key is available to the public; the private key is available only to an individual.

RSA

The most common public-key algorithm is called the **RSA method** after its inventors (Rivest, Shamir, and Adleman). The private key here is a pair of numbers (N, d); the

Figure 28.8 *Public-key cryptography*

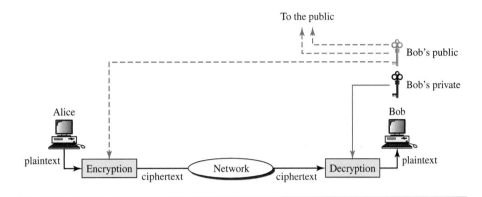

public key is also a pair of numbers (N, e). Note that N is common to the private and public keys.

The sender uses the following algorithm to encrypt the message:

$$C = P^e \bmod N$$

In this algorithm, P is the plaintext, which is represented as a number; C is the number that represents the ciphertext. The two numbers e and N are components of the public key. Plaintext P is raised to the power e and divided by N. The mod term indicates that the remainder is sent as the ciphertext.

The receiver uses the following algorithm to decrypt the message:

$$P = C^d \bmod N$$

In this algorithm, P and C are the same as before. The two numbers d and N are components of the private key. Figure 28.9 shows an example.

Figure 28.9 *RSA*

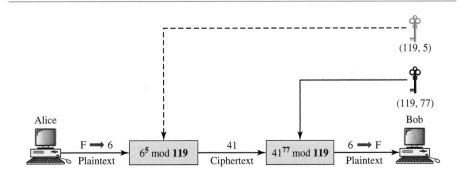

Imagine the private key is the pair (119, 77) and the public key is the pair (119, 5). The sender needs to send the character F. This character can be represented as the number 6 (F is the sixth character in the alphabet). The encryption algorithm calculates $C = 6^5$ mod 119 = 41. This number is sent to the receiver as the ciphertext. The receiver uses the decryption algorithm to calculate $P = 41^{77}$ mod 119 = 6 (the original number). The number 6 is then interpreted as F.

The reader may question the effectiveness of this algorithm. If an intruder knows the decryption algorithm and $N = 119$, the only thing missing is $d = 77$. Why couldn't the intruder use trial and error to find d? The answer is yes, in this trivial example an intruder could easily guess the value of d. But a major concept of the RSA algorithm is to use very large numbers for d and e. In practice, the numbers are so large (on the scale of hundreds of digits) that the trial-and-error approach of breaking the code takes a long time (months, if not years) even with the fastest computers available today.

Choosing Public and Private Keys   One question that comes to mind is, How do we choose the three numbers N, d, and e for encryption and decryption to work? The inventors of RSA used number theory to prove that using the following procedure will guarantee that the algorithms will work. Although the proof is beyond the scope of this book, we outline the procedure:

1. Choose two large prime numbers p and q.
2. Compute $N = p \times q$.
3. Choose e (less than N) such that e and $(p-1)(q-1)$ are relatively prime (having no common factor other than 1).
4. Choose d such that $(e \times d)$ mod $[(p-1)(q-1)]$ is equal to 1.

Comparison

Before closing the section on cryptography, let us do a brief comparison between the two categories.

Advantages and Disadvantages of Symmetric-Key Cryptography

Symmetric-key algorithms are efficient; it takes less time to encrypt a message using a symmetric-key algorithm than it takes to encrypt using an asymmetric-key algorithm. The reason is that the key is usually smaller. For this reason, symmetric-key algorithms are used to encrypt and decrypt long messages.

Symmetric-key cryptography is often used for long messages.

A symmetric-key algorithm has two major disadvantages. Each pair of users must have a unique symmetric key. This means that if N people in the world want to use this method, there needs to be $N(N-1)/2$ symmetric keys. For example, for 1 million people to communicate, 500 billion symmetric keys are needed. The distribution of the keys between two parties can be difficult.

Advantages and Disadvantages of Asymmetric-Key Cryptography

Asymmetric-key encryption/decryption has two advantages. First, it removes the restriction of a shared symmetric key between two entities (e.g., persons) who need to communicate with each other. A shared symmetric key is shared by the two parties and cannot be used when one of them wants to communicate with a third party. In public-key encryption/decryption, each entity creates a pair of keys; the private one is kept, and the public one is distributed. Each entity is independent, and the pair of keys created can be used to communicate with any other entity. The second advantage is that the number of keys needed is reduced tremendously. In this system, for 1 million users to communicate, only 2 million keys are needed, not 500 billion, as was the case in symmetric-key cryptography.

Public-key cryptography also has two disadvantages. The big disadvantage is the complexity of the algorithm. If we want the method to be effective, the algorithm needs large numbers. Calculating the ciphertext from plaintext using the long keys takes a lot of time. That is the main reason that public-key cryptography is not recommended for large amounts of text.

Asymmetric-key algorithms are more efficient for short messages.

The second disadvantage of the public-key method is that the association between an entity and its public key must be verified. If Alice sends her public key via an email to Bob, then Bob must be sure that the public key really belongs to Alice and nobody else. We will see that this certification is really important when we use public-key cryptography for authentication. However, this disadvantage can be overcome using a certification authority (CA) that we discuss later in the chapter. We use the terms *symmetric-key* and *secret-key* interchangeably. We also use the terms *asymmetric-key* and *public-key* interchangeably.

28.2   PRIVACY

The first service we expect from a secure system is privacy. **Privacy** means that the sender and the receiver expect confidentiality. The transmitted message must make sense to only the intended receiver. To all others, the message must be unintelligible.

The concept of how to achieve privacy has not changed for thousands of years: The message must be encrypted. That is, the message must be rendered unintelligible to unauthorized parties. A good privacy technique guarantees to some extent that a potential intruder (eavesdropper) cannot understand the contents of the message.

Privacy with Symmetric-Key Cryptography

Privacy can be achieved using symmetric-key encryption and decryption, as shown in Figure 28.10. As we discussed before, in symmetric-key cryptography the key is shared between Alice and Bob.

Using symmetric-key cryptography is very common for achieving privacy. Later in this chapter, we will see how to manage the distribution of symmetric keys.

Figure 28.10   *Privacy using symmetric-key encryption*

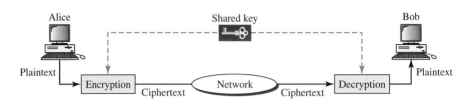

Privacy with Asymmetric-Key Cryptography

We can also achieve privacy using asymmetric-key (public-key) encryption. There are two keys: a private key and a public key. The private key is kept by the receiver. The public key is announced to the public. This is shown in Figure 28.11.

Figure 28.11   *Privacy using asymmetric-key encryption*

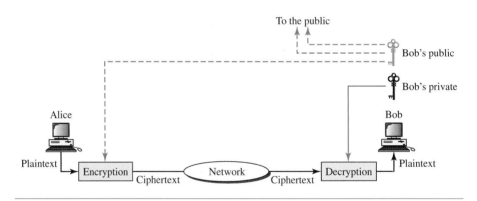

The main problem with public key encryption is its owner must be verified (certified). We will see how to solve this problem shortly.

28.3   DIGITAL SIGNATURE

Other services we expect from a secure system are message authentication, message integrity, and nonrepudiation. **Message authentication** means that the receiver needs to be sure of the sender's identity and that an imposter has not sent the message. **Message integrity** means that the data must arrive at the receiver exactly as they were sent. There must be no changes during the transmission, either accidental or malicious. As more and more monetary exchanges occur over the Internet, integrity is crucial. For example, it would be disastrous if a request for transferring $100 changed to a request for $10,000 or $100,000. The integrity of the message must be preserved in a secure communication. **Nonrepudiation** means that a receiver must be able to prove that a received message came from a specific sender. The sender must not be able to deny sending a message that he or she, in fact, did send. The burden of proof falls on the receiver. For example, when a customer sends a message to transfer money from one account to another, the bank must have proof that the customer actually requested this transaction. These three services can be achieved by using what is called **digital signature.**

> **Digital signature can provide authentication, integrity, and nonrepudiation for a message.**

The idea is similar to the signing of a document. When we send a document electronically, we can also sign it. We have two choices: We can sign the entire document, or we can sign a digest (condensed version) of the document.

Signing the Whole Document

Public-key encryption can be used to sign a document. However, the roles of the public and private keys are different here. The sender uses her private key to encrypt (sign) the message just as a person uses her signature (which is private in the sense that it is difficult to forge) to sign a paper document. The receiver, on the other hand, uses the public key of the sender to decrypt the message just as a person verifies from record another person's signature.

In digital signature, the private key is used for encryption and the public key for decryption. This is possible because the encryption and decryption algorithms used today, such as RSA, are mathematical formulas and their structures are similar. Figure 28.12 shows how this is done.

Figure 28.12   *Signing the whole document*

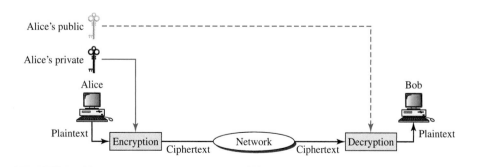

Digital signatures can provide integrity, authentication, and nonrepudiation. The integrity of a message is preserved because if Eve intercepted the message and partially or totally changed it, the decrypted message would be unreadable.

We can use the following reasoning to show how a message can be authenticated. If Eve sends a message while pretending that it is coming from Alice, she must use her own private key for encryption. The message is then decrypted with the public key of

Alice and will therefore be nonreadable. Encryption with Eve's private key and decryption with Alice's public key result in garbage.

Digital signature also provides for nonrepudiation. However, we need a trusted third party. The trusted party saves the message received from Alice. If Alice later denies sending the message, Bob can appeal to the third party and show that encrypting and decrypting the saved message with Alice's private and public key can create a duplicate of the saved message.

Digital signature does not provide privacy. If there is a need for privacy, another layer of encryption/decryption must be applied.

Signing the Digest

We said before that public-key encryption is efficient if the message is short. Using a public key to sign the entire message is very inefficient if the message is very long. The solution is to let the sender sign a digest of the document instead of the whole document. The sender creates a miniature version or **digest** of the document and signs it; the receiver then checks the signature on the miniature.

To create a digest of the message, we use a **hash function.** The hash function creates a fixed-size digest from a variable-length message, as shown in Figure 28.13.

Figure 28.13   *Hash function*

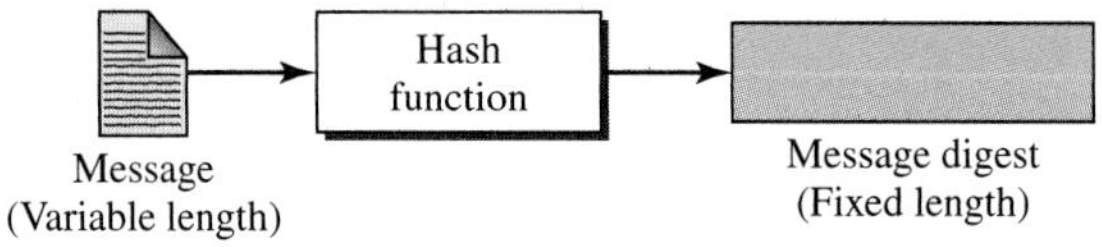

Message
(Variable length)

Hash
function

Message digest
(Fixed length)

The two most common hash functions are called MD5 (Message Digest 5) and SHA-1 (Secure Hash Algorithm 1). The first one produces a 120-bit digest. The second produces a 160-bit digest.

Note that a hash function must have two properties to guarantee its success. First, hashing is one-way; the digest can only be created from the message, not vice versa. Second, hashing is a one-to-one function; there is little probability that two messages will create the same digest. We will see the reason for this condition shortly.

After the digest has been created, it is encrypted (signed) using the sender's private key. The encrypted digest is attached to the original message and sent to the receiver. Figure 28.14 shows the sender site.

The receiver receives the original message and the encrypted digest. He separates the two. He applies the same hash function to the message to create a second digest. He also decrypts the received digest, using the public key of the sender. If the two digests are the same, all three security measures are preserved. Figure 28.15 shows the receiver site.

Figure 28.14   *Sender site*

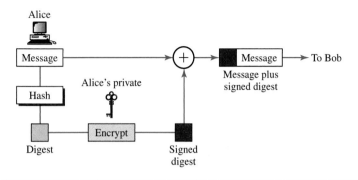

Figure 28.15   *Receiver site*

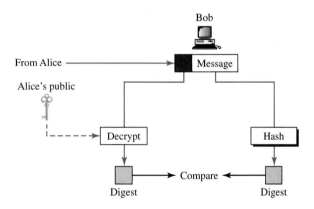

According to Section 28.1, we know that the digest is secure in terms of integrity, authentication, and nonrepudiation, but what about the message itself? The following reasoning shows that the message itself is also secured:

1. The digest has not been changed (integrity), and the digest is a representation of the message. So the message has not been changed (remember, it is improbable that two messages create the same digest). Integrity has been provided.

2. The digest comes from the true sender, so the message also comes from the true sender. If an intruder had initiated the message, the message would not have created the same digest (it is improbable that two messages create the same digest).

3. The sender cannot deny the message since she cannot deny the digest; the only message that can create that digest, with a very high probability, is the received message.

28.4 ENTITY AUTHENTICATION

The main issue in security is key management, as we will see later. However, key management involves **entity authentication.** We, therefore, briefly discuss this issue before talking about key management.

Entity Authentication with Symmetric-Key Cryptography

In this section, we discuss authentication as a procedure that verifies the identity of one entity to another. An *entity* can be a person, a process, a client, or a server; in our examples, entities are people. Specifically, Bob needs to verify the identity of Alice and vice versa. Note that entity authentication, as discussed here, is different from the message authentication that we discussed in the previous section. In message authentication, the identity of the sender is verified for each single message. In entity authentication, the identity is verified once for the entire duration of system access.

First Approach

In the first approach, Alice sends her identity and password in an encrypted message, using the symmetric key K_{AB}. Figure 28.16 shows the procedure. We have added the padlock with the corresponding key (shared key between Alice and Bob) to show that the message is encrypted with the key.

Figure 28.16 *Using a symmetric key only*

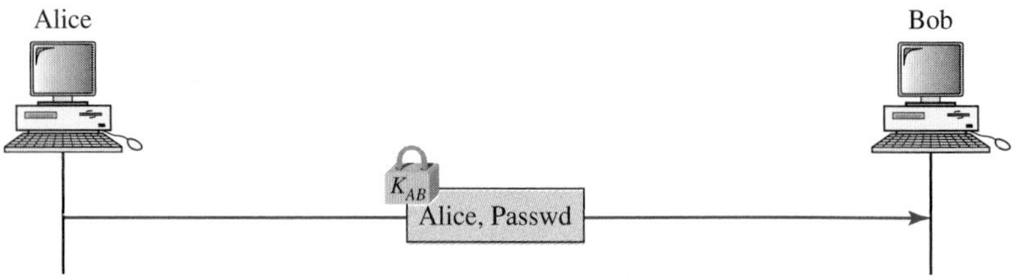

Is this a safe approach? Yes, to some extent. Eve, the intruder, cannot decipher the password or the data because she does not know K_{AB}. However, Eve can cause damage without accessing the contents of the message. If Eve has an interest in the data message sent from Alice to Bob, she can intercept both the authentication message and the data message, store them, and resend them later to Bob. Bob has no way to know that this is a replay of a previous message. There is nothing in this procedure to guarantee the freshness of the message. As an example, suppose Alice's message instructs Bob (as a bank manager) to pay Eve for some job she has done. Eve can resend the message, thereby illegally getting paid twice for the same job. This is called a **replay attack.**

Second Approach

To prevent a replay attack (or playback attack), we add something to the procedure to help Bob distinguish a fresh authentication request from a repeated one. This can be done by using a **nonce.** A nonce is a large random number that is used only once, a one-time number. In this second approach, Bob uses a nonce to challenge Alice, to make sure that Alice is authentic and that someone (Eve) is not impersonating Alice. Figure 28.17 shows the procedure.

Figure 28.17   *Using a nonce*

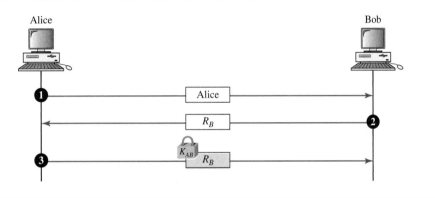

Authentication happens in three steps. First, Alice sends her identity, in plaintext, to Bob. Bob challenges Alice by sending a nonce, R_B, in plaintext. Alice responds to this message by sending back the nonce and encrypting it using the symmetric key. Eve cannot replay the message since R_B is valid only once.

Bidirectional Authentication

The second approach consists of a challenge and a response to authenticate Alice for Bob. Can we have **bidirectional authentication?** Figure 28.18 shows one method.

In the first step, Alice sends her identification and her nonce to challenge Bob. In the second step, Bob responds to Alice's challenge by sending his nonce to challenge her. In the third step, Alice responds to Bob's challenge. Is this authentication totally safe? It is on the condition that Alice and Bob use a different set of nonces for different sessions and do not allow multiple authentications to take place at the same time. Otherwise, this procedure can be the target of a **reflection attack;** we leave this as a research activity.

Entity Authentication with Public-Key Cryptography

We can use public-key cryptography to authenticate an entity. In Figure 28.18, Alice can encrypt the message with her private key and let Bob use Alice's public key to decrypt the message and authenticate her. However, we have the man-in-the-middle

Figure 28.18 *Bidirectional authentication*

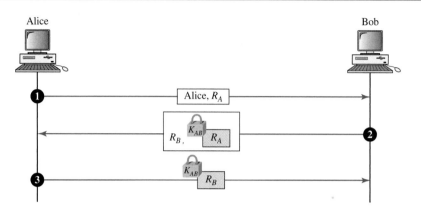

(see next section) attack problem because Eve can announce her public key to Bob in place of Alice. Eve can then encrypt the message containing a nonce with her private key. Bob decrypts it with Eve's public key, which he believes is Alice's. Bob is fooled. Alice needs a better means to advertise her public key; Bob needs a better way to verify Alice's public key. We discuss public-key certification next.

28.5   KEY MANAGEMENT

We discussed how secret-key and public-key cryptography can be used in message security and entity authentication. However, we never explained how symmetric keys are distributed and how public keys are certified. We explore these two important issues here.

Symmetric-Key Distribution

There are three problems with symmetric keys.

1. First, if n people want to communicate with one another, there is a need for $n(n-1)/2$ symmetric keys. Consider that each of the n people may need to communicate with $n-1$ people. This means that we need $n(n-1)$ keys. However, symmetric keys are shared between two communicating people. Therefore, the actual number of keys needed is $n(n-1)/2$. This is usually referred to as the n^2 **problem.** If n is a small number, this is acceptable. For example, if 5 people need to communicate, only 10 keys are needed. The problem is aggravated if n is a large number. For example, if n is 1 million, almost half a trillion keys are needed.

2. Second, in a group of n people, each person must have and remember $n-1$ keys, one for every other person in the group. This means that if 1 million people want to communicate with one another, each must remember (or store) almost 1 million keys in his or her computer.

3. Third, how can two parties securely acquire the shared key? It cannot be done over the phone or the Internet; these are not secure.

Session Keys

Considering the above problems, a symmetric key between two parties is useful if it is dynamic: created for each session and destroyed when the session is over. It does not have to be remembered by the two parties.

A symmetric key between two parties is useful if it is used only once; it must be created for one session and destroyed when the session is over.

Diffie-Hellman Method   One protocol, the **Diffie-Hellman (DH) protocol,** devised by Diffie and Hellman, provides a one-time session key for two parties. The two parties use the session key to exchange data without having to remember or store it for future use. The parties do not have to meet to agree on the key, it can be done through the Internet. Let us see how the protocol works when Alice and Bob need a symmetric key to communicate.

Before establishing a symmetric key, the two parties need to choose two numbers N and G. The first number, N, is a large prime number with the restriction that $(N - 1)/2$ must also be a prime number; the second number G is also a prime number, but it has more restrictions. These two numbers need not be confidential. They can be sent through the Internet; they can be public. Any two numbers, selected properly, can serve the entire world. There is no secrecy about these two numbers; both Alice and Bob know these magic numbers. Figure 28.19 shows the procedure.

Figure 28.19   *Diffie-Hellman method*

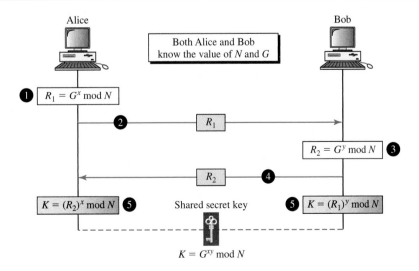

The steps are as follows:

- ❏ **Step 1**   Alice chooses a large random number x and calculates $R_1 = G^x \bmod N$.
- ❏ **Step 2**   Alice sends R_1 to Bob. Note that Alice does not send the value of x; she only sends R_1.
- ❏ **Step 3**   Bob chooses another large number y and calculates $R_2 = G^y \bmod N$.
- ❏ **Step 4**   Bob sends R_2 to Alice. Again, note that Bob does not send the value of y; he only sends R_2.
- ❏ **Step 5**   Alice calculates $K = (R_2)^x \bmod N$. Bob also calculates $K = (R_1)^y \bmod N$. And K is the symmetric key for the session.

The reader may wonder why the value of K is the same since the calculations are different. The answer is an equality proved in number theory.

$$(G^x \bmod N)^y \bmod N = (G^y \bmod N)^x \bmod N = G^{xy} \bmod N$$

Bob has calculated $K = (R_1)^y \bmod N = (G^x \bmod N)^y \bmod N = G^{xy} \bmod N$. Alice has calculated $K = (R_2)^x \bmod N = (G^y \bmod N)^x \bmod N = G^{xy} \bmod N$. Both have reached the same value without Bob knowing the value of x or Alice knowing the value of y.

The symmetric (shared) key in the Diffie-Hellman protocol is $K = G^{xy} \bmod N$.

Example 1

Let us give an example to make the procedure clear. Our example uses small numbers, but note that in a real situation, the numbers are very large. Assume $G = 7$ and $N = 23$. The steps are as follows:

1. Alice chooses $x = 3$ and calculates $R_1 = 7^3 \bmod 23 = 21$.
2. Alice sends the number 21 to Bob.
3. Bob chooses $y = 6$ and calculates $R_2 = 7^6 \bmod 23 = 4$.
4. Bob sends the number 4 to Alice.
5. Alice calculates the symmetric key $K = 4^3 \bmod 23 = 18$.
6. Bob calculates the symmetric key $K = 21^6 \bmod 23 = 18$.

The value of K is the same for both Alice and Bob; $G^{xy} \bmod N = 7^{18} \bmod 23 = 18$.

Man-in-the-Middle Attack   The Diffie-Hellman protocol is a very sophisticated symmetric-key creation algorithm. If x and y are very large numbers, it is extremely difficult for Eve to find the key knowing only N and G. An intruder needs to determine x and y if R_1 and R_2 are intercepted. But finding x from R_1 and y from R_2 are two difficult tasks. Even a sophisticated computer would need perhaps a long time to find the key by trying different numbers. In addition, Alice and Bob change the key the next time they need to communicate.

However, the protocol does have a weakness. Eve does not have to find the values of x and y to attack the protocol. She can fool Alice and Bob by creating two keys: one between herself and Alice and another between herself and Bob. Figure 28.20 shows the situation.

Figure 28.20   *Man-in-the-middle attack*

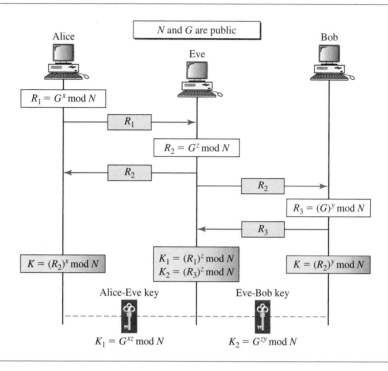

The following can happen:

1. Alice chooses x, calculates $R_1 = G^x$ mod N, and sends R_1 to Bob.
2. Eve, the intruder, intercepts R_1. She chooses z, calculates $R_2 = G^z$ mod N, and sends R_2 to both Alice and Bob.
3. Bob chooses y, calculates $R_3 = G^y$ mod N, and sends R_3 to Alice. R_3 is intercepted by Eve and never reaches Alice.
4. Alice and Eve calculate $K_1 = G^{xz}$ mod N, which becomes a shared key between Alice and Eve. Alice, however, thinks that it is a key shared between Bob and herself.
5. Eve and Bob calculate $K_2 = G^{zy}$ mod N, which becomes a shared key between Eve and Bob. Bob, however, thinks that it is a key shared between Alice and himself.

In other words, two keys, instead of one, are created: one between Alice and Eve and one between Eve and Bob. When Alice sends data to Bob encrypted with K_1 (shared by Alice and Eve), the data can be deciphered and read by Eve. Eve can send the message to Bob encrypted by K_2 (shared key between Eve and Bob); or she can even change the message or send a totally new message. Bob is fooled into believing that the message has come from Alice. The same scenario can happen to Alice in the other direction.

This situation is called a **man-in-the-middle attack** because Eve comes in between and intercepts R_1, sent by Alice to Bob, and R_3, sent by Bob to Alice. It is also known as a bucket brigade attack because it resembles a short line of volunteers passing a bucket of water from person to person.

Key Distribution Center (KDC)

The flaw in the previous protocol is the sending of R_1 and R_2 as plaintext which can be intercepted by any intruder. Any private correspondence between two parties should be encrypted using a symmetric key. But this can create a vicious circle. Two parties need to have a symmetric key before they can establish a symmetric key between themselves. The solution is a trusted third party, a source that both Alice and Bob can trust. This is the idea behind a **key distribution center (KDC).**

Alice and Bob are both clients of the KDC. Alice has established one symmetric key between herself and the center in a secure way, such as going to the center personally. We call Alice's symmetric key K_A. Bob has done the same; we call his symmetric key K_B.

First Approach Using a KDC   Let us see how a KDC can create a session key K_{AB} between Alice and Bob. Figure 28.21 shows the steps.

Figure 28.21   *First approach using KDC*

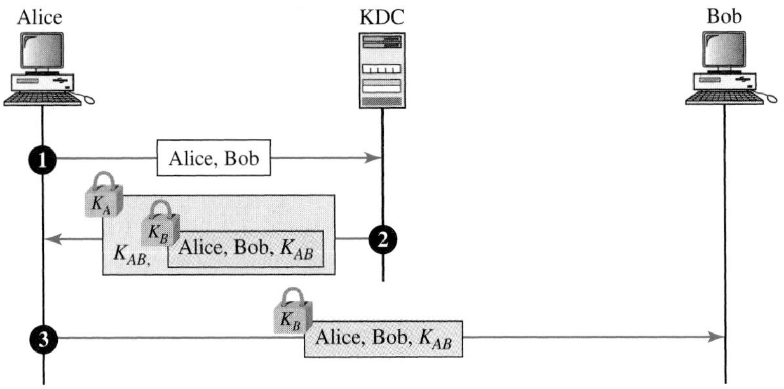

- ❏ **Step 1**   Alice sends a plaintext message to the KDC to obtain a symmetric session key between Bob and herself. The message contains her registered identity (the word *Alice* in the figure) and the identity of Bob (the word *Bob* in the figure). This message is not encrypted; it is public. KDC does not care.
- ❏ **Step 2**   KDC receives the message and creates what is called a **ticket.** The ticket is encrypted using Bob's key (K_B). The ticket contains the identities of Alice and Bob and the session key (K_{AB}). The ticket with a copy of the session key is sent to Alice. Note that Alice receives the message, decrypts it, and extracts the session key. She cannot decrypt Bob's ticket; the ticket is for Bob, not for Alice. Note also that we have a double encryption in this message; the ticket is encrypted, as well as the entire message.
- ❏ **Step 3**   Alice sends the ticket to Bob. Bob opens the ticket and knows that Alice needs to send messages to him using K_{AB} as the session key.

❏ **Sending data.**   After the third step, Alice and Bob can exchange data using K_{AB} as a one-time session key. Eve can use the replay attack we discussed previously. She can save the message in step 3 as well as the data messages and replay all.

Needham-Schroeder Protocol   Another approach is the elegant **Needham-Schroeder protocol,** a foundation for many other protocols. This protocol uses multiple challenge-response interactions between parties to achieve a flawless protocol. In the latest version of this protocol, Needham and Schroeder use four different nonces: R_A, R_B, R_1, and R_2. Figure 28.22 shows the seven steps of this protocol.

Figure 28.22   *Needham-Schroeder protocol*

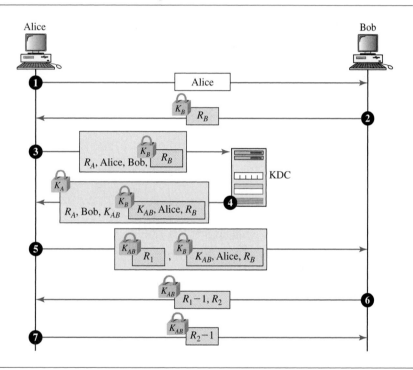

The following are brief descriptions of each step:

❏ **Step 1**   Alice sends her identity to Bob, thereby declaring that she needs to talk to him.

❏ **Step 2**   Bob uses nonce R_B and encrypts it with his symmetric key K_B. Nonce R_B is intended for the KDC, but it is sent to Alice. Alice sends R_B to the KDC to prove that the person who has talked to Bob is the same person (not an imposter) who will talk to the KDC.

❏ **Step 3**   Alice sends a message to the KDC that includes her nonce, R_A, her identity, Bob's identity, and the encrypted nonce from Bob.

❑ **Step 4**   The KDC sends an encrypted message to Alice that includes Alice's nonce, Bob's identity, the session key, and an encrypted ticket for Bob that includes his nonce. Now Alice has received the response to her nonce challenge and the session key.

❑ **Step 5**   Alice sends Bob's ticket to him along with a new nonce, R_1, to challenge him.

❑ **Step 6**   Bob responds to Alice's challenge and sends his challenge to Alice (R_2). Note that the response to Alice's challenge is the value $R_1 - 1$; this ensures that Bob has decrypted the encrypted R_1. In other words, the new encryption ensures that an imposter has not sent the exact encrypted message back.

❑ **Step 7**   Alice responds to Bob's challenge. Again, note that the response carries $R_2 - 1$ instead of R_2.

Otway-Rees Protocol   A third approach is the **Otway-Rees protocol,** another elegant protocol, that has fewer steps. Figure 28.23 shows this five-step protocol. The following briefly describes the steps.

Figure 28.23   *Otway-Rees protocol*

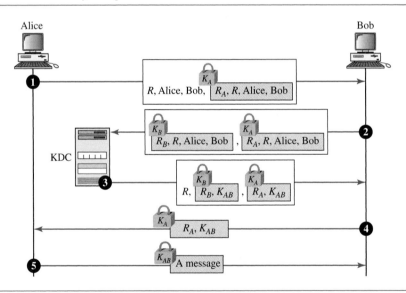

❑ **Step 1**   Alice sends a message to Bob that includes a common nonce R, the identities of Alice and Bob, and a ticket for KDC that includes Alice's nonce R_A (a challenge for KDC to use), a copy of the common nonce R, and the identities of Alice and Bob.

❑ **Step 2**   Bob creates the same type of ticket, but with his own nonce R_B; both tickets are sent to KDC.

❑ **Step 3**   KDC creates a message that contains R, the common nonce, a ticket for Alice and a ticket for Bob; the message is sent to Bob. The tickets contain the corresponding nonce, R_A or R_B, and the session key K_{AB}.

❏ **Step 4**   Bob sends Alice her ticket.

❏ **Step 5**   Alice sends a message encrypted with her session key K_{AB}.

Public-Key Certification

In public-key cryptography, people do not need to know a symmetric shared key. If Alice wants to send a message to Bob, she only needs to know Bob's public key, which is open to the public and available to everyone. If Bob needs to send a message to Alice, he only needs to know Alice's public key, which is also known to everyone. In public-key cryptography, everyone shields a private key and advertises a public key.

> **In public-key cryptography, everyone has access to everyone's public key.**

The Problem

In public-key cryptography, everybody who expects to receive a message from someone else needs to somehow advertise his or her public key to the sender of the message. The problem is how to advertise the public key and make it safe from Eve's interference. If Bob sends his public key to Alice, Eve may intercept it and send her (Eve's) own public key to Alice. Alice, assuming that this is Bob's public key, encrypts a message for Bob with this key and sends it to Bob. Eve again intercepts and decrypts the message with her private key and knows what Alice has sent to Bob. Eve can even put her public key online and claim that this is Bob's public key.

Certification Authority

Bob wants two things: He wants people to know his public key, and he wants no one to accept a public key forged as Bob's. Bob can go to a **certification authority (CA),** a federal or state organization that binds a public key to an entity and issues a certificate. The CA has a well-known public key itself that cannot be forged. The CA checks Bob's identification (using a picture ID along with other proof). It then asks for Bob's public key and writes it on the certificate. To prevent the certificate itself from getting forged, the CA creates a message digest from the certificate and encrypts the message digest with its private key. Now Bob can publicly announce the certificate as plaintext and the encrypted message digest. Anybody who wants Bob's public key gets the certificate and the encrypted digest. A digest can then be created from the certificate; the encrypted digest is decrypted with the CA's public key. The two digests are then compared. If they are equal, the certificate is valid and no imposter has posed as Bob.

X.509

Although the use of a CA has solved the problem of public-key fraud, it has created a side effect. Each certificate may have a different format. If Alice wants to use a program to automatically download different certificates and digests belonging to different people, the program may not be able to do so. One certificate may have the public key in one format and another in another format. The public key may be in the first line in one certificate, and in the third line in another. Anything that needs to be used universally must have a universal format.

To remove this side effect, ITU has devised a protocol called **X.509,** which has been accepted by the Internet with some changes. Protocol X.509 is a way to describe the certificate in a structural way. It uses a well-known protocol called ASN.1 (Abstract Syntax Notation 1) that we discussed in Chapter 21. Some of the fields and their meanings defined by X.509 are listed in Table 28.1.

Table 28.1 *X.509 fields*

Field	Explanation
Version	Version number of X.509
Serial number	The unique identifier used by the CA
Signature	The certificate signature
Issuer	The name of the CA defined by X.509
Validity period	Start and end period that certificate is valid
Subject name	The entity whose public key is being certified
Public key	The subject public key and the algorithms that use it

Public-Key Infrastructure (PKI)

When we want to use public keys universally, we have a problem similar to one concerning DNS (Domain Name System) in Chapter 17. We found that we cannot have only one DNS server to answer the queries. We need many servers. In addition, we found that the best solution is to put the servers in a hierarchical relationship. If Alice needs to get Bob's IP address, Alice sends a message to her local server that may or may not have Bob's IP address. The local server can consult its parent server, up to the root, until the IP address is found.

Likewise, a solution to public-key queries is a hierarchical structure called a **public-key infrastructure (PKI).** Figure 28.24 shows an example of this hierarchy.

Figure 28.24 *PKI hierarchy*

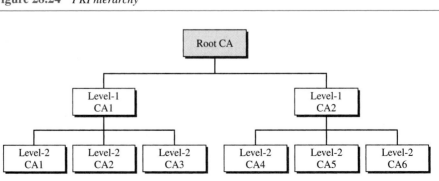

At the first level, we can have a root CA that can certify the performance of CAs in the second level; these level-1 CAs may operate in a large geographic area or logical area. The level-2 CAs may operate in smaller geographic areas.

In this hierarchy, everybody trusts the root. But people may or may not trust intermediate CAs. If Alice needs to get Bob's certificate, she may find a CA somewhere to issue the certificate. But Alice may not trust that CA. In a hierarchy Alice can ask the next-higher CA to certify the original CA. The inquiry may go all the way to the root.

PKI is a new issue in the Internet. It will undoubtedly broaden in scope and change in the next few years.

Kerberos

Kerberos is an authentication protocol, and at the same time a KDC, that has become very popular. Several systems including Windows 2000 use Kerberos. Kerberos is named after the three-headed dog in Greek mythology that guards the gates of Hades. Originally designed at MIT, it has gone through several versions. We discuss only version 4, the most popular, and we briefly explain the difference between version 4 and version 5, the latest.

Servers

Three servers are involved in the Kerberos protocol: an **authentication server (AS),** a **ticket-granting server (TGS),** and a real (data) server that provides services to others. In our examples and figures, *Bob* is the real server and *Alice* is the entity requesting service. Figure 28.25 shows the relationship between these three servers.

Figure 28.25 *Kerberos servers*

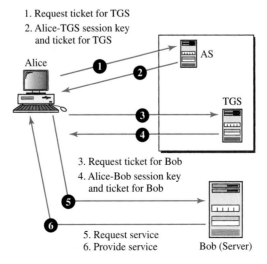

1. Request ticket for TGS
2. Alice-TGS session key and ticket for TGS

Alice

AS

TGS

3. Request ticket for Bob
4. Alice-Bob session key and ticket for Bob

5. Request service
6. Provide service

Bob (Server)

Authentication Server (AS)   The AS is the KDC in the Kerberos protocol. Each entity registers with the AS and is granted an identity and a password. The AS has a database with these identities and the corresponding passwords. The AS verifies the entity, issues a session key to be used between Alice and the TGS, and sends a ticket for the TGS.

Ticket-Granting Server (TGS)   The TGS issues a ticket for the real server (Bob). It also provides the session key (K_{AB}) between Alice and Bob. Kerberos has separated the entity verification from ticket issuing. In this way, although Alice verifies her ID just once with AS, she can contact TGS multiple times to obtain tickets for different real servers.

Real Server   The real server (Bob) provides services for the entity (Alice). Kerberos is designed for a client-server program such as FTP, in which an entity uses the client process to access the server process. Kerberos is not used for person-to-person authentication.

Operation

A client process (Alice) can receive a service from a process running on the real server (Bob) in six steps, as shown in Figure 28.26.

Figure 28.26   *Kerberos example*

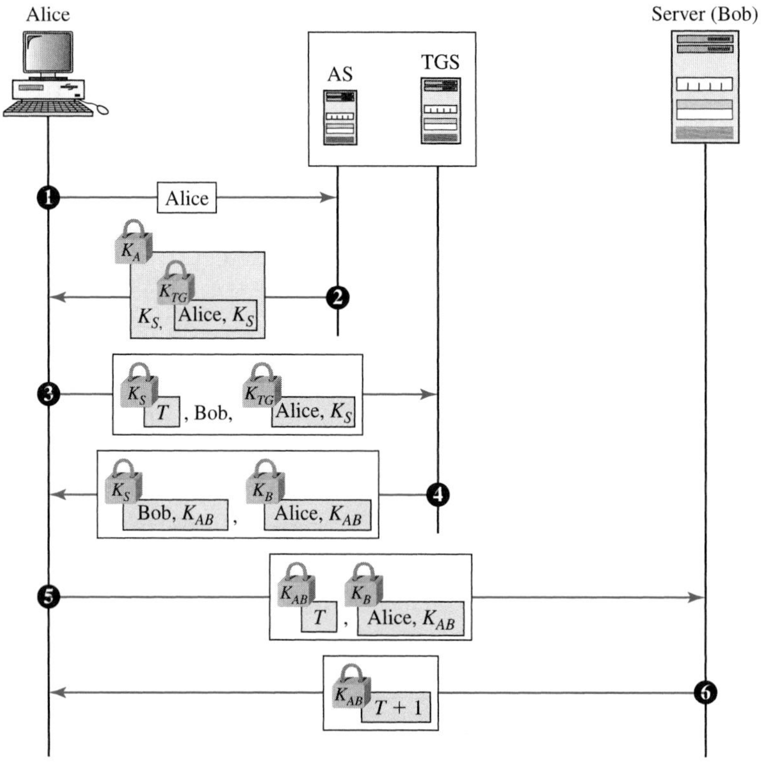

❏ **Step 1** Alice sends her request to AS in plaintext, using her registered identity.

❏ **Step 2** The AS sends a message encrypted with Alice's symmetric key K_A. The message contains two items: a session key K_S that is used by Alice to contact TGS and a ticket for TGS that is encrypted with the TGS symmetric key K_{TG}. Alice does not know K_A, but when the message arrives, she types her password. The password and the appropriate algorithm together create K_A if the password is correct. The password is then immediately destroyed; it is not sent to the network, and it does not stay in the terminal. It is only used for a moment to create K_A. The process now uses K_A to decrypt the message sent; K_S and the ticket are extracted.

❏ **Step 3** Alice now sends three items to the TGS. The first is the ticket received from AS. The second is the name of the real server (Bob), and the third is a timestamp which is encrypted by K_S. The timestamp prevents a replay by Eve.

❏ **Step 4** Now, TGS sends two tickets, each containing the session key between Alice and Bob K_{AB}. The ticket for Alice is encrypted with K_S; the ticket for Bob is encrypted with Bob's key K_B. Note that Eve cannot extract K_{AB} because she does not know K_S or K_B. She cannot replay step 3 because she cannot replace the timestamp with a new one (she does not know K_S). Even if she is very quick and sends the step 3 message before the timestamp has expired, she still receives the same two tickets that she cannot decipher.

❏ **Step 5** Alice sends Bob's ticket with the timestamp encrypted with K_{AB}.

❏ **Step 6** Bob confirms the receipt by adding 1 to the timestamp. The message is encrypted with K_{AB} and sent to Alice.

Using Different Servers

Note that if Alice needs to receive services from different servers, she need repeat only the last four steps. The first two steps have verified Alice's identity and need not be repeated. Alice can ask the TGS to issue tickets for multiple servers by repeating steps 3 to 6.

Kerberos Version 5

The minor differences between version 4 and version 5 are briefly listed below:

1. Version 5 has a longer ticket lifetime.
2. Version 5 allows tickets to be renewed.
3. Version 5 can accept any symmetric-key algorithm.
4. Version 5 uses a different protocol for describing data types.
5. Version 5 has more overhead than version 4.

Realms

Kerberos allows the global distribution of ASs and TGSs, with each system called a **realm.** An entity may get a ticket for a local server or a distant server. In the second case, for example, Alice may ask her local TGS to issue a ticket that is accepted by a distant TGS. The local TGS can issue this ticket if the distant TGS is registered with the local one. Then Alice can use the distant TGS to access the distant real server.

28.6   SECURITY IN THE INTERNET

All the security principles and concepts discussed so far can be used to provide all aspects of security for the Internet model. In particular, security measures can be applied to the network layer, transport layer, and application layer.

At the IP layer, implementation of security features is very complicated, especially since every device must be enabled. IP provides services not only for user applications, but also for other protocols such as OSPF, ICMP, and IGMP. This means that implementation of security at this level is not very effective unless all devices are equipped to use it. We discuss a protocol called IPSec that provides security at the IP level.

At the transport layer, security is even more complicated. We could modify the application or modify the transport layer for security. Instead, we discuss a protocol that "glues" a new layer to the transport layer to provide security on behalf of the transport layer.

At the application layer, each application is responsible for providing security. The implementation of security at this level is the simplest. It concerns two entities: the client and the server. We discuss a security method at the application layer called PGP.

IP Level Security: IPSec

IP Security (IPSec) is a collection of protocols designed by the IETF (Internet Engineering Task Force) to provide security for a packet at the IP level. IPSec does not define the use of any specific encryption or authentication method. Instead, it provides a framework and a mechanism; it leaves the selection of the encryption, authentication, and hashing methods to the entity.

Security Association

IPSec requires a logical connection between two hosts using a *signaling protocol,* called **Security Association (SA).** In other words, IPSec needs the connectionless IP protocol changed to a connection-oriented protocol before security can be applied. An SA connection is a simplex (unidirectional) connection between a source and destination. If a duplex (bidirectional) connection is needed, two SA connections are required, one in each direction. An SA connection is uniquely defined by three elements:

1. A 32-bit security parameter index (SPI), which acts as a virtual circuit identifier in connection-oriented protocols such as Frame Relay or ATM.
2. The type of the protocol used for security. We will see shortly that IPSec defines two alternative protocols: AH and ESP.
3. The source IP address.

Two Modes

IPSec operates at two different modes: transport mode and tunnel mode. The mode defines where the IPSec header is added to the IP packet.

Transport Mode   In this mode, the IPSec header is added between the IP header and the rest of the packet, as shown in Figure 28.27.

Figure 28.27   *Transport mode*

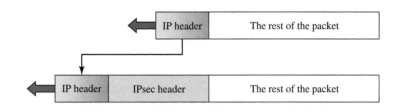

Tunnel Mode   In this mode, the IPSec header is placed in front of the original IP header. A new IP header is added in front. The IPSec header, the preserved IP header, and the rest of the packet are treated as the payload. Figure 28.28 shows the original and the new IP packet.

Figure 28.28   *Tunnel mode*

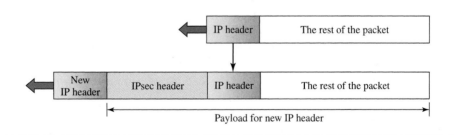

Two Security Protocols

IPSec defines two protocols: Authentication Header (AH) protocol and Encapsulating Security Payload (ESP) protocol. We discuss both of these protocols here.

Authentication Header (AH) Protocol   The **Authentication Header (AH) protocol** is designed to authenticate the source host and to ensure the integrity of the payload carried by the IP packet. The protocol calculates a message digest, using a hashing function and a symmetric key, and inserts the digest in the authentication header. The AH is put in the appropriate location based on the mode (transport or tunnel). Figure 28.29 shows the fields and the position of the authentication header in the transport mode.

Figure 28.29 *AH*

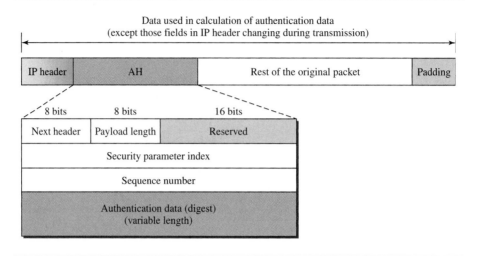

When an IP datagram carries an authentication header, the original value in the protocol field of the IP header is replaced by the value 51. A field inside the authentication header (next header field) defines the original value of the protocol field (the type of payload being carried by the IP datagram). Addition of an authentication header follows these steps:

1. An authentication header is added to the payload with the authentication data field set to zero.
2. Padding may be added to make the total length even for a particular hashing algorithm.
3. Hashing is based on the total packet. However, only those fields of the IP header that do not change during transmission are included in the calculation of the message digest (authentication data).
4. The authentication data are included in the authentication header.
5. The IP header is added after changing the value of the protocol field to 51.

A brief description of each field follows:

❏ **Next header.** The 8-bit next-header field defines the type of payload carried by the IP datagram (TCP, UDP, ICMP, OSPF, and so on). It has the same function as the protocol field in the IP header before encapsulation. In other words, the process copies the value of the protocol field in the IP datagram to this field. The value of the protocol field in the IP datagram is changed to 51 to show that the packet carries an authentication header.

❏ **Payload length.** The name of this 8-bit payload-length field is misleading. It does not define the length of the payload; it defines the length of the authentication header in 4-byte multiples, but it does not include the first 8 bytes.

❑ **Security parameter index.** The 32-bit security parameter index (SPI) field plays the role of a virtual circuit identifier and is constant for all packets sent during a Security Association connection.

❑ **Sequence number.** A 32-bit sequence number provides ordering information for a sequence of datagrams. The sequence numbers prevent playback. Note that the sequence number is not repeated even if a packet is retransmitted. A sequence number does not wrap around after it reaches 2^{32}; a new connection must be established.

❑ **Authentication data.** Finally, the authentication data field is the result of applying a hash function to the entire IP datagram except for the fields that are changed during transit (e.g., time-to-live).

The AH protocol provides message authentication and integrity, but not privacy.

Encapsulating Security Payload   The AH protocol does not provide privacy, only message authentication and integrity. IPSec later defined an alternative protocol that provides message authentication, integrity, and privacy called **Encapsulating Security Payload (ESP).** ESP adds a header and trailer. Note that ESP's authentication data are added at the end of packet which makes its calculation easier. Figure 28.30 shows the location of the ESP header and trailer.

Figure 28.30   *ESP*

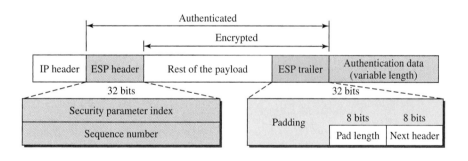

When an IP datagram carries an ESP header and trailer, the value of the protocol field in the IP header changes to 50. A field inside the ESP trailer (the next-header field) holds the original value of the protocol field (the type of payload being carried by the IP datagram, such as TCP or UDP). The ESP procedure follows these steps:

1. An ESP trailer is added to the payload.
2. The payload and the trailer are encrypted.
3. The ESP header is added.
4. The ESP header, payload, and ESP trailer are used to create the authentication data.
5. The authentication data are added at the end of the ESP trailer.
6. The IP header is added after changing the protocol value to 50.

The fields for the header and trailer are as follows:

❏ **Security parameter index.** The 32-bit security parameter index field is similar to that defined for the AH protocol.

❏ **Sequence number.** The 32-bit sequence number field is similar to that defined for the AH protocol.

❏ **Padding.** This variable-length field (0 to 255 bytes) of 0s serves as padding.

❏ **Pad length.** The 8-bit pad length field defines the number of padding bytes. The value is between 0 and 255; the maximum value is rare.

❏ **Next header.** The 8-bit next-header field is similar to that defined in the AH protocol. It serves the same purpose as the protocol field in the IP header before encapsulation.

❏ **Authentication data.** Finally, the authentication data field is the result of applying an authentication scheme to parts of the datagram. Note the difference between the authentication data in AH and ESP. In AH, part of the IP header is included in the calculation of the authentication data; in ESP, it is not.

ESP provides message authentication, integrity, and privacy.

IPv4 and IPv6   IPSec supports both IPv4 and IPv6. In IPv6, however, AH and ESP are part of the extension header.

AH versus ESP   The ESP protocol was designed after the AH protocol was already in use. ESP does whatever AH does with additional functionality (privacy). The question is why do we need AH? The answer is that we don't. However, the implementation of AH is already included in some commercial products, which means that AH will remain part of the Internet until these products are phased out.

Transport Layer Security

Transport Layer Security (TLS) was designed to provide security at the transport layer. TLS was derived from a security protocol called Secure Sockets Layer (SSL), designed by Netscape to provide security on the WWW. TLS is a nonproprietary version of SSL designed by IETF. For transactions on the Internet, a browser needs the following:

1. The customer needs to be sure that the server belongs to the actual vendor, not an imposter. For example, a customer does not want to give an imposter her credit card number. In other words, the server must be authenticated.

2. The customer needs to be sure that the contents of the message are not modified during transition. A bill for $100 must not be changed to $1000. The integrity of the message must be preserved.

3. The customer needs to be sure that an imposter does not intercept sensitive information such as a credit card number. There is a need for privacy.

There are other optional security aspects that can be added to the above list. For example, the vendor may need to authenticate the customer. TLS can provide additional features to cover these aspects of security.

Position of TLS

TLS lies between the application layer and the transport layer (TCP), as shown in Figure 28.31.

Figure 28.31   *Position of TLS*

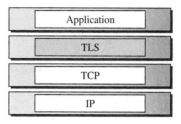

The application layer protocol, in this case HTTP, uses the services of TLS, and TLS uses the services of the transport layer.

General Idea

TLS allows two parties to exchange messages in a secure environment. To accomplish this goal, TLS requires that

1. Two parties agree on three protocols: an entity authentication protocol, a message authentication protocol, and an encryption/decryption protocol.
2. The entity authentication protocol is used to authenticate two parties to each other and establish a secret between them.
3. Each party uses a predefined function to create session keys and parameters for the message authentication protocol and encryption/decryption protocol.
4. A digest is calculated and appended to each message to be exchanged using the message authentication protocol and the corresponding keys/parameters.
5. The message and digest are encrypted using the encryption/decryption protocol and the corresponding keys/parameters.
6. Each party extracts the necessary keys and parameters needed for the message authentication and encryption/decryption.

Two Layers

TLS has two layers. The top layer includes three protocols, one for session setup (handshaking), one for alerting the other party of an unusual situation, and one for informing the establishment of security parameters. The lower layer, the record protocol, is used to encapsulate messages from the upper layer and the application layer. Figure 28.32 shows the two layers.

Handshake Protocol   The handshake protocol uses several messages; they authenticate the client for the server and the server for the client, negotiate the encryption cipher and hash algorithm, and create cryptographic keys for data exchange. The handshaking is done in four phases as shown in Figure 28.33.

Figure 28.32   *TLS layers*

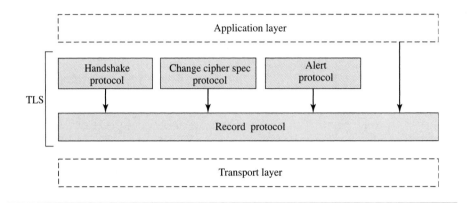

Figure 28.33   *Handshake protocol*

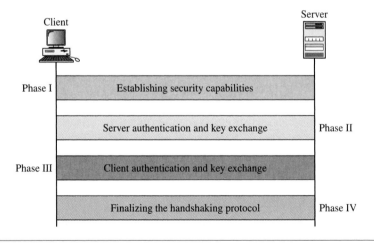

❑ **Phase I**   In Phase I, the client and the server announce their security capabilities and choose those that are agreeable to both. In this phase, a session ID is established, and a cipher suite is chosen. A compression method is agreed upon. Finally, two random numbers are selected, one by the client and one by the server, for creating security parameters.

❑ **Phase II**   In phase II, the server authenticates itself. The server may send its certificate, its public key, and may also request a certificate from the client.

❑ **Phase III**   Phase III is designed to authenticate the client if required by the server. Depending on the selection of the cipher suite, the client may send a secret number, called a pre-master secret to be used for calculating the session keys.

❏ **Phase IV**   In Phase IV, the client and server send messages to establish cipher specifications, which allow them to start using the keys and parameters.

Change Cipher Spec Protocol   This protocol is designed to activate the security services (message authentication and encryption/decryption) after all of the agreements are confirmed in the handshake protocol. After exchanging the one message defined in this protocol, the two parties can use the services.

Alert Protocol   The Alert Protocol is used to signal an error or a potential error to other party. The packet exchanged defines the severity level of the condition (warning or error) and the description of the alert.

Record Protocol   The Record Protocol accepts a message (or a fragment of a message if it is large) from the application layer or other three protocols, compresses it (optional), creates a digest out of it, encrypts it, and adds the record protocol header to it. The result is delivered to TCP for transmission as shown in Figure 28.34.

Figure 28.34   *Record Protocol*

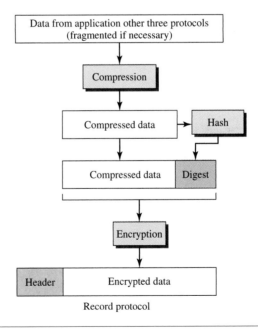

Record protocol

However, note that some of the messages from the three other protocols cannot be compressed, authenticated, or encrypted because, at the time the message is sent, the cipher suite and the parameters may have not been negotiated. These messages simply bypass the steps shown in the figure.

Application Layer Security: PGP

The implementation of security at the application layer is more feasible and simpler, particularly when the Internet communication involves only two parties, as in the case of email and TELNET. The sender and the receiver can agree to use the same protocol and to use any type of security services they desire. In this section, we discuss one protocol used at the application layer to provide security: PGP.

Pretty Good Privacy (PGP) was invented by Phil Zimmermann to provide all four aspects of security (privacy, integrity, authentication, and nonrepudiation) in the sending of email.

PGP uses digital signature (a combination of hashing and public-key encryption) to provide integrity, authentication, and nonrepudiation. It uses a combination of secret-key and public-key encryption to provide privacy. Specifically, it uses one hash function, one secret key, and two private-public key pairs. See Figure 28.35.

Figure 28.35   *PGP at the sender site*

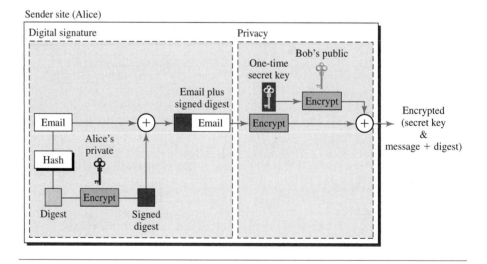

The figure shows how PGP creates secure email at the sender site. The email message is hashed to create a digest. The digest is encrypted (signed) using Alice's private key. The message and the digest are encrypted using the one-time secret key created by Alice. The secret key is encrypted using Bob's public key and is sent together with the encrypted combination of message and digest.

Figure 28.36 shows how PGP uses hashing and a combination of three keys to extract the original message at the receiver site.

The combination of encrypted secret key and message plus digest is received. The encrypted secret key first is decrypted (using Bob's private key) to get the one-time secret key created by Alice. The secret key then is used to decrypt the combination of the message plus digest.

Figure 28.36 *PGP at the receiver site*

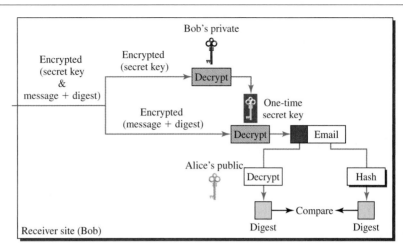

28.7   FIREWALLS

All previous security measures cannot prevent Eve from sending a harmful message to a system. To control access to a system we need firewalls. A **firewall** is a device (usually a router or a computer) installed between the internal network of an organization and the rest of the Internet. It is designed to forward some packets and filter (not forward) others. Figure 28.37 shows a firewall.

Figure 28.37 *Firewall*

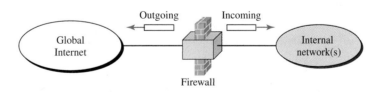

For example, a firewall may filter all incoming packets destined for a specific host or a specific server such as HTTP. A firewall can be used to deny access to a specific host or a specific service in the organization.

A firewall is usually classified as a packet-filter firewall or a proxy-based firewall.

Packet-Filter Firewall

A firewall can be used as a packet filter. It can forward or block packets based on the information in the network layer and transport layer headers: source and destination

IP addresses, source and destination port addresses, and type of protocol (TCP or UDP). A **packet-filter firewall** is a router that uses a filtering table to decide which packets must be discarded (not forwarded). Figure 28.38 shows an example of a filtering table for this kind of a firewall.

Figure 28.38   *Packet-filter firewall*

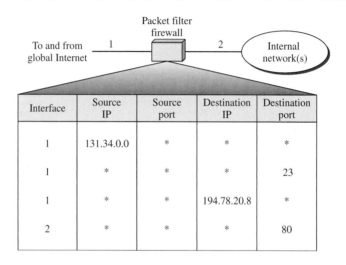

Interface	Source IP	Source port	Destination IP	Destination port
1	131.34.0.0	*	*	*
1	*	*	*	23
1	*	*	194.78.20.8	*
2	*	*	*	80

According to the figure, the following packets are filtered:

1. Incoming packets from network 131.34.0.0. are blocked (security precaution). Note that the * (asterisk) means "any."

2. Incoming packets destined for any internal TELNET server (port 23) are blocked.

3. Incoming packets destined for internal host 194.78.20.8. are blocked. The organization wants this host for internal use only.

4. Outgoing packets destined for an HTTP server (port 80) are blocked. The organization does not want employees to browse the Internet.

> **A packet-filter firewall filters at the network or transport layer.**

Proxy Firewall

The packet-filter firewall is based on the information available in the network layer and transport layer headers (IP and TCP/UDP). However, sometimes we need to filter a message based on the information available in the message itself (at the application layer). As an example, assume that an organization wants to implement the following policies regarding its Web pages: Only those Internet users who have previously established business relations with the company can have access; access to other users must be blocked. In this case, a packet-filter firewall is not feasible because it cannot distinguish between different packets arriving at TCP port 80 (HTTP). Testing must be done at the application level (using URLs).

One solution is to install a proxy computer (sometimes called an application gateway), which stands between the customer computer and the corporation computer. When the user client process sends a message, the application gateway runs a server process to receive the request. The server opens the packet at the application level and finds out if the request is legitimate. If it is, the server acts as a client process and sends the message to the real server in the corporation. If it is not, the message is dropped and an error message is sent to the external user. In this way, the requests of the external users are filtered based on the contents at the application layer. Figure 28.39 shows an application gateway implementation for HTTP.

Figure 28.39 *Proxy firewall*

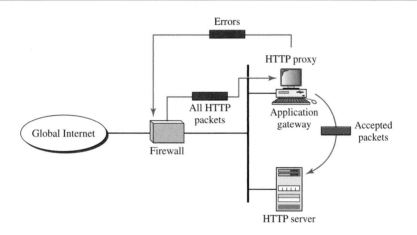

A proxy firewall filters at the application layer.

28.8 KEY TERMS

Authentication Header (AH) protocol	cryptography
authentication server (AS)	Data Encryption Standard (DES)
bidirectional authentication	decryption
block cipher	digest
certification authority (CA)	digital signature
cipher	Encapsulating Security Payload (ESP)
ciphertext	entity authentication

firewall	private key
handshake protocol	proxy firewall
hash function	public key
IP Security (IPSec)	public-key cryptography
Kerberos	public-key infrastructure
key	realm
key distribution center (KDC)	reflection attack
man-in-the-middle attack	replay attack
message authentication	RSA method
message integrity	Security Association (SA)
n^2 problem	substitution
Needham-Schroeder protocol	symmetric-key cryptography
nonce	ticket
nonrepudiation	ticket-granting server (TGS)
Otway-Rees protocol	Transport Layer Security (TLS)
packet-filter firewall	transpositional cipher
plaintext	triple DES
Pretty Good Privacy (PGP)	X.509
privacy	

28.9   SUMMARY

❑ Cryptography is the science and art of transforming messages to make them secure and immune to attack.

❑ Encryption renders a message (plaintext) unintelligible to unauthorized personnel.

❑ Decryption transforms an intentionally unintelligible message (ciphertext) into meaningful information.

❑ Cryptography algorithms are classified as either symmetric-key methods or public-key methods.

❑ In symmetric-key cryptography the same secret key is used by the sender and the receiver.

❑ DES is a symmetric-key method adopted by the United States.

❑ In public-key cryptography, the public key is used by the sender to encrypt the message; the private key is used by the receiver to decrypt the message.

❏ One of the commonly used public-key cryptography methods is the RSA algorithm.

❏ The issues involved in single-message security are privacy, authentication, integrity, and nonrepudiation.

❏ Message privacy is achieved through encryption of the plaintext and decryption of the ciphertext.

❏ Message authentication, integrity, and nonrepudiation are achieved through a method called digital signature.

❏ We can use digital signature on the entire message or on a digest of the message. A hash function creates the digest from the original document.

❏ Encryption of a message using a shared symmetric key is vulnerable to a replay attack. The use of a nonce can prevent this type of attack.

❏ The use of symmetric keys for entity authentication requires too many shared keys if the user population is large.

❏ The Diffie-Hellman method provides a one-time session key for two parties. However, it is vulnerable to a man-in-the-middle attack.

❏ A key distribution center (KDC) is a trusted third party that assigns a symmetric key to two parties.

❏ The Needham-Schroeder protocol for user authentication uses multiple challenge-response interactions between communicating parties. The Otway-Rees protocol for user authentication uses even fewer challenge-response interactions.

❏ A certification authority (CA) is a federal or state organization that binds a public key to an entity and issues a certificate.

❏ A public-key infrastructure (PKI) is a hierarchical system to answer queries about key certification.

❏ Kerberos is a popular authentication protocol that requires an authentication server and a ticket-granting server.

❏ Security methods can be applied in the application layer, transport layer, and IP layer.

❏ IP Security (IPSec) is a collection of protocols designed by the IETF to provide security for an Internet packet.

❏ The Authentication Header protocol provides integrity and message authentication.

❏ The Encapsulating Security Payload protocol provides integrity, message authentication, and privacy.

❏ Transport Layer Security (TLS) provides security at the transport layer through its handshake protocol and data exchange protocol.

❏ Pretty Good Privacy (PGP) provides security for the transmission of email.

❏ A firewall is a router installed between the internal network of an organization and the rest of the Internet.

❏ A packet-filter firewall blocks or forwards packets on the basis of information in the network and transport layers.

❏ A proxy firewall blocks or forwards packets based on information in the application layer.

28.10   PRACTICE SET

Exercises

1. Using substitution with key = 4, encrypt the following message

    THIS IS A GOOD EXAMPLE

2. Using substitution with key = 4, decrypt the following message

    IRGVCTXMSR MW JYR

3. Using substitution without knowing the key, decrypt the following message

    KTIXEVZOUT OY ROQK KTIRUYOTM G YKIXKZ OT GT KTBKRUVK

4. Use the following encrypting algorithms to encrypt the message "GOOD DAY."
    a. Replace each character with its ASCII code.
    b. Add a 0 bit at the left to make each character 8 bits long.
    c. Swap the first 4 bits with the last 4 bits.
    d. Replace every 4 bits with its hexadecimal equivalent.
    What is the key in this method?

5. Use the following encrypting algorithm to encrypt the message "ABCADEFGH" (assume that the message is always made of uppercase letters).
    a. Treat each character as a decimal number, using ASCII code (between 65 and 90).
    b. Subtract 65 from each coded character.
    c. Change each number into a 5-bit pattern.

6. Using the RSA algorithm, encrypt and decrypt the message "BE" with key pairs (3, 15) and (5, 15).

7. Given the two prime numbers $p = 19$ and $q = 23$, try to find N, e, and d.

8. To understand the security of the RSA algorithm, find d if you know that $e = 17$ and $N = 187$.

9. In the RSA algorithm, we use $C = P^e \bmod N$ to encrypt a number. If e and N are large numbers (each hundreds of digits), the calculation is impossible and creates an overflow error even in a supercomputer. One solution (not the best one) using number theory involves several steps, where each step uses the result of the previous step:
    a. $C = 1$.
    b. Repeat e times: $C = (C \times P) \bmod N$.
    In this way, a computer program can be written that calculates C using a loop. For example $6^5 \bmod 119$, which is 41, can be calculated as follows:

    $$(1 \times 6) \bmod 119 = 6$$
    $$(6 \times 6) \bmod 119 = 36$$
    $$(36 \times 6) \bmod 119 = 97$$
    $$(97 \times 6) \bmod 119 = 106$$
    $$(106 \times 6) \bmod 119 = 41$$

    Use this method to calculate $227^{16} \bmod 100$.

10. Add a layer of symmetric-key encryption/decryption to Figure 28.12 to provide privacy.

11. Add a layer of public-key encryption/decryption to Figure 28.12 to provide privacy.

12. Show that G^{xy} is the same as $(G^x)^y$ using $G = 11$, $x = 3$, and $y = 4$.

13. Prove that the result of G^{xy} mod N is the same as the result of $(G^x \bmod N)^y$ mod N, using $G = 7$, $x = 2$, $y = 3$, and $N = 11$.

14. The fact that the result of G^{xy} mod N is the same as the result of $(G^x \bmod N)^y$ mod N can tremendously simplify the calculation of G^{xy} mod N. Use this fact to calculate 7^{18} mod 11. *Hint:* Factor 18 and do three calculations.

15. What is the value of the symmetric key in the Diffie-Hellman protocol if $G = 7$, $N = 23$, $x = 3$, and $y = 5$?

16. What are the values of R_1 and R_2 in the Diffie-Hellman protocol if $G = 7$, $N = 23$, $x = 3$, and $y = 5$?

17. In the Diffie-Hellman protocol, what happens if x and y have the same value? That is, have Alice and Bob accidentally chosen the same number? Are the values of R_1 and R_2 the same? Is the value of the session key calculated by Alice and Bob the same? Use an example to prove your claims.

18. In the first approach using KDC, what happens if the ticket for Bob is not encrypted in step 2 with K_B, but is encrypted by K_{AB} in step 3?

19. In the bidirectional approach to authentication, if multiple-session authentication is allowed, Eve intercepts the R_B nonce from Bob (in the second session) and sends it as Alice's nonce for a second session. Bob, without checking that this nonce is the same as the one he sent, encrypts R_B and puts it in a message with his nonce. Eve uses the encrypted R_B and pretends that she is Alice, continuing with the first session and responding with the encrypted R_B. This is called a *reflection attack*. Show the steps in this scenario.

20. Draw AH in the tunnel mode.

21. Draw ESP is used in the tunnel mode.

22. Draw a figure to show the position of AH in IPv6.

23. Draw a figure to show the position of ESP in IPv6.

24. The PGP protocol uses three keys. Explain the purpose of each.

25. Does the PGP protocol need the services of a KDC? Explain your answer.

26. Does the PGP protocol need the services of a CA? Explain your answer.

Research Activities

27. Why is there a need for four nonces in the Needham-Schroeder protocol?

28. In the Needham-Schroeder protocol, how is Alice is authenticated by the KDC? How is Bob authenticated by the KDC? How is the KDC authenticated for Alice? How is the KDC authenticated for Bob? How is Alice authenticated for Bob? How is Bob authenticated for Alice?

29. Can you explain why in the Needham-Schroeder protocol, Alice is the party that is in contact with the KDC; but in the Otway-Rees protocol, Bob is the party that is in contact with the KDC?

30. There are four nonces (R_A, R_B, R_1, and R_2) in the Needham-Schroeder protocol, but only three nonces (R_A, R_B, and R_1) in the Otway-Rees protocol. Can you explain why there is a need for one extra nonce, R_2, in the first protocol?

31. Why do we need only one timestamp in Kerberos instead of four nonces in Needham-Schroeder or three nonces in Otway-Rees?

32. Find information about a symmetric-key cipher called AES.

33. Find information about a public-key cipher called ElGamal.

34. The digital signature scheme discussed in this chapter is based on RSA. Find information about a digital signature scheme called ElGamal.

APPENDIX A

ASCII Code

The American Standard Code for Information Interchange (ASCII) is the most commonly used code for encoding printable and nonprintable (control) characters.

ASCII uses seven bits to encode each character. It can therefore represent up to 128 characters. Table A.1 lists the ASCII characters and their codes in both binary and hexadecimal form.

Table A.1 *ASCII table*

Decimal	Hexadecimal	Binary	Character	Description
0	00	0000000	NUL	Null
1	01	0000001	SOH	Start of header
2	02	0000010	STX	Start of text
3	03	0000011	ETX	End of text
4	04	0000100	EOT	End of transmission
5	05	0000101	ENQ	Enquiry
6	06	0000110	ACK	Acknowledgment
7	07	0000111	BEL	Bell
8	08	0001000	BS	Backspace
9	09	0001001	HT	Horizontal tab
10	0A	0001010	LF	Line feed
11	0B	0001011	VT	Vertical tab
12	0C	0001100	FF	Form feed
13	0D	0001101	CR	Carriage return
14	0E	0001110	SO	Shift out
15	0F	0001111	SI	Shift in
16	10	0010000	DLE	Data link escape

Table A.1   *ASCII table (continued)*

Decimal	Hexadecimal	Binary	Character	Description
17	11	0010001	DC1	Device control 1
18	12	0010010	DC2	Device control 2
19	13	0010011	DC3	Device control 3
20	14	0010100	DC4	Device control 4
21	15	0010101	NAK	Negative acknowledgment
22	16	0010110	SYN	Synchronous idle
23	17	0010111	ETB	End of transmission block
24	18	0011000	CAN	Cancel
25	19	0011001	EM	End of medium
26	1A	0011010	SUB	Substitute
27	1B	0011011	ESC	Escape
28	1C	0011100	FS	File separator
29	1D	0011101	GS	Group separator
30	1E	0011110	RS	Record separator
31	1F	0011111	US	Unit separator
32	20	0100000	SP	Space
33	21	0100001	!	Exclamation mark
34	22	0100010	"	Double quote
35	23	0100011	#	Pound sign
36	24	0100100	$	Dollar sign
37	25	0100101	%	Percent sign
38	26	0100110	&	Ampersand
39	27	0100111	'	Apostrophe
40	28	0101000	(	Open parenthesis
41	29	0101001	)	Close parenthesis
42	2A	0101010	*	Asterisk
43	2B	0101011	+	Plus sign
44	2C	0101100	,	Comma
45	2D	0101101	-	Hyphen
46	2E	0101110	.	Period
47	2F	0101111	/	Slash
48	30	0110000	0	
49	31	0110001	1	
50	32	0110010	2	

Table A.1   *ASCII table (continued)*

Decimal	Hexadecimal	Binary	Character	Description
51	33	0110011	3	
52	34	0110100	4	
53	35	0110101	5	
54	36	0110110	6	
55	37	0110111	7	
56	38	0111000	8	
57	39	0111001	9	
58	3A	0111010	:	Colon
59	3B	0111011	;	Semicolon
60	3C	0111100	<	Less than sign
61	3D	0111101	=	Equal sign
62	3E	0111110	>	Greater than sign
63	3F	0111111	?	Question mark
64	40	1000000	@	At sign
65	41	1000001	A	
66	42	1000010	B	
67	43	1000011	C	
68	44	1000100	D	
69	45	1000101	E	
70	46	1000110	F	
71	47	1000111	G	
72	48	1001000	H	
73	49	1001001	I	
74	4A	1001010	J	
75	4B	1001011	K	
76	4C	1001100	L	
77	4D	1001101	M	
78	4E	1001110	N	
79	4F	1001111	O	
80	50	1010000	P	
81	51	1010001	Q	
82	52	1010010	R	
83	53	1010011	S	
84	54	1010100	T	

Table A.1   *ASCII table (continued)*

Decimal	Hexadecimal	Binary	Character	Description
85	55	1010101	U	
86	56	1010110	V	
87	57	1010111	W	
88	58	1011000	X	
89	59	1011001	Y	
90	5A	1011010	Z	
91	5B	1011011	[	Open bracket
92	5C	1011100	\	Backslash
93	5D	1011101	]	Close bracket
94	5E	1011110	^	Caret
95	5F	1011111	_	Underscore
96	60	1100000	`	Grave accent
97	61	1100001	a	
98	62	1100010	b	
99	63	1100011	c	
100	64	1100100	d	
101	65	1100101	e	
102	66	1100110	f	
103	67	1100111	g	
104	68	1101000	h	
105	69	1101001	i	
106	6A	1101010	j	
107	6B	1101011	k	
108	6C	1101100	l	
109	6D	1101101	m	
110	6E	1101110	n	
111	6F	1101111	o	
112	70	1110000	p	
113	71	1110001	q	
114	72	1110010	r	
115	73	1110011	s	
116	74	1110100	t	
117	75	1110101	u	
118	76	1110110	v	

Table A.1 *ASCII table (concluded)*

Decimal	Hexadecimal	Binary	Character	Description
119	77	1110111	w	
120	78	1111000	x	
121	79	1111001	y	
122	7A	1111010	z	
123	7B	1111011	{	Open brace
124	7C	1111100	|	Bar
125	7D	1111101	}	Close brace
126	7E	1111110	~	Tilde
127	7F	1111111	DEL	Delete

APPENDIX B

Numbering Systems

We use different numbering systems: base 10 (decimal), base 2 (binary), base 8 (octal), base 16 (hexadecimal), base 256, and so on. All of the numbering systems examined here are positional, meaning that the position of a symbol in relation to other symbols determines its value. Each symbol in a number has a position. The position traditionally starts from 0 and goes to $n - 1$, where n is the number of symbols. For example, in Figure B.1, the decimal number 14782 has five symbols in positions 0 to 4.

Figure B.1   *Positions and symbols in a number*

Decimal Number: 14782

1	4	7	8	2	Symbols
4	3	2	1	0	Positions

As we will see, the difference between different numbering system is based on the *weight* assigned to each position.

B.1   BASE 10: DECIMAL

The base 10 or decimal system is the one most familiar to us in everyday life. All of our terms for indicating countable quantities are based on it, and, in fact, when we speak of other numbering systems, we tend to refer to their quantities by their decimal equivalents. The term *decimal* is derived from the Latin stem *deci,* meaning ten. The decimal system uses 10 symbols to represent quantitative values: 0, 1, 2, 3, 4, 5, 6, 7, 8, and 9.

Decimal numbers use 10 symbols: 0, 1, 2, 3, 4, 5, 6, 7, 8, and 9.

Weights

In the decimal system, each weight equals 10 raised to the power of its position. The weight of the symbol at position 0 is 10^0 (1); the weight of the symbol at position 1 is 10^1 (10); and so on.

B.2   BASE 2: BINARY

The binary number system provides the basis for all computer operations. Computers work by turning electrical current on and off. The binary system uses two symbols, 0 and 1, so it corresponds naturally to a two-state device, such as a switch, with 0 to represent the off state and 1 to represent the on state. The word *binary* derives from the Latin stem *bi,* meaning two.

Binary numbers use two symbols: 0 and 1.

Weights

In the binary system, each weight equals 2 raised to the power of its position. The weight of the symbol at position 0 is 2^0 (1); the weight of the symbol at position 1 is 2^1 (2); and so on.

Binary to Decimal

To convert a binary number to decimal, we use the weights. We multiply each symbol by its weight and add all of the weighted results. Figure B.2 shows how we can change binary 1001110 to its decimal equivalent 78.

Figure B.2   *Binary to decimal transformation*

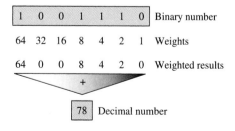

Decimal to Binary

A simple division trick gives us a convenient way to convert a decimal number to its binary equivalent as shown in Figure B.3. To convert a number from decimal to binary, divide the number by 2 and write down the remainder (1 or 0). That remainder is the least significant binary digit. Now, divide the quotient of that division by 2 and write down the new remainder in the second position. Repeat this process until the quotient becomes zero.

Figure B.3   *Decimal to binary transformation*

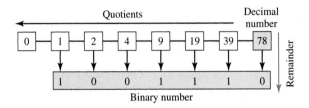

B.3   BASE 16: HEXADECIMAL

Another system used in this text is base 16. The term *hexadecimal* is derived from the Greek term *hexadec,* meaning 16. The hexadecimal number system is convenient for identifying a large binary number in a shorter form. The hexadecimal system uses 16 symbols, 0, 1, . . . , 9, A, B, C, D, E, and F. The hexadecimal system uses the same first ten symbols as the decimal system, but instead of using 10, 11, 12, 13, 14, and 15, it uses A, B, C, D, E, and F. This prevents any confusion between two adjacent symbols.

> **Hexadecimal numbers use 16 symbols: 0, 1, 2, 3, 4, 5, 6, 7, 8, 9, A, B, C, D, E, and F.**

Weights

In the hexadecimal system, each weight equals 16 raised to the power of its position. The weight of the symbol at position 0 is 16^0 (1); the weight of the symbol at position 1 is 16^1 (16); and so on.

Hexadecimal to Decimal

To convert a hexadecimal number to decimal, we use the weights. We multiply each symbol by its weight and add all of the weighted results. Figure B.4 shows how hexadecimal 3A73 is transformed to its decimal equivalent 14963.

Decimal to Hexadecimal

We use the same trick we used for changing decimal to binary to transform a decimal to hexadecimal. The only difference is that we divide the number by 16 instead of 2. Figure B.5 shows how 14963 in decimal is converted to hexadecimal 3A73.

Figure B.4   *Hexadecimal to decimal transformation*

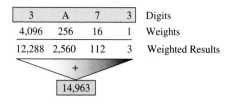

Figure B.5   *Decimal to hexadecimal transformation*

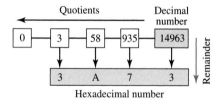

B.4   BASE 256: IP ADDRESSES

One numbering system that is used in the Internet is base 256. IPv4 addresses use this base to represent an address in dotted decimal notation. When we define an IPv4 address as 131.32.7.8, we are using a base 256 number. In this base, we could have used 256 unique symbols, but remembering that many symbols and their values is burdensome. The designers of the IPv4 address decided to use decimal numbers 0 to 255 as symbols and, to distinguish between the symbols, a *dot* is used. The dot is used to separate the symbols; it marks the boundary between the positions. For example, the IPv4 address 131.32.7.8 is made of four symbols 8, 7, 32, and 131 at positions 0, 1, 2, 3 respectively.

> **IPv4 addresses use the base 256 numbering system.**
> **The symbols in IPv4 are decimal numbers between 0 and 255; the separator is a dot.**

Weights

In base 256, each weight equals 256 raised to the power of its position. The weight of the symbol at position 0 is 256^0 (1); the weight of the symbol at position 1 is 256^1 (256); and so on.

IP Addresses to Decimal

To convert an IPv4 address to decimal, we use the weights. We multiply each symbol by its weight and add all of the weighted results. Figure B.6 shows how the IPv4 address 131.32.7.8 is transformed to its decimal equivalent.

Figure B.6   *IPv4 address to decimal transformation*

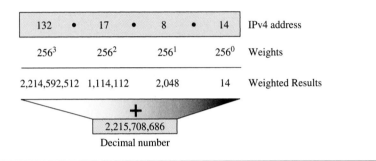

Decimal to IP Addresses

We use the same trick we used for changing decimal to binary to transform a decimal to an IPv4 address The only difference is that we divide the number by 256 instead of 2. However, we need to remember that the IPv4 address has four positions. This means that when we are dealing with an IPv4 address, we must stop after we have found four values. Figure B.7 shows an example for an IPv4 address.

Figure B.7   *Decimal to IPv4 address transformation*

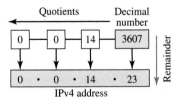

B.5   A COMPARISON

Table B.1 shows how systems represent the decimal numbers 0 through 15. As you can see, decimal 13 is equivalent to binary 1101, which is equivalent to hexadecimal D.

Table B.1   *Comparison of three systems*

Decimal	Binary	Hexadecimal
0	0	0
1	1	1
2	10	2
3	11	3
4	100	4
5	101	5
6	110	6
7	111	7
8	1000	8
9	1001	9
10	1010	A
11	1011	B
12	1100	C
13	1101	D
14	1110	E
15	1111	F

B.6   OTHER TRANSFORMATIONS

There are other transformations such as base 2 to base 16 or base 16 to base 256. It is easy to use base 10 as the intermediate system. In other words, to change a number from binary to hexadecimal we first change the binary to decimal and then change the decimal to hexadecimal. We discuss some easy methods for common transformations.

From Binary to Hexadecimal

To change a number from binary to hexadecimal, we group the binary digits from the right by fours. Then we convert each four bit group to its hexadecimal equivalent using Table B.1. In Figure B.8, we convert binary 1010001110 to hexadecimal.

Figure B.8   *Transformation from binary to hexadecimal*

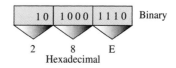

From Hexadecimal to Binary

To change a hexadecimal number to binary, we convert each hexadecimal digit to its equivalent binary number using Table B.1 and concatenate the results. In Figure B.9, we convert hexadecimal 28E to binary.

Figure B.9   *Transformation from hexadecimal to binary*

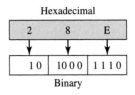

From Base 256 to Binary

To convert a base 256 number to binary, we first need to convert the number in each position to an 8-bit binary group and then concatenate the groups.

From Binary to Base 256

To convert from binary to base 256, we need to divide the binary number into groups of 8 bits, convert each group to decimal, and then insert separators (dots) between the decimal numbers.

APPENDIX C

Checksum

This appendix briefly describes three common checksum techniques: traditional, Fletcher, and Adler.

C.1 TRADITIONAL

Traditionally, the checksum calculation for IP, UDP, and TCP uses *one's complement* arithmetic. We use three number systems, binary, hexadecimal, and decimal. The first two are done manually to show the concept; we use a flowchart for the third.

Calculation in Binary

To show a binary checksum calculation, we use the data in Figure 11.9 in Chapter 11. First we calculate the partial sum as shown in Figure C.1. We add each column and carry to the next columns, if necessary. We then calculate the sum. Finally, we get the checksum, which is the one's complement of the sum (each 0 is changed to 1 and each 1 to 0). We step through the calculations:

❑ When we add the first (rightmost) column, we get 7. The number 7 in binary is 111. We keep the rightmost 1 and carry the rest to columns 2 and 3.

❑ When we add the second column, we include the carry from the first column. The result is 8, which is 1000 in binary. We keep the first bit (rightmost) and carry the rest (100) to columns 3, 4, and 5.

❑ We repeat the above procedure for each column.

❑ When we finish adding the last column, we have two 1s for which there are no columns left for addition. We add these two 1s to the partial sum in the next step.

❑ If there is no carry from the last or previous columns, the partial sum is the sum. In this example, there are carries; these are added to the partial sum to obtain the final sum.

❑ After the sum is calculated, we complement each bit to get the checksum.

Figure C.1   *Traditional checksum using binary numbers*

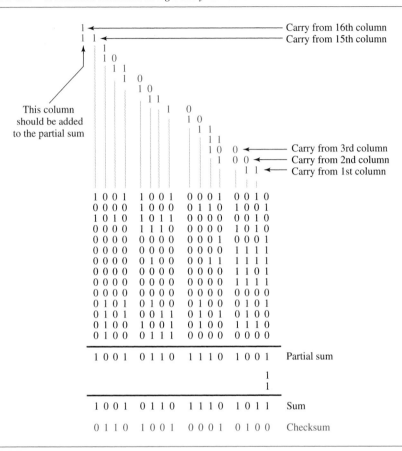

Calculation in Hexadecimal

Now let us do the same calculation in hexadecimal. First we calculate the partial sum as shown in Figure C.2. We add each column and carry to the next columns, if necessary. Note the following points:

- ❏ We use 10, 11, 12, 13, 14, and 15 instead of A, B, C, D, E, and F when we add hexadecimal digits.

- ❏ When we add the first column, we get 105. This number in hexadecimal is 69_{16}. We keep the first digit (9) and carry the second digit (6) to column 2.

- ❏ We repeat the same procedure for each column.

- ❏ When we add the last column, we get 41. This number in hexadecimal is 29_{16}. We keep the first digit (9) and add the second digit to the partial sum in the next step.

- ❏ If there are no carries from the last or previous columns, the partial sum is the sum. In this example, there is a carry; this is added to the partial sum to obtain the sum. Figure C.2 shows this calculation. Now we have the sum.

❏ After the sum is calculated, we complement each hexadecimal digit to get the checksum. Figure C.2 also shows the checksum. Note that when we calculate the complement, we subtract each digit from 15 to get the complement (one's complement in hexadecimal). The figure also shows the checksum in binary.

Figure C.2   *Traditional checksum using hexadecimal numbers*

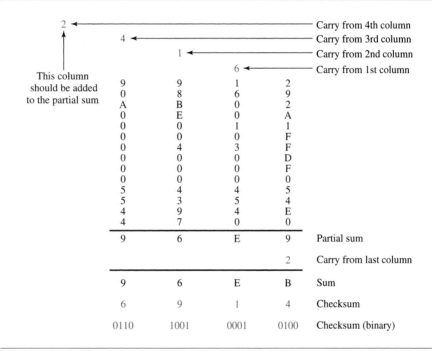

Decimal Calculation

We can also calculate the checksum in decimal. In this system, each 16-bit data section is treated as an unsigned integer. The integers are added together to find the sum using one's complement arithmetic. However, note that the one's complement arithmetic calculation is modulo $2^{16} - 1$ (65535). This means that the result needs to be divided by 65535 with only the remainder kept. The modulo calculation is done at each iteration and held in a 16-bit variable. After we exit from the loop, we have the sum. The checksum is the difference between the sum and 65535. Several efficient algorithms have been designed for this calculation; we show a simple one in Figure C.3. D_i is the ith data item (integer).

Table C.1 shows the step by step calculation of sum and the checksum for the data in Figure C.1. Note that in each step, the result is calculated modulo 65535.

The checksum, 26900, is 0x*6914* in hexadecimal and *0110 1001 0001 0100* in binary. This confirms our previous results.

Figure C.3   *Traditional checksum using decimal*

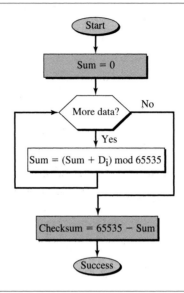

Table C.1   *Example of a traditional checksum*

Hex	Decimal (D_i)	Sum = 0
9912	39186	39186
0869	2153	41339
AB02	43778	19582
0E0A	3594	23176
0011	17	23193
000F	15	23208
043F	1087	24295
000D	13	24308
000F	15	24323
0000	0	24323
5445	21573	45896
5354	21332	1693
494E	18766	20459
4700	18176	38635

Sum = 38635
Checksum = 65535 − 38635 = 26900

C.2   FLETCHER

There is one major problem with the traditional checksum calculation. If two 16-bit items are transposed in transmission, the checksum cannot catch this error. The reason is that the traditional checksum is not weighted: it treats each data item equally. In other words, the order of data item is immaterial to the calculation. The Fletcher checksum was devised to weight each data item according to its position.

Fletcher has proposed two algorithms: 8-bit and 16-bit. The first, 8-bit Fletcher, calculates on 8-bit data items and creates a 16-bit checksum. The second, 16-bit Fletcher, calculates on 16-bit data items and creates a 32-bit checksum.

Eight-Bit Fletcher

The eight-bit Fletcher is calculated over data octets (bytes) and creates a 16-bit checksum. The calculation is done modulo 256 (2^8), which means the intermediate results are divided by 256 and the remainder is kept. The algorithm uses two accumulators, A and B. The first simply adds data items together; the second adds a weight to the calculation. There are many variations of the 8-bit Fletcher algorithm; we show a simple one in Figure C.4.

Figure C.4   *Eight-bit Fletcher*

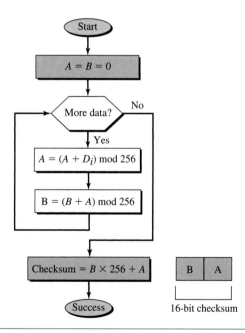

It can be proved that the accumulator B is a weighted sum of the data items. We have

$$A = D_1 + D_2 + \cdots + D_n$$
$$B = nD_1 + (n-1)D_2 + \cdots + D_n$$

If, for example, D_1 and D_2 are swapped during the transmission, the calculation of B at the receiver is different from the one done at the sender.

As an example, let us calculate the eight-bit Fletcher checksum for the string "Forouzan". We change each character to its equivalent ASCII value and calculate the values of A and B in Table C.2.

Table C.2   *Example of a 8-bit Fletcher checksum*

Byte	D_i	$A = 0$	$B = 0$
F	70	$A = 0 + 70 = 70$	$B = 0 + 70 = 70$
o	111	$A = 70 + 111 = 181$	$B = 70 + 181 = 251$
r	114	$A = 181 + 114 = 39$	$B = 251 + 39 = 34$
o	111	$A = 39 + 111 = 150$	$B = 34 + 150 = 184$
u	117	$A = 150 + 117 = 11$	$B = 184 + 11 = 195$
z	122	$A = 11 + 122 = 133$	$B = 195 + 133 = 72$
a	97	$A = 133 + 97 = 230$	$B = 72 + 230 = 46$
n	110	$A = 230 + 110 = 84$	$B = 46 + 84 = 130$
			Checksum $= B \times 256 + A = 33364$

The 16-bit checksum in this case is 0x8254 in hexadecimal. Note that the checksum is actually the concatenation of B (82) and A (54). In other words, when A and B are calculated, B goes to the left-most byte and A to the right-most byte.

Sixteen-Bit Fletcher

The sixteen-bit Fletcher checksum is calculated over 16-bit data items and creates a 32-bit checksum. The calculation is done modulo 65536, which means the intermediate results are divided by 65536 and the remainder is kept.

Let us calculate the sixteen-bit Fletcher checksum for the string "Forouzan". We change each character to its equivalent ASCII value, combine two bytes together, and calculate the values of A and B in Table C.3.

Table C.3   *Example of 16-bit Fletcher*

Byte	D_i	$A = 0$	$B = 0$
Fo	18031	$A = 18031$	$B = 18031$
ro	29295	$A = 47326$	$B = 65357$
uz	30074	$A = 11864$	$B = 11685$
an	24942	$A = 36806$	$B = 48491$
			Checksum $= B \times 65{,}536 + A = 3{,}177{,}942{,}982$

The 32-bit checksum in this case is 0xBD6B8FC6. Note that the checksum is actually the concatenation of B (BD6B) and A (8FC6). In other words, when A and B are calculated, A goes to the right-most two bytes and B to the left-most two bytes.

C.3   ADLER

The Adler checksum is a 32-bit checksum. It is similar to the 16-bit Fletcher with three differences. First, calculation is done on single bytes instead of two bytes at a time. Second, the modulus is a prime number (65521) instead of 65536. Third, A is initialized to 1 instead of 0. It has been proved that a prime modulo has a better detecting capability in some combinations of data. Figure C.5 shows a simple, though inefficient, algorithm in flowchart form.

Figure C.5 *Adler checksum*

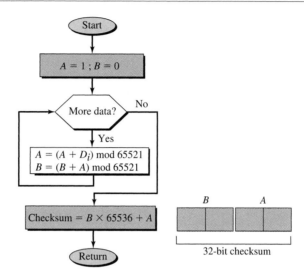

It can be proved that the accumulator *B* is the weighted sum of data items. We have

$$A = D_1 + D_2 + \cdots + D_n + 1$$
$$B = nD_1 + (n-1)D_2 + \cdots + D_n + n$$

Let us calculate the Adler checksum for the string "Forouzan". We change each character to its equivalent ASCII value and calculate the values of *A* and *B* in Table C.4.

Table C.4   *Example of Adler checksum*

Byte	D_i	A = 1	B = 0
F	70	A = 1 + 70 = 71	B = 0 + 71 = 71
o	111	A = 71 +111 = 182	B = 71 + 182 = 253
r	114	A = 182 + 114 = 296	B = 253 + 296 = 549
o	111	A = 296 + 111 = 407	B = 549 + 407 = 956
u	117	A = 407 + 117 = 524	B = 956 + 524 = 1,480
z	122	A = 524 + 122 = 646	B = 1480 + 646 = 2,126
a	97	A = 646 + 97 = 743	B = 2126 + 743= 2,869
n	110	A = 743 + 110 = 853	B = 2869 + 853 = 3,722
			Checksum = 3722 $\times$ 65,536 + 853 = 243,925,845

The 32-bit checksum in this case is 0E8A0355. Note that the checksum is actually the concatenation of *B* (0E8A) and *A* (0355). In other words, when *A* and *B* are calculated, *A* goes to the right-most two bytes and *B* to the left-most two bytes.

Error Detection

Networks must be able to transfer data from one device to another with complete accuracy. A system that cannot guarantee that the data received by one device are identical to the data transmitted by another device is essentially useless. Yet any time data are transmitted from one node to the next, they can become corrupted in passage. Many factors can alter or wipe out one or more bits of a given data unit. Reliable systems must have a mechanism for detecting and correcting such errors.

> **Data can be corrupted during transmission. For reliable communication, errors must be detected and corrected.**

D.1 TYPES OF ERRORS

Whenever bits flow from one point to another, they are subject to unpredictable changes because of interference. This interference can change the shape of the signal. In a single-bit error, a 0 is changed to a 1 or 1 to a 0. In a burst error, multiple bits are changed. For example, a 0.01-s burst of impulse noise on a transmission with a data rate of 1200 bps might change all or some of 12 bits of information.

Single-Bit Error

The term single-bit error means that only one bit of a given data unit (such as a byte, character, data unit, or packet) is changed from 1 to 0 or from 0 to 1.

> **In a single-bit error, only one bit in the data unit has changed.**

Figure D.1 shows the effect of a single-bit error on a data unit. To understand the impact of the change, imagine that each group of 8 bits is an ASCII character with a 0 bit added to the left. In the figure, 00000010 (ASCII *STX*) was sent, meaning *start of text,* but 00001010 (ASCII *LF*) was received, meaning *line feed.* (For more information about ASCII code, see Appendix A.)

Figure D.1   *Single-bit error*

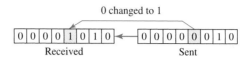

Single-bit errors are the least likely type of error in serial data transmission. To understand why, imagine a sender sends data at 1 Mbps. This means that each bit lasts only 1/1,000,000 s, or 1 μs. For a single-bit error to occur, the noise must have a duration of only 1 μs, which is very rare; noise normally lasts much longer than this.

However, a single-bit error can happen if we are sending data using parallel transmission. For example, if eight wires are used to send all 8 bits of 1 byte at the same time and one of the wires is noisy, one bit can be corrupted in each byte. Think of parallel transmission inside a computer, between CPU and memory, for example.

Burst Error

The term **burst error** means that 2 or more bits in the data unit have changed from 1 to 0 or from 0 to 1.

A burst error means that 2 or more bits in the data unit have changed.

Figure D.2 shows the effect of a burst error on a data unit. In this case, 0100010001000011 was sent, but 0101110101000011 was received. Note that a burst error does not necessarily mean that the errors occur in consecutive bits. The length of the burst is measured from the first corrupted bit to the last corrupted bit. Some bits in between may not have been corrupted.

Figure D.2   *Burst error of length five*

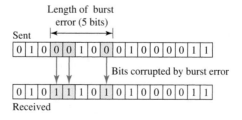

Burst error is most likely to occur in a serial transmission. The duration of noise is normally longer than the duration of one bit, which means that when noise affects data, it affects a set of bits. The number of bits affected depends on the data rate and duration of noise. For example, if we are sending data at 1 kbps, a noise of 1/100 s can affect 10 bits; if we are sending data at 1 Mbps, the same noise can affect 10,000 bits.

D.2   DETECTION

Although the goal of error checking is to correct errors, most of the time we first need to detect errors. Error detection is simpler than error correction and is the first step in the error correction process.

Redundancy

One **error detection** mechanism would be to send every data unit twice. The receiving device would then be able to do a bit-for-bit comparison between the two versions of the data. Any discrepancy would indicate an error, and an appropriate correction mechanism could be set in place. This system would be completely accurate (the odds of errors being introduced onto exactly the same bits in both sets of data are infinitesimally small), but it would also be insupportably slow. Not only would the transmission time double, but also the time it takes to compare every unit bit by bit must be added.

The concept of including extra information in the transmission for error detection is a good one. But instead of repeating the entire data stream, a shorter group of bits may be appended to the end of each unit. This technique is called **redundancy** because the extra bits are redundant to the information; they are discarded as soon as the accuracy of the transmission has been determined.

> **Error detection uses the concept of redundancy, which means adding extra bits for detecting errors at the destination.**

Figure D.3 shows the process of using redundant bits to check the accuracy of a data unit. Once the data stream has been generated, it passes through a device that analyzes it and adds on an appropriately coded redundancy check. The data unit, now enlarged by several bits, travels over the link to the receiver. The receiver puts

Figure D.3   *Redundancy*

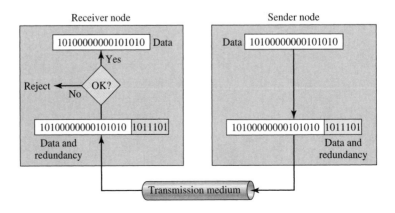

the entire stream through a checking function. If the received bit stream passes the checking criteria, the data portion of the data unit is accepted and the redundant bits are discarded.

Parity Check

The most common and least expensive mechanism for error detection is the **parity check.** In this technique, a redundant bit, called a **parity bit,** is added to every data unit so that the total number of 1s in the unit (including the parity bit) becomes even (or odd). Suppose we want to transmit the binary data unit 1100001 [ASCII *a* (97)]; see Figure D.4. Adding the number of 1s gives us 3, an odd number. Before transmitting, we pass the data unit through a parity generator. The parity generator counts the 1s and appends the parity bit (a 1 in this case) to the end. The total number of 1s is now 4, an even number. The system now transmits the entire expanded unit across the network link. When it reaches its destination, the receiver puts all 8 bits through an **even-parity** checking function. If the receiver sees 11000011, it counts four 1s, an even number, and the data unit passes. But what if the data unit has been damaged in transit? What if, instead of 11000011, the receiver sees 11001011? Then when the parity checker counts the 1s, it gets 5, an odd number. The receiver knows that an error has been introduced into the data somewhere and therefore rejects the whole unit. Note that for the sake of simplicity, we are discussing here even-parity checking, where the number of 1s should be an even number. Some systems may use **odd-parity** checking, where the number of 1s should be odd. The principle is the same.

Figure D.4 *Even-parity concept*

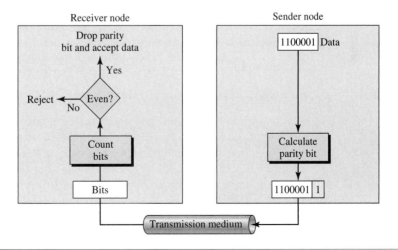

In parity check, a parity bit is added to every data unit so that the total number of 1s is even (or odd for odd-parity).

Example 1

Suppose the sender wants to send the word *world*. In ASCII (see Appendix A), the five characters are coded as

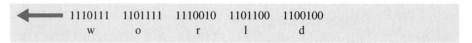

$$\text{1110111} \quad \text{1101111} \quad \text{1110010} \quad \text{1101100} \quad \text{1100100}$$
$$\text{w} \qquad\quad \text{o} \qquad\quad \text{r} \qquad\quad \text{l} \qquad\quad \text{d}$$

Each of the first four characters has an even number of 1s, so the parity bit is a 0. The last character (d), however, has three 1s (an odd number), so the parity bit is a 1 to make the total number of 1s even. The following shows the actual bits sent (the parity bits are underlined).

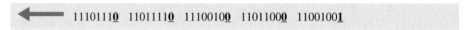

$$\text{1110111}\underline{\text{0}} \quad \text{1101111}\underline{\text{0}} \quad \text{1110010}\underline{\text{0}} \quad \text{1101100}\underline{\text{0}} \quad \text{1100100}\underline{\text{1}}$$

Performance

Simple parity check can detect all single-bit errors. It can also detect burst errors as long as the total number of bits changed is odd (1, 3, 5, etc.). Let's say we have an even-parity data unit where the total number of 1s, including the parity bit, is 6: 1000111011. If any 3 bits change value, the resulting parity will be odd and the error will be detected: 1*111*111011:9, 0*11*0111011:7, 1*1*00010011:5—all odd. The checker would return a result of 1, and the data unit would be rejected. The same holds true for any odd number of errors.

Suppose, however, that 2 bits of the data unit are changed: 1*1*10111011:8, 1*1*00011011:6, 1000011010:4. In each case the number of 1s in the data unit is still even. The parity checker will add them and return an even number although the data unit contains two errors. This method cannot detect errors where the total number of bits changed is even. If any two bits change in transmission, the changes cancel each other and the data unit will pass a parity check even though the data unit is damaged. The same holds true for any even number of errors.

Simple parity check can detect all single-bit errors. It can detect burst errors only if the total number of errors in each data unit is odd.

Cyclic Redundancy Check (CRC)

The most powerful of the redundancy checking techniques is the **cyclic redundancy check (CRC).** Unlike the parity check, which is based on addition, CRC is based on binary division. In CRC, instead of adding bits to achieve a desired parity, a sequence of redundant bits, called the CRC or the CRC remainder, is appended to the end of a data unit so that the resulting data unit becomes exactly divisible by a second, predetermined binary number. At its destination, the incoming data unit is divided by the same number. If at this step there is no remainder, the data unit is assumed to be intact and is therefore accepted. A remainder indicates that the data unit has been damaged in transit and therefore must be rejected.

The redundancy bits used by CRC are derived by dividing the data unit by a predetermined divisor; the remainder is the CRC. To be valid, a CRC must have two qualities: It must have exactly one less bit than the divisor, and appending it to the end of the data string must make the resulting bit sequence exactly divisible by the divisor.

Both the theory and the application of CRC error detection are straightforward. The only complexity is in deriving the CRC. To clarify this process, we will start with an overview and add complexity as we go. Figure D.5 provides an outline of the three basic steps.

Figure D.5 *CRC generator and checker*

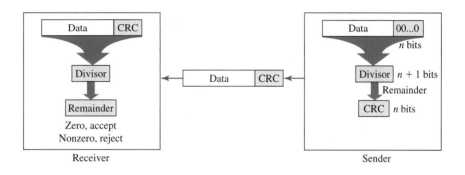

First, a string of n 0s is appended to the data unit. The number n is 1 less than the number of bits in the predetermined divisor, which is $n + 1$ bits.

Second, the newly elongated data unit is divided by the divisor, using a process called binary division. The remainder resulting from this division is the CRC.

Third, the CRC of n bits derived in step 2 replaces the appended 0s at the end of the data unit. Note that the CRC may consist of all 0s.

The data unit arrives at the receiver data first, followed by the CRC. The receiver treats the whole string as a unit and divides it by the same divisor that was used to find the CRC remainder.

If the string arrives without error, the CRC checker yields a remainder of zero and the data unit passes. If the string has been changed in transit, the division yields a non-zero remainder and the data unit does not pass.

The CRC Generator

A **CRC generator** uses modulo-2 division. Figure D.6 shows this process. In the first step, the 4-bit divisor is subtracted from the first 4 bits of the dividend. Each bit of the divisor is subtracted from the corresponding bit of the dividend without disturbing the next-higher bit. In our example, the divisor, 1101, is subtracted from the first 4 bits of the dividend, 1001, yielding 100 (the leading 0 of the remainder is dropped). The next unused bit from the dividend is then pulled down to make the number of bits in the remainder equal to the number of bits in the divisor. The next step, therefore, is 1000 − 1101, which yields 101, and so on.

In this process, the divisor always begins with a 1; the divisor is subtracted from a portion of the previous dividend/remainder that is equal to it in length; the divisor can only be subtracted from a dividend/remainder whose leftmost bit is 1. Anytime the leftmost bit of the dividend/remainder is 0, a string of 0s, of the same length as the divisor,

---

Figure D.6   *Binary division in a CRC generator*

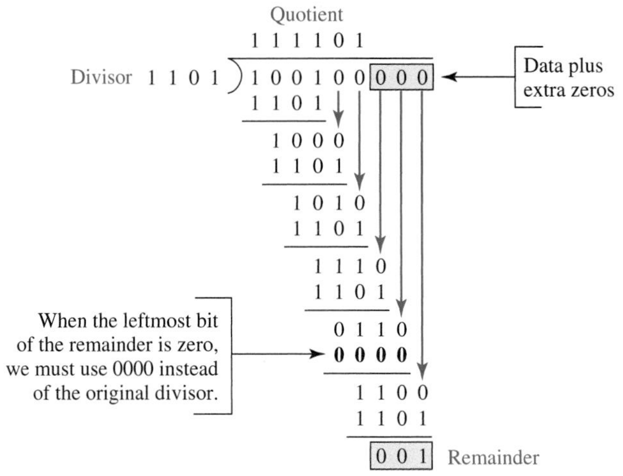

Quotient
1 1 1 1 0 1

Divisor 1 1 0 1) 1 0 0 1 0 0 0 0 0 ← Data plus extra zeros
1 1 0 1 ↓

1 0 0 0
1 1 0 1 ↓

1 0 1 0
1 1 0 1 ↓

1 1 1 0
1 1 0 1 ↓

When the leftmost bit of the remainder is zero, we must use 0000 instead of the original divisor. →
0 1 1 0
0 0 0 0 ↓

1 1 0 0
1 1 0 1

0 0 1   Remainder

---

replaces the divisor in that step of the process. For example, if the divisor is 4 bits long, it is replaced by four 0s. (Remember, we are dealing with bit patterns, not with quantitative values; 0000 is not the same as 0.) This restriction means that, at any step, the leftmost subtraction will be either $0 - 0$ or $1 - 1$, both of which equal 0. So, after subtraction, the leftmost bit of the remainder will always be a leading zero, which is dropped, and the next unused bit of the dividend is pulled down to fill out the remainder. Note that only the first bit of the remainder is dropped—if the second bit is also 0, it is retained, and the dividend/remainder for the next step will begin with 0. This process repeats until the entire dividend has been used.

The CRC Checker

A **CRC checker** functions exactly as the generator does. After receiving the data appended with the CRC, it does the same modulo-2 division. If the remainder is all 0s, the CRC is dropped and the data are accepted; otherwise, the received stream of bits is discarded and data are resent. Figure D.7 shows the same process of division in the receiver. We assume that there is no error. The remainder is therefore all 0s, and the data are accepted.

Polynomials

The divisor in the CRC generator is most often represented not as a string of 1s and 0s, but as an algebraic **polynomial** (see Figure D.8). The polynomial format is useful for two reasons: It is short, and it can be used to prove the concept mathematically.

The relationship of a polynomial to its corresponding binary representation is shown in Figure D.9.

Figure D.7   *Binary division in a CRC checker*

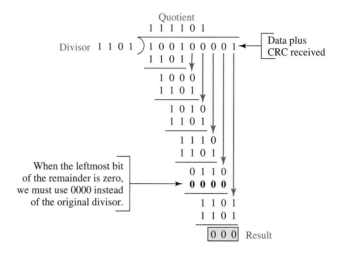

Figure D.8   *A polynomial*

$$x^7 + x^5 + x^2 + x + 1$$

Figure D.9   *A polynomial representing a divisor*

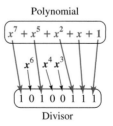

A polynomial should be selected to have at least the following properties:

- ❑ It should not be divisible by x.
- ❑ It should be divisible by $x + 1$.

The first condition guarantees that all burst errors of a length equal to the degree of the polynomial are detected. The second condition guarantees that all burst errors affecting an odd number of bits are detected.

Example 2

It is obvious that we cannot choose x (binary 10) or $x^2 + x$ (binary 110) as the polynomial because both are divisible by x. However, we can choose $x + 1$ (binary 11) because it is not divisible by x, but is divisible by $x + 1$. We can also choose $x^2 + 1$ (binary 101) because it is divisible by $x + 1$ (binary division).

Standard Polynomials

Some standard polynomials used by popular protocols for CRC generation are shown in Table D.1.

Table D.1   *Standard polynomials*

Name	Polynomial	Application
CRC-8	$x^8 + x^2 + x + 1$	ATM header
CRC-10	$x^{10} + x^9 + x^5 + x^4 + x^2 + 1$	ATM AAL
ITU-16	$x^{16} + x^{12} + x^5 + 1$	HDLC
CRC-32	$x^{32} + x^{26} + x^{23} + x^{22} + x^{16} + x^{12} + x^{11} + x^{10} +$ $x^8 + x^7 + x^5 + x^4 + x^2 + x + 1$	LANs SCTP

Performance

CRC is a very effective error detection method. If the divisor is chosen according to the previously mentioned rules,

1. CRC can detect all burst errors that affect an odd number of bits.
2. CRC can detect all burst errors of length less than or equal to the degree of the polynomial.
3. CRC can detect, with a very high probability, burst errors of length greater than the degree of the polynomial.

Example 3

The CRC-12 ($x^{12} + x^{11} + x^3 + x + 1$), which has a degree of 12, will detect all burst errors affecting an odd number of bits, will detect all burst errors with a length less than or equal to 12, and will detect, 99.97 percent of the time, burst errors with a length of 12 or more.

Checksum

The third error detection method is called the **checksum.** Like the parity checks and CRC, the checksum is based on the concept of redundancy. We discuss several checksum methods in Appendix C.

APPENDIX E

Project 802

In 1985, the Computer Society of the IEEE started Project 802, a drive to set standards to enable intercommunication between equipment from a variety of manufacturers. Project 802 does not seek to replace any part of the OSI model. Instead, it is a way of specifying functions of the physical layer, the data link layer, and to a lesser extent the network layer to support interconnectivity of major LAN protocols.

> **In 1985, the Computer Society of IEEE developed Project 802. It covers the first two layers and part of the third level of the OSI model.**

The relationship of Project 802 to the OSI model is shown in Figure E.1. The IEEE has subdivided the data link layer into two sublayers: logical link control (LLC) and media access control (MAC).

Figure E.1 *LAN compared with the OSI model*

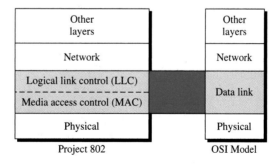

The LLC is non-architecture-specific; that is it is the same for all IEEE-defined LANs. The MAC sublayer, on the other hand, contains a number of distinct modules; each carries proprietary information specific to the LAN product being used.

> **Project 802 has split the data link layer into two different sublayers: logical link control (LLC) and media access control (MAC).**

The strength of Project 802 is modularity. By subdividing the functions necessary for LAN management, the designers were able to standardize those that can be generalized and isolate those that must remain specific. Each subdivision is identified by a number: 802.1 (internetworking); 802.2 (LLC), and the MAC modules 802.3 (CSMA/CD), 802.4 (Token Bus), 802.5 (Token Ring), and others (see Figure E.2).

Figure E.2   *Project 802*

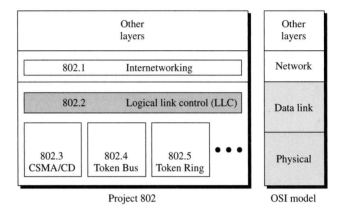

E.1   PROJECT 802.1

802.1 is the section of Project 802 devoted to internetworking issues in LANs. It seeks to resolve the incompatibilities between network architectures without requiring modifications in existing addressing, access, and error-recovery mechanisms, among others.

> **IEEE 802.1 is an internetworking standard for LANs.**

E.2   PROJECT 802.2

802.2 is the section of Project 802 related to the physical and data link layers. It divides the data link layer into two sublayers: LLC and MAC.

LLC

In general, the IEEE Project 802 model takes the structure of an HDLC frame and divides it into two sets of functions. One set contains the end-user portions of the frame: the logical addresses, control information, and data. These functions are handled by the IEEE 802.2 LLC protocol. LLC is considered the upper layer of the IEEE 802 data link layer and is common to all LAN protocols.

IEEE 802.2 logical link control (LLC) is the upper sublayer of the data link layer.

PDU

The data unit at the LLC level is the protocol data unit. The PDU contains four fields familiar from HDLC: a destination service access point (DSAP), a source service access point (SSAP), a control field, and an information field (see Figure E.3).

Figure E.3   *PDU format*

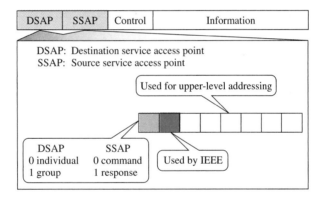

- ❏ **DSAP and SSAP.**   The DSAP and SSAP are addresses used by the LLC to identify the protocol stacks on the receiving and sending machines that are generating and using the data. The first bit of the DSAP indicates whether the frame is intended for an individual or a group. The first bit of the SSAP indicates whether the communication is a command or response PDU (see Figure E.3).
- ❏ **Control.**   The control field of the PDU is identical to the control field in HDLC. As in HDLC, PDU frames can be I-frames, S-frames, or U-frames and carry all of the codes and information that the corresponding HDLC frames carry (see Figure E.4).

MAC

The second set of functions, the media access control sublayer, resolves the contention for the shared media. It contains the synchronization, flag, flow, and error control specifications necessary to move information from one place to another, as well as the physical address of the next station to receive and route a packet. MAC protocols are specific to the LAN using them.

Figure E.4   *Control fields in a PDU*

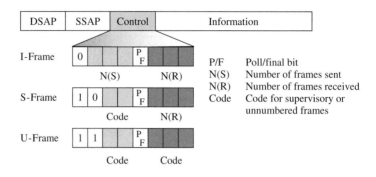

The media access control (MAC) layer is the lower sublayer of the data link layer.

In the MAC layer, Project 802 is itself divided into several projects in response to the de facto standards used by the industry. Three of them are related to the LANs we discussed in Chapter 3.

APPENDIX F

Contact Addresses

The following is a list of contact addresses for various organizations mentioned in the text.

❑ **ATM Forum**

Presidio of San Francisco

P.O. Box 29920 (mail)

572B Ruger Street (surface)

San Francisco, CA 94129-0920

Telephone: 415.561-6275

E-mail: info@atmforum.com

www.atmforum.com

❑ **Federal Communications Commission (FCC)**

445 12th Street S.W.

Washington, DC 20554

Telephone: 1-888-225-5322

E-mail: fccinfo@fcc.gov

www.fcc.gov

❑ **Institute of Electrical and Electronics Engineers (IEEE)**

Operations Center

445 Hoes Lane

Piscataway, NJ 08854-1331

Telephone: 732.981-0060

www.ieee.org

❑ **International Organization for Standardization (ISO)**

1, rue de Varembe

Case postale 56

CH-1211 Geneve 20

Switzerland

Telephone: 41 22 749 0111

E-mail: central@iso.ch

www.iso.org

❏ **International Telecommunication Union (ITU)**
Place des Nations
CH-1211 Geneva 20
Switzerland
Telephone: 41 22 730 5852
E-mail: tsbmail@itu.int
www.itu.int/home

❏ **Internet Architecture Board (IAB)**
E-mail: IAB@isi.edu
www.iab.org

❏ **Internet Corporation for Assigned Names and Numbers (ICANN)**
4676 Admiralty Way, Suite 330
Marina del Rey, CA 90292-6601
Telephone: 310.823-9358
E-mail: icann@icann.org
www.icann.org

❏ **Internet Engineering Steering Group (IESG)**
E-mail: iesg@ietf.org
www.ietf.org/iesg.html

❏ **Internet Engineering Task Force (IETF)**
E-mail: ietf-infor@ietf.org
www.ietf.org

❏ **Internet Research Task Force (IRTF)**
E-mail: irtf-chair@ietf.org
www.irtf.org

❏ **Internet Society (ISOC)**
1775 Weihle Avenue, Suite 102
Reston, VA 20190-5108
Telephone: 703.326-9880
E-mail: info@isoc.org
www.isoc.org

RFCs

In Table G.1, we list alphabetically by protocol the RFCs that are directly related to the material in this text. For more information go to the following site: *http://www.rfc-editor.org*.

Table G.1 *RFCs for each protocol*

Protocol	RFC
ARP and RARP	826, 903, 925, 1027, 1293,1329, 1433, 1868, 1931, 2390
BGP	1092, 1105, 1163, 1265, 1266, 1267, 1364, 1392, 1403, 1565, 1654, 1655, 1665, 1771, 1772, 1745, 1774, 2283
BOOTP and DHCP	951, 1048, 1084, 1395, 1497, 1531, 1532, 1533, 1534, 1541, 1542, 2131, 2132
CIDR	1322, 1478, 1479, 1517, 1817
DHCP	See BOOTP and DHCP
DNS	799, 811, 819, 830, 881, 882, 883, 897, 920, 921, 1034, 1035, 1386, 1480, 1535, 1536, 1537, 1591, 1637, 1664, 1706, 1712, 1713, 1982, 2065, 2137, 2317, 2535, 2671,
FTP	114, 133, 141, 163, 171, 172, 238, 242, 250, 256, 264, 269, 281, 291, 354, 385, 412, 414, 418, 430, 438, 448, 463, 468, 478, 486, 505, 506, 542, 553, 624, 630, 640, 691, 765, 913, 959, 1635, 1785, 2228, 2577
HTML	1866
HTTP	2068, 2109
ICMP	777, 792, 1016, 1018, 1256, 1788, 2521
IGMP	966, 988, 1054, 1112, 1301, 1458, 1469, 1768, 2236, 2357, 2365, 2502, 2588
IMAP	See SMTP, MIME, POP, IMAP

Table G.1 *RFCs for each protocol (concluded)*

Protocol	RFC
IP	760, 781, 791, 815, 1025, 1063, 1071, 1141, 1190, 1191, 1624, 2113
IPv6	1365, 1550, 1678, 1680, 1682, 1683, 1686, 1688, 1726, 1752, 1826, 1883, 1884, 1886, 1887, 1955, 2080, 2373, 2452, 2463, 2465, 2466, 2472, 2492, 2545, 2590,
MIB	See SNMP, MIB, SMI
MIME	See SMTP, MIME, POP, IMAP
Multicast Routing	1584, 1585, 2117, 2362
NAT	1361, 2663, 2694
OSPF	1131, 1245, 1246, 1247, 1370, 1583, 1584, 1585, 1586, 1587, 2178, 2328, 2329, 2370
POP	See SMTP, MIME, POP, IMAP
RARP	See ARP and RARP
RIP	1131, 1245, 1246, 1247, 1370, 1583, 1584, 1585, 1586, 1587, 1722, 1723, , 2082, 2453
SCTP	2960, 3257, 3284, 3285, 3286, 3309, 3436, 3554, 3708, 3758
SMI	See SNMP, MIB, SMI
SMTP, MIME, POP, IMAP	196, 221, 224, 278, 524, 539, 753, 772, 780, 806, 821, 934, 974, 1047, 1081, 1082, 1225, 1460, 1496, 1426, 1427, 1652, 1653, 1711, 1725, 1734, 1740, 1741, 1767, 1869, 1870, 2045, 2046, 2047, 2048, 2177, 2180, 2192, 2193, 2221, 2342, 2359, 2449, 2683, 2503
SNMP, MIB, SMI	1065, 1067, 1098, 1155, 1157, 1212, 1213, 1229, 1231, 1243, 1284, 1351, 1352, 1354, 1389, 1398, 1414, 1441, 1442, 1443, 1444, 1445, 1446, 1447, 1448, 1449, 1450, 1451, 1452, 1461, 1472, 1474, 1537, 1623, 1643, 1650, 1657, 1665, 1666, 1696, 1697, 1724, 1742, 1743, 1748, 1749
TCP	675, 700, 721, 761, 793, 879, 896, 1078, 1106, 1110, 1144, 1145, 1146, 1263, 1323, 1337, 1379, 1644, 1693, 1901, 1905, 2001, 2018, 2488, 2580
TELNET	137, 340, 393, 426, 435, 452, 466, 495, 513, 529, 562, 595, 596, 599, 669, 679, 701, 702, 703, 728, 764, 782, 818, 854, 855, 1184, 1205, 2355
TFTP	1350, 1782, 1783, 1784
UDP	768
VPN	2547, 2637, 2685
WWW	1614, 1630, 1737, 1738

APPENDIX H

UDP and TCP Ports

Table H.1 lists the common well-known ports ordered by port number.

Table H.1   *Ports by port number*

Port Number	UDP/TCP	Protocol
7	TCP	ECHO
13	UDP/TCP	DAYTIME
19	UDP/TCP	CHARACTER GENERATOR
20	TCP	FTP-DATA
21	TCP	FTP-CONTROL
23	TCP	TELNET
25	TCP	SMTP
37	UDP/TCP	TIME
67	UDP	BOOTP-SERVER
68	UDP	BOOTP-CLIENT
69	UDP	TFTP
70	TCP	GOPHER
79	TCP	FINGER
80	TCP	HTTP
109	TCP	POP-2
110	TCP	POP-3
111	UDP/TCP	RPC
161	UDP	SNMP
162	UDP	SNMP-TRAP
179	TCP	BGP
520	UDP	RIP

Table H.2 lists the ports, ordered alphabetically by protocol.

Table H.2   *Port numbers by protocol*

Protocol	UDP/TCP	Port Number
BGP	TCP	179
BOOTP-SERVER	UDP	67
BOOTP-CLIENT	UDP	68
CHARACTER GENERATOR	UDP/TCP	19
DAYTIME	UDP/TCP	13
ECHO	TCP	7
FINGER	TCP	79
FTP-CONTROL	TCP	21
FTP-DATA	TCP	20
GOPHER	TCP	70
HTTP	TCP	80
POP-2	TCP	109
POP-3	TCP	110
RIP	UDP	520
RPC	UDP/TCP	111
SMTP	TCP	25
SNMP	UDP	161
SNMP-TRAP	UDP	162
TELNET	TCP	23
TFTP	UDP	69
TIME	UDP/TCP	37

Glossary

1000BASE-CX   Gigabit Ethernet using copper.

1000BASE-LX   Gigabit Ethernet using optical fiber and long-wave laser signals.

1000BASE-SX   Gigabit Ethernet using optical fiber and short-wave laser signals.

1000BASE-T   Gigabit Ethernet using four twisted-pair cables.

100BASE-FX   Fast Ethernet using optical fiber.

100BASE-T4   Fast Ethernet using four twisted-pair cables.

100BASE-TX   Fast Ethernet using two twisted-pair cables.

100BASE-X   Fast Ethernet using two wires.

10BASE-FL   Traditional Ethernet using optical fiber.

10BASE-T   Traditional Ethernet using twisted-pair cable.

10BASE2   Traditional Ethernet using thin coaxial cable.

10BASE5   Traditional Ethernet using thick coaxial cable.

A

abbreviation   A method to shorten the IPv6 address by eliminating certain 0 digits.

abstract syntax notation 1 (ASN.1)   A language used in SNMP, SSL, and TSL.

access control   A method to determine which device has control over a link.

active close   Closing a TCP connection by a process.

active document   In the World Wide Web, a document executed at the local site.

active open   Opening a TCP connection by a process.

additive increase   Congestion avoidance strategy used by TCP.

address mask   A 32-bit number that extracts a network or subnet address.

Address Resolution Protocol (ARP)   A protocol mapping logical addresses to physical addresses.

address space   The total number of addresses used by a protocol.

Advanced Networks and Services (ANS)   The owner and operator of the Internet since 1995.

Advanced Networks and Services Network (ANSNET)   The high-speed Internet backbone.

Advanced Research Project Agency (ARPA)   The government agency that funded ARPANET.

Advanced Research Project Agency Network (ARPANET)   The packet switching network that was funded by ARPA.

agent   A router or a host that runs the SNMP server process.

agent advertisement   A process in which a router informs a mobile host of its address.

agent discovery   A process through which a mobile host on its home network learns the address of a home agent.

agent solicitation   A process in which a mobile host on a foreign network uses ICMP to learn an agent's address.

alias   In SMTP, a name that represents a group of recipients.

American National Standards Institute (ANSI)   A national standards organization that defines standards in the United States.

American Standard Code for Information Interchange (ASCII)   A character code developed by ANSI.

anonymous FTP   FTP without user name or password.

anycast address   A group address in which only one member is reached.

applet   A computer program in Java for creating an active Web document.

application adaptation layer (AAL)   A layer in ATM protocol that breaks user data into 48-byte payloads. Implementations are AAL1, AAL2, AAL3/4, and AAL5.

application layer   The seventh layer in the OSI model. The fifth layer in TCP/IP suite.

area   A collection of networks, hosts, and routers within an autonomous system.

area border router   A router that disseminates routing information about an area.

association   A connection in SCTP.

asymmetric digital subscriber line (ADSL)   A version of DSL.

asynchronous transfer mode (ATM)   A WAN protocol featuring high data rates.

ATM consortium   A group of ATM software and hardware vendors.

ATM forum   A group of parties interested in rapid development of ATM.

ATM switch   An ATM device providing both switching and multiplexing functions.

ATMARP   A protocol that applies ARP to an ATM WAN.

attended bulk data traffic   Traffic in which the user is waiting to receive data.

authentication   Verification of the sender of a message.

Authentication Header Protocol   A protocol in IPSec that provides integrity and authentication.

automatic tunneling   Tunneling in which the receiving host has an IPv6 compatible address.

autonomous system (AS)   A group of networks and routers under the authority of a single administration.

autonomous system boundary router   A router that disseminates routing information about an autonomous system.

B

backbone router   A router inside the backbone area.

background data   In IPv6, traffic consisting of data that is usually delivered in the background; low priority data.

bandwidth on demand   Allocation of bandwidth based on the demand.

Basic Encoding Rules (BER)   A standard that encodes data to be transferred through a network.

Basic Service Set (BSS)   The building block of a wireless LAN as defined by the IEEE 802.11 standard.

Bellman-Ford algorithm   An algorithm used to calculate routing tables in the distance vector routing method.

best-effort delivery   The unreliable transmission mechanism by IP that does not guarantee message delivery.

block mode   In FTP, delivery of the data in blocks.

Bootstrap Protocol (BOOTP)   The protocol that provides configuration information from a table (file).

Border Gateway Protocol (BGP)   An interdomain system routing protocol based on path vector routing.

bridge   A network device operating at the first two layers of the OSI model.

broadcast address   An address that allows transmission of a message to all nodes of a network.

broadcasting   Transmission of a message to all nodes in a network.

browser   An application program that displays a WWW document.

C

cable modem   A technology in which channels in cable TV provide Internet access.

cable modem transmission system (CMTS)   A cable modem devise installed in the distribution hub.

caching   The storing of information in a small, fast memory to hold data items that are being processed.

care-of address   The temporary address of a mobile host on its foreign network.

carrier sense multiple access (CSMA)   A contention access method in which each station listens to the line before transmitting data.

carrier sense multiple access with collision avoidance (CSMA/CA)   An extension of CSMA in which collision is avoided.

carrier sense multiple access with collision detection (CSMA/CD)   An extension of CSMA in which collisions are detected and data are retransmitted.

cell   A small, fixed-size data unit.

cell   In cellular telephony, a geographical area served by a cell office.

cell network   A network using the cell as its basic data unit.

Certification Authority (CA)   A trusted party that issues certificates in public-key cryptography.

channel   A communications pathway.

character mode   A TELNET operation mode in which each character typed is sent by the client to the server.

checksum   A method for error detection.

cipher   An encryption/decryption algorithm.

ciphertext   The encrypted data.

Clark's solution   A solution to prevent the silly window syndrome.

classful addressing   An IPv4 addressing mechanism in which the IP address space is divided into 5 classes: A, B, C, D, and E.

classless addressing   An addressing mechanism in which the IP address space is not divided into classes.

Classless InterDomain Routing (CIDR)   A technique to reduce the number of routing table entries.

client process   A running application program on a local site that requests service from a running application program on a remote site.

collision   The event that occurs when two transmitters send at the same time on a channel designed for only one transmission at a time.

co-located care-of address   A care-of address of a mobile host acting as a foreign agent.

common gateway interface (CGI)   A standard for creating dynamic documents.

compatible address   An IPv6 address consisting of 96 bits of zero followed by 32 bits of IPv4 address.

community antenna TV (cable TV)   A cable network service that broadcasts video signals to locations with poor or no service.

compression   The reduction of a message without significant loss of information.

configuration file   A file containing information needed when a computer is booted.

configured tunneling   Tunneling in which the receiving host does not support an IPv6-compatible address; reconfiguration is necessary.

congestion   Excessive network or internetwork traffic causing a general degradation of service.

congestion-controlled traffic   Traffic in which a source adapts itself to traffic slowdown when there is congestion.

connecting device   A tool that connects computers or networks.

connection establishment   The preliminary setup necessary for a logical connection prior to actual data transfer.

connection resetting   A procedure that terminates the existing connection and establishes a new one.

connection termination   A procedure that terminates a connection.

connectionless protocol   A protocol using connectionless services.

connectionless service   A service for data transfer without connection establishment or termination.

connection-oriented protocol   A protocol using connection-oriented services.

connection-oriented service   A service for data transfer involving establishment and termination of a connection.

Consultative Committee for International Telegraphy and Telephony (CCITT)   An international standards group now known as the ITU-T.

contiguous mask   A mask composed of a run of 1s followed by a run of 0s.

control character   A character that conveys information about the transmission rather than the actual data.

control connection   The FTP connection used for exchanging control information.

control traffic   Highest priority traffic such as routing and management messages.

cookie   A string of characters that holds some information about the client and must be returned to the server untouched.

Core-Based Tree (CBT)   A group-shared multicasting protocol that uses a center router as the root of the tree.

corrupted segment   A data segment with errors.

country domain   A subdomain in the Domain Name System that uses two characters as the last suffix.

crossbar switch   A switch consisting of a lattice of horizontal and vertical paths. At the intersection of each path, there is a crosspoint that connects the paths.

crosspoint   The junction of an input and output in a crossbar switch.

cryptography   The science and art of transforming messages to make them secure and immune to attacks.

Computer Science Network (CSNET)   A network sponsored by the National Science Foundation.

D

data connection   The FTP connection used for data transfer.

data encryption standard (DES)   The block, symmetric-key cipher adopted by the U.S. government.

data link layer   The second layer in the OSI model and TCP/IP suite.

datagram   In packet-switching, an independent data unit.

de facto standard   A protocol not legislated by an authority, but in widespread use.

de jure standard   A protocol legislated by an authority.

deadlock   A situation in which a sender and receiver are waiting for information from each other.

decapsulation   Removal of a header and trailer from a message.

decryption   Recovery of the original message from the encrypted data.

default mask   The mask in classful addressing for class A to C.

default mode   A TELNET operation mode used when no other mode is invoked.

default routing   Routing a packet when no specific route is defined.

Defense Advanced Research Projects Agency (DARPA)   A government organization, which, under the name of ARPA funded ARPANET and the Internet.

Defense Data Network (DDN)   The military portion of the Internet.

delayed response strategy   A technique in IGMP to prevent unnecessary traffic.

delivery   The physical forwarding of packets.

denial-of-service attack   A form of attack in which the site is flooded with so many phony requests that eventually force the server to deny responses.

designated parent router   In distance vector multicast routing, the router that distributes a multicast packet to downstream networks.

destination address   The address of the receiver of the data unit.

dialog   The communication between two devices.

dialog control   The technique used by the session layer to control the dialog.

digest   A condensed version of a document created by a hash algorithm.

digital signature   A method to authenticate the sender of a message.

digital subscriber line (DSL)   A technology using existing telecommunication networks to accomplish high-speed delivery of data, voice, video, and multimedia.

Dijkstra's algorithm   In link state routing, an algorithm that finds the shortest path to each destination.

direct broadcast address   A special address used by a router to send a packet to all hosts in a specified network.

direct delivery   A delivery in which the final destination of the packet is a host connected to the same physical network as the deliverer.

direct sequence spread spectrum (DSSS)   A wireless transmission method in which each bit to be sent by the sender is replaced by a sequence of bits called a chip code.

discrete cosine transform (DCT)   A JPEG phase in which a transformation changes the 64 values so that the relative relationship between the pixels are kept but the redundancies are revealed.

Distance Vector Multicast Routing Protocol (DVMRP)   A multicast routing protocol based on distance vector routing.

distance vector routing   A routing method in which each router sends its neighbors a list of networks it can reach and the distance to that network.

distributed database   Information stored in many locations.

DNS server   A computer that holds information about the name space.

domain   A subtree of the domain name space.

domain name   In DNS, a sequence of labels separated by dots.

domain name space   A structure for organizing the name space in which the names are defined in an inverted-tree structure with the root at the top.

Domain Name System (DNS)   A service that converts user-friendly names to IP addresses.

dotted-decimal notation   A notation for IPv4 addresses; each byte is converted to its decimal equivalent and then set off from its neighbor by a decimal.

double crossing   An inefficient situation that results when a remote host communicates with a mobile host that has moved to the same network.

dual stack   Two protocols (IPv4 and IPv6) on the same station.

duplex mode   See *full-duplex mode.*

duplicate segment   A segment identical to another.

dynamic configuration protocol   A protocol that features tables that are automatically updated as changes occur.

dynamic document   A Web document created at the server site.

Dynamic Domain Name System (DDNS)   DNS in which domain names are updated automatically.

Dynamic Host Configuration Protocol (DHCP)   An extension to BOOTP that dynamically assigns IP addresses and updates configuration files.

dynamic mapping   Mapping physical and logical addresses dynamically.

dynamic port number   A port number that is neither controlled nor registered and can be used by any process.

dynamic routing   Routing in which the routing table entries are updated automatically by the routing protocol.

dynamic routing table   A routing table that has its entries updated automatically by the routing protocol.

E

electronic mail (email)   A method of sending messages electronically based on mailbox addresses rather than a direct host-to-host exchange.

Electronics Industries Association (EIA)   An organization that promotes electronics manufacturing concerns.

Encapsulating Security Payload (ESP)   A protocol defined by IPSec that provides privacy as well as a combination of integrity and message authentication.

encapsulation   Adding a header and/or trailer to a data unit.

encryption   Converting a message into an unintelligible form that is unreadable unless decrypted.

end-to-end message delivery   Delivery of the whole message from the sender to the receiver.

entering-point router   In an ATM network, the router from which the cell begins its transmission.

entity   Anything capable of sending or receiving information.

envelope   The part of the email that contains the sender address, the receiver address, and other information.

ephemeral port number   A port number that is used for a short period of time.

error control   The detection and correction of errors in data transmission.

error correction   The process of correcting bits that have been changed during transmission.

error detection   The process of determining whether or not some bits have been changed during transmission.

Ethernet   A local area network protocol that has gone through many generations.

exiting-point router   In an ATM network, the router from which the cell ends its transmission.

expiration timer   A timer that governs the validity of a route.

extended binary coded decimal interchange code (EBCDIC)   An 8-bit character code developed and used by IBM.

Extended Service Set (ESS)   A wireless LAN service composed of two or more BSSs with APs as defined by the IEEE 802.11 standard.

extension header   Extra headers in the IPv6 datagram that provide additional functionality.

external link   An advertisement that allows a router inside an autonomous system to know which networks are available outside the autonomous system.

extranet   A private network that uses the TCP/IP protocol suite and allows authorized access from outside users.

F

Fast Ethernet   The second generation of Ethernet with a data rate of 100 Mbps.

Federal Communications Commission (FCC)   A government agency that regulates radio, television, and telecommunications.

file transfer, access, and management (FTAM)   In the OSI model, an application layer service for remote file handling.

File Transfer Protocol (FTP)   In TCP/IP, an application layer protocol that transfers files between two sites.

finite state machine   A machine that goes through a limited number of states.

firewall   A device (usually a router) installed between the internal network of an organization and the rest of the Internet to provide access control.

flat namespace   A name space with no hierarchical structure.

flooding   Forwarding a packet through all interfaces except the one from which the packet has arrived.

flow control   A technique to control the rate of flow of frames (packets or messages).

flow label   An IPv6 mechanism to enable the source to request special handling of a packet.

foreign agent   A host attached to a foreign network that receives and delivers packets sent by the home agent to the mobile host.

foreign network   The network to which a mobile host moves.

forum   An organization that tests, evaluates, and standardizes a new technology.

four-way handshake   A sequence of four events for connection establishment or termination.

fractional T line   A service that allows several subscribers to share one T-line by multiplexing their transmissions.

fragmentation   The division of a packet into smaller units to accommodate a protocol's MTU.

frame   A packet in the data link layer.

Frame Relay   A packet-switching protocol defined for the first two layers of the OSI model.

Frame Relay Forum   A group formed by some corporations to promote the acceptance and implementation of Frame Relay.

frequency hopping spread spectrum (FHSS)   A wireless transmission method in which the sender hops to different frequencies.

frequency masking   A phenomenon in which a loud sound in a frequency range can partially or totally mask a softer sound in another frequency range.

full-duplex Ethernet   An Ethernet implementation in which every station is connected by two separate paths to the central hub.

full-duplex mode   A transmission mode in which communication can be two way simultaneously.

fully qualified domain name (FQDN)   A domain name consisting of labels beginning with the host and going back through each level to the root node.

G

garbage collection timer   A timer that advertises the failure of a route.

gateway   A connecting device operating at all five layers of the Internet model.

generic domain   A subdomain in the domain name system that uses generic suffixes.

geographical routing   A routing technique in which the entire address space is divided into blocks based on geographical areas.

Gigabit Ethernet   The third generation of Ethernet with a data rate of 1000 Mbps.

grafting   Resumption of multicast messages.

groupid   The multicast address of a group.

group-shared tree   A multicast routing feature in which each group in the system shares the same shortest path tree.

H

H.323   A standard designed by ITU to allow telephones on the public telephone networks to talk to computers connected to the Internet.

half-duplex mode   A transmission mode in which communication can be two-way but not at the same time.

handshaking   A process to establish or terminate a connection.

hardware address   An address used by a data link layer to identify a device. Physical address.

hash function   An algorithm that creates a fixed-size digest from a variable-length message.

header   Control information added to the beginning of a data packet or a message.

header translation   Conversion of the IPv6 header to IPv4.

hexadecimal colon notation   In IPv6, an address notation consisting of 32 hexadecimal digits, with every four digits separated by a colon.

hidden terminal problem   A situation in which a terminal may be hidden from another in a wireless environment (due to natural obstacles).

hierarchical name space   A tree-like name space, with each succeeding level becoming more and more specific.

hierarchical routing   A routing technique in which the entire address space is divided into levels based on specific criteria.

high bit rate digital subscriber line (HDSL)   DSL service with a higher data rate.

home address   A mobile host's permanent address on its home network.

home agent   A host attached to the home network of the mobile host that receives and sends packets (for the mobile host) to the foreign agent.

home network   A network that is the permanent home of the mobile host.

homepage   A unit of hypertext or hypermedia available on the Web that is the main page for an organization or an individual.

hop count   The number of nodes along a route. It is a measurement of distance in RIP.

host   A station or node on a network.

host file   A file that maps host names to host addresses.

host-specific routing   A routing method in which the full IP address of a host is given in the routing table.

hostid   The part of an IP address that identifies a host.

host-to-host protocol   A protocol that can deliver a packet from one physical device to another.

hybrid network   A private network with access to the global Internet.

hypermedia   Information containing text, pictures, graphics, and sound that is linked to other documents through links (URLs).

hypertext   Information containing text that is linked to other documents through links (URLs).

Hypertext Markup Language (HTML)   The computer language for specifying the contents and format of a Web document. It allows additional text to include codes that define fonts, layouts, embedded graphics, and hypertext links.

Hypertext Transfer Protocol (HTTP)   An application service for retrieving a Web document.

I

image file   In FTP, the default format for transferring binary files.

inbound stream   The input stream for a host in the SCTP protocol.

indirect delivery   A delivery in which a packet goes from one router to another.

Institute of Electrical and Electronics Engineers (IEEE)   A group consisting of professional engineers with committees that prepare standards.

integrity   Preserving the original data.

interactive traffic   Traffic in which interaction with the user is necessary.

interdomain routing   Routing among autonomous systems.

interface   The boundary between two pieces of equipment. A set of commands for communication between two layers.

International Organization of Standardization (ISO)   A worldwide organization that defines and develops standards on a variety of topics.

International Telecommunications Union–Telecommunication Standardization Sector (ITU–T)   A standards organization formerly known as the CCITT.

internet   A collection of networks connected by internetworking devices such as routers.

Internet   The global internet.

Internet address   A 32-bit or 128-bit network-layer address used to uniquely define the connection of a host to the Internet.

Internet Architecture Board (IAB)   The technical adviser to the ISOC; oversees the continuing development of the TCP/IP protocol suite.

Internet Assigned Numbers Authority (IANA)   A group supported by the U.S. government that was responsible for the management of Internet domain names and addresses until October 1998.

Internet Control Message Protocol (ICMP)   A protocol in the TCP/IP protocol suite that handles error and control messages.

Internet Corporation for Assigned Names and Numbers (ICANN)   A private, nonprofit corporation managed by an international board that assumed IANA operations.

Internet draft   A working Internet document (a work in progress) with no official status and a six-month lifetime.

Internet Engineering Steering Group (IESG)   An organization that oversees the activities of IETF.

Internet Engineering Task Force (IETF)   A group working on the design and development of the TCP/IP protocol suite and the Internet.

Internet Group Management Protocol (IGMP)   A protocol in the TCP/IP protocol suite that handles multicasting.

Internet Mail Access Protocol (IMAP)   A complex and powerful protocol to handle the transmission of electronic mail.

Internet Network Information Center (INTERNIC)   An agency responsible for collecting and distributing information about TCP/IP protocols.

Internet Research Task Force (IRTF)   A forum of working groups focusing on long-term research topics related to the Internet.

Internet service provider (ISP)   A company that provides Internet services.

Internet Society (ISOC)   The nonprofit organization established to publicize the Internet.

Internet standard   A thoroughly tested specification that is useful to and adhered to by those who work with the Internet. It is a formalized regulation that must be followed.

internetworking   Connecting several networks together using internetworking devices such as routers and gateways.

internetworking devices   Electronic devices such as routers and gateways that connect networks together to form an internet.

Internetworking Protocol (IP)   The network-layer protocol in the TCP/IP protocol suite governing connectionless transmission across packet-switching networks.

Internetworking Protocol, next generation (IPng)   Another term for the sixth version of the Internetworking Protocol, IPv6.

intracoded frame (I-frame)   In MPEG, an independent frame that is not related to any other frame and appearing at regular intervals.

intranet   A private network that uses the TCP/IP protocol suite.

inverse domain   A subdomain in the DNS that finds the domain name given the IP address.

IP address   See *Internet address.*

IP address class   In IPv4, one of the five groups of addresses: A, B, C, D, and E.

IP datagram   The Internetworking Protocol data unit.

IP Security (IPSec)   A collection of protocols designed by the IETF to provide security for a packet carried on the Internet.

iterative resolution   Resolution of the IP address in which the client may send its request to multiple servers before getting an answer.

J

Java   A programming language used to create active Web documents.

jitter   A phenomenon in real-time traffic caused by gaps between consecutive packets at the receiver.

K

Karn's Algorithm   An algorithm that does not include the retransmitted segments in calculation of round-trip time.

keepalive timer   A timer that prevents a long idle connection between two TCPs.

key distribution center (KDC)   In symmetric-key cryptography, a trusted third party that shares a key with each user.

L

layered architecture   A model based on ordered tiers.

lexicographic ordering   Ordering based on a dictionary.

limited broadcast address   A destination address defining all hosts on a network.

line mode   A TELNET operation mode in which line editing is done by the client.

Link Control Protocol (LCP)   A PPP protocol responsible for establishing, maintaining, configuring, and terminating links.

link local address   An IPv6 address used by a private LAN.

link state database   In link state routing, a database common to all routers and made from LSA information.

local address   The part of an email address that defines the mailbox.

local area network (LAN)   A network connecting devices inside a single building or inside buildings close to each other.

local host   The user computer.

local login   Using a terminal directly connected to the computer.

local loop   The link that connects a subscriber to the telephone central office.

logical address   An address defined in the network layer.

logical IP subnet (LIS)   A grouping of nodes of an ATM network in which the connection is logical, not physical.

longest mask match   The technique in CIDR in which the longest prefix is handled first when searching a routing table.

loopback address   An address used by a host to test its internal software.

M

magic cookie   In BOOTP, the number in the format of an IP address indicating that options are present.

mail exchanger   Any computer capable of receiving email.

Management Information Base (MIB)   The database used by SNMP that holds the information necessary for management of a network.

manager   The host that runs the SNMP client program.

mapped address   An IPv6 address used when a computer that has migrated to IPv6 wants to send a packet to a computer still using IPv4.

mask   For IPv4, a 32-bit binary number that gives the first address in the block (the network address) when ANDed with an address in the block.

masking   A process that extracts the address of the physical network from an IP address.

maturity level   The phases through which an RFC goes.

maximum transfer unit (MTU)   The largest size data unit a specific network can handle.

media player   An application that plays an audio/video file.

media server   A server accessed by a media player to download an audio/video file.

message   Data sent from source to destination.

message access agent (MAA)   A client-server program that pulls the stored email messages.

message transfer agent (MTA)   An SMTP component that transfers the message across the Internet.

metric   A cost assigned for passing through a network.

Military Network (MILNET)   A military network originally part of ARPANET.

mixer   A device that combines real-time signals from different sources into one signal.

mobile host   A host that can move from one network to another.

multicast address   An address used for multicasting.

multicast backbone (MBONE)   A set of internet routers supporting multicasting through the use of tunneling.

Multicast Open Shortest Path First (MOSPF)   A multicast protocol that uses multicast link state routing to create a source-based least cost tree.

multicast router   A router with a list of loyal members related to each router interface that distributes the multicast packets.

multicast routing   Moving a multicast packet to its destination.

multicasting   A transmission method that allows copies of a single packet to be sent to a selected group of receivers.

multihomed device   A device connected to more than one network.

multimedia traffic   Traffic consisting of data, video, and audio.

multiple unicasting   Sending multiple copies of a message, each with a different unicast destination address, from one source.

multiplexing   The process of combining signals from multiple sources for transmission across a single data link.

multiplicative decrease   A congestion avoidance technique in which the threshold is set to half of the last congestion window size, and the congestion window size starts from one again.

Multipurpose Internet Mail Extension (MIME)   A protocol that allows non-ASCII data to be sent through email.

N

Nagle's algorithm   An algorithm that attempts to prevent silly window syndrome at the sender's site.

name server   A computer that maps computer names to IP addresses.

name space   All the names assigned to machines on an internet.

name-address resolution   Mapping a name to an address or an address to a name.

National Science Foundation (NSF)   A government agency responsible for Internet funding.

National Science Foundation Network (NSFNET)   A backbone funded by NSF.

netid   The part of an IP address that identifies the network.

network   A system consisting of connected nodes that share data, hardware, and software.

Network Access Point (NAP)   A complex switching station that connects backbone networks.

network address   An address that identifies a network to the rest of the Internet; it is the first address in a block.

network address translation (NAT)   A technology that allows a private network to use a set of private addresses for internal communication.

Network Control Protocol (NCP)   In PPP, a set of control protocols that allows the encapsulation of data coming from network layer protocols.

network file system (NFS)   A TCP/IP application protocol that allows a user to access and manipulate remote file systems as if they were local. It uses the services of remote procedure call protocol.

Network Information Center (NIC)   An agency responsible for collecting and distributing information about TCP/IP protocols.

network interface card (NIC)   An electronic device, internal or external to a station, with circuitry that connects stations to the network.

network layer   The third layer in the OSI model and the TCP/IP suite.

network support layers   The physical, data link, and network layers.

network-specific routing   Routing in which all hosts on a network share one entry in the routing table.

network-to-network interface (NNI)   In ATM, the interface between two networks.

Network Virtual Terminal (NVT)   A method that allows remote login.

next-hop address   The address of the first router to which the packet is delivered.

next-hop routing   A routing method in which only the address of the next hop is listed in the routing table instead of a complete list of the stops the packet must make.

node-to-node delivery   Transfer of a data unit from one node to the next.

noise   Random electrical signals that result in degradation or distortion of the data.

noncontiguous mask   A mask composed of a series of bits that is not a string of 1s followed by a string of 0s, but a mixture of 0s and 1s.

nonpersistent connection   A connection in which one TCP connection is made for each request/response.

nonrepudiation   A security aspect in which a receiver must be able to prove that a received message came from a specific sender.

O

object   A variable in an SNMP packet.

object identifier   A hierarchical method used by SMI to name variables managed by SNMP.

octet   Eight bits.

one's complement   A representation of binary numbers in which the complement of a number is found by reversing each bit.

open shortest path first (OSPF)   An interior routing protocol based on link state routing.

open systems interconnection (OSI)   A seven-layer model for data communication defined by ISO.

optical carrier (OC)   The hierarchy of fiber-optic carriers defined in SONET.

option negotiation   In TELNET, a client and server interaction to decide which options to use.

orthogonal frequency-division multiplexing (OFDM)   A multiplexing method similar to FDM, with all the subbands used by one source as a given time.

out-of-band signaling   A method of signaling in which control data and user data travel on different channels.

outbound stream   An output stream in a host using SCTP.

P

packet   Synonym for data unit, mostly used in the network layer.

Packet Internet Groper (PING)   An application program to determine the reachability of a destination using an ICMP echo request and reply.

packet-filter firewall   A system that forwards or blocks packets based on the information in the network-layer and transport-layer headers.

page   A unit of hypertext or hypermedia available on the Web.

parent server   A server running infinitely and accepting connections from the clients.

partially qualified domain name (PQDN)   A domain name that does not include all the levels between the host and the root node.

passive open   The state of a server as it waits for incoming requests from a client.

path   The channel through which a signal travels.

Path MTU Discovery technique   An IPv6 method to find the smallest MTU supported by any network on a path.

path vector routing A routing method on which BGP is based; in this method, the ASs through which a packet must pass are explicitly listed.

perceptual encoding An encoding technique used for audio compression in which some flaws in our auditory system are used to encode audio signals.

peer-to-peer process A process on a sending and a receiving machine that communicate at a given layer.

periodic timer A RIP timer that controls the sending of messages.

permanent virtual circuit (PVC) A virtual circuit transmission method in which the same virtual circuit is used between source and destination on a continual basis.

persistence timer A technique to handle the zero window-size advertisement.

persistent connection A connection in which the server leaves the connection open for more requests after sending a response.

physical address The address of a device used at the data link layer (MAC address).

physical layer The first layer of the OSI model and TCP/IP suite.

physical topology The manner in which devices are connected in a network.

piggybacking The inclusion of acknowledgment on a data frame.

plaintext In encryption/decryption, the original message.

playback buffer A buffer that stores the data until they are ready to be played.

point-to-point link A dedicated transmission link between two devices.

Point-to-Point Protocol (PPP) A protocol for data transfer across a serial line.

poison reverse A feature added to split horizons in which a table entry that has come through one interface is set to infinity in the update packet.

policy routing A path vector routing feature in which the routing tables are based on rules set by the network administrator rather than a metric.

port address In TCP/IP protocol an integer identifying a process.

port number See port address.

Post Office Protocol (POP) A popular but simple SMTP mail access protocol.

PPP over Ethernet (PPPoE) Use of the PPP protocol over an Ethernet network.

predicted frame (P-frame) An MPEG frame which contains only the changes from the preceding frame.

prefix For a network, another name for the common part of the address range.

presentation layer The sixth layer of the OSI model.

Pretty Good Privacy (PGP) A protocol that provides all four aspects of security in the sending of email.

primary server A server that stores a file about the zone for which it is an authority.

privacy A security aspect in which the message makes sense only to the intended receiver.

private key In asymmetric-key cryptography, the key that is kept secret.

private network A network that is isolated from the Internet.

process A running application program.

process identification A number that uniquely defines a process.

process-to-process communication Communication between two running application programs.

protection against wrap sequence (PAWS)   Using timestamps to prevent one delayed or lost packet from reappearing in the next round of sequence numbers.

protocol   Rules for communication.

Protocol Independent Multicast (PIM)   A multicasting protocol family with two members, PIM-DM and PIM-SM; both protocols are unicast-protocol dependent.

Protocol Independent Multicast, Dense Mode (PIM-DM)   A source-based routing protocol that uses RPF and pruning/grafting strategies to handle multicasting.

Protocol Independent Multicast, Sparse Mode (PIM-SM)   A group-shared routing protocol that is similar to CBT and uses a rendezvous point as the source of the tree.

protocol suite   A stack or family of protocols defined for a complex communication system.

proxy ARP   A technique that creates a subnetting effect; one device answers ARP requests for multiple hosts.

proxy firewall   A system that filters a message based on the information available in the message itself (at the application layer).

proxy server   A computer that keeps copies of responses to recent requests.

pruning   Stopping the sending of multicast messages from an interface.

pseudoheader   Information from the IP header used only for checksum calculation in UDP and TCP packets.

public key   In asymmetric-key encryption, a key known to everyone.

public-key cryptography   A method of cryptography with two keys: public and private; asymmetric-key cryptography.

push data   Data that must be sent with minimum delay; marked by setting the push bit in the TCP header.

Q
queue   A waiting list.

R
radio frequency wave   Electromagnetic energy in the 3-kHz to 300-GHz range.

rate adaptive asymmetrical digital subscriber line (RADSL)   A DSL-based technology that features different data rates depending on the type of communication.

raw socket   A structure designed for protocols that directly use the services of IP and use neither stream sockets nor datagram sockets.

read-only memory (ROM)   Permanent memory with contents that cannot be changed.

real-time multimedia traffic   Traffic consisting of data, audio, and video that is simultaneously produced and used.

Real-Time Streaming Protocol (RTSP)   An out-of-band control protocol designed to add more functionality to the streaming audio/video process.

real-time traffic   Traffic in one form that is simultaneously produced and used.

Real-time Transport Control Protocol (RTCP)   A companion protocol to RTP with messages that control the flow and quality of data and allow the recipient to send feedback to the source or sources.

Real-time Transport Protocol (RTP)   A protocol for real-time traffic; used in conjunction with UDP.

receiver   The target point of a transmission.

recursive resolution   Resolution of the IP address in which the client sends its request to a server that eventually returns a response.

registered port   A port number, ranging from 1,024 to 49,151, not assigned or controlled by IANA.

registrar   An authority to register new domain names.

registration   A phase of communication between a remote host and a mobile host in which the mobile host gives information about itself to the foreign agent.

registration request   A packet sent from the mobile host to the foreign agent to register its care-of address and also to announce its home address and home agent address.

relay agent   For BOOTP, a router that can help send local requests to remote servers.

relay MTA   An MTA that can relay email.

remote host   The computer that a user wishes to access while seated physically at another computer.

remote login   The process of logging on to a remote computer from a terminal connected to a local computer.

remote server   A program run at a site physically removed from the user.

rendezvous router   A router that is the core or center for each multicast group; it becomes the root of the tree.

rendezvous-point tree   A group-shared tree method in which there is one tree for each group.

repeater   A device that extends the distance a signal can travel by regenerating the signal.

Request for Comment (RFC)   A formal Internet document concerning an Internet issue.

requirement level   One of five RFC levels.

reserved address   IP addresses set aside by the Internet authorities for future use.

resolver   The DNS client that is used by a host that needs to map an address to a name or a name to an address.

retransmission timer   A timer that controls the waiting time for an acknowledgment of a segment.

Reverse Address Resolution Protocol (RARP)   A TCP/IP protocol that allows a host to find its Internet address given its physical address.

reverse path broadcasting (RPB)   A technique in which the router sends the packet out of the interface for which it is the designated parent.

reverse path forwarding (RPF)   A technique in which the router forwards only the packets that have traveled the shortest path from the source to the router.

reverse path multicasting (RPM)   A technique that adds pruning and grafting to RPB to create a multicast shortest path tree that supports dynamic membership changes.

ring topology   A topology in which the devices are connected in a ring.

root label   In DNS, a null (empty) string.

root server   In DNS, a server whose zone consists of the whole tree.

round-trip time (RTT)   The time required for a datagram to go from a source to a destination and then back again.

router   An internetworking device operating at the first three OSI or TCP/IP layers.

routing   The process performed by a router; finding the next hop for a datagram.

Routing Information Protocol (RIP)   A routing protocol based on the distance vector routing.

routing table   A table containing information a router needs to route packets.

RSA encryption   A public-key cryptography method by Rivest, Shamir, and Adleman.

S

secondary server   In DNS, a server that transfers the complete information about a zone from another server (primary or secondary) and stores the file on its local disk.

secret-key encryption   A security method in which the key for encryption is the same as the key for decryption; both sender and receiver have the same key.

security   The protection of a network from unauthorized access, viruses, and catastrophe.

security association (SA)   An IPsec signalling protocol that creates a logical connection between hosts.

segment   The packet at the transport layer.

segmentation   The splitting of a message into multiple packets; usually performed at the transport layer.

semantics   The meaning of each data unit or part of a data unit.

sender   The originator of a message.

sequence number   The number that denotes the location of a frame or packet in a message.

server   A running application program (process) on a remote site that gives services to clients.

service-point address   See *port address*.

session layer   The fifth layer of the OSI model.

shortest path   The optimal path from the source to the destination.

silly window syndrome   A situation in which a small window size is advertised by the receiver and a small segment sent by the sender.

simple and efficient adaptation layer (SEAL)   An AAL level designed for the Internet (AAL5).

simple data type   An atomic SMI data type from which other data types are constructed.

Simple Mail Transfer Protocol (SMTP)   The TCP/IP protocol defining electronic mail service on the Internet.

Simple Network Management Protocol (SNMP)   The TCP/IP protocol that specifies the process of management in the Internet.

simplex mode   A transmission mode in which communication is one way.

site local address   An IPv6 address used if a site having several networks uses the Internet protocols but is not connected to the Internet for security reasons.

slash notation   A shorthand method to indicate the number of 1s in the mask.

sliding window protocol   A protocol that allows several data units to be in transition before receiving an acknowledgment.

slow convergence   A RIP shortcoming apparent when a change somewhere in the internet propagates very slowly through the rest of the internet.

slow start   A congestion-control method in which the congestion window size increases exponentially at first.

socket address   A structure holding an IP address and a port number.

sorcerer's apprentice bug   A TFTP problem for a delayed packet in which every succeeding packet is sent twice and every succeeding acknowledgment is received twice.

source address   The address of the sender of the message.

source quench   A method, used in ICMP for flow control, in which the source is advised to slow down or stop the sending of datagrams because of congestion.

source routing   Routing predefined by the sender of the packet.

source-based tree   A tree used for multicasting by multicasting protocols in which a single tree is made for each combination of source and group.

source-to-destination delivery   The transmission of a message from the original sender to the intended recipient.

spanning tree   A tree with the source as the root and group members as leaves; a tree that connects all of the nodes.

spatial compression   Compression of an image by removing redundancies.

specific host on this network   A special address in which the netid is all 0s and the hostid is explicit.

split horizon   A method to improve RIP stability in which the router selectively chooses the interface from which updating information is sent.

spread spectrum   A wireless transmission technique that requires a bandwidth several times the original bandwidth.

standard   A basis or model to which everyone has agreed.

star topology   A topology in which all stations are attached to a central device (hub).

state transition diagram   A diagram to illustrate the states of a finite state machine.

static configuration protocol   A protocol, such as BOOTP, in which the binding between the physical and IP addresses is static and fixed in a table until changed by the administrator.

static document   On the World Wide Web, a fixed-content document that is created and stored in a server.

static mapping   A technique in which a manually configured list of logical and physical addresses is used for address resolution.

static routing   A type of routing in which the routing table remains unchanged.

static-routing table   A routing table used in static routing; usually manually updated.

stationary host   A host that remains attached to one network.

stop-and-wait protocol   An error control protocol using that sends a message and waits for the acknowledgment.

Stream Control Transmission Protocol (SCTP)   The new transport layer protocol designed for Internet telephony and related applications.

stream identifier (SI)   The identity of a stream in a multi-streamed protocol such as SCTP.

stream sequence number (SSN)   In SCTP, the sequence number of a chunk in a stream.

stream mode   An FTP transmission mode in which data is delivered as a continuous stream of bytes.

Structure of Management Information (SMI)   In SNMP, a component used in network management.

structured data type   An SMI data type composed of a combination of simple data types.

stub link   A network that is connected to only one router.

subdomain   A part of a DNS domain.

subnet address   The network address of a subnet.

subnet mask   The mask for a subnet.

subnetting   Dividing a network into smaller units.

subnetwork   A part of a network.

suboption negotiation   In TELNET, the interaction between a client and server to decide on the suboption to use.

suffix   For a network, the varying part (similar to the hostid) of the address. In DNS, a string used by an organization to define its host or resources.

supernet   A network formed from two or more smaller networks.

supernet mask   The mask for a supernet.

supernetting   The combining of several class C blocks to create a larger range of addresses.

switch   A device connecting multiple communication lines together.

switching fabric   The switching mechanism in a router to send an input packet to the output packet.

switched Ethernet   An Ethernet in which a switch, replacing the hub, can direct a transmission to its destination.

switched virtual circuit (SVC)   A virtual circuit transmission method in which a virtual circuit is created and in existence only for the duration of the exchange.

symmetric digital subscriber line (SDSL)   A DSL-based technology similar to HDSL, but using only one single twisted-pair cable.

symmetric-key cryptography   A cipher in which the same key is used for encryption and decryption. Secret-key cryptography.

synchronization points   Reference points introduced into the data by the session layer for the purpose of flow and error control.

synchronous digital hierarchy (SDH)   The ITU-T equivalent of SONET.

Synchronous Optical Network (SONET)   A standard developed by ANSI for fiber-optic technology that can transmit high-speed data. It can be used to deliver text, audio, and video.

synchronous transport module (STM)   A signal in the SDH hierarchy.

synchronous transport signal (STS)   A signal in the SONET hierarchy.

syntax   The structure or format of data, meaning the order in which they are presented.

T

T-lines   A hierarchy of digital lines designed to carry speech and other signals in digital form. The hierarchy defines T-1 and T-3 lines.

tag   A formatting instruction embedded in an HTML document. In SCTP, the session identifier.

TCP timer   The timers used by TCP to handle retransmission, zero window-size advertisements, long idle connections, and connection termination.

TCP/IP protocol suite   A group of hierarchical protocols used in an internet.

teleconferencing   Audio and visual communication between remote users.

temporal compression   An MPEG compression method in which redundant frames are removed.

Terminal Network (TELNET)   A general purpose client-server program that allows remote login.

this host on this network   A special address in which the netid and hostid are all 0s; used by a host at bootstrap time when it does not know its IP address.

three-way handshake   A sequence of events for connection establishment or termination consisting of the request, then the acknowledgment of the request, and then confirmation of the acknowledgment.

time to live (TTL)   See *packet lifetime*.

time-sharing   Multiple users sharing the resources of a large computer.

time-waited timer   A TCP timer used in connection termination that allows late segments to arrive.

timing   Referring to when data must be sent and how fast it can be sent.

topology   The structure of a network including physical arrangement of devices.

trailer   Control information appended to a data unit.

transient link   A network with several routers attached to it.

translation   Changing from one code or protocol to another.

translation table   A table used by a NAT router to resolve a private address with an external address.

translator   A computer that can change the format of a high-bandwidth video signal to a lower quality narrow-bandwidth signal.

Transmission Control Protocol (TCP)   A transport protocol in the TCP/IP protocol suite.

Transmission Control Protocol/Internetworking Protocol (TCP/IP)   A five-layer protocol suite that defines the exchange of transmissions across the Internet.

transmission sequence number (TSN)   In SCTP, the sequence number of each chunk.

transparency   The ability to send any bit pattern as data without it being mistaken for control bits.

transport layer   The fourth layer in the OSI model and the TCP/IP suite.

Transport Layer Security (TLS)   A security protocol at the transport level designed to provide security on the WWW.

transport mode   Encryption in which a TCP segment or a UDP user datagram is first encrypted and then encapsulated in an IPv6 packet.

transpositional cipher   A cipher method in which the position of characters or bits are changed.

tree   A hierarchical data structure in which each node on a tree has one single parent, and zero or more children.

triangle routing   An inefficient routing that occurs when a remote host sends a packet to the mobile host; the packet goes from the remote host to the home agent and then to the mobile host.

triggered update process   A RIP feature to remedy instability in which an update is sent immediately following a change.

Trivial File Transfer Protocol (TFTP)   An unreliable TCP/IP protocol for file transfer that does not require complex interaction between client and server.

tunnel mode   Encryption in which the entire IP datagram with its base header and extension headers is encrypted and then encapsulated in a new IP packet using the ESP extension header.

tunneling In multicasting, a process in which the multicast packet is encapsulated in a unicast packet and then sent through the network. In VPN, the encapsulation of an encrypted IP datagram in a second outer datagram. For IPv6, a strategy used when two computers using IPv6 want to communicate with each other when the packet must pass through a region that uses IPv4.

type of service (TOS) A criteria or value that specifies the handling of the datagram.

U

unattended data traffic Traffic in which the user is not waiting (attending) for the data.

unicast address An address defining one single destination.

unicast message A message sent to just one destination.

unicasting The sending of a packet to just one destination.

Uniform Resource Locator (URL) A string of characters (address) that identifies a page on the World Wide Web.

unsolicited response A RIP response sent periodically, every 30 seconds that contains information about the entire routing table.

unspecified address An IPv6 address consisting entirely of 0s.

update binding packet A packet that binds the care-of address to the home address of a mobile host.

urgent data In TCP/IP, data that must be delivered to the application program as quickly as possible.

urgent pointer A pointer to the boundary between urgent data and normal data.

user agent (UA) An SMTP component that prepares the message, creates the envelope, and puts the message in the envelope.

user datagram The name of the packet in the UDP protocol.

User Datagram Protocol (UDP) A connectionless TCP/IP transport layer protocol.

user interface The interface between the user and the application.

user network interface (UNI) The interface between a user and the ATM network.

user support layers The session, presentation, and application layers in the OSI model.

V

variable-length subnetting The use of different masks to create subnets on a network.

verification tag The tag in SCTP that defines a session.

very high bit rate digital subscriber line (VDSL) A DSL-based technology for short distances.

videotex The process of accessing remote databases interactively.

virtual channel identifier (VCI) A field in an ATM cell header that defines a channel.

virtual circuit (VC) A logical circuit made between the sending and receiving computer. The connection is made after both computers do handshaking. After the connection, all packets follow the same route and arrive in sequence.

virtual connection identifier A VCI or VPI.

virtual link An OSPF connection between two routers that is created when the physical link is broken.

virtual path identifier (VPI) A field in an ATM cell header that identifies a path.

virtual private network (VPN)   A technology that creates a network that is physically public, but virtually private.

voice over IP   A technology in which the Internet is used as a telephone network.

W

warning packet   A packet sent by the home agent to inform the remote host that a mobile host has moved.

Web   Synonym for World Wide Web (WWW).

well-known attribute   Path information that every BGP router must recognize.

well-known port   A port number that normally identifies a process on the server.

wide area network (WAN)   A network that uses a technology that can span a large geographical distance.

window scale factor   A multiplier that increases the window size.

wireless transmission   Communication using unguided media.

working group   An IETF committee concentrating on a specific Internet topic.

World Wide Web (WWW)   A multimedia Internet service that allows users to traverse the Internet by moving from one document to another via links that connect them together.

X

X.25   An ITU-T protocol that defines the interface between a data terminal device and a packet-switching network.

Z

zone   In DNS, what a server is responsible for or has authority over.

References

Comer, Douglas E. *Internetworking with TCP/IP,* vol. 1, 4th ed. Upper Saddle River, NJ: Prentice-Hall, 2000.

————. *Internetworking with TCP/IP,* vol. 2. Upper Saddle River, NJ: Prentice-Hall, 1999.

————. *Internetworking with TCP/IP,* vol. 3. Upper Saddle River, NJ: Prentice-Hall, 1996.

Dickie, Mark. *Routing in Today's Internetworks.* New York, NY: Van Nostrand Reinhold, 1994.

Forouzan, Behrouz. *Data Communications and Networking,* 3rd ed. Burr Ridge, IL: McGraw-Hill, 2004.

Forouzan, Behrouz. *Local Area Networks.* Burr Ridge, IL: McGraw-Hill, 2003.

Gerd, Keiser. *Local Area Networks.* Burr Ridge, IL: McGraw-Hill, 2nd ed. 2002.

Halsall, Fred. *Data Communications, Computer Networks and Open Systems,* 4th ed. Reading, MA: Addison-Wesley, 1995.

Huitema, Christian. *Routing in the Internet.* Upper Saddle River, NJ: Prentice-Hall, 1995.

Johnson, Howard W. *Fast Ethernet.* Upper Saddle River, NJ: Prentice-Hall, 1996.

Kurose, James F., and Ross, Keith W. *Computer Networking,* 3rd ed. Reading, MA: Addison-Wesley, 2004.

Leon-Garcia, Albert, and Widjaja, Indra. *Computer Networks,* 2nd ed. Burr Ridge, IL: McGraw-Hill, 2nd ed. 2004.

Moy, John. *OSPF.* Reading, MA: Addison-Wesley, 1998.

Partridge, Craig. *Gigabit Networking.* Reading, MA: Addison-Wesley, 1994.

Perlman, Radia. *Interconnections,* 2nd ed. Reading, MA: Addison-Wesley, 2000.

Peterson, Larry L., and Davie, Bruce S. Computer Networks, 3rd ed. 340 Pine Street, San Francisco, CA: Morgan Kaufmann, 2003.

Stallings, William. *Data and Computer Communication,* 7th ed. Upper Saddle River, NJ: Prentice-Hall, 2004.

Stallings, William. *High-Speed Network,* Upper Saddle River, NJ: Prentice-Hall, 1998.

Stevens, W. Richard. *TCP/IP Illustrated,* vol. 1. Reading, MA: Addison-Wesley, 1994.

———. *TCP/IP Illustrated,* vol. 3. Reading, MA: Addison-Wesley, 1996.

Stewart, Randall R., and Xie, Qiaobing. *Stream Control Transmission Protocol (SCTP),* Reading, MA: Addison-Wesley, 2002.

Tanenbaum, Andrew S. *Computer Networks,* 4th ed. Upper Saddle River, NJ: Prentice-Hall, 2003.

Wright, Gary R., and W. Richard Stevens. *TCP/IP Illustrated,* vol. 2. Reading, MA: Addison-Wesley, 1995.

Index

Numerics

1000BASE-LX, 49
1000BASE-SX, 49
1000BASE-T, 49
1000BASE-X, 49
100BASE-FX, 48
100BASE-T4, 48
100BASE-TX, 48
2MSL, 325
2X, 646
56K modem, 55
802.1, 800
802.11, 54
802.2, 800
802.3, 800
802.4, 800
802.5, 800

A

AAL, 68, 69
AAL1, 68
AAL2, 68
AAL3/4, 69
AAL5, 69, 622
  ATM, 626
  ATM layer, 623
  CRC field, 623
  Internet, 622
  length field, 623
  packet size, 622
  pad field, 623
  padding, 622
  trailer, 622
  type field, 623
  user-to-user ID field, 623
ABORT chunk, 362, 369

Abstract Syntax Notation 1.
  See ASN.1
AC value, 655
access control
  data link layer, 23
access method
  CSMA/CD, 44
access point. *See* AP
accumulative acknowledgment, 307
ACK, 286
  block number field, 535
  delayed, 539
  duplicate, 307
  opcode field, 535
  SIP, 671
  TFTP, 535
acknowledgment number, 280, 281
acknowledgment policy, 315
acknowledgment, 305
  accumulative, 307
  delayed, 305
  generation, 306
  rules, 306
  SCTP, 352
  TCP, 306
active document, 608
  client site, 608
  Java, 608
active open, 285, 295
  FTP control connection, 520
  FTP data connection, 521
additive increase, 317
address
  broadcast, 101
  direct broadcast, 96
  IP, 35
  limited broadcast, 97
  link, 34

  logical, 24
  loopback, 99
  multicast, 100
  need for multiple, 159
  network, 96
  physical, 34
  port, 36
  private, 99
  service-point, 26
  special, 96
  specific host on this network, 98
  this host on this network, 98
  types, 33
  unicast, 100
address aggregation, 126, 143–144
address allocation, 126
address mask
  ICMPv6, 714
address mask message, 224
Address Resolution Protocol.
  See ARP
address space, 82
  IPv6, 692
address to name
  resolution, 481
addressing, 33
  ATM WAN, 627
  classful, 115
  classless, 115
  Ethernet, 46
  levels of, 33
  mobile IP, 637
Adler checksum, 788
Adobe PostScript, 558
ADSL, 56, 58
  actual bit rate, 57
  vs. HDSL, 58
  vs. VDSL, 58

Advanced Research Projects
    Agency. *See* ARPA
advertised receiver window
    credit, 357
agent, 575–576
    database, 576
    function, 589
    MIB, 585
    passive open, 595
    trap, 576
agent advertisement, 640
    care-of address field, 641
    code field, 641
    length field, 641
    lifetime field, 641
    sequence number field, 641
    type field, 641
agent discovery, 640
    phases, 640
agent solicitation, 642
AH, 755
    authentication data, 756
    authentication data field, 757
    vs. ESP, 758
    header, 756
    IP header, 756
    next header field, 756
    payload length field, 756
    sequence number, 757
    SPI field, 757
Alert Protocol, 761
alias, 555
allocation of resources, 364
American National Standards Institute.
    See ANSI
American Standard Code for
    Information Interchange.
    See ASCII
AMI, 58
mplifier, 70
AND operation, 92
anonymous FTP, 532
ANSI, 7–8
ANSNET, 3
anycast address, 692
AP, 50, 54
APNIC, 693
applet, 608
application adaptation layer. *See* AAL
application layer, 28
    directory services, 29
    file manipulation, 28
    mail services, 29
    NVT, 28
    responsibilities, 28

security, 754
services, 28
TCP/IP, 30, 32
application layer security
    PGP, 762
    proxy firewall, 765
area, 404
    id, 404
    virtual link, 404
area border router, 404, 415
    backbone router, 404
ARP, 31, 159–161
    ATMARP, 630
    broadcast physical address, 160
    broadcast query, 161
    direct delivery, 132
    dynamic mapping, 161
    encapsulation, 163
    four cases, 164
    hardware length field, 162
    hardware type field, 162
    host to host, 164
    ICMPv6, 689, 715
    indirect delivery, 133
    IP to physical address
        mapping, 161
    operation, 163
    package, 166
    packet components, 161
    packet format, 162
    process, 163
    protocol length field, 162
    protocol type field, 162
    proxy, 166
    query packet, 161
    response packet, 161
        components, 161
    router to host on different
        network, 165
    router to host on same
        network, 165
    sender hardware address
        field, 163
    sender protocol address field, 163
    steps involved, 163
    target hardware address field, 163
    target protocol address field, 163
    unicast physical address, 160
    unicast response, 161
ARP design, 171–172
ARP package
    cache table, 167
    cache-control module, 170
    components, 167
    FREE state, 170

    input module, 169
    output module, 168
    PENDING state, 168–169
    queues, 168
    RESOLVED state, 168–169
ARP packet
    reply, 169
    request, 169
ARPA, 2
ARPANET, 2
    original nodes, 2
    TCP/IP, 3
AS, 386, 751–752
    area, 404
    backbone, 404
    graphical representation, 407
    multihomed, 424
    speaker node, 421
    stub, 424
    transit, 424
    types, 424
ASCII, 771
    FTP, 523
    HTML, 604
ASN.1, 580
    X.509, 750
ASP, 607
association, 347–348, 362
    packets exchanged, 364
    termination, 368
association abortion, 368
association establishment, 363
asymmetrical DSL. *See* ADSL
asymmetric-key cryptography
    certification, 749
    entity authentication, 741
    privacy, 736
    problem, 749
asynchronous TDM
    ATM, 66
Asynchronous Transfer Mode.
    See ATM
ATM, 65–66
    AAL1, 68
    AAL2, 68
    AAL3/4, 69
    AAL5, 69, 626
    architecture, 66, 621
    asynchronous TDM, 66
    ATM layer, 69
    backward compatibility, 65
    connection-oriented, 65
    cost considerations, 65
    current compatibility, 65
    design goals, 65

example, 66
Internet, 621
layers, 68, 621
medium, 65, 69
movement toward hardware, 65
multiplexing, 66
physical layer, 69, 625, 633
SONET, 69
virtual connection, 66
WAN, 621
ATM Forum, 9
address, 803
ATM layer
cell size, 69, 623
CLP field, 625
congestion control, 625
function, 69, 623
header for NNI, 623
header, 623
HEC field, 625
NNI level flow control, 623
payload type field, 624
priority for discard, 625
UNI level flow control, 623
VCI field, 624
VPI, 623, 624
ATM switch
layers, 621
ATM WAN, 621
address, 621
address binding, 627
addressing, 627
ATM layer, 623
encapsulation, 621, 625
fragmentation, 621
IP address, 627
physical address, 627
physical layer, 625
router, 621, 626
switch, 621
VPI, 627
ATMARP, 621, 627
ARP, 630
client, 630
connecting to server, 630
establishing virtual circuit, 630
hardware length field, 628
hardware type field, 628
inverse operation, 631
LIS, 632
operation, 628
packet format, 628
physical address, 630
protocol length field, 629
protocol type field, 628

PVC, 629
router exchange example, 629
sender hardware address
    field, 629
sender protocol address field, 629
server, 629–630
server table, 631
SVC, 629
target hardware address field, 629
target hardware length field, 629
target protocol address field, 629
target protocol length field, 629
virtual circuit, 630
virtual connection, 630
attenuation, 70
audio, 652
analog, 652
compression, 653
digitizing, 652
authentication, 707
AH protocol, 757
algorithm, 707
bidirectional, 741
digital signature, 736
of entity, 740
IPv4, 689
Kerberos, 751
receiver, 707
RIP, 398
RIPv2, 398
security key, 707
security parameter index field, 707
sender, 707
Authentication Header protocol.
    See AH
authentication server. *See* AS
automatic tunneling, 720
autonomous system. *See* AS

B

back pressure, 315
backbone, 404
backbone router, 404
bandwidth, 64
    real-time traffic, 666
bandwidth on demand, 64
banyan switch, 152
    internal collision, 153
base 256, 776, 779
    to binary, 782
    weight and value, 779
    weights, 779
base header
    IPv6, 698

Basic Encoding Rules. *See* BER
basic service set. *See* BSS
Batcher-banyan switch, 68, 153
BER, 582
class subfield, 582
format, 582
IP address example, 584
length field, 583
number subfield, 582
SNMP, 592
tag field, 582
value field, 583
best-effort delivery, 31, 179
B-frame, 658
BGP, 385, 424
CIDR, 424
encapsulation, 430
external, 425
header, 426
internal, 425
keepalive message, 429
length field, 426
marker field, 426
notification message, 429
open message, 427
packet format, 426
path attributes, 424
path vector routing, 424
port, 807
session, 425
type field, 427
types of packets, 426
update message, 428
bidirectional authentication, 741
bidirectional edge, 406
bidirectional frame, 658
binary file
FTP, 523
binary notation, 82
finding the class, 85
binary system, 776–777
to base 256, 782
to decimal, 777
to hexadecimal, 781
symbols, 777–778
weights, 777
block descriptor, 524
BOOTP, 457, 459
binding, 463
boot filename field, 462
broadcast message, 458
client hardware address
    field, 462
client IP address field, 462
client port, 458

BOOTP—*Cont.*
   configuration, 464
   different network, 459
   error control, 460
   gateway IP address field, 462
   hardware length field, 461
   hardware type field, 461
   hop count field, 461
   number of seconds field, 462
   operation, 458
   operation code field, 461
   options, 462, 463
   packet format, 461
   relay agent, 459
   same network, 458
   server IP address field, 462
   server name field, 462
   server port, 458
   static configuration protocol, 463
   static protocol, 463
   TFTP, 460, 542
   transaction ID field, 462
   UDP port, 459
   your IP address field, 462
bootstrap process, 457
Bootstrap Protocol. *See* BOOTP
Border Gateway Protocol. *See* BGP
bridge, 71
   connecting LANs, 72
   dynamic, 73
   as a filter, 71
   function, 71
   router, 74
   transparent, 72
   two-layer switch, 74
broadcast address, 100, 459
broadcast physical address, 34
broadcasting, 439
browser, 600
   client protocol, 600
   controller, 600
   dynamic document, 605
   HTML, 603
   interpreter, 600
   markup language, 603
   streaming stored audio/video, 659
BSS, 50
bucket, 147
bucket brigade attack, 745
buffer
   circular, 277
   receiver site, 278
   router, 151
   TCP, 277
burst error, 790–791

bursty data, 64
bus topology, 22
BYE message, 671
byte number, 280
byte-oriented protocol, 346

C

CA, 735, 749, 767
   X.509, 750
cable modem. *See* CM
cable modem transmission system.
       See CMTS
cable TV, 58
cache
   WWW, 600
cache table, 167
   ARP, 167
   attempts, 168
   hardware address, 168
   hardware length, 168
   hardware type, 168
   interface number, 168
   protocol address, 168
   protocol length, 168
   protocol type, 168
   queue number, 168
   space, 167
   state, 168
   time-out, 168
cache-control module, 170
caching, 482
   counter, 483
   problems, 482
   time-to-live, 483
   unauthoritative source, 482
Caesar cipher, 729
CANCEL message, 671
care-of address, 638
   co-located, 639
carrier sense, 44
carrier sense multiple access with
       collision avoidance.
       See CSMA/CA
carrier sense multiple access with
       collision detection. *See* CSMA/CD
CATV, 58
CBT, 449
   autonomous system, 449
   core router, 451
   DVMRP and MOSPF, 450
   encapsulation, 451
   leaving the group, 450
   multicast packet, 450
   rendezvous router, 449

CCITT, 8
cell, 65, 68
   ATM, 68
   ATM WAN, 625
   definition, 65
   header, 68
   payload, 68
   size, 68
   structure, 68
cell loss priority, 625
cell network, 65
   multiplexing, 66
   VC, 67
cell relay, 65
center router, 443
Cerf, Vint, 2
certification authority. *See* CA
CGI, 605
   body, 607
   form, 606
   header, 607
   output, 606
   parameter passing, 606
   query string, 606
   script, 607
Change Cipher Spec Protocol, 761
checksum, 200, 262, 305, 783, 798
   Adler, 788
   BOOTP, 461
   calculation, 262
   complement, 200, 783
   complement in hex, 785
   decimal, 785
   Fletcher, 786
   fragmentation, 188
   header coverage, 201
   hexadecimal, 784
   ICMP, 226
   IP packet, 201
   method, 200
   one's complement
       arithmetic, 263
   partial sum, 783
   partial sum in hex, 784
   protocol field, 262
   at receiver, 200
   SCTP, 350
   at sender, 200
   sum, 783
   sum in hex, 784
   TCP, 305
   UDP, 262–264
   weighted, 786
chip code, 51
choke point, 315

chunk, 349, 354
  data, 355
  flag field, 354
  format, 354
  identifier, 352
  length field, 355
  protocol payload identifier, 356
  SI field, 356
  SSN field, 356
  TSN, 349
  TSN field, 356
  type field, 354
  user data field, 356
CIDR, 107–108
  BGP, 424
  IPv6, 691
CIDR notation, 117
cipher, 728
  public, 728
  substitution, 729
  traditional, 729
  transpositional, 730
ciphertext, 728
  RSA, 733
circular buffer, 277
Clark's solution, 305
class A, 88
class B, 88
class C, 90
class D, 91, 100
class E, 91
classful addressing, 81, 84, 108, 115
  blocks, 88
  classes, 88
  forwarding, 136
  obsolescence, 108
  mask, 117
  RIP, 397
  searching, 147
  subset of classless, 118
  sufficient information, 92
classless addressing, 81, 84, 115
  address allocation, 126
  address space, 115
  addresses in block, 120
  block, 118
  first address, 116, 118–119
  forwarding, 141
  last address, 120
  mask, 117
  modern routers, 148
  number of addresses, 116
  prefix, 117
  restrictions, 116
  RIPv2, 397

routing table, 149
  search, 148
  subnet, 122
  subnet example, 123
  suffix, 118
  variable-length blocks, 115
classless interdomain routing.
      See CIDR
client, 256
  Web, 600
client process, 99
client program
  port number, 257
client-server
  definitions, 257
  email, 550
  remote login, 499
  WWW, 599
client-server paradigm, 256
clock synchronization, 224
CLOSED state, 295–296, 298, 370
closed-loop congestion control, 315
CLOSE-WAIT state, 295, 297
CM, 59
CMTS, 59
coaxial cable
  cable TV, 58
  HFC, 58
codepoint, 183
ColdFusion, 607
collision domain, 45
co-located care-of address, 639
Common Gateway Interface. *See* CGI
community antenna TV, 58
compatible address, 695
complement, 200, 783
compression, 653
  audio, 653
  DNS, 489
  FTP, 524
  MPEG, 657
  spatial, 657
conferencing, 101
confidentiality, 735
configured tunneling, 720
congestion, 312
  additive increase, 317
  buffer, 217
  destination host, 217
  ICMPv6, 711
  multiplicative decrease, 318
  prevention, 315
  queue, 313
  routers, 217
  TCP, 313

congestion avoidance, 317, 319
congestion control, 281, 315
  closed-loop, 315
  network role, 316
  open-loop, 315
  SCTP, 352, 380
congestion detection, 319
congestion policy, 316
congestion window, 300, 316
congestion-controlled traffic, 699
connecting device, 24, 69
connection
  nonpersistent, 616
  persistent, 616
  transport layer, 256
connection control, 26
connection establishment
  procedure, 285
  SMTP, 566
  TFTP, 537
  three-way handshaking, 285
connection resetting, 291
connection termination, 368
  SMTP, 567
  TFTP, 537
connectionless, 155
connectionless protocol, 132
connectionless service, 132
  UDP, 264
connectionless transport layer, 26
connection-oriented
      service, 131, 279, 348
  SCTP, 348
  TCP, 32
connection-oriented transport layer, 26
Consultative Committee for
      International Telegraphy and
      Telephony. *See* CCITT
contact addresses, 803
contention, 801
control chunk, 352
control field
  PDU, 801
control information
  SCTP, 351
control-block table, 268
controller, 600
cookie, 287, 363–364, 601–602
  access, 602
  advertising agency, 602
  shopping, 602
COOKIE ACK chunk, 359, 363
COOKIE-ECHO chunk, 359, 363, 371
COOKIE-ECHOED state, 370
COOKIE-WAIT state, 370

core router, 443, 449
Core-Based Tree. *See* CBT
country domain, 479
    mapping, 481
CRC, 794–795
    ATM layer, 625
    basis, 794
    checker, 796
    division, 795
    divisor, 795–796
    example, 798
    generator, 795
    modulo-2 division, 795
    overview, 794
    performance, 798
    polynomial, 796
    PPP, 62
    receiver, 795
    receiver function, 794
    redundancy bit, 794
    remainder, 794
    remainder at receiver, 794
    sender, 795
    sender function, 794
    standard polynomials, 796, 798
CRC generator, 796
CRC-32, 46
    Ethernet, 46
    wireless, 54
crossbar, 152
crossbar switch, 152
crosspoint, 152
cryptography, 727
CSMA/CA, 53
CSMA/CD, 44–45
    Project 802.3, 800
CSNET, 3
curTSN, 374
cwnd, 316
cyclic redundancy check.
        See CRC

D

DATA, 535
    block number field, 535
    data field, 535
    opcode field, 535
DATA chunk, 352, 355
data compression, 28
data connection, 521
data delivery, 367
Data Encryption Standard. *See* DES
data link layer, 22
    access control, 23

    addressing, 23
    error control, 23
    flow control, 23
    framing, 23
    function, 22
    LLC, 801
    physical addressing, 23
    PPP, 62
    Project 802, 799
data link processor, 151
data transfer, 367
    vs data delivery, 367
    mobile IP, 640, 645
    multihoming, 366
    remote host, 645
    SCTP, 365
    TCP, 287
    TFTP, 537
data transmission rate, 45
database
    DHCP, 464
    multicasting, 440
database description message, 419
    B flag field, 420
    E flag field, 419
    I flag field, 420
    LSA header field, 420
    M flag field, 420
    M/S flag field, 420
    message sequence number
        field, 420
datagram, 32, 180
    format, 180
    in IP, 180
    IP, 31
    version field, 534–535
DCE, 64
DCF, 52
DCT, 655
    AC value, 655
    gradient case, 656
    sharp change case, 655
    uniform gray scale case, 655
DDNS, 493
de facto standard, 7
de jure standard, 7
deadlock, 312, 324
debugging tools, 227
decapsulation
    UDP, 265
decimal system, 776
    to binary, 777
    to hex, 778
    to IP address, 780
    symbols, 776
    weights, 777

decryption, 728
default forwarding, 136
default mask, 93, 106
default router, 220
delay, 313
    load, 313
    real-time traffic, 663
delayed response, 242
DELAYING state, 248
delivery, 131–132
    connection type, 131
    direct, 132
    end-to-end, 24
    indirect, 133
    source-to-destination, 23–24
    station-to-station, 23
demultiplexing
    UDP, 267
denial of service attack, 287
Department of Defense.
        See DOD
DES, 730–732
designated parent router, 448
destination option, 709
Destination Service Access Point.
        See DSAP
destination unreachable, 214, 216
    ICMPv6, 711
    code field, 711
DHCP, 457, 463
    BOOTP, 463
    bound state, 466
    database, 463
    DDNS, 493
    dynamic configuration
        protocol, 464
    exchanging messages, 467
    flag field, 464
    initializing state, 465
    mobile host, 638
    options field, 464
    packet format, 464
    rebinding state, 467
    renewing state, 467
    requesting state, 466
    selecting state, 466
    TFTP, 542
    transition states, 465
DHCPACK, 466–467
DHCPDISCOVER, 465–466
DHCPNACK, 467
DHCPOFFER, 466
DHCPREQUEST, 466
dialog control, 26, 27
differentiated services, 181
Diffie-Hellman method, 743, 744

digest, 737–738
  hash function, 738
  PGP, 762
  receiver site, 738
  security, 739
  sender site, 738
  signing, 738
digital signature, 736–737
  hash function, 738
  integrity, 737
  nonrepudiation, 738
  PGP, 762
  private key, 737
  public key, 737
  signing the digest, 738
  signing the whole document, 737
digital subscriber line. *See* DSL
digital subscriber line access
  multiplexer. *See* DSLAM
digitizing audio, 652
Dijkstra algorithm, 399, 401
  multicast link state routing, 445
  steps, 401
direct broadcast address, 96
direct delivery, 132
direct sequence spread spectrum.
  See DSSS
directory services, 29
discarding policy, 315
discrete cosine transform. *See* DCT
diskless machine, 173, 255, 457, 533
  booting, 173
  physical address, 173
  RARP, 457
diskless station, 225
diskless workstation, 457, 533
distance learning, 441
Distance Vector Multicast Routing
  Protocol. *See* DVMRP
distance vector routing, 387
  initial tables, 388
  instability, 390
  RIP, 392
  sharing, 388
distributed coordination function.
  See DCF
distribution system, 50, 64
DMT, 56, 58
DNS, 471
  caching, 482
  compression, 489
  country domain, 479
  divisions, 477
  domain, 475
  encapsulation, 493

generic domain, 478
  Internet, 477
  inverse domain, 480
  inverted-tree structure, 472
  labels, 472
  levels, 472
  offset pointer, 489
  primary server, 477
  question record, 486
  record types, 486
  registrar, 481
  resolver, 481
  resource record, 488
  root server, 476
  secondary server, 477
  server, 475
  TCP, 494
  UDP, 494
  updating, 493
  zone, 475
DNS message, 483
  additional information
    section, 486
  additional records field, 485
  answer records field, 485
  answer section, 486
  authoritative records field, 485
  authoritative section, 486
  flags field, 484
  header, 484
  identification field, 484
  question records field, 485
  question section, 486
DNS response
  answer records field, 486
  question records field, 486
DO command, 506
do not fragment bit, 188
DOD, 2
dog-leg routing, 646
domain, 474, 475
  country, 479
  generic, 478
  inverse, 480
domain name, 472–473, 554
domain name space, 472
domain name system. *See* DNS
DONT command, 506
dotted-decimal notation, 82
double-crossing. *See* 2X
downloading, 56
DSAP, 801
DSL, 56–58
DSLAM, 57
DSSS, 51

DTE, 64
dual stack, 718
duplicate ACKs, 307
DVMRP, 445, 449
  CBT, 450
  MBONE, 453
  PIM-DM, 452
dynamic configuration protocol, 463
dynamic database, 464
dynamic document, 605
  example, 605
  script, 607
Dynamic Domain Name System.
  See DDNS
Dynamic Host Configuration
  Protocol. *See* DHCP
dynamic mapping, 160–161
dynamic port, 259
dynamic routing, 148

E

eavesdropping, 708
EBCDIC
  FTP, 523
  IBM, 771
echo request and reply messages, 221,
  222, 714
ECN, 380
e-commerce, 602
EIA, 8
Electronic Industries Association.
  See EIA
electronic mail. *See* email
elm, 553
email, 547
  alias, 555
  architecture, 547
  composing, 552
  domain name, 554
  forwarding, 552
  local part, 554
  mailboxes, 552
  PGP, 762
  reading, 552
  replying, 552
  scenario 1, 547
  scenario 2, 548
  scenario 3, 549
  scenario 4, 550
  web-based, 571
encapsulation, 398
  ARP, 163
  ATM WAN, 625

encapsulation—*Cont.*
  BOOTP, 458
  DNS, 493
  IGMP, 244
  OSI model, 21
  OSPF, 421
  RARP, 175
  UDP, 265
  VPN, 683
encryption, 728
  DES, 730
  IPv4, 689
  presentation layer, 28
  symmetric-key, 728
  tunneling, 683
end-of-option option, 193, 325
entering-point router, 626–627
entity authentication, 740
  asymmetric-key
    cryptography, 741
  first approach, 740
  vs message authentication, 740
  second approach, 741
  steps, 741
envelope, 553
EOP, 325
ephemeral port
  FTP control connection, 520
  FTP data connection, 521
  TFTP, 540
ephemeral port number, 257
  queue, 266
ERROR, 536
  error datafield, 536
  error number field, 536
  opcode field, 536
  RRQ, 536
  TFTP, 536
  WRQ, 536
error, 790
  example, 790
  types, 790
ERROR chunk, 361
error control, 26, 281, 305
  BOOTP, 461
  SACK chunk, 379
  SCTP, 352, 376
  TCP, 276
  TFTP, 538
  transport layer, 24, 256
  UDP, 264
  X.25, 64
error detection, 790, 792
  checksum, 200, 798
  CRC, 795

Ethernet, 46
  parity check, 793
  tools, 305
error message
  ICMP package, 233
error reporting, 710
  ICMP, 212, 213
  ICMP v4 and v6, 711
escape character, 511
ESP, 708, 757
  AH protocol, 758
  authentication data field, 758
  format, 708
  next header field, 758
  pad length field, 758
  padding field, 758
  procedure, 757
  sequence number field, 758
  SPI field, 758
  transport mode, 708
  tunnel mode, 708
ESS, 50
  communication, 50
  composition, 50
  stations, 50
ESTABLISHED state, 295, 372
Ethernet, 44
  802.2 frame, 46
  acknowledgment, 46, 216
  addressing, 46
  broadcast address, 160
  CRC, 46
  Fast, 48
  fields, 46
  frame format, 46
  Gigabit, 48
  implementations, 47
  IPv6 address, 694
  length/type PDU, 46
  MAC frame, 46
  multicasting, 245
  physical address, 46
  preamble, 46
Ethernet address, 34
Eudora, 553
even-parity, 793
exiting-point router, 626–627
expiration timer, 396
explicit congestion notification.
  See ECN
explicit signal, 315
exponential backoff, 323
exponential increase, 316
extended service set. *See* ESS
extension header, 702

authentication, 707
destination option, 709
ESP, 708
fragmentation, 706
hop-by-hop option, 703
source routing, 705
external BGP (E-BGP), 425
external link LSA, 416

F

Fast Ethernet, 48
  collision domain, 48
  data rate, 48
  implementation, 48
fast retransmission, 308
FCC, 9
  address, 803
Federal Communications
  Committee. *See* FCC
FHSS, 51
fiber, 61
fiber-optic cable
  bandwidth capabilities, 61
file transfer, 519
File Transfer Protocol.
  See FTP
filter
  ADSL, 57
filtering, 71
FIN segment, 289–290
FIN+ACK segment, 289
finite state machine, 292
  SCTP, 369
FIN-WAIT-1 state, 295–296
FIN-WAIT-2 state, 295–296
firewall, 763
  packet filter, 763
  proxy, 764
flat name space, 472
Fletcher, 410, 787, 788
flickering, 653
flooding, 400, 409
  multicast distance vector routing, 446
  RPF, 446
flow control, 26, 281, 370
  congestion, 217
  definition, 299
  in IP, 216
  SCTP, 352, 373
  sliding window, 300
  TCP, 276, 299
  TFTP, 538
  transport layer, 24, 256
  UDP, 264

flow label, 690, 698, 701
  faster processing, 701
  real-time transmission, 701
  rules for use, 701
foreign agent, 639
  agent discovery, 640
  home agent, 639, 645
  mobile host, 645
  registration, 642
foreign network, 638
forum, 7–8
forwarding, 131, 133
  classful addressing, 136
  classless addrressing, 141
  no subnet, 136
  subnet, 139
forwarding module, 137
forwarding techniques, 134
four-way handshake, 289, 296, 362
FQDN, 473
  DNS server, 474
fractional T services, 61
fragmentation, 186–187, 367, 706
  checksum, 188
  do not fragment bit, 188
  fields copied, 188
  flags field, 188
  fragmentation offset, 188
  header fields, 188
  ICMP error message, 188
  identification field, 188
  IPv6, 706, 711
  more fragment bit, 188
  offset, 189
  reassembly, 187
  reassembly steps, 189
  SCTP, 367
frame, 23, 64
  MPEG, 657
Frame Relay, 9, 62, 64
Frame Relay Forum, 8
FREE state, 248
frequency hopping spread
  spectrum. *See* FHSS
frequency masking, 654
FTP, 519
  access commands, 525
  active open, 520
  anonymous FTP, 532
  ASCII file, 523
  attributes of communication, 523
  binary file, 523–524
  binary file storage example, 531
  block mode, 524
  browser, 600

client components, 520
client definitions, 523
client in data connection, 521
command, 524–525
communication, 521
compressed mode, 524
connections, 519–520
control connection, 519–520, 522
data connection, 519–521, 523
data formatting commands, 526
data structure, 524
EBCDIC file, 523
ephemeral port, 520–521, 526
file management commands, 525
file printability, 523
file retrieval, 529
file storage, 529
file structure, 524
file transfer, 529
file transfer commands, 526
file type, 523
first digit of response, 527
HTTP, 609
image file, 523
minimize delay TOS, 520
miscellaneous commands, 527
nonprint attribute, 523
NVT, 522
page structure, 524
passive open, 520–521
port number, 526
port-defining commands, 526
ports, 519, 807
record structure, 524
response, 524, 527
second digit of response, 527
sending a directory or file name, 529
server components, 520
stream mode, 524
TELNET, 524
text file, 524
third digit of response, 528
transmission mode, 524
URL, 601
full domain name, 472
full-duplex, 22
  SCTP, 348
full-duplex service, 278
fully qualified domain name. *See* FQDN

G

G.71, 674
G.723.1, 674

G.723.3, 653
G.729, 653
garbage collection
  timer, 396
gatekeeper, 673
gateway, 2, 75
  H.323, 673
general header
  SCTP, 353
general query message, 242
generic domain, 478, 481
geographical routing, 147
GET message, 659
GIF, 558
  HTML, 605
Gigabit Ethernet, 48
  frame length, 48
  implementation, 49
  MAC layer, 48
Gopher, 601, 807
government regulatory
  agencies, 7
graceful termination, 368
grafting, 448–449
granted block, 121
Graphics Interchange Format. *See* GIF
gray scale, 654
grep, 276
group address, 438
group membership, 237
group membership, 716
group table, 248
  group address, 249
  interface number, 249
  reference count, 249
  state field, 248
groupid, 239
group-shared tree, 443
GSM, 653
guest password, 532

H

H.225, 674
H.245, 674
H.248, 346
H.323, 346, 671, 673
half-close, 289, 290
half-duplex, 22
handshake
  TLS, 759
hash function, 738
hashing
  AH protocol, 756

HDLC
  Ethernet comparison, 46
  PDU, 801
  PDU control field
      similarities, 801
  Project 802, 800
HDSL, 58
header, 20
  CGI, 607
  SCTP, 350, 353
header error, 219
header error correction, 625
header translation, 720
  procedure, 721
  rules, 721
HEARTBEAT ACK chunk, 360
HEARTBEAT chunk, 360
hello message, 418
  backup designated router
      IP address, 419
  dead interval field, 419
  designated router IP address, 419
  E flag, 418
  hello interval field, 418
  neighbor IP address field, 419
  network mask field, 418
  priority field, 418
  T flag, 418
hexadecimal colon notation, 691
hexadecimal notation, 47, 84
hexadecimal system, 776, 778
  to binary, 782
  to decimal, 778
  weights, 778
HFC
  bands, 58
  bandwidth, 58
  data rate, 59
  downstream data band, 59
  sharing, 59
  transmission medium, 58
  upstream data band, 59
  upstream sharing, 59
  video band, 59
HFC network, 58
hidden terminal problem, 53
hierarchical name space, 472
hierarchical routing, 146
hierarchy
  IP address, 103
  name server, 475
  subnet, 103
high bit rate digital subscriber line.
      See HDSL
High Rate DSSS. *See* HR-DSSS

HMAC
  TLS, 759
home address, 638
home agent, 639, 645
  agent discovery, 640
  foreign agent, 639, 645
  registration, 642
home network, 638
hop count, 385
  RIP, 393
hop-by-hop option, 703
  jumbo payload, 705
  Pad1, 703
  PadN, 703–704
  payload, 703
host
  ARP query, 161
  routing table, 220
host configuration, 457
host file, 471
hostid, 87, 103
  masking, 93
host-specific forwarding, 134
host-specific routing, 135
host-to-host communication, 256
host-to-host protocol, 32
Hotmail, 571
HR-DSSS, 52
HTML, 603
  anchor, 605
  attribute, 604
  browser, 604
  example, 603
  graphic image, 605
  interpreter, 600
  markup language, 603
  tag, 604
HTTP, 571, 599, 609
  body, 614
  browser, 600
  client, 609
  email, 571
  embedded commands, 609
  entity header, 614
  FTP similarity, 609
  general header, 613
  header, 612
  header categories, 612
  message format, 609
  MIME, 609
  multimedia, 659–660
  port, 807
  proxy server, 616
  request header, 613
  response header, 613

  server, 609
  SMTP similarity, 609
  status code, 611
  status phrase, 611
  transaction, 609
  URL, 601
  version, 610
  WWW, 609
hub, 71
hybrid network, 680–681
  IP address, 681
hybrid-fiber-coaxial network. *See* HFC
HyperText Markup Language.
      See HTML
Hypertext Transfer Protocol. *See* HTTP

I

IAB, 12
  address, 804
  IETF, 12
  IRTF, 12
  RFC, 13
IANA, 13
  range, 258
ICANN, 13
  address, 804
ICMP, 31–32, 211
  address mask messages, 224
  checksum, 226
  checksum at receiver, 226
  checksum at sender, 226
  checksum field, 213
  code field, 213
  data section, 213
  debugging, 227
  destination unreachable
      message, 214
  diagnostics, 221
  echo request, 223
  echo request and reply messages, 221
  encapsulation, 211
  error correction, 213
  error handled, 214
  error handling, 32
  error message, 213
  error reporting, 213
  error-reporting message, 212
  fragmentation problem, 215
  host unreachable, 215
  ICMP type field, 213
  IP header, 214
  isolated source host, 216
  message format, 213

message types, 212
messages, 32
network unreachable, 214
nongeneration of message, 214
parameter problem error, 712
parameter problem message, 219
ping, 227
port numbers, 214
port unreachable, 215
precedence probelm, 216
prohibited communication, 216
protocol unreachable, 215
purpose, 213
query message, 212, 221
redirect message, 219
restricted by filter, 216
router solicitation and
    advertisement, 225
source quench message, 216
source routing problem, 215
time exceeded error, 712
time exceeded message, 218
timestamp messages, 223
TOS problem, 216
traceroute, 229
tracert, 229
unknown destination host, 215
unkown destination network, 215
violation of host precedence, 216
icmp object, 585
ICMP package, 232
input module, 232
modules, 232
output module, 233
ICMPv4
comparison with v6, 711
ICMPv6, 689, 709
checksum field, 710
code field, 710
compared to ICMPv4, 710–711
destination unreachable message, 711
echo request and reply, 714
error packet, 710
error reporting, 710
format, 710
group membership, 716
IGMP, 716
neighbor solicitation and
    advertisement, 715
packet too big, 712
parameter problem, 712
query messages, 713
redirection, 713
router solicitation and
    advertisement, 715

time exceeded, 712
type field, 710
IDLE state, 248
IEEE, 8, 800
address, 803
Project 802, 799
IEEE 802.11, 50–51
IEEE 802.3, 46
IESG, 13
address, 804
IETF
address, 804
working group, 13
if object, 585
ifconfig, 150
I-frame, 658
IGMP, 31–32, 237
address conversion, 245
address mapping, 245
checksum field, 239
data-link layer, 245
delayed response, 242
destination IP address, 245
distributing router, 240
domain, 244
encapsulation, 244
Ethernet address, 245
function, 237
group address field, 239
host list, 240
host membership, 240
ICMPv6, 689, 716
IP layer, 244
IP protocol, 237
joining a group, 240
leave report, 238
leaving a group, 241
loyal member, 239
maximum response type
    field, 239
membership report, 238
message format, 238
message types, 238
monitoring group
    membership, 241
multicast routing, 445
netstat, 247
in network layer, 237
operation, 239
physical multicast
    addressing, 245
protocol field, 244
query for membership
    continuation, 242
query message, 238

query router, 243
router list, 240
router membership, 240
states, 248
TTL field, 244
tunneling, 246
type field, 239
WAN, 246
IGMP package, 247
components, 247
group table, 248
group-joining module, 249
group-leaving module, 249
input module, 250
output module, 251
timers, 249
IMAP4, 569–570
IMP, 2
inbox, 552
incarnation, 295, 364
indirect delivery, 133
address mapping, 133
infinity
distance vector routing, 391
RIP, 393
information technology, 7
infrastructure network, 50
INIT ACK chunk, 356, 358, 363
INIT chunk, 356, 363
initiation tag field, 357
rwnd, 357
INIT-ACK chunk, 371
initial sequence number
    (ISN), 282
initiation tag, 371
input module
ARP, 169
IGMP, 250
input port, 151
input queue, 205
instability
distance vector routing, 390
instance suffix, 586
Institute of Electrical & Electronics
    Engineers. *See* IEEE
integrity
AH protocol, 757
digital signature, 736
interactive audio/video, 651
interconnectivity, 7
interdomain routing, 386
path vector routing, 421
interface
LSP, 400
OSI model, 19

interface message processor.
    See IMP
interface number, 137
internal BGP (I-BGP), 425
international Internet service
    providers, 5
International Organization for
    Standardization. *See* ISO
International Standards
    Organization. *See* ISO
International Telecommunications
    Union. *See* ITU
International Telecommunications
    Union–Telecommunication Stan-
    dards Sector. *See* ITU-T
Internet, 1
    ATM WAN, 621
    birth of, 2
    current, 4
    definition, 1, 385
    DNS, 477
    draft, 9
    example, 101
    history, 1
    IP address, 159
    logical address, 159
    packet, 159, 385
    packet delivery, 159
    physical address, 159
    purpose, 499
    security, 727, 754
    standard, 9
    timeline, 5
Internet address, 81
Internet Architecture Board.
    See IAB
Internet Assigned Numbers
    Authority. *See* IANA
Internet Control Message Protocol.
    See ICMP
Internet Corporation for Assigned
    Names and Numbers. *See* ICANN
Internet Engineering Steering Group.
    See IESG
Internet Engineering Task Force.
    See IETF
Internet Group Management
    Protocol. *See* IGMP
Internet Mail Access Protocol,
    version 4. *See* IMAP4
Internet phone, 662
Internet Protocol. *See* IP
Internet Protocol, next generation.
    See IPng
Internet Protocol, version 6. *See* IPv6

Internet radio, 652
Internet Research Steering Group.
    See IRSG
Internet Research Task Force.
    See IRTF
Internet service providers. *See* ISP
Internet Society. *See* ISOC
internet standards, 9
Internet TV, 652
internetwork protocol. *See* IP
internetworking, 800
    Project 802, 800
    Project 802.1, 800
Internetworking Protocol. *See* IP
INTERNIC, 693
interoperability, 7
interpreter, 600
intracoded frame, 657
intradomain routing, 386
inTransit, 374
inverse domain, 480
    mapping, 481
    server, 480
inverse query, 480, 481
inverse reply message, 629
inverse request message, 629
INVITE message, 671
IP, 2, 31, 179
    advantages, 31
    analogy, 180
    ATM, 621
    best-effort delivery, 179
    congestion, 217
    congestion handling, 181
    connectionless, 132, 180
    connectionless protocol, 31
    datagram, 31, 180
    deficiencies, 211
    flow control, 216
    host-to-host communication, 256
    host-to-host protocol, 32
    incomplete delivery, 256
    lack of error handling, 211
    lack of management
        communication, 211
    multiplexing, 185
    network layer protocol, 31
    paired with TCP, 180
    protocols, 31
    reliability, 180
    routing, 32
    TCP/IP, 179
    unreliable, 179
    X.25, 63
IP address, 33, 81

ARP, 31, 161
ATM WAN, 627
binary notation, 82
broadcast, 35
classful addressing, 84
to decimal, 780
depletion, 95
diskless machine, 173
dotted decimal notation, 82
format, 35
hierarchy, 102–103
host, 258
hostid, 87
hybrid network, 681
location, 173
mobile host, 638
multicast, 35
need for, 35
netid, 87
node location, 95
node's connection, 95
notation, 82
private network, 681
RARP, 31
special address, 96
stationary host, 637
unicast, 35
unique, 81
universality, 81
IP algorithm, 203
IP datagram
    checksum field, 185
    destination address field, 185
    destination protocol, 185
    differentiated services, 181, 183
    flag field, 184
    fragmentation, 183–188
    header length calculation, 183
    header length field, 181
    hop limit field, 699
    hops allowed, 184
    identification field, 184
    loop problem, 184
    need for total length field, 184
    option error, 219
    options, 191
    padding, 184
    precedence subfield, 181
    priority, 181
    protocol field, 185
    reassembly, 187
    segment encapsulation, 278
    size, 183
    source address field, 185
    time-to-live field, 184

TOS bits subfield, 182
total length field, 183
version field, 181
IP design, 204
IP layer security, 754
ip object, 585
IP package, 203
    forwarding module, 205
    fragmentation module, 206
    header-adding module, 204
    MTU table, 205
    processing module, 204
    queues, 205
    reassembly module, 207
    reassembly table, 206
    routing table, 205
IP packet, 131
IP Security. *See* IPSec
IP telephony, 346
IPng. *See* IPv6
IPSec, 754
    AH, 682
    ESP, 682
    modes, 755
    protocols, 755
    SA, 754
    VPN, 682
IPv4, 37
    address space problems, 689
    automatic tunneling, 720
    base 256, 779
    compared to IPv6 header, 702
    comparison to IPv6, 709
    configured tunneling, 720
    deficiencies, 689
    header translation, 720
    IPSec, 758
    real-time traffic problems, 689
    security problems, 689
    transition to IPv6, 718
    tunneling, 719
IPv6, 38, 689
    address, 690, 695
    address abbreviation, 691
    address notation, 691
    address space, 690
    address space assignment, 692
    authentication, 707
    automatic tunneling, 720
    base 256, 779
    CIDR, 691
    compared to IPv4 header, 702
    comparison to IPv4, 709
    configured tunneling, 720
    destination option, 709

ESP, 708
extension header, 702
extension of the protocol, 690
features, 690
flow label, 701
flow of packets, 701
fragmentation, 706
header format, 690
header translation, 720
hop-by-hop option, 703
improvements, 38
IPSec, 758
jumbo payload, 705
local address, 696
new features, 689
new options, 690
node ID, 694
Pad1, 703
PadN, 704
provider ID, 693
registry ID, 693
reserved address, 694
resource allocation, 690
routing protocols, 689
runs of zero, 691
security, 690
source routing, 705
subscriber ID, 693
transition from IPv4, 718
transport mode, 708
tunnel mode, 708
tunneling, 719
IPv6 address
    abbreviation example, 691
    categories, 692
    consecutive zeros, 691
    IPv4, 695
    IPv4 compatible, 695
    link local, 696
    loopback address, 695
    mapped, 695
    multicast, 697
    provider-based, 693
    reserved, 694
    shorthand notation, 691
    site local, 697
    type field, 693
    type prefix, 692
    unicast, 693
    unspecified, 695
IPv6 packet, 698
    base header, 698
    base header fields, 698
    destination address field, 699
    extension header, 698

flow label field, 698
format, 698
hop limit field, 699
next header field, 699
payload, 698
payload length field, 699
priority field, 698–699
source address field, 699
version field, 698
IPv6 priority
    attended bulk data traffic, 700
    background data, 700
    control traffic, 700
    interactive traffic, 700
    no specific traffic, 700
    unattended data traffic, 700
IPv6 traffic, 699
    congestion-controlled, 699
    flow label, 701
    noncongestion-controlled, 700
    priority, 700
    priority assignments, 699
    redundancy, 700
IRSG, 13
IRTF, 13
    address, 804
ISO, 7, 17
    address, 803
    Frame Relay, 9
    purpose, 17
ISOC, 12
    address, 804
ISP, 115, 146
    address range, 115
    address allocation, 126
    granted block, 121
    local, 146
    national, 146
    regional, 146
iterative resolution, 482
ITU, 8
    address, 804
ITU-T, 7
IUA, 345

J

Java, 608
    interpreter, 600
Java applet, 608
JavaScript, 608
jitter, 663
    timestamp, 663
Joint Photographic Experts Group.
    See JPEG

JPEG, 558, 654
  DCT, 655
  gray scale, 654
  HTML, 605
  image compression, 657
  quantization, 656
  redundancy, 655
  spatial compression, 657
JSP, 607
jumbo payload, 703, 705

K

Kahn, Bob, 2
Karn's algorithm, 323
KDC, 746
  AS, 752
  Kerberos, 751
  session key creation, 746
  symmetric key, 746
  ticket, 746
keepalive message, 427, 429
keepalive timer, 324
Kerberos, 751
  AS, 752
  different servers, 753
  operation, 752
  real server, 752
  realm, 753
  Version 5, 753
key, 728
  secret, 728
  symmetric, 734
key distribution center. See KDC

L

label, 472
  country domain, 479
  generic domain, 478
LAN, 44
  Frame Relay, 64
  TCP/IP, 31
lastack, 328–329
LAST-ACK state, 296
LCP, 62
  function, 62
lease, 464
leave report, 238, 241
lexicographic ordering, 588
lifetime field, 641
limited broadcast address, 97
link, 24
  address, 34
  OSPF, 405

point-to-point, 405
stub, 406
transient, 405
virtual, 407
Link Control Protocol. See LCP
link local address, 696
link state acknowledgment
  packet, 421
link state packet. See LSP
link state request packet, 420
link state routing, 398, 400
  hello message, 418
link state update packet, 409
LIS, 632
  ATMARP, 632
LIST command, 529
LIST message, 530
LISTEN state, 295, 298
LLC, 799–800
  addressing, 801
  data link layer, 801
  Project 802.2, 800
load, 312–313
local address, 696
local area network. See LAN
local Internet service provider, 5
local ISP, 5, 146
local login, 500
  mechanism, 500
  procedure, 501
local part, 554
LocalTalk address, 34
locator, 601
logical address, 159
logical IP subnet. See LIS
Logical Link Control. See LLC
login, 500, 501
long fat pipe, 327
longest mask matching, 145
longest match searching, 148
loop, 184
  multicast distance vector
    routing, 446
  RPB, 447
  time exceeded message, 218
loop prevention, 423
loopback, 204
loopback address, 99, 695
loose source route option, 196
loose source routing, 705
lossy compression, 656
LSA
  advertising router field, 410
  checksum field, 410
  E flag field, 410

external link, 416
length field, 410
link state age field, 409
link state ID field, 410
link state type field, 410
network link, 412
router link, 410
sequence number field, 410
summary link to AS
  boundary, 416
summary link to network, 415
T flag field, 410
LSP, 400
  flooding, 400
  generation, 400

M

M2UA, 345
M3UA, 346
MAA, 550
MAC, 799–801
  functions, 801
  modules, 800
  protocol specific, 801
MAC sublayer
  wireless LAN, 52
magic cookie
  BOOTP, 462
mail, 553
mail access agent. See MAA
mail exchanger, 554
mail server, 548
mailbox, 547, 554
mailing list, 555
Management Information Base.
  See MIB
manager, 575–576
  active open, 595
  database, 576
  function, 576, 589
  passive open, 595
  remote reboot, 576
man-in-the-middle attack, 744–745
mapped address, 696
mapping
  address to name, 481
  dynamic, 160
  host file, 471
  logical to physical address,
    159, 161
  name to address, 481
  static, 159
markup language, 603

mask, 92
AND operation, 94
classful addressing, 117
classless addressing, 117
default, 93, 106–107
subnet, 106–107
supernet, 107–108
masking, 92
purpose, 225
subnet, 105
maximum inbound stream, 357
maximum segment lifetime
(MSL), 295
maximum segment size (MSS), 316
maximum segment size option, 326
format, 326
window scale factor, 327
maximum transfer unit. *See* MTU
maximum transmission unit.
See MTU
MBONE, 453
MD5, 738
measured RTT, 321
media access control. *See* MAC
media gateway control, 346
media player, 659
media server, 660
membership report, 238, 240
destination IP address, 245
mesh topology, 22
message access protocol, 569
message transfer agent. *See* MTA
message-oriented protocol, 346
metafile, 659
metric, 385, 404
OSPF, 404
TOS, 385
type of service, 404
MIB, 576, 585
accessing a variable, 585, 586
accessing simple variable, 586
agent, 585
indexes, 587
instance definition, 587
lexicographic ordering, 588
network management, 578
object categories, 585
object identifier tree, 585
role, 577
SNMP, 577
table identification, 586
variable, 585
mib object, 580
MIB2, 585
microswitch, 152–153

MILNET, 3
MIME, 555
7bit encoding, 559
8bit encoding, 559
alternative multipart
subtype, 557
application data type, 558
audio data type, 558
base64 encoding, 559
binary encoding, 559
content subtype, 556
content-description header, 561
content-Id header, 560
content-transfer-encoding
header, 558
content-type header, 556
digest multipart subtype, 557
external-body subtype, 557–558
headers, 555
image data type, 558
message data type, 557
message/RFC822, 557
mixed multipart subtype, 557
MPEG, 558
multipart data type, 557
NVT ASCII, 555
octet-stream application
subtype, 558
parallel multipart subtype, 557
partial message subtype, 557
postscript application
subtype, 558
quoted-printable encoding, 560
RFC822 message subtype, 557
text data type, 556–557
types of data, 556
version header, 556
video data type, 558
minimize delay, 520
minimum frame length, 45
mixer, 666
mixing, 666
mobile host, 637–638
foreign host, 645
remote host, 645
triangle routing, 647
mobile IP, 637
address change, 638
addressing, 637
agent, 639
agent advertisement, 640
agent discovery, 640
agent solicitation, 642
co-located care-of address, 640
data exchange, 638

data transfer, 640, 644
double crossing, 646
foreign agent, 639
inefficiency, 646
inefficiency solution, 647
registration, 640
registration request, 642
transparency, 646
triangle routing, 647
more fragment bit, 188
MOSPF, 444–445
CBT, 450
Motion Picture Experts Group.
See MPEG
MP3, 653
compression, 654
data rates, 654
MPEG, 558, 654, 657
B-frame, 658
frame types, 657
I-frame, 657
MIME, 558
P-frame, 658
temporal compression, 657
versions, 658
MPEG audio layer 3, 653
MSL, 295
MSS, 316, 326
MTA, 548, 561
client, 561
server, 550, 561
MTU, 186, 712
fragmentation, 706
IP design, 206
maximum length, 187
minimum size, 706
SCTP, 379
values for protocols, 187
multicast address, 34, 100, 692
assigned, 100
conferencing, 101
IPv6, 697
scope field, 697
multicast backbone.
See MBONE
multicast distance vector
routing, 445
DVMRP, 449
multicast link state routing, 444
Multicast Open Shortest Path First.
See MOSPF
multicast packet, 450
multicast router, 238–239
groupid, 240
purpose, 241

multicast routing, 441
  designated parent, 448
  grafting, 449
  pruning, 448
  shortest path tree, 441–442
  source-based tree, 442
multicasting, 237, 437–438
  applications, 237, 440
  database, 440
  dissemination, 440
  distance learning, 441
  emulation, 440
  multimedia, 665
  news dissemination, 440
  real-time traffic, 665
  RIPv2, 398
  router interface, 438
  teleconferencing, 441
  tunneling, 453
  UDP, 268
  unicasting, 440
multihomed AS, 424
multihomed computer, 95
multihoming, 348
  SCTP, 348
multimedia, 651
  multicasting, 665
multiple access, 44
multiple unicasting, 439
  vs. multicasting, 440
multiple-stream delivery, 347
multiplexing, 66, 267
multiplicative decrease, 318–319
multipoint configuration, 22
Multipurpose Internet Mail
    Extensions. See MIME
multistage switch
  banyan, 152
multistream service, 347
music
  sampling rate, 652

N

n^2 problem, 742
Nagle's algorithm, 304
name server
  hierarchy, 475
name space, 471
  central authority, 472
  distribution, 475
  flat, 471–472
  hierarchical, 471–472
name-address resolution, 481
NAT, 684

national ISP, 5, 146
NCP, 2, 62
Needham-Schroeder, 747
neighbor solicitation and
    advertisement message, 715
netid, 87, 102
  masking, 93
Netscape, 553
netstat, 247
network, 1
  foreign, 638
  hybrid, 681
  private, 680
network access point (NAP), 5
network address, 88, 90–91, 96
  properties, 91
network address translation.
    See NAT
network capacity, 313
Network Control Protocol.
    See NCP
Network Information Center.
    See NIC
Network Interface Card. See NIC
network layer, 23
  logical Addressing, 24
  packet, 23
  Project 802, 799
  responsibilities, 24
  routing, 24
  TCP/IP, 31
network link
  attached router field, 412
  fields, 412
  network mask field, 412
network link LSA, 412
network management, 578
  MIB, 578
  programming analogy, 578
  SMI, 578
network security, 727
network service
  connectionless, 131
network support layers, 19
network to network interfaces. See NNI
network virtual terminal. See NVT
network-specific forwarding, 134
next-hop address, 137
next-hop forwarding, 134
NIC, 13, 46
  as device id, 161
  Ethernet, 46
  station address, 31
NNI, 66
  ATM, 623

no operation (NOP) option, 95, 325–326
node
  IP address, 95
node functionality, 222
nonce, 741
  Needham-Schroeder, 747
nonpersistent connection, 616
non-repudiation
  digital signature, 736, 738
NOP, 326
notification message, 429
  error code field, 430
  error data field, 430
  error subcode field, 430
NSFNET, 3
nslookup, 493
null suffix, 474
number system, 776
  comparison, 780
  transformation, 781
NVT, 28, 501
  ASCII, 502
  character set, 502
  control characters, 502
  data characters, 502
  FTP, 522
  TCP/IP stack, 501
  TELNET, 501
  tokens, 501
Nyquist theorem, 652

O

OACK, 541
object identifier, 579
octal system, 776
octet, 82
odd parity, 793
OFDM, 52
on-demand audio/video, 651
one's complement arithmetic,
    200, 226, 263, 783
one-time session key, 747
one-to-all communication, 101
one-to-many communication, 100
one-to-one communication, 100
open message, 427
  my autonomous system field, 427
  BGP Identifier, 427
  hold time field, 427
  option parameter length field, 427
  option parameters field, 428
  version field, 427
Open Shortest Path First. See OSPF

open system, 17
Open Systems Interconnection.
    See OSI
open-loop congestion control, 315
operating system
    local login, 500
    NVT, 501
optical fiber
    ATM, 65
    HFC, 58
optimum path, 423
option
    max segment size, 326
    no-op, 326
    SACK, 331
    SACK-permitted, 331
    window-scale, 327
Option Acknowledgment. *See* OACK
option negotiation, 505
options
    class subfield, 191
    code field, 191
    copy subfield, 191
    data field, 192
    end of option, 193
    format, 191
    function, 191
    IP datagram, 191
    length field, 192
    loose source route, 196
    no operation option, 193
    number subfield, 191
    record route option, 193
    strict source route, 195
    timestamp, 196
    types, 192
OPTIONS message, 671
Orthogonal Frequency Division
    Multiplexing. *See* OFDM
OSI
    interoperability, 18
    layer communication, 18
    Project 802, 799
OSI model, 7, 17, 20, 30
    application layer, 28
    architecture, 18
    data link layer, 22
    grouping of functions, 18
    header, 20
    layer interface, 19
    layer overview, 20
    layers, 17–18, 21
    layers traversed, 18
    network layer, 23
    network support layers, 19

organization, 19
peer-to-peer process, 18
physical layer, 18, 21
presentation layer, 27
session Layer, 26
summary of layers, 29
vs. TCP/IP, 17, 30
trailer, 20
transport layer, 24
user support layers, 20
OSPF, 385–386, 404
    database description message, 419
    encapsulation, 421
    hello message, 418
    link state acknowledgment packet, 421
    link state request packet, 420
    link state update packet, 409
    link types, 405
    metric, 404
    network as a link, 405
    packet, 408
    packet header, 408
    packet types, 418
    point-to-point link, 405
    stub link, 406
    transient link, 405
    virtual link, 407
OSPF header
    area identification field, 409
    authentication data field, 409
    authentication type field, 409
    checksum field, 409
    message length field, 409
    source router IP address, 409
    type field, 409
    version field, 408
Otway-Rees, 748
outbound stream, 357
outbox, 552
Outlook, 553
out-of-band signaling, 510
out-of-order segment, 308
output module
    ARP, 168
output port, 151
output queue, 205

P

packet, 385
    OSPF, 408
    router, 75
    SCTP, 350
packet format
    SCTP, 353

Packet Internet Groper. *See* ping
packet priority, 699
packet switching
    IP, 180
packet-filter firewall, 764
packet-too-big message, 712
Pad1 option, 703, 704
padding, 325
    AH protocol, 756
    chunk, 354–356
    end of option option, 193
    RTP, 667
PadN option, 703
page, 600
parallel, 791
parallel transmission
    single-bit error, 791
parameter problem message, 219, 712
    code field, 219, 712
    header ambiguity, 219
    missing option, 219
parity bit, 793
parity check, 793
    even number of errors, 794
    odd number of errors, 794
    performance, 794
partial sum, 783
partially qualified domain name.
    See PQDN
PASS command, 529, 531
passive open, 285
    FTP control connection, 520
    FTP data connection, 521
PASV command, 521, 526
path, 601
path attribute, 425
    AS_PATH, 425
    NEXT-HOP, 425
    non-transitive, 425
    ORIGIN, 425
    transitive, 425
Path MTU discovery
    technique, 706
path vector routing, 421
    loops, 423
    optimum path, 423
    policy routing, 423
    sharing, 422
PAWS, 329
PDU, 801
    control field, 801
    format, 801
    in Ethernet, 46
    length or type field, 46
    types, 801

peer-to-peer process, 18
perceptual encoding, 653
performance, 798
periodic timer, 396
    operation, 396
periodic update, 390
Perl, 607
permanent virtual circuit. *See* PVC
persistence timer, 312, 323
    operation, 324
persistent connection, 616
P-frame, 658
PGP, 762
    application layer, 762
    hash, 762
PHP, 607
physical address, 33–34, 159
    ARP, 31, 161
    ATM WAN, 627
    authority, 34
    Ethernet, 34
    multicast, 34
    need for, 161
    RARP, 31
    size and format, 34
    unicast, 34
physical layer, 21
    ATM, 68, 69
    ATM WAN, 625
    bit representation, 21
    bit synchronization, 22
    data rate, 22
    Frame Relay, 64
    line configuration, 22
    OSI model, 18
    purpose, 21
    TCP/IP, 31
    topology, 22
    transmission Mode, 22
physical layer processor, 151
piggybacking, 280, 282
PIM, 451
PIM-DM, 451–452
    RPF, 452
PIM-SM, 452
    CBT, 452
    strategy, 452
pine, 553
ping, 222, 227
pixel, 653
    MPEG, 657
PKI, 750
plaintext, 728
    RSA, 733
playback attack, 741

playback buffer, 664
pointer query, 480
point-to-point
    sample network, 101
point-to-point configuration, 22
point-to-point link, 405
Point-to-Point Protocol.
    See PPP
point-to-point WAN, 55
    physical layer, 55
poison reversed, 391
policy routing, 423
polynomial, 796–797
    binary representation, 796
    CRC, 796
    example, 798
    properties, 797
POP, 569
    modes, 570
port, 68, 161, 459, 595, 644
    registered, 259
    SNMP, 595
    well-known, 259
port 68, 459
port 161, 595
port 162, 595
port 434, 644
port address, 33, 36
    example, 36
    size, 36
PORT command, 521, 526,
    530–531
port number, 256–257
    ephemeral, 257
    example, 257
    ICMP, 214
    process, 258
    universal, 257
    well-known, 257, 259
Post Office Protocol. *See* POP
PPP, 61
    address field, 62
    control field, 62
    data field, 62
    FCS, 62
    flag field, 62
    layers, 62
    physical layer, 62
    protocol field, 62
PPP over Ethernet. *See* PPPoE
PPPoE, 63
PQDN, 474
    suffix, 474
predicted frame, 658
predictive encoding, 653

prefix, 637
    classless addressing, 117
    subnet, 122
prefix length, 117
presentation layer, 27
    compression, 28
    encryption, 28
    responsibilities, 27
    translation, 27
Pretty Good Privacy.
    See PGP
primary address, 366
primary server, 477
priority field, 699
privacy, 735
    AH protocol, 757
    asymmetric-key cryptography, 736
    symmetric-key
        cryptography, 735
private address, 99
    NAT, 684
private key, 732
    asymmetric-key cryptography,
        736, 749
    digital signature, 737
    PGP, 762
    RSA, 734
private network, 680
    IP address, 680–681
probe, 324
processing module, 204
process-to-process
    communication, 256, 276, 346
    TCP, 276
Project 802, 799
    modularity, 800
    OSI model, 799
Project 802.1, 800
Project 802.2, 800
    LLC, 801
Project 802.3, 802
Project 802.5, 802
protection against wrapped
    sequence numbers (PAWS), 329
protocol, 6, 18
protocol data unit. *See* PDU
Protocol Independent Multicast.
    See PIM
Protocol Independent Multicast, Dense
    Mode. *See* PIM-DM
Protocol Independent Multicast, Sparse
    Mode. *See* PIM-SM
Protocols, 6
provider-based address, 693
    subnet identifier field, 694

proxy ARP, 166
 example, 166
 mobile IP, 645
proxy firewall, 765
proxy server, 616
pruning, 448
pseudoheader, 262
 purpose, 262
pseudoterminal driver, 501
PSH flag, 287
psychoacoustics, 654
PTR query, 480
public key, 732
 asymmetric-key
  cryptography, 736, 749
 certification, 742
 digital signature, 737
 RSA, 734
public key infrastructure (PKI), 750
public-key
 asymmetric-key, 728
public-key cryptography, 732
 advantages, 735
 disadvantages, 735
 key verification, 735
 keys, 732
 RSA algorithm, 732
pull program, 551
pull protocol, 569
push operation, 288
push program, 551
push protocol, 569
PVC, 629
 ATMARP, 629

Q

Q.931, 674
quantization
 image compression, 656
query
 DNS, 483
query message, 221, 238
 destination IP address, 245
 ICMP, 212
 ICMP v4 and ICMPv6, 714
 ICMPv6, 713
 response time, 242
 special, 241
query router, 242–243
question record, 486
 format, 486
 query class field, 487
 query name field, 486
 query type field, 487

queue, 313
 ARP, 168
 input, 313
 output, 313
 overflow in UDP, 266
 UDP, 265–266
QUIT command, 530, 532

R

RARP, 31, 159–160, 173, 175
 alternative solutions, 175
 encapsulation, 175
 first boot, 31
 ICMPv6, 689
 IP address, 457
 logical address, 173
 masking, 225
 packet format, 174
 physical broadcast address, 160
 physical machine, 173
 purpose, 31
 server, 175
 unicast address, 160
RARP reply, 173
RARP request, 173
Read Request. *See* RRQ
realm, 753
real-time audio/video
 example, 662
real-time delay, 663
real-time interactive
 audio/video, 662
Real-Time Streaming Protocol.
  See RTSP
real-time traffic
 characteristics, 662
 error control, 666
 Internet, 689
 mixer, 666
 multicasting, 665
 ordering, 665
 playback buffer, 664
 RTP, 667
 sequence number, 665
 TCP, 666
 threshold, 664
 time relationship, 662
 timestamp, 663
 translation, 666
 translator, 666
 UDP, 666
Real-time Transport Control
  Protocol. See RTCP

Real-time Transport Protocol.
  See RTP
reassembly module, 207
reassembly table, 206
receiver window
 (rwnd), 300
receiving buffer, 277
Record Protocol, 761
record route option, 193
 pointer, 194
recursive resolution, 481
redirect message, 219
 code field, 220
 example, 220
 host-specific route, 221
 ICMP package, 233
 network-specific route, 221
 purpose, 220
 TOS, 221
redundancy, 655, 792
 checksum, 798
 CRC, 794
 send data twice, 792
redundancy check, 792
reflection attack, 741
regional ISP, 5, 146
REGISTER message, 671
registered port, 259
registrar, 481
registrar server, 672
registration, 642
 care-of address field, 643
 extension field, 644
 flag field, 643
 home address field, 643
 home agent field, 643
 identification field, 644
 lifetime field, 643
 mobile IP, 640
 port number, 644
 type field, 643
registration reply, 642, 644
registration request, 642
registration/administration/status
  (RAS), 674
regulatory agencies, 9
relay agent, 459
reliable service
 SCTP, 349
remote host
 mobile host, 646
remote login, 500–501
 problems, 500
rendezvous router, 443, 449
 selection, 450

repeater, 70
    amplifier, 70
    vs. HDSL, 58
    hub, 71
    location, 71
    segment, 70
replay attack, 740
    KDC, 747
Request for Comment. *See* RFC
resolution
    iterative, 482
    name to address, 481
    recursive, 481
resolver, 481
resource record, 488
Resource Reservation Protocol
    (RSVP), 701
response
    DNS, 483
RETR command, 529
retransmission, 307
    SCTP, 379
    TCP, 307
retransmission policy, 315
retransmission time-out (RTO), 307, 321
retransmission timer, 312, 320
Reverse Address Resolution
    Protocol. *See* RARP
reverse path broadcasting. *See* RPB
reverse path forwarding. *See* RPF
reverse path multicasting. *See* RPM
RFC, 9, 805
    draft standard, 10
    elective level, 11
    experimental, 10
    historic, 10
    informational, 10
    Internet standard, 10
    limited use level, 11
    maturity levels, 9
    not recommended level, 11
    proposed standard, 9
    recommended level, 11
    required level, 11
    requirement level, 11
ring topology, 22
RIP, 385, 392
    address field, 394
    broadcasting, 398
    command field, 394
    distance field, 394
    encapsulation, 398
    entry, 394
    expiration timer, 396
    family field, 394

garbage collection timer, 396
    message format, 394
    periodic timer, 396
    port, 807
    port assignment, 398
    request, 394
    requests and responses, 394
    response, 394
    shortcomings, 397
    solicited response, 394
    timers, 396
    unsolicited response, 394
    version 2, 397
    version field, 394
RIP v2, 397
    authentication field, 398
    classless addressing, 397
    message format, 397
    multicasting, 398
    next hop address field, 397
    route tag field, 397
    subnet mask field, 397
RIPNIC, 693
rlogin, 499, 515
root, 401
root server, 476
round-trip time, 321
router, 24, 74, 385
    address, 75, 225
    addresses, 75
    area border, 404
    ATM, 621
    backbone, 404
    bridge, 74
    components, 151
    designated parent, 448
    fragmentation, 186
    function, 74–75
    input port, 151
    multicast, 239
    as multihomed device, 95
    as network station, 75
    output port, 151
    packets, 75
    vs. repeater, 74
    structure, 151
    subnet, 103
    switching fabric, 152
    three-layer switch, 75
router advertisement
        message, 225
    address preference level, 225
    default router, 225
    format, 225
router hierarchies, 75

router link
    data field, 410
    identification field, 410
    metric field, 412
    metric for TOS 0, 412
router link LSA, 410
router solicitation and
        advertisement message, 225
    format, 225
    function, 225
    ICMPv6, 715
routing, 131, 148
    distance vector, 387
    multicast, 441
    network layer, 24
    subnet, 105
Routing Information Protocol. *See* RIP
routing processor, 151–152
routing protocol, 385, 444
    multicast, 437
routing table, 133, 149, 385
    added by redirection flag, 149
    classless addressing, 141
    distance vector routing, 389
    dynamic, 148, 385
    flags field, 149
    gateway flag, 149
    hierarchy, 146
    host-specific flag, 149
    interface field, 149
    link state routing, 400
    mask field, 149
    modified by redirection flag, 149
    network address field, 149
    next hop address field, 149
    reference count field, 150
    search, 147
    search algorithm, 147
    shortest path tree, 403
    static, 148
    up flag, 149
    updating of, 220
    use field, 150
RPB, 447
RPC
    port, 807
RPF, 446
RPM, 448
    graft message, 449
    grafting, 449
    prune message, 448
RRQ, 534
    filename field, 534
    mode field, 534
    opcode field, 534

RSA, 732
  choosing the keys, 734
  number size, 734
RST flag, 291
RST+ACK, 299
RSVP, 701
RTCP, 669
  application specific message, 670
  bye message, 670
  message types, 669
  port number, 670
  receiver report, 670
  RTP, 669
  sender report, 670
  source description message, 670
RTO, 307, 321
RTP, 666–667, 701
  contributor count, 668
  contributor ID, 669
  extension header, 668
  header, 667
  marker field, 668
  padding, 667
  payload type field, 668
  port number, 669
  RTCP, 669
  sequence number field, 668
  synchronization source, 669
  timestamp, 668
  UTP, 667
  version field, 667
RTSP, 660
RTT, 321
  deviation, 321
  Karn's algorithm, 323
  measured, 321
  measuring, 328
  smoothed, 321
run-length encoding, 524
rwnd, 316, 374

S

SA, 46
SACK, 307
SACK chunk, 359, 367, 379
SACK option, 331
SACK-permitted option, 331
sampling rate
  voice, 652
script
  CGI, 607
SCTP, 32, 306, 345
  acknowledgment number, 352
  association, 347

association establishment, 362
chunk, 349
congestion control, 380
cookie, 364
data ransfer, 365
data transfer vs data delivery, 367
ECN, 380
features, 346
flow control, 373
four SACKs, 379
header, 353
multihoming, 348
multistream delivery, 367
packet format, 353
position in suite, 345
reliable service, 349
retransmission timer, 379
sender site, 378
services, 346
state transition diagram, 369
stream, 351
verification tag, 354, 364
SCTP association, 362
SCTP header, 350
  checksum field, 354
  destination port address field, 354
  source port address field, 354
SCTP packet, 350
  vs TCP segment, 350
SDSL, 58
SEAL, 69, 622
search algorithm, 147
searching, 147, 148
secondary server, 477
Secure Sockets Layer. *See* SSL
security, 754
  application layer, 754
  authentication, 736
  firewall, 763
  integrity, 736
  network layer, 754
  nonrepudiation, 736
  transport layer, 754
Security Association (SA), 754
security parameter index (SPI), 754
segment, 26, 70, 278, 281–282
  header fields, 282
  IP datagram, 32
  size, 282
  TCP, 32
  TCP/IP, 32
selective acknowledgment (SACK), 307
semantics, 6
sending buffer, 277
sequence number, 280

ICMP, 214
serial transmission
  burst error, 791
server, 256
  primary, 477
  root, 477
  secondary, 477
  UDP queue, 266
  WWW, 600
server program, 257
service type, 181
service-point addressing, 25
Session Initiation Protocol. *See* SIP
session key, 743
  Diffie-Helman, 743
  KDC, 746
  TGS, 752
session layer, 26, 27
SFD, 46
  function, 46
SHA-1, 738
shared-group tree
  CBT, 451
sharing, 388
  distance vector routing, 388
  path vector routing, 422
shift count, 327
shortest path tree, 401
  link state routing, 400
  multicast routing, 441–442
  root, 401
  routing table, 403
  unicast routing, 441
SHUTDOWN ACK chunk, 361
SHUTDOWN chunk, 361, 372
SHUTDOWN COMPLETE
  chunk, 361
SHUTDOWN PENDING, 372
SHUTDOWN-ACK-SENT, 372
SHUTDOWN-ACK-SENT
  state, 370
SHUTDOWN-PENDING
  state, 370
SHUTDOWN-RECEIVED
  state, 370
SHUTDOWN-SENT
  state, 370, 372
SI, 349
silly window syndrome, 304
  cause, 304
  Clark's solution, 305
  created by receiver, 304
  created by sender, 304
  delayed acknowledgment, 305
  Nagle algorithm, 304

simple and efficient adaptation
    layer. *See* SEAL
simple data type, 581
Simple Mail Transfer Protocol.
    See SMTP
Simple Network Management
    Protocol. *See* SNMP
simplex, 22
simultaneous close, 372
simultaneous open, 287, 370
single-bit error, 790
    frequency, 791
SIP, 346, 671
    addresses, 671
    communication, 672
    messages, 671
    modules, 671
    session establishment, 672
    termination, 672
    tracking, 672
site local address, 697
sliding window, 300, 327
    buffer, 300
    silly window syndrome, 304
sliding window size
    formula, 327
slow start, 316, 319, 616
slow start threshold, 317
SMI, 576, 579
    ASN.1, 580
    BER, 582
    data type, 579
    encoding, 582
    encoding method, 579
    functions, 579
    network management, 578
    objects, 579
    role, 577
    sequence data type, 581
    sequence of data type, 582
    simple data type, 580–581
    SNMP, 577
    structured data types, 580, 581
    tree structure, 580
SMIv2, 579
smoothed RTT, 321
SMTP, 561
    commands, 561–562
    connection establishment, 566
    connection termination, 567
    DATA command, 563
    EXPN command, 564
    HELO command, 562
    HELP command, 564
    HTTP, 609

MAIL FROM command, 563
mail transfer phases, 566
message transfer, 566
NOOP command, 563
permanent negative completion
    reply, 565
port 25, 566, 807
positive completion reply, 564
positive intermediate reply, 565
QUIT command, 563
RCPT TO command, 563
responses, 561, 564
RSET command, 563
SEND FROM command, 564
service not available, 566
service ready, 566
SMAL FROM command, 564
SMOL FROM command, 564
transient negative completion
    reply, 565
TURN command, 564
VRFY command, 563
SNMP, 575, 589
    agent, 575
    agent database, 576
    analogy, 578
    BER, 592
    client program, 576
    client/server mechanism, 595
    data, 592
    error index field, 592
    error status field, 591
    error types, 591
    format, 591
    function, 575
    GetBulkRequest, 590
    GetNextRequest, 589
    GetRequest, 589
    header, 592
    InformRequest, 590
    management basics, 576
    manager, 575–576
    max-repetition field, 592
    message elements, 592
    non-repeater, 591
    overview, 578
    PDU, 589
    port, 595, 807
    report, 591
    request ID, 591
    response, 590
    role, 577
    security parameters, 592
    server program, 576
    SetRequest, 590

SMI, 577
tag, 593
trap, 590
UDP port, 595
VarBindList field, 592
version, 592
snmp object, 585
SNMPv3, 592
    security, 595
    SNMPv2, 595
socket address, 260, 460
    definition, 260
    IP header, 260
    pair, 260
    port number, 260
SONET, 61
    video, 653
sorcerer's apprentice bug, 539
source quench message, 216, 711
    purpose, 217
    recipient, 217
    usefulness of, 218
source quench packet, 315
source routing, 705, 706
Source Service Access Point.
    See SSAP
source-based tree, 442
    multicast distance vector
        routing, 445
spatial compression, 657
speaker node, 421
    initialization, 422
special address, 96
    subnet, 106
special query message, 241
specific host on this network, 98
SPI, 754, 757
split horizon, 391
SQL, 607
SSAP, 801
SSN, 349
SSL, 758
ssthresh, 317
standards, 7, 8
standards organizations, 7
star topology, 22
state transition diagram
    SCTP, 369
    TCP, 292
static database, 464
static document, 603
static mapping, 159, 161
    limitations, 159
    overhead, 160
    table, 161

static routing table, 148, 385
station address, 31
stationary host, 637
STOR command, 529, 531
stream
    definition, 32
    SCTP, 351
Stream Control Transmission
    Protocol. *See* SCTP
stream delivery, 277
stream identifier. *See* SI
stream sequence number. *See* SSN
streaming, 659
streaming live audio/video,
    651, 662
streaming stored audio/video,
    651, 659
    media server, 660
    streaming server and RTSP, 660
    web server, 659
    web server and meta file, 659
strict source route, 705
strict source route option, 195
    rules, 195
STRU command, 531
Structure of Management
    Information. *See* SMI
structured data type, 581
stub AS, 424
stub link, 406
subdomain, 474
subnet, 102
    address, 106
    address range, 123
    classless addressing, 122
    forwarding, 136, 139
    hostid, 103
    prefix, 122
    router, 103
    special address, 106
    subnetid, 103
    three levels of hierarchy, 103
    variable length, 124
subnet address, 106
subnet mask, 105, 107
    classless addressing, 122
    contiguous, 105
    ICMPv6, 714
    non-contiguous, 105
    vs supernet mask, 108
subnetting
    IPv4, 689
    need for, 102
subnetwork. *See* subnet
substitution cipher, 729

suffix, 118, 474, 637
suffix length, 118
summary link to AS boundary
    LSA, 416
summary link to network, 415
    metric field, 416
    network mask field, 416
    TOS field, 416
supernet, 102, 107
supernet mask, 107–108
    IPv4, 689
SVC, 629
    ATMARP, 629
switch, 24, 152
    banyan, 152
    Batcher-banyan, 154
    crossbar, 152
    three-layer, 75
    two-layer, 74
switched virtual circuit. *See* SVC
switched WAN, 63, 101
switching fabric, 151–152
symmetric digital subscriber line.
    See SDSL
symmetric key, 740
    Diffie-Hellman, 744
    distribution, 742
    KDC, 746
    n^2 problem, 742
    PGP, 762
    secret-key, 728
symmetric-key cryptography, 728
    advantages, 734
    disadvantages, 734
    key, 728
    privacy, 735
SYN flooding attack, 287, 364
SYN segment, 285
SYN+ACK, 286
synchronization points, 27
SYN-RCVD state, 295, 297
SYN-SENT, 295
SYN-SENT state, 295, 297
syntax, 6
sys object, 585

T

T line, 60
T-1 line, 61
T-3 line, 61
table lookup, 152
tag, 604
TCB, 333–334, 364

TCP, 2, 32, 180, 255, 275
    abort a connection, 292, 299
    acknowledgment number, 281
    acknowledgment type, 307
    buffer, 277, 288
    byte numbering, 280
    checksum, 283
    congestion control, 281
    connection establishment,
        285, 293
    connection reset, 291
    connection termination, 289
    connection-oriented, 279, 284
    deadlock, 312
    delayed segment scenario, 311
    denying a connection, 292, 297
    DNS, 493
    duplicate segment scenario, 311
    encapsulation, 284
    error control, 281, 305, 376
    fast retransmission scenario, 310
    flow control, 281, 299
    full-duplex, 278, 285
    function, 32
    ICMP, 214
    idle connection, 292
    and IP, 180
    lost acknowledgment scenario, 311
    lost segment scenario, 309
    network performance, 313
    normal scenario, 308
    numbering system, 280
    OSI model, 30
    ports, 807
    position in suite, 275
    pseudoheader, 283
    push bit, 288
    push operation, 288
    pushing data, 288
    real-time traffic, 666
    reliable service, 279
    resending a segment, 311
    vs SCTP, 346
    segment, 278, 281
    segment re-ordering, 32
    segmentation, 32, 524
    sequence number, 32, 280
    server state, 295
    simultaneous close, 297
    simultaneous open, 297
    SIP, 671
    sliding window, 300
    state transition diagram, 293
    stream delivery, 277
    stream transport protocol, 32

TCP—*Cont.*
  streaming live audio/video, 662
  stream-oriented protocol, 289
  termination, 293
  timers, 320
  transport layer protocol, 30
  urgent data, 289
  well-known port numbers, 259
  window shutdown, 303
TCP header
  acknowledgment number
    field, 282
  checksum field, 283
  control field, 283
  destination port address
    field, 282
  header length field, 283
  options, 325
  options field, 284
  reserved field, 283
  sequence number field, 282
  source port address field, 282
  urgent pointer field, 283
  window size field, 283
tcp object, 585
TCP option
  end-of-option, 325
  maximum segment size, 325
  multiple-byte option, 325
  no operation, 325
  one-byte option, 325
  timestamp, 325
  window scale factor, 325
TCP package, 333
  input processing module, 338
  main module, 334
  output processing module, 338
  TCB, 333
  timer, 334
TCP segment
  vs SCTP packet, 350
TCP/IP, 1–2, 30
  addresses, 33
  application layer, 30, 32
  application layer and OSI
    model, 32
  ARPANET, 3, 37
  data link layer, 31
  datagram format, 180
  file transfer, 519
  hierarchical structure, 30
  IP, 179
  layers, 30
  network layer, 31
  NVT, 501

  OSI model, 17, 30
  physical and data link layers, 31
  physical layer, 31
  standard file transfer, 519
  transport layer, 30, 32
  UDP, 32
  UNIX, 3
  v4 problem, 37
  Version 5, 37
  Version 6, 38
teleconferencing, 441, 652
telephony, 652
telephony signalling, 346
TELNET, 499
  abort output, 509
  are you there, 509
  binary option, 505
  browser, 600
  character mode, 512
  client, 502
  client abort, 511
  control characters, 502
  controlling the server, 509
  default mode, 512
  disabling an option, 506
  DONT command, 506
  echo option, 505
  embedding, 503
  enabling an option, 505
  erase character, 509
  go ahead, 512
  IAC, 508
  infinite loop, 510
  interrupt process, 509
  line mode, 512
  line mode option, 505
  mode of operation, 512
  offer to disable, 506
  offer to enable, 506
  option negotiation, 505
  options, 504
  out-of-band signaling, 510
  port, 503, 807
  pseudoterminal driver, 501
  remote login, 501
  request to enable, 506
  security, 515
  sending data, 503
  server, 502
  status option, 505
  suboption character, 508
  suboption negotiation, 508
  suppress go ahead option, 505
  symmetry, 508
  synchronization character, 510

  temporal compression, 657
  temporal masking, 654
  terminal, 499
  terminal speed option, 505
  terminal type option, 505
  timesharing, 499
  timing mark option, 505
  urgent TCP segment, 510
  URL, 601
  user interface, 513
  WILL command, 506
  WONT command, 506–507
terminal network.
    See TELNET
termination
  SCTP, 368
  TFTP, 533
  ACK, 535, 537
  ACK message, 535
  applications, 542
  BOOTP, 460, 542
  connection, 536
  connection establishment, 537
  connection termination, 537
  damaged message, 538
  DATA, 535, 537
  DATA message, 535
  data transfer, 537
  DHCP, 542
  duplicate message, 538
  duplication of messages, 538
  ephemeral port, 540
  ERROR, 536–537
  error control, 538
  file retrieval, 538
  file storage, 538
  flow control, 538
  lack of checksum field, 538
  lost acknowledgment, 538
  lost message, 538
  messages, 534
  need for, 533
  options, 541
  port, 807
  port usage, 539
  reading a file, 533, 537
  RRQ, 534, 537
  security, 542
  sorcerer's apprentice
    bug, 539
  termination, 537
  timeout, 538
  UDP, 536
  well-known port, 540
  WRQ, 534–535, 537

TGS, 751
    AS, 752
    Kerberos, 752
this host on this network, 98
three-ACKs, 319
three-layer switch, 74
three-node instability, 391
three-way handshaking,
        285, 289, 362, 396
    example, 285
throughput, 313–314
    load, 314
ticket, 746
ticket-granting server. *See* TGS
time exceeded message, 218, 712
    code field, 218
    late fragments, 218
    time-to-live field, 218
time-out, 305
timer
    expiration, 396
    garbage collection, 396
    keepalive, 324
    periodic, 396
    persistence, 323–324
    retransmission, 320
    retransmission SCTP, 379
    RIP, 396
timesharing, 499
    login, 500
    password checking, 500
timestamp
    ICMPv6, 714
    real-time traffic, 663
    RTCP, 670
    RTP, 668
timestamp message
    clock synchronization, 223
    original timestamp field, 223
    receive timestamp field, 223
    reply, 223
    request, 223,
    round-trip time, 223
    transmit timestamp field, 223
    trip times, 223
timestamp option, 196, 328
    flags field, 197
    format, 328
    operation, 328
    overflow field, 197
timestamp request and reply
        messages, 223
    clock synchronization, 224
time-to-live
    caching, 483

TIME-WAIT state, 295
time-wait timer, 325
timing, 6
T-line
    bursty data, 64
    fractional, 61
TLS, 758
    general idea, 759
    handshake, 759
    HMAC, 759
    layers, 759
    phase I, 760
    phase II, 760
    phase III, 760
    phase IV, 761
    position, 759
Token Bus
    Project 802, 800
Token Ring
    Project 802.5, 800
TOS, 182
    categorizing, 182
    interpretations, 182
    values for application
        programs, 182
TP, 66
traceroute, 199, 227
tracert, 229
trailer, 20
    ATM cell, 625
transceiver, 47
transient link, 405
    cost assignment, 406
    graphical representation, 406
transit AS, 424
transition
    IPv4 to IPv6, 718
transition strategy, 718
    dual stack, 718
    header translation, 720
    tunneling, 719
translation, 666
    presentation layer, 27
    real-time traffic, 666
translator, 666
transmission control block.
        See TCB
Transmission Control Protocol.
        See TCP
transmission media
    quality, 64
transmission paths. *See* TP
transmission sequence number.
        See TSN
transparent bridge, 72

transport layer, 24, 32, 256
    connection control, 26
    connection mechanism, 256
    delivery to application
        program, 256
    error control, 26
    flow control, 26
    protocols, 32, 255, 275
    real-time traffic, 666
    reassembly, 26
    receiving process, 256
    responsibilities, 24, 32, 256
    security, 754
    segmentation, 26
    service-point addressing, 25
    TCP, 32
    TCP/IP, 30, 32
transport layer security. *See* TLS
transport mode, 755
transpositional cipher, 730
trap, 576
triangle routing, 646
triggered update, 390
triple DES, 732
Trivial File Transfer Protocol.
        See TFTP
TSN, 349
    initial, 358
tsrecent, 328–329
TTL, 204, 295
tunnel mode, 755
tunneling, 246
    automatic, 720
    configured, 720
    multicasting, 453
    VPN, 683
twisted pair, 58
two-layer switch, 74
two-node loop instability, 391
TYPE command, 531
type of service. *See* TOS
type prefix, 692

U

UA, 547, 551
    command-driven, 552
    envelope, 554
    envelope info, 554
    GUI-based, 553
    mail format, 553
    mail summary, 554
    message, 554
    message body, 554

UA—*Cont.*
  message header, 554
  receiving mail, 554
  types, 552
UDP, 30, 32, 255, 275
  advantages, 256
  checksum, 262, 264–265
  compared to TCP, 32
  connection establishment, 536
  connectionless, 256
  connectionless service, 264
  data link layer, 265
  decapsulation, 264–265
  demultiplexing, 267
  DNS, 493
  encapsulation, 264
  flow and error control, 264
  for simple communication, 267
  function, 256
  ICMP, 214
  incoming queue, 266
  internal control mechanism, 268
  IP, 265
  management programs, 268
  multicasting and
    broadcasting, 268
  multiplexing, 267
  operation, 264
  outgoing queue, 266
  package, 268
  physical layer, 265
  port creation, 265
  port unreachable, 266
  ports, 807
  position in TCP/IP suite, 255
  process-to-process protocol, 32
  queuing, 265
  real-time traffic, 666
  route-updating protocols, 268
  RTP, 667
  RTP port, 669
  vs SCTP, 346
  SIP, 671
  size restriction, 264
  SNMP, 595
  socket address, 260
  termination, 536
  TFTP, 536–537
  transport layer protocol, 30
  unreliable, 256
  uses, 267
  well-known port number, 259
UDP design, 270–271
udp object, 585
UDP package

  components, 268
  control-block module, 269
  control-block table, 268
  example, 270
  input module, 269
  input queue, 269
  output module, 270
UDP port
  RTCP, 670
  TFTP, 539
underlying technologies, 43, 621, 637
UNI, 66
  ATM, 623
unicast address, 34, 100, 692
unicast routing, 441
  shortest path tree, 441
unicast routing protocols, 385
unicast routing table
  RPF, 446
unicasting, 237, 437
  multiple, 439
  router interface, 438
uniform resource locator. *See* URL
UNIX, 3
unspecified address, 695
update binding packet, 647
update message, 428
  network layer reachability
    information field, 429
  path attributes field, 428
  path attributes length field, 428
  unfeasible routes length
    field, 428
  withdrawn routes field, 428
updating
  distance vector routing, 388
  path vector routing, 422
URG bit, 289
urgent byte, 289
URL, 601
  alias, 601
  anchor, 605
  components, 601
  host, 601
  HTTP, 601
  locator, 601
  multimedia, 660
  pathname, 601
  port number, 601
  protocol, 601
user agent. *See* UA
USER command, 529, 531
user datagram, 260
  checksum example, 263
  checksum field, 261

  destination port number
    field, 261
  format, 260
  length calculation, 261
  length field, 261
  pseudoheader, 262
  source port number field, 261
user datagram protocol. *See* UDP
user network interface. *See* UNI
user support layers, 20

V

V.90, 56
VC, 66
  cell network, 67
VCI
  ATM, 624
  ATM WAN, 627
VDSL, 58
verification tag, 351, 363–364
very high bit rate digital subscriber line.
    See VDSL
video, 652
  compression, 654
  digitizing, 652
  frame rate, 653
  real-time traffic, 689
  resolution, 653
video conferencing, 662
virtual circuit identifier. *See* VCI
virtual circuits. *See* VC
virtual link, 404, 407
virtual path. *See* VP
virtual path identifier. *See* VPI
voice
  sampling rate, 652
voice over IP, 662, 670
VP, 66
VPI, 67
  ATM, 624
  ATM WAN, 627
VPN, 680–681
  IPSec, 682
  security, 682
  tunneling, 682–683
VRC, 793

W

WAN, 64
  ATM, 621
  Frame Relay, 64
  TCP/IP, 31

warning packet, 647
Web
   cookie, 602
   functions, 601
Web page, 600
   body, 604
   head, 604
   HTML, 603
   structure, 604
   tag, 604
Web site, 599
well-known attribute, 425
well-known port, 259
   BOOTP, 459
   list, 807
   queue, 266
   TFTP, 540
well-known port number, 257
   TCP, 276
   SCTP, 346

WILL command, 506
window scale factor, 327
window scale factor option
   connection setup, 327
   shift count, 327
window size, 316
   basis of, 316
wireless
   addressing mechanism, 54
   frame control field, 54
   MAC layer frame, 53
   MAC sublayer, 52
   physical layer, 51
wireless Ethernet, 50
wireless LAN, 53
World Wide Web. *See* WWW
Write Request. *See* WRQ
WRQ, 534
WWW, 599, 601–602

X

X.25, 63, 64
   IP, 63
X.509, 749
   CA, 750
xDSL, 56

Y

Yahoo, 571

Z

zone, 475

NSFNET	National Science Foundation Network	**RTCP**	Real-time Transport Control Protocol
NVT	network virtual terminal	**RTP**	Real-time Transport Protocol
OC	optical carrier	**RTSP**	Real-Time Streaming Protocol
OFDM	orthogonal frequency-division multiplexing	**RTT**	round-trip time
OSI	Open Systems Interconnection	**SA**	security association
OSPF	open shortest path first	**SCTP**	Stream Control Transmission Protocol
PAWS	protection against wrap sequence	**SDH**	synchronous digital hierarchy
PGP	Pretty Good Privacy	**SDSL**	symmetric digital subscriber line
PIM	Protocol Independent Multicast	**SEAL**	simple and efficient adaptation layer
PIM-DM	Protocol Independent Multicast, Dense Mode	**SFD**	start frame delimiter
		SI	stream identifier
PIM-SM	Protocol Independent Multicast, Sparse Mode	**SMI**	Structure of Management Information
PING	Packet Internet Groper	**SMTP**	Simple Mail Transfer Protocol
POP	Post Office Protocol	**SNMP**	Simple Network Management Protocol
PPP	Point-to-Point Protocol		
PPPoE	PPP over Ethernet	**SONET**	Synchronous Optical Network
PQDN	partially qualified domain name	**SSH**	secure shell
PVC	permanent virtual circuit	**SSN**	stream sequence number
RADSL	rate adaptive asymmetrical digital subscriber line	**STM**	synchronous transport module
		STS	synchronous transport signal
RARP	Reverse Address Resolution Protocol	**SVC**	switched virtual circuit
RFC	Request for Comment	**TCP**	Transmission Control Protocol
RIP	Routing Information Protocol	**TCP/IP**	Transmission Control Protocol/ Internetworking Protocol
ROM	read-only memory		
RPB	reverse path broadcasting	**TELNET**	Terminal Network
RPF	reverse path forwarding	**TFTP**	Trivial File Transfer Protocol
RPM	reverse path multicasting	**TLS**	Transport Layer Security